The Religious Bodies
of
AMERICA

The Religious Bodies

of

AMERICA

By

F. E. MAYER

(1892—1954)

PROFESSOR OF SYSTEMATIC THEOLOGY
Concordia Seminary, St. Louis, Mo.

FOURTH EDITION

Revised by Arthur Carl Piepkorn

SAINT LOUIS

To Martha

Preface to the First Edition

This book has grown out of more than twenty-five years of classroom activity at the two theological seminaries of The Lutheran Church — Missouri Synod, Concordia Seminary at Springfield, Ill., and Concordia Seminary at St. Louis, Mo., teaching courses in the distinctive doctrines of American churches. In this text the author has endeavored to observe the following theological principles: an unqualified submission to the divine truth as it is revealed in the sacred records of Holy Scripture; acceptance of the Word of God as the absolute and final standard and rule of all Christian proclamation; the conviction that the Lutheran Confessions are a full and correct witness to this divinely revealed truth; a deep concern to preserve and cultivate the true ecumenical spirit which recognizes the spiritual unity of all Christians through faith in Christ, transcending all denominational lines, but which at the same time is conscious of the obligation to censure and to correct every doctrinal trend which threatens to undermine or destroy the unity of faith.

The text is intended primarily for the theological student and the parish minister. However, many laymen are vitally interested in the doctrines and practices of the several church bodies and seek information which enables them to discuss intelligently and sympathetically the differences between the various denominations. The author attempted to keep these two classes of readers in mind. The professional theologian no doubt will frequently turn to the bibliography, the footnotes, and the references listed for further research. The layman, however, may ignore this scholarly apparatus. A glossary of technical theological terms has been added to assist him in reading the text.

The author has at all times endeavored to interpret objectively and without prejudice or bias the doctrines and practices of each religious group in the light of its historical development and on the basis of its official creedal statements. In this effort many individuals have assisted him by collecting, analyzing, and evaluating the materials basic for this study. The author has in mind particularly the several graduate students of Concordia Seminary, St. Louis, Mo., who did a great deal of research work, Walter Bartling, Herbert T. Mayer, Henry Reimann, Robert M. Raabe, Richard Z. Meyer, Hans Boehringer. The author wishes to thank the manager, the editors and proofreaders, the layout department, and the staff of the composing room of Concordia Publishing House for their painstaking care in producing this book. Especial thanks are due to my colleague Professor Arthur Carl Piepkorn, Ph. D., for critically reading the entire manuscript and for making many helpful suggestions.

We now send forth this volume in the hope and with the prayer that a careful study of the text will help Christians to contend for and to preserve the faith once delivered to the saints.

Festival of the Reformation, 1953

F. E. MAYER

Preface to the Second Edition

The unexpectedly enthusiastic welcome accorded to THE RELIGIOUS BODIES OF AMERICA exhausted the large first printing within nine months of the date of publication. In a work so extensive and written over so long a period some minor errors of fact and interpretation inevitably crept in. Where published reviews and private communications called such inadvertent errors to the author's and the publisher's attention, it was the desire of both to make appropriate correction in the second edition. After the lamented death of the author shortly after the publication of the first edition, Dr. Otto A. Dorn, the manager of Concordia Publishing House, requested me to accept responsibility for making the necessary changes in the second edition. Moved by devotion to a sainted colleague to whom I owe very much and for whom I have vast regard and deep affection, I have accepted Dr. Dorn's invitation. In preparing the second edition, I have had the benefit of the late Dr. Mayer's own notes for a revision and the constructive suggestions of reviewers of the first edition as well as the generous assistance of many colleagues and friends, of the Concordia Publishing House staff, and — by no means least — of the students of my classes in comparative symbolics at Concordia Seminary. To all these belongs largely the credit for any improvement which this second edition exhibits. At the same time the responsibility for the changes made is mine alone.

Soli Deo gloria!

St. Mary Magdalene's Day, 1955

ARTHUR CARL PIEPKORN

Prefatory Note to the Fourth Edition

As in the case of the third edition, published in 1958, the necessity of reprinting THE RELIGIOUS BODIES OF AMERICA affords a welcome opportunity to bring the work up to date once more. The basic structure of the book remains intact. The union of the General Council of Congregational and Christian Churches and the Evangelical and Reformed Church into the United Church of Christ has necessitated some reorganization of Parts IV and VI, while the unions that have taken place among various Lutheran and Presbyterian bodies and between the Unitarians and the Universalists have brought about corresponding changes in Chapter 5 of Part III, Chapter 5 of Part IV, and Chapter 1 of Part X. Likewise some 350 additions have been made in the bibliographical references beyond those introduced into the second and third editions. A projected comprehensive revision still lies a number of years in the future.

St. Gregory's Day, 1961

ARTHUR CARL PIEPKORN

Acknowledgments

The author gratefully acknowledges his indebtedness to the following owners of copyrights for permission to quote from their copyrighted publications.

Abingdon-Cokesbury Press, Nashville, Tenn.: *The American Churches, an Interpretation,* by W. W. Sweet (1948).

Baker Book Store, Grand Rapids, Mich.: *The Westminster Assembly and Its Work,* by B. B. Warfield (1931).

Christian Board of Publication, St. Louis, Mo.: *An American Religious Movement,* by W. E. Garrison (1945).

The Christian Century Foundation, Chicago, Ill.: *Christian Century,* June 7, 1944, p. 690.

Trustees under the Will of Mary Baker Glover Eddy, Boston, Mass.: *Science and Health, With Key to Scriptures,* by Mary Baker Eddy (1934).

Dodd, Mead and Co., New York, N. Y.: *Mind Remakes Your World,* by Ernest Holmes (1944).

Eden Publishing House, St. Louis, Mo.: *The German Church on the Frontier,* by Carl Schneider (1939).

Wm. B. Eerdmans Publishing Company, Grand Rapids, Mich.: *Evangelical Quarterly,* October, 1944, p. 275.

Gospel Publishing House, Springfield, Mo.: *The Spirit Himself,* by R. M. Riggs (1949).

Harper and Brothers, New York, N. Y.: *Creeds of Christendom,* by Philip Schaff (1896–1899).

B. Herder Book Company, St. Louis, Mo.: *The Pohle-Preuss Series of Dogmatic Textbooks,* sixth edition, by Arthur Preuss, editor (1930).

National Council of the Churches of Christ in the United States of America, New York, N. Y.: *Yearbook of American Churches,* 1960.

Nazarene Publishing House, Kansas City, Mo.: *Holiness and Power,* by A. M. Hills (1897).

Philosophical Library, Inc., New York, N. Y.: *Encyclopedia of Religion,* by V. Ferm (1945).

Pilgrim Press, Boston, Mass.: *Our Christian Faith, Congregationalism Today and Tomorrow,* by Walter Horton, 1945.

Fleming H. Revell Company, Westwood, N. J.: *The Modern Movement in American Theology,* by F. H. Foster (1939).

ix

Charles Scribner's Sons, New York, N. Y.: *History of Philosophy,* by Alfred Weber (1925); *Creeds and Platforms of Congregationalism,* by Williston Walker (1893).

The Sunday School Board of the Southern Baptist Convention, Nashville, Tenn.: *The Baptist Faith,* by E. Y. Mullins (1935).

The University of Chicago Press, Chicago, Ill.: *Finality of the Christian Religion,* by G. B. Foster (1907).

The Westminster Press, Philadelphia, Pa.: *The Christian Sacraments,* by Hugh Thomson Kerr (1944).

World Council of Churches, New York, N. Y.: *Ecumenical Review,* October, 1952, p. 67.

Yale University Press, New Haven, Conn.: *The Rise of the Social Gospel in American Protestantism,* by C. H. Hopkins (1940).

Contents

The Religious Bodies

of

AMERICA

INTRODUCTION

Introduction

The Christian church has always found it necessary to express its faith in creeds. As an antithesis to Judaism and paganism the early Christian church formulated its baptismal creeds. Subsequently the several Ecumenical Councils had to proclaim their various creedal dicta against the many errorists and heretical views which disturbed the church. Some creeds, because of their wide acceptance, are called Ecumenical Creeds. But in the course of time the various churches have adopted specific creeds. The churches of the Eastern Rite profess allegiance to the creeds adopted by the seven ecumenical councils. In 1530 the political protectors of the Lutheran movement adopted and submitted to the Holy Roman Emperor the *Augsburg Confession*. In 1563 the Roman Catholic church fixed its doctrines in the *Canons and Decrees of the Council of Trent*. The several Calvinistic Reformed church bodies adopted a number of creedal statements during the 16th and 17th centuries. Many newer religious bodies have subsequently formulated some creedal platform setting forth their respective doctrinal tenets.

For the most part, such creedal declarations are in theory the witness of a specific group to its understanding of the Word of God. Therefore churches usually consider their creeds not as the sources and judges of the divine truth, but only as witnesses to the truth as revealed by Christ and given to man in the Sacred Record. In the light of this truth the Christian must examine his creedal position, and thus each succeeding generation will make the creed its own.

A comparative study of the creeds adopted by the major churches holds a prominent place in the majority of the European theological curricula. Since the creeds are often designated as "symbols," this study is known as Comparative Symbolics. It is designed to set forth on the basis of the various creeds the doctrinal differences that divide the churches. In most European countries the churches were grouped according to the four traditional creedal systems and granted legal and political status.

In America the situation is totally different. With the establishment of our United States a significant change occurred also in the popular attitude toward creeds. A concomitant of the American principle of separation of church and state is the principle of free-churchism. This manifests itself, among other things, in the division of the historical churches into separate groups and in the founding of independent church bodies, so that today more than 250 such bodies are listed in the census report. However, one must not lose sight of the fact that all but a few of these can be grouped into several larger families, each with the same basic historic background, the same creedal position, and the same church practices. Therefore, in spite of the apparent divisions and multiplications, the historic churches remain, and the creeds are still relevant.

A second factor in changing the average churchman's approach to the creeds was the pragmatic principle expressed in the shibboleth "Not creeds, but deeds." Proponents of this slogan advocate the complete removal of all creedal barriers and the establishment of a united Christendom which would foster a fellowship not necessarily predicated on the unity of faith and confession, but on the opportunity it affords to share diverse religious experiences. This unionistic principle, advocating unity in essentials, toleration in nonessentials, and charity in all things, hopes to bring about the New Testament fellowship of faith. However, the New Testament fellowship reveals itself in the unity of faith and confession. This unity implies that the Christian church must necessarily censure and reject all views and tenets which threaten to undermine the faith once delivered to the saints. Contrary to the false pragmatic and unionistic principle, Christian fellowship demands a comparative study of the various creeds in the light of God's Word and, on the basis of such studies, the sifting of truth from error.

A third factor in causing creeds to be relegated to the background in American church life was the rise of liberal theology. Liberal theology held that truth is found in the experiences of the individual and of society and that therefore it constantly fluctuates and no creedal statement can fix it permanently. At best, creeds are viewed only as the record of past religious experiences and are held to be constantly in need of revision and reinterpretation.

The anticreedal bodies on the American scene present a peculiar problem. They reject every creedal statement and insist that the free Christian goes directly to the New Testament and accepts only such doctrines, practices, and even terms as are specifically mentioned in the New Testament. However, the very rejection of creeds, ecclesiastical terms, denominational names, postulates a creedal position. In addition, these bodies usually make a literal and atomistic interpretation of some New Testament reference or incident the very center of their proclamation.

Some observers distinguish between church and sect. However, it is extremely difficult to make such a distinction, since each one's theological orientation will determine his concept of a church and a sect. Generally the term "church" is employed to denote the large historic churches of the Christian tradition, whereas the term "sect" is applied to such groups as advocate some novel doctrine or practice, often allegedly given by direct divine revelation.

Actually, the various esoteric, healing, and metaphysical cults do not belong to the American churches. But since these cults play an important role on the American religious scene, we devote the concluding chapters of this text to the more prominent among them.

The material presented in this book may be grouped according to various methods. Some writers have employed the topical method and have catalogued the teachings of each church body under the various heads of Christian dogmatics. This method, however, is rather unsatisfactory. Some American writers list the various church bodies alphabetically and offer a brief encyclopedic statement concerning the doctrines and practices of each body. This text, however, endeavors to classify all bodies, to trace the historical origin and development of each denominational family, and to show how each related family, apparent innovations notwithstanding, maintains certain basic theological premises and observes certain practices that figured prominently in historical development. This procedure enables the reader to understand and to appreciate why each church body believes and practices as it does.

The statistical data are in a constant state of flux and for that reason are not included in this text. Up-to-date annual statistics can be obtained through the *Yearbook of American Churches,* published by the National Council of the Churches of Christ in the U. S. A.

GENERAL BIBLIOGRAPHY

1. *Comparative Symbolics*

Marheinecke, Philippus. *Institutiones symbolicae, doctrinarum catholicarum, protestantium, socinianorum, ecclesiae Graecae minorumque societatum Christianarum summam et discrimina exhibentes*, 2d ed. Berlin: Libraria Vossiana, 1825.

Moehler, J. A. *Symbolism or Exposition of the Doctrinal Differences Between Catholics and Protestants*, trans. J. R. Robertson. London: Gibbings & Co., 1906.

Molland, Einar. *Christendom: The Christian Churches, Their Doctrines, Constitutional Forms, and Ways of Worship.* New York: Philosophical Library, 1959.

Schaff, Philip. *The Creeds of Christendom.* New York: Harper & Bros., 1896—1899.

Walther, Wilhelm. *Lehrbuch der Symbolik, die Eigentümlichkeiten der vier christlichen Hauptkirchen.* Leipzig: Scholl, 1924.

Winer, Johann Georg Benedikt. *Comparative Darstellung des Lehrbegriffs der verschiedenen Kirchenparteien*, 2d ed. Leipzig: Carl Heinrich Reklam, 1837.

2. *Religious Bodies in America*

Bilheimer, Robert S. *The Quest for Christian Unity.* New York: Association Press, 1952.

Burr, Nelson R. *A Critical Bibliography of Religion in America.* 2 vols. Princeton, N. J.: Princeton University Press, 1961.

Carroll, H. K., ed. *American Church History Series.* 12 vols. New York: Christian Literature Company, 1893.

Cobb, John B., Jr. *Varieties of Protestantism.* Phila.: The Westminster Press, 1960.

Engelder, Theo., W. F. Arndt, Theo. Graebner, and F. E. Mayer. *Popular Symbolics.* St. Louis: Concordia Publishing House, 1934.

Ferm, Vergilius. *The American Church of the Protestant Heritage.* New York: Philosophical Library, 1953.

Guenther, Martin. *Populäre Symbolik.* Saint Louis: Concordia Publishing House, 1872.

Klotsche, E. H. *Christian Symbolics.* Burlington, Iowa: Lutheran Literary Board, 1929.

Lambert, Richard D., ed. *Religion in American Society.* Phila.: The American Academy of Political and Social Sciences, 1960.

Marty, Martin E. *The New Shape of American Religion.* New York: Harper & Bros., 1959.

Mead, Frank S. *Handbook of Denominations in the United States*, 3d ed. New York: Abingdon Press, 1961.

Neve, J. L. *Churches and Sects of Christendom*, rev. ed. Blair, Nebr.: Lutheran Publishing House, 1944.

Olmstead, Clifton E. *History of Religion in the United States.* Englewood Cliffs, N. J.: Prentice-Hall, 1960.

Phelan, M. *Handbook of All Denominations.* Nashville: Cokesbury Press, 1933.

Poovey, William A. *Your Neighbor's Faith: A Lutheran Looks at Other Churches.* Minneapolis: Augsburg Publishing House, 1961.

Rhodes, Arnold Black, Frank H. Caldwell, and L. C. Rudolph, eds. *The Church Faces the Isms.* New York: Abingdon Press, c. 1958.

Smith, H. Shelton, Robert T. Handy, and Lefferts A. Loetscher. *American Christianity: An Historical Interpretation with Representative Documents.* New York: Charles Scribner's Sons, 1960—.

Smith, James Ward, and A. Leland Jamison, eds. *Religious Perspectives in American Culture.* Princeton, N. J.: Princeton University Press, 1961.

———, eds. *The Shaping of American Religion.* Princeton, N. J.: Princeton University Press, 1961.

Spitz, Lewis W., Sr. *Our Church and Others.* St. Louis: Concordia Publishing House, 1960.

Sweet, William Warren. *The American Churches, an Interpretation.* New York: Abingdon-Cokesbury Press, 1948.

————. *The Story of Religions in America.* New York: Harper & Bros., 1930.

The U. S. Department of Commerce, Bureau of the Census. *Census of Religious Bodies.* Washington, D. C., 1936. Failure to provide the necessary Congressional appropriation prevented the 1946 and 1956 publication of this highly valuable study on the history, doctrine, practice, and statistics of each religious group.

Williams, J. Paul. *What Americans Believe and How They Worship.* New York: Harper & Bros., 1952.

Yearbook of American Churches, published regularly by the National Council of the Churches of Christ in the U. S. A. New York.

The following encyclopedias contain much significant material:

Die Religion in Geschichte und Gegenwart. 3d ed. Tübingen: J. C. B. Mohr (Paul Siebeck), 1957—.

Encyclopaedia Britannica.

Hastings, J. *Encyclopaedia of Religion and Ethics.* New York: Charles Scribner's Sons, 1928.

Jackson, Samuel Macaulay, ed. *The New Schaff-Herzog Encyclopedia of Religious Knowledge.* 12 vols. Grand Rapids: Baker Book House, 1949—50.

Loetscher, Lefferts A., ed. *Twentieth Century Encyclopedia of Religious Knowledge.* Grand Rapids: Baker Book House, 1955. A 2-volume supplement to *The New Schaff-Herzog Encyclopedia.*

Lueker, Erwin L., ed. *The Lutheran Cyclopedia.* St. Louis: Concordia Publishing House, 1954.

The Religious Bodies
of
AMERICA

The Holy Oriental Catholic and Apostolic Church

SECTION I

European Background

The flourishing period of Eastern Christianity is roughly coextensive with the era of the great Trinitarian and Christological controversies. The Eastern theologians to a very large degree assumed the theological leadership in the seven great ecumenical councils: Nicaea, 325; Constantinople, 381; Ephesus, 431; Chalcedon, 451; Second Council of Constantinople, 553; Third Council of Constantinople, 680; and Second Council of Nicaea, 787. In the latter part of this period the Filioque, the Easter, and the iconoclastic controversies marked a growing breach between the East and the West. The end of the first period is usually associated with the death of John of Damascus (d. 752?), considered by many the greatest dogmatician of Eastern Orthodoxy.

The second period, covering approximately the years 750–1500, witnessed the rise of the papacy and the Eastern church's bitter struggle with Islam and the Tartars. This is the era of the evangelization of the Slavic peoples and, as a result of the violent mistreatment of the Eastern Christians by the Crusaders from the West, of the final break between the two parts of Christendom.[1]

In the Reformation period the Eastern Orthodox church came in contact with Lutheran and Reformed theologians. Almost immediately after its publication the Augsburg Confession was translated into Greek and later sent to the patriarch of Constantinople for an opinion, but with no apparent effect. In 1575 the Tübingen theologians requested Jeremiah II to give an official opinion on the Lutheran confession. In his reply Jeremiah rejected all the distinctive doctrines of the Augsburg Confession.[2]

NOTE: For key to abbreviations see Appendix C; for Bibliography, the end of Part I.

[1] The Byzantine church brought the Gospel to the Slavs in the ninth century, and since the tenth the Orthodox church has been the national church of Russia. Until 1453 the Russian Orthodox church was under the patriarch of Constantinople. In 1589 the latter agreed to the creation of a Russian patriarchate in Moscow. Peter the Great vested all ecclesiastical authority in a "Spiritual College," later called the "Holy Synod" (1721).

[2] *Wort und Mysterium: Der Briefwechsel über Glauben und Kirche 1573 bis 1581 zwischen den Tübinger Theologen und dem Patriarchen von Konstantinopel* (Witten: Luther-Verlag, 1958). Georges Florovsky, "An Early Ecumenical Correspondence," in Yngve Brilioth, ed., *World Lutheranism of Today: A Tribute to Anders Nygren, 15 November 1950* (Stockholm: Svenska Kyrkans Diakonistyrelses Bokförlag, 1950), pp. 98—111, and "The Greek Version of the Augsburg Confession," *Lutheran World*, VI (1959), 153—155. See also Eduard Steinwand, "Lutheranism and the Orthodox Church," ibid., pp. 122—139.

Cyril Lucar (1568–1638) was patriarch of Alexandria and Constantinople and in this position carried on an extensive correspondence with leading Calvinist theologians. Jesuit intrigue not only checked his efforts to introduce Calvinistic views but finally led to his death. In opposition to the Jesuits who endeavored to bring about a reconciliation between the Eastern and the Western churches, and especially against the Calvinistic movement of Lucar, a number of confessions were drafted, particularly the confession of Peter of Mogila, metropolitan of Kiev (1640–1643), and the important confession of Dositheus (1672).

Other important confessional writings of this era are the catechism of Platon (ca. 1800), metropolitan of Moscow, and the catechism of Philaret, approved by the Holy Synod of St. Petersburg, 1839, and subsequently by all Eastern patriarchs.

The modern era is marked by the *rapprochement* of the Anglican churches and the Orthodox churches of Russia and Greece. As early as 1862 Anglicans and Episcopalians asked the Russian Orthodox church to recognize the validity of the Anglican ministry, in order that Anglicans might minister to the Russian immigrants in Alaska and the West Coast and, in turn, the Eastern church could minister to the Anglicans who traveled in the East. The Russians, however, questioned the validity of Anglican orders, rejected the idea of a second marriage of priests, and demanded that the Anglican churches accept the seven sacraments, trine immersion, veneration of icons, prayers for departed.

However, with the terrific and catastrophic experiences of the Russian Orthodox Christians in the Bolshevist Revolution of 1917, a new era of *rapprochement* between the two bodies occurred. Many of the leaders of the Russian church made peace with the Bolshevist regime. Several leading theologians fled to Paris, where the Anglicans assisted these refugees to establish the Theological Oriental Institute. Through the professors at this seminary, chiefly Nikolai Berdyaev and Father Sergius Bulgakoff, the Western world became familiar with the theological thinking of the Russian Orthodox church.[3]

The attitude of European and Asiatic orthodoxy toward the ecumenical movement is somewhat ambivalent. Many of the leaders have been ready to cooperate, primarily to bear witness to their belief that in both doctrine and liturgy they must set before the eyes of the heterodox "the splendor and majesty of orthodox adoration." But the

---

3 Berdyaev, the interpreter of Russia's great novelist Dostoevski, represents a semi-Gnostic philosophy. Berdyaev, like Dostoevski, held that our age needs a new spirituality based on the rights of man as a free man. Man receives this spiritual freedom when the Holy Spirit dwells in man as the principle of freedom and life and thus links God and His world. See Berdyaev, *The Destiny of Man* (Scribner's, 1937); *Spirit and Reality* (Scribner's, 1939); Horton, pp. 8—30; Hromadka (1944), pp. 18—33. For a biography of Berdyaev, see Donald A. Lowrie, *Rebellious Prophet: A Life of Nicolai Berdyaev* (New York: Harper & Bros., 1960). — Sergius Bulgakoff, until his death in 1944 dean of the Orthodox Theological Institute in Paris, was the chief exponent of sophiology ("divine wisdom"). He held that the creature world, which cannot exist by itself, must be united with the divine world. This takes place in *sophia*, and only in this union the world and man receive their real meaning. Bulgakoff, *The Wisdom of God.* — On the Institute itself, see Lowrie, *Saint Sergius in Paris: The Orthodox Theological Institute* (New York: The Macmillan Co., [1951]).

present political situation makes their active participation somewhat precarious and limited.[4]

The Fellowship of St. Alban and St. Sergius – a society chiefly of Anglicans and exiled Orthodox founded in 1928 – is cultivating cordial relations among the denominations represented by its members.[5]

In the United States five Orthodox bodies belong to the National Council of the Churches of Christ in the U. S. A.

SECTION II

The Formal and Material Principles [6]

The Formal Principle

Orthodox theology maintains that the source of religion, the formal principle of its theology, is the Holy Scriptures and the "sacred tradition"; and it says that thereby it is taking a mediating position between Rome, which adds "pious opinions" and papal decrees to the "holy traditions," and those Christians who reject tradition wholly.

The Orthodox church accepts the books of the Old Testament in the Septuagint version, including the Apocrypha and the books of the New Testament, as given by divine inspiration. Its teachers distinguish between inspiration, an internal energy operating within man's mind, and illumination, the Spirit's assistance guarding men against error.

In the widest sense, traditions include the teachings of Jesus and the apostles, handed down from generation to generation and collected in the Holy Scriptures and other documents of the past. The Holy Scriptures therefore are not considered the final and complete source of doctrine.

In the final analysis the Holy Orthodox church is the source of all matters of faith. The church, that is, the undivided church prior to the schism and since then the Eastern Orthodox church, is viewed as the depository of the truth given by Christ and the apostles and the authentic and infallible interpreter of divine revelation as contained in the Scriptures and the "sacred traditions." The laity is discouraged from reading

---

[4] (Archbishop) Iakovos, "The Contribution of Eastern Orthodoxy to the Ecumenical Movement," *Lutheran World*, VI (1959), 140—147; (Bishop) Dorotheos of Pringiponisson, "The Ecumenical Patriarchate and the Ecumenical Movement," *Ecumenical Review*, XIII (1960/1961), 96—99. The 1920 Message of the Ecumenical Patriarch calling for a fellowship of churches has been newly translated in *Ecumenical Review*, XII (1959/1960), 79—82. In 1961 the Patriarchate of Moscow applied for membership in the World Council of Churches.

[5] Patriarch Athenagoras, *Ecumenical Review*, V (1953), 167 f. — Roger Lloyd, II, 277 ff. Cp. Neve, pp. 63—65.

[6] We have leaned heavily on Frank Gavin's *Some Aspects* in presenting Orthodox theology. In his Hale Lectures of 1922 this Anglo-Catholic professor of the Episcopalian Nashotah House gives a good summary of the writings of modern Orthodox dogmaticians, 1875—1925, especially of Chrestos Androutsos. — See also the two articles in *Ecumenical Review*, XII (1959/1960), by Panagios P. Bratsiotis, "The Fundamental Principles and the Main Characteristics of the Orthodox Church," 154—163, and by Georges Florovsky, "The Ethos of the Orthodox Church," 183—198.

the Scriptures, since they are not considered capable of penetrating into the profound spiritual truths.[7] The following, in varying degrees, are the authorities for the faith for the Orthodox churchman: (1) the ancient creeds; (2) the writings of the Fathers; (3) the decrees of the ecumenical councils; (4) the decrees of the councils subsequent to the separation of the Eastern and Western churches, especially those of Constantinople (1672) and Jerusalem (1672); (5) the Orthodox confessions, such as that of Peter of Mogila; (6) the encyclicals, such as the letter of Patriarch Jeremiah II, 1570; (7) the authorized catechisms of the Eastern church.[8]

In describing the relation of faith and reason to each other, and the place of reason in theology, the Eastern church differs from Rome by denying that there is a real development of doctrine and holds that all Christian doctrine is contained in the Gospel and like a bud awaits full unfolding. The Orthodox church objects particularly to the adoption of the Filioque, papal infallibility, and the immaculate conception of Mary, as cases of a false development of doctrine.[9]

In its formal principle one of the distinctive characteristics of all Eastern Orthodox churches comes to the surface. This is the tenacious adherence to the old. It seems that the terms "ancient" and "orthodox" are viewed as synonyms. They regard themselves as the Orthodox, the "right-teaching," church because they have uniformly maintained the ancient doctrines and cultus. The first Sunday in Lent is observed as the Sunday of Orthodoxy by a dramatization of the hoped-for "eighth ecumenical council," in which all controversies are to be settled. This tenacious adherence to the old has had its wholesome effects. The Eastern churches experienced no dogmatical development as did the Western Catholic church, and by and large they are closer to evangelical churches than to the Roman Catholic church. This clinging to old customs provided in part the dynamics in large sections to withstand heroically the bitter persecutions by the Turks and the Bolshevists. Unfortunately, however, the Eastern churches do not go back sufficiently far, but base their doctrines and practices to a very large degree on traditions which arose after A. D. 200. This tenacious adherence to the old tends to rob the Christian faith of its really soteriological significance, and theology has been reduced to a mere body of fixed truth which the faithful are expected to accept intellectually. Eastern Orthodoxy places all emphasis on orthodoxy — right teaching — and on its corollary, right knowing.[10]

---

[7] Confession of Dositheus, Qu. 1.

[8] Ph. Schaff, Creeds, I, 43—73; II, 275—542; the Orthodox Confession, 1643; Confession of Dositheus, 1672; the Longer Catechism, 1839. — Philaret's Longer Catechism explains the manner in which "holy tradition" and Holy Scripture are said to be the source of religious knowledge (Qus. 16—61). The modern dogmaticians have not deviated materially from the position held for almost 1500 years. Cp. Gavin, pp. 17—25; 206—18; Sergius Bulgakoff, in Revelation, Ch. iv, presents the modern Orthodox position, which views revelation under the fourfold aspect of (1) holy tradition, (2) Holy Scripture, (3) authority of the church, (4) a continuous process.

[9] Gavin, pp. 42—53. On the papacy in particular, see Nicolas Afanassieff, Nicolas Koulomzine, Jean Meyendorff, and Alexandre Schmemann, La primauté de Pierre dans l'Église orthodoxe (Neuchâtel: Delachaux et Niestlé, c. 1960).

[10] Walther, pp. 36—41. Neve, Churches: "Rechtgläubigkeit" is more important than "Rechtgläubigkeit." — An Eastern Orthodox convert to the

The Material Principle

The material principle of Greek Orthodoxy, the central theological idea, may be summarized in the words of St. Athanasius: "Christ became man that we might become divine." In accord with its principle of adhering to the old, Eastern Orthodoxy follows the teachers of the second and third centuries who viewed Christ's work largely as *theopoiesis*, i. e., the ultimate deification of man. This is based on the Neoplatonic view of man's final destiny. The Eastern Orthodox Christians seek eternal life in a permanent rooting in the ultimate reality. They hold that in Christ a new divine principle has been implanted in human nature, and through the church this is imparted to all who are in Christ's mystical body. Man is therefore viewed as being incomplete rather than inherently sinful. Salvation is presented more as a vitalistic matter, a new life in Christ, than as deliverance from the penalties attaching to sin. The material principle of Eastern theology is that man is saved less *from* sin than *for* service to God; not from finitude which leads to sin, but for the infinity of God, who keeps man from sinning; in brief, salvation is the ennobling, the purification, the rebirth of man. This material principle is reflected both in the theology and in the cultus of the Eastern church.

SECTION III

Theological Emphases

In theology the material principle manifests itself in the Neoplatonic view of God and man; in the concept of Christ's work; in the peculiar significance of the church as the human side of Christ's life; in the sacraments, which are considered as the "medicine of immortality"; in the emphasis on the resurrection as a joyful experience.[11]

The Doctrine of God. The theology of Eastern epistemology is oriented much more in philosophical thought patterns than that of Western theology. This is evident in its approach to the doctrine of God.

Eastern theologians hold that the knowledge of God is by intuition, experience, and reason; and as such it is the common heritage of all men. But this is complemented by the revelation of God in Christ. Orthodox theologians marshal seven arguments for the existence of God and develop each in great detail: the cosmological, psychological, physioteleological, ethical, ontological, historical, apologetic.[12]

Eastern churches have always been champions of the Athanasian soteriological emphases — not the Augustinian metaphysical ones against the Unitarians — in the doctrine of the Trinity. Under the influence of the Neoplatonic

Roman Catholic church is not asked to abjure heresies, as must other converts. He is required only to make a profession of the "full faith," including both the "ancient" teachings and the later dogmas.

[11] Pittenger, p. 503. Unlike the Eastern and the Lutheran churches, Roman Catholicism through its emphasis on penance and purgatory leaves little room for joy.

[12] Gavin, pp. 61—80.

philosophy that God as the Absolute is the cause of everything, they view thé Father as the source of the Trinity. Against the charge of subordinationism the Orthodox theologians maintain that the Father is the only source and cause, the Son and Spirit the effects of this cause or principle. The Greek Orthodox theologians oppose the procession of the Holy Spirit from the Father and the Son (Filioque), not only because it was added to the Constantinopolitan Creed of 381 as late as 589 but also because it is contrary to their concept of the Father. They admit that the Spirit proceeds *through* — but not *from* — the Son.[13]

The Doctrine of Man. Elements of Neoplatonic philosophy are clearly discernible in the entire doctrine of creation and of man in particular. The cosmos is said to be dual, consisting of the visible and the invisible. Man likewise is a mixture, in whom spiritual and material forces are united, and in the union of his rational soul and his material body man is viewed as a microcosm, the capstone and end of the material creation. According to his body he belongs to the physical order; and according to his soul, or spirit, he belongs to the spiritual order. This view has several significant theological implications: (1) The prevalent view concerning the

origin of man is creationism.[14] (2) Since the body is considered far inferior to the soul, in reality a prison house of the soul, Greek Orthodoxy views man's salvation primarily as the soul's gradual liberation from the body and its return to God by a process of mystical union.[15] (3) Like Rome, Eastern Orthodoxy distinguishes between the image of God and the likeness, or similitude, of God. The former is said to consist in the sum total of the powers which were given to man at his creation, and the latter in a potential or future perfection which becomes a reality only when man correctly exercises his created and native powers. In his fall man lost the likeness, but not the image. (4) This means that Eastern Orthodoxy maintains man's natural ability to do good and denies his total depravity.[16]

Original sin is described negatively as the loss of original righteousness and positively as an injury to man's spiritual and ethical nature. Original sin is man's guilt; he somehow sinned with Adam and must make reparation for this sin.

The Person and Work of Christ. In describing the theanthropic person of Christ the Eastern church uses the terminology which the church has employed in the various Christological controversies. The Eastern church is in agreement with the dogmatical formula-

13 In support of this assertion the Eastern theologians refer to John 15: 26, 27, but they ignore such references as John 14:26; 16:7; Gal. 4:6; Rom. 8:9. — Cp. Gavin, pp. 124—33. Walther, pp. 7, 8. Neve, p. 56 f. In the Bonn conferences of 1874 and 1875 the Anglican church made concessions to Eastern theology in defining the Filioque. Schaff, *Creeds,* I, 77 f.; II, 545—54.

14 *Orthodox Conf.,* Qu. 28. However, some maintain that the soul is the result of both divine and human activity and support both creationism and traducianism. Gavin, p. 161.

15 In this view Eastern Orthodoxy has maintained the soteriology of ancient church Fathers, especially of Irenaeus, also Augustine, in his famous phrase *per illum* [Christ, the man] *ad illum* [Christ in glory]. Cp. J. L. Neve, *History of Christian Thought,* I, 80 f.

16 *Orthodox Conf.,* Qu. 27. *Conf. of Dositheus, Decretum* XIV. Cp. Gavin, p. 161 ff.

tions used by the Creed of Chalcedon to express the personal union.

The work of Christ is presented in various ways. The Neoplatonic principle manifests itself in the view that the sincere acceptance of Christ's doctrine becomes the seed of immortality. Neoplatonism becomes evident especially in the so-called *anakephalaiosis*, or recapitulation, theory, which holds that Adam is by nature the head of the human race and responsible for its depravity, but that Christ has graciously made Himself the new Head of mankind.[17] Some lean toward the Origenian theology that our Lord's death is chiefly man's redemption from the power of the devil. The majority of Greek dogmaticians speak of the work of Christ under the threefold office of Prophet, Priest, and King. In His priestly office Christ is said obediently to have taken our nature and by this act of obedience to have compensated for man's guilt; and by His death He is said to have counterbalanced our eternal death. According to this view, the work of Christ is primarily the act of propitiation. This was accomplished objectively when Christ died; and subjectively it is accomplished when the grace of God flows from the Cross and each man dies to sin and follows the example of Christ's life. Only he who strives and conquers in this struggle by following Christ's example and using his free will is said to be redeemed, justified, sanctified, and saved. The death of Christ has removed every obstacle for the rehabilitation of man and opened the way of salvation and eternal life. But since man has fallen into the depths of destruction and

is unable to raise himself, he stands in need of divine assistance.[18]

In the main it is true that Eastern Orthodoxy has tenaciously adhered to the theological formulations of the Ancient Church. Nevertheless, Eastern theologians did not escape entirely the impact of the 16th-century Reformation. There has been a slight modification or shift of emphasis in theological orientation, noticeable especially in the areas of grace, the church, the sacraments. The antitheses to Roman, Lutheran, and Calvinistic theology are quite sharply drawn.

Salvation by Grace. "Grace" has become more central in Oriental thinking since the Reformation. It is used to denote God's essential goodness, which prompts Him to give man all he needs for reinstatement into his original state of righteousness. The concept may also denote the divine power by which man appropriates the redemptive work of Christ. This "grace," or the divine saving energy, is given to the church and distributed through the Sacraments so that man may cultivate the life in Christ and prepare himself for eternal life. According to modern Orthodox dogmaticians, grace is, properly speaking, a process in the development of the individual life covering the following states: conversion, regeneration, justification, sanctification, and the mystical union. In direct opposition to the Lutheran and Calvinistic concept of justification as a forensic act, the Greek theologians define justification as an actual change in man and place the chief emphasis upon the continuous sanctification. Justification is said to

[17] *Longer C.*, Qus. 196, 197, 208, 212.

[18] Cp. Gavin, p. 202. — Eastern theologians specifically reject the Roman doctrine that Christ has gained "superabundant satisfactions" and that the sacrifice of the cross requires constant repetition. They hold that the sacrifice of the cross is indeed repeated in the sacrifice of the Eucharist; however, not to make propitiation, but to make intercession for man. Gavin, p. 196.

remain "potential," and not to become "actual," until the final completion in the mystical union with God.[19]

The Doctrine of the Church. Since the Reformation the Eastern dogmaticians have formulated their doctrine of the church in sharp antithesis to Rome and especially to Lutheranism, stating expressly that the Lutheran definition of the church as the communion of saints reduces the church to a Platonic idea. They say that the church is both visible and invisible: visible, because her Founder became incarnate and visible, because she ministers the grace of God under visible signs, because she is outwardly united in one faith, because she has a visible organization, and because her members are visible men. The church is invisible, because she is the bearer of divine gifts and is engaged in transforming mankind into the kingdom of God. The union of Christ's two natures — visible and invisible — is said to be analogous to the holy union in the church between the divine, life-giving principle and its human, external manifestation.

Orthodox theologians maintain that only the Eastern church has remained faithful to the ancient ecumenical councils, that therefore it alone represents the true and infallible catholic church of Christ, and that outside this church there is, strictly speaking, no salvation.[20]

The ecclesiastical office is considered necessary as the means to administer the grace of God. The Roman Catholic theory of the ministry as an office of jurisdiction is rejected; likewise the primacy of one bishop over all others. The apostolic succession is considered to be of the very *esse* of the church.[21] There are four minor orders and three orders of the ministry: deacon, priest, bishop. Celibacy is restricted to the members of religious orders. The second marriage of priests is not forbidden, but disqualifies from the administration of the sacraments.

The Sacraments. English-speaking Orthodox theologians prefer the term "mystery" to "sacrament." Orthodox theology holds that through these "mysteries" God enters into the world to transform it and specifically enters into

19 Cp. Gavin, pp. 219—32. *Orthodox Conf.,* Qu. 1: "What must an Orthodox Christian man believe to obtain eternal life? Answer: The right faith and good works." The *Conf. of Dositheus, Decretum IX, XIII,* states that faith active in good works justifies. This is the Roman *fides per caritatem formata.* The third part of the *Orthodox C.* is devoted to the "union between faith and love" and discusses in detail the Law and the Commandments. Cp. Schaff, *Creeds,* II, 519—42. The distinction between "potential" justification — God pronounces a man just in view of what he will become — and "actual" justification — man by his own free will actually attains the righteousness before God — is said to do justice to Paul's doctrine of "potential" and James' presentation of "actual" justification.

20 See *Longer C.,* Qus. 252, 261, 272, 274. The encyclicals of 1848 and 1902, likewise the Synod of 1872, state that the Orthodox Churches of the East alone constitute the Holy Apostolic Church, the pillar and ground of truth. Gavin, p. 253. This doctrinal position seems to make it impossible for the Eastern church to take part in the ecumenical movement. Ancient and modern decisions declare that only the Orthodox church can consider herself as the whole and only catholic church and that acceptance of her entire teachings and her sacraments is essential to unity of doctrine. Patriarch Athenagoras, *Ecumenical Review,* January, 1953, p. 165 f., lists the reasons why Orthodox churches should participate in the ecumenical movement as well as the conditions under which these churches can participate.

21 *Conf. of Dositheus, Decretum X, XII.*

men to make them divine. In the mystery of the incarnation, God not only entered the world in the one event, but also continues this process in the church through the sacraments.[22] The sacraments are defined as rites instituted by Christ to convey through visible signs invisibly the grace of God and bring to men the regenerating, justifying, and sanctifying grace. The Lord Himself instituted the seven sacraments: Baptism, the Eucharist, Chrism, Penance, Orders, Marriage, and Unction, the first two personally, the others mediately through the apostles. The sacraments are said to be necessary to salvation. The argument runs as follows: Grace, absolutely necessary to salvation, is conveyed only through the sacraments, each sacrament having a specific sacramental virtue for man's seven defects. Therefore each must use those sacraments which are necessary for him, and failure to use them means loss of salvation.[23] The opinions vary whether all sacraments, or only some, or only Baptism, implant an indelible character. Rome's often exaggerated sacerdotalism is not accepted in Eastern Orthodoxy, and the lofty concept of the minister of the sacrament prevalent in Roman Catholicism is not present in the Orthodox church. Christ is considered the real Minister, while the priest is the instrument through which the proper outward sign is performed. However, the Eastern church shares with the Roman church the belief that the priest must have the interior intention to do what the church has prescribed. The *ex opere operato* theory is not prominent.

Baptism is performed by trine — triple — immersion. It is said to convey the forgiveness of sins not only negatively by the removal of sin and its guilt and punishment but also positively by effecting the regeneration and justification of the soul. Baptism restores man to his original righteousness. Orthodoxy maintains that the lust, or concupiscence, which remains in the baptized, is not sinful and remains without spiritual damage, even as pain and death remain in the baptized.[24] The sacrament of Chrism, or Holy Anointing, or Confirmation, is said to complete baptism and is administered immediately after baptism.

The Eucharist is viewed both as a sacrament and as a sacrifice. Until the Reformation period various views concerning the real presence of the body and blood of Christ were entertained, and agreement seems to exist only in the use of the term *metousiōsis*. No attempt is made to explain the mystery of the change which takes place.[25]

Unlike the Roman Catholic church, the Eastern church celebrates the Eucharist under both kinds. The elements are distributed by intinction, i. e., the particles of consecrated bread, dipped into the consecrated wine, are administered to the communicants. On the assumption that according to John 18:28 Christ instituted the Lord's Supper on the 13th of Nisan rather than on the 14th the Eastern church uses leavened bread.[26] As a sacrament the Eucharist is said to be necessary to salvation; therefore also infants are admitted to the Lord's Supper. As a sacrifice it is viewed as a continuation of the sacrifice

---

[22] George P. Michaelides, pp. 96—107.

[23] Gavin, pp. 277, 303. *Longer C.*, Qu. 286.

[24] *Orthodox Conf., Quaestio CIII.* Gavin, p. 310 f. The Eastern church knows of no "baptism of desire," as does the Roman Catholic church.

[25] *Longer C.*, Qu. 340.

[26] A. Edersheim, *Life and Times of Jesus, the Messiah* (Grand Rapids: Eerdmans) II, 481 ff. J. W. Ylvisaker, *The Gospels* (Minneapolis: Augsburg Publ. House, 1932), pp. 636—646.

on the cross. In the Eucharist, Christ as Priest and Victim offers to the Father His body and blood under the forms of bread and wine.[27]

The essential parts of the sacrament of Penance are said to be contrition, confession, punishment, and in this respect the Eastern church is in virtual agreement with Rome. However, it rejects the Roman view which makes the priest the judge with power to impose "punishments" and to grant indulgences.

Holy orders is the sacrament in which the Holy Ghost, through the imposition of the Bishop's hands, ordains men to administer the sacraments and to instruct the people in faith and piety. Much is made of the "apostolic succession." [28]

Holy Unction is a sacrament in which the body of the sick is anointed with oil and the grace of God is invoked for the healing of bodily and spiritual infirmities. Unlike Rome, the Eastern church does not practice Holy Unction in preparation for death, but primarily for healing.

Matrimony is included among the sacraments, or "mysteries," because Eph. 5:31 f. uses the term "mystery" in describing the union of Christ and His church. The marriage may be dissolved in case of adultery, treason, and apostasy. Mixed marriages are discouraged.[29]

Eschatology. Eastern theology distinguishes between the particular and the general judgment. The former occurs at the time of death, when the soul of the faithful enters "paradise," or "Abraham's bosom," and the soul of the unbeliever enters Hades, "outer darkness," or "eternal fire." Orthodoxy rejects the theory of purgatory for the cleansing of the soul, because no sacraments are available in the intermediate state. The Orthodox theologians maintain that there are various degrees of reward and that prior to the general judgment the soul will be assigned to a degree of bliss corresponding to its merits. Prayers for the dead are retained because of the antiquity of this custom. In the final judgment all righteous souls will be eternally blessed in fullest measure and the unrighteous consigned to the full punishment.

The Cultus. The material principle — the sacraments implant the divine life — comes to the surface particularly in the cultus. At first glance the folk piety of Eastern Orthodoxy seems to be no more than mere formalism and dead ritualism. However, it must be kept in mind that — in every form of service and in all the mysteries (sacraments), in the liturgy, in the sacramentals, in the worship of relics and icons — the one purpose is to effect the mystical union between the believer and God. In its thinking the Eastern mind holds that the goal of man's life is the union with the Deity. The establishment of this union is said to require a visible and tangible means to lift man up to the Deity. Thus every form of the liturgy, every part of the service, is viewed as having a sanctifying purpose.[30]

---

[27] *Orthodox Conf., Quaestio CVII, Conf. of Dositheus, Decretum XVII.* Longer C., Qus. 315—50; Gavin, p. 347.

[28] *Conf. of Dositheus, Decretum X. Longer C.,* Qus. 357—60. Kokkinakis, pp. 91—178.

[29] Kokkinakis, pp. 23—90.

[30] To the Western mind many of the ceremonies observed by the Eastern Orthodox Christians seem to border on superstition. It is not uncommon that worshipers depart when their spiritual needs have been met by the emotional reaction. When ecclesiastical wedding ceremonies or funerals became highly dangerous in Russia, the faithful would secretly

The "holy liturgy" is in reality a religious drama in which the entire plan of salvation is dramatized by the priest and the choir. In the Eastern liturgy the resurrection of Christ constitutes the climax and culmination of the entire service. The Passion of Christ is portrayed when the consecrated elements are carried about in the church and deposited on the altar, which in this portion of the liturgy is viewed as Christ's burial place. But immediately after this the altar is made the symbol of the empty tomb. The dramatization of the resurrection is designed to be a truly joyous experience. This is followed by the distribution of the elements to the congregation.[31] In order to carry out the drama of the death, resurrection, and ascension of Christ, the sanctuary of the typical Eastern Orthodox church contains two compartments. In the section closest to the congregation are pews for the singers. Immediately next to this section is the altar space. Between the two sections is the iconostasis, a partition with three openings allowing for four panels each with an icon: the icon of

the local saint, of Mary, of Jesus, and of Joseph respectively. The center opening brings the altar *(bēma)*, or the "holy of holies," into view, where the priest performs the rites to symbolize the work of Christ.[32]

The veneration of icons is also considered essential for effecting the mystical union with God.[33] As the holy liturgy makes the invisible Christ tangible, so the icons bring the worshiper into the closest association not only with Christ, but especially with those who were closest to Christ, His "immaculate" mother, Joseph, and the other saints. The prototype is said to be truly present in the icon, provided it has been painted in conformity with the ancient rules. The faithful adorn their homes with icons, and in venerating them they are instructed to kiss the icon (the feet of Christ's icon, the hands of Mary's, the face of others) and to burn candles and incense before them. Like Rome, the Eastern church distinguishes between *latreia* (the worship of God) and *douleia (hyperdouleia)*, the veneration of saints.[34]

have the wedding rings blessed in lieu of an ecclesiastical ceremony and a handful of dirt consecrated for the committal service. — In a state of complete physical relaxation, brought about by proper breathing, the Neptic Fathers assert that they can effect a recollection *(nepsis)*. In this state they chant incessantly: "Lord Jesus Christ, have mercy"; and in this way their spirit is said to free itself from any attacks of the enemy and to succeed in rising day after day to the love and desire of God. In this condition the neptic is said to experience incredible joys and triumphs. See Attwater, pp. 71—73.

31 *Longer C.*, Qus. 315—50.

32 Cp. Walther, pp. 26—28; 41—44.

33 The Eastern church maintains that graven images are idols and their worship is forbidden in the Decalog. But icons or painted surfaces are said to be typified by the sacred representations of the cherubim. *Longer C.*, Qus. 516—22.

34 Walther, pp. 28—30.

SECTION IV

The Eastern Orthodox Bodies in America

The Eastern Orthodox church is represented in Europe and Asia by four ancient patriarchates: (1) Constantinople, with jurisdiction over Turkey; (2) Alexandria, over Egypt; (3) Antioch, over Syria, except Palestine, Galatia, and Mesopotamia; (4) Jerusalem, over Jerusalem and Palestine. A number of modern patriarchates have also been created. Each patriarchate is autonomous, and although the Patriarch of Constantinople bears the style of Ecumenical Patriarch, each of the patriarchs is sovereign in his jurisdiction.

There are a number of autocephalous national churches, such as those of Greece, Albania, Bulgaria, Cyprus, Romania, the Soviet Union, and Yugoslavia. Practically all the European and Asiatic sections of the Orthodox church are represented by branches in the United States. There are about a dozen separate organizations of the Orthodox church, some of them under the jurisdiction of the church in their homeland to some extent, others completely autonomous.

The Albanian Orthodox Diocese in America. Organized in 1908, this church is completely self-governing under its own bishop, whose see city is Boston.

The Bulgarian Eastern Orthodox Church traces its history back to 1907, when the first church was built in Madison, Ill. The Holy Synod of Bulgaria erected a bishopric in New York in 1938. It is now a metropolitical see, whose incumbent exercises jurisdiction over all the Bulgarian Orthodox Christians of this hemisphere and Australia. In 1945 full communion was restored between the Bulgarian Orthodox Church and the Ecumenical Patriarch, who had excommunicated the Bulgars in 1872.

The American Carpatho-Russian Orthodox Greek Catholic Church has only one diocese. The see city is Johnstown, Pa. In 1886 extensive immigration of Roman Catholics of the Greek rite from Central Europe began to take place. About five years later many of these immigrants started to return to the Orthodox obedience of their fathers. By 1936 this tide had achieved such proportions that a diocese could be organized; it received canonical recognition in 1938, when the Ecumenical Patriarch consecrated its first bishop in Istanbul.

The Romanian Orthodox Episcopate of America has Detroit as its see city and includes parishes in Canada as well as in the United States. The first parishes in North America were organized in 1901. From 1911 on repeated efforts were made to organize an American diocese, but the Patriarch of Romania consecrated no bishop for his American subjects until 1935. The political complications introduced by World War II and its aftermath resulted in the assertion by the American diocese of its autonomy.

The Serbian Eastern Orthodox Church grew out of the immigration that began around 1890 and that led to the founding of St. Sava's Church in Jackson, Calif., in 1894. The Patriarch of Serbia consecrated the first bishop for the American diocese in 1926. His see city is New York.

The Syrian Antiochian Orthodox Church came into existence through two American missions to immigrants from the jurisdiction of the Orthodox Patriarch of Antioch, the Syrian mission of the Russian Orthodox Church (founded in 1902) and the mission of the Patriarchate of Antioch in 1914. Since 1936 all of the Syrian Orthodox parishes have had a single bishop, who in 1940 was elevated to the rank of Metropolitan Archbishop of New York and All North America and whose jurisdiction extends from Canada to Mexico.

There are three Ukrainian Orthodox bodies in the United States. The *Ukrainian Orthodox Church of the U. S. A.* was formally organized in 1919. It consisted at first both of Ukrainian Orthodox immigrants and of former Roman Catholic Uniate Ukrainians. The metropolitan resides in South Bound Brook, New Jersey. *The Ukrainian Orthodox Church of America under the Ecumenical Patriarch* is governed immediately by a metropolitan-primate who is technically a suffragan of the Greek Archbishop of North and South America and whose see city is New York. *The Holy Ukrainian Autocephalic Orthodox Church in Exile* was organized in 1954 by refugee bishops, clergy, and people; it has its headquarters in New York. The metropolitical see of the *Independent Ukrainian Orthodox Church in Canada* is in Winnipeg, Manitoba.

The two largest Eastern Orthodox communities in this hemisphere are the Greek and the Russian.

The first parish of what is now called the *Greek Archdiocese of North and South America,* the archbishop of which has his see in New York, was founded in New Orleans in 1866. From 1908 to 1922 the Greek parishes in this country were technically under the jurisdiction of the Holy Synod of Athens, but in the latter year the Ecumenical Patriarch asserted direct jurisdiction; the conflict between the two was finally composed in 1930, when the Greek Archbishop of North and South America was given hemispheric jurisdiction under the Ecumenical Patriarch.

The Russian Orthodox Greek Catholic Church of America has been in the Western Hemisphere since the colonization of Alaska in the eighteenth century, and Sitka became the see city of the first Orthodox diocese erected on this continent. In 1871 diocesan headquarters were transferred to San Francisco and in 1901 to New York. In 1903 it became an archdiocese with jurisdiction over all North America. The first Sobor (general council) was held at Pittsburgh in 1919; at the second Sobor, held in Detroit in 1924, the American jurisdiction asserted its autonomy. In addition to the large Russian church, there are several smaller bodies: *The Russian Orthodox Church Outside Russia,* with headquarters in New York; the *Russian Orthodox Catholic Church, Archdiocese of the Aleutian Islands and North America,* loyal to the Holy Synod of Moscow; and an American branch of the *Estonian Orthodox Church in Exile,* administered by an archpriest. All three have their headquarters in New York.

There are a number of small church bodies that profess to be Orthodox but are not recognized by the authentic Eastern Orthodox churches. Frank Mead has called them "autogenic (self-starting)" churches in distinction to the autonomous and autocephalous churches of historic Orthodoxy. They include the *American Orthodox Church,* the *Apostolic Episcopal Church,* the *Holy Orthodox Church in America (Eastern Catholic and Apostolic),* and the *Syrian Orthodox Church of Antioch (Archdiocese of the U. S. A. and Canada).*

SECTION V

The Separated Far Eastern Churches

There were a number of schisms in the early church, dating chiefly from the era of the Christological controversies. Some of these still survive, among them the "Assyrian" (sometimes miscalled "Nestorian") church, which stressed vehemently the two natures of our Lord and was widely accused of teaching that there are in Christ two persons; and, at the opposite theological extreme, the Monophysite churches (which assert that in our Lord there is but one nature, or *physis*), namely, the Armenian church, the Syrian Jacobites (including the — originally Assyrian — Christians of St. Thomas on the Malabar Coast of India), the Coptic church of Egypt, and the church of Abyssinia. Although they may use the term "Orthodox" in their titles, they are not in communion with the Ecumenical Patriarch.

Legitimate representatives of these ancient "schismatic" churches in America are:

The Church of the East and of the Assyrians. A few thousand members of this church live in this country, chiefly in Connecticut, Philadelphia, Chicago, and Michigan. The Catholicos of the whole church, whose see was at Kudshanes prior to World War I, resides in Turlock, California. The close contact between Anglicans and the Assyrians since 1886 is reflected in the extensive use by the Assyrians of Protestant Episcopal churches for their services. Technically they accept only the first two ecumenical councils, and they refuse the title "Mother of God" to the Virgin

Mary, although they teach that from the first moment of His conception our Lord was both perfect man and perfect God. Their sacramental theory is less developed than that of other Eastern bodies.

The Assyrian Orthodox Church is the North American branch (established in 1907) of the Syrian Jacobite Patriarchate of Antioch. The archbishop resides at Central Falls, R. I. The faith of the church is expressed in the Eastern version of the "Nicene" Creed. It counts seven sacraments; administers Holy Baptism by pouring or immersion; believes that the bread and wine in the Holy Eucharist are the body and blood of Christ; and venerates the blessed Virgin Mary and the saints.

The Armenian Apostolic Orthodox Church in America is the American province of the church of Armenia. The archbishop, who resides in New York, is under the spiritual jurisdiction of the Catholicos of Echmiadzin, Armenia. His (arch)diocese covers all of the United States except California, which is a separate diocese. Like other Monophysite churches, the Armenian church denies the two natures in our Lord, rejects the decrees of the Council of Chalcedon and subsequent councils, counts seven sacraments, and requires all candidates for holy orders to be elected by the people.[35]

A number of heads of small church bodies claim to derive their orders from Far Eastern sources, usually through Joseph Réné Vilatte, who claimed to

---

[35] See Karekin Sarkissian, "The Ecumenical Problem in Eastern Christendom," *Ecumenical Review*, XII (1959/1960), 436—454.

have been consecrated as "Archbishop of North America" in 1892 by Julius Alvares, who called himself Archbishop of the Independent Catholic Church of Goa and Ceylon and who had been consecrated by the Syrian Antiochene Bishop of Kottayam, India, in 1889. These bodies — none of which have been acknowledged by the authentic separated Far Eastern prelates — include the "Old Catholic" *American Catholic Church, Archdiocese of New York,* the *African Orthodox Church* (organized in 1921 to provide Negro Episcopalians with churches of their own), the *American Holy Orthodox Catholic Apostolic Eastern Church* (affiliated with *The Orthodox Catholic Patriarchate of America*), and the *American Catholic Church (Syro-antiochean).*

BIBLIOGRAPHY

PART I   SECTIONS I—V

Alivisatos, Hamilcar S. "Church, State, and Society — An Orthodox View," *Lutheran World,* VI (1959), 148—152.

Anderson, Paul. *People, Church, and State in Modern Russia.* New York: The Macmillan Co., 1944.

Attwater, Donald. *The Dissident Eastern Churches.* Milwaukee: Bruce Publishing Co., 1937.

Benz, Ernst. *Geist und Leben der Ostkirche.* Hamburg: Rowohlt, 1957.

————. *Die Ostkirche im Lichte der protestantischen Geschichtschreibung von der Reformation bis zur Gegenwart.* Freiburg: Verlag Karl Alber, 1952.

Brandreth, Henry R. T. *Episcopi Vagantes and the Anglican Church.* London: Society for Promoting Christian Knowledge, 1947.

Bratsiotis, Panagiotis, ed. *Die orthodoxe Kirche in griechischer Sicht.* Stuttgart: Evangelisches Verlagswerk, 1959—1960. 2 vols.

Bulgakoff, Sergius, in John Baillie and Hugh Martin, eds., *Revelation.* New York: The Macmillan Co., 1937. Pp. 125—180.

————. *The Wisdom of God.* New York: Paisley Press, Inc., 1938.

Callinicos, Constantine N. *The Greek Orthodox Catechism.* New York: Greek Archdiocese of North and South America, 1953.

Evdokimov, Paul. *L'Orthodoxie.* Paris: Delachaux et Niestlé. 1959.

Florovsky, Georges. "The Legacy and Task of Orthodox Theology," *Anglican Theological Review,* XXXI (1949).

Gavin, Frank. *Some Aspects of Contemporary Greek Orthodox Thought.* (The 1922 Hale Lectures.) New York: Morehouse Publishing Co., 1923.

Hadjiantoniou, George A. *Protestant Patriarch: The Life of Cyril Lucaris (1572—1638), Patriarch of Constantinople.* Richmond, Va.: John Knox Press, c. 1961.

Hromadka, Joseph L. "Civilization's Doom and Resurrection," *Theology Today,* I (1944).

Horton, W. *Continental European Theology.* New York: Harper & Bros., 1938. "The Rediscovery of Orthodox Theology," ch. iv.

Janin, Réné. *The Separated Eastern Churches.* St. Louis: Herder, 1933.

Klostermann, R. A. *Probleme der Ostkirche: Untersuchungen zum Wesen und zur Geschichte der griechisch-orthodoxen Kirche.* Göteborg: Elanders Boktryckeri, 1955.

Kokkinakis, Athenagoras. *Parents and Priests as Servants of Redemption: An Interpretation of the Doctrines of the Eastern Orthodox Church on the Sacraments of Matrimony and Priesthood.* New York: Morehouse-Gorham Co., 1958.

Lloyd, Roger. *The Church of England in the Twentieth Century.* New York: Longmans, Green & Co., 1950.

Lossky, Vladimir. *The Mystical Theology of the Eastern Church.* London: James Clarke and Co., 1957.

Manning, C. "Khomyakov and the Orthodox Church," *Review of Religion,* January, 1942.

Michaelides, G. P. "Sacraments from the Eastern Orthodox Point of View," *Christendom,* Winter, 1941.

Nassar, Seraphim, ed. *Book of Divine Prayers and Services of the Catholic Apostolic Church of Christ.* New York: The Blackshaw Press, 1938.

Neve, J. L. *Churches and Sects of Christendom.* Blair, Nebr.: Lutheran Publishing House, 1944.

Pittenger, W. N. "The Spirit of Eastern Orthodoxy," *Christendom,* Autumn, 1943.

Schaff, Philip. *Creeds of Christendom,* New York: Harper & Bros., 1919.

Schlink, Edmund. "Changes in Protestant Thinking about the Eastern Church," *Ecumenical Review,* X (1957/1958), 386 to 400.

————. "The Significance of the Eastern and Western Traditions for the Christian Church," *Ecumenical Review,* XII (1959 and 1960), 133—153.

Soroka, Leonid, (Dean) Umw, and Stan W. Carlson. *Faith of Our Fathers: The Eastern Orthodox Religion.* Minneapolis: The Olympic Press, 1954.

Spinka, Matthew. *The Church and the Russian Revolution.* New York: The Macmillan Co., 1927.

————. *The Church in Soviet Russia.* New York: Oxford University Press, 1956.

Timasheff, N. S. *Religion in Soviet Russia.* New York: Sheed and Ward, 1942.

Walther, Wilhelm. *Lehrbuch der Symbolik.* Leipzig, Erlangen: Deichertsche Buchhandlung, W. Scholl, 1924.

PART TWO

The Holy Catholic Apostolic Roman Church

SECTION I
Introductory Overview

Dogmatico-Historical Survey

The Holy Catholic Apostolic Roman Church is that branch of Christendom which "recognizes the bishop of Rome as pope, vicar of Christ on earth, and the visible head of the church."[1] Though this church is vulgarly called the Catholic church, the proper designation is the Roman church, because according to the Tridentine Profession of Pius IV all its teachers must pledge true obedience to the pope as the bishop of Rome. The dominant characteristic of this church can best be stated as unconditional obedience to the hierarchy and through them to the pope. The hierarchical tendencies of the Roman church manifested themselves at a very early period. The Anglican scholar Lightfoot saw in the First Epistle of Clement (96) "the first step toward papal domination." Victor of Rome (190) excommunicated the Asiatic churches for keeping Easter on a date different from that of Rome. Innocent I (417) claimed authority for his see to decide on doubtful matters for the whole church.[2] The "father of the medieval Papacy," Gregory the Great (d. 604), viewed the church as *civitas Dei*, a temporal state in which the hierarchy controls all areas of human life, and he succeeded in embodying the claim of the supremacy of the Roman bishop in the church's dogma. Rome's hierarchical pretensions were pronounced in their most complete form by Gregory VII (1077), later by Boniface VIII in the bull *Unam sanctam* (1302), in which the pope claimed to be the source of all spiritual and secular authority, and finally by Pius IX in the bull *Pastor aeternus* (1870), which explicitly demands unconditional obedience to the pope's pronouncements *ex cathedra*.[3] For more than fifteen centuries the bishop of Rome has claimed supremacy for himself and his see, and there is

NOTE: For key to abbreviations see Appendix C; for Bibliography, the end of this Part.

[1] *Census of Religious Bodies* (Washington, D. C.: U. S. Gov't Printing Office, 1936) II, 1542. The statement was prepared for the Department of Commerce by the Rt. Rev. Msgr. Michael J. Ready. The official name of the pope is His Holiness the Pope, Bishop of Rome and Vicar of Jesus Christ, Successor of St. Peter, Prince of the Apostles, Supreme Pontiff of the Universal Church, Patriarch of the West, Primate of Italy, Archbishop and Metropolitan of the Roman Province, Sovereign of the Temporal Dominions of the Holy Roman Church and Sovereign of Vatican City.

[2] E. Giles, ed., *Documents Illustrating Papal Authority A. D. 96—454* (London: Society for Promoting Christian Knowledge, 1952), pp. 1—3, 14—19, 201—203. J. L. Neve, *History*, I, 71—75. A. L. Graebner, "Die Anfänge des Papsttums," *Lehre und Wehre*, St. Louis, XXVIII (1892), 365—70.

[3] Cp. Adolf Harnack, *Lehrbuch der Dogmengeschichte* (Freiburg, 1890) III, 127—51; 405.

25

no appreciable difference between the fifth and the twentieth century in Rome's dominant characteristic.

This fixed attitude is clearly seen also in Rome's doctrinal system. At the conclusion of the sixth century, Gregory systematized and popularized the various doctrines and practices which were introduced into the church during the many controversies of the preceding four centuries: authority of the traditions, Semi-Pelagianism, justification ' by infused grace, satisfactions, meritoriousness of works, the church as a visible organization, the hierarchical system, the sacrificial character of the Mass, monasticism, veneration of saints, purgatory.[4] The later increasingly rigid enforcement of clerical celibacy and the sale of indulgences, obligatory auricular confession and transubstantiation (1215), withholding of the cup (1414), the further development of the penitential system, the Mary cult, and monasticism did not materially change the basic theological principles of Roman theology. Nor did the schoolmen from the tenth to the fifteenth century inaugurate any radical departures from the theology current in the Roman church since Gregory. All scholastics started with the premise that the teachings of the church are divinely revealed and therefore true. But they held that not only "divine revelation" but also reason is a divine gift and that faith and reason are two paths which must lead to the same goal, namely, the beatific vision of God. The schoolmen therefore sought to combine Aristotelian metaphysics and Christian theology, though the individual leaders were poles apart in their theological orientation (Anselm: *credo ut intelligam,* and Abelard: *intelligo ut credam*), and though there was great theological rivalry and dissension among the various orders, all schoolmen were determined to validate the teachings of the church by keen logical argumentation.[5]

In the sixteenth century the Council of Trent (1545—63) summarized the basic theological tenets of Rome in direct opposition to the Lutheran Reformation and in part to Calvinistic theology. Because of the basic theological differences between Thomists and Scotists this council failed to speak with finality on many important doctrines. Nevertheless it was agreed in condemning summarily the Lutheran *sola gratia* and *sola fide* and in declaring in unmistakable terms its own chief doctrines, such as justification by infused grace, sacramentalism, sacerdotalism. At the same time Rome closed her ranks and with a united front took measures not only to stop the spread of the evangelical message but also to regain lost territory. The newly organized Society of Jesus became the chief instrument in carrying through the Counter Reformation according to the decrees of the Council of Trent. This was done so effectively that with but very slight modifications the decrees of this council are still in effect today.[6] This fact has become evident in subsequent theological controversies within the church, particularly in the Jansenist controversy. The

[4] H. H. Howarth, *Gregory the Great* (New York: E. P. Dutton & Co., 1912).

[5] Cp. R. Seeberg, *Lehrbuch der Dogmengeschichte,* 4th ed. (Leipzig: A. Deichert, 1920), III, chs. iii—v. *Cath. Encyc.,* s. v. "Scholasticism."

[6] B. J. Kidd, *The Counter Reformation 1550—1600.* (London: S. P. C. K., 1933). See also the definitive, multivolume work of Hubert Jedin, *A History of the Council of Trent,* trans. Ernest Graf (St. Louis: B. Herder Book Co., 1957—), and his *Papal Legate at the Council of Trent: Cardinal Seripando,* trans. Frederick C. Eckhoff (St. Louis: B. Herder Book Co., 1957).

bull *Unigenitus* (1713) settled this controversy by condemning 101 statements of the Jansenist Quesnel, some of which were Biblical and others Augustinian.[7] Toward the end of the nineteenth century several French theologians, especially Alfred Loisy (d. 1941), submitted the theological claims of the papacy to a radical criticism. This liberal movement, known as Modernism, was condemned by Pius X in the bull *Pascendi dominici gregis* (1907) as the "synthesis of all heresies." [8]

Through the long centuries the Roman pontiff has claimed absolute authority in the spiritual and secular realms.[9] True, Rome's authority in the secular realm has been seriously challenged, especially in Europe. In 1870, the year in which the pope declared his infallibility, the secular power of Rome came to an end in Italy. It was partly restored by the Concordat of 1929, which recognized the Vatican City as an independent state. In 1906 church and state were separated in France, and all church property was declared to be property of the state. In the subsequent decades the membership of the Roman Catholic church in France has dwindled considerably. In Spain the entire property of the church was nationalized in 1933; also in Mexico the temporal prestige of the Roman Catholic clergy has suffered irreparable damage. In 1948 the political influence of the Roman hierarchy in the Balkan States, especially through the so-called Uniate churches, was checked by the Communists.

While Rome has suffered a contraction of its political powers, it has expanded its spiritual pretensions. At present there are especially two movements in Romanism which are designed to spread the spiritual and moral influence of Rome in areas outside its own fold: Catholic Action and Neo-Thomism.

CATHOLIC ACTION

Pius XI defined Catholic Action:[10] "The part taken by the Catholic laity in the apostolic mission of the church with

---

[7] This infamous bull condemns, among other Jansenist teachings, the statements that the reading of the Bible is for all, that without grace the will is capable of everything evil and incapable of anything good, and that the first grace that God gives to a sinner is forgiveness. See Schaff, *Creeds*, I, 105—107.

[8] E. R. Hardy, "Liberalism and Catholic Thought in England, 1860 to 1940." Van Dusen and Roberts, *Liberal Theology, an Appraisal* (New York: Scribner's, 1942).

Johannes Kübel, *Geschichte des katholischen Modernismus* (Tübingen: Mohr Verlag, 1909). *Der Katholizismus, sein Stirb und Werde*, ed. Gustav Mensching (Leipzig: Hinrichs Verlag, 1937). Karl Holl, "Der Modernismus," *Gesammelte Aufsätze zur Kirchengeschichte* (Tübingen: Mohr Verlag, 1938), III, 437, 459.

[9] The claims of the bull *Unam sanctam* have not been rescinded, as will be shown in a later section.

[10] Suggested bibliography for Catholic Action:

Confrey, Burton, *Catholic Action: A Textbook for Colleges and Study Clubs*. New York: Benziger Bros., 1935.

Fitzsimmons, John, and Paul McGuire, *Restoring All Things: A Guide to Catholic Action*. New York: Sheed & Ward, 1938.

Lelotta, F., *Fundamental Principles of Catholic Action*. South Bend, Ind.: Fides Publishers.

Lord, Daniel. Various Tracts. Queen's Work, 3115 S. Grand Ave., Saint Louis, Mo.

Zimmermann, Paul. *Catholic Action*. Unpublished B. D. Thesis. Pritzlaff Library, St. Louis. Contains an exhaustive bibliography.

the object of defending the principles of faith and morals and of spreading a sane and beneficial social action and to restore Catholic life in the home and society. This is to be done under the guidance of the hierarchy of the church."[11] According to the advocates of Catholic Action, the members of the church constitute the lay apostolate. As lay apostles they have a twofold obligation.

1. Through the administration of the seven sacraments, particularly of the Mass, the ordained priest is able to establish the one perfect society in the world, the mystical body of Christ, the Catholic church.[12] The layman, as an unordained priest, should be not only a "spectator" but also an active participant in the "liturgy," i. e., the sacrificial part of the Roman service. By communing frequently the lay apostle will foster the growth of the mystical body of Christ;[13] and by re-enacting the entire liturgy of the church year in his home life he will share in the priesthood of all believers (1 Peter 2:9, 10).[14]

2. Only the priest, by virtue of his ordination, has the power to make people members of the Roman Catholic church; only the pope, by virtue of his alleged primacy, can speak a final word on all spiritual, theological, moral, and social problems. But the lay apostles must become "the long hand of the priest to reach fields where the priest has no access."[15] By participating in the apostolate of the hierarchy for the defense of religion and moral principles, the laity, under the direction of the hierarchy, is to aid in restoring Roman Catholic life in the family and in society.[16] Catholic Action is not merely "the pursuit of personal Christian perfection . . . but also a true apostolate in which Catholics of every social class participate, coming thus to be united in thought and activity."[17] In short, Catholic Action is an attempt to enlist and to unify the Roman Catholic laity in an aggressive program to widen the influence of the Roman church by applying Rome's moral theology to society's many problems. Catholic Action is, of course, only one means through which the Roman church hopes to make an impact on society. It appears that the clergy has not everywhere supported this movement with equal enthusiasm. But the clergy as a whole and the hierarchy in particular are determined in every way possible to reconstruct our society according to the principles laid down in the papal encyclicals dealing with social problems.[18]

To accomplish this purpose, Rome

11 Herbert Kildany, "The Meaning of Catholic Action," *Catholic World,* CXL (October 1934), 105.

12 Wm. McGarry in J. Maritain, *Religion and the Modern World* (Philadelphia: University of Pennsylvania Press, 1941), p. 35.

13 Fitzsimmons, p. 18; Maynard, p. 604.

14 Confrey, p. 40 f.

15 Stanley B. James, "The Basis of Catholic Action," *Ecclesiastical Review,* August, 1941, p. 104.

16 Confrey, p. 44.

17 P. J. Lydon, *Ready Answers,* p. 18.

18 Pius XI is known as the pope of Catholic Action, because he gave impetus to the movement by the encyclicals *Non abbiamo bisogno* (June 29, 1931), *Firmissimam constantiam* (March 28, 1937), and especially *Quadragesimo anno* (May 15, 1931), published in commemoration of the fortieth anniversary of *Rerum novarum* in which Leo XIII had dealt with the reconstruction of the social order. Leo affirmed the right of private property but

has selected nine areas of activity: (1) the undergirding of the home by making the same principles which govern a Roman Catholic society operative in the family, the basic unit of society; (2) vocational guidance by Roman Catholic laymen to direct the youth into such professions as will redound to the welfare of the Roman church;[19] (3) instruction in the proper use of leisure time *ad maiorem gloriam ecclesiae;* (4) training in citizenship to the end that the members of the various professions (the medical, legal, etc.) might bring Roman Catholic thought to bear on the problems of the professions; (5) thorough indoctrination in Rome's moral theology on the supposition that "Protestantism as a Christian influence is almost dead. . . . The future of American and of Christian civilization depends upon Catholic college graduates";[20] (6) a publicity program which will accentuate Roman Catholic principles; (7) active participation in social service with the proper emphasis on "the supernatural motive in Christian charity"; (8) establishment of proper relations between capital and labor by organizing the Association of Catholic Trade Unionists,[21] whose aim is to gain all Roman Catholic wage earners for unionism and all Roman Catholic unionists for membership in the A. C. T. U.

according to the principles enunciated by Leo XIII in his encyclical "On the Condition of Labor" (1891) (incidentally this document claims that all attempts to settle the question of capital and labor will be in vain if the Roman church is ignored);[22] (9) a determined effort to gain rural America through the Rural Life Program by planting Roman Catholic missions in predominantly Protestant areas.[23]

From the point of view of Roman Catholicism, Catholic Action is highly commendable, since it is designed to make the Romanists conscious of the obligations of church membership and primarily to give them an absolute and final answer on every moral issue.[24] It must be borne in mind, however, that the entire program is predicated on Rome's basic error, that the solution of our spiritual and moral problems lies within the powers of human reason and man's inherent capacity for good. In this respect the entire movement is a counterpart of the social gospel of Modernism. The program is further based on the presumptuous claim that our civilization is doomed unless the pope's voice is heeded. In the Middle Ages secular power was in the hands of the nobility, and the church therefore addressed itself to the princes; but the seat of power now is with the common

condemned the abuses of capitalism as a yoke of slavery laid upon the masses. He advocated control of private property for the common good, socialized hospitalization for expectant mothers, adequate wages to forestall birth control. Maynard, pp. 429, 595. McKnight, ch. vii.

[19] Confrey, p. 112.

[20] M. F. Walsh, secretary of state, New York, quoted in *New York Times,* Dec. 9, 1940.

[21] *Nation,* Jan. 4, 1941, pp. 11—13. Also Harold Fey, "Catholicism and the Worker," *Christian Century,* Dec. 27, 1944, p. 1498 f. Jules Weinberg, "Priests, Workers, Communists," *Harper's Magazine,* Nov., 1948.

[22] *Five Great Encyclicals* (New York: The Paulist Press, c. 1939), pp. 1—30.

[23] Fey, *Can Catholicism Win America?* ch. vii.

[24] See, for example, Francis J. Connell, *Father Connell Answers Moral Questions,* ed. by Eugene L. Weitzel (Washington: The Catholic University of America Press, 1959).

man, and therefore Rome today appeals to the common man. This is true particularly in democratic America. Confrey has without camouflage stated the objectives of Catholic Action as follows: "If Catholics will but follow the teaching of the Church, practicing their religion publicly as well as privately and cooperating on the basis of equality with their fellow Americans, instead of two Americas — the one small and Catholic, the other large and pagan, each completely ignorant of the other, and the eventual failure of the Catholic Church to exercise any appreciable influence upon the major destinies of the American republic — we shall have the unchanging morality of the Catholic Church accepted more widely as the standard of our country. As Augustine Birrell has said: 'It is the mass that matters,' and Carlton Hayes, 'The mass, which nourishes virtue and inspires beauty, is the ultimate obligation of America.' " [25]

Neo-Thomism [26]

Neo-Thomism recommends a middle course between the anthropocentric philosophy, which has virtually identified God and man, and the dialectic philosophy, which sees an insoluble tension between reason and faith. Neo-Thomism affirms both "the divine order and the unshakable intrinsic value of nature and reason," [27] and it finds in Thomas Aquinas the solution for our modern disorder. In the encyclical *Aeterni Patris* (1879) Leo XIII, an advocate of Neo-Thomism, said that "on the wings of St. Thomas' genius human reason has reached the most sublime heights it can probably

[25] Confrey, p. 157.

[26] Suggested bibliography on Thomism and Neo-Thomism:

Aubrey, Edwin E. *Present Theological Tendencies.* New York: Harper & Bros., 1936, ch. iv (a keen analysis by a Protestant theologian).

Bandas, Rud. G. *Contemporary Philosophy and Thomistic Principles.* Milwaukee: Bruce Publishing Co., 1932.

Bretscher, Paul M. "Neo-Thomism Once More." *C. T. M.,* XXII (1951), 357—64.

Farrell, Walter. *A Companion to the Summa.* New York: Sheed & Ward, 1940.

Gilson, Etienne. *Christianity and Philosophy,* trans. Ralph MacDonald. New York: Sheed & Ward, 1939.

Hornig, Gottfried. "Recent Studies of Thomas Aquinas," *Lutheran World,* V (1958), 38—51.

Horton, Walter. *Contemporary Continental Theology.* New York: Harper & Bros., 1938, ch. ii (the author deals with the views of Christopher Dawson, Etienne Gilson, and Erich Przywara).

Maritain, Jacques. *Scholasticism and Politics,* trans. Mortimer J. Adler. New York: Macmillan, 1940.

———. *Ransoming the Time.* New York: Charles Scribner's Sons, 1941.

———. *On the Philosophy of History,* ed. Joseph W. Evans. New York: Charles Scribner's Sons, 1957.

———. "Contemporary Renewals," in *Religion and the Modern World.* Univ. of Pa. Bicentennial Conference. Phila.: University of Pennsylvania Press, 1941. Pp. 8 to 20 (see also pp. 27—40).

Pegis, Anton C. *Introduction to Saint Thomas Aquinas.* New York: Modern Library, 1948.

Siegel, William. "The Revival of Thomist Philosophy," *Augustana Lutheran Quarterly,* Jan., 1940, pp. 38—45.

[27] J. Maritain, *Religion and the Modern World,* p. 11.

ver attain," and Pope Pius XI in the ncyclical *Studiorum ducens* (1923) reffirmed that Thomas Aquinas is *the* heological teacher of the Roman Catholic church.

The Neo-Thomists maintain that our utonomous culture has lost unity, direcion, and depth and has become the prey)f agnosticism, naturalism, and individualism.[28] In scholastic theology every ictivity in society, culture, and art was inified and integrated to serve the church. Ultimately man's body and pirit, reason and faith, were directed oward one goal, the beatific vision of God. Today the prevalent world view s atomistic. All human activities are compartmentalized without a unitive purpose so that business is divorced rom government, art from the church, iationalism from a world brotherhood, philosophy from theology, the natural rom the supernatural, and man from God. This world view has produced an ignostic society. The naturalistic philosophy of the modern era leaves no room or absolute criteria of moral behavior ind offers no final purpose for human existence. An autonomous culture bases ill truth on the individual's subjective experience. Will-o'-the-wisp impulses — he will to live (Schopenhauer), the will o power (Nietzsche), *élan vital* (Bergson) — are a shallow explanation of life's purpose. To smother man's doubts, modern activism, under the guise of "busyness," is advocated as a substitute for he real purpose of life.

Neo-Thomists maintain that the only inswer to modern man's anthropocentric ind autonomous humanism is an "integral humanism." Maritain describes this as a humanism "which considers man in the wholeness of his natural and supernatural being and which sets no *a priori* limit to the descent of the divine into man." This he believes to be in full accord with the principles of Thomas.[29] According to Thomas, God is pure essence and as such the first cause and the only unifying cause of all possible interactions and relations. There is no escape from the tensions of these interactions and no possibility of attaining an integrated personality unless there is in man a happy combination of reason and faith, the natural and the supernatural, science and metaphysics, philosophy and theology. When this occurs, man is able to know God and his real purpose in life.[30] The Neo-Thomistic integral humanism is based on the scholastic premise that both reason and faith are divine gifts and can therefore never be at variance with each other.[31] According to Maritain, this humanism recognizes the worth and dignity of man, for it does full justice to his alleged inherent capacities. At the same time it gives proper credit to the "light" which comes by nature to all men at their birth and supernaturally to reborn men at their baptism. By combining the highly speculative with the profoundly religious convictions, and by reconciling the newly discovered truths with philosophy and reason, Neo-Thomism claims to resolve the tensions which arise from the dual fact that man, created out of nothing, is inclined toward nothingness, and that this same man, created in the image of God, is really more than man.[32] By re-

[28] Aubrey, pp. 115—49; Horton, p. 55 ff.

[29] Maritain, *Scholasticism and Politics*, p. 9.

[30] Some Neo-Thomists employ the term "existentialism" in this connection; not, however, in the sense of Kierkegaard, Heidegger, Jaspers, and certainly not in the spirit of Sartre.

[31] McGarry, "Modern Trends in Catholic Theology," in Maritain, p. 31 f. (See fn. 12.)

[32] Maritain, p. 12. Cp. also Robert E. Brennan, "The Thomist Revival," *Ecclesiastical Review*, Phila., Jan., 1941, pp. 12—25.

solving this tension Neo-Thomism claims to unify man's total activity and thereby to direct him toward his ultimate goal, namely, the beatific vision of God.[33] Neo-Thomism offers the Roman scientist and philosopher a philosophy which sacrifices none of the theological premises of Romanism and in which the theories of science and philosophy receive their due. Neo-Thomism also has a strong appeal for those non-Roman intellectuals who feel that they must disavow a purely secularistic philosophy but are offended at a theology which teaches total depravity and monergism.[34]

There is probably no other church which has the capacity for harboring so many widely divergent theological points of view as the Roman church. It condemned the modernist Loisy, but not Abelard, who outliberalized the most radical liberal theologian of modern Protestantism.[35] In one country Rome

will unrelentingly enforce the principles of *Unam sanctam;* in another country it will accommodate itself to the prevalent political or religious views.[36] Leo XIII proscribed participation in interdenominational conferences, but in a letter to the bishop of Grenoble, 1892, he states that Christian prudence suggests interchurch co-operation in the interest of social welfare.[37] The priests of some Uniate churches may marry while others must be celibates. There is still greater divergence on strictly theological questions. This makes it difficult for anyone not trained in this theological system objectively to evaluate its doctrines and practices. In challenging a specific Roman Catholic error the non-Romanist may receive the reply that the church does not teach that particular doctrine. The problem lies in the fact that, as Friedrich Heiler points out, the Roman Catholic church is really a complex of seven dif-

---

33 Aubrey, p. 147.

34 Maritain delivered the lectures on "Scholasticism and Politics" at the University of Chicago, and Mortimer J. Adler, a member of its faculty, edited the translation.

35 Alfred Weber says: "The more familiar we become with Scholastic literature, the less apt are we to exaggerate the progress of free thought from the thirteenth to the nineteenth century. The historians who endeavor to trace all modern negations to the Reformation ignore, or affect to ignore, the fact that in the ninth century the Catholic Scotus Erigena denied eternal punishment; that in the twelfth, the Catholic Abelard declared the teachings of the Greek philosophers to be superior to those of the Old Testament; that in the thirteenth, a great number of Catholics refused to believe in the miraculous conception and in the resurrection of Christ; that in the same century, or two hundred years before the Reformation, and at a time when the power of the Holy See was at its height, St. Thomas and Duns Scotus found themselves obliged to prove, with all the arts of logic, the need of revelation and the credibility of the Divine Word; finally, that these submissive, devoted, and orthodox doctors of the Church combined with their Catholic convictions a freedom of thought, the like of which is but rarely met with in the Protestant theology of the seventeenth century." *History of Philosophy,* trans. Frank Thilly, expanded by R. B. Perry (New York: Chas. Scribner's Sons, 1925), p. 196. On diversity in Roman theology see Skydsgaard in *Man's Disorder and God's Design* (New York: Harper & Bros., 1948), I, 162 f.

36 Gustav Voss, "Missionary Accommodation and Ancestral Rites in the East," *Theological Studies,* IV (Dec., 1943), 525—60.

37 Wilfred Parsons, S. J., "Intercreedal Cooperation in the Papal Documents," *Theological Studies,* June, 1943, pp. 159—82. Cp. "The R. C. and the First Assembly of W. C. C.,"*Ecumenical Review,* Winter, 1949, pp. 197 to 212.

ferent types of religion. It is a religion of primitive superstition, a legalistic religion, a political-social religion, a rationalistic religion of theological doctrines, an esoteric mystery religion, a mystical religion, and even an evangelical religion of salvation.[38] The Roman church can take various forms without ever relinquishing one iota of its basic characteristic: obedience and submission to the Roman pontiff as the indispensable condition of salvation.[39]

Organization

The Roman pontiff is the head of the Roman Catholic organization and is the supreme authority in matters of faith and morals. Next to the pope is the College of Cardinals, whose number has been raised by John XXIII to seventy-five, and who until 1945 were selected primarily from Italy. There are eleven "congregations" or boards, with headquarters in Vatican City, who deal with such duties as guarding doctrines and practices, regulating legislation concerning the sacraments, supervising the various orders, granting dispensations, propagating the faith. There are also three tribunals, or courts: (1) the Sacred Penitentiary (decides questions of conscience), (2) the Sacred Roman Rota (deals with civil and criminal cases), and (3) the Apostolic Segnatura (determines legal procedure). The bishop is invested with authority over all souls and property in his diocese and is responsible directly to the pope. An archbishop has essentially the same rights

and duties, only that his competence is of a higher order. Cardinals, archbishops, and bishops constitute the hierarchy. The parish priest is the final link between pope and people. The laity has no voice in the conduct of church matters nor in the choice of the priest.

In the United States the organization of the church includes an apostolic delegate, 43 archbishops, of whom 5 are cardinals, 224 bishops, and 53,796 priests. The special province of the apostolic delegate is the settling of difficulties that may arise in the conduct of the dioceses. An archbishop has the care of his archdiocese, and he has precedence and a certain limited competence in his province. There are 26 provinces. Within each diocese authority is vested in the bishop, although appeal may be made to the apostolic delegate and in the last resort to one of the congregations in Rome. In addition to the bishop, the organization of a diocese includes a vicar-general, who, under certain conditions, acts as the bishop's representative; a chancellor, or secretary; a council of consulters, usually six in number, three of whom are nominated by the bishop and three by the clergy of the diocese; and different boards of examination and superintendence.[40]

There are numerous religious orders, male and female. Some are devoted to teaching, others to one of the many charitable endeavors of the Roman church, others to preaching and missionary activity, still others to the contemplative life.[41]

[38] Wilhelm Pauck, "Romanism and Catholicism," *Theology Today*, Jan., 1948, p. 458. — Heiler, *Der Katholizismus*, pp. 159—592.

[39] L. W. Spitz, "*Roma Semper Eadem*," *C. T. M.*, XIX (1948), 801—23. But see also Carl Umhau Wolf, "Reform in Roman Catholicism," *Lutheran Quarterly*, XIII (1961), 47—66.

[40] Michael Williams, loc. cit. Cp. Census Report, II, 1547 f. — On the organization of the Roman headquarters of the church, see Heinrich Scharp, *How the Catholic Church Is Governed*, trans. Annelise Derrick (New York: Herder and Herder, 1960).

[41] For an introductory study to the monastic and religious orders see the following general references: *Cambridge Medieval History* (New York:

The Roman Catholic Church in the United States [42]

The first Roman Catholic parish in the United States was established at St. Augustine, Fla., in 1565. The English did not begin to colonize America until Protestantism had been firmly established in England (1603), and providentially the United States remained predominantly, almost exclusively, Protestant until late in the nineteenth century.[43] Lord Baltimore (George Calvert), a Roman Catholic, desirous to provide a haven for his disenfranchised and persecuted *English* coreligionists founded Maryland in 1633, the first colony to guarantee religious liberty. There is, however, no historical basis for Rome's assertion that the Roman church is responsible for the American principle of separation of church and state. The Maryland experiment is proof for no more than that Rome grants religious tolerance wherever the Roman church constitutes a minority. Nor dare one forget that the Jesuits violently opposed Lord Baltimore's liberal principles.[44] At the conclusion of the Revolutionary War the Roman Catholic population was not much in excess of 20,000, 15,800 of whom lived in Maryland. Beginning with the nineteenth century, great waves of Irish and German immigrants settled in the seaboard cities, and under the wise leadership of Bishop (later Archbishop) Carroll of Baltimore (1790 to 1815) the Roman Catholic church engaged in its program of expansion. Carroll successfully combated "trusteeism" (a proposal to establish each congregation as an independent and autonomous unit under a board of trustees) and "nationalism" (a plan to organize each language group into separate congregations); and thus he maintained, on the one hand, the absolute authority of his episcopal office over every parish and, on the other hand, welded his coreligionists with divergent backgrounds into an Americanized unit. The Roman Catholic church has experienced a tremendous growth, primarily through immigration. From approximately 150,000 members in 1807 it had grown to about 41,000,000 by 1960.[45] Its membership is still about 80 per cent urban, a factor which, in part, explains the tremendous power which this church wields in many of our larger cities. While the hierarchy formerly fostered this urban concentration, it has found that urban society often proves baneful to the church and in recent years has given much concern to rural Roman Catholicism. Until 1893 the American church was organized as "mission territory," but since the establishment of the Apostolic Delegation at Washington the American hierarchy enjoys greater independence. American Romanism does not differ

Cambridge Univ. Press, 1903), I, 521—42; V, 658—96. *Encyclopaedia Britannica* (Chicago: Encyc. Brit. Press, 1951), XV, 687—89. *Encyc. of Religion and Ethics,* ed. Hastings (New York: Scribner's, 1928), VII, 781—94; X, 693—713. *The New Schaff-Herzog Encyc.* (Grand Rapids: Baker Book House, 1950), VII, 465—68. Also see Dom Cuthbert Butler, *Benedictine Monachism* (New York: Longmans, Green & Co., 1924).

[42] O'Gorman and Maynard, loc. cit. See also Bibliog. below, § 4.

[43] William Warren Sweet, *The Story of Religion in America* (New York: Harper & Bros., 1930), pp. 11—37. Charles and Mary Beard, *The Rise of American Civilization* (New York: Macmillan, 1931), I, 11 ff.

[44] William Warren Sweet, *Religion in Colonial America* (New York: Charles Scribner's Sons, 1942), pp. 167—81.

[45] This number includes all who have been baptized in the Roman Catholic faith and have not formally renounced such membership. *Census of Rel. B.,* II, 1528.

from European in doctrine or organization. Naturally, certain points of practice will receive greater emphasis here than in Europe. Likewise there are certain agencies which are more suitable for American conditions, notably the National Catholic Welfare Conference, an agency of the hierarchy for supervising education, the press, social action, legal matters, and lay organizations. The Roman church is compelled to make adjustments in democratic America which it need not make in authoritarian lands where it is the established church.

Diplomatic relations between Washington and the Vatican were broken off in 1867, when Pius IX ordered Protestant worship to be removed outside the walls of Rome. Relations were again established in 1940 when President Roosevelt appointed Myron C. Taylor as his personal representative, and continued through his administration.

There is sufficient ground for the assumption that Rome is determined to gain a dominant position in the United States.[46]

The Doctrinal Standards

Viewed historically, Roman Catholic standards of doctrine fall into three definite categories: those adopted by both the Eastern and the Western church before the Eastern schism; namely, the ecumenical creeds and the decisions of the seven ecumenical councils; those accepted by all Roman Catholics prior to 1870, namely, the decrees of the ten councils from 1123 until 1563; those decrees accepted by all Romanists who subscribe to the absolutistic powers of the papacy.[47]

It is extremely difficult to determine, with any degree of certainty, the exact position of Rome on many significant points of doctrine. True, Rome has adopted a number of doctrinal standards as binding upon the faithful: the Word of God, the traditions, and the solemn decrees of the councils. The Vatican Council, however, demands that in addition to these the faithful must accept those teachings which the church "by her ordinary and universal *magisterium* proposes for belief as having been divinely revealed." [48] All such as are not members of this church must judge by the authoritative standards when they seek to determine the church's position on any given point.

a) *The Canons and Decrees of the Council of Trent* (1545–63) was the first Roman confessional statement to codify the doctrines of medieval theology.[49] Its significance for Lutherans lies in its anathemas against the Lutheran doctrine of justification. On this point there was unanimity in 1563; there still is today. Trent, however, was unable to resolve the deep differences between the Dominicans and Franciscans concerning sin and grace, Mary's immaculate conception, and papal supremacy.

b) The *Tridentine Profession,* also known as the Creed of Pius IV (1564), contains a summary of specific Romanist doctrines, declares the Roman church to be the mother and mistress of all churches, and demands of the *ecclesia docens* the oath of allegiance to the pope. The Creed of Pius IV is also called the Profession of Converts, because converts are obligated to subscribe to it and to renounce and anathematize

---

[46] Fey, *Can Catholicism Win America?* Cp. McKnight, ch. xvii. — Blanshard, loc. cit.

[47] Schaff, *Creeds,* I, 84.

[48] *Dogmatic Constitution of the Catholic Faith,* Third Session, April 24, 1870, quoted in Schaff, *Creeds,* II, 244. Cp. the introductory chapter of Joseph Neuner and Heinrich Rood, *Der Glaube der Kirche in den Urkunden der Lehrverkündigung* (Regensburg, 1938), pp. 17, 20 f.

[49] For literature see Bibliog.

all heresies which the church has condemned.[50]

c) *Catechismus Romanus* (1566), although prepared at the direction of the council and the pope, did not gain universal approval. It reflects the Augustinian theology of the Dominicans, who leaned toward Thomistic theology, and not the theology of the Franciscans, which, especially with respect to grace, followed Scotus. The chief opposition to this catechism came from the Jesuits, and the Roman catechism was supplanted in many sections by the catechisms of Peter Canisius and Robert Bellarmine.

Tridentine theology found its most able defender in Robert Bellarmine (1542–1621) in his *Disputations on the Controversies of the Christian Faith* (1587–90). Bellarmine's defense of Trent and his attack on Martin Chemnitz (1522–86) were ably answered by the Lutheran dogmatician John Gerhard (1582–1637) in his *Loci*.

d) A significant source of doctrine is found in the collections of canon law. In Roman theology canon law is "the body of laws and regulations made and adopted by ecclesiastical authority for the government of the Christian Church and its members." As Christ's representatives the apostles and their successors are said to be endowed with legislative and disciplinary powers; hence their laws concerning faith and morals are considered binding. In 1148 Gratian published *Concordia discordantium canonum*, a codified collection of the many decrees and regulations (including also the notorious Pseudo-Isidorian decretals), which had been issued by popes and councils during the preceding centuries. Since 1870 the legislative powers of the church are vested in the pope and the Congregations of the Holy Office. Pius X ordered a complete revision of canon law, and in 1917 Benedict XV published the *Codex iuris canonici*.[51] It should be noted that additional revisions and changes are published from time to time.[52]

[50] The first part of the Tridentine Profession is the Nicene Creed. The second part is a synopsis of Tridentine theology. Some of the statements are: "I most steadfastly admit and embrace the apostolic and ecclesiastical traditions and all other observances and constitutions of the same Church." "I also admit the Holy Scriptures according to that sense which our holy Mother Church has held, and does hold, to which it belongs to judge of the true sense and interpretation of the Scriptures; neither will I ever take and interpret them otherwise than according to the unanimous consent of the Fathers." The third part contains the oath of allegiance. Schaff, *Creeds*, I, 98 f. The new formula for the abjuration and profession of faith to be made by converts is based upon the Tridentine Profession. See *Emanuel*, published by the Fathers of the Blessed Sacrament, 184 E. 76th St., New York, July, 1942, p. 216.

[51] *Cath. Encyc.*, s. v. "Law," "Canon"; *Encyclopaedia Brit.*, s. v. "Canon Law"; *Religion in Geschichte und Gegenwart*, s. v. "Kirchenrecht." A summary of the significant canons is contained in Lydon, *Ready Answers in Canon Law*. The important part which canon law plays in Roman theology is reflected in the many references which Philipp Melanchthon makes to the canonists, the canon, and canon law in the Apology of the Augsburg Confession. The Pritzlaff Library, Concordia Seminary, has a reprint of *Corpus iuris canonici*, published by Gregory XIII, 1582.

[52] E. g., Sec. B, par. 2, of can. 1099 has been "rescripted" and is no longer in force. This regulation had exempted from the regulations covering mixed marriages such non-Roman Catholics as had been baptized in the Roman Catholic faith. The new rule is that all who are born of a mixed marriage and baptized as Roman Catholics, though brought up in the Protestant faith, must submit to the Roman Catholic rules concerning marriage, even when marrying a non-Roman Catholic. *C. T. M.*, XX (1949), 223.

e) The many bulls, decrees, and encyclicals published by councils, and in modern times by the popes, are received by Romanists as binding, some even being considered "divinely inspired." The most significant documents are the following:

Unam sanctam (1302), by Boniface VIII, declares that submission to the papacy in all spiritual and secular matters is necessary to salvation. This bull is the classic expression of Rome's claim to world supremacy, a claim which has not been rescinded.

Unigenitus Dei Filius (1713), by Clement XI, condemns 101 sentences of the Jansenist Pasquier Quesnel, thus committing the Roman church in unmistakable terms to an antievangelical position. The bull rejects as false such Jansenist teachings as these: The sinner is not free — except to evil — without the grace of the Liberator (38); the will . . . is capable of all evil and incapable for any good (39); all may read the Sacred Scriptures (80).[53]

Ineffabilis Deus (1854), by Pius IX, declares "that the most blessed Virgin Mary, in the first moment of her conception, by a special grace and privilege of Almighty God, in virtue of the merits of Christ, was preserved immaculate from all stain of original sin."[54]

The encyclical *Quanta cura* and the *Syllabus* (1864), by Pius IX, are directed against the "dangerous heresies" of modern secularism and Protestantism, such as Communism, socialism, Bible societies, contemporary liberalism. In ten chapters the *Syllabus* condemns eighty errors. By implication Romanists must believe the direct opposite of the views branded as errors.[55]

The Vatican Decrees of 1870 restate the *Dogmatic Constitution of the Catholic Faith*, which treats of God as Creator, of revelation, of faith, and of faith and reason and in 18 canons condemns errors on pantheism and naturalism. The Vatican Council adopted the First Dogmatic Constitution of the Church of Christ, known also as *Pastor aeternus*, climaxing the teaching of Rome on the primacy of St. Peter and his successors by declaring the infallibility of the pope.[56]

---

[53] Schaff, *Creeds*, I, 106.

[54] Ibid., II, 213.

[55] Ibid., II, 213—53. Schaff publishes the Latin text with an English translation. Of particular interest are the errors condemned in ch. v. Schaff summarizes twenty errors (19—38): "The Church is subject to the State; the Church has no right to exercise her authority without the leave and assent of the State; the Church has not the power to define dogmatically that the religion of the Catholic Church is the only true religion; Roman Pontiffs and ecumenical Councils have exceeded the limits of their power, usurped the rights of princes, and have erred even in matters of faith and morals; the Church has no power to avail herself of force, or any temporal power, direct or indirect; besides the inherent power of the Episcopate, there is another temporal power conceded expressly or tacitly by the civil government, which may be revoked by the same at its pleasure; it does not exclusively belong to the jurisdiction of the Church to direct the teaching of theology; nothing forbids a general council, or the will of the people, to transfer the supreme Pontiff from Rome to some other city; national Churches, independent of the authority of the Roman Pontiff, may be established; the Roman Pontiffs have contributed to the Greek schism." I, 131.

[56] *The Vatican Decrees* are published by Schaff, *Creeds*, II, 234. For the story of the Vatican Council and a critical examination of this papal decree see ibid., I, 134—38; Janus, loc. cit.

Aeterni Patris (1879), by Leo XIII,[57] recommends the restoration of Thomistic theology.

Rerum novarum (1891), by Leo XIII, declares that the problem of capital and labor cannot be solved unless the voice of the church is heeded, for the church by divine command directs human conduct (capital and labor) by its precepts.[58]

Providentissimus Deus (1893), by Leo XIII, concerns the study of the Scriptures.[59]

Pascendi dominici gregis (1907) and the *Syllabus* (1909), by Pius X, condemn the views of Roman modernism.[60]

Quadragesimo anno (1931), by Pius XI, lays down principles for reconstructing the social order.[61]

Munificentissimus Deus, the Apostolic Constitution by which is defined the dogma of faith that Mary, the Virgin Mother of God, has been assumed into heaven bodily (1950).

The official liturgical works: the *missale, rituale, manuale, pontificale, breviarium.*

The standard works on dogmatic and moral theology, especially those of Thomas Aquinas, Robert Bellarmine, J. A. Moehler, and W. Wilmers.

Publications which bear the *nihil obstat* and the *imprimatur* are considered free of doctrinal or moral error. Those who grant the *nihil obstat* or *imprimatur* do not thereby express their agreement with the contents, opinions, or statements.

SECTION II

The Formal and Material Principles

The Roman church is the most dogmatic and at the same time the least doctrinal church. There is a fixed dogmatic limit, but within this limit there is room for divergent and often contradictory opinions. It is difficult to understand how Rome sometimes can be extremely dogmatic in certain theological matters, and sometimes very tolerant. This enigma resolves itself when one understands both the formal and the material principle of Roman theology. In discussing points of doctrine with Romanists it is therefore essential to know the source and norm of Rome's doctrines (formal principle) as well as the central theological thought which controls the entire doctrinal system (material principle).

---

[57] Leo XIII published many encyclicals, as did also his immediate successors. The 144 encyclicals published between 1878 and 1937 are registered chronologically, and the subject matter of each is briefly mentioned, by Sister M. Claudia Carlen, I. H. M., *A Guide to the Encyclicals of the Roman Pontiffs from Leo XIII to the Present Day* (New York: the H. W. Wilson Co., 1939).

[58] Treacy, p. 30 ff.

[59] Reprinted as Preface to the Douay Version of the Bible. See Bibliog.

[60] Mirbt, No. 652.

[61] Treacy, p. 168 ff.

The Formal Principle

In the Fourth Session (April 8, 1546) the Council of Trent declared that the Gospel is

the fountain of all, both saving truth and moral discipline, [and that] this truth and discipline are contained in the written books and the unwritten traditions which, received by the Apostles from the mouth of Christ Himself, or from the Apostles themselves, the Holy Ghost dictating, have come down even unto us, transmitted as it were from hand to hand . . . and preserved in the Catholic Church by a continuous succession.[62]

The church, bound by this decree, teaches the dictation theory of inspiration and accepts the canonical writings as divinely inspired and therefore as God's message to man. Pope Leo XIII encouraged the reading of the Bible by granting an indulgence of 300 days to the faithful who read the Scriptures at least fifteen minutes a day. He stated in addition that the Scriptures have "been bestowed upon the human race for their instruction in divine things." [63] This seems to be a radical departure from Rome's position prior to Trent. The fact is that Luther had so successfully defended the *sola Scriptura* that the Council of Trent was compelled to modify the late medieval position and to appear to champion the *sola Scriptura* principle.

In actuality, however, Rome's formal principle must still be summarized in the words of the Smalcald Articles:

The Papacy also is nothing but sheer enthusiasm by which the Pope boasts that all rights exist in the shrine of his heart, and whatever he decides and commands within his church is spirit and right, even though it is above and contrary to Scripture and the spoken Word.[64]

Appealing to 1 Tim. 3:15, Rome claims that the *ecclesia docens,* i. e., the hierarchy, more specifically the pope, is the infallible teacher in determining both the scope of the subject matter to be accepted and also the sense in which this is to be believed. The Council of Trent states that the "Gospel" is contained in the written books (the Scriptures of the Old and New Testaments) as well as in the unwritten traditions (the extra-Scriptural statements on faith and morals contained in the writings of the fathers, the decrees of the councils, and the official pronouncements of the papal see). It must be kept in mind, however, that both groups of writings come under the general heading of "tradition." Since the days of Bellarmine, Rome distinguishes between "objective," or "material," and "formal" tradition. The former term denotes the subject matter transmitted; the latter, the act of transmission. The church hands down (Latin: *tradit*) the "Gospel" as it is allegedly contained either in the Scriptures or in the traditions. However, the teaching office, not the Scriptures and the traditions, is the final source and norm of faith and discipline. As judge and interpreter of both, the *ecclesia docens* is bound neither by traditions nor by Scriptures. Anthony C. Cotter states that the ultimate explanation of the obscurity of the Bible is God Himself, who purposed to make the *magis-*

---

[62] Council of Trent, Sess. IV. See Richard Baepler, "Scripture and Tradition in the Council of Trent," *C. T. M.,* XXXI (1960), 341—362.

[63] See Preface to New Testament (Paterson, N. J.: St. Anthony Guild Press, 1941). Wilmers: "Die h. Schrift *enthält* nicht nur Gottes Wort, d. h., einzelne geoffenbarte Wahrheiten, sondern sie *ist* auch Gottes Wort, d. h., alles in ihr Enthaltene ist der Ausspruch des Heiligen Geistes." I, 130.

[64] Part III, Art. VIII, 4. These articles, drafted by Luther in 1537 for a proposed general council, bring into sharp relief the points of difference between Lutherans and Romanists.

terium the primary recipient of all revelation, the Bible included, so that the *magisterium* may properly be called the primary and even the only channel of revelation.[65] Rome's *formal principle* therefore is (1) Scripture, (2) the traditions, and (3) reason. Theologically these three are considered of equal validity as sources of religious knowledge.

CHURCH ABOVE BIBLE

Rome avers that its high regard for the Bible is evidenced by the fact that most of the New Testament authors were members of the Catholic church, that this church has given the Bible to Christendom, and that it considers the Bible a precious storehouse of dogmatic and moral instruction. Rome nevertheless insists that the church has authority over the Scriptures, but that the Bible has none over the church.

Rome teaches that the Bible is inadequate and insufficient and needs the supplementation which only the church can provide. Bellarmine stated that the New Testament Epistles were written only to meet certain local conditions; and Andrada, the official interpreter of Trent, declared that the New Testament books served only as "notes" to aid the apostles' memory. On the basis of Jer. 31:33 he argues that the chief difference between the two Testaments is that the Old was written on tablets of stone and paper, whereas the New was written almost entirely into the heart of the church. The Roman apologists usually argue as follows:

> Christ did not say, Sit down and write Bibles and let everyone judge for himself. That injunction was left for the 16th century, and we have seen the result of it in the founding of 500 religions all quarreling with one another about the interpretation of the Bible.[66]

Thomas F. Coakley writes:

> The Catholic Church existed before the Bible; it is possible for the Catholic Church to exist without the Bible, for the Catholic Church is altogether independent of the Bible. The Bible does not give any systematic, complete, and exhaustive treatment of the doctrines of

---

[65] "The Obscurity of the Bible," *The Catholic Biblical Quarterly,* IX (1947), 453—64. Fathers Rumble and Carty (*Bible Quizzes* [St. Paul: Radio Replies Press, 1943], 2,500,000 circulation) in 86 questions and answers set forth clearly that Rome considers the *magisterium* (the *ecclesia docens*) the only and final norm of divine truth. Cp. esp. Qus. 71, 77. For a detailed presentation of the formal principle of Rome see Wilmers, I, 171 ff.; Moehler, ch. v, pp. 255—310; K. Adam, *Spirit of Catholicism,* p. 168 ff. Cp. advertisement of Knights of Columbus, "No . . . The Bible Is Not Our Sole Guide," *Atlantic Monthly,* May, 1952.

[66] Tract, *Truth About Catholics* (Los Angeles: Cath. Lit. Board, 1936), p. 2. See Gibbons, pp. 77—94. It should be noted that "500 religions" is a gross exaggeration. Statistics can be used to prove almost anything. Also to be observed is the fact that there is as much doctrinal division within the Roman church as among non-Romanists. Cp. Samuel M. Cavert, "A Look at the American Churches," *Religion in Life,* Summer, 1949: "This fragmentation is not quite as serious as the tabulation of 256 separate and independent bodies seems to indicate. A better perspective on the situation is gained when it is explained that ninety-seven per cent of all the church members of the United States are found in the fifty larger denominations, each with a membership of 50,000 or more. Two hundred of the groups listed in the census are so small that they count for less than three per cent of the church membership of the nation. As a further corrective of first impressions, it may be pointed out that approximately eighty per cent of American Protestantism is embraced within eight denominational families: Baptist, Methodist, Lutheran, Presbyterian and Reformed, Disciples, Episcopal, Congregational, Evangelical United Brethren."

Christ. In many respects it is, like a stenographer's notebook, partial and fragmentary, to be supplemented later on in more elaborate detail by other agencies. Christ never wrote a word of the Bible. One might naturally expect Him to have set the example by writing at least some portions of the Bible if He intended His followers to take their entire religion from it. Christ never ordered His apostles to write any part of the Bible. We might well expect such a command from Him if He desired the members of His Church to have recourse to the Bible for their religion. Christ could not have intended that the world should take its religion from the Bible, since so many millions of the human race today, to say nothing of past ages, cannot read or write.[67]

The Roman Catholic church claims the authority to determine the Scriptural canon and has decreed that the *Vulgate is to "be held as authentic* and that no one is to dare, or presume, to reject it under any pretext whatever." [68] A number of significant Roman doctrines have been defended on the basis of faulty Vulgate renderings of the original, e. g., Gen. 3:15 (*ipsa tibi conteret caput* ["she shall bruise thy head"]); Eph. 5:32 (the Greek word *mysterion* [mystery] is rendered *sacramentum); 1* Cor. 4:1 (*dispensatores sumus* ["we are stewards"] has been used as an argument to prove that the hierarchy may dispense the laity from the cup). Furthermore, Trent decreed that the *Apocrypha belong to the canon* and must be accepted as inspired and dictated by the Holy Ghost.[69] Some of the apocryphal writings are extremely valuable to Rome, since it makes use of them to support such doctrines as the expiatory power of good works (Tob. 4:11 f.) and meritorious sacrifices and prayers for the dead (2 Macc. 12: 44 ff.).

Rome views the Bible and the traditions as the "law or constitution of the Church," and therefore American Romanists frequently argue that as the Supreme Court must interpret the Federal Constitution, so there must be a living authority which determines the meaning of the church's constitution. Appealing to 2 Peter 1:20 — but completely ignoring the context as well as Acts 17:11 — Rome states that as little as any citizen may put his own construction on the law of the land, so little is a member of the church permitted to exercise the right of "private interpretation." Rome's claim to be the official "supreme court" is a clear case of such "private interpretation" as is forbidden in 2 Peter 1:20. Rome claims furthermore that the Bible is a dark book, hard to understand, and in need of official interpretation. Even if it is granted that the sections in Paul's Letters which St. Peter (2 Peter 3:16) declared to be hard to understand contain doctrines which are essential to salvation, the Romanists overlook the fact that these doctrines are dark only for

---

[67] *Inside Facts About the Catholic Church,* p. 21 f.; quoted in *Popular Symbolics* (St. Louis: C. P. H., 1934), p. 155 f. Cp. F. E. Mayer, "Romanism, Calvinism, Lutheranism, on the Authority of Scripture," *C. T. M.,* VIII (1937), 260 ff.

[68] Sess. IV, "Decree Concerning the Edition and Use of the Sacred Books." This position was reaffirmed in 1870. On the history of the Vulgate see *Realenzyklopädie,* s. v. *"Bibelübersetzung";* Schaff-Herzog, s. v. "Bible Versions." The translation of the New Testament prepared in 1941 is based on the Vulgate.

[69] Geo. A. Vogel, "A Comparison of the King James and the Douay Version," *C. T. M.,* VI (1935), 18 and especially 102 ff. — On the Rom. Cath. Canon of the Old Testament, including Apocryphal Books, cp. John E. Steinmueller, *A Companion to Scripture Studies,* 2d ed. (New York: Joseph F. Wagner, c. 1941), II.

the unlearned and the unstable. According to the Tridentine Profession the right to judge the true sense and interpretation of the Scriptures belongs only to the church, and no layman nor theologian dare interpret them otherwise than in the sense which Mother Church has held and does hold.[70] "Mother Church," however, defies all hermeneutical principles. The Council of Trent uses Luke 13:5; Acts 2:38 to prove that penance is a sacrament; Communion under one kind is justified on the basis of 1 Cor. 4:1; 11:34. The explanatory notes in the Douay Version show the arbitrary manner in which Rome employs the Scriptures.[71]

Rome's attitude toward Holy Scripture can probably be gauged best by its regulations concerning the reading of the Bible by the laity. Rome denies the charges frequently made that it proscribes Bible reading by the laity, asserting, on the one hand, that the church has never issued an absolute and categorical interdiction of Bible reading, and pointing, on the other hand, to the encyclicals of Benedict XV (*Spiritus Paraclitus*, 1920) and of Pius XII (*Divino*

afflante Spiritu, 1943), which encourage Bible reading. Both claims must be carefully evaluated. In 1199 Innocent III declared that the desire to read the Bible is to be commended, but that the reading in "conventicles" (without the supervision of the duly appointed priest) is not to be tolerated, because the profundity of the Scriptures is such that not only the unlearned but also the *docti et prudentes* cannot grasp its meaning. By an allegorical interpretation of Ex. 19:13 (the animal which touched the holy mountain Sinai was to be stoned) unsupervised Bible reading was prohibited lest any unlearned person (*aliquis et indoctus*) dare presume to delve into the sublimity of the Scriptures and preach it to others.[72] In 1229, the synod of Toulouse decreed that the laity should not be permitted to have the books of the Old and the New Testament, with the exception of the Psalter, the breviary for the holy office, and *horae beatae Mariae* for devotional purposes.[73] In accord with the resolution of Trent that a commission be established to prepare an index of prohibited books Pius IV

70 Wilmers, p. 200 ff.; 217 ff. Gibbons, p. 77 ff. Moehler, p. 261 f.

71 Council of Trent, Sess. XIV, ch. 1; Sess. XXI, ch. 1; Sess. XXII, ch. 1. Chemnitz in *Examen Concilii Tridentini* exposes Rome's use of the Scriptures. — The New Testament published by the Confraternity of Christian Doctrine in 1941 has greatly reduced the number of notes as compared with the Douay Version. But those which are supplied show the sense in which the Roman Catholic church interprets certain significant texts of the Scriptures. The explanatory note to Rome. 5:12 ("all have sinned") reads in part: "The Church, the official interpreter of the Scriptures, teaches us also that in view of the future sufferings of Christ, His blessed Mother was preserved from original sin." Rom. 3:21 is made to teach that "the justice of God through faith is not that holiness whereby God is just, but that grace which He imparts to the soul to make it really, intrinsically pleasing and holy in His sight. The necessary condition for obtaining the infusion of this divine gift is faith, not a bare speculative faith, but a practical faith which through the love of God effects the observance of the commandments and the performance of other good works." — On Roman Catholic versions of the Bible in English since the Reformation, see Hugh Pope, *English Versions of the Bible*, ed. Sebastian Bullough (St. Louis: B. Herder Book Co., 1952), Parts III and IV, and Frederick F. Bruce, *The English Bible: A History of Translations* (New York: Oxford University Press, 1961), pp. 113—126, 201—210.

72 Mirbt, No. 173.

73 Ibid., No. 194.

in 1564 laid down ten rules to guide the *Congregatio indicis* (now the Congregation of the Holy Office) in establishing the *Index librorum prohibitorum et expurgandorum*. The fourth rule reads:

> Since it is manifest by experience that, if the Holy Bible in the vulgar tongue be suffered to be read everywhere without distinction, because of men's rashness (*temeritas*) more evil than good arises, let the judgment of the bishop or inquisitor stand in this respect, so that, after consulting with the parish priest or the confessor, they may grant permission to read translations of the Scriptures, made by Catholic writers, to those whom they understand to be able to receive no harm, but an increase of faith and piety from such reading; which permit (*facultas*) let them have in writing. But whosoever shall presume to read these Bibles or have them in possession without such permit shall not be capable of receiving absolution for their sins, unless they have first given up their Bibles to the ordinary [the bishop].[74]

Significant are the statements of the bull *Unigenitus* (1713), in which Clement XI condemned the propositions of Quesnel that the Bible should be read by all and that the obscurity of the Bible does not exempt the laity from reading the Word of God.[75] When the newly organized Bible societies developed great activity at the beginning of the nineteenth century, the popes in unmistakable language condemned them.[76] Pius VII not only condemned the Protestant Bible societies as a pestilence, a snare prepared for man's eternal ruin, tares sown by the adversaries, but also dissolved the Roman Catholic Bible societies. Leo XII spoke of the Bibles published by the Protestant Bible societies as poisonous pastures; Pius IX in the *Syllabus* of 1864 condemned them as being on the same level with Communism, socialism, and secret societies; and Leo XIII in the index of 1897 proscribed all except officially approved and annotated versions. Thus, although it is true that Rome has never issued an absolute prohibition of Bible reading by the laity, it is equally true that the recent encouragements to read the Bible are restricted and qualified. The regulations of Pius IV in Rule Four still stand. Rome still affirms that the reading of approved Bibles is not necessary. For though the Bible is a precious treasure, it may be misused.[77] Inasmuch as indulgences can be gained by the mere reading of the Bible, one is prompted to ask whether such reading is considered a work of supererogation.

TRADITIONS A SOURCE OF DOCTRINE

Rome teaches that the "Gospel" is contained also in the "unwritten traditions," the writings of the Fathers and the pronouncements of the church through the centuries. The last verse of John's Gospel teaches that not everything is set down in the Scriptures. Rome interprets this to mean that part of Christian doctrine must be sought elsewhere, namely, in the "traditions" (2 Thess. 2:14; Acts 2:42).[78] These traditions (*traditio materialis*) were given to the apostles and their rightful successors, deposited in the shrine of the

---

[74] Bull *Dominici gregis custodiae*, March 24, 1564. Mirbt, No. 481.

[75] Ibid., No. 398.

[76] The bulls *Postremis litteris* (June 4, 1816) and *Magno et acerbo* (Sept. 3, 1816) by Pius VII. Mirbt, No. 427.

[77] Wilmers, I, 238 ff. Gibbons, loc. cit.; cp. Innocent III: *Quia multi defecerunt scrutantes scrutinio*. Mirbt, No. 173. But see also Ernest B. Koenker, "The New Role of the Scriptures in Roman Catholicism," *Lutheran Quarterly*, X (1958), 248—254.

[78] Fathers Rumble and Carty, p. 28.

church, and are to be proclaimed by the infallible church. *(traditio formalis)* as the occasion demands. Rome's doctrinal system is not complete, for there are such important doctrines as that of original sin on which there is no full agreement. Even its ecclesiology is, as Dominicus Coster said in 1941, still in the "pretheological state." [79]

To the non-Romanist this appears to be a clear case of development of doctrine. But Rome answers that it is impossible for her to proclaim new doctrines. "It can, however, develop more and more the truth entrusted to it, can define it more exactly and develop the entire wealth of revelation with increasing clarity. By this process not one of the dogmas previously held is rejected, nor are any added which have not been previously taught implicitly." [80] Francis J. Connell states: "Nothing can be added to the deposit of divine revelation since the death of the last apostle, because the truths proclaimed by Christ and the apostles were intended as the completion of the message of God to the human race." He continues to set forth that the pope's infallibility does not imply the pronouncement of new doctrines. It extends to the explanation of the revealed truth and to those doctrines which are intimately connected with, though not actually contained in, "the deposit of truth." [81] Rome says there can be no development of doctrine, for according to John 16:12 all doctrines have always been believed implicitly even though not taught explicitly. A view held by only some in the church, as a *pia sententia,* will not be elevated to an official doctrine until sufficient tradition has been found to support it. "The policy of the Church is to be cautious and slow in taking novel views such as tend to shock and alarm the simple-minded, until such views have been firmly established by evidence." [82] In defense of the new doctrine of papal infallibility Cardinal Gibbons stated:

> The Council did not create a new creed, but rather confirmed the old one. It formulated into an article of faith a truth which in every age had been accepted by the Catholic world because it had been *implicitly* [italics ours] contained in the deposit of revelation. [83]

Cardinal Newman in his essay on *The Development of Christian Doctrine* and Johann Moehler in his *Einheit in der Kirche* present virtually the same views in answering the charge of development. Moehler says:

> The Divine Spirit, to whom is entrusted the guidance and vivification of the Church, becomes by His union with the human spirit in the Church a peculiarly Christian intuition, a deep sure guiding

---

79 Edm. Schlink, "Die Kirche in Gottes Heilsplan," *Theologische Literaturzeitung,* Nov., 1948, p. 646; republished in the *Ecumenical Review,* 1949, 150 ff.

80 Wilmers, II, 694.

81 "Does Catholic Doctrine Change?" *American Ecclesiastical Review,* CXVII (July—Dec., 1947), 322 f. Wilmers, I, 127. Moehler, 288 f. A recent discussion of the history of doctrinal development in the modern Roman Catholic church is Owen Chadwick, *From Bossuet to Newman* (Cambridge: University Press, 1957).

82 Father Hull in Julius A. Weber, *Religions and Philosophies in the United States* (Los Angeles: Wetzel Publ. Co., 1931), p. 60. In *Die römische Lehre von der unbefleckten Empfängnis Mariä* (Berlin, 1865), Ed. Preuss shows from the sources how Rome employed the traditions to elevate the *pia sententia* to a *dogma of the church.* Roman apologists will, of course, answer that Preuss recanted his book in 1871.

83 Gibbons, p. 130.

feeling, which, as it abides in truth, leads also into all truth . . . is not purely an internal act, but is always based on external testimony and outward authority, preceded by an outward certainty. . . . The Church, therefore, as representing Christ, is the living exposition of the divine revelation and thus invested with Christ's own authority and infallibility. . . . If the Church is not the authority representing Christ, then everything relapses into darkness, uncertainty, doubt, distraction, unbelief and superstition. Revelation becomes null and void, fails in its real purpose and must henceforth be even called in question and finally denied. . . . All developments in dogma as well as in morality can be considered as resulting from formal acts of the whole community.[84]

Paradoxically Rome forbids the teaching of any new doctrine, whereas Rome itself certainly has promulgated many new doctrines. This constitutes no contradiction for Roman theologians, who insist that the *ecclesia docens* is infallible and that all doctrines were deposited in one shrine of the church and were implicitly held since the death of the last apostle. The Vatican Council in the dogmatic decree on faith declares:

All those things are to be believed with divine and Catholic faith which are contained in the Word of God, written or handed down (*in verbo Dei scripto vel tradito*), and which the Church either by a solemn judgment, or by her ordinary and universal magisterium proposes for belief as having been divinely revealed.[85]

This is "sheer enthusiasm" and grants the church unlimited reign in promulgating "new doctrines." And that is the real meaning of *traditio*.

REASON A SOURCE OF DOCTRINE

Finally Roman theologians make reason a source of religious knowledge. Following the example of the early Apologists (especially Justin Martyr in his *Logos spermatikos* theory) and the later scholastics, these theologians maintain that both reason and revelation are divine gifts and can therefore never be at variance with each other.[86] The later scholastics, especially Thomas Aquinas, introduced the empirical method and inductive logic of Aristotle into the realm of theology and repudiated Platonic idealism with its emphasis on intuitive knowledge, which had been held by earlier scholastics. Thomas "Christianized Aristotle and Aristotelianized Christian theology." Anselm's "ontological argument," as Kant called it, runs thus: We have the *idea* of an absolutely perfect being. But to be perfect a being must have existence. Therefore an absolutely perfect being must exist.[87] This is Platonic idealism. Thomas, however, employing Aristotelian dialectics, alters the process and uses the following four steps to prove the existence of God: (1) demonstration by natural reason of the existence of God; (2) the establishment by reason of the existence of freedom and immortality of the soul; (3) transition from reason to faith in revelation; and (4) recognition of the church as the authoritative interpreter

[84] Gustav Voss, "Johann Adam Moehler and the Development of Dogma," *Theological Studies*, September, 1943, 420—44.

[85] Schaff, *Creeds*, II, 244 f.

[86] The Vatican Council said: "Not only can faith and reason never be opposed to one another, but they are of mutual aid one to another." Schaff, *Creeds*, II, 249. Burtt, loc. cit. Seeberg, *Dogmengeschichte*, III, 143 ff., discusses the three prominent views held by scholastics: realism, nominalism, conceptualism.

[87] See A. C. Welch, *Anselm and His Work* (Edinburgh: T. & T. Clark, 1901), p. 72.

of the true revelation.[88] Roman Catholic theologians maintain that human reason is competent up to a certain point and that it is also competent to determine where its competence ends; otherwise it could not be competent anywhere. Thomas gave a high rank to reason and the intellect, and he is today the recognized teacher of Roman theology.[89] It is therefore not surprising that the entire theology of Rome is supported by rationalistic arguments, specious though they often are.

While Rome frequently alleges that she employs logic primarily for apologetic reasons, standard dogmatic works of Rome prove conclusively that throughout her theological system reason is considered a legitimate source of divine truths. This rationalist principle becomes evident not only in such points of doctrine as are accepted by all Christians,[90] but especially also in those Roman teachings which have been elevated from pious opinions to dogmas of the church. Roman Catholics argue for their cult of Mary thus: Jesus is a true man, and as such loves His mother. If He did not love His mother more than any other creature, He would not be true man. The blessed Mother is therefore nearer to Jesus than any creature. She has the position of Mother in heaven.[91] The dogma of Mary's assumption is supported by the following syllogism: It is not fitting that the Mother of God be contaminated by sin. In view of His future suffering, Christ preserved her from original sin. Having no sin, she was immortal by absolute right, but sharing in all the work of Christ, she was united with Him in His death and likewise in His ascension.[92]

Rome will probably never repeat the Galileo incident, since its rationalistic principle enables the church today to adjust itself to current scientific knowledge — in so far as there is no conflict with fixed dogmas of the church. The church will accept the findings of modern psychology so long as they are not contrary to its views concerning the freedom and immortality of the soul.[93] But while Rome insists on maintaining the supernatural origin of each soul (creationism), it holds that

the general theory of evolution is not only unobjectionable, it becomes a necessary conclusion from sound Catholic principles. Christian philosophy does not admit supernatural interference where the natural order suffices. . . .

[88] The fivefold argument for the first step is presented by Thomas in *Summa theologica*, I, Qu. 2, Art. 3.

[89] See "Neo-Thomism" above.

[90] While the Bible-centered theologian believes the doctrine of the Trinity, though it is contrary to natural reason and above the enlightened reason, the Roman theologian argues as follows: It must be granted that this doctrine is not contrary to *divine* reason and therefore cannot conflict with *human* reason. Since the doctrine is not contrary to divine reason, it cannot contain any contradiction; and since it actually does not contain any contradiction, human reason cannot find any contradiction where there is none. Wilmers, I, 484.

[91] A Paulist Father, *Devotion to Mary* (New York: the Paulist Press, 1913), p. 7.

[92] O'Connell, ch. iv. See also F. E. Mayer, "The Dogma of Mary's Assumption: A Symptom of Antichristian Theology," *C. T. M.*, XXI (1950), 181.

[93] M. Maher, *Psychology: Empirical and Rational* (New York: Longmans, Green & Co.), Preface. Wm. A. Kelly, *Educational Psychology* (Milwaukee: Bruce Publ. Co., 1938).

Man's *body* is the result of natural forces put into the world by God.[94] The various encyclicals on social and moral problems, on the relation of church and state, on capitalism and labor, reflect throughout the rationalistic principle. If one grants the major premises, then one is compelled by cold logic to accept the inevitable conclusions.[95]

A theology based on reason appeals to man, since it is on man's level. It is, as Philip Melanchthon points out, a theology of the Law, a theology of the natural man.[96] At first glance a theology of reason should lead to certainty; in reality it is a theology of doubt. There are violent differences among leading theologians on important points of doctrine; there are even different trends of thought.[97] Finally Romanists expressly deny that a Christian can attain to absolute assurance in matters of faith. Roman dogmaticians usually speak of three types of assurance: metaphysical, theological, and absolute.[98] Since no man can be certain that his reason and intellect has correctly interpreted the empirical theological data, he is compelled to transfer to the church the responsibility of rightly interpreting all religious facts.[99]

Whether Rome appeals to the Scriptures, or to the traditions, or to reason as the source of doctrine, its formal principle is, in the final analysis, *sola ecclesia, solus papa.*

The Material Principle

Although Rome can shelter a variety of religious views, some of which appear to the Protestant to be mutually exclusive, there is a central thought which controls the entire system. This may be summarized briefly as follows: Man's soul, since it comes directly from God, is good and strives for reunion with God, realized in the beatific vision of God. Man's body is subject to sin and is alienated from God. Therefore man must be progressively justified, i. e., be made just. This result is effected when through the sacraments man enters into the "state of grace" and observes the commandments which the church, i. e., the hierarchy, by her "divine commission," imposes upon the "faithful." Rome's material principle is an extreme type of legalism, a system of "works-righteousness." [100]

---

[94] W. A. Hauber, "Evolution and Catholic Thought," *Ecclesiastical Review*, March, 1942, p. 161—77.

[95] Paul Blanshard has attacked Rome's ethical principles in government, industry, labor, medicine, law, etc., outside the religious frame of reference. This is a basic mistake in dealing with Romanists.

[96] Ap., IV (II), 36 ff.; 130 ff.

[97] In Europe, for example, there was at the turn of the century a sharp clash between liberalism and scholasticism; cp. Walter Horton, "The Revival of Catholic Theology," *Continental European Theology* (New York: Harper & Bros., 1938), pp. 41—84.

[98] On "certainty" see Pohle-Preuss, VII, 379 ff.; also George D. Smith, I, 13 ff.

[99] K. Adam, *The Spirit of Catholicism*, pp. 24, 32 f., 42 ff., 224 ff.

[100] W. Walther speaks of Rome's Judaism (nomism), pp. 160—66.

SECTION III

Basic Doctrines

The discussion of Rome's theology will be restricted to the theological formulations in which Rome differs from other churches, especially the Lutheran.

Doctrine of God

With some other Western Christian churches, Rome accepts the Quicunque and on the basis of the amended *Constantinopolitanum* confesses the procession of the Holy Spirit from the Father and the Son. In the Dogmatic Constitution of the Church the Vatican Council sets forth the commonly accepted propositions concerning God's being and attributes.[101] It defines God as "being one, sole, absolutely simple and immutable spiritual substance" and ascribes to God all the Scriptural divine attributes. Nevertheless Roman theologians place an undue emphasis on God's sovereignty and justice.[102] True, they also speak of God's love, but God's love tinged with legalism. This becomes evident from Rome's definition of love as that attribute which prompts God to communicate His treasures to man, not as a free gift but as a reward in accord with man's works.[103]

All of God's works (creation, preservation, redemption, justification) are said to flow not so much from God's love, beneficence, grace, and goodness as from His sovereignty and His purpose of self-glorification. Some Roman theologians have held that creation flows from God's love, but the Vatican Council anathematized those who say that God created the world "by a necessity equal to the necessity whereby He loves Himself and deny that the world was made for the glory of God."[104] Especial emphasis is placed on God's justice. Scholasticism has drawn a picture of God which is based on a system which places God and man on a contractual basis.[105] Trent in Sess. VI, Canon 21, anathematizes anyone who says that Christ Jesus was given of God to men only as a Redeemer in whom to trust and not also as a Legislator whom to obey. God is viewed as Judge, whose primary attribute is justice. This accounts for the many juridical terms and the frequency with which they are employed (merit, reward, the forum of the church) and for the entire penitential system, with its inquisition, satisfactions, dispensations, indulgences, including the theological premises for the theory of purgatory. If this emphasis on divine justice were granted, then the reasonableness of some

---

101 Schaff, *Creeds,* II, 239.

102 1 John 4:9; cp. M. Luther, Large C., the Creed, p. 63 f.

103 W. Walther, pp. 51 ff., 161, and cp. E. Klotsche, p. 68 ff. (See Bibliog.)

104 Schaff, *Creeds,* II, 252. The election, and even the reprobation, of individuals is ascribed to God's sovereignty and self-glorification. Cp. below, "Eschatology."

105 Seeberg, *Lehrbuch der Dogmengeschichte,* 3d ed., III (Leipzig: A. Deichertsche Verlagsbuchhandlung Nachfolger, 1913), 368 f., 402 ff.

extra- and non-Scriptural theories, such as the existence of *limbus infantum*, must also be granted. Rome argues that because of God's justice unbaptized children, tainted with original sin, cannot come into His presence, nor can He permit them to be damned, since they have committed no actual sin. God must therefore prepare for them a "state of perfect *natural* happiness." [106] God's justice is also the basis for the scholastic distinction between *meritum de congruo* (a reward corresponding to man's use of his natural endowments) and *meritum de condigno* (the reward due him who in "the state of grace" performs the divinely prescribed works). The one-sided emphasis on God's justice prompts Romanists to view grace as that infused supernatural quality whereby man can perform "supernatural" works which are rewarded "supernaturally." This undue emphasis on divine justice is reflected in Rome's view that though God remits the eternal punishment of sin, His justice requires some compensation, to be rendered in the form of satisfactions.[107]

Doctrine of Man

Neoplatonic tendencies, clearly discernible in the theology of the Eastern church, are evident also in the theology of the Western church.[108] According to Neo-Platonism, the world and man came into being by a process of emanations from the Absolute. The soul of man comes directly from God and is perfect, whereas the body, which represents the last emanation, is evil and in constant conflict with the soul. Although the Vatican Council (Canon I, 4) condemned this extreme view, it does leave room for a modified form of dualism; and since the church has not spoken officially on this point, various views are held. It seems that the Thomistic teaching, which advocates a dualistic view of man, has gained general assent. All organic things, including the body of man, are said to be created out of organic and perishable matter, whereas the immaterial soul is, by a special creative act of God, made out of nothing. For this reason Rome considers traducianism — an open question elsewhere in Christendom — a heretical view and accepts creationism as *sententia certa*. To guard against extreme dualism, the theologians state that God forges soul and body into an indissoluble union, the soul imparting its immortality to the embryo and the body giving its individuality to the rational soul. Theologians are not agreed when this union takes place; some say when the child is conceived, others when the fetus is four and a half months old.[109] This modified dualism has serious implications for Rome's teachings concerning the nature of man, both in the state of integrity and since the Fall.

Rome distinguishes between the nat-

---

[106] *Cath. Encyc.*, II, 267.

[107] Trent, Sess. VI, ch. xiv, Can. 30; XIV, ch. viii, Can. 12, 13. — Luther and his co-workers had to deal largely with this concept. This is reflected in the Ap. Cp. Philip Watson, *Let God Be God* (London: Epworth Press, 1947), p. 51 ff. H. Boehmer, *Road to Reformation* (Philadelphia: Muhlenburg Press, 1946), p. 141 f.

[108] See the section on the Eastern Orthodox church. Augustine, the father of much of Western theology, did not entirely free himself from his Neoplatonic environment. Cp. J. L. Neve, *A History of Christian Thought* (Philadelphia: The Muhlenberg Press, c. 1946), I, 101.

[109] Walther, p. 57 f. *Cath. Encyc.*, s. v. "Creationism." Karl Vossler, *Medieval Culture* (New York: Harcourt, Brace & Co., 1929), I, 100—20. Wilmers, I, 588 ff., 651 ff. Smith, pp. 295 ff., 349 ff. Moehler, p. 51.

ural and supernatural gifts bestowed upon man in the state of integrity. The image of God is said to consist in the bestowal of such *natural* endowments as freedom of the will, right emotions, great scientific knowledge, and immortality of the soul. According to his natural constitution, Adam's body, even before the Fall, was the seat of concupiscence, i. e., his sensuous desires or his interest in, and love for, the beauties of creation. These natural gifts enabled him to lead a rich mundane life, but were insufficient for the attainment of the beatific vision of God. Therefore God endowed him also with such *supernatural* gifts as perfect control over concupiscence, *immortality of the body*, and chiefly "sanctifying grace," called the *donum gratiae superadditum*, which enabled Adam to attain the similitude according to both body and spirit. Because of these supernatural gifts there were no inordinate desires in Adam, there was no conflict between flesh and spirit, but rather complete conquest of concupiscence (which, according to Trent, is not sin, though it may lead to sin).[110] J. A. Moehler says:

> The schoolmen say: "His inferior faculties of soul and bodily impulses acted unresistingly under the guidance of his reason, and therefore everything in him was in obedience to reason, as his reason was in obedience to God," and accordingly lived in blessed harmony with himself and with his Maker. . . . This relation of Adam to God, as it exalted him above human nature and made him participate in that of God (including immortality of the body) is hence termed a supernatural gift of divine grace, superadded to the endowments of nature.[111]

The teachers are not agreed as to the time when nor as to the reason why

Adam received this superadded gift. The Scotists held that Adam "merited" this "grace" and therefore received it sometime after creation; Thomists taught that it was a concreated gift. The council dodged the issue by stating that Adam was *constituted* in holiness and justice.[112] This raises the question as to the extent of the loss which Adam incurred through the Fall. Roman theologians are not in full accord; some follow the Scotists, who held that Adam is again in the state in which he was prior to receiving the *donum superadditum*, thus leaving man's "nature" virtually unimpaired. Others incline to the Thomistic view that the loss of holiness and justice affected also the "nature" of man. Trent satisfied both parties by decreeing in the Fifth Session that Adam "lost the holiness and justice wherein he had been constituted and that the entire Adam through that offense of prevarication was changed in body and soul for the worse." Bellarmine says that Adam's condition after the Fall differs from his constitution *in puris naturalibus* (before the bestowal of the superadded gift) in the same manner in which a man robbed of his clothes is distinguished from a naked person. After the Fall Adam is deprived of that which he had not as yet received at his creation.[113]

Like Adam, his descendants lost the similitude, but not the divine image. Accordingly man is still endowed, even as Adam *in puris naturalibus*, with a free will and with reason, whereby he is able to know and to worship God as far as these powers allow. In chapter I of Sess. VI Trent declares that in Adam all men have lost their holiness, and have become subject to death, the wrath

---

110 Wilmers, I, 637. Smith, I, 320 ff.

111 Pp. 27, 29.

112 In the first draft the word "created" *(conditus)* was employed, but changed to *constitutus* at the suggestion of Pacecus; ibid., p. 29.

113 Walther, p. 61; also Klotsche, p. 78.

of God, and the devil. Nevertheless, "free will, weakened though it was in its powers, and bent down, was by no means extinguished in them." Moreover, in Canon V, Trent specifically condemns the Lutheran doctrine of the bondage of the will. Moehler, a strong advocate of the theory that natural man still has *facultas se applicandi ad gratiam,* denounces the definition of original sin in the Augsburg Confession (*sine metu Dei et cum concupiscentia*) as being contrary to human experience, for he finds that "in superstition [of the heathen] faith lies concealed." The idolatry of the heathen is considered by him as evidence that man still has spiritually good aspirations.[114]

There is an irreconcilable clash between Romanism and Lutheranism on the entire doctrine of sin. Luther declares that original sin is the capital sin and "is so deep and thorough a corruption of nature that no reason can understand it." [115] The Council of Trent did not describe the essence of original sin, except in so far as it views original sin primarily as deprivation and not as total depravity. Rome specifically condemned the Scriptural view that concupiscence is sin when it decreed that although Paul sometimes calls concupiscence sin, it is not really sin, but only an incentive to sin (*fomes,* "tinder") which remains in man for his exercise. Moeller states that a carnal emotion (concupiscence)

in conflict with the will does not contaminate the will.[116] Hence Rome views only voluntary transgression as sin. Whereas Lutheran theology sees in every sin a rebellion against God, Roman theologians deal with individual sins and thoroughly atomize the concept of sin. Depending on the attendant circumstances, the intention, and other considerations, Rome has fixed various categories and catalogs of sin, such as nine foreign sins, six sins against the Holy Ghost, four sins which cry for vengeance, seven mortal sins. In particular she distinguishes between mortal and venial sins.[117] When non-Roman theology speaks of mortal sins in distinction from venial sins, it has in mind such sins as destroy faith. But Rome's distinction between venial and mortal refers only to the alleged degree of gravity of sins committed by the "faithful." The distinction between venial and mortal sins is set forth by Di Bruno:

> Mortal and venial sins differ fundamentally in their effect on the soul; mortal brings immediate spiritual death, or separation from God, venial inflicts wounds more or less severe, but not immediately fatal; it cools, but does not dissolve the friendship of God. . . . Mortal sin is a thorough violation, or breaking, of a commandment of God with full knowledge and deliberation. . . . Venial is either a slight infringement of the Law, or it may be in some cases a great violation of the Law, but ren-

---

[114] Ch. vi: "Doctrine of the Lutherans Respecting Original Sin" (pp. 54 to 66); ch. vii: "Considerations of Heathenism" (pp. 66—72). While the Lutheran Reformers stated that in those things which are subject to reason the heathen can do good works but that in spiritual matters man's totality is depraved, Moehler states that "history [of the pagan religions] confirms the Catholic doctrine of original sin and incontrovertibly demonstrates that, deep as his fall might have been, man lost not his freedom, nor was despoiled of the image of God" (p. 72).

[115] S. A., P. III, Art. I, 3. By "*Hauptsünde*" Luther denotes that original sin is the source of all other sin. See, below, "Lutheran Church."

[116] Pp. 63 f., 107; Wilmers, I, 668 f.; Smith, I, 332 f.

[117] Cp. Luther, W. A., 10, 2, p. 334 ff.; also A. Urban, *Teacher's Handbook to the Catechism* (New York: Joseph F. Wagner), I, 198 ff.

dered slight in the person who commits it through his want of sufficient knowledge, deliberation, or freedom. Venial sin is not a complete breaking of a commandment, but a tendency towards breaking it. . . . Venial sin, although an offense against God, does not cause the forfeiture of God's friendship nor the loss of justifying grace, as mortal sin does; but it diminishes God's love towards us. . . . It causes a stain and a guilt in the soul, of which we can easily obtain pardon; and therefore it is in that sense called venial, from the Latin *venia*, pardon. . . . Mortal sin offends God grievously, causes death to the soul, and deserves everlasting punishment.[118]

Rome has, however, been unable to find a fully satisfactory definition of a mortal sin. The catechisms usually define a mortal sin as comprising three elements: a sinful act in an important matter, committed with full understanding of the evil, and the entire consent of the will.[119]

Rome's anthropology is of far-reaching importance for its entire theology. Its teaching concerning sin denies the absolute need of a divine Redeemer, and its views concerning the freedom of man's will ascribe to man the ability to co-operate in his own salvation.

Christ's Person and Work

With the ancient symbols, including the Chalcedonian, Rome confesses the true deity and full humanity of Christ in one Person. Its concept of the personal union, however, is colored by its modified dualism, which makes a distinction between the natural and supernatural constitution of man and places a relatively low estimate on human nature. For this reason Roman theologians can say that the holiness of the human nature in Christ is predicated on a twofold grace: the grace of the personal union, which did not confer all holiness, and sanctifying grace, and immediate infusion of the same virtues which other men receive through the sacraments mediately. Furthermore, the dogmaticians maintain Christ's impeccability not only on the basis of the personal union, but also by rational arguments, such as that peccability is incompatible with His dignity and with the enjoyment of the beatific vision during His earthly life.[120] And specifically the theologians deny the *genus maiestaticum*, more particularly the communicated omnipresence of the human nature, stating that the glorified body of Christ is enclosed in heaven and is not on earth except in a special manner, such as in the Sacrament of the Altar. Roman dogmaticians have debated whether the humanity of Christ is entitled to *latreia* or only to *hyperdulia*, the veneration accorded to Mary.[121]

Rome's doctrine concerning Christ's work contains strange contradictions for the evangelical Christian. These come to the surface in the statement that Christ's work is twofold, namely, to redeem and to teach. But in both phases of Christ's work the material principle is the dominant factor. In defining the redemptive work Roman dogmaticians state that, by His active and passive obedience rendered in our stead, Christ redeemed mankind from all sin, death,

---

[118] Quoted in *Popular Symbolics*, p. 168 f.; cp. Smith, II, 925 ff.; 945 ff.; Christian Pesch, *Praelectiones dogmaticae* (Freiburg-im-Breisgau: Herder & Co., 1923), IX, *Tractatus* II *(De peccato)*, 309—70; Wilmers, III, 531 ff.

[119] Walther, p. 66.

[120] Wilmers, II, 225 ff., 238.

[121] Ibid., p. 339 f. Smith, I, 379 f., resolves the problem by distinguishing between the formal and material objects of worship; cp. Pohle-Preuss, IV, 279 ff. and especially 287 f.

and eternal damnation.[122] At the same time, Rome's undue emphasis on the justice of God and the idea of merit permeates its views concerning Christ's redemptive work. Neither the Anselmic satisfaction theory of the atonement, nor the Scotist acceptilation theory, is generally accepted, but rather the Thomistic view that Christ earned a *superabundant* merit by His infinite love, unspeakable suffering, and the divine character of His person. Franks summarizes Thomas' view as follows:

> To Christ was given "grace," not only as to a single person but in so far as He is Head of the Church, in order that from Him it might overflow to the members; and therefore the works of Christ have the same relation both to Himself and to His members, as the works of another man established in grace have to himself. Now it is manifest, that whoever being established in grace suffers for righteousness' sake, by this very thing merits for himself salvation: wherefore Christ by His passion merited salvation, not only for Himself, but also for all His members.[123]

This superabundant merit, like the superabundant merits of other saints, is deposited in the "treasury of the Church" to be dispensed by the church to its members. Following Thomas, Roman theologians view Christ's work under a fourfold aspect: (1) through His innocent life and death Christ rendered to God a *satisfaction* in the stead of man; (2) the death upon the cross is the *sacrifice* which reconciles God and reestablishes the pristine state of grace; (3) *redemption* delivers man from the power of sin, death, devil; and (4) through His work He earned the *merit* to be exalted and to confer upon men the "graces" necessary for their justification. A Romanist may understand this in the truly evangelical sense. No doubt many do so and rely solely on grace as God's favor in Christ's all-sufficient work. But the leading dogmaticians understand it to mean that Christ has gained sufficient graces (or virtues) for man, whereby men are enabled to acquire holiness and salvation by their own works. Thus they remain true to Rome's material principle and all doctrines derived from it.[124] While Rome today teaches that Christ is the Propitiation for both original and actual sins, it nevertheless states that Christ purposed *primarily* to remove original sin not because it is the greater sin, but because it is universal. Accordingly Roman theologians can still maintain that although Christ has removed the guilt of original sin, the expiation of actual sins is primarily man's own obligation.[125]

The material principle of Rome's theology is evident particularly in the second phase of Christ's work, His teaching office. Trent asserts (Sess. VI, Can. 21) that man's justification rests as much on Christ the "new Legislator" as upon Christ the Redeemer. Many theologians favor the *anakepha-*

---

[122] Wilmers, II, 283 ff.; *C. Rom.*, 51; cp. The Council of Trent, Sess. VI, ch. ii, Canons 2, 10, 26; Smith, I, 62 f.; Wilmers quotes approvingly from the hymn *Adoro devote:*
Pelican of mercy, Jesu, Lord and God,
Cleanse me, all unclean, in Thy most precious blood:
Blood, whereof one drop, for humankind outpoured,
Might from all transgression have the world restored.

[123] Robert S. Franks, *A History of the Doctrine of the Work of Christ in Its Ecclesiastical Development* (London: Hodder & Stoughton [1918]), I, 269.

[124] Walther, p. 65 f.; Wilmers, II, 305 ff.; Smith, I, 495, 564, 577.

[125] Wilmers, II, 291 f.; Smith, I, 491 f., 565 f. The Lutheran Confessions specifically condemned this view. A. C., III, 3; XXIV, 24—33.

laiōsis theory, a mystical theory of the atonement held by Irenaeus, and teach that Christ became the Second Adam in order to restore the union between God and man through His incarnation. In line with this theory they teach that Christ by word and deed gave an example of all those virtues whereby man himself can effect his ultimate union with God.[126]

Justification

In Section VI the Council of Trent, in theses and strong antitheses directed against the Lutherans, sets forth its views on justification. Modern dogmaticians dare not deviate from Trent. But as a result of various controversies, particularly the Molinist and Congruist (*ca.* 1600) and the Jansenist (*ca.* 1700), the distinction between *actual* and *sanctifying* grace seems to receive greater emphasis. Justification is presented as the application of (1) actual grace, "a supernatural gift by which rational creatures are enabled to perform salutary acts," and (2) habitual or sanctifying grace, "a habit, a more or less enduring state, which renders men pleasing to God." Pohle summarizes Rome's doctrine as follows:

> Humanity was reconciled to God by the Redemption. This does not mean that every individual human being was forthwith justified, for individual justification is wrought by the application to the soul of grace derived from the inexhaustible merits of Jesus Christ.[127]

The first phase of justification is the bestowal of *actual* grace. Actual grace is said to be "prevenient, co-operating, merely sufficient, accidentally efficacious, intrinsically efficacious, congruent, external, internal, natural, supernatural, calling, sanctifying, healing." The two chief categories under which actual grace is viewed are "prevenient" or "illuminating grace" and "co-operating grace." Actual grace is prevenient inasmuch as it is the divine assistance which communicates to the will the power (*posse*) to perform a salutary act and thus precedes the spontaneous act of the soul. It may also be called "merely sufficient" grace. Prevenient grace is bestowed upon *all* men. Actual grace is co-operating grace when it prompts deliberate consent on the part of the will and results in the action itself (*agere*) and may therefore also be called efficacious grace. Peronne defines actual grace as

> that unmerited interior assistance which God, by virtue of the merits of Christ, confers upon fallen man, in order, on the one hand, to remedy his infirmity resulting from sin and, on the other, to raise him to the supernatural order and thereby to render him capable of performing supernatural acts, so that he may attain justification, persevere in it to the end, and thus enter into everlasting life.[128]

Although Trent vacillated between Scotist Pelagianism, which ascribed virtually unimpaired power to man, and Thomist Semi-Pelagianism, which ascribed as much as possible to God and as little as possible to man, modern theologians generally hold that for all "salutary acts" actual grace is absolutely necessary. In their opposition to all forms of naturalistic theology they maintain that while man is able without the aid of grace to arrive at the knowledge of God and to perform some naturally good works, actual grace is absolutely necessary not only for faith but for the very begin-

---

[126] Wilmers, II, 267 ff., 299 ff. See Smith, I, Ch. xii: "Jesus Christ, the Model of Manhood," 401—39; Pohle-Preuss, V, 143 f.

[127] Pohle-Preuss, VII, 1.

[128] Ibid., pp. 18, 32 ff., 41.

ning of faith. This beginning of faith, "whether we call it faith itself or speak, as the Semi-Pelagians did, of certain preambles of faith . . . wherever the supernatural domain of salutary action begins, there it is God who begins, there is prevenient grace." [129] This seems to be a departure from pre-Reformation theology. The term "grace" no longer seems to denote primarily the "infused virtues" whereby man works out his justification, but a gratuitous gift of God. Whereas in Semi-Pelagianism man is viewed as making the beginning of his justification, modern Romanists ascribe the beginning exclusively to God's grace. Nevertheless the standard doctrine that man's justification is dependent on his good works is not in the least modified. In the first place, the concept of grace is presented in such a way that it does not exclude human merit. The apparent conflict between the dogma of the absolute gratuity of grace and the teaching that man can merit justification and earn eternal glory is resolved by stating that the *prima gratia* and all graces based on it are unmerited by nature in strict justice. Rome therefore also retains the distinction between *meritum de congruo* and *de condigno,* though in a somewhat modified form. Whereas formerly man was said to be able to earn *meritum de congruo* with his natural endowments and *meritum de condigno* only with "infused grace," some leading modern dogmaticians teach that both types of merit can be earned only in the "state of grace," congruous merit being measured on the basis of fitness, condign merit on the ground of justice. [130] In the

second place, "man may prepare himself negatively for the reception of supernatural grace by not putting any obstacles in the way," or, in positive terms "by faithfully co-operating with the grace of God, man is able to merit additional grace, and this holds true even of infidels and sinners." [131] In the third place, God's grace is in reality not the gratuitous favor of God, but primarily a good quality in man. Pohle declares:

> God gives all men sufficient graces. But He is not obliged to give to each *efficacious* graces, because all that is required to enable man to reach his supernatural destiny is co-operation with sufficient grace, especially with the *gratia prima vocans,* which is the beginning of all salutary operation.

In expanding this, he states that not only "all just men," not only "ordinary sinners" and "obdurate" men, but even the heathen receive sufficient graces for salvation. It is held as a *certa opinio* that since God does not permit anyone to perish for want of grace, the heathen as *fideles negativi* receive sufficient graces so that by an "implicit faith" they obtain a "supernatural belief" in those cardinal truths which the church demands as necessary for salvation. [132] In short, actual grace illuminates all men's reason, excites their will, and thereby offers them the possibility to use their powers to choose between evil and good. If man chooses the evil, grace in his case was "merely sufficient"; if the good, he prepares himself for the reception of sanctifying grace. Thus the dogmaticians can say that God alone

---

[129] Ibid., p. 104 f.

[130] Ibid., pp. 130 ff., 430 ff. Thomas already advocated the now more commonly accepted distinction. Cp. Heinrich Rinn, *Dogmengeschichtliches Lesebuch,* p. 273. — In the Ap., Melanchthon shows that no matter which distinction is used, either concept destroys the doctrine of *sola fide.* — It seems that the scope of the state of grace is broadened.

[131] Pohle-Preuss, VII, 147 f.

[132] Ibid., pp. 167, 168, 172, 179 ff.

makes conversion a possibility, but man makes it a reality, or in the words of Pohle:

> Actual grace is a transient supernatural help given by God from the treasury of the merits of Jesus Christ for the purpose of enabling man to work out his eternal salvation.[133]

The second and essential phase of justification is the application of sanctifying grace, which, according to Trent, comprises three steps: (1) the preparation *(iustificatio in fieri)*; (2) the essence *(in esse)*; (3) the fruit of justification or the merits of good works *(in facto esse)*.[134] The Scriptural distinction between conversion (the sinner's acceptance of the complete atonement) and justification (God's pronouncement of the complete absolution) has no place in Roman theology. In fact, Roman dogmatics has no place for the *locus* on conversion. Trent speaks of justification as the change in man, a process running through certain well-defined stages.

The first, or preparatory, step is faith. Both Evangelical and Roman theologians teach that man is justified by faith, but disagree fundamentally as to the nature and place of faith in justification. In Lutheran theology faith is the divinely wrought assurance which knows, accepts, and trusts in Christ's all-sufficient sacrifice. In Rome's theology faith is purely intellectual, "a dogmatical or theoretical belief in the truths of Divine Revelation," a belief which may be either implicit or explicit. A person "makes an act of implicit faith when he says: 'I believe whatever the church teaches'" (collier's faith). Explicit faith is "an express and fully developed belief in the truths of revelation," but on the basis of Heb. 11:6 many theologians hold that only two doctrines must be accepted explicitly: the existence of God and eternal retribution.[135] Naturally, this faith cannot "justify." Trent (Sess. VI, 8, 6) therefore teaches that faith is the "root" of justification, in fact the source of four additional preparatory or dispositive steps to justification: (1) fear of divine justice; (2) hope; (3) initial love; (4) contrition. These four acts change the *fides informis* to *fides caritate formata*, and this "faith active in good works," *prepares* man for justification and *precedes* justification.[136]

The essence of justification is defined by Trent (Sess. VI, ch. iv) as that renewal of the soul whereby negatively sins are blotted out and positively the sinner is actually made just. Roman as well as Evangelical theology teaches that man is justified for Christ's sake. In Lutheran theology this means that God imputes Christ's all-sufficient sacrifice to the sinner and thereby forgives all his sin or declares him just. Rome specifically condemns this forensic, or juridical, justification, and carefully distinguishes between forgiveness, or the eradication of sin, and justification, a moral change. It teaches that because

---

133 Ibid., p. 3; Walther, op. cit., p. 130 f.

134 Pohle-Preuss, VII, Part II. — A large portion of this section (pp. 271 to 435) is devoted to a refutation of the Lutheran principles *sola fide* and *sola gratia*. Cf. Moehler, pp. 101 ff.; 119 f.; Smith, I, Ch. xvi: "Sanctifying Grace," 549—83; Pesch, V, *"De gratia habituali,"* 194 ff.; Wilmers, IV, 113—205.

135 Pohle-Preuss, VII, 273—84; not even the knowledge that there is a Redeemer is regarded as absolutely necessary; see also Pesch on *"fides dogmatica,"* V, 230; Smith, I, 26 f.; Wilmers, IV, 133.

136 Pohle-Preuss, VII, 295 ff. Some theologians hold that if the sinner's contrition is dictated by perfect love and he has an implicit desire for the sacrament, contrition accomplishes justification. — Moehler attacks Luther's justification by faith alone, p. 101 f.; Wilmers, IV, 135 f.

of the merits of Christ (*causa meritoria*) God infuses sanctifying grace, a supernatural quality bestowed upon the soul, which makes man just and an heir of heaven. The meaning of the verb "justify" is based on the Vulgate *iustificare* (to make just), and Roman theologians go to great lengths in their attempt to show that "justify" in the Bible must not be understood in a forensic sense.[137] The infusion of grace so completely transforms the sinner that he is changed from an unjust to a just person. Sanctifying grace "is a splendor and light that effaces all the stains of the soul," establishes a supernatural friendship between God and the soul, elevates man to the rank of an adopted child with the claim on the beatific vision, and even infuses the divine nature. The "deification of the soul," whereby man "is raised above himself to a quasi-divine dignity," is an article of faith. The manner of this *apotheōsis*, however, is variously understood, since the theologians cannot agree which of God's attributes are communicable. Thomas held that the soul's deification consists in the ability to understand God's being.[138] In addition to effecting justification, sanctifying grace infuses as "supernatural concomitants" the three divine virtues faith, hope, charity; the four cardinal moral virtues

prudence, justice, fortitude, temperance; the seven gifts of the Holy Spirit of Is. 11:2 f.; and finally the indwelling of the Holy Ghost.[139]

Rome's doctrine of the sinner's justification through his "love" or good works must of necessity be a theology of doubt. Ordinarily no one, unless he has received a special revelation, as had the thief on the cross, can obtain a "metaphysical," let alone a "theological," certainty of salvation. There is only a moral certainty, which admits of varying degrees and may, as in the case of Paul (Rom. 8:38 f.), become so great as to exclude all reasonable doubt.[140] Since grace is not viewed as God's favor toward man for Christ's sake, but as an inherent quality in man, Rome teaches that sanctifying grace is present in varying degrees and may be increased by man either *ex opere operantis* (good works) or *ex opere operato* (the sacraments). It may also be lost entirely by mortal sin. Faith, on the other hand, being merely an intellectual *habitus,* cannot be destroyed by mortal sin.[141]

According to Trent, the fruit of justification consists in this, that all good works performed in the state of sanctifying grace are meritorious *de condignò,* i. e., gain merit in the strict sense of

---

137 Pohle-Preuss, VII, 313—22; Moehler, p. 101 ff.; Wilmers, IV, 117 to 126; Smith, I, 550 f.; Pesch, V, 220 ff. But the brilliant young Swiss Roman Catholic theologian Hans Küng, in his book *Rechtfertigung: Die Lehre Karl Barths und eine katholische Besinnung* (Einsiedeln: Johannes Verlag, c. 1957), asserts that there is substantial identity between the doctrine of justification of Karl Barth, which is basically that of the Reformation, and the correctly understood position of the Council of Trent.

138 Pohle-Preuss, VII, 337—62, esp. 340—46; 405. The *apotheōsis* theory is no doubt responsible for the strong emphasis on mystical experience. Thomas said that he had experienced revelations which made all his writings seem nothing but straw. See Josef Pieper, *The Silence of Saint Thomas: Three Essays*, trans. John Murray and Daniel O'Connor (New York: Pantheon Books, c. 1957), 38—41.

139 Pohle-Preuss, VII, 362—77. — Some of these views are "theologically certain," others are "probable" opinions, and still others "more probable."

140 Ibid., pp. 379—83. Cp. Moehler on certainty, pp. 152—61; Pesch, V, 231 ff.; Smith, I, 582 f.

141 Pohle-Preuss, VII, 384—96.

the word. Our quarrel with Rome is not whether good works are necessary, nor whether good works will be rewarded, but whether good works are necessary to earn and merit salvation. Rome teaches that man cannot merit "actual grace" (which precedes justification), but Trent (Can. 32) anathematizes those who deny that man "truly merits an increase of grace, eternal life and the attainment of that eternal life and also an increase of glory." [142] But again an element of grave uncertainty is injected, for the dogmaticians list seven conditions and restrictions. A work to be meritorious must be (1) morally good, (2) free, (3) performed with the assistance of actual grace; (4) inspired by a supernatural motive; it must be performed by (5) a wayfarer prior to death who is (6) in the state of grace; and (7) it must be acceptable to God as deserving of merit. [143] Lutheranism and Romanism are poles apart in the doctrine of justification, and there can never be *rapprochement* as long as this wide theological chasm remains concerning such vital points as the author of our justification; the nature and function of faith; the meaning of grace; the Scriptural definition of justification; the relation of justification to sanctification.

SECTION IV

The Sacramental System

In Roman theology the justification of the sinner is "ordinarily not a purely internal and invisible process or series of acts, but requires the instrumentality of external visible signs, which either confer or augment grace. . . . The redemptive power [emanating from the Cross] flows into the souls of men through the Sacraments and the Cross."

Fra Di Bruno defines a sacrament as an outward sign of a corresponding invisible grace ordained by Jesus Christ as a permanent means in the Church and which, by virtue of Christ's infinite merits, has power to convey to the worthy receiver the grace which it signifies. The object of the sacraments is to apply the fruit of our Savior's redemption to men by conveying, through their means, to our souls either the "habitual grace" of justification or an increase of the same and a pouring in of other graces or the recovery of justification when lost. [144]

The sacraments contain and confer "the grace which they signify." In other words, they impart sanctifying grace and all its concomitants, viz., the divine virtues of faith and the infused moral

---

[142] Pohle-Preuss, VII, 423 ff. "An unattainable life would be a chimera, but the attainment of eternal life does not coincide with the gaining of the merit, but must be put off until death," and therefore Trent uses both phrases: "eternal life" and "attainment of that eternal life," p. 427.

[143] Ibid., pp. 410—22.

[144] Fra Di Bruno, *Catholic Belief*, edited from the Italian by L. A. Lambert (New York, 1884), p. 61. Quoted in *Popular Symbolics*, p. 175. Pohle-Preuss, VIII, 1, 8, 67. In this dogmatic series four volumes are devoted to the sacraments. Cp. Council of Trent, Sess. VII, esp. the canons on the sacraments in general. Wilmers, IV, pp. 209—857; Moehler, 202 ff.; Smith, II, 733—1100; Pesch, all of Vols. VI and VII.

virtues. In addition, each sacrament confers its own specific sacramental grace. Justification is therefore obtainable only through the sacraments appointed by the church. The sacraments play such a prominent role in Roman theology that many consider sacramentalism to be the heart and core of Rome's theology. The fact is, however, that Rome's doctrine on the sacraments stands in an intimate relation to its material principle in general and, in particular, to its views concerning (1) man, (2) faith and grace, and (3) the church.

Rome's view that man's soul and body belong to two different spheres prompts the view that "if man were a pure spirit, then would the divine powers, which produce justice and holiness, require no visible medium." Because of "the entanglement of man with the lower world, which is subjected to a curse," man must be "raised up to a world of higher order." This is accomplished by the specific graces conveyed through each of the seven sacraments.[145]

Rome's view of faith as a mere intellectual assent and its definition of grace as an infused quality in man becomes evident in a twofold manner in its sacramental theology. In the first place, only the sacraments are means of "grace." The Word is not. The sacraments are never viewed as the proclaimed Word, for in 1 Cor. 1:17 St. Paul is said to distinguish very sharply between preaching and baptizing. The hearing of the Mass in a foreign tongue (despite a widespread desire for greater use of the vernacular) has been fixed generally as a commandment of the church, while the sermon has been relegated to the background.[146] In the second place, Rome vigorously defends the *ex opere operato* efficacy of the sacraments. In Art. XIII of the Augsburg Confession the Lutherans declared that the sacraments

are signs and testimonies of the will of God toward us, instituted to awaken and confirm faith in those who use them. Wherefore we must so use them that faith be added to believe the promises which are offered and set forth through the Sacraments.

Trent anathematized this view and declared that the sacraments contain the grace which they signify and that they confer it "in virtue of the act performed," *ex opere operato*, independently of the merits and disposition of the recipient. The use of the Latin language is maintained in the Mass, not only because there is no solid argument for the use of the vernacular, but primarily because those ignorant of the Latin lose nothing of the sacramental effect, since the sacraments produce their effect *ex opere operato*. Rome says that the words of institution are not properly a proclamation (*verbum concionale*), but a consecratory word (*verbum consecratorium*). As such the words confer sanctifying grace by the mere act performed and do not require faith. This seems to give the sacraments a power and an efficacy *sine bono motu cordis* and *sine fide*. Rome, however, strenuously objects to this implication. It teaches that there must be a "dispositive preparation" on

---

[145] Moehler, p. 210 ff. The theory that, since the flesh is the seat of sin, justification is effected by subduing the flesh through asceticism seems to be reflected in the emphasis which the dogmaticians place on the specific grace of each sacrament. John A. O'Brien, *Modern Psychology and the Mass* (New York: The Paulist Press, 1927), p. 30, states: "The philosophical basis of the use of ceremonies in religious service is found in the composite nature, physical and mental, with which the Creator has endowed man."

[146] Pohle-Preuss, VIII, 112, 140; Walther, p. 90. Cp. Theo. Graebner, "The Means of Grace in Roman Theology," *C. T. M.*, X (1939), 241 ff.

the part of the recipient to "produce the full effect." This preparation consists in "not placing an obstacle (*obex*) to grace." In other words, sacramental grace is effective *ex opere operato* when man is not living in mortal sin. Rome furthermore teaches expressly that the Old Testament sacraments derived their efficacy from faith (*ex opere operantis*), whereas the New Testament sacraments do not require faith.[147] The real point is that Rome objects to the doctrine of justification by faith, which it has summarized falsely: *Pecca fortiter, crede fortius* ("sin courageously, believe still more courageously").

Finally there is an integral relation between Rome's sacramentalism and sacerdotalism. The sacraments are absolutely necessary to salvation. But, according to Trent (Sess. VII, Can. 10), the sacraments, with the possible exception of Baptism and Matrimony can be administered only by Christ's appointed administrants who through Holy Orders have received the necessary qualifications. This places the salvation of man into the hands of the hierarchy. Through the sacramental system the priesthood is said to supply every need of man from the cradle to the grave. If the laity becomes recalcitrant, the hierarchy has the powerful instrument of the interdict. When imposed on an individual (e. g., a divorced person), a parish, a diocese, or a nation, the interdict makes the performance of any of the seven sacraments impossible and automatically deprives the interdicted person of the only means of salvation.

The three constituent elements of a sacrament are said to be the visible sign, the invisible grace, and the divine institution. The dogmaticians say that the matter (*materia*) of the sacrament is indeterminate until the word determines its form (*forma*). An example will illustrate: There are many symbolic ablutions. These are not Baptism until the words of institution determine the form to be Baptism. The word must be recited as prescribed by the church. Since it is in the administrant's power to corrupt the *forma,* either inadvertently or deliberately, the intention is listed by some as a third part of the visible sign. Both Romanists and Lutherans employ Augustine's famous dictum: "The word comes to the element, and thus it becomes a sacrament"; the Lutherans, because the word requires "all hearts to believe," the Romanists because the efficacy lies in the mere act performed by the administrant.[148]

"Invisible grace" is conferred by each of the seven sacraments. Ordinarily the sacraments of the dead (Baptism and Penance) begin sanctifying grace, while the sacraments of the living increase it. In addition, each sacrament confers a special grace, the sacramental grace. Baptism, for example, effects regeneration; Confirmation, spiritual manhood. Three sacraments — Baptism, Confirmation, and Holy Orders — imprint an indelible character on the soul. This special sacramental character is said to be a distinctive sign which sets the baptized, confirmed, or ordained apart from those who have not received these sacraments; an obligatory sign, which unites man indissolubly with Christ; a configurative sign, which constitutes the image of God; a dispositive sign, which disposes the soul to receive grace and therefore the right to claim grace. With

---

147 Pohle-Preuss, VIII, 124—142; see also pp. 118, 146, 202; Pesch, VI, 46 ff.; Wilmers, IV, 218 ff.; Smith, II, 746 f.; Moehler, p. 203. The *opus operatum* efficacy of Baptism is proved from John 3:5: *ex aqua et Spiritu Sancto.* The principal cause of spiritual birth is said to be the Holy Ghost and the instrumental cause the water.

148 Pohle-Preuss, VIII, 58 ff., 110.

Thomas the church holds that this indelible character endures throughout eternity; in the good by adding to their glory and in the wicked by increasing their shame.[149]

The third element of a sacrament is Christ's institution. According to Trent, it is an article of faith that Christ personally and immediately instituted seven sacraments. For the immediate institution of Baptism and the Eucharist there is said to be direct Scriptural evidence; for that of Penance and Holy Orders, good Scriptural ground; and for the remaining sacraments, justifiable assumption. However, the argument that Christ instituted no fewer than seven sacraments is based largely on certain assumptions and deductions. For his bodily perfection the individual must experience birth, growth, nourishment, healing, and the restoration of physical powers; and for his social development the power to govern and to propagate the race are necessary. In order that man may attain spiritual perfection, both as an individual and as a member of the community, Christ instituted seven sacraments. Following Thomas, the Roman church teaches:

> Baptism, by which we are born again to Christ; confirmation by which we grow up and are strengthened in the grace of God; the Eucharist, that true bread from heaven which nourishes our souls to eternal life; penance, by which the soul which has caught the contagion of sin is restored to spiritual health; extreme unction, which obliterates the traces of sin and invigorates the powers of the soul; holy orders for the public administration of the sacraments; and finally, matrimony, a sacrament instituted for the legitimate and holy union of man and woman, for the conservation of the human race and the education of children in the knowledge of religion and the love and fear of God.[150]

Roman apologists charge that Lutherans destroy the objectivity of the sacraments when they teach that faith is necessary for a salutary use of the sacraments. They claim that the only guarantee for true objectivity lies in the *opus operatum* theory. Lutherans teach that the validity and objectivity of the sacraments rests entirely upon the inviolable promises of God in the words of institution. The Roman theologians are not consistent. On the one hand they teach that through the sacraments God infallibly infuses grace by the mere act performed, but, on the other hand, they make the efficacy dependent on the disposition of both the administrant and the recipient. The validity of a sacrament depends on the "interior disposition" of the administrant. He need not be in a state of grace, nor have faith, nor be orthodox, but he must have the

---

[149] Pohle-Preuss, VIII, 66—96, esp. 88 ff.

[150] *Popular Symbolics*, p. 175. Pohle-Preuss, VIII, 46 ff., 97 ff.; Wilmers, IV, 260 f.; C. Rom., P. II, Cap. 1, qu. 10. Cp. Pesch, VI, 27 ff. Roman Catholic textbooks state that "even without Scriptures and tradition we can recognize that the Catholic teaching about the number of the sacraments corresponds most aptly to the demands of reason and the necessities of human life" and usually quote with approval Goethe's encomium of the sacramental system in his *Autobiography* I, 245 ff. Cp. Konrad Algermissen, p. 475. Another argument is as follows: "The sanctity demanded by the New Law demands more perfect Sacraments than those given to the Old Testament dispensations." Pohle-Preuss lists four dispensations, each with its specific sacramental system: (1) the quasi sacrament of Paradise, probably the tree of life and marriage; (2) the sacrament of nature, from Adam to Moses, probably the parents' prayer for the cleansing of their children from the stain of original sin; (3) the sacraments of the Mosiac Law, namely, circumcision, the paschal meal, the sacrifices, the priesthood; (4) the seven sacraments of the new Law, pp. 18—31.

right intention. The Council of Trent decreed that "in ministers, when they effect and confer the Sacraments, there [must be] required the intention at least of doing what the Church does." The administrant is a minister of Christ (1 Cor. 4:1) and must intend to exercise the powers delegated to him by Christ. Since the church acts in the name of Christ, the administrant must have the intention to do "at least what the Church does." Rome argues as follows: The union of the *materia* and the *forma* constitutes the sacrament; but the purpose for the combination of matter and form is determined by the intention of the priest; hence his intention determines whether the action is a sacrament or not. This theory may raise serious doubts in the mind of the recipient. Some dogmaticians have therefore attempted to allay these doubts, at least in part, by defending the thesis that "a minister who has the intention of performing the external rite, but withholds his interior assent from the mind of the church, validly confers a sacrament." The majority of dogmaticians have held that this proposition runs counter to conciliar and papal decisions, especially Trent, Sess. XIV, ch. vi and Can. 9. They say that "a minister who while carefully observing the prescribed rite would withhold interior assent to the mind of the Church could have no other intention than to play the hypocrite." This means that no one can be certain, "with the certainty of faith," that he receives a true sacrament, because the sacrament cannot be valid without the intention of the minister and no man can see another's intention. Leo XIII modified this interpretation in the bull *Apostolicae curae* (1896). He declared that when the minister seriously and correctly administers the matter and the form, he is considered as having intended to do what the church does.[151] The validity of the sacraments depends further on the recipient's *intentio*, "a positive intention to receive the sacrament validly." Most theologians are agreed that only Matrimony and Orders require a "virtual intention" based on mature deliberation. The remaining sacraments are received validly if the recipient has an interpretative or habitual intention, i. e., a subconscious, implicit, and an abiding wish to do what the church has prescribed. For a worthy reception, however, the recipient must also have the right disposition. Baptism and Penance require faith, fear, hope, contrition. The other sacraments increase grace and require only that the recipient be in the state of grace. The "contrition" required for the first two need not be perfect. Attrition, a supernatural sorrow motivated by fear or love, is sufficient. For the other sacraments the condition is virtually

---

151 *Popular Symbolics*, p. 176 ff.; Pohle-Preuss, VIII, 163 ff., esp. pp. 183 to 186; Wilmers, IV, 240—44; Mirbt, No. 492; cp. Moehler, p. 205 ff. Rome rejects the Donatist error, but it also teaches that a priest living in mortal sin commits a sacrilege when "he solemnly and officially confers a sacrament," and Cardinal de Lugo claims that "the value of the Mass is dependent on the greater or lesser holiness of the reigning Pope, the bishops, and the clergy throughout the world." Pohle-Preuss, VIII, 188. The Pastoral Letter to the Clergy of the First Provincial Council of Baltimore (1829) states: "You are the ministers of the sacraments whose efficacy, it is true, is derived not from your virtue, but from the power of God, the merits of the Saviour, the institution of Christ, the influence of the Holy Ghost and the dispositions of those who receive them. But you are well aware that those dispositions are more or less excited as your conduct is more or less beneficially influential." Peter Guilday, ed., *The National Pastorals of the American Hierarchy (1792—1919)* (Westminster: The Newman Press, 1954), p. 48 f.

only a negative one; viz., not to be in mortal sin.[152] The *ex opere operato* is no guarantee to the recipient that he has validly or worthily received the sacraments. In the first place, the church teaches that "the amount of grace conferred by a sacrament depends on the disposition of the recipient." [153] In the second place, the sincere Romanist is troubled by such a question as: Was I free from every mortal sin and really in the state of grace? A scrupulous Roman Catholic may ask: Was my attrition properly motivated? Did I observe all the requirements of the church, such as those pertaining to the Eucharistic fast? True objectivity and real certainty can be obtained only when the heart trusts with firm reliance on the promises of God.

The Several Sacraments

BAPTISM

Roman Catholic theologians define Baptism as a "sacrament instituted by Christ, in which, by the outward washing of the body with water, with invocation of the Three Persons of the Most Holy Trinity, man is spiritually reborn and sanctified unto life everlasting." [154] The matter is water applied by immersion, or aspersion, or, most commonly, by effusion, in sufficient quantity to warrant the term "washing." The form is: "I baptize thee in the name of the Father and of the Son and of the Holy Ghost." If the words "I baptize thee" are omitted, or if the form is otherwise changed, Baptism is considered invalid. The sacramental effects are threefold: the grace of justification, the forgiveness

of all the penalties of sin, and the conferring of the sacramental or indelible character. First, Baptism, as a means of justification, forgives sin and sanctifies the soul. Trent declared (Sess. V, Can. 5) that through Baptism the guilt of both original and actual sin is wiped out. The concupiscence which remains after Baptism no longer partakes of the nature of guilt. Second, Baptism remits not only the eternal but also the temporal punishment due to sins committed prior to Baptism. According to Trent, there is in the baptized "nothing whatever to retard their entry into heaven." For this reason the church imposes no satisfactions at Baptism as is done at the time of Penance. The penalties which remain after Baptism, e. g., sickness and death, are merely medicinal.[155] The third effect of Baptism is the bestowal of the sacramental or indelible character. This "character," in the first place, separates those who through Baptism belong to the "body of the [Roman Catholic] Church" from the unbaptized. In this respect the baptismal character is a "distinctive sign." The baptismal character, in the second place, subjects all baptized persons to the jurisdiction of the Roman church and obligates them to keep all her ecclesiastical precepts (*signum obligativum*). Accordingly Rome views all properly baptized persons as legitimate members of the Roman Catholic church. In 1873 Pius IX demanded that the German Emperor Wilhelm take measures to stop the anti-Roman tendencies of his government, because "everyone who has received Baptism is in some way and degree subject to the Pope." [156]

---

152 Pohle-Preuss, VIII, 191—203.

153 Ibid., p. 73.

154 Ibid., p. 204.

155 Ibid., p. 231 f.; Wilmers, IV, 286.

156 The correspondence between Pius IX and Emperor Wilhelm is reprinted as the Preface to Robert Hoffmann's edition of Luther's *Passional Christi und Antichristi* (Leipzig, n. d.); Pohle-Preuss, VIII, 236 f. See Trent,

Ordinarily baptism by water is necessary for salvation. Under certain conditions Baptism of Desire (baptismus flaminis) is sufficient, provided there is "perfect contrition" and the firm resolve — held at least implicitly — to receive Baptism at the earliest opportunity. Perfect contrition is said to effect immediate justification. Through Baptism of Desire non-Romanists can on their deathbed become members of the "Church" even without baptism by water.[157] The Baptism of Blood (baptismus sanguinis) is more nearly perfect than the preceding two because it incidentally cleanses the soul from all venial and mortal sin. Prayers for the souls of martyrs are therefore "an insult to the martyrs." [158]

The Roman church insists on the necessity of infant baptism for the removal of original sin. Trent (Sess. VII, Can. 13) teaches that faith cannot be presumed in infants, and they must therefore be baptized in the faith of the church. Unbaptized infants are excluded from heaven and the beatific vision because they lack justifying grace,

but they cannot be classified with the reprobate. Therefore the justice of God has provided the limbus infantum, where, in the opinion of many theologians, they enjoy a beatitude based on their natural love of God.[159]

Rome distinguishes between "solemn" and "private" baptism. The former can be administered only by a priest; the latter by anyone, even a heretic. Rome does not permit re-baptism. In the case of converts the priest either recognizes the previous baptism or administers a conditional baptism.[160]

CONFIRMATION

In this sacrament, "those already baptized, through the imposition of hands, anointment, and the prayer of the bishop, receive the power of the Holy Ghost, by which they are enabled to believe firmly and to profess the faith boldly." Confirmation, like Baptism, confers an indelible character. The majority of theologians hold that the "baptismal character" makes a person a subject of Christ and the "confirmation

Sess. XIV, ch. ii. On membership of heretics in the church see the section on "The Church"; see also canon laws covering baptized non-Roman Catholics, s. v. "Mixed Marriages" in Lydon, p. 361 f.

157 R. Raphael J. Markham, in Apostolate to Assist Dying Non-Catholics, Cincinnati, recommends to members of the "Apostolate to Assist Dying Non-Catholics" to make an attempt to prepare the non-Roman Catholic for a happy death by placing in his hands in any way possible a little ornamented card which has no appearance of Roman Catholicity, but which "contains all the acts necessary and sufficient for the soul. . . . Their [unbaptized persons'] only salvation lies in making an act of perfect love of God or of perfect contrition. . . . Any non-Catholic, whether or not he be baptized, who sincerely makes the acts on the card, will have done all that is necessary for his justification. It is understood, of course, that, if not baptized, he does not know of the necessity of Baptism, and then this act of perfect love or perfect contrition is for him Baptism of Desire." (Pp. 1—3.) Cp. Pohle-Preuss, VIII, 243.

158 Ibid., p. 251 f.

159 Gibbons, p. 273; Wilmers, IV, 302; I, 691 ff.; Smith, II, 355 ff.

160 An interrogatory submitted by a Roman priest to a non-Roman pastor concerning the baptism of a convert to Roman Catholicism contains questions such as these: Is water used by pouring, sprinkling, or immersion in the administration of baptism in your church? What are the exact words that are pronounced when baptism is administered? Do you teach that baptism is absolutely necessary for salvation? That baptism really, effectively, of itself confers grace? What is your intention in baptizing?

character" a *soldier* of Christ. The
majority hold that the *matter* of this
sacrament is the imposition of hands
and the *form*, the words pronounced by
the bishop: "I sign thee with the sign
of the cross and 'confirm thee with the
chrism of salvation," etc. Normally, only
a bishop may administer this sacrament.
Although infant confirmation is still upheld in theory, in usual practice the
recipient must have acquired the rudi-
ments of Christian knowledge and have
previously received the sacrament of
Penance. Hence, "as a rule, Confirmation is not administered until a child
has reached the use of reason." [161]

THE EUCHARIST

The dogmatic works present this
doctrine under three headings: (1) the
Real Presence; (2) the Eucharist as
a sacrament (Communion); (3) the Eucharist as a sacrifice (Mass).[162]

The Real Presence. Roman theology
places a relatively low estimate not only
upon human nature in general, but tends
to denigrate even Christ's human nature.
Some theologians hold that His humanity
does not receive the *latreia* given to God,
but only the *hyperdulia* given to Mary.
Rome believes that the human nature of
Christ, also after His ascension, is
limited to a specific place in *heaven*.
However, according to Trent (Sess. XIII,
Can. 1), the whole Christ is really and
substantially present in the Eucharist.
On the one hand, it denies the *genus
maiestaticum*, and on the other it vigor-

ously defends the Real Presence. The
Scholastics tried to solve this tension by
arguing that multilocation does not multiply the object, but only affects its external relation to and presence in space.
They speak of a continuous, discontinu-
ous, mixed, and circumscriptive multilocation – all miraculous, of course, but
making it possible from a rational point
of view for "Christ with His natural
dimensions to reign in heaven, whence
He does not depart, and at the same
time to dwell in sacramental presence
on numberless altars throughout the
world." [163]

In Roman theology the basis for the
Real Presence is the dogma of transubstantiation. According to Rome, "transubstantiation" signifies not an accidental
change, such as occurs when a wax
figure is changed from a ball to a cube,
nor a material conversion, as when wood
is changed to ashes; for in the one only
the accidents are changed, the substance
remaining the same, and in the other the
matter remains the same. Rather "transubstantiation" is such a conversion
where the substance of bread and wine
ceases to exist. All that remains of the
bread and wine are their accidents, such
as color, taste, smell, form. Trent (Sess.
XIII, ch. iv) defines the doctrine as
follows:

> By the consecration of bread and wine
> a conversion is made of the whole sub-
> stance of the bread into the substance
> of the body of Christ, and of the whole
> substance of the wine into the substance

[161] Smith, II, 836 f. On Confirmation in general see Pohle-Preuss, VIII,
276—303, and other sources listed in fn. 144, above.

[162] This section is a revision of F. E. Mayer's treatise "The Roman Doctrine of the Lord's Supper" in *C. T. M.*, X, 801—16. Cp. Pohle-Preuss, IX
(408 pages); Wilmers, IV, 375—576; *Catholic Encyclopedia*, s. v. "Eucharist" and "Mass"; *C. Rom.;* Jean de Puniet, *The Mass*, trans. by the Benedictines of Stanbrook (New York: Longmans, Green and Co., 1930); Smith,
II, 839—918; Pesch, VI, 261—452. Attention is directed to Luther's treatises
against the Roman Mass and to Ap. XXII, XXIV.

[163] Pohle-Preuss, IX, 175—84. Cp. "Christ's Person and Work," above.
See Wilmers, II, 339 f.; IV, 380 f.

of His blood; which conversion is by the Holy Catholic Church suitably and properly called transubstantiation.[164]

The theologians are not agreed as to the manner in which the body and blood enter into the species of bread and wine. According to the Thomists, the glorified body of Christ is reproduced in such a way that the change "has something in common with creation and transmutation." Transubstantiation is virtually both an annihilation and a creation, and the only reason why the body of Christ is not created is that the body already exists. Bellarmine explains transubstantiation as a conversion which does not cause the body to begin to exist, but to begin to exist under the species of bread and wine. While the theologians today usually avoid the term "creation," they nevertheless believe that "the power inherent in the words of consecration is so great that if the substance of the Eucharistic body did not already exist, these words would as surely call it into being as the fiat of the Almighty created the universe." [165]

By virtue of the words of consecration the body and the blood are present,

but that is not all, for by reason of a natural concomitance there is simultaneously present all that is physically inseparable from the body and the blood, namely, the soul and the humanity of Christ and, because of the personal union, also His divinity. Christ, whole and entire, with His flesh and blood, His body and soul, His deity and humanity, is present. The presence of the "entire Christ" *(Christus totus in toto)* is the basis for the dogma of concomitance. Trent says (Sess. XIII, ch. iii) that Christ, whole and entire, is received under either species and "that as much is contained under either species as under both." Not only is the entire Christ present under each species, but also under each and every particle of each species. This has been variously interpreted. Some believe that even before the division the body of Christ is present as many times as the host can be divided into separate particles; others say that as an unbroken mirror reproduces one reflection, a broken mirror, however, as many complete reflections as there are fragments, so also the body of Christ is present whole and

---

[164] Pohle-Preuss offers the following explanation of the decree in the form of Aristotelian dialectics: "In the Holy Eucharist we have a true conversion. There are, first, the two extremes of bread and wine as the *terminus a quo* and the body and blood of Christ as the *terminus ad quem*. There is, secondly, an intimate connection between the cessation of the one extreme and the appearance of the other, in that both events result not from two independent processes (e. g., annihilation and creation), but from one single act. At the words of consecration the substance of the bread vanishes to make room for the body and blood of Christ. Lastly, there is a *commune tertium* in the unchanged appearances of the *terminus a quo*. Christ, in assuming a new mode of being, retains these appearances in order to enable us to partake of His body and blood. The *terminus totalis a quo* is not annihilated, because the appearances of bread and wine continue. What disappears is the substance of bread and wine, which constitutes the *terminus formalis a quo*. Nor can the *terminus totalis ad quem* be said to be newly created, because the body and blood of Christ, and in fact the whole Christ, as *terminus formalis ad quem*, pre-exist both in His divinity (from eternity) and in His humanity (since the Incarnation). What begins to exist anew in the *terminus ad quem* is not our Lord as such, but merely a sacramental mode of being, in other words, the sacrament of the body and blood of Christ." (IX, 109)

[165] Pohle-Preuss, IX, 127. See Tract No. 30, Our Sunday Visitor Press. Cp. the bull *Exultate Deo* by Eugene IV, Nov. 22, 1439, Mirbt, Nos. 234 to 237.

entire under each fragment of the host.[166] According to Trent (Sess. XIII, Can. 4), it is, furthermore, an article of faith that the "substantial" body and blood of Christ are present in the Eucharist before, in, and after the use of the elements. The so-called "permanence of the Real Presence" raises the problem as to what happens to the body and blood in the Eucharist in case the species are destroyed by fire, mold, evaporation. The accepted answer is as follows: The body and blood is present under the appearances of bread and wine as long as these are really appearances and ordinarily capable of containing the substance of bread and wine.[167]

The dogma of the Real Presence and Transubstantiation is said to rest on the words of institution, which "can only mean that when Christ had spoken, the substance of the bread was gone and there was the body of Christ." Commenting on John 6:52 ff., Pohle says:

> If we take the manna of the desert [v. 49 ff.] . . . as a type of the Eucharist, we can argue as follows: Assuming that the Eucharist contained merely consecrated bread and wine . . . the original would not excel the type by which it was prefigured. But St. Paul teaches that the original must transcend its type in the same way in which a body excels its shadow, and consequently the Eucharist contains more than mere bread and wine.[168]

The dogma of transubstantiation rests chiefly on tradition and is supported by "probable, proper, and reasonable arguments." Wilmers establishes the necessity of the Real Presence by following two analogies from the Old Testament: (1) The Old Testament was a type of the New. In the Old Testament the presence of God was indicated through the Ark of the Covenant. The peculiar presence of God among Israel must be fulfilled in richer form in the New Testament. The incarnation was only a partial fulfillment of the Old Testament type, since Christ withdrew His physical presence at the ascension. Therefore the presence of Christ in the Eucharist is necessary if the type is to have its complete fulfillment. (2) Essentially Christianity is the religion of love. Love manifests itself in a desire to associate with those whom one loves. There is a desire both on the part of God and of man to be near each other. This is possible in the Eucharist. But in order to exercise man's faith, Christ does not come in His real form, but under the species of bread and wine.[169]

The dogma of transubstantiation and the permanence of the Real Presence is the basis for views and practices which obtain only in the Roman Catholic church. There is a definite trend of Romanticism in Roman theology, which attempts to objectify and materialize the

---

[166] Council of Trent, Sess. XIII, ch. iii, Pohle-Preuss, IX, 88 f. What would the disciples have received had they celebrated the Lord's Supper while Christ was in the grave? Answer: His body as it then existed, namely, separated from His soul, though not from His deity. Wilmers, IV, 458 f.

[167] Pohle-Preuss, IX, 133—35; Wilmers, IV, 434 f.

[168] Pohle-Preuss, IX, 15—16. Cp. Wilmers, IV, 382.

[169] Wilmers, ibid., p. 415 ff. After quoting from Thomas Aquinas, the author adds significantly: "Das sind Gründe, die der einfache Gläubige mehr mit dem Gefühle als mit dem Verstand erfasst, und vielleicht haben wir es diesem richtigen, wenn auch dunklen, Ahnen teilweise zuzuschreiben, dass der Glaube an die wirkliche Gegenwart auch bei den vorkommensten Sekten des Orients sich erhalten hat." Wilmers devotes 20 pages of small type to statements from tradition to prove the dogma of transubstantiation (395 ff.). Pohle-Preuss devotes 42 pages to the chapter "Speculative Discussion of the Mystery of the Real Presence" (IX, 143—84).

spiritual without sacrificing the mysterious and miraculous. Moehler states:

> To this inferior order of things (the world of sense) the Church opposes a higher order, not to annihilate the former but to bestow on it the blessings of redemption, to explain its significance, and to purify by heavenly influences all the stages of earthly and sinful existence. . . . Symbolical signs bring the higher world more immediately within the perception of sense and withal convey from that world the capacity for its influence.[170]

The Eucharist is said to bring the supernatural Christ physically into the world. This is the chief purpose of Catholic Action. By reading Masses the priest brings the physical Christ into the lives of his members, whereas the laity, through its participation in the liturgy, makes the entry of Christ into human lives more general.[171] Since Christ is present whole and entire in the Eucharist, Trent (Sess. XIII, Canons 5, 6) demands that its members "adore" the "Eucharistic Christ" in the same manner as the exalted Christ at God's right hand. When non-Romanists ask for Scripture proof, Pohle answers that "in the absence of Scripture proof this proposition must be demonstrated from tradition." When the charge is preferred that this view is tantamount to *artolatreia,* the Roman apologists answer that there can be no worship of the bread because the bread has ceased to exist. At the same time Rome admits that the adoration extends both to Christ and to the appearances and does not hesitate to say:

> The adoration which Catholics give to Christ under the appearances of bread and wine is not separate and distinct from that which they give to the sacred species as such. . . . We give no *separate* adoration to the accidents. . . . The object of our adoration is the *totum sacramentale.* . . . In practice neither the Church nor the faithful pay any attention to this subtle distinction [between the Eucharistic Christ and the species].[172]

The Roman cultus offers many opportunities to "adore" the Eucharistic Christ: (1) the reservation of the host in a specially ornate tabernacle on the altar under the "eternally" lit sanctuary lamp; (2) the elevation of the host after the consecration; (3) the exposition of the sacrament providing an opportunity to "look upon and to salute the body of Christ"; (4) the establishment of societies for the perpetual adoration so that somewhere throughout the world at all times someone is rendering adoration to the species, an honor which according to Rome belongs to God alone; (5) the celebration of the Corpus Christi Festival on the Thursday after Trinity. The purpose of the festival is to prepare a royal entry for Christ and, by taking the host into the open, to proclaim Christ as King of Creation and to make all nature a temple of God. It is, furthermore, a testimony of the faith against heretics, especially against Berengar of Tours (1050), who held to a symbolical interpretation of the sacrament. And lastly it is viewed as a satisfaction for all the indignities inflicted on the Eucharistic Christ;[173] (6) the Eucharistic Congresses similar to the Corpus Christi; (7) the Devotion of the Sacred Heart, which is based on the theory that since the flesh of Christ may be adored, much more so the noblest part of it, especially

---

170 Moehler, p. 203 ff.

171 Confrey (fn. 10 above), 59—62.

172 Pohle-Preuss, IX, 136 f., 141.

173 Wilmers, IV, 467. The German word *Fronleichnamsfest* is derived from *Fron* ("master") and *Leichnam* ("corpse").

since it is the seat of His love and of the eternal Word.[174]

The Eucharist as a Sacrament. The leading theologians do not agree in describing the nature of this sacrament. Deharbe defines the essence of the Eucharist thus:

[The Holy Eucharist] is the true body and blood of our Lord Jesus Christ, who is really and substantially present under the appearances of bread and wine for the nourishment of our souls.[175]

The *Catechismus Romanus* states that the consecration (a sacrificial act) and the communion (the reception of an already existing sacrament) do not belong to the. *essence* of the Eucharistic sacrament, but rather that the sacramental essence is the species of bread and wine. The majority hold that the *matter* of the Sacrament is "the bread and wine which are to be converted into the body and blood of Christ," and the *form* is "the word of consecration which effects this conversion." The difficulty in defining the essence of this sacrament lies in the fact that the Eucharist is viewed both as a sacrament and as a sacrifice, the sacrificial idea predominating. Applying this to the withholding of the cup, the theologians state that the use of the two species was instituted by Christ. Although the use of *both* kinds need not be observed in the Eucharist as a *sacrament*, it is essential for the Eucharist as a *sacrifice*, i. e., in the Mass, for in every sacrifice there must be a real slaying of the victim. The "unbloody" sacrifice of the Mass is effected when, by virtue of the consecration as "a two-edged mystical sword," the priest separates the body and the blood of Christ under the elements of bread and wine.[176] The reasons for withholding the cup are popularly stated as follows:

1. because the apostles did not always give the wine to the people, as in cases of sickness and in prisons, where the wine could not be administered; 2. because of the danger of spilling the blood of Jesus in administering it; 3. because of the great aversion to drink of the same cup of which the diseased drink; 4. because in some countries it is hard to preserve or to procure wine; 5. because some people cannot drink wine; 6. because Jesus gave to His Church the power to regulate these things.[177]

The sacramental effects are said to be fourfold: (1) It unites the soul with Christ. The physical consumption of the host effects a sacramental union, and this results *ex opere operato* in a mystical union through the "theological virtue of love." (2) Since Communion is only for those who already have remission of mortal sins, it can only increase sanctifying grace, that is, convey powers to avoid sin and to perform good works. (3) It blots out venial sins and preserves

[174] Ibid., p. 472 ff.

[175] De Harbe, Q. 566.

[176] Pohle-Preuss, IX, 185, 188, 347.

[177] Quoted in *Popular Symbolics*, p. 186. Gibbons, p. 300 f. The Council of Trent devoted an entire session (XXI) to the vexing problem of "both kinds" and finally left the matter to the pope, who granted "both kinds" in Austria and Bavaria under special conditions. Pohle-Preuss, IX, 246—54. The Papalist Confutation of 1530 argued for "one kind" by stating that the early church practiced "lay Communion." However, the Confutation did not state that in the early church this term denoted that an unfrocked priest might no longer consecrate the Eucharist, but merely took the Lord's Supper with the laity, nor did the Confutation state that the modern connotation of the term lay Communion as Communion under one kind was introduced much later. Georg D. Fuchs, *Bibliothek der Kirchenversammlungen* (Leipzig, 1780), I, 47. Ap., XXII, 26 ff.

from mortal sin. (4) According to John 6:55, it is a pledge of the body's resurrection, for by its contact with the Eucharistic Christ the body has a moral right to the future resurrection.[178]

To receive Holy Communion worthily a communicant must be free from mortal sin and must comply with the church's rule of fasting, recently relaxed to a considerable degree. The communicant should also strive to free himself from deliberate venial sin and should prepare himself by meditation and by making fervent acts of faith, hope, love, and contrition.

The resolution of Trent and the encyclical of Pius X admonish the people to commune frequently. The decree of the Fourth Lateran Council (1215), which required all Christians to commune at least once a year at Easter, is perpetuated in the modern Roman Catholic church. In the United States the "Easter Communion" period is 99 days. This is a commandment of the church, and failure to observe it carries with it the penalty at least of mortal sin.

The Eucharist as a Sacrifice. In the sacrament, God is the Giver and the sinner the recipient. In a sacrifice the order is reversed. In accord with Rome's material principle, the Mass as the highest sacrifice offered by man to God is the heart and core of the Roman cultus. Man is said to stand in a threefold relationship of obligation to God: (1) As a creature of soul and body, man owes God mental and physical adoration, physical sacrifice *(sacrificium latreuti-*

cum); (2) as a sinner before the Judge, he must appease God's wrath *(propitiatorium);* (3) as the *recipient of many blessings,* man has the twofold duty of thanking God for past favors and imploring Him for future help *(sacrificium eucharisticum et impetrarium).* A "figurative" sacrifice (prayers, good works) is insufficient. The history of comparative religions and divine revelation are said to show that a sacrifice is "the external offering of a sensible gift, in recognition of God's supreme dominion and in order to appease His anger." Jews and Gentiles in the pre-Christian era had sacrifices and from this it follows that

> the professors of the Christian faith, in order to be able to satisfy their duty of worshiping God, must have a permanent sacrifice just as well as the Old Testament Jews. This craving of the heart, which has deeply imbedded itself in all religions, is not satisfied by the sacrifice of the cross, since that was offered "once for all" and in one place only. The Catholic Church, being the "mystical Christ," must have a sacrifice of her own, because otherwise she could not fulfill her duty of worshiping God in the most perfect manner possible. Without a sacrifice the Christian cult would be inferior to the Levitic ceremonies, nay, even to the feeble manifestations of natural religion.[179]

Rome adduces three arguments for its contention that the Mass is *the* sacrifice: (1) The words of institution "Given and shed for you" refer not to the sacrifice on the *cross,* but to the sacrifice He was then and there offering in the

---

[178] Pohle-Preuss, IX, 218—34; Wilmers, IV, 548—76. Rome's Neoplatonism comes to the surface in this entire discussion, for some dogmaticians have gone so far as to speak of a "conversion of the human flesh into that of the God-Man." There is a vast difference between Rome's view and that expressed by Luther, viz., that the mouth which orally receives Christ does not know what the heart receives. The mouth must live on account of the heart which will live through the Word. (See *Dass diese Worte etc. noch feste stehen,* W. A., XX, 178—191; Large Cat., V, pars. 68, 45.)

[179] Pohle-Preuss, IX, 286, 293.

Last Supper;[180] (2) the early Communion liturgies contain the consecration, which is said to be the act of the Eucharistic sacrifice; (3) tradition teaches so.

The Mass is described as the highest religious act, because Christ here in an unbloody manner offers His body and blood, given and shed on the cross. All Roman dogmaticians declare that in essence there is no difference between the offering on the cross and the sacrifice of the Mass, for in each Christ is both Priest and Victim. The difference between the two consists only in the manner of the sacrifice, the one being bloody or real, and the other unbloody, or sacramental. The theologians are not agreed on how or at what precise moment the "unbloody immolation" occurs. Is the sacrificial act the consecration, or the breaking of the bread, or the priest's eating the host and consuming the wine? The view held by the majority, that the words of consecration separate the blood from the body, is summarized by Pohle as follows:

Since it was no mere death from suffocation that Jesus suffered, but a bloody death, in which His veins were emptied of their blood, this condition of separation must receive visible representation on the altar. This condition is fulfilled only by the double consecration, which brings before our eyes the body and blood in the state of separation and thus represents the mystical shedding of the blood. It is this consideration that suggested to the Fathers the idea, which

was adopted into some liturgies, of the double consecration as a two-edged "mystical sword." [181]

But many questions remain unanswered. Is there a real slaying of Christ or only a representative, a dramatic, repetition of the slaying of Christ? Does the sacrificial act culminate in a *kenōsis*, a real self-abasement, or in glorification? If it is a *kenōsis*, how does the impassibility of the transfigured Lord permit His body and blood to be reduced to the condition of food and thus be placed at the mercy of mankind? Does the glorified Lord experience a physical or a metaphysical suffering? According to Trent (Sess. XXII, ch. i), the death of Christ occurs mystically and by representation. In the Mass the same body and blood are offered as a sacrifice to God as were sacrificed on the cross. Moehler states correctly that in the sacrifice on the cross Christ's entire active obedience is, as it were, epitomized. He then continues to say that in the Mass this objective sacrifice becomes subjective and is appropriated by man. For

Christ on the cross is still an object strange to us: Christ, in the Christian worship, is our property, our victim. There he is the universal victim — here he is the victim for us in particular, and for every individual amongst us; there he was only the victim; — here he is victim acknowledged and revered: there the objective atonement was consummated; — here the subjective atonement is partly fostered and promoted, partly expressed.[182]

---

[180] While many ancient codices of the Vulgate have *fundetur* (future), some, in accordance with the Greek *ekchynnomenon* (present tense), have *funditur*. This is said to prove that Christ shed His blood in "an unbloody manner" for the first time on Maundy Thursday. Ibid., p. 308.

[181] Ibid., p. 347.

[182] Moehler, p. 239. — Pohle-Preuss analyzes seven theories advanced by Roman theologians to explain the metaphysical essence of the Mass, i. e., how and in what degree the concept of the sacrifice is realized in the "double" consecration of the bread and the wine (IX, 349—70). William J. McGarry writes: "How the Mass was truly a sacrifice was a question which vexed and still vexes Catholic theologians. The doctrine asserting the

By participating in the Mass man offers to God a eucharistic and a propitiatory sacrifice. In the former he discharges his obligation of adoration and thankoffering, in the latter the obligation of propitiation and impetration. The Mass is viewed primarily — it seems almost exclusively — as a propitiatory and impetratory sacrifice. This is in accord with Trent (Sess. XXII, ch. ii and Can. 3), which teaches

that this sacrifice is truly propitiatory and that by means thereof this is effected, that we obtain mercy and find grace in seasonable aid, if we draw nigh unto God contrite and penitent, with a sincere heart and upright faith, with fear and reverence. For the Lord, appeased by the oblation thereof and granting the grace and gift of penitence, forgives even heinous crimes and sins. For the victim is one and the same, the same now offering by the ministry of priests who then offered Himself on the cross, the manner alone of offering being different. . . . If any one says that the sacrifice of the Mass is only a sacrifice

of praise and thanksgiving or that it is a bare commemoration of the sacrifice consummated on the cross, but not a propitiatory sacrifice, or that it profits him only who receives and that it ought not to be offered for the living and the dead for sins, pains, satisfactions, and other necessities, let him be anathema.

The Mass is called a propitiatory sacrifice because it gains remission of guilt and other blessings "by entreaty" and is therefore really an impetratory sacrifice. As such the Mass, according to Trent (Sess. XXII, ch. iii and Can. 5) is offered also to the saints, in order to gain their intercession. The distinction between propitiation and impetration is more theoretical than real, as becomes evident from the liturgical prayers. In the prayer after the offertory the priest raises the paten and says:

Accept . . . this spotless Host, which I, Thy· unworthy servant offer unto Thee . . . for my numberless sins, offenses, and negligences; on behalf of all here present and likewise for all faithful

fact was always clear; the explanations differed. All admitted that one and the same Victim was offered, that the priest offered the Victim ministerially for Christ, that the number of separate offerings of the Victim increased each day. Two principal explanations of the problem were offered. One school held that a mystical immolation sufficed to constitute the Mass a real sacrifice. Hence, there was one real death and immolation on Calvary, only a mystical and repeated immolation in the Mass. An opposite school held that, to have a real sacrifice, the quality of victimhood must here and now in each Mass be assumed by Christ. They saw the Victim endue this quality of victimhood because Christ in the Mass is present without the visible accompaniment of the qualities He has in His risen Body in heaven. To these opinions a third view, not new, but allegedly bearing patristic thought on the Eucharist, was added by Father de la Taille. It held that for the reality of a sacrifice no real immolation is here and now required. What is required is a real victim in the hands of an offerer. Thus, as Christ at the supper offered the sacrifice of a victim to be immolated on the morrow, so priests now offer the sacrifice of a victim immolated on the yesterday of Calvary. Further, this present offering in the Mass repeats dramatically and re-enacts mystically and in an unbloody manner the bloody Sacrifice of Calvary. None of these theories has been raised to the dignity of an article of faith. In the seminaries one or other of the three views with minor modifications is being taught" (*Religion and the Modern World*, p. 37). Pohle holds that an acceptable theory must recognize the following: (1) The Mass is both an absolute and a relative sacrifice; (2) the sacrificial action of double consecration relates to the Eucharistic Christ, not to the elements; (3) the sacrificial act must culminate in a real self-abasement; (4) since Christ is impassible, the "slaying" is sacramental or mystical. (IX, p. 359)

Christians living and dead, that it may profit me and them as a means of salvation unto life everlasting.[183]

In short, in the Mass the priest is said to repeat the sacrifice on the cross and offers it to God as an act of adoration and especially as a sacrifice of propitiation. The congregation by attending the Mass fulfills its obligations of adoration, reparation, impetration, and thanksgiving.

The effects of the Mass as a propitiatory sacrifice are chiefly twofold: (1) In the sacrament God is said to forgive sins *immediately*, in the sacrifice *mediately*. According to Trent (Sess. XXII, ch. ii, Can. 3), God is "appeased by the oblation" and is prompted to change His attitude toward the sinner and to grant him the "grace and gift of penitence," whereby man is reconciled to God. Thus the Mass is offered to prompt God to "forgive even heinous crimes and sins." For as Old Testament sacrifices frequently turned the temporal punishments from Israel, so the Mass, an infinitely better sacrifice, remits the satisfactions and temporal punishments. In the catechism for children the purpose of the Mass is summarized thus: "to obtain the remission of sins and of the temporal punishments due them." [184] (2) Trent says that the Mass is offered to obtain also "other necessities of life." Trent is not specific, but in the popular literature on the Mass these "necessities" include "any temporal good that is not hurtful to the soul." Cochem lists seventy-seven graces and virtues which result from a pious hearing of the Mass.[185]

The beneficiaries of every Mass are all of the members of the Church Militant and Triumphant. The priest, who is nearest the source of grace and for whom — as is indicated in the words "for you" — the Lord especially shed His blood, is the chief beneficiary. All who in union with the priest devoutly "assist at Mass" are also assured of its blessings. The Mass may be offered for special persons, even for the dead as long as they are in purgatory. If the dead for whom a Mass is spoken should be either in hell or in heaven, the benefit of the Mass will be directed to some other "poor" soul.[186]

The efficacy of the Mass is both infinite and limited. Inasmuch as Christ, who is both the Victim and the Priest, is infinite, the Mass is efficacious *ex opere operato*, and its intrinsic value is infinite.[187] Its *extensive* value, however, is finite, because it is also contingent on the celebrant and on the active participants. Some theologians assume that the celebrant's own dignity affects the value of the Mass; likewise, that the satisfactory value of the Mass for the release of temporal punishments varies according to the number of passive participants for whom the Mass is offered. In other words, a Mass read for ten souls gives to each participant only one tenth of the benefits.[188] The participant receives the blessings *ex opere operato*, but the degree of the benefits depends

---

[183] Father Stedman, *My Sunday Missal*, 42d printing, p. 43. Cp. prayers from ancient liturgies in Pohle-Preuss, IX, 376, 378, in which the Mass is allegedly viewed as a propitiatory sacrifice.

[184] Wilmers, IV, 515.

[185] Pohle-Preuss, IX, 292 ff. Martin v. Cochem, *Erklärung des heiligen Messopfers*, 5th ed. (Cologne: J. P. Bachem, 1870), p. 106 ff.

[186] Wilmers, pp. 519 ff., 522.

[187] Pohle-Preuss, IX, 381 f., 387 f. Wilmers, IV, 516 f.

[188] Since ordinarily a priest can read only one Mass a day, the orders for Masses at certain shrines exceed the facilities. They cannot be read at other shrines if the purchaser is to receive full value.

on the participant's devotion, disposition, and purity of motives, and thus the benefits are acquired also *ex opere operantis*.[189]

Canon law gives detailed instructions concerning the many required ceremonies, e. g., the use of Latin, the number of Masses to be read a day, the prescribed vestments. All the essential ceremonies must be observed if the Mass is to be valid.[190]

In the doctrine and the cultus of the Mass Rome's entire theology is epitomized and reaches its climax. Therefore, as Campegius stated at Augsburg in 1530, the Roman church can under no condition give up the Mass.[191]

PENANCE

The Council of Trent devoted the entire Session XIV to formulating the decrees and canons concerning the sacrament of Penance. Pohle summarizes the fifteen canons as follows:

I. Penance is a true Sacrament, instituted by Christ for the forgiveness of post-baptismal sins.

II. Penance is a Sacrament distinct from Baptism.

III. The words of Christ recorded in John XX, 23, are to be understood of the power of forgiving and retaining sins in the Sacrament of Penance, not of preaching the Gospel.

IV. For the remission of sins there are required three acts by the penitent, which are as it were the matter of the Sacrament of Penance, viz.: contrition, confession, and satisfaction. The terrors with which the conscience is smitten upon being convinced of sin, and the fiduciary faith generated by the Gospel, are not sufficient to obtain forgiveness.

V. Imperfect contrition, which is acquired by means of the examination, recollection, and detestation

---

[189] Pohle-Preuss, p. 390. Wilmers, IV, 518, 546 ff.

[190] C. C. Smyth, *The Ceremonies of the Mass* (New York: Paulist Press). Lydon, *Ready Answers*, pp. 371—79. On "Dialogue Mass," Francis B. Donnelly, "Dialogue Mass in the Vernacular," *Ecclesiastical Review* (1941), pp. 115—23. The practice of receiving "stipends" for private Masses is based on Paul's maxim that he who serves the altar shall live thereof. The following are the more regular forms of the Mass (cp. *Cath. Encyc.*, s. v. "Mass"):

(Solemn) High Mass: the norm of all Masses. The rubrics of the Ordinary always presuppose a Mass to be high. Celebrant assisted by deacon and subdeacon.

Low Mass: said by celebrant without aid of deacon and subdeacon.

Sung Mass (missa cantata): a modern compromise. Really a Low Mass, since the essence of a High Mass is not the music but the assistance of deacon and subdeacon.

Pontifical Mass: in which one or more bishops (or prelates with assimilated episcopal rank) participate. May be either high or low.

Votive Mass: A Mass offered for a *votum*, a special intention (e. g., Nuptial, Requiem). The Votive Mass does not, as is normally the rule, correspond to the office of the day. Hence it may not be said at certain times and seasons.

Nuptial Mass: a Mass "for a groom and bride," incorporating special prayers and ceremonies. It may not be celebrated on certain days (e. g., Sundays and the penitential seasons).

Requiem Mass: a Mass for the dead, either at death, on anniversary of death, or, in general, for all dead (e. g., All Souls' Day). Also a Votive Mass.

[191] Karl A. Hase, *Handbuch d. Protestantischen Polemik gegen die röm. Kirche* (Leipzig, 1863), p. 487.

of sins, is a true and profitable sorrow, and does not make a man a hypocrite and a greater sinner.

VI. Sacramental confession is of divine institution and necessary to salvation, and auricular confession is not a human invention.

VII. Auricular confession comprises by divine right all mortal sins, even those which are secret, and may lawfully extend also to venial sins.

VIII. The confession of all sins, as demanded by the Church, is not impossible, but a duty incumbent on all the faithful of both sexes.

IX. The sacramental absolution given by the priest is a judicial act, not a bare declaration, and must be preceded by confession on the part of the penitent.

X. Priests alone have the power of binding and loosing, and can exercise it even if they are in a state of mortal sin.

XI. Bishops have the right of reserving cases to themselves, and from such reserved cases no priest may absolve except with proper faculties.

XII. God does not always remit the whole punishment together with the guilt of sin, and the satisfaction of penitents does not consist in the faith wherewith they apprehend that Christ has satisfied for them.

XIII. Satisfaction for sins, as to their temporal punishment, is made to God through the merits of Christ, partly by the penance which the priest imposes and partly by those voluntarily undertaken by the penitent himself. Consequently, Penance is more than merely a new life.

XIV. The works of satisfaction performed by the penitent do not obscure the doctrine of grace, the true worship of God, and the benefit of Christ's death.

XV. The power of the keys which Christ gave to the Church is not merely the power to loose, but also to bind, and therefore enables priests to impose punishments on those who confess.[192]

The penitential system rests upon two basic principles of Roman theology: the absolute authority of the church and the Semi-Pelagian theory that man is able and obligated to co-operate in his own justification. Trent teaches that according to John 20:20 f.; Matt. 16:19; 18:18, Christ gave to Peter and his successors "supreme power to govern the Church, to admit into and exclude from it, to make and execute laws, to impose and remit penalties," in short, the "faculty of forgiving and retaining the guilt and the punishment of sin." [193] One pervading principle prevails throughout the long history of the penitential system, namely,

that the Church has the power not only to impose penalties for the violation of her laws and the reparation of public scandal, but also, and principally, to forgive the sins of those who are contrite and ready to give satisfaction, and that her judicial decision in each case is ratified by God.

The theologians maintain the absolute necessity of this ecclesiastical power, because, as Trent (Sess. XIV, canon 6) teaches, no Christian guilty of a mortal sin can be saved unless he obtains pardon from the church through Penance. But it must also be stated that a person may have "perfect contrition" without the sacrament of Penance and thereby gain immediate justification. This is said to be possible because such "perfect contrition" is always accompanied by the desire to receive Penance. Also venial sins, which allegedly do not destroy

[192] Pohle-Preuss, X, 23—25. The entire volume of 264 pages is devoted to Penance.

[193] Ibid., pp. 8—13.

grace and entail damnation, come under the power of the keys. According to Trent, however, the church cannot retain venial sins.[194]

In Penance the priests exercise judicial power. In ch. ii of the *Canons and Decrees of the Council of Trent,* the church declared that the Lord wanted those who through Baptism had become members of the household of faith but had again fallen into mortal sin "to be placed as criminals before the Church's tribunal." And in ch. v the Council declared that Penance is a sort of trial court with Christ's apostles and their successors sitting as judges, "to whom all mortal crimes must be carried, so that they may pronounce the sentence of forgiveness or retention." This is the heart of the penitential system, and, in the words of Atzberger, a leading modern theologian, "the pivot around which the whole Catholic doctrine of Penance revolves." [195]

In line with its Semi-Pelagian theology, Rome speaks of penance as *baptismus laboriosus,* also as the "second plank after shipwreck." The thought behind these terms is the following: The church is the ship surrounded by drowning men. In her generosity the church through Baptism rescues men without any effort on their part. But when men through mortal sin fall overboard, the church throws out the life line of Penance, and man must by his own efforts regain the safety of the church.

The Lutheran Reformers directed some of their sharpest polemics against the Roman penitential system because of these two basic premises. The universal priesthood of all believers is diametrically opposed to the absolute power over consciences exercised by the priest in Penance. The Reformers condemned compulsory confession as practiced in the sixteenth century as an unbearable torture of consciences. Probably at no point is the antithesis between Rome's doctrine of man's co-operation in salvation and the Lutheran principle of *sola gratia, sola fide,* so apparent as in their respective doctrines on penance.[196]

Since Rome has decreed that Penance is a sacrament, it must also ascribe to it matter and form. Rome has experienced considerable difficulty in determining the nature of matter. Theologians are agreed that anything perceptible to the senses may be viewed as the matter of a sacrament. The Scotists held that the words of absolution constitute both the matter and the form in Penance. The Thomists, whom the majority follows today, hold that the three acts of the penitent constitute the matter. The form is the word of absolution: *"Ego te absolvo a peccatis tuis in nomine Patris et Filii et Spiritus Sancti."*

Each sacrament is said to produce a particular sacramental effect which is not present in the other sacraments. According to Trent (ch. iii) the particular effect of Penance is twofold: (1) to reconcile man with God, more particularly, "to heal the soul infirm through sin," and thus to confer peace of conscience; (2) to effect the restoration of the supernatural merits which the penitent has lost through mortal sin, since it would not be fair for these merits to be irretrievably lost. It is evident that Rome does not think of justification in terms of forgiveness of sins, but of personal sanctification. Trent specifically

---

[194] Ibid., pp. 62, 63.

[195] Ibid., p. 65. See also Trent, Sess. XIV, ch. v.

[196] See Luther's treatises against Eck, Emser, Catharinus, and esp. *Von der Beichte, ob die der Papst Macht habe zu gebieten,* W. A. VIII, 138 to 185. Cp. Ap. XI, XII.

condemns the view that the absolution spoken by the priest is declaratory. The priestly absolution is a judicial action which actually abolishes sin. In short, as W. Walther points out, the Lutheran Christian says: "Where there is forgiveness of sin, there is life and salvation"; Rome inverts this statement and says: "Where there is new life, there is forgiveness of sin." [197]

Since Penance is both a sacrament and a tribunal of justice, only he can validly administer this sacrament who has been granted the power of order and jurisdiction *(potestas ordinis et iurisdictionis)*. The jurisdiction of the pope extends over the entire church, that of the bishops over the respective dioceses; that of the priest over his own parish. Penitents can obtain a valid and licit absolution only at the tribunal which has jurisdiction over them. There are higher and lower courts with specific powers. The bishops, as the higher court, have the right to limit the jurisdiction of the lower court and "reserve" certain cases for their jurisdiction. Some cases are "reserved" for the papal court.[198]

On the one hand, Rome teaches that Penance, as do all sacraments, confers its effects *ex opere operato*. On the other hand, the penitent's three acts: contrition, confession, and satisfaction, occupy such a central position [199] that the *ex opere operato* efficacy of the sacraments seems to be entirely discarded. These acts are said to be not only "dispositions"

to indicate the recipient's worthiness, but "conditions of the validity of the sacraments, since in Penance worthiness and validity coincide." [200] The "virtue of Penance" (the ability of any upright person to be sorry for sin, to confess his sin, and to make amends) is said to be the very heart of Penance. By "adding the sacramental *opus operatum* Christ merely increased the efficacy of repentance." [201] The non-Romanist finds it impossible to follow these fine distinctions. Does Rome teach that there is a non-sacramental and a sacramental Penance — one for non-members and the other for members, one for callous and one for pious Romanists?

The sacrament of Penance is treated by the Roman dogmaticians under the aspects of contrition, absolution, and satisfaction.

Contrition. The Council of Trent defines contrition as the sorrow of the heart and detestation of sin committed, with the resolve to sin no more. The term "contrition" is taken from the Latin *conterere* (to pulverize, to grind), and the Vulgate uses "contrite" to denote complete compunction of the heart, which "grinds the sinner to dust." When this feeling of utter helplessness arises from perfect love of God, it is called "perfect contrition"; when it is prompted by fear of punishment or other motives, it is called "imperfect contrition," or "attrition." Attrition "merely softens the

---

197 Pohle-Preuss, X, 111—18; Walther, p. 103 f.

198 Pohle-Preuss, X, 128. Cp. Lydon, *Ready Answers*, p. 326 ff. As to the Lutheran understanding of *potestas ordinis et iurisdictionis* see Ap., XXVIII, 13.

199 Pohle-Preuss, X, 133. Pohle devotes 130 pages and Wilmers 80 pages to a discussion of these three acts. Wilmers subdivides contrition into five acts, exploration of the conscience, contrition, amendment, confession, satisfaction. Wilmers views the exploration as preparatory to contrition. The penitent is expected to examine his life according to the commandments of God and the church. (IV, 633 ff.)

200 Pohle-Preuss, X, 133.

201 Ibid., p. 3.

heart," whereas perfect contrition reconciles the sinner with God before the sacrament is actually received.[202] This definition of perfect contrition raises a number of troublesome questions. Does the "act of perfect love" abolish sin immediately, without the sacrament of Penance? The *Catechismus Romanus* (Part II, cap. 5, Qu. 34) teaches that with "perfect love" man at once receives pardon. But if that were the case, why are confession and satisfaction still required? A common answer is: The church cannot dispense from confession, because confession is an integral part of the office of the keys, and without the exercise of this power the sinner cannot obtain remission. Therefore it is assumed that the "act of perfect love" implies the desire to make confession. Again, Roman Catholic theologians are agreed that no one can be certain if he has perfect love or not. Nor is perfect love a dispensation from satisfactions, since this act of love is in itself the satisfaction and gains an indulgence. A second question is: Does perfect contrition always justify immediately? Trent cautiously uses the word "sometimes." On the basis of 1 Peter 4:8, however, many answer the above question affirmatively.[203] A third problem is: What constitutes the act of "perfect love"? The answer: To love God for His own

sake, i. e., because of His own essential goodness. To love Him because He is good to us would be a form of self-interest. This raises the further question: Can man with his natural self-interests love God perfectly? The answer given is that man is expected to love God only with such intensity as the grace of God provides.[204]

The definition of attrition as given by Trent in ch. iv has been the occasion for much theological discussion, and, if taken seriously, must lead the penitent either to great anxiety or to a false security. Attrition is said to be valid for penance if it springs from fear, hope, or other motives. Trent (ch. iv) specifically condemned Luther's teaching that sorrow over sin motivated by fear of hell is hypocrisy and a sin and decreed in Canon V that attrition may be motivated either by the fear of hell and punishment or by a consideration of the turpitude of sin.[205] The majority of theologians are agreed that mere fear of hell is sufficient for a valid sacrament. Many problems arise in this connection. Is the fear of purely temporal punishments, such as purgatory, famine, war, sufficient? The attritionists answer affirmatively, though some add the proviso that the affliction must be viewed as coming from God; the contritionists an-

---

[202] Ibid., p. 134 f. *Attritio* is derived from *atterere*, to rub against. It does not occur in the Vulgate.

[203] Ibid., p. 139 ff. According to Pallavicini, *Historia Concilii Tridentini*, XII, 10, 27, the council in deference to the pope's views deleted the word "always" and substituted "sometimes" (loc. cit.)

[204] Ibid., p. 135 ff.

[205] Ibid., 157 ff. The core of Lutheran hamartiology is that every sin is rebellion against God, an extreme form of egocentricity, *cor incurvatum in se*. As long as contrition is no more than remorse, it is truly sin, viz., hatred of God, who punishes so severely, and self-love, which seeks its own welfare. Cp. Luther, *Commentary on Psalm 90 (91)*, W. A., XL/3, 484—594. Theo. Harnack, *Luthers Theologie* (Munich: Chr. Kaiser Verlag, 1927), discusses such topics as the sinner and the divine Law; the cause of divine wrath; the essence and effect of God's wrath; liberation from divine wrath. Theo. Engelder, "Zur Lehre von der Reue," *C. T. M.*, V (1934), 218 ff., 369 ff., 497 ff., 584 ff., 657 ff.

swer negatively.[206] Since fear is sufficient for penance, the theologians have debated the nature of this fear: Is it *timor simpliciter servilis* or *serviliter servilis?* In other words, does fear come from "moral self-love" or only from inordinate egotism? from the injury done to the soul or merely from the harm inflicted upon the body?

Confession. In sacramental confession the penitent submits himself and his sins to the judicial power of the keys. Sacramental confession consists of the following parts: the sinner's self-accusation; declaration of all mortal sins with the attendant circumstances; confession before the properly authorized priest; absolution as a judicial act, effective *ex opere operato.*[207] The theologians readily admit that there is only indirect Scriptural testimony for *sacramental* confession and that the references to confession in Scripture do not apply. The sacramental confession is said to be necessarily implied in the institution of the office of the keys as a judicial power to which the penitent must submit his crime.[208] Innocent III in the Constitution *Omnis utriusque sexus* (1215) decreed that every member of the church must make confession of his sins at least once a year. Failure to do so was defined as a mortal sin.[209] The Roman Catholic church has perpetuated this requirement. The Council of Trent prescribes that all mortal sins must be confessed.[210] Since the priest as a judge must impose a sentence commensurate with the greatness of the crime, he must know all such attendant circumstances as either diminish or aggravate, or even alter, the crime. For example, under certain conditions theft of a carpenter's tools may be a venial sin, but if the carpenter is thereby deprived of a day's wages, it may become a mortal sin.[211] Rome realizes that auricular confession places a tremendous, onerous, and often a distasteful burden on its members and that the "confessional box" may be

---

[206] Pohle-Preuss, X, 162. — Pohle, an attritionist, discusses the still unsettled controversy between attritionism and contritionism. The former school maintains that sorrow based on fear of hell is salutary; the latter says it is insufficient unless accompanied by an act of "initial charity." This section contains valuable information on the tensions between various schools of thought at Trent, which are reflected in the careful wording of the decrees and canons (pp. 170—79). — Bellarmine taught that in attrition the *will* to sin may continue, but later popes have branded this as a motive "hardly sufficient" for penance. Cp. *Cath. Encyc.,* XI, 619.

[207] Pohle-Preuss, X, 181—84. The confession is viewed as a penalty for sin and as a means to win back God's friendship. *Cath. Encyc.,* XI, 618 ff.

[208] Pohle-Preuss, X, 185—91. The chief argument is based on "prescription," viz., the church always had the penitential system (ibid., pp. 192 to 215). Wilmers, pp. 597—619.

[209] Mirbt, p. 181. The Council of Trent decreed that penance is as necessary for those who have fallen into sin after baptism as is baptism for the unregenerated. Sess. XIV, Can. 2. Cp. E. Boyd Barrett, "The Drama of Catholic Confession," *Journal of Religion,* VII (1928), p. 188 ff. But note what Smith has to say: "Since only mortal sins must be submitted to the sacramental tribunal, this precept does not bind those who are not in mortal sin." He goes on to say that an anxious Christian will normally confess mortal sin at his earliest convenience, the inference being that the Easter Confession is meant primarily for the lax (p. 975). Easter Communion is absolutely obligatory.

[210] Trent, Sess. XIV, Can. VII on Penance.

[211] Wilmers, IV, 663 f. Pohle-Preuss, X, 187 f.

frightfully abused. It therefore reminds the penitents that the priest is under an absolute seal of silence, that confessing disgraceful sins before one man obviates the greater shame of confessing them before all the angels and that the confessor has heard the confession of worse crimes.[212]

Evangelical churches do not object to private confession. In fact, the Lutheran Confessions advocate it on account of the private absolution.[213] The chief objection to the compulsory papal confession is that the hearts of men are left in doubt. When has a penitent made a full and honest confession? If he is unable to recall all mortal sins, an incomplete, a "virtual," confession (the desire to confess all) will suffice.[214] But did the penitent really endeavor to remember everything? A full confession of all mortal sins with all attendant circumstances is said to be essential. But if this should prove very difficult or impossible, a partial confession is said to be sufficient. Physical weakness may be a mitigating circumstance. The preservation of the good name of a third party, e. g., a partner in the crime, may under certain conditions exempt from revealing all details.[215] Non-Romanists wonder how "an honest confession can be good for the soul" if the confessional box can become a torture chamber in which the penitent is at once defendant, prosecutor, and witness. There can be no objective peace of soul, neither for him who is scrupulously honest nor for him who perfunctorily goes to penance, trusting in its *ex opere operato* efficacy.[216]

Satisfaction. Every mortal sin involves both guilt and punishment. Baptism removes both, but Penance removes only the guilt and the eternal punishment. The temporal punishment remaining after Penance is canceled in part by such satisfactions as the priest imposes. Trent (Sess. VI, Can. 30; XIV, Can. 12) specifically condemned the Lutheran doctrine that in justification God cancels the guilt and *all* punishment. To support this view the Roman theologians appeal not only to tradition, but also to Scripture, particularly to such cases as Adam and Eve, and especially to David (2 Sam. 12:13).[217] In reality the doctrine of satisfactions rests upon several basic principles of Rome's theology.

---

212 Walther, p. 107. Lydon, *Ready Answers*, p. 154. James P. Kelly, *The Jurisdiction of the Confessor* (New York: Benziger Bros., 1929).

213 A. C., XXV; Ap., VI, 6.

214 Ibid.

215 Wilmers, IV, 661 ff.

216 Pohle-Preuss, X, 168.

217 Ibid., p. 217 ff. Wilmers, IV, 676 ff. It is not clear why the temporal penalties which remain after Baptism are said to be medicinal and not real punishments, while those remaining after Penance are vindictive. — Cp. Ap. XII, 133—173 (VI, 36—76), where Melanchthon argues that the Biblical references which the adversaries produce do not refer to canonical satisfactions; that the death of Christ is a satisfaction not only for guilt but also for eternal death; that true prayers, alms, and fasting have God's command and cannot therefore be omitted without sin; that vindictive punishment is necessary in repentance, not as merit or consideration, but formally, that is, because regeneration itself takes place through a perpetual mortification of our old self; that contrition is more truly a punishment than satisfactions; that while canonical satisfactions do not take away public calamities, we can profitably teach on the basis of the Sacred Scriptures that total repentance, that is, contrition, faith, and good works, done out of faith, bring about the mitigation of both public and private disasters; and that the Lutheran position on these points is demonstrably Biblical and Catholic.

1. It is a necessary corollary of the undue emphasis placed on the justice of God. God in His sovereignty could forgive the temporal as well as the eternal punishment, but it is only proper and just that through imposed satisfactions man receives what he properly has deserved and restores to God the obedience he has withheld.[218] 2. The "just" man is credited with the ability to acquire not only supernatural merits but also satisfactions *de condigno,* i. e., as a just reward. The merits effect eternal beatitude, the satisfactions, either as satis*factions (doing* enough in this life) or as satis*passions (suffering* enough in purgatory), blot out the temporal punishments.[219] 3. The priest functions as a judge and according to Trent (Sess. XIV, Canons 8, 15) must therefore impose — not merely suggest — an adequate work of penance. And finally the efficacy of penance is primarily *ex opere operato,* not *ex opere operantis.*[220]

The customary satisfactions are praying, fasting, almsgiving, the three "good works" which are said to lend themselves to serve as satisfactions for the three cardinal sins, pride, lust of the flesh, and lust of the eyes. The Evangelical Christian, who believes that the essence of a good work is that it is done joyfully and willingly, cannot understand that a God-pleasing work can "partake of the character of punishment," or how prayer can be an *opus poenale, laboriosum,* a "bitter" work.[221] Lest the priest should impose such "punishments" as might make penance distasteful, Trent (ch. viii) advises the confessor to consider not only the grievousness of the crime, but also the ability of the penitent. The handbooks on moral theology contain specific instructions to guide the confessor in imposing satisfaction justly and also prudently, i. e., with proper regard for the penitent's social position, economic status, occupation, temperament. The penitent is obligated to accept the satisfactions and to fulfill them as prescribed. Failure to do so means that the satisfactions must be made in purgatory under much more difficult conditions, unless the penitent has inadvertently forgotten the specific instructions or is legitimately hindered from carrying them out. The penitent may respectfully request the confessor to change the satisfaction if it exceeds his ability. The Roman catechism even grants the penitent the right to engage a substitute to render the satisfaction if he is prevented from doing so himself.[222] The penitential system administered according to ecclesiastical instructions is an acceptable program of moral righteousness. It appeals to reason because it emphasizes self-examination and encourages man to make amends for his sin. But as a way of salvation it is totally inadequate.

Indulgences. An "indulgence" is a remission of the temporal punishments

---

[218] Wilmers, IV, 676, 678.

[219] Pohle-Preuss, X, 226 f.

[220] Ibid., pp. 228—31.

[221] Ibid., p. 228. *C. Rom.,* Part II, ch. 5, Qu. 58 f. Satisfaction is not like contrition and confession an *essential* part of the sacrament. But it is an integral part because it is necessary to obtain the remission of temporal punishment. *Cath. Encyc.,* XI, 628.

[222] Walther, p. 109. *C. Rom.,* II, ch. 5, Qu. 61. Pesch, p. 135. Smith, II, 975, remarks that the modern penances are very slight; hence substitution would hardly appear necessary. See also footnote on same page: "The actual performance of the penance imposed is not necessary for the validity of the Sacrament; it is sufficient if at the time of absolution the will to do the penance is present."

which a penitent has yet to undergo either here or in purgatory; this remission is granted by the church through the power of the keys from "the treasury of the superabundant merits of Christ and His saints." An indulgence is granted outside the sacrament and is called an extrasacramental complement to Penance.[223] But will not the theory that an indulgence releases the penitent from the satisfactions imposed by the priest completely undermine all morality, the very thing which the satisfactions are said to foster? The answer is that the sacramental penance blots out punishments *ex opere operato*, whereas the extrasacramental indulgence is valid only *ex opere operantis*. In other words, it requires the recipient's worthiness and the performance of certain acts. The indulgence doctrine is not, as it might appear at first glance, contrary to the emphasis which Rome places on the justice of God. According to Trent, it is an article of faith *(propositio fidei proxima)* that there is an inexhaustible treasury of superabundant merits from which the penitent may draw to compensate for his sin and to satisfy the justice of God. A number of propositions are advanced to prove the existence of such a treasury and the church's right to dispense the accumulated merits. Every good work is viewed as having a twofold effect, the one satisfactory, the other meritorious. Christ's life and death were not only propitiatory and sufficient to cancel guilt but also meritorious. Since Christ did not require these merits for

Himself, they are said to be superabundant and, according to Rom. 5:19 ff., flow into the thesaurus. Because Christ's person is infinitely worthy, His merits are infinite and make the thesaurus inexhaustible. The dogma of the communion of saints is said to indicate that also the merits of the saints flow into this treasury. Because of her sinlessness, Mary was not required to make satisfactions. Her good works, particularly her sorrows, gained superabundant merit. The saints' works of supererogation, such as works of penance beyond the amount required for the expiation of their sins, and especially martyrdom, were more than sufficient for their own satisfaction, and are deposited with the church for the common good.[224] The existence of such a treasury is simply taken for granted, since tradition is said to have unanimously taught it.[225] The argument that the church is the divinely appointed custodian of this treasury runs as follows: The church has the greater power to remit eternal punishment, it must also have the lesser power to remit totally or partially the temporal punishments; further, the church has always exercised this power, both in the sacrament of Penance and in the extrasacramental indulgence; according to the law of prescription it must therefore be presumed that Christ gave to the church t' e unconditional jurisdiction of the treasury.

The granting of indulgences does not release man from his obligation to work

---

223 Pohle-Preuss, X, 234. Wilmers discusses indulgences, IV, 692 to 714. — Cp. *Cath. Encyc.*, s. v. "Indulgence." The chief official sources are: *Unigenitus Dei Filius*, of Clement VI, 1343; *Inter cunctas*, of Martin V, 1418, which condemned the Wycliffite and Hussite doctrines; *Exsurge, Domine*, of Leo X, 1520, which condemned forty-one alleged errors of Luther; Council of Trent, Session XXV, "Resolutions on Indulgences," Dec. 4; *Censures of 79 Sentences of M. Baius* (1567). For text of these documents see Mirbt, No. 223 ff. Cp. Pohle-Preuss, X, 233.

224 Wilmers, IV, 694 f. Pohle-Preuss, X, 253 ff. *Indulgence Quizzes to a Street Preacher* (a tract), p. 1 ff.

225 Pohle-Preuss, X, 244—54.

out his own salvation. Roman theologians are virtually unanimous in the opinion that indulgences do not destroy, but rather foster morality. For the church will grant indulgences only upon the fulfillment of three conditions. The recipient must be in the state of grace, must conscientiously perform the prescribed good works, and must really have the intention to gain an indulgence. The Roman Catholic doctrine of indulgences is said to be

> severity itself compared with the Protestant all-embracing act of faith, which alone suffices to wash away all man's sins, and to put him at once, without penance or purgatory, into the assembly of the elect.[226]

This was unfamiliar language in the days of the indulgence traffic, and there is no doubt that some exaggerated views have been corrected, e. g., that indulgences can be sold and bought, that an indulgence is a remission of past sins or permission for a future sin, though it is difficult to explain why several papal bulls have used the expression "an indulgence for the remission of sins." The standard teaching today is that indulgences cannot be obtained gratis, for free indulgences would be contrary to God's justice and destructive of morality.

If one grants the premises for indulgences, then one is not surprised at their popularity. On the basis of the existence of "the treasury of the Church" and the church's power to draw on this inexhaustible fund, the penitent is given the choice of removing the temporal punishments either by satisfactions (in this life) and satispassions (in purgatory) or by obtaining an indulgence. The choice is obvious, and all the more so since an indulgence may be obtained with a minimum of effort on the part of the penitent.

> What is easier than to have the holy name of Jesus on our lips as we go from hallowed mound to mound and from row to row? Indulgenced ejaculations are hardly valued enough. "My Jesus, mercy!" 100 days each time; "Jesus, Mary!" 300 days each time; "Heart of Jesus, in Thee I trust!" 300 days each time; "Sweet Heart of Jesus, be Thou my love!" 300 days each time. In less than a minute's time, if you have the proper dispositions of contrition and love, you have a thousand days' indulgence, a remission of temporal punishment that could have been acquired in olden centuries only by ten hundred days of penitential sackcloth and ashes.[227]

There are many indulgences, usually classified as follows: (1) universal, which may be gained anywhere, and local, available at a specified church or shrine; (2) perpetual, available at all times, and temporary, restricted to a certain day of the week or month; (3) real and personal, the first attached to material objects, e. g., a rosary, crucifix, the second to be gained by classes of persons, e. g., members of a religious community; (4) solemn and plain; (5) plenary and partial indulgences; [228]

---

[226] Ibid., p. 257 f. *Quizzes*, p. 25.

[227] Quoted in *Popular Symbolics*, p. 182. Gibbon, p. 375 ff. Cf. W. Faerber, *Commentary on the Catechism*, ed. F. Girardey (St. Louis: Herder Book Co., 1937), p. 388 f. Lydon, *Ready Answers*, pp. 304—10, discusses canons 911—36, which deal with various phases and details of indulgences, e. g., the acts required for a plenary indulgence; only one plenary indulgence can be gained on one day; indulgenced beads, when destroyed or sold, lose their indulgence, but not when loaned.

[228] The "plenary indulgence" is remission of the whole debt of temporal punishments. Among the many plenary indulgences participation in a jubilee, celebrated every 25 years, grants the ideal indulgence. To receive a plenary indulgence one must be free from "all affection for sin." A partial indulgence remits a part of the temporal punishments, e. g., an indulgence of

(6) indulgences for the living and indulgences for the dead.[229]

Apostolic indulgences are those which the pope attaches to crosses, crucifixes, chaplets, rosaries, scapulars, images, medals, provided these have been blessed by the pope or his delegate and provided they are used by the original owner. In the transfer to another person the blessed object loses its power. When one considers that there are several types of rosaries, hundreds of scapulars, medals, images, etc., one can understand why Trent in Session XXV instituted the Congregation of Indulgence to guard against many abuses which "gave occasion to heretics to blaspheme this honorable name of indulgences." Particularly offensive were the traffic in indulgences and the introduction of "apocryphal" or spurious indulgences. Lutherans, the Reformed, and the Eastern Orthodox church reject the entire system, not because of the abuses, but because they cannot accept Canon 926, which bases the granting of indulgences on the Roman doctrines of the communion of saints, the treasury of superabundant satisfactions, and the power of the church to draw on this treasury.[230]

EXTREME UNCTION

The teaching of Trent on this sacrament (Sess. XIV) is summarized by Pohle as follows:

Extreme Unction is a Sacrament of the New Testament instituted by Jesus Christ, in which the sick, who are seriously ill, by the anointing with holy oil and the prayer of the priest, receive the grace of God for the good of their souls, and often also for their bodies.[231]

The Council (Sess. XIV, ch. i, Can. 1) said that it has been

instituted by Christ, our Lord, as truly and properly a sacrament of the new law, insinuated indeed in Mark [6:13], but recommended and promulgated to the faithful by James the Apostle [James 5:14] and brother of the Lord.

It is admitted that there is no Scriptural statement nor an express patristic tradition to prove that Christ instituted Extreme Unction as a sacrament. The doctrine is based on an assumption (Extreme Unction confers grace; therefore Christ "very probably" instituted it after His resurrection); on later tradition; on the *Decretum pro Armenis* by Eugene IV (1439); on the Tridentine decree; and on an *ad hominem* argument:

It is impossible to believe that He who soothed the last hours of a dying sinner with the assurance of an immediate entrance into the kingdom of heaven, would be unmindful of the needs of His faithful followers in the final hours of their earthly pilgrimage.[232]

The matter of this sacrament is "pure olive oil blessed by a bishop" at Mass

---

40 days (a quarantine) or 300 days. The partial indulgence is "gauged by the penitential canons of the ancient Church." An indulgence of seven years remits as much of the temporal punishments as was remitted in the ancient church by seven years of ecclesiastical penance.

229 *Cath. Encyc.*, VII, 788 f. Since an indulgence can be granted only "by an act of ecclesiastical jurisdiction," and since the "poor" souls in purgatory are no longer under this jurisdiction, they can obtain the benefit of an indulgence only through the intercession of the living.

230 Cp. Schwiebert, *Luther and His Times*, Ch. x, pp. 303—30. Bainton, *Here I Stand*, pp. 71—83.

231 Pohle-Preuss, XI, 3. The standard dogmatic works discuss Extreme Unction in connection with Penance, because Trent views it as the consummation of penance and of the entire Christian life.

232 Francis J. Connell, *Death Can Be Joyous* (New York: Paulist Press), pp. 3, 5 f.

on Maundy Thursday. This oil is applied to the "organs of the five external senses" (eyes, ears, nostrils, lips, hands) and to the feet. The form, according to the *Decretum pro Armenis,* is:

> Through this holy anointing and His most benign mercy, may the Lord pardon thee whatever transgression thou hast committed by sight (or "hearing," "smell," "taste and speech," "touch" and "walking"). Amen.[233]

The theologians are not agreed as to what constitutes the sacramental grace in Extreme Unction. Some hold that it enables

> the faithful to pass directly from the present life to everlasting happiness without being obliged to remain even for a moment in purgatory.

But others object to this view, since it would make prayers for the dead unnecessary; nor can anyone be certain that his devotion is so ardent that he will enter heaven without purgatory. Following Trent, the majority teach that Extreme Unction (1) increases "grace"; (2) remits venial sins and, according to many theologians, also mortal sins, thus not only completing Penance but in certain cases taking its place; (3) comforts the sick and helps them meet death calmly; (4) conditionally restores health.[234] Theoretically Extreme Unction is administered only to baptized persons (1) who are in "the state of grace" and properly disposed; (2) who are dangerously ill (condemned criminals and soldiers before battle are excluded, though they are entitled to the Eucharist as a viaticum); (3) who are "morally responsible."[235] According to the *opus operatum* theory, however, Extreme Unction may be administered to

a Catholic bereft of consciousness in the very act of sin and in danger of death. For despite his transgressions he would in all likelihood desire the sacraments if he knew that death were at hand. . . . It is now a recognized medical principle that real death may not take place until several hours after apparent death. The Catholic Church allows priests to act on this principle by administering Extreme Unction to one who has been suddenly stricken down and has apparently been dead for three or four hours, on condition that life still remains.[236]

HOLY ORDERS

In Rome's theology sacerdotalism is the indispensable correlative of sacramentalism. The theologians must therefore establish by "reason" and "revelation" the two propositions of Trent that "there is in the New Testament a visible and external priesthood" (Sess. XXIII, Can. 1); and "whereas it is clear that grace is conferred by sacred ordination, which is performed by words and outward signs . . . orders is truly and properly one of the seven sacraments of Holy Church" (ch. iii and Can. 3). The first proposition is established by the following line of argument: Ethnic religions recognized the need of propitiatory sacrifices; the Old Testament had sacrifices; the New Testament church, being far superior to either, has a superior sacrifice, the unbloody sacrifice of the Mass; a sacrifice requires a priesthood; since the apostles and their successors were commissioned to offer the Mass as a daily and continuous sacrifice (Heb. 5:1), there must be a visible priesthood. The second proposition is established as follows: The purpose of Christ's work was to gain "grace" *(gratia infusa)* for man-

---

[233] Ibid., pp. 10—13. Cp. Pohle-Preuss, XI, 16—23.

[234] Connell, pp. 21—24; Pohle-Preuss, XI, 24—34. Wilmers, IV, 722 to 724; Girardey, p. 391 f.

[235] Pohle-Preuss, XI, 44—50.

[236] Connell, pp. 25, 26, 28.

kind's sanctification; this "invisible grace" is offered only through "visible signs," the sacraments; Christ gave these to the apostles to be administered by them and their successors; it must be assumed that the transfer of so important an authority was accompanied by such visible solemnities as would clearly indicate that with the bestowal of authority the apostles also received the "invisible grace" to administer their powers properly; in short, in "orders" there are both, the invisible grace and the visible sign: therefore ordination is a sacrament.[237] The argument for the sacramental character of ordination is said to rest on "revelation" (Scripture and tradition). The "imposition of hands," mentioned in 2 Tim. 1:6 and in the early patristic writings, is said to be the visible sign of the invisible grace. Since "no one but the God-man could establish this connection," it may be assumed that Christ instituted ordination as a sacrament during the forty days prior to His ascension.[238] The universal priesthood of believers is regarded as essentially different from the priesthood imparted by holy orders.[239]

Since ordination is a Roman sacrament, it must have matter and form. The imposition of hands is considered the matter, and the invocation of the Holy Ghost the form. The theologians are not agreed which of the three impositions

and accompanying prayers constitute the sacrament.[240] According to Trent (Sess. XXIII, ch. iv., and Can. 4), the chief sacramental effect is the bestowal of the indelible character, "which can neither be effaced nor taken away." Ordination is said to elevate the priest above the laity and to entitle him to many prerogatives, such as immunity from civil court action, special honors in life and death. The tonsure is the "clerical crown" and is enlarged as the priest is elevated to higher orders. It is not commonly used in America.[241]

The hierarchy, an order of governors with various ranks, is considered as essential for the church as various ranks of offices are necessary for the state. Therefore it must be assumed that Christ provided for the establishment of grades in the ministry.[242] In the Roman church there are eight orders: bishop, priest, deacon, subdeacon, acolyte, exorcist, lector, and porter; the first three were instituted by Christ, the others by the church and therefore are not sacramental. The episcopate is the highest, because, according to tradition and by decree of Trent (Sess. XXIII, ch. iv), the bishop has peculiar functions not assigned to lower ranks, for example, confirmation, and especially the powers to ordain and to appoint priests and through them to govern the diocese *(potestas ordinis et iurisdictionis).* This

---

237 Wilmers, IV, 729—33.

238 Pohle-Preuss, XI, 55—61.

239 Wilmers, IV, 736—42. In an address on the "Priesthood of Our Laity," delivered at the International Marian Congress in Rome on November 2, 1954, Pius XII declared: "Whatever is the full meaning of this honorable title and claim [to 'priesthood' which St. Peter ascribed to the faithful in his First Letter, II, 5. 9], it must be firmly held that the 'priesthood' common to all the faithful, high and reserved as it is, differs, not only in degree but in essence also, from priesthood fully and properly so called, which lies in the power of offering the Sacrifice of Christ Himself, since he [the ordained celebrant] bears the Person of Christ, the Supreme High Priest" (the *St. Louis Register,* XIV, 46 [Nov. 12, 1954], Section One, 11).

240 Pohle-Preuss, XI, 62—71.

241 Ibid., p. 72 ff. — Walther, p. 115 f.

242 Wilmers, IV, 742 f.

includes the power of excommunication and the granting of dispensations. The pope is *summus episcopus*. The priesthood has power to administer all sacraments, except Confirmation and Ordination, and to offer the unbloody sacrifice. The diaconate is said to be the lowest or the first sacrament of orders, granting the right "to serve at the altar, to baptize, to teach." [243] The other five orders, the so-called minor orders, are said to be of ecclesiastical origin and therefore do not have sacramental character. The "election" to minor orders may be exercised by priests. But the "ordination" of higher clerics is the sole prerogative of the bishop, and according to Trent the sacramental character of ordination by its very nature excludes the consent and vocation of the people.[244]

Though celibacy is said not to be a divine law, but merely an ecclesiastical precept, Gregory VII and Trent (Sess. XXIV, Can. 9) made celibacy binding upon bishops, priests, deacons, and subdeacons. The usual arguments are that "virginity" is a higher estate than matrimony; that as the spouse of Christ the church must be free from all secular influences, e. g., the cares and interests of a family; the Old Testament priests observed abstinence during their time of Temple service; the priest is the spiritual father of his parish.[245]

MATRIMONY

The Council of Trent (Sess. XXIV, Can. 1) has condemned all who deny that matrimony is a sacrament. This canon is said to rest upon Eph. 5:23-32, in which Christ employs marriage to illustrate His mystical union with the Church. Wilmers finds the following points of analogy: Christ left His Father and cleaves to the church until the end of time; in this union He creates a spiritual progeny under the fostering care of "Mother Church"; for nineteen centuries the church has been His obedient spouse, whom He loves in spite of the failings of its members. Wilmers concludes that by making matrimony a symbol of the mystical union Christ elevated matrimony to a "mystery" (*sacramentum*). Matrimony is said to be a sacrament because St. Paul further attributes to it the three essential notes of a sacrament: an external sign, invisible grace, Christ's institution.[246] Accordingly Rome teaches that in the pre-Christian era

[243] Trent, Sess. XIV, ch. vii; XXIV, ch. i; XXV, ch. xxi; XXIII, Can. 1 — Pohle-Preuss, XI, 78 ff., 94 ff., 99 ff.

[244] Trent, Sess. XXIII, Can. 7. Wilmers, IV, 752 f. The validity of Anglican ordination is treated on pp. 761—72. Leo XIII in *Apostolicae curae* (1896) decided against Anglican Orders. Pohle-Preuss, XI, 70 f. The practice of ordaining infants is said to be valid though illicit (ibid., pp. 128, 130 ff.). — John Bligh, *Ordination to the Priesthood* (New York: Sheed and Ward, c. 1956), pp. 8, 9, holds that "it is almost certain that with Papal authorization he [a simple priest] can validly ordain even to the diaconate and priesthood," inasmuch as the *Decretum pro Armenis* (1439) "would seem to imply that in extraordinary circumstances the minister of either [Confirmation or Ordination] can be a priest" and inasmuch as Boniface IX in 1400 and 1403, Martin V in 1427, and Innocent VIII in 1489 empowered abbots who were only simple priests to ordain their subjects to sacred orders.

[245] Ibid., 130 ff. Roman historians are ready to admit the long history of the abuses incident to celibacy which have been laid to the charge of the medieval priesthood (Ap., XXIII). Cp. Lortz, and Adam (*One and Holy*), Ch. ii, in Bibliog., below.

[246] Wilmers, IV, 810 f. Pohle-Preuss follows the same line of argumentation. "Christian marriage is a sacred sign which produces internal grace, because St. Paul calls it a great mystery and symbol of Christ's union with the Church. . . . The sacraments of the New Law produce grace *ex opere*

matrimony was indeed a valid contract, but not a sacrament. In the New Testament, however, "every legitimately contracted marriage is *eo ipso* a sacrament, and vice versa, when the sacrament is received there is a nuptial contract . . . for it is always a great mystery (i. e., a sacrament) among Christians when a man leaves his father and mother and cleaves to his wife." [247]

The sacramental effects are said to be an increase of sanctifying grace and the bestowal of the special grace necessary to perform the functions of matrimony. Since marriage symbolizes the indissoluble mystic union of Christ and the church, matrimony imprints a quasi-sacramental character and, like all sacraments, bestows special sacramental effects. These are as follows:

As members of the bride of Christ, married people are wedded with Christ Himself. When they join themselves together, they can do so legally only for the purpose which Christ pursues in His union with the Church, namely, to propagate the mystical body of Christ. Thus the marital union is a participation in the union between Christ and His Church. [248]

In matrimony the *matter* and the *form* are contained in the nuptial contract or the signs used to express the mutual consent. In so far as the consent signifies "the mutual surrender of the bodies," the contract is the matter; and in so far as it "signifies the acceptance,"

it is the form. [249] From this it follows that the priest is not the "minister" of this sacrament. Since the contract contains both the matter and the form, only the contracting parties can administer this sacrament to each other. As "ministers" of the sacrament they must have "the intention of doing what the Church does, i. e., contracting a Christian marriage." Marriage is therefore called "the lay sacrament." The priest as official representative of the church is the chief witness and "the minister of the solemn ceremonies with which the Church surrounds marriage," e. g., the ecclesiastical solemnization and the nuptial blessing. The recipients of matrimony must be baptized persons who are not hindered by impediments. [250]

Rome's definition concerning matter, form, minister, and recipient in this sacrament leads to deductions which appear contradictory to anyone untrained in Roman canon law. On the one hand, Trent decreed (Sess. XXIV, ch. i) that any marriage not performed in the presence of the parish priest, for example, by a Lutheran pastor, must be declared null and void. On the other hand, Canon 1012 states that since the contract, not the blessing, is in itself the sacrament, the valid marriage of two baptized non-Romanists is a sacrament. Pius X solved this conflict in the *Ne temere* (effective since 1908), in which he ruled that the Tridentine decree is binding only on members of the papal church. [251] The

operato. Hence, if matrimony is a true symbol of the mystic union between Christ and the Church, it must produce grace in those who receive it." The teachers are not agreed whether Christ instituted this "sacrament" at Cana, after the resurrection, or when He restored "the pristine indissolubility of marriage, Matt. 19:8 ff." (XI, 148—51.) — Cp. the exhaustive study by George H. Joyce, *Christian Marriage* (see Bibliog.).

247 Pohle-Preuss, XI, 157 ff. Cp. Geo. D. Smith, II, 1064—68.

248 Pohle-Preuss, XI, 168—71. M. J. Scheeben, *Die Mysterien des Christentums* (1912), p. 517, quoted in Algermissen, p. 501.

249 Pohle-Preuss, XI, 165 ff.

250 Ibid., pp. 214—18.

251 Mirbt, No. 551 f. Cp. Lydon, *Ready Answers*, p. 352.

code of May 19, 1918, liberalized the decree still more, by ruling that since 1918 all marriages of baptized persons are valid. It is significant that Pius XII, in a rescript effective January, 1949, rescinded Section B, par. 2 of Canon 1099, which excluded all non-Romanists and heretical Roman Catholics from observing the canonical marriage celebrations. This indicates that Rome considers all baptized persons as coming under her jurisdiction.[252] Rome's teaching that only marriages among baptized persons are a sacrament, while all others are merely a contract, raises such questions as these: Does the marriage of an unbaptized couple become a sacrament when both become Christians? What happens when only one is baptized?[253] Since the proper intention of both contracting parties is required, can either spouse be certain of a valid matrimony?

In a day of "easy divorces" the Roman church is to be commended for its emphasis of the indissolubility of marriage. Rome, however, goes beyond the Scriptures on two points: (1) it recognizes no grounds for divorce, and (2) it claims authority to establish diriment impediments. Trent (Sess. XXIV, Can. 7) teaches that matrimony is indissoluble even in case of adultery. Matt. 5:32 and especially 19:9 are said to allow only a separation from bed and board. This interpretation is supported by the proposition that in Matt. 19:9 Christ revoked the Mosaic Law permit-

ting divorce and thereby elevated the New Testament marriage above the pre-Christian marriage; for if Matt. 19:9 were understood to allow divorce and remarriage, the New Testament would become inferior to the Old Testament.[254] Nevertheless Rome teaches that under two conditions there is an "extrinsic dissolubility: (1) Trent (Sess. XXIV, Can. 6) gave the pope the right to dissolve an "unconsummated marriage" between Christians when one party makes a "solemn profession of religion" and by relinquishing all worldly things actually suffers "a kind of spiritual death" in entering into a religious order; (2) A marriage between non-baptized persons may be dissolved by virtue of the "Pauline privilege" (1 Cor. 7:10 ff.), i. e., if one party becomes a Christian and the other refuses to live with the baptized in peaceful wedlock.[255]

The Tridentine Council (Sess. XXIV, Can. 4) condemns all who deny that the Roman church has the authority to establish impediments to marriage. The assumption is that Christ elevated matrimony to a sacrament, but left it to the church to establish the specific conditions under which marriage is to be performed. Some theologians find proof for this authority in the church's power to bind and to loose, the majority, however, in the law of prescription. That is to say, the church has exercised this authority for at least fifteen centuries, and the infallible church could not have

---

252 The canon declares: "Every contract validly made by any baptized couple, whether Catholics are not, is *ipso facto* and always a sacrament of the New Law, giving a title to grace and actually producing grace if no obstacle to it is consciously placed by the parties. Grace sanctifies and strengthens the lives of the parties. *The contract itself is the sacrament, not the blessing.* The valid marriage of two baptized non-Catholics is a sacrament even though the parties do not realize it or believe it." Lydon, *Ready Answers*, p. 343. — Cp. also H. A. Ayrinhac, revised P. J. Lydon, *Marriage Legislation* (New York: Benziger Bros., 1949), p. 238.

253 Pohle-Preuss, XI, 162 f.

254 Ibid., pp. 192—98. Wilmers, IV, 798—810.

255 Pohle-Preuss, XI, 203 f., 208 f.

done so if it did not *possess* this right.[256] In the course of the centuries Rome has established many impediments in addition to those prescribed in God's Word. Some of these have been modified, others suspended, and therefore canon law is subject to periodic revisions. It must also be noted that there is no apparent uniformity in the observance of all the rules laid down in the 132 canons on marriage. This is very confusing.[257] The church further claims authority to grant dispensations from any *ecclesiastical* impediment. This power presupposes the authority of "haling into court" and of passing a judicial judgment. Since the entire church is subject to the matrimonial laws, the pope is the only competent authority to adjudicate all marital cases and to grant dispensations. On the basis of the Tridentine canon (Sess. XXIV, Can. 12) no Roman Catholic is "permitted to doubt" that only the church has the right to control the administration of marriage, even in such matters as *sanatio in radice,* which validates an invalid marriage and legitimatizes the children born before validation. The claim for this all-inclusive authority rests on two dogmas: (1) Marriage is a sacrament, and therefore only the Church can regulate its administration. The state can claim no jurisdiction whatsoever. If both

church and state had jurisdiction, there would be constant conflict between two courts. (2) The marriage of baptized non-Roman Catholics is a sacrament, and the state must restrict itself to purely civil and nonessential legislation, e. g., regulations concerning property rights. Civil marriages between baptized persons under state control and without regard for the laws of the church are said to be "contrary to divine law," i. e., in the light of *Ne temere,* they are illicit, though valid. For its nonbaptized members the state may establish impediments as long as they are of a purely civil character.[258]

The church has established fifteen impediments to marriage, four of which are prohibitory, the rest diriment, i. e., divisive. The former make marriage illicit, but not invalid, the latter invalidate marriage. The prohibitory impediments are marriage in the closed seasons (Trent, Sess. XXIV, ch. x); any ecclesiastical prohibition, such as marriage to a baptized non-Romanist, known as "mixed marriage"; the "simple" vow of chastity; an unjustly broken engagement. The most significant divisive impediments are insufficient age, impotence, the existence of a former valid marriage with a surviving partner, and forbidden degrees of consanguinity and affinity.[259]

---

[256] Martin S. Scott, *Marriage Problems* (New York: Paulist Press), p. 17; and especially Wilmers, IV, 834 f. Pohle-Preuss, XI, 221 ff. Council of Trent (Sess. XXIV, ch. ii, Canons 2, 3, 8).

[257] Roman Catholics often charge non-Romanist writers with misrepresenting the Roman position, and they insist that they never heard of such rules, nor were these observed in their specific case of a mixed marriage. But the non-Romanist is compelled to judge Rome's position on the basis of official documents and not upon the whims of a priest or the ignorance of the parishioners. Cp. Walther, p. 147. — At Luther's time the medieval church had 18 impediments. See Luther, *Vom ehelichen Leben,* W. A., X/2, 275—304.

[258] Pohle-Preuss, XI, pp. 225—40. *Sanatio in radice,* ibid., p. 228. Wilmers, IV, 834—41.

[259] *Cath. Encyc.,* s. v., "Impediments." Wilmers, IV, 831—34. On divisive impediments in the most recent canonical legislation, see *Codex Juris Canonici Pii XII Pontificis Maximi* (Westminster: Newman Press, 1952), Ch. iv, "De impedimentis dirimentibus," Canons 1067—1080, pp. 357—362.

No other church in Christendom can accept Rome's fundamental premise that the church as the divinely appointed agent has authority to establish extra-Biblical impediments and *eo ipso* the judicial power (1) to annul marriage and (2) to grant or refuse dispensations. Other Christians recognize the Biblical distinction between divorce (dissolution of a valid marriage) and annulment (declaration that no marriage existed). Their complaint against Rome is that this church will not permit the innocent party to remarry, though, according to Matt. 19:9, the bond has actually been dissolved by malicious desertion or adultery; and, again, that she will declare a marriage null even though there is no Scriptural ground. Nor can non-Romanists accept the principles of casuistry which empower a bishop to grant a dispensation from the church's express prohibition if — as the church asserts — such regulation "causes undue hardship." In a small, isolated, and interrelated community, for example, the bishop may permit marriages between third cousins, a relationship which ordinarily invalidates a marriage.

In recent years the prohibitory impediment of disparity of religion ("mixed marriage") has become a vexing problem. The church has forbidden mixed marriages, i. e., the marriage of a member of the church with a *baptized* nonmember.[260] But, according to canon law, the bishop may grant a dispensation from this prohibition if the following promise is signed by the non-Roman Catholic:

(1) That he will recognize the principle of the indissolubility of marriage;

(2) That he will not prevent the Roman Catholic party from exercising his faith;

(3) That all children, of either sex, born to the couple shall be baptized and brought up in the Roman Catholic faith, even though the Roman Catholic party should be taken away by death;

(4) That the marriage shall be performed before a priest.

Canon law prescribes that the Roman Catholic must promise to work for the conversion of his or her non-Roman Catholic spouse. The church, however, is "ashamed of such marriages," and according to canon law such a marriage is not performed in the church and is not blessed. But if greater evil to the parties concerned or to the church would result from carrying out this rule, the bishop may permit the marriage in the church.[261] It is reported that in more than thirty per cent of the American dioceses this dispensation is a standing rule. From reports it appears that there is no uniformity in the observance of the various marriage canons.

The Roman Catholic church has

---

[260] Paul Blanshard, "The Catholic Church and Annulment," *Christian Century*, April 27, 1949, p. 523. According to *America*, July 2, 1949, p. 393, the Sacred Roman Rota decided 124 cases in 1948; in 76 cases the marriage was declared valid, in 48 a declaration of nullity was issued. More than one third of the cases were handled gratuitously. — Cp. Lydon, *Ready Answers*, pp. 352—67; also George H. Joyce, pp. 208—14, for list of canonical impediments. See also *Cath. Encyc.*, XIII, 141.

[261] On Mixed Marriages see Wilmers, IV, 844 ff., and the following tracts: John O'Brien, *Why Not a Mixed Marriage?* Paulist Press, N. Y. — Anthony L. Ostheimer, *Instructions for Non-Catholics Before Marriage.* — Fathers Rumble and Carty, *Marriage Quizzes* (St. Paul: Radio Replies Press). — F. E. Mayer, *To Sign or Not to Sign* (St. Louis: C. P. H.). — *If I Marry a Roman Catholic*, National Council of the Churches of Christ, N. Y. — James A. Pike, *If You Marry Outside Your Faith* (New York: Harper & Bros., 1954).

taken a very determined stand against "unnatural planned parenthood," or birth control. Its opposition is said to be based on the principle that "it is always sinful to oppose or to check any force of nature." The church which claims to be charged with the right to fix the moral standards of its people, itself will not tamper with the laws of nature nor permit its members to do so. The church does not oppose "planned parenthood" *per se,* and it claims to give proper consideration to the problems of family economics and the mother's health as factors for limiting the number of children. But the church teaches that such limitation must be solved solely either by the law of biological sterility and fertility — the rhythm method — or by self-denial. Some Roman Catholic writers attack the use of contraceptives also on the ground that their use constitutes a mental, physical, and even social hazard.

The Roman hierarchy encourages the clergy to give premarital counseling according to the church's moral theology. The members are advised to consult their physicians (Romanists) for instruction in the rhythm method, as the only system for a God-pleasing means of control over conception.[262]

[262] Francis J. Connell, "Birth Control: "The Case for the Catholic," *Atlantic,* CLXIV (Oct., 1939), 469 ff. Cp. F. W. Rice, M. D., "A Catholic Physician's Views on Family Limitation," *Ecclesiastical Review,* CIII (July, 1940), p. 62 ff. See also Harold Gardiner, "Enemy of the West — Birth Control," *America,* LXXVII (Aug. 9, 1947), 513 f. H. A. Seifert, C. S. S. R., "Marriage Instruction Regarding Birth Control," *Ecclesiastical Review,* Vol. XCVI, No. 4 (April, 1937), 401—5. Gerald J. Schnepp and Joseph Mundi, "What Doctors Think of the Rhythm Method" (a Survey in St. Louis), *Ecclesiastical Review,* Vol. CXXIII, No. 2 (Aug., 1950), pp. 111—16. The use of a pessary or any permanent obstacle to conception is wrong under all conditions, even in view of miscarriage or danger of abortion. If used, the church refuses to grant absolution. Cp. "Birth Control and Refusing the *Debitum,*" *Ecclesiastical Review,* Vol. 106, No. 2 (Feb., 1942), pp. 142—43; Joseph A. M. Quigly, "The Use of Contraceptives," *Ecclesiastical Review,* Vol. CIX, No. 5 (Nov., 1952), pp. 386—90, a case study. The vehemence of the Roman Catholic reaction in Holyoke, Mass., in 1940 to the action of the First Congregational Church of that city in making its facilities available to Margaret Sanger for a discussion of birth control supplies the backdrop for the careful study made by Kenneth Wilson Underwood in 1947 (subsequently supplemented with other studies through 1956) and published as *Protestant and Catholic: Religious and Social Interaction in an Industrial Community* (Boston: Beacon Press, c. 1957).

There have been strong protests against this teaching by members of the church. E. Boyd Barrett, *Rome Stoops to Conquer* (New York: Julian Messner, Inc., 1935), pp. 126—44. He states that the Roman Catholic people are irritated as much as others over this emphasis by their church (p. 131 ff.). He attacks Rome's attempt to force this doctrine on the whole American public (pp. 127—28). Cp. Paul Blanshard, *American Freedom and Catholic Power,* p. 135 ff.; and *Communism, Democracy and Catholic Power* (Boston: Beacon Press, 1951).

SECTION V

The Sacramentals

Rome teaches that the sacramentals, like the sacraments, are external rites capable of conferring special blessings, but that, unlike the sacraments, they have not been instituted by Christ, but by the church; do not confer sanctifying grace, but other salutary blessings; are not effective *ex opere operato* (by the mere act performed), but *ex opere operantis*, that is, their efficacy is dependent upon the pious disposition of the recipient and the intercession of the church.[263] The American hierarchy seems to follow a threefold classification: exorcisms, blessings, objects.[264]

EXORCISM

This is viewed as a command given to the devil, ordering him in the name of God to depart from a specific person, place, or things and to desist from interfering maliciously in human affairs. The church is said to have attached such exorcisms to many sacramentals, e. g., to holy water, the sign of the cross. In the case of actual diabolical possession special permission must be obtained from the bishop before the priest may exorcise a person actually possessed of the devil.[265]

BLESSINGS

These are prayers which draw God's favor upon persons and things. There are two kinds of blessings, the constitutive and the invocative. The former, also known as consecration, dedicates a person or thing to the special service of God. In the latter type things are blessed for the benefit of the person in whose behalf the blessing is invoked, such as a wheel chair, silkworms, autos, fields, fishing tackle, bread, cattle, pets, etc. The Roman manual is said to have made provisions to bless even the most commonplace happenings in man's life.

263 H. Leclercq, *Cath. Encyc.*, XIII, s. v. "Sacramentals." Cp. Council of Trent, Sess. VII. Some theologians predicate the entire system of sacramentals on Platonic philosophical principles. Platonism maintains that only the "idea" is perfect; in other words, only abstract and metaphysical concepts are good, but all material and tangible things are more or less sinful. Before Christians can use these, they must be cleansed by consecrations. *Cath. Encyc.*, IV, 276 f. Pohle-Preuss, VIII, 111 ff.

264 Roman Catholics use various methods of classifying the many sacramentals. *The Cath. Encyc.* classifies them according to acts and things. Pohle-Preuss follows Thomas' distinction between consecrations and blessings.

265 J. T. Mueller, *Christian Dogmatics* (St. Louis: C. P. H., 1934), p. 501. — Luther saw no objection to the exorcism in the baptismal office, retaining it in his own of 1523, but abbreviating it further in that of 1526. The latter edition of the *Taufbüchlein* was widely incorporated in the Lutheran Symbols as an appendix to the Small Catechism. Most Lutheran service books retained the exorcism, to excite a bitter controversy within Lutheran ranks and to be the subject of reproach on the part of Calvinists. When not forced by such attacks to defend the practice, the Lutheran theologians freely admitted that it was a nonessential. It disappeared from general use in the era of the Enlightenment at the end of the 18th century.

BLESSED OBJECTS

Such are holy water, rosaries, scapulars, when used devoutly according to the prescriptions of the church. They are said to bring various blessings to the faithful. In certain sections of the Roman church, especially in countries which are predominantly Roman, sacramentals, especially as "blessed objects," play a highly important part in the life of its members. The sign of the cross and holy water are probably the most widely used sacramentals.

The sign of the cross with the accompanying Trinitarian profession is an ancient Christian symbol of the church's most holy faith and was never intended to be more than that. But today in many sections of the Roman church it is considered a means of securing God's protection against the assaults of the devil.

Romanists say that *holy water* when properly used,

> confers actual graces, remits venial sin, restrains the power of Satan and secures temporal blessings, such as bodily health and protection against temporal evils. It is also an effective means for the relief of the suffering souls in purgatory. . . . One drop of holy water is often more efficacious than a long prayer. Our prayers are frequently full of distractions. This, however, is not the case with the prayer of the Church attached to the holy water. This prayer, being the prayer of the pure and holy bride of Christ, is perfect. For this

reason the poor souls in purgatory so ardently long for holy water.[266]

Candles play a prominent part in the Roman cultus. The wax is said to represent the body of Christ, the wick His soul, and the flame His divinity. Romanists are instructed to have blessed candles available in the home at all times, for unexpected emergencies, particularly for Extreme Unction.[267] The pious use of the Agnus Dei, a disk of wax with the imprint of a lamb, is said to deliver from a sudden and "unprovided" death — without benefit of the clergy — and to give assurance that Christ will include the bearer in His intercession.

Scapulars are originally strips of woolen cloth worn over the shoulder and hanging down in front and in back, symbolizing the yoke of Christ. Only members of the respective order may wear the scapular and receive the specific blessings, both physical and spiritual, attached to the scapulars of the various orders. No layman is permitted to wear such a scapular.[268] The church, however, permits the laity to wear small reproductions of the monk's garments under ordinary clothing, whereby a layman becomes a quasi-member of the respective religious order and participates in the respective blessings.[269] The most popular scapulars seem to be those of the Benedictine, the Dominican, and especially the Carmelite Order.[270]

---

[266] From tract *Holy Water*, published by Benedictine Convent of Perpetual Adoration, Clyde, Mo.

[267] Candles are blessed on Candlemas Day, Feb. 2, the festival of Christ's presentation in the Temple, Luke 2:31.

[268] It was not uncommon in the Middle Ages that laymen who had been unable to wear the scapular during their lifetime requested that they be clothed in a monk's garment rather than the customary shroud. Ap., III, 240, esp. German text.

[269] The lay scapular is a small strip of woolen cloth worn directly on the skin. Since this may prove uncomfortable and unhygienic, a medal may be substituted under certain conditions.

[270] Cp. Haffert (see Bibliog.). According to tradition, the Virgin Mary directed Simon Stock (d. 1265) on Mount Carmel to wear the Carmelite

There are various forms of the *rosary*, ranging in size from five to fifteen decades. A bead contains a large Our Father pearl and ten Hail Mary pearls. The pendant is composed of a crucifix, which the faithful holds in his hand, of a large Our Father pearl and three small pearls at which the Ava Maria, the Gloria Patri, and the Credo are recited. The Dominican rosary contains fifteen decades.[271] The use of blessed ashes on Ash Wednesday is to remind the faithful that they must return to dust; and the display of the blessed palms on Palm Sunday is to them a constant reminder that by using the palms regularly they will merit by their good works to meet Christ when He returns in glory.

Romanists are cautioned not to despise these sacramentals as of no religious value or to consider them as having inherent miraculous powers.[272] Neither caution is really necessary for devout Romanists. The highly intellectual Romanist sees great symbolic meaning in the sacramentals. The Neoplatonic background prompts Roman theologians to teach that in Adam's fall Satan gained dominion over the created world, particularly the inanimate objects. All material things are Satan's working tools and must be exorcised, blessed, and sanctified for the Christian's use.[273] But in vulgar Romanism the sacramentals are used in such a way that they seem to be endowed with almost supernatural powers. Though the church teaches that the efficacy of the sacramental is contingent on the personal devotion of

scapular in her honor. In return Mary promised untold physical and spiritual blessings culminating in the Sabbatine Indulgence, i. e., on Saturday (Mary's special day) she would free from purgatory all the souls of Carmelites who had died during the previous week. This glorious promise, while intended at first only for the Carmelite monks, is made available to all lay people who wear with devotion a small reproduction of the garment properly blessed by the church.

271 In reciting the Dominican rosary the faithful are expected to meditate on the fifteen so-called "mysteries." The first five are the *joyful:* the Annunciation; the Visitation; the Nativity; the Presentation of the Child Jesus in the Temple; the Finding of the Child Jesus in the Temple. The second five are the *sorrowful:* The Agony in the Garden; the Scourging at the Pillar; the Crowning with the Thorns; Jesus Carries His Cross; the Crucifixion. The third five are the *glorious* mysteries: the Resurrection; the Ascension; the Descent of the Holy Ghost on the Apostles; the Assumption of Our Blessed Lady into Heaven; the Coronation of Our Blessed Lady. Each mystery requires ten Ave Marias, making a total of 150, plus the first three Ave Marias before starting the rosary. Cp. Bishop Challoner, *The Garden of the Soul* (Westminster, Md.: The Newman Press, 1945).

272 In 1866 the Second Council of Baltimore addressed the clergy: "Let them persuade those who trust too much in their wisdom and cleverness that these things, insignificant and unimportant though they may seem, are not to be despised, since they are of no little assistance toward right living and the attainment of salvation. Let them admonish the less educated persons — who are apt to fall into the contrary error — that they must not attribute too great efficacy to sacramentals nor think that these of themselves can avail much, without pious dispositions. Let them especially reprehend those who use these sacred things like charms, such as heathen have, to preserve them from the wrath of God, even when they are sunk in the mire of the most hideous vices."

273 It was Luther's contribution to show that according to the Bible all created things are God's precious gifts to man and therefore "holy" when used by "holy people."

the users (*ex opere operantis*), the church has clothed the more than 100 various benedictions and the numerous exorcisms in Latin formulae. But how can faith and devotion be engendered by a formula which is meaningless to him who recites it? The Romanist need not be surprised that the non-Romanist views the entire devotion to sacramentals as a pagan superstition.[274]

SECTION VI
Rome's Doctrine of the Church

Pius XII inaugurated several significant shifts of emphasis in Rome's traditional position concerning the doctrine of the church. According to Rome's theory of the development of doctrine, Rome's ecclesiology may undergo some additional changes,[275] however, none which would affect the heart and core of Roman theology, particularly the intimate relation between ecclesiology on the one hand and Rome's sacerdotalism and sacramentalism on the other.

The Nature of the Church

Until recently Roman dogmaticians presented the doctrine of the church with an introductory thesis defining the nature of the church. The majority of the catechisms followed Bellarmine's definition:

The Church is a body of men united together by profession of the same Christian faith, and participation in the same sacraments under the governance of lawful pastors, more especially the Roman Pontiff, the sole Vicar of Christ on earth.[276]

Modern Roman dogmaticians have felt keenly that every definition of the church according to the standard dogmaticians places the primary emphasis on the visible character of the church, and they feared that this emphasis must lead to a complete ignoring of the mysterious character of the church as the "mystical body of Christ." To set forth the mysterious character of the church, Roman dogmaticians have given new and more spiritual meaning to the terminology "the body and the soul of the Church." [277]

274 J. A. Phillip, *Papal Paganism* (Nashville, Tenn.: Cokesbury Press, 1924), p. 69 ff.

275 Schlink, loc. cit. McKnight, loc. cit., credits Pius XII with inaugurating several significant theological changes, particularly in three encyclicals: *Divino afflante Spiritu*, 1943, which encourages Bible reading; *Mystici corporis Christi*, 1943, which is directed against a false mysticism and espouses Roman Catholic activism; *Mediator Dei*, 1947, which denounces a false use of ancient liturgical forms, p. 246 ff. But the author also shows that Pius XII proved to be a reactionary on other points.

276 Bellarmine as quoted in the *Cath. Encyc.*, s. v. "Church." See Walther, p. 68 f., for a summary of the definitions according to Roman standard catechisms.

277 This is evidently the concern of Pius XII in *Mystici corporis Christi*. Roman Catholic dogmatics textbooks since 1943 are written in the spirit of this encyclical, which aims to stress the spiritual character of the church without yielding one point in the traditional position of Rome. Cp. E. Myers, "The Mystical Body of Christ," in Smith, II, 659 ff.

THE BODY AND THE SOUL OF THE CHURCH

Modern Roman dogmaticians initiate the study of the church with an analysis of the purpose and function of the church rather than with a definition of its nature. The purpose of the church is said to be to remove the effects of the corporate fall of mankind, i. e., man's separation from God, through the corporate redemption, i. e., man's blissful reunion with God. In His incarnation in the flesh, Christ made this reunion with God possible. But this possibility does not become an actuality unless Christ continues His incarnation in the church. The church is therefore the mystical body of Christ, the "prolongation of the incarnation." In the church the grace which Christ brought is said to link all the members together as the body of Christ, of which He is the Head.[278] It is therefore no longer quite correct to say with Bellarmine that the Catholic church is as visible as the kingdom of Venice. Roman theologians are endeavoring to find a mediating position between such coarse externalism and a transcendent view of the church. They say that as there was a synthesis of the visible with the invisible in the incarnate Christ, so also in the mystical body of His continued incarnation, the church. The invisible side is said to be the salutary operation of the Holy Spirit in the teaching, sacerdotal, and pastoral offices. The visible side is said to include the bearers of the threefold office as well as the faithful in their daily (visible) activity. The papal encyclical of 1943 seems to require some modification in Rome's ecclesiology, particularly in the description of the "soul" and "body" of the church and the former threefold classification of membership: (1) All those faithful who are in the state of sanctifying grace belong to the body and soul of the church; (2) Those who are in mortal sin belong only to the body of the church; (3) Those sincere non-Roman Catholics who are unaware of the demands of the Roman church belong to the soul of the church.[279]

Much more significant is the current description of the "soul" and the "body" of the church. Romanists aver that this terminology has been completely misunderstood and misused by Protestants, as though it allowed for the view that it is not necessary to belong to the visible body of the (papal) church as long as a person belonged to the "soul of the Church." Leo's statement: "Let it suffice to state that as Christ is the head of the Church, the Holy Spirit is the soul of the Church,"[280] has been given new emphasis by Pius XII. He taught that the spirit is the "life force" of the mystical body of Christ, i. e., the "soul of the mystical body. The "soul" of the church is therefore not the total of those who somehow are connected with the church without actual membership in the visible church, but the "soul" is said to be the gracious activity of the Spirit, the animating principle of the church dwelling in the church and in everyone individ-

---

[278] Adam, *Spirit of Catholicism*, loc. cit.

[279] Algermissen, p. 21 ff. In spite of the shift of emphasis Roman Catholics may still retain their Platonic approach in defining the church, i. e., view the church as an *idea* before it is a *res*. A Roman Catholic may define the church as an institution, an office, which exists prior to one's becoming a member of the church. Such a view places great emphasis upon the priesthood as an authority. And even when the church is described as a body of men united by the profession of the same Christian faith and participation in the same sacraments, the basic idea is that such union is always dependent upon the authority of lawful pastors, more specifically of the Roman pontiff, the sole vicar of Christ.

[280] Leo XIII, encyclical *Divinum illud munus*, 1897.

ually. From Him proceed all the charismata in the church, even — so say Roman theologians — such a small supernatural act as to call Jesus Lord.[281]

THE CONTINUOUS INCARNATION OF CHRIST IN THE THREEFOLD OFFICE

The purpose of the church is to transform the fellowship of misery which is the lot of all mankind since Adam's fall into a fellowship of grace established through the sacraments and effected in the mystical body of Christ. The mystical body of Christ can be established only if the grace of God is restored to mankind. Only a threefold office can remedy or remove the threefold damage of Adam's sin, namely, man's sin, his spiritual ignorance, and his weakness to do what is right.[282] The "continuous incarnation" of Christ in the mystical body requires the continuation of Christ's threefold office. Every textbook on Roman dogmatics states in effect that Christ bestowed upon the apostles and their successors the threefold authority: to teach (prophetic office), to administer the sacraments (priestly office), and to rule (the pastoral, or shepherd, office).[283] All three offices are indispensable for the "prolongation of the incarnation," i. e., for the mystical body of Christ, or the "Catholic" church. This is said to be true especially of the sacerdotal office. Roman dogmaticians maintain that as Mary conceived the Son of God and brought the Invisible One to earth in visible form, so the priest by the same Holy Spirit conceives the incarnate Son of God and gives Him existence in the bosom of the church under the consecrated host. Thus the priest becomes for the Eucharistic body what Mary was for the incarnate Son of God, and He becomes as it were the agent whereby the mystical body of Christ is established.[284] The sacerdotal office (as the *ministerium*) deals directly with the "sanctification" of the church and is considered the most important function. Since this function has been discussed previously,[285] only the doctrinal authority (*magisterium*) and jurisdictional authority (*regimen*) remain for consideration, the first especially because it implies the infallibility of the teaching office and the second because it is basic for the primacy of the pope.

The Infallibility of the Pope. The Roman church maintains that for the proper performance of the first office Christ endowed the church, more specifically the Roman pontiff, with the grace of infallibility. It is argued — though not convincingly to non-Romanists — that the Roman church has always claimed infallibility and that by this claim it has actually established her infallibility. In 1870 the Vatican Council at the insistence of Pius IX decreed:

> We, the sacred council approving, teach, and so define as a dogma divinely revealed, that the Roman Pontiff, when

---

281 *Mystici corporis Christi*, §§ 60—62; Myers, in Smith, II, 672.

282 Algermissen, p. 26 ff.

283 Wilmers, II, 371. Pohle-Preuss, V, 146 ff., 159 ff. Smith, II, 710, speaks of the doctrinal, the ministerial, and the jurisdictional authority. The terms *magisterium* and *ministerium* are also frequently employed, the former embracing the teaching and ruling functions of the clergy, and the second the administration of the sacraments, in other terms, the power of order and of jurisdiction. The twofold classification seems to have been employed at the time of the Reformation.

284 Cp. M. J. Scheeben, p. 467, quoted by Algermissen, p. 33 f.

285 Cp. "Sacraments," esp. "Holy Orders."

he speaks ex cathedra — that is to say, when in the discharge of the office of pastor and teacher of all Christians, by virtue of his supreme apostolic authority, he defines a doctrine regarding faith and morals to be held by the universal Church — is through the divine assistance promised to the blessed Peter himself, possessed of the infallibility with which the divine Redeemer wills that His Church should be endowed for defining doctrine concerning faith and morals; and that therefore such definitions of the Roman Pontiff are of themselves, and not from the consent of the Church, unalterable. But if any one shall venture (which may God avert!) to contradict our definition, let him be accursed.[286]

Prior to 1870 the infallibility was allegedly the prerogative of the church and was said to be vested in the bishops and councils. Since 1870 infallibility is the special *charisma* of the supreme pontiff. But Roman theologians point out that, in line with the Creed of Pius IV, the pope is but the mouthpiece of the church and that he can never define anything infallibly "apart from the Church," since infallibility belongs fundamentally to the church. The church therefore is said to possess an active infallibility in the teaching office and a passive infallibility in the believing of its members.[287]

Not only the alleged truths of revelation themselves, such as the dogma of Mary's assumption, but also all matters which are connected with such truths are said to fall within the scope of infallibility. Thus the pope may speak infallibly on a great variety of theological and moral issues, e. g., when he fixes dogmatical definitions, condemns false philosophical trends, establishes such dogmatic facts as the ecumenicity and validity of a certain council, canonizes saints, determines theological conclusions, such as man's freedom, Christ's impeccability. It is difficult to understand how the theory of papal infallibility can have any real value for devout Romanists, because a Roman Catholic usually has no way of determining when the pope has spoken infallibly. Furthermore, Roman dogmaticians distinguish among revelation (exclusively God's prerogative), inspiration (a divine-human activity), and infallibility (a human activity in which God assists).[288] Roman dogmaticians claim that not only faith in the continuity of the church rests upon an infallible pope but that even faith in God rests upon faith in the infallible church.[289]

The Primacy of the Pope. To fulfill the third divinely appointed office, that of the government, Christ is said to have given to the church jurisdictional authority. More specifically, Christ appointed Peter as primate of the church. Matt. 16:15 is said to teach that Peter is not a stone, not even the best stone in the church, but he is the rock on whom

286 There was much opposition to this decree prior to its adoption. Cp. esp. Janus (*nom de plume* for Bishop Döllinger) pp. 49—65, 436—48, who lists many contradictions among various popes as an argument against papal infallibility. George Salmon, *The Infallibility of the Church*, 2d ed. (Grand Rapids: Baker Book House, 1951). See Schaff's interesting description of the events connected with the Vatican Council, *Creeds*, I, 134—47.

287 Aelred Graham, "The Church on Earth," in Smith, II, 702 ff. Gibbons, p. 125; cp. p. 65 ff.

288 Graham, in Smith, II, 712.

289 On the theological grades of certainty, see Ludwig Ott, *Fundamentals of Catholic Dogma*, trans. James Bastible, ed. Patrick Lynch (St. Louis: B. Herder Book Co. [1954]), pp. 9—10.

the church is built.[290] Romanists find Peter's jurisdictional authority confirmed in the post-Easter command to feed the sheep and lambs, i. e., to guide and rule the faithful; sanctioned in the Apostolic church; and taken for granted in the entire Christian era.[291] Since Christ established the church as a visible body, He also had to provide the church with a visible head.[292] Non-Romanists wonder whether the church has two heads, Christ and Peter. Pius XII answers:

> Nor against this may one argue, that the primacy of jurisdiction established in the Church gives such a Mystical Body two heads. For Peter in virtue of his Primacy is only Christ's Vicar; so that there is only one chief Head of this Body, namely, Christ. He never ceases personally to guide the Church by an unseen hand, though at the same time He rules it externally, visibly through him who is His representative on earth. After His glorious Ascension into heaven this Church rested not on Him alone, but on Peter, too, its visible foundation stone. That Christ and His Vicar constitute one only Head is the solemn teaching of Our predecessor of immortal memory, Boniface VIII, in the Apostolic Letter *Unam sanctam;* and his successors have never ceased to repeat the same.[293]

Rome teaches that Christ established the pope as His personal, visible representative and committed to him the jurisdictional authority. The pope judges all, but himself is judged by none. The papal authority is absolute, and the papal primacy is specifically not a primacy of honor, but of jurisdiction.[294]

The pope's jurisdictional authority extends over the entire church; the bishop's only over his respective diocese. The pope's unconditional jurisdiction is said to be (1) a legislative authority, exemplified in the conciliar action of Acts 15:28 ff. or in the Pauline privilege of 1 Cor. 7:12 ff.; (2) a judicial authority based on Matt. 18:15 ff. and 1 Cor. 5:3;[295] (3) coercive or punitive power, which imposes on the pope the duty and authority to punish the disobedient by depriving them of temporal or spiritual blessings, sometimes by excommunication, sometimes by the interdict.[296]

From the standpoint of its purpose and function the church may be defined as the mystical body of Christ and a visible congregation incorporated and nourished by the sacraments, governed by designated shepherds under one supreme shepherd, and brought to ultimate reunion with God through the government

---

[290] The Vatican Council, ch. i, declares specifically that Peter was endowed directly and immediately with the primacy of jurisdiction, and ch. ii states that this primacy is continued in the popes.

[291] Cp. Wilmers, II, 423. Whether or not Peter ever was in Rome is entirely irrelevant.

[292] Cp. ibid., p. 385.

[293] *Mystici corporis Christi,* § 42; Council of Trent, Sess. XIV, ch. vii; Sess. XXIII, Can. 8.

[294] Papal authority is so total that a contemporary high-ranking German churchman compared *das geheimnisvolle Rom* with *das unheimliche Moskau.* Cp. "Passionary of Christ and Antichrist," published with an epilog by Luther in 1521. Reprinted in W. H. T. Dau, *At the Tribunal of Caesar* (St. Louis: Concordia Publishing House, 1921), pp. 253—79.

[295] Since it is impossible for the pope to sit as judge in all cases requiring the interpretation of the church's law or the pronouncing of a verdict, Rome has an elaborate system to take care of the countless cases. There are, however, so-called "reserved cases," which can be determined only by the pope.

[296] Cp. Graham, in Smith, II, 714 f.

of ecclesiastical offices, particularly the Roman pontiff, the visible representative of Christ.

The Four Visible Characteristics of the Visible Church

Roman theologians teach that men can be incorporated into the mystical body of Christ only through obedience to the teaching office, constant use of the ministerial office in the dispensation of the sacraments, and submission to the jurisdictional authority of the church. Therefore the church must be visible so that man can find this church in the pastoral office or, more exactly, in the bearers of this office.[297] Roman theologians argue that as the incarnate Christ established His divine sonship by visible evidence, so the church, Christ's mystical body, must also have visible characteristics; in fact, the church's claims for her divine origin must be as visible as were those which Christ produced for His divine mission.

This assertion has given rise to the charge that the Roman concept of the church as a visible society is devoid of true spirituality. The papal encyclical of 1943 intended to remove this charge.[298] It claims, for example, that the soul of the church (the invisible church) does not differ greatly from the body of Christ (the visible church), since both continue the work of God in and through the visible church. The encyclical argues that there can be no conflict between the invisible church — the work of the Holy Spirit — and the visible church — the pastors and the teachers in their threefold office. Rather as body and soul complement and perfect each other, so the soul of the church (inasmuch as the church has received the Spirit) and the body of the church (inasmuch as Christ has established a visible office) are in reality the two component parts of the church. Thus the papal encyclical retains the centuries-old claim that the Roman church as the mystical body of Christ points to four visible qualities to warrant the claim for her divine origin.[299]

Unity is the first mark which is said to establish the claim that the Roman church is the only church. This unity is said to manifest itself visibly by the unanimous profession of one and the same faith, the unanimous performance of the same acts of worship, and the acceptance of one and the same system of government. The Roman theologians identify the visible Roman Catholic church with the holy catholic church. Therefore they maintain that the unity is not only a unity of Christ with redeemed humanity, but also an outward, unmistakable, and visible unity. Pius XII declares:

> Since this social Body of Christ has been designed by its Founder to be visible, this co-operation of all its members must also be externally manifest through their profession of the same faith, and their

---

[297] Cp. Walther, p. 69, and other sources. It appears that modern Rome has not deviated very far from Bellarmine, after all. — Smith, II, 701—10.

[298] Cp. *Mystici corporis Christi*, § 8, 9, 64—73. In the early years of the Reformation the issue between Luther and the Romanists was very largely Luther's teaching that the holy Christian church is not a visible kingdom, but the congregation of believers. Cp. Karl Holl, *Gesammelte Aufsätze* (Tübingen, 1932), I, 288—301. Pius XII very specifically condemned the "Lutheran error" which "invents an imaginary church." (*Mystici c. C.*, § 15, 70 ff.)

[299] Graham, in Smith, II, 701 f. The Knights of Columbus' advertisement "Meet the Living God or Die an Eternal Death" invites non-Romanists to find the church in Peter, whom one cannot miss because Christ has placed four clear marks upon the church built on Peter.

sharing the same sacrifice and practical observance of the same laws. Above all, everyone must be able to see the Supreme Head, who gives effective direction to what all are doing in a mutually helpful way towards attaining the desired end, that is, the Vicar on earth of Jesus Christ. As the Divine Redeemer sent a Paraclete, the Spirit of Truth, who in His name should govern the Church in an invisible way; similarly He commissioned Peter and his Successors, to be His personal representatives on earth and to assume the visible government of the Christian community.[300]

Holiness is the second visible sign and characteristic of the church. Romanists insist that their church is the church, because she alone sets forth nothing but the Gospel of Christ and therefore her teaching must be holy, and because through the infusion of divine grace by means of her sacramental system the church alone can produce holiness in her members.

The Roman theologians claim catholicity for their church, because she is spread throughout the world, has always existed, will never cease, is diffused among all nations, is found in every stratum of society, possesses the entire doctrine of Christ, has means of salvation against the spiritual ills of all men, and rightfully claims the allegiance of all.[301]

Apostolicity is said to be a mark of the Roman church, because this body has preserved the Apostolic doctrine and cultus and especially because in her midst the Apostolic office is present by an unbroken succession.

Extra Ecclesiam Salus Non Est

The Fourth Lateran Council (1215) states expressly that there is only one catholic church, outside which there is no salvation. This statement is correct if the term "catholic" is used as meaning universal. But the Roman theologians insist that the word must be understood as referring solely to the Roman Catholic church. Pius IX, in the consistorial allocution *Singulari quadam,* December 9, 1854, defined the Roman church as the single ark of salvation, outside which all who do not enter will perish. Speaking of the Roman church, Pius XII declared:

Only those are really to be included as members of the Church who have been baptized and profess the true faith and who have not unhappily withdrawn from Body-unity or for grave faults been excluded by legitimate authority. "For in one Spirit," says the Apostle, "were we all baptized into one Body, whether Jews or Gentiles, whether bond or free." As therefore in the true Christian community there is only one Body, one Spirit, one Lord and one Baptism, so there can be only one faith. And so if a man refuse to hear the Church, let him be considered — so the Lord commands — as a heathen and a publican. It follows that those who are divided in faith or government cannot be living in one body such as this, and cannot be living the life of its one divine Spirit.[302]

This means that complete and unconditional obedience to the authority of the church — since 1870 to the pope — is necessary to salvation. Submission to the church also demands membership in the visible church because the church

---

[300] *Mystici c. C.,* § 76. K. Adam holds that the pope is the suprapersonal expression and guarantee of the unity which the visible organism requires. Christ did not intend that the pope should be one, even the best, of the many stones which constitute the church, but the rock on which all stones are built, because Christ had decreed that the pope should embody that unity which invites mankind to find in the church its redemption. (*Spirit of Catholicism,* pp. 40—45.)

[301] Graham, in Smith, II, 705, fn. 1.

[302] *Mystici corporis Christi,* § 23.

as the supreme authority demands such membership.

The Roman theologians argue that the legitimacy of Rome's claim is unmistakably evident from the four visible characteristics of the church. These are said to prove that only in the Roman church the incorporation into the mystical body of Christ can take place, for only this church has the means to bestow sacramental grace on men and the threefold office to effect the ultimate reunion of mankind with God. For the Romanist it follows with irrefutable logic that outside this church there is no salvation.

This claim, so contrary to the Biblical doctrine of the church, raises two significant problems for Roman theologians: (1) Does salvation require explicit or implicit membership in the Roman church? In other words, can a sincere non-Romanist be saved? (2) Can Rome participate in any ecumenical endeavors, and if so, on what conditions?

1. Rome's distinction between the body and soul of the church was frequently understood to imply that non-Romanists "in faith" constitute the soul of the church and professing Roman Catholics the body of the church. Pius XII frowned on this view because it was misused in the interest of making a false distinction between the invisible and the visible church. He therefore taught that full and explicit membership in the Roman Catholic church must be the ultimate goal. He declared:

We desire nothing more ardently than that they [the whole non-Roman Catholic world] may have life and have it more abundantly. . . . From a heart overflowing with love We ask each and every one of them to be quick and ready

to follow the interior movements of grace, and to look to withdrawing from that state in which they cannot be sure of their salvation. For even though unsuspectingly they are related to the Mystical Body of the Redeemer in desire and resolution, they still remain deprived of so many precious gifts and helps from heaven, which one can only enjoy in the Catholic Church.

May they then enter into Catholic unity, and united with us in the organic oneness of the Body of Jesus Christ may they hasten to the one Head in the society of glorious love. With persevering prayer to the Spirit of love and truth We wait for them with open arms to return not to a stranger's house, but to their own, their Father's house.[303]

In only two cases is salvation possible without explicit membership in the church of Rome. But even in these cases there must be a membership "by desire" (in voto).

According to Roman teaching, baptism is always necessary for membership and, when correctly performed, always effects legitimate membership in the Roman church.[304] But if it should be impossible to receive a water baptism the "baptism of desire" is said to suffice for the regeneration of the soul.[305]

The church teaches that membership in the Roman Catholic church is not necessary in case one is in invincible ignorance of the true nature of the church. Invincible ignorance excuses from membership when through no culpable negligence one does not recognize the Roman church as the true church and believes that though he is not explicitly a member of the true church, he nevertheless belongs to the true church.[306] Any Christian who is sincerely and honestly convinced that

---

[303] Ibid., §§ 117, 118.

[304] See "Baptism," above, esp., notes 156, 157.

[305] Council of Trent, Sess. VI, ch. iv.

[306] "Ignorance is absence of knowledge that should be present. . . . In general, inadvertence, thoughtlessness, error, are classed in law with invin-

Rome's authority is a usurpation and who is unable to recognize the papal claims is "invincibly ignorant" and therefore implicitly a member of the Holy [Roman] Catholic church. However, it must be noted that it is not correct to say that the explicit member belongs to the body of the church and the implicit member only to the soul of the church. The papal encyclical of 1943 ruled out such an antithesis between "body" and "soul." It teaches that the Holy Spirit as the animating and indwelling principle is the "soul of the church." Thus all, both explicit and implicit members, are under the Spirit's gracious activity and thus may be viewed as belonging to the "soul of the church." [307]

2. Rome's fundamental principles make it impossible for her to enter upon any intercommunion or ecumenical relations except on her own terms. [308] Rome states:

> The Roman Catholic Church, convinced, through its divine prerogatives, of being the only true Church, must demand the right to freedom for herself alone, because such a right can only be possessed by truth, never by error. As to other religions, the church will certainly never draw the sword, but she will require that by legitimate means they shall not be allowed to propagate false doctrine. . . . In some countries (like the U. S. A.) Catholics will be obligated to ask full religious freedom for all, resigned at being forced to cohabitate where they alone should rightfully be allowed to live. [309]

In recent years not a few Roman theologians, especially in Europe, sought a *rapprochement* with the evangelical churches. [310] As early as 1895 the encyclical *Provida matris* suggested prayer for the reconciliation and ultimate reunion of all churches with Rome. In 1919 Benedict XV appeared to encourage the Protestants who suggested his participation in the World Conference on Faith and Order. Roman Catholic historians and dogmaticians seemed to

cible ignorance. Ignorance is vincible or invincible according as it could, or could not, be removed." The individual is not held responsible for invincible ignorance. Lydon, *Canon Law*, p. 295. Cp. Pius IX, in allocution *Singulari quadam*. This applies only to a "material" heretic, e. g., a sincere Lutheran or Methodist, but not to a "formal" heretic nor to a schismatic. *C. Rom.*, Part I, ch. x., Qu. 1.

307 *Mystici corporis Christi*, § 61. Cp. Myers, in Smith, II, 672 ff., 697.

308 In the opinion of some writers the Lutheran position is the same as the Roman Catholic. Williams, *What Americans Believe and How They Worship*, p. 161.

309 F. Cavalli, S. J., in *Civiltá Cattolica*, official Jesuit organ published in Rome and quoted in *Christian Century*, (June 23, 1948). Cp. also Francis J. Connell, *Freedom of Worship*, tract published by Paulist Press, N. Y., 1944. This tract states that according to the Law of God no one has the right to accept any religion except the Roman Catholic religion, or to be a member of any other church, or to practice any divine worship, excepting that sanctioned by the Roman church (4). In predominantly Roman Catholic countries the rulers are justified in restricting or even preventing any denominational activity contrary to the Roman religion (10). In a country like the U. S. A., however, where there is such a diversity of religious views, complete equality for all religions is undoubtedly as yet the wisest policy (15). Cp. M. Searle Bates, *Religious Liberty: An Inquiry*, (New York: International Missionary Council, 1945).

310 The Rev. Charles Boyer, S. J., organized *Unitas*, including in its membership a few Protestants, for interfaith meetings. Reported in *Christian Century*, (Jan. 2 and 30, 1946), 26, 133.

take an entirely new attitude toward the significance of the Reformation.[311] But a *rapprochement*, not to say a reunion, is out of the question unless the non-Roman Catholics submit to the infallible teaching office of the pope. Leo XIII granted permission to participate in interdenominational discussions only if the topic dealt with individual and social welfare.[312] Pius XI stated very emphatically in *Mortalium animos* (January 6, 1926), that the Roman church could not participate in ecumenical endeavors because he could not consider any denomination as a legitimate partner to a theological discussion.[313] Piux XII declared in 1943 that those who have severed the bonds with the visible head of the church have left the mystical body of Christ and cannot find the haven of eternal salvation.[314] The *Monitum* of June 5, 1948, permitted the Romanists to take part in the public discussion of religious questions.[315] But in his Christmas message of 1949 Pius XII invited all Christendom to participate in the 1950 jubilee year and to return to Rome, where men will find "the immovable rock to which their faith is anchored." [316] On December 20, 1949, the Sacred Congregation of the Holy Office published the Instruction *De motione oecumenica*, addressed to the bishops of the Roman Catholic church throughout the world, which stressed that, while the truth of revelation is not to be sought in some kind of higher synthesis of Roman Catholic and non-Roman teaching, the divided state of Christendom is a breach of the divine order which Christians by their very faith in Jesus Christ are obligated to repair. The Instruction also attributes the desire for unity among non-Roman Christians to the work of the Holy Spirit.[317]

[311] Roman historians are using a new approach to the Reformation story. Cp. esp. Lortz, II, *passim.* Adam, *One and Holy*, pp. 67—76, has gone so far as to say that Lutheran Christianity could help to understand Roman Catholic Christianity, for both stress an objective teaching authority, the Lutheran church by making much of her Confessions. Rome has also approached Evangelical Christianity in its new interest in and study of the Bible. Karl Adam therefore suggests a reunion might be effected if the Lutherans would take the "real" Luther seriously and view the primacy of the pope in Matt. 16:18, 19 purely as a Biblical problem.

[312] Wilfred Parsons, loc. cit. (fn. 37).

[313] This significant encyclical was published in England as *True Religious Unity* by Catholic Truth Society, 1928.

[314] *Mystici corporis Christi*, § 43.

[315] *Acta Apostolicae Sedis*, XL (1948), 257.

[316] Cp. "The Pope's Christmas Message" in *C. T. M.*, XXI (1950), 134—36. "Rome and the Ecumenical Movement," ibid., p. 625. "Rome's Basis for Theological Rapprochement," ibid., p. 384.

[317] *Acta Apostolicae Sedis*, XLII (1950), 142—147; see Thomas Sartory, *Die Ökumenische Bewegung und die Einheit der Kirche* (Meitingen: Kyrios-Verlag, 1955), 93—99, and the report in *America*, March 11, 1950. — Cp. the excellent study of K. E. Skydsgaard: "The Roman Catholic Church and the Ecumenical Movement," and "A Supplementary Note" by the Roman Catholic writer Maurice Villain, in *Man's Disorder and God's Design*, I, 155 to 177, and René Pache, "Rome and the Ecumenical Movement," *Bibliotheca Sacra*, Vol. CVIII, January, 1951. Several Roman reactions to the Amsterdam meeting are published in *Ecumenical Review*, Vol. I, No. 2 (Winter, 1949), pp. 202—12. The number of works by Roman Catholics on the Ecumenical Movement is growing rapidly. The list which follows is representative: Gregory Baum, *That They May Be One: A Study of Papal Doctrine (Leo XIII—Pius XII)* (London: Bloomsbury Publishing Co., 1958);

Church and State

In the Bull *Unam Sanctam* (1302) Boniface VIII summarized — and ironically enough also terminated — the long history of the papal political aspirations.[318]

Among the modern popes it was particularly Pius IX who in his encyclical *Quanta cura* and the *Syllabus of Errors* (December 8, 1864) restated the position of Gregory VII and Boniface VIII. Like his predecessors, he claimed that submission to the pope is necessary for salvation; denied, on the one hand, every authority of the state over the church, particularly also over church property; but, on the other, under no condition exempted the princes from obedience to the Pontiff; reiterated that the material sword must be drawn for the church, the spiritual by the church, and that the secular power must submit to the spiritual as the higher. In the *Syllabus* he claimed authority not only over family life and the educational system, but also the right to interfere in legislation and, if necessary, to demand its altera-

tion. Pius IX declared war on the whole modern social order and endeavored to hurl society back into medieval history with its religious tyranny and intolerance.[319]

Leo XIII was not as bitter but just as emphatic as Pius IX in his denunciation of the claims of the modern state, especially as developed in the United States of America. In his encyclical *Immortale Dei*, November 1, 1885, he seemingly grants that there are two distinct powers, one charged with the ecclesiastical and the other with the civil affairs. But he maintained that

it would be very erroneous to draw the conclusion that in America is to be sought the desirable status of the Church, or that it would be universally lawful or expedient for the state and church to be, as in America, dissevered and divorced. [The principle of religious freedom is a] license from which would flow the consequence that the judgment of each one's conscience is independent of all [papal] law, and that everyone has a right to think whatever he chooses, and to publish whatever he thinks.[320]

C. J. DuMont, *Approaches to Christian Unity*, trans. Henry St. John (Baltimore: Helicon Press, 1959); George H. Tavard, *Two Centuries of Ecumenism*, trans. Royce W. Hughes (Notre Dame, Ind.: Fides Publishers Association, c. 1960); John M. Todd, *Catholicism and the Ecumenical Movement* (London: Longmans, Green and Co., 1956); Maurice Villain, *Introduction à l'Oecuménisme* (Tournai: Casterman, 1958); Gustave Weigel, *A Catholic Primer on the Ecumenical Movement* (Westminster, Md.: Newman Press, 1957). See also the last named's "American Roman Catholicism and Ecumenism," *Lutheran World*, V (1958), 28—37.

318 At the height of the clash between the pope and the French king, Boniface claimed the following: "There are two swords, the spiritual and the temporal. . . . Both are in the power of the church; the one, the spiritual, to be used *by* the church, the other, the material, *for* the church; the former that of the priest; the latter that of kings and soldiers, to be wielded at the command and by the sufferance of the priest. One sword must be under the other, the temporal under the spiritual. . . . The spiritual instituted the temporal power and judges whether that power is well exercised. . . . If the temporal power err, it is judged by the spiritual. . . . We, therefore, assert that it is necessary to salvation to believe that every human being is subject to the Pontiff of Rome "

319 Cp. John P. McKnight, pp. 198—207.

320 Ibid., p. 271. In 1899 the pope addressed to Cardinal Gibbons a letter known as *Festem benevolentiae*, in which he condemns the "American heresy."

Pius XI stated:

The church can never relinquish the God-given task of interposing her authority . . . in all those matters that have a bearing on moral content. For the deposit of truth entrusted to us by God and awaiting the office of propagating . . . the entire moral law, demand that both social and economic questions be brought within our supreme jurisdiction insofar as they refer to moral issues.[321]

Non-Romanists find it hard to see how a strict application of these pronouncements can avoid leading to a divided loyalty, the one toward the papal supreme authority and the other to the United States. And non-Romanists have grounds for the fear of a clash between the ecclesiastical power and the state and of the loss of the priceless gift of religious liberty. Rome insists that it is the only true religion and that all other religions may at best be only tolerated. This assertion is certainly contrary to the American ideal of religious liberty.[322] No doubt the vast majority of Romanists resent any questioning of their loyalty. They have shown in time of war and otherwise that they are loyal American citizens, with no divided loyalty. And not a few theologians as well as representative American Roman Catholics have denied that they desire the union of church and state in America.[323]

Nevertheless the Roman apologists are confronted by the stubborn fact that Leo XIII stated in unmistakable terms

that the state must not only have a care for religion, but that it dare recognize only the true religion, that professed by the Roman Catholic church. The argument continues: the state is under moral obligation to support only the religion which is true; no state is justified in supporting error, since thereby the state would grant to error the same recognition which it is morally obliged to give only to the true religion. This means that the state must officially recognize the Roman Catholic religion as the religion of the commonwealth, that no citizen has the "natural right" to propagandize his form of religion; that no person may practice his own form of worship — at least in public — lest he injure the faith of the "true believer," an injury against which the state must protect Roman Catholics.[324]

In reply to the charge that Rome's principles are undemocratic and unAmerican, Roman apologists cite Maryland as the first colony to grant religious liberty. But Lord Baltimore, a devout Roman Catholic, initiated Maryland's Act of Toleration (1649), in spite of papal displeasure, not as an experiment in a new political philosophy, but to make Maryland an asylum for his persecuted coreligionists, who were tolerated in no colony, not even in Rhode Island.[325] Again, Roman Catholic authors not infrequently paint the political and social philosophy of the Roman church

[321] See *Quadragesimo anno,* 1931, and *Rerum novarum,* 1891, both in *Five Great Encyclicals,* published by the Paulist Press, New York, 1939.

[322] Cp. Harold Fey, *Can Catholicism Win America?*

[323] See Williams, p. 83. James M. O'Neill, *Catholicism and American Freedom* (New York: Harper & Bros., 1952), pp. 33—37.

[324] John A. Ryan and Francis G. Boland, p. 313 ff.; cp. also p. 135. — See also the report of a conference of distinguished French Roman Catholic theologians at LaSarte, published as *Tolerance and the Catholic: A Symposium,* trans. George Lamb (New York: Sheed and Ward, 1955), and the World Council of Churches study by A. F. Carillo de Albornoz, *Roman Catholicism and Religious Liberty* (Geneva: World Council of Churches, 1960).

[325] Theodore Maynard, p. 120, makes extravagant claims for Rome's championing religious liberty. But cp. W. W. Sweet, *Religion in Colonial America,* p. 180 f.

entirely in the colors of American Roman Catholicism and put aside completely the exclusive claims to the right of being recognized as the state church.[326]

As far as is known, Rome has not deviated in the least from the principles held by the popes since Boniface VIII. Roman theologians have, however, changed their approach to this problem. They begin by asking: What is the purpose of the ecclesiastical and of the temporal power? The answer reads about as follows: The church's purpose is to accomplish man's ultimate sanctification; whatever human thing is of a sacred character belongs to the salvation of the soul and the worship of God and is subject to the power and judgment of the church. The state is instituted to look after the temporal welfare of man, and to the state are assigned all those matters which are of a civil and political authority. However — and this is the new point of emphasis — there are matters of a "mixed nature." The marriage contract obviously belongs in this category: as a sacrament, marriage belongs only to the church of Christ; as a social contract, the state may determine some regulations for those contracting it. But the church must always have the higher authority.[327] Education is another item of "mixed matters." The state is responsible for the welfare of its future citizens and may therefore legislate within the sphere of education. However, Rome maintains that the state dare not ignore nor set aside anything

that fosters the potential incorporation into the mystical body of Christ, i. e., the Roman Catholic church.[328] The implications of this premise are obvious. The theory of "mixed matters" can ultimately be applied to every sphere of activity in the temporal realm. The Romanist will grant that the modern state may legislate in all social, political, or private matters and promote the temporal good of its citizens. But since man's final goal is the beatific vision and since the church's mission is to help man reach this goal, the state dare not disregard the spiritual aspirations; it must, at least indirectly, help its citizens to realize them.[329] Such a patent mingling of the secular and spiritual realms is possible only under a theological system based on legalistic concepts. Roman theologians maintain that it is the express mission of the state to foster the work of the church, the Roman Catholic church. Though the state must foster the common good of all its citizens, it must also consider that man is so constituted that he cannot be happy unless his heart is set on God, man's ultimate goal. Therefore the state must, at least indirectly, encourage whatever will assist the realization of this goal.

The Roman church has found a way of living side by side with the modern state. Rome insists that the church has no design to interfere with the affairs of the modern state, except that the church must maintain the right to judge politics in its ethical and religious bearing and

---

[326] Cp. W. E. Garrison (in his review of James O'Neill's *Catholicism and American Freedom*), *Christian Century*, July 15, 1952, p. 828.

[327] On Dec. 7, 1949, the pope declared that no Roman Catholic judge is permitted to preside in any case of civil divorce where the marriage is valid before God and the church. The church thus determines, in the final analysis, the rules and regulations for the court, in the case of marriages. See *Christian Century*, 1949, Nov. 21, p. 1,380; Nov. 30, p. 1,413; Dec. 21, p. 1,509.

[328] Graham, in Smith, II, 727 ff. The Roman Catholic campaign in 1961 to secure Federal aid for their denominational system of education once more touched off a wave of controversy on this issue.

[329] Ibid., p. 728.

especially to disapprove and to protest against all that might make her unable to carry out her mission. In the situation where Rome's ideal relation between church and state is unobtainable, the Roman church is willing to accept much that is imperfect, so that the good may be preserved. If necessary, the church will arrange concordats with governments which in many ways are opposed to the interests of the church.[330] This flexibility which enables the church to effect a *modus vivendi* with almost any political regime is said to be a sign — not of opportunism — but of Rome's independence of all political machines.[331]

With the rise of the modern state the Roman pontiffs, especially since Leo XIII, have directed their attention less to political problems and more to ethics, social ethics in particular. This area is viewed as being of a "mixed nature," and the church claims the right to demand that society — industry, capital, labor — so organize the social structure that Christian ethics as interpreted by the church can prevail.

The encyclicals of Leo XIII and Pius XI on the "social order" testify to Rome's deep interest in social ethics, but the tenor in which they are issued makes it unmistakably clear that the pontiffs assume without qualification that it is their province to speak with authority on social ethics.[332]

Rome will not change its dogmatical position relative to church and state. But Rome can adjust its policies to meet the changing conditions, and thus its policy — not the principle — is different in countries where the Roman church is the state-recognized church, from countries where she is a minority, as in the United States of America. But it must be kept in mind that not a few writers state quite frankly that they consider the present situation obtaining in America a temporary arrangement, which will be changed when Rome no longer is in the minority. But the realization of this ideal, they hasten to add, is so remote that no one need be alarmed about it.[333]

The same church which could reach an agreement with a totalitarian state [334] will find a *modus vivendi* to operate in the modern democracy. Leo XIII and Pius XI went a long way to find a solution, and Pius XII and John XXIII seem to have come still closer to a way in which the Roman church sacrifices none of her age-old principles and yet is able to retain the good will of Americans.[335]

[330] Cp. the Concordat with Mussolini, Feb. 11, 1929. McKnight, pp. 283 to 290.

[331] See Graham, in Smith, II, 726—30.

[332] The *Five Great Encyclicals*. See especially Leo XIII, *Rerum novarum* (1891), and Pius XI, *Quadragesimo anno* (1931). Cp. above, "Catholic Action," and esp. Philip Hughes, *The Pope's New Order*, which presents the tremendous shift of emphasis that has taken place in Roman thinking. Paul Blanshard, *American Freedom and Catholic Power*, shows the extent to which the Roman Catholic church presumes to speak in ethical questions. Unfortunately Blanshard's argumentation is weakened by his attempt to present Rome's political and social philosophy as completely divorced from Rome's theology. This is a complete distortion of Rome's ecclesiology and commits Blanshard to an ethical system which is completely humanistically orientated.

[333] Ryan and Boland, p. 320.

[334] See McKnight, ch. xv, "The Papacy and Fascism," and ch. xvi, "The Papacy and Communism."

[335] Cp. ibid., ch. xvii, "The Papacy and American Democracy," an accurate and a charitable interpretation of the position of Pius XII. — For a summary of developments in the papacy since Pius IX, see Carl S. Meyer, "The Modern Papacy," *C. T. M.*, XXIX (1959), 241—260.

SECTION VII

Veneration of the Saints

Of Saints in General

Probably at no other point in Roman Catholic doctrine does the enigmatic and contradictory character of this church become more patent than in its doctrine of the veneration and invocation of saints. Theological theories and the practices of the people seem to be in diametrical opposition to each other. The veneration of saints has come down from the early church, and there is sufficient evidence that the martyrs were revered in special services at a very early age.[336] By the seventh century the veneration of saints had assumed the nature of the invocation of saints. Since Trent Rome teaches that

> the saints who reign together with God, offer up their own prayers to God for men, that it is good and useful suppliantly to invoke them and to have recourse to their prayer, aid, and help for obtaining benefits from God. They think impiously who assert that they [the saints] do not pray for men or that the invocation of them to pray for each of us in particular is idolatry.[337]

The theological basis is found in the words of the Creed "communion of saints." The perfected saints in heaven are said to assist those who in their wayfaring require the saints' intercessions and a share in their works of supererogation.

Rome rightly feared that veneration and invocation might easily lead to adoration and pagan idolatry. For that reason Roman theologians insist on carefully distinguishing between veneration (*dulia*) and adoration (*latria*), the former given to saints alone, the latter to God alone. However, it is quite evident that the average Romanist does not observe this distinction. The same outward forms of worship employed in the adoration of God are used in the veneration of saints. The evangelical Christian views Rome's veneration of the saints' images and relics as a superstitious and idolatrous practice, though he is well aware of Rome's claim that the veneration is intended for the saint and not for the image and that help is expected from the saint and not from the relic. But he cannot reconcile Rome's theory and its practice at certain shrines erected in honor of specific saints. If the altars and images themselves are not to be worshiped, then why do Romanists make pilgrimages to certain shrines to obtain help from a saint which is not available at another shrine for this same saint? Officially Rome agrees with St. Augustine, who denounced Faustus' charge that the Christians had erected altars to the glory and memory of the martyrs by showing that these altars had been erected to the glory of God.[338] But in practice it fosters a cultus which non-

---

[336] Cp. A. C., XXI.

[337] Council of Trent, Sess. XXV.

[338] *Contra Faustum*, I, 20, c. 21.

Romanists are constrained to view as pagan.[339]

Rome teaches officially that in reality saints only intercede but do not actually help. In practice Rome has a large list of saints, each endowed with a specific qualification.[340] The church permits the public veneration of those saints only whose sanctity has been publicly proclaimed by the Congregation of Sacred Rites and whom the pope has placed into the canon of saints. Rome says it is very careful in its procedure of canonizing saints. Two attested miracles are required before beatification, and two additional miracles are necessary for canonization, except in the case of martyrdom.[341]

Mariology

The Roman cultus of the saints reaches its climax in the veneration accorded to the Virgin Mary. According to Roman dogmaticians, she is entitled not only to *dulia* but also to *hyperdulia*, the same honor which most Romanists ascribe to the human nature of Christ. By willingly becoming the "Mother of God" Mary has earned more merit than any other saint and is therefore entitled to the highest degree of veneration. Through her divine motherhood, whereby she became the mother of God and actually received the infinite Son of God into the community of her life, she has performed the most sublime of all works performed by human beings, and she excels in nobility and dignity all other persons. As motherhood always presupposes marital union — the most intimate of all mutual relations — so Mary by her divine maternity entered into the closest communion with God Himself. In fact, Mary is spoken of as the "spiritual vessel" of the Trinity, since through her instrumentality the eternal Son of the Father was carried to earth by the Holy Ghost and born into the human race. Therefore Mary is viewed as the "mystic rose," the flower of humanity, since from her Christ grew as the First Fruit and subsequently also Christ's mystical body. Thus as the mother of Christ she is also the mother of the church.[342]

As the Mother of God Mary is said to have been chosen from eternity to be the "mother of grace" and to be "full of grace," and to have been endowed from

---

[339] In 1903 the pope suggested that it might be useful to roll paper images of the Virgin Mary into small pills and swallow them to regain one's health. Mirbt, No. 497. For the superstitions of Lourdes and Fatima cp. *New Schaff-Herzog Encyc.*, VII, 47—49; "Pax Christi Pilgrimage to Lourdes," by J. I. Malloy, *Catholic World*, No. 167, p. 563, September 1948. "Miracles of Fatima," *Life*, II, 25, Dec. 20, 1948, pp. 33—36.

[340] For a detailed list of the various professions and stations in life and the corresponding saint for each profession, such as blind men, bookbinders, common women, confectioners, drunkards, glaziers, grocers, horsedealers, jockeys, nurses, pilgrims, spinners, theologians, see the *Lutheran Witness*, LI (Jan. 19, 1932), 32.

[341] The first step in the process of canonization is to establish the practice of heroic virtue and to declare the subject "venerable"; the second is beatification, which requires that at least two miracles be proved to have taken place through his (her) intercession, except in the case of true martyrdom. See *The Catholic Encyclopedia*, II, 364—369, s. v. "Beatification and Canonization."

[342] Algermissen, p. 435 ff. Through Mary people are said to become members of the church. In commenting on John 3:3-5, B. J. Le Frois states that Baptism symbolizes a virginal birth. As Mary conceived Christ by the Holy Spirit, so in Baptism — a symbol of Mary's Spirit-fructified womb — all the children of the church are born. "The Spiritual Motherhood of Mary," *Catholic Biblical Quarterly*, April, 1952.

infancy with a grace surpassing that given to saints and angels. This is in part the basis for the dogma of Mary's immaculate conception. But Rome goes beyond this. Through her divine motherhood Mary was able to increase her grace to such a measure that it surpasses the sum total of "sanctifying grace" of all saints and angels. Her participation in Christ's work is said to be the foundation for Rome's dogma of Mary's assumption.[343] Since the proclamation of the bull *Ineffabilis Deus* (1854) Roman Catholics must believe

> that the doctrine which holds that the Blessed Virgin Mary, at the first instance of her conception, by a singular privilege and grace of the Omnipotent God, in virtue of the merits of Jesus Christ, the Savior of Mankind, was preserved immaculate of all stain of original sin, was revealed by God and therefore should firmly and confidently be believed by the faithful.[344]

But more important still is the view that because of her sinlessness Mary could share in Christ's redemptive work. By her voluntary surrender to become the mother of God, Mary's flesh and blood shared in Christ's atoning sacrifice. From the moment that the Redeemer of mankind rested beneath the heart of Mary she offered Him to the Father and joined Him in the sacrificial gift to God.

Mary's entire life is viewed as sharing the Savior's redemptive work, especially in the so-called mystical experiences — the joyful, especially the birth and presentation in the Temple; the sorrowful, especially Christ's death; and the glorious, Christ's resurrection and ascension.[345] Romanists make the most extravagant statements concerning her and address her as *salvatrix, reparatrix, restauratrix, liberatrix, reconciliatrix, redemptrix.* Theologically Rome holds that Mary is not the cause of man's salvation, but the mediatrix of Christ's redemptive work. She is therefore not considered the primary, but the intermediate cause of man's redemption. Nevertheless she is regarded as co-operating with Christ, who alone is the Redeemer, and she is spoken of as a "ministering partner" in the execution of His work. As Eve participated in mankind's fall, so Mary the "second Eve" is the helpmate *(adiutrix)* of the "second Adam." As both Adam and Eve, though in a different manner, are the cause of mankind's sin, and as both were conquered by the devil, so both sexes must co-operate in restoring mankind. True according to Scripture, Adam's guilt was the greater because he was the head of the race; but since Eve initiated the sin, the work of redemption must also be initiated by a woman.[346]

---

[343] Cp. Pohle-Preuss, VI, p. 28 ff.

[344] There had been violent controversies among Romanists, particularly between the Scotists who championed the doctrine of Mary's immaculate conception and the Thomists who opposed it. In the opinion of many one of the most able refutations of the immaculate conception was written by Eduard Preuss (see Bibliog.). Unfortunately this able defender of the truth later on defected to the Roman Catholic church and renounced his book against the papal decree of Mary's immaculate conception. — Roman theologians say that Mary enjoyed such freedom from sin that she had the character of impeccability. But this is not a dogma, but a "doctrine of probability." Algermissen, p. 441 f.

[345] On the mystical experience see "Rosary" above.

[346] Scheeben supports this theory with the following four propositions: (1) Man's redemption is the work of the Triune God; therefore the two Persons proceeding from the Father must be represented by a created agent; (2) the honor of man's redemption is to be shared not only by a human

By her co-operation with Christ's sacrifice Mary has become the mediatrix through whom alone mankind now can receive the blessings of Christ's sacrifice. Some extravagant statements go so far as to say that Mary's soul remained in Christ's lifeless body; that when the side of Christ was pierced, Mary assumed all the power of Christ's death to bestow new life on mankind; that Mary received the lifeless body of Christ in her bosom and has thereby symbolized the truth that she is the depository of Christ's merits. Mary is considered to be the spiritual mother of the redeemed.[347]

In the plenitude of grace Mary was able to gain such a measure of grace that she would share with Christ also in His ascension. It had been a "pious opinion" for centuries that only as the resurrected and ascended "queen of heaven" can Mary open the portals of heaven *(felix coeli porta),* and only as the "Mother of our Judge" can she quiet the fears of the redeemed as in death they are brought before the judgment seat of Christ. On November 1, 1950, Pius XII, in spite of considerable opposition, pronounced the dogma of the assumption, that is, that Mary was bodily received into heaven.[348]

Because of the total lack of Scriptural and of historical evidence for this dogma, most Roman theologians establish the dogma on purely "theological" grounds. The church has "proximate, definite, and decisive" reasons to argue that, because of her sinlessness, worthiness, and dignity, Mary enjoyed a threefold freedom from the bondage of death: (1) from the necessity of death; (2) from the penal consequences of sin, e. g., the law of decomposition; (3) from the duration of death until the general resurrection. Many theologians hold that, because of her complete sinlessness, Mary was not subject to death as a punishment. True, Mary had a mortal nature. This does not mean that she was subject to the necessity of death, as the rest of mankind, since, by virtue of her divine motherhood, Mary possessed a "supernatural claim." This claim implied complete exemption from death, except for the fact that in the economy of redemption her death was necessary — necessary not as a means of canceling man's sin, but as an evidence that she was not greater than her Son and that as her nature was truly human, so was also the nature of her divine Son. It is argued further that under certain circumstances death can be something dignified and glorious. The degrading thing about death is the concomitant decomposition, the penalty and curse of sin. Through her union with Christ as His spouse and mother,

nature but also by a human person; (3) at least one human being as a representative of mankind must passively take part in the redemption to assure its procurement for mankind in general; (4) through her participation in the redemption, Mary, as the maternal bride of Christ, has become the mother of the redeemed, and they are assured of sharing in the merits of Christ. Cp. M. J. Scheeben, *Mariology,* trans. T. Geukers (St. Louis: Herder, 1947), Vol. II, ch. vii.

[347] It is but natural that a Marian cultus of a very extreme form would evolve. Raphael V. O'Connell, S. J., *Our Lady,* p. 105 ff., shows clearly that no intercessory prayer will open the treasures of divine grace except via the three "degrees," i. e., Mary to Jesus, Jesus to the Father. For prayers used to invoke Mary see the tract *Prayers to the Blessed Virgin Mary* (401 West 59th St., New York: The Pulpit Press). For information concerning the scapular devotions see Haffert, esp. pp. 54 ff., 92 ff.

[348] Cp. O. R. Vassal-Phillips, "Mary, Mother of God," in Smith, I, 548 f. F. E. Mayer, "Dogma of Mary's Assumption," *C. T. M.,* XXI (1950), p. 187 ff.

Mary could not see corruption. The incorruption of Mary's body is said to be supported by the incorruption of her virginity, since she was not contaminated by another's sinful flesh when she conceived Christ; since her womb was not violated in any way; and her freedom from the *fomes* of sin was perfected through Christ's conception. Since incorruptibility and resurrection are correlative concepts, death could not hold Mary's body until the general resurrection; on the contrary, her bodily resurrection and assumption must have taken place in the shortest possible time. According to one tradition, the disciples found Mary's grave empty on the third day. Sometimes Romanists support the theory of Mary's bodily assumption by the alleged fact that no relics of Mary have been found anywhere.

The dogma of Mary's bodily assumption is the climax of Rome's entire Mariology, specifically of her participation in man's redemption. In fact, the entire premise of Mary's mediating work as taught by Rome climaxes in her bodily ascension. Some theologians advance the following points: (1) Mary is the Mother of God through and in her body. and therefore a permanent separation of her body from her soul is as impossible as in Christ; (2) Mary is the bride of Christ, and without the resurrection of her body the intimate and complete union of Christ and His church portrayed in Ephesians 5 could not be effected; (3) the Fourth Commandment demands that Christ honor His mother, which He can do best by having her share in His own bodily resurrection and glorification; (4) since Mary has been appointed as mankind's mediatrix, she must herself experience the fruits of the work of Christ and become the perfect surety that Christ's work is complete. In fact, as the "second Eve," she now stands at the side of Christ.[349]

349 Since the proclamation of the encyclical *Munificentissimus Deus* in 1950, several important studies pro and con have appeared. Joseph Duhr, *The Glorious Assumption of the Mother of God* (trans. from the French by John M. Fraunces; New York: Cath. Book Publ. Co., 1950). Paul F. Palmer, S. J., *Mary in the Documents of the Church*. Herm. Volk, *Das neue Mariendogma* (Regensburg, 1950). Volk is a Roman Catholic theologian. Edm. Schlink *et al.*, *Evangelisches Gutachten zur Dogmatisierung der leiblichen Himmelfahrt Mariens*, published in English, *Lutheran Quarterly*, May, 1951. Friedrich Heiler, *Das Neue Mariendogma im Lichte der Geschichte und im Urteil der Ökumene* (Munich-Basel, 1951), a comprehensive presentation of all relevant material. Heinrich Bornkamm, "Motive und Konsequenzen des neuen Mariendogmas," *Arbeit und Besinnung*, No. 12, (1951).

In honor of Mary's assumption Pius XII composed the following prayer: "O Immaculate Virgin, mother of God and mother of men, we believe with all the fervor of our faith in thy triumphant assumption, in soul and in body, into heaven, where thou art acclaimed queen by all the choirs of the angels and by all the legions of the saints;

"And we unite with them to praise and bless the Lord, who hath exalted thee above all other pure creatures, and to offer thee the breath of our devotion and of our love.

"We know that thy gaze, that maternally caressed the humble and suffering humanity of Jesus on earth, satiates itself with the sight of the glorious humanity of the uncreated Knowledge [the divine knowledge, i. e., God], and that the joy of thy soul in contemplating face to face the adorable Trinity causes thy heart to throb with tenderness.

"And we, poor sinners, we, for whom the body weighs down the flight of the soul, we beseech thee to purify our senses that we may learn, from here below, to enjoy God, God alone, amidst the enchantment of creatures.

"We confide that thine eyes of mercy look down upon our miseries and upon our sorrows, upon our struggles and upon our weaknesses; that thy

SECTION VIII

Eschatology

Roman theology devotes more space and gives greater attention to eschatological problems than do most theological systems.[350] This emphasis on eschatology is fully in accord with Rome's chief theological principle, that the Christian religion is a system of good works and merits, wrongdoing and punishment. Accordingly Roman theologians frequently view justice as the predominant divine characteristic and say that no activity is more constantly predicated of God than judgment, i. e., God's punitive interference with the works of evil men and His providential intervention in the course of the universe as a reward for the virtuous action of God's children. However, this view is again modified by the several conflicting theories on predestination. There is as yet no dogma on this point. But the view of Thomas Aquinas seems to prevail. Thomas holds that election is not determined so much by man's good or evil deeds and God's justice as by God's free act whereby He showed mercy to some and only justice to others. But there are many who hold contradictory views. The only point of agreement is that the destiny of the soul is determined by the decree of predestination. The basis for such a decree, whether man's works or God's

lips smile upon our joys and upon our victories; that thou hearest the voice of Jesus say of each one of us, as He did of His beloved disciple (John): behold thy son;

"And we, who invoke thee (as) our mother, we take thee, as (did) John, for guide, strength, and consolation in our mortal life.

"We have the vivifying certainty that thine eyes which wept on the earth bathed with the blood of Jesus, yet turn toward this world, prey to wars, to persecutions, to oppressions of the just and the weak;

"And we, from the shadows of this vale of tears, await from thy heavenly light and thy sweet pity surcease from the griefs of our hearts, from the trials of the Church and of our fatherland.

"We believe, finally, that in the glory over which thou reignest, robed with sun and crowned with stars, thou art, after Jesus, the joy and the gladness of all the angels and of all the saints;

"And we, from this earth, through which we pass as pilgrims, comforted by the faith in the future resurrection, look toward thee, our life, our sweetness, our hope; lead us with the gentleness of thy voice, to show us one day, after this our exile, Jesus, the blessed fruit of thy womb, O clement, O pious, O sweet Virgin Mary." Published in *St. Louis Post-Dispatch*, Oct. 29, 1950.

350 In *The Teaching of the Catholic Church*, G. D. Smith devotes about 10 per cent to eschatology. — Lutheran theology has been charged with focusing everything on that "blessed last hour" of the individual and thus losing sight of the over-all history of the Kingdom. There is, of course, the danger of a false emphasis. But it does remain a fact that in death each stands alone and that unless he knows how to die in peace, for him death is dreadful. To prepare for a blessed departure is the objective of the Christian message. Cp. A. Koeberle, "Reconciliation and Justification," *C. T. M.*, XXI (September, 1950), p. 657 ff.

mercy (or justice or free will) is not determined.[351]

Rome teaches that death closes the time of merit and demerit and places man either under God's temporal or His eternal judgment, since he who dies in sanctifying grace can no longer sin after death and he who dies in mortal sin can no longer repent. After death man can be in only one of two lots, either in the state of love or of enmity toward God. He is either judged worthy to attain the beatific vision or he is doomed to a state of eternal, conscious, and complete separation from God.

Heaven is described as the beatific vision of God, where the perfected soul will possess God and all the fullness of His truth, goodness, and beauty and where every yearning of the soul is satisfied in perfect rest and endless peace.[352] Hell is viewed not so much as a place of physical torment as rather a place where the special burden of the direct act of divine justice and judgment is borne. Nevertheless Roman theologians find a somewhat mitigating circumstance in the alleged Christian principle that God's vindictive justice is never so comprehensive as His remunerative justice.[353]

The Roman doctrine of salvation by works and the overemphasis of God's justice at the expense of His grace and mercy in Christ nowhere becomes so evident as in Rome's eschatology, especially in Rome's teaching that in addition to heaven and hell there are three more places for the souls after death: (1) limbus infantum for unbaptized children who had no mortal sins and therefore were not guilty of any punishment, but who because of the lack of baptism have no sanctifying grace and are unable to earn the beatific vision;[354] (2) the limbus patrum, the place where some Old Testament saints were detained until Christ liberated them at His descent to hell; and (3) purgatory, the final step in the soul's way to the beatific vision of God. Some theologians maintain that few, if any, souls are ready at death for the beatific vision, with the exception of the Virgin Mary and baptized infants. The line of theological thinking is the following: This life is given to us to win our place in heaven. At death everyone in the state of grace has won the right to have everything removed which would hinder him from entering the beatific vision of God. Therefore we have won the right to have especially all venial sins forgiven and those affections removed which have taken root in our souls. This cleansing will take place in purgatory. But God is a God of justice, and He can never forgive the sins without adequate compensation or satisfactions. Very few, if any, will have rendered all the satisfactions imposed in the sacrament of Penance. The satisfactions still due will be rendered in purgatory.[355]

---

[351] Anscar Vonier, "Death and Judgment," in Smith, II, 1105, 1122 ff. Cp. Thomas Aquinas, Summa, I, Qu. 23, Art. 5 ad 3.

[352] J. P. Arendzen, "Heaven, or the Church Triumphant," in Smith, II, 1248, 1282, lists two primary sources of the joy of heaven: the vision of God as the satisfaction of the mind and the love of God as the satisfaction of the will. Among the secondary sources of happiness in heaven he lists the contemplation of Christ's human nature, of Mary and the angels, the wonders of heaven, and the glorification of the body.

[353] Vonier, in Smith, II, 1133.

[354] Smith, I, 356—58. This limbo (or limbus, i. e., fringe) is sometimes portrayed as a children's playground with all facilities to meet the natural appetites of its occupants. Occasionally a waft of smoke from hell or purgatory may enter this limbo.

[355] J. B. McLaughlin, "Purgatory," in Smith, II, 1140 ff.

Rome's doctrine of purgatory is based on reason, traditions, and some Scriptural references, and primarily on the final and absolute authority of the church. Purgatory is said to be taught in the apocryphal Book of Maccabees (2 Macc. 12:40-46) and in Matt. 12:32 (the sin against the Holy Ghost will not be forgiven in this or the future world; therefore there are sins that will be forgiven in the future world); Matt. 5:25, 26 (until thou hast paid the uttermost farthing); 1 Cor. 3:12-15 (the Christians' work will be tested by fire). Rome claims that no tradition is so old as the traditions for the alleged doctrine of purgatory. These traditions are said to go back to earliest Apostolic times. And finally Rome's doctrine of purgatory appeals to reason.[356]

Rome's teaching of purgatory is not merely a doctrinal appendage but part and parcel of the basic principles of its theology. (1) Only in purgatory is man supposed to be able to meet the various requirements of God's specific attributes of justice, wisdom, goodness. (2) Only in a theological system which fails to deal with the infinite gravity of sin, which distinguishes between mortal and venial sin, is a purgatorial system possible. (3) It is but natural that a theology which ascribes so large a part to man's ability to co-operate in his salvation would find a way whereby man could complete the satisfactions which he was unable to complete in his earthly life. Rome specifically teaches that through their own efforts the suffering souls have gained the right to complete the punishments and cleansings in purgatory.[357]

Concerning the condition of the souls in purgatory, Romanists admit that the sufferings of purgatory are real and great; some theologians hold there is no difference between the suffering of purgatory and of hell in essence, but only in quantity, the punishments of purgatory being temporal and those of hell infinite. The suffering souls are said to be on their way to heaven and to have reached that stage where their salvation is sure and they are no longer assailed by any doubts concerning their ultimate salvation. Their time of trial is said to be over, and their love therefore can now no longer go to greater heights or fall below the present degree.

They are said to be in a state of such great love of God that they long to make atonement for sin and that the soul actually derives untold happiness from the suffering which it must endure, because it sees the great end and purpose of the suffering, namely, the beatific vision of God.

The suffering souls are usually spoken of as the "poor souls." They are "poor" inasmuch as the soul cannot earn merits in purgatory. If, says Rome, that were possible, then the soul could claim a higher degree of salvation than God has allotted. This would imply, says Rome, a third judgment, while Scripture knows only two judgments, one at death and one at the resurrection. On the contrary, Scripture (John 9:4) is said to teach that

---

[356] Many ancient philosophical systems had a purgatorial system. In fact, every system which was predicated on the assumption that man can in part or in whole work out his salvation requires some sort of purgatory.

[357] *Ibid.*, II, 1148—55. There are some inconsistencies in Rome's teaching. If, as many teachers hold, the flesh is the seat of sin, why is the soul and not the body punished and purified? If the soul, which, according to a large number of Roman teachers, comes directly from God and is virtually free from sin, why does it not return to God directly instead of being detained and purified in purgatory?

in purgatory the souls have entered the night in which no man can work. It is therefore impossible to render satisfactions and to earn additional merit in purgatory. The soul must endure satispassions to pay its debts and to be cleansed. It is very difficult to follow the logic of Rome's teaching. On the one hand, Rome states that the soul in purgatory loves God so perfectly that it gladly suffers the satispassions in order to gain the beatific vision. On the other hand, Rome teaches that since the "poor" souls are unable to do anything themselves, they most earnestly desire the help of the Church Militant. Intercession for the departed souls has been made one of the daily obligations of the Church Militant. Immediately upon death the church begins to pray for the soul's release from purgatory. The church prescribes various prayers addressed to Mary, the office for the dead, the regular prayers for the departed, and especially the Masses for the dead, which are viewed as the most important to release the souls from purgatory.[358]

The question as to the duration of a soul's stay in purgatory is left unanswered. The church allows perpetual Masses to be arranged for one soul, since the church does not know how long a soul must suffer, nor how much atonement God will allow for each Mass. The visions of souls begging for help indicate that some souls may be in purgatory for a century or longer. In this life the church has jurisdiction and determines how many satisfactions are required. In the case of the poor souls in purgatory, however, the church no longer has this power, and she can only intercede for them.[359] Those who are alive at the end of the world must also go through the required purgation. But in their case God will somehow concentrate into a moment of time the required satispassion.

Probably at no point does the basic difference between the Roman Catholic and the evangelical way of salvation become so apparent as in the doctrine of purgatory. The one is the way of human effort, the other is the way of grace and faith.

---

[358] Ibid., II, 1169 ff. Cp. *Cath. Encyc.*, "Requiem Masses," "Vigils," etc. Roman theologians have considerable difficulty to make the following points clear to the non-Romanist and, no doubt, to their members who are paying for soul Masses. By its very nature as the sacrifice of Christ's body and blood the value of the Mass is infinite, and one Mass ought to suffice to liberate a soul. But at the same time the actual effect produced by a Mass is limited; otherwise Mother Church would not allow hundreds of Masses to be said for one soul in purgatory. B. V. Miller, "The Eucharistic Sacrifice," in Smith, II, 914. Only a Platonic philosopher and an obedient child of the Roman church can follow these niceties of distinction. — The belief that it is possible to do something for the departed may also help to quiet the conscience of such children as failed to do their duty toward their parents.

[359] McLaughlin, in Smith, II, 1159, 1171.

SECTION IX

Uniate Churches

From the era of the Crusades to the Reformation, the Western church put forth repeated efforts to heal the breach between it and the various churches of the East, but reunions effected by the Second Council of Lyons (1274) and the Council of Ferrara-Florence (1437 to 1439) were transient and superficial. After the Reformation, the Roman Catholic church made diligent attempts to persuade Eastern Christians to accept the primacy of the pope, offering in return for this capitulation the preservation of the respective church's traditional rite, liturgical language, ceremonial (such as Communion under both kinds), and discipline (such as the privilege of marriage for the parochial clergy).

Most of the Uniate churches (the term comes via the Polish *unia* from the Russian *uniya,* "union," i. e., with the Roman church) are small dissident groups which have split off from the parent body.[360] Exceptions are the Maronite Patriarchate of the Lebanon, which has no non-Uniate counterpart and which has been in communion with Rome since the twelfth century, and the Chaldean church, which probably outnumbers its Assyrian counterpart and which has been in communion with Rome since the fifteenth century. The present reunion with the Malabarese Uniates of India dates back to the seventeenth century, with the Armenian, the Coptic, and the Syrian Uniates to the eighteenth century, and with the Ethiopian Uniates to the nineteenth

century. The most recent reunion is with the so-called Malankarese Christians of the Malabar Coast in India, which took place in 1930. The Byzantine (Greek-Slavonic) rite is represented by the Italo-Greeks of Italy (in communion with Rome since the great Eastern schism, although frequently in peril of extinction), the Melkite Uniates of Syria (since the seventeenth century), the Greek Uniates of Greece (since the nineteenth century), and the Uniates of the Slavic countries. Since World War II the Uniate churches of the Byzantine rite in Romania, Bulgaria, Czechoslovakia, Hungary, and Yugoslavia have for the most part returned to their original Orthodox obedience, in part at least under the pressure of the Communist regimes in the Balkan countries. By far the largest Uniate community — prior to World War II it accounted for nearly two thirds of the 8,200,000 Uniate Christians in the world — is the Ruthenian (Carpatho-Russian) church of Polish Galicia and the ethnically related Podcarpathian Ruthenians of Czechoslovakia. The reunion of the former with Rome dates back to the Synod of Brest, then in Lithuania, in 1596; the reunion of the latter took place in the next century.

In this country there are Italo-Greek, Romanian, Melkite, Maronite, and Armenian Uniate parishes under American ordinaries; the Ruthenian Uniates are numerous enough to have bishops of their own. The general effect of the

---

[360] The over-all ratio of Uniate to non-Uniate Eastern and Far Eastern Christians is about 1:19.

administrative policies followed since 1929 — such as the prohibition of marriage to American-trained candidates for the priesthood and the refusal to admit additional married Uniate priests from abroad to parishes in this hemisphere — points to the ultimate Latinization of the Uniates in this country.

Uniates accept the entire Roman Catholic faith and acknowledge without reservation the supreme jurisdiction of the bishop of Rome. They are thus — in spite of differences of rite and discipline — Roman Catholics in the fullest sense. At the same time it should be noted that the term "Uniate" is no longer in favor with Roman Catholic authorities. Instead, Roman Catholic writers now describe them as "Ruthenian Catholics," "Armenian Catholics," etc.

SECTION X

Old Catholic Churches

Old Catholic Churches. As a generic term "Old Catholic" churches denotes those church bodies which have retained certain distinctive doctrines and customs of the Roman Catholic church, while rejecting the authority of the pope and repudiating those decisions of the Council of Trent and later councils which conflict with "ancient Catholic principles." Ever since 1723 the Chapter of Utrecht, as a result of the Jansenist controversy, has been electing archbishops independent of the church of Rome. After the Vatican Council of 1870, dissenting Roman Catholics of Germany and Switzerland organized the Old Catholic church under the leadership of Ignaz Döllinger and obtained episcopal succession from the See of Utrecht, with which the German and Swiss Old Catholics have since remained in communion. Old Catholics reject such Roman Catholic innovations as papal infallibility and the dogmas of the immaculate conception and the assumption of the Blessed Virgin Mary. Their clergy may marry. They encourage Bible reading and use the vernacular in worship. Theologically they range from conservative to liberal.

Early in this century abortive efforts were made to establish Old Catholic missions in Great Britain and in the United States, as a result of which a number of bishops claim to stand in the Old Catholic episcopal succession. The Old Catholics of Europe, however, have repudiated all these claimants and the bodies which they head, such as the *North American Old Roman Catholic Church (The North American Catholic Church),* the *Old Catholic Church in America,* the *Old Catholic Archdiocese of the Americas and Europe,* and *The Reformed Catholic Church (Utrecht Confession), Province of North America,* as well as other "Old Catholic" bodies which claim episcopal orders from other sources, such as the *American Catholic Church, Archdiocese of New York.* The only Old Catholic body in this country that European Old Catholics acknowledge as such is the *Polish National Catholic Church of America.*

The Bonn Agreement of 1931 provides for intercommunion between the Old Catholic church and the Anglican communion (including in this country the Protestant Episcopal church) on the basis of mutual recognition. The Old Catholic church has displayed a consistent interest in ecumenical movements.

Polish National Catholic Church of

America. This organization originated at Scranton, Pa., in 1897, when Polish immigrants became restive under the "absolute religious, political, and social power over the parishioners" given by the Third Plenary Council of Baltimore (1884) to the Roman Catholic priesthood and by the rather free exercise of that power on the part of certain Polish Roman Catholic priests. The secession represented about 20,000 Roman Catholic parishioners, chiefly in the East. The first synod was held at Scranton in 1904, which resolved to translate all Latin worship books into Polish and to establish a theological seminary. In 1921 the rule of celibacy was abrogated, and marriage of the clergy was allowed, but only with the knowledge and permission of the bishop and lay members of the respective congregations.

The Profession of Faith asserts that "man, by following the Supreme Being, is in this life capable of attaining a certain degree of the happiness and of the perfection which is possessed of God in an infinite degree"; that "faith is helpful to man toward his salvation, though not absolutely necessary," which is especially true of "blind faith." Good deeds, however, it holds, "bring us nearer to God and to His Mediator, Jesus Christ, and make us worthy of being His followers and brothers and of being children of the heavenly Father." It rejects the doctrine of eternal punishment. Sin is regarded as a "lack of perfection in the essence of man; and as mankind progresses in this knowledge of the causes of life and the nature of God and comes nearer and nearer to Him, sin will gradually grow less and less until it vanishes entirely. Then man will become the true image and child of God, and the kingdom of God will prevail upon earth."

The Lithuanian National Catholic Church. This church was organized at Scranton, Pa., in 1914, under the direction of Bishop Hodur of the Polish National Catholic Church.

BIBLIOGRAPHY

PART II   SECTIONS I—X

1. *Doctrine*

The Holy Bible. Trans. from the Latin Vulgate. St. Louis: Herder, 1912. The New Testament was first published at Rheims (1582) and the Old Testament at Douay (1609). This Bible is known as the Douay Version. It is annotated in the interest of Roman doctrine.

The New Testament. Trans. from the Vulgate. Paterson, N. J.: St. Anthony Guild Press, 1941. This is a revision of the Challoner-Rheims (Douay) Version.

Canons and Decrees of the Council of Trent. Original Text with English Translation by H. J. Schroeder. St. Louis: B. Herder Book Co., 1941.

Catechismus Romanus. Many editions. We have followed the Latin-German edition of Adolf Buse, Bielefeld-Leipzig, 1867.

Catholic Dictionary. Revised edition. New York: Macmillan Co., 1950.

Catholic Encyclopedia. New York: Robert Appleton Co., 1907. 15 volumes and Index. — An authoritative and indispensable reference work on all phases of Roman history, doctrine, cultus, law, practice, organization.

Asmussen, Hans, and Thomas Sartory. *Lutheran-Catholic Unity?* Baltimore: Helicon Press, 1960.

Adam, Karl. *The Spirit of Catholicism.* Trans. Justin McCann. New York: Macmillan Co., 1937.

————. *One and Holy.* Trans. Cecily Hastings. New York: Sheed & Ward, 1951.

Algermissen, Konrad. *Christian Denominations.* Trans. Joseph W. Grunder. St. Louis: Herder Book Co., 1945.

Bivort de la Saudée, Jacques de. *God, Man and the Universe: A Christian Answer to Modern Materialism.* New York: P. J. Kenedy and Sons, 1953.

Bosc, Jean, Jean Guitton, and Jean Daniélou. *The Catholic Protestant Dialogue,* trans. Robert J. Olsen. Baltimore: Helicon Press, 1960.

Carlen, (Sister) M. Claudia. *Dictionary of Papal Documents, Leo XIII to Pius XII (1878—1957).* New York: P. J. Kenedy and Sons, 1958.

A Catholic Catechism. New York: Herder and Herder, c. 1959. The official English version of the epochal Roman Catholic catechism for children authorized in 1957 by the German hierarchy.

Chinigo, Michael, ed. *The Pope Speaks: The Teachings of Pope Pius XII.* New York: Pantheon Books, c. 1957.

Connell, Francis J. *The New Confraternity Edition of the Revised Baltimore Catechism No. 3.* New York: Benziger Brothers, 1952.

Cristiani, Leon, and Jean Rilliet. *Catholics and Protestants: Separated Brothers.* Trans. Joseph I. Holland and Gilbert V. Tutungi. Westminster, Md.: The Newman Press, 1960.

Daniel-Rops, Henry [pseudonym] ed. *The Twentieth Century Encyclopedia of Catholicism.* New York: Hawthorn Books, 1959—. A 150-volume series on all aspects of contemporary Roman Catholicism.

Deharbe, J. *Catechism of Christian Doctrine.* Approximately 25 different editions by various publishers. We used the edition of Benziger, N. Y., 1882. Originally written in German. Translated into many languages.

De Lubac, Henri. *Catholicism: A Study of Dogma in Relation to the Corporate Destiny of Mankind.* New York: Sheed and Ward, 1958.

Denzinger, Heinrich. *The Sources of Christian Dogma (Enchiridion Symbolorum et Definitionum,* 30th ed.). Trans. Roy J. Defferari. St. Louis: B. Herder Book Co., 1957.

Fremantle, Anne, ed. *The Papal Encyclicals in Their Historical Context.* New York: Mentor Books, c. 1956.

Gibbons, James. *The Faith of Our Fathers.* Many editions; Baltimore, Md.: John Murphy Co. We used the 110th edition (1917).

Hardon, John A. *The Protestant Churches of America.* Westminster, Md.: The Newman Press, 1956.

————. *Christianity in Conflict: A Catholic View of Protestantism.* Westminister, Md.: The Newman Press, 1959.

Heiler, Friedrich. *Der Katholizismus, seine Idee und seine Erscheinung.* Munich: Ernst Reinhardt, 1923.

Hughes, Philip. *The Pope's New Order.* New York: The Macmillan Co., 1944. A systematic summary of the social encyclicals and addresses, from Leo XII to Pius XII. Probably the best source on the social thinking of the modern papacy. The author covers practically all current social problems.

Journet, Charles. *The Primacy of Peter from the Protestant and from the Catholic Point of View.* Trans. John Chaplin. Westminster, Md.: The Newman Press, 1954.

Joyce, George H. *Christian Marriage.* London: Sheed & Ward, 1948.

Leeming, Bernard. *The Churches and the Church: A Study of Ecumenism.* London: Darton, Longman and Todd, c. 1960.

Lortz, Joseph. *Die Reformation in Deutschland,* 3d ed., Freiburg: Verlag Herder, 1948.

Mirbt, Carl. *Quellen zur Geschichte des Papsttums und des roemischen Katholizismus.* Tübingen: Mohr, 1924. Contains the relevant decrees of Councils on doctrine and discipline, papal encyclicals, decisions concerning canon laws, etc.

Moehler, J. A. *Symbolism, or Exposition of the Doctrinal Differences Between Catholics and Protestants.* Trans. J. B. Robertson. London: Gibbings & Co., 1906.

Ott, Ludwig. *The Fundamentals of Catholic Dogma.* Trans. Patrick Lynch; ed. James Bastible: St. Louis: B. Herder Book Co., 1954.

Palmer, Paul F., ed. *Sacraments and Worship.* Westminster, Md.: The Newman Press, 1955—1959. 2 vols.

Preuss, Arthur. Editor of "The Pohle-Preuss Series of Dogmatic Textbooks," 6th ed.; St. Louis: B. Herder Book Co., 1930. This is an adaptation of Joseph Pohle's (died 1921) *Lehrbuch der Dogmatik,* 1902. — Vol. I: *God, His Knowability, Essence, Attributes;* II: *The Divine Trinity;* III: *God, the Author of Nature and the Supernatural;* IV: *Christology;* V: *Soteriology;* VI: *Mariology;* VII: *Grace, Actual and Habitual;* VIII, IX, X, XI: *The Sacraments;* XII: *Eschatology.*

Rahill, Peter James. *The Catholic in America: From Colonial Times to the Present Day.* Chicago: Franciscan Herald Press, c. 1961.

Smith, Geo. D. *The Teaching of the Catholic Church, a Summary of Catholic Doctrine.* 2 vols. New York: Macmillan, 1948. A collection of essays by recognized Roman theologians.

Tavard, George H. *The Catholic Approach to Protestantism.* New York: Harper and Bros., c. 1955.

Theological Studies, quarterly published by the theological faculties of the Society of Jesus in the United States. Woodstock, Md.

Theology Digest, published three times annually by St. Mary's College, St. Marys, Kans., the School of Divinity of St. Louis University. Begun in 1953.

Treacy, G. C. *Five Great Encyclicals.* New York: Paulist Press, 1939.

Whalen, William J. *Separated Brethren: A Survey of Non-Catholic Christian Denominations in the United States.* Milwaukee: The Bruce Publishing Co., c. 1958.

Wilmers, W. *Lehrbuch der Religion: Ein Handbuch zu Deharbe's katholischem Katechismus.* 4 vols. Münster. The seventh edition was prepared by Jos. Hontheim, 1907. We followed the 1894 edition. There is also a one-volume edition.

2. *History and American Roman Catholicism*

Brown, Robert McAfee, and Gustave Weigel. *An American Dialogue: A Protestant Looks at Catholicism and a Catholic Looks at Protestantism.* Garden City, N. Y.: Doubleday and Co., 1960.

Brezzi, Paolo. *The Papacy: Its Origin and Historical Evolution.* Trans. Henry J. Yannone. Westminster, Md.: The Newman Press, 1958.

Browne, Henry J. "American Catholic History: A Progress Report on Research and Study,"

in *Church History,* XXVI (1957), 372 to 380.

Burn-Murdoch, H. *The Development of the Papacy.* London: Faber and Faber, 1954.

Christ, Frank L., and Gerard E. Sherry, eds. *American Catholicism and the Intellectual Ideal.* New York: Appleton-Century-Crofts, c. 1961.

Cogley, John, ed. *Religion in America: Original Essays on Religion in a Free Society.* New York: Meridian Books, 1958.

Ellis, John Tracy. *American Catholicism.* Chicago: The University of Chicago Press, c. 1956.

Hastings, Adrian, ed. *The Church and the Nations: A Study of Minority Catholicism.* New York: Sheed and Ward, 1959.

Hughes, Philip. *A History of the Church.* New York: Sheed & Ward, 1935—1947. Vol. I (The Early Church); Vol. II (From 7th to 13th Centuries); Vol. III (Aquinas to Luther).

McAvoy, Thomas T. *The Great Crisis in American Catholic History, 1895—1900.* Chicago: Henry Regnery Co., 1957.

——— (ed.). *Roman Catholicism and the American Way of Life.* Notre Dame, Ind.: University of Notre Dame Press, 1960.

Maynard, Th. *The Story of American Catholicism.* New York: The Macmillan Co., 1941. The author is a convert to Romanism, and his book is definitely biased.

McDonald, Donald, ed. *Catholics in Conversation: Seventeen Interviews with Leading American Catholics.* Philadelphia: J. B. Lippincott Co., c. 1960.

McSorley, Joseph. *An Outline of History of the Church by Centuries.* 2d ed.; St. Louis: Herder, 1948.

Murray, John Courtney. *We Hold These Truths.* New York: Sheed and Ward, 1960.

O'Dea, Thomas F. *American Catholic Dilemma: An Inquiry into the Intellectual Life.* New York: Sheed and Ward, 1958.

O'Gorman, Thomas. *History of the Roman Catholic Church in the United States.* New York: The Christian Literature Co., 1895. (In the "American Church History Series.")

Ong, Walter J. *Frontiers in American Catholicism: Essays on Ideology and Culture.* New York: The Macmillan Co., 1957.

————. *American Catholic Crossroads: Religious-Secular Encounters in the Modern World.* New York: The Macmillan Co., 1959.

3. Cultus, Organization, Canon Law

Abbo, John A., and Jerome D. Hannan. *The Sacred Canons: A Concise Presentation of the Current Disciplinary Norms of the Church.* 2d ed. St. Louis: B. Herder Book Co., 1960. 2 vols. A summary commentary on the 2414 canons of the 1917 *Codex Iuris Canonici.*

Attwater, Donald. *The Catholic Eastern Churches.* Milwaukee: The Bruce Publishing Co., 1935.

Bouyer, Louis. *Liturgical Piety.* South Bend: University of Notre Dame Press, 1955.

Cabrol, Fernand. *The Books of the Latin Liturgy,* trans. by the Benedictines of Stanbrook. St. Louis: B. Herder Book Co., 1932.

Connell, Francis L. *Father Connell Answers Moral Questions.* Washington: The Catholic University of America Press, 1959.

Eisenhofer, Ludwig, and Joseph Lechner. *The Liturgy of the Roman Rite.* Trans. A. J. and E. F. Peeler, ed. H. E. Winstone. New York: Herder and Herder, 1961.

Ellard, Gerald. *The Dialog Mass.* New York: Longmans, Green & Co., 1942.

Haffert, John Matthias. *Mary in Her Scapular Promise.* Sea Isle City, N. J.: Scapular Press, 1942.

Liturgical Catechism: A Catechism on the Divine Liturgy of the Byzantine-Slavonic Rite. Pittsburgh: Byzantine-Slavonic Rite Catholic, Exarchate of Pittsburgh, 1954.

Lydon, P. J. *Ready Answers in Canon Law for the Parish Clergy.* New York: Benziger, 1934.

Missale Romanum. Regensburg: Fridericus Pustet, [1942].

National Catholic Almanac, The. Paterson, N. J.: St. Anthony Guild Press, 1960.

O'Connell, Raphael V. *Our Lady Mediatrix of All Graces.* Baltimore: John Murphy, 1926.

Parsch, Pius. *The Church's Year of Grace.* Trans. William G. Heidt et al. Collegeville, Minn.: Liturgical Press, 1953—1959. 5 vols.

Peil, Rudolf. *A Handbook of the Liturgy.* Trans. H. E. Winstone. New York: Herder and Herder, 1960.

Ryan, John A., and Francis J. Boland. *Catholic Principles of Politics.* New York: The Macmillan Co., 1940. The authors show how the papacy can accommodate itself to political principles without yielding any of its basic principles.

Short Breviary for Religious and Laity. Collegeville, Minn.: Liturgical Press, 1942.

Woywod, Stanislaus. *A Practical Commentary on the Code of Canon Law,* revised by Callistus Smith. New York: J. F. Wagner Co., 1952.

4. Non-Roman Catholic Sources

Barrett, E. B. *While Peter Sleeps.* New York: Ives Washburn, 1929.

Berkouwer, Gerritt C. *The Conflict with Rome.* Trans. David H. Freeman. Philadelphia: The Presbyterian and Reformed Publishing Co., 1958. A European Reformed view.

Blanshard, Paul. *American Freedom and Catholic Power.* Boston: Beacon Press, 1949.

Boehmer, Heinrich. *The Jesuits.* Trans. P. Z. Strodach. Phila.: Castle Press, 1928. Probably the best treatise on the Jesuit Order.

Burtt, Edwin A. *Types of Religious Philosophy.* New York: Harper & Bros., 1939. Ch. ii: "The Catholic Philosophy of Religion," comes to grips with the main propositions of scholastic, more specifically Thomist, theology.

Chemnitz, Martin. *Examen Concilii Tridentini.* 1565—73. The best edition, Frankfurt, 1707, republished by Eduard Preuss, Berlin, 1861.

Cross, Robert D. *The Emergence of Liberal Catholicism in America.* Cambridge, Mass.: Harvard University Press, 1958.

Eckhardt, C. C. *The Papacy and World Affairs.* Chicago: University of Chicago Press, 1937.

Fairweather, A. M. *Nature and Grace: Selections from the Summa Theologica of Thomas Aquinas.* Philadelphia: The Westminster Press, 1954.

Fey, Harold. *Can Catholicism Win America?* Pamphlet. A series of articles reprinted from the *Christian Century,* Nov. 29, 1944, to Jan. 17, 1945.

Garrison, W. E. *Catholicism and the American Mind.* New York: Willett, Clark & Colby, 1928.

Guettée, René-François. *The Papacy.* Trans. A. Cleveland Coxe. New York: Minos Publishing Co., n. d. (reprint of the 1866 edition).

Janus. *Der Papst und das Konzil.* Leipzig: C. F. Steinacker, 1869. Janus (Bishop Döllinger) sets forth all the arguments against the infallibility.

Koenker, Ernest Benjamin. *The Liturgical Renaissance in the Roman Catholic Church.* Chicago: The University of Chicago Press, 1954.

McKnight, John P. *The Papacy, a New Appraisal.* New York: Rinehart and Co., 1952.

Neve, J. L. *A History of Christian Thought.* Phila.: United Lutheran Publication House, 1943. Vol. I contains the history of dogma, including the Tridentine theology. Vol. II contains two short sections on modern phases of Roman theology.

Pelikan, Jaroslav Jan, Jr. *The Riddle of Roman Catholicism.* New York: Abingdon Press, 1959.

Preuss, Eduard. *Die römische Lehre von der unbefleckten Empfängnis.* Berlin: Verlag von G. Schlawitz, 1865.

Schaff, Philip. *Creeds of Christendom.* New York and London: Harper & Bros., 1896, 1899. Vol. I contains excellent historical material on Roman history of dogma.

Vol. II contains the official Latin text (and English translation) of the *Symbola Romana* of 1563; 1564; 1854; 1864; 1870.

Scharper, Philip, ed. *American Catholics: A Protestant-Jewish View.* New York: Sheed and Ward, c. 1959.

Sperry, W. L. *Religion in America.* New York: The Macmillan Co., 1946. The chapter "American Catholicism" is based largely on Maynard's history and unfortunately did not eliminate Maynard's evident bias.

Sweet, William Warren. *The American Churches: An Interpretation.* Nashville: Abingdon-Cokesbury, 1948.

Von Loewenich, Walther. *Modern Catholicism.* Trans. Reginald H. Fuller. New York: St. Martin's Press, 1959.

Walther, Wilhelm. *Lehrbuch der Symbolik.* Leipzig: Scholl, 1924. The section on the Roman church is considered one of the best evaluations of Roman Catholic theology. E. Klotsche, in *Christian Symbolics,* follows Walther quite closely, and thus offers the English readers a synopsis of Walther's keen and detailed analysis.

5. *Polish National Catholic Church of America*

Andrews, Theodore. *The Polish National Catholic Church in America and Poland.* London: S. P. C. K., 1953.

Zielinski, Thaddeus, Louis Orzech, and Albert Tarka. *A Catechism of the Polish National Catholic Church.* Scranton: Mission Fund of the Polish National Catholic Church, 1955.

The Lutheran Church

Approximately seventy-one million persons in Christendom bear the name Lutheran. That so large a segment of the visible church is named after the man Martin Luther is really a historical accident. The papal bull of 1521 which excommunicated Luther from the official church applied the name "Lutheran" to Luther's adherents to stigmatize them as heretics and schismatics. Luther and his followers protested against the use of a personal name under such conditions.[1] During the first fifty years the followers of Luther were known as Evangelicals or "Reformed churches." When the line of demarcation was sharply drawn between Lutherans and Reformed, after 1580, the name Lutheran came into more frequent use, and by the end of the Thirty Years' War it was in general use.[2]

SECTION I

Luther's Theological Development

In seeking the answer to life's most important question: How can I find a forgiving God? Luther initiated a "Copernican revolution" in theology. As Copernicus revolutionized scientific thought by substituting a heliocentric for the age-old geocentric world view, so Luther's rediscovery of the Gospel proved to be the undoing of the popular egocentric or anthropocentric theology of the Law and human righteousness and re-established the theocentric or Christo-

NOTE: For key to abbreviations see Appendix C; for Bibliography, the end of this Part.

[1] When in 1522 some overzealous followers of Luther called themselves Lutherans, Luther wrote: "Please do not use my name; do not call yourselves Lutherans, but Christians. . . . The doctrine is not mine; I have not been crucified for anyone. . . . Why should I, a miserable bag of worms, give my meaningless name to Christ's children?" W. A., VIII, 684—685. When, however, the Romanists resorted to name calling in an attempt to discredit the Lutheran Reformation (cp. Ap. XV, 42 German), then Luther yielded to the use of his name. Cp. W. H. T. Dau, in V. Ferm, What Is Lutheranism? pp. 199—207. J. P. Williams, What Americans Believe (New York: Harper and Bros., 1952), on p. 152, unfortunately quotes Dau completely out of context. — For a Roman Catholic analysis of the Lutheran attitude toward Luther see Ernst Walter Zeeden, The Legacy of Luther, trans. Ruth Mary Bethell (Westminster: The Newman Press, 1954).

[2] In Germany, as in other parts of Europe, several provincial churches, notably in Wuerttemberg, though subscribing to the A. C. and Luther's Catechisms, are known as "Evangelical." In the Scandinavian countries, where the Lutheran church is the state church, the word "Lutheran" is not in the official title.

centric message of man's salvation by divine grace for Christ's sake.[3] Many factors brought about this "Copernican revolution" and helped to direct it into the greatest religious and theological reformation in the history of Christendom. As is frequently the case, God employs "creative controversies" to fashion His instruments. In Luther's case these "creative" controversies came both from within and from without and his theological development is intimately connected with these.

Conflicts from Within

The dominant thought during Luther's formative years, especially as a young monk in Erfurt, seemed to center in a deep guilt consciousness and correspondingly in his concern to find some human device to eradicate the sin which harassed him. On the road to the rediscovery of the Gospel Luther went through four major stages: his encounter with Occamism, Augustinianism, mysticism, Christ-centered faith.[4]

OCCAMISM

During his university days Luther came under the influence of the great English scholastic, William of Occam. Especially two phases in Occamist thinking were of significance for Luther. First, Occam departed radically from the epistemology of most scholastics. They held that since reason and revelation are both gifts of God, both are of equal significance as the source of divine truth. Occam and the nominalists [5] held that reason cannot apperceive the

supranatural, since it is completely outside the realm of reason. Only faith can apprehend, though not comprehend, the mysteries, the miracles, and even the dogmas of the church. This teaching undoubtedly affected Luther deeply in his evaluation of the whole structure of Roman theology. His contacts with Occam increased both Luther's loathing for the Aristotelian dialectical method and his faith in the divinely revealed Scriptures as the only source of Christian truth. Second, Occam's concept of God proved to be frightening for Luther. Occam thought of God as Absolute Will; more specifically, he held that God is entirely responsible for man's "justification." In Luther's effort to silence his accusing conscience, he heeded the Occamist teaching that in contrition God would cleanse man of his inbred sin, whereas scholasticism held that man earns God's grace by his own effort. But when Luther failed to gain assurance that he had obtained the infused grace — the means to attain righteousness — he feared that the Absolute God by an unconditioned act of predestination had excluded him from salvation, and thus the Occamist concept of God as the Absolute Will drove him to despair. It was in this frame of mind that he was receptive for the Gospel.

AUGUSTINIANISM

In his study of Occam, Luther became familiar with Augustine's writings. Among the many impacts on his theological development, Augustine's views on sin and grace were of the greatest

---

[3] Philip Watson, p. 33 ff.

[4] Tschackert, *Die Enstehung der luth. u. ref. Kirchenlehre* (Göttingen, 1910), p. 34 ff.; Boehmer, chs. iii, v; R. Seeberg, IV; Edgar Carlson, loc. cit.; cp. also U. Saarnivaara, *Luther Discovers the Gospel* (St. Louis: C. P. H., 1950).

[5] Occam was a nominalist, and Luther called himself a nominalist. On the main points of nominalism, esp. in its distinction from realism, see Seeberg, *Lehrbuch der Dogmengeschichte* (3d ed., 1913), IV, 63 ff.

significance for Luther, because they differed fundamentally from the Pelagian view of sin, especially the Pelagian denial of original sin. From Augustine, Luther learned that concupiscence is truly sin, that original sin is man's total lack of all goodness and his constant inclination toward all that is evil. Luther's understanding of the grim reality that original sin is the "capital" sin was a most significant step on the road to the Reformation.[6] He saw the main prop of scholastic theology crumbling away when he learned that man does not possess the capacity to merit "grace" and to work out his own salvation. The chief lesson from Augustine was that "grace" is not an acquired quality in man, but God's favor, which alone can begin and complete man's justification.[7]

MYSTICISM

A third factor which deeply affected Luther's theological development was mysticism, especially German mysticism. Some types of mysticism are the highest forms of an egocentric philosophy. True, they seem to demand complete self-negation. But abnegation is in reality the acme of self-interest because it flows from the hope of attaining a higher bliss. Many mystics assert that the soul has the right and the capacity to enter directly into union with "the naked God," with God in His transcendence. The famous mystic Tauler[8] urged complete mortification, total surrender to God, conquest of every form of egocentricity, even the desire to be saved, and for a time mysticism seemed to offer Luther an escape from his guilt consciousness. But the mystical way served only to aggravate Luther's spiritual condition, for it emphasized the pious life, complete abnegation, total passivity, the very things which Luther was unable to accomplish. The mystical way seeks direct union with God, to hear the "uncreated Word," while Luther felt that the impurity of his heart excluded such a mystical union. Thus mysticism served in a negative way to direct Luther to the Incarnate Word as He is revealed in Holy Scripture. However, the Tauler type of mysticism also made several positive contributions to Luther's theological development. The Roman sacramental and sacerdotal system relegates the personal relation of man and his God into the background. In mysticism the spotlight is directed not upon an altar or an intermediary but on the individual who seeks personal union with God. Scholasticism can be a logical, abstract system of thought, but the mystic is concerned with his own personal problems and is inclined to introspection. Scholasticism has an elaborate system of cataloguing sins according to their greatness, their nature, their effect. Mysticism reduces all sin to the one grievous concept of egocentricity. And, finally, in scholasticism God is pictured as a God of justice who metes out punishments and rewards with inexo-

---

[6] Roman Catholic historians formerly pictured Luther's guilt consciousness as the result of secret sins. The fact is — and fair Romanists agree — that Luther's anxiety was caused not so much by "actual" sins as rather by the deep awareness of the extent and gravity of man's original sin or his inherent depravity. Cp. Seeberg, op. cit., IV, 84—96. Theo. Harnack, I, 193 ff. A. Hamel, *Der junge Luther u. Augustin* (Gütersloh, 1934), I, 98 ff.

[7] During the early period Luther's understanding of justification was entirely in Augustinian thought patterns, i. e., he believed that justification is accomplished by progressive sanctification and that the sinner is "made holy." Ibid., p. 115 ff.

[8] In 1516 Luther published the anonymous *Deutsche Theologie* because he claimed to have learned immeasurably much from it. Cp. Koestlin-Hay, I, 125 ff.

rable righteousness, whereas mysticism thinks of God primarily in terms of infinite love.

CHRIST-CENTERED FAITH

The man who more than anyone else helped Luther to escape from his labyrinth of anxiety, doubt, and despair, was the prior of his Augustinian community, John Staupitz. In the hours of despair Staupitz turned Luther away from his sin, from the inadequacy of his monastic life, from an arbitrary decree of election, to "the wounds of Christ." In his previous experience Luther had seen Christ only as a new Legislator; the Gospel as a "new law," with countless "evangelical counsels"; the righteousness of God only as God's condemning and punitive justice. But when Luther beheld the "wounds of Christ," then he saw the Scriptures in an entirely new light, as Gospel, as good news. Christ became the focal point through which he now saw the concepts *justification, justify, righteousness of God*. Luther describes his experience as follows:

At last I perceived that the "righteousness of God" is the perfect obedience of Christ and that the believer shall live before God, not through his own righteousness, but solely through Christ's complete righteousness. It seemed to me that I was born anew and that I had entered into the open gates of Paradise.

The whole Bible suddenly took on new meaning for me. I ran through it — as much as came to mind — and found that everywhere my interpretation was confirmed. . . . Thus the word "righteousness," which had been odious to me, now became the very entrance into heaven.[9]

The inward struggles with sin and a frightening guilt consciousness came to a conclusion in the rediscovery of the Gospel. This rediscovery of the Gospel has been summarized in the threefold *sola* of the Reformation: *sola Scriptura, sola gratia, sola fide.*[10]

In Luther's thinking the *sola Scriptura* principle is exclusively Christocentric. The "Scriptures alone" is the same as "the Gospel alone," and "the Gospel alone" is Christ alone. The Christocentric approach to the Sacred Scriptures revolutionized Luther's entire theology. The Word of Christ in the Gospel became an objective reality for Luther and the Gospel promises a "given," a "constant," a *datum*, which remains ever the same regardless of his own personal experiences. The important point for Luther was that in Christ God's gracious promises are an eternally abiding "Yea" and "Amen."[11] *Sola Scriptura* meant for Luther that God had spoken His absolution in the Scriptures, and thus the Scriptures had opened Par-

---

[9] Pref. to Vol. I of Luther's Latin works. March, 1545. W. A., LIV, 186, 3—16. It is a matter of conjecture whether this is Luther's description of his "tower experience," to which he refers in later life. Hanns Lilje, p. 68, places the "tower experience" into the spring of 1513. Saarnivaara, pp. 35, 49, places the "tower experience" as late as 1518.

[10] Theodore Engelder, "The Three Principles of the Reformation," in W. H. T. Dau, ed. *Four Hundred Years* (St. Louis: C. P. H., 1917).

[11] It is sometimes assumed that the *sola Scriptura* principle of the Reformation implies first and foremost Luther's firm insistence that the Scriptures are the only source of doctrine. It is that, too, of course, but that never was an issue in Luther's own theological development. As an Occamist he had always accepted the absolute authority of the Bible. (Seeberg, op. cit., IV, 80 ff.) This phase of the *sola Scriptura* principle became an issue in his later conflicts with the Pope's representatives and the "heavenly prophets." — See also Lewis W. Spitz, Sr., "Luther's *Sola Scriptura*," in *C. T. M.*, XXXI (1960), 740—745; Jaroslav J. Pelikan, Jr., *Luther the Expositor* (St. Louis: C. P. H., c. 1959).

adise to him. Scripture alone is the Gospel alone. After Luther had learned the true meaning of *sola Scriptura,* the Gospel was no longer a new law — *nova lex* — nor Christ the new Legislator who has established in the papacy a reign of commandments. Formerly the "Gospel" had been *cacangelium* (bad news), because it was only Law, but now it became *evangelium* (good news). The deep chasm between Law and Gospel, and the correct distinction between the two, is for Luther the basis of true theology and summarizes the sharp antithesis of Lutheran teaching to Romanism and incidentally also to Calvinism as well.[12]

The basic difference between Romanist and Lutheran theology may also be summarized in *sola gratia.* This watchword means that salvation is ours solely by God's unmerited grace in Christ's all-sufficient work. "By grace alone," "for Christ's sake alone," "through faith alone, without any human merit" — or any of a number of variations — express the one central article of the Christian faith. In Luther's view this article permeates all theology:

This one article, namely, faith in Christ, rules my heart. All my theological thoughts, day or night, proceed from

this article, revolve about it, and always return to it.[13]

Roman theologians, however, refuse to accept this Lutheran watchword. Either Rome defines grace as some infused quality, virtue, or power in man, or Rome objects to the word "alone" and ascribes man's justification in part to God and in part to man. But grace is not grace unless it is entirely grace.[14] Grace cannot be quartered, or halved, or treated in any piecemeal fashion. We obtain everything by grace, or we get nothing at all.

The *sola fide* principle flows inevitably from *sola gratia.* They stand in relation to each other as the convex and concave of a sphere. If the sinner's justification is by grace, it can be only by faith, since grace excludes every meritorious cause in man, even faith as a meritorious cause. The fact that man is justified by faith without any work on his part, that faith is the hand which receives gratuitously God's pardon, that great fact was the heart of Luther's new experience. The Romanists were willing to accept the letter but not the spirit of the *sola fide.* They held that man is saved by faith, but it must be a faith active in good works and therefore meritorious.[15]

---

12 All three are ardent advocates of a *sola Scriptura* principle, but for basically different reasons. Romanism hears in the Scriptures the commandments of the God of justice; Calvinism, the stern voice of the God of sovereignty; the Lutheran church, the gracious voice of Christ. Consequently there is a basic difference in their theology and even in their *Weltanschauung.* Luther offers suggestions to correct the social and ecclesiastical abuses of his day in the light of the Gospel, in the Christ-centered Scripture, not according to the Law, as Zwinglian and Calvinistic theology does. Cp. especially the "reformatory" writings of 1520.

13 Pref. to *Commentary on Galatians,* W. A., XL/1, 33.

14 Augustine: *Gratia, nisi gratis sit, non est gratia.*

15 Roman theologians call this faith *fides formata.* In the final analysis this is not faith, since man is not justified by faith, but his own good works. Because Rome defines "faith" differently from the Lutheran church (cp. footnotes to Rom. 3:28 in Douay Version), Luther inserted the word "alone" in his translation of Rom. 3:28 and vigorously defended this "alone" against the charge that he had tampered with the Bible. Cp. *Vom Dolmetschen,* W. A., XXX/2, 640—643.

Conflicts from Without

It was inevitable that the emergence of the three Reformatory principles as a result of Luther's spiritual conflicts would soon bring on conflicts from without. But these new controversies only helped to bring into sharp relief the basic Reformatory principles and to focus them upon specific theological points. These "creative" controversies may best be classified as (1) anti-Roman, in the areas of religious authority, the way of salvation, the nature and function of the church; (2) antispiritualistic, in the doctrinal areas of the means of grace and the ministry.[16]

THE ANTI-ROMAN CONTROVERSIES

The introductory statement of the Ninety-five Theses: "When our Lord and Master Jesus Christ says," summarizes Luther's faith as to religious authority, the first area in which he clashed with Rome. During the years of his inner conflicts he had learned that Scripture is God's dynamic and creative Word bringing Christ to man's heart. It is this Christocentric approach which prompted Luther to state as early as 1512 that faith places itself captive to Christ's Word.[17] In his early conflicts with Rome, Luther — even as late as 1518 — accepted the papal decrees as a secondary authority.

But in the controversy with the famous Professor Eck of Ingolstadt in the Leipzig Disputation (1519) he came to see clearly that Christ's Word in the Scriptures is the only religious authority. Now he declared boldly that he would pit one word of Scripture against all the teachers,[18] and at Worms he declared defiantly and triumphantly that his conscience is bound only by God's Word. For the same reason he refused to bind anyone's conscience to anything but Christ's Word in matters of faith, since the eternal weal and woe of souls is at stake and one needs an absolutely reliable word when man must appear before God's judgment. Luther's Christocentric approach to the Scriptures is reflected in his paradoxical position which gave him freedom to determine the Scriptural canon and at the same time demanded complete submission to the Scriptures.[19] As a result of his Christocentric faith he evaluated the Old Testament in its Christological content, not in its legal or historical lessons, and saw in it "Christ's swaddling clothes and the manger." In the light of this faith, Luther boldly examined the dogmas, pious opinions, rites, ceremonies, commandments, and traditions of the church, and discarded everything which in his opinion was anti-Christian.[20]

---

[16] There were many more controversies, such as the one brought on by the antinomian views of Agricola. It is not the purpose of this chapter to delineate Luther's theology in detail, but to show the factors which led to the formulation of Lutheran theology in the Lutheran Confessions.

[17] W. A., I, 77. Cp. Tschackert, 57 ff.

[18] W. A., I, 384. Cp. Boehmer, Ch. XII; W. H. T. Dau, *The Leipzig Debate in 1519* (St. Louis: C. P. H., 1919).

[19] Cp. M. Reu, *Luther and the Scriptures* (Columbus, Ohio, ca. 1944). Neither Luther nor the Lutheran Confessions established an official list of the sacred writings, as was done in the Reformed Confessions and at Trent.

[20] A good case in point is Luther's critique of the theological method of the scholastics. Luther rejected the entire Aristotelian method, not because of obscurantism in himself, but because "philosophy" had silenced Christ. J. J. Pelikan, *From Luther to Kierkegaard* (St. Louis: C. P. H., 1950), p. 10 ff., discusses Luther's attitude toward philosophy. Another case in point is Luther's attitude toward the monastic orders, which he

The second anti-Roman controversy revolved about the way of salvation. Here the antitheses between Roman and Lutheran theology are sharply drawn and definitely set forth.

In the opinion of many the basic difference between Roman and Lutheran theology is most clearly set forth in the totally divergent views concerning sin. Rome thinks of sin chiefly in terms of isolated acts, some more, others less grievous; some venial, others mortal.[21] Luther's early insights into the true nature of sin as man's rebellious, spirit, as man's inborn wickedness, came into sharp relief in his controversies with Dr. Eck and Erasmus of Rotterdam. He learned to know that sin, viewed negatively, is the total lack of the fear and love of God and, viewed positively, nothing but evil concupiscence. In fact, it became increasingly clear that Luther actually thought almost exclusively in terms of man's "capital" sin, the sin of his origin, his total corruption, his complete alienation from God, his concupiscence, his inborn egotistic drive, the sin which embraces everything that man thinks and does without faith in God, the sin that subjects man to God's wrath.[22]

Luther's divergent view on the nature and consequence of sin lies at the bottom of practically all his theological controversies with Rome, especially in the areas of Christ's work, of justification, and of faith. Luther's understanding of Christ's work deepened and broadened as the controversies with Rome brought home to him ever more clearly the twofold character of sin, namely, as guilt and as bondage. Therefore Luther portrays Christ's work both as the payment of man's debt by his perfect life and innocent death and as man's liberation from the dreadful powers which held him captive. This twofold emphasis of Christ's work made the doctrine of Christ's theanthropic person — the God-man — so meaningful for Luther. Only as God-man has Christ "become my Lord" and removed "the tyrants and jailers," namely, sin, the devil, death, and all evil.[23]

condemned because these religious orders had crowded out Christ's Word and work. See *On Monastic Orders*, 1521, W. A., VIII, 573—669. Seeberg, op. cit., IV, 332—54 discusses Luther's view on the relation of the dogmas to the Scriptures.

[21] Cp. "Sin" and "Grace" in P. II.

[22] Luther's theological insights regarding the nature of man as a sinner and God's attitude toward man, the sinner, are some of the most penetrating in all theological literature. Cp., for example, *De servo arbitrio* and the *Exposition of Psalm 90 (91)*. Cp. Theo. Harnack, I, 135—48. Seeberg, pp. 163—76. On distinction between Law and Gospel, cp. ibid., pp. 201—14.

[23] Exposition of Second Article, *Large C.* Cp. Seeberg, IV, 188—190, where the author discusses Christ's work as propitiation and liberation. The idea has recently been advanced in certain Lutheran circles that Luther in reality emphasized only "the classical theory" of the Atonement, i. e., that Christ's work consisted in liberating man from his enemies. Cp. G. Aulén, *Christus Victor;* the same author, *The Faith of the Christian Church*, trans. Eric H. Wahlstrom, 2d English ed. (Philadelphia: Muhlenberg Press, c. 1960), pp. 196—213. This theory is said to supply the real dynamics to Christ's work. Cp. T. A. Kantonen, *Resurgence of the Gospel* (Phil.: Muhlenberg Press, 1948), ch. ii. But this theory overlooks the fact that Luther always kept in mind that God is the Author both of the judgment and of the Redemption. Luther understood the words *"pro nobis"* to mean first of all that Christ suffered the curse of God for us, in our stead. Cp. especially Luther's comments on Gal. 3:13 in the large *Commentary*

This aspect of Christ's work was a complete departure from the Roman view, oriented entirely in the doctrine of righteousness by man's work as a complement to Christ's sacrifice. Roman theology rejects the forensic character of justification and views it as progressive sanctification.[24]

In his polemics against this Neoplatonic concept, Luther saw with increasing clarity the necessity of maintaining a sharp distinction between justification and sanctification, without, however, in any way separating them. The Romanists maintained that Luther's doctrine of justification by faith alone lacked all dynamics; in fact, undermined morality. Therefore Luther found it necessary to expand the epigrammatic statement: *Sola fides iustificat, sed fides non est sola.*[25] Faith brings true liberty, for —

so Luther maintained — it brings liberation from the curse of sin and from the burden of the Law so that man always has a "good conscience" in God's sight. In this liberty the believer is free to serve his fellow man. Thus the entirely free man becomes the servant of all.[26] These insights changed Luther's entire view of the Christian life. His ethics is such that it can be applied only by him who through faith is free from every coercion and whose concept of the Christian vocation is oriented in justifying faith. Thus Christian ethics in Lutheran theology is always spontaneous and requires no legalistic orientation nor motivation.[27]

The third area of anti-Roman controversies which helped to crystallize Luther's theological thinking centered in the doctrine of the church. Two points

on *Galatians*, W. A., XL/1, 432—52. Cp. Theo. Harnack, II, 195 ff. Adolf Koeberle (see P. II, fn. 350, above), pp. 641—58. M. H. Franzmann, "Reconciliation and Justification," *C. T. M.*, Vol. XXI, No. 2 (February, 1950), pp. 81—93. Theo. Laetsch ed., *The Abiding Word* (St. Louis: C. P. H., 1946 [R. C. Rein, "Forgiveness of Sin"]), I, 146. Francis Pieper, *Christian Dogmatics* (St. Louis: C. P. H., 1951), II, 344 ff., 503 ff.

24 In Roman teaching "justification" is taken in its original Latin etymology, *iustum facere*, to make a person just by a metaphysical process. Cp. Martin Chemnitz (see P. II, Bibliog., above). The English "justify" is a contraction of *iustificare*. The forensic idea is absent from the etymological sense, although it is a part of the original Greek term represented by *iustificare* in the Latin New Testament.

25 "Faith alone justifies, but faith is never alone." In the Preface to Romans he wrote: "Oh, faith is a living, vital thing! It does not ask whether good works are to be done. Before one asks, it has already done them and is always active." W. A., *Bibel*, VII, 11, 9—12.

26 These thoughts are set forth most adequately in his treatise *On Christian Liberty*, W. A., VII, 20—38. Cp. F. E. Mayer, "Human Will in Bondage and Freedom," *C. T. M.*, XXII (Oct. and Dec. 1951), pp. 719—47, 785—819.

27 Cp. Einar Billing, *Our Calling*, trans. C. Bergendoff (Rock Island, 1950). Cp. Oliver Rupprecht, "A Remedy for Modern Chaos," *C. T. M.*, XXII (1951), p. 820 ff. Werner Elert, *The Christian Ethos*, trans. Carl J. Schindler (Philadelphia: Muhlenberg, c. 1957), Part II. Large C., "The Decalog." The so-called "Third Use of the Law" will be discussed later. Cp. W. Elert, *Morphologie des Luthertums*, Vol. II, *passim*. A. Koeberle, "The Social Problem in the Light of the Augsburg Confession," *Lutheran Church Quarterly*, July, 1945. E. Brunner, *The Divine Imperative*, trans. by Olive Wyon (Phil.: Westminster Press, 1947), is a study in Christian ethics which devotes considerable space to an evaluation of Luther's "ethics" from the Reformed point of view. Cp. pp. 68—81; 588—91.

in particular demanded Luther's close scrutiny: the nature of the church and the authority of the hierarchy. The climactic "tower experience" he speaks about gave him a clear insight into the *sola fide* principle and with it an understanding — though still vague — that the church is the total number of believers, and believers only, whose great treasure is the Gospel of Christ.[28] In his controversy with Dr. Eck he came to see clearly that the hierarchy did not possess the authority which it had claimed for centuries; in fact, that there are no ranks at all in the holy Christian church. For through Baptism all are priests; all have the Gospel, the sacraments, the absolution.[29] The fact that Luther did not become an anarchist in his revolt against the usurpation of power on the part of the hierarchy was due in no small measure to his new insights gained in the controversies with the "enthusiasts."

THE ANTISPIRITUALIST CONTROVERSY

In controversies an extreme position frequently provokes an equally extreme reaction, with the result that people may pour out the child with the bath water. In their opposition to the Roman Catholic rites, ceremonies, church organization, some followers of Luther went to the opposite extreme. Some became "enthusiasts," others mystics, many even anarchists. In their opposition to Rome's

sacramentalism and sacerdotalism they rejected every means of grace. They held that the Holy Spirit works directly in man and gathers a congregation of saints without the Word or the sacraments. In their protest against the social abuses brought on by ecclesiastical and secular princes, some even rejected all forms of government. In short, there was danger that the Reformation might end in a revolution.

Luther encountered three types of "enthusiasts" or spiritualists. In his controversies with these between 1522 and 1528 he saw with increasing clarity the necessity of emphasizing the objectivity of the means of grace.[30]

The earliest of the spiritualists whom Luther encountered was Karlstadt. He initiated the iconoclastic revolution in Wittenberg during Luther's stay at the Wartburg. Without instructing the congregation he abolished the celebration of the Holy Communion under one kind, did away with confession, and renounced his vow of celibacy. Karlstadt's theology is probably best described as mysticism. He believed that by perfect union with God he could obtain complete moral perfection. As a result of his extreme mysticism he considered the means of grace a hindrance to find God. He held that man learns to know God by intuition. This is the height of subjectivism. Karlstadt taught that every congregation

---

[28] Cp. Thesis 62 of Ninety-five Theses. Karl Holl (see P. II, fn. 8), I, 288—301, shows that Grisar is wrong in charging that Luther invented a theory of the church to justify his defection from the church. The fact is that Luther's controversy with Rome grew out of his newly discovered concept of the church. Cp. F. E. Mayer, "The *Una Sancta* in Luther's Theology," *Christendom*, XII (1947), 315 (reprinted in *C. T. M.*, XVIII [1947], 801 ff.).

[29] *The Papacy at Rome Against Alveld* (1520) W. A., VI, 285—324. Cp. also *Open Letter to the Nobility*, W. A., VI, 404—469. Boehmer, ch. xxiv, discusses the significance of these writings for Luther's concept of the church. E. Rietschel, *Das Problem der unsichtbaren-sichtbaren Kirche bei Luther*, Leipzig, 1932. Herman Preus, *The Communion of Saints* (Minneapolis, Minn.: Augs. Publ. H., 1948), pp. 75—94. Seeberg, op. cit., IV, 278—307, discusses Luther's new understanding of the church.

[30] See Tschackert, pp. 121—200. See Schwiebert, pp. 535—70.

as a group of holy people is supreme, i. e., supreme to introduce a theocratic form of government with all the Old Testament laws.

Luther's second encounter with "enthusiasm" occurred in December, 1521, when some Anabaptists, known as the "Zwickau prophets," seriously disturbed the people of Wittenberg. They maintained that they had special revelations. A little later Thomas Muenzer with similar interests initiated a social revolt. This collapsed in the Peasants' War of 1525, when the princes resorted to strong measures to suppress the uprising. One result of this unfortunate affair was the common man's distrust of the political and ecclesiastical authorities. This distrust may have been responsible in part for the rise and spread of the Anabaptist movement.[31] The Anabaptists differed widely on important doctrines. Some were anti-Trinitarian, others restorationists, practically all were Pelagians. But they were united in their opposition to infant baptism, on the theory that the Holy Spirit works directly in the hearts of man without any means of grace. The Anabaptists were typical mystics and held that God speaks to man directly and that man obtains his knowledge of God immediately and intuitively. Such a view invariably leads to subjectivism and individualism. It isolates the individual, usually advocates the conventicle system, ignores the ecumenicity and continuity of the holy Christian church. The Anabaptists disparaged all social institutions, since they considered these only secular and external. Many Anabaptists held that civil government as well as domestic and commercial life lacks all spirituality and therefore is in reality an impediment to man's union with God. Thus the Anabaptists became ecclesiastical and social anarchists.

The third form of "enthusiasm" which confronted Luther was represented by Zwingli and Schwenkfeld.[32] Zwingli's "enthusiastic" inclinations came to the surface especially in his controversy with Luther concerning the Real Presence in the Holy Communion. Schwenkfeld, in his attempt to mediate between Zwingli and Luther, resorted to an extreme form of mysticism.

In his controversies with these various types of "enthusiasts" Luther was determined to set forth clearly both the objectivity of the means of grace and the necessity of ecclesiastical orders. The main issue in the antienthusiastic controversies centered in the meaning and significance of the means of grace. The 16th-century "enthusiasts" fully agreed with Luther that "the Holy Spirit calls, gathers, enlightens, and sanctifies the whole Christian church on earth and keeps it with Jesus Christ in the one true faith." But they disagreed totally as to the manner in which the Holy Spirit does His work. Several points of view converge in Luther's conflict with the "enthusiasts." First, Luther had freed himself from all dualistic Neoplatonism, which attempts to place man's body and his soul into two neatly fixed compartments and has devised one way to deal with the soul and another with the body. Luther had discarded such a division and always preached to the total man. Second, in his controversies with the "enthusiasts," Luther was led to lay increasingly greater emphasis on the historic Word and the incarnate Christ, the "only ladder to God."[33] The

---

31 Cp. Mennonites for bibliog.; Tschackert, p. 132 ff.

32 See "Zwingli" and "Schwenkfeld," P. IV, below.

33 Cp. Luther, *Against the Heavenly Prophets*, W. A., XVIII, 62—214, esp. Part Two, 134 ff. "Outwardly God works through the Word and internally through the Spirit."

Neoplatonic "division" of man was largely responsible for Rome's theory that the body is benefited by the mere performance of the sacramental rite. Against this view Luther emphasized the oral proclamation of the Word.[34] The "enthusiasts" claimed to hear God's Word directly. Against these Luther stressed the objective Word, whether written or spoken, as in absolution or fraternal admonition, or visible, as in the sacraments. Against the false objectivity of Rome with its *ex opere operato* theory, Luther maintained that it is only through faith that man receives the salutary benefits of the sacraments. Against the subjectivity of the Donatists and "enthusiasts," Luther insisted that the efficacy of the sacrament resides solely in the Word, not in the faith of the administrant or the recipient of the sacrament. In his defense of infant baptism, Luther had to bring out clearly the objectivity of Baptism, without, however, in any way denying that faith is necessary indeed for its salutary use. In short, Baptism is an act of God and not of the recipient of Baptism.[35] While the same principles were involved in the various debates concerning the Lord's Supper, the chief question in the latter centered about the sacramental union.

The second important result of the controversies with the "enthusiasts" was the Lutheran emphasis on the necessity of ecclesiastical orders, more specifically *the public ministry*. In Luther's opinion the establishment of the public ministry of the Word is the most important matter confronting the church, since God wills to give the Holy Spirit to those only who receive it through the sacred ministry.[36]

Against the hierarchical claims of Roman theology Luther stressed the doctrine of the universal priesthood of all believers. This doctrine not only conveys to all Christians the Gospel of Jesus Christ but also imposes on them the obligation to dispense these treasures in the Christian church.[37] In opposition to the "enthusiasts," however, Luther sharply distinguished between the universal priesthood, which commissioned

---

[34] *"Das Wort muss geschrienn werden."* The Gospel is nothing but a proclamation of the grace of God. W. A., XII, 259; I, 89—113. Much has been made of the fact that Luther strongly emphasized the oral proclamation and that he seemingly deplores the fact that the New Testament was written at all. True, he stated that the writing of the New Testament is an evidence of the lack of the Holy Spirit. But he adds that if wishing would remedy the situation, one could wish nothing more desirable than that all books would be abolished except the Bible. He stated that the Holy Spirit wanted the Gospel not only to be proclaimed orally but also to have it written so that if the shepherds failed in their proclamation, Christ's sheep might be led into the Scriptures to find pasture and protection. W. A. X, 625—27. In his comment on 1 John 5:13 Luther states that St. John's written letter is to serve as a means to come to faith and eternal life (John 20:31), and that we are to know that God's testimony comes to us through the oral voice or through the Scriptures (2 Tim. 3:16, 17; 1 Tim. 4:13). W. A., XX, 788—790. See S. A. Cp. Karl Barth, *Kirchliche Dogmatik* (Zürich, 1947), I, Part One, 89—113.

[35] See "The Means of Grace," and "Mennonites and Baptists," P. IV, below.

[36] W. A., XVII/2, 135, 20.

[37] Cp. C. F. W. Walther, *Kirche und Amt* (Erlangen: Andreas Deichert, 1865), pp. 30—54, 178—215. Th. Engelder, ed., *Walther and the Church* (St. Louis: C. P. H., 1938), pp. 58 f., 71 ff. L. W. Spitz, "The Universal Priesthood of Believers, with Luther's Comments," *C. T. M.*, XXIII (1952), p. 1 ff.

all Christians to administer the Office of the Keys, and the public ministry, instituted by God for the public and official exercise of this office. And in the appointment of men for this office, Luther held to the principle that God uses means to call and ordain men for this office. Therefore Luther considered the ministry the highest and most glorious office within the Christian church. He saw in the minister the instrument through which God performs the highest miracles, the conversion and salvation of men. In Luther's opinion the office of the local pastor is the highest office in the church. Luther is not concerned with the type of outward organization, and he was willing to return to the episcopal form of church government, provided the bishops permitted the preaching of the Gospel. His ideal, no doubt, was a congregation of genuine Christians. But he soon learned, especially from the Anabaptist attempt to establish visible groups of holy people, that his ideal could not be realized.[38] Luther's concern was primarily with the congregation, according to the principle that wherever the Word (i. e., the Gospel and the sacraments) is, there is the congregation; and, conversely, wherever the congregation is, there is preaching and administration of the sacraments. Luther expressed this in the epigrammatic formula: The Word is never without God's people, and God's people are never without the Word.

Luther was well aware of the danger lurking in a misuse of the supremacy of the local congregation. In the Anabaptist movement it led to anarchistic separatism and an unbridled individualism, which made the subjective opinion not only of the congregation but ultimately of the individual the absolute and final authority in matters of religion. Against a false congregationalism, Luther early advocated a form of supervision of the local congregation which would assure as far as possible the pure preaching of the Word and the correct administration of the sacraments. Luther did not favor the so-called *Landeskirche*, and when he called on the princes to assist in the supervision of the churches, he thought of them merely as "emergency bishops." Furthermore, the financial situation of the common people was such that they could not support the public ministry, but had to depend upon the right of patronage. No doubt, the danger of a general revolution throughout Germany prompted Luther to urge the government to exercise its authority also in the area of church government in order to maintain order and decency in those turbulent days.[39]

In his controversy with both Rome and the Anabaptists, Luther advocated the principle of the proper distinction between church and state, without an absolute separation of the two. Against the Roman view that there is only one seat of power and that secular power is subject to the spiritual power, Luther maintained the sovereignty of each in its sphere. The Anabaptists disenfranchised themselves completely from the state and thought only in terms of a spiritual kingdom. Against their complete denial of the need for a secular

[38] This is still a basic principle with the Mennonites.

[39] See Seeberg, p. 295 ff. Luther, Pref. to Small C.; *Address to Christian Nobility*, 1520, W. A., VI, 404—469; *Secular Authority, to What Extent It Should Be Obeyed*, W. A., XI, 245—281. George F. Hall, "Church and State," *What Lutherans Are Thinking* (Columbus: Wartburg Press; 1947), pp. 500 ff. P. F. Siegel, "Civil Government," in Laetsch (see fn. 23), I, 508 ff. F. Edward Cranz, *An Essay on the Development of Luther's Thought on Justice, Law and Society* (Cambridge, Mass.: Harvard University Press, 1959).

state, Luther maintained that the state is indispensable.

Luther's distinction between church and state was the practical application of the distinction between Law and Gospel, and accordingly he held that the secular government is concerned with the physical welfare of man, including also the punishment of the evildoer. The church deals only with spiritual matters, such as the forgiveness of sins, eternal life and salvation.

SECTION II
The Lutheran Confessions

The Lutheran particular creeds were prepared and adopted during the fifty-year period 1528—1579 and are comprehended in the *Book of Concord*.[40] This collection of creedal statements contains the answer of Lutheranism to the many controversies which disturbed the church during the 16th century. This century saw a revival of practically every view and aberration which had occurred during the preceding centuries of the Christian church: Anti-Trinitarianism and humanism; Pelagianism and synergism; determinism and Manichaeanism; spiritualism and "enthusiasm"; sacerdotalism and sacramentalism; mysticism and asceticism; perfectionism and antinomianism; chiliasm and apocalypticism; Donatism and Novatianism. The *Book of Concord* deals either explicitly or implicitly with every doctrinal aberration of the contemporary period and, for that matter, of every period in the church's history.

THE VARIOUS CONFESSIONS

The signers of the *Book of Concord* included the three ecumenical creeds in their creedal statements as a public testimony of their being in the continuity of the Christian church of the West and of their conviction that their doctrine was in accord with the consensus of the holy Christian church.[41]

The *Augsburg Confession of 1530* is the basic Lutheran confession. It was submitted to Charles V, Emperor of the Holy Roman Empire, by the Elector of Saxony and other German princes and cities to give a summary of the doctrines which were preached in their territories and to give the reasons why certain rites had been abolished. The first twenty-one Articles set forth very briefly the doctrines of God (I), Man (II, XVIII, XIX), Redemption (III, XXI), Justification (IV), the Ministry (V), the New Obedience (VI, XX), the Church (VII, VIII), the Sacraments (IX—XIII), Ecclesiastical Order (XIV), Church Rites (XV), the Government (XVI), Last Things (XVII). In Articles XXII to XXVIII the reasons are given why the Evangelicals had abolished such "abuses" as the Holy Communion under one element, the compulsory celibacy of

---

[40] First German edition, 1580; official Latin edition, 1584. Lutherans frequently designate their confessions as symbols. On the interpretation of the Book of Concord see Arthur Carl Piepkorn, "Suggested Principles for a Hermeneutics of the Lutheran Symbols," *C. T. M.*, XXIX (1958), 1—24.

[41] Cp. F. Bente, p. 91 ff. For further historical material on the Catholic Creeds see F. J. Badcock, *The History of the Creeds*, 2d ed. (London: S. P. C. K., 1938), and J. N. D. Kelly, *Early Christian Creeds*, 2d ed. (London: Longmans, 1960).

the clergy, the Mass as a propitiatory sacrifice for the living and the dead; monastic vows.[42]

Melanchthon is usually considered the author of the Augsburg Confession, though the document is based to a large extent on the Schwabach and Marburg Articles of October, 1529, prepared by Luther, and the Torgau Articles, prepared by a committee in April, 1530. Melanchthon took the liberty of making changes in virtually every subsequent printing. Some changes were in the interest of greater clarity. But in the 1540 edition, known as the *Variata*, he seems to have made at least one change to make the document more acceptable to the Calvinist party.[43]

The *Apology of the Augsburg Confession* was prepared by Melanchthon upon his return from Augsburg and published in April, 1531, as the Evangelicals' answer to the papalist Confutation. This Roman document, drawn up by the Emperor's theological advisers, asserted that it had refuted all major points of the Augsburg Confession, and on this basis the Emperor demanded in effect that the Evangelicals cease and desist from their preaching and practice. In four-teen articles Melanchthon showed that (1) the papal Confutation had failed to refute the Augsburg Confession and (2) that the issues between the Romanists and Evangelicals were much more basic than a mere difference concerning ceremonies. The Apology shows that the two parties were oriented in basically different theologies: the one in a theology of the Law, teaching that man must seek his salvation in his own good life; the other in the theology of the Gospel, teaching that man is justified only by faith in the "foreign" righteousness of Christ.[44]

The *Smalcald Articles* were drafted in 1536 by Luther at the request of the Saxon Elector; they were to serve as the Evangelical statement of faith at the council which Pope Paul III had convoked by Mantua in 1537. The Elector's original plan, to have the representatives of the Smalcald League formally adopt the Articles at the February, 1537, assembly, failed. Nevertheless, all but six of the theologians at the meeting subscribed the Articles for their own persons. Subsequently many provincial *corpora doctrinae* reproduced them, and

---

[42] Gustav Plitt, *Einleitung in die Augustana* (Erlangen, 1867). M. Reu, *The Augsburg Confession* (Columbus: Wartburg Press, 1930). F. Pieper, *Das Grundbekenntnis der ev.-luth. Kirche* (St. Louis: C. P. H., 1880 and 1930). Wilhelm Maurer, "Melanchthon as Author of the Augsburg Confession," in *Lutheran World*, VII (1960), 153—167; Heinrich Bornkamm, *Der authentische lateinische Text der Confessio Augustana* (Heidelberg: Carl Winter, 1956).

[43] Art. X. See F. E. Mayer, "Artikel X der Variata," in *C. T. M.*, II (1931), 594 ff., and "Ist die Variata synergistisch und majoristisch?" ibid., VI (1935), 254 ff. — On Melanchthon, see H. Engelland, *Melanchthon, Glauben und Handeln;* Clyde Leonard Manschreck's somewhat uneven *Melanchthon, the Quiet Reformer* (Nashville: Abingdon Press, 1958); Robert Stupperich, "The Development of Melanchthon's Theological-Philosophical World View," *Lutheran World*, VII (1960), 168—180; R. R. Caemmerer, "The Melanchthonian Blight," *C. T. M.*, XVIII (1947), 321 ff.; and the papers read at the Melanchthon quadricentennial convocations at Concordia Seminary, St. Louis, in 1960 and published in *C. T. M.*, XXXI (1960), 468—481, 553—546.

[44] In some editions of the Lutheran Confessions the articles are numbered to correspond as far as possible with those of the A. C.; others use two numbers, thus II(I), the first indicating the article of the A. C., and the second the sequence of the Ap. For abbreviations see Appendix C.

the *Book of Concord* gave them full symbolical status.[45]

The *Tract Concerning the Authority and Primacy of the Pope* was written by Melanchthon in six days during and at the direction of the February, 1537, meeting of the Smalcald League. The tract is designed as an appendix to the Augsburg Confession and the Apology in rejecting explicitly the pretensions of the pope and his hierarchy.[46]

Luther's *Large and Small Catechisms* were written simultaneously and appeared on the market in the spring of 1529. Both are an exposition of the three traditional chief parts, the Decalog, the Creed, the Our Father, to which Luther added two chief parts, Baptism and the Lord's Supper.[47]

The *Formula of Concord* is a carefully prepared doctrinal summary in answer to the several controversies which disturbed the German Lutheran church from 1548 to 1578. In eleven articles it sets forth and defends the position of Luther in the various intra-Lutheran controversies.

The Synergistic Controversy raised the question whether man in any way has the native ability to co-operate in his conversion. The Formula of Concord followed Luther's *De servo arbitrio* in setting forth that it is not man's concern to solve the apparent contradiction between God's universal grace and human responsibility, nor is it man's business to answer the question: "Why some, others not?" Article I is directed against those overzealous Lutherans who held that original sin is actually man's essential nature, and Article II defends divine monergism against those who held that man has native powers to co-operate in his conversion. Article III sets forth the Lutheran doctrine on justification by faith and rejects the view which ascribes justification to Christ's indwelling. Article IV is directed against those who confuse the doctrines of justification and sanctification.

The proper distinction between Law and Gospel has been called the "especial brilliant light of the Reformation." The Formula of Concord maintains this proper distinction against the antinomians, who held that contrition is not wrought by the Law, but by the Gospel (Art. V), and against the perfectionists, who ignored completely that throughout his life the justified man is a sinner still and in need of the preaching of the Law (Art. VI).[48] The Formula of Concord devotes much space to a clear presentation of the Lutheran doctrine of the Real Presence against some followers of Melanchthon, who for rationalistic and unionistic reasons secretly favored the Calvinistic view that Christ is present in

---

[45] Hans Volz and Heinrich Ulbricht, eds., *Urkunden und Aktenstücke zur Geschichte von Martin Luther's Schmalkaldischen Artikeln 1536—1574* (Berlin: Walter de Gruyter und Co., 1957).

[46] Luther (W. A., L, 160 ff.). *Die Bekenntnisschriften,* pp. XXIV to XXVII.

[47] The Small Catechism also includes a section on "How the Unlearned Should Be Taught to Confess" and two appendices, one consisting of forms for table and private daily prayers, the other the "Table of Duties." Complete editions of the *Book of Concord* include as supplements to the Small Catechism the *Traubüchlein* of 1529 and the *Taufbüchlein* of 1526. — W. A., XXXI, 123 ff. contains a summary of the research done in this area. Cp. M. Reu, *Quellen zur Geschichte des kirchl. Unterrichts im ev. Deutschland* (Guetersloh, 1904—1927), 8 vols. The Large C. is chiefly a collection of catechetical sermons preached by Luther in Wittenberg.

[48] The heading "The Third Use of the Law" has led to serious misunderstandings of the meaning of Art. VI, Cp. "Law and Gospel," below.

the Holy Supper only in a spiritual manner (Art. VII). Inasmuch as the denial of the Real Presence was predicated on a false Christology, the Formula of Concord was compelled to present the doctrine of Christ's personal union in considerable detail, especially that phase of Christology called "communication of attributes" (Art. VIII).[49]

Article IX briefly sets forth that the manner of Christ's descent into hell is a mystery, but that its purpose is to comfort us. After the Lutheran armies had been defeated in 1548, some Lutheran theologians advocated the reintroduction of such abolished rites and ceremonies as were considered indifferent in order to obviate worse consequences. The Formula of Concord, however, maintained that a church rite ceases to be indifferent when it is introduced or dropped to avoid persecution (Art. X). Article XI deals with the doctrine of God's gracious election. This doctrine was not in dispute among Lutherans, though it could easily have become a very controversial matter.[50] The Formula of Concord (Art. XI) directs all who have questions concerning their election to the serious, efficacious, and universal will of God revealed in the Gospel.

The Confessional Principle of Lutheranism

The confessional principle of Lutheranism differs basically from that of the Reformed bodies. Lutheranism accepts its Confessions as a joint and unanimous reply to God's message in the Scriptures and as the doctrinal norm and standard for its teachers and members.

In its confessional loyalty Lutheranism accepts wholeheartedly and without equivocation the confessional writings prepared by Luther or his close associates or his loyal followers. Non-Lutherans especially in the anticreedal churches, may interpret the Lutheran confessional loyalty as mere hero worship. It is of course true, as the Worms Luther monument and as Kaulbach's famous fresco of the Reformation point out, that Luther occupies a unique and singular position among all the great reformers. This is not due to his magnetic personality.[51] The Lutheran's loyalty to the Lutheran Confessions is justified only by a personal conviction that they clearly state the Gospel message, which assures the sin-burdened conscience of God's unmerited grace in Christ, and correctly portray the nature and function of the Christian's faith. For this reason the Lutheran Confessions are accepted as the standard of the Christian proclamation; however, not as though Lutherans had two sources of doctrine, the Scriptures and the Confessions. Lutherans accept only the Scriptures as the source and norm of truth. But they believe that their Confessions are in full conformity with the Scriptures, and in that sense are a "derived" rule and standard according to which

---

[49] This was the work chiefly of Martin Chemnitz, considered by many the prince of Lutheran dogmaticians. Cp. *De duabus naturis in Christo* (Jena, 1570). He also compiled the "Catalog of Testimonies," an appendix to the Lutheran Confessions, which shows that Lutheran Christology is in harmony with Scripture and the ancient fathers. Cp. C. P. Krauth, p. 316 ff. Philip Schaff is mistaken in his stricture that Lutheran Christology, specifically the communication of divine attributes to the Man Christ Jesus, starts from the preconceived view of the Real Presence (*Creeds*, I, 285 ff.).

[50] In America this doctrine led to a long and bitter controversy between the Ohio and Missouri Synod and divided practically all German and Norwegian American Lutherans into two opposing groups.

[51] Cp. W. Walther, *Charakter Luthers* (Leipzig, 1917), *passim*.

the preaching in Lutheran churches is judged.[52]

Wherever Lutherans have accepted the Confessions in this way they also have demanded that their churches and teachers commit themselves to the doctrinal content of the Confessions *quia*, i. e., "because" they are in accord with the Scriptures, not *quatenus*, i. e., "in so far as" they agree with Scripture. A *quatenus* subscription is in reality no subscription at all.[53] There is no uniform practice in all parts of Lutheranism as to the extent of the confessional pledge. In not a few sections of the Lutheran church the confessional "oath" covers only the Augsburg Confession. Since World War II European Lutherans have taken the Confessions more seriously than they had at the turn of the century.[54]

The Lutherans consider the Confessions not only a doctrinal standard; they are more than a body of truth; they become a public confession, a confessional act. They are, in the first place, the believer's joyful response to God's gracious offer in the Gospel. The Lutheran Confessions are kerygmatic and prayable, i. e., they belong in the pulpit and the pew. They are a doxology. In the second place the Confessions estab-

[52] In the "Comp. Sum." '(Th. D.) of the F. of C., nearly 8,200 theologians and leading laymen declared in 1580 that in their churches the Lutheran Confessions "have always been regarded as the summary and norm of the pure doctrine, which Dr. Luther, of blessed memory, has drawn from God's Word and firmly established against the Papacy and other sects," and they add the solemn declaration that the Sacred Scriptures alone are the source and norm of doctrine, a position granted to no human writing. From the conviction that their confessional statements were in full accord with God's Word the signers to the *Book of Concord* publicly avowed before God's judgment throne and in the presence of the entire Christian church that they would abide by this unanimously approved rule and norm of doctrine. In the Preface to the *Book of Concord* these same men declared: "We are determined not to depart even a finger's breadth either from the subject matter or the terminology of these [the Lutheran Confessions], but with the Holy Spirit's aid to abide by the unanimous agreement and to examine all controversies according to this norm." Cp. C. P. Krauth, Ch. v: "The Confessional Principle of the Conservative Reformation," esp. pp. 167—79; also Schmauck and Benze, chs. xvii, xviii; Engelder et al., *Popular Symbolics*, p. 16; F. Bente, p. 8. See also Nils A. Dahl, "The Lutheran Exegete and the Confessions of His Church," *Lutheran World*, VI (1959), 2—10, and Erwin L. Lueker, "Functions of Symbols and of Doctrinal Statements," *C. T. M.*, XXXII (1961), 274—285.

[53] The *quia* subscription is not to be understood as giving an infallible character 'to the Confessions. It does not cover historical facts, specific interpretations, lines of argument. Cp. C. F. W. Walther, "Why Should Our Pastors and Teachers Subscribe Unconditionally to the Symbolical Writings of Our Church?" trans. and condensed by A. C. W. Guebert, *C. T. M.*, XVIII (1947), 241 ff.; Krauth, 179 ff.; Edm. Schlink, p. 50 ff.; Willard D. Allbeck, p. 8 ff. See also Piepkorn (fn. 40 above)

[54] The German theologians have always manifested a deep academic interest in the history of the Lutheran Confessions and have produced a tremendous literature in this area. The *Kirchenkampf* in Germany seemingly made the Lutheran Confessions a really relevant factor. The ecumenical movement also helped to arouse new interest in the Lutheran Confessions. The first Bad Boll Conference in 1948 was devoted entirely to a discussion of the significance of the Augsburg Confession. Cp. F. E. Mayer, *The Story of Bad Boll* (St. Louis: C. P. H., 1948). During the paper shortage after the war the U. S. Military Government granted the necessary paper for a 5,000-copy edition of Schlink, op. cit., (1946 ed.).

lish the consensus with the fathers and with their own contemporaries. The act of confessing places the present church in the continuity of faith and is a public testimony that she shares the conflicts and conquests of the faithful of all ages. And finally Lutherans believe that loyalty to the confessions is a precious heritage which each generation must recapture for itself and transmit to its descendants. Lutherans believe that divine truth is absolute, has not changed since Apostolic times, will not change during future generations, in accord with Jesus' saying that His words shall never pass away.[55] The permanence of the Lutheran confessional principle is expressed in the slogan:

God's Word and Luther's doctrine pure
Shall to eternity endure.

SECTION III

The Formal and Material Principles of Lutheran Theology

The Formal Principle

The source of doctrine, or the formal principle of Lutheran theology, is *sola Scriptura*, Scripture alone. It does seem strange that with its alleged emphasis on the sole authority of Scripture the Lutheran church nowhere has a specific article setting forth its attitude toward Holy Scripture. By contrast the early Reformed Confessions have an elaborate statement concerning the place and the scope of Scripture, including even a list of all the books which are considered canonical. The Lutheran Confessions have no specific article dealing with Holy Scripture for three reasons.

1. The medieval Western church had never questioned the divine inspiration and authority of the canonical writings of the Old and the New Testament.[56] In their conflict with Rome the Lutherans could take for granted that they and their opponents accepted the Bible as God's Word. For this reason the Augsburg Confession states repeatedly that the doctrines proclaimed among the Evangelicals are taken solely from Holy Scripture and asks that all criticisms of the Lutheran preaching be examined in the light of Scripture.[57] Throughout the Apology, Melanchthon constantly appeals to Sacred Scripture, pleads with the Romanists to compare the Evangelicals' doctrines with Scripture, and complains that they simply ignore the many clear passages which show that faith alone justifies man; in short, says Melanchthon, all of Scripture supports the

[55] The Lutheran church believes that the symbols in the *Book of Concord* are a correct formulation of the doctrinal content of the Sacred Scriptures. This conviction accounts in part for the fact that German scholars have spared no effort to establish the original text and to direct the reader to the pertinent material which will enable him to understand the Confessions.

[56] See the relevant sections in P. II, above.

[57] See Pref. to A. C. In the concluding paragraph of the doctrinal part of the A. C. the confessors state that the foregoing 21 articles contain about the sum of their doctrine, in which there is nothing that varies from the Holy Scriptures or the Catholic church or the Roman (i. e., the Western) church.

doctrine proclaimed by the Evangelicals.[58] Likewise the Smalcald Articles declare most emphatically that God's Word alone, and no one else, not even angels, shall determine the doctrine.[59] The authors of the Formula of Concord state specifically that the only rule and norm to judge doctrines are the prophetic and apostolic Scriptures of the Old and the New Testament, the pure fountain of Israel. All other writings of ancient and modern teachers are in no wise equal to Scripture, but subject to it, and at best only witnesses to the truth.[60] And, finally, the Preface to the entire Book of Concord is in reality only a further exposition of the doxology in the opening paragraph that in the last days of the world's history God has granted a reappearance of the light of His Gospel and Word, "through which alone we receive true salvation." In this Preface the authors of the Book of Concord describe the Augsburg Confession as having been prepared from the Word of God and the most holy writings of the prophets and apostles and as having been accepted as the norm and guide for teachers. They deplore the various controversies within the Lutheran church, which would have been avoided if all had faithfully persevered in the pure doctrine of God's Word and regulated their teaching according to the rule of the divine Word handed down to posterity in a godly and excellent way through its publicly approved symbols. And of the Formula of Concord, the last of the Lutheran symbols, the leaders of Lutheranism stated that they accepted it because it agreed with the Word of God and also with the Augsburg Confession. Like a red thread the sole authority of the Scriptures runs throughout the Lutheran Confessions.

2. Lutheran theology usually distinguishes carefully between symbolics and dogmatics. "Symbolics" takes many things for granted which "dogmatics" must discuss in detail. In particular, "symbolics" is the study of the theses and antitheses in a given controversy and the examination of the church's answer to the specific problem, not only as a statement of truth but also as a confessional act. Symbolics has a doxological [61] and a somewhat existential character. It deals with actual life situations and makes no attempt to present the Christian faith in every point nor in a systematic and comprehensive manner.

3. The Lutheran Confessions have no special article on the divine character of Scripture, because their interest was centered so prominently on a Christocentric approach to Scripture. They have no interest in an atomistic, proof-text, concordance approach to the Scriptures. The Confessions state that Scripture must always be presented according to its two main parts, Law and Gospel, for God's two most significant works are first to frighten and slay man and then to justify and vivify the frightened person. Thus, according to the Lutheran Confessions, the main thought of all the Gospels and Epistles of the entire Scriptures is that we should believe that in Christ Jesus through faith we have a gracious God.[62] The Apology points out that "enthusiasts," humanists, and rationalists dissect the Scriptures into individual Bible texts and explain the articles concerning the righteousness of

---

[58] Ap. XII, 66; IV, 102; 107 ff.; XX, 2; II, 50.

[59] S. A., P. II, 15, 10.

[60] See F. C. Ep., Of the Summary Concept, 2.

[61] The title page of the A. C. contains the quotation: "I will speak of Thy testimonies also before kings and will not be ashamed," Ps. 119:46. Cp. Allbeck, 3 ff.

[62] Ap., IV, 87, 102; XII, 53; XX, 2.

faith in a philosophical and a Jewish manner. But in this atomistic Biblicist manner they actually abolish the doctrine of Christ as Mediator. Without the knowledge of the Gospel the Bible remains a meaningless and useless book.[63] But when the Scriptures are seen as Gospel, as *evangelium*, the Word of God becomes the sanctuary above all sanctuaries, which sanctifies the person and everything he does.[64]

Wherever this Word is preached, it becomes the power of God, an active and creative Word, and engenders the faith which accepts the Bible as Christ's inerrant and final Word. This belief does not depend on rational arguments, but it is a divinely wrought faith.[65] The Lutheran Confessions take for granted that a Christian accepts the Scriptures as God's Word, both as God speaking in this Word here and now and as God's Word spoken in times past through the holy writers.[66] In Lutheran theology the believer does not accept the absolute authority of the Scriptures as an a priori truth, but because he has learned to know Christ as his divine Savior; has experienced the power of His Word in the Scriptures upon his heart; and relies implicitly on Christ's own statement concerning the divine character of the Scriptures. It is therefore proper to say that the formal principle of Lutheran theol-

ogy is entirely Christological. This holds true with the same force also of the material principle, or the central thought.

Justification by faith is usually referred to as *articulus stantis et cadentis ecclesiae*, the article by which the church stands and falls. When speaking of the material principle of theology, Lutherans do not have in mind a basic principle according to which a body of doctrines may be developed. The material principle of Lutheran theology is in reality only a synopsis and summary of the Christian truth. When Lutheran theologians speak of justification by faith as the material principle of theology, they merely wish to indicate that all theological thinking must begin at this article, center in it, and culminate in it. As the various facets of the diamond catch, refract, reflect, the light, so the phrase "justification by faith alone" gives brilliance to every phase of Christian revelation, and in turn each facet of Christian truth sheds new brilliance on this so-called central doctrine, whether it is viewed as justification by faith, or as the work of Christ, or as the distinction between Law and Gospel, or as faith in Christ, or as the doctrine of the "righteousness before God."[67]

In the Confessions this doctrine is usually presented either as the doctrine

[63] Ap., IV, 376.

[64] Large C., 3d Com., 91, 92, 100, 101.

[65] H. Echternach, "The Lutheran Doctrine of the '*Autopistia*' of Holy Scripture," trans. J. T. Mueller, *C. T. M.*, XXIII (1952), 241, 272.

[66] In Lutheran theology the Scriptures are both *Deus locutus* and *Deus loquens* (God who has spoken and God now speaking). Dialectical theology also employs this terminology. But it views the Scriptures as *Deus loquens* primarily in such a way as virtually to deny the objectivity of the Scriptures. Cp., for instance, Emil Brunner, *The Divine-Human Encounter*, trans. A. W. Loos (Phila.: Westminster Press, 1943). Another approach to Luther's concept of the Scriptures is discussed by T. A. Kantonen, pp. 113—24. On the attitude of the dogmaticians of the era of Lutheran Orthodoxy to the Sacred Scriptures, see Robert Preus, *The Inspiration of Scripture*, 2d ed. (Mankato: Lutheran Synod Book Co., 1957).

[67] See Luther, *Pref. to Galatians*, W. A., XL/1, 33—37 also *Pref. to Latin Works*, 1545, W. A., LIV, 179—187.

>f Christ's work or the doctrine of justi-
ication. The Formula of Concord states:

> This article concerning justification by
> faith is the chief article in the entire
> Christian doctrine, without which no
> poor conscience can have any firm con-
> solation or can truly know the riches of
> the grace of Christ.[68]

The Apology summarizes the entire
Scriptures in terms such as "the Gospel
message," "absolution," "the forgiveness
of sin," "justification," or in such concepts as God's new relation to man and
man's new relation to God. Melanchthon
states:

> In this controversy [that men obtain the
> remission of sin through faith alone and
> are justified] the chief topic of Christian
> doctrine is treated, which, when rightly
> understood, illumines and amplifies the
> honor of Christ and brings necessary
> and most abundant consolation to de-
> vout consciences.[69]

When in 1537 the Lutherans were confronted by the question whether for the
sake of peace they could yield anything,
Luther states concerning the "office and
work of Jesus Christ, or our redemption":

> Of this article nothing can be yielded or
> surrendered, even though heaven and
> earth, and everything should sink to
> ruin (Acts 4:12; Is. 53:5). Upon this
> article all things depend which we teach
> and practice in opposition to the pope,
> the devil, and the world. Therefore we
> must be sure concerning this doctrine
> and not doubt; otherwise all is lost,
> and the pope and the devil in all things
> gain the victory and suit over us.[70]

Only within the frame of reference of
the doctrine of justification can any
Christian doctrine be considered in a
salutary way. The doctrine of justification is, as it were, the strand on which
all the pearls of Christian revelation are
strung.[71]

SECTION IV

The Soteriological Approach to Christian Doctrine

The Lutheran Confessions present all
Christian doctrine from the soteriological standpoint, that is, from the meaning each has for our salvation. Each and
every doctrine of Christian revelation
must be viewed *in actu*, not only *in
statu;* it must be within the focus of
a real spiritual problem and be presented only in its soteriological significance.[72]

---

[68] F. C., Th. D., III, 6.

[69] Ap., IV, 2. Cp. A. C., XXVI, 4; XXVIII, 48.

[70] S. A., P. II, 5.

[71] The charge is sometimes made that Lutheranism overstresses the
doctrine of justification by faith alone so much that it loses sight of the
significance of other doctrines, such as sanctification. There have been
periods in the history of Lutheranism when the theologians' exclusive
concern seemed to be to present the doctrine of justification precisely and
as a result treated all doctrines in a vacuum. But genuine Lutheran
theology, while maintaining a careful distinction between the various doctrines, e. g., justification and sanctification, will never permit a separation
of Christian doctrines into isolated compartments.

[72] Symbolics may therefore serve admirably as an introduction to
Lutheran dogmatics. Cp. Schlink, op. cit. (Appendix: "Anleitung zur
dogmatischen Arbeit"), pp. 398—432.

Theology

The Lutheran Confessions make no attempt to define God. This may be due in part to the antipathy of the Reformers during the early days against the scholastic method, which tried to define God in purely metaphysical terminology without any regard or reference to the soteriological implications. The Lutheran Confessions recognize that it is impossible to define the Infinite, chiefly because the transcendent God reveals Himself only as He enters into a personal relationship with man, i. e., God confronts man either as the Lawgiver or as the Law Remover. And conversely man's relation to God is either that of being under God's wrath because of man's transgressions or that of being under God's grace because of Christ's redemptive work in freeing man from the demand and the threats of the Law.[73]

The Lutheran Confessions lay great emphasis on the reality of the wrath of God, not as an academic question, but as real life experience. The Lutheran Confessions say that God's Law is man's dreadful enemy either inasmuch as the Law makes presumptuous hypocrites, or inasmuch as it causes rebellion against God, or because it creates terrors of conscience and leads to despair. At any rate it always increases man's enmity against God. The Law demands perfect obedience of man without in any way helping man to render it, and at the same time reveals the wrath of God and constantly accuses man and shows man the "angry God."[74] Thus the Law becomes a dreadful thunderbolt (*Donneraxt*) with which God knocks into a heap both the manifest sinners and the vaunted hypocrites and drives them all together into terrors and despair. Only from the revelation of God's Word does man fully understand the greatness of God's wrath, when the Law shows man his dreadful condition and the reality of the wrath of God.[75]

But God terrifies and slays the sinner in order to come to His real work, namely, to quicken and comfort the frightened sinner, to whom God under the Law is the object of his fear and terror, but under the Gospel becomes a lovable object, *obiectum amabile*.[76] Lutheran theology holds that unless this distinction between the Law and the Gospel is strictly observed, and unless the fact is kept in mind that God is both a God of wrath and a God of love, terrible confusion will result. The resultant description of God will be a caricature of God and lead the sinner either to false security or to despair. On occasion the Lutheran Creeds picture God as the God of wrath (Law); and again as One who "has opened to us the depth of His paternal heart and His absolute, perfect indescribable love."[77] In Lutheran theology even the words "to have a God

---

[73] F. E. Mayer, "Reflections on Trinity Sunday," *C. T. M.*, XXI (1950), p. 451 ff.; John Theodore Mueller, "The Concept of God in the Lutheran Confessions," *C. T. M.*, XXVI (1955), 1—16; L. W. Spitz, "The Soteriological Aspect of the Doctrine of the Holy Trinity According to the Lutheran Confessions," ibid., pp. 161—171.

[74] See Large C., I, 16, 31, 37, 38. *Ap.*, II, 42; IV, 9, 79; XII, 34 (cp. the German text). Melanchthon complains that his opponents were "inexperienced theologians," for they could not understand the doctrine of the grace of God, because they had never experienced the "terrors of conscience."

[75] Ap., IV, 36, 37, 40, 62, 295 (*lex semper accusat*); S. A., P. III, Arts. I, II, III (Of Sin, the Law, Repentance).

[76] Ap., IV, 129. Cp. XII, 51 f.; F. C., Th. D., V, 12—15.

[77] Large C., Creed, 64.

are given a soteriological meaning, for these words are said to mean that the Christian has someone to whom he can flee for refuge in every trial, and from whom he can seek good for every life situation; in short, that he trusts implicitly in God's never-ending love. Such faith is well anchored, according to the Confessions, because God is like a fountain whose supply becomes the richer and purer, the more water it gushes forth.[78]

The doctrine of the Holy Trinity is not presented as a cold dogmatic proposition, nor has it been included in the Augsburg Confession merely to give historic and "legal" standing to the Evangelical party. Lutherans affirm the Quicunque (Athanasian Creed), which maintains that whoever will be saved must worship the Unity in Trinity and the Trinity in Unity. The Confessions carefully distinguish the three Persons and yet maintain the absolute Unity. However, the Trinity in Unity and the Unity in Persons is not presented for mere contemplation, but for our salvation. Soteriologically this means, on the one hand, that the One Eternal has redeemed us, and, on the other hand, that all three Persons have co-operated in each specific phase of the divine work. The Confessions state:

[In the Three Articles God reveals that] He has created us for the purpose that He might redeem and sanctify us; furthermore that He might bestow everything upon us in heaven and on earth,

He has given us His Son and the Holy Ghost, through whom He brought us to Himself. We could never have been able to know the Father's grace without our Lord Jesus Christ, who is a mirror of the paternal heart and outside of whom we behold only an angry and dreadful Judge. But of Christ we could know nothing either except the Spirit had revealed it to us.[79]

The Christian is instructed to view the divine work of creation in its soteriological significance, since God is our Creator that we may benefit from Christ's work. For that reason the Confessions are concerned, not with describing the creation of the world as a historic fact in the distant past, but rather with establishing the significance of the creation for the individual: "God has created me and all creatures."[80] It is this soteriological emphasis, which prompts the Lutheran Confessions to say that God has done this not from any motive of self-glorification, from *eros*, an egotistic love, but as a loving Father who provides His children with all they need in temporal and spiritual blessings.[81]

Anthropology

MAN AS GOD'S CREATION

The Lutheran Confessions present the doctrine of man under two aspects: (1) man as God's creation, (2) man as a sinner. Against all Neoplatonic theories the Lutheran Confessions maintain that the total man — body and soul —

---

[78] Ibid., I, 1, 4, 14, 15; Sec. Pet., 56.

[79] Ibid., Creed, 64. The nineteenth-century German liberals held that by retaining the ancient doctrine of the Trinity the Lutheran Reformers only caused confusion. See esp. A. Harnack, *Dogmeng.*, III, 741. The fact is, of course, that Athanasius long before had won the battle against all forms of monarchianism by setting forth the soteriological significance of the Trinity. J. L. Neve, *History*, I, 114 ff.

[80] At this point Lutheranism departs basically from the position of Rome's philosophy, from the Calvinistic doctrine of God's sovereignty, and from liberalism's anthropological motto of the universal fatherhood of God and brotherhood of man. See the respective sections.

[81] Large C., Creed, 17—24, 28—30, 63, 69; Lord's Prayer, 51. Cp. Koestlin-Hay, II, 208, 284. A Nygren, *Agape and Eros*, I, 108 ff.; II, 463 ff.

is God's handiwork and that the body, no less than the soul, must be held in high regard.[82] This means in the first place that, in spite of his sin and corruption, man is still God's creation.[83] Though subject to bondage because of man's sin, the entire creation is given to man for his use and enjoyment.[84] Lutheranism holds that all creatures, including social institutions, are God's means for man's temporal welfare. This applies especially to the estate of matrimony, based upon the "attraction" of husband and wife to each other.[85]

This means, secondly, that the total man, body and soul, has been redeemed by Christ, has been sanctified by the Holy Spirit. Lutheranism teaches that Baptism is one of God's means by which He brings the blessings won by Christ not only to the soul but to the body as well. Baptism benefits the entire person; in particular, it assures the total man not only that his soul shall live forever, but that in the resurrection of the body the Holy Spirit will complete His work of sanctifying the entire person.[86]

MAN AS SINNER

In agreement with all branches of Christendom the Lutheran Confessions declare that man lost his original righteousness, or the image of God. However, the Confessions refer to man's original state only in passing and describe it briefly as the state in which man knew, feared, and trusted in God. The lost image will be restored again in man's regeneration, when he receives the true knowledge of God.[87]

The Confessions approach the doctrine of sin solely from the soteriological aspect, never as a mere academic question or even as a problem in sociology or biology. The apparent overemphasis on or preoccupation with sin in Lutheran theology has led some to view Lutheran theology as rather morbid; however, the detailed discussion of sin was necessary not only because of the antithesis in Roman and Zwinglian theology, but primarily because of man's natural inclination to deny his utter corruption and to boast of his own worth and dignity.[88]

---

[82] Neoplatonic views are largely responsible for the ascetic practices in Roman theology and the heavy emphasis in Calvinism on mortification and contemplation of the future life as means to subdue the "body." This view prevails in some modern cults which see sin primarily as residing in the body, while the soul is considered good and able to return to God. See Jaroslav Pelikan, "The Doctrine of Creation in Lutheran Confessional Theology," *C. T. M.* XXVI (1955), 569—579, as well as Paul Meehl, Richard Klann, Alfred Schmieding, Kenneth Breimeier and Sophie Schroeder-Sloman, *What, Then, Is Man? — A Symposium of Theology, Psychology, and Psychiatry* (St. Louis: C. P. H., c. 1958), especially chs. ii, ix—xiii.

[83] See F. C., Th. D., I, 33 ff.

[84] Large C., Com. I, 26.

[85] Ibid., Com. IV, 116, 109; Com. VI, 206—8. Ap., XXIII, 3, 7, 19, 32, 52 f., 63, where mandatory celibacy is condemned. Cp. A. C., XXIII.

[86] Large C., Art. III, 57 f. The Confessions state: "For this reason these two things are done in Baptism, the water is poured on the body because it cannot comprehend more than the water, and the Word is spoken that also the soul may comprehend it. Since both water and the Word constitute one Baptism, also body and soul must live eternally. The soul through the Word and the body because it is united with the soul." Ibid., Baptism, 45. Cp. the Lord's Supper, 68, and W. A., XXIII, 178—181.

[87] Ap., II, 15 ff.; IV, 230; F. C., Ep., I, 10.

[88] On Luther's theology concerning sin see Th. Harnack, I, 193 ff. Koestlin-Hay, II, 338—58. Concerning Melanchthon's doctrine of sin see H. Engelland, *Melanchthon, Glauben und Handeln* (Munich, 1931), *passim*.

The adherents of the Augsburg Confession teach

that after Adam's fall all men, propagated in the natural way, are born with sin, that is, without fear of God, without trust in God, and with concupiscence; and that this sickness and disease of our birth [originis] is really and truly sin, condemns us, and brings with it eternal death to those who have not been born again by Baptism and the Holy Spirit.[89]

The Lutheran Confessions view sin as the total and deep corruption of every man. They do not separate original sin from actual sins as though each belonged into a specific compartment, as was done by later Lutheran dogmaticians. The Confessions call "original sin" the "capital sin," from which the so-called actual sins proceed.[90]

In their antithesis to Roman Semi-Pelagianism (and subsequently to Lutheran synergism) the Confessions were constrained to present original sin both negatively, namely, as a complete lack of fear of God and trust in God, and positively, as concupiscence or constant evil inclination. The sin with which man is born is not only a lack of righteousness but also an active rebellion against the Creator. By nature man has no faith in God, no love toward God, and at the same time hates God, despairs of God's grace, and puts his trust in temporal things, preferably his own wisdom, power, and moral goodness. Original sin is not a single act, but the inherent and constant sinful inclination, or concupiscence, which drives man to rebel against God and His will and, contrariwise, to seek only his own interests.[91]

In the controversy between the synergists and the Flacians it became necessary to stress particularly the fact that the total person is corrupted so that there is nothing whole or uncorrupt in man's body or soul, in his interior or exterior powers.[92] Against the Zwinglian view, shared by the later Arminians, that original sin is a sickness, a kind of infection, an imposed burden, the Confessions stress that all of man's powers in his reason, will, and affections are totally and continually corrupted. In the words of Luther:

Original, or natural, or personal sin is the real chief sin. If this were not true, there would be no real sin. This sin is not committed like all other sins, but it exists, it lives, and it commits all sins, and it is the essential sin, which does not sin for an hour or for a time: but where and how long the person exists, there, too, is the sin.[93]

[89] A. C., II (Latin text).

[90] S. A., P. III, Art. I: "Dies heisst die Erbsünde oder Hauptsünde" *(hoc nominatur originale, haereditarium, principale, et capitale peccatum).* Cp. F. C., Ep. I, 21; Th. D., I, 5.

[91] Ap., II, 3, 8, 25, 26. Because of original sin man is not only *aversus a Deo* but *adversus Deum,* turned from God and turned against God. The papal Confutation rejected the Lutheran description of original sin. It held that concupiscence, or evil inclination, is a deed and therefore an actual sin (ibid., II, 1).

[92] F. C., Ep. I, 8. On the Flacian Controversy see Bente, p. 144 ff., Frank, *Theologie der Concordienformel,* I, 50 ff., W. Preger, *Matthias Flacius Illyricus und seine Zeit* (Erlangen, 1861), Lauri Haikola, *Gesetz und Evangelism bei Matthias Flacius Illyricus* (Lund: C. W. K. Gleerup, 1952). — The terms "substance" and "accident" were employed in this controversy to set forth in philosophical concepts the distinction between nature, which is the handiwork of God, and man's original sin, which is in nature. The theological emphasis of the terms was to maintain both that man is totally corrupted and that he is responsible for his rebellion.

[93] W. A., X, I, 508 ff. Emil Brunner, *Man in Revolt,* trans. O. Wyon (New York, 1939), p. 150, quotes this passage.

Because of the sin of our origin, we are under the wrath of God and the tyranny of the devil. The Confessions present this as a Scriptural fact, without any attempt to explain the mystery of the transmission of Adam's sin to his descendants.[94] The most deplorable thing about man's sinful condition is the fact that he is unable to know God's wrath over sin or the depth of his own wicked condition, in fact, man's ignorance of this his condition constitutes his gravest sin. Strictly speaking, man is ignorant of God, and at best he has only a faint spark of knowledge that there is a God. He cannot know God's wrath nor His grace, because original sin is essentially ignorance of God. When the Confessions state that human reason understands the Law in a certain way they refer to the external work of the Law, not to the real meaning of God's Law, which implies fear and love of Him above all things and trusting Him in all afflictions. Man recognizes that there is a divine law, but he fails to understand the real meaning of the fact that it is God's Law which confronts him. Original sin is described as such a deep corruption of our nature that we cannot understand it. And the greatest detriment is not only that we have to suffer the wrath of God but also that we fail to understand what we are suffering. Nor does man understand his own nature and its corruption. He does not realize that the Law of God in its accusations only increases his inherent enmity and rebellion against God. He does not recognize the Law as the ever-accusing Word of God, the thunderbolt which destroys both the manifest sinners and the vaunted hypocrites. Only the revelation of God's wrath in the Law shows us the reality of God's wrath over sin, the total incapacity of man to do something about his sin.[95]

In describing the wrath of God and the deplorable condition of man in such detail, the Lutheran Confessions are not motivated by a psychopathic exaggeration of man's sinfulness — a type of religious masochism — but entirely by a soteriological interest. The Confessions express the faith of men who had experienced the terrors of conscience, wrought by the Law, and the grace of God, revealed in the Gospel. They wanted others to share their experiences with them. The authors of the Lutheran Confessions present the depth of sin and the infinite greatness of God's wrath in order that man might see the greatness of his redemption through the Person and work of the Redeemer.[96]

The Person and Work of Christ

THE PERSON OF CHRIST

The Lutheran Confessions give expression to the Chalcedonian Christology. In presenting this doctrine they use such terms as the personal union, the communion of natures, and the commu-

---

[94] F. C., Th. D., I, 13, 19; Ap., II, 46. The Lutheran Confessions apparently favor the theory of traducianism as more nearly in conformity with the doctrine of man's original corruption than is possible when creationism is maintained. See F. C., Th. D., I, 7, 9, 27 f., 38.

[95] Ap. II, 7 f., 13 f., 17, 51, 81, 131, 159; IV, 295. Large C., Com. I, 17—19; Creed, 52; F. C., Th. D., II, 9. See Robert Hoeferkamp, "Natural Law and the New Testament," *C. T. M.*, XXIII (1952), 645 ff. Cp. Schlink, p. 82 ff. Karl Barth rejects natural theology entirely. Cp. Hermann Sasse, *Here We Stand*, pp. 156—59. The position of Melanchthon on the natural knowledge of God is treated by Friedrich Huebner, *Natürliche Theologie und theokratische Schwärmerei bei Melanchthon* (Gütersloh, 1936), pp. 15—25.

[96] F. C., Th. D., I, 3; Ap., II, 34; IV, 5, 46 f., 147 ff., 186—188; XII, 44.

nication of attributes. This terminology became necessary in the controversy concerning the Real Presence of Christ's body in the Lord's Supper.[97] The Lutheran Confessions, however, present Christology solely for its soteriological significance. They ask: "What does it mean that Jesus Christ has become my Lord?" and answer:

It is this, that Christ has redeemed me from sin, the devil, death, and all evil. Formerly I had no Lord nor master, but was held captive under the power of the devil, condemned to death, enmeshed in sin and blindness. . . . The devil came and led us into disobedience, sin, death, and all evil, so that we were under God's wrath and displeasure and doomed to eternal damnation, as we had deserved and merited. We were without counsel, help, or comfort, until the only-begotten Son of God had mercy on our dreadful condition and came from heaven to help us. Now all the tyrants and jailers are expelled, and in their place Jesus Christ, the Lord of life, righteousness, of all good and salvation, has delivered us poor lost human beings out of the jaws of hell, has liberated us and restored us to the Father's grace and mercy as His own, and has taken us under His protection so that He can govern us by His righteousness, wisdom, power, life, and salvation.[98]

Therefore the Lutheran Confessions state:

It is not enough to believe that Christ was born, that He suffered, that He was quickened again, unless we also add this article, which states why all this was done, namely, the forgiveness of sin [*causa finalis historiae: remissio peccatorum*].[99]

The Lutheran Confessions bring every Christian doctrine into the focus of Christ's saving work. To know Christ means to know and accept His benefits.[100] There is no Christology without soteriology. This applies particularly to every facet of the rich, mysterious, and inscrutable doctrine of the person of Christ, the God-man. The doctrine of the Personal Union is the very foundation of Christ's redemptive work. Any Nestorian attempt to separate the two natures is a negation of Christ's work.[101] This is true also when the Person of Christ is viewed under the aspect of the communion of natures, since it is to emphasize particularly that in the theanthropic person (God-man) a true union and communion exists between the divine nature of Christ and His human nature so that it can truly be said of Him that in Him dwelleth all the fullness of the Godhead bodily. Thus alone could He become my Lord, the Lord of Life, the

---

[97] The Lutheran Symbols, here as elsewhere, are concerned wholly with reproducing and defending Biblical and Catholic teaching. Thus, for instance, Article VIII argues: "The created gifts given and imparted to the human nature in Christ . . . do not attain the majesty which the Scriptures and the ancient Fathers on the basis of the Scriptures ascribe to the assumed human nature in Christ. . . . That Christ received such [majesty] and that it was given and imparted to the assumed human nature is something that we should and must believe on the basis of the Scriptures. But . . . this doctrine must also be rightly explicated and diligently defended against all heresies." (Th. D., VIII, 54. 60.)

[98] Large C., Creed, 27—30.

[99] Ap. IV, 51.

[100] Cp., for example, Ap., II, 50; IV, 46, 101; VII, 33; XXIV, 72; Large C., Creed, 43; F. C., Th. D., I, 3. — In the *Loci* of 1521 Melanchthon wrote: "*Hoc est Christum cognoscere, beneficia eius cognoscere* (This is to know Christ, to know His benefits)."

[101] F. C., Th. D., III, 56; VIII, 43, 84, 20.

Book of Life.[102] The authors of the Formula of Concord devote much space to the so-called threefold communication of attributes, especially to the second mode of communication of attributes, known to dogmaticians as the *genus maiestaticum*, that is, the divine glory is communicated to the human nature, not as an essential, but as a communicated attribute, so that the human nature of Christ from the moment of the incarnation shares in all divine properties. The detailed presentation of this doctrine in the controversy with the Zwinglians and later the crypto-Calvinists concerning the real presence of Christ in the Holy Supper may at first glance appear to be no more than a logomachy, a mere sparring with metaphysical concepts.[103] But according to the Lutheran viewpoint the *genus maiestaticum* is of great soteriological significance. This doctrine guarantees that in His threefold office Christ is present with His church not only according to His deity but also and especially according to His human nature. This means that Christ speaks to us as man to man; sympathizes with us as one who has experienced in His assumed human nature all temptations which come to us; rules the entire universe also according to the nature whereby He is our brother and we are flesh of His flesh.[104] The doctrine concerning the two states is presented in the Lutheran Confessions only in its relevance to Christ's redemptive work. They teach that though Christ possessed all divine properties in the state of humiliation,[105] He used His divine glory only when it was necessary to accomplish the work of our redemption. Also the state of glorification is presented primarily from its soteriological significance.[106]

---

[102] Cp., for example, Large C., Creed, 30 f.; F. C., Th. D., XI, 13 ff., 65 f., 70.

[103] F. C., Th. D., VIII, 76—87; cp. also 12, 18, 28 ff., 64, 66. Some modern Lutheran theologians say that the Lutheran Confessions went beyond the traditional position of the church and therefore strenuously object to the doctrine of the *genus maiestaticum*. Cp. Paul Althaus, *Christliche Wahrheit* (Bertelsmann, 1949), II, 223 f. Althaus contends that Lutheran dogmaticians lost the Christ faith in the interest of a Christ theory and apparently believes that Melanchthon's complaint in the 1521 *Loci* against the Romanists is applicable against the later Lutheran theologians. Melanchthon wrote: "To know Christ is to know His benefits, not to look at His natures and the modes of His incarnation." Consult the exhaustive treatment of Christology in Francis Pieper (op. cit., fn. 22, above), II, 85—305. Cp. also "Catalogue of Testimonies," an appendix to the Lutheran Confessions. This is a catalog of Scripture references and quotations from the church Fathers to show that Lutheran Christology is in accord with Scriptures and ancient tradition.

[104] See especially F. C., Th. D., VIII, 76—87. The Lutheran Confessions maintain that a denial of the Real Presence is the denial of significant soteriological facts. VIII, 41 ff.

[105] The German text, F. C., Th. D., VIII, 26, has *"völlige Possess,"* which seems to imply that the man Christ did not fully possess the divine properties until His glorification. Cp. *Bekenntnisschriften*, p. 1025, fn. 4, p. 1032, fn. 5. It must be kept in mind that *"Possess"* is undoubtedly derived from the Latin *possidere* and denotes to exercise one's authority.

[106] Modern kenoticists hold that Christ emptied Himself of all divine attributes in such a way that He did not possess them, but gradually regained them as a reward for His perfect obedience. They charge that the Lutheran Confessions maintain a Christology in which Christ's deity no longer is a true deity and His humanity no longer a real humanity. Althaus, 229 ff.

THE WORK OF CHRIST

The Lutheran Confessions teach that a knowledge of the history of Christ is meaningless unless the purpose of His life, death, and resurrection are immediately added, namely, that Christ lived and died to gain the forgiveness of sin, upon which faith each individual Christian must lay hold.[107]

In Lutheran dogmatics the work of Christ is usually presented under Christ's threefold office as Prophet, Priest, and King. This is a very effective way to present soteriology. The Lutheran Confessions do not make this distinction, though they use the terms "Mediator," "Prophet," "Priest," and "Head of the Church," to describe Christ's work.[108] The Augsburg Confession and the Apology present the work of Christ under the concept of Mediator, namely, as Mediator of satisfaction and of intercession. The life, Passion, and death of Christ are viewed as His satisfaction for all sins and His sacrifice to reconcile God; and His glorification as the means to bring these blessings to us.[109]

The doctrine of Christ's redemptive work runs as a golden thread through all the Confessions [110] and is presented in variegated hues. Christ is both the Victim, the Lamb that bears the sin of the world, and the Priest. He is both the Mercy Seat before God and the High Priest, who intercedes for us. He is the Mediator and the Mediation; the Treasure — in Roman theology the "thesaurus" is the alleged depository of Christ's and the saints' superabundant merits — and the Treasurer; the Payment and the Payer; the Redeemer and the Redemption.

Christ has redeemed us from the curse of the Law, being made a curse for us, that is, the Law condemns all men. Christ was without sin, but because the sinless Christ assumed the punishment of sin and became a victim for us, He removed the power of the Law. It can now no longer accuse us and condemn those who believe in Christ, because He Himself is the Propitiation for them, and on account of this propitiation they are now counted just.[111]

The Confessions emphasize the vicarious character of Christ's work. As the Mediator of all redemption, Christ is presented as having fully and completely kept the Law in our stead, paid the penalty of our guilt, placated the wrath of God for us, and as the perfect and complete Propitiation for the sins of the world. Christ's work is absolutely complete both intensively and extensively. It requires no complement in any respect. It needs only to be accepted in faith.

Faith gratuitously accepts the forgiveness of sins, because it pits the Mediator and Propitiator Christ — never our own merits — against the wrath of God. This

---

[107] See Ap., IV, 46, 51; XXIV, 72 f.

[108] F. C., Th. D., VIII, 47. Calvin's Christology employs the distinction of the threefold office. See *Evangelical Quarterly*, 1948, p. 233. W. Elert, *Der christliche Glaube* (Furche Verlag, Berlin, 1940), pp. 405—10. T. G. Voigt, "The Speaking Christ in His Royal Office," *C. T. M.*, XXIII (1952), p. 161 ff. — The Eastern Orthodox theologians also use the terminology "threefold office."

[109] A. C., III: *ut reconciliaret nobis patrem et hostia esset*. Cp. IV; XX, 9; XXI, 4; XXIV, 21. Cp. also Ap., IV, 53, 57, 81, 162, 165, 179, 317; XII, 76; XV, 12; XXI, 14, 17 ff.; XXIV, 19—24, 58; S. A., P. II, Art. I; Large C., Creed, II, 31.

[110] It is treated *ex professo* only in A. C., III, and in Large C., Creed, II.

[111] Ap., IV, 179; cp. also XII, 140; XXIV, 8, 56; XXI, 41 f., Large C., II, 31; F. C., Th. D., III, 57.

is the true knowledge of Christ. It appropriates for its own use all the benefits of Christ, regenerates the heart, and precedes the fulfilling of the Law.[112]

Any attempt on the part of man to supplement Christ's work by his own effort is condemned as contrary to divine revelation, as an insult to Christ's work, and as a denial of Christ's honor.[113] The Lutheran Confessions concentrate on the vicarious work of Christ for man's redemption and reject the view that Christ is primarily man's Exemplar and man's new Lawgiver. All those who would like to harmonize the promises of Christ with the sentences of Socrates are charged with crucifying and burying Christ anew, darkening His glory, insulting His honor, and completely obscuring His benefits.[114] The denial of the vicarious character of what dogmaticians call Christ's active obedience — as was done by Anselm and the Lutheran George Karg (Parsimonius) — and the Calvinistic tendency to overemphasize Christ's

active obedience prompted the Lutherans to present the whole work of Christ as obedience and to discuss in particular the place of what dogmaticians call Christ's "active" obedience in the plan of our redemption.[115] They present the whole work of Christ as an act of obedience and show that from His holy and innocent birth to His ignominious death upon the cross He rendered to God a perfect and full obedience to recompense for our disobedience. This complete and full obedience of Christ both in His life and in His death is accounted to the believer for righteousness.[116]

Justification

The Augsburg Confession declares: Men cannot be justified before God by their own virtues, merit, or work, but are justified freely for Christ's sake through faith, when they believe that they have been received into grace, that their sins have been forgiven for Christ's

---

[112] Ap., IV, 47. The German text reads: "That faith which receives the forgiveness of sins freely by grace is a genuine faith which will not place against the wrath of God its own works and merits. These amount to no more than a tiny feather in a hurricane (*ein Federlein gegen den Sturmwind*), but faith places over against God's wrath the Mediator Christ. And such faith is truly knowing Christ."

[113] The A. C. and the Ap. rejected the propitiatory sacrifice of the Mass, the propitiatory power of fasting, the obligatory observance of human traditions, the satisfactory character of monastic vows, not because these were humanly ordained ordinances, but because they were observed as a necessary supplement to Christ's work. Cp. A. C., XX, 9; XXV, 14 ff.; XXVI, 1, 21; XXVII, 38.

[114] Ap., IV, 3, 15, 81. In a letter to the Christians at Strasbourg, Dec. 15, 1524, Luther points out that Christ as an Exemplar does not differ greatly from the saints. W. A., XV, 396, 18—19.

[115] Anselm's satisfaction theory is presented in his *Cur Deus Homo?* Cp. A. C. Welch (P. II, fn. 87, above), ch. ix. — George Karg taught that according to His human nature Christ was subject to the Law and thus obligated to keep it and hence His perfect life in conformity with God's will has no vicarious value. Without realizing it, Karg actually separated Christ's two natures. He ignored that since Christ is both God and man, He is at the same time subject to, and Lord of, the Law. Cp. Bente, p. 160; Frank, II, 29; also Schaff, *Creeds*, I, 274.

[116] Th. D., III, 22, 56, 58. The Formula of Concord uses neither the term "active obedience" nor the term "passive obedience"; instead it speaks of Christ's *einigen, ganzen, volkummnen Gehorsam* and of *der ganzen Person Christi ganzen Gehorsamb.* Cp. Th. Engelder, "The Active Obedience of Christ," *C. T. M.*, I (1930), 810 ff.

sake, who rendered satisfaction for our sins by His death. This faith God counts for righteousness before Himself. Rom. 3:4.[117]

The doctrine of justification is considered the most important article of the Christian faith.[118]

In presenting this doctrine the Confessions stress two central thoughts: Justification is solely for Christ's sake and solely by faith.

"FOR CHRIST'S SAKE"

Justification is the imputation of Christ's perfect obedience. The Confessions present justification as a forensic act, i. e., God declares the sinner righteous. Justification is always God's, never man's act. The Apology declares:

Justification in this article is to be used in the forensic meaning, that is, to absolve the guilty and declare him just; however, not because of his own righteousness, but because of Christ's, which is a foreign righteousness and is communicated through grace. Therefore in this article righteousness is always the imputation of a foreign righteousness.[119]

This "foreign" righteousness is a divinely established constant, an invariable, a *datum*, a permanent reality, regardless of man's personal piety, emotion, and experience.

The Confessions use several concepts promiscuously and synonymously: "forgiveness of sins," "justification by faith," "renewal," "adoption," "imputation of Christ's righteousness."[120] This has occasioned the question whether the doctrine of justification is really central. The fact is that a specific antithesis requires a specific emphasis. This is true of the apparent contradiction in Melanchthon's own presentation, when he describes justification as a forensic action and then adds "justification means to make righteous people out of unrighteous." There is no problem, however, since Melanchthon is speaking antithetically to Rome's theory that justification is a process by which sin is eradicated progressively. Against this false view Melanchthon must point out that through justification man enters into a new relation with God in which he also becomes righteous.[121]

The believer accepts the "entire Christ" and is therefore always perfectly justified in the presence of God. There is no room in Lutheran theology for the view that justification is progressive, through the infusion of some supernatural quality (the *gratia infusa* of Pelagian theologians) or through the indwelling of Christ (Andrew Osiander and his party).[122] It is a Lutheran theological axiom that justification is always complete and dare never be equated with a progressive sanctification.

"BY FAITH ALONE"

Faith plays a central role in the Lutheran doctrine of justification. Therefore it is essential to keep in mind that

---

[117] A. C., Art. IV. See Henry W. Reimann, "Vicarious Satisfaction: A Study in Ecclesiastical Terminology," *C. T. M.*, XXXII (1961), 69—77; Henry P. Hamann, Jr., *Justification by Faith in Modern Theology* (St. Louis: Concordia Seminary School for Graduate Studies, 1957).

[118] Ap., IV, 2, 238; S. A., P. II, Art. I; F. C., Th. D., III, 7.

[119] Ap., IV, 305, cp. 252. F. C., Th. D., III, 17.

[120] Cp. F. C., Th. D., III, 17—21.

[121] Cp. Ap., IV, 72. Among the many monographs on this difficult section see H. Engelland (above, fn. 88), p. 541 ff.; R. Seeberg, p. 403 ff.; W. Walther, pp. 366—71, 376—83; Schlink, p. 134 ff.

[122] F. C., Th. D., III, 6, 30, 56; Andreas Osiander ascribed man's justification to the "Christ *in* us" rather than to the "Christ *for* us" Bente, p. 152 ff.; Preger, I, 205—98; Tschackert, 489 ff.

faith, according to the Lutheran Confessions, is described as "to want and to accept the offered promise of the forgiveness of sins." Faith is to receive, to accept, to reach for, the full mercy of God in Christ Jesus. Faith is always a dynamic activity, a running after, a seeking; it is to "dare" God to give Christ and His complete redemption. Faith is praised so highly, not because it is a good work, but because it has so glorious an object. Faith is said to be the highest worship because it accepts God at His gracious promise. Faith is actually the righteousness which avails before God, because by faith — not on account of faith — Christ's righteousness is imputed to us as our own.[123]

In Lutheran theology the term *sola fide* is used to exclude all works from the doctrine of justification. Faith is said to be the beginning, middle, and end of justification. The Confessions point out that the sinner's justification is in no way effected or affected by man's good works, either before or subsequent to God's act of justification.[124] Man cannot prepare himself for God's activity by a deep sorrow, an earnest longing, or partly by faith and partly by good works. Man is justified solely by faith for Christ's sake, not by Christ for faith's sake. Therefore the Lutheran Confessions made the somewhat bold statement that God imputes this faith for righteousness in His own sight. This does not mean that God justifies the sinner because He considers his faith such a fine and morally excellent work, but solely because faith accepts the promise of Christ's all-sufficient work.[125]

The Lutheran emphasis on the centrality of the doctrine of justification by faith has led to two charges. The first is that Lutheran theology has so stressed the exclusion of good works from justification that it has surrendered the dynamics for Christian piety. It is true

---

[123] Ap., IV, 48: [*Fides*] *est velle et accipere oblatam promissionem remissionis peccatorum et iustificationis.* A. C., XX, 26. Cp. also Ap., IV, 49, 57—59, 106, 182. Roman Catholic dogmaticians sometimes define faith merely as an intellectual knowledge of and assent to the historic facts of redemption and distinguish between such assent and confidence. The Lutheran Confessions also employ the terms "knowledge, assent, confidence"; not, however, as three distinct steps leading to a full faith, but merely as three aspects of faith. The assent which devils and the godless give to the history of Christ is faith in no sense of the word, and it is actually condemned. The Lutheran Confessions describe saving faith as "special faith," which knows, believes, and accepts unconditionally that Christ is our Righteousness. Ap., IV, 45—48, 50; XII, 45, 60; XIII, 20 f.; A. C., XX, 23. — The term "special faith" is used against the Roman Catholic view of *fides informis*, a mere knowledge of God's existence and acceptance of the church's authority, in distinction from the *fides formata*, when faith is said to be active in love and takes on form. Ap., IV, 182, 215—217.

[124] The synergists in the Lutheran church held that some are converted and justified and others not because the conduct of some prior to God's activity is better than that of the others. The issues in this question were resolved in F. C., II. See Robert D. Preus, "The Significance of Luther's Term *Pure Passive* as Quoted in Article II of the Formula of Concord," *C. T. M.*, XXIX (1958), 561—570. The Majorists held that subsequent to justification good works are necessary to retain faith and salvation. Cp. ibid., IV.

[125] The Confessions state that men are justified *propter Christum per fidem*, not *per Christum propter fidem*. Ap., IV, 45, 46, 48, 56, 106, 113, 194, 308; F. C., Ep., III, 19, 20; Th. D., III, 11, 28. In the several instances where the Apology does employ the formula *propter fidem*, as in IV, 177, "faith" is taken metaphorically for its object, viz., "Christ." Cp. Schlink, p. 178 ff.

that the Lutheran Confessions make a sharp distinction between justification and everything that precedes or follows justification.[126] This, however, is only a logical distinction, not a chronological differentiation; a distinction, not a separation; the one an act in the heart of God and the other an act in and by man; the one the complete and present victory over every foe, the other the continuous battle between the Christian and his enemies; the one as the "already," the other as the "not yet." This distinction maintains the *sola gratia* of justification and the believer's obligation to be active in sanctification, expressed in the epigrammatic statement *Sola fides iustificat, et tamen numquam est sola* (Faith alone justifies, but faith is never alone).[127]

There is no ground for the second charge that the Lutheran Confessions present the *sola fide* in such a way that faith is viewed as a static, intellectual assent to a body of Christian truth and that consciences are lulled to sleep. The Confessions prepared by Luther and Melanchthon speak of that faith which

is not merely an idle thought, but such a new light, life, and power in the heart as renews the heart, the mind, and the emotions, as makes an entirely different person and a new creature of us. . . .

[And when we speak of this faith], then everybody understands that we do not speak of a faith which can coexist with mortal sin.[128]

The Formula of Concord was compelled to enter upon the problem of the proper relation of faith and works. In their concern to defend the Lutheran doctrine against every form of antinomianism and to find a stimulus for good works, some Lutheran theologians maintained that "good works are necessary to salvation." [129] Against this view the Formula of Concord stresses two points. First, any mingling of man's good works into the doctrines which deal with Christ's work, with the sinner's justification and our eternal salvation, leads to despair or to false security.[130] Second, the Christian must perform good works, not to merit salvation, but for other reasons. It is the very nature of faith to do good works, because

faith is a divine work in us that changes us and regenerates us of God and puts to death the old Adam, makes us entirely different men in heart, spirit, mind, and all powers, and brings with it the Holy Spirit. Oh, it is a living, busy, active, powerful thing that we have in faith, so that it is impossible for it not to do good without ceasing!

---

[126] This point had to be stressed both against the Romanists and against Andrew Osiander, who taught that Christ so dwells in the believer that by this divine indwelling sin gradually disappears as a drop of ink is dissolved in the ocean. This theory failed to observe the distinction between justification and sanctification. Cp., above, fn. 122.

[127] See F. C., Ep., III, 10, 19, 20; Th. D., III, 19, 22—24, 26, 27, 30, 32 35, 36, 43; Par. 41 quotes Luther: "There is a beautiful harmony between faith and good works. But it is faith alone which apprehends the blessings, yet faith is never alone." Cp. also IV, 15, 31; Ap., IV, 125.

[128] Ap., IV, 64. Cp. A. C., XX, 27—40; Small C., Baptism, Qu. 4. The Confessions reject in unmistakable terms the theory of "once in grace, always in grace." Cp. S. A., P. III, Art. IV, 42 ff. Cp. Ap., IV, 143, 144; F. C., Th. D., IV, 15, 31.

[129] George Major, who was the chief exponent of this "Romanizing" maxim, modified it to read: "Good works are necessary to retain faith." Nevertheless the formula was rejected as paving the way for making good works a condition of justification and salvation instead of a consequence. Cp. Bente, p. 112 f.; Frank, II, 148 ff.; 216 ff.; Preger, 351 ff.

[130] Th. D., IV, 22, 23, 37.

Nor does it ask whether good works are to be done; but before the question is asked, it has wrought them and is always engaged in doing them. But he who does not do such good works is void of faith, and gropes and looks about after faith and good works, and knows neither what faith or good works are, yet babbles and prates with many words concerning faith and good works. Faith is a living, bold trust in God's grace, so that a man would die a thousand times for it. And this trust and knowledge of divine grace renders joyful, fearless, and cheerful towards God and all creatures, which the Holy Ghost works through faith; and on account of this, man becomes ready and cheerful, without coercion, to do good to everyone, to serve everyone, and to suffer everything for love and praise to God, who has conferred this grace on him, so that it is impossible to separate works from faith, yea, just as impossible as it is for heat and light to be separated from fire.[131]

Lutheran confessional theology insists that a Christian must do good works because God wills them; they are fruits of the Spirit; they show forth God's praise; they are a constant exercise of faith and a testimony of our faith to the world.[132] That we are justified by grace for Christ's sake through faith is so central in Lutheran confessional theology that it is the *leitmotiv* of every doctrine. As this theme is central in justification, so also in the doctrine of conversion, or regeneration, and sanctification in both the wide and the narrow sense.

Conversion

The early Lutheran Confessions contain no article which deals specifically with the doctrine of conversion.[133] Nevertheless they devote much space to the subject matter in connection with justifying faith. In their antithesis to Rome they had to fill the well-known dogmatical terms with an entirely new meaning. Justification is described as the change in the heart of God; regeneration, or conversion, as the complete change in the heart of man. Justifying faith is described as the newly created will which wants the promised grace of God, or as the God-given hand which accepts the divine reconciliation. Faith and regeneration are virtually identified. In the terrors of conscience faith accepts God's promise to justify, and such faith is said to quicken, to comfort, to engender new life, to be the beginning of eternal life.[134]

The Lutheran Confessions describe conversion in various ways, which may be summarized under the twofold concept of contrition and faith: sometimes merely as repentance, or faith in Christ, sometimes as embracing the renewal of life.[135] But the concern of the Confes-

---

[131] Luther in Pref. to Romans quoted in F. C., Th. D., IV, 10—12; VI, 17. Cp. Ap., IV, 262, 274; XII, 58 (German text).

[132] Ap., IV, 189. Cp. 349: The Christian is admonished to make his calling and election sure by his own good works. F. C., Th. D., IV, 33.

[133] This may be due in part to the fact that Roman Catholic dogmaticians do not devote a special section to conversion, as do Protestant dogmaticians, for the simple reason that from their point of view man is by nature turned toward God and no conversion really occurs. See "Grace," P. II.

[134] Ap., IV, 125; XII, 28—38. Faith is that change whereby the God of Sinai, of anger, becomes a lovable object. *Ita demum [Deus] fit obiectum amabile,* Ap. IV, 129. Faith is said to free from death, bring forth new life. Ap., IV, 64, 65; XII, 46, 50; S. A., P. III, Art. XIII, 1. Faith is the liberation of the bound will; it makes unwilling hearts obedient and recalcitrant wills willing. Cp. F. C., Th. D., II, 83, also 65—68, 70.

[135] Ap., XII, 28, 46, 56; S. A., P. III, Art. III.

sions is soteriological throughout, and this leads them to make such bold statements as "Justification is regeneration."[136]

In presenting the doctrine of conversion the Lutheran Confessions dwell not so much on the nature as rather on the cause, or source, of conversion. This emphasis was necessary because of the encounter with two basically wrong views, Semi-Pelagianism and synergism. Both ascribe inherent spiritual powers to natural or unconverted man. The former holds that in his natural state man can do some spiritually good works, but requires God's "grace" to complete his justification. The latter holds that God must begin the process of conversion by awakening man's latent and dormant powers, but man must complete the divine work.[137]

In its antithesis to the Semi-Pelagianism of the scholastic theologians the Lutheran Confessions stress the absolute necessity of a complete change, because of man's constant and determined rebellion against God and his native inclination either to a false security (work-righteousness) or to a hopeless despair (terrors of conscience).[138]

In antithesis to every form of synergism the confessions maintain the *sola gratia*. In strongest terms possible they deny any spiritual powers to man, such as a *facultas se applicandi ad gratiam*, a *modus agendi*, i. e., any inclination toward accepting the Holy Spirit's invitation, or even a positive activity toward one's conversion. The Lutheran Confessions teach that

in His immeasurable grace and mercy God comes to us before (*zuvorkommen, praevenit*) we have done anything; provides for the preaching of the Gospel, through which the Holy Ghost effects our conversion and renovation; and through the proclamation and meditation of His Word He kindles faith and other God-pleasing virtues.[139]

Thus, according to Lutheran theology, the *sola gratia* accompanies the Christian all the way. Justification and conversion are God's free gift to man, unmerited, undeserved. As man's own work, in whole or in part, both would be no more than the self-righteousness of civic uprightness and as such blasphemy. But when the *sola gratia* is placed into the center, God is glorified. The *sola gratia*, however, is possible only *sola fide* and requires "all hearts to believe." Thus the Lutheran Confessions constantly revert to the correlative of *sola gratia*, namely, *sola fide*.

136 F. C., Th. D., III, 19; *Iustificatio est regeneratio;* cp. Ap., IV, 72, 78, 117.

137 There is essentially little difference between the two views. When Luther first noted the synergist aberrations of his co-workers, he is alleged to have said: "*Haec est ipsissima theologia Erasmi.*" Kolde, *Analecta,* p. 266, quoted in Bente, p. 128.

138 A. C., II; Ap., II, 6, 25; S. A., P. III, Art. I, 2; F. C., Th. D., II, 10, 11, 25—39, 19, 59. See the references to the "Pelagianizing" theology of scholastic theologians, Ap., IV, 19, 29; XVIII, 1 ff. This emphasis is still necessary against modern Romanist theologians, against Arminianism, and, of course, against all egocentric cults.

139 F. C., Th. D., II, 71; cp. II, 5, 7, 12, 18, 25, 44, 85. On the Synergistic Controversy see Preger, II, 181—227; Frank, I, 113—240; Bente, pp. 124—43; R. R. Caemmerer, pp. 321—28, and F. E. Mayer, pp. 254—67 (fn. 43, above). The synergistic leanings of the Melanchthonians were prompted largely by humanistic and rationalistic attempts to solve the insoluble mystery expressed in the question, Why some, others not? Of course, neither synergism nor Semi-Pelagianism provides the answer, for the question, Why do some employ the alleged native ability, while others do not? still remains. Cp. F. C., Th. D., II, 78; XI, 26.

The Means of Grace

In order that we may obtain such faith God has ordained the ministry, has given the Gospel and the Sacraments. Through these, as through means, He bestows the Holy Spirit, who works faith where and when He wills, in those who hear the Gospel, which teaches that because of Christ's merits, not our own, we have a gracious God if we believe this.[140]

In the terminology of the Lutheran Confessions the means of grace designate the God-appointed means or instruments *(Werkzeug)* through which (1) God offers and conveys His grace in Christ to me, and through which (2) He engenders faith to accept this grace.[141]

THE GOSPEL

The Gospel, in the first place, actually brings Christ to men. It is much more than a historical record of God's great work in Christ. It actually makes us contemporaries of the great events and partakers of the great blessings which Christ accomplished. The Gospel is not only a promise of a future blessing, but it actually conveys to us the entire Christ with the totality of His gifts as a present possession. In effect the Confession can say: We are reconciled through the Gospel. In his exposition of the Third Commandment Luther states:

> The Word of God is the sanctuary above all sanctuaries; in fact, it is the Christian's only sanctuary. . . . The Word of God is the treasure which sanctifies all things. . . . At what-

ever hour a person uses God's Word, preaches, listens, reads, or meditates, he . . . is sanctified.[142]

The Confessions assert again and again that eternal things, eternal righteousness, the Holy Spirit, and eternal life can be bestowed only through the God-appointed means, the Word and the sacraments. They state with equal emphasis that in and through the Gospel God offers and conveys to man everything that he needs for his eternal salvation. The Gospel is not only the promise of the forgiveness, but in reality the absolution itself, as certainly as if Christ Himself pronounced it. The Gospel is more than a doctrine about the reconciliation; it is the gift of a reconciled God.[143]

The Gospel, in the second place, actually creates faith. By nature — this is the consistent teaching — man is blind, deaf, ignorant, spiritually dead, and therefore incapable of seeing the grace of God, hearing the Gospel, understanding and wanting divine grace. Therefore the Holy Spirit must work saving faith. This He does solely and only through the Gospel. In the offer and invitation to accept God's grace lies also the power to create faith to accept it. According to Lutheran theology, two facts must be kept in mind: (1) The Holy Spirit is given only through the Word, and without the Word — as far as man knows — the Holy Spirit uses no vehicle to reach man; (2) the Holy Spirit is always in the Word, and therefore the Gospel in all its various forms is always divinely efficacious. The Gospel not only commands us to come to Christ, but is the

---

[140] A. C., V (German). See also the Latin text.

[141] Accordingly Lutheran dogmaticians usually ascribe a twofold power to the means of grace: the *vis collativa* and the *vis effectiva*.

[142] Large C., Com. III, 91; Creed, III, 38.

[143] A. C., XXVIII, 9; cp. XVIII, 3 (the Holy Spirit is given through the Word); Ap., IV, 67 f., 120; VII, 36; XXVII, 11, 40. S. A., P. III, Art. IV. F. C., Th. D., II, 5.

power of the Holy Spirit to create in man every necessary faculty to come to Christ.[144] The Lutheran Confessions protest against every form of "enthusiasm," which teaches that the Holy Spirit operates outside the specified means. They condemn all religious views which are not based upon Scripture as devil's doctrines designed to mislead men.[145]

In its antithesis to Rome's theory that the sacraments are efficacious *ex opere operato*, the Lutheran Confessions stress the necessity of faith to appropriate the Gospel and state that the Word both requires and engenders faith. In antithesis to all forms of "enthusiasm," Lutheranism maintains that the Spirit is always in the Word and the sacraments and that they are efficacious regardless of man's attitude, but that the salutary use requires "all hearts to believe." [146]

The Lutheran Confessions are not consistent in listing the various means of grace. Sometimes they use the generic term "Gospel," then merely the term "Word," then Word and sacraments. At times the Confessions place the total emphasis on the oral proclamation, *Predigt*. In describing the Gospel the Con-

fessions state that God in His richness has provided that the Gospel come to us

first, through the oral word, whereby the forgiveness of sin is proclaimed in all the world, which is the proper office of the Gospel; second, through Baptism; third, through the Sacrament of the Altar; fourth, through the Office of the Keys and through the conversation and consolation by brethren among one another.[147]

The claim is sometimes made that Lutheran theology holds that the Holy Spirit is operative and effective only in the oral proclamation. The fact is that both the preached and the written Word are said to be the means of grace.[148]

THE SACRAMENTS

The sacraments are frequently mentioned as separate means of grace. This applies in a measure, for they are called the "visible" Word in distinction from the proclaimed Word. The Confessions declare that the "visible Word" is intended for the eyes, as the audible or spoken Word is intended for the ears. But they point out that the effect of both is the same, namely, to incite the heart to believe.[149] It is sometimes said that

144 C. A., V; XXVIII, 8; Ap., XII, 40: *Deus vere per verbum vivificat;* XXIV, 79: *per verbum operatur Spiritus Sanctus.* Cp. IV, 67, 81, 85 (German text, *Triglot*, p. 212, or *Bekenntnisschriften*, p. 224); VII, 15. S. A., P. III, Art. VIII, 3, 10, 11. Large C., 2d Pet., 53: the kingdom comes only through the Word and faith; Baptism, 30. See extensive discussion in F. C., II, 48—57; XI, 26, 33, 44.

145 Ap., XII, 141; S. A., P. III, Art. III, 5; F. C., Th. D., II, 4, 5, 80; XII, 30.

146 The statement in A. C., V: "Where and when God wills" does not imply that the Word is efficacious only at certain times, but is meant rather as an admonition to employ the means at all times, since we do not know when and what God will do through the means.

147 S. A., P. III, Art. IV.

148 S. A., P. III, Art. II, 15, where the context indicates that "Word of God" is the written Word. See Ap., XII, 42 ff. See also Fred Kramer, "*Sacra Scriptura* and *Verbum Dei* in the Lutheran Confessions," *C. T. M.*, XXVI (1955), 81—95.

149 Ap., XIII, 5. See Arthur Carl Piepkorn, *What the Symbolical Books of the Lutheran Church Have to Say About Worship and the Sacraments* (St. Louis: C. P. H., 1952), pp. 15—41. It is in the spirit of the Lutheran

the sacrament serves as a sign and seal of God's grace to the individual and may be viewed as the "individualized Word." From this view it is in order to call "private," or individual, absolution a sacrament and to urge its retention for the individual's necessary assurance. The Confessions point out that man's need is so great and his trouble so manifold that God has provided several ways and means to bring the divine promises to man.[150] The Lutheran emphasis on the sacraments as the "visible Word" is motivated in part by the conviction that the Holy Spirit converts the total person, body and soul. Both the Neoplatonism of Rome (and of Calvin) and the "enthusiasm" of the spiritualists place a low estimate upon the body. The Lutheran Confessions, however, maintain that the entire person, body and soul, must be converted and saved. This is effected in Baptism, where water and God's Word are united in one action to save both body and soul, the body through the water (which cannot comprehend more) and the soul through the promise.[151]

According to the Lutheran Confessions the sacraments are means of grace in no less nor in any greater degree than the spoken or written Word. However, in antithesis to both the sacramentalism of Rome and the "enthusiasm" of the spiritualists the Confessions present the doctrine on Baptism and the Lord's Supper in some detail.[152] During the early years of the Lutheran Reformation there was no uniform practice regarding the number of sacraments. The Confessions written by Luther and Melanchthon list three: Baptism, Absolution, and the Sacrament of the Altar. Among the dogmaticians the view prevailed that Baptism in its significance and efficacy embraces also the "third sacrament," repentance.[153]

BAPTISM

The Essence of Baptism. Baptism is described both as water comprehended in the Word and conversely as the Word encased in water. Baptism is said to be nothing but God's Word in the water, so that the two dare never be separated.[154] The specific divine word in

Confessions to speak of the means of grace as the threefold Word, the written, the spoken, the signed (visible) Word. Cp. F. E. Mayer, "De ministerio ecclesiastico," *C. T. M.*, XXI (1950), 881—95; Herman A. Preus, "The Written, Spoken, and Signed Word," ibid., XXVI (1955), 641—656.

150 Ap., XIII, 2—4; XI, 2; XXIV, 18 ff., 49, 69. Large C., Baptism, 74; Lord's Supper, 22, 29. See esp. F. C., Th. D., XI, 37, 38. — S. A., P. III, Art. IV.

151 Large C., Baptism, 44 ff. Cp. also Lord's Supper, 68. A person must view the Lord's Supper as a genuinely wholesome medicine which will help him and give him life for body and soul.

152 Roman theologians hold that each of the seven sacraments confers some specific "sacramental grace" necessary to aid man in his justification. Cp. P. II, above, "The Sacraments." Most Reformed theologians subscribe in some degree to Zwingli's maxim "The Holy Spirit requires no vehicle" and consider the sacraments merely as outward badges of men's profession to be Christian. Cp. "Means of Grace," P. IV, below.

153 The sequence of Articles IX—XII in the A. C. is significant: IX, Baptism; X, Lord's Supper; XI, Confession; XII, Repentance; XIII, The Use of the Sacraments. Even orders and marriage are called sacraments, Ap., XIII, 11, 14. At the same time the Confessions point out that the important question is not the number, but the essence, of the sacraments. Ap. XIII, 2, 17.

154 S. A., P. III, Art. V, 1. Large C., Baptism, 22, 29, 31. Cp. Schlink, pp. 204—16; Piepkorn, pp. 23—26.

Baptism is threefold. There is first God's command in the words of institution. This command gives Baptism its glory and power, for wherever God ordains anything — even if it were such an insignificant thing as picking up a piece of straw — He puts His divine glory and majesty behind His institution.[155] There is, second, God's name. Baptism is God's work, since it is done in the name of the Triune God. God, not man, baptizes and through Baptism makes us His own.[156] And, third, in Baptism we have God's promise that "whosoever believes and is baptized shall be saved."

The Blessings of Baptism. According to the Small Catechism, Baptism "works forgiveness of sins, delivers from death and the devil, and gives eternal salvation." Baptism is not only a symbol of the new birth, not only a promise of the new life, but it actually creates what it symbolizes. The baptized Christian has died in his Baptism and is already in possession of eternal life. Paradoxically he is both a dying man according to his corrupt nature and a resurrected man according to his new nature. Baptism permits us to see in the mortal frame of our body the glorified body. Baptism is liberation from Satan and adoption as God's sons and heirs of life. It bestows forgiveness of the entire guilt of sin, but not the destruction of the essence of original sin, as Rome teaches.[157]

The Efficacy of Baptism. Since God has put His Word into Baptism, He has placed His divine power into the sacramental washing. Therefore Baptism — the Word encased in the water — is a saving bath, a washing of regeneration. The Lutheran Confessions call the Word of God a *Tätelwort*, a creative word, a dynamic word, and its efficacy never subsides or diminishes. Therefore the efficacy of Baptism is lifelong, and the baptized Christian is advised to return to his Baptism when he falls into sin, since the words of institution remain efficacious in spite of man's sin and unbelief.[158] Faith does not belong to the essence of Baptism. Faith is indeed necessary, not to make Baptism efficacious, but to receive its blessings. Hence both statements are correct: "Baptism creates faith," and "Baptism requires faith." [159]

In antithesis to the Anabaptists the Lutheran Confessions emphatically de-

---

[155] Ap., IX, 2; Large C., Baptism 6—9.

[156] Ibid., 10; Ap. XXIV, 8.

[157] Cp. Ap., IX, 2; Large C., Baptism, 2, 6, 10, 12, 23, 24, 65. The blessings of Baptism are symbolized both in baptism itself and in some of the ceremonies accompanying the rite. Immersion was still practiced in many sections of the church at the beginning of the 16th century, and in the Lutheran Confessions this mode of baptism — immersion and emergence — is viewed as symbolizing the mortification of the Old Adam and the resurrection of the new man. Large C., Baptism, 64 f. Cp. F. C., Th. D., II, 67. The formulary for Baptism contains the renunciation of the devil and all his works and all his ways, and prescribes several ceremonies to symbolize the blessings of Baptism, notably exorcism. The prescribed formulary for exorcism reads: "I adjure thee, thou unclean spirit, in the name of the Father, Son, and Holy Ghost, to come out of, and to depart from this servant of Jesus Christ." See "Taufbüchlein," *Bekenntnisschriften*, pp. 538—39.

[158] Roman theology directs the baptized person who has fallen into mortal sin to penance, *baptismum laboriosum*. In Lutheran theology there is no room for a repetition of baptism or a substitute for baptism. Even if the candidate for baptism did not believe at the time of his baptism, he was validly baptized. Large C., Baptism, 74—82.

[159] A. C., XIII; Ap., XIII, 5; Large C., Baptism, 27, 53, 56.

fend infant baptism chiefly in the interest of the perpetuity of the church.[160] The psychological problem as to an infant's capability to believe is ruled out of order, for even if children could not believe, Baptism still would remain God's ordinance. The Lutheran teaching is: The child is brought to Baptism, first, because it is God's ordinance and command, and, second, because the church believes and prays that God will engender faith.[161]

THE LORD'S SUPPER [162]

In Lutheran theology both Baptism and the Lord's Supper are viewed as the "visible Word," through which God offers and conveys His blessings to man. In this respect the Lutheran Confessions see no difference between the two. At the same time they point to distinctive characteristics and functions of each. Baptism is described as being not simple water only, but the water comprehended in God's command. The Lord's Supper, however, is defined not only as the bread and wine comprehended in God's command, but also as the body and blood of Christ. In Baptism the earthly element because of its union with the Word becomes the washing of regeneration. In the Lord's Supper, however, the earthly elements do not become nourishment for the soul, but because of the union with the Word are the body and blood of Christ. The formulation "The bread and wine are the body and blood" rules out every symbolical interpretation of the words of institution.[163] A further distinction is that Baptism as the washing of regeneration engenders the spiritual life; the Lord's Supper, which is the body and blood of Christ, nourishes and sustains it.[164] Finally, the Lord's Supper, in distinction from Baptism, is viewed as our eucharistic sacrifice of thanksgiving for God's great deliverance and the public profession of our faith in Christ's death and resurrection.[165]

The Essence. The Lutheran formulation of the essence of the Lord's Supper received point and emphasis chiefly from the antithesis to both the Roman Catholic and the Zwinglian-Calvinist doctrine concerning the Real Presence, the former maintaining a starkly physical presence of Christ and the second a purely spiritual presence of Christ according to His divine nature.[166] It is

---

[160] Ibid., 49—51.

[161] Ibid., pp. 55—57. See "Taufbüchlein," *Bekenntnisschriften,* pp. 535—539.

[162] Piepkorn, pp. 26—39. — There is some fluctuation as to the terminology. "The Sacrament of the Altar," "the Holy Supper," "the Eucharist," "the Mass," are used interchangeably.

[163] Cp. Small C.; Large C., 8—10; Schlink, p. 221. See Jaroslav J. Pelikan, *Luther the Expositor* (St. Louis: C. P. H., 1959); Hermann Sasse, *This Is My Body: Luther's Contention for the Real Presence in the Sacrament of the Altar* (Minneapolis: Augsburg Publishing House, c. 1959).

[164] Large C., Lord's Supper, 23 ff. Some Lutherans call Baptism *sacramentum initiationis* and Holy Communion *sacramentum confirmationis.*

[165] Ap., XXIV, 74, 77; IV, 210.

[166] The Roman theory of transubstantiation is said to be basic not only for Communion under one kind, but also for the doctrine that the Mass is the unbloody sacrifice of Christ; in fact, for the entire system of sacramentalism and sacerdotalism. Cp. P. II, Sec. IV, above. Luther's insistence on the Real Presence at Marburg, 1529, is often viewed as the occasion for the allegedly uncalled-for division of Protestantism, since it is said that the points of divergence between Luther and Zwingli were only superficial. The fact is that in the opinion of Lutheran theologians basic issues were at stake, of which the denial of the Real Presence was only symptomatic.

charged occasionally that Lutheran theology makes so much of the Real Presence that people are afraid to partake of the Lord's Supper, since the body and blood of Christ may prove to be poison to kill them. The fact is that Lutheran theology has only a soteriological and sacramental interest in the Real Presence and considers the Lord's Supper as a wholesome medicine for the soul and the body.[167]

In antithesis to the views which reduce the Real Presence either to a mere physical or a mere spiritual presence the Lutheran Confessions have urged three points: (1) the union of the earthly and heavenly elements is a sacramental union *(unio sacramentalis);* (2) the communicants receive the body and blood of Christ orally *(manducatio oralis);* (3) the unbelievers truly receive the body and blood of Christ *(manducatio indignorum).*

The Reformed charge that the Lutheran doctrine of the Real Presence comes very close to Rome's theory of transubstantiation, that at best it is consubstantiation or impanation.[168] In sharp antithesis both to the Romanist and to the Reformed theologians the Lutheran Confessions declare that "in, with, and under" the bread and wine the body and blood of Christ are present. But the prepositions are to be used merely antithetically and not as an attempt to explain the mystery of the Real Presence.[169] Lutheran theology insists on taking Christ's words as they read and gladly admits that Christ's words are an unusual mode of expression.[170] Since nowhere else but in the Sacrament of the Altar such a miraculous union of earthly and heavenly elements occurs, the Confessions have called it a sacramental union. But they make no attempt to explain the "how" of this sacramental union.

The symbolic view, which recognizes only a spiritual union, has always been the favored one.[171] Lutheran theology cannot accept it for two reasons. First, the symbolic view is predicated on the axiom: *Finitum non est capax infiniti,* "the finite body of Christ is incapable of omnipresence," and therefore can be present "locally" only at one place at one

---

[167] Large C., Lord's Supper, 67, 68.

[168] "Transubstantiation" implies that the earthly elements retain only their external appearances (color, taste, etc.) and are changed into Christ's body and blood. "Consubstantiation" usually denotes the theory — erroneously charged against Lutheranism — that the earthly and heavenly elements are united into one substance. "Impanation" is the theory that the body of Christ is somehow encased in the consecrated host.

[169] Large C., 28, 10; S. A., P. III, Art. VI, 1; F. C., Th. D., 35, 37 ff.

[170] F. C., Th. D., VII, 35, 37, 38, 115 ff. *The Apology of the F. C.* (published by the Lutherans against the Calvinistic attacks on the Lutheran doctrine of the Real Presence), states: "The expression [This is My Body, Th. D., 38] is called an unusual *(inusitata)* mode of speech, because in the ordinary figures of speech there is none which is just like the one Christ employs" (quoted in *Bekenntnisschriften,* p. 984, fn. 4).

[171] Some of the early church Fathers, including Augustine, can be interpreted as leaning toward a symbolical view. In 1530 Melanchthon wrote his *Sententiae veterum aliquot scriptorum de coena Domini* (*C. R.,* XXIII, 733—751) to demonstrate that the Lutheran position was that of the Fathers of the church, The Swiss Reformer John Oecolampadius replied with his *Dialogus,* an effort to show that the Zwinglian view was universally held until the 7th century. Cp. F. E. Mayer, "Artikel X der Variata," *C. T. M.,* II (1931), 594 ff. Reformed theologians today hold a large variety of views concerning the Lord's Supper; probably the most prevalent one is that a mystical union between the believer and Christ takes place.

time. The Lutheran Confessions consider this a denial of the personal union of Christ and in effect a total negation of Christ's saving work.[172] Secondly, Lutheranism holds that every word of God is a creative word. Christ's word of institution, "This is My body," is a mighty fiat. When — so Lutherans maintain — the officiant today speaks the words of consecration, his words are effective by virtue of Christ's command and institution.[173] The Lutheran Confessions refrain from entering upon the discussion at which precise moment the sacramental union begins or ends, except to state that there is no sacramental union outside the entire sacramental action or use, which comprises the consecration, the distribution, and the reception of the elements.[174]

In the Crypto-Calvinist Controversy it became necessary to maintain, secondly, the oral manducation and to state in unequivocal terms that the communicant partakes of Christ's body and blood orally, with the mouth, but that the manner is "spiritual," supernatural. The Reformed recognize only the "spiritual" eating and drinking described in John 6: 53 ff., which is symbolical language for believing. The Lutherans maintain that such a spiritual eating and drinking is indeed necessary for a salutary Communion. But in contrast to the Reformed view they maintain that in the

oral partaking of bread and wine the communicant also partakes orally of Christ's body and blood. The Lutherans strenuously renounce the Reformed charge of a "Capernaitic" eating and reject all idle and blasphemous questions, because the words of institution compel us to take our reason captive.[175]

The third emphasis which, according to Lutheran theologians, is inherent in the Real Presence is the fact that also unbelievers orally receive the body and blood of Christ (*manducatio indignorum*). Since the words of institution are Christ's creative words, they alone — not faith — effect the presence of His body and blood. Both the believer and the unbeliever receive the heavenly elements. But, unlike the believer, the unbeliever receives it for judgment. Far from deterring sincere Christians from partaking of Communion, this doctrine in reality assures the communicant that the Real Presence rests not upon his own worthiness or faith, but solely on the power of Christ's word.[176]

The Blessings. According to the Lutheran Confessions the Real Presence is of great soteriological and sacramental significance. In the words of institution the communicant is assured that he receives the body and blood of Christ and in this heavenly gift an unspeakably great treasure, since it is unthinkable that the body of the glorified God-man

---

172 The express purpose of Article VIII of the F. C. is to answer the Reformed hypothesis that Christ cannot be present "sacramentally" in the Supper. For the Lutherans the Real Presence is a soteriological question of the greatest significance. Cp. esp. Th. D., VIII, 38—47.

173 Th. D., VII, 75—78.

174 Ibid., 79—87.

175 F. C., Th. D., 105—28; 61—67; Ep., VII, 41, 42. The term "Capernaitic" is merely a euphemism for cannibalistic.

176 Large C., Lord's Supper, 15, 16, 69, 72. Lutheran theology recognizes only two classes of communicants, the worthy and the unworthy, both receiving the body and blood of Christ. Reformed theology asserts that there are three classes, the worthy (strong believers), the unworthy (doubting believers), and the godless (unbelievers). The first two receive Christ's body and blood "spiritually"; the third receive only bread and wine.

should be a futile and fruitless thing.[177] In the Lord's Supper Christ offers Himself, His entire Person, life, and work, in the words and the elements to all communicants.[178] This means that we share the life of the God-man from His holy incarnation to His innocent death and burial. The words "Given and shed for you" are not merely a report of a historical event, but actually make the communicant a contemporary and participant of this glorious fact. Thus Christ offers us the entire treasure which as God-man He has brought from heaven.[179]

"Where there is forgiveness of sins, there is also life and salvation." The sacrament offers and gives Christ not only in His death, but also in His resurrection and glorified life. The Lutheran Confessions maintain that every celebration of the Lord's Supper is in effect an anticipation of our own resurrection and the glorification of our body. At every Communion the ancient antiphon of Notker the Stammerer: "In the midst of life we are surrounded by death" must be inverted to read: "In the midst of death we are surrounded by life." In Baptism the Christian has died and arisen to the new life; in the Lord's Supper he receives the true body and blood of Christ as food, medicine, refreshment, for body and soul. The Confessions point out that those Christians who are negligent in their Communion attendance soon become callous and spiritually rude and coarse. On the other hand, in frequent Communion Christ offers the necessary gifts to lead a God-pleasing life.[180] Like Baptism, the Lord's Supper is a "wholesome and salutary medicine" to bestow life upon our body and soul. For where the soul is restored, the body, too, is helped.

The Salutary Use. In opposition to Rome's theory that the efficacy of the sacraments lies in the mere performance according to the rites of the church, *ex opere operato,* the Lutheran church teaches that faith is unconditionally necessary for the salutary use of the Lord's Supper. The true worthiness of the communicants consists not in any outward bodily preparation, not in the resolution to lead a better life, not even in strong faith, but simply in faith.[181]

Law and Gospel

The proper distinction between Law and Gospel is called the most brilliant light of the Reformation.[182] This statement has significance only in the light of the Lutheran understanding of the Gospel as the means of grace. Lutheran dogmaticians usually speak of the Gospel as the power of God to bring us Christ and His treasures (*vis dativa*) and also the power to create faith, which makes these treasures our own (*vis effectiva*). Any mingling of the Law into the Gospel message is viewed not only as poor theology but as actually obscuring the Gospel and robbing Christians of the Gospel comfort.

[177] Large C., Lord's Supper, 29, 30.

[178] F. C., Th. D., VII, 6.

[179] Ap., XXIV, 49, 90; Large C., Lord's Supper, 28, 29, 33—35.

[180] Ibid., 70, 78, 54, 68, 23 f.; Ap., XXII, 10; F. C., Th. D., VII, 44, 59. Cp. Th. D., VIII, 76 ff. In fact, the entire Christology is presented in the F. C. from the soteriological viewpoint. More specifically, the believing communicant receives the entire Christ.

[181] Small C., Ques. 4. Large C., Lord's Supper, 33, 57 f., 72—78; A. C., XXIV, 30 f.; Ap., IV, 210; XXII, 10; XXIV, 71—73, 77; F. C., Th. D., 69—71.

[182] F. C., Ep. V, 2; Th. D., V, 1.

The danger of mingling and confounding the two doctrines is very real, because both doctrines must always be preached side by side. In fact, the entire Scriptures must be divided into these two parts, Law and Gospel. God can be viewed only in one or the other of His works, either as Lawgiver or as Law Remover; either as the God who strikes terror into man's heart, who threatens, who kills, or the God who has prepared comfort for us, who quickens, who heals, who saves.[183]

The Lutheran Confessions declare that the mingling of Law and Gospel is an ever-present and a real danger to Christian theology. Throughout the Scriptures both doctrines are presented side by side, in fact, so closely that the two doctrines are contained in one sentence.[184] To maintain the proper distinction between the two doctrines, it is mandatory to understand clearly the nature and function of each. Some theologians reduce the Gospel to a "new Law" when they impose on men the "evangelical counsels" and "commandments of the church" as necessary for salvation. The antinomians, on the other hand, pretend to elevate the Gospel by doing away with the Law entirely,[185] and thereby unwittingly they also reduce the Gospel to Law. While there is an inseparable conjunction between the Law and the Gospel, the functions of the two dare never be confounded, lest the Gospel be changed into Law and the whole Christian proclamation be turned topsy-turvy.[186]

The Lutheran Confessions present the function of the Law as twofold: (1) to restrain sin, and (2) to reveal original sin and its fruits. Actually the Law increases sin and thus makes men worse, because the Law forbids the very things that they want to do, and they respond in open mutiny and violent rebellion. Sometimes this rebellion manifests itself in haughty pride. The Law shows how comprehensively sin has corrupted man and how unable he is to do God's will. But proud man assumes the right to cut down God's holy demands to his own standard and capacity. This procedure implies that man completely ignores God's holy demands in the First

---

[183] Ap., IV, 5, 102, 186, 257; XII, 53; F. C., Th. D., V, 23. Lutheran dogmaticians usually present the Christian doctrine under larger headings, such as bibliology, theology, anthropology, etc. But it would be fully in accord with the Lutheran Confessions to divide all dogmatical material under the two major headings, Law and Gospel, and to treat every phase of Christian revelation from the twofold aspect of Law and Gospel; for example, man under the Law and under the Gospel. Cp. fn. 73, above.

[184] Ap., XII, 44, refers to Matt. 11:28, where the burden of sin (Law) and coming to Christ (Gospel) are mentioned in the same breath.

[185] Some antinomians in the Lutheran church, like Agricola, maintained that no preaching of the Law dare to be tolerated in the Christian pulpit because the Christian must learn the way of salvation only from the "Gospel." Other Lutherans showed antinomian trends by stating that the Law knows nothing of faith and therefore cannot reveal the sin of unbelief; it is therefore the function of the Gospel to reveal the greatest of all sins, man's unbelief. These two views were condemned in F. C., V, VI. Cp. Frank, II, 148 ff., 243 ff. W. Preger, I, 336 ff.; P. Tschackert, 478 ff., 514 ff.; F. Bente, 161 ff.; Lauri Haikola, Gesetz und Evangelium bei Matthias Flacius Illyricus (Lund: C. W. K. Gleerup, 1952).

[186] There is also a semantic problem, since both terms are used in a narrow and broad sense. The term "Law" may denote the Law written into man's heart, the image of God, even "the good counsel" of God, Ap., IV, 351; F. C., Ep., V, 2; Th. D., I, 10; II, 50; VI, 5. The Gospel is spoken of as the entire New Testament message, the proclamation of both God's wrath over sin and His pardon for the sinner.

Table and so changes the demands of the Second Table that at best no more remains than a mere outward conformity with the letter of the Law.[187] In short, the chief function of the Law is to drive man to despair, to a realization of total bondage to his sin and of his enslavement under Satan.[188]

The Law, secondly, reveals God's wrath. The theme of a large section of the Apology is: The Law constantly accuses us and shows us only God's wrath. The two adverbs "constantly" and "only" occur again and again. By revealing God's wrath over sin the Law can produce only hatred of God. And this endures throughout eternity, for the verdict "Depart from Me" is a word effective not only in the moment when God pronounces it, but it is an eternally active and effective word.[189] And this revelation and knowledge of God's wrath is an actual experience of God's wrath; it is the terrors of conscience, it is an actual state of eternal dying under the curse of God.[190] The real and proper function of the Law is to reveal sin and God's wrath. Whatever therefore reveals God's wrath is Law, be it in the Old or the New Testament. Thus even the Passion history is Law in so far as it shows the greatness of God's wrath.[191]

The Apology speaks of only one chief purpose of the Law, to condemn; the Smalcald Articles speak of two and the Formula of Concord even of three "uses" of the Law.[192] The term "third use" of the Law is used primarily to designate the preaching of the Law to the Christian, in so far as and because he is still at all times the sinner. The Christian according to his old man has his own ideas as to what is sin and what is a God-pleasing work. For that reason the old Adam, the recalcitrant and bucking bronco that remains in the Christian, must be forced to do good works not only with coaxing and threatenings, but also with the heavy stick of afflictions and punishments. Until we strip off the body of sin in death and are perfectly renewed in the glorious resurrection, the Christian is under the demands, threats, and punishment of the Law. What is sometimes called the "third use" is in reality the "chief use" of the Law in its proclamation to the regenerate in so far as he still has the old Adam.[193]

The only purpose of preaching the Law as the proclamation of God's wrath is to lead man to a knowledge of sin. This is the "alien office" which enables the Holy Spirit to come to His real and proper office, namely, to preach the Gospel, which, strictly speaking, is nothing but the proclamation of what man should believe in order to obtain forgiveness for his sins, which the Law has

---

[187] S. A., P. III, Art. II, 1 ff. Cp. Ap., IV, 35, 130, 131; XII, 145 (see the German text). F. C., Th. D., V, 10—17.

[188] Ap., IV, 20, 212.

[189] S. A., P. III, Art. III, 7. Ap., IV, 40. The phrase *lex semper accusat* occurs in several variations in the Ap., IV, 249, 295, etc.

[190] S. A., P. III, Art. III, 2; Ap., IV, 37, 47, and many other references.

[191] Luther: "What more terrible preaching of God's wrath than the suffering and death of His own Son?" F. C., Th. D., V, 12.

[192] S. A., P. III, Art. II (twofold); F. C., Ep., VI, 1 (threefold). Werner Elert, *The Christian Ethos*, pp. 294—303, declares that the later Lutheran dogmaticians have no ground for appealing to Luther in their view of the "third use" of the Law, but that this concept came into Lutheran theology from Calvinistic theology, where the "third use" is considered the primary use of the Law.

[193] F. C., Th. D., VI, 6—9, 18—25.

revealed.[194] Therefore both Law and Gospel must be preached in the Christian church until the end of human history. This juxtaposition, however, dare never lead to a mingling of the two. For though they always go together, they are as far apart as heaven and earth.[195] They stand in a dialectical relation to each other, so that the one always and categorically denies what the other affirms. The Law announces to man: "God demands everything of you if you hope to be saved." The Gospel declares: "Christ has done everything for you." The Law declares: "You are a sinner; God hates you; you are eternally lost." The Gospel proclaims the very opposite: "You are righteous; God loves you; you are eternally saved." According to the Lutheran Confessions both pronouncements must always be proclaimed. If the church proclaims: "Do the best possible, and you will be saved," she dishonors Christ and His work and actually abolishes the Gospel. If, on the other hand, she proclaims: "It is God's nature to overlook and pardon man's weaknesses," she dishonors God's holiness, abolishes the Law, and thus negates Christ's vicarious work. Both Law and Gospel must therefore always be preached together, but in such a way that the fact that they are diametrical opposites is always observed.[196]

The Christian Life

Some later Lutheran dogmaticians present all Christian doctrines sequentially, beginning with regeneration and concluding with glorification (the order of salvation). The Lutheran Confessions of the 16th century do not systematize so precisely. Their chief concern is to retain the Christological implication of the Christian proclamation in its central position. The article concerning Christ, His Person and works, is the primary and principal article also in the doctrine of sanctification.

It is frequently charged that the Lutheran Confessions failed to evaluate accurately the significance of sanctification or the Christian life and that the best they could do was to use the term "fruits of faith." [197] However, the term "fruits of faith" is good, for it points out that good works never have an independent purpose, e. g., to serve as merits whereby to gain eternal life. Man's good moral behavior has no value by itself. Nevertheless Lutheran theology esteems good works highly, but for other reasons than in the Roman system. This becomes evident in the fact that Lutheran theology has no "system of ethics" in the usually accepted definition of the term.[198] Without attempting to prescribe a detailed catalog of "dos" and "don'ts," the Lutheran Confessions de-

194 Ibid., V, 11—17; 20—22.

195 Ibid., V. 24. Ap., IV, 186.

196 F. C., Th. D., V, 1, 23 ff. Cp. C. F. W. Walther, *The Proper Distinction Between Law and Gospel*, trans. W. H. T. Dau (St. Louis: C. P. H., 1929). Theo. Harnack, I, 444 ff.

197 Hans Asmussen, pp. 95—105. *"Aus der Unterscheidung* [between justification and sanctification] *wird leicht eine Scheidung,"* i. e., the "and" in "justification and sanctification" may easily prove to be fatal.

198 In Lutheran theology Christian ethics is usually not treated as a separate and distinct phase of dogmatics. Cp. Adolph Harless, *Christliche Ethik*, 1845; Johann Michael Reu and Paul H. Buehring, *Christian Ethics* (Columbus: Lutheran Book Concern, 1930); W. Elert, *The Christian Ethos;* Eric H. Wahlstrom, *The New Life in Christ* (Phila.: Muhlenberg Press, 1950), ch. iv; George W. Forell, *Ethics of Decision* (Philadelphia: Muhlenberg Press, c. 1955); Joseph Sittler, *The Structure of Christian Ethics* (Baton Rouge: Louisiana State University Press, 1958).

scribe in broad terms the implications of "the new life in Christ." A frequent charge is to the effect that the Lutheran emphasis of *sola gratia* and *sola fide* destroys every incentive for good works or will inevitably lead to antinomianism. This charge is wholly false.

FAITH AND GOOD WORKS INSEPARABLE

In accord with their central doctrine the Lutheran Confessions point to the indissoluble union between faith and good works. They affirm the axiom "Good works do not make a man pious, but a pious man does good works." Paradoxically Lutheran theology teaches that man is saved *sola fide* and at the same time not only requires good works, but also shows how good works can be done. By properly stressing both the *sola gratia* and the necessity of good works it makes the Christian life rich and meaningful.[199]

The statement "Good works are necessary" is directed against the Roman Catholic theologians and against the Majoristic trends within the Lutheran church.[200] Some Lutherans held that the phrase "good works are necessary" involves compulsion and coercion. The Lutheran Confessions answer that good works are indeed necessary, not by a necessity of coercion, but of immutability, since it is the very essence and nature of faith to be active constantly and willingly in good works.[201]

The prime requisite of a good work is that it be in conformity with the will of God. Therefore the Lutheran Confessions reject the whole battery of human-devised works as being no better than pagan idolatry.[202] At the same time the Confessions point out that mere outward conformity with the letter of the commandment does not constitute a good work. Since the summary of all commandments is love of God, and since love is the actual fulfilling of the Law, the attitude of the heart determines the character of a work. Without such love all worship, no matter how holy it may appear, is an empty shell without any kernel, yes, it is an abomination in the sight of God and the dead, cold, ineffective work of a hypocrite. The Christian's good works are never coerced, but always flow from a willing spirit, because the Law is written into his heart.[203]

In antithesis to the Roman and Arminian views which consider good works necessary for man's salvation, the Apol-

[199] A. C., VI; XX; XXVII; Ap., IV, 124, 125, 136, 140; S. A., P. III, Art. IV, 40, and many other references.

[200] For bibliog. on Georg Major's extreme statement and its Romanizing trends cp. fn. 129.

[201] A. C., XXVII; Ap., IV, 189; XII, 77; F. C., Ep., Art. IV; Th. D., IV, 7, 14. The Christian "must" do good works by a *necessitas ordinis mandati et voluntatis Christi ac debiti nostri, non autem necessitas coactionis,* Th. D., IV, 16.

[202] A. C., XX, 3; XXVII, 36; Ap., XV, 14 ff.; XXVII, 54; XIII, 77; Large C., Decalog, 102, 115, 116, 311; F. C., Th. D., IV, 7; VI, 5, 25.

[203] Ap., II, 15—22; IV, 123—125, 130, 131, 136—144, 219, 289. Cp. the entire article against monastic vows, esp., XXVII, 25. F. C., IV, 12, 17 f. Lutheran theology holds that civic righteousness is necessary for successful social living and that man is able to render it. Lutheranism teaches that such outward and civic righteousness is a divine ordinance whereby God checks the evil designs of the devil and wicked men and maintains decency in the world. Though God has promised to reward such civic righteousness, this philosophic righteousness remains only a Pharisaic righteousness, and its sphere is exclusively secular and temporal. Ap., IV, 14—16, 22—24, 28, 130, 288.

ogy in the German text summarizes the significance of good works as follows:

One must do good works, because God wills it; they are fruits of faith, as St. Paul says Eph. 2:10; therefore good works must follow faith as an expression of gratitude toward God; furthermore, that faith may exercise itself, grow and increase, and that through our confessions and godly conduct others may be admonished.[204]

SPHERE OF CHRISTIAN ACTIVITY

The sphere of Christian activity does not consist in self-appointed and unnatural practices. The Christian life is "new obedience" in whatever sphere of activity the Christian finds himself. This means, first of all, that in his every activity the Christian devotes his service entirely to God and to his fellow man and is never prompted to seek his own welfare. The Christian life cannot be viewed atomistically, as though it consisted in observing certain canonical hours, exercising oneself in specific virtues, performing certain prescribed works perfunctorily. The Christian's entire life is simply "new obedience." Therefore also affliction or the "holy cross" is part of the Christian life in so far as the Christian for God's sake will gladly and willingly endure the persecutions incident to his state as a believer.[205]

Lutheran theology has, secondly, a deep interest in God's creation. True, Lutheranism is otherworldly. Paradoxically, for this very reason, it is truly this-worldly in a God-pleasing manner. To confess: "I believe in God the Father, Creator of heaven and earth," means that I must and will find joy in the things which God has created and use everything which God has created for me and in which He reveals His fatherly heart toward me. The Christian worships and serves not only the "Redeemer God," but also the "Creator God."[206]

Lutheranism, thirdly, always deals with the total person. It allows for no conflict between the this-worldly and otherworldly view in the Christian life; it grants no double standard of morality, one motivated solely by the Holy Spirit, and the other controlled by reason, personal advantage, or some social factor. The Christian as a total person is active in good works, and his one standard is love toward God and toward the fellow man. Thus the Christian's good works are called "fruits of the Spirit," while the unbeliever's are "works of the Law."[207]

A fourth phase which Lutheranism stresses in the doctrine of sanctification is the high value which Holy Scripture places upon the vocation. In antithesis to monasticism the Lutheran Confessions maintain that by divine ordinance and creation God has ennobled every Christian vocation. The Lutheran Confessions repeatedly contrast the works of "the saint" who attempts to serve God in his self-appointed labors of fasting, men-

[204] Ap., IV, 189. The Christian's good works serve as an admonition to others, since Christ displays His glorious kingdom and celebrates His victory over Satan, not only in the missionary and pastoral successes of a Paul or Augustine, but also in the humblest good work of every Christian. Good works are said to be necessary also to assure us of the state of grace and to make our calling and election sure, inasmuch as they are an evidence of the Christian's faith. Ap., XX, 12 f.; cp. F. C., Th. D., IV, 33.

[205] See A. C., XXVII, 31, 32; Large C., Lord's Prayer, 65. Cp. W. Walther, pp. 394—422. The Lutheran Confessions were written to a large extent against the exaggerated and sinful views of the "religious" life in distinction from the "secular" life.

[206] Large C., Creed, 12—24. See Arthur Carl Piepkorn, "Christ and Culture: A Lutheran Approach," *Response*, II, 1 (Pentecost, 1960), 3—16.

[207] A. C., XVI, 5; F. C., Th. D., VI, 10—16.

dicancy, pilgrimages, whereby he serves neither God nor man, and the Christian who sees God's command in every form of labor and state of life and therefore knows that his work is nobler than that of any monk or nun.[208] In vocational counseling the Lutheran will observe only the principle that in his vocation the Christian serve God and his fellow man. He rejects the false notion that a specific command given to a specific person, for instance, the Savior's injunction to the rich young ruler, is a universally binding command. The Christian's concern is to occupy himself with such holy works as are Christ's victories over Satan and thus most glorious works in the sight of God.[209]

CHRISTIAN PERFECTION

The Lutheran Confessions set forth the Scriptural view on Christian perfection in antithesis to the flight from the world advocated by scholastics and Anabaptists. The former held that Christian perfection is obtainable by a specific mode of living, preferably the "religious" life with the careful observance of the various rules of the respective religious order. Lutheranism maintains that "Christian perfection" consists in this, that the heart trusts God, believes that for Christ's sake God is gracious and merciful, seeks everything from God, and confidently asks God for whatever is necessary in our trials and tribulations.[210] The Anabaptists and Schwenkfeldians maintained that in conversion the Holy Spirit works such a change that man becomes completely holy in this life. Against this false view the Lutheran Confessions point out that Christians must indeed lead righteous lives, but that the incipient righteousness of Christians is very imperfect and pleases God only for Christ's sake.[211]

Antinomianism is another type of perfectionism. It anticipates the perfected and glorified state of the Christian when it claims that because the Christians are the temples of the Holy Spirit, they require no preaching of the Law. The Lutheran Confessions maintain that while the Christian is free from the Lord according to the new man, according to the old Adam he is still under the demands, coercion, threats, and curse of the Law; that although the Christian's sins are covered by the perfect obedience of Christ, and although he daily mortifies the old Adam, nevertheless the Christian retains the old Adam as long as he dwells in the flesh, and he is therefore always *simul iustus et peccator*, at the same time a just man and a sinner.[212]

---

[208] See Large C., Decalog, 120, 117, 143, 148. See Oscar E. Feucht et al., eds., *Engagement and Marriage: A Sociological, Historical, and Theological Investigation* (St. Louis: C. P. H., c. 1959), chs. 5—7, 10, and the same editors' *Sex and the Church* (St. Louis: C. P. H., c. 1961), chs. vi to ix, xii.

[209] Ap., IV, 191 ff. See Billing and Rupprecht, fn. 27, above.

[210] A. C., XXVII, 44—50; Ap., XXVII, 24—33, 49, 50. See entire Article XXVII, on "Monastic Vows." The Lutheran Confessions brand the whole theory of the meritoriousness of the works of supererogation as devils' doctrine, because it actually suppresses the doctrine of the Gospel. Ap., XII, 45, 65.

[211] Ap., IV, 161, 293, 308, and many other references. Some of the early Quakers adopted the Anabaptist principle. Currently the position of the Anabaptists is shared in a large measure by the Holiness bodies.

[212] F. C., Th. D., VI, 2—8; Ap., IV, 160 f. The doctrine of perfectionism is predicated on the denial of the true nature of sin, particularly the theory that nothing is really sin unless it is a conscious and voluntary action. Ap., II, 42 ff.; IV, 166—171.

The Church and the Ministry

THE CHURCH

The Nature and Essence of the Church. In Lutheran theology the doctrine of the church (*ecclesiology*) is always Christology and soteriology. In reality, this doctrine is an epitome of all Christian doctrine. It is true that the central article from which all theological thinking must issue, and to which it must return, is the article of Christ. But this applies equally well to the doctrine of the church, for the church is the congregation of those whom Christ has rescued from the power and tyranny of Satan, sin, and eternal death and in whose hearts He has established His glorious rule.[213] As a member of the church the Christian possesses eternal life as an "already." Unless this is maintained, the concept of the church will degenerate into a mere external organization, as in all Romanizing theology; or into a spiritualized and metaphysical fellowship that is no more than a Platonic idea, as in the Anabaptist movement. Lutheranism defines the church in the strict sense as the congregation of saints and believers among whom the Gospel is purely preached and the sacraments rightly administered.[214] A child of seven years is said to know that the church is the holy believers. In a broad sense the Christian church is composed of all those who profess Christianity and is essentially an empirical domain in which unbelievers and believers mingle freely until the great separation on Judgment Day. But in spite of their outward association with Christians the unbelievers belong to the kingdom of the devil and have no part in the kingdom of Christ. The unbelievers know as little about Christ's kingdom and its nature as they do of Christ's true glory, which is hidden until His glorious manifestation.[215] Though the church is hidden under the cross, *cruce tecta*, and its true essence and glory are known only to faith, Lutheran theology maintains against "enthusiastic" and spiritualistic principles that membership in the church is possible only by the Holy Spirit's call through the external means of grace. In brief, Lutheranism maintains both that the church is the congregation of holy people, *congregatio sanctorum*, and that it is the congregation of called people, *congregatio vocatorum*.[216]

The Marks of the Church. Though the church does not consist in external things, such as ceremonies and rites, and though her true essence remains unknown to the unbeliever, the presence of the church can be established by the proclamation of the Gospel and the administration of the sacraments. The church and the means of grace stand

---

[213] Large C., II, 27; Ap., VII, 13; XXVII, 27.

[214] A. C., VII. — Some take the *sanctorum* of *sanctorum communio* to be the neuter gender and understand the phrase as a sharing of holy things. So, for instance, Werner Elert, *Abendmahl und Kirchengemeinschaft in der alten Kirche hauptsächlich des Ostens* (Berlin: Lutherisches Verlagshaus, 1954), pp. 5—16, 116—181.

[215] Ap., VII, 9—22. On the whole subject, see Arthur Carl Piepkorn, "What the Symbols Have to Say About the Church," *C. T. M.*, XXVI (1955), 721—763; Anders Nygren, ed., *This Is the Church*, trans. by Carl C. Rasmussen (Philadelphia: Muhlenberg Press, 1952); Conrad Bergendoff, *The Doctrine of the Church in American Lutheranism* (Philadelphia: Board of Publication of the United Lutheran Church in America, c. 1956); Vilmos Vajta et al., eds., *The Unity of the Church, A Symposium: Papers Presented to the Commission on Theology and Liturgy of the Lutheran World Federation* (Rock Island: Augustana Press, c. 1957).

[216] A. C., VII, VIII.

in an indissoluble union with each other, and the one is unthinkable without the other. Thus preaching and administration of the sacraments are marks *(notae)* of the church.[217]

The statement: "In which [the Christian church] the Gospel is rightly taught and the sacraments are rightly administered," [218] causes difficulty only when the holy Christian church is confounded with a specific external organization. The word "rightly" denotes that qualitatively there is only one Gospel, but that quantitatively it can be present in a greater or lesser degree. Likewise the sacraments are rightly administered, or they are not sacraments. The church — in its truest sense, or "strictly speaking" — is found in the "empirical" or "visible" church — the church "broadly speaking." [219]

The Attributes of the Church. The church is the one *holy* catholic church. The church is holy because all members are adorned with the "foreign righteousness of Christ" and with their own incipient righteousness of life. The holiness is predicated on the doctrines of justification and sanctification. The holiness of the church is not marred by the evil works of the nominal Christians, for the godless men and hypocrites who are mingled with the true believers are not the church and share only its outward signs and marks.[220]

Unity and catholicity are two glorious aspects of the church. The unity consists solely in the unity of faith in the one Lord,[221] and its catholicity only in the universality of sharing in Christ. The Lutheran interpretation of "catholic" is Christological, and the term can be reproduced with "Christian." [222]

The holy Christian church is infallible. This applies only to the true church, not to the empirical church. Membership in the true church is absolutely necessary to salvation. Outside the church there is no Holy Spirit, and without Him it is impossible to come to Christ. Outside the church there is no forgiveness of sins and no holiness, but in the church everything is designed to bring forgiveness, life, and salvation.[223]

---

[217] Large C., II, 41—45, 61, 37, 56.

[218] A. C., VII. The word "rightly" was purposely added in the A. C. It is not in the Schwabach Articles or the earlier drafts of the A. C.

[219] Cp. F. E. Mayer, "The Proper Distinction Between Law and Gospel and the Terminology Visible and Invisible Church," *C. T. M.*, XXV (1954), 177—198.

[220] Large C., II, 37, 39, 51, 53; Ap., VII, 5, 14—16, 28 f.

[221] The Lutherans hold that no end of confusion arises when this spiritual unity is confounded with external uniformity in rites or church activities. Eph. 4:5 applies to the true inner unity and not to an outward union in ecumenical church work or even in the establishment of a denominational doctrinal agreement. Cp. A. C., VII, 4; Ap., VII, 33 f. See Paul M. Bretscher, "The Unity of the Church," *C. T. M.*, XXVI (1955), 321—340.

[222] Ap., VII, 10, 20. The word "Christian" was used instead of "catholic" prior to Luther's time, e. g., in an exposition of the Creed in 1485 and in Surgant, *Manuale Curatorum*, 1506.

[223] Ap., VII, 14, 27, 22; Large C., II, 45, 55 f., 66. Unfortunately some authors interpret such statements as if Lutherans identified the holy Christian church with the Lutheran church. Cp., for example, J. Paul Williams (fn. 1, above), p. 152. Lutherans do not unchurch those bodies with whom they are not in communion; this is true with reference even to the Roman Catholic Church. See Kristen Ejner Skydsgaard, *One in Christ*, trans. Axel C. Kildegaard (Philadelphia: Muhlenberg Press, c. 1957); Skydsgaard, "On Dialogues Between Roman Catholic and Lutheran Theologians," *Lutheran World*, VII (1960), 126—141; and George A. Lindbeck,

The Ministry

The Lutheran Confessions present this doctrine against the background of sacerdotalism and "enthusiasm." Against sacerdotalism Lutherans make much of the priesthood of all believers. They maintain that according to 1 Peter 2:9 all Christians have the right and authority to call and ordain ministers. According to the Lutheran doctrine of the church, the command to preach is given to the church, the congregation of believers. Wherever the church is, there is therefore *eo ipso* the authority to preach. According to the very heart of Lutheran theology the one and only function of the ministry is to preach the Gospel and administer the sacraments; in other words, to absolve penitent sinners, to guide Christians, to judge doctrine, and, if necessary, to condemn error, to excommunicate impenitent sinners, and to ordain ministers.[224]

Against the "enthusiasm" of the Anabaptists and others the Lutheran Confessions emphasize the God-ordained institution of the public ministry. No one is to preach or administer sacraments in the church unless he is *rite vocatus*. The Lutheran Confessions esteem the call into the ministry so highly that they are willing to call both the ministry and ordination a sacrament if it is understod to mean that the ministry has been established by God, who has given His promise that through the appointed ministers He will work in the hearts of men.[225]

The Christian and Civil Government

The opinion generally prevailed prior to the Reformation period that true piety was obtainable only in the monastic orders, as many Romanists claimed; or in strict asceticism, as later asserted by the Anabaptists, since all secular things, such as one's calling, or vocation, matrimony, government, were considered more or less sinful or at least impure. The Lutheran Confessions support the principle that all civil orders have been established by God and as such are God's precious gifts to us, whereby He maintains order and decency in the world, nourishes and supports us, governs and protects us. Luther suggested that the prince's coat of arms should contain a loaf of bread rather than a lion, to remind the subjects that it is through the office of the government that they obtain peace, protection, and daily bread. It is the government's duty to enact laws, to serve as judge, to regulate civil affairs, and — if necessary — to conduct just wars. And all Christians are to participate in these activities directly if qualified and called upon; otherwise indirectly by giving obedience to the government and constantly making intercession for it. The Lutheran Confessions maintain that all legitimate governments are ordained, retained, and defended by God to protect men against the devil.[226] The Lutheran position on the doctrine of the state has been charged with developing a *laissez-faire* attitude. Worse still, some have com-

---

"The Evangelical Possibilities of Roman Catholic Theology," ibid., 142 to 152.

[224] A. C., XXVIII, 5, 21, 30. Cp. S. A., *Tract on the Authority and Primacy of the Pope*, pp. 66—70. Ap., XVI, 42—44 (German text). See also Hans H. Kramm, *Bischof, Pastor und Gemeinde: Die lutherische Lehre vom Amt* (Berlin: Lutherisches Verlagshaus, 1954).

[225] A. C., XIV: *Nemo debeat in ecclesia publice docere aut sacramenta administrare nisi rite vocatus.* Cp. Ap., XIII, 5—13; XXVIII, 9—11. The efficacy of the means of grace is not dependent upon the faith or unbelief of the minister (A. C., VIII; Ap., VII, 19 ff., 28).

[226] Ap., XVI, 1—5, 7; XIII, 75; Large C., Com. IV, 150. See also H. Richard Klann, "Luther on War and Revolution," *C. T. M.*, XXV (1954), 353—366.

pletely misunderstood the Lutheran distinction between the spiritual and the secular realms and have actually separated them in the fashion of the Anabaptists. The Lutheran doctrine on the Christian's duty toward civil government can be understood only in the light of the Gospel. The Christian knows that the Gospel has sanctified everything he does, including his activity in the social order. The Gospel grants true Christian liberty, enabling the Christian to make free decisions concerning his social and civil activities in accordance with the supreme commandment of love.[227]

During the Reformation period the proximity of the Last Day was a great reality, in fact, so much so that every social order seems to be viewed only as an "interim" instrument. True, the Christian is admonished to possess all things as though he did not possess them. But at the same time the Lutheran Confessions stress that the Christian lives in two realms, the state and the church. While he keeps them distinctly apart as two independent powers, he uses each in its specific sphere of function and activity: each with its peculiar means, the church with the means of grace, the government with external force. In its sphere, and using its God-given means, the government is said to perform "holy works," to "serve God." The better to serve God and man the state has the jurisdiction to enact laws, to gather scientific and technological information, to foster education and culture, and the power to punish the evildoer. It is therefore not improper to say that government is the greatest earthly benefit of God given to man.[228] But the state deals only with temporal and external things. The state fosters the righteousness which elevates man in the sight of men. The church alone brings the righteousness which "prevails" in God's sight.[229]

Eschatology

The Lutheran Confessions devote only two short articles to the second coming of Christ and refer to it in passing in a few instances. However, there is an eschatological overtone throughout the Confessions, and all doctrines are presented in this eschatological setting. The authors of each confessional book make their confessions before contemporary society and posterity in the full consciousness that they must give an account before the judgment seat of Christ. Lutheran theology views all Christian doctrine in the light of eter-

---

[227] This statement seems to answer the charge that the Lutheran pronouncement on civil government in the Confessions is completely inadequate today, because it does not come to grips with such modern questions as pacifism, capital punishment, nuclear war, etc. The Lutheran Confessions simply enunciate basic principles. The application of these must be left to the enlightened and sanctified conscience of the Christian. See Warren Quanbeck, ed., *God and Caesar: A Christian Approach to Social Ethics* (Minneapolis: Augsburg Publishing House, c. 1959); Harold C. Letts, ed., *Christian Social Responsibility* (Philadelphia: Muhlenberg Press, c. 1957), 3 vols.; Edgar M. Carlson, *The Church and the Public Conscience* (Philadelphia: Muhlenberg Press, c. 1956); Howard Hong, *This World and the Church: Studies in Secularism* (Minneapolis: Augsburg Publishing House, c. 1955); Eivind Berggrav, *Man and State*, trans. George Aus (Philadelphia: Muhlenberg Press, c. 1951); Richard R. Caemmerer, *The Church and the World* (St. Louis: Concordia Publishing House, 1949).

[228] A. C., XVI, XVIII, 4. Ap., XVII, 59; IV, 22. Tract on the Authority and Primacy of the Pope, 31.

[229] Ap., IV, 22. Cp. Schlink, Ch. vii.

nity, *sub specie aeternitatis.*[230] This is true of the doctrine of the church, and the eschatological overtone enables Lutheran theology to distinguish between the church in the strict sense and the empirical church. Now the hypocrites are mingled with the church, but in the revelation at Christ's return the true church and the hypocrites will be forever separated.[231] Likewise the doctrine of man can be understood most clearly in the light of eschatology. In this life we know man only in his corruption and are prone to make his corruption a part of his very being and thus blame God for man's sin. At Christ's second coming the corruption in every saint will forever be removed from his nature to the glory of God, and the invisible conflict between man in his new nature and man in his old nature will forever be ended.[232] Then also the absolute distinction between Law and Gospel will be publicly demonstrated. In this life the Christian is *iustus,* fully justified through faith in the Gospel, and at the same time *peccator,* a sinner, under the Law. At Christ's second coming the Law in its eternal verdict "Depart!" will apply only to those on Christ's left, and the Gospel in its eternally effective "Come!" will concern only the saints.[233]

The Lutheran Confessions condemn every form of chiliasm. They maintain that the earth is experiencing a gradual degeneration, a process of senescence.[234]

Lutheran theology includes the doctrine of God's gracious election under eschatology, because it views predestination as the summary of all Christian revelation; not only as a synopsis of God's gracious revelation but also as the final gracious truth, the capstone of all Christian revelation. In Lutheran theology predestination is exclusively soteriological and comprehends every gracious act for His elect children. Lutherans describe God's eternal decree of grace as follows: God has in eternity decreed to do for me all that He in time has done, is doing, and will continue to do for my eternal salvation. Usually eight points are listed as comprising God's gracious activity as decreed for me from eternity: redemption, vocation through the means of grace, conversion, justification, sanctification, protection against enemies, preservation in faith, and ultimately glorification.[235] These points comprise the entire order of salvation and are the Gospel in a nutshell. They cover my salvation from eternity to eternity. Lutheran theology advises that in contemplating the doctrine of election one should first occupy himself with the Gospel and there obtain the forgiveness of sins; second, contend with sin; and then in time of trials go to the

---

[230] A. C., XVII; Ap., XVII; Pref. to A. C.; F. C., Th. D., XII, 40; Schlink, ch. viii; F. E. Mayer "Foreword," *C. T. M.,* XXII (1951), 1—7.

[231] Ap., VII, 19.

[232] F. C., Ep., I, 10.

[233] Large C., II, 57 ff.; F. C., Th. D., VI, 6.

[234] A. C., XXIII, 14; Ap., XXIII, 53, 54. A sign of the world's senility is the activity of the antichristian powers, sometimes identified with Islam, sometimes with the papacy, because of its lies concerning the Mass, purgatory, etc. S. A., II, 4, 14; Tract on Authority and Primacy of the Pope, 39, 57; Ap., VII, 48; XXIV, 51; XV, 18. Luther concludes the Pref. to the S. A. with the prayer: "Dear Lord Jesus, do Thou convoke a council, and deliver Thy servants by Thy glorious advent." On purgatory, the intermediate state, prayer for the dead, see S. A., II, 2, 12; Ap., XXIV, 94, 96.

[235] F. C., Th. D., XI, 14—22.

doctrine of predestination and there learn that God in His grace has decreed my eternal election from all eternity.[236] This doctrine is truly Christological, for it directs the sinner to seek his election only in Christ, "the Book of Life," drives the sinner to the means of grace, motivates and activates Christian living, assures the believer of his salvation, and guarantees the existence of the church.[237] According to Lutheran theology, the doctrine of election stresses nothing but the *sola gratia*. It assures the Christian that his eternal welfare has been taken out of his own impotent hands and placed into the mighty hand of God and that eternal salvation is as certain as God's promises are irrevocable. And thus all doctrines in Lutheran theology revolve about the one central principle of *sola gratia*.

Cultus and Polity

The Lutheran cultus is both sacramental and sacrificial: sacramental because Lutheran theology holds that God's grace comes only through the means of grace, sacrificial because the Christian seeks opportunity to worship, praise, and serve God for His unmerited grace.[238] The Lutheran liturgy for the public worship is designed in the first place to assure the worshiper of the grace of God through the Office of the Keys. Therefore it is correct to say that the highest form of worship is the proclamation of the Gospel, be that in the sermon, the lessons, Baptism, the Lord's Supper, absolution, the singing of hymns and chants, prayers, or even through external ceremonies. The Christian who has received the forgiveness of sins wishes to find an opportunity to bring his sacrifice of praise for the blessings received. The cultus must therefore also be truly sacrificial. Throughout, the Lutheran service is designed to offer the reconciled Christian an opportunity to bring his eucharistic sacrifice in the chants and hymns, in the prayers, in his witness, and even in the celebration of the Holy Eucharist.[239]

The Lutheran church retains all such ceremonies as serve the Christian in his worship, as help to establish the historical continuity of the church, as are pedagogically useful and promote outward decency and order in the public worship. While the Lutheran church has never aimed to establish absolute

[236] F. C., XI, 33. Calvinism, in its theocentric approach to all theology and its principle of God's absolute sovereignty, uses predestination as the focal point of theology. According to the Lutheran Confessions, the doctrine of election is exclusively soteriological. They definitely reject any mistaking of God's prescience for God's predestination as a mingling of Law and Gospel. The former is Law and extends over all creatures, good and evil; the doctrine of predestination, however, is concerned only with the believers and deals only with and through the Gospel.

[237] Ibid., 65—77. The Lutheran Confessions refuse to answer questions which are not answered in Scripture. Ibid., 40—42, 58—62, 78, 83—85.

[238] P. Brunner, Luther D. Reed, and Christian Georg Rietschel (see Bibliog., below). The similarity between the Lutheran and Roman cultus is largely historical. The underlying principles are basically different. On some details, see Henry W. Reimann, "The Liturgical Movement: An Appraisal," *C. T. M.*, XXX (1959), 421—431; Piepkorn, "What About Vestments for Pastors?" ibid., 482—493, 582—594; Walter F. Fischer, "Fasting and Bodily Preparation — A Fine Outward Training," ibid., 887—901.

[239] Ap., XXIV, 18, 19, 31—34, 38—44, 52—56. See also Piepkorn, *What the Symbolical Books of the Lutheran Church Have to Say About Worship and the Sacraments* (St. Louis: C. P. H., 1952).

liturgical uniformity, it does condemn such innovations as give offense or are made to avoid persecution.[240]

The principle governing church polity is simply that the highest authority rests with the Christians. The execution of this authority is considered of secondary importance, since the only concern in determining church polity is whether the congregation is properly served with Word and sacrament. But whether the episcopal or the synodical form of government is adopted as of human right, the church in the strict sense is not an earthly monarchy under a visible head, but a communion of saints under Christ, whose highest law for faith and life is the Holy Scriptures.[241]

SECTION V

The Lutheran Church in America

General History

Dutch Lutherans brought their church to Albany and New Amsterdam in the first half of the sixteenth century. St. Matthew's Church of New York and the parish at Albany both date their beginnings to 1649; both have remained Lutheran congregations uninterruptedly since their organization. Almost all the churches founded by Swedish Lutherans on the Delaware (from 1638 on) later became Episcopalian.[242]

Lutheranism became firmly established about fifty years later, when large groups of German Lutheran immigrants came to New York, Pennsylvania, Delaware, Maryland, and the Carolinas. In response to a request to help the widely scattered German Lutheran congregations toward a better organization and a more adequate ministerial supply, the Rev. Henry Melchior Mühlenberg was sent to America in 1742. He was an excellent organizer, a good theologian, a polished gentleman, a remarkable scholar, and soon organized the scattered Lutherans into congregations, obtained worthy pastors, founded schools for the education of the young, and in 1748 organized the Evangelical Lutheran Ministerium of Pennsylvania, the first Lutheran synod in America.[243] Müh-

240 Ap., XV, 49; XXVIII, 17; XV, 51, 52; Large C., I, 85; A. C., XV, 1. See Piepkorn, pp. 11—13.

241 A. C., XXVIII; Ap., VII, 45, 33; XIV, 1 ff.; VII, 5 ff., 17, 23; XXVIII, 15—27, 53—57; Large C., II, 51; S. A., P. II, Art. 4; Tract on the Authority and Primacy of the Pope, 24, 54—56, 67, 68; F. C., Th. D., X, 9—18, 21. In most European countries the church polity is episcopal; in America it is basically congregational, though it may also be viewed as synodical, since in many instances the separate congregations entrust the synodical organization with considerable authority.

242 H. E. Jacobs, The Evangelical Lutheran Church in the U. S. Vol. IV of the American Church series (New York, 1893), pp. 80 ff. See also Harry J. Kreider, History of the United Lutheran Synod of New York and New England, I (Philadelphia: Muhlenberg Press, 1954). The congregation at Wilmington prepared an edict against slavery and advocated religious tolerance as early as 1638 and 1642.

243 Although they have been credited with organizing "the first Lutheran Synod in America," the sixty congregations of the Raritan Valley

lenberg has rightly been called the "patriarch of the Lutheran church in America." In the subsequent decades other synods were organized: New York Ministerium (1786), the synods of North Carolina (1803), of Ohio (1818), of Maryland and Virginia (1820), and of Tennessee (1820). With the exception of the Ohio and Tennessee synods these bodies formed the General Synod or Conference (1820).

During the second period of its history, American Lutheranism experienced a tremendous expansion, due in part to the westward trek after the Revolutionary War, but chiefly to the tremendous influx of immigrants from Germany and the Scandinavian countries, who settled in the Middle West. In 1839 the first Lutheran immigrants from Germany to come to Missouri settled in Perry County and St. Louis. They came from Saxony and were fleeing from the rationalism that was rampant in the state church of their homeland at that time.

They were imbued with a double portion of the spirit of confessionalism. Their fiery zeal for the whole body of Lutheran doctrine was made even more intense by the ardor of their piety. This union of denominational zeal and religious fervor gave them extraordinary power of propagandism, so that the few shiploads of Saxon pilgrims have grown into one of the largest Lutheran bodies, the Missouri Synod. This body was organized in 1847, with headquarters at St. Louis, under the powerful leadership of C. F. W. Walther.[244]

While the early Lutheran colonists were readily integrated into the social and political life of America, the later Lutheran immigrants retained their European cultural background and also their language. This provincialism proved to be not without some blessings, for these Lutheran immigrants retained their confessional loyalty and their deep concern for a thorough religious instruction of the youth. This in turn safeguarded them against the influence of revivalism and subsequently of liberalism. In 1870 the Lutheran church in America had something less than half a million confirmed members; through an energetic "home mission" program among Lutheran immigrants the Lutheran church had by 1910 become the fourth-largest church in America, with nearly two and a quarter million members.

This period, however, also witnessed several divisions among the Lutheran groups. The General Synod experienced the first rift during the Civil War, when in 1863 seven synods organized the United Synod of the South. The second division within the General Synod occurred in 1866 over the doctrinal position of some of its leaders, especially S. S. Schmucker, the "father of the Evangelical Alliance" (1855) and the author of the "Definite Platform," a compromise between the theology of the Augsburg Confession and the Reformed position. When the Melanchthon and the Franckean Synods, in spite of their un-Lutheran character, were admitted to the General Synod, such leaders as Charles Porterfield Krauth, William J. Mann, and J. A. Seiss separated from the General Synod, organized a seminary at Philadelphia (Mount Airy), approved Krauth's "Fundamental Principles of Faith and Church Polity," and organized the General Council at Fort Wayne in 1867. The Synodical Conference (1872), a federation of midwestern synods known for their confessional position also experienced controversies and

which united in 1735 formed a conference rather than a synod. Jacobs, 125 ff. Karl Kretzmann in *Concordia Historical Institute Quarterly*, VIII (1935), 33—36, 76—84; IX (1936), 3—9, 83—90.

[244] A. R. Wentz, in *Census Report*, II, 850.

divisions. In 1881 the Ohio Synod withdrew because of doctrinal differences with the Missouri Synod; so did the Norwegian Synod, partly in order to adjust a difficulty among its own members, but chiefly because of the predestinarian controversy with Missouri.

The third period of American Lutheranism, beginning with the. First World War, was an era of *rapprochement* among American Lutherans. This accounts for several mergers. In 1917 most of the Norwegian bodies united on the basis of the Madison Theses. Shortly thereafter 45 separate district synods, mainly members of the General Synod, the General Council, and the United Synod of the South, joined to organize the United Lutheran Church. In 1930 five Midwest synods formed a federation, the American Lutheran Conference,[245] and in the same year the Ohio, Iowa, and Buffalo Synods merged as the American Lutheran Church.

The Several Bodies

Nineteen out of every 20 American Lutherans are (or will soon be) members of one of three bodies: The Lutheran Church in America (which will combine the United Lutheran Church, the Augustana Church, the American Evangelical Lutheran Church, and the Suomi Synod); The Lutheran Church — Missouri Synod; and the American Lutheran Church.

THE UNITED LUTHERAN CHURCH IN AMERICA

This church is currently the largest body of Lutherans in America. It came into being in 1918 through a merger of the General Synod, the General Council, and the United Synod of the South, ratified by all the constituent synods except the Augustana Synod. These three bodies, united prior to 1860 and separated because of doctrinal and Civil War differences, were brought together through several joint endeavors: a joint mission program, the adoption of a uniform liturgy, and a large-scale celebration of the 400th anniversary of the Lutheran Reformation. The doctrinal position is summarized as follows:

As its doctrinal basis the United Lutheran Church receives the canonical Scriptures of the Old and New Testaments as the inspired Word of God and the only infallible rule of faith and practice, the three ecumenical creeds as important testimonies drawn from the Holy Scriptures, the Unaltered Augsburg Confession as a correct exhibition of the faith and doctrine of the Evangelical Lutheran Church and the generic creed of Lutheranism, and the other confessions as in harmony with one and the same pure Scriptural faith. All district synods are pledged to the same basis. One of the stated objects of the Church is "to preserve and extend the pure teaching of the Gospel and the right administration of the sacraments." [246]

---

[245] The American Lutheran Church, the Augustana Evangelical Lutheran Church, the Evangelical Lutheran Church, the Lutheran Free Church, and the United Evangelical Lutheran Church. The conference, which was created to facilitate co-operation among its member bodies in matters of common interest and responsibility, such as missions, social service, education, publications, and theological education, had as its doctrinal basis the Minneapolis Theses of November 18, 1925, reproduced in *Doctrinal Declarations: A Collection of Official Statements on the Doctrinal Position of the Various Lutheran Bodies in America* (St. Louis: C. P. H., 1957), pp. 107—110. With the organic union of three of its constituent bodies in early prospect, the conference was dissolved on November 10, 1954.

[246] Cp. Abdel R. Wentz, ed., *The Lutheran Churches of the World* (Geneva: Lutheran World Federation, 1952), p. 293 ff.

The ULCA deems this an adequate statement of the confessional Lutheran position and a sufficient basis for union. It permits liberty of opinion on matters which it does not regard as conclusively defined in the symbols, such as "theories" of the ministry or of the inspiration of the Sacred Scriptures.[247] The form of organization of the ULCA is such that it conducts the publications, missionary and other work of the whole church. The constituent synods conduct their own affairs; operate colleges, theological seminaries, and institutions of mercy; and are responsible for the discipline of pastors and congregations. Synods differ in some respects because of their history and constituency. The 1920 ULCA statement on pulpit and altar fellowship and on membership in fraternal orders is used more as an ideal than as a norm for discipline. The ULCA holds full membership in the National Council of the Churches of Christ in the United States of America.[248] Among the constituent synods of the United Lutheran Church is the *Icelandic Evangelical Lutheran Synod of North America* (1885). Its strength is chiefly in Canada. The projected merger with the Augustana Church, the American Evangelical Lutheran Church and the Suomi Synod is scheduled to take place in 1962.

THE LUTHERAN CHURCH — MISSOURI SYNOD

This synod was organized by the Saxon immigrants of Missouri (Martin Stephan), the Hanoverians of Indiana (Frederick Wyneken) and the Franconians of Michigan (William Loehe).[249]

These three groups were deeply interested in Lutheran orthodoxy. Their settlement in America was due largely to religious interest. The Saxons had left Europe because of the rationalism in the state church; the Franconians settled in Frankenmuth, Mich., in order to do mission work among the Indians by word and by deed as a Christian community. After repudiating their former hierachical ideas and practices, the Saxons emphasized the sovereignty of the local congregation, still a characteristic feature of the Missouri Lutherans. The deep interest in re-establishing Lutheran orthodoxy prompted C. F. W. Walther to publish *Der Lutheraner* (1844), which prepared the way for the formation of the Synod of Missouri,

---

[247] The "Pittsburgh Agreement," a statement on the doctrine of inspiration proposed to ULCA and the old ALC for adoption, reads in part:

By virtue of a unique operation of the Holy Spirit (2 Tim. 3:16; 2 Peter 1:21), by which He supplied to the holy writers content and fitting word (2 Peter 1:21; 1 Cor. 2:12, 13), the separate books of the Bible are related to one another and, taken together, constitute a complete, errorless, unbreakable whole, of which Christ is the center (John 10:35). They are rightly called the Word of God. This unique operation of the Holy Spirit upon the writers is named inspiration. We do not venture to define its mode, or manner, but accept it as a fact. Believing, therefore, that the Bible came into existence by this unique co-operation of the Holy Spirit and the human writers, we accept it (as a whole and in all its parts) as the permanent divine revelation, as the Word of God, the only source, rule, and norm for faith and life, and as the ever fresh and inexhaustible fountain of all comfort, strength, wisdom, and guidance for all mankind.

[248] Wentz, *Luth. Churches*, p. 297.

[249] See Chr. Hochstetter, *Die Geschichte der ev.-luth. Missouri Synode* (Dresden, 1885). Theo. Graebner, *Church Bells in the Forest* (St. Louis: C. P. H., 1945). Walter O. Forster, *Zion on the Mississippi* (St. Louis: C. P. H., 1953).

Ohio, and Other States in 1847. In its confessional statement The Lutheran Church — Missouri Synod accepts the Holy Scriptures as the infallible and inspired Word of God; [250] and the three ecumenical creeds, the Augsburg Confession, the Apology of the Augsburg Confession, the Smalcald Articles, Luther's two Catechisms, and the Formula of Concord as correct expositions of the Word of God. According to its constitution, the purpose of this body is:

(1) The conservation and continuance of the unity of the true faith (Eph. 4: 3-16; 1 Cor. 1:10) and a united effort to resist every form of schism and sectarianism (Rom. 16:17); (2) the extension of the kingdom of God; (3) the training of ministers and teachers for service in the Evangelical Lutheran Church; (4) the publication and distribution of Bibles, churchbooks, schoolbooks, religious periodicals, and other books and papers; (5) the endeavor to bring about the largest possible uniformity in church practice, church customs, and, in general, in congregational affairs; (6) the furtherance of Christian parochial schools and of a thorough catechetical instruction preparatory to admission to the Sacrament; (7) supervision of the ministers and teachers of the Synod with regard to the performance of their official duties; (8) the protection of pastors, teachers, and congregations in the fulfillment of their duties and maintenance of their rights.

Many believed that the strict adherence to all the Lutheran Confessions bordered on symbololatry and a return to the 17th-century dogmaticians could produce only a repristination theology, and they predicted the early doom of this new synod. However, it enjoyed a tremendously rapid expansion, largely because the "practical seminary" at Springfield, Ill., prepared consecrated men quickly

to minister to the German Lutheran immigrants on the frontier to supplement the supply of candidates prepared at St. Louis, Mo.

The confessional solidarity for which this body is known is due in part to the extensive Christian elementary school system for the training of its youth and in part to the uniform training of its ministers. The synod was disturbed by several controversies with other Lutheran bodies, particularly concerning the ministry and the doctrines of conversion and predestination.

Until the outbreak of the First World War this body was so engrossed in establishing congregations among immigrants and developing its inner growth that it seemed to become self-centered, insular, and provincial in its outlook. But by the end of the First World War, English had increasingly become the medium of church work, and the members awakened to their responsibility toward their unchurched neighbors. World War II intensified and widened the missionary program. This body has become known for its zeal to maintain purity of doctrine and at the same time for its zeal to fulfill its universal mission obligation.

THE AMERICAN LUTHERAN CHURCH

On January 1, 1961, the American Lutheran Church came into being through the corporate union of three former member bodies of the American Lutheran Conference: (1) the American Lutheran Church; (2) the Evangelical Lutheran Church; and (3) the United Evangelical Lutheran Church.

(1) The former American Lutheran Church was itself the result of a merger in 1930 of three Synods: the Ohio Synod, the Buffalo Synod, and the Iowa Synod.

---

[250] See Richard R. Caemmerer, Arthur Carl Piepkorn, Martin H. Franzmann, and Walter R. Roehrs, "Essays on the Inspiration of Scripture," in C. T. M., XXV (1954), 738—753.

The Ohio Synod was organized in 1818 by pastors of the Pennsylvania Ministerium and some Tennessee clergymen to serve more effectively the many German Lutherans who had crossed the Alleghenies at the turn of the 19th century. In 1830 a seminary was opened in Columbus, Ohio. Under the leadership of Professors W. F. Lehmann and M. Loy the Ohio Synod became a charter member of the Synodical Conference, but severed its connection in 1881 at the outbreak of the bitter predestinarian controversy. This body always had a deep concern for Lutheran confessional theology.

The Buffalo Synod was organized in 1845 by J. A. Grabau, known for his strong confessionalism and his hierarchical bent.

The Iowa Synod was founded at St. Sebald, Iowa, in 1854 by several Loehe emissaries and was very successful in establishing congregations among the German Lutheran immigrants in the Midwest. During its early history it sought union both with the Missouri Synod and the General Council. But it disagreed with the former on the doctrine of the church and ministry, the second coming of Christ, the binding character of the subscription to the Symbolical Books, and, after the outbreak of the predestinarian controversy, on the doctrines of conversion and election. Its attempt to unite with the General Council was thwarted by the latter's failure to give an unqualified statement on the "Four Points" (altar and pulpit fellowship, lodges, chiliasm).

(2) The *Evangelical Lutheran Church*, known until 1946 as the Norwegian Lutheran Church of America, had been formed in 1917 by the union of the Hauge's Norwegian Evangelical Lutheran Synod (1876; originally organized as the Evangelical Lutheran Church of America in 1846 by Elling Eielsen and Oster Hansen), the Synod for the Norwegian Evangelical Lutheran Church of America, founded by J. A. Ottesen, H. A. Preus, A. C. Preus, and C. L. Clausen in 1853,[251] and the United Norwegian Lutheran Church in America, founded by Gjermund Hoyme, J. N. Kildahl, M. O. Bockmann, and F. A. Schmidt in 1890. This church accepts and confesses the Holy Scriptures as the revealed Word of God and the only source and rule of faith, doctrine, and life. It accepts only the three ecumenical creeds, the Unaltered Augsburg Confession, and Luther's Small Catechism. This synod has succeeded to a very marked degree in making each local congregation conscious of its responsibility for evangelism.

(3) The *United Evangelical Lutheran Church*, until 1946 the United Danish Evangelical Lutheran Church, was organized by Norwegian and Danish immigrants in 1870. It remained close to the Lutheran Church in Denmark in theology and liturgy.

THE EVANGELICAL LUTHERAN AUGUSTANA CHURCH OF NORTH AMERICA

In the fall of 1851 groups of Swedish, German, Norwegian, and Danish extraction in Illinois and Iowa organized the Synod of Northern Illinois. In 1860 the Swedes and Norwegians withdrew to organize the Scandinavian Lutheran Augustana Synod of North America, from which the Norwegians withdrew in 1870. In its constitution the Augustana Church accepts the Scriptures as the revealed Word of God and the only infallible rule of faith and practice and the ecumenical creeds, and it accords symbolic status to the whole *Book of Concord*. Among the early leaders were such men as

251 See Gerhard L. Belgum, *The Old Norwegian Synod in America, 1853—1890* (New Haven: Unpublished Yale University Ph. D. dissertation, 1957); cf. *Church History*, XXIX (1960), 93.

Pastors Lars P. Esbjörn and T. M. Hasselquist, the former professor at the Illinois State University, a Lutheran institution at Springfield, Ill.; and the latter the president both of the synod and of what is now the Augustana Seminary and College at Rock Island, Ill. While today many of its members live in the Middle West, it is spread across the country; it is the largest Lutheran body in New England, and its greatest recent growth has been in New England, New York, Texas, and California. It was in fellowship with the General Council until 1918, when it declined to enter into the merger resulting in the ULCA.

The Augustana Church has retained closer ties with its European mother church than probably any other major Lutheran group. This fact is reflected in its liturgy; to some extent in the centralization of considerable power in the conference and the synodical organization; in its ecumenical outlook; and in its attitude toward the Lutheran Confessions. (The Church of Sweden accepts as of symbolical authority only the Augsburg Confession and the Small Catechism.) Pietism of the Rosenius type became dominant in many Augustana congregations. However, the subjectivism of this form of revivalism was counteracted in part by the theology of Henrik Schartau, who renounced his early Herrnhut pietism and urged pastors to rely on doctrinal instruction — not emotional preaching — to promote Christian growth.[252] This church is a member of the National Council of the Churches of Christ in the United States of America and the World Council of Churches. It is negotiating an organic union with the ULCA, the American Evangelical Lutheran Church, and the Suomi Synod.

THE WISCONSIN EVANGELICAL LUTHERAN SYNOD

This synod — known until 1959 as the Joint Synod of Wisconsin and Other States — came into being in 1917 as the result of a merger of the former Michigan Synod, organized in 1840, chiefly by emissaries of the Basel Mission Society, the Wisconsin Synod, organized in 1850 by adherents of the Prussian Union, and the Minnesota Synod, which was brought into being by the General Synod but later joined the General Council and ultimately entered into fraternal relations with the Synodical Conference. Under the leadership of Adolf Hoenecke and his associates the Wisconsin Synod took a very definite stand against its early unionistic practices in favor of sound Lutheran confessional theology.[253]

THE LUTHERAN FREE CHURCH

The Lutheran Free Church was organized in 1897 by former members of the United Norwegian Lutheran Church. As the name indicates, this body emphasizes the independence and autonomy of the congregation and frowns upon extra-congregational governing bodies. It allows great latitude in doctrine, maintaining that Christian unity is based on a religious experience rather than on unity of doctrine.[254] It accepts the Holy Scriptures as the revealed Word of God and unreservedly subscribes to the ecumenical symbols, the Small Catechism, and the Augsburg Confession. It stresses the autonomy of the local congregation, personal Christian experience, and vital congregational life.

In 1957 a referendum of congregations on joining the merger of the Ameri-

---

252 Wentz, *Luth. Churches,* pp. 266—73.

253 M. Lehninger, *Continuing in His Word* (Milwaukee: Northwestern Publishing House, 1951).

254 Wentz, *Census,* II, 989 f.; *Luth. Churches,* pp. 280—84. *Guiding Principles and Rules for Work* (Minneapolis: Lutheran Free Church, n. d.).

can, Evangelical, and United Evangelical Lutheran churches failed by 1.29 per cent to give the requisite two-thirds majority in favor. The church will again vote on the issue in 1961.

THE FINNISH EVANGELICAL LUTHERAN CHURCH OF AMERICA (SUOMI SYNOD)

Some of the congregations of this body in Upper Michigan, where much of its strength is still concentrated, were founded as far back as 1867; it was organized as a synod in 1890. It is a member of the National Lutheran Council and is planning to unite with the United Lutheran Church, the Augustana Church, and the American Evangelical Lutheran Church in the Lutheran Church in America in 1962.[255]

THE AMERICAN EVANGELICAL LUTHERAN CHURCH

This body, formerly the Danish Evangelical Lutheran Church, goes back to 1894. Historically its theology is "Grundtvigian"; theologically it is less conservative than most Lutheran bodies in this country. It plans to unite in 1962 with the United Lutheran Church, the Augustana Church, and the Suomi Synod.

THE SYNOD OF EVANGELICAL LUTHERAN CHURCHES

Organized in 1902, this synod embraces chiefly the Slovak Lutherans who immigrated to the United States during the last decades of the 19th century. It was known until 1959 as the Slovak Evangelical Lutheran Church of the U. S. A.

THE EVANGELICAL LUTHERAN SYNOD

This body came into being when a substantial minority separated from the Norwegian Lutheran Church of America in 1917.[256] Until 1958 it was called the Norwegian Synod of the American Evangelical Lutheran Church.

OTHER BODIES

Lutheran Brethren of America is a small body of Norwegian Lutherans who remain independent, chiefly because they could not find in any existing synod sufficiently stringent rules governing the reception and disciplining of church members. It was organized in 1900.

The Evangelical Lutheran Church of America (Eielsen Synod) is an old (1846) and very small Norwegian body.

The Finnish Apostolic Church of America is made up chiefly of Finnish immigrants who had been deeply influenced by the revival led by Lars Levi Laestadius in 1846, and who organized their body at Calumet, Mich., in 1872.

The National Evangelical Lutheran Church came into being when a part of the Finnish congregation at Calumet, Mich., did not join the Suomi Synod for fear that it would lose its congregational autonomy. Today it has clergy in eleven states, Canada and Australia. Closely related to the Missouri Synod, it utilizes the facilities of that synod in the training of its pastors.

The Protest'ant Conference (Lutheran) is a society of pastors and congregations who in 1926 protested against alleged deviations of the Wisconsin Synod.

The Orthodox Lutheran Conference was organized in 1951 by former members of the Missouri Synod in protest against this body's alleged deviations from its earlier doctrinal position.

The Concordia Lutheran Conference is the name taken by one of the two

---

[255] See Walter J. Kukkonen, "The Suomi Synod's Stream of Living Tradition," *Lutheran Quarterly*, X (1958), 26—53.

[256] Sigurd C. Ylvisaker, ed., *Grace for Grace*, (Mankato, Minn.: Lutheran Synod Book Co., 1943).

groups into which the Orthodox Lutheran Conference split in 1956.

The Church of the Lutheran Confession is an ultra-conservative body formally organized in January, 1961, at Sleepy Eye, Minn., by congregations and clergymen that had withdrawn from the Wisconsin Evangelical Lutheran Synod, the Evangelical Lutheran Synod, and the Orthodox Lutheran Conference because of dissatisfaction with an alleged lack of doctrinal discipline in the Synodical Conference.

The Lutherans in Canada and Alaska are affiliated with the major synods in the United States. In 1958 representatives of all seven bodies then operating in Canada engaged in exploratory conversations looking toward creation of a united Canadian Lutheran church. Subsequently, three of the Canadian districts of The Lutheran Church — Missouri Synod were reorganized as the *Lutheran Church — Canada*, but it was stressed that the formation of the new body, the components of which continue to retain their status in The Lutheran Church — Missouri Synod, would not stand in the way of further union discussions with the other Lutheran bodies in Canada, which co-ordinate their activities through the *Canadian Lutheran Council*.

In South America there are nine independent bodies (the United Evangelical Lutheran Church in Argentina; the Synodal Federation of the Evangelical Church of Lutheran Confession in Brazil; the Evangelical Lutheran Church in British Guiana; the German Evangelical Church in Chile; the German Evangelical Synod of the River Plate; the Evangelical Lutheran Church of Colombia; the Evangelical Lutheran Church of Ecuador; the Evangelical Lutheran Church of Peru; the Evangelical Lutheran Church in Venezuela) and two synodical Districts of the Missouri Synod. The Lutheran work in Central America is largely on a missionary basis.

The Synodical Conference

The Evangelical Lutheran Synodical Conference of North America, organized in 1872, comprises four synods: The Lutheran Church — Missouri Synod, the Wisconsin Evangelical Lutheran Synod, the Synod of Evangelical Lutheran Churches, and the Evangelical Lutheran Synod. Each constituent synod carries on its independent program of education, publication, and missions. However, they jointly promote "Negro Missions," both in the United States and, since 1936, in Africa (Nigeria, Ghana). In 1955 the Evangelical Lutheran Synod severed fellowship relations with The Lutheran Church — Missouri Synod, but did not withdraw from the Conference. Actual withdrawal is currently (1961) under consideration by both this body and the Wisconsin Evangelical Lutheran Synod.[257]

The National Lutheran Council

This is an agency organized in 1918 by the majority of Lutheran synods to deal with the Federal Government in such matters as looking after the spiritual welfare of the Armed Forces in World War I and to carry on relief work among the victims of war. The constitution lists the following purposes and objectives:

1. To witness for the Lutheran Church on matters which require an expression of common faith, ideals, and program.

2. To bring to the attention of the Participating Bodies matters which in its

---

[257] See Alfred O. Fuerbringer and Martin H. Franzmann, "A Quarter-Century of Interchurch Relations: 1935—1960," in *C. T. M.*, XXXII (1961), 5—14.

judgment may require utterance or action on their part.

3. To represent Lutheran interests in America in matters which require common action,

(a) before national and state governments,

(b) before organized bodies and movements outside the Lutheran Church.

4. To emphasize the continuing importance of a right relation between Church and State.

5. To further the interests and the work of the Lutheran churches in America.

6. To undertake and carry on such work as may be authorized by the Participating Bodies in fields where co-ordination or joint activity may be desirable and feasible, such as publicity, statistics, welfare work, missions, education, student work, and other fields.

7. To take the necessary steps to meet emergencies requiring common action, each Participating Body to determine the extent of its co-operation in emergency work.

8. To undertake additional work with the specific consent of the Participating Bodies.[258]

Currently the National Lutheran Council includes all the major Lutheran bodies in the United States except the synods belonging to the Synodical Conference. During 1960 discussions were initiated between the Council and The Lutheran Church — Missouri Synod on the doctrinal basis for co-operation between church bodies not in pulpit and altar fellowship. The first two discussions indicated that the differences between the two sides were not as great as had generally been supposed.

The Lutheran World Federation

According to a 1961 estimate there are approximately 71,000,000 baptized Lutherans in the world. Lutheranism thus embraces about 10 per cent of the world's Christian population. The majority of Lutherans are found in central and northern Europe. There are ethnical and sociological differences among the various groups of Lutherans, but there is also a marked theological diversity. The purpose of the Lutheran World Federation is to bring the various elements of world Lutheranism more closely together for a united testimony of Lutheran principles.

The first meeting of the Lutheran World Convention was held in Eisenach, Germany, in 1923 and was attended by 147 delegates, representing 22 different nations in Europe, Asia, Africa, and America. At this first meeting the discussions centered in the ecumenical character of the Lutheran church, the Confessions as the indispensable foundation of the Lutheran church, the importance of unity, the challenge of missions.[259] A second meeting was held in Copenhagen in 1929 and a third in Paris in 1935.

Shortly after the cessation of hostilities in 1945 plans were laid to revive the Lutheran World Convention. This was done at Lund in 1947 by forming the Lutheran World Federation. The doctrinal basis is as follows:

> The Lutheran World Federation acknowledges the Holy Scriptures of the Old and New Testaments as the only source and the infallible norm of all church doctrine and practice, and sees in the Confessions of the Lutheran Church, especially the Unaltered Augs-

[258] Osborne Hauge and Ralph H. Long, *Lutherans Working Together: A History of the National Lutheran Council* (New York: National Lutheran Council, n. d.).

[259] *The Lutheran World Convention*, the minutes, addresses, and discussions of the Conference at Eisenach, Aug. 19, 1923, issued by American Committee on Arrangements (Phila.: United Luth. Publ. H., 1925).

burg Confession and Luther's Catechism, a pure exposition of the Word of God.

According to its constitution

1. The Lutheran World Federation shall be a free association of Lutheran Churches. It shall have no power to legislate for the Churches belonging to it or to interfere with their complete autonomy, but shall act as their agent in such matters as they assign to it.

2. The purposes of The Lutheran World Federation are:

a) To bear united witness before the world to the Gospel of Jesus Christ as the power of God for salvation;

b) To cultivate unity of faith and confession among the Lutheran Churches of the world;

c) To promote fellowship and cooperation in study among Lutherans;

d) To foster Lutheran participation in ecumenical movements;

e) To develop a united Lutheran approach to responsibilities in missions and education; and

f) To support Lutheran groups in need of spiritual or material aid.[260]

The second Assembly of the Federation met at Hanover in 1952, the third at Minneapolis in 1957.[261] The fourth Assembly is to meet in Helsinki, Finland, in 1963. Currently (1961), the Federation includes 62 bodies in 33 countries with a total membership exceeding 50,000,000 baptized persons.[262]

BIBLIOGRAPHY

PART III   SECTIONS I—V

1. *Works of Martin Luther*

The standard edition is the Weimar edition (W. A.), begun in 1883 and scheduled for early completion. When completed this critical edition will comprise over 100 volumes. The Erlangen edition (1826—1857) was used extensively by scholars prior to the W. A. The Lutheran Church — Missouri Synod published a *Volksausgabe* of the chief works of Luther. Prof. F. A. Hoppe revised the famous Walch edition, including a translation into German of all Latin writings. It is known as the St. Louis edition, published by Concordia Publishing House, 1880—1910. The Holman edition, United Lutheran Publishing House, in six volumes offers Luther's chief writings in English; and the Lenker edition, begun in 1903, contains fourteen volumes of Luther's exegetical and homiletical writings. Other English versions include *Luther's Primary Works* by Wace and Buchheim; the translations of Luther's early writings by Bertram Lee Woolf; the American translation project of Concordia Publishing House and the Muhlenberg Press, edited by Jaroslav Jan Pelikan, Jr., and Helmut Lehmann, the first volume of which was issued in 1955; and Vols. XV—XVIII of the Library of Christian Classics (Philadelphia: The Westminster Press, 1955—); in addition to translations of individual writings by various persons.

[260] Wentz, *Luth. Churches*, p. 433.

[261] See Carl E. Lund-Quist, ed., *The Proceedings of the Third Assembly of the Lutheran World Federation* (Minneapolis: Augsburg Publishing House, 1958).

[262] On the Lutheran World Federation in general, see Carl E. Lund-Quist, ed., *Lutheran Churches of the World* (Minneapolis: Augsburg Publishing House, c. 1957), and Siegfried Grundmann, *Der Lutherische Weltbund: Grundlage, Herkunft, Aufbau* (Cologne: Böhlau Verlag, 1957).

2. *Martin Luther and the Reformation*

Bainton, Roland. *Here I Stand.* Nashville: Abingdon-Cokesbury, 1950

Belgum, Gerhard L., ed. *The Martin Luther Lectures.* Decorah, Iowa: Luther College Press, 1957—. The Martin Luther Lectures are given annually by a panel of lecturers on the campus of Luther College, Decorah, Iowa, and treat some aspect of Luther's thought and influence.

Blayney, Ida Walz. *The Age of Luther: The Spirit of the Renaissance — Humanism and the Reformation.* New York: Vantage Press, 1957.

Boehmer, H., *Road to Reformation.* Trans. John W. Dobberstein and Theodore G. Tappert. Phila.: Muhlenberg Press, 1946.

Bornkamm, Heinrich. *Luther's World of Thought.* Trans. Martin H. Bertram. St. Louis: C. P. H., c. 1958.

Carlson, Edgar M. *The Reinterpretation of Luther.* Phila.: Westminster Press, 1948.

Forell, George Wolfgang. *Faith Active in Love.* New York: The American Press, 1954.

Grimm, Harold J. *The Reformation Era.* New York: The Macmillan Co., 1954.

Harnack, Theodosius. *Luthers Theologie.* Munich: Chr. Kaiser Verlag, 1927.

Holl, Karl. *The Cultural Significance of the Reformation.* Trans. Karl and Barbara Hertz and John H. Lichtblau. New York: Meridian Books, 1959.

Jorgensen, Alfred T. *Martin Luther.* Minneapolis: Augsburg Publishing House, 1953.

Kerr, H. T., *Compend of Luther's Theology.* Phila.: Westminster Press, 1943.

Koestlin, J. *The Life of Martin Luther.* Trans. from the German. New York: Charles Scribner's Sons, 1913.

————. *Theology of Luther.* Trans. Charles E. Hay. Phila.: Lutheran Publ. Society, 1897.

Kooiman, Willem J. *By Faith Alone: The Life of Martin Luther.* London: Lutterworth Press, 1954.

Kramm, Hans Herbert W. *The Theology of Martin Luther.* London: James Clarke, 1947.

Lilje, Hanns. *Luther Now.* Trans. Carl J. Schindler. Phila.: Muhlenberg Press, 1952.

Lortz, J. *Die Reformation in Deutschland.* Freiburg: Herder, 1939. The author, a member of the Roman Church, attempts to give an objective evaluation of the Lutheran Reformation.

Mackinnon, J. *Luther and the Reformation.* New York: Longmans, 1930. 4 vols.

Plass, Ewald M., ed. *What Luther Says: An Anthology.* St. Louis: C. P. H., 1959. 3 vols.

Prenter, Regin. *Spiritus Creator.* Trans. John M. Jensen. Philadelphia: Muhlenberg Press, 1953. A monograph which proposes to set forth systematically Luther's doctrine of the Holy Spirit and His work.

Rupp, Gordon. *The Righteousness of God: Luther Studies.* New York: Philosophical Library, 1953.

Schwiebert, E. G. *Luther and His Times.* St. Louis: C. P. H., 1950.

Thiel, Rudolph. *Luther.* Trans. Gustav E. Wiencke. Phila.: Muhlenberg Press, 1955.

Tillmanns, Walter G. *The World and Men Around Luther.* Minneapolis: Augsburg Publishing House, c. 1959.

Vajta, Vilmos. *Luther on Worship: An Interpretation.* Trans. U. S. Leupold. Phila.: Muhlenberg Press, c. 1958.

Watson, Philip. *Let God Be God.* Phila.: Muhlenberg Press, 1949.

Zeeden, Ernst Walter. *The Legacy of Luther: Martin Luther and the Reformation in the Estimation of the German Lutherans from Luther's Death to the Beginning of the Age of Goethe.* Trans. Ruth Mary Bethell. Westminster, Md.: Newman Press, 1954. An abbreviated English version of the first volume of the author's 2-volume *Martin Luther und die Reformation im Urteil des deutschen Luthertums* (Freiburg-im-Breisgau: Verlag Herder, 1950—1952). The documentation, contained in the second volume, is not available in English.

3. *The Lutheran Confessions*

Among the many editions of the Lutheran Confessions the following deserve special mention:

Die Bekenntnisschriften der Evangelisch-Lutherischen Kirche, 1930. 4th ed. Göttingen: Vandenhoeck und Ruprecht, 1959. This critical edition, known as *Jubiläumsausgabe,* was prepared by a group of scholars and contains all relevant bibliographical materials as to text and content.

Bente, F., and W. H. T. Dau. *Concordia Triglotta*, with "Historical Introductions." St. Louis: C. P. H., 1921.

Tappert, Theodore G., ed. *The Book of Concord: The Confessions of the Evangelical Lutheran Church.* St. Louis: C. P. H., c. 1959. Based on the critical text of the *Jubiläumsausgabe.*

Among the many works on sixteenth and seventeenth century Lutheran theology the following deserve special mention:

Allbeck, Willard D. *Studies in the Lutheran Confessions.* Phila.: Muhlenberg Press, 1952.

Asmussen, Hans. *Warum noch Lutherische Kirche? (Ein Gespräch mit der Augsburgischen Konfession).* Stuttgart: Evangelisches Verlagswerk, 1949.

Brunstaed, Friedrich. *Die Theologie der Lutherischen Bekenntnisschriften.* Gütersloh: Bertelsmann Verlag, 1951.

Elert, W. *Morphologie des Luthertums.* Rev. edition. Munich: C. H. Beck'sche Verlag, 1952. 2 vols.

Gensichen, Hans-Werner. *Damnamus: Die Verwerfung von Irrlehre bei Luther und im Luthertum des 16. Jahrhunderts.* Berlin: Lutherisches Verlagshaus, 1955.

Krauth, Chas. P. *The Conservative Reformation.* Phila.: The United Lutheran Publ. House, 1871.

Little, C. H. *Lutheran Confessional Theology.* St. Louis: C. P. H., 1943.

Neve, J. L., and George J. Fritschel. *Introduction to the Symbolical Books of the Lutheran Church.* 2d ed., revised. Columbus: Wartburg Press, 1956.

Sasse, Herman. *Here We Stand.* Trans. Theodore G. Tappert. New York: Harper and Bros., 1938.

Schaff, Ph. *Creeds of Christendom,* I. New York: Harper, 1899.

Schlink, Ed. *Die Theologie der Lutherischen Bekenntnisschriften.* 2d ed. Muenchen: Chr. Kaiser, 1950. An English translation by Herbert J. A. Bouman, under the title, *The Theology of the Lutheran Confessions,* is scheduled for early publication by Muhlenberg Press, Philadelphia.

Schmauck, Th., and Benze, G. *The Confessional Principle.* Phila.: Muhlenberg Press, 1911.

Schmid, Heinrich. *The Doctrinal Theology of the Evangelical Lutheran Church, Verified from the Original Sources.* Trans. Charles A. Hay and Henry E. Jacobs. 4th ed. Phila.: Lutheran Publication Society, c. 1899.

Walther, Wilh. *Lehrbuch der Symbolik.* Erlangen-Leipzig: Deichertscher Verlag, 1924.

4. Cultus

Brunner, Peter. "Zur Lehre vom Gottesdienst der im Namen Jesu versammelten Gemeinde," in *Leiturgia — Handbuch des evangelischen Gottesdienstes.* Editors: Karl Ferdinand Mueller and Walter Blankenburg. Kassel: Johannes Stauda, 1952 to 1953.

Koenker, Ernst B. *Worship in Word and Sacrament.* St. Louis: C. P. H., c. 1959.

Piepkorn, Arthur Carl. "The Protestant Worship Revival and the Lutheran Liturgical Movement," in Massey Hamilton Shepherd, Jr., ed., *The Liturgical Renewal of the Church* (New York: Oxford University Press, 1960), pp. 53—97.

Reed, Luther Dotterer. *The Lutheran Liturgy.* 2d ed. Philadelphia: Muhlenberg Press, 1960.

————. *Worship: A Study of Corporate Devotion.* Philadelphia: Muhlenberg Press, c. 1959.

Response: In Worship, Music, the Arts. The semiannual publication of the Lutheran Society for Worship, Music, and the Arts. Begun in 1959.

Rietschel, Christian Georg. *Lehrbuch der Liturgik.* 2d ed. by Paul Graff. Göttingen: Vandenhoeck und Ruprecht, 1951.

Una Sancta. A quarterly journal published in the interest of the liturgical life and worship of the Lutheran church. Begun in 1942.

5. American Lutheranism

a. General

Bente, F. *American Lutheranism.* St. Louis: C. P. H., 1919.

Doctrinal Declarations: A Collection of Official Statements on the Doctrinal Position of Various Lutheran Bodies in America. St. Louis: C. P. H., 1957.

Fendt, E. C., ed. *What Lutherans Are Thinking*. Columbus, Ohio: Wartburg Press, 1947.

Ferm, Vergilius. *The Crisis in American Lutheran Theology*. New York: Century Co., 1927.

———. *The American Church of the Protestant Heritage*. New York: Philosophical Library, 1953. Chapter iii.

Graebner, A. L. *Geschichte der lutherischen Kirche in Amerika*. St. Louis: C. P. H., 1892.

Jacobs, Henry Eyster. *Lutherans* (American Church History Series, Vol. IV). New York: The Christian Literature Co., 1893.

Kraushaar, C. O. *Verfassungsformen*. Gütersloh: C. Bertelsmann, 1911. Portrays the polity of all the American churches.

Kunstmann, John G., ed. *The Church and Modern Culture*. Valparaiso: Valparaiso University Press, 1953.

Lueker, Erwin L., ed. *Lutheran Cyclopedia*. St. Louis: Concordia Publishing House, 1954.

Meyer, Carl S. "Lutheran Immigrant Churches Face the Problems of the Frontier," *Church History*, XXIX (1960), 440—462.

Neve, J. L. *History of the Lutheran Church in America*, 3d ed., rev. by Willard D. Allbeck. Burlington, Iowa: Lutheran Literary Board, 1934.

Qualben, L. P. *Lutheran Church in Colonial America*. New York: Thomas Nelson and Sons, 1940.

Seilhamer, Frank H. "The New Measure Movement among Lutherans," *Lutheran Quarterly*, XII (1960), 121—143.

Spaude, Paul W. *The Lutheran Church Under American Influence*. Burlington: The Lutheran Literary Board, 1943.

Tappert, Theodore G., and John W. Doberstein, eds. *The Journals of Henry Melchior Muhlenberg*. Phila.: Muhlenberg Press, 1942—1958. 3 vols. A 1-vol. abridgement by the same editors has been published under the title, *The Notebook of a Colonial Clergyman, Condensed from the Journals of Henry Melchior Muhlenberg* (Phila.: Muhlenberg Press, 1959).

Wentz, A. R. *Lutheran Church in American History*. Phila.: United Lutheran Publ. House, 1923; 2d ed., 1933.

———. *A Basic History of Lutheranism in America*. Philadelphia: Muhlenberg Press, 1955.

Wiederaenders, Robert C. "The Lutheran Church in North America: A Bibliography, 1945—1957," *Lutheran Quarterly*, X (1958), 339—51.

Concordia Historical Institute Quarterly, published by Concordia Historical Institute, St. Louis, Mo.

Concordia Theological Monthly, ed. by the faculty of Concordia Seminary, St. Louis. This journal continues *Lehre und Wehre* (1855—1929), *Theological Quarterly* (1897—1920), *Theological Monthly* (1920 to 1929), and *Magazin für Ev. Luth. Homiletik* (1877—1929). Saint Louis: C. P. H.

Lutheran Quarterly, published quarterly by the Editorial Council of Lutheran Theological Seminaries and continuing the *Lutheran Quarterly*, founded in Gettysburg as the *Evangelical Review*, in 1849; the *Lutheran Church Review*, founded in Philadelphia in 1882; the *Lutheran Church Quarterly*, Philadelphia and Gettysburg, since 1928; and the *Augustana Quarterly*, Rock Island, Ill., since 1922.

Lutheran World, official English quarterly of the Lutheran World Federation. Edited in Geneva; published by Sonntagsblatt, Hamburg-Kleinflottbeck, Germany. Begun in 1954.

b. Synodical Histories

Baepler, W. A. *A Century of Grace*. St. Louis: C. P. H., 1947.

Carlson, C. J. *Years of Our Church*. Minneapolis: Lutheran Free Church Publ. Co., 1942.

Deindorfer, J. *Geschichte der ev.-luth. Synode von Iowa*. Columbus: Lutheran Book Concern, 1897.

Eglands, Valdimar J. *Lutherans in Canada*. Winnipeg: The Icelandic Evangelical Lutheran Synod in North America, 1945.

Forster, Walter O. *Zion on the Mississippi*. St. Louis: C. P. H., 1953.

Henkel, S. *History of the Tennessee Synod*. New Market, Va.: Henkel Co., 1890.

Koehler, J. P. *Geschichte der Wisconsin Synode*. Vol. I. Milwaukee: Northwestern Publ. House, 1925.

Lillegard, George O., ed. *Faith of Our Fathers.* Mankato: Lutheran Synod Book Co., 1953.

Meuser, Fred W. *The Formation of the American Lutheran Church.* Columbus: Wartburg Press, 1958.

Mundinger, C. S. *Government in the Missouri Synod.* St. Louis: C. P. H., 1947.

Nelson, Clifford, and Eugene L. Frevold. *The Lutheran Church among Norwegian-Americans: A History of the Evangelical Lutheran Church.* Minneapolis: Augsburg Publishing House, 1960.

Olson, Oscar N. *Century of Life and Growth.* Rock Island, Ill.: Augustana Book Concern, 1940. A history of the Augustana Lutheran Church.

Polack, W. G. *The Building of a Great Church,* 2d ed. St. Louis: C. P. H., 1941.

Preus, J. C. K., T. F. Gullixson, and E. C. Reinertson, eds. *Norsemen Found a Church.* Minneapolis: Augsburg Publishing House, 1953.

Repp, Arthur, C., ed. *Hundred Years of Christian Education.* River Forest: Lutheran Education Association, 1947.

Sheatsley, S. V. *Joint Synod of Ohio.* Columbus: Lutheran Book Concern, 1919.

Ylvisaker, S. C. *Grace for Grace.* Mankato, Minn.: Bethany Press, 1943.

PART FOUR

The Reformed Bodies

SECTION I

Introduction

The Term "Reformed Churches"

Originally "Reformed churches" denoted all the groups of the 16th century which protested against the spiritual tyranny of Rome and finally were compelled for conscience' sake to separate from the Roman Catholic church. In this sense the Formula of Concord describes the Augustana as a "common confession of the Reformed Churches, whereby our Reformed [i. e., Lutheran] Churches are distinguished from the papists and other repudiated and condemned sects and heresies."[1] The followers of Zwingli, and especially of Calvin, early adopted the term to denote their churches also. In 1561 Theodore Beza, Calvin's successor, submitted the *Confessio Gallicana* of 1559, a faithful summary of Calvin's theological system, to Charles IX as the confession of the Reformed church.[2] In Europe the term is generally used to denote the Zwinglian or Calvinistic bodies of Switzerland, France, Holland, England, and Germany. In American Lutheran circles the term has usually been employed in a wider sense to include also the Arminian bodies.

Basic Differences Between Lutherans and Reformed

At first there were many points in which Zwingli (and Calvin) seemed to be in agreement with Luther. Nevertheless, there was a basic difference in theological orientation, which usually manifests itself in three areas. The first concerns the cultus, or worship. Both groups protested against the "papal abuses," but from a different motivation. The Lutherans abolished those papal abuses which they considered contrary to the central doctrine of the Gospel. At the same time, from a deep sense of the historical continuity of the true church, the Lutherans retained all ceremonies which could be cleansed from the Roman ballast and be filled with their true evangelical meaning. And these "reformed" ceremonies they gladly placed into the service of proclaiming the pure doctrine of God's Word. Zwingli, motivated largely by humanistic interests, viewed Rome's cultus as superstition and contrary to the "new spirit." Calvin was a Biblicist and accepted the Scriptures in a literalistic sense. He felt that a thorough reforma-

NOTE: For abbreviations see Appendix C; for Bibliography, the end of the sections.

[1] Preface to *Formula of Concord*.

[2] Neve, *Churches and Sects*, p. 237. Schaff, *Creeds*, I, 358 f., speaks of inadequacy of the term.

197

tion of the church required the complete abolition of all ceremonies for which there was no specific Scriptural command. Outwardly therefore the Zwinglian and Calvinian reformation seemed to be much more thorough and radical than the Lutheran.

But "the different spirit" of Zwingli — and in a similar degree that of Calvin[3] — manifested itself, secondly, in another and more basic manner; namely, in the divergent view concerning the means of grace. Lutheran theology emphasizes the objective character of the means of grace as the only foundation for faith; Christian assurance is based solely upon the objective promises of the Gospel. Reformed theologians have sometimes mistakenly characterized the Lutheran objectivity of the means of grace as "contemplative quietism" or even as passivism. Reformed theology professes to be activistic and therefore directs the Christian to seek the assurance of his being in the state of grace in a program of Christian activity rather than in the means of grace. Question 86 of the Heidelberg Catechism: "Why must we do good works?" is answered: "That with our whole life we may show ourselves thankful to God for His blessings and that He may be glorified through us; then also that we ourselves be assured of our faith by the fruits thereof, and by our godly walk may bring our neighbors also to Christ."[4] Activism has become a characteristic of Reformed theology. Lest the Christian trust in his Christian activity as the *sign* of his state of grace, Reformed theologians put great emphasis on divine monergism, evident in the Calvinistic principle of an absolute predestination and the resultant "once in grace, always in grace" theory.[5] From the Lutheran viewpoint Reformed theology errs in two directions. First, it attempts to penetrate the secret and sovereign counsels of God and thus seeks to obtain an a priori view of God as a basis of assurance. In other words, it investigates the *deus absconditus*, who has not revealed Himself to us in the Scriptures, and it fails to find the sought assurance. Second, it stresses Christian sanctification in order to find an a posteriori basis for the assurance of being in the state of grace. Calvinism has fused these two views into a single controlling theme, the glorification of God. And this is the driving force in the Calvinistic churches for a tremendous activity extending to every area of life, including politics and commerce. It is a matter of inner necessity so to organize the congregation that the conduct of all its members can be controlled to the glory of God; and to unite the various congregations into an organization which will make Christ the Lord in all areas of human life, if necessary even by force. In the implementation of its basic principle Reformed theology has always appealed to the Bible as the divinely given codex for both doctrine and life. It is not incorrect to say that the major premise of Calvinistic theology is the proposition that the Bible interpreted in a strictly literalistic sense is the norm in every area of human life.[6] Philip Schaff summarizes the difference between Lutheran and Reformed theology as follows:

[3] Koehler, *Kirchengeschichte*, par. 192; W. Walther, *Lehrbuch der Symbolik*, p. 282; Merle W. Boyer, "Lutheran *Geist* and Protestant World View," *Christendom*, Summer, 1945.

[4] Schaff, III, 338. Cp. also The Westminster Confession, p. 631.

[5] Cp. for example, Abraham Booth, *The Reign of Grace*, reprinted by Eerdmans, Grand Rapids, 1949, ch. x.

[6] Meusel, *Kirchliches Handlexikon*, s. v. "Die Reformierte Kirche"; W. Walther, *Eigenart der Reformierten Kirche*, p. 272 f.

The Lutheran Confessions start from the wants of sinful man and the personal experience of justification by faith alone and find, in this "article of the standing and falling church," comfort and peace of conscience and the strongest stimulus to a godly life. The Reformed churches (especially the Calvinistic sections) start from the absolute sovereignty of God and the supreme authority of His holy Word and endeavor to reconstruct the whole church on this basis. The one proceeds from anthropology to theology; the other, from theology to anthropology. . . . The Lutheran church has an idealistic and contemplative, the Reformed church a realistic and practical, spirit and tendency. The former aims to harmonize church and state, theology and philosophy, worship and art; the latter draws a sharper line of distinction between the Word of God and the traditions of man, the church and the world, the church of communicants and the congregation of hearers, the regenerate and the unregenerate, the divine and the human.[7]

In the third place, Reformed theological principles allow and actually call for a great variety of theological trends. True, there is a unifying principle which can be traced through the theology of all the Calvinistic-Reformed church bodies, as they are laid down in Calvin's *Institutes*, the Heidelberg Catechism, and other standard confessional statements of the Reformed bodies. But within this framework there is relatively wide theological latitude and room for various theological trends. This latitude is due in no small degree to Calvin's view that "common grace" is that inherent quality in man which permits the various racial and national groups to develop their culture and theology according to their respective and specific needs.[8] This accounts in part for the fact that there is a large number of confessional standards

of equal standing though of divergent doctrinal viewpoints. The Reformed church experienced serious doctrinal controversies, and as a result there have been many divisions within the Reformed orbit. At this point attention is directed to those movements which have most significantly modified or changed Reformed theology.

Movements That Modified Reformed Theology

1. The Arminian controversy at the beginning of the 17th century was the first to divide the Reformed church. This controversy helped to crystallize the main tenets of Calvinism, known as the Five Points, and paved the way for a rational approach to theology. Because of their extreme radicalism the early Arminians were unable to gain a foothold. A century later John Wesley advocated a modified form of Arminianism as it is represented in the theology of the Methodist family. Since then it is historically proper to classify the Reformed churches as either Calvinistic, with a theocentric theology, or Arminian, with an anthropocentric theology. In spite of this basic difference these two branches of Reformed theology reach similar conclusions. Both place a low estimate on the means of grace and great emphasis on subjectivism, the former because of their theocentric and the latter because of their anthropocentric orientation. Both incline toward legalism and asceticism, the one to the glory of God, the other in the interest of perfectionism.

2. In the 18th century, philosophical systems — notably deism, naturalism, romanticism, and idealism — greatly modified the position of stark Calvinism, especially in England. These philosophical systems in part explain the rise of

---

7 Schaff, I, 216 f.

8 Meeter, H. H., *Calvinism*, p. 184 f.

such mystical and spiritualistic movements as Quakerism, which in turn also helped to modify and to change Calvinism.[9]

3. In America more so than in Europe, revivalism resulted in deep and essential changes in Reformed theology. In particular, revivalism set in motion a reaction against the Calvinistic doctrine of God's absolute sovereignty and His decree of a double election. This is true especially of the great revival of 1734, which marked the beginning of New England theology. In the Great Awakening of 1800, "Deeds rather than creeds" was the shibboleth. This revival gave rise to anticreedalism, and members of both Calvinistic and Arminian bodies joined in organizing several union churches.

4. On the surface the Reformed churches seemed to be rent asunder by the modernist-fundamentalist controversy of the 20th century. But the unbiased observer is impressed by the fact that both movements express aspects of the basic Reformed, more specifically, Calvinistic principles of theology. Modernism seeks to magnify the glory of God in a social and economic revolution; fundamentalism in the establishment of a millennial kingdom.

5. The theological revival in its American form appears as a determined effort to steer a middle course between the prewar modernism and fundamentalism.

6. A few leaders are working toward a pan-Protestant union on a basis sufficiently wide to unite all Reformed bodies. Whether ultimately such a reunion is possible, and whether the historic differences can be completely erased, is a matter of conjecture. One great obstacle to such a complete reunion seems to be a matter of church polity rather than of doctrine.

Classification of Reformed Groups

Because of the horizontal and vertical divisions among the Reformed churches in America, it is extremely difficult to group the many bodies into clearly defined families. The Census Bureau of the United States Department of Commerce makes no attempt to classify the various Reformed bodies, but lists them alphabetically. Since the theological orientation of a church body is frequently reflected in its church polity, it has been suggested that one could group the Reformed bodies according to the form of government:

(1) The Episcopalian bodies (hierarchical); (2) the Presbyterian bodies (presbyterial); (3) the Congregational churches (congregational); (4) the anticreedal groups (individual).

Obviously such a classification cannot take cognizance of the many shades of theological opinions. The most satisfactory grouping, and the one adopted in this text, is to classify the bodies in theologically related families.

1. *The Calvinistic Bodies:* The Reformed and Presbyterian churches; the Calvinistic Baptist churches; the Protestant Episcopal Church; several small bodies.

2. *The Arminian Bodies:* The Methodists; the United Brethren; the Free Will Baptists; the Salvation Army; the Holiness bodies; the Pentecostal groups.

3. *The Unionistic Bodies:* The Christian Churches; the Disciples; a large number of small groups, such as the several Churches of God; the United Church of Christ.

4. *The Adventist Groups.*

It must be observed that this classification does not do justice to several larger bodies, notably the Protestant Episcopal Church in the U. S. A. and the United Church of Christ. Other bodies,

---

[9] J. L. Neve, *History of Christian Thought*, II, 50—66.

especially the smaller sects, cannot well be grouped in one or the other "theological" family, because their basic principle is unique or because several theological trends are merged; for example, the Moravians, the Mennonites, and some of the Dunkers.[10] It is also impossible in the above classification to reflect some of the recent phenomena in the larger Reformed bodies, such as the conflict between liberalism and fundamentalism, the widespread acceptance of premillennialism, and the revival of Reformation theology.

SECTION II

Genetic History of Reformed Theology

The *Monument International de la Reformation* in Geneva very properly places John Calvin into the center of those 16th-century theologians who were primarily responsible for developing Reformed theology. At first there were two distinct and independent movements in Switzerland, the one in the German section of Switzerland and southwestern Germany inaugurated by Huldreich Zwingli (1484–1531) and his co-workers Oecolampadius, Bullinger, and Bucer; and the other in French Switzerland, at Geneva, spearheaded by John Calvin (1509–1564). For a time it seemed that the two movements would remain separate and distinct, until Calvin effected a union between the two in the *Consensus Tigurinus* of 1549.[1] Calvin, of course, is the man who gave his impress to Reformed theology. However, to evaluate fully Reformed principles it is necessary to understand Zwingli's theological development and the main points of his system.[2]

Zwingli's Theology

The extent of Luther's influence on Zwingli's theological development is a matter of debate. The fact is that Zwingli's religious interests differed fundamentally from those of Luther. Zwingli had been trained in the humanistic spirit, and he remained a humanist throughout his life. Intellectual moralism, a modified scholasticism, rationalism, and "enthusiasm" characterize his theology. Zwingli, moreover, was motivated largely by an ardent patriotism. It was this latter motive which first aroused in him a revulsion against the papacy. While priest at Glarus (1506 to 1516), he protested against the practice of the Swiss youths who hired themselves out as soldiers to foreign princes, including the pope. His opposition to Rome took definite shape during his brief ministry at Mariä-Einsiedeln, a popular shrine with all the pomp and circumstance of relic worship. In his opposi-

---

[10] Clark in *Small Sects of America* classifies the so-called small sects as charismatic, perfectionistic, pessimistic.

[1] J. T. Mueller, "Notes on the Consensus Tigurinus," *C. T. M.*, XX (December, 1949), 894—909.

[2] Paul Tschackert, pp. 228—57 (see P. III, fn. 4), a thorough presentation, whom we have followed. George W. Richards, "Theology of Zwingli," *Lutheran Church Quarterly*, XXI, 153—71. See Neve (P. III, Bibliog.). Cp. Bromiley, pp. 31—40.

tion to the superstitious view that God deals with men through relics, he went to the other extreme, for it was here that he first conceived his "enthusiastic" principle expressed in his theological axiom "The Holy Spirit requires no vehicle." In 1519 Zwingli was transferred to Zurich, and here he soon put into practice the reformatory principles which had gradually ripened. It was, however, a reformation of the cultus and of morals rather than of theology; a reformation by legislation rather than by Gospel preaching; a reformation which, though outwardly much more radical than that of his Wittenberg contemporary, was, after all, oriented in German humanism and therefore was interested primarily in restoring the church according to the Apostolic pattern. Between 1523 and 1525 Zwingli, in co-operation with the Zurich canton government, abolished saint worship, Masses for the dead, the Lord's Supper under one kind, the use of Latin in the service, the worship of relics, holy orders. But more, with one fell swoop the entire liturgical heritage of the church was cast aside. The fact that Zwingli did not become a victim of the iconoclasm of the Anabaptists was due not so much to theological considerations as to his intense nationalism. His ardent patriotism could not countenance the communistic and anarchistic principles of the Swiss Anabaptists nor their arrogant claim that they alone constituted the chosen people of God. When they demanded rebaptism of adults as a token of membership in their "spiritual kingdom,"

Zwingli vigorously defended infant baptism. He did so because he viewed baptism as a parallel to circumcision and as the outward token that children are received into the socio-ecclesiastical community. His interest in defending infant baptism was therefore sociological rather than theological. The only really theological controversy in which Zwingli became involved was precipitated by Carlstadt's attack on the Real Presence. Luther's treatises of 1526 and 1527 against Carlstadt and Oecolampadius prompted Zwingli to write against Luther. The Colloquy at Marburg in 1529 failed to bring about a reconciliation because the two theologians had less in common than had been assumed, and is still being assumed, in many quarters.[3] In the meantime Zwingli's unfortunate attempt to fuse religion and his socio-political principles had misled him and his followers in Zurich, Bern, and Basel to advocate the use of force in "reforming" the still Romanist cantons of Switzerland. Zwingli had entrusted the government of the church to the state and expected the state to foster the spreading of the Gospel. In 1531 the Romanist cantons attacked the Zurich canton at Kappel, in retaliation for the blockade which Zurich had imposed on them to force them into the Reformed camp. Zwingli was mortally wounded in the battle.[4]

Zwingli's theological system is summarized in his *Commentarius de vera et falsa religione* (1525), his *Ratio fidei* (submitted at Augsburg in 1530), and his *Fidei expositio* (1531).[5] His human-

---

[3] Walther Koehler, *Zwingli und Luther*, II (Gütersloh: C. Bertelsmann Verlag, 1953), Roland Bainton, pp. 318—22; E. G. Schwiebert, pp. 695 to 714 (P. III, Bibliog.).

[4] Oecolampadius and Bucer expressed in varying degrees the Zwinglian theological emphases.

[5] Oskar Farner, *Huldrych Zwingli*. (Zurich: Zwingli-Verlag, 1943—), a multivolume work still in process; S. M. Jackson, *Huldreich Zwingli, the Reformer of German Switzerland* (New York: G. Putnam's Sons, 1901). Koehler, op. cit. Rudolph Staehelin, *Huldreich Zwingli: Sein Leben und Wirken nach den Quellen dargestellt.* 2 vols. (Basel: Benno Schwabe,

istic training prompted him to seek the origin and the nature of the Christian faith in the Greek New Testament. Tschackert is undoubtedly correct when he thinks Zwingli's theological principle to be that the Bible is the sole authority.[6] But this is true only in so far as Zwingli viewed the Bible as the sole norm and standard in regulating the external life of the Christian community. For in spite of the emphasis which he placed on scientific and literal interpretation, his "enthusiastic" principle prompted him to place "the spirit" above the letter. Furthermore, Zwingli failed to distinguish between Law and Gospel, for both are considered by him as the revelation of God's gracious will. He viewed God's Word as the guide and rule by which man's life is to be regulated, and he so completely erased the difference between Law and Gospel that he could speak of the Law as "good news." Zwingli's approach to the Scriptures was definitely legalistic, and in this respect he has deeply influenced the Reformed church.

The material principle of Zwingli's theology is absolute divine causality.[7] He is a consistent determinist and finds the exclusive cause of evil in God; however, with this modification, that what appears evil to us is not evil for God,

since as the absolute Sovereign He is above all law. According to Zwingli, the sole cause of man's salvation lies in God's absolute predestination. Faith, which is wrought immediately by God, is the infallible sign of election and can never be lost. Since predestination is absolute and immediate, it may also extend beyond the boundaries of the Christian church and her proclamation and include the upright heathen. Unlike Calvin, Zwingli does not teach an election to reprobation. Nor does he teach man's total depravity. He holds that original sin is indeed a serious damage, but not an irreparable damage. In Christology Zwingli follows the philosophic principle *finitum non est capax infiniti*. His theory of the *alloeosis*, i. e., an artificial attempt to maintain the unity of Christ's person and yet to separate the divine and the human, has not found acceptance in Reformed theology. In his opinion the value of Christ's work consisted in this, that God had appointed Christ as the pledge of our election.[8]

According to Zwingli, the separation between the Creator and the creature is such that God does not employ means of grace. Nor are means necessary, for the believer receives all spiritual blessings immediately through divinely wrought

1895—1897). This was the standard work until Koehler and Farner. Bard Thompson, "Zwingli Study Since 1918," *Church History*, XIX—2 (June, 1950), pp. 116—28. This contains a complete bibliog. Cp. J. L. Neve, *History of Christian Thought*, I, 243—48, for a fine overview of Zwingli's theology; Gottfried W. Locher, *Die Theologie Huldrych Zwinglis im Lichte seiner Christologie* (Zürich: Zwingli-Verlag, 1952—); W. Walther, *Symbolik*, on some of the excesses in Swiss churches; *Catholic Encyc.*, s. v. "Zwingli."

6 P. 239.

7 This is not the place to investigate whether his view of a sovereign God resulted from his antipathy to the relic worship at Einsiedeln, which gave the glory due to God to creatures, or to Neoplatonic influences, or to scholastic determinism. — Neither can we here trace the various points of Zwingli's theological system. Only so much is of interest here as has influenced the Reformed church. And in this respect Zwingli's influence is far less than that of Calvin.

8 This became an issue in the Luther-Zwingli controversy on the Lord's Supper. Cp. F. C., Art. VII.

faith. The Christian's assurance does not rest on creaturely means, such as Word and sacraments, but solely on faith itself, which is implanted directly by the Holy Spirit. Having no collative power, the Word is to be preached merely as a "sign of God's grace." The sacraments are viewed as signs and badges whereby men outwardly indicate that they are through faith already the recipients of God's grace.[9] The sacraments do not possess a sacramental, but a sacrificial character. Baptism is merely the public profession that God has already acted. The Lord's Supper is primarily eucharistic in character, inasmuch as it provides the Christians an opportunity to thank God publicly for the gift of the Savior.[10] Zwingli is consistent when he rejects the Lutheran doctrine of the Real Presence, for it is contrary not only to his Christology, but also to his tenet concerning the immediacy of the Spirit's working. He is therefore compelled to view the entire Lord's Supper as a symbolic action, the elements being regarded as symbols of Christ's body and blood and the oral manducation, or eating, no more than a symbol of the spiritual eating. Zwingli's views on the sacraments have been considerably modified and given a deeper spiritual meaning by Calvin and the English Reformed churches.

An evaluation of Zwingli's theology would be incomplete without stating that his interests were more sociological than soteriological. These interests prompted him to view the congregation as a socio-religious community and the state as God's handmaiden, both to further piety.[11] Thus Zurich became a republican state church. The German-Swiss Reformation was of tremendous significance during the time of the Reformation. It remained, however, for the French-Swiss reformers, especially John Calvin, to systematize the Reformed theology and to give it the vitality whereby it became the dominant force on two continents.

Calvin's Theology

There is no doubt that Calvin (1509 to 1564) did more to shape Reformed theology than any other individual. Schaff says:

He belongs to the small number of men who have exerted a moulding influence, not only upon their own age and country, but also upon future generations in various parts of the world; and not only upon the Church, but indirectly also upon the political, moral, and social life. The history of Switzerland, Germany, France, the Netherlands, Great Britain, and the United States for the last three hundred years bears upon a thousand pages the impress of his mind and character. He raised the small republic of Geneva to the reputation of a Protestant Rome. . . . His spirit stirred up the Puritan revolution of the seventeenth century, and his blood ran in the veins

---

[9] A. C., XIII, is directed against this Zwinglian view.

[10] In rejecting infant baptism Karl Barth follows in the Zwinglian tradition. John C. Mattes, "A Reply to Karl Barth on Baptism," *Lutheran Church Quarterly*, 1947, pp. 173—86. "A German Lutheran Declaration of the Doctrine of Baptism," *C. T. M.*, XXI (1950), 855—60.

[11] Zwingli believed that a church without the secular arm is maimed and incomplete. In the *"Sittenmandat"* of 1530 he uses the civil arm to enforce religious functions; he *orders* church attendance and punishes religious transgressions, not only with excommunication but also with banishment from the community. Roger Ley, *Kirchenzucht bei Zwingli* (Zurich: Zwingli-Verlag, 1948), reviewed in *Anglican Theological Review*, XXXI (1949), p. 252. Geo. W. Richards, "Zwingli and Reformed Tradition," in W. K. Anderson, ed., *Protestantism* (Nashville, 1944), pp. 52 to 66.

of Hampden and Cromwell, as well as Baxter and Owen. He may be called, in some sense, the spiritual father of New England and the American republic. Calvinism, in its various modifications and applications, was the controlling agent in the early history of our leading colonies (as Bancroft has shown); and Calvinism is, to this day, the most powerful element in the religious and ecclesiastical life of the Western world.[12]

The basic principles of Calvinism still are the very lifeblood of the historic Calvinistic churches. Likewise fundamentalism has its taproots in the soil of Calvinism. Even in liberalism certain principles of Calvinism can be detected. It is generally admitted that neo-orthodoxy to a very marked degree moves in the thought patterns of Calvinism. It is therefore apparent that a study of Calvin's theology and of historic Calvinism is indispensable for a proper evaluation of the American theological scene.

By temperament and training Calvin inclined toward austere asceticism. His schoolmates nicknamed him "the Accusative Case." For a brief time he studied law. Unlike Luther, he does not seem to have experienced a deep soul struggle. Little is known as to the reasons for his conversion to Protestantism. The persecution of Protestants by Francis I compelled Calvin to flee to Basel, where at the age of 27 he published the *Institutio Religionis Christianae,* the *magna charta* of Calvinistic theology, as a defense of the Reformed doctrine. The Preface, addressed to Francis I, is a literary masterpiece filled with pathos and eloquence.[13] During an overnight stay at Geneva, Calvin was persuaded by William Farel to remain in this city and to complete the reformatory program which Farel had inaugurated but was unable to complete. Under Calvin's leadership the former license and frivolity in Geneva gave way to strict moral severity. But the libertine party did not take kindly to this austere manner of living and initiated a rebellion against Calvin's rule, which culminated in the expulsion of the reformer. From 1538 to 1541 Calvin lived in exile at Strasbourg, where he came into close contact with Bucer and signed the Augsburg Confession "in the sense in which its author understood it." Here he served as professor at the Academy of Strasbourg and devoted himself especially to New Testament interpretation. But by 1541 the moral conditions in Geneva had so deteriorated that Calvin was asked to return. Upon his return he established a plan of government in which the College of Pastors and the Consistorial Court of Discipline, with himself at the head, aimed not only to direct the affairs of the city, but also to control the social life of its citizens. To all intents and purposes Geneva became a theocracy. After the execution of the anti-trinitarian Michael Servetus, the expulsion of the libertines, and violent clashes with

---

[12] Schaff, *Creeds,* I, 445, fn. It is providential that England did not colonize America until the first decades of the 17th century. By this time Protestantism, though Calvinistic, had been firmly established in England. Thus by God's providence most of what became the United States was colonized by Evangelical nations, unlike Canada, which was settled by French Roman Catholics, and Central and South America, which were colonized by Spanish and Portuguese Roman Catholics. Cp. Charles Beard, *The Reformation of the Sixteenth Century* (Hibbert Lectures, 1883), p. 300 ff.

[13] The first (1536) and second (1539) editions must be studied in the light of the final edition (1559). The third edition is available in English, translated by John Allen, 2 vols. (Eerdmans, 1949). Volumes XX and XXI in the Library of Christian Classics (Philadelphia: The Westminster Press, 1960) also reproduce the *Institutes.*

those who opposed him, Calvin became the undisputed head of Reformed Protestantism. Calvin performed a double function: he systematized Reformed theology, and he organized its ecclesiastical discipline. He must be regarded as the father of Reformed theology and the founder of Presbyterian church polity.

THE MATERIAL AND FORMAL PRINCIPLES OF CALVIN'S THEOLOGY [14]

THE MATERIAL PRINCIPLE

It is very frequently assumed that Calvin's material principle, the center of his theology, is the theory of the double election. This is not the case. A modern Calvinist states:

> Election concerns itself with *man*, whereas Calvin places *God* into the center; election concerns itself with man in the *fallen* estate, whereas Calvinism considers man also in the estate of *integrity*. Election deals only with *moral beings*, whereas Calvinism deals with the *entire universe*.[15]

Nor is justification the material principle, as has recently been asserted.[16] The central and controlling thought of Calvinism is Calvin's concept of the glory of God. It may also be stated in the form of the question: What must I do for the greater glory of God? Calvin is so theocentric in his theology that he has been called "the God-intoxicated" theologian and the best representative of theocentricism.[17] For Calvin God is the beginning, the means, the end of everything. This principle prompts Calvin to systematize every phase of theology around the "greater glory of God" concept and to integrate all areas of life — ecclesiastical, cultural, political, social, economic, scientific — with this God-centered concept.[18]

In order to make His own glorification possible God is said to bestow His grace upon all men. The grace of God "which hath appeared to all men" is called "common grace," i. e., common to all men. But according to Calvin this

---

[14] This section on Calvin's theology does not attempt to present primarily only Calvin's own theological development, but rather the main principles of Calvin's theology in their cumulative effect upon Reformed theology. Therefore such references to the leading Reformed confessions will be adduced as represent either modifications of, or accretions to, Calvin's theology. In this section we leaned heavily on W. Walther, as did also Klotsche (General Bibliog.), pp. 203—41.

[15] Meeter, p. 34.

[16] Wilhelm Albert Hauck, esp. p. 39 ff. Wilhelm Niesel, pp. 234, 117 f., points out that for Calvin the mystical union with Christ is determinative in the doctrine of justification. For a critique of Hauck's thesis see *C. T. M.*, XI (1940), 153.

[17] P. G. Fuhrmann, *God-centered Religion* (Grand Rapids, 1942), p. 164 f.

[18] It is often stated, and correctly so, that all forms of Pelagianism are anthropocentric, that Lutheranism is Christocentric, and that Calvinism is theocentric. Pelagianism asks: What am I able to do for my salvation? Lutheranism asks: What has Christ done for my salvation? Calvinism asks: What must I do for the greater glory of God? In this connection the question arises whether Calvin's apparent emphasis of theocentricity is not actually a case of egocentricity. The constant stress on what man is obligated to do is more in line with an *eros* religion than the *agape* theology of Scripture. At any rate Lutheranism finds an inner conflict and an irreconcilable clash in Calvin's high theocentricity. Cf. A. Nygren, *Agape and Eros*, trans. Philip Watson (Philadelphia: The Westminster Press, 1953), pp. 532—48, where Nygren analyzes the apparent contradiction between theocentricity and egocentricity in Augustine.

grace is not God's pardoning grace in Christ. It is rather that gift which enables men to live to the glory of God in the areas of culture, industry, politics, science.[19] The sovereign will of God manifests itself also in the bestowal of "special grace." This grace is given only to the elect and irresistibly works their salvation. If man could resist this grace, God's will would no longer be sovereign and absolute. Thus the irresistibility of "special grace" is a necessary corollary of Calvin's theocentric theology.[20]

THE FORMAL PRINCIPLE

In accord with this material principle Calvin developed his formal principle, i. e., the source of religious truth. Calvin views the universe as a system of beautiful harmony, both in the realm of the spirit and of nature, and he therefore concludes that God's will is revealed in nature and in history. In the state of integrity man clearly understood and followed God's will.[21] As a result of sin, however, man no longer sees this system of perfect order, and therefore God has given the Bible as a corrective and as the absolute standard and norm for all conduct both in the moral and the spiritual realms. God has given the Bible to direct man's thinking and conduct in the fields of science, culture, business, society, the home, and in politics. There is no area of human conduct for which the Bible does not serve as the norm according to which all men are to pattern their conduct for the greater glory of God.[22] It is man's duty to embrace with gentle docility and without any exception all that is delivered in the Scriptures. This applies especially to all points of doctrine.[23] Thus the Bible is made the code for right belief. This is reflected, for example, in the etymology of the word "miscreant," which originally denoted one who believed falsely and by his false belief commits a crime, like the anti-trinitarian Michael Servetus, whose crime of false belief was subject to capital punishment.

It is therefore not incorrect to say that Calvin's formal principle is *sola Scriptura*. He asserted that he never knowingly twisted the Scriptures.[24] Nevertheless there is a significant difference

---

[19] Kerr, loc. cit.; Meeter, pp. 63—67.

[20] Some early American Calvinists went so far as to declare that the withholding of special grace is also to the glory of God. Throughout eternity the damned will glorify God that they were made instruments on whom God exercised and manifested His absolute and sovereign will. Foster, *The Genetic History of New England Theology*, p. 157.

[21] Nature and history contain vestiges of God's activity, "certain signs of His glory" (*Calvini opera selecta*, 3, 45, 6). Niesel asks: "Is nature and history a sort of second Bible, a second source of revelation?" He does not think that Calvin teaches a natural theology understood in the commonly accepted use of this term (pp. 36—50). Nevertheless it is correct to say that Calvin viewed all law as one, though less clearly understood by the unbeliever than by the believer. Calvin can identify the Natural Law as perceived by the unbeliever with the commandments of Moses and the ethical injunctions of the New Testament. Otto A. Piper, "What Is Natural Law?" *Theology Today*, Jan., 1946, p. 476.

[22] *Inst.*, III, xxi, 3.

[23] Ibid., I, xviii, 4.

[24] Cp. J. T. Mueller, "Luther oder Calvin?" in *C. T. M.*, IV, 255 ff. Niesel (p. 27) states that while it is true that Calvin held the Bible to be the only rule and norm for the Church's doctrine (*Op. sel.*, 5, 140, 1), it is false to call this his formal principle. Calvin's theology is Bible-

between Lutheranism and Calvinism in making *sola Scriptura* the formal principle. And this difference is due to the divergent concepts as to the purpose and scope of the Bible.

Differences in Understanding the "Sola Scriptura." Lutheran theology asks: What has God done for my salvation? and finds the answer in the Scriptural revelation of God's grace. Calvin asks: What must I do to the greater glory of God? and sees in the Bible the Sovereign's will for man's conduct and belief. In the papacy men must submit blindly to the voice of the church; in Calvinism men are required to submit obediently to the Bible. Calvin's approach to the Bible appears to be legalistic rather than evangelical and reveals a mingling of Law and Gospel.[25]

Since Calvin views the Bible as the divinely given codex of doctrine and ethics, his view of inspiration is static and not dynamic and comes very close to a theory of mechanical inspiration. In fact, some of his followers, notably Prof. Johannes Buxtorff, maintained that also the vocalization of the Masoretic text is divinely inspired. The conviction that the Bible is God's verbally inspired Word is created by the inner illumination of the same Spirit who inspired the Scriptures.[26] Lutheranism holds that this conviction is wrought by the Spirit through the Word itself and thereby avoids the Calvinistic danger of approaching the Scriptures with an a priori

conviction of its divine character. Calvinism maintains furthermore that since the Bible is the absolute and only authority for Christians, they must know with certainty which books constitute the Bible and which books must be eliminated. Therefore the Reformed confessions not only developed a well-defined teaching on the inspiration of the Scriptures, but also fixed the extent of the Biblical canon.[27]

The hermeneutical principles of Lutheranism cannot be applied to Biblical interpretation where Calvin's principles are consistently followed. Calvinism does not allow for different degrees of value in the individual books of the Bible and practically denies any distinction between the two Testaments. It is no doubt correct that Calvin sees a distinction between the two Testaments, inasmuch as the New Testament presents in full colors the same Christ whom the Old only foreshadowed. But it is also true that Calvin's legalistic principle prompted him virtually to erase the distinction between the two Testaments. This is evident particularly from his concept of the Law as the basis for, and the ground of, the divine-human covenant relation. This covenant relation obligates man to fulfill the requirements of God's Law. Though Christ has come to free us from the coercion of the Law, He has not abolished it, for "the doctrine of the Law, which remains inviolate after Christ, prepares us for every

centered because its sole function is to direct men to the scope of the Bible, Jesus Christ. Cp. also *The Word of God and the Reformed Faith*, ed. by the Public Commission of the Second American Calvinistic Conference (Grand Rapids: Baker Book Store, 1943).

25 W. Walther, pp. 217 ff., 274 f.; for a synopsis of Walther see Klotsche, p. 205 (fn. 14, above).

26 *Inst.*, I, vii, 1, 5; IV, viii, 8, 9. Some Calvin scholars deny this. Cp. Niesel, p. 28 f. *Inst.*, I, vii, 5. L. Boettner, *The Inspiration of the Scriptures* (Grand Rapids, 1940). Paul T. Fuhrmann, "Calvin, The Expositor of Scripture," *Interpretation*, VI (1952), 188—209.

27 Cp. the *West. Conf.* (see below, "The Pres. Church"). The Ref. editions of the Bible do not contain the Apocryphal Books.

good work with its doctrine, admonition, rebuke, and reprimand." [28] According to Calvin, the chief function of the Law is to serve not as a mirror, but as a rule. This principle prompted Calvin to maintain that the Old Testament rites have been abolished only as to their use, but not as to their significance. Thus Baptism and the Lord's Supper have supplanted only the form but not the purpose of circumcision and the Passover. The legalistic emphasis in Calvin's theology is reflected not only in his approach to the Scriptures, but also throughout his theology, especially in the realm of sanctification, in the nature and function of the church, and in his philosophy of life.[29]

Calvinism is frequently charged with rationalism. It must be granted that theoretically Calvin fully subscribed to the *sola Scriptura* principle; that he never wanted to develop his own ideas about God and man. His motto was *Ad verbum est veniendum.* Nevertheless Calvin also held that apparent contradictions in God's revelation can be solved by "sanctified" reason. He believed that "reason is the instrument which the believer uses in examining the object of faith. Reason and faith are not opposed to each other. Hence, even in religious matters nothing contrary to right reason may be admitted." [30]

THE CHIEF ARTICLES OF FAITH

Calvin's basic theological principles are reflected in his theocentric theology, his presbyterian church polity, and his Reformed cultus. While no one group among modern Calvinists follows Calvin in all points, nevertheless in their totality the various Calvinist bodies represent a fairly complete picture of Calvin's position on the chief doctrines of the Christian faith. A résumé of Calvin's views on the chief articles of the Christian faith in distinction from Lutheranism, and to some extent from Arminianism and Romanism, should prove helpful in properly evaluating the theological orientation of modern Calvinistic bodies.

OF GOD

The overemphasis on the sovereignty of God stamps Calvinism as a theocentric theology. In both Calvinism and Lutheranism the theological slogan is *soli Deo gloria.* But the motivation differs: in the former, because man must fear and glorify the sovereign Lord; in the latter, because man is privileged to trust and serve the gracious and forgiving God. In the one the emphasis lies on what God expects of man for His own glory, in the other on what God has done for man.[31] Calvin's undue emphasis on God's sovereignty endangers

[28] Niesel, pp. 98—103. R. Seeberg, *Dogmengeschichte*, 3d ed., IV (Erlangen, 1920), 565 f.

[29] Literalism usually goes hand in hand with legalism. This is evident among some of the Pres. bodies, who not only interpret the "Second" and the "Fourth" Commandments literalistically, but who insist on the exclusive use of Psalms in public worship or the specific mention of the Triune God in the Federal Constitution. Dispensationalism, advocated particularly by Calvinists, is based on a very literalistic understanding of the Bible. Many of the smaller sects in America are the natural outcome of a coarse literalism.

[30] Calvin's differentiation of three kinds of reason in "The Clear Explanation of Sound Doctrine Concerning the True Partaking of the Flesh and Blood of Christ in the Holy Supper to Dissipate the Mists of Tileman Heshusius" (J. K. S. Reid, *Calvin: Theological Treatises* [Phila.: The Westminster Press, 1954], pp. 272—74) is illuminating.

[31] The Lutheran view has been called egocentric, similar in some respects to Romanism. Lutheran theology is not anthropocentric, but Christocentric and in a sense also theocentric. On the theocentricity of Luther's theology see Philip Watson (P. III, above, Bibliog.), ch. ii.

the centrality of God's love in Christ Jesus.[32] This overemphasis on the sovereignty of God becomes most patent in Calvin's doctrine of a double election. God is the Absolute, subject to no law. In His absolute sovereignty He has predetermined that the salvation of some is to be to the glory of His grace; the reprobation of others likewise to the glory of His name. Under Calvin's successor, Theodore Beza, supralapsarianism was developed as the best way to set forth God's absolute sovereignty.[33]

OF MAN

Calvin distinguishes sharply between man's corporeality and his spirituality. This view of man may be in part due to the overemphasis on God's sovereignty, which prompted Calvin to say that God made our body of clay to keep us humble. It seems more likely, however, that he did not break completely with Neoplatonic dualism, which had dominated Christian thought for long cen-

turies. He viewed the soul not only as essentially distinct from the body, but also as the far more glorious part of man.[34] He speaks of the body as the prison house of man. Therefore man's goal in this life is to seek liberation from the body. Calvin goes so far in his dualism as to claim that the pleasant experiences of life, e. g., culture, art, sports, natural beauties, are not to gladden our hearts but to make us more conscious of the greater glory of God and to increase our yearning for the time when our souls shall be liberated from the restrictions of this mundane body. As long as we are in the body, we are far from God, and only when we are liberated from the body, can we really enjoy God.[35] Calvin's somewhat pessimistic view of man's body has several very significant theological implications. In the first place, it puts a low estimate on the doctrine of the resurrection of the body.[36] In the second place, it affects his entire philosophy of life. This is

32 The work of Christ is viewed in this perspective (*Inst.*, II, xvii, 1).

33 *Inst.*, III, xxi, 5; xxii, 3; xxiv, 12, 14; it is a horrible decree, xxvii, 7. Calvin does not recognize the Lutheran distinction between the antecedent, or universal, will of God, and His consequent, or punishing, will toward those who spurn God's grace. The consistent Calvinist arrives at a view of election which cannot but view God as the Cause of man's reprobation as well as his salvation. This is the case in supralapsarianism, which views the divine decrees in the following sequence: (1) to glorify Himself by man's salvation and reprobation; (2) to create man; (3) to permit the Fall so that God's glory would not suffer harm; and (4) to send Christ for those whom He has already decreed to save. In this sequence the decree of salvation or reprobation precedes the decree of man's fall (*supra lapsum*). According to infralapsarianism (*infra lapsum*), which triumphed at the Synod of Dort, the decrees occurred in the following order: (1) to create man in holiness; (2) to permit the Fall; (3) to save some; (4) to pass by the others. L. Berkhof, *Reformed Dogmatics* (2d ed.), I, 118—25; cp. *Inst.*, II, iii, 6. Neither view can do justice to the Scriptural concept of grace as God's loving favor toward all men available only in Christ Jesus. At best, grace is God's work in us by exciting in our hearts a love, desire, and ardent pursuit of righteousness.

34 *Inst.*, I, xv, 1, 2. O. S., 3, 176, 1. See also Thomas F. Torrance, *Calvin's Doctrine of Man* (Grand Rapids: Wm. B. Eerdmans Publishing Co., 1957; British edition, 1947).

35 *Inst.*, loc. cit. Cp. Koeberle, *The Quest for Holiness*, p. 130 ff.

36 While modern Calvinists do not accept Calvin's dualistic view of men (cp. Klotsche [P. II, Bibliog.] p. 215), they do not share Luther's deep insights into the soteriological significance of the resurrection of the body.

evident especially in his thesis that man's vocation or calling in life is a means to mortify the flesh. In accord with his dominant motif of the sovereign will and sovereign decree Calvin presents a view of the vocation which has led to asceticism and legalistic pietism.[37] The profession or vocation into which a person has been "called" is his sphere of activity for the greater glory of God, and he dare not have any earthly or carnal ambitions beyond those of his immediate and direct vocation.

Calvin and the historic Calvinistic confessions teach the total depravity and the complete culpability of man because of original sin. But Calvin finds no solution for the dilemma which arises in maintaining both the absolute sovereignty of God and man's accountability for sin. On the one hand, he maintains that man's corruption is due in part to God's sovereign decree. He states that the cause of contagion is that it was ordained by God that the gifts which He had conferred on Adam should by him be preserved or utilized both for himself and for his posterity. Calvin held that according to God's sovereign will all men were in Adam and through his disobedience all men were corrupted in Adam's sin. On the other hand, Calvin rejects a fatalistic view by maintaining that man does not sin by coercion, but by a free choice.[38]

CHRIST'S PERSON AND WORK

The sovereignty of God has influenced Calvin's Christology as to both the person and the work of Christ. The charge of Nestorianism is often raised against Calvinism. But this charge must be qualified as much as the charge that Lutheran Christology is Eutychian. Calvin repudiated both Nestorianism and Eutychianism.[39] Calvin and the Reformed have maintained the true deity and the true humanity of Christ and the personal union. But it is difficult, if not impossible, to hold the personal union and at the same time question or even deny the communion of natures and the communication of attributes, especially

---

Luther sees in the resurrection of the body the Holy Spirit's activity to sanctify completely the total person according to both body and soul. Cp. Large C., Creed, III, 59—61. Luther holds that in Baptism the application of water to the body is in God's economy the assurance that the body, together with the soul, is to be eternally with God (Ibid., Baptism, pp. 44—46).

[37] Georgia Harkness, p. 178 ff., a résumé of Max Weber, loc. cit. R. H. Tawney, pp. 240 ff. W. Walther, p. 263. Einar Billing, *Our Calling*, trans. Conrad Bergendoff, pp. 14—16.

[38] *Inst.*, II, i, 7; *Corpus Reformatorum*, 23, 62; 47, 57; 33, 660 f. Cp. Westm. Conf., VI, 1. Later Calvinistic theologians wrestled with this problem. Some solved it by the so-called federal headship theory, according to which Adam was the head of the first covenant, a covenant of works, and he acted as our representative; others, notably Jonathan Edwards, by the theory that God is the author of the situation in which man acts, but man is the author of his reaction to the specific situation. Cp. Foster, p. 69 ff. (fn. 20). Reason is unable to find a satisfactory solution of this problem. — The federal headship theory views original sin as the transgression of a specific commandment by mankind's representative in Paradise. Lutheran theology in distinction from both the Roman and the Calvinistic holds that original sin is both a total lack of trust in God and a vicious rebellion against God inherited from our first parents. Cp. Ap., II. Original sin is therefore spoken of as the "capital" sin. S. A., P. III, Art. I, 1.

[39] Niesel, pp. 109—111. Cp. L. Boettner, *Studies in Theology* (Grand Rapids, 1947), p. 200 ff. B. B. Warfield, *The Person*, etc., p. 211 ff.

the so-called *genus maiestaticum*.[40] As a result of his emphasis on the sovereignty and transcendence of God, Calvin holds that it is necessary for God Himself to condescend to man. Such a condescension can take place only in the incarnation. But at the same time he maintains that Christ "miraculously descended from heaven, but in such a way that He never left heaven." Under the aspect of the personal union this statement could probably be correctly understood. But from the viewpoint of the communion of natures it actually spells the separation of the natures. According to the axiom *finitum non est capax infiniti*, the humanity of Christ could not be a true humanity if it could partake of the divine properties.[41] The humiliation is therefore considered as being essentially the incarnation, and the exaltation as being the bestowal of great powers to the human nature. The denial of a real communion of natures is evident in the Reformed view of the Real Presence in the Lord's Supper.

It is difficult to maintain the intrinsic value of Christ's work if God's sovereign decrees are given such priority as is done by Calvin. According to him, God has first decreed to embrace the elect in His gratuitous favor. This God could do, because men are His creatures, and as such He finds something in us to love. Nevertheless, as long as we are sinners, He cannot receive us entirely. Therefore to reconcile us completely to Himself, He abolishes all our guilt by the expiation exhibited in the death of Christ. . . . The love of God the Father therefore precedes our reconciliation in Christ; or rather it is because He first loves, that He afterwards reconciles us to Himself.[42]

The divine decree of the Absolute Sovereign rather than the infinite grace in Christ is the "first cause" of God's "remarkable good pleasure to appoint Christ Mediator to procure salvation for us." This basic concept is also expressed in the view that "God could have redeemed us through angels, but the death of Christ shows more adequately the greatness of sin." This view has given rise to the charge that Calvin was an advocate of the declaratory theory of the atonement. However, Calvin did not draw the expected conclusions. On the contrary, he speaks of the necessity of an objective reconciliation.[43]

In speaking of the effect of Christ's work Calvin seems to come near to the ancient *theopoiēsis* concept. Irenaeus and other church Fathers leaned toward the Neoplatonic view that the soul which had emanated from God finds its ultimate goal in the return to God and reunion with God by a kind of "deification." In speaking of Christ's incarnation Calvin states that the Son of God became man in order to "receive to Himself what belongs to us and transfer to us

---

[40] This was the real issue between Lutherans and Calvinists in the 16th century. Cp. F. C., VII and esp. VIII, 39—44.

[41] Niesel, p. 111. The Admonition of Neustadt of 1581, a defense of Calvin's Christology against Chemnitz and the Lutheran Confessions, states: "If something human is attributed to God (Christ) and something divine to man (Christ), this is nothing but a figure of speech as far as the two natures are concerned." Cp. W. Heyns, *Manual of Ref. Doctrine* (Grand Rapids, 1926), p. 93; *Pop. Symb.*, p. 212.

[42] *Inst.*, II, xvi, 3. Cp. xvii, 1 ff.

[43] Ibid., II, xi, 1, 2. II, xvii, 2. Walther, 202. Cp. Franks, *History of the Doctrine of the Work of Christ* (London: Hodder and Stoughton, [1918]), 2 vols. The New England theologians were outspoken advocates of the Acceptilation theory.

what is His and make that which is His by nature ours by grace." [44]

Finally, compelled by the logic of his major premise, Calvin teaches the limited atonement. In His absolute sovereignty God chooses what disposal He will make of Christ's redemptive work. And He has decreed that Christ's death is only for the elect, His people. For the reprobate Christ's death had only an incidental reference in so far as they share in "common grace." [45]

JUSTIFICATION

Calvin maintains the forensic character of justification by faith. He states:

The believer apprehends by faith the righteousness of Christ, invested in which he appears in the sight of God not as a sinner, but as a righteous man. Thus we simply explain justification to be an acceptance by which God receives us into His favor and esteems us as righteous persons; and we say that it consists in the remission of sins and the imputation of the righteousness of Christ.[46]

In recent years it has been argued that justification is Calvin's chief article, the article without which the Christian religion cannot stand, and that in this respect there is a great similarity between Luther and Calvin.[47] This is only partially true. In fact, a close examination reveals that Calvin's concept of justification and its significance differs fundamentally from Luther's. In Calvin's theological thought not justification, but sanctification to the glory of God is the predominant motif. It is for this reason that Calvin lays great emphasis on our being "ingrafted into the body of Christ." Again he states "that we are justified, not without works, yet not by works, since union with Christ, by which we are justified, contains sanctification as well as righteousness." This sentence can be rightly understood. However, it must be kept in mind that in Calvin's theology the *Christus in nobis* is emphasized more than the *Christus pro nobis*.[48] Accordingly faith is defined, not primarily as the hand which appropriates Christ's objective work of reconciliation, but as the bond which unites us with Christ.[49] From another point of view faith is the conviction that one has been elected and is "in the state of grace"; and since the election is unalterable, therefore faith really is the belief that "once in grace, always in grace." Again, Calvin defines faith as a knowledge of the will of God respecting us, received from His Word.[50] Accordingly Calvin defines the nature of pure and genuine religion as "consisting in faith united with a serious fear of

---

[44] *Inst.*, II, xii, 2.

[45] L. Boettner, *Studies in Theology*, 315 ff.

[46] *Inst.*, III, xi, 2. The Ref. standards, esp. the *Westm. Conf.*, follow Calvin.

[47] Niesel, p. 125. Wilhelm Albert Hauck, p. 17. See also Parker, "Calvin's Doct.," p. 101 ff.

[48] *Inst.*, III, xiii, 5. He seems to approach Osiander, who held that justification is effected by a *physical* indwelling of the Son of God in the believer. Calvin, however, holds that it is through the mystical indwelling of Christ. In Calvin's opinion a physical union with Christ is impossible, because Christ's body is now confined to heaven. In his opinion the mystical union signifies that Christ through the power of the Holy Spirit destroys the curse of sin residing in our bodies and infuses the power of His life into ours so that we no longer live unto ourselves but unto Him. J. Bohatec, *Staat u. Kirche*, p. 300.

[49] *C. R.*, VII, 599; Niesel, pp. 116 f., 130.

[50] *Inst.*, III, ii, 6.

God, comprehending a voluntary reverence and producing legitimate worship agreeable to the injunction of the Law." [51]

REPENTANCE AND SANCTIFICATION

According to Calvin, mortification stands in a causal relation to justification. In his exposition of the Third Article of the Apostles' Creed he discusses the Christian life under the following heads: (1) religion and life; (2) Christian self-denial; (3) the good life and the life to come; (4) rules for Christian living; (5) justification by faith. This sequence — a complete reversal of the order in Lutheran theology — is in accord with Calvin's entire theology. It is predicated on the overemphasis which Calvin places upon the relation of the creature to the sovereign God, on man's obligation of obedience. This accounts for the fact that repentance is called "evangelical grace." [52] Repentance, manifest in self-denial and meditation upon the future life, is the ground of the assurance that the believer is in the state of grace and thereby in the possession of a certain sign of his election. The basis of faith is therefore not, as in Lutheran theology, the universal promise of God contained in the Gospel, but the Holy Spirit's activity evident in producing self-denial and observance of the rules for Christian living. [53]

The Calvinistic principle for Christian ethics is nomistic and in a sense atomistic. The idea of obligation predominates. Calvin's ethics operates predominantly with such concepts as law, ordinances, commandments, obedience. An action is ethical and moral not because it conforms to an ethical standard, but because it is an act of obedience. [54] The emphasis on obedience has moved Calvin to teach that the third use of the Law more clearly sets forth the real purpose of the Law than the other two uses. For the same reason Calvin can compare the Christian's attitude toward God to that of a slave, who is ready to serve his master, but must constantly learn what is expected of him; or that Calvin could say that the unwilling flesh of the Christian can be incited to good works by the Law, even as a lazy mule is goaded by the whip. [55]

Calvin's ethics has resulted in an ascetic and puritanical view of life. As was pointed out previously, his modified dualism prompted Calvin to think very disparagingly of the functions of the body. There is here a morbid view of life, bordering almost on pessimism. Man is to use life's goods only as far as they further his course toward heaven and serve the greater glory of God. In this interest Calvin established a strict code of right and wrong, as will be shown in the next section.

[51] *Ibid.*, I, ii, 2.

[52] *Ibid.*, III, iii, 7, 20. *Westm. Conf.*, XV, 1. See also Ronald S. Wallace, *Calvin's Doctrine of the Christian Life* (Grand Rapids: Wm. B. Eerdmans Publishing Co., 1959).

[53] For a detailed discussion of the difference between the Lutheran and the Calvinistic definitions of "repentance" see Engelder (P. II, fn. 205). *C. T. M.*, V (1934), 445—55, 497—509. In Lutheran theology the redeemed child of God says: "Because God has showered such blessings upon me, therefore I will gladly and freely serve Him."

[54] *Inst.*, II, xix, 4; II, vii, 12. The Ref. principles of ethics are clearly reflected in Emil Brunner (P. III, fn. 27, above), pp. 148 ff., 605.

[55] *Inst.*, II, vii, 12. In Lutheran theology the "third use" of the Law is the application of the Law to the Christian in so far as he still has the old Adam. Cp. F. C., V. W. Walther, 254 ff. F. E. Mayer, "The Function of the Law in Christian Preaching," *C. T. M.*, XX (1949), 123. Werner Elert, *The Christian Ethos* (P. III, fn. 27, above), pp. 294—30.

THE CHURCH

Calvin's doctrine of the church must be viewed in the light of his emphasis on the sovereignty of God. Calvin defines the church as the entire number of the elect. He makes election — not faith as in Lutheran theology — the ground for membership in the church. He alleges that in this way he is destroying all human self-assertion and placing the power and the victory of the church solely into the hands of God.

While Calvin has little to say about the "spiritual" phase of the church, he gives over 200 pages of the *Institutes* to the "visible" church. This is in reality the phase of the church which primarily interests him.[56] The establishment of the visible church is God's ordinance, and the visible church is the means through which He will speak to the world. For if God would speak to the world directly, all men would flee from Him. Since the visible church is God's spokesman, Calvin lays great emphasis on a sharp distinction between the true visible church and all false visible churches. The true church possesses the Office of the Keys, and its main function is to interpret the Bible and to compel all men to live according to the precepts of the Bible. This view accounts for his emphasis on the presbyterian form of church government with its "teaching" and "ruling" elders. All offices in the church are to serve but one purpose, the lordship of Christ. The chief office is that of the pastor, who is to preach and administer the sacraments; next in order is that of the doctors, who are to watch the purity of the proclamation in the church. The presbyters and deacons,

respectively, are to curb the frivolous and to alleviate the suffering of the needy.

In order to compel all citizens to live to the glory of God, Calvin in 1541 proposed a stringent system of church discipline, known as Ecclesiastical Ordinances. These were adopted by the city council and were made the civil law for Geneva. There was the closest possible relation between church and state in establishing a code of ethics and in forcing the Genevans to conform to this standard. The church was viewed as the conscience of the state. To fulfill her mission, God provided the ministry and the consistory, the former to function as an authoritative teaching office and the latter as an effective disciplining agency. The secular and spiritual authorities were viewed as the two arms working jointly to establish Christ's undisputed lordship in every area. This is usually called the Genevan theocracy. However, it was a theocracy only in so far as the ecclesiastical authority was to assist the secular power as a spiritual guide. There seems to have been rather a co-operation between the two than a subordination of the secular to the spiritual. The secular authority was charged with regulating the conduct of men according to the Decalog, while the spiritual power had the duty to interpret the Decalog. The state was the will of God in action, according to the counsel and direction of the consistory. Calvin was the undisputed head of the Genevan government, not, however, *ex officio*, but because of his recognized leadership in both the ecclesiastical and the secular council.[57]

---

[56] The Lutheran Confessions speak of the church in a strict and wide sense (Ap., VII, VIII). Calvin early employed the terms "invisible" and "visible." This terminology is much more suitable to his concept of the church than to the Lutheran. Niesel, 177 f.

[57] The question: Was Geneva a theocracy? is answered affirmatively by H. Hausherr, p. 16, and negatively by Schaff, *Hist.*, etc., p. 471. On Calvin's views concerning the power and authority of the state see A. Hyma, *Christianity and Politics*, pp. 142—52; Georgia Harkness, pp. 222—26;

It was Calvin's conviction that though Christ has fulfilled the Law, the basic principles of the Mosaic Law were not abrogated. This meant that he prescribed the punishment for such sins as blasphemy, adultery, and witchcraft on the basis of the Mosaic Law. Indeed, Calvin went beyond this Law and established economic principles, introduced price control, and laid down specific rules for the choice of one's vocation and the discharge of one's obligations in it.[58] In the various social relations the church carefully prescribed the limits for everyone's conduct; for example, the church prescribed the menus for the various income groups; the style and color of dress. Card games and all luxury items were forbidden. In short, the private life of every citizen of Geneva was minutely prescribed and closely watched.

The punishments for infractions of the Ecclesiastical Ordinances were extremely harsh. Within two years 58 persons were condemned to death and 76 were exiled. This in a community of 20,000 inhabitants! During the pestilence of 1546, 34 women were burned at the stake on charges of having practiced sorcery. In two years 400 people were punished for laughing during the sermon or for dancing.[59]

Finally Calvin's basic principle, and his view of the church in particular, prompted him to maintain that membership in the visible church is an indispensable cause of salvation. He went even farther and insisted that also the nonelect must belong to the church in order to promote the glorification of God. This may account in part for the tremendous church activity which has characterized Calvinistic church bodies.

THE MEANS OF GRACE

Calvin's view of the Scriptures and the sacraments is dominated by his emphasis on the sovereignty and transcendence of God. This emphasis is reflected in three points.

1. Calvin holds that a revelation of the majesty of God would completely crush man, the finite creature. To reveal His will to man, God condescended to man's level. This condescension took place in the incarnation of Christ, when God confronted man in the finitude of

William A. Mueller, *Church and State in Luther and Calvin* (Nashville: Broadman Press, 1954), pp. 73—163. On the organization of the Genevan Consistory see C. Bergendoff, loc. cit. The Geneva pattern of a theocracy was not fully realized anywhere in the Reformed church. On early Reformed ecclesiology see Geddes MacGregor, *Corpus Christi: The Nature of the Church According to the Reformed Tradition* (Philadelphia: Westminster Press, 1959). On the influence of Calvinistic theocratic theorizing in early American Protestantism, see John R. Bodo, *The Protestant Clergy and Public Issues 1812—1848* (Princeton: Princeton University Press, 1954).

58 Cp. Einar Billing, loc. cit. It is no doubt difficult to prove the thesis of Max Weber that Calvin's ethics are responsible for the rise of capitalism. Nevertheless it is true that Calvin's insistence on such virtues as industry and frugality, coupled with the principle that one dare not use the fruits of one's labor for one's enjoyment, became a contributory factor in the establishment of the Dutch and British industrial and financial empires. Calvin did not countenance the retirement of anyone, no matter how old, nor did he permit that the savings should ever lie idle. Everybody and everything must be active to the glory of God. Cp. Weber, ch. v; Harkness, ch. ix; Tawney, p. 211 ff. — In their attacks on Communism — and on the National Council of Churches — some neo-Calvinists have virtually made Anglo-Saxon capitalism part of the Christian culture.

59 Cp. Schaff, *History*, VII, 490 ff. W. Walther, pp. 212 ff.; 260 f. But see also Ernst Pfisterer, *Calvins Wirken in Genf* (Essen: Lichtweg-Verlag, 1940), 27—52.

human flesh. It takes place today when God condescends to prattle, as it were, and to speak so that man can bear to hear the declaration of His will.[60]

2. Calvin not only distinguishes between the Word and the Spirit, but separates the two. True, Calvin never went as far as Zwingli, who said that the Spirit requires no vehicle. He definitely maintained that ordinarily the Spirit employs the Word in the calling of the elect and that the Spirit is present conjointly with the proclamation of the Word.[61] His concept of God's absolute will prompted him to reason as follows: Experience shows that man can and does resist the outward call of the Gospel. If the Holy Spirit were really in the Gospel, this resistance would be impossible unless it were assumed that finite and impotent man were actually stronger than the absolute God. He therefore made a careful distinction between the outward Gospel, which can be resisted, and the Spirit who comes immediately and irresistibly to the elect.[62]

3. Calvin holds that the primary function of the Word and the sacraments is that of teaching man the will of the sovereign Lord of the universe. Man is therefore obligated to use both regularly in order to be thoroughly acquainted with its teaching and fully persuaded of the claims which this teaching makes upon him.

Calvin's Concept of the Sacraments. This is much higher than that of Zwingli, who considered the sacraments only as badges whereby Christians may recognize one another as Christians. In Calvin's opinion the sacraments are a "visible" word; in fact, they even excel the Word in so far as they present to us the Word in a painting. He speaks of the sacraments as the mirror, which reflects what the Word offers, or as the seal, which authenticates a document. The sacramental signs proclaim the Gospel visibly so that men may be able the more readily to believe the Gospel. This is essentially the Augustinian symbolic interpretation of the sacrament. Calvin could therefore fully and in the sense of its author subscribe to Augustine's famous epigrammatic statement, *Verbum accedit ad elementum et fit sacramentum,* i. e., the ceremony is a meaningless symbol until the accompanying word explains its meaning. According to Calvin,

Baptism assures us that we have been washed and cleansed; the Lord's Supper, that we have been redeemed. The water symbolizes the cleansing, the blood the satisfaction. We find both in

---

[60] *C. R.,* XXVI, 387. Calvin likens God to a nurse who employs one form of speech in dealing with children and another when speaking to adults.

[61] *Inst.,* IV, i, 1. Cp. Kerr, p. 93.

[62] From the Lutheran viewpoint, the fact that the Gospel can be resisted by man is proof that the Holy Spirit is always active in the Word and the sacraments. There can be no resistance (Matt. 23:37; Acts 7:51), unless there is a real power present and operative. W. Albrecht, *"Non est vis magica,"* C. T. M., VII (1936), 175. Reformed dogmatics have quite consistently accepted Calvin's theory of the immediacy of the Spirit's operation. Charles Hodge, *Syst. Theol.,* II, 684. Henry Thiesen, *Introductory Lectures in Systematic Theology* (Grand Rapids, 1949): "The Scriptures produce spiritual results only as attended by the Spirit of God," p. 394. Whether Calvinism has always been consistent in the practical application is another question. The Arminians say that God gives sufficient light to every human being and that man by his native powers can decide to accept or reject the measure of light given him.

Christ, who, as St. John says, came with water and blood to cleanse and to redeem.[63]

Calvin held that God ordained the public ministry so that pastors can instruct God's people, and the sacraments have been appointed as useful aids to maintain and strengthen faith. Sometimes it appears that Calvin is ready to ascribe to the sacraments themselves — not to the immediately operative power of the Holy Spirit — the power to engender faith. He says that the fruit of Baptism is our incorporation into Christ and that thereby Christ Himself becomes the power of Baptism. Again he states that the command to take the body of Christ indicates that God wants the communicants to share Christ and to be united with Him. In the Lord's Supper we have the promise of Christ's presence, and we must therefore believe that we receive Christ as though He were truly present. But it must be kept in mind that Calvin does not ascribe collative and effective power to the sacraments. He maintains that faith must precede the use of the sacrament, for "a vessel must be open to receive the oil, and thus faith must be present when the Word and the sacraments come to us." They are signs that the Holy Spirit has already wrought faith prior to the use of the sacraments. Therefore participation in the sacraments is after all not for the purpose of thereby obtaining the promises of God, but it is a public profession of faith. For this reason Baptism is administered in the majority of Calvinistic churches as "believer's baptism," i. e., only such are considered candidates for Baptism as are already believers or are at least in a "covenant-relation" through their birth of Christian parents.[64] The Lord's Supper is said to be in every case a congregational celebration. When house-communions are celebrated, the congregation must be represented by the elders, because the Lord's Supper is thought to be an act of profession of faith, and such a profession is meaningless unless it is made in public.[65]

The Real Presence. It is rather difficult to establish what Calvin actually understood by the term "the Real Presence."[66] Many scholars believe that Calvin occupied a mediating position between Zwingli and Luther and that in the *Consensus Tigurinus* he made an

[63] Cp. Niesel, p. 204. *Op. sel.*, V, 279, 37.

[64] Cp. Niesel, pp. 207, 210. Hugh Thompson Kerr, *The Christian Sacraments* (Phila., 1944), esp. chs. ii, iv, vii. Cp. Shedd, *Dogmatic Theology*, II, 574: "Baptism is the sign and seal of regeneration . . . not a means of it. It does not confer the Holy Spirit as a regenerating Spirit, but is the authentic token that the Holy Spirit has been, or will be, conferred; that regeneration has been, or will be, effected." The Geneva Catechism answers the question, What is the significance of Baptism? thus: "In it forgiveness of sins and spiritual regeneration are symbolized."

[65] Walther, p. 37.

[66] This question is much more relevant in Continental Europe than in the U. S. A., because the Reformed and the Lutherans have attempted since 1818 to find a satisfactory compromise between their respective views of the Real Presence. The most recent effort climaxed in the "Arnoldshain Theses" of 1957 (see Keith R. Bridston, "Survey of Church Union Negotiations, 1957—1959," *Ecumenical Review*, XII [1959/1960], 244; Paul M. Bretscher, "The Arnoldshain Theses on the Lord's Supper," *C. T. M.*, XXX [1959], 83—91). On an earlier effort, the "Halle Resolutions" of 1937, see Matthias Schulz, "The Question of Altar Fellowship According to the Halle Resolutions," *C. T. M.*, XVIII, 534—37. On the whole issue, see M. Reu, *Can We Still Hold to the Lutheran Doctrine of the Lord's Supper?* (Columbus: Wartburg Press, 1941), p. 86 ff.

honest attempt to give to the Lord's Supper a much deeper spiritual significance than Zwingli had done. Zwingli held that the bread and wine are only symbols of Christ's body and blood. Calvin, however, viewed the entire act of eating and drinking the physical elements as a symbol of an actual spiritual eating and drinking. He held that as food nourishes the body, so the spiritual power of Christ's body nourishes our souls; as we receive the elements with the mouth, so we receive the heavenly gifts by faith. Calvin states that we truly receive the body and blood of Christ and grow into one body with Christ so that He dwells within us and we in Him. While Calvin undeniably ascribes a much higher spiritual significance to the Lord's Supper than Zwingli, he agrees with the German-Swiss Reformer that the communicant does not receive the same body and blood which Christ gave and shed on the cross. Calvin interprets the "Real Presence" as a spiritual union between the believing communicant and the ascended Christ and rejects the view of a sacramental union between the elements in the Lord's Supper and the body and blood of Christ. Calvin's doctrines concerning the human nature of Christ and the immediate working of the Holy Spirit constrain him to view the words of institution symbolically.

1. Calvin asserted that the true humanity of Christ could be safeguarded only if one stoutly maintained that according to His human nature Christ is as far distant from us as heaven and earth are separated from each other. He held that since Christ withdrew His body from the earth, the pious souls can be united with the body of Christ only by ascending spiritually through faith to Christ's body which is locally confined in heaven. He rejected the so-called *genus maiestaticum,* the doctrine that the divine properties are communicated to Christ according to the human nature. This doctrine, he said, ascribes to the human nature of Christ so much majesty that the similarity between His nature and ours would be completely erased and thereby His worth and value as our Redeemer endangered, if not actually denied.[67]

2. Calvin held, furthermore, that the chasm between the ascended Christ, who is now in the uncreated realm of eternity, and the believers, whose abode is in this finite world, is so infinite that only God Himself can bridge this gulf. According to Calvin, God can close the infinite gap between Himself and man solely through the secret and incomprehensible power of the Holy Spirit. By His immediate working the Holy Spirit becomes the link between Christ and the believer, and He unites them so intimately that we become bone of His bones and flesh of His flesh. In and through the spiritual eating the Spirit bestows upon the believer those prerogatives which the Father communicated to Christ's flesh.[68] This intimate union occurs not only during the cele-

---

[67] *Consensus Tigurinus,* 21—25. *Inst.,* IV, xvii, 10, 18, 30, 36. Calvin therefore rejected the Lutheran view of *unio sacramentalis* (the communicant receives both, the earthly elements and at the same time the body and blood of Christ; however, not by a transubstantiation, nor impanation, nor "consubstantiation," but by the sacramental union) and the *manducatio oralis* (the communicant receives with his mouth the body and blood of Chist), and the *manducatio indignorum* (also the unbelieving truly receive the body and blood of Christ, but for their judgment). The advocates of a symbolic view of the Lord's Supper speak of three classes of communicants: the worthy, the unworthy or those whose faith is weak, and the godless. The former two receive spiritually the body and blood of Christ, the latter receive nothing but bread and wine.

[68] Calvin's views are probably expressed most fully and adequately

bration of the sacrament but is a process constantly going on. Calvin's definition of the "Real Presence" is entirely spiritual, highly metaphysical, or, probably, existential and dynamic.

There is a wide divergence among the Reformed bodies in the definition of the Real Presence. In some Reformed circles the Zwinglian view is upheld, and the Lord's Supper is spoken of merely as a memorial, or a symbol of the unity of the church, or as an act of joint profession in a common faith. In other Reformed circles, for example, in the Heidelberg Catechism, Qu. 79, terminology is employed which creates the impression that the 16th-century issues between Calvinism and Lutheranism have been completely removed. However, an examination of the context in which such phrases as "we receive the true body of Christ" occur, reveals that the Reformed churches have not deviated materially from Calvin's position. Even in such Reformed circles as ascribe to the Lord's Supper a highly spiritual significance, the Real Presence is viewed only as a "spiritual" presence.[69]

Summary

Calvin's theology has left its unmistakable imprint on the various Reformed bodies. The chief characteristics may be summarized under (1) spiritualism, (2) nomism, (3) sovereignty of the divine will. To a greater or lesser degree these chief features are discernible in the historic Calvinistic bodies.

in the Scotch Confession of Faith (1560), Art. XXI, which contains the following: "In the Supper, rightly used, Christ Jesus is so joined with us that He becomes the very Nourishment and Food for our souls. . . . This union is wrought by the operation of the Holy Ghost, who by true faith carries us above all earthly things that are visible, carnal, and earthly, and makes us to feed upon the body and blood of Christ Jesus, which was once broken and shed for us but is now in heaven and appears in the presence of His Father for us. And yet, notwithstanding the far distance of place which is between His body, now glorified in heaven, and us, now mortal in this earth, we must assuredly believe that the bread and the cup is the communion of His body and blood so that we confess . . . that the faithful in the right use of the Sacrament do so eat the body and drink the blood of the Lord Jesus that He remains in them and they in Him; yea, they are so made flesh of His flesh and bone of His bone that as the eternal Godhead has given to the flesh of Christ Jesus (which of its own condition and nature was mortal and corruptible) life and immortality, so does Christ Jesus, His flesh and blood eaten and drunk by us, give unto us the same prerogatives." Quoted in Scotch and Latin (Schaff, *Creeds*, III, 468 f.) and translated by the author of this textbook.

[69] Theodore Engelder, "The Reformed Doctrine of the Lord's Supper," *C. T. M.*, X, 641—56. The Presbyterians, probably more than any other Reformed body, wish to elevate the significance of the Lord's Supper. Yet they teach a spiritual manducation only and reject both the oral manducation and manducation on the part of the unworthy. Cp. *Westm. Conf.*, XXIX, 5, 7, 8. Commenting on Qu. 170 of the *Westm. Larger C.*, a Presbyterian pastor and scholar states that the Real Presence occurs when the communicants by faith experience the presence of Christ. "The Real Presence is not discovered in the elements, but in Him of whom the elements speak. . . . When we say that Christ is present in the Sacrament, we assert that in the entire ordinance — in the words of the institution, which are His words; in the act of breaking the bread and pouring out the wine; in the act of *receiving by faith* what is blessed in His name; in the action of the Holy Spirit in making everything embodied in the Sacrament efficacious — in all that is said and done Christ manifests Himself to the *believer*." (Italics ours). H. T. Kerr, *Sacr.*, pp. 90, 91.

BIBLIOGRAPHY

PART IV   SECTION II

Barth, Karl. "Gott erkennen, Gott ehren, Gott vertrauen nach Calvins Katechismus," *Theologische Existenz Heute,* XXVII (1935), 25—44.

Bergendoff, Conrad. "Church and State in the Reformation Period," *Lutheran Church Quarterly,* III (January, 1930), 36—62.

Bohatec, J., ed., *Festschrift zum 400jährigen Geburtstage Johann Calvins.* Leipzig: Rudolf Haupt, 1909.

———. *Calvins Lehre von Staat u. Kirche.* Breslau, 1937.

Bratt, John H. *The Rise and Development of Calvinism: A Concise History.* Grand Rapids: Wm. B. Eerdmans Publishing Co., 1959.

Bromiley, G. W. *Zwingli and Bullinger.* Phila.: Westminster Press, 1953.

Brown, Robert McAfee. *The Spirit of Protestantism.* New York: Oxford University Press, 1961.

Calvin, John. *Institutes of the Christian Religion.* 2 vols. Trans. John Allen. Grand Rapids: Wm. B. Eerdmans Publishing Co., 1949.

———. *Opera* in the *Corpus Reformatorum,* Vols. 29—88.

———. *Commentaries.* Edited by David W. and Thomas F. Torrance. Grand Rapids: Wm. B. Eerdmans Publishing Co., 1959—. 30 vols.

———. Selected works. Library of Christian Classics, Vols. XX—XXIII. Phila.: Westminster Press, 1954—1960.

Cobb, John B., Jr. *Varieties of Protestantism.* Phila.: Westminster Press, 1960.

Dakin, Arthur. *Calvinism.* Phila.: Westminster Press, 1940.

De Moor, Leonard. "Calvin's View of Revelation," *Evangelical Quarterly,* III (April, 1931), 172—92.

Dillenberger, John and Welch, Claude. *Protestant Christianity Interpreted through Its Development.* New York: Charles Scribner's Sons, 1954.

Doumergue, Emile. *Jean Calvin. Les hommes et les choses de son temps.* 5 volumes. Lausanne: G. Budel et Cie., 1899—1917. — This is the standard biography and evaluation.

Dower, Edward A., Jr. "Continental Reformation: Works of General Interest; Studies in Calvin and Calvinism," *Church History,* XXIV (1955), 360—367; XXIX (1960), 196—204. The former article covers the period 1948—1955, the latter 1955—1960.

Ferm, Vergilius. *The American Church of the Protestant Heritage.* New York: Philosophical Library, 1953.

Forell, George W. *The Protestant Faith.* Englewood Cliffs, N. J.: Prentice-Hall, 1960.

Harkness, Georgia. *John Calvin, the Man and His Ethics.* New York: Holt, c. 1931.

Hauck, Wilhelm Albert. *Calvin und die Rechtfertigung.* Guetersloh: C. Bertelsmann Verlag, 1938.

Hausherr, Hans. "Der Staat in Calvins Gedankenwelt," *Verein für Reformationsgeschichte,* cxxxvi (1923).

Holl, Karl. "J. Calvin," 1909. *Gesammelte Aufsätze* (see P. II, fn. 8) III, 254—84.

Hunter, A. Mitchell. *The Teaching of Calvin.* New York: Fleming H. Revell, 1950.

Kerr, Hugh Thompson. *A Compend of Calvin's Institutes.* Phila.: Presbyterian Board of Education, 1939.

Koehler, Walther. *Zwingli und Luther.* Leipzig: Verein für Reformationsgeschichte, 1924 to 1953. 2 vols.

Lindsay, Thomas. "The Reformation in Geneva Under Calvin," *A History of the Reformation.* N. Y.: Scribner's, 1925. Pp. 61—136.

Macgregor, Geddes. *Corpus Christi: The Nature of the Church According to the Reformed Tradition.* Phila.: The Westminster Press, 1958.

McNeill, John T. "Thirty Years of Calvin Study," *Church History,* XVII (1948), 207—40, with an "Addendum," ibid., XVIII (1949), 241.

———. *The History and Character of Calvinism.* New York: Oxford University Press, 1954.

Meeter, H. Henry. *The Fundamental Principle of Calvinism.* Grand Rapids: Wm. B. Eerdmans Publishing Co., 1930.

Mielke, Arthur W. *This Is Protestantism.* Westwood, N. J.: Fleming H. Revell Co., c. 1961.

Niebuhr, H. Richard. *The Kingdom of God in America.* New York: Harper & Bros., 1959.

Niesel, Wilhelm. *Die Theologie Calvins.* Munich: Chr. Kaiser Verlag, 1938. In English: *The Theology of Calvin,* trans. Harold Knight (Phila.: Westminster Press, 1956).

Nixon, Leroy. *John Calvin, Expository Preacher.* Grand Rapids: Wm. B. Eerdmans Publishing Co., 1950.

Parker, T. H. T. "A Bibliography and Survey of British Study of Calvin," *Evangelical Quarterly* (April, 1946), pp. 123 to 132 and 199—208.

Pauck, Wilhelm, "Calvin's Institutes," in *The Heritage of the Reformation.* Boston: Beacon Press, 1950.

Schaff, Philip. *Creeds of Christendom.* New York: Harper & Bros., 1919.

———. *History of the Christian Church,* VII, 255.

Stuermann, Walter E. *A Critical Study of Calvin's Concept of Faith.* Tulsa, Privately printed, 1952.

Tawney, R. H. *Religion and the Rise of Capitalism.* New York: Harcourt Brace & Co., 1926.

Wallace, Ronald S. *Calvin's Doctrine of the Word and Sacrament.* Grand Rapids: Wm. B. Eerdmans Publishing Co., 1957 (British ed., 1953).

———. *Calvin's Doctrine of the Christian Life.* Grand Rapids: Wm. B. Eerdmans Publishing Co., 1959.

Warburton, Ben A. *Calvinism.* Grand Rapids: Wm. B. Eerdmans Publishing Co., 1955.

Warfield, Benjamin B. *Calvin and Calvinism.* New York: Oxford University Press, 1931.

———. Ed. Sam G. Craig. *The Person and Work of Christ.* Phila., 1950.

Weber, Max. *The Protestant Ethic and the Spirit of Capitalism,* 1904. Trans. Talcott Parsons. London: George Allen and Unwin, 1930.

Whale, J. S. *The Protestant Tradition: An Essay in Interpretation.* New York: Cambridge University Press, 1959.

SECTION III

The Reformed Confessions

The Significance of Confessions in the Reformed Churches

It has often been said that the Reformed churches hold the Bible in such high esteem that they pay relatively little attention to confessional statements, some having gone so far as to reject the use of all creeds. There are several reasons why the Reformed

churches, unlike the Lutheran church, do not regard their confessions as the theological norm of their teaching.[1] Although Calvinism, from the days of Dort and Westminster to the present, has had and still has distinguished dogmaticians, the formulating of, and subscription to, confessional standards is not taken nearly so seriously as in the Lutheran church.[2] Calvinistic theology, furthermore, grants

[1] Schaff, *Creeds*, I, 356.

[2] Tschackert, p. 410.

considerable latitude in establishing local confessional standards according to the varying cultural and political environments of each country or province in which the Reformed church was established.[3] In the majority of Reformed bodies the confessions have virtually lost all significance. Only a few Reformed churches require the clergy to subscribe to the standards. The study of the Reformed standards is nevertheless necessary, since they have given point and emphasis to the current theological orientation, cultus, and government of the respective bodies.

European theologians usually group the fifty-eight Reformed confessions according to their Zwinglian or Calvinian origin. This grouping has no significance for the American situation, for in transplanting the Reformed churches to America the language and cultural background of Europe proved of far greater significance in the development of the many Reformed bodies. The most logical procedure for the proper understanding of the American Reformed churches demands that these standards be classified as either Continental or British.[4]

The Principal Confessions

THE CHIEF CONTINENTAL CONFESSIONS

a) *Geneva Catechism,* 1545, composed by Calvin, is largely an abstract of his *Institutes.*

b) *Consensus Tigurinus,* 1549, removed the misunderstanding between the Zwinglians and the Calvinsits concerning the means of grace, the Lord's Supper in particular, and was largely responsible for the adoption of Calvinism in Switzerland.[5]

c) *Consensus of Geneva,* 1552, is chiefly Calvin's defense of his doctrine of predestination against the charges of the Roman Catholic Pighius.

d) *Gallican Confession,* 1559, is a faithful summary of Calvin's theology.

e) The *Heidelberg Catechism,* 1563, is probably, next to the Westminster Confession, the most significant Reformed confession, representing a rather moderate view of the formulations of Calvin's theology.[6] It was intended to a large degree to compose the theological controversies among the Lutherans, Melanchthonians, and Calvinists of the Palatinate. The Elector Frederick leaned

---

[3] In Andover Seminary the theological professors were required to pledge their adherence to the Westminster Shorter Catechism every five years (D. D. Williams, *The Andover Liberals,* New York, 1941, p. 5 f.). The Presbyterian church requires that its clergy accept the Westminster Confession not in so many words, but in spirit.

[4] Some historians include the Thirty-Nine Articles and the *Book of Common Prayer* among the Reformed Confessions.

[5] J. T. Mueller, "Notes on the Consensus Tigurinus of 1549," *C. T. M.,* XX (1949), pp. 894—909.

[6] Karl Barth, *Die christliche Lehre nach dem Heidelberger Katechismus* (Muenchen: Christian Kaiser Verlag 1949), reviewed in *Evangelische Theologie,* April, 1949. Henry Hoeksema, *The Heidelberg Catechism, an Exposition* (Grand Rapids: Eerdmans, 1944). Leonhard Fendt, "Die achtzigste Frage des Heidelberger Katechismus" in *Theologische Literaturzeitung,* 1950, 282 f. Schaff, *Creeds,* I, 529 f. Boeckel, pp. 395—425. August Lang, "Der Heidelberger Katechismus," *Verein für Reformationsgeschichte,* CXIII, 1913. Philip Vollmer, "Evaluation of the Heidelberg Catechism," *Theol. Mag.* (March, 1928), pp. 90—97.

toward Melanchthonianism and finally embraced the Calvinistic doctrine of the Lord's Supper and, in general, Reformed theology. In 1563 he instructed Zacharias Ursinus (1534–1583) and Caspar Olevianus (1536–1585) to prepare the Heidelberg Catechism as a doctrinal norm unfettered by the theological discussions in his territory. The leitmotif of the Catechism is given in Question 1.[7] The first part, anthropology, treats of man's misery and reflects Lutheran thinking; the second discusses redemption and the sacraments and bears a definite Calvinistic stamp; the third part deals with man's gratitude under the heading of the Decalog and the Lord's Prayer.[8] It emphasizes practical religion more than doctrine.

f) The *Belgic Confession*, 1561, was prepared by Guido de Brès (Bray) and was adopted by the Synod of Antwerp in 1566 and by the Synod of Dort in 1619. It is the recognized standard of the Reformed churches in Holland and Belgium and of the Dutch Reformed church in the United States. It follows the Gallican Confession and is considered next to this confession the best statement of Calvinistic theology.

g) The *Second Helvetic Confession* of 1566 was prepared by Bullinger and published by Frederick III of the Palatinate. Its spirit is that of the Bucer and Bullinger type of mediating theology. This fact is evident in the doctrine of election, where the confession attempts to avoid Pelagianism and Augustinianism, and particularly in the definition of the "Real Presence" and the "sacramental eating," where the confession harmonizes Zwingli's and Calvin's views.[9]

[7] Schaff, *Creeds*, III, 307, 308: "Question 1. What is the only comfort in life and death? Answer. That I, with body and soul, both in life and in death, am not my own, but belong to my faithful Savior Jesus Christ, who with his precious blood has fully satisfied for all my sins, and redeemed me from all the power of the devil; and so preserves me that without the will of my Father in heaven not a hair can fall from my head; yea, that all things must work together for my salvation. Wherefore, by his Holy Spirit, he also assures me of eternal life and makes me heartily willing and ready henceforth to live unto him. Question 2. How many things are necessary for thee to know, that thou in this comfort mayest live and die happily? Answer. Three things: First, the greatness of my *sin* and *misery*. Second, how I am *redeemed* from all my sins and misery. Third, how I am to be *thankful* to God for such redemption."

[8] The Decalog is given according to Exodus 20. The "third" rather than the "second" use of the Law is emphasized in accord with Melanchthon's and especially Calvin's view. See W. Elert, *Zwischen Gnade und Ungnade;* see also *Lutheran World Review*, January, 1949; F. E. Mayer (above, fn. 55, P. IV, Sec. I) — Calvin's doctrine of election did not find acceptance in the German Reformed church. The only reference to election is found in Qu. 54, "What is the Holy Christian Church?" and the answer is Scriptural and truly comforting. It stresses that from the foundation of the world unto the end of time the Son of God, out of the human race, gathers, protects, and preserves an elect congregation unto eternal life, and that "I am and shall be a living member" of this church. — The Catechism is divided into 52 lessons, a lesson for each Sunday of the year.

[9] Tschackert, p. 403. Schaff, *Creeds*, I, 390—420. On the "sacramental eating" see Art. XXI, E. F. C. Mueller, p. 211 f. The "Real Presence" is presented under the analogy of the sun, which is far distant from us in the sky, yet effectively present to us. Thus Christ is present, not corporeally but spiritually by His life-giving operation.

h) *The Canons of Dort* were prepared in answer to the Arminian or quinquarticular theologians.[10] James Arminius (1560–1609), a strict supralapsarian, was commissioned to refute an infralapsarian treatise.[11] His studies led him to the conclusion that he could not defend a system which leaves no room for the universal grace of God and the freedom of man, but which places "God's will above His character" and pictures God as coming with a sovereign decree rather than an invitation.[12] Thus he became a vehement opponent of Beza's supralapsarianism. Arminius held that Calvin's description of God as the only free agent in a universe of puppets actually made God the author of sin; in fact, "the only sinner." Arminius directed his attacks especially against unconditional election, which destroys the glory of God and dishonors Christ because it teaches that prior to Christ's saving death and prior to God's invitation man's eternal fate is already determined. Contrary to both supralapsarianism and infralapsarianism Arminius taught "a universal salvation to all who

accept Christ and human freedom to hear and accept God's invitation in responsive loyalty and faith." [13]

In the hope of obtaining religious toleration the Arminians in 1610 submitted their "Five Points," known as the "Remonstrance," to the estates of Holland. In the subsequent theological as well as political controversies the contra-remonstrants gained the upper hand and convened the Synod of Dort (1618 to 1619), to which representatives of the Reformed churches of England, Switzerland, the Palatinate, and Scotland were invited. This synod, the most ecumenical in the Reformed church's history, had already prejudged the Arminians and had invited them only as defendants.[14]

THE FIVE POINTS OF CALVINISM
AND ARMINIANISM COMPARED

1. *Election.* Calvinism teaches an absolute, unconditional election inasmuch as God, according to His sovereignty, has decreed to give a certain number to Christ to be saved by Him. — Arminianism teaches that election is

---

[10] Schaff, *Creeds*, I, 508—23, discusses the Arminian Decrees of Dort in detail. The article by Lowell N. Atkinson, "The Achievement of Arminius," in *Religion in Life* (1950), pp. 418—30, will prove helpful in presenting a correct interpretation of the Canons of Dort.

[11] Hodge (*Syst. Theol.*, II, 316) thus defines supralapsarianism: "According to this view, God in order to manifest His grace and justice selected from creatable men [i. e., from men to be created] a certain number to be vessels of mercy and certain others to be vessels of wrath. In the order of thought, election and reprobation precede the purpose to create and to permit the Fall."

[12] Atkinson, p. 422.

[13] There seems to be a marked similarity between Arminius and Melanchthon in the doctrines of anthropology and soteriology. The followers of Arminius, however, esp. Simon Episcopius (1583—1644) and Hugo Grotius (1583—1645), the author of the rectoral theory of the atonement, developed Arminian theology along latitudinarian and liberal trends. See Robert S. Franks (P. IV, Sec. I, fn. 43, above). *The Writings of James Arminius*, trans. James Nichols and W. R. Bagnall (Grand Rapids: Baker Book House, 1956), 3 vols.

[14] For a detailed summary of the "Five Points" of Calvinism see Schaff, *Creeds*, p. 519 ff. The Five Points of Calvinism are presented under the acrostic *t-u-l-i-p*, *t*otal depravity, *u*nconditional election, *l*imited atonement, *i*rresistible grace, *p*erseverance in grace.

conditioned by the foreseen faith or unbelief.

2. *Atonement.* Calvinism teaches that the saving efficacy of the atoning death of Christ extends to all the elect, but only to the elect, so as to bring them infallibly to salvation. Intrinsically the work of Christ is of infinite worth because Christ is the eternal Son of God, but extensively its efficacy is restricted to the elect.[15] Arminianism teaches not only that Christ died for all but also that the benefits of His death are made available to all.

3. *Total Depravity.* Calvinism teaches that all men are conceived in sin, are by nature children of wrath, incapable of any saving good, and that without the Holy Spirit's work they are neither willing nor able to seek God. — Arminianism holds that fallen man is indeed unable to come to faith without the Holy Spirit. At the same time the Remonstrants denied total depravity and made the Holy Spirit's gracious operation contingent on man's co-operation.[16]

4. *Irresistible Grace.* The Dort theologians maintain that, through the power of the regenerating Spirit, God irresistibly penetrates into the innermost parts of man and infuses new powers into man's will.[17] — The Arminians held that God's grace and man's will are concurrent causes of conversion and that man has the power not only to resist but also to accept God's grace.

5. The Dort Synod reiterated the Calvinistic doctrine that God's persevering grace so delivers the elect from the dominion of sin that, once they have been assured of their election, they cannot finally fall from grace. — Arminianism holds that since man's final salvation is contingent in part on God's grace and in part on man's will, no one can be certain of his final salvation.

CHIEF BRITISH REFORMED CONFESSIONS

The *Anglican Thirty-nine Articles* and the *Book of Common Prayer* are frequently listed among the Reformed confessions. This statement is not quite correct inasmuch as the influence of the Lutheran Augsburg Confession and the Lutheran church orders is quite evident.

The *Scotch Confession of Faith,* 1560, is Calvinistic. However, the emphasis on the sovereignty of God's will and the theory of the double election are not so prominent in this confession as in most of the Continental confessions or in the Westminster Confession.

The *Westminster Confession,* the *Larger* and the *Smaller Catechism,* 1647.[18]

The *Savoy Declaration,* 1658, is the standard of the English Dissenters, or Congregationalists, and follows the Westminster Confession except that it rejects the authority of the presbytery and the synod.[19]

---

[15] On the limited atonement and the arguments in support of it see the standard Reformed dogmatics textbooks of Charles Hodge, Karl Heppe, Lorraine Boettner, Lewis Berkhof.

[16] "Opinion" of Remonstrants, Mueller, LVI; see also the "rejection of errors" in Boeckel, p. 531. Conrad Wright, "Edwards and the Arminians on the Freedom of the Will," *Harvard Theol. Review,* XXXV (October, 1942), 241—62.

[17] Canons, *Third and Fourth Heads,* Art. XI, XIV.

[18] This Confession is discussed in connection with Presbyterianism.

[19] See A. G. Matthews, ed. *The Savoy Declaration of Faith and Order, 1658* (London: Independent Press, 1959).

BIBLIOGRAPHY

PART IV   SECTION III

Collections of the Reformed Confessions

Boeckel, E. G. A. *Die Bekenntnisschriften der evangelisch-reformierten Kirche.* Leipzig, 1847. This is an annotated edition of the Reformed confessions in the German language.

Fabricius, Caius. *Corpus Confessionum. Die Bekenntnisse der Christenheit.* Leipzig and Berlin: Walter de Gruyter Co., 1928. Only Vols. X and XX were available to us. In addition to the confessions, this work contains the agenda, hymnbook, significant resolutions, in short, everything which will give an insight into the church life of each denomination.

Mueller, Ernst Friedrich Karl. *Die Bekenntnisschriften der Reformierten Kirche.* Leipzig: A. Deichert, 1903. This edition contains all the fifty-eight Reformed confessions, including the later ones.

Niemeyer, H. A. *Collectio confessionum in ecclesiis reformatis publicatarum.* Leipzig, 1840.

Niesel, Wilhelm. *Bekenntnisschriften und Kirchenordnungen der nach Gottes Wort reformierten Kirche.* München: Chr. Kaiser, 1938. This edition contains the *Düsseldorfer Thesen,* 1933, and the *Barmen Erklärung,* 1934.

Schaff, Philip. *Creeds of Christendom.* Vol. I contains the historical introductions and Vol. III the text of the confessions, both in the original and in the English translation. (Cp. P. II, Bibliog., above.)

Summaries and Evaluations of Reformed Theology

Heppe, Heinrich. *Die Dogmatik der evangelisch-reformierten Kirche dargestellt und aus den Quellen belegt.* Ed. Ernst Bizer. 2d ed. Neukirchen: Neukirchener Verlag, 1958. (An unauthorized and rather unsatisfactory English translation of the 1st ed. [1934—35] was published in 1950 by G. T. Thomson.)

Jacobs, Paul. *Theologie reformierter Bekenntnisschriften in Grundzügen.* Neukirchen: Neukirchener Verlag, 1959.

Klotsche, E. H. *Christian Symbolics.* Burlington: Luth. Literary Board, 1929. Pp. 203 to 241. See below, under Walther.

Schneckenburger, M. *Vergleichende Darstellung der lutherischen und reformierten Kirchenbegriffe.* Stuttgart: Metzler, 1855.

Walch, Johann Georg. *Historische und theologische Enleitung in die Religionsstreitigkeiten ausserhalb der evangelisch-lutherischen Kirche,* Jena, 1736. 5 vols.

Walther, Wilhelm. *Lehrbuch der Symbolik.* Leipzig, 1924. The third part (pp. 180 to 290) is an excellent summary and incisive critique of Reformed theology on all points of faith and practice. Walther's work is based directly on Calvin's writings and the Continental and British Reformed confessions. Klotsche has made Walther's material available, in condensed form, to the American student.

SECTION IV

The Reformed Churches

There are more than 125 separate Reformed and Presbyterian bodies in the world. These bodies follow Calvin's theological and ecclesiastical principles and constitute the largest Protestant group under the same form of church government. The similarity in doctrine and polity among the Reformed and Presbyterian groups has led to the formation of "The Alliance of the Reformed Churches Throughout the World Holding the Presbyterian Order," also known by the brief title of the World Presbyterian Alliance. It includes practically all of the more than 46,000,000 adherents of Presbyterianism.[1] There is no essential difference in doctrine and polity between the Reformed and the Presbyterian bodies. The points of divergence are due largely to the difference in the social, cultural, and political conditions under which the two groups came into existence, the Reformed churches being of Continental and the Presbyterian churches of British origin. In America these differences have been perpetuated, and it is therefore necessary to discuss the two groups separately.

European Background

The American Reformed churches trace their origin to the Reformed churches of Switzerland, France, Holland, Western Germany, and Hungary. In Switzerland the Zwinglian type of theology was modified by Henry Bullinger and Martin Bucer and brought more closely into conformity with Calvin's theological principles.

In France the Protestants, later known as the Huguenots, were severely persecuted. In 1559, they organized the Protestant Synod and adopted the Gallican Confession and the Presbyterian form of church government. For various reasons the church of the Reformation was unable to gain a firm and permanent foothold in France.[2]

In the Netherlands Calvin's principles found the warmest and stanchest supporters. Fifty years prior to the Lutheran Reformation, Evangelical ideas had been promulgated by such men as John Wesel Gansevoort, John Wessel, and Rudolf Agricola; by 1520 Evangelical groups with Lutheran leanings had become established in many of the Dutch provinces in spite of bitter persecutions.[3] The Dutch Protestants, however, accepted Calvinism rather than Lutheranism, largely because the former justified armed resistance to tyranny on theological grounds. In 1571 the first General Synod of the Dutch Reformed church convened at Emden; it accepted the Belgic and French Confessions as

---

[1] The executive secretary's office is in Geneva, Switzerland.

[2] Roland H. Bainton, *The Reformation of the Sixteenth Century* (Boston: Beacon Press, 1952), pp. 160—82. *The Cambridge Modern History* (Cambridge: Univ. Press, 1903), II, ch. 9, esp. p. 283 ff., pp. 346—84; III, ch. 1, p. 491 ff. *New Schaff-Herzog Encycl.* (Grand Rapids: Baker Book House, 1950), V, 393—400.

[3] Cp. Luther's hymn in memory of the Dutch martyrs Esch and Voes, in 1523. J. Koestlin, *Martin Luther* (5th ed.; 1903) I, 606 ff. Bainton, *The*

well as the Geneva and the Heidelberg Catechism, and introduced a presbyterian polity. A plan to merge the Lutherans and the Reformed was opposed by Theodore Beza. In 1618 the Synod of Dort definitely committed the Dutch Reformed church to Calvinistic theology when it adopted the "Five Points of Calvinism" and introduced a form of church polity and a liturgy along the lines advocated by Calvin.[4] It was due largely to the Dutch Reformed that Holland became the first asylum for persecuted dissenters, particularly the Huguenots, the Waldenses, the English Separatists, and the Scottish Covenanters.

Reformed theology was introduced into Germany when Frederick of the Palatinate in 1559 accepted Calvin's views on the Lord's Supper [5] and a modified form of Calvinism as it is represented in the Heidelberg Catechism, prepared by Caspar Olevianus and Zacharias Ursinus. The German Reformed gained a foothold in Western Germany and to some extent also in Prussia. At several German universities within Lutheran territories provision was made for a Reformed theological professorship, for example, at Erlangen and Göttingen. The Prussian Union and, more recently, the formation of the Evangelische Kirche in Deutschland (EKID) were attempts to fuse the Lutherans and the Reformed into one church body.[6]

Reformed theology was introduced into Poland, Hungary, Romania, and Czechoslovakia. In these areas the Reformed church has suffered persecution from the Roman church in the Counter Reformation and more recently from Communism.[7]

The Reformed Churches in America

The Reformed Church in America was founded by emigrants from Holland who formed the colony of the New Netherlands, under the authority of the States-General and under the auspices of the Dutch East India Company. Unlike other colonists, the early Knickerbockers came to America not to escape persecution, but rather to pursue business interests. With Governor Minuit, in 1626, came two *Krank-Besoeckers*, or *Zieken-Troosters*, that is, comforters of the sick. The first minister, Jonas Michaelius, arrived in 1628, and a church was organized with at least 50 communicants, consisting both of Walloons and Dutch. At first the work was in charge of the Synod of Holland, but the American colonists sought greater freedom from the mother church and, under the leadership of T. J. Frelinghuysen, arranged for the training of their own clergy by founding Rutgers College in 1766 at New Brunswick, N. J. The retention of the Dutch language retarded its growth, and, in fact, alienated its youth. Attempts to unite with the German Reformed church failed very largely because the Dutch Reformed demanded that, in addition to

---

Ref., etc., pp. 176—78. *Encycl. Brit.* (Chicago: Encycl. Brit. Press, 1951), XIX, p. 39. *New Schaff-Herzog*, IX, 422. *Cambr. Mod. Hist.*, II, iii, James Mackinnon (Bibliog., above, P. III), pp. 337—38.

[4] *American Church History*, VIII, 18.

[5] The Palatinate was Melanchthon's homeland. On this important chapter of church history see "Hist. Introd.," *Triglotta*, p. 184 ff. Cp. General Bibliog., Bente, Dau.

[6] See section on Ev. and Ref. church. — The Lutherans in Germany insist that EKID is not a church, but only a federation, while Reformed and United church leaders assert that EKID is a union church.

[7] *Cambr. Mod. Hist.*, III, 719 ff.; IV, 1 ff. Cp. *Census*, 1936, II, 1727.

the Heidelberg Catechism, the Dort Articles and the Belgic Confession be accepted as confessional standards. From 1848 on large numbers of Hollanders, in some instances entire congregations with their pastors, migrated to Michigan and Iowa, many of them, notably those who came under the leadership of Van Raalte and Scholte, to escape persecution.[8]

This body's theological position has been summed up in these words:

> The doctrinal standards of the Reformed Church in America are the Belgic Confession, the Heidelberg Catechism, and the Canons of the Synod of Dort. The church is thus a distinctively Calvinistic body. It has a liturgy for optional use in public worship, with forms of prayer. Some parts of the liturgy, as those for the administration of baptism and the Lord's Supper and for the ordination of ministers, elders, and deacons, are obligatory; the forms of prayer, the marriage service, etc., are not obligatory. Children are "baptized as heirs of the Kingdom of God and of His Covenant"; adults are baptized (by sprinkling or immersion, as preferred) on profession of repentance for sin and faith in Christ. All baptized persons are considered members of the church, are under its care, and are subject to its government and discipline. No subscription to a specific form of words being required, admission to communion and full membership is on confession of faith before the elders and the minister.[9]

Its church polity is presbyterian and conforms to that of the Presbyterian church except for the nomenclature. In recent years this body has relaxed some of its strict rules against Freemasonry and has adopted an aggressive mission policy. Its two theological seminaries are located at New Brunswick, N. J., and at Holland, Mich. (Hope College).

The Netherlands Reformed Congregations constitute a body organized in 1907 by immigrants from Holland who had seceded from the established church of that country.

The Christian Reformed Church was organized in 1857 by such Dutch immigrants to Michigan and Iowa as did not approve of the doctrinal and disciplinary position of the older Dutch Reformed groups. This body has remained conservative and adheres strictly to the Calvinistic theology as laid down in the Belgic Confession, the Canons of Dort, and the Heidelberg Catechism. In using Psalms in the public service, it follows the custom of the Reformed Presbyterian church. However in recent years this rule has been relaxed. In addition to Calvin College and Seminary at Grand Rapids, Mich., its members support a flourishing system of Christian elementary schools.[10] Recent immigration has contributed to a rapid growth in Canada.

The Protestant Reformed Churches of America is a small group of churches which separated from the Christian Reformed Church in 1924 under the leadership of Herman Hoeksema.

The Hungarian Reformed Church in America is a small body of Hungarian Reformed who did not accept the "Tiffin Agreement," which sought to

---

[8] Cp. the histories in the Bibliography on p. 26, and Henry S. Lucas, *Netherlanders in America* (Ann Arbor: The University of Michigan Press, 1955).

[9] *Census*, 1936, II, p. 1506.

[10] The National Union of Christian Schools has over 200 elementary and 27 high schools with a total enrollment of over 57,000. Co-operating with members of the Christian Reformed Church in the Union are members of the Reformed Church in America and of the Protestant Reformed Church. A quite separate organization, with a broader denominational base, is the National Association of Christian Schools with nearly 150 elementary and 34 high schools; the total enrollment exceeds 18,000.

transfer them from the mother church in Hungary[11] to the Reformed church in the United States. It accepts the Reformed confessions, but as to church polity it occupies middle ground between episcopacy and presbyterianism. It adopted the present name in 1958; before that it was called the *Free Magyar Reformed Church in America.*

The Reformed Church in the United States, of German origin, became part of the Evangelical and Reformed Church (1934), which in turn became part of the *United Church of Christ* (q. v.).

BIBLIOGRAPHY

PART IV SECTION IV

Beets, Hy. *Christian Reformed Church in North America.* Grand Rapids, Mich.: Eastern Avenue Book Store, 1923.

Corwin, E. T., et al. "A History of the Reformed Church, Dutch, the Reformed Church, German, and the Moravian Church in the United States." *American Church History Series,* VIII.

Demarest, D. D. *The Reformed Church in America.* New York: Bd. of Publ. of Ref. Dutch Ch., 1884.

Heyns, W. *Manual of Reformed Dogmatics.* Grand Rapids, 1926.

Hoffman, Milton J. "The Reformed Church in America," in Vergilius Ferm, ed., *The American Church of the Protestant Heritage* (New York: Philosophical Library, 1953). Pp. 131—45.

Hoogstra, Jacob T., ed. *American Calvinism: A Survey.* Grand Rapids: Baker Book House, 1957.

Hyma, Albert. *Van Raalte and His Dutch Settlements in the U. S. A.* Grand Rapids: Wm. B. Eerdmans Publishing Co., 1947.

Kromminga, D. H. *The Christian Reformed Tradition from the Reformation to the Present.* Grand Rapids, Mich.: Wm. B. Eerdmans Publishing Co., 1943.

Kromminga, John. *The Christian Reformed Church, a Study in Orthodoxy.* Grand Rapids: Baker Book House, 1949.

Schooland, Marian M. *Children of the Reformation: The Christian Reformed Church, Its Origin and Growth.* Grand Rapids: Wm. B. Eerdmans Publishing Co., 1958.

SECTION V

Presbyterianism

Calvin's two basic principles, the sovereignty of God and the absolute authority of the Bible in all matters of faith and life, are said to find their fullest and best expression in Presbyterianism. The term "Presbyterian" is usually understood to refer to a specific form of church government, and rightly so. But today this term is, as a rule, employed to denote a type of Calvinism which emphasizes four clearly defined fundamental principles: (1) the undivided

[11] See Imre Revesz, *History of the Hungarian Reformed Church,* trans. George A. F. Knight (Washington: The Hungarian Reformed Federation of America, 1956), a history of Hungarian Calvinism from the Reformation to after World War II.

sovereignty of God in His universe; (2) the sovereignty of God in salvation; (3) the sovereignty of the Scriptures in faith and conduct; (4) the sovereignty of the individual conscience in the interpretation of the Word of God.[1]

Presbyterianism in Scotland

The life and activity of John Knox (1505–1572), the Reformer of Scotland, typifies the chief characteristics of Calvin's theology. At the age of forty he became an ardent convert to Protestantism and an uncompromising advocate of English Puritanism. Persecuted by Queen Mary, he fled to Geneva (1554 to 1559), where he became more Calvinistic than John Calvin. Upon his return to Scotland he devoted himself to a thorough reformation of the doctrine, church government, and discipline according to Calvin's principles. These were embodied in the Scotch Confession of Faith, 1560. Knox was not an original thinker — his only contribution is the introduction of a strict observance of the Sabbath — but an excellent organizer; and the Scottish church, largely because of Knox's work, may be considered the most consistent Calvinistic body to this day.[2]

Covenanting, patterned after the Old Testament practice in Joshua 24:25 and 2 Kings 11:17, is a distinctive feature of Scotch Presbyterianism. The Covenants of 1581, 1638, and 1643 were politico-religious agreements in which the people pledged to maintain their religious and national interests against the papacy and later against the episcopacy. The practice of covenanting is based on Calvin's principle of the sovereignty of God and on his distinction between common and special grace. Accordingly the Scotch Presbyterians maintained that Christian citizens must insist that in all its institutions human society must be organized upon a distinctively Christian basis.[3] This comes very close to Calvin's theocratic ideals. According to one authority,[4] the Covenanters held that government as a *function* belongs to the area of "common grace" and has nothing to do with religion. But as an *institution* it is a moral agent. As such it is under Christ's mediatorial office, and the state owes allegiance to Christ. The church, which has the divine duty to proclaim the entire counsel of God, must therefore fix the Scriptural qualifications also for civil offices. However, the church does not have authority to enforce its prescriptions, for as every Christian, so also the state as a moral agent has the right to interpret Scripture, including the sections on civil government. In case of an irreconcilable clash between the state's

---

[1] *Census*, II, 1382 (see P. II, fn. 1).

[2] Attempts at reconciling the differences between the Church of England and the Church of Scotland have been persistently unsuccessful; on the most recent efforts see Keith Bridston, "Survey of Church Union Negotiations 1957—1959," *Ecumenical Review*, XII (1959/1960), 246 to 248.

[3] *The Scottish National Covenant* of 1581 and *A Solemn League and Covenant for Reformation and Defense of Religion* are reprinted in Thompson, p. 317 ff. See also Schaff, pp. 685 ff. 3,690; *Schaff-Herzog Encycl.*, s. v.; *Census*, II, 1462 f. (Cp. P. II, fn. 1) On the whole matter of covenanting see Lewis B. Schenk, *The Presbyterian Doctrine of Children in the Covenant* (New Haven: Yale U. Press, 1940). The significance of covenanting is said to be similar to the confirmation vow practiced by Lutherans. This is not the case.

[4] Johannes G. Vos, *The Scottish Covenanters*, reviewed in *Presbyterian Guardian*, Dec. 25, 1940. See also quotation from A. A. Hodge, *Popular Lectures on Theological Themes*, in the same periodical, 1942, p. 72.

and the individual's interpretation the Covenanter has the right to remain aloof from participating in any civil affairs.[5]

Presbyterianism in England

The establishment of Presbyterianism in England is a result of the Puritan conflict.[6] There were two major parties in the Established Church of England at the turn of the 17th century: (1) The Anglican party, consciously Catholic in its theology, worship, and church government, supported by James I (1603 to 1625) and especially by Charles I (1625 to 1649) and Archbishop Laud, who vigorously defended the principle of the divine right of kings and bishops; and (2) the Puritan party, intensely Calvinistic in theology and worship and opposed to the hierarchical form of church government.[7] In 1638 Charles endeavored to force conformity to the *Book of Common Prayer* upon the Scots, who retaliated by forming the National Covenant of Scots in defense of Presbyterian theology and church polity. The tyrannical manner in which the king attempted to outlaw Calvinistic doctrine in England and to compel the English Puritans to adopt the *Prayer Book* and Arminian theology was a contributing factor in the Civil War (1642–1649). In its opposition to the political and religious tyranny of the crown and the bishop, Parliament was supported by Oliver Cromwell, under whose leadership the army overthrew the Episcopal hierarchy, exiled the royalist clergymen, deposed and executed Archbishop Laud (1645) and finally the king (1649). Amidst these turbulent times Parliament convened the Westminster Assembly (1643) to effect a thorough reformation of the Established Church in theology and church government according to the Presbyterian principles of the "Scotch League and Covenant" of 1643. The Westminster Assembly prepared the Westminster Confession (1647) and the Shorter and Longer Catechisms as the doctrinal standards for the Established Church. Presbyterianism, however, was short-lived in England, for in 1660 the Puritan Commonwealth was forced to give way to the restoration of the monarchy and to the reintroduction of the Anglican episcopacy and the liturgy. Westminster theology and church polity had relatively little significance in England. However, Westminster theology gained a firm foothold in American Presbyterianism, to a large degree among English and American Congregationalism, and to a certain extent among the early American Baptists.[8] It can be stated that no other religious document had so significant a bearing on American church life, and incidentally also on many of American political ideals, as the Westminster Confession. For this

---

[5] On the basis of this principle some groups among the Reformed Presbyterians refuse to go to the ballot box because the Federal Constitution does not specify allegiance to the Triune God. See below.

[6] For details of this important and complicated phase of church history, in which political intrigue and expediency played so large a role, see Theodore Hoyer, "The Historical Background of the Westminster Assembly," *C. T. M.*, XVIII (1947), 572—91.

[7] Two other parties, the Separatists and the Independents, can also be identified, the former led by Robert Browne, the latter by William Ames and Henry Jacob. They were the forebears respectively of the English Baptists and of the Congregationalists, and will be discussed later.

[8] The *Savoy Declaration* (1658) of the English Congregational churches and the *New Hampshire Confession* of the American Baptists follow the *Westm. Conf.* very closely, except with regard to the Presbyterian form of church government.

reason a relatively large amount of space must be given to Westminster theology.

Schaff states:

The Westminster Confession sets forth the Calvinistic system in its scholastic maturity after it had passed through the sharp conflict with Arminianism in Holland, and as it had shaped itself in the minds of Scotch Presbyterians and English Puritans during their conflict with High-Church prelacy.[9]

The controlling theme, or material principle, of Westminster theology is the sovereignty of God,[10] and this principle is reflected throughout the confession.

Bibliology. The Westminster Confession (Art. I, 1) maintains the absolute necessity of the Bible because natural revelation in creation and history is in-sufficient to convey such knowledge of God and of His will as is necessary for salvation and because supernatural revelation has ceased. The revelation of God's will is extant only in the canonical books of the Old and New Testaments,[11] which "are given by inspiration of God to be the rule of faith and life." The Confession states furthermore that the original text was "immediately inspired," which according to a leading Westminster theologian means that it "comes directly from God the Father, by the Holy Ghost, without any means."[12] The Westminster Confession accepts the Bible as the absolute and final authority "concerning all things necessary for God's own glory, man's salvation, faith, and life." This authority is said to rest not on the Bible's own intrinsic value

---

[9] P. 760. In the following analysis we have leaned heavily on Schaff and on Warfield, *Westm. Assembly.* See also George S. Hendry, *The Westminster Confession for Today: A Contemporary Interpretation of the Confession of Faith* (Richmond: John Knox Press, 1960).

[10] The term "sovereign" has often been equated with "arbitrary." This, however, is not true. Lutherans also speak of the sovereignty of God, in fact, the term "Lord," which is so frequently ascribed to God, denotes God's separateness, sovereignty. But it is theologically incorrect when the sovereignty of God is emphasized at the expense of His love and other attributes.

[11] In its listing of the canonical books the *Westm. Conf.* does not include the Apocryphal Books of the Old Testament. The English versions from Tyndale to the British Revised Version contain the Apocrypha as an appendix to the Old Testament. J. Paterson Smyth, *The Bible in the Making,* p. 162. E. J. Goodspeed, *The Apocrypha in the Bible,* p. 5 ff. After 1629, on account of Puritan influence, the Apocrypha are often omitted.

[12] John Ball, *A Short Treatise,* 1656, quoted in Warfield, p. 204. Another representative theologian stated: "Both the understanding and will of man, as farre as they were meerly naturall, had nothing to doe in this holy work, save onely to understand, and approve that which was dictated by God himselfe, unto those that wrote it from his mouth, or the suggesting of his Spirit. . . . Thus, then, the holy Ghost, not only assisted holy men in penning the Scriptures, but in a sort took the work out of their hand, making use of nothing in the men, but of their understandings to receive and comprehend, their wills to consent unto, and their hands to write downe that which they delivered." John White, *A Way to the Tree of Life* (London, 1647), quoted in Warfield, *l. c.,* p. 207 f. Warfield devotes an entire chapter (pp. 261—333) to "Westminster Divines on Inspiration," from which it is evident that many of them held views on inspiration which come very close to the mechanical theory of inspiration, a theory which was not entirely foreign to Calvin. *Institutes* I, vi, 1, 2; vii, 7. These views on inspiration have been widely accepted by the strict Fundamentalists, usually under the term "Plenary Inspiration."

and the testimony of the church, but on "the inward work of the Holy Spirit bearing witness in and by the Word." [13]

An evaluation of the Westminster Confession's Bibliology from the Lutheran viewpoint suggests a number of observations.[14]

1. Lutheran theology also maintains the absolute authority of the Bible; however, not on the basis of an a priori assumption that it is divinely inspired, but on the basis of a Christocentric approach to the Bible.[15]

2. The Westminster Confession states that the Bible is the only rule for faith and life. But a careful study of the confession creates the impression that the Bible is viewed not so much as the rule of faith as rather of life and that a legalistic trend permeates the entire confession, evident especially in the espousal of the "covenant theology." [16] A legalistic spirit manifests itself also in the

frequent recurrence of such terms as "duty to His revealed will," "to be under obligation," "obedience to Christ," "covenant," [17] and in the imposition of Old Testament laws upon New Testament Christians, such as the observance of the "Sabbath," [18] specific commands of Ex. 20:4, 5, proscription of false religions.[19] A modern Scottish theologian writes that the Westminster Confession is

> more concerned with correct belief than with faith itself, and it must bear some blame for the emphasis so long laid on "soundness" of doctrine as the mark of the true believer. With its emphasis also on law, its view of the Sabbath, its legalistic trend, its doctrine of good works, it has to be admitted that it gave more place to the law than to the prophets.[20]

3. And the Westminster Confession assigns an unwarranted place to rea-

---

[13] *Westm. Conf.*, I, 4, 5, 6.

[14] See P. III, Sec. III.

[15] Cp. W. Walther, *Lehrbuch der Symbolik*, p. 223.

[16] See *Westm. Conf.*, Art VII. Qu. 32 of the Larger C.: "How is the grace of God manifested in the second covenant?" The answer is given: "The grace of God is manifested in a second covenant in that He freely provideth and offereth to sinners a Mediator and life and salvation by Him; and requiring faith as the condition to interest them in Him . . . and to enable them unto all holy obedience as the evidence of the truth of their faith." Cp. also Qus. 33—35. In Qu. 91 the answer is: "The duty which God requireth of man is obedience to His revealed will."

[17] Art. XX, dealing with Christian liberty, is concerned primarily with the Christian's liberty from the imposition of man-made commandments. Cp. also the Larger C., Qus. 91—148.

[18] Schaff, *Creeds*, III, 648. The Larger C. states, Qu. 116: "What is required in the fourth commandment? A. The fourth commandment requireth of all men the sanctifying or keeping holy to God such set times as he hath appointed in his Word, expressly one whole day in seven; which was the seventh from the beginning of the world to the resurrection of Christ, and the first day of the week ever since, and so to continue to the end of the world; which is the Christian Sabbath, and in the New Testament called *The Lord's Day*." Cf. Shorter C., Qus. 58—62.

[19] Larger C., Qu. and Ans. 109. The American Presbyterians deleted the latter from the Catechism to conform to the American principles of religious toleration.

[20] John McConnachie, "The Westminster Confession of Faith: Its Greatness and Some Defects in the Light of Today," in the *Evangelical Quarterly*, October, 1944, p. 274 ff.

son.[21] Though the Westminster divines undoubtedly believed that they had safeguarded the Biblical principle sufficiently against the encroachment of rationalism, nevertheless the Westminster Confession represents a high type of "Calvinistic scholasticism." In the words of Philip Schaff:

[It] approaches the deepest mysteries of faith, such as the Trinity, the Incarnation, the eternal decrees of election and reprobation of men and angels, with profound reverence indeed, yet with a boldness and assurance as if they were mathematical problems or subjects of anatomical dissection. It shows usu-ally a marvelous dexterity in analysis, division, subdivision, distinction, and definition, but it lacks the intuition into the hidden depths and transcending heights where the antagonisms of partial truths meet in unity.[22]

Election. The Westminster theology maintains both divine sovereignty and human responsibility. It avoids the supralapsarianism of Beza, which virtually makes the decree of reprobation the cause of damnation, and inclines to infralapsarianism, which views the foreordination to damnation as a "permissive" act, in which God "passed by the others." [23] Though the Westminster di-

21 *Westm. Conf.,* I, 6. *Reformed Dogmatics,* by Heinrich Heppe, ed. by Ernst Bizer (1934—1935), trans. by G. T. Thomson, with a foreword by K. Barth, London, 1950. Barth states that while Heppe is out of date, he nevertheless showed him [Barth] the way for his lectures in dogmatics. Warfield quotes approvingly Heppe, *Die Dogmatik der evangelisch-reformierten Kirche,* to show how reason is to be employed in theology. Heppe states: "Since theology is to recognize and present what belongs to natural religion too, a distinction may be drawn between *articuli simplices (puri),* which rest simply on revelation, and *articuli mixti,* in the presentation of which reason also has its material part. Only we must hold fast to the fact that the fundamental doctrines of theology (of the Trinity, of the fall of the human race, of the Redeemer, of the true blessedness and of the only way to it) can be apprehended only out of revelation and that, therefore, the holy Scriptures are of absolute authority in all the sections of the system of doctrine." Warfield, *Westm. Assembly,* p. 163 f.

22 Schaff, *Creeds,* I, 790 f. McConnachie states (p. 277): "I consider as more than a defect, as a real demerit of the Westminster Confession of Faith, its persistent tendency to subject faith to logical explanation and to rationalize the Gospel." And concerning the controlling idea of Westminster theology McConnachie writes (p. 275): "The Westminster Confession took an unfortunate step in being led away, in its doctrine of Divine Sovereignty, from the earlier insight of the Scots Confession that predestination has to be interpreted through Christology. It is not apart from, or before Christ, but *in Christ* that men's destinies are determined. 'For that same eternal God and Father elected us in Christ Jesus, before the foundation of the world, and appointed Him to be our Head and Brother, our Pastor and great Bishop of our souls' (*Scots Confession,* Art. VIII). In separating between the decree of God and the existence of Jesus Christ, and in conceiving of election as taking place in some sort of eternity before and without Christ, with a complete mathematical precision, the Westminster Confession steps off the Christian ground of election. Instead of interpreting the sovereignty of God as sovereign Fatherhood, and sovereign grace, by which all men are elected in Christ, it relates it with the idea of omnipotence, and leaves its doctrine of predestination as a dark patch within the sphere of Christian doctrine. Actually it makes God the prisoner of His own predestination."

23 Schaff, *Creeds,* III, 608 f.: "God from all eternity did, by the most wise and holy counsel of His own free will, freely and unchangeably ordain whatsoever comes to pass; yet so as thereby neither is God the author of

vines expressly state that "God is not the approver of sin," though they recognize so-called "second causes" and speak of a "hypothetical universalism," [24] no one can read the Westminster Confession without finding in it the Calvinistic doctrine of a double election.[25]

Soteriology. The Westminster Confession teaches that Christ's redemptive work is all-sufficient intensively, but not extensively, for in the interest of its controlling principle of God's sovereignty it limits the work of Christ to the elect.[26] Faith is described as the *medium lepticum*, as the hand which receives Christ's righteousness. At the same time the Confession states that faith is "believing to be true what is revealed in the Word, yielding obedience to the commandments . . . trembling at its threatenings." [27] In the article on justification good works are excluded, but repentance unto life is called "an evangelical grace." [28] This has commonly

been understood to mean that the believer must gain the assurance of his salvation from his repentance. And when the believer has once gained this assurance, it is impossible for him "totally or finally to fall away from the state of grace." [29]

The Means of Grace. In accord with its controlling principle Westminster theology teaches that the "effectual calling by His Word and Spirit" is restricted to "all those whom God hath predestinated unto life," on whom the Holy Spirit works "immediately" in the case both of infants dying before baptism and of "all other elect persons who are incapable of being outwardly called by the ministry of the Word." "Others not elected, although they may be called by the ministry of the Word . . . never truly come to Christ and cannot be saved." [30]

The Church. The Westminster Confession defines the "invisible church" as "the whole number of the elect" and the

sin, nor is violence offered to the will of the creatures, nor is the liberty or contingency of second causes taken away, but rather established. . . . By the decree of God, for the manifestation of His glory, some men and angels are predestined unto everlasting life, and others foreordained to everlasting death."

[24] Some of the Westminster divines (compare Art. III, 6 and VIII, 8 with VII, 3) leaned toward a doctrine proposed by the French theologian Moïse Amyraut (Amyraldus). In his *Traité de la prédestination* (1634) he taught a purely theoretical universalism, according to which God wills the salvation of all men on the condition that they believe — a condition that they can meet abstractly, but, because of their inherited corruption, not in fact — with a real particularism, according to which the elect will inevitably be saved. See *New Schaff-Herzog Encyclopedia*, I, 161.

[25] It is for this reason that the Northern and Southern Presbyterians have added the Declaratory Statement, reprinted in fn. 57 below.

[26] Art. VIII, 4, 5; cp. XI, 4.

[27] Cp. Art. XI, 1, 2 with XIV, 2.

[28] Art. XV, 1. See also the explanatory note. Cp. Art. XVI: "By good works believers strengthen their assurance." Cp. the thoroughgoing analysis of the doctrines of repentance, Christian assurance, the purpose of sanctification, in Reformed theology, with the pertinent references to the *Westm. Conf.*, in Walther, *Lehrbuch der Symbolik*, pp. 245—79.

[29] Art. XVII, 1; XVIII, 2, 3, 4.

[30] Art. X, 1, 3, 4. The Confession seems to imply that it would be unworthy of the sovereign God to employ means which man can resist.

"visible church" as "consisting of all who profess the true religion and their children, outside of which church there is ordinarily no salvation." To this visible church Christ has given the ministry, the oracles, and the ordinances of God for the perfecting of the saints, and of this church Christ is the Head.[31]

Church Government. The Westminster Assembly advocated the Presbyterian church government, but was unable to introduce it permanently in England.[32]

Presbyterianism in North America

Probably in no Protestant church in American are theology and ecclesiastical procedure so closely interrelated as in Presbyterianism.[33] The American Presbyterian system is described in the *Manual* as a unit in which all parts of doctrine and practice stand in a logical relation to a controlling idea. This controlling principle — Lutheran theologians would speak of this as the dogmatic foundation, or the material principle — is the doctrine of the divine sovereignty, or "the absolute control of the universe . . . by the one supreme, eternal, omniscient, omnipresent, and omnipotent Spirit for wise, just, holy, and loving

ends known fully to Himself alone." The Presbyterian system is defined as "that body of religious truths and laws of which the sovereignty of God is the germ and nexus, the life and soul." The organic principle — in Lutheran theology the terms organic foundation, or formal principle are used — is "the sovereignty of the Word of God as the supreme and infallible principle and rule of faith and practice." [34]

The Presbyterian system is fixed in the Westminster Standards,[35] known as the *Constitution*, and

> this is the law of the whole Church, the common rule and guide in theology, duty, worship, and government. The jurisdiction of the *Constitution* extends over all persons and bodies within the Church, whether church members, church officers, or church judicatories. The instant a person becomes a member of the Church or a new judicatory is established, that instant, by virtue of the facts, they come under the jurisdiction of the *Constitution*.[36]

All officers must subscribe to the Standards and at their ordination thereby declare that they are in full agreement with all "essential and necessary articles." A subscription of the *ipsissima verba* is no longer required.[37]

---

[31] Art. XXV, 1—4.

[32] Schaff, *Creeds,* I, 732. See also G. D. Henderson, *Presbyterianism* (Aberdeen: The University Press, 1954).

[33] *The Constitution of the Presbyterian Church in the United States of America* and the *Manual of Presbyterian Law for Church Officers and Members,* revised in 1937 and prepared for publication by L. S. Mudge and W. P. Finney, served as basis for the analysis of American Presbyterianism. — The references to the *Westm. Conf.* are quoted according to the American revised form of the Confession.

[34] *Manual,* 31, 32.

[35] The Presbyterian standards, comprising the *Westminster Confession* and the two *Catechisms;* and the administrative standards, comprising the *Form of Government,* the *Book of Discipline,* and *Directory for Worship.*

[36] *Manual,* p. 27. "Its [Presbyterianism's] first task is the construction of a constitution or fundamental law. For this step it utilized the Old Testament notion of a covenant." (Zenos, p. 14)

[37] Ibid., 29, 30.

WESTMINSTER STANDARDS

The *Manual* presents Presbyterianism under four main topics.

Theology. With all Christians Presbyterians accept the great truths of the three ecumenical creeds; with all Protestants, they accept the supremacy of the Scriptures, the sole lordship of God over consciences, the all-sufficiency of Christ's work, justification by faith alone; and with all Calvinists they maintain the Five Points of Calvinism as "the affirmation of the sovereignty of God in its relation to the salvation of the individual," which excludes any human effort in the individual's redemption, justification, perseverance, and ultimate glorification.[38]

Duty. Under this heading Presbyterians put all those obligations which they find implied in the doctrine of God's sovereignty. According to the *Manual*

Presbyterians believe that because God is sovereign, therefore man's free agency is a foreordained element of his being and involves his responsibility to God; that the moral law as contained in the Ten Commandments and amplified in

the New Testament is always binding upon men; . . . that faith in Christ is obligatory upon all who hear the gospel; . . . that Christians must show forth by godly living the truth of their profession of religion; that good works are the test and evidence of adoption into the household of God, not a ground for salvation; . . . that God's name is ever to be held in supreme reverence.[39]

Form of Government. The Presbyterian view concerning the church may be summarized under three points: the unity of the church as a visible body;[40] the necessity of efficient control over all members;[41] and the delegation of authority to representatives.[42] Presbyterian polity is minutely described in the *Form of Government* (26 chapters) and in the *Book of Discipline* (14 chapters).[43] The government is vested in the teaching elder (pastor) and the ruling elders (laymen); the former is God's representative and the latter the representatives of the people.[44] The heart of Presbyterian polity lies in the authority given to the several judicatories, congregational, presbyterial, synodical, and general. Each judicatory has competence

[38] *Ibid.*, p. 34.

[39] *Ibid.*, p. 35.

[40] *Westm. Conf.*, rev. ed., Art. XXV. Such an identification of the visible church with Christ's kingdom was no doubt partly the reason which prompted Charles Stelzle to "bring the kingdom of God" down into the factories, the community, and to become one of the early advocates of the social gospel. See F. E. Mayer, "The Presbyterian Church," *C. T. M.*, XV (Dec., 1944), 808 ff., and S. Hopkins, *Rise of the Social Gospel*, p. 282.

[41] "Christ has appointed a government in His Church; the right inheres in all members to participate in church affairs; the Church possesses authority to discipline and to administer government." *Manual*, p. 37 f.

[42] Zenos, pp. 26, 27. According to Zenos, the first step in church government is the construction of a constitution based on the concepts of the Old Testament covenant. Christ has given authority to the church, that is, to all those who profess His religion and submission to His laws. Zenos holds that congregationalism breaks the visible church into units; that Presbyterianism maintains the visible unity of the church by its representative government, a type of representative democracy, in which the whole body, though it is divided into sections, is again united by the interrelation of "higher bodies, courts, or judicatories." Pp. 14—18.

[43] See the *Constitution*, pp. 331—382 and 385—436.

[44] This form of polity is said to be derived from 1 Tim. 5:17; 1 Cor. 12:28; and the Old Testament precept.

in its area to require obedience to the laws of the church and to exclude the disobedient. The congregational authority is vested in the session, consisting of the pastor and the ruling elders of the local church. It has the duty and authority to receive, examine, admonish, and suspend members.[45] The presbytery consists of the pastors and one ruling elder from each congregation in a certain district. Its functions are to examine, license, and ordain candidates for the ministry and to supervise the various congregations in its district.[46] The synod comprises all pastors and ruling elders in a larger district, for example, a state. It has no legislative authority and is concerned with the welfare of parishes in each district.[47] The General Assembly is the highest judicatory. It can receive complaints only from the next lowest judicatory. It deals with doctrinal matters and has legislative authority.[48]

Worship. The *Constitution* prescribes in detail both the principle and the manner of divine worship.[49] The *Manual* describes Presbyterianism as follows:

> In its theology it honors the divine sovereignty without denying human freedom; in its views of human duty, while insisting upon obedience to God, it emphasizes human responsibility; in its worship it magnifies God while it brings blessing to man, by maintaining the right of free access on the part of every soul to Him whose grace cannot be fettered in its ministrations by any human

ordinance whatsoever; and in its government it exalts the Headship of Christ, while giving full development to activities of the Christian people. From its beginning to its close the system acknowledges God as Sovereign, and in its every part it is affirmed to be in harmony with the teachings of God's Word. Its twin symbols are "an Open Bible" and "the Burning Bush," burning yet not consumed.[50]

The Presbyterian Bodies

The Presbyterian church constitutes the fourth largest evangelical denomination in America, represented in eleven bodies, of which seven are of English origin and four of Scotch origin. The English groups total about 3,600,000 and the Scotch 380,000 (1956). In Canada a majority of the Presbyterians united with the *United Church of Canada* in 1925; approximately 784 congregations, about one third of the total membership, did not join the United Church of Canada.

THE UNITED PRESBYTERIAN CHURCH IN THE U. S. A.

This body, the largest church in the worldwide Presbyterian family, came into being in 1958 through the merger of the Presbyterian Church in the U. S. A. ("Northern Presbyterians") and the United Presbyterian Church of North America. Letters have since been sent to nine American sister churches in the

---

[45] *Form of Government,* IX.

[46] Ibid., X. The Presbyterians will not tolerate any disregard of the prerogatives of the presbytery. An example: Alexander Campbell entered another presbytery to minister to neglected people and was ousted from the Church. See Disciples.

[47] Ibid., XI.

[48] Ibid., XII. This fourth judicatory was added to the *Form of Government* by American Presbyterians. In continental Europe and in the Reformed churches of America virtually the same system is followed, under a different nomenclature: The session is called the consistory; the presbytery, the classis; the synod, the provincial synod; the assembly, the general synod.

[49] *Manual,* p. 46.

[50] Ibid., p. 47.

Reformed and Presbyterian traditions inviting them to enter into unity discussions with the new body.[51]

Presbyterianism was transplanted to America in the early decades of the 17th century by Puritan ministers of the Established Church of England who held Presbyterian views. The first presbytery, however, was organized at Philadelphia in 1706 by seven ministers representing about ten congregations of various European antecedents, such as British, Scotch, Puritans, and Dutch Reformed. By 1716 the presbytery had increased to such an extent that it was organized as a synod with four presbyteries. In 1729 it formally adopted the Westminster Standards.

The Great Awakening under Jonathan Edwards and George Whitefield (1734) divided the Presbyterians into "New Side" and "Old Side" parties. The former, under the leadership of William Tennent, Sr., and his son Gilbert, endorsed the revivalism of Edwards and maintained that evidence of religious experience was more essential in a candidate for the ministry than a college education. The "New Side" pastors, active especially in the New Brunswick presbytery, advocated in addition a more liberal interpretation of the Westminster Standards.[52] In 1758 the breach between the New and Old Side parties was healed.

The adoption of the Federal Constitution after the Revolutionary War prompted the Presbyterians in 1788 to reorganize the church government in accord with the new American ideals. The most important change was the creation of a new judicatory, the General Assembly. The *Constitution* and the *Form of Government* were revised accordingly. The section in the Second Commandment of the Westminster Confession which charged the state not to tolerate false religions was deleted.[53]

The great revival of the first decades of the 19th century led to the Cumberland secession; and the slavery question, to the separation of the Northern and Southern Presbyterians.

The plan of Union adopted in 1801 by the Presbyterian church and the Association of Congregational Churches provided that Congregational ministers could serve Presbyterian churches and vice versa, and congregations with members in both denominations were granted the right of representation in the general meetings of both bodies. But the plan soon proved disadvantageous to both parties. The Congregationalists lost numerically because of the cohesive organization of the Presbyterian church, and the Presbyterians suffered confessionally because of the doctrinal laxity among Congregational ministers and their patent interest in New England theology.[54]

---

[51] Keith R. Bridston, "Survey of Church Union Negotiations 1957 to 1959," in *Ecumenical Review*, XII (1959/1960), 254—255.

[52] In 1736 William Tennent founded the Log College for the training of pastors according to his ideals. He died in 1746, the year in which a charter was secured for the College of New Jersey, now Princeton University. Witherspoon, who became its president in 1768, was its first professor of divinity and did much for the development of American Presbyterianism. — See Alan Simpson, *Puritanism in Old and New England* (Chicago: University of Chicago Press, 1956).

[53] Zenos, p. 69. Cp. Schaff, *Creeds*, I, 806—9.

[54] The New England theology was advocated primarily by N. W. Taylor, whose so-called "New Haven theology" was branded as Arminian by the strict Presbyterians. Cp. F. H. Foster, *Genetic History of New England Theology* (Chicago, 1907), pp. 430 ff. Albert Barnes, the author of *Barnes' Notes*, was also accused of leaning toward the "new theology."

A large number of Presbyterians with a strong denominational loyalty and doctrinal consciousness, known as the "old school," succeeded at the Assembly in 1837 in abolishing the Plan of Union and to exscind the four synods whose members leaned toward a more liberal interpretation of the Westminster Standards. These synods, known as the "new school," met at Auburn, adopted a defense document, the Auburn Affirmation of 1837,[55] and organized their own General Assembly. In the succeeding decades greater flexibility in the interpretation of the confessional standards gained the ascendancy, and by 1869 the differences between the old and the new school had largely disappeared. The more liberal spirit, however, did not immediately gain the upper hand, because Presbyterians have always insisted on thorough indoctrination in the confessions, and doctrinal innovations do not easily take root.[56] Nevertheless, the church finally yielded to the pressure to revise the confessions in the interest of bringing the doctrine of God's decree into harmony with God's universal grace. In 1903 the general assembly adopted the Declaratory Statement.[57] This marked a new attitude toward the historic confessional standards. Almost simultaneously came the movement to apply the principles of higher criticism to the Old and New Testaments, spearheaded by Professors Charles Briggs, Arthur Cushman McGiffert of Union Seminary, and H. Preserved Smith of Lane University.[58] The outcome of the debate revolving about this issue may be summarized as follows:

> The Church does not undertake to pronounce judgment on any scientific, literary, or historical problem [in the Bible]. The Church's verdicts are limited at the most to the doctrinal implications of literary or historical or scientific views. . . . In doing this [judging the unsoundness of the im-

---

[55] Reprinted in Thompson, pp. 357—62. See also Elwyn A. Smith, "The Role of the South in the Presbyterian Schism of 1837—1938," *Church History*, XXIX (1960), 44—63.

[56] Heresy trials have been relatively frequent among Presbyterians during the last century. A notable case was that of Dr. Swing, who was brought to trial in Chicago in 1878 because he deviated from the current interpretation of the confessional standards.

[57] "First, with reference to chap. III, Sec. i and vii of the Confession of Faith: that concerning those who are saved in Christ the doctrine of God's eternal decree is held in harmony with the doctrine of His love to all mankind, His gift of His Son to be the propitiation for the sins of the whole world, and His readiness to bestow His saving grace on all who seek it; and concerning those who perish the doctrine of God's eternal decree is held in harmony with the doctrine that God desires not the death of any sinner, but has provided in Christ a salvation sufficient for all, adapted to all, and freely offered in the Gospel to all; that men are fully responsible for their treatment of God's gracious offer; that His decree hinders no man from accepting that offer; and that no man is condemned except on the ground of his sin. Second, with reference to Chap. X, Sec. 3, of the Confession of Faith, that it is not to be regarded as teaching that any who die in infancy are lost. We believe that all dying in infancy are included in the election of grace and are regenerated and saved by Christ through the Spirit, who works when and where and how He pleases." (*Pop. Symb.*, p. 245, footnote.)

[58] Briggs was suspended from the ministry in 1893. But Union Theological Seminary, no longer under Presbyterian control, did not remove him from office.

plications] the Church is not condemning the historical or scientific theories themselves, but only the implications.[59]

The inroads of liberal theology, especially among the younger clergy, prompted the Assembly of 1910 to decide that candidates for the ministry were to be examined on the "five essential doctrines of the Word of God and our Standards." These "five essentials" are:

1) that the Holy Spirit did so inspire, guide, and move the writers of Holy Scripture as to keep them from error;

2) that our Lord Jesus Christ was born of the Virgin Mary;

3) that Christ offered up Himself a sacrifice to satisfy Divine justice and to reconcile us to God;

4) that our Lord Jesus Christ on the third day rose again from the dead with the same body with which He suffered, with which also He ascended into heaven, and there sitteth at the right hand of His Father, making intercession;

5) that our Lord Jesus showed His power and love, working mighty miracles. This work was not contrary to nature, but superior to it.[60]

These five fundamentals were reaffirmed by the assemblies of 1911, 1916, and 1923. One party took the position that the assemblies' declarations on these Five Points were binding on all ministers; the other party said that they were only an opinion which, while valuable, had no binding force, because the *Constitution* made no provision that the ordained was to be examined according to this procedure. The controversy came to a head when the Philadelphia Presbytery protested against Harry Emerson Fosdick's ministry in the First Presbyterian Church of New York.[61] The 1923 Assembly condemned modernism and reaffirmed the Five Points. Thereupon the modernistic party drafted the Auburn Affirmation, asserting (1) that the General Assembly lacked constitutional authority to bind a presbytery to any "essential" doctrine, and (2) that the Five Points are not essential to the Scriptural and Westminster system of doctrine.[62] Gradually modernism gained

---

[59] Zenos, p. 97.

[60] Reprinted in H. M. Griffiths, *The Case for Compromise*, n. d., p. 16.

[61] See Harry Emerson Fosdick, *The Living of These Days: An Autobiography* (New York: Harper and Brothers, 1956).

[62] Cp. ibid. "This opinion of the General Assembly attempts to commit our Church to certain theories concerning the inspiration of the Bible, and the Incarnation, the Atonement, the Resurrection, and the Continuing Life and Supernatural Power of our Lord Jesus Christ. We all hold most earnestly to these great facts and doctrines; we all believe from our hearts that the writers of the Bible were inspired of God; that Jesus Christ was God manifest in the flesh; that God was in Christ, reconciling the world unto Himself, and through Him we have redemption; that having died for our sins He rose from the dead and is our ever-living Savior; that in His earthly ministry He wrought many mighty works, and by His vicarious death and unfailing presence He is able to save to the uttermost. Some of us regard the particular theories contained in the deliverance of the General Assembly of 1923 as satisfactory explanations of these facts and doctrines. But we are united in believing that these are not the only theories allowed by the Scriptures and our standards as explanations of these facts and doctrines of our religion and that all who hold to these facts and doctrines, whatever theories they may employ to explain them, are worthy of all confidence and fellowship." (Reprinted from "That Famous Auburn Affirmation," *Christian Faith and Life*, Vol. 41, No. 4.) *Christianity Today*, Fall, 1939; *Presbyterian Guardian*, 1941, Nov. 10th and following issues.

control of the church administration, and such liberal theologians as George A. Buttrick and Henry Sloane Coffin became the administrative and theological leaders of the Presbyterian church.[63]

A merger between the Northern Presbyterians and the Protestant Episcopal Church, often proposed during the '30s and '40s, foundered chiefly because the compromise on ordination satisfied neither the Episcopalians, who ordain in the "apostolic succession," nor the Presbyterians, for whom the validity of the ministry rests upon Presbyterian ordination.

In 1920 the *Welsh Presbyterian Church* united with the Presbyterian Church in the U. S. A.

While the Presbyterian Church in the U. S. A. was strongly English in its origins, the other party to the 1958 merger, the United Presbyterian Church of North America, traces its history back to the Covenanter and Secession movements in Scotland during the 18th century. Scottish Covenanters entered into an agreement among themselves to oppose every attempt on the part of secular and ecclesiastical rulers to foist Roman Catholic doctrine and practice upon their church. The first secession was occasioned by the Law of Patronage, which deprived the people of any voice in the choice of a pastor and led to the organization of the Associate Synod of Scotland. The second secession was occasioned by the question whether a seceder could honestly take the burgess' (Burghers') oath. According to ancient custom, a citizen at his reception into the corporate community took an oath of allegiance to the religion of the country and to the crown and the magistracy.

The Burghers said that a seceder could take such an oath. The Antiburghers held the opposite view and formed separate congregations independent of the church of Scotland. These divisions were transferred to this country, and similar questions have been the occasion of much internal strife. In the course of time there were various realignments, and some groups have disappeared completely by mergers.[64]

The United Presbyterian Church of North America was a relatively successful attempt to merge the various groups of Covenanters and Seceders in 1858 when the greater part of the Associate Synod and the Associate Reformed Synod united. The merged body was very conservative theologically. However, the Scottish influence was evident in so far as this body, in distinction from British Presbyterians, held that the free offer of salvation is for all and went so far as to teach the unequivocal universal salvation of infants. In its Confessional Statement of 1929 it changed its stand on "close Communion," lodge membership, and exclusive use of Psalms.

THE PRESBYTERIAN CHURCH IN THE U. S. *(Southern Presbyterians)*

The separation of the Southern from the Northern Presbyterians is usually attributed to a division of views on the question of slaveholding. The issue, however, was deeper and involved questions of theology, ethics, and ecclesiastical procedure. A large number of Northern churches were adherents of the "New School" theology with its "more progressive" social orientation. In this spirit the Northern presbyteries

---

[63] Coffin presents his attitude toward the Bible in David Roberts and Henry Van Dusen, *Liberal Theology*, in Ch. xiv, "The Scriptures." On Buttrick see G. R. Post, *Is Our Faith a Grand Perhaps?* a tract quoting from Buttrick, *The Christian Fact and Modern Doubt*.

[64] See *Encycl. Brit.*, s. v. "United Presbyterian Church." *The Reformed Principles Exhibited by the Reformed Presbyterian Church* (Phila., 1875), pp. 65—146.

asked the Southern presbyteries as early as 1853 to state their views on the slavery question, whereupon a number of presbyteries in the South withdrew and organized a separate synod. At the outbreak of the Civil War the Geneva Assembly pledged its wholehearted support to the Federal Government in its fight for the abolition of slavery. The Southern presbyteries protested on the basis that according to Presbyterian church law the Assembly had no right to introduce and to decide a political question, still less to make its decision in this question a condition of membership, since slaveholding was not viewed by them as a sin. The Southern presbyteries withdrew and organized The Presbyterian Church in the United States. Several unsuccessful attempts at reunion of the Northern and Southern Presbyterians were undertaken. The failure of these efforts at reunion is due in part to the difference in treating the Negro members, the Southern Presbyterians in distinction from the Northern church having organized the Negro members in separate congregations and presbyteries. Another prominent reason is the greater theological conservatism of the Southern Presbyterians, manifest in their strict adherence to the spirit and letter of their creeds.[65]

OTHER PRESBYTERIAN BODIES

The Cumberland Presbyterian Church. During the great revival in Kentucky, at the beginning of the 19th century, the Cumberland presbytery approved of the excessive practices so prominent in this revival and ordained men to the ministry who in the opinion of the Synod of Kentucky were not qualified by learning or sound doctrine.[66] The Synod of Kentucky dissolved the Cumberland presbytery, and in 1809 the General Assembly confirmed this action, whereupon a number of ministers in the Cumberland presbytery organized an independent presbytery, which ultimately developed into the Cumberland Presbyterian Church as a separate denomination. This body has retained the Presbyterian polity. In theology it has adopted a moderate Calvinism, rejecting the decree of reprobation and stressing human responsibility. In fact, it may be called a sort of *via media* between Calvinism and Arminianism. The hope that the 1903 revision of the Westminster Confession would lead to a union with the Northern Presbyterians was not wholly realized, for while a large section of the Cumberland Presbyterians united with the Northern Presbyterians, a dissident majority has continued the Cumberland tradition.

The Cumberland Presbyterian Church in the United States and Africa was organized after the Civil War, in 1869, to give the Negro members of the Cumberland Presbyterian Church an opportunity to establish their own separate congregations and ecclesiastical organizations. In doctrine and polity they are in full accord with the parent organization. A presbytery in Liberia merged with it in 1940.

The Orthodox Presbyterian Church. This body was organized in 1936 as a result of the bitter contentions between those who affirmed and those who in the Auburn Affirmation denied that strict adherence to the "Five Fundamentals"

---

[65] However, in 1939 the General Assembly deleted from the *Westm. Conf.* the paragraph on the decree of election as well as the paragraph in which the pope is expressly called the Antichrist.

[66] Doctrinal indifference, a usual concomitant of revivalism, was particularly evident in the Kentucky revival, where this indifference led to the organization of a number of anticreedal and antidenominational bodies, the so-called "Christians." See, below, "Christian Church."

was a necessary requisite for the examination and ordination of ministers for the Presbyterian church. J. Gresham Machen of Princeton Seminary, an outspoken leader of the antimodernistic school,[67] charged that the Auburn Affirmation theology had gained control of the church, its seminaries, and especially its Board for Foreign Missions.[68] Machen and the so-called "orthodox group" urged the laity to withhold funds from this board and to support the newly organized Independent Board. When this group refused to dissolve the Independent Board, they were charged with insubordination and in 1936 suspended from the ministry. Thereupon they formed the Presbyterian Church of America. Since this name was very similar to the name of the parent organization, the latter secured a court injunction against its use.[69] The name Orthodox Presbyterian Church was adopted to indicate that the Machen followers were "in the true succession of the Presbyterian church," which had been abandoned, so they felt, by the parent Presbyterian church.

The Bible Presbyterian Church. This church was organized by a group of men who with Machen were suspended from the ministry, but who took a more rigid position than the leadership of the Orthodox Presbyterian Church in favor of total abstinence and premillennialism. The first synod of the Bible Presbyterian Church was held in 1938; subsequently the antitheses referred to have been moderated to some extent. Currently conversations are being held looking toward organic union with the Reformed Presbyterian Church in America, General Synod.

The Collingswood Synod of the Bible Presbyterian Church was organized in 1956 by a group representing approximately one fifth of the membership of the Bible Presbyterian Church. A major issue between the two groups revolved about the methods to be used in opposing ecumenical associations like the National Council of Churches and the World Council of Churches. The leadership of the Collingswood Synod has been largely instrumental in organizing the minuscule "American Council of Churches" and "International Council of Churches" (q. v.).

The Synod of the Associate Presbyterian Church of North America, a very small group, is a direct descendant of the first seceder movement in Scotland. It encourages public covenanting, opposes secret societies, prescribes the exclusive use of Psalms in the public worship.

The General Synod of the Associate Reformed Presbyterian Church, formerly the Associate Reformed Presbyterian Church, is the result of a number of re-alignments among the Presbyterian Covenanters.

The Synod of the Reformed Presbyterian Church of North America (Old School), sometimes known as Covenanters, maintains the obligation of covenanting for the purpose of reforming the United States by "a constitutional recognition of God as the source of all power, of Jesus Christ as the Ruler of Nations, of the Holy Scriptures as the

---

[67] Machen is the author of such fundamental theological works as *The Virgin Birth* and *Christianity and Liberalism.*

[68] The Presbyterians were represented on the commission which conducted the "Laymen's Foreign Missions Inquiry" and ultimately published *Rethinking Missions* (New York: Harper & Brothers, 1932). This report reflects liberal theology.

[69] Frank S. Mead, *Handbook of Denominations in the U. S.,* rev. ed. (New York: Abingdon Press, 1955), p. 177.

supreme rule, and of the true Christian religion." [70] Until the Federal Constitution is revised according to these principles, the members of this body are not permitted to cast their ballots or to hold public office.

The Reformed Presbyterian Church in North America, General Synod, was established in 1833 through a separation from the foregoing body on the question of a member's relation toward the United States Government. This body leaves it to the individual whether or not he wishes to vote and to hold office.

The Presbyterian Church of Canada comprises those Presbyterian churches which did not enter the United Church of Canada when that body was formed.[71]

BIBLIOGRAPHY

PART IV   SECTION V

Armstrong, Maurice W., Lefferts A. Loetscher, and Charles A. Anderson, ed. *The Presbyterian Enterprise: Sources of American Presbyterian History.* Phila.: Westminster Press, 1956.

Clark, Gordon H. *What Presbyterians Believe.* Phila.: Presbyterian and Reformed Publishing Co., 1956.

Drury, Clifford Merrill. "The Presbyterian Church in America," in Vergilius Ferm, ed., *The American Church of the Protestant Heritage.* New York: Philosophical Library, 1953, pp. 69—89.

Hodge, Charles. *Systematic Theology.* 3 vols. New York, 1873.

Klett, Guy Soulliard. *Presbyterians in Colonial Pennsylvania.* Phila.: University of Pennsylvania Press, 1937.

Loetscher, Lefferts A. *The Broadening Church: A Study of Theological Issues in the Presbyterian Church since 1869.* Phila.: University of Pennsylvania Press, 1954.

McCulloch, W. E. "The United Presbyterian Church in America," in Vergilius Ferm, ed., op. cit., pp. 209—22.

McDonald, B. W., *History of the Cumberland Presbyterian Church.* Nashville, 1888.

McKinney, William Wilson, ed. *The Presbyterian Valley.* Pittsburgh: Davis and Warde, 1958. (Essays on the history of Presbyterianism in the Upper Ohio River Valley from colonial times to 1870.)

Reed, R. C. *History of the Presbyterian Churches of the World.* Phila., 1905.

Rian, Edward H. *The Presbyterian Conflict.* Grand Rapids: Wm. B. Eerdmans Publishing Co., 1940.

Roberts, W. H. A. *A Concise History of the Presbyterian Church in the United States of America.* Phila., 1920.

Slosser, Gaius J. *They Seek a Country: The American Presbyterians, Some Aspects.* New York: The Macmillan Co., 1955.

Stephens, J. Vant. *The Presbyterian Churches, Divisions and Unions in Scotland, Ireland, Canada and America.* 1910.

Sweet, William. *Religion on the American Frontier.* Chicago: University of Chicago Press, 1931—46. 4 vols.

Thompson, R. E. *A History of the Presbyterian Churches in the United States* ("American Church History Series," Vol. VI). New York: Christian Literature Co., 1895.

Warfield, Benjamin B. *Revelation and Inspiration.* New York: Oxford University Press, 1927.

——. *Studies in Theology.* New York: Oxford University Press, 1932.

——. *The Westminster Assembly and Its Work.* New York: Oxford University Press, 1931.

Zenos, Andrew C. *Presbyterianism in America.* New York: Thomas Nelson and Sons, 1937.

[70] *Census,* II, 1463.
[71] See below, Part Six, Section III.

SECTION VI

The Baptists

The 23,000,000 (1960) Baptists of the world, united in the Baptist World Alliance,[1] represent a variety of divergent theological views. At first glance there seems to be no unifying factor to serve as a common bond for the various groups of Baptists. It is sometimes assumed that the basic principle which unites all Baptists is their distinctive doctrine of "believers'" or "adult" baptism performed by immersion. This, however, is not the case, for adult baptism and immersion are observed also by other groups. Nor do all Baptists insist on immersion as the only form of baptism.[2] Strictly speaking, the name "Baptist" is misleading. The competency of the soul of man in matters religious is the basic principle on which all Baptists are united and out of which all Baptist beliefs grow.[3] For want of a better term this principle can best be defined as "theological individualism." For this reason Baptists acknowledge no human founder, recognize no human authority, and subscribe to no human creed.[4] Baptists have always maintained that every believer has "absolute liberty under Christ," for as a member of Christ he has the right to interpret Christ's will for himself.[5]

It is therefore not surprising that widely divergent theological views are current among the various Baptist groups, among the individual local churches, and logically also among the members of the local church. Calvinism and Arminianism, fundamentalism and liberalism, separatism and unionism, flourish side by side. No other religious body seems to be so hopelessly divided into parties and schisms as the Baptists. And yet few religious bodies have so tenaciously, consistently, and loyally held to their basic principle as the Baptists. The Baptist emphasis on the sovereignty of the individual has made a strong appeal to the "common man," to the socially and economically "disinherited," and has been an important factor in making the Baptists, originally a despised sect, one of the largest religious bodies in America.

The English Baptists

Three theories are advanced concerning the historic origin of Baptist bodies. The first, not generally held, is that the Baptist principles had their beginning in the work of John the Baptist, Christ's

---

[1] *1961 Britannica Book of the Year* (Chicago: Encyclopaedia Britannica, c. 1961), p. 96. The alliance was organized in 1905 in London to unite all Baptists throughout the world and to create and express Baptist world consciousness. The Russian Baptists, estimated to have numbered between two and four million before the Bolshevist Revolution, are not included in the total. Torbet, p. 501 ff.

[2] The name "Baptist," *Täufer, Dunker,* dates from the Reformation and is of Anabaptist origin.

[3] E. Y. Mullins, quoted by A. C. Archibald, "When Is a Baptist a Baptist?" *Watchman-Examiner,* March 1, 1945, p. 205.

[4] *Census,* II, 83.

[5] A. H. Strong, *Christ in Creation and Ethical Nomism* (Phila., c. 1899), pp. 252, 257. Cp. Schaff, *Creeds,* I, 853.

public ministry, and the outpouring of the Holy Spirit on Pentecost. The second theory is that modern Baptists owe their origin to the Swiss and German Anabaptist movement, which, in turn, is said to be the continuation of the principles enunciated by the Donatists, the Novatians, the Lollards, the Cathari, and the Waldensians.[6] The Baptist historian A. H. Newman believes that the early English Baptists were directly influenced by the Mennonites, especially during the time of their exile in the Netherlands.[7] These early English Baptists were Free-Will Baptists, shared some of the views of the Anabaptists, and, like the Mennonites, were bitterly persecuted. The majority of Baptist historians advocate a third theory, namely, that the origin of the Baptists, particularly the Calvinistic Baptists, has no connection with the Mennonites, but is intimately associated with the Separatist movement in England during the closing decades of the sixteenth century. This view seems to be historically correct. On the one hand, the majority of the English Baptists repudiated such Mennonite errors as soul sleep, "inner light," extreme pacifism, refusal to hold public office, and, on the other, shared with the Separatists, or the Congregationalists,

a common theology and essentially the same polity.[8] Robert Browne, often spoken of as the founder of English Particular Baptists, and John Smyth, one of the early rebaptizers, strongly influenced John Robinson, the spiritual father of American Congregationalism. As early as 1609 John Smyth drafted a statement of his beliefs, but it was not until 1644 that the seven London Particular Baptist churches drew up the London Confession, in which they set forth their antithesis to what they considered the erroneous doctrine of the Anabaptists and the General Baptists.[9] 1644 is therefore frequently given as the year of the origin of the Baptist churches.

It must be kept in mind that since the sixteenth century there always have been two groups of Baptists, the General (Arminian) Baptists, who believe in universal atonement and salvation and in the freedom of human will. This branch of Baptists is related to the Anabaptists. The Particular Baptists have always favored Calvin's theology of a limited, or particular, atonement. The Particular Baptists by far outnumber the Free Will, or General, Baptists. John Bunyan is probably the best representative of the General Baptists, while Andrew Fuller

[6] Torbet, p. 60.

[7] He states: "The historical relations of modern Baptists to the Anabaptists of the sixteenth century are close and direct. . . . A still more direct influence was exerted by the Mennonites of the Netherlands upon the English refugees so that these became antipedobaptist (from 1609 onward)." *Schaff-Herzog Encyc.*, I, 457.

[8] Torbet, p. 61 f. See "Presbyterianism" and "Congregationalism," Secs. V, VI. No doubt some of the confusion about early Baptist history arises from the fact that the distinction between General, or Arminian, and Particular, or Calvinistic, Baptists is not always observed. Newman lists the similarities and differences between the Baptists and Mennonites and demonstrates the unwillingness of the latter to enter into a union with the former. Schaff-Herzog, s. v. "Baptists." He finds the differences in such matters as oaths, magistracy, warfare, and the weekly celebration of the Lord's Supper. However, he does not mention other doctrinal differences between the two groups. *A History*, p. 46 f. In the fundamental principle of the responsibility of the individual conscience the Mennonites and the Baptists are agreed. Stokes, I, 112 f.

[9] Torbet, p. 74.

and Charles Haddon Spurgeon are among the outstanding Calvinist or Particular Baptists. To present a solid front against the Anglican state church and to maintain their principal convictions, the General and the Particular Baptists of England united in 1891.

The American Baptists

HISTORICAL BACKGROUND

Some Baptist historians believe that the first Baptist church on the American continent was established by Roger Williams, at Providence, R. I., in 1639; others, that John Clarke planted the first Baptist congregation in American soil at Newport, R. I., in 1638. Roger Williams, originally a clergyman in the Anglican church, was a typical Separatist, a rugged individualist, and an ardent advocate of the principle of "soul liberty." His political philosophy dealt the doctrine of the divine right of the English kings and their bishops a really telling blow.[10] Because of his opposition to Bishop Laud, Williams was compelled to migrate to America in 1631, where he became assistant pastor at Plymouth

and two years later pastor at Salem. But his advocacy of the right of the individual, especially of complete religious toleration and liberty, brought him into conflict with the New England ecclesiastical and civil authorities.[11] He denied that a civil court had any jurisdiction to legislate in matters of conscience as to punish sins against the First Table, e. g., nonconformity in religion. He advocated complete "soul liberty" and full religious freedom.[12] In 1635 Williams was expelled from the Salem colony and with five families founded Providence, R. I., whose charter guaranteed complete liberty of conscience. Rebaptism was not introduced until 1638 or 1639, when a church of rebaptized members was established.[13] Modern Baptists are divided as to Williams' place in Baptist history. The fact is that he considered "believers' Baptism" and immersion minor matters, and for that reason he does not rate high in some Baptist quarters. But as an ardent advocate of soul liberty he exerted a deep influence on the development of Baptist political philosophy.

Most of the early colonial Baptist

[10] James Ernst, op. cit. Cotton Mather compared Williams to a windmill which, driven by a violent storm, whirled the millstone with such speed that it became ignited, and set the mill and ultimately the whole town on fire. See also Perry Miller, *Roger Williams: His Contribution to the American Tradition* (Indianapolis: Bobbs-Merrill, 1953).

[11] Cp. Stokes, I, 194 ff.

[12] His principles are laid down in *The Bloudy Tenent of Persecution:* (1) God requireth not an *uniformity of Religion* to be *inacted in any civill state;* which inforced *uniformity* (sooner or later) is the greatest occasion of *civill Warre, ravishing of conscience, persecution of Jesus Christ* in His servants, and of the *hypocrisie* and destruction of millions of souls. (2) It is the will and command of God, that . . . a *permission of the most Paganish, Jewish, Turkish, or Antichristian consciences and Worships,* bee granted to *all* men in all *Nations* and *Countries;* and they are only to be fought against with the *Sword* which is onely (in Soule *matters*) *able to conquer,* to wit, the *Sword* of *God's Spirit, the Word of God.* (3) True *civility* and *Christianity* may both flourish in a *State* or *Kingdome,* notwithstanding the *permission of divers* and contrary consciences, either of Jew or *Gentile.* Sweet, *Story of Rel. in Am.,* p. 103. (Sec. VI, fn. 13.)

[13] See R. E. Harkness, "Principles of the Early Baptists of England and America," *Crozer Quarterly,* V (1928), 440—60, quoted in Sweet, *Story of Rel. in Am.,* p. 102.

churches were small groups of English Baptists. Though their views infiltrated a few New England Puritan and Congregational colonies, these groups met with such strong opposition that their growth was extremely slow. After a century had elapsed, there were only eleven Baptist churches in Connecticut, eight in Massachusetts, and four in Rhode Island. The Baptists fared better in the Central colonies, especially in Pennsylvania. In 1762 the Philadelphia Association numbered twenty-nine churches. The Baptists experienced their greatest expansion in the Southern colonies during the last third of the 18th century.

The majority of the early Baptists were Particular or Calvinistic Baptists. For a time, however, Arminianism and Unitarianism threatened to make strong inroads. Therefore in 1742 the Baptist Association adopted a strong Calvinistic confession.[14] The Arminian, or Free Will, Baptists gained a foothold in Carolina and throughout the South, but they have always remained a relatively small group.[15]

BASIC THEOLOGICAL TENETS

Baptists have consistently maintained that it is anti-Biblical to establish doctrinal unity by means of "man-made" creeds and doctrinal formulations. This assertion does not mean that Baptists do not have a unifying, basic theological emphasis, a so-called theological material principle. On the contrary, diverse as the Baptist churches are, they nevertheless have a fixed theological principle that determines the doctrines and practices of all of them. This basic principle is like a gem with two facets.

The first facet is the doctrine of the absolute lordship of Jesus Christ, who has revealed His will in the Bible. Baptists consider the Bible "as the supreme standard by which all human conduct, creeds, and opinions must be tried." Baptists always have been, and most of them still remain, strong advocates of "verbal inspiration," and the complete inerrancy of the Bible, and therefore also of the absolute authority of all its injunctions.[16]

The second facet of their basic belief is the complete sovereignty and the full competency of the soul under God in all religious matters. For Baptists "the crown jewel of humanity is the right of private judgment." [17] In their antithesis to every form of ecclesiastical authority they maintain that the New Testament

---

[14] During the early decades of the 18th century Arminian influence was rather strong in the New England colonies, but it was firmly opposed by Welsh Baptists with a Calvinistic background, who assumed a dominant position in the Philadelphia Association. This association in 1742 adopted the Philadelphia Confession, essentially the same as the one set forth by the English Baptists in 1677, 1688, and 1689, which in turn is virtually identical with the Westm. Conf. Henry C. Vedder, *A History of the Baptists in the Middle States* (Phila.: Am. Bapt. Publ. Co., 1898), p. 91 f.; cp. Newman, p. 239.

[15] Free Will Baptists total approximately 200,000 (1960).

[16] Torbet, p. 476. Art. I of the N. H. Conf. reads: "We believe that the Holy Bible was written by men divinely inspired, and is a perfect treasure of heavenly instruction; that it has God for its Author, salvation for its end, and truth without any mixture of error for its matter; and therefore is, and shall remain to the end of the world, the true center of Christian union, and the supreme standard by which all human conduct, creeds, and opinions should be tried."

[17] Georg W. Truett, *Baptists and Religious Liberty*, a tract published by the First Baptist Church, Dallas, Tex., pp. 9—15. See also "Dr. Truett's Great Presidential Address," *Watchman-Examiner*, August 10, 1939, p. 900.

everywhere places the emphasis on the individual as a sovereign and free person; that Christ requires the individual to detach himself in all religious matters from the family, the church, the state, from society, his dearest friends, and all institutions, and to enter into a direct and personal relationship with God; that it is every Christian's privilege and duty to determine what is right or wrong for and by himself from the Bible alone, without benefit of sacraments, clergy, creeds, and the like.[18] Baptists maintain furthermore that every regenerate soul is fully competent to know the will of God and therefore requires no mediation whatsoever in establishing or maintaining the right relations with God. Such competency is said to be derived from the indwelling Christ and is said to be directly implied in the doctrine of the priesthood of believers.[19] The two basic theological tenets have been summarized as follows:

The Word of God as the sole standard of faith and conduct; the immediacy of the soul's approach to God without the aid of any intermediary; baptism by immersion of the believer upon a pro-

fession of his faith; repudiation of baptismal regeneration; a regenerated church membership; the church a spiritual democracy; the liberty of the soul to worship God according to the dictates of its own conscience without any interference from church or state; and the separation of church and state in all matters of religion and church work.[20]

This basic theological position has had several very significant implications for Baptist theology and church polity.

Anticreedalism. Baptists have consistently refused to be bound by any man-made creeds. They have, of course, from time to time formulated standards or confessions to indicate the general principles underlying their theology.[21] But they consider it contrary to their basic tenet of Christ's sovereign lordship to demand subscription to any man-made creed. Any pressure to accept another man's formulation of Christian doctrine they hold to be an infringement on the individual's right and competence. To them it is of the essence of Christianity to believe that spiritual truth is addressed immediately to the individual soul and demonstrated to it directly by

---

[18] Torbet, p. 16. Truett, p. 13.

[19] E. Y. Mullins, W. H. Tribble, *The Baptist Faith* (Nashville: The S. S. Bd. of So. Bapt. Conv., 1935), pp. 22—26. The same authors maintain that in the Baptist principle of the sovereignty and competence of the individual there is a happy combination of the Renaissance principle of intellectual freedom, the Anglo-Saxon ideal of personal and political liberty, and the Reformation doctrine of justification by faith.

[20] C. A. Hagstrom, "What About the Baptist Distinctive?" *Watchman-Examiner*, April 4, 1940, p. 354. Another Baptist writer summarizes the basic propositions under six axioms: "(1) The theological axiom: The holy and loving God has a right to be Sovereign. (2) The religious axiom: All souls have an equal right to direct access to God. (3) The ecclesiastical axiom: All believers have a right to equal privileges in the church. (4) The moral axiom: To be responsible, man must be free. (5) The religio-civic axiom: A free church in a free state. (6) The social axiom: Love your neighbor as yourself." Mullins, p. 31.

[21] The following creeds are held in high esteem: (1) The Confession of the Seven Churches in London, 1644; (2) The Baptist Confession of 1688, known in America as the Philadelphia Confession. This is identical with the *Westm. Conf.* except for the articles dealing with church polity and Baptism. It is reprinted in Schaff, III, 738—41. (3) The New Hampshire Baptist Confession of 1833. In 18 short articles this confession presents a moderate Calvinistic theology. It is reprinted ibid., 742—48.

the Spirit. They cite Heb. 8:10 to prove that God directly writes His laws into the believer's heart and that all spiritual enlightenment comes immediately from God and therefore not from men, not from a priest, not from an ecclesiastical organization, not even from the brethren, let alone man-made creeds.[22] In their one-sided emphasis on the believer's spiritual freedom Baptists have ignored three facts. (1) Baptists after all do have a creed. The basic theological axioms and the implications derived from them are essentially a creed. In reality their protestation that they refuse to be bound by creeds is itself a binding creed. (2) The comforting reality of the historical continuity of the Christian church is not maintained — as Baptists sometimes argue — by such negatives as anticreedalism, antipedobaptism, but by loyal adherence to those sacred Scripture truths which have been believed "always, everywhere, and by all." (3) There is a real necessity for creeds. The history of Christian doctrine gives ample evidence that there is in man an inherent tendency to mistake "his own preconceived notions for the voice of God." Among many of the Baptist churches, for instance, a false emotionalism and "enthusiasm" similar to that found among the Mennonites and the Quakers is rampant. The majority of the Baptists believe in the immediacy

of the Spirit's operation, and some come close to the theory of the "inner light." [23]

Anticreedalism has taken a heavy toll among the Baptists, not statistically but theologically. The conservative Baptists are in danger of falling victims to ecclesiastical atomism and a puerile dogmatism because of a false loyalty to the Scriptures. The liberal Baptists are completely indifferent to doctrine and view the Scriptures merely as a record of outstanding and unique religious experiences. And yet, in spite of the seemingly insurmountable barrier between the liberal and the fundamental Baptist, the two are essentially united in the espousal of the same basic Baptist principle, viz., the sovereignty of Christ and the spiritual competence of the individual. Both regard doctrinal disunity as less undesirable than the ecclesiastical adoption and domination of a creed. G. B. Foster, one of the most liberal among the Baptist liberals, describes the Baptist principles as follows:

> Strictly speaking, there can be no heresy, technically so called, in the Baptist denomination, for the reason that there is no creed subscription; no creed subscription, for the reason that there is no formal creed; no formal creed, for the reason that Baptist churches, unlike the hybrid of ecclesiastical Protestantism, hold to the right of private judgment, of freedom of conscience, and of freedom of thought and

---

[22] Mullins, p. 46.

[23] This "enthusiasm" has become evident particularly in the Pentecostal movement. While the emphasis on perfectionism is attributable to Methodist influence, the high emotional type of religion in the Pentecostal groups stems from Baptist elements. But also among the various Baptist churches emotionalism is rather prevalent and manifests itself in opposing any form of ritualism. "When a Baptist church exchanges its flaming prophet and evangelist for a polished performer [question of pulpit-centered vs. chancel-centered churches], the days of decay and decline are at hand. An American will freeze to death more quickly in the Arctic circle than an Eskimo. Baptists will not survive long in the Arctic winters of ritualism, sacramentalism, and sacerdotalism. The chancel type of church has developed in this spiritual atmosphere and is an architectural expression of it. Baptists may find that it is a 'spiritual igloo.'" The *Watchman-Examiner*, Sept. 5, 1940, p. 956.

speech. It is not that creed is a matter of indifference to religion from the Baptist point of view; it is that the right of the individual to form his own creed is inalienable, and that this right which was exercised by Baptists in the past, resulting in a certain set of beliefs, carries therewith the right today of either accepting or modifying, or replacing those past beliefs.[24]

And George W. Truett, a conservative among the conservative Baptists, could declare in his presidential address to the Sixth Congress of the Baptist World Alliance:

> The competency of the individual, under God, "is the keystone truth of Baptists. . . . Religion is a matter of personal relationships between the soul and God, and nothing extraneous may properly intrude here — no ecclesiastical or civil order, no church, no ordinance, nor sacrament, nor preacher, nor priest may dare to stand between the individual soul and Christ." [25]

Literalism and Legalism. The Particular Baptists lay great emphasis on the sovereignty of Christ and on the New Testament as the complete and perpetual law of Christ's kingdom. In their approach to the Bible, particularly to the New Testament, the Particular Baptists follow Calvin and more specifically the Westminster divines.[26] A literalistic and legalistic overtone manifests itself more or less explicitly throughout Baptist theology. Some sections of the Baptist churches are extremely literalistic in their interpretation of the New Testament. They follow the principle that whatsoever is not specifically commanded in the New Testament is sinful. They condemn every form of ecclesiastical organization because they can find no command for it. Since the apostles

did not establish mission societies to solicit and collect funds, the "antimission" Baptists separated from their brethren who had organized mission societies; some forbid the payment of salaries to missionaries; others the opening of Sunday schools; another group insists on Sabbatarianism, others on the rite of foot washing, and some on trine immersion.

So far as Calvinism is legalistic, the Particular Baptists view the Christian life as a "life of law." One leading Baptist summarizes these "laws of the Kingdom" in the following seven statements:

> 1. The law of salvation, that is, salvation is by personal faith in Christ without works, without the acceptance of formal creeds, without membership in a church organization or use of humanly administered sacraments. 2. The law of worship, that is, there must be a free and direct intercourse between the Father and the believer. 3. The law of filial society, that is, every child of God has a place in the service of God with all other believers. 4. The law of liberty, that is, every regenerate person has liberty and autonomy under God and is free to worship and to serve God. 5. The law of brotherhood, that is, the free soul is in fellowship with all other free souls. 6. The law of edification, that is, Christian growth must be in conformity with the essential principles of the laws of the Kingdom. 7. The law of holiness, that is, everything in the church must serve personal and social righteousness.[27]

"No Sponsorial Religion." In using this slogan the Baptists do not mean to imply that some teach the possibility of salvation by proxy, but to undergird their basic doctrine that every individual soul is sovereign and that no ecclesiastical or civil order, no church organiza-

---

[24] Foster, p. xviii (Pref. to 2d ed.).

[25] *Watchman-Examiner*, Aug. 10, 1939, p. 900.

[26] The Bapt. Conf. of 1688 follows the *Westm. Conf.* quite closely in the article on the Bible. Cp. Sec. V, "Presbyterianism in England."

[27] Mullins, p. 23 f.

tion and creed, no ordinance, no sacrament, no preacher or priest, dare stand between God and the individual. It is for this reason that Baptists reject pedobaptism, or infant baptism. Baptists do not, as is sometimes assumed, reject infant baptism on the ground that children are innocent and free from original sin. Rather, the Particular Baptists teach that children are in need of divine grace.[28] But they do maintain that Baptism is only a symbolic act, which signifies that through Christ the believer is now in vital connection with the Father, and that he has accepted Christ's commandments as the law of his life.[29] Hence only such may be baptized as have professed repentance toward God, faith in, and obedience to, the Lord Jesus. Obviously, say the Baptists, an infant is incapable of such profession. To baptize an infant and then to pledge him without his will and consent to assume the obligations symbolized in baptism is contrary to the principle of the soul's inherent sovereign right to determine for itself whether or not to accept the supreme lordship of Christ.[30] Some Baptists for the same reason protest against the "consecration" of children, a custom which is currently observed by some Baptist churches.

Baptists are nearly unanimous in their belief that the only proper mode of baptism is immersion. Some Baptists seem to consider immersion the article by which the church stands or falls. At least among non-Baptists the opinion frequently obtains that immersion is the distinctive doctrine of the Baptists and the reason for their name. No Christian church denies that immersion is a proper mode of baptism.[31] But the basic question is whether Baptism is a means of grace or merely a sign. In agreement with all Reformed bodies Baptists believe that Baptism is "an ordinance of the New Testament which must be unto the party baptized a sign of his fellowship with Him in His death and resurrection."[32] But by insisting on immersion the Baptists show greater consistency than other Reformed bodies. For if Baptism, as they say, is only a symbol of our fellowship in Christ's death and resurrection, then immersion, submersion, and emergence would be logically the proper form of baptism "to show forth in a solemn and beautiful emblem our faith in the crucified, buried, and risen Savior,

---

[28] N. H. Bapt. Conf., Art. III (Schaff, III, 743), states: Man was created in holiness, under the law of his Maker; but by voluntary transgression fell from that holy and happy state; in consequence of which all mankind are now sinners, not by constraint, but choice; being by nature utterly void of that holiness required by the law of God, positively inclined to evil; and therefore under just condemnation to eternal ruin, without defense or excuse.

[29] Torbet, p. 413. Cp. Wallace, pp. 151—56; Mullins, p. 76 f. See also the Bapt. Conf., Art. XXVIII (Schaff, III, 741).

[30] Oscar Cullmann, *Die Tauflehre des N. T.* (Zurich, 1948); Joachim Jeremias, *Hat die Urkirche die Kindertaufe geübt?* (Göttingen, 1938, 1949); trans. by J. K. S. Reid, *Baptism in N. T.* (Chicago: Henry Regnery Co., 1950); John C. Mattes, "A Reply to Karl Barth on Baptism," *Luth. Ch. Quart.*, 1947, pp. 173—86.

[31] In his 1519 treatise on Baptism, as well as in the *Taufbüchlein* (1523, 1526), Luther advocates baptism by immersion. W. A., II, 727; *Bekenntnisschriften*, p. 540; Schwiebert, p. 447 f. But it must be kept in mind that Luther held that Baptism is not only a symbol but also a means of grace and that therefore it works and effects what it symbolizes.

[32] Bapt. Conf. of 1688, XXVIII, 1 (Schaff, III, 741).

with its effect in our death to sin and resurrection unto life." [33]

Scripture, however, does not teach that Baptism is merely a symbol, but rather that Baptism produces in us what it symbolizes. The important thing in Baptism therefore is that it effects faith, or regeneration, which is symbolized by any of the modes of baptism. Accordingly the New Testament terms for "baptize" do not denote immersion in every instance.[34] And, finally, there is no conclusive proof either in the New Testament or in the Apostolic church that immersion was generally used.

The Church. Among Baptists the term "church" tends in ordinary usage to be restricted to the local and visible congregation of the regenerate. Baptists say:

The distinctive contribution of Baptists to [the discussion of] "the Church Universal" is to be found in their insistence on the individual soul in relation to God, without human mediation of parent, priest, church, or sacrament, and in the conception of the entire ecclesiastical autonomy of the church. Their root belief and life principle has been and remains individualism and voluntarism in religious experience, relation and responsibility.[35]

In accord with their basic assumption, Baptists hold that

A Gospel church is an organized body of believers, equal in rank and privileges, administering its affairs under the headship of Christ, united in the belief of what He has taught, covenanting to do what He has commanded, and cooperating with other like bodies in kingdom movements.[36]

Baptists are well aware of the danger which inheres in their "separatism," "individualism," "come-outism." If the principle of the complete autonomy of every individual soul is strictly applied, there could be no joint worship, not even in the local congregation. Against such anarchic separatism the Baptists maintain a voluntary fellowship of the separate churches in local associations, in state and national conventions, and in the Baptist World Alliance. They have attempted to temper their separatism by a larger loyalty to the spirit of the New Testament.[37] The majority of Baptists believe that the church is both a fellowship and an organization. As a fellowship they believe that entrance into the church is by the experience of regeneration and is thus a fellowship of saints without any reference to the particular denomination to

---

[33] N. H. Conf., Art. XIV (Schaff, III, 747).

[34] Cp. Charles Porterfield Krauth, *Cons. Ref.*, Ch. XI.

[35] W. O. Carver, "The Baptist Conception of the Church," in *The Nature of the Church*, a report of the American Theol. Committee of the World Conference of Faith and Order (New York, 1945), p. 71 f. Cp. also H. E. Dana and M. L. Sipes, *A Manual of Ecclesiology* (Kansas City, 1944); Duke K. McCall, ed., *What Is the Church?: A Symposium of Baptist Thought* (Nashville: Broadman Press, c. 1958); Winthrop Still Hudson, *Baptist Concepts of the Church: A Survey of the Historical and Theological Changes Which Have Produced Changes in Church Order* (Phila.: The Judson Press, 1959); Franklin M. Segler, *A Theology of Church and Ministry* (Nashville: Broadman Press, c. 1960), esp. Part I. — For references to the "Church Universal" in Baptist statements of conviction see, for example, Article 33 of the London Confession of 1644, Article 26 of the London Confession of 1677, and Article 12 of the New Hampshire Confession of 1833.

[36] Torbet, pp. 25, 26.

[37] Hillyer Straton, "What Is Disturbing the Baptists?" *Christian Century*, March 29, 1944, p. 394 f. Mullins, p. 59.

which the individual Christian belongs. Most Baptists believe that once a person is in this fellowship, he is always in it. Only those are received into the organized church who have made a profession of Jesus as Lord and Savior. Admittance into this local church is by vote of the congregation and by immersion.[38]

The Baptist church polity is sometimes viewed as being congregational. Strictly speaking, it goes beyond congregationalism, for even in the congregation the sovereign right of the individual must be duly respected, and no ecclesiastical legislation dare ever come between the individual and his God. Since the individual deals with Christ directly, Baptists speak of their church polity as a perfect spiritual democracy without any kind of human headship, such as bishops, presbyters, synodical officials, or congregational elders and pastors. But also the term "spiritual democracy" seems inadequate, for Baptists insist that the complete autonomy under Christ is based upon obedience to Christ's supreme law given to the church in the Scriptures.[39] It is difficult to find an adequate term which does full justice to the following principles:

A local Baptist church comes into existence through the action of a group of Christian believers, all having obeyed the command of Christ to be baptized in accordance with the mode the New Testament requires, and the action they collectively take in forming a local Baptist church is the free and voluntary dedication of each and all of them to the realization of certain common purposes that they hold to be the outline of the Christian way of life. This is called by them "Our Covenant." This body may or may not have a confession of faith. It has no set forms of worship. Each of these churches is sovereign, independent, varying in doctrinal views, free to frame its own program of Christian activities as it pleases. The dominant desire is to live so that others may see in their conduct the meaning of the Christian way of life. . . . There are items in this covenant which cannot be carried out unless there be co-operation of Baptist churches with other Baptist churches. The bodies that are thus formed, made up of these independent Baptist churches, are called Associations and Conventions. The first has to do with the promotion of Christian fellowship among the churches in a given section. The second deals with the raising of funds contributed for the carrying on of a program which no local church can successfully conduct by itself. This program includes evangelism, education, benevolence, and missions. . . . Each of these bodies may pass resolutions, but these are binding only upon the persons present.[40]

Baptists are therefore consistent when they refuse to participate in any movement which tends toward the establishment of any organization which they fear may become a superchurch. This explains the attitude of the Southern Baptists toward the National Council of the Churches of Christ in the United States or the World Council of Churches, and the refusal of Canadian Baptists to unite with the United Church of Canada. The American (formerly Northern) Baptists are an exception, since in recent years this convention has become more and more denominationally minded.[41]

[38] Carver, pp. 68, 69.

[39] *Census*, II, 89.

[40] Rufus W. Weaver, in *Watchman-Examiner*, Nov. 5, 1942.

[41] The Southern Baptist Convention and The Lutheran Church — Missouri Synod are the only large Evangelical bodies not participating formally in contemporary ecumenical organizations. However, the basic reasons for non-participation are different in the case of the Baptists from what they are for the Lutherans.

Religious Freedom and the Separation of Church and State. Baptists have always insisted on the principle "a free church in a free state." Beginning with Roger Williams, the Baptists have advocated religious liberty. In their espousal of the separation of church and state they had a point in common with the Quakers. The Baptists of Virginia were no doubt largely responsible for the adoption of the First Amendment to our Constitution.[42] The Baptists have protested against a tax-supported church and were probably the first American group to advocate support of the church on a purely voluntary basis. They accepted the principle of tax-exemption for church property only because they believed that the state benefits from religion. The Baptists' opposition to the Roman Catholic church is based primarily on Rome's dogma that it is the only legitimate church and therefore alone entitled to state recognition and support.

In their insistence on the separation of church and state the Baptists did not accept the Anabaptist views that the state is inherently wrong. They believe that the church must aid and assist the state, especially by serving as the conscience of the state. Baptists have often been called the champions of the "common man" and of the socially and economically disinherited people. In more recent times, under the leadership of Walter Rauschenbusch and Shailer Mathews, many Baptists have become strong advocates of the "social gospel."

The Priesthood of Believers. The Baptists have made one phase of the priesthood of believers a functional reality to a greater degree than probably any other body. This phase is the great missionary activity which the Baptists have demonstrated throughout their history. Not only have they been active in foreign mission work, but they have also succeeded in making Christians realize their individual responsibility toward their fellow men.

The Baptist Bodies

THE PARTICULAR BAPTISTS

Baptists are in principle opposed to all ecclesiastical organizations. While the majority of Baptist congregations are loosely banded together in national conventions, many go no farther than to practice fellowship in local associations, without any formal organization. Some even limit the fellowship to a mere exchange of the minutes of their local meetings. For this reason it is rather difficult to classify and to describe the various Baptist bodies. It must further be kept in mind that the missionary, educational, and publication programs are not carried on by the convention or association as such, but rather by societies organized for this purpose. These societies are usually made up of individual Baptists from various conventions and associations, without delegated authority from their local congregation or the respective association.[43]

The American Baptist Convention.[44] During the first two centuries of their American history the Baptists of the Northern States showed little growth, largely because of their "separatistic"

---

[42] Mullins, pp. 89, 95; Sweet, *Story of Rel. in Am.,* 274 f.; *Rel. in Col. Am.,* chs. iv, x. Cp. Stokes, I, 368—75.

[43] Baptist statistics are not always complete because they are sometimes given in such a way as "to avoid disclosing the statistics of any individual church" (*Census,* II, 256).

[44] See Paul M. Harrison, *Authority and Power in the Free Church Tradition: A Social Case Study of the American Baptist Convention* (Princeton University Press, 1959). Until 1950 this body was known as the Northern Baptist Convention.

principle. After the Revolutionary War, however, a number of factors compelled the Baptists to draw more closely together. The desire to raise the standards of ministerial training led to the founding of the Baptist Educational Society in 1812. The zeal of the Judsons for a concerted Baptist effort in foreign mission work proved to be a large factor in awakening Baptist denominational consciousness and, in 1814, led to the organization of the General Missions Convention for Foreign Mission Work. The challenge of the newly opened Western frontier and the need of ministering to Baptists on this new frontier resulted in the formation of the Home Missions Society in 1832. However, in 1844 the Baptists of the Northern and Southern States split over the question of raising and distributing missionary funds. Many Southern Baptists thought any organizational and denominational effort to raise funds was anti-Scriptural because it was not expressly commanded in the New Testament. Hence the Northern Baptists are often spoken of generically as missionary Baptists, whereas many among the Southern Baptists were known as antimission Baptists.[45]

The American Baptists, unlike other Baptist groups, have virtually become a denomination in the generally accepted definition of this term. In 1907 the Northern Convention was organized as a corporation, a rather significant departure from the historic position of most Baptists. Though the local church still retains its autonomy, the Convention is now so organized that duly elected delegates through interlocking boards conduct the various activities formerly conducted by the various societies. Furthermore the American Convention differs from many Baptist groups, particularly the Southern Baptists, in taking an active part in all ecumenical movements.[46]

The sovereignty and competence of every soul has proved to be a two-edged sword among the Northern Baptists. This principle permitted the rise of liberalism and resulted in a division of the Northern Baptists into two opposing theological camps. Colgate-Rochester Seminary and the Divinity School of the University of Chicago became the theological centers for the new liberal theology.[47] At Colgate-Rochester William Newton Clarke[48] and Walter Rauschenbusch[49] and at Chicago William Rainey Harper, the first president, George Burndon Foster, and Shailer Mathews[50] spearheaded the liberal

---

[45] Cp. Newman, pp. 432—42.

[46] Proposals to merge the American Baptists and Disciples have met with several obstacles, e. g., the suspicion on the part of some Baptists that the Disciples teach "baptismal regeneration."

[47] Mayer, "Lib. Theol. and Ref. Ch.," *C. T. M.*, XV (1944), 798—802.

[48] See esp. his *Outline of Christian Theology*, 1898, and *The Christian Doctrine of God* (New York, 1909).

[49] Walter Rauschenbusch, *Christianity and the Social Crisis* (New York: The Macmillan Co., 1907), and *Christianizing the Social Order* (New York: The Macmillan Co., 1913); Dores Robinson Sharpe, *Walter Rauschenbusch* (New York: The Macmillan Co., 1942). For a discussion of Rauschenbusch and a complete bibliog. cp. P. E. Kretzmann, "The Social Gospel," *C. T. M.*, XV (July, 1944), 459—71. Also Hopkins, *Rise of Social Gospel*, pp. 215—32, and Ralph L. Moellering, "Rauschenbusch in Retrospect," *C. T. M.*, XXVII (1956), 613—633.

[50] See G. B. Foster, loc. cit. Shailer Mathews, *The Faith of Modernism*, 1924, *Atonement and Social Progress*, 1930. See also E. E. Aubrey, "Shailer Mathews," *Journal of Religion*, 1942, pp. 341—45. A. H. Newman, "Recent Changes in the Theology of the Baptists," *American Journal of Theology*, X (1906), 587—609.

movement. As a final recourse the fundamentalist opened several opposition seminaries.[51] They also protested against the Foreign Mission Society's "inclusive" policy, which granted the Board the right to commission missionaries who had accepted the social gospel and all its premises.[52] The Fundamentalist Fellowship in the Northwestern Convention endeavored to establish an "exclusive" policy and to formulate a creedal statement to which all foreign missionaries were to subscribe. They failed in this endeavor, since even conservative Baptists held that the subscription to any creedal statement is contrary to the basic principle of the Baptist churches, who throughout their history have considered the New Testament as a sufficient guide. The Northern Baptist Convention stated that "creedal statements are the beginning of the reign of ecclesiasticism and dogmatism and will sound the death knell of individual religious freedom and will lead to intellectual dishonesty, because individual religious concepts are never static for those who search the Scriptures with open mind and heart." [53]

Many churches of the American Baptist Convention no longer insist on immersion and close Communion. It is impossible to establish the ratio of conservative and liberal churches. The influence of contemporary theological movements is evident.

In 1958 the *Danish Baptist General Conference* merged with the American Baptist Convention.

The Southern Baptist Convention. The history and theology of this convention is essentially the same as that of the American Convention. The chief occasion for separation was the slavery question, more specifically the Northern Baptists' declaration that they would not appoint a slaveholder as a missionary. Some believe that an organized method of raising funds for missions also played a role in the separation. Apparently at the time of the separation the antimissionary spirit was quite strong in the South. Today the Southern Baptists must be classified as missionary Baptists. The Primitive Baptists, strongly represented in the South, are still antimission. They fear that mission societies will lead to ecclesiasticism.

The Southern Baptists have remained much more conservative in theology than the American Baptists and in general have remained loyal to the summary of a modified Calvinism as it is contained in the New Hampshire Confession. Many of its clerical and lay leaders are known for their espousal of verbal inspiration, for which reason they are frequently, but mistakenly, identified theologically with The Lutheran Church — Missouri Synod. Southern Baptist Seminary at Louisville, Ky., is its chief theological school.[54] Fearing that the federation of denominations in larger organizations will lead to ecclesiasticism, they have refused to join the National Council of the Churches of Christ and the World Council of Churches. Southern Baptists exchange "messengers" with the American Baptists, and some Baptist congregations hold membership in both conventions.

---

[51] Hillyer Straton, loc. cit. (fn. 37).

[52] A number of Northern Baptists had been members of the Commission of Appraisal, which published *Re-thinking Missions, a Laymen's Inquiry After One Hundred Years* (New York, 1932). This report reflected the thinking of the comparative religions school and advocated a social gospel.

[53] Taken from the "Report of the Coleman Committee," *Watchman-Examiner,* April 6, 1944, pp. 325—27. Cp. also Sept. 30, 1943, p. 929, and March 23, 1944, pp. 273, 274.

[54] See *A History of Southern Baptist Theological Seminary* (Nashville: Broadman Press, 1959).

The Conservative Baptist Association of America, organized in 1947, regards the Bible as the inspired Word of God and hence infallible and of supreme authority, and stresses the freedom and autonomy of the local congregation.

The National Baptist Conventions.[55] Immediately after the Civil War the various Baptist mission societies entered upon such an active mission program among the emancipated Negroes that within three decades about one million were gathered into Baptist churches. These Negro Baptists organized the two National Baptist Conventions, differentiated by the fact that one uses the suffix "Incorporated" after the name. In doctrine and polity they are theoretically in full harmony with the American and the Southern Convention. In polity their antiecclesiasticism is so pronounced that it is extremely difficult to classify the various local churches.

The Baptist General Conference, functioning since 1879, is composed of Swedish Baptist immigrants and their descendants.

National Baptist Evangelical Life and Soul Saving Assembly of the U. S. A. This body concentrates on evangelistic work.

Primitive Baptists. At the beginning of the nineteenth century the majority of Baptists in the South held that all church practices not specifically commanded in the New Testament are contrary to the Scriptures. Therefore they were opposed to the establishment of Sunday schools, the formal training of pastors, and the remuneration of pastors for missionary work. These Baptists were nicknamed "Hard-shell" Baptists. In particular they directed their opposition against the forming of any society for foreign or home mission work, not because they were opposed to mission work, but because they could not find any directive in the New Testament for such societies. Hence they are commonly known as Antimission Baptists. Baptists rightly consider the "antimission movement" the saddest chapter of Baptist history,[56] because this literalistic and narrow approach to the New Testament would have definitely thwarted the greatest contribution of the Baptists, a very successful missionary effort.

The Primitive Baptists are extremely Calvinistic in theology and rigidly separatistic in polity. Fellowship between the various churches and local associations is maintained merely by the exchange of the minutes. Any association or church deviating from Baptist principles is dropped from fellowship.

The National Primitive Baptist Convention of the U. S. A. is a Negro body with local associations and a national convention.

Two-Seed-in-the-Spirit-Predestinarian Baptist. This small group is of interest chiefly because of the Manichean error that all mankind falls into two classes. One class is endowed with a good spiritual seed, implanted by God into Adam. All descendants who have this implanted seed in their spirit constitute a "spiritual generation existing in Christ before the creation" and are gathered into the church, which is the resurrected body of Christ. These are saved by "grace" — they had nothing to do with the implanting of the spiritual seed — and are absolutely sure of their salvation. Satan implanted an evil seed in the spirit of the rest of mankind. These are irrevocably doomed to damnation.

American Baptist Association. The

---

[55] *The National Baptist Convention* was organized in 1880 and incorporated in 1915. *The National Baptist Convention of America,* often called the "unincorporated" group, withdrew in 1916. *The National Baptist Convention of the U. S. A., Incorporated,* perpetuates the parent body.

[56] A. H. Newman, p. 433.

main tenets emphasized by this group are the verbal inspiration of the Bible, the premillennial coming of Christ, the complete autonomy and equality of every local congregation, which alone has the commission to do mission work. For this reason they have been known as "equality" Baptists. They advocate extreme separatism, asserting that only they are the custodians of divine truth, especially in perpetuating the "landmark" of the apostolic succession, namely, believers' baptism.[57]

Seventh Day Baptists. There are two groups, one of English, the other of German origin. The English *Seventh Day Baptist General Conference* goes back to a church organized in 1671 at Newport, R. I. They are in full agreement with the principles of the Calvinistic Baptists except for their view that Saturday and not Sunday must be observed as the Sabbath, because Christ and His apostles observed the Old Testament Sabbath. William Miller, the spiritual forebear of the Seventh-day Adventists, originally belonged to this group. The German *Seventh Day Baptists* were founded by the mystic Conrad Beissel in 1728. This group originally was organized as a celibate and communistic settlement at Ephrata, Pa.[58]

The General Association of Regular Baptist Churches left the Northern Baptists in 1932. In theology they follow the New Hampshire Confession with strong premillennial leanings; in polity they are extremely congregational.

THE GENERAL BAPTISTS

The General Baptists are Arminian in their theology. In distinction from the Particular Baptists they maintain universal atonement and free will. The first Baptists in England were General or Arminian Baptists and no doubt reflected the early Mennonite influence.

The North American Baptist General Conference is composed of German immigrants and their descendants. Many of the churches in this conservative, evangelistically-minded body are still bilingual.

General Baptists. This is both a generic term denoting all so-called Free Will Baptists and also the specific name of a small group of Baptist churches. The origin of the latter is difficult to trace. Some say that the origin of this group goes back to 1607. As a distinct group they do not appear until Benoni Stinson organized them in 1823 in Indiana. Several unsuccessful attempts were made to bring about closer affiliation with other Free Will Baptist churches. In theology this group of Baptist churches is Arminian. Open Communion is advocated, and foot washing is practiced.

The Christian Unity Baptist Association. This is a very small group in which there has been much dissension regarding open Communion.

Regular Baptists. Under this heading a number of associations are included who claim the honor of representing the original English Baptists before the distinction between Particular and General Baptists became an issue. They have no confessions, and Arminian as well as Calvinistic views are prevalent among them. There is no church organization, though there are more than 20 associations. They observe close Communion, generally practice foot washing, and advocate the principles which underlie perfectionism. This group of Baptist churches is related to the preceding group.

---

[57] Torbet, p. 298.

[58] This very small group is of interest chiefly for historical reasons. For a complete bibliog. cp. Eugene E. Doll and Anneliese Funke, *The Ephrata Cloisters*, Phila., 1944.

The North American Baptist Association is strong chiefly in Arkansas, Texas, and Mississippi. Its theology is evangelical, fundamental, missionary, predominantly premillennial.

The Free Will Baptists. A number of Baptist groups are represented under this heading who have in common their opposition to Calvinistic doctrine. It is extremely difficult to trace their history.[59] They are highly emotional, extremely separatistic. In 1910 there were over 50 separate associations. In 1911, however, many of the New England associations affiliated with the Northern Baptists. *The National Association of Free Will Baptists* currently has 200,000 members.

The United Free Will Negro Baptist Church. This group of Negro Baptist churches is similar in theology to the previous body.

The Evangelical Baptist Church Incorporated, composed of Free Will Baptists, was organized in 1935.

United Baptists. In 1801 a union of Particular and Arminian Baptists was effected as the United Baptists. Many of these churches have in recent years affiliated with other Baptist bodies.

The Separate Baptists in Christ trace their origin to the separatist movement in England at the close of the sixteenth century. Most of the Separate Baptists have united with other Baptists, especially with the Southern Baptist Convention.

Duck River (and some six kindred) Associations. These associations are found chiefly in the hill country of Alabama and Tennessee. Some lean toward a liberalist Calvinism, others toward a modified Arminianism. They are related to the Separate, Regular, and United Baptists. They object to the paying of a stated salary to pastors and the publication of statistics. Fellowship among associations is by letter only.

The General Six-Principle Baptists were organized in Rhode Island in 1653. Their distinctive doctrine is the view that according to Heb. 6:1, 2 "six principles," esp. the laying on of hands, are essential to church membership.

The Independent Baptist Church of America is of Swedish origin and in theology similar to the preceding group.

In Canada the *Baptist Federation of Canada* acts as co-ordinating agency for the *Baptist Convention of Ontario and Quebec,* the *Baptist Union of Western Canada* and the *United Baptist Convention of the Maritime Provinces.* Not associated with the Federation is *The Fellowship of Evangelical Baptist Churches in Canada.*

BIBLIOGRAPHY

PART IV

SECTION VI

Aldredge, E. P. *Southern Baptist Handbook.* Nashville: 1940.

Barnes, William W. *The Southern Baptist Convention, 1845—1953.* Nashville: Broadman Press, 1954.

Baxter, Norman A. *History of the Freewill Baptists: A Study in New England Separatism.* Rochester: American Baptist Historical Society, 1957.

Boyd, Jesse L. *A History of Baptists in America Prior to 1845.* New York: American Press, 1957.

Ernst, J. *Roger Williams, the New England Firebrand.* New York: The Macmillan Co., 1932.

Foster, G. B. *The Finality of the Christian Religion.* Chicago: University of Chicago Press, 1909.

[59] Cp. Torbet, pp. 273 f., 302 f.

Hughey, J. D. Jr. "Baptists and the Ecumenical Movement," *Ecumenical Review,* X (1957/1958), 401—410.

Leavenworth, Lynn, ed. *Great Themes in Theology: Study Papers Prepared for American Baptist Theological Conferences.* Chicago: The Judson Press, c. 1958.

Mullins, E. Y. *The Christian Religion in Its Doctrinal Expression.* Phila., 1917.

Newman, A. H. *History of Baptist Churches.* "American Church History Series." The Christian Literature Co., 1894.

Posey, Walter Brownlow. *The Baptist Church in the Lower Mississippi Valley, 1776 to 1845.* Lexington: University of Kentucky Press, 1957.

Stokes, Anson Phelps. *Church and State in the United States.* New York: Harper & Bros., 1950.

Sweet, William Warren. "The Baptist and Quaker Elements," *Religion in Colonial America.* New York: Charles Scribner's Sons, 1942.

————. *Religion on the American Frontier. The Baptists, 1783—1830.* Chicago: Henry Holt, 1931.

Torbet, Robert G. *A History of the Baptists.* Phila.: The Judson Press, 1950.

————. "Baptist Churches in America," in Vergilius Ferm, ed., *The American Church of the Protestant Heritage.* New York: Philosophical Library, 1953, pp. 187 to 206.

Wallace, O. C. S. *What Baptists Believe.* Nashville: The S. S. Bd. of So. Bapt. Conv., 1913.

SECTION VII

The Protestant Episcopal Church

Anglicanism is "more a loyalty than a doctrinal position." Since it is not a confessional denomination, it is very difficult to evaluate its doctrinal stand and to determine its proper place among the historic churches. Its liturgy reveals strong Lutheran influence at many points. Its ethic bears the imprint of both Zwinglianism and Calvinism. It has deliberately supplemented its historic Western heritage with importations from Eastern Orthodoxy in the interest of a more comprehensive Catholicity. This accounts for the fact that in the United States many Anglicans or Episcopalians object to their church's official name, the Protestant Episcopal Church, since "Protestant" is popularly regarded as antithetic, rather than complementary, to "Catholic," and the name for that reason fails to indicate that the

Episcopal church is "a portion of the Holy Catholic church." Others object to the sharp antithesis contained in the term "Protestant," because the liturgy and canon law of the Anglican and Episcopal church is said to follow very closely the ancient Roman church before the great schism between the Eastern and Western churches.[1] Yet many, possibly even a majority of, Episcopalians and their fellow Anglicans are sympathetic to the Reformed rather than to the Western Catholic position. It is significant, for instance, that the perennial efforts which extremely vocal minorities in the Protestant Episcopal church have made to have "Protestant" formally eliminated from their denomination's official style have been consistently defeated.

The Anglican communion consists of

[1] William Wilson Manross, p. 315. Kenneth Mackenzie, Pref., p. vi., and *passim.*

fourteen national provincial churches and a number of extraprovincial dioceses. While even Anglican leaders regard the theological variety inside the Anglican communion as "astonishing," it is held together by a common standard of worship and life in *The Book of Common Prayer*, a common post-Reformation historical tradition in which the Thirty-Nine Articles are a prominent milestone, a common episcopal ministry, a common recognition of the pre-eminence of the primatial see of Canterbury, and such modern structural institutions as the Lambeth Conference and the Anglican Congress.[2]

An appreciation of the history of Anglicanism is helpful for a proper evaluation of the Protestant Episcopal church.[3]

The Anglican Church

IN ENGLAND

England produced few great theologians and reformers, but it did furnish the church a relatively large number of able Christian statesmen and aggressive church leaders. The English spirit of independence, even prior to the Reformation, due in part to England's insular position, was largely responsible for the development of the principle of religious and civil liberty. Thus in God's providence the British Empire became an important instrument in the spread of the Protestant Reformed religion.

In its early stages the English Reformation was a rejection of papal authority rather than of papal errors. Henry VIII (1509—1547) inaugurated a partial reformation; however, not from religious convictions as much as for personal and political reasons.[4] His break with Luther and his attempt to exterminate the Lutheran movement in England came very largely as a result of the unhappy issue of his literary conflict with the Wittenberg Reformer.[5] In the Six Articles of 1539, Henry reaffirmed the Roman doctrine and practice on transubstantiation, withholding of the cup, priestly celibacy, the vow of chastity, private Masses, and auricular confession. Under Edward VI (1547—1553), Archbishop Thomas Cranmer succeeded in introducing wholesome reforms in doctrine and cultus. Two prayer books – the first (1549), with strong Lutheran elements – were published and the Edwardine Articles, 42 in number, adopted. These Articles reflect Lutheran influence and are patterned largely after the Augsburg Confession.[6]

[2] Philip Carrington, "The Structure of the Anglican Communion" in Powel Mills Dawley, ed., *Report of the Anglican Congress 1954* (Greenwich: The Seabury Press, 1954), pp. 45—48.

[3] A. D. Innes, *England Under the Tudors* (New York: Putnam's, 1937); James Gairdner, *The English Church in the 16th Century*, Vol. IV in Stephens and Hunt, *History of the English Church* (London, New York: The Macmillan Co., 1903). For a modern Roman Catholic interpretation, see Philip Hughes, *The Reformation in England*, 3 vols. (New York: The Macmillan Co., 1954).

[4] W. Norman Pittenger, "What Is an Episcopalian?" in Leo Rosten, ed., *A Guide to the Religions of America* (New York: Simon and Schuster, 1955) p. 49.

[5] Schaff, *History*, VI, 396 ff. See also Erwin Doernberg, *Henry VIII and Luther: An Account of Their Personal Relations* (Stanford, Calif.: Stanford University Press, c. 1961), pp. 3—59.

[6] Theodore Graebner, "When England Almost Became Lutheran," in *Four Hundred Years*, p. 269 ff. See also Mackinnon (see P. III, Bibliog.),

Under Queen Mary I (1553–1558) England witnessed a period of Protestant martyrdom and a return to Romanism. Under Elizabeth (1558–1603), the theology and cultus of Anglicanism, as we now know it, became the official doctrinal position of the Established Church. It was her aim to make the Established Church sufficiently comprehensive to satisfy the majority of her subjects.[7] Seeking to function as a *via media* between Continental Protestantism and Romanism, the Church of England endeavors to be Catholic but not Roman in its cultus; it is episcopal in its government, though subject in temporalities to the crown; it is Reformed in doctrine, though it carefully avoids at most points a Lutheran or Calvinistic preference.[8] The Act of Supremacy gave the crown the right to nominate the prelates, summon and dissolve convocations, sanction creeds, and punish heresies, but did not officially invest the crown with a sacerdotal character. By act of Parliament and with the sanction of Elizabeth the Edwardine Articles were revised. As an official formulation of Anglican theology the Thirty-Nine Articles (Latin version of 1563 and of 1571) have never been superseded. Today they have merely a historical significance. Through Elizabeth's influence Anglicanism developed an eclecticism and comprehensiveness which enables Calvinistic

Puritans, Arminian Methodists, liberal rationalists, and Romanizing churchmen to worship side by side; which has room for medieval and modern ideas, evangelical doctrine and Catholic cultus, uniformity in church government and elasticity in doctrine.[9]

Under the Stuarts, James I (1603 to 1625) and Charles I (1625–1649), Calvinism made strong inroads into the Established Church, and the "Five Points" adopted at Dort were vehemently debated pro and con. Both kings proscribed this discussion and, on the advice of Archbishop Laud, Charles I issued His Majesty's Declaration in 1628, which restricted all theological discussions on the Five Points to "the literal and grammatical sense of the Thirty-Nine Articles." The High Church party, which defended the divine right of kings — and of bishops — was pleased with this turn of events, but the Puritans were all the more determined to root out popery and Arminianism. In the ensuing conflict between the crown and the Puritans the royal office was abolished, Charles and Archbishop Laud were executed, the Presbyterian form of government was introduced, and Calvinistic theology was adopted by the Westminster Assembly, 1643–1647. For a short period Presbyterianism was established as the official religion of the Commonwealth (1649–1660).[10]

IV, 352 ff.; Schaff, *Creeds,* I, 600 ff.; Henry Eyster Jacobs, *The Lutheran Movement in England,* 2d ed. (Phila.: General Council Publication House, 1916); E. George Pearce, "Luther and the English Reformation," *C. T. M.,* XXXI (1960), 597—606; Carl S. Meyer, "Cranmer's Legacy," ibid., XXVII (1956), 241—268.

[7] Carl S. Meyer, *Elizabeth I and the Religious Settlement of 1559* (St. Louis: C. P. H., 1960); Charles F. Mullet, "The Elizabethan Settlement and the English Church," *C. T. M.,* XXX (1959), 643—658; Lowell H. Zuck, "The Influence of the Reformed Tradition on the Elizabethan Settlement," ibid., XXXI (1960), 215—226.

[8] Neve, p. 300.

[9] Schaff, I, 598 ff. The influence of the Swiss Reformers on sixteenth-century Anglican thought is documented in Helmut Kressner, *Schweizer Ursprünge des anglikanischen Staatskirchentums* (Gütersloh: C. Bertelsmann Verlag, 1953).

[10] See Sec. V, "Presbyterianism."

In 1660, with the restoration of the royal office under Charles II, who became a Roman Catholic on his deathbed, Anglicanism was re-established as the official religion. In the subsequent decades several acts of Parliament granted greater toleration to dissenting and Nonconformist groups. Anglicanism is still the established religion in England.[11]

IN THE UNITED STATES [12]

For our purposes the history of Anglicanism may be divided into three periods: 1609–1785; 1785–1845; 1845 to 1950.

1609–1785. A huge cross in Golden Gate Park, San Francisco, marks the spot where the first Anglican service was conducted on American soil by the chaplain of Sir Francis Drake in 1579. The colonization charters granted Sir Humphrey Gilbert (1598) and Sir Walter Raleigh (1584) provided for public services according to the Anglican rite. A Church of England chaplain among the colonists at Jamestown, Va., began his ministrations there in 1607, over a decade before the founding of Plymouth. According to its charter, the chief purpose of the colony was to convert the natives, and for this purpose all colonists were required to take the Oath of Supremacy and to give evidence of being free from "papal superstition."[13] The later colonies of Virginia and Maryland were also predominantly Anglican. The Virginia colonies formed a legislative assembly which enacted not only the political laws, but also such laws as regulated the religious life of all colonists: the assessment of taxes for the

Established Church, uniformity in doctrine and worship, the imposition of fines for nonattendance at divine services. The Quakers and Puritans in the Virginia colonies were taxed for the support of the "Established Church," but were not persecuted, as was the case in England. In Virginia, and to some extent in Maryland, the Anglican church was the state church and flourished numerically and financially. This flourishing condition was not so general in the other Southern colonies. In the New England colonies the Anglicans became the victims of an intolerance similar to that which the English church had displayed toward the Independents and Separatists. However, the intolerance of the Massachusetts Congregationalists led to the revocation of their charter, whereupon the Anglicans organized in Boston and built King's Chapel in 1689. In Connecticut the resignation of the two Congregationalist professors of Yale in order to receive Anglican orders enabled the Anglicans to gain a foothold in 1722. The first church to be established in New York was Trinity Parish, 1695. George Berkeley was deeply interested in establishing a Christian university in New York and was largely responsible for the founding in 1754 of King's College (now Columbia University) and the College of Philadelphia (now University of Pennsylvania).[14] Nevertheless the Anglican church was faced by a serious obstacle, the failure of the English church to supply competent ministers along with the antagonism of the Dissenters, who were suspicious of the establishment of a state church.[15]

[11] From time to time the tensions between the Established Church and the so-called Free churches come to the surface rather violently. See, for instance, *Time,* Jan. 23, 1951.

[12] Manross' excellent one-volume history has been used extensively in this section.

[13] Sweet, *Rel. in Col. Am.,* p. 28 ff.

[14] Manross, chs. iii, viii.

[15] *Census,* II, 1,487.

1785–1845. The Anglicans of Virginia and Maryland, financially and organizationally independent of England, supported the revolutionary cause. The majority of the Anglican clergymen in the other colonies were loyalists. After the war they lost the financial support of the British Society for the Propagation of the Gospel, and their congregations were impoverished. When the colonists gained independence from England, the Anglicans lost their episcopal supervision, which had been vested in the Bishop of London.

The first significant step in the reorganization of Anglicanism was taken when Anglican churchmen applied to the Maryland Legislature for a charter. The petitioners adopted the name "Protestant Episcopal Church," the term "Protestant" to distinguish it from the Roman church, and the term "Episcopal" to distinguish it from the Presbyterian and Congregational bodies. This name was ultimately adopted by American Anglicans in spite of considerable protest. In Connecticut the establishment of an American episcopacy was initiated when the clergy elected Samuel Seabury as their bishop and instructed him to seek episcopal consecration in London. The Archbishop of Canterbury refused to omit the oath of allegiance to the English crown from the consecration rite, and Seabury finally obtained the consecration from the nonjuring bishops in Scotland in 1784. The Rev. William White of Philadelphia, an ardent supporter of the Revolutionary cause and an advocate of constitutional government, assumed the leadership in rallying the scattered Anglican forces. In 1784 he submitted seven proposals for a projected general convention. The most significant were:

IV. That the Episcopal Church shall maintain the doctrines of the gospel as now held by the Church of England and shall adhere to the liturgy of said church, as far as shall be consistent with the American Revolution and the constitution of the respective States.

VI. That the clergy and laity assembled in convention shall deliberate in one body, but shall vote separately, and the concurrence of both shall be necessary to give validity to any measure.[16]

These proposals were adopted in 1785, a revision of *The Book of Common Prayer* was ratified at the General Convention of 1789, and a petition was dispatched to the English bishops requesting recognition of the Protestant Episcopal church as a distinct branch of the Holy Catholic church. During the subsequent decades both church and state passed through trying times, largely because of the antireligious spirit imported from France and the general moral decadence. After the death of John Wesley in 1791, his followers drifted rapidly toward their ultimate secession from the Anglican church. The American revisions in *The Book of Common Prayer* were viewed by many as a departure from the teaching of the Anglican church and caused serious dissensions.

Under the leadership of such men as Bishop John Henry Hobart of New York and the Rev. William Augustus Muhlenberg, who had been reared a Lutheran, the Episcopal church established church schools, fostered theological training, initiated a missionary program, and founded eleemosynary institutions.

THE MODERN PERIOD, 1845–1950

During the past century Anglicans on both sides of the Atlantic felt the impact of several trends in theological thought which modified some views peculiar to Anglicanism and accentuated others.

The Tractarian, or Oxford, Movement. The Oxford Movement was a re-

16 Ibid., p. 1,488 f.

action against the spiritual decadence of the Anglican clergy and laity. We find this summary of its aims:

The objects of the Oxford Movement (and for the most part still operative) were: (1) To vindicate the Catholic position of the Church of England; (2) to reassert its identity with the pre-Reformation Church in England; (3) to insist on the continuity of its apostolic succession; (4) to exalt episcopal order; (5) to emphasize the importance of the sacraments; (6) to enhance the ideal of the priesthood.[17]

The leaders were John Keble, Edward Pusey, and John Henry Newman. Many Tractarians, particularly Newman, went beyond the High-Churchmanship of the seventeenth and eighteenth centuries.[18] They defended the necessity of remaining at peace with the Roman Catholic tradition and decried the Reformation. In particular they maintained that the Thirty-Nine Articles actually were Catholic rather than Protestant, since they did not condemn purgatory itself, but only its abuses, did not sanction the right of private judgment, and did not deny the infallibility of the church councils. They presumed the right to consider Roman Catholic dogmas which were adopted in the modern period as being within the bounds of "permissible opinions."[19]

In America the Evangelical party at first strenuously opposed the "Romanizing" tendencies of the English Tractarians. But from 1840 onward the Anglo-Catholic views received increased recognition.[20] Gradually the "comprehensive policy" led to the adoption, in 1874, of the "Ritual Canon." This compromising canon advocated tolerance of conflicting views and championed the possibility of two traditions living together and enriching each other.[21]

Liberal Theology. Anglicanism has always been sympathetic to an intellectual approach to Christianity. During the early decades of the nineteenth century the Platonic and Kantian poet-philosopher Samuel Taylor Coleridge advocated a modified use of reason, but held that the validity of spiritual truths is determined not by an intellectual process, but by the degree in which these truths meet man's moral needs, a view similar to Schleiermacher's principle that *das fromme Gottesbewusstsein* is the source of religious truth.[22] Many consider the

---

[17] Stowe, p. 12. The following books will prove helpful in evaluating Anglo-Catholicism: Yngve Brilioth, *The Anglican Revival* (Longmans, 1925); C. P. S. Clarke, *The Oxford Movement and After* (New York: Morehouse, 1932); Geo. E. De Mille, *The Catholic Movement in the American Episcopal Church* (Phila.: Church Historical Society, 1941); S. L. Ollard, *A Short History of the Oxford Movement* (New York: Morehouse, 1932); H. L. Stewart, *A Century of Anglo-Catholicism* (Oxford U. Press, 1929); Owen Chadwick, ed., *The Mind of the Oxford Movement* (Stanford, Calif.: Stanford University Press, 1960).

[18] See George Every, *The High Church Party, 1688—1718* (London: S. P. C. K., 1956).

[19] Manross, p. 268—73.

[20] Nashotah House, a High Church seminary, was founded 1841 at Waukesha, Wis., and moved to Nashotah, Wis., in 1842.

[21] Manross, pp. 294 ff., 306 f.

[22] Charles Richard Sanders, *Coleridge and the Broad Church Movement* (Durham, N. C.: Duke University Press, 1943). A reviewer of this study (*Christian Century*, March 24, 1943, p. 362) states: "Anglican liberalism in the nineteenth century included two groups, associated respectively with Oxford and Cambridge, the former predominately Aristotelian and, in some measure, heir to the method of the Enlightenment, the latter

Schleiermacher-Coleridge influence, next to the rationalizing element inherent in Anglicanism, the strongest factor in the rise of Broad-Church-ism. While the Broad Church men differed widely on many points, they were agreed in their efforts to maintain a liberal attitude in theology and to minimize the importance of definite dogmas. Liberalism usually manifests itself first in a liberal attitude toward the Bible. Such an attitude dominates *Lux Mundi* (1890), a collection of essays edited by the English Anglo-Catholic leader Charles Gore. Liberal theology gained a foothold in the Protestant Episcopal church in this country during the last quarter of the nineteenth century, chiefly through Phillips Brooks of Boston (elevated to the episcopate in 1892) and Charles Briggs, who after his suspension from the Presbyterian church because of his liberal views was ordained an Episcopal priest in 1899. Many liberals openly denied the Virgin Birth, some the historicity of Jesus, and a few even the existence of a personal God.[23] In recent years the sharp antitheses between the liberals

and the Anglo-Catholics have been modified. The Anglo-Catholics have become more liberal, and the liberals more appreciative of the traditional position of the church. A similar phenomenon is reflected in the so-called "liberal Evangelical" movement, which "endeavors to combine freedom with historical study and theological interpretation as well as with reverent experimentation in worship."[24]

The Rise of the Social Gospel. In England "the Social Message" of the Anglican church may or may not accord with the policies of Parliament and the social consciousness of the monarch. Under the late Archbishop William Temple the "social gospel" received some emphasis.[25] In the United States a number of Episcopalians were among the earliest advocates of the "social gospel."[26] The extreme form of the social gospel movement, as urged by Walter Rauschenbusch, did not find many adherents among the Episcopalians. In recent years the Episcopal church has concerned itself with many social prob-

having a Platonic and Kantian coloration and combining a free and progressive spirit with a reverence for the wisdom of the past. Coleridge, whose affinities were with the second, is credited by the author with being 'the chief source of the Broad Church movement.' He was a liberal-minded conservative, a representative of 'Platonic old England' (the sort of thing Dean Inge discusses in his *Platonic Tradition in English Religious Thought*), with a profound distrust of science's reliance on hard facts and cold logic and of its distrust of metaphysics. He was for the free use of reason, but held that 'spiritual truths are not addressed primarily to the intellective faculty of man,' but 'are substantiated by their correspondence to the wants, cravings, and interests of the moral being.'"

[23] Manross, p. 348. George P. Fisher, *History of Christian Doctrine* (New York: Charles Scribner's Sons, 1923), p. 446 ff. E. Clowes Chorley, *Men and Movements in the American Episcopal Church* (New York: Charles Scribner's Sons, 1946), p. 425 ff.

[24] Manross, p. 394 f.; Gardiner M. Day, *A Prayer Manual*, p. 210.

[25] For a concise statement of William Temple's social thinking see Charles H. Lowry, Jr., "William Temple," *Christendom*, VIII (Winter, 1943), 26—41.

[26] Hopkins (Sec. VII, fn. 49), p. 287 f. Cp. Winston Churchill, *The Inside of the Cup* (New York: Macmillan, 1913), a tendential novel, revolves about the attempts of an Episcopalian rector to implement a social gospel program in his parish.

lems, such as world peace, capital and labor, marriage and divorce.[27]

The Ecumenical Movement. Both the Anglican and the Episcopalian churches opened negotiations with the Russo-Greek church in 1862 for the purpose of establishing an agreement which would recognize the validity of the sacraments and the orders of both churches. This attempt was not initially successful; nevertheless the Episcopal church supported the Russian seminary at Paris after World War I. More recently the Greek Orthodox and the Anglican churches have established fraternal relations, each recognizing the ministry and the sacraments of the other body.[28] Since 1920 limited mutual recognition has existed between the Anglican churches and the Lutheran state church of Sweden.[29] The Anglicans were among the prime movers in the organization of the World Council of Churches. The Protestant Episcopal church did not join the Federal Council of Churches until 1942. Some of their leaders argued that in accord with the Savior's prayer they should not commit themselves by joining an organization which did not embrace all Christians and which might stand in the way of a larger unity. Yet the first president of the National Council of the Churches of Christ (1950) was Presiding Bishop Henry Knox Sherrill. To date the protracted attempts to unite the Episcopalians and the Presbyterians have been in vain, largely because neither group is ready to accept the other's view of Orders.[30] This, in turn, may reflect basic disagreement at a profounder theological level.

THE GENIUS OF ANGLICANISM

From the preceding historical sketch it is evident that the distinctive characteristic of Anglicanism is its comprehensiveness.

Latitudinarianism. Lutherans appreciate the treasures of Anglicanism: the King James Version of the Bible; *The Book of Common Prayer;* an excellent hymnody; a tradition of superior ecclesiastical architecture; a large number of outstanding Biblical scholars. But Lutherans by and large cannot understand the doctrinal ambiguity of the Anglican church. To them Anglicanism is an enigma. They cannot understand how some Anglicans stand at the front door bidding a genuine welcome to the Reformed churches, while other members of the same household, at the same time and with the same sincerity, as it were, pour cold water from an upper window on the unsuspecting visitors.[31] The confessionally conscious Lutheran finds entirely unacceptable a theological principle which tolerates mutually exclusive views. He cannot understand how a leader of the Episcopal church can invite the "religious seeker" to escape the Babel of confusion by "finding his faith" in a church which tolerates diametrically divergent views and grants

---

[27] Miller and others, *Christianity and Conscience,* p. 178 ff. Manross, p. 318 f.

[28] Schaff, *Creeds,* I, 74—78. Percy V. Norwood, "Reunion with the Eastern Church," *Anglican Theol. Review,* Jan. 1941, pp. 47—66. Cp. also P. 1, "Eastern Orthodox Church."

[29] W. Arndt, "Conference of Episcopalians and Augustana Synod Lutherans," *C. T. M.,* VII (1936), 461—464. Conrad Bergendoff, "The Holy Christian Church," *Lutheran Companion,* Feb. 22, 1936, p. 236 ff.

[30] Cp. Bishop William Thomas Manning in *The Living Church,* Oct. 4, 1939; Oct. 15, 1941.

[31] Angus Dun, "The Ambiguous Episcopal Church," *Christendom,* VI, 13. Dun is bishop of the diocese of Washington, D. C.

all the right to worship God according to their conscience.[32] It has been said of the Church of England – and this applies in part to the Episcopal church – that it

> is the most enigmatic and baffling of national institutions. It is the very embodiment of paradox. Theoretically it is the Church of the English nation; actually its effective membership is claimed by no more than a petty fraction of the citizens. It is a reformed Church, but it refuses fellowship with all other reformed churches with the partial exception of the Church of Sweden. It is at once the most authoritative and the least disciplined of all Protestant churches, the proudest in corporate pretension, the feeblest in corporate power.[33]

The Three Theological Parties. In appraising itself, the Episcopal church finds itself in the same dilemma as a boy in the laughing gallery. Viewing himself in the first mirror, he exclaims: "How high I am!" in the second: "How low I am!" and in the third: "How broad I am!"[34] Anglicanism is simultaneously Low, High, and Broad Church, although to the vast majority of the Protestant Episcopal clergy and laity these designations are probably no more binding than equivalent partisan labels in political life.

The Low Church men, now also known as the Evangelicals, were formerly considered orthodox in theology, tolerated no departure from the essentials of religion, emphasized "Gospel preaching" — hence the designation "Evangelicals" — and accepted the Apostolic origin of the episcopacy without denying the validity of nonepiscopal ministerial offices. Many Low Church men were identified with the Wesleyan movement and with its emphasis on a deep personal religious experience. Some Low Church men superimposed the Methodist revival techniques upon the devotional system presented in *The Book of Common Prayer.* Justification by faith, usually in the Wesleyan sense, and the need of conversion became their watchwords in the conflict with the Tractarians. The sacraments and order were given a secondary position; the Lord's Supper was viewed as a memorial, and "baptismal regeneration" was rejected. They resembled the Puritans in their moral standard and sought the consciousness of the supernatural not in worship and ritualism, but in the divinely guided experiences of everyday life.[35] During the past half century they have coalesced more and more with the Broad Church party.

The High Church party, now commonly known as Anglo-Catholicism, wishes to be neither Protestant nor Roman Catholic, but a movement which contends that it is perpetuating the ideals of pre-Roman Western Catholicism.[36] In its moderate form American

---

[32] Theodore Will, pp. 38—45, 129. This comprehensive or indifferent spirit accounts for the fact that Buchmanism obtained its foothold in America under the aegis of Samuel M. Shoemaker while he was rector of Calvary Episcopal Church, N. Y. Shoemaker promoted the Oxford Group Movement by the following books: *The Conversion of the Church; Twice-Born Ministers; A Confident Faith; If I Be Lifted Up; Religion That Works.*

[33] H. H. Henson, the *Church of England,* quoted in a review of his book by P. V. Norwood in the *Anglican Theological Review,* XXII (1940), 143.

[34] Dun (fn. 31), p. 4.

[35] Manross, 214—17, 270. Chorley, p. 435 ff.

[36] Stowe, loc. cit., presents a brief but satisfactory study of this movement. Much of the recent devotional literature of the Episcopal church is written in the spirit of Anglo-Catholicism. Mackenzie, op. cit.; Dearmer, op. cit.; Damrosch, op. cit.; Day, op. cit.

Anglo-Catholics emphasize the personal element in the devotional life and oppose a cold and dead ritualistic formalism. However, in distinction from their more "Protestant" coreligionists, Anglo-Catholics deny that a definite religious experience is necessary and maintain that the spiritual development can take place only within the church through the sacraments. Anglo-Catholics hold that Christ founded the visible church with a threefold ministry as the only official institution to carry on His work. Certainty of salvation requires submission to the church and the use of her offices. With Rome and Eastern Orthodoxy, the Anglo-Catholics believe that the church is the author of the Bible, has fixed the canon, and is the Bible's only rightful interpreter.[37]

In its extreme form, Anglo-Catholicism defines the "Catholic tradition" according to the "canon" of St. Vincent of Lerins as "that which has been believed everywhere, always, and by all." The seven General Councils are held to be quasi-infallible. The Eastern Orthodox, Roman Catholic, and Anglican churches are viewed as the legitimate heirs of the undivided church; the apostolic succession is considered the "article by which the church stands or falls." [38] Some Anglo-Catholics have restored pre-Reformation elements of both theology and cultus, such as purgatory,

the veneration of the virgin Mary, Communion under one kind, the cult of the saints and transubstantiation. The *American Missal,* which is widely used by "advanced" Anglo-Catholics, contains interpolations from Roman sources.[39] Actual conversions to Rome have not been infrequent. Up to 1938, according to reports, 1,016 Anglican priests entered the Roman Catholic church.[40] Of course, there have been a comparable number of conversions to Anglicanism.

Broad Churchmanship has usually aimed to minimize the doctrinal differences in the Anglican church and to find an intellectual approach to Christianity. It tends to be represented in both the High and the Low Church parties. In its theology this school espouses the same basic principles as modernism, or liberal theology.[41]

The Unifying Principle. The non-Anglican often fails to comprehend how a church with such widely divergent and mutually exclusive views can maintain its organizational unity. What is the unifying principle of Anglicanism? It is sometimes stated mistakenly that the tie which unites all Anglicans is the belief in the apostolic succession. But this view is not shared by all Anglicans. Some Anglicans have suggested that the Anglican communion is particularly qualified to serve as God's instrument to

---

[37] Chorley (fn. 23), p. 426 ff.

[38] Manross, p. 271. See esp. Stowe, pp. 26—61.

[39] Thomas J. Williams, "The Revival of the Religious Life," *Living Church,* Feb. 25, 1945, p. 12 f. Evelyn A. Cummins, "The Anglo-Catholic Tightrope," *Christian Century,* Nov. 24, 1937, p. 1454 ff. Dun (fn. 23), pp. 3—13. "One of the characteristics by which the Church really is the Church is the sprouting of monastic communities according to the pattern of Christ's own life." See unsigned editorial "The Monastic Ideal," *Living Church,* Feb. 25, 1945, p. 14 f. — "Guild of All Souls" prays for the repose of all souls, *Living Church,* Sept. 2, 1945. In a defense of the invocation of saints it is said that their knowledge of our invocation is only a "reflected knowledge." Canon Marshall M. Day, *The Living Church,* Oct. 28, 1945, p. 4.

[40] *Christianity Today,* April 1, 1938.

[41] See, above, "Liberal Theol."

unite all Christendom.[42] Others have suggested that the common cultural tradition of Anglo-Saxons is the unifying factor in the several Anglican churches. This suggestion is not in accord with either the history of English and American Anglicanism or the history of the Christian church, which has generally broken down cultural, economic, and social barriers.

A major unifying principle among Anglicans is their "comprehensiveness," which enables the Anglican church to give shelter to almost every type of Christian expression from Anglo-Catholicism to traditional Evangelicalism.[43] The various theological traditions of Christendom are given equal standing in this church body. It is granted that the "comprehensive policy" is a part of the English tradition. To some extent the American Episcopalians have inherited this comprehensiveness. In 1951 Anglo-Catholics of England clashed with the Evangelicals over the attitude of the Established Church toward the English Protestant Free churches, such as Congregationalism. The London *Church Times* reminded both parties that, after all, the genius of the English church, and perhaps of the English nation, is that it has held these two strains of tradition together. They are held in tension, but the tension need not be an unhealthy one. The mischievous thing is to suppose that the two traditions are in opposition. The simple truth is that any true Catholic must be evangelical. Any true Evangelical must be Catholic.[44] From the Lutheran point of view the "comprehensive policy" is the Anglican church's greatest weakness. In spite of large cathedrals, long traditions, impressive ceremonials, fine educational institutions, the Established Church of England has only a very tenuous hold on the English people. And many American Anglicans see the dangers inherent in doctrinal indifference.[45] Tolerance of error will sound the deathknell of true religion. The Christian religion is a religion of convictions, not of compromises. Christian charity does not dissimulate, temporize, or compromise.

THE DOCTRINAL STANDARDS

The Thirty-Nine Articles have given direction and emphasis to the latitudinarian, eclectic, and comprehensive policy which characterizes English and American Anglicanism. The Thirty-Nine Articles attempted to unify to some extent the various continental theological principles of the German, Swiss, and French reformations. The Melanchthonian-Brentian influence is seen especially in the doctrines of justification and baptism. The Thirty-Nine Articles bear great similarity to the Augsburg Confession and Brenz's Württemberg Confession of 1551.[46] The royal supremacy in religious matters, the close union of

[42] Theodore Will, *The Episcopal Church,* p. 77 f. and *passim.*

[43] W. Norman Pittenger, "What Is Disturbing Episcopalians?" *Christian Century,* May 10, 1944, p. 586. See also the splendid summary in Schaff, *Creeds,* I, 599.

[44] Quoted in *Time,* July 23, 1951.

[45] Several Protestant Episcopal chaplains are reported to have indicted their own church severely because of the disastrous results of this comprehensive policy.

[46] Schaff reprints in parallel columns the Thirty-Nine Articles and the two German confessions. *Creeds,* I, 623—29. Zwinglian-Bucerian influence is reflected in the articles on Man and Election. On Original Sin the Articles take a mediating position between Rome's Semi-Pelagianism and the Augustinian-Lutheran doctrine of total depravity. In the doctrine of Election the Articles carefully avoid the infralapsarian view of Calvinism

church and state, espiscopacy, and particularly the "comprehensive policy" are typically Anglican. After the Revolutionary War the American Episcopalians made slight revisions in the Thirty-Nine Articles to conform to the political changes brought about by the Declaration of Independence.

The Book of Common Prayer expresses Anglican theology and is generally viewed not only as containing the ritual law of the church but also as setting forth its theology. Several revisions of the *Prayer Book* to satisfy the various theological trends have been made in all churches of the Anglican communion.[47]

On the principle *lex orandi lex credendi,* the one norm accepted by Anglicans is *The Book of Common Prayer.* Subscription to the Thirty-Nine Articles is not required in the Protestant Episcopal Church. At their ordination priests make the following declaration:

I do believe the Holy Scriptures of the Old and New Testaments to be the Word of God, and to contain all things necessary to salvation, and I do solemnly engage to conform to the doctrine, discipline, and worship of the Protestant Episcopal Church in the United States of America.

Anglicans hold that the points of the Lambeth Quadrilateral, adopted in 1888, are sufficient for the unity of Christendom:

a) The Holy Scriptures of the Old and New Testaments as "containing all things necessary to salvation," and as being the rule and ultimate standard of faith.

b) The Apostles' Creed as the baptismal symbol, and the Nicene Creed as the sufficient statement of the Christian faith.

c) The two sacraments ordained by Christ Himself — baptism and the Supper of the Lord — ministered with unfailing use of Christ's words of institution and of the elements ordained by Him.

d) The historic episcopate, locally adapted in the methods of its administration to the varying needs of the nations and peoples called of God into the unity of His church.[48]

In the English church the Thirty-Nine Articles are looked upon as representing the doctrinal and historical position of Anglicanism in relation to both Rome and the other churches of the Reformation. An Anglican theologian is permitted to disregard a particular formulary if he considers it not wholly adequate; but he is expected to preserve whatever truth that formulary was trying to secure. He must also carefully distinguish between the normal teachings of the church and his own "pious opinion." [49]

and reject the limited atonement, unconditional election, and the inamissibility of faith. However, Calvinism is very evident in the article on the Lord's Supper. Bicknell discusses the various Articles in their historical and theological significance.

[47] The last revision of the *American Prayer Book* occurred in 1928. See Manross, p. 352. The Athanasian Creed was deleted by the Episcopal church as early as 1785.

[48] *Census,* II, 1492. See also "The Lambeth Conference and the Ecumenical Movement," *Ecumenical Review,* XI (1958—1959), 107—108; Louis A. Haselmayer, *Lambeth and Unity* (New York: Morehouse-Gorham Co., c. 1948); H. W. Montefiore, "The Historic Episcopate," in Kenneth M. Carey (ed.), *The Historic Episcopate in the Fulness of the Church* (Westminster: Dacre Press, 1954), pp. 105—108.

[49] *Doctrine in the Church of England* (see Bibliog.), pp. 37—39. This study was recommended by the National Council of the Protestant Episcopal Church as setting forth doctrines generally accepted in the Church of England. The Bishops of the Provinces of Canterbury and York had

THE FORMAL AND MATERIAL PRINCIPLES

By virtue of the comprehensive policy Anglicanism has found it possible to present both its formal and its material principle in such a way as to avoid open clashes.

THE FORMAL PRINCIPLE

The Thirty-Nine Articles state (Article VI) that the canonical books of the Old and New Testaments are the only source of doctrine, and they expressly forbid (Article XX) the church to retain anything contrary to the Word of God. In reality, however, Anglicanism recognizes two additional sources of religious truth: the authority of the church and reason.

In accord with the historic position of Anglicanism many Episcopalians consider the Bible the only source and the all-sufficient norm of religious truth. This has been, generally speaking, the position of Low Church-ism. The adherents of the High Church party hold that doctrinal authority rested successively in Christ, in the teaching church, in the Scriptures, and in the councils.[50] The High Church party makes a great deal of the consensus fidelium, that is, the brief summary of doctrines believed everywhere, at all times, by all, and this consensus is considered the real standard and norm of Christian doctrine.[51] To satisfy the Broad Church men, Anglican theology admits a third source of truth, namely, God's self-disclosure in the religious and moral development of the human race as a whole, in the religion of Israel, the person of Christ, and the life of His mystical body, the church.[52] Thus the comprehensive policy is said to make room in one household for such disparate views as those held by the three "schools" in the Protestant Episcopal church.

THE MATERIAL PRINCIPLE

It is impossible to speak of a uniformly accepted material principle, a central doctrine which constitutes the core of its theology. The Low Church tended to place into the center of its theology the doctrine of God's grace which faith apprehends without the addition of human works, and thereby remained in the Reformation tradition; the High Church considers the corporate worship of the church the center of its theology. In accord with this material principle it has extolled the apostolic succession as essential for the assured administration of the sacraments and a God-pleasing worship and developed

appointed a commission to show the agreement of doctrine in the Anglican church and to work for the diminution of disagreements, and after several years of study the commission published its report, which sets forth the doctrines held by the various "schools" in Anglicanism. — We shall refer to this simply as Commission.

50 Commission, p. 31. This does not mean that High Church theologians seek an absolute authority in matters of faith and life. The church must always allow for different varieties of Christian emphases. While the church has the right to determine articles of faith, it dare not regard them as infallible. A heretic should, of course, be condemned; however, always with the proviso that the future may prove him to have been right. The authority for doctrine is the Christian tradition, a "living experience," a true "evangelical catholicism." Percy L. Urban, "Authority and Freedom in Doctrine," Anglican Theol. Review, Oct., 1946, pp. 192—202. See also Sherman E. Johnson, "The Episcopal Church and the Bible," Anglican Theol. Review, October, 1942, p. 307 f.; Cyril C. Richardson, "By What Authority?" Anglican Theol. Review, July, 1942, pp. 245—55.

51 Commission, p. 35. Cp. Flew, Jesus and His Church (1938), p. 257 ff.

52 Commission, p. 43.

a view of the church which makes membership in a church with the historic episcopate almost indispensable to full Christianity. The Broad Church sees the heart of religion in a life which conforms to the ethical teachings of Jesus. The eclectic and comprehensive character of Anglicanism becomes very evident in a survey of the opinions held on the basic Christian doctrines.

God. Anglican theology demands faith in a personal Supreme Being, to whom man owes worship and the service of righteousness of life [53] and with the ancient church confesses the doctrine of the Trinity. However, there have been attempts to explain this doctrine in terms of experience, for example, the term "Trinity" as the Christian's threefold experience of God as a loving Father, as the Lord and Savior, and as the dynamic power in the Christian's life.[54]

Anthropology. The Thirty-Nine Articles (IX and X) rejected Pelagianism. Total depravity is neither avowed nor denied, for man is said to be "very far gone from original righteousness." Anglicans seem to be agreed on the reality of original sin, its evil effect on man, its guilt, but otherwise allow great latitude in describing the cause and nature of original sin. Some say that it is due to social environment, some to a biological

transmission, some to the transcendental solidarity of the human race, and others to the fact that man is by nature a finite being.[55]

Christ's Person and Work. While the Thirty-Nine Articles (II, III, and IV) restated the Chalcedonian Christology, it is obvious that among modern Anglicans there is no agreement concerning the person of Christ. While some hold to the real personal union, many favor kenoticism — the theory that Christ did not possess the fullness of divine majesty before His glorification — and not a few hold a humanitarian view of Christ and give a symbolical interpretation to His incarnation, virgin birth, and resurrection.[56] There is no agreement among Anglicans concerning the nature of Christ's work. The only point on which they are agreed is that Christ demands our discipleship and worship.[57]

The Church and the Ministry. Article XIX of the Thirty-Nine Articles states:

> The visible Church of Christ is a congregation of faithful men, among the which the pure Word of God is preached, and the Sacraments duly ministered according to Christ's ordinance in all those things that of necessity are requisite to the same.

The majority of Anglicans hold that the one, holy, catholic, apostolic church is

[53] *Commission,* pp. 42, 44 f. The radical pantheistic principles of some Broad Church men found no following.

[54] *Commission,* p. 97 f. Two contemporary Anglican discussions of the Trinity are: Leonard Hodgson, *The Doctrine of the Trinity* (New York: Charles Scribner's Sons, 1944), and Cyril C. Richardson, *The Doctrine of the Trinity* (New York: Abingdon Press, 1958).

[55] *Commission,* pp. 62—67, 223 f. Bicknell states: "If a man were totally corrupt, there could be no moral struggle and man could not be aware of his corruption," p. 231. This is a fallacy, for finitude does not imply sinfulness. The angels and man in the state of integrity were finite, but not sinful. Dialectical theology sometimes seems to equate creatureliness and sinfulness, or, at least, imperfection.

[56] *Commission,* pp. 81 f., 86.

[57] *Commission,* p. 73. Franks, *History,* shows how far some recent Anglicans have deviated (II, 391 ff., 428). Cp. Leonard Hodgson, *The Doctrine of the Atonement* (New York: Charles Scribner's Sons, 1951).

a "visible" society with an unbroken line of institutionalized officers, regulations, and powers, and established in England at least since 314. Accordingly Anglicans believe that the oneness of the church consists in the fusion of Christian doctrine and worship within the framework of the church's sacramental ministry;[58] that the holiness of the church is the response to the divine purpose of the church; that her catholicity consists in retaining the ecumenical creeds, the sacraments, and the historic succession of the episcopacy; and that her apostolicity is established by an unbroken connection with the apostolic church by means of a continuity of doctrine and duly consecrated bishops.[59] All Anglicans maintain some form of the continuity of the ministry, usually expressed in the term "apostolic succession." For some this denotes an unbroken succession of episcopal consecration as indispensable for the validity of all official acts. Others regard it only as the continuity of doctrine and view an unbroken consecration merely as helpful.[60] How deeply the idea of a continuity of persons rather than of doctrine only is rooted appears from the opposition to the proposed merger between Presbyterians and Episcopalians. The main objection to the "Proposed Agreement for Joint Merger" has been that it undermines the doctrine of the apostolic succession, so clearly stated in The Book of Common Prayer.[61]

The Anglicans hold that there are three grades of the ministry: bishop, priest, deacon. The bishop is viewed as the whole church's living representative in his diocese, where he maintains the apostolic mission and authority by his episcopal office. He is the chief pastor, and he alone administers confirmation and orders and exercises the Office of the Keys.[62] The priests are the clergy ordained to preach and administer the sacraments in the local parish. The deacons usually devote themselves exclusively to spiritual activities in the parish, assist at Communion, and may be licensed to preach.

It should be noted that many consider the apostolic succession and the three grades of the ministry to be not of divine right, but merely a historical development, and say that the apostolic succession is of the bene esse, not of the esse of the church. Archbishop Laud argued for the divine right of bishops when the Puritans claimed the divine

58 Commission, p. 103. Leicester C. Lewis, "The Anglican Concept of the Church," in The Nature and Function of the Church, G. W. Richard, ed. (New York: Willett, Clarke & Co., 1945), pp. 85—87. Since the time of Bishop Hooker many Anglicans view the church primarily as a social unit based upon a salvation viewed primarily as social and corporate. Cp. Cyril C. Richardson, The Church Through the Centuries (New York: Chas. Scribner's Sons, 1938), pp. 168—76.

59 Commission, pp. 104—11.

60 Commission, p. 19. Cp. J. L. Ainslie, "The Doctrines of Ministerial Order in the Reformed Churches," summarized in Charles S. Macfarland, Current Religious Thought (New York: Fleming H. Revell, 1941). Claude Jenkins and K. D. Mackenzie, eds., Episcopacy, Ancient and Modern (London: S. P. C. K., 1930).

61 For the union document see Living Church, Oct. 15, 1941, pp. 12—15.

62 Article XXIII, Commission, p. 122 f. Kenneth E. Kirk, The Apostolic Ministry (New York: Morehouse-Gorham, 1946), and Felix L. Cirlot, Apostolic Succession and Anglicanism (Lexington, Ky.: Trafton Publ. Co., 1946). Both books are reviewed in Anglican Theol. Review, January, 1948, pp. 68—81.

right for the presbytery. Later the Tractarians maintained the apostolic succession in the interest of divorcing the authority of the church from the state.[63]

The Sacraments. The Episcopalians are agreed neither as to the place nor as to the significance of the sacraments. The corporate life of the church is so emphasized that the sacramental benefit for the individual's personal life recedes into the background. The Thirty-Nine Articles (XXV) stated that the sacraments are not only badges of Christian men's profession, but also "sure witnesses and effectual signs of grace . . . by which He doth work invisibly in us." But since the days of Hooker many Anglicans consider the sacraments "the social and corporate rites of the Church in which by means of divinely appointed signs the spiritual life flows from God." [64] As to the manner in which sacramental grace is bestowed, some hold that it is given directly, others that the sacraments "convey opportunity for grace," and still others, that the sacraments express a state of mind and will which prepares men to receive the gift of God with profit.[65] The Thirty-Nine Articles (XXVII) allow for teaching baptismal regeneration. However, most Episcopalians seem to view Baptism as the sacrament of initiation, whereby a person is grafted into the corporate, visible church.[66]

Many divergent views are entertained concerning the Lord's Supper. Officially the Anglican church repudiates the Roman Catholic theories of transubstantiation and of the Mass as a propitiatory sacrifice. It appears that for most Anglicans the Holy Communion is a eucharistic sacrifice, an act of worship, in fact, the central act of worship, "the corporate act of the church towards God, performed for the body by the priesthood." [67] Officially the Anglican church adopted a symbolic view of the Lord's Supper, denying oral manducation by the wicked and faithless, and taught the reception of Christ's body and blood by faith alone. Today many Anglo-Catholics speak of "the Real Presence," which denotes to some that the bread and wine somehow become the body and blood of Christ; to others that the body and blood of Christ are really present in the hearts of the recipients, but not in the elements themselves, hence the term "receptionalism"; and to still others, that through consecration the elements receive a "spiritual virtue" — hence the term "virtualism" — and that the elements may therefore really be called "sacramental body and blood." [68]

The Book of Common Prayer provides formularies for absolution, ordination, confirmation, marriage, and unction. These are spoken of as "sacred rites," though many Anglo-Catholics speak of them as sacraments and ascribe to them sacramental graces.

ORGANIZATION AND GOVERNMENT

The Protestant Episcopal Church is organized along hierarchical lines. Not the congregation, but the bishop is considered supreme. The American church

---

[63] Richardson, pp. 211—20. See also Norman Sykes, *Old Priest and New Presbyter: Episcopacy and Presbyterianism since the Reformation* (Cambridge: University Press, 1956) and J. V. Langmead Casserley, "The Apostolic Ministry," *Christian Century,* LXXVIII (1961), 419—421.

[64] *Commission,* p. 128.

[65] *Commission,* p. 130.

[66] *Commission,* p. 137 f. On the Lutheran influence on the Thirty-Nine Articles in this doctrine, see Bicknell, pp. 463—78.

[67] *Commission,* pp. 156—65. Cp. Bicknell, pp. 515—26.

[68] *Commission,* pp. 168—83.

differs from the Established Church in England in so far as the laity is represented in the government of the church. In the local parish the priest is assisted by the vestry, but the direction of the spiritual functions is in the hands of the rector exclusively. The diocese is governed by the bishop, assisted by the diocesan convention, which is composed of clergymen and laymen. The General Convention consists of two houses, one of bishops and one of deputies, the latter being constituted of an equal number of clergymen and laymen; each body deliberates separately. The General Convention meets every three years, and in the interim the affairs are handled by the National Council. The presiding bishop is the highest ecclesiastical administrative authority for the General Convention.

The Anglicans are opposed to rigid regulations in their religious life, such as govern the Roman Catholics or the Calvinistic Puritans. Nevertheless, according to Article XXXIV, the traditions and ceremonies of the church are to be observed and offenders are to be punished. These precepts of the church are said to be "interpretations of the divine law put forth by the authority of the church." There is no final and complete list of traditions extant. The Anglo-Catholic Congress has agreed on the following regulations: The observance of Sunday and holy days, frequent Communion, annual confession, fasting, observance of marriage laws, support of the ministry.[69] The Episcopalians have experienced considerable difficulty in the establishment of a canon on marriage which maintains the indissolubility of marriage and also grants the right of annulments. The last revision seems to have liberalized the canon by expanding the list of impediments.[70]

In short, the Anglican church can satisfy churchmen of practically all descriptions: the ritualist, the formalist, the sacramentalist, the biblicist, the pietist, the legalist, the moralist, the ecumenist, the intellectual. Yet its very inclusiveness mystifies anyone who desires a trumpet to give a distinct sound.

Since 1942 discussions have been going on between the Protestant Episcopal Church and The Methodist Church, exploring the possibilities of intercommunion as an approach to organic union. "Tentative suggestions for reaching intercommunion" were set forth by the two commissions in 1958.

The Canadian counterpart of the Protestant Episcopal Church in the U. S. A. was formerly known as the Church of England in Canada. Since 1955, however, it bears the name *The Anglican Church of Canada.*

Reformed Episcopal Church

This small body came into being when Bishop George David Cummins of Kentucky seceded from the Protestant Episcopal Church because of its ritualism and exclusiveness. In 1873 he and the then Dean of Canterbury took part in an interdenominational communion service in the Fifth Avenue Presbyterian Church, New York. For this action Bishop Cummins was severely censured. Together with a number of Low Church men he seceded, and in 1876 organized the Reformed Episcopal church. In the Declaration of Principles this body confesses its adherence to the Thirty-Nine Articles — with a few minor revisions — accepts the episcopacy as "a very ancient and desirable form of church polity," allows freedom in the form of worship, and expressly rejects the following

[69] Cp. Mackenzie, p. 20. The various precepts or laws are described in detail, pp. 121—22.

[70] *The Living Church*, Oct. 13, 1946, p. 20.

iews: the divine and exclusive right of the episcopacy; the exaltation of the clergy over the "royal priesthood"; baptismal regeneration; the sacrificial char-

acter of the Lord's Supper and any doctrine of a Real Presence.[71] There are two Reformed Episcopal dioceses in Canada.

BIBLIOGRAPHY

PART IV   SECTION VIII

Anson, Peter F. *The Call of the Cloister*. London: S. P. C. K., 1956. A description of religious communities in various parts of the Anglican Communion.

Balleine, G. R. *A History of the Evangelical Party in the Church of England*. London: Church Book Room Press Ltd., 1951.

Bicknell, E. J. *A Theological Introduction to the Thirty-Nine Articles of the Church of England*. Third edition by H. J. Carpenter. London: Longmans, Green & Co., 1955.

Book of Common Prayer and Administration of the Sacraments and other Rites and Ceremonies of the Church, published by the Church Pension Fund of the Protestant Episcopal Church.

Coburn, John B., and W. Norman Pittenger, eds. *Viewpoints: Some Aspects of Anglican Thinking*. Greenwich: The Seabury Press, 1959.

Damrosch, Frank, Jr. *The Faith of the Episcopal Church*. New York: Morehouse-Gorham Co., 1946.

Dawley, Powel Mills. *The Episcopal Church and Its Work*. Greenwich: The Seabury Press, 1955.

Day, Gardiner M., ed. *A Prayer Book Manual*. Louisville: Cloister Press, 1943.

Dearmer, Percy. *The Parson's Handbook*. 12th ed. London, New York, Toronto: Geoffrey Cumberlege, 1932.

De Mille, George E. *The Episcopal Church Since 1900: A Brief History*. New York: Morehouse-Gorham, 1955.

Doctrine in the Church of England. New York: The Macmillan Co. The Report of the Commission on Christian Doctrine appointed by the Archbishops of Canterbury and York in 1922.

Dunlop, Colin. *Anglican Public Worship*. London: SCM Press, 1953.

Knox, Wilfred L., and A. R. Vidler. *The Development of Modern Catholicism*. Milwaukee: Morehouse Publishing Co., 1933.

Mackenzie, Kenneth D. *The Catholic Rule of Life*. Milwaukee: Morehouse Publishing Co., 1933.

Manross, William Wilson. *A History of the American Episcopal Church*. New York, Milwaukee: Morehouse Publishing Co., 1935.

Manual of Catholic Devotion for Members of the Church of England. London: Lord Halifax House, the Church Literature Association.

More, Paul Elmer, and Cross, Frank Leslie. *Anglicanism*. Milwaukee: Morehouse Publishing Co., 1935.

Neill, Stephen. *Anglicanism*. Baltimore: Penguin Books, 1958.

Pike, James Albert, and W. Norman Pittenger. *The Faith of the Church*. New York: The National Council of the Protestant Episcopal Church, 1951.

Prayer Book Studies. New York: The Church Pension Fund, 1953—. A multivolume series by the Standing Liturgical Commission of the Protestant Episcopal Church in the U. S. A. on proposed revisions of the American *Book of Common Prayer*.

---

[71] Schaff, *Creeds*, I, 665; *Census*, II, 1526.

Schaff, Philip. *Creeds* (see Bibliog., P. III).

Shepherd, Massey Hamilton, Jr. *The Oxford American Prayer Book Commentary.* New York: Oxford University Press, 1950.

———. *The Reform of Liturgical Worship: Perspectives and Prospects.* New York: Oxford University Press, 1961.

———, ed. *The Liturgical Renewal of the Church.* New York: Oxford University Press, 1960.

———, ed. *The Eucharist and Liturgical Renewal.* New York: Oxford University Press, 1960.

Stowe, Walter Herbert. *The Essence of Anglo-Catholicism.* New York: Morehouse-Gorham Co., 1942.

———. "The Protestant Episcopal Church in the United States of America," in Vergilius Ferm, ed., *The American Church of the Protestant Heritage.* New York: Philosophical Library, 1953, pp. 93 to 128.

Will, Theodore. *The Episcopal Church.* New York: Morehouse Publishing Co., 1935.

Wilson, Frank E. *Faith and Practice.* New York: Morehouse-Gorham Co., 1945.

PART FIVE

The Arminian Bodies

All Arminian bodies share with James Arminius (1560—1609) his bitter opposition to Calvin's theory of an absolute and sovereign double election. Toward the close of the sixteenth century a number of leading Dutch theologians questioned the Scriptural basis for Calvin's and Beza's supralapsarianism, and Arminius was appointed to vindicate the alleged Scriptural correctness of Calvinism. But in his endeavor to defend the theological premises of Calvin, especially the limited atonement and unconditional election, Arminius became convinced that Calvin's basic principles were anti-Scriptural, and he became an outspoken advocate of universal grace and the freedom of the will. After the early death of Arminius in 1609 Simon Episcopius and Hugo Grotius drafted their objections to Calvinism in the so-called Five Points of Arminianism. This document, also called the Remonstrance, teaches: (1) God's knowledge of man's faith or unbelief the condition of election; (2) the universality of God's grace and Christ's redemptive work; (3) human freedom and responsibility under prevenient grace; (4) the resistibility of divine grace; (5) the possibility of final and total apostasy. The Synod of Dort (1619) rejected these Articles and condemned its subscribers, the so-called Remonstrants.[1] Gradually Arminianism, especially under Philip van Limborch, took a turn toward latitudinarianism, rationalism, moralism, and liberalism. This radical form of Arminianism, however, was not adopted by any church body, though advocated by individual theologians in Holland, England, and Germany.[2]

The following groups identify themselves as Arminian: (1) All the Methodist bodies, which trace their origin directly or indirectly to the Wesleyan revival of the eighteenth century; (2) the large number of Holiness bodies which originated during the present century; (3) several bodies which are related to Methodism in doctrine and practice, though of independent origin, notably the United Brethren and the Evangelical Association; (4) the Salvation Army and kindred organizations. — The Mennonites and the General Baptists hold many views similar to those of Arminianism. Both groups, however, antedate Arminianism, and their theological emphases are different.

NOTE: For key to abbreviations see Appendix C; for Bibliography see end of the sections.

[1] See P. IV, Sec. III, Ref. Doctr. Standards.

[2] Cp. Neve, *Ch. and Sects*, p. 325 f. The radical form of Arminianism is part of the history of Christian thought rather than a part of the dogmatical evaluation of each denomination. Cp. Walch, *Streitigkeiten ausserhalb der lutherischen Kirche*, III, 540 ff. Neve, *Hist. of Chr. Thought* (Phila.: Muhlenberg Press, 1946), II, *passim*. On links with England, see Rosalie L. Colie, *Light and Enlightenment: A Study of the Cambridge Platonists and the Dutch Arminians* (Cambridge: University Press, 1957).

SECTION I

Methodism

The Formative Years of Methodism

The history of Methodism is the lengthened shadow of John Wesley (1703–1791), one of England's greatest religious organizers and a prince among English pulpiteers. He and his brother Charles (1707–1788) preached and sang religious fervor into the heart of a religiously starved nation.

English deism and French rationalism had devitalized Christianity, enthroned reason as the only source of religious knowledge, and led large areas of the Established Church of England back into paganism. The Anglican, or Established, church suffered from "suspended animation" and was unable to attract the English people with the dead formalism that characterized it in many places. Tremendous social and economic upheavals contributed to the alienation of the people from the church. Moreover, the sharp contrast between the newly established rich class, usually members of the Established Church, and the great masses of the poor and underprivileged, only served to estrange the latter still more from the church. A reaction against the prevailing conditions was inescapable. That the reaction in England did not develop into a civil war, as was the case in France, was no doubt in large measure due to the Wesley revival.[3]

Next to Luther and Calvin no other Protestant leader has exerted such a wide, deep, and lasting influence on so many people as John Wesley. This fact is all the more remarkable since Wesley, unlike Luther or Calvin, was not a theologian. Wesley was the counselor of anxious souls and sought for himself and others the answer to man's basic religious question: What must I do to be saved? That was, of course, the basic concern also of Luther, who found the answer to the quest of the anxious soul in the Scriptural doctrine of justification by grace, through faith. This was also the concern of Calvin, who directed the searching soul to the sovereign God. Wesley, however, attempted to silence the restless heart by directing it to its own experience of Christian perfection. The basic difference between Luther, Calvin, and Wesley may be stated as follows: In Lutheranism the Christian is viewed as the justified sinner; in Calvinism as the obedient servant; in Methodism as the perfect man.[4]

All biographers of Wesley are agreed that Wesley's theological development reached its climax in the doctrine of perfection. All other theological points were subservient to this article of Wesley's theology. To understand Wesley and the entire Methodist movement, it is essential to follow Wesley's theological development from early childhood up to the Aldersgate experience in 1738.[5]

1. The first steps toward Wesley's view of the nature and significance of Christian perfection can be traced to the strict training which Wesley received

---

[3] Cp. Arnold Nash, "The England to Which John Wesley Came," in *Methodism*, ed. Anderson. Maimin Piette, p. 117 ff. Lee, p. 18 ff.

[4] Schaff, *Creeds*, I, 892.

[5] Cp. esp. Lee, loc. cit., and Cell, loc. cit.

under the tutelage of his highly gifted mother in the parsonage at Epworth. She was the daughter of one of London's most noted dissenting clergymen, a theologian in her own right, the authoress of a treatise on predestination. In the large household each child at an early age learned to live according to a carefully defined "method" of prescribed rules for conduct. Hence Mrs. Wesley has been called "the mother of Methodism." Her famous sons were convinced that a system of method, a life according to definite rules and regulations, was the only way to self-improvement and ultimately to perfection.[6]

2. Three authors made a great impact on Wesley's theological development toward Christian perfection. Jeremy Taylor's *Holy Living and Holy Dying* deeply disturbed Wesley. He felt that he was not prepared for death, since he lacked the holiness without which no man can see the Lord. The medieval *Imitatio Christi* deeply impressed Wesley, chiefly because of the author's discipline and rules for holy living.[7] Probably the most significant single factor in Wesley's theological development was William Law's *Christian Perfection*. This book helped materially to crystallize in Wesley's mind the theological idea which later became the dominant article of his faith. In the opinion of some this book also laid the foundation for Wesley's mysticism and Romanticism.[8]

In 1729 John Wesley and a number of other Oxford students, notably his brother Charles and George Whitefield, began to meet regularly for the systematic exercise in all such Christian virtues as might lead them to attain that perfection and holiness which they considered indispensable to salvation. They engaged not only in methodical Bible study and in prayer but also in acts of charity. But try as he would, Wesley failed to obtain peace through his activities in the so-called "Holy Club." He undertook a missionary journey to Georgia, hoping that by observing the religious rites of the pagan Indians he might find the answer to his earnest searching. On his American journey he made contact with the Moravians, who convinced him that, contrary to his experience, it is possible to obtain holiness and perfection. He therefore spent six months at the Moravian settlement at Herrnhut, Saxony, to observe the "choir" system as an instrument toward perfection. But the antinomian views of the Moravians, which seemed to free them from all legal restraints, were contrary to his entire training.[9] Nevertheless it was the Moravian Peter Boehler who urged Wesley to pray for the experience of the peace and joy which he sought so earnestly. Wesley himself believed that he gained the desired assurance in the Aldersgate Street experience on May 24, 1738. Methodists usually consider this date the beginning of their church body. Wesley described the experience as follows:

In the evening I went very unwillingly to a society in Aldersgate Street, where

[6] Piette, p. 212 ff.

[7] Some of Wesley's opponents later charged him with Pelagianism and called him a "Jesuit in disguise." It has been suggested that the *Imitatio Christi* influenced Wesley toward Romanism. However, it is more likely that Wesley's opponents among Anglican theologians identified his Arminianism with Pelagianism in order to discredit him.

[8] Flew, p. 314, and Brazier Greene, *John Wesley and William Law* (London: Epworth Press, 1945), reviewed in *Religion in Life*, 1946, p. 624, question these views.

[9] See the "Moravian Church."

one was reading Luther's preface to the Epistle to the Romans. About a quarter before nine, while he was describing the change which God works in the heart through faith in Christ, I felt my heart strangely warmed. I felt I did trust in Christ, Christ alone, for salvation; and an assurance was given me that He had taken away my sins, even mine, and saved me from the law of sin and death.

I began to pray with all my might for those who had in a more special manner despitefully used me and persecuted me. I then testified openly to all there what I now first felt in my heart. But it was not long before the enemy suggested, "This cannot be faith; for where is thy joy?" Then was I taught that peace and victory over sin are essential to faith in the Captain of our salvation; but that as to the transports of joy that usually attend the beginning of it, especially in those who have mourned deeply, God sometimes giveth, sometimes withholdeth them, according to His own will.

After my return home I was much buffeted with temptations, but cried out, and they fled away. They returned again and again. I as often lifted up my eyes, and He sent me help from His holy place. And herein I found the difference between this and my former state chiefly consisted. I was striving — yea, fighting with all my might under the law, as well as under grace; but then I was sometimes, if not often, conquered; now I was always conquered.[10]

It is rather difficult to analyze Wesley's experience psychologically and still more difficult to define it theologically. It was not his conversion, since Wesley considered himself a Christian before

1738. In the light of his basic theological principles it seems that Wesley considered the Aldersgate experience as that moment in which by a personal and subjective conviction the Spirit's witness was written directly upon his soul to the effect that he was now assured of the necessary faith and strength to lead a life of holiness. This assurance did not mean that Wesley said that he was completely free from sin.[11] Wesley never claimed perfection for himself. It is probably best to describe Wesley's Aldersgate experience as the deep emotional assurance that Christ was his Savior. This seems to have given Wesley the firm and steady conviction that he was no longer subject to voluntary sins and therefore able to free himself from the wrath of God by a life of holiness in the service of Christ and the world. The heart of Wesley's experience — and of his theology — was the subjective conviction that he now possessed a constant and intensive love of Christ. Therefore Wesley's experience has been called a "mystical" rather than an "evangelical" conversion. In other words, Wesley had attained a higher and more constant state of religious devotion.[12]

One of the distinctive characteristics of Wesley's theology is subjectivism. After his "religious experience" Wesley continued to use regularly the "means of grace." But to these he added prayer and discipline. In Lutheran theology the assurance is based on the objective character of the means of grace apart from any personal and subjective feeling. Wesley, however, rested his assurance on his own intense religious experience

---

[10] From Wesley's *Journal*, reprinted in *Christian Advocate*, May 19, 1938, p. 464. The section from Luther's Preface which so deeply moved Wesley contains the well-known sentence: "Faith is a living, busy, active, powerful thing and does not ask whether good works are to be done; but before one asks, it has already done them and is always doing them."

[11] The Holiness Bodies maintain that Wesley's basic assumption was complete perfection. This assertion is not correct.

[12] Lee, Ch. v, pp. 87—103.

rather than upon the objective promises of God. In the Anglican church, worship was primarily a corporate activity and had become completely ritualistic and formalistic. Wesley's religious experience was individualistic, and he held each individual must personally experience his escape from the wrath of God and for himself seek after holiness. Wesley did not seek the holiness in solitude as does one type of mystic, but in society, in social activity.

Wesley immediately endeavored to persuade others to share his own religious experience. But although he was an ordained clergyman in the Anglican church, the average church was closed to him, partly because the clergy questioned his methods and partly because they distrusted his theology. Wesley and his co-workers therefore had to resort to other means to reach the great masses, such as preaching in the open fields or barns, protracted watch meetings, and especially the class system. In the fall of 1739 a group of some ten men, who seemingly had shared Wesley's religious experience, were organized by Wesley as the United Society, "a company of men having the form and seeking the power of godliness, united in order to pray together, to receive the work of exhortation, and to watch over one another in love, that they may help each other work out their salvation." [13] As the Wesleyan movement spread, Wesley felt that the newly gained converts could not be entrusted to the spiritual care of their regular pastor. Therefore he established the class system, patterned after the Moravian "choirs." Ten or twelve members were placed under the supervision of a class leader, whose duty it was to investigate once a week each member's spiritual growth and to advise as the occasion demanded as well as to receive the weekly freewill offering for the support of the work. The separate societies or classes constituted a circuit and were under the supervision of a lay preacher. This is the beginning of the circuit system with the circuit rider, which proved so effective in the establishment of Methodism on the American frontier. Wesley was convinced that the lay preachers were not sufficiently qualified to be placed permanently in charge of a parish, and he therefore early introduced the Methodist itinerancy. In 1744 Wesley convened the first general conference of all workers and thereby established the system of "annual conferences." Thus within about five years all the salient features of Methodism had been established by John Wesley, and the founder of the new religious movement was ready to carry out his principle: "The world is my field."

The Wesleys were untiring workers, as is evident especially from John Wesley's *Journal*. It is estimated that he traveled 225,000 miles and preached 40,000 sermons, besides carrying on a tremendous correspondence and preparing his writings for publication. His brother Charles composed some 6,000 hymns. George Whitefield, whom Benjamin Franklin considered one of the world's greatest orators, was closely associated with the Wesleys until his Calvinistic views compelled him to go a separate way.[14] Within fifty years Methodism had become firmly established in England and to some extent in the American colonies. With its many branches and offshoots the Methodist family has become the largest Protestant body of English origin. The Wesleyan revival was probably the greatest religious awakening since the sixteenth-century Reformation. Like all great religious awakenings the Wesleyan

[13] *B. of Disc.,* par. 92.

[14] See Stuart C. Henry, *George Whitefield: Wayfaring Witness* (New York: Abingdon Press, 1957).

movement has had a tremendous impact also on the social, economic, and political life. It was in no small measure responsible for the transformation of English society from a factious, slave-trading aristocracy to a free and educated democracy.[15]

The Doctrinal Standards

The *Twenty-Five Articles of Religion,* based on the Thirty-Nine Articles and *The Book of Common Prayer* of the Established Church, were prepared by Wesley in 1784 for the American Methodists. Wesley's Arminianism becomes quite evident in the articles on original sin, free will, and prevenient grace. In other points the Twenty-Five Articles remain very close to Anglican theology.

Wesley's *Sermons and Notes on the New Testament* are usually accepted as a doctrinal standard. In the "Deed of Declaration" (1784) Wesley bequeathed the 359 Methodist chapels to the "Legal Hundred" on the condition that they accept his *Notes on the New Testament* — a popular version of Bengel's *Gnomon* — and his published sermons dealing with such doctrines as salvation by faith, original sin, free grace, the witness of the Spirit.[16]

The Book of Discipline, as the title indicates, contains the ethical and practical rules of life which are considered essential for membership in the Methodist church. A study of this manual is essential to a proper evaluation of Methodism. The constitution of the first Methodist society lists a large number of negative and positive injunctions whereby the members were to indicate that they really were desirous "to flee from the wrath to come and to be saved from their sins."[17] These rules play such a prominent part in Methodist church life that this church body may be called a church with a discipline rather than with a doctrinal platform. To say that the Wesleys were not interested in doctrine is, of course, contrary to fact, as their hymns amply testify. But John Wesley was evidently interested more in deeds than in creeds. It must be remembered that his movement was a reformation of life, not of doctrine. This explains in part why the "discipline" has played such a prominent role throughout the history of Methodism.[18] Wesley himself was averse to all theological discussions which emphasized doctrine at the expense of Christian life. In "Character of a Methodist" he states:

> I will not quarrel with you about any mere opinion. Only see that your heart be right toward God; that you know and love the Lord Jesus Christ; that you love your neighbor and walk as your Master walked; and I desire no more. I am sick of opinions; I am weary to hear them. My soul loathes this frothy food. Give me solid and substantial religion; give me an humble and gentle lover of God and man; a man full of mercy and good fruits, without partiality and without hypocrisy; a man laying himself out in the work of faith, the patience of hope, the labor of love. Let my soul be with these Christians, who-

---

[15] Brady, op. cit. W. H. Fitchett, *Wesley and His Century* (New York: Eaton and Mains, 1908), p. 283 ff.

[16] The Methodists say that theirs is the only denomination whose theology is confessed in the form of preached sermons. However, Luther's Large C. is to a large extent composed of Luther's catechetical sermons preached at Wittenberg.

[17] *B. of Disc.*, Nos. 94—97.

[18] The significance of the discipline in the Methodist parsonage was well portrayed in Alyene Porter, *Papa Was a Preacher* (New York, Nashville: Abingdon-Cokesbury, 1944). Hartzell Spence, *One Foot in Heaven* (London: Whittlesey House; New York: McGraw-Hill Book Co., Inc., 1940).

soever they are, and whatsoever opinion they are of.[19]

Wesley and his adherents believe that the genius of Methodism is its ability to make dogma completely subordinate to life.[20] Bishop Rowe has stated the Methodist position correctly: "To put it epigrammatically, the distinguishing doctrine of Methodism is that it has no distinguishing doctrine."[21] Strictly speaking, this statement is a half-truth; for Methodism has a doctrinal system, and Methodists indeed have very definite doctrinal convictions, as became quite evident in the fundamentalist-modernistic controversy.

The Doctrinal System

THE FORMAL PRINCIPLE

Wesley and his adherents believe that the Scriptures, reason, and the teachings of the ancient church are the three sources of Christian doctrine.[22] It seems that Wesley took the term "reason" in a rather wide sense, namely, as the cumulative experience of adult Christians.[23] At this point Wesley comes dangerously close to the Quaker "inner light" theory and in reality makes the *vox populi Christiani* the *vox Dei*. It is therefore not surprising that Wesley's adherents among the Holiness bodies and Pentecostal groups very frequently make their own religious experiences the final religious authority, while Wesley's adherents among the liberal theologians make a controlled religious experience the exclusive source of religious truths.[24]

THE MATERIAL PRINCIPLE

The material principle of Wesley's theology is the "perfected" man. Christian perfection is the heart and center of Methodism. It is here that Wesley parts company with both Luther and Calvin. It has been pointed out that whereas Lutheran theology is concerned with the justified man and Calvinism with the obedient servant, the concern of Wesleyanism is with the perfected Christian.[25] The heart of Wesley's theology can best be presented under four points: universal, free, full, and sure salvation.[26]

Universal Salvation. When applied to Wesleyan theology, the term universal salvation has a wider meaning than in its original Arminian setting, where it was employed primarily to refute the

---

[19] Quoted from Rowe, p. 24, in Neve, *Ch. and Sects*, p. 323.

[20] Sheldon, X, 31—52.

[21] Rowe, p. 123, quoted in Neve, *Ch. and Sects*, p. 409.

[22] Cf. Lee, pp. 130—36. Article V of the Twenty-Five Articles states expressly that the Holy Scriptures as contained in the canonical books of the Old and New Testaments contain all things necessary to salvation.

[23] Lee, pp. 136—46.

[24] See below under "The American Methodist Bodies."

[25] Schaff, *Creeds*, I, 891, 897 ff.

[26] Paul Sloan summarizes Wesley's theology under the following four points: Justification by faith alone; true freedom of human personality; the doctrine of the pure heart; the witness of the Spirit or Christian assurance. *Christian Advocate*, May 19, 1939, p. 473. Cp. Mayer, "Lib. Theol. and Ref. Ch.," (P. IV, Sec. VII, fn. 47). Anderson, loc. cit., devotes Part II to a discussion of nine "distinctive emphases" in Methodism, the first four of which are of doctrinal concern: (1) "Salvation for All," by Robert E. Cushman, pp. 103—15; (2) "God Can Be Experienced," by Nels F. S. Ferré, pp. 116—27; (3) "Freedom from Rigid Creed," Lee, pp. 128—38; (4) "The Search for Perfection," Harris F. Rall, pp. 139—48.

theory of a limited atonement. Wesley believed not only that salvation has been procured for all, but also that salvation is actually offered to all, regardless of whether or not they hear the Gospel proclamation. Wesley inclined strongly to the theory of "universality of opportunity" as advocated by Origen. Like Origen he believed that God's kingdom is really threefold, represented best by three concentric circles. The Father's kingdom is the most extensive and embraces all men. In this realm men are guided in their actions only by the light of reason and therefore will be judged solely by the use they made of their opportunities. In the Son's kingdom the standard of judgment is the Gospel. The Spirit's realm is restricted exclusively to those who have had an "experiential knowledge" of Christ. As the degree of knowledge varies in each of the three dispensations, so also the standard of judgment. For Wesley the important point is that God never requires more than that man live according to the measure of light given to him. In Wesley's opinion "universal salvation" is tantamount to "universal opportunity." [27] As a theologian Wesley is frequently an enigma. At times he extols the grace of God most beautifully, as in the hymn "Jesus, Thy Blood and Righteousness." But again he will describe God's grace merely as a divine initiative which kindles such love toward God and men in our hearts as will provide salvation. This is not merely Arminianism, but Semi-Pelagianism. It is difficult to state how consistently Wesley held these tenets.[28]

Free Salvation. The Calvinistic overemphasis of the sovereignty of God and the virtual denial of human freedom and responsibility was entirely foreign to Wesley's thinking. Extreme Calvinists have pictured God as the "wholly other," in whose sight man is nothing but a contemptible worm. Wesley, however, found the goodness of God reflected everywhere in creation, particularly in man. According to Wesley, man still bears the image of his Maker, and God still deigns to dwell in man. Wesley therefore placed great emphasis on the sovereignty and dignity of man.[29] It was only natural that Wesley ascribed to this "sovereign man" freedom of choice. In Wesley's use of the term

---

[27] In his *Journal* Wesley made this entry: "I read today part of the meditations of Marcus Antonius. . . . I doubt but what this is one of those many who shall come from the East and West and sit down with Abraham." Quoted in Robert Southey, *Life of John Wesley* (New York: Everet Duye Kinck and George Long, 1820), II, 8, 9, fn.

[28] An entry in his *Journal* reads: "A mystic who denies justification by faith may be saved. But if so, what becomes of the *articulus stantis vel cadentis ecclesiae?* If so, is it not high time for us to reject bombast and words half a yard long to return to the plain words: 'He that feareth God and worketh righteousness, is accepted of Him'?" Quoted in Lee, p. 161. See the entire Ch. vii in Lee. Schaff quotes Wesley: "No man living is without some 'preventing' grace, and every degree of grace is a degree of life. There is a measure of free will supernaturally restored to every man, together with that supernatural light which enlightens every man that cometh into the world. That by the offense of one judgment came upon all men (all born into the world) unto condemnation, is an undoubted truth, and affects every infant as well as every adult person. But it is equally true that by the righteousness of One, the free gift came upon all men (all born into the world — infants and adults) unto justification."

[29] Wesley was the bitter foe of every form of oppression and was one of the first advocates of the abolition of slavery. Cp. Lee, p. 289 f.

"free salvation" the accent lies on the word "free," to wit, man is a free agent and able to accept or to reject salvation.

It is at this point that Wesley departs entirely from the sixteenth-century Reformers and follows Arminianism, which in many points resembles Rome's Semi-Pelagianism. Wesley held that man did not entirely lose the divine image. The image, he said, is both a moral and a natural endowment, the former consisting in perfect righteousness, the latter in reason and free will. In the Fall, man lost the former, but not the latter. However man's will was weakened in the Fall, and he is incapable of making the right choice unaided. God therefore approaches man with "prevenient grace." Wesley teaches that no human being is entirely devoid of this prevenient grace, which he describes as follows:

> There is no man that is in a state of mere nature; there is no man, unless he has quenched the spirit, that is wholly void of the grace of God. No man living is entirely destitute of what is vulgarly called natural conscience. But this is not natural: it is more properly termed, preventing [prevenient] grace. Every man has a greater or less measure of this, which waiteth not for the call of man. Every man has, sooner or later, good desires, although the generality of men stifle them before they can strike deep root, or produce any considerable fruit. Everyone has some measure of that light, some faint glimmering ray, which sooner or later, more or less, enlightens every man that cometh into the world. And everyone, unless he be of the small number whose conscience is seared as with a hot iron, feels more or less uneasy when he acts contrary to the light of his own conscience. So that no

man sins because he has not grace, but because he does not use that grace which he hath.[30]

This view demonstrates that Wesley's definition of original sin and original guilt differs radically from that of the sixteenth-century Reformers. The Lutheran Confessions describe original sin negatively as the loss of the concreated righteousness and positively as a pervasive and constant inclination toward all that is evil and state further that because of this condition man is subject to God's eternal wrath.[31] Wesley indeed states that man is very far gone from his original righteousness, but denies specifically that this inherent departure is truly sin and guilt. He holds that, strictly speaking, sin is a willful transgression of a known law. The heathen, for example, who are only in the dispensation of the Father cannot be held responsible for actions committed in total ignorance of the divine Law as it is revealed in the Son's or the Spirit's dispensation. In fact, Wesley held that in so far as the Christians are still subject to ignorance, mistakes, and infirmities, their sins are not really sins and do not involve guilt.[32]

Full Salvation. The two preceding points are basic for an understanding of Wesley's doctrine of "full salvation," or Christian perfection. The doctrine of the perfected man "according to the stature of Christ" is in Wesley's opinion the heart and core of the Gospel message. He compared repentance to the porch and faith to the door of a house, but found the house itself in Christian perfection. From its inception the distinctive feature of Methodism was the emphasis on the Christian's desire to flee

---

[30] Sermon LXXXV, quoted in Lee, p. 124. The entire section, pp. 118—30, discusses this matter in great detail. Lee points out that since man has not totally lost the divine image, the term "natural man" is, according to Wesley, a mere abstraction.

[31] The A. C. and the Ap., Art. II.

[32] It is very difficult to state precisely what Wesley actually taught. Sangster, ch. ix, offers a very satisfactory analysis.

from the wrath to come and to be saved from sin. Wesley's watchword was: "Without holiness no man shall see the Lord" (Heb. 12:14). In a sermon Wesley describes the average Christian's outward conduct and then continues:

> This is only the outside of that religion which he insatiably hungers after. The knowledge of God in Christ Jesus; "the life which is hid with Christ in God"; the being "joined unto the Lord in one spirit"; the having "fellowship with the Father and the Son"; the "walking in the light as God is in the light"; the being "purified even as He is pure" — this is the religion, the righteousness he thirsts after; nor can he rest till he thus rests in God.[33]

Wesley's idea of the "perfected man" is probably best summarized in his description of a Methodist as

> one who lives according to the method laid down in the Bible; who loves the Lord with all his heart and prays without ceasing; whose heart is full of love toward all mankind and is purified from envy, malice, wrath and every unkind affection; who keeps all God's commandments from the least unto the greatest; who follows not the customs of the world; who cannot speak evil of his neighbor any more than he can lie;

who does good to all men. . . . These are the marks of a Methodist. By these alone do Methodists desire to be distinguished from other men.[34]

The great goal in Wesleyanism is the attainment of "pure love." Wesley's views may be summarized thus:

> Salvation means the forgiveness of the sinner by grace. . . . But it also means a new kind of life. Here Wesley's emphasis on the ethical came in, taking at times with some of his followers a form of perfectionism which has evoked sharp criticism. In principle it was what Paul had insisted upon: forgiveness meant not only a new life, but the "law of the Spirit of life in Christ Jesus." God demands a new life, and He gives what He demands. With Wesley that took the form of an emphasis on the doctrine of sanctification, which he felt the Reformers had neglected. Grace meant for him not only forgiveness, but transforming power.[35]

Though Wesley wrote a great deal on the central theme of his theology, it is almost impossible to state exactly what he actually taught, and the views of historians as well as those of Wesley's adherents differ widely, especially on such questions as these: Did Wesley teach sinless perfection? Is sin eradi-

---

[33] Quoted in Lee, p. 194.

[34] Quoted in *Christian Advocate*, May 19, 1938, p. 38.

[35] H. F. Rall, "The Methodist Church," *The Nature of the Church* (New York: Willett, Clark & Co.), p. 105. Paradoxical as it may appear, Wesley, on the one hand, was close to Luther, and, on the other, his theological principles were the very antithesis of Luther's. Sangster, p. 100, presents this fact clearly. He quotes Wesley thus: "Who wrote more ably on Justification by Faith alone than Martin Luther, and who was more ignorant of the doctrine of Sanctification or more confused in his conception of it? On the other hand, how many writers of the Roman Church (as Francis Sales and Juan de Castzniza in particular) have written strongly and scripturally on Sanctification, who, nevertheless, were entirely unacquainted with the doctrine of justification. . . . How blasphemously does Luther [in *Commentary on Galatians*] speak of good works and of the law of God — constantly coupling the law with sin, death, hell, or the devil; and teaching that Christ delivers us from them all alike. Whereas it can no more be proved by Scripture that Christ delivers us from the law of God than that He delivers us from the holiness or from heaven. Here (I apprehend) is the real spring of the grand error of the Moravians. They follow Luther, for better, for worse. Hence their 'No works; no law; no commandments.' "

cated or suppressed? Is entire sanctification an instantaneous or a progressive experience? Is perfection absolute or relative?

1. Wesley believed that the essence of perfection is not some emotional experience, but love.[36] He writes:

> A will steadily and uniformly devoted to God is essential to a state of sanctification, but not a uniformity of joy or peace or happy communion with God. . . . Rapturous joy is a great blessing; but it seldom continues long before it subsides into calm, peaceful love.[37]

2. Wesley believed that the Christian is so perfect that he does not commit sin. He held that Christian perfection implies being so crucified with Christ that the believer loves God with all his heart, that no wrong temper, none contrary to love, remains, but that the Christian is motivated by pure love. While Wesley did not contend for the term "sinless" perfection, he did not object to it.[38] In *Plain Account of Christian Perfection* Wesley states that a man filled with pure love may still be subject to a mistake of judgment. But though such a mistake requires the atoning blood, since it is a departure from perfect love, it is not, properly speaking, a sin, since it is not contrary to love. Here Wesley departs completely from the Lutheran Reformation. Luther never fails to emphasize that as long as the Christian is in this world, he is at once both just and sinful (*simul iustus et peccator*), that he has

the new and the old man, that he is engaged in a constant conflict between the flesh and the spirit (Rom. 7:14-25). Wesley, however, mistook the temporary volition for a permanent attitude and actually anticipated the perfection of the saints in heaven. Nevertheless Wesley did not contend that it was possible in this life to attain absolute perfection, nor angelic, and not even Adamic, perfection, but only a relative perfection, depending on the measure in which the Christian is free from voluntary sin. It is not clear whether Wesley believed that sin is merely suppressed or that it is eradicated.[39]

3. Wesley held that Christian perfection is both an instantaneous act — the exact moment of which must be known — and a progressive development. He wrote:

> I believe this perfection is always wrought in the soul by a simple act of faith; consequently in an instant. . . . But I believe a gradual work, both preceding and following that instant. As to the time, I believe this instant generally is the instant of death, the moment before the soul leaves the body. But I believe it may be ten, twenty, or forty years before. I believe it is usually many years after justification; but that it may be within five years or five months after it. I know no conclusive argument to the contrary.[40]

4. Wesley believed that a regulated way of life is indispensable for the attainment of Christian perfection. There-

---

[36] The best studies on this problem are: Sangster, loc. cit.; Lee, ch. viii; Flew, p. 313 ff. The Holiness bodies claim that the modern Methodist church has deviated from Wesley's doctrine of perfection and believe themselves commissioned to restore Wesley's original doctrine. Cp. Mayer, "Entire Sanctification," *C. T. M.*, III (1932), p. 417 ff.

[37] Quoted in Sangster, p. 80.

[38] Ibid., p. 81.

[39] Cp. Lee, p. 186.

[40] Quoted in Lee, p. 188. Cp. also Sangster, pp. 30 f.; 79; 81; 84 f.; McConnell, ch. vii. The Holiness bodies aver that Wesley viewed entire sanctification as an instantaneous act without any further progress. This does not seem to have been Wesley's view.

fore he prescribed the "discipline" in which every phase of the Christian's life is carefully outlined. Wesley held that religion must be a ruling habit of the soul. To achieve this habit, he introduced the class system and divided the members into probationary and full members, a distinction which is still observed.[41]

Sure Salvation. In Lutheran theology the sinner is directed to the objective and certain promises of God as the only basis of assurance. In Calvinism the assurance is based on God's unconditional decree and the elect's perseverance in grace. Wesley, however, based the assurance of salvation on the inner witness of the spirit, a twofold witness, namely, that of God's Spirit, which is objective and comes first, and man's own spirit, which is immediate and a result of the Spirit's direct witness.[42] In the final analysis Wesley rested his faith on his faith, a highly subjective procedure. There is, however, no evidence that Wesley employed the methods of many later Methodist revivalists, who endeavored to bring the hearers first to the point of nervous and physical collapse and then to a state of ecstasy in which they experienced direct revelations of God's pardoning love. Wesley warned against such excesses to gain the witness of the Spirit. Nevertheless, he did advocate the use of "means" like prayer and especially protracted watch meetings — sometimes lasting to the point of exhaustion.[43]

The basic principles underlying Wesley's fourfold salvation are evident in all modern Arminian bodies, and come to the surface in one form or another and with varying emphasis in all the spiritual descendants of Wesley from the most conservative member of a Holiness body to the most radical exponent of liberal theology. These basic theological principles have furthermore given the Arminian bodies definite characteristics which distinguish them from Lutheranism and to a large degree from Calvinism.

ARMINIAN CHARACTERISTICS

Latitudinarianism. This is of course a characteristic of the Established Church in England, with which Wesley remained in fellowship throughout his life. Nevertheless, Wesley's latitudinarianism did not stem from expediency nor indifference toward doctrine as in the Established Church, but from his all-consuming interest in the doctrine of Christian perfection. Methodism seeks the unifying factor for all Christian churches not in unity of doctrine, but in the common effort to help men attain the "stature of Christ." [44]

Legalism. The prominence given to the "discipline" is an evidence of the legalistic trend in Methodism. The "discipline" is the constitution and body of laws which govern the faith and life of the individual and the ritual and organizational procedure of the local congregation and the conferences. There is

41 The place of discipline in Wesley's theology is discussed by Lee, Ch. ix.

42 In three sermons on "Witness of the Spirit" Wesley describes the assurance of the direct witness of the Spirit as "an inward impression on the soul" that the believer is God's child. The indirect witness is the testimony of our soul assuring us of the reliability of the Spirit's direct witness. Cp. Schaff, *Creeds*, I, 899.

43 He commended the action of two boys who did not sleep for two days, until the Lord "poured the riches of His grace upon these children." Cp. Lee, p. 231 ff.

44 Neve, *Ch. and Sects*, p. 336 f. The doctrinal basis for the merger of the three largest Methodist bodies in 1939 required no more than a short sentence. *B. of Disc.*, 1944 ed., p. 12.

probably no other church family which has such an elaborate system of rules and regulations for its pastors and members, both probationary and full members, as the Methodist church. It is of course true that all Reformed bodies, both of Calvinistic and Arminian leanings, are legalistic in varying degrees. At first glance it may appear as if Wesleyanism advocates a legalism even more austere and rigorous than that of the Calvinistic Puritans. Nevertheless, there is a basic difference between Calvinist and Methodist legalism. In Calvinism the observance of the Bible's ethical injunctions is viewed as the obligation which man as a finite creature and a bond servant owes to the sovereign Lord. It is therefore extremely difficult ever to associate a spirit of joy with Calvinistic legalism. In Methodism, however, the discipline is viewed as the means whereby the Christian — a free man and more or less master of his own destiny — seeks and attains Christian perfection. It is difficult to imagine that the Methodist type of legalism leads to a morbid spirit, though, like all forms of legalism, it frequently leads to uncertainty.[45]

Emotionalism and "Enthusiasm." An outstanding characteristic of Methodism has always been its emotionalism. The Methodist church has proved to be a good army for conquest because in its appeal to the emotions it develops crusaders, but it is a poor army for occupation, because its members usually lack doctrinal solidity. Experience shows that one cannot sustain or rekindle a fire of religious fervor merely by an appeal to the emotions, any more than a forest fire can be started in a "burnt-over" area.[46] Wesley, sensing the danger of overemphasizing emotionalism and enthusiasm, always urged the use of "means," such as prayer, Christian conversation, reading the Scriptures, attendance on preaching. Nevertheless, there *is* a strong emotional trend throughout Wesley's and his co-workers' ministry. Wesley held that the goal of the Christian is a type of mysticism or "enthusiasm" which manifests itself in a joyous religious experience. Wesley's mysticism was not of the contemplative type — he severely criticized Luther because he considered him to be "deeply tinctured with mysticism." Wesley sought the mystical union with God in a life of joyful service to God and his fellow man, a mysticism somewhat similar to that of Bernard of Clairvaux and Francis of Assisi.[47] This mysticism determined his attitude toward the sacraments as means of grace. Calvinism

[45] The contrast between Calvin's and Wesley's view on vocation is adequately presented by Max Weber, trans. R. H. Tawney, *The Protestant Ethic and the Spirit of Capitalism* (London: George Allen and Unwin Ltd., 1930), p. 139 ff. See also McConnell, ch. ix: "Spreading Social Righteousness," esp. on Wesley's view regarding the daily calling, p. 269 ff.

[46] The strong appeal to the emotions was undoubtedly one of the chief reasons why the Methodist circuit rider was so extremely successful on the frontier in the early decades of the nineteenth century. Cp. Sweet, *Rel. on the Am. Fr., 1783—1840.* Vol. IV. *The Methodists.* (Univ. of Chicago Press, 1946), p. 41 ff. One of the best examples of the futility to start a revival in a "burnt-over area" is Jonathan Edwards' attempted second revival in 1740.

[47] Lee, ch. xii; McConnell, pp. 149—63. Arthur Cushman McGiffert, *Protestant Thought Before Kant* (New York: Chas. Scribner's Sons, 1922), p. 162 ff. Wesley could not have charged Luther with antinomian mysticism if he had actually read Luther's *The Liberty of a Christian Man.* Watson, p. 101 (see P. II, fn. 107).

denies that the sacraments have any collative and effective power, since it would be beneath the dignity of the sovereign God to work through visible and resistible means. Wesley, however, denies the regenerative power of the means of grace because in his opinion man is by nature endowed with spiritual gifts and able to attain mystic union with God without sacramental regeneration.[48]

Social Consciousness. At the beginning of Wesley's career the Established Church had little or no interest in the problems of the individual. Wesley, however, held that there could be no religion and no holiness unless it were social. Wesley undoubtedly did much

to reduce the social ills of English society, such as the drink evil. Philanthropy, the abolition of slavery, and child-labor legislation may be traced indirectly to Wesley's efforts. In the tradition of Wesley the modern leaders in Methodism have drafted the social creed of the Methodist church.[49]

The doctrines and theological points of view described in the previous section constitute what is known today as Arminianism. In America the following groups espouse the Arminian theology: (1) the large Methodist family; (2) the approximately sixty Holiness and Pentecostal groups; (3) the Evangelical United Brethren Church; (4) the Salvation Army and related groups.

SECTION II

The American Methodist Bodies

In 1939 the Methodist Episcopal Church, the Methodist Episcopal Church South, and the nonepiscopal Methodist Protestant Church united and organized as The Methodist Church. This merger brought into one body approximately 85 per cent of all American Methodists. The three large Negro bodies total close to 10 per cent of the total of Methodists. They do not differ from The Methodist Church in doctrine or polity. It is therefore correct — at least organizationally — when Methodists assert that since 1939 they are "a united people." True, there are a score of additional separate Methodist organizations, but they are all small and total no more than approximately 135,000 of the 12,359,000 Methodists (1960).

The Methodist Church

John and Charles Wesley served as spiritual advisers to the colonists at Savannah, Ga., 1735–1738. This service, however, cannot be considered as establishing Methodism in America, since it antedates the founding of the first Methodist society in London. Methodism was brought to America by Philip Embury of New York in 1760 and subsequently by Robert Strawbridge of Maryland. Later Wesley sent Thomas Rankin, Francis Asbury, and several itinerant preachers to minister to the Methodist colonists. The first annual Methodist conference was held in Philadelphia in 1773. The Methodist preachers were not in sympathy with the cause of the American colonists, and all except As-

[48] Cf. Neve, *Ch. and Sects*, p. 338.

[49] McConnell, pp. 233—310.

bury returned to England during the Revolutionary War. To provide for the 15,000 spiritually orphaned American Methodists, Wesley, completely ignoring Anglican ecclesiastical procedure, ordained ministers for the colonies, appointed Thomas Coke and Francis Asbury as superintendents, prepared a liturgy and articles of faith, and declared the American Methodist societies free and independent of the Anglican hierarchical control. At the "Christmas Conference" of Baltimore in 1784 some sixty lay preachers agreed to accept Wesley's proposals and formed the Methodist Episcopal Church.

The phenomenal growth of the Methodist church was due, in part, to the itinerancy which enabled the Methodist preachers to follow, if not to anticipate, the frontiersman on his westward trek; in part, to the emotional type of religion, which compensated somewhat for the loneliness of the frontier; in part, to the ceaseless drive of the Methodist preachers, to whom Bishop Asbury granted no "winter quarters." [50]

Theological differences have generally not been considered ground for divisions among Methodists. Questions of polity, however, have brought about separations. The two German Methodist bodies, the United Brethren and the Evangelical Church, were excluded from membership in the Methodist church by Bishop Asbury merely because of their language. More serious was the schism over the episcopal form of government. When Asbury assumed what some considered autocratic powers, James O'Kelly led a secession to establish a nonepiscopal body. In 1827 the Methodist Protestant Church was organized on the principle that ecclesiastical authority rests with the people and not with the clergy. Subsequently other nonepiscopal bodies were formed. [51] Another vexing problem was occasioned by the Negro question. As early as 1800 the Negroes of the North formed separate organizations because they believed that they were not fairly treated in the white churches. The most significant division was caused by the slavery question. The early Methodists had opposed slavery; in fact, the General Rules of 1784 forbade the purchase of slaves and demanded the gradual emancipation of slaves. For alleged economic reasons the Southern Methodists defended the institution of slavery and finally in 1845 broke with the Northern Methodists. [52]

During the first quarter of the present century liberal theology gained a strong foothold among the Northern Methodists and to a limited degree also among Southern Methodists. But the introduction of liberalism among the Methodists did not cause such a violent controversy as did the infiltration of liberalism in the Calvinistic Presbyterian church. Theologians who had been brought up in the Calvinistic tradition had to do a complete turnabout in theology before they could accept liberal theology, while liberalism is somewhat congenial to the theological atmosphere of Methodism. This fact becomes apparent from a com-

[50] Sweet, *Rel. on Am. Fr.*, p. 51 ff. (see fn. 46); also his *C. Rider Days.* Elizabeth K. Nottingham, *Methodism and the Frontier* (New York: Columbia Univ. Press, 1941). See also Charles A. Johnson, *The Frontier Camp Meeting: Religion's Harvest Time* (Dallas: Southern Methodist University Press, 1955).

[51] J. Minton Batten, "Division in American Methodism" in Anderson, pp. 51—64; Paul N. Garber, *The Methodists Are One People* (Nashville: Cokesbury Press, 1939), pp. 21—33. — James O'Kelly was prominently identified with the establishment of the Christian Church.

[52] Garber, pp. 37—71. Cp. Buckley, p. 407 ff. See also J. Beverly F. Shaw, *The Negro in the History of Methodism* (Nashville: Parthenon Press, 1954).

parison of the theological premises of Methodism with the three basic assumptions of modernism.[53]

1. The source of religious knowledge as well as the standard of religious values is religious experience. Reliance on religious experience was one of Wesley's principles, and in this respect Schleiermacher's basic premise bears considerable similarity to Wesleyanism. A prominent Methodist points out that in the 18th century Wesley had taught the preachers to listen to the voice of religious experience, and less than a century later Schleiermacher trained the scientific theologians to do the same thing.[54]

2. Certain cosmic and divine factors assure man's growth into a meaningful personality. This basic assumption is predicated on the belief that the universe is controlled by a law-abiding order and that in man the forces for good are stronger than the forces for evil. Wes-

ley's views concerning the Father's universal love and man's own freedom of choice are not too far removed from the second basic assumption of liberalism.

3. Religion has the responsibility to transform all social institutions according to the social ethics promulgated by Jesus. It seems to be only a short step from Wesley's ideal of individual perfection to the liberal's ideal of social perfection.[55] The liberal theologians within the Methodist church could justifiably consider themselves to be in the tradition of Wesleyanism; however, they drew conclusions far beyond those which Wesley drew. The conservative Methodists were stymied in their efforts to check the inroads to modernism, for, on the one hand, the Methodist discipline applies no doctrinal test to its clergy,[56] and, on the other, Methodist polity grants almost unlimited powers to the episcopacy in dealing with dissenting

[53] Cf. Edwin A. Burtt, *Types of Religious Philosophy* (New York: Harper & Brothers, 1939), ch. viii, esp. 348 f. Cp. also Mayer, "Lib. Theol. and the Ref. Ch." (fn. 26).

[54] Cp. Lee, p. 302. Clarence Seidenspinner, "Church for Tomorrow," *The Christian Century*, Oct. 4, 1944: "The sermon fifty years hence will be the result of a community of thought. It will reflect the fact that the church is a research foundation where groups of people are at work exploring human experience."

[55] For an analysis by Methodists on the impact of Wesley's theology on liberalism, see Lee, ch. xii.

[56] For admission to the ministry the preacher is to be asked the following questions:

1. Have you faith in Christ?
2. Are you going on to perfection?
3. Do you expect to be made perfect in love in this life?
4. Are you earnestly striving after it?
5. Are you resolved to devote yourself wholly to God and His work?
6. Do you know the General rules of our church?
7. Will you keep them?
8. Have you studied the doctrines of The Methodist Church?
9. After full examination do you believe that our doctrines are in harmony with the Holy Scriptures?
10. Will you preach and maintain them?
11. Have you studied our form of church discipline and polity?
12. Do you approve our church government and polity?
13. Will you support and maintain them?
14. Will you diligently instruct the children in every place?
15. Will you visit from house to house?
16. Will you recommend fasting or abstinence, both by precept and example?

members.[57] In the Methodist church the issue between the modernists and the fundamentalists centered in the areas of religious publications and the training of ministers. The publication of the Sunday school literature and of the practical and devotional literature for the laity was and still is in the hands of liberals.[58] The same seems to be true of the Commission on Ministerial Training, which is instructed to guide the reading of such men as prepare by private study for the Methodist ministry. The list of required and suggested books is predominantly in the liberal tradition.[59] In recent years The Methodist Church has emphasized the need of formal theological training of its ministers. Of its ten accredited seminaries the best known are no doubt the Boston University School of Theology, Drew Theological Seminary, and Garrett Biblical Institute. These schools have largely taught the traditional liberal theology.[60] However,

17. Are you determined to employ all your time in the work of God?
18. Are you in debt so as to embarrass you in your work?
19. Will you observe the following directions?
    a. Be diligent. Never be unemployed. Never be triflingly employed. Never trifle away time; neither spend any more time at one place than is strictly necessary.
    b. Be punctual. Do everything exactly at the time. And do not mend our rules, but keep them; not for wrath, but for conscience' sake.

[57] Cole, ch. viii: "'The Essentialists' and the Methodist Episcopal Church." Cole is much prejudiced against fundamentalism.

[58] In October, 1941, the *Abingdon Quarterly* — the Sunday school lessons for the entire Methodist church — initiated a new series of lessons under the title "Some Great Christian Teachings," which contain extremely radical statements concerning the person and work of Christ. The *Christian Advocate,* the well-known Methodist weekly, has consistently carried articles written entirely in the liberal tradition.

[59] For a list of these prescribed readings see B. of Disc., 1944, pp. 585 to 591.

[60] Cp. Anderson, pp. 185—87. Since the days of Borden Parker Bowne the Boston Univ. School of Theol. has advocated a philosophical doctrine known as "Personalism."

"Personalism" is a philosophical system in which persons are the sole metaphysical realities as well as the only ultimate intrinsic values. . . . In the main personalism has appeared in theology as a liberal "modernistic" force, defending the concept of an omnipotent and absolute God but more recently developing the idea of a God whose will is limited by factors not created by that will. . . . Liberal personalists incline toward an ethical, personal, rational reinterpretation of Christian thought about the Trinity (modalism), the incarnation (rejecting the two natures), inspiration, revelation (denying the revelation of fixed dogmas), the sacraments, conversion, and salvation. Personalists tend toward Semi-Pelagianism and toward Arminian rather than Calvinistic views.

Cp. Vergilius Ferm, ed., *An Encyclopedia of Religion* (New York: The Philosophical Library, 1945), p. 576. Henry Nelson Wieman and Bernard E. Meland, *American Philosophies of Religion* (Chicago: Willett, Clark & Co., 1936), pp. 132—45; 318—25. The theology of Garrett Biblical Institute has been determined very largely by Harris F. Rall, whose liberalism is clearly evident in his *Christianity* (New York: Scribner's, 1940), his *Religion as Salvation* (New York: Abingdon-Cokesbury Press, 1953), and in his *The God of Our Faith* (New York: Abingdon Press, c. 1955); see also David Wesley Soper, *Men Who Shape Belief* (Phila.: The Westminster Press, 1955), "Harris Franklin Rall: A Theology of Rational Faith," pp. 112—28.

there has been a reaction against the coarse liberalism of the first twenty-five years of this century both among Methodists and among leaders of other denominations.[61]

No other American denomination supported the social gospel as wholeheartedly as did the Methodist church. Undoubtedly Wesley's strong views on individual perfection became the springboard for advocating social perfection. The adherents of Wesley have always considered it the duty of the church not only to stress the infinite worth of each person as a child of God but also to save him from every influence in his personal and social life which would harm or destroy his personality. The Methodist Church has adopted an elaborate "social creed" which sets forth both the premises and the program of the social gospel.[62] Some of the more liberal theologians adopted the Ritschlian principle that Christ's kingdom of the New Testament is primarily a worldly kingdom, the coming of which is dependent on the improvement of our social, industrial, political, and economic life. The 1944 Episcopal address insisted that the Christian ethic must be applied to the economic order and that co-operation in government, industry, labor, and agriculture would lead toward a guaranteed annual income and hasten the coming of the kingdom of God on earth.[63] It is true that the Christian church has frequently

---

[61] This is true esp. in Edwin Lewis, Drew Theological Seminary, who in his *Christian Manifesto*, published in 1943, challenged a purely humanistic type of religion as advocated by many liberal theologians and who spearheaded neo-orthodoxy in the Methodist church. See also Soper, *Major Voices in American Theology* (Philadelphia: The Westminster Press, c. 1953), pp. 15—36, and Carl Michalson, "The Edwin Lewis Myth," *The Christian Century*, LXXVII (1960), 217—219.

[62] In 1912 the Methodist Church adopted the following social creed: We stand for equal rights and complete justice for all men in all stations of life; for the principle of conciliation and arbitration in industrial dissensions; for the protection of the worker from dangerous machinery, occupational diseases, injuries, and mortality; for the abolition of child labor; for such regulations of the conditions of labor for women as shall safeguard the physical and moral health of the community; for the suppression of the "sweating system"; for the gradual and reasonable reduction of the hours of labor to the lowest practical point, with work for all; and for that degree of leisure for all which is the condition of the highest human life; for a release from employment one day in seven; for a living wage in every industry; for the highest wage that each industry can afford and for the most equitable division of the products of industry that can ultimately be devised for the recognition of the Golden Rule and the mind of Christ as the supreme law of society and the sure remedy for all social ills.

C. H. Hopkins, *The Rise of the Social Gospel in American Protestantism, 1865—1915* (New Haven: Yale University Press, 1940), p. 291. See also Charles C. Cole, Jr., *The Social Ideas of the Northern Evangelists 1826 to 1860* (New York: Columbia University Press, 1954); Timothy L. Smith, *Revivalism and Social Reform in Mid-Nineteenth Century America* (New York: Abingdon Press, 1957); Robert Moats Miller, *American Protestantism and Social Issues, 1919—1939* (Chapel Hill, N. C.: The University of North Carolina Press, 1958), a very solid inquiry; and Paul A. Carter, *The Decline and Revival of the Social Gospel: Social and Political Liberalism in American Protestant Churches, 1920—1940* (Ithaca: Cornell University Press, 1954).

[63] *B. of Disc.*, 1944 ed., p. 577 f. E. Stanley Jones, *The Christ of the American Road* (cp. *C. T. M.*, XV [1944], p. 808). Neve, *Ch. and Sects,*

failed to instruct her members concerning the social implications of the Gospel. But it is tantamount to a denial of the Christian Gospel when a church body goes to the opposite extreme and finds the heart of the Christian message in a plan of action which will so change our social institutions that every human being will have ample opportunity to develop into a strong Christian personality.

Since 1939 the Methodists regard themselves a united people. After many futile efforts to unite all Methodists into one body the Plan of Union was prepared in 1934. This plan looked toward the merger of the two large episcopal bodies (commonly known as Northern and as Southern Methodists) and the nonepiscopal Methodist Protestant Church. The three bodies differed purely in matters of church polity. The theological basis for the union could therefore be summed up in the brief statement: "The Articles of Religion shall be those historically held in common by the three uniting churches." [64] The two episcopal bodies had separated because of the slavery question and its implications, and a reunion of the two was predicated very largely on the place to be assigned to the Negro conferences in the plan of unification. The two episcopal bodies and the nonepiscopal Methodist Protestant Church differed as to the form of church government, particularly the participation of the laity. The episcopal bodies maintained that ecclesiastical authority should be vested in "conferences" under the jurisdiction of a superintendent who makes the pastoral appointments for a designated area, but is under the bishops, whose responsibility covers the entire church. The nonepiscopal body held that church authority is not vested in the clergy, but emanates from the people "upward to

p. 343 ff. Mayer, "The Kingdom of God According to the New Testament," in *Proceedings of the Texas District* (St. Louis: C. P. H., 1942). In *By This Sign Conquer*, Bishop G. Bromley Oxnam stated in 1943 that the Kingdom to seek is the rule of God in human society, in "a co-operative social order" in which "the sacredness of every personality is recognized" and in which "every individual finds opportunity for the fullest self-expression of which he is capable." In this kingdom "each individual" gives himself "for ends that are socially valuable." The impulse to serve will be stronger than the impulse to acquire. Differences in talent and capacity mean "proportional responsibilities and ministry" to the common good. Quoted by Charles Macfarland, *A Survey of Religious Literature*, 1943, p. 98 f. In *The Church and Contemporary Change* (New York: Macmillan Co., 1950), Bishop Oxnam maintains that the tensions of our society must be dissolved by the democratic process, but with due recognition of the social and economic forces now at work. He maintains that capitalistic individualism is on the way out and that the welfare state is approaching. In this change the minister must lead the procession. However, he dare "never forget that in an hour of changing environment the central message of Christianity is one of salvation. . . . All social change in which the minister labors has as its final objective the salvation of the human soul, the reconciliation of man with man, and man with God." Oxnam maintains that in reconstructing the social order the primary task of the church is to convert the individual. Naturally the question arises: How will the church act in reconstructing our order if either capital or labor does not yield to the influence of the Gospel? Cp. *The Luth. Q.*, Aug., 1951, p. 319 f., and *C. T. M.*, Feb., 1952, p. 159.

[64] *B. of Disc., Constitution*, Art. III. The Articles of Religion referred to are the Twenty-Five Articles prepared by Wesley. There were a few voices of protest against the Northern Methodists' toleration of liberalism, and ultimately not all joined the new union.

the pastor." To meet the practical problems, the Plan of Union provided for the following types of conferences: (1) The General Conference, composed of an equal number of clergymen and laymen and constituting the supreme legislative body. (2) Five jurisdictional conferences for the white churches — one for each larger section of the U. S. A. — and one Negro jurisdictional conference overlapping the white conferences. The jurisdictional conference functions in the promotional and administrative affairs and actually constitutes the center of Methodist activity. (3) The annual conference is the major unit for governing the local parishes. (4) The judicial conference is the final authority in all constitutional matters. The participation of laymen in all conferences is a distinct departure from the former practice in the episcopal bodies. The Council of Bishops continues the historic itinerant general superintendency and supervises the spiritual and physical affairs of the entire church.[65]

Methodists contend that in the tradition of Wesley the Methodist church is probably the most ecumenical-minded body. Some of its leaders envision the organic union of all Christian bodies, at least of all non-Roman bodies.[66] Because of its historical and psychological approach to religion, Methodism is said to be especially well qualified to serve as a sort of pivotal point for the union of

all churches. Wesley and his adherents are said to have retained the great liturgical treasures as these were preserved in the Anglican church. He also placed great emphasis on a personal religious experience of God's love and the saving grace of Christ, and by this psychological approach Methodism is said to recognize the significance of the individual. Methodists played a prominent part in forming the Federal Council of Churches and have participated in the various conferences which ultimately led to the forming of the World Council of Churches.[67]

The Methodist church has been characterized as follows:

In many ways it is our most characteristic church. It is short on theology, long on good works, brilliantly organized, primarily middle-class, frequently bigoted, incurably optimistic, zealously missionary, and touchingly confident of the essential goodness of the man next door.[68]

Exploratory discussions looking to eventual union are being carried on between The Methodist Church and both the Protestant Episcopal Church in the U. S. A. and the Evangelical United Brethren Church.

The Southern Methodist Church. This body is a continuation of the Methodist Episcopal Church South. It came into being when several thousand

---

[65] *B. of Disc., Constitution.* Cp. John M. Moore, *The Long Road to Methodist Union* (Nashville: Abingdon-Cokesbury, 1938). Ch. x, esp. p. 192. Paul N. Garber, ch. vii. The *Christian Advocate*, May 19, 1938, pp. 486—90, offers a comprehensive picture of the Methodist church polity.

[66] E. Stanley Jones has advocated a union of all churches throughout the world, patterned somewhat after our country's Federal Union, in which each denomination would retain certain rights as the separate states in the Union and the church of the world would constitute the uniting factor. The Methodist Ecumenical Conference, comprising the Methodists of the world, was organized in 1881.

[67] Ivan Lee Holt, "Methodism and Ecumenical Christianity," Anderson, pp. 283—90.

[68] Editorial in *Life*, Nov. 19, 1947. On the various denominational activities, cf. *B. of Disc.*, Part VII and Appendix.

Southern Methodists declined to take part in the 1939 merger.[69]

The Fundamental Methodist Church, Incorporated, withdrew from The Methodist Church in 1942.

The African Methodist Episcopal Church. This church was organized by Richard Allen in 1816 in Philadelphia because of prevailing racial discriminations. It is now the second largest Methodist body.

The African Methodist Episcopal Zion Church. This church was founded in 1796 in New York on account of the humiliating treatment accorded Negroes in the white churches.

The Christian Methodist Episcopal Church, established in 1870, when the white and colored congregations of the Methodist Episcopal Church South amicably agreed to separate. Until 1956 this body was officially known as the Colored Methodist Episcopal Church.

The Union American Methodist Episcopal Church. This small body was founded in 1813, in Wilmington, Del.

The Independent African Methodist Episcopal Denomination, a small body which separated from the African Methodist Episcopal Church on questions of administration.

The Reformed Zion Union Apostolic Church, a small Negro body, founded in 1869 at Boydton, Va.

The Reformed Methodist Union Episcopal Church was founded in 1885.

Most of the following churches separated from the former Methodist Episcopal Church in protest against the episcopalian form of church government. As a result they are all congregational and nonepiscopal in church government. Practically all these smaller Methodist groups stress the doctrine of entire sanctification, and some are highly emotional.

The Congregational Methodist Church was organized in 1852 in protest against episcopal church polity.

The Congregational Methodist Church of the U. S. A. is an unincorporated counterpart of the former body.

The Cumberland Methodist Church withdrew from the Congregational Methodist Church in 1950.

The New Congregational Methodist Church is a small nonepiscopal body founded in 1881.

The Wesleyan Methodist Church of America came into existence in 1843 partly in opposition to episcopacy, but primarily in protest against slavery. This body continues its separate existence because of the conviction that entire sanctification as a specific Wesleyan doctrine does not receive proper emphasis in other Methodist groups. Members dare not use or manufacture intoxicants nor hold membership in secret societies. In 1958 the *Missionary Bands of the World, Incorporated,* organized among Free Methodist Church young people by Vivian A. Dake in 1885, merged with the Wesleyan Methodist Church of America. Negotiations for union of the merged body with the Pilgrim Holiness Church are under way.

The Free Methodist Church of North America was organized by B. T. Roberts at Pekin, N. Y., in 1860, because he and his associates believed that worldliness, a strong ecclesiastical machinery, toleration of slavery, and membership in secret societies were doing great harm to true Methodism. The members of this group are fundamentalists in theology and very emotional in their worship. They stress entire sanctification. Other features are the insistence that the members do not use or manufacture intoxicants and the exclusion of instrumental music and choir singing from the churches. Their superintendents, corresponding some-

[69] Elmer T. Clark, *The Small Sects in America* (Nashville: Abingdon-Cokesbury, 1949), pp. 60—68.

what to the bishops in the Methodist Episcopal churches, are elected for a term of four years. In the conferences laymen have the same representation as ministers.

The Primitive Methodist Church. This church had its origin in England in 1812, after Lorenzo Dow, an American revivalist, had conducted a series of camp meetings according to the American pattern. Because their meetings were extremely emotional, they were known as "Ranters." They became established in America during the first half of the last century. In polity this body is congregational.

The African Union First Colored Methodist Protestant Church, Incorporated, and the *Free Christian Zion Church of Christ* are small Negro bodies.

The Evangelical Methodist Church

was organized in 1946 in protest against modernism.

The Bible Protestant Church was organized in 1939 by the Eastern Conference of the Methodist Protestant Church as a protest against the Kansas City merger, particularly the implied fellowship with liberal theologians. It tends more toward Calvinism in its acceptance of verbal inspiration, eternal security, premillennialism, rejection of infant baptism.

The Holiness Methodist Church, a small body organized at Grand Forks, N. Dak., in 1909. The present name was adopted in 1920.

The Lumber River Annual Conference of the Holiness Methodist Church was formed in North Carolina in 1900. It is not a part of the Holiness Methodist Church described in the preceding paragraph.

BIBLIOGRAPHY

PART V

SECTION I AND II

John Wesley

Burtner, Robert W., and Robert E. Chiles, eds. *A Compend of Wesley's Theology.* New York: Abingdon Press, 1954.

Cell, George C. *The Rediscovery of John Wesley.* New York: Henry Holt and Co., 1935.

Deschner, John. *Wesley's Christology.* Dallas: Southern Methodist University Press, 1960.

Haddal, Ingvar. *John Wesley.* London: The Epworth Press, 1961.

Lee, Umphrey. *John Wesley and Modern Religion.* Nashville: Cokesbury Press, 1936.

McConnell, Frances J. *John Wesley.* New York: Abingdon Press, 1939.

Piette, Maximin. *John Wesley in the Evolution of Protestantism.* New York: Sheed and Ward, 1937.

Turner, George Allen. *The More Excellent Way: The Spiritual Basis of the Wesleyan Message.* Winona Lake: Light and Life Press, 1952.

Williams, Colin W. *John Wesley's Theology Today.* New York: Abingdon Press, c. 1960.

History of Methodism

Brady, J. W. *England: Before and After Wesley.* New York: Harper & Bros., 1939.

Buckley, J. M. *History of Methodists in the U. S. A.* ("American Church History Series"). New York: The Christian Literature Co., 1894. Vol. V.

Luccock, Halford E., and Paul Hutchinson. *Story of Methodism.* Nashville: Cokesbury Press. Rev. ed., 1950.

Norwood, Frederick A. "Methodist Historical Studies, 1930—1959," *Church History,* XXVIII (1959), 319—417, and XXIX (1960), 74—88.

Sweet, William Warren. *Circuit Rider Days Along the Ohio.* New York: Methodist Book Concern, 1923.

———. *Methodism in American History,* 2d ed., Nashville: Abingdon Press, 1954.

Doctrinal Emphases

Anderson, William K., ed. *Methodism.* New York: Methodist Publ. House, 1947. Twenty-five essays by leading Methodists on important phases of Methodist beliefs and practices.

Flew, R. Newton. *The Idea of Perfection in Christian Theology.* New York: Oxford University Press, 1934.

Goodloe, Robert W. *The Sacraments in Methodism.* Nashville: The Methodist Publishing House, 1953.

Harmon, Nolan B. *The Organization of the Methodist Church,* 2d ed., Nashville: The Methodist Publishing House, 1953.

———. *Understanding the Methodist Church.* Nashville: The Methodist Publishing House, 1955.

———, ed. *Book of Discipline.* New York: Methodist Publ. House. Published quadrennially.

Rowe, J. T. *The Meaning of Methodism.* Nashville: Cokesbury Press, 1926.

Sangster, W. E. *Path to Perfection.* American ed. Nashville: Abingdon-Cokesbury Press, 1943.

Sheldon, H. C. "Changes in Theology Among the American Methodists," *American Journal of Theology,* X, 31—52.

Modern Methodism

Clark, Elmer T. "Methodism," in Vergilius Ferm, ed. *The American Church of the Protestant Heritage.* New York: Philosophical Library, 1953. Pp. 313—30.

Cole, Steward G. *The History of Fundamentalism.* New York: Richard R. Smith Co., 1931.

Garber, P. N. *The Methodists Are One People.* Nashville: Abingdon-Cokesbury Press, 1939.

Schilling, S. Paul. *Methodism and Society in Historical Perspective.* Nashville: Abingdon Press, c. 1960. A social history of Methodism to 1908, emphasizing how the church interacted with its secular environment.

Schofield, Charles E. *We Methodists.* New York: Methodist Publ. House, 1939. Written after the merger of the three largest Methodist bodies.

Straughn, James H. *Inside Methodist Union.* Nashville: Abingdon Press, 1958.

SECTION III

The Holiness Bodies

In this section the term "Holiness bodies" is used in the wider sense to include all those denominations and associations which in some form owe their origin to the Holiness Movement inaugurated shortly after the Civil War. Two wings were represented in this movement. The one was composed of the Holiness bodies, i. e., all those groups who claimed loyalty to the true Wesleyan tradition. They believed that the New Testament baptism of the Holy Spirit was the Spirit's act of "entire sanctification," an instantaneous and total cleasing from sin and an entire and abiding devotion to God. The other wing was composed of those who taught that ordinarily the baptism with the Holy Ghost is a natural accompaniment of so-called speaking in other tongues. The latter group was, and still is, given more or less to the ecstatic, sometimes manifesting itself in shouting, dancing, and trances.[1] Frequently these two wings are distinguished by the designations "holiness" and "Pentecostal," also "perfectionist" and "charismatic." The two groups sometimes also are distinguished as to their original historical background. The former are said to be rooted in Wesleyan theology, while the latter owe their Pentecostal propensity to the highly developed subjectivism of the Baptists. This differentiation is only partly correct, since each branch shares, at least to a certain extent, some basic characteristics of the other.[2] For the purpose of this book it will do to classify them as perfectionist and Pentecostal bodies. In addition to these two larger groupings, there are several loosely organized fellowships that have dedicated themselves to the spreading of the doctrine of entire holiness, the so-called Evangelical Associations.

History

MODERN PERFECTIONISTS

The history of the present American perfectionist bodies is intimately associated with several important revivals during the nineteenth century. Chief among these was undoubtedly the revival under Charles Finney, who more than any other man was responsible for formulating and popularizing the doctrine of entire sanctification during the nineteenth century. Finney, an Arminian theologian, maintained that man inherits sin solely by his own free choice; that conversion is man's personal surrender, effected by his own choice and effort, usually under a great emotional strain; that entire sanctification includes complete freedom from evil thoughts and is an instantaneous act subsequent to conversion; and that this perfect liberation from sin is the normal experience of Christians.[3]

However, the modern Holiness bodies were brought into being chiefly by the national Holiness Movement. After the Civil War, a spirit of worldliness entered the churches. To counteract this downward trend several local revivals were initiated. These revivals, held for the most part under the auspices of Methodists, were designed to lead to the experience of entire sanctification and to engender the usual emotional phenomena.

---

1 Redford, Foreword. The widely-publicized practices of some mountaineer extremists, such as snake-handling and drinking poison, are discountenanced by the organized Pentecostal bodies.

2 Clark, *Small Sects*, p. 16 ff., distinguishes between the perfectionist, or subjectivist, sects (ch. iii) and the Pentecostal, or charismatic, sects (ch. iv). This Methodist leader and scholar includes among the perfectionist sects: fifteen small Methodist bodies, the Methodist-related bodies, Church of the Nazarene and other more conservative holiness denominations, the Evangelistic Associations, the Quakers, the Oxford Group Movement. As Pentecostal, or charismatic, bodies Clark classifies those groups whose worship is characterized by glossolalia and trances. Frequently these movements attract the socially and economically "disinherited." It seems, however, that as the social and economic conditions improve, the extremely emotional and the unconventional elements in their beliefs and practice gradually disappear. Walter G. Muelder "From Sect to Church," *Christendom*, 1945, pp. 450—62.

3 Charles Finney (1792—1875) was originally a Presbyterian minister, but disavowed the principles and implications of Calvinism. After a tremendously successful period of revivalism, 1824—1832, he became professor of theology at Oberlin (Ohio) College and prepared large numbers of students for evangelistic and revivalistic work. He is called the founder of "Oberlin theology," the center of which is the Arminian principle of

It is one of the paradoxes of history that the doctrine for which in Wesley's opinion the Methodist people had been raised up had all but disappeared from this church body. In practice and gradually also in theory the Methodist church no longer championed Wesley's doctrine of perfection.[4] This was indirectly one of the causes for several schisms in Methodism. In their reaction against the alleged departure from Methodist doctrine the majority of small Methodist bodies, especially the Holy Rollers, espoused a theory of sanctification more extreme than Wesley's.[5] By 1867 the national Holiness Movement had gained such a large following among the Methodists that "holiness" became the watchword in theory and practice. Between 1880 and 1900 the Methodist family was divided into holiness and antiholiness groups. The bishops of the Methodist churches viewed these movements with alarm and in 1894 stated in their Pastoral Letter:

There has sprung up among us a party with "holiness" as a watchword. . . . Religious experience is represented as though it consisted of only two steps, the first step out of condemnation into peace and the next into Christian perfection. The effect is to disparage the new birth and all stages of spiritual growth if there be not professed perfect holiness. Such terms as "saints," "sanctified," are restricted to the few who have reached the height of perfect purity and improperly denied to the body of believers.[6]

A relatively large number of preachers and laymen in several other Protestant groups and in widely scattered sections of our country shared the views of these "holiness" groups. At first they organized only prayer bands within their respective denominations and local churches, *ecclesiolae in ecclesia*. But they felt ill at ease among the "antiholiness" people of their respective bodies and therefore formed separate church bodies with "holiness" as their watchword.

MODERN PENTECOSTALS

Manifestations akin in one way or another to modern Pentecostalism have appeared throughout the church's history. The stress has been on "a theology of the Holy Spirit," a theology in which the Holy Spirit is said to manifest His presence and immediate operation by the so-called Pentecostal gifts. The earliest

man's freedom in spiritual matters. Foster, *Gen. Hist.* Richard E. Day, *Man of Like Passions* (Grand Rapids: Zondervan Publishing House, 1942), is a popular and extremely sympathetic biography. — J. H. Noyes, founder of the Oneida Community, was converted in one of Finney's revival meetings and seems at first glance to have advocated some of Finney's principles of perfection. However, the notorious excesses at Oneida had nothing in common with the Finney movement. Cp. Beardsley, *Hist. of Chr. in Am.*, p. 150 ff. — See also William G. McLoughlin, Jr., *Modern Revivalism: Charles Grandison Finney to Billy Graham* (New York: Ronald Press, 1959). — For a critique of the Oberlin theology by a modern perfectionist see Hills, ch. iii.

[4] Indicative of the theological shift which has occurred in the Methodist church is the 1935 revision of the second stanza of "Love Divine," which now reads, "Let us find the promised rest," instead of "that second rest," i. e., a second work of grace. Clark, *Sm. Sects*, p. 58. — See also John Leland Peters, *Christian Perfection and American Methodism* (New York: Abingdon Press, c. 1956).

[5] See "The Methodist Bodies," P. V., Sec. II. Cp. also Clark, *Small Sects*, pp. 56—68.

[6] Du Bose, *History of Methodism*, II, 90 ff. . Clark, *Small Sects*, p. 72 ff.

and in many respects the most typical form of Pentecostalism was Montanism. In the course of history Pentecostalism has appeared in various forms, notably in the mystic's ecstatic experiences of levitation, visions, trances, and in the weird physical and psychical phenomena of numerous cults. But basically ancient and modern Pentecostalism fosters a theology of the Holy Spirit which lays greater emphasis on exhibiting the alleged charismatic gifts than on the person and work of the Holy Spirit. Some have even professed to see a set pattern of social, economic, and religious behavior in the rise and growth of Pentecostalism. Periods of economic prosperity, these say, secularize the church and provide no stimulus for a charismatic movement. Such a movement, they hold, arises during or immediately after great national or cosmic catastrophes, when there is a yearning for Christ's early return; or during periods of widespread religious apathy, when the "groaning after holiness" is more in evidence.[7]

The Jonathan Edwards Revival of 1734 is frequently listed as the first American manifestation of Pentecostalism. However, it is first only in so far as it was accompanied by unusual and violent physical reactions expressing both fear and joy.[8] The Kentucky Revival, especially at Cane Ridge, at the beginning of the nineteenth century, manifested psychological phenomena of a greater variety, deeper intensity, and more weird emotionalism than any other similar movement in modern times.[9]

The modern Pentecostal movement in the United States and Canada began toward the close of the last century. It was at first known as the Latter Rain Movement. It seems that this term originated with the adherents of the elder and the younger R. G. Spurling, revivalists, who conducted meetings in Tennessee and North Carolina. These

---

[7] These generalizations have been disputed. The depression of the thirties apparently did not usher in the great revival many expected. Kincheloe, pp. 92—96. Nor did the great revival of religion which was anticipated as a certain sequel to World War II materialize.

[8] See Clark, *Sm. Sects,* p. 89. Ola E. Winslow, *Jonathan Edwards* (New York: The Macmillan Co., 1940), pp. 96—267. It is extremely difficult to explain the physical phenomena under Edwards' ministry, inasmuch as they seem entirely foreign to his manner of preaching and especially to his theology. He read his carefully prepared manuscript with little or no modulation and, contrary to revivalist technique, made his appeal to the intellect rather than to the emotions. The first revivalist outburst in 1734 resulted largely from the series of sermons on "Justification," which "seem to be less sermons than highly theological disquisitions." Furthermore, he was a Calvinist and his theology was therefore not at all congenial to revivalism, which usually flourishes in the soil of the Arminian doctrine of man's spiritual freedom. But he found himself constrained to modify his Calvinistic position of divine determinism after the experiences of 1734. A strict Calvinist could not have preached the famous sermon "Sinners in the Hands of an Angry God," delivered in 1741, with its strange combination of deterministic and freewill theology. Edwards reminds those who "may have reformed your life in many things" but "were never born again" that God's "sovereign pleasure, His arbitrary will," may cast them to hell at any moment. "The God that holds you over the pit of hell, much as one holds a spider over the fire, abhors you. . . . 'Tis a great furnace . . . that you are held over in the hand of that God whose wrath is provoked. . . . You hang by a slender thread with flames of divine wrath ready every moment to singe it." H. Norman Gardiner, ed., *Selected Sermons of Jonathan Edwards* (New York: Macmillan Co., 1904), p. 88.

[9] This revival was in a large measure responsible for the organization of several unionizing bodies. Cp. P. VI, Sec. IV.

people believed that the "former rain" in Joel 2:28 ff. was a prophecy of the speaking in tongues on the first Pentecost, the beginning of the Christian era. The "latter rain" in this prophecy was said to refer to another widespread "speaking in tongues" at the end of the Christian era and immediately prior to Christ's premillennial coming. Early in the twentieth century Pentecostal revivals occurred in various parts of the United States and among entirely unrelated groups. These revivals were characterized by a strong emphasis upon the presence of the "spiritual" gifts, especially the speaking in an unknown tongue and divine healing as an evidence of having received the baptism with the Holy Spirit. Premillennialism also received much emphasis, and the belief in the proximity of the end of the present era developed a tremendous evangelistic and missionary enthusiasm. Pentecostal revivals occurred simultaneously in North Carolina, Tennessee, Minnesota, New England, and Ohio. The most noteworthy were the revivals under A. J. Tomlinson in Tennessee; under Charles F. Parham in Topeka, Kans., beginning in 1901; and at the Azusa Street Methodist Church, a Negro congregation in Los Angeles, in 1906 under Charles Seymour. By 1910 the term "Pentecostal Movement" was applied to all groups who taught the need for the experience of the baptism in the Holy Spirit evidenced by the speaking in tongues. Since there were a large number of independent movements, serious and essential differences in matters of doctrine and practice developed. In 1914 E. N. Bell and several representative Pentecostal preachers organized the General Council, which ultimately became the Assemblies of God, the largest of the Pentecostal groups.[10]

Doctrinal Emphases

There is a basic doctrinal affinity between the perfectionist and the Pentecostal wings of the Holiness bodies. The dogmatical points of emphasis among the perfectionist bodies are expressed adequately in the doctrinal statement of the Church of the Nazarene:

We deem belief in the following sufficient: (1) in one God, the Father, Son, and Holy Ghost; (2) in the plenary inspiration of the Old and New Testaments; (3) that man is born with a fallen nature and is therefore inclined to evil, and that continually; (4) that the finally impenitent are hopelessly and eternally lost; (5) that the atonement through Jesus is for the whole human race and that whosoever repents and believes on the Lord Jesus Christ is justified and regenerated and saved from the dominion of sin; (6) that the believers are to be sanctified wholly, subsequent to regeneration through faith in the Lord Jesus; (7) that the Holy Spirit bears witness to the new birth and also to entire sanctification of believers; (8) in the return of our Lord,

---

[10] Frodsham contains the most detailed history of the modern Pentecostal movement. Clark, *Sm. Sects*, p. 100 ff., and W. Gordon Brown, p. 82, describe certain phases of the movement. See also Ethel E. Goss, *The Winds of God: The Story of the Early Pentecostal Days (1901—1914) in the Life of Howard A. Goss* (New York: Comet Press, 1958); Homer A. Tomlinson, ed., *Diary of A. J. Tomlinson, Founder of the Church of God, General Overseer 1903—1943 — Outstanding Leader of the Pentecostal and Holiness Movement* (Queens Village, N. Y.: The Church of God World Headquarters, c. 1949), 3 vols. — Pentecostalism became widespread in the Scandinavian countries. In England it was at first identified with the Keswick Conference and was known as the Oxford Holiness Movement. C. E. Beardman and R. Pearsall Smith, two American revivalists, popularized Pentecostalism in Continental Europe, esp. in Germany.

in the resurrection of the dead, and in the final Judgment.[11]

Typical of the theology current among the Pentecostal groups is the Statement of Faith contained in the Constitution of the Pentecostal Fellowship of North America:

(1) We believe the Bible to be the inspired, the only infallible, authoritative Word of God; (2) that there is one God, eternally existent in three persons: Father, Son, and Holy Ghost; (3) in the deity of our Lord Jesus Christ, in His virgin birth, in His sinless life, in His miracles, in His vicarious and atoning sacrifice through His shed blood, in His bodily resurrection, in His ascension to the right hand of the Father, and in His personal return in power and glory; (4) that for the salvation of lost and sinful men regeneration by the Holy Spirit is absolutely essential; (5) that the full gospel includes holiness of heart and life, healing for the body and the baptism in the Holy Spirit with the initial evidence of speaking in other tongues as the Spirit gives utterance; (6) in the present ministry of the Holy Spirit, by whose indwelling the Christian is enabled to live a godly life; (7) in the resurrection of both the saved and the lost; they that are saved unto the resurrection of life and they that are lost unto the resurrection of damnation; (8) in the spiritual unity of believers in our Lord Jesus Christ.[12]

These doctrinal summaries reveal that the difference between the two wings among the Holiness bodies lies primarily in the description of the "baptism of the Holy Ghost." The adherents of the Pentecostal wing maintain that the baptism of the Holy Ghost is the bestowal of the Pentecostal charismatic gifts. Some Pentecostals believe that all the signs mentioned in Mark 16:17, 18 are promised to the New Testament church as an abiding gift, while the majority restrict this promise to the speaking in an unknown tongue. Frequently the Pentecostals designate their message as the "full Gospel," the "foursquare Gospel." Relatively wide latitude is granted in Scripture interpretation, but the various Pentecostal groups are agreed on the following four points as constituting the essence of the Gospel: Christ the Savior, the Sanctifier, the Healer, the Coming King.[13] The perfectionist wing, on the other hand, gives less heed to the so-called Pentecostal blessing, including the speaking in tongues, and directs its attention almost exclusively to the doctrine of entire sanctification. While individual members of the perfectionist groups may advocate divine healing, the official doctrinal statements contain no reference to it.

All Holiness bodies profess the fundamental doctrines proclaimed by the

---

[11] *Manual of the History, Doctrine, Government and Ritual of the Church of the Nazarene*, 4th ed. (Kansas City, Mo.: Nazarene Publishing House, c. 1924), p. 29. Cp. Redford, p. 54 ff.

[12] Furnished by the Executive Office, General Council, Assemblies of God, Springfield, Mo.

[13] Cp. Simpson, *Fourfold Gospel*. Simpson was the founder of the Christian and Missionary Alliance. The Pilgrim Holiness Church describes the full Gospel as comprising the following four points: (1) justification for the removal of actual sins and entire sanctification for the eradication of original sin; (2) the premillennial coming of Christ; (3) divine healing; (4) the evangelization of the entire world. Aimee Semple McPherson declared that Ezekiel's vision (Ezek. 1:5 ff.) contains the cornerstones in the "Gospel Foursquare." The man in the vision is Christ, man's Savior; the lion is the power of Christ's baptism with the Holy Ghost; the ox is Jesus as Burden-bearer and Healer; and the eagle is the symbol of His premillennial coming. Cp. Marcus Bach, *They Have Found a Faith* (Indianapolis: Bobbs-Merrill, 1946), p. 76 f.

conservative Arminian bodies, and, like the fundamentalists, they are strongly premillennial.[14] The distinctive doctrines of the Holiness bodies are (1) entire sanctification as an instantaneous experience, distinct from and subsequent to conversion and regeneration; (2) the baptism with the Holy Ghost and fire. The Pentecostal wing adds (3) the baptism with the Holy Ghost manifest in the Pentecostal signs, at least in the speaking in an unknown tongue, and (4) Christ's provision for healing also of the body.

ENTIRE SANCTIFICATION

Perfectionism is the *raison d'être* of several pagan religions. It is the heart and core of several philosophical systems, and in some form it has been advocated in virtually every era of the Christian church. There are basically two roots from which perfectionism grows. The one is the Pelagian and, in part, pagan principle that man is inherently good and inherently capable of perfectibility. This is the basic principle of all New Thought cults. The other is the Arminian principle that though God requires perfection, this perfection need not be absolute and that by a special divine act He so subdues and eradicates sin that man no longer voluntarily yields to it. Frequently the modern perfectionists claim affinity with the Anabaptists, the Quakers, the Quietists, and the Pietists.[15] But the greatest impetus to the modern holiness movement was provided by the Wesleyan theology.[16] In full accord with Wesley,

the modern Holiness bodies teach that "regeneration removes the love of sin, justification the guilt of sins already committed, and sanctification the inclination to sin in the future." But modern perfectionists deviate from Wesley in several points. Wesley taught that although the evil propensities continue in the sanctified believer, they are involuntary and therefore no absolute barrier to entire holiness. The modern Holiness people, however, maintain that in the act of entire sanctification God completely frees the regenerated believers from inbred sin. Furthermore, Wesley favored the view that perfection is attained progressively. The modern perfectionists teach that entire sanctification is instantaneous and complete; it is not "*at*tainment," a gradual increase in sanctification, but "*ob*tainment," i. e., an instantaneous and perfect deliverance from all sinful inclinations.[17] Wesley held that perfection is a necessary prerequisite for entry into heaven, but he granted that ordinarily perfection is gained progressively, "moment by moment," until the hour of death. The modern perfectionists differ from Wesley and insist that since sin is in the heart and not in the body, death cannot have anything to do with the believers' perfect sanctification. The heart must be made holy now. They also say that they distinguish between "consecration" and "sanctification." Consecration is said to be entirely man's part, man's "act of devotement to God" and only a condition of sanctification, whereas sanctification is said to be the cleansing from inbred

---

[14] On the distinction between conservative Christianity and fundamentalism and on the fundamentalists' doctrine concerning the premillennial coming of Christ see P. VIII, Sec. I; P. IX, Sec. II.

[15] Redford, pp. 26, 27. C. E. Brown, p. 62 ff. Brown, the historian of the Church of God, quotes a lengthy section from Robert Barclay's *Apology* in support of the contention that the early Quakers advocated the theory of entire sanctification.

[16] Cp. Mayer, "Entire Sanctification," *C. T. M.*, III (1932), 417—29.

[17] Simpson, *Fourfold Gospel*, p. 30.

sin, an act which God alone can perform, since only the God of peace Himself can sanctify us wholly (1 Thess. 5:23).[18] Entire sanctification is described as:

A second definite work of grace in the heart, whereby we are thoroughly cleansed from all sin. Only those who are justified and walking in the favor of God can receive this grace. It is not absolute perfection; that belongs to God alone. It does not make a man infallible. It is perfect love — the pure love of God filling a clean heart. . . . It is capable of increase. It prepares for more rapid growth in grace. It may be lost, and we need to continually watch and pray. It is received by faith. It is accomplished by the baptism with the Holy Ghost and fire, which is the baptism of Jesus Christ, foretold by John the Baptist. It is loving the Lord, our God, with all the heart, soul, mind, and strength and our neighbor as ourselves. This is what the Apostles and Disciples received in the upper room at Jerusalem on the day of Pentecost. It is the inheritance of the Church, and with it comes preparation and anointing and power for the work to which God has called us. Our preachers are to definitely preach it and urge it upon all believers. It is the privilege and duty of all believers to seek and obtain it. It is this to which we are called, "That we might be made partakers of His holiness." [19]

Modern holiness preachers expressly state that entire sanctification implies and presupposes complete eradication of all inbred sin.[20] This view is based on the claim that original sin does not involve guilt until it is approved by the free agent. Nevertheless, God is not pleased with the unlovely fruits which are produced by our "moral disease."

Therefore it is not sufficient that man has forgiveness of his actual or voluntary sins, but "he must have relief in the 'basement story' of his moral nature." Regeneration, in the opinion of the Holiness bodies, can only correct the evil will and renew man's free will, so that the Christian is inclined to good. But it does not eradicate nor entirely remove the wayward tendencies. Therefore Christ has procured, they say, "a full salvation," "salvation to the uttermost," not only covering our voluntary transgressions by His forgiveness, or by justification, but also destroying sin by "sanctification." In a similar vein some writers maintain that God in his justification of sinners

cannot reach original sin, since justification is pardon; and original sin cannot be pardoned, since it involves no guilt. The conclusion, then, is: I stand a justified man with inherited depravity within me. Nor can regeneration correct man's inherited depravity, for it affects only man's personal depravity, man's personal evil will. But original sin is more than an act of the will. It is the involuntary waywardness of the flesh. But since God demands not only an actual obedience, but also holy dispositions, therefore only entire sanctification, an obedience of acts, can separate the sinner from all involuntary tendencies. . . . A fully saved heart can look up into the face of Jesus and without mental reservation say, "Thy will be done," while the whole nature responds, "Amen." . . . But if depravity remain, it will rebel and refuse to yield.[21]

The doctrine of entire sanctification rests furthermore upon the premise that Christ has gained a twofold salvation,

---

[18] Ibid., p. 31. Hills, ch. iii, esp. p. 54.

[19] The first *Manual of the Church of the Nazarene*, 1898, in Redford, pp. 55, 56.

[20] Wesley's exact position on this point is difficult to establish. See, above, Sec. I.

[21] Hills, pp. 39, 83, 89, 97 ff.

justification and sanctification, because man needs both forgiveness for voluntary sins and liberation from the secret sinful yearnings of the consecrated, but not yet sanctified Christian. Each of these blessings is said to be instantaneously complete, appropriated solely by faith, and in no wise to be complemented by man's activity. The affirmation of the modern perfectionists that a sanctified believer keeps Christ's law perfectly seems preposterous until one is informed that entire sanctification implies only a relative perfection, not an "absolute perfection" (since only God is absolutely holy), not a "sinless perfection" (since it is possible to fall), nor the perfection of the believer's glorified state. Nor must one paint sin so dark as to offend every conception of divine goodness in the heart of man. Nor dare one, conversely, set the standard of holiness too high. Entire sanctification is said to be "entire" when the Christian serves Christ according to the knowledge he possesses and when he prays: "Lord, I give Thee all I know to give, just as well as I know how. . . . If I do not give all, it is because I do not know how, and Christ cannot hold me responsible for what I do not know." In the words of Simpson: "God adapts the standard of our duty to our circumstances, ability, and growth, and we are fully obedient as God calls us forward step by step." [22]

In the opinion of some Holiness writers, sanctification is tantamount to an infusion of Christ. Simpson writes:

"When we are dedicated to God [entirely sanctified], Christ comes to live in us as truly as though we were visibly dwelling under His wing. God is again manifest in the flesh." The same writer affirms that the "saint's" mental faculties can successfully shut out all mundane thoughts and be unaffected by sinful pleasures, yes, even by esthetically beautiful things of this world. He pictures the act of sanctification as the emptying of a skull, which is then filled with God's penetrating fire so that all mental faculties become the willing servants of God. Many Holiness teachers declare that in sanctification the "living physical Christ comes into our life, sharing His physical life with ours in a union which is closer than the connubial life" and that because of this union "we shall have the power of Christ in our bodies." [23]

The Holiness people cannot ignore the temptations with which they, too, are beset. But they emphatically declare that their evil inclinations do not come from within, but are entirely from without, "for the heart is made pure, the enemies are without, and the fort royal is all friendly to the King." Since the temptations allegedly come entirely from without, in the main from Satan, and the "saint" overcomes them, therefore God can credit him with an obedience all the more pleasing because the temptations had been so strong.[24]

The perfectionists base their teaching of entire sanctification to a large extent on the alleged cumulative experience of "sanctified" Christians. Therefore tes-

---

[22] Hills, pp. 287 ff.; 55, 93, 41, 248. Simpson, *Wholly Sanctified*, p. 110 ff.

[23] Simpson, *Wholly Sanctified*, p. 129; *Fourfold Gospel*, pp. 39 f., 61; Hills, p. 229 f. Simpson and the early advocates of modern perfectionism predicated "divine healing," physical regeneration, and even intellectual rehabilitation, on entire sanctification. The modern Pentecostals have a different theological basis for this tenet, as will be shown later.

[24] Hills, p. 90; Simpson, *Wholly Sanctified*, p. 105. The Council of Trent teaches that the stronger the concupiscence, the greater the reward for conquering it (*Sess.* V, ch. 5). Allegations of complete freedom from evil propensities are not infrequent.

timonial meetings usually play a large part among the perfectionist bodies. The advocates of perfectionism maintain that there are five times as many prooftexts for the doctrine of entire sanctification as there are for the doctrine of conversion, and ten times as many as for the doctrine of Christ's deity. The contention that entire sanctification is the central doctrine of Holy Writ rests partly on a literalistic and partly on an arbitrary interpretation of the Scriptures. Many of the passages are adduced merely because they contain the word "holy" or one of its cognates, though they clearly refer not to entire sanctification, but to justification, the new obedience, and God's help in temptations; others are torn out of their context and interpreted rather arbitrarily.[25] The theory of entire sanctification is based primarily on the scholastic axiom *a debere sequitur posse,* that is, if God demands holiness of His children, then they must be able to render such holiness.

God never gives a "must" without a "may." . . . What shall we say of these commands in Eph. 1:4; Col. 1:22? Is God a heartless tyrant issuing commands to a race of moral beings that none are able to keep? If holiness is not attainable, then God commands what is impossible. But God's commands are enabling. If He [Christ] is able to come to our aid and to remove all inbred sin, will He refuse to remove this evil? . . . Jesus taught His disciples to pray, "Thy will be done on earth as it is in heaven." No one will deny that the angels are sanctified. Then Jesus prays that believers may be sanctified on earth. . . . Who will be rash enough to affirm that the Son of God was praying for something that was not according to the will of God and was therefore impossible? . . . If entire sanctification is unattainable, then God of choice induces imperfect moral and spiritual purity, when He might just as well effect perfect purity; that Jesus abides in believers who are filled with warring lusts, when He might render their hearts clean temples of the Holy Ghost; that God commands us to be holy, though He knows we cannot keep this command, thus making Himself an unjust tyrant.[26]

Perfectionism will lead to a false security, because it completely ignores the relevance of the Law for the Christian, who is always *iustus et peccator,* a justified person and a sinner still, dispenses with daily repentance, promotes pride and conceit, and anticipates the heavenly perfection. Or perfectionism leads to doubt and despair because sooner or later God's Law will reveal the complete inadequacy of man's own holiness in the judgment of God.

---

25 Such passages as Col. 1:22; 2:10; Eph. 5:26, 27; and 1 Thess. 5:23 do not teach entire sanctification as perfectionists aver. In 1 John 3:9 the present tense is used, which denotes durative action, i. e., the Christian cannot keep on sinning; sin is no longer the ruling principle. In Rom. 7: 14-25 Paul is said to present himself as an example of those who are living below their privilege as believers; and Phil. 3:11-15, esp. in the light of Luke 13:32, is said to refer exclusively to the perfection in the resurrection state. (Hills, pp. 174, 178.) 1 John 1:8 compared with 3:9 allegedly does not describe Christians, but the docetists. (Ibid., p. 181.) Matt. 23:19 (the altar sanctifies the gift) is said to mean that Jesus makes entirely holy the regenerated though still unsanctified believer. (Ibid., p. 264.) Clarence T. Craig, "Paradox of Holiness," *Interpretation,* VI (1952), pp. 146—61, discusses the objection of the perfectionists to the R. S. V. in translating ἁγιάζω twenty-two out of thirty times with "consecrate" rather than "sanctify." They say that "consecrate" denotes man's activity and "sanctify" God's. This is not tenable; but later editions of the R. S. V. have restored "sanctify."

26 Hills, pp. 101—124; 126; 131; 165; 279.

THE BAPTISM OF THE HOLY GHOST

The Pentecostals hold that

All believers are entitled to, and should ardently expect, and earnestly seek, the promise of the Father, the Baptism in the Holy Ghost and fire, according to the command of our Lord Jesus Christ. This was the normal experience of all in the early Christian Church. With it comes the enduement of power for life and service, the bestowment of the gifts and their uses in the work of the ministry (Luke 24:49; Acts 1:4; 1:8; 1 Cor. 12:1-31). This wonderful experience is distinct from and subsequent to the experience of the new birth (Acts 10: 44-46; 11:14-16; 15:7-9).[27]

In varying degrees Pentecostalism views the baptism of the Holy Spirit as the central doctrine of the Scriptures and the climax in the Christian life. It is often said, and correctly so, that Calvinism is theocentric and that Lutheran theology is Christocentric. By the same token Pentecostalism may be described as a pneumatocentric theology. Pentecostals teach that the baptism of the Spirit is more to be desired than the new birth, since the new birth concerns man only in so far as he is a sinner, while the baptism of the Spirit is only for such as are already saints. They state:

The teaching of the entire Bible is that the new birth has to do with the sinner. . . . It is the one way into God's family. The Baptism with the Holy Spirit has to do solely with those who have already repented and believed, and are already God's children. It [the Baptism with the Spirit] is that "which the world cannot receive." To receive it, we must "love Jesus and keep His commandments." It is for "My servants and handmaidens, saith the Lord." It is the enduement of power upon the yielding, confiding disciple, as is beautifully portrayed to us in that loving, happy, worshipful company in the upper room, as well as at Samaria and elsewhere. Then let us not confuse these two glorious mountain peaks in the Christian experience [repentance and the Baptism with the Spirit].[28]

Some Pentecostals speak of three great spiritual experiences or works of grace in the Christian life: (1) repentance, (2) entire sanctification, (3) baptism with the Spirit.[29]

a. The centrality which Pentecostalism assigns to the baptism of the Spirit is most intimately associated with the basic and central doctrine of the Holiness bodies. "Entire sanctification" is said to occupy the central position in the economy of salvation. And this central work is ascribed by the perfectionists to the Holy Spirit, whose very name (Holy) indicates "that in Him rests the blazing fire of the purity and holiness of almighty God," that it is His work to condemn sin, to enable the believer to conquer sin, and to impart Christ's life and power.[30] Pentecostals hold that at the believers' conversion the Spirit begins to be *with* them, but that not until their Pentecostal experience is He also *in* them (John 14:17).[31] Even as Jesus had to wait for His anointing with the Holy Spirit before He was endowed with power from on high for His witnessing ministry, so no Christian can live the full Christian life nor render Christian serv-

---

[27] Art. VII, *Statement of Fundamental Truths* (Springfield, Mo.: Gospel Publ. House).

[28] W. T. Gaston, *The New Birth and the Baptism in the Holy Spirit,* tract publ. by the Gospel Publ. House, Springfield, Mo.

[29] One group listed its statistics as follows: 7,458, saved; 4,591, sanctified; 4,316, filled with the Holy Ghost.

[30] Riggs, pp. 10—17.

[31] Ibid., p. 45.

ice until the Spirit has done the same thing for him (Luke 24:49). Conversion is said to be a grand experience in which Christ comes to the believer. But an incomparably greater blessing, the gift of "so great a salvation," the baptism of the Spirit, is conferred only when the Spirit Himself comes to the believer in the so-called Pentecost experience. In that experience

> the sanctified partake of Christ's nature and in a measure of the qualities which Christ has. Even as Christ Himself received a mighty Baptism in the Spirit which marked a great change in His ministry, so the Baptism in the Spirit today anoints a person with power and confers upon him the full complement of the gifts of the Spirit.[32]

b. Many Pentecostals consider the Holy Spirit's work an important factor in the dispensational scheme of world history. On the basis of Joel 2:23 f. and Acts 2:16-21, Pentecostals aver that in the fifth dispensation the Holy Spirit was poured out only on some, but that in the sixth dispensation, the New Testament era, He would be poured out on all. As the former rain, or the fall rain, and the latter, or spring, rain marked the beginning and end of the Jewish harvest, so the New Testament is opened and concluded by a special outpouring of the Spirit accompanied by the gift of speaking in tongues. The "former" rain is identified with the first Pentecost, and the "latter rain" with the events of the closing period of the sixth dispensation, beginning about 1890, when a great outpouring of the Holy Spirit occurred.[33] This "latter rain," evidenced by the speaking in unknown tongues, is said to indicate that the Spirit is concluding

His work during the remaining period of the sixth dispensation. He is now active in forming the body of Christ and preparing it for the rapture, when He will raise the dead in Christ (Rom. 8:11) and transform the living Christians (Phil. 3:21). During the subsequent tribulation period the Holy Spirit will deal with the 144,000 Jews which are sealed to Him. This sealing is to be followed by the millennium, the seventh and final dispensation, when Christ and the Holy Spirit will reclaim and transform the earth according to Joel 2:28, 29; Is. 32:15; 44:33; Ezek. 36:27. The grand climax of the Holy Spirit's work will come during the millennium, when He will pervade the earth with His presence and teach men to glorify God, remove all sickness, liberate the groaning creation of its travail, and bring everything into subjection to Christ.[34]

c. There is no agreement among the Holiness bodies as to the real nature of the baptism of the Holy Spirit. The perfectionist wing of the Holiness group usually defines the baptism of the Holy Spirit as the second work of grace following conversion. The Pentecostal wing, however, as a rule describes the baptism of the Holy Spirit as a rather esoteric and even ecstatic experience. Commenting on Acts 1:8, a Pentecostal states:

> The room was filled. They were overwhelmed, submerged, baptized, filled, and saturated; brought fully under the sway and control of the blessed Spirit; mind, soul, and body completely carried away by the torrent of Divine power, which came like a mighty landslide from the hills of Glory, until they burst forth in rapturous, heavenly, ecstatic utterance in the Holy Spirit, one hundred

[32] Ibid., p. 79 ff.

[33] Ibid., p. 92 ff. Frodsham, ch. xxiii, esp. p. 261 ff. W. G. Brown, p. 92 ff. The early Pentecostals spoke of this movement as the "Latter Rain Movement."

[34] Riggs, pp. 187—91. The dispensational system is described in detail under "Premillennialism."

per cent supernatural. Oh, who would not covet such a baptism? [35]

All Holiness people, perfectionist and Pentecostal, are agreed that the baptism of the Holy Spirit is an experience distinct from and subsequent to conversion.

Therefore it is evident that the reception of the Holy Ghost, as here spoken of, has nothing whatever to do with bringing men to believe and repent. It is a subsequent operation; it is an additional and separate blessing; it is a privilege founded on faith already actively working in the heart. . . . I do not mean to deny that the gift of the Holy Ghost may be practically on the same occasion, but never in the same moment. The reason is quite simple, too. The gift of the Holy Ghost is grounded on the fact that we are sons by faith in Christ, believers resting on redemption in Him. Plainly, therefore, it appears that the Spirit of God has already regenerated us.[36]

As the apostles waited ten days for Pentecost, so Christians today must be ready to await their baptism with the Holy Spirit. During this "waiting period" one's eternal salvation is not in jeopardy, for

a man may be regenerated by the Holy Spirit and still not be baptized with the Holy Spirit. In regeneration, there is the impartation of life by the Spirit's power, and the one who receives it is saved: in the Baptism with the Holy Spirit, there is the impartation of power, and the one who receives it is fitted for service. . . .[37]

The vast majority of Christians have always taught that the significance of the first Pentecost was the divine public demonstration that the New Testament church was fully equipped for the great task of witnessing for Christ among all nations. Biblical interpreters have advanced at least two acceptable interpretations of the references to the baptism with the Holy Ghost and Baptism with fire (Luke 3:16). The one is that Christ here describes the Holy Spirit's saving work of regenerating, justifying, sanctifying, and preserving the Christian, or bestowing upon him all those spiritual powers which are necessary for his Christian calling (Acts 2:17; Is. 44:3; Zech. 12:10; Titus 3:6; 1 Cor. 12:3; Eph. 5:18). This view takes the term "fire" as a description of the purifying work of the Holy Spirit. The other view is that in the light of v. 17 Christ is here speaking of His own condemnatory work, the "fire" symbolizing God's wrath over man's rejection of the Gospel. Whatever specific meaning this text may have, there is no warrant in the Scriptures for the Pentecostal theory that the Holy Spirit does His saving work apart from the means He has given to the church, the Word and the sacraments.[38]

The assertion that the baptism of the Holy Spirit is a second act of grace subsequent to conversion, and not enjoyed by all Christians, requires considerable wresting of the Scriptures and an arbitrary interpretation such as the following:

The message of 1 Cor. 12:13 is not that all Christians have received the Holy Ghost, but that all Christians who *have* received the Holy Ghost are filled with the *selfsame Spirit,* and that fact should urge them to unity and not to isms.[39]

d. Virtually all Holiness bodies maintain that there is always some evidence of the Spirit's baptism. The Pentecostal wing maintains that this evidence is

---

[35] Gaston, p. 14.

[36] William Kelley, quoted by Riggs, p. 55.

[37] R. A. Torrey, quoted by Riggs, p. 48.

[38] Engelder, et al., pp. 69, 85.

[39] Harold Horton, quoted by Aldrich, p. 174.

tangible and manifests itself at least in the gift of tongues, frequently in the presence of all the charismatic gifts enumerated in Mark 16:17, 18.[40] The most commonly accepted view is that

the Baptism of believers in the Holy Ghost is witnessed by the initial physical sign of speaking with other tongues as the Spirit of God gives utterance (Acts 2:4). The speaking in tongues in this instance is the same in essence as the gift of tongues (1 Cor. 12:4-10, 28) but different in purpose and use.[41]

On the basis of 1 Corinthians 12 the Pentecostals frequently speak of a threefold classification of charismatic gifts: (1) three gifts of revelation, namely, wisdom, knowledge, and discerning of spirits; (2) three gifts of power, namely, faith, miracles, and healing; and (3) three gifts of utterance, namely, prophecy, tongues, and interpretation.[42] The third is the most common. When asked why God would employ tongues after He has given His message directly in one's own language, they answer that it does not behoove man to criticize God's plan. The assertion is made that by the bestowal of this gift, God undoes the confusion and separation of Babel and restores world unity (John 11:52); gives a strong sign to unbelievers (1 Cor. 14:21); indicates the universality of His grace; gives His people a means to pray according to Rom. 8:26 and with "a thou-

---

[40] In reply to the statement that God restores all charismatic gifts the following observations are in place:

(1) Possessing and employing the means of grace, the church is fully equipped to do its work (Matt. 28:19 f.; Rom. 10:17; 1 Cor. 11:26; Luke 16:29). (2) The spirit of "enthusiasm," which rejects the external Word as futile, assumes only another form when it declares that the Word and sacrament alone are incapable of building the church. (3) Scripture warns against miracle-mindedness (John 4:48; 1 Cor. 1:22; 12:31). (4) It is not for us to prescribe to God when and to what degree He must bestow His gifts (1 Cor. 12:11). (5) The signs were given for the confirmation of the pure Gospel; signs performed by errorists are works of Satan (Deut. 13:1-3; Matt. 24:24; 2 Thess. 2:9 ff.). (6) Those churches which allege that the extraordinary, miracle-working gifts of the apostolic age have been revived among them must demonstrate them, even such as the innocuous use of poison (Mark 16:18), and the raising of the dead (Matt. 10:8). (7) Mark 16:17-20 teaches that, having received the fullness of the Holy Ghost at Pentecost, believers possess also the power to perform miracles. Where the need for it arises, in the judgment of God, He will perform miracles through any believer. The need existed in the beginning of the preaching of the Gospel and was met by the abundance of charisms in the church. But the text does not state that wherever there are believers, in every age, in every community, there shall be a display of miraculous powers. Those who take it in any such absolute sense would have to apply it to every single one of "them that believe." But not even in the apostolic days did every believer speak with new tongues, etc. Besides, if Jesus had promised the recurrence of the extraordinary charisms to every age of the church, He would have uttered an unfulfilled prophecy. — V. 20 does not state that the Lord "will confirm" the Word with signs following in every age of the church. It states that the Lord "confirmed" the Word with signs following. He confirmed it for the benefit of the first age and of every following age. Engelder, *Pop. Symb.*, p. 104 ff. — The Pentecostals usually ignore the fact that Mark 16:8 ff. does not occur in the better attested New Testament texts.

[41] Art. VIII, *Statement* (fn. 27, above).

[42] Riggs, pp. 11, 30, 117. Such gifts in Rom. 12:16 ff. as teaching and exhorting are said to supplement the charismatic gifts of 1 Corinthians 12.

sand tongues to sing my great Redeemer's praise"; and furnishes a vehicle to express His message to the church, provided an interpretation is also given.[43]

Relatively little space is given in the New Testament to speaking in tongues. In the light of this fact it seems rather strange that such extreme Biblicists as the Pentecostals can consider this phenomenon indispensable for the church and the Spirit's work. It is noteworthy that when St. Paul describes the Spirit's work, e. g., Gal. 5:22, 23, he makes no reference whatsoever to speaking in tongues. In fact, this phenomenon was not present in every New Testament church. It is mentioned only three times in the Book of Acts, and only in 1 Corinthians 14 does St. Paul discuss it. The three references to this phenomenon in Acts indicate clearly that it was given purely as a witness to the Gospel proclamation. On Pentecost Day it was one of the signs to convince Israel that the crucified Jesus is Savior and Lord. In the home of Cornelius the phenomenon helped to show Peter that the Gospel is for the Gentiles as well as for the Jews. At Ephesus (Acts 19:1-7) this charismatic gift served to persuade the disciples of John the Baptist that the Christian era had replaced the Johannine era. In Corinth the speaking in tongues seems to have done more harm than good. It led to spiritual pride and perhaps to wrong participation by women in the public worship. In the words of St. Paul this charism is the least among several spiritual gifts, inasmuch as it does not edify the entire body and at best is

[43] Riggs, pp. 162—68. Frodsham, pp. 263—79. Frodsham summarizes the Pentecostal teachings concerning the speaking of tongues as follows:

1. That God Himself would speak with the people by this means (stammering lips and another tongue) to whom He said, "This is the rest wherewith ye may cause the weary to rest, and this is the refreshing, yet they would not hear." Is. 28:11, 12.

2. That "this [glossolalia] is that" prophesied by Joel concerning the outpouring of the Spirit in the last days. Joel 2:28-32; Acts 2:16-20.

3. That it is one of the five signs the Lord Himself declared should follow them that believe. Mark 16:16-18.

4. That all the apostles and the women and others with them spoke in other tongues when they were filled with the Holy Ghost on the day of Pentecost (Acts 2:4) according to the promise of Christ. Acts 1:5, 8.

5. That the Gentiles both in Caesarea and Ephesus also spoke in tongues when they received the like gift. Acts 10:46; 19:6.

6. That it is described in 1 Corinthians as one of the manifestations of the Spirit given for profit.

7. That he that has this gift speaks, converses, or communes with God in a language no man can understand. 1 Cor. 14:2.

8. That "he that speaketh in an unknown tongue edifieth himself." 1 Cor. 14:4.

9. That the apostle, speaking at the commandment of the Lord, declares, "I would that ye all spake with tongues." 1 Cor. 14:5, 37.

10. That the peer of apostles speaks in definite gratitude concerning his speaking in tongues more than all the voluble Corinthians. 1 Cor. 14:18.

11. That it is a sign to them that believe not that God Himself uses. 1 Cor. 14:21, 22.

12. That the apostle gives the final injunction, "Forbid not to speak with tongues," 1 Cor. 14:39. (P. 271.)

a highly ecstatic form of prayer and praise for private use.[44]

Various attempts have been made to analyze the tongues movement. The theologian will immediately grant that if this charism were essential at any moment in God's economy, the Spirit would supply it. But in its manifestation among the Pentecostals it is an extreme form of "enthusiasm," the theory that an intuitive and experiential knowledge of divine things supersedes the written Word. The majority of psychologists who have written on this subject consider the movement a case of religious paranoia, megalomania, or an escape mechanism from frustration, or even as an indication of mental instability, or simply as a case of spiritual intoxication. They usually point out that the techniques employed and the conditions prevailing in the "waiting meetings" are such as may and frequently do lead to the complete exhaustion of the body and the total distraction of the mind. The reactions of these experiences are said to be such that psychological phenomena simulating the charismatic gifts are not uncommon. In particular the use of speech may be completely divorced from thought. During such periods of emotional shock the individual may utter sounds which he sincerely believes to be an unknown tongue and which another under a similar nervous shock may feel capable of interpreting, neither of the two actually understanding what allegedly has been said in the unknown tongue. It is, of course, also probable that in a moment of high tension an individual's subconscious mind is at work recalling the language employed in childhood, but long since forgotten.[45] Finally, one dare never forget that God may send "strong delusions" as punishments for not accepting the truth of the Gospel and what seem to be charisms are in reality the deceiving signs of Satan. (2 Thess. 2:9-12; 2 Cor. 11:13-15)[46]

---

[44] Cp. Stolee, chs. iii—v, vii. Cp. A. Robertson and A. Plummer, *A Critical and Exegetical Commentary on the First Epistle of St. Paul to the Corinthians* (Edinburgh: T. &. T. Clark, 1911); "Report on Spiritual Speaking," by a committee of the Protestant Episcopal Diocese of Chicago, *C. T. M.*, XXXII (1961), 217—220, and William H. Nes, "Glossolalia in the New Testament," ibid., pp. 221—223.

[45] Pratt, p. 172 ff. Davenport, loc. cit. Clark, *Psychology*, pp. 243—57, 119 ff. Cutten, p. 129 f. Unfortunately during tremendous psychological reactions sexual sins are not uncommon. H. A. Ironside, at one time a strong advocate of perfectionism and its emotionalism, states the following:

"And as to downright wickedness and uncleanness, I regret to have to record that sins of a positively immoral character are, I fear, far more frequently met within holiness churches and missions than the outsider would think possible. I know whereof I speak; and only a desire to save others from the bitter disappointments I had to meet leads me to write as I do." *Holiness, The False and True* (New York: Loizeaux Brothers, 1912), p. 36.

[46] The handling of snakes is often listed as a charismatic gift. However, the following statistics shed some light on the alleged divine character of this practice:

"The bites of rattlesnakes are 10 per cent fatal, of copperheads only 7 per cent, of the cottonmouth moccasins 24 per cent. Snake handlers use only copperheads and rattlesnakes in their meetings. Furthermore, they have gradually immunized themselves by receiving the venom in small portions — some as high as 200 times." (*Field and Stream Magazine*, July, 1938.)

CHRIST THE HEALER

Divine healing is the third plank of the foursquare Gospel. Briefly stated, the theological premise for the Pentecostal theory of divine healing is the assumption that in His atonement Christ provided not only for the removal of our sin, but of our sicknesses as well. Faith healing as practiced by the Pentecostals dare not be identified with other forms of immediate healings, such as the miraculous healings at celebrated shrines or the mental or metaphysical healings of modern cults.[47] The Pentecostal healing is said to be available to faith as unconditionally and as readily as is the pardon for sin. Of all the charismatic gifts faith healing is said to be the most common, for when Jesus was unable to do any mighty works in Nazareth because of the natives' unbelief, He was still able to perform several healings. Since Christ always remains the same (Heb. 13:8), His healing power, transferred to Spirit-baptized believers, is as available today as during His earthly ministry, and divine healings are as common now as then.[48]

The theological premise for faith healing is summarized in the statement: Christ has provided a double cure for a double curse. The Pentecostals usually advance two arguments to establish their thesis that healing is provided in the Atonement.

1. They affirm that every sickness, disease, deformity of body or mind, is the direct result of a specific sin. To be complete, Christ's atonement must remove not only the sin, but also in every case the result of the sin, human illness. But if healing is provided for in the atonement and available to all, does it not follow that man will never die? The Pentecostal answer is in substance:

> Not necessarily. There is no need that we should die of disease. The system might just wear out and pass away as the apple ripens and falls in autumn or the wheat matures and dies in June. It has simply fulfilled its natural period. "Thou shalt come to thy grave in a full age like as a shock of corn cometh in in his season," Job 5:26. This is very different from the apple falling in June with a worm in it. This is disease. The promise of healing is not physical immortality, but health until our life work is done. "With long life will I satisfy him," Psalm 91:16. We may not all live to fourscore, but we may all be "satisfied."

The favorite prooftexts are Psalm 103:3; 1 Peter 2:24; esp. Is. 53:4, 5. Aimee Semple McPherson comments on Is. 53:5 as follows:

> Was He whipped that my sins might be washed away? No, child, the blood of the cross was sufficient for that. Why, then, did they whip Him so? 'Twas thus He bore our suffering, and "By His stripes we are healed." At the whipping post He purchased your healing.

P. J. McCrossan says:

> Much of His precious blood was doubtless shed while receiving that awful bruise (stripes) for our physical healing, but the rest of His precious blood was reserved to be shed on the Cross for our sins.

---

[47] This distinction between divine and faith healing may be observed:

In the former a healer is considered necessary as the agent to bring healing to the patient; in the latter, the patient may receive healing immediately by an act of faith. Throughout the history of the church there have been periods when divine healing received a great deal of attention. Cp. Biederwolf, pp. 157—216. On the overall question of the healing ministry of Christ and His disciples and its relation to the healing ministry in the church today, see Bernard Martin, *The Healing Ministry in the Church* (Richmond: John Knox Press, c. 1960).

[48] Riggs, p. 139 ff.

And F. F. Bosworth states:

> You can be healed when you put the bread in your mouth, if not before, by discerning the Lord's body broken for your healing. It is just as easy to be healed of a cancer as it is to be forgiven of sins.[49]

Gal. 3:13 is another favorite prooftext with many advocates of divine healing. They say that Christ freed us from the curse of the Law, i. e., the curses enumerated in Deut. 28:15-62, especially the loathesome diseases mentioned in v. 27. Some go so far as to say that to free us from our physical ailments Christ was actually afflicted with these Egyptian diseases, the botch, the scab, the itch, the emerods. Consistency would compel them to ascribe to Christ also the curses of v. 28 — a blasphemous thought.[50]

2. They declare that all diseases can be healed by a "complete surrender to Christ" and that healings are always available to the Spirit-filled believer. One of the writers states:

> When the soul is walking in harmony and obedience, the life of God can fully flow into the body. . . . The living, physical Christ must come into our life sharing His physical life with you in a union which is nearer than the connubial life, so near that the very life of His veins is transferred into yours. . . . The sanctified Christian receives the healing in Christ's body by faith and as he abides in Christ's living body.[51]

But the theory that healing has been procured in the atonement and is always available to faith ignores several express Scriptural teachings. (1) Sickness is not always a direct consequence of sin (John 9:3). (2) Christ's healings were always instantaneous, complete, but not always — as the Pentecostals teach — dependent upon the patient's personal faith (Luke 22:51). (3) The consistent Pentecostal will not use any physical remedy for sickness. St. Paul, however, admonished Timothy to drink wine to relieve his frequent infirmities, and he commended Luke, the "beloved physician." Christians employ every means which God has put at their disposal: not only prayer, but also medicine. God wants us to employ His means as the regularly appointed channels and not to rely presumptuously on self-appointed means.[52] (4) The teaching that healing is always available to faith leads to doubt or despair. If the Pentecostals are correct, then such ailing Christians, be it Paul, Timothy, Epaphroditus, Trophimus, must have been "holding back some of the full testimony or service to Christ" or have failed "to fulfill one of God's conditions." (5) How could Christ commend the Good Samaritan for doing a deed which is actually contrary to God's will? (6) The alleged Scriptural argumentation for the healing theory is based to a very large extent on the use

---

[49] Quoted in Biederwolf, pp. 9, 10. Wilbur Glenn Voliva of Zion, Ill., the successor of Alexander Dowie, also maintained that divine healing is available in the atonement. See *Leaves of Healing*, Jan. 14, 1939.

[50] Biederwolf, p. 125. This author examines the dozens of Scripture references which are adduced to prove that healing is provided in the atonement, e. g., Ex. 15:26 (though nothing is said in this passage about the atonement); Lev. 14:18 (the atonement of the leper was ceremonial). Ibid., pp. 217—305.

[51] Simpson, *Fourfold Gospel*, pp. 60, 61, 64.

[52] The first article of the Creed requires even more faith than the divine healers, for it teaches the Christian to believe that God places the entire creation at our disposal for our well-being. This doctrine of God's benevolent providence through the ordinary means seems too simple for some people.

of figurative language drawn particularly from the agricultural and medicinal customs among the Children of Israel. In most instances the word "heal" does not refer to physical but to spiritual restoration. (7) Christians do not generalize from the isolated case of anointing and blessing handkerchiefs (Acts 19:11, 12; 28:2). (8) But more basic than all this reasoning is the fact that faith healing ignores the true nature of sin and thus vitiates the true value of Christ's redemptive work. The demonic power which Satan exercises over men is not so much physical as spiritual. The result of sin is not so much a physical ailment as rather eternal separation from God. Therefore Christ bore our infirmities and our sicknesses not primarily to free us from our physical ailments, but to conquer Satan (Luke 10:17-20; Matt. 8:16, 17). By placing physical healing into the center, the divine healer actually relegates Christ's real work into the background, and ultimately the believer in his unsuccessful quest for physical health may lose his eternal health.

In dealing with divine healers we must not overlook the fact that medical science and psychology are agreed that strong and persistent impressions and suggestions — such as invariably precede the supposed divine curses — modify the patient's functional disposition. An abnormal mental state invariably affects the patient's metabolism and ultimately his entire physical condition. If it is furthermore kept in mind that according to medical science a large percentage of ailments are attributable to a neurosis, then one can easily understand the success of divine healers. In discussing divine healing we must give due con-

sideration also to the dynamic force of such basic emotions as joy and fear. Such emotions may be engendered by endlessly repeating such refrains as "I Come, I Come," or by playing martial music in a progressively higher pitch. The "crowd psychology" is a valuable ally to the divine healers. The "crowd" not only restricts the individual's freedom but also serves as a reservoir of individual courage. A healing meeting may also serve as an escape mechanism for a frustrated life, for there the patient is the center of attraction. One rarely hears of healings performed in a private meeting. It must also be kept in mind that a neurotic can simulate all symptoms of a disease. For that reason it is correct to say that mental attitudes make physical invalids. Conversely the mental attitude will also cure a mental disease, and on occasion a real disease can be arrested — though not cured — by one's mental attitude.[53]

THE PREMILLENNIAL COMING OF CHRIST

This fourth plank of the full Gospel plays a very prominent part in much of the perfectionist and Pentecostal literature; however, frequently either the doctrine of sanctification or the baptism of the Holy Spirit so predominates their thinking that this particular point of view recedes into the background.[54]

The Several Bodies

The Holiness bodies can be divided into the following classes: (1) The denominations constituting the perfectionist wing. Their chief doctrinal emphases are conversion, entire sanctification, and the premillennial coming of Christ. The "gifts" of speaking in tongues and of

---

[53] Dr. E. Podolsky, *The Doctor Prescribes Music* (Phila.: F. A. Stokes, 1936), states that certain sounds produce several changes in the glands and the nerves. Fast music increases the metabolism, and shrill music is said to affect the chemical elements in the body. Quoted in *Time*, Feb. 20, 1939, p. 41. Sadler, p. 79. J. B. Morgan, *Keeping a Sound Mind* (New York: The Macmillan Co., 1937), p. 291.

[54] For "Premillennialism" see P. IX, Sec. II.

divine healing and other typical Pentecostal features are usually not taught by these bodies. (2) The denominations constituting the Pentecostal wing. In addition to the emphasis on entire sanctification, these center their proclamation on the "Pentecostal experience," manifested particularly in the gift of tongues and healing. (3) The Evangelistic Associations. These are not denominations, but, as the name indicates, organizations to propagate the doctrine of entire sanctification. Some are also "Pentecostal." [55]

THE PERFECTIONIST BODIES

The Christian and Missionary Alliance has its origin in the revivalistic work of Dr. A. B. Simpson, a Presbyterian minister, among the unchurched masses of New York in 1881. Originally this group was — and in the opinion of many of its members still is — no more than a mission society to propagate the main tenets of Simpson's theology, expressed in the formula of the fourfold Gospel: Christ the Savior, the Sanctifier, the Healer, and the Coming King.[56] One section of the movement seems to place greater stress on these theological emphases,[57] and another on the church's missionary obligation.

The Christian Nation Church is a very small body, extremely legalistic. It features the fourfold Gospel.[58]

Christ's Sanctified Holy Church (Negro) came into being when white evangelists brought the doctrine of "entire sanctification as a distinct experience" into the Negro Methodist church in Louisiana.

Church of Christ (Holiness) U. S. A. was at first interdenominational and antisectarian, but gradually developed into a new denomination, being represented chiefly in Mississippi and Virginia. In addition to the Arminian doctrines, it emphasizes entire sanctification, baptism by immersion, the gift of the Holy Ghost, foot washing, and divine healing.

Church of God (Anderson, Ind.) is one of the many groups which will use no other name than this "Biblical" term.[59] To differentiate itself from others of the same name, it inserts parenthetically the location of its headquarters. D. S. Warner, a minister in the Winebrennerian Church of God, believed that

> the doctrine of justification by faith seems to have spent itself in the early sixteenth century in the formation of iron-clad sects and technical creeds which were designed by their founders as vessels to hold the water of life. The founding of sects and creeds used up the force of the evangelical impulse, and there was a long period of spiritual dullness in Protestantism.

In his opinion the church was revived in three stages — when Pietism restored the doctrine of justification as a personal experience; when Wesley restored entire sanctification to the church; and when the Plymouth Brethren, the Winebren-

---

[55] The list of Holiness bodies in this chapter is based on the information contained in the current *Yearbook of the Churches*, published by the National Council of the Churches in the U. S. A. and on other sources.

[56] A. B. Simpson was one of the first, if not the first, to popularize this type of theology in his publication *The Fourfold Gospel*. See above, "Divine Healing."

[57] So the Manual of 1931. According to a tract entitled *What Is the Christian and Missionary Alliance?* the teaching on "deeper spiritual truth" is outlined in Simpson's *The Fourfold Gospel*.

[58] Clark, *Sm. Sects*, p. 82 f.

[59] The list of the Churches of God in the *Yearbook of the Churches* is incomplete because some of them refuse to submit any information.

nerians, and the Campbells sought to establish the unity of the church. In 1877 Warner became an ardent advocate of "entire sanctification as the second work of grace," for which he was brought to trial in the Winebrennerian church.[60] In his heresy trial and ultimate expulsion he maintained that he

> simply discovered one great spiritual principle, which was the identification of the visible and invisible church in a spiritual congregation of Christians from which no Christian was excluded by any man-made rules or corporate forms of organization.[61]

The Church of God is described by its adherents first as a "reformation movement" designed to affect ultimately the entire church and bring it to the realization of the grand Scriptural ideal that spiritual fellowship with Christ and with one another and devotion to Scriptural ideals constitute a sufficient bond for the followers of Christ. They insist that originally the church of God was not a congregation of individuals but the concrete embodiment of the spiritual body of Christ. In this state the church was perfect, having both purity of doctrine and a theocratic form of government. These two characteristics were lost in the Roman church, but they are being restored: the purity of doctrine through the Lutheran Reformation, and the theocratic form of government through the Church of God reforma-tion movement, which rejects all ecclesiasticism and has established the ideal of a Spirit-filled and Spirit-directed church. The Church of God rejects all creeds as "a system of human authority in church relationships and in spiritual operations." It contends that it "recognizes the Lord's people in all communions and feels an irresistible drawing in the Spirit toward them." It therefore demands that its members give up the unscriptural systems of ecclesiasticism and recognize the principle of theocracy in the church and accept only such authority in the Church of God as "exists in the individuals by virtue of their divine gifts and qualifications."[62] Warner's unique and peculiar emphasis was "the identity, at least possible identity, of the visible and the invisible church."[63] His second chief theological emphasis was "entire sanctification," with such related doctrines as divine healing and a strict form of asceticism.[64]

The Church of the Nazarene is the largest Holiness body and represents the merger over many years of the following perfectionist movements and groups:

> The Church of the Nazarene in the West, the Central Evangelical Holiness Association, and the Pentecostal Churches of America in the East, the New Testament Church of Christ, the Independent Holiness Church, and the Pentecostal Mission in the South, the Pentecostal Churches of Scotland and

---

[60] Charles E. Brown, pp. 63—72.

[61] Ibid., p. 100.

[62] F. C. Smith, *Brief Sketch of the Origin, Growth, and Distinctive Doctrine of the Anderson, Ind., Church of God* (1927). See also Charles Ewing Brown, "The Church of God (Anderson, Indiana)," in Vergilius Ferm, ed., *The American Church of the Protestant Heritage* (New York: Philosophical Library, 1953), pp. 435—54.

[63] Charles E. Brown, p. 68.

[64] *The Gospel Trumpet* was Warner's chief instrument to spread his unique beliefs. The antimedicine tradition is strongly developed in the Church of God. Ibid., p. 172. Until quite recently the wearing of neckties was forbidden, and in 1910 a split occurred over this question. Ibid., p. 364. There is no denominational church polity, since every local church is viewed as *the* Church of God. Cp. the Plymouth Brethren.

England, and the Laymen's Holiness Association.[65]

Some of these bodies, in turn, were the result of prior mergers. In distinction from most other Holiness bodies this denomination is found in practically all parts of the United States. In doctrine and cultus the Nazarene church represents the conservative element in the perfectionist wing of the Holiness bodies. [66] It is essentially in accord with historic Methodism, both in doctrine and polity. Its distinctive mark is the emphasis which it places upon the doctrine that in His atonement Jesus has made provision not only to save men from their sins but also to perfect them in love. Its doctrinal position is very broad. The Nazarene church "requires only such avowals of belief as are essential to Christian experience" (entire sanctification). It grants liberty to its members in the doctrine of Christ's second coming, in the mode of baptism, and in divine healing. The Nazarene church has explicitly disavowed the speaking in tongues.[67]

The Church of the Living God is represented by two Negro groups. The parent group is known by the added motto "Christian Workers for Fellowship." It was organized in 1889 as a fraternal order. Its founder, Wm. Christian, "who, by virtue of a divine call, created the office of chief," held that the "Freemason religion is the true mode of religion" and that his "organism shall be known as operative Masonry and its first

three corporal degrees shall be Baptism, Holy Supper, and feet washing." Dues in the nature of tithes are collected; the churches are known as temples; the sick are anointed. The seceding group, which withdrew in 1919 and is episcopal in polity, calls itself the *House of God, Which Is the Church of the Living God, the Pillar and Ground of the Truth, Incorporated.*

Kodesh Church of Immanuel, composed chiefly of dissidents from the African Methodist Episcopal Church, is a second-blessing Holiness body as the designation "kodesh" (Hebrew for "holy") indicates.

The Pilgrim Holiness Church is a fusion of a number of Holiness churches, notably of the International Apostolic Holiness Union and of the Pilgrim Holiness Church, which had been a district of the Nazarene church. Its doctrinal motto is: "In essentials unity, in nonessentials liberty, in all things charity." According to its manual, the specific purpose of the Pilgrim Holiness Church is to preach the so-called "full Gospel," i. e., salvation from actual sins through justification and from original sin through entire sanctification; the premillennial coming of Christ; divine healing; and evangelization of the entire world.[68] In 1958 the General Conference of this body approved a merger with the Wesleyan Methodist Church of America.

United Holy Church of America, Incorporated, is a perfectionist body

---

[65] Redford, pp. 82—170. Cp. *Census,* II, 458—60.

[66] The description of the doctrine of entire sanctification in the preceding section is drawn very largely from material published by the Nazarene church.

[67] Both Gaddis and Clark point out that the Nazarene church no longer seems to advocate perfectionism with the former fervor. All the Nazarene colleges have in recent years elided the term "holiness" from their name. Clark, *Sm. Sects,* pp. 75, 224. However, in some sections the Nazarenes are very emotional in their worship.

[68] *Census,* II, 137.

founded at Method, N. C., in 1886. It proclaims the fourfold Gospel, including divine healing.[69]

Triumph the Church and Kingdom of God in Christ, founded in 1902, teaches the cleansing from sin in all "justified" believers, entire sanctification as an instantaneous work of second grace, and baptism by fire as an experience obtainable by faith.

The Fire Baptized Holiness Church was organized as a holiness association in 1898 at Atlanta, Ga.

The Fire Baptized Holiness Church (Wesleyan), known until 1945 as the Southeast Kansas Fire Baptized Holiness Association, is evangelistic, episcopal, and strongly Wesleyan in doctrine.

The Holiness Church of God, Incorporated, was established at Madison, N. C., in 1920 and incorporated in 1928.

The Church of the Gospel is a small Holiness body.

THE PENTECOSTAL CHURCHES

The baptism of the Holy Spirit as a special work of grace and evidenced by one or more charismatic gifts is said to be the common possession of all Pentecostal churches. They make no attempt to fix a uniform standard for the degree of intensity of the Pentecostal experience, and there are varying degrees of ecstasy in which the religious fervor manifests itself. To the observer this ecstasy may appear as religious frenzy, sometimes bordering on the bizarre, and again as a more or less controlled ecstatic manifestation.

There seem to be two main groupings of Pentecostal churches. The one group of churches places great emphasis on the Pentecostal experience, especially the gift of tongues, and usually embodies the term "Pentecostal" in its official title. The other group emphasizes, in addition to Pentecostalism, an extreme form of antidenominationalism, manifest in its refusal to accept any other title than "Church of God."

PENTECOSTAL FELLOWSHIP OF NORTH AMERICA

The majority of the so-called "Pentecostal" churches are members of the *Pentecostal Fellowship of North America.* It is a loose organization, but co-ordinates effort in matters common to all members.[70]

The General Council of the Assemblies of God is the largest Pentecostal body. It was organized in 1914 in Hot Springs, Ark., and in 1916 it established its headquarters at Springfield, Mo. Its doctrinal position is typically Pentecostal. It features speaking in tongues as evidence of the baptism of the Spirit and stresses Christ's premillennial coming.[71] Local churches are urged to use "Assembly of God" as a title.[72]

Calvary Pentecostal Church, Incorporated, founded in 1931, is confined to the Pacific Northwest.

[69] Ibid., II, 1649.

[70] According to information supplied by J. Roswell Flower, general secretary of General Council, Assemblies of God, in correspondence, Feb. 6, 1952, the following bodies constitute this fellowship: Assemblies of God, Springfield, Mo.; Church of God, Cleveland, Tenn.; International Church, Foursquare Gospel, Los Angeles, Calif.; Pentecostal Assemblies of Canada, Toronto, Ont., Canada; Pentecostal Holiness Church, Franklin Springs, Ga.; Open Bible Standard Churches, Des Moines, Iowa; International Pentecostal Assemblies, Newcastle, Wyo.; Zion Evangelistic Fellowship, Providence, R. I.

[71] See the publications of Gospel Publ. House, Springfield, Mo.

[72] Churches are currently located in every state of the Union and in 72 foreign countries.

The Congregational Holiness Church withdrew from the Pentecostal Holiness Church in protest against strict superintendency, which allegedly interfered with the spontaneous response to the Spirit's guidance.

International Church of the Foursquare Gospel is the work of Mrs. Aimee Semple McPherson. In spite of her unconventional career she attracted thousands. She proclaimed the fourfold Gospel with every means at her disposal, her magnetic personality, her great artistic and dramatic gifts, and her ability to utilize even unfavorable publicity to her advantage. Mrs. McPherson was one of the most ardent advocates of the "tongues" charism. She said that the Spirit inspired not only the interpretation of her utterances in a foreign tongue, but also her writings in English.[73] Her son Ralph is continuing the work of his late mother. The Elim Foursquare Church in England has no organic connection with the McPherson group.

The Pentecostal Holiness Church, Incorporated, combines Wesleyan perfectionism with belief in the Pentecostal baptism with the Holy Spirit and the gift of speaking in tongues.

The Pentecostal Free Will Baptist Church, Incorporated, resulted from a merger in 1959 of two North Carolina Free Will Baptist Conferences.

The Pentecostal Church of Christ, founded in 1917 and incorporated a decade later, has its main strength in Kentucky and Ohio.

The Emmanuel Holiness Church was organized in 1953 by participants in the General Conference of the Pentecostal Fire-Baptized Holiness Church held at Whiteville, N. C.

The Pillar of Fire, organized in 1901 by Mrs. Alma White as the Pentecostal Union, adopted the present name in 1917. It is a Methodistic holiness group.

The Open Bible Standard Churches, Incorporated, is a merger dating back to 1935 of the Bible Standard Churches and the Open Bible Evangelistic Association. It is a "full Gospel" body which emphasizes evangelism and missions.

The Church of Our Lord Jesus Christ of the Apostolic Faith, Incorporated, was founded in Columbus, Ohio, and moved its headquarters to New York in 1919.

The Bible Way Churches of Our Lord Jesus Christ World Wide, Incorporated, was organized in 1957 by a group which withdrew from the previously named body because of dissatisfaction with its "authoritarian organization."

The International Pentecostal Assemblies stresses tithing and nonresistance.

The Pentecostal Church of God of America, Incorporated, was organized in 1919.

The Pentecostal Fire-Baptized Holiness Church had its origin in the Fire-Baptized movement shortly prior to 1900 and espouses an extremely rigorous asceticism.

The Christian Church of North America was known until 1948 as the Italian Christian Churches, Unorganized.

Pentecostal Assemblies of Canada is an organization of the Pentecostal groups of Canada.

THE CHURCHES OF GOD

There are relatively many Pentecostal churches which spurn the use of any title except the New Testament term "Church of God." In fact, some state that the majority of Pentecostals are affiliated with one of the many parties known only by the name Church

[73] Marcus Bach, ch. iii (*supra,* fn. 13).

of God.[74] This type of Pentecostalism goes back to the activities of R. G. Spurling in Cherokee County, N. C. His work was revived and popularized by A. J. Tomlinson, who took over the movement in 1896. In 1907 Tomlinson organized the Church of God with headquarters at Cleveland, Tenn. In January, 1908, this group, until then a "Holiness" body, adopted the Pentecostal message and began to advocate an extreme asceticism. The distinctive feature was Tomlinson's allegation that this body was the ideal church, patterned after the New Testament church. He used the terms "Church of God" and "the Holy Christian Church" promiscuously as denominational designations. The Church of God maintains that its church government is like that of the apostolic church, for "as the first church had its headquarters at Jerusalem," so the Churches of God have their headquarters at Cleveland, Tenn. As the apostolic church was "theocratic in its government, James speaking with the counsel and perfect agreement of the council, Acts 15:19," so the will of God is said to be recognizable today when "the church strictly adheres to the leadings of the holy church." [75]

There have been many divisions in the course of less than half a century. The following is a partial list:[76]

The Church of God of Prophecy, M. A. Tomlinson, general overseer.

The Church of God (Cleveland, Tennessee).

The Church of God (Queens Village, New York), Homer A. Tomlinson, general overseer.

The (Original) Church of God.

Founded by R. G. Spurling in 1886, it claims to be the first to use this "Bible name."

The Church of God (Greenville, South Carolina).

The Church of God by Faith, founded in Florida in 1919.

The Church of God (Seventh Day) (Denver, Colorado) keeps Saturday as Sabbath, believes in Christ's imminent return, and holds that the earth will be the everlasting home of the righteous.

Church of God and Saints of Christ. This group was organized by William S. Crowdy in 1897 at Lawrence, Kans. He had a revelation, he stated, in which he received "Seven Keys": repentance of sin; baptism into water; receiving the unleavened bread and water for Christ's body and blood; foot washing; the keeping of the Ten Commandments; the breathing upon with a holy kiss; and the Disciples' or Lord's Prayer. Later Crowdy had a second revelation to the effect that the Negro race is descended from the Ten Lost Tribes of Israel — hence the nickname "Black Jews" — and that the Negro people must keep the Ten Commandments and adhere literally to the teachings of the Bible, the Old and the New Testament constituting man's positive guide to salvation.

Of the several hundred congregations affiliated with this body only the church at Belleville, Va., is established as a communistic settlement. This is also the headquarters.[77]

The Church of God (Apostolic) is a small perfectionist body which maintains that it is the true church according to the apostolic basis.

---

[74] Mead, pp. 54 ff., 143 (*supra*, fn. 55); Clark, *Sm. Sects,* p. 100 ff. Confusion is worse confounded inasmuch as there are Mennonite, Brethren, Holiness, and Adventist bodies with no further designation than Church of God.

[75] Minutes of Annual Assembly of the Churches of God, Cleveland, Tenn., 1931, pp. 13—17.

[76] Clark, *Sm. Sects,* pp. 100—104.

[77] Cp. Bishop H. Z. Plummer, in *Census,* 1936, II, p. 438 ff.

NEGRO PENTECOSTAL BODIES

No adequate census of the Holiness groups among Negroes has ever been made. In every larger city with a strong Negro population there are independent congregations, sometimes with weird-sounding names, which resemble the Pentecostal church in theology and in worship. Only the most significant can be mentioned here. In the following all but the first three are Pentecostal in the Tomlinson tradition.

The Pentecostal Assemblies of the World, Incorporated, was organized as an interracial body in 1914. The white members withdrew in 1924.[78]

The United Holy Church of America, Incorporated, was founded in 1886 at Raleigh, N. C.

The Apostolic Overcoming Holy Church of God was founded in 1916 at Mobile, Ala.

The Church of God in Christ, a large Negro body, founded in 1897 by C. H. Mason, asserts that it is divinely instituted as the church of God and that its name was directly revealed to Mason.

The Churches of God, Holiness, who, like the other bodies bearing this name, hold that "the body of believers in any one place is the church in that place, for on account of the unity of Christ there can be but one church in a particular place, though there may be several meeting places." [79]

The Free Christian Zion Church of Christ.

National David Spiritual Temple of Christ Church Union (Incorporated) of the U. S. A.

UNITARIAN PENTECOSTALS

There are several Unitarian offshoots of Pentecostalism. They are known as "Jesus Only" groups, because they baptize in the name of Jesus only on the basis of their premise that Christ is All and that the names Father, Son, and Holy Spirit are names of the Lord Jesus Christ. This view is held by:

The United Pentecostal Church, Incorporated, with headquarters at Saint Louis, a merger, completed in 1945, of elements that go back to 1914.

The Apostolic Church of Pentecostals of Canada.

Pentecostal Assemblies of the World, a biracial body with headquarters in Indianapolis.[80]

THE EVANGELISTIC ASSOCIATIONS

These are not denominational bodies but associations of congregations or of individual members. They have in common the desire to spread the doctrine of entire sanctification.[81]

The Apostolic Christian Churches of America, a small group of German-Swiss churches founded by Benedict Weyeneth about 1847. The group is strongly perfectionistic and nonresistant.

The Apostolic Christian Church (Nazarean), a loose association of 53 German-Swiss congregations. It was founded by S. H. Froehlich. The body teaches entire sanctification; the Novatian error that he who has arrived at the state of perfection and again enters the state of sin cannot receive forgiveness; that in Baptism sins are not only for-

---

[78] Mead, p. 144.

[79] K. H. Burruss, *Star Book and Discipline* (no place or date of publication), p. 11 ff.

[80] J. Roswell Flower (fns. 12, 70). Cp. Clark, *Sm. Sects,* p. 104. Clark states that there are also "Father Only" Churches of God, so called because they baptize only in the name of the Father (p. 105).

[81] *The Apostolic Faith Mission,* disbanded in 1957, belonged to this classification.

given, but "entirely burnt away"; and opposition to war and oaths.

The Christian Congregation is related to the Barton Stone Movement and centers its message and work in John 13: 34, 35.

The Church of Daniel's Band is a very small group.

The Church of God (Apostolic) was formed in Danville, Ky., in 1897.

The Church of God as Organized by Christ, organized by the Mennonite P. J. Kaufman, takes an extreme position in its opposition to denominationalism and congregationalism.

The Metropolitan Church Association, an outgrowth of the missionary activity of the Metropolitan Methodist Church of Chicago, carries on an aggressive missionary program in all parts of this country and in foreign countries to proclaim the full Gospel. Believing that

Matt. 19:21 must be understood literally, no one connected with the organization, not even the teachers at the large Bible school in Waukesha, Wis., receives a regular salary.

The Missionary Church Association is a group of co-operating evangelical churches which seek "better opportunities for cultivating deeper spiritual life and engaging in aggressive work." Most of its missionaries, trained at the Fort Wayne Bible Training School, are sent to foreign mission fields. It stresses in particular entire sanctification, the premillennial coming of Christ, divine healing, nonresistance, baptism by immersion.

The American Evangelical Christian Churches. This ministerial association and fellowship, whose churches are known as American Bible Churches, was founded in 1944 and has its headquarters in Chicago.

BIBLIOGRAPHY

PART V

SECTION III

Primary Sources:

Bosworth, F. *Christ the Healer.* Chicago: F. Bosworth, 1924.

Brown, Charles E. *When the Trumpet Sounded.* Anderson, Ind.: Warner Press, 1951. A history of the Church of God (Anderson, Indiana).

Frodsham, Stanley J. *With Signs Following.* Rev. ed., Springfield, Mo.: Gospel Publ. House, 1946. Contains a history of modern Pentecostalism, esp. of the "tongues" movement, by an early advocate.

Hills, A. M. *Holiness and Power.* Cincinnati, Ohio: Revivalist Office, 1897.

Redford, M. E. *The Rise of the Church of the Nazarene.* Kansas City, 1951.

Riggs, R. M. *The Spirit Himself.* Springfield,

Mo.: Gospel Publ. House, 1949. This Pentecostal study of the nature and effect of the "Baptism of the Holy Spirit" is almost indispensable for an understanding of the theology of Pentecostalism.

Simpson, A. B. *The Fourfold Gospel.* New York: Christian Alliance Publ. Co., 1925.

————. *Wholly Sanctified.* New York: Christian Alliance Publ. Co., 1925. Simpson was one of the chief exponents of the so-called fourfold Gospel.

Secondary Sources:

Aldrich, Roy L. "Is the Pentecostal Movement Pentecostal?" *Bibliotheca Sacra*, CVIII (1951).

Beardsley, Frank G. *The History of Christianity in America.* New York: American Tract Society, 1938.

————. *Religious Progress Through Religious Revivals.* New York: American Tract Society, 1943.

Biederwolf, Wm. E. *Whipping Post Theology.* Grand Rapids: Eerdmans Publ. Co., 1934. A very exhaustive treatment and critique of the theological premises of "faith healing."

Brown, W. Gordon. *Pentecostalism,* mimeographed manuscript, Toronto Baptist Seminary, n. d. It shows the Pentecostals' arbitrary use of Scripture texts.

Buskirk, James D. *Religion, Healing, and Health.* New York: Macmillan Co., 1952.

Clark, Elmer T. *The Psychology of Religious Awakening.* New York: Macmillan Co., 1929.

————. *The Small Sects in America.* Rev. ed.; Nashville: Abingdon-Cokesbury, 1949. Chs. iii and iv deal mainly with the psychological aspects of the "perfectionist" and "charismatic" sects.

Cutten, George B. *Speaking with Tongues.* New Haven: Yale Univ. Press, 1927.

Davenport, F. M. *Primitive Traits in Religious Revivalism.* New York, 1905.

Gaddis, M. E. *Christian Perfectionism in America.* Unpubl. doctor's dissertation, Univ. of Chicago Library. Contains excellent, well-documented source material.

Graebner, Theo. *Faith Cure.* St. Louis: C. P. H., 1929.

Ironside, H. A. *Holiness, the False and the True.* 10th ed. New York: Loizeaux Brothers, 1942. A former adherent of "entire sanctification" points out its unscripturalness and its spiritual as well as moral dangers.

Kincheloe, Samuel C. *Religion in the Depression.* New York: Social Science Research Council, 1937.

McKenzie, John G. *Psychology, Psychotherapy and Evangelicalism.* New York: Macmillan Co., 1940.

Niebuhr, H. Richard. *The Social Sources of Denominationalism.* New York: Henry Holt Co., 1929.

Norborg, Sverre. *Varieties of Christian Experience.* Minneapolis: Augsburg Publ. House, 1937.

Pratt, James B. *The Religious Consciousness.* New York: Macmillan Co., 1920. Considered one of the best psychological analyses of the so-called modern "charismatic" phenomena.

Sadler, Wm. *The Truth About Mind Cure.* Chicago: A. C. McClurg & Co., c. 1928.

Stolee, H. J. *Pentecostalism.* Minneapolis: Augsburg Publ. House, 1936. A good critique of the "tongues" phenomenon.

Stolz, K. R. *The Psychology of Religious Living.* Nashville: Cokesbury Press, 1937.

Sweet, W. W. *The American Church.* New York: Abingdon-Cokesbury Press, 1948.

————. *Revivalism in America: Its Origin, Growth and Decline.* New York: Chas. Scribner's Sons, 1944.

Warfield, Benjamin. *Perfectionism.* Phila.: The Presbyterian and Reformed Publishing Co., 1958.

Weatherhead, Leslie D. *Psychology and Life.* New York: Abingdon Press, c. 1935.

————. *Psychology, Religion and Healing.* Nashville: Abingdon-Cokesbury, 1951. A succesful London minister examines man's search for health of body and mind and concludes that both religion and psychology are essential to the success of healing methods.

Weisberger, Bernard A. *They Gathered at the River: The Story of the Great Revivalists and Their Impact on Religion in America.* Boston: Little, Brown and Co., c. 1958.

SECTION IV

The Evangelical United Brethren Church

The Evangelical United Brethren Church came into being through a merger in 1946 of the United Brethren Church and the Evangelical Church. These bodies have very similar historical, cultural, and doctrinal backgrounds and are closely related to Methodism in theology and polity.

The United Brethren. Philip William Otterbein (1726–1814), the founder of the United Brethren, had been trained for the Reformed ministry in Germany and came to America in 1752 at the invitation of Michael Schlatter, a Dutch Reformed pastor, to minister to the spiritually neglected and scattered Germans of Reformed antecedents. About 1754 Otterbein purported to have had a deep religious experience which prompted him to oppose strenuously the "educational religion" of his denomination. His doctrinal principle of "the assurance of personal salvation" and his revivals and protracted prayer meetings, love feasts, and the class system aroused the opposition of his coreligionists. About this time he and the Mennonite preacher Martin Boehm (1725–1813), who also preached "experimental religion," began to conduct revival meetings among the Germans in Pennsylvania, Maryland, and Virginia. In 1774 Otterbein accepted a call to an independent German congregation at Baltimore. In 1789 a conference of several ministers, formerly lay workers under Otterbein, was held, and in 1800 a definite organization was formed, with Otterbein and Boehm as bishops. Though such divergent theological tendencies as those of the Reformed, Lutheran, Mennonite, and Dunkard were represented, Arminian theology and Methodist church polity prevailed. But for the language question the new body would have been received by the Methodist church. The United Brethren Church experienced no theological controversies except one concerning man's conversion, but a schism resulted from a matter of discipline. In 1889 an article forbidding "connection with secret combinations" was modified to apply only to secret societies "which infringe upon the rights of those outside their organization and whose principles and practices are injurious to the Christian character of their members." Since this change was interpreted as permitting membership in fraternal and benevolent orders, a protesting minority withdrew and became known as Old Constitution Brethren.

In doctrine the United Brethren were strict Arminians and followed Wesley's theological principles rather closely. After a long controversy the conference of 1853 defined "depravity" as "absence of holiness, which unfits man for heaven, but does not involve guilt." They emphasized the doctrine of sanctification as "the work of God's grace by which those who have been born again are separated in their acts, words, and thoughts from sin." Like some Methodists they believed that in sanctification the desire to sin is removed. The Christian Sabbath was said to be divinely appointed. The mode of baptism, the manner of celebrating the Lord's Supper, the practice of infant baptism and foot washing, were left to the judgment of the individual.

The United Brethren adopted definite rules and regulations governing the conduct of their members. Like the Methodists they employed the class system. "In case of neglect of duty of any kind or disobedience to the order and discipline of the church, admonition and, if necessary, expulsion is to take place." Intoxicating drinks and slaveholding were strictly forbidden; the use of tobacco was discountenanced; social and political reforms, such as prohibition and the abolition of child labor, played a prominent part in the church activities.

The church polity was quasi-episcopal, the "stationing" committee, composed of the bishop and the conference superintendents, supplying the charges with pastors. The General Conference was the court of highest appeal.

The Evangelical Church. This body had a similar development. It is rightly considered one of the branches of Methodism. Its founder was Jacob Albright (Albrecht, 1759–1808), a Lutheran layman, who after his "conversion" in 1796 began to preach among the German people of eastern Pennsylvania. He was so thoroughly in accord with Methodist principles that he planned to establish a German branch of Methodism, a move which the Methodist bishops vetoed. Nevertheless in 1803 he effected a permanent organization. His adherents were called Albright People or Brethren (*Albrechtsleute, Albrechtsbrüder*), or German Methodists. The name of their own choosing was Evangelical Association (*Evangelische Gemeinschaft*). Later they adopted the name Evangelical Church. Working at first only in German, they later carried on their work predominantly in English. After the model of the Methodist Episcopal Church they adopted the circuit system and the itinerant ministry. In 1891, a number of churches withdrew and founded the United Evangelical Church. In 1922,

the latter body merged again with the Evangelical Church. Certain groups, however, remained apart.

The doctrine of the Evangelical Church was Arminian, and perfectionism was a prominent feature. Christian perfection was described as a state in which sin has lost its power over us and we rule over the flesh, the world, and Satan, yet in watchfulness.

The Methodist influence on Albright's doctrinal position is evident throughout his Articles of Faith. The visible church of Christ is described as the communion of the true believers. The decrees of the church are considered binding by divine right. Infant baptism is not universally practiced, and if a person baptized in infancy earnestly desires rebaptism, this may be granted him. Baptism is considered a sign whereby Christians obligate themselves to perform all Christian duties, and a symbol of the washing that has taken place inwardly. The polity Albright adopted for his organization has the essential features of Methodist church government — the circuit system, the itinerant ministry, a general, an annual, and a quarterly conference. Pastors were appointed annually by the bishop and the presiding elders. Through reappointment a pastor might serve a parish seven consecutive years. The bishops served four years.

The merger of the United Brethren and the Evangelical Churches required no essential changes in the doctrine or polity of either church, since their doctrine and polity were essentially Methodist. Church government is by conferences under the supervision of bishops or superintendents. The general conference, which meets every four years, is the highest authority. There are two conferences in Canada. Conversations are being carried on looking toward eventual union with The Methodist

Church and toward closer co-operation with the Church of the Brethren.

In addition to the merged body, there are three small related bodies.

The United Brethren in Christ (Old Constitution) does not differ from the larger body doctrinally, but only in matters of discipline, particularly concerning the lodge question.

The United Christian Church is a very small dissident group.

The Evangelical Congregational Church was formed by a small group which favored a more congregational polity than was provided for in the 1922 merger of the Evangelical and the United Evangelical Churches.

BIBLIOGRAPHY

PART V

SECTION IV

Drury, A. W. *History of the Church of the United Brethren.* Dayton: U. B. Publ. House, n. d.

Eller, Paul H. "The Evangelical United Brethren Church," in Vergilius Ferm, ed., *The American Church of the Protestant Heritage.* New York: Philosophical Library, 1953. Pp. 353—68.

Spreng, S. P. *The United American Brethren in Christ and the Evangelical Association.* ("American Church History Series XII.") New York: The Christian Literature Co., 1894.

Weaver, J. *Practical Comment on the Confession of Faith.* Dayton: U. B. Publ. House, n. d.

SECTION V

The Salvation Army

Its History

The Salvation Army was founded by William Booth (1829 to 1912), who at the age of seventeen became a lay preacher in the Wesleyan Methodist Church at Nottingham, England. In 1853 he entered the ministry of the New Connexion Methodists as pastor and evangelist. Supported by his wife, "the mother of the Army," he decided, over the protest of his superiors, to become an evangelist and met with remarkable success as an itinerant evangelist in various parts of England. In 1865 he began to preach to the neglected masses of London's East End, where his unconven-

tional methods, e. g., street preaching, processions, bands, emotional singing, etc., aroused the enmity of the ministers, but gained for him many loyal and enthusiastic followers. In the most uncomfortable and disreputable buildings the roughest, most ignorant, and wildest men and women of London were brought together and accepted the ministrations of Booth and his wife. By 1878 the number of stations had grown to eighty, and the work which had been known as the "Christian Mission" was officially organized and called the "Salvation Army." The organization is quasi-military, and its orders and regulations are modeled after those of the British army. Booth became its commander in chief and introduced a strictly autocratic form of government, demanding unquestioning obedience of all subordinates. The doctrinal summary is known as Articles of War; the mission halls are known as citadels. Such military terms as unit, corps, post, division, cadet, lieutenant, captain, general, indicate that the Salvation Army is organized for crusade and conquest. In 1880 the Salvation Army "opened its campaign" in America, but two years later the first defection under Thomas Moore occurred, which resulted in the organization of the American Rescue Workers. In 1896 the General's son, Commander Ballington Booth, and his wife seceded from the Army and organized the Volunteers of America. The Salvation Army survived these losses, however; currently it operates over 8,400 "centers of operation" in the United States, in addition to its activities in 85 foreign countries.

The work of the Army is twofold. Its prime purpose is said to be the spiritual regeneration of fallen mankind by endeavoring to persuade fallen men and women to lead clean lives. But Booth's belief was that a hungry man must first be fed before he would hunger for God. From the very beginning Booth's basic principle was that social and spiritual work must go hand in hand. He believed that the moral ills of London's "submerged tenth" were directly and exclusively the result of three social ills: pauperism, the white-slave trade, and the drink evil; and that at the bottom of these were the overcrowded conditions of London's East End. He hoped to reestablish broken men and women by a grand social rehabilitation program. He proposed to establish a city colony as a harbor of refuge and a place of employment within the city; a farm colony

where the rehabilitated might produce vegetables for the city colony; an overseas colony to absorb all those not provided for in the first colonies. The key to the entire scheme was that each colonist would be fully and honorably employed. The underlying principles of this program of social work are still the heart and core of the Salvation Army's social program. In many quarters the Army is considered the best agency to deal with social delinquency and the problems of the underprivileged. The Army has established "shelters" for men and women, boardinghouses for young women, maternity hospitals for unmarried mothers, orphanages, settlements in the poor quarters of the great cities. Prison work and parole, family relief, aid to stricken areas, and similar humanitarian endeavors are so prominent that the Salvation Army is frequently treated solely as a social agency. However, as a matter of fact, the Army workers in their social service aim to bring the "gospel of salvation by character to the neglected masses."

Its Theological System

The Salvation Army must therefore be considered a religious movement. Although it has no formal creed, it has a very definite theological system, which is summarized in the eleven articles of the *Foundation Deed,* the legal charter granted the society in 1878 and expanded in the catechisms and in the handbooks of doctrine.[1] William Booth, a Methodist by training, loyally followed Arminianism, more specifically, the emphases of Wesley. Like Wesley he believed that salvation is (1) "universal," inasmuch as also the heathen have the benefit of Christ's work without the preaching of the Gospel; is (2) "free," that is, man of his own

---

[1] The references in this section are to Bramwell Booth, *Handbook of Doctrine,* 1927.

choice both accepts or rejects God's grace; is (3) "full," since entire sanctification, or perfection, should be the goal of all Christians; and is (4) "sure," inasmuch as there is a direct witness to one's salvation. The formal and material principles of Booth's theology are practically identical with Wesley's.

In establishing his formal principle, or the source of religious truth, Booth and his followers manifest a spiritualism and a principle of the Spirit's immediacy similar to that underlying the Quaker theory of the "Inner Light." This fact is evident in his attitude toward the Scriptures and particularly toward the sacraments. On the one hand the Salvation Army teaches that

> the Scriptures of the Old and New Testaments were given by inspiration of God and that they only constitute the divine rule of Christian faith and practice.

On the other hand the Army actually holds that the Bible is not absolutely necessary, since God reveals His will immediately, speaks to men directly, goes straight to the heart, and speaks to His people through their spiritual leaders.[2] The extreme spiritualism of the Salvation Army appears especially in its attitude toward the two sacraments. It holds that since the religion of Jesus is spiritual, ceremonials "are sometimes a hindrance rather than a help to spiritual life." And for that reason, so they teach, Christ "did not leave any direction as to any outward ceremonial (sacrament) to replace that of the old dispensation." Baptism and the Lord's Supper are placed on a par with the abrogated Jewish ceremonies, are said to be unnecessary for salvation or the development of spiritual life and evidently

not intended to be perpetually observed. The all-important baptism is said to be the baptism with the Holy Spirit, which "results in the purifying of the heart and in power for service." The dedication of children, testimony, wearing uniforms, pledging total abstinence, being sworn in, and regulations are said to accomplish the same ends which the advocates of "water Baptism" claim for Baptism. Concerning the Lord's Supper the Army contends that "John's silence in this matter both in his Gospel and in his epistles is evidence that no new and essential ceremonial was instituted." The true observance of the Lord's Supper is said to consist in remembering Christ's death by engaging in spiritual conversation, "particularly in connection with (the regular) eating and drinking."[3]

The Salvation Army holds the Arminian view relative to the fall and sinfulness of man. The *Handbook* states that "all men are born with a sinful nature, which early leads to wrongdoing." But it also declares that man is a free agent and that man's "spiritual powers were marred, but not destroyed. God speaks through man's conscience, kindles in him good desires, and is at hand to make him more than superior to the evil in his dispositions and surroundings." "Free will enables man, by choosing the good, to rise to the highest heights of holiness or, by choosing evil, to sink to the lowest depths of sin." Man is not a child of wrath by nature, for "no one will perish for the sins of his forefathers who does not make such sins his own." In some sections of the *Handbook* the doctrine of total depravity seems to be taught: "He is born with an inclination to sin," and in others denied: "Spiritual death is, in some meas-

---

[2] Ibid., pp. 3—8, 114.

[3] Ibid., Appendix, pp. i—x. Cp. Bramwell Booth, *Echoes and Memoirs,* ch. xxii. He takes the Quaker attitude toward the sacraments. The allegedly "neutral position" toward the sacraments is tantamount to a rejection of the sacraments.

ure, the condition of all by nature . . .
however, is not at once complete and
. . . does not imply the absence of will
power." Hence man is able to work out
his own salvation, for "God commands
the sinners to repent; and this implies
that they are able to do so." In discussing the doctrine of election the *Handbook* declares that "God chooses those
who themselves choose to do what He
says." [4]

The Salvation Army holds a view of
the atonement which is largely the rectoral theory developed by the Arminian
Hugo Grotius. In accord with basic
Arminian principles the Salvation Army
views the work of Christ as being a revelation of the greatness of man's guilt
and of God's love. On the one hand the
Handbook declares that Christ "delivers
us from sin and its bondage"; but, on
the other, it states that "the death of
Jesus Christ should not be represented
as the literal or actual payment of the
sinner's debt." This view of Christ's
work is largely nomistic, inasmuch as
the Salvation Army considers the death
of Christ to have been sufficient to make
amends for the damage done the honor
of the Law and to induce men, because
of Christ's sacrifice, to "entertain a far
more profound respect for the Law and
justice of God than would have been
the case had He sent the human race
to hell." The greatness of our guilt and
the justice of God having been demonstrated by the death of Christ, the way
has been opened whereby that debt can
rightly be forgiven and pardoned. The
death of Christ revealed God's mercy
and permitted God "to let His love and
mercy flow out in forgiveness to those
who repent and trust the Savior." And
in this sense "Christ is a Propitiation for

sin, or Satisfaction to divine justice."
The Salvation Army attempts to reconcile its view of man's free will and God's
unmerited grace in Christ's redemption
by stating that "God's promises always
have some condition attached. . . . However, no man can do or suffer anything
to merit salvation. The only ground of
salvation is to be ascribed to love of God
as revealed in the work and sacrifice of
Christ. . . . But man is free to accept or
reject the salvation which he in no way
merits." [5] Regeneration, or conversion,
is described as a "change of character
by which we are once more made in
goodness and truth and love after the
likeness of God . . . the beginning of
a new spiritual life, the soul starting life
afresh with everything new," so that
"the ruling principle of life has been
changed from selfishness to love of God
and the fellowman." Justification is
viewed as a forensic act, for God "in
virtue of Christ's sacrifice does justice
to that sacrifice by pardoning the believing penitent." But in accord with
the Grotian theory of the atonement it
is not the vicarious work performed in
man's stead which is actually the ground
of God's justifying act, but the love of
God as shown in the sacrifice of Christ." [6]
The first condition for salvation is repentance, "the sincere determination to
forsake sin and to obey God, to long for
pardon, to make restitution as far as
possible." [7] Faith is a second requisite.
In its description of faith the Salvation
Army at times seems to come close to
the definition of the sixteenth-century
reformers, who viewed faith as the hand
which appropriates Christ's work. But
the *Handbook,* in accord with Arminian
theology, views faith primarily as trusting obedience, as "that act of personal

[4] *Handbook,* pp. 54, 58, 96, 79.

[5] Ibid., pp. 72, 65, 73, 68, 81.

[6] Ibid., pp. 100—105.

[7] Ibid., pp. 93—96.

heart trust by which the sinner commits himself to God and accepts the forgiveness which God so freely offers." Obviously the Salvation Army views faith primarily as obedience, for it teaches that the heathen can be saved without knowledge of, or faith in, Christ. According to John 1:9 the heathen are said to "have a measure of light," know "something of God's love, mercy, and Fatherhood," and "will be dealt with according to the light they possess." Even though they have no knowledge of Christ, "they will be accepted on the ground of Christ's atoning sacrifice" (which has vindicated God's justice and made reconciliation possible). "Obeying the light is the condition of their salvation, just as faith in Jesus is the condition of ours." [8]

The Salvation Army teaches entire sanctification. Artile X of the *Foundation Deed* reads as follows:

> We believe that it is the privilege of all believers to be wholly sanctified, and that their whole spirit, and soul, and body may be preserved blameless unto the coming of our Lord Jesus Christ (1 Thess. 5:23). That is to say, we believe that after conversion there remain in the heart of the believer inclinations to evil, or roots of bitterness, which, unless overpowered by Divine grace, produce actual sin; but that these evil tendencies can be entirely taken away by the Spirit of God and the whole heart, thus cleansed from everything contrary to the will of God, or entirely sanctified, will then produce the fruit of the Spirit only. And we believe that persons thus entirely sanctified may, by the power of God, be kept unblamable and unreprovable before Him.

Accordingly Booth's description of Christian perfection seems to be in accord with that of the modern Perfectionists rather than that of Wesley. The *Hand-book* declares that the entirely sanctified person's "disposition is entirely purified; inborn sin is done away with, or destroyed." It seems to be self-understood that "no really efficient [Salvation Army] officer is without this blessing." [9] The central theme of the Salvation Army is holiness of life. Its material principle is the rebuilding of character. This is so central that it lists among the joys of heaven the further development of character.[10]

The Salvation Army in Canada conducts the body's activities in that country and in Bermuda.

American Rescue Workers

In 1882 Thomas E. Moore was placed in charge of Salvation Army work in the United States, but differences of opinion as to administration caused him to withdraw from the London headquarters. In 1896 he organized the American Rescue Workers. These say that they are thoroughly American in their principles and methods and stress the right of separate existence on the premise that the work of the Salvation Army "is of such character and importance that it can best be done under American methods and rule." The organization of the American Rescue Workers follows a military pattern. The activities of the group are of the typical "rescue mission" kind. Its workers must "give every evidence of a change of heart and must live for the bettering and saving of humanity." The cardinal doctrines are emblematized in the American Rescue Workers' banner, the background of white representing purity, the five-pointed red star symbolizing the blood of Christ, the border of blue representing the heavenliness, and the fringe of yellow typifying the fire of the Holy Ghost. Its theology is virtually

[8] Ibid., pp. 109—11.

[9] Ibid., p. 123.

[10] Ibid., p. 169.

identical with that of the Salvation Army, except, perhaps, that the Rescue Workers want to be not only a philanthropic and evangelistic society but also a Christian church, in which the sacraments of Baptism and the Lord's Supper are administered.

The Volunteers of America

In 1896 Commander and Mrs. Ballington Booth organized the Volunteers of America, in response to a desire to establish a philanthropic and evangelistic society which "recognizes the spirit and justice of the Constitution of the United States, and it is not, and never shall be, controlled or governed by any foreign power whatsoever." Whereas the Salvation Army was absolutely autocratic in its discipline and government, the Volunteers wanted to espouse the democratic principles of self-government. But in methods, doctrines, and aims they have patterned their society after the parent organization. It is "a movement military in its methods, organized for the reaching and uplifting of all sections of people and bringing them to the immediate knowledge and service of God." The spiritual work is considered its real work, while its benevolent, philanthropic, and humanitarian endeavors are of secondary importance, being considered only a means to the end of bringing the Gospel to the neglected and unchurched. No charitable work may be done at a given place unless spiritual work is first established. The Volunteer movement must therefore be considered a church. Doctrinally the Volunteers are closely related to the Salvation Army, of which they are in a sense an offshoot, for they have adopted the same fundamental principles. They differ from the Army in so far as they do not treat the sacraments disparagingly. The Constitution prescribes that the sacraments shall be administered to all who desire them, but "the observance of the sacraments is not to be considered as an essential condition of membership." [11] The society is active in various phases of social relief. But its outstanding philanthropic work is done among prisoners. They also assist the families of prisoners and the paroled and the discharged prisoners.

BIBLIOGRAPHY

PART V   SECTION V

Booth, Bramwell. *Salvation Army Handbook of Doctrine.* London, 1927.

――――. *Echoes and Memoirs.* New York: Geo. H. Doran, 1925.

Booth, Maud B. *Beneath Two Flags.* New York: Funk & Wagnalls, 1891.

Booth, William. *In Darkest England and the Way Out.* Chicago, 1890.

Ervine, St. John. *God's Soldier, General William Booth.* New York: Macmillan Co., 1935.

Manual of Rules for the Volunteers of America. New York: National Headquarters, n. d.

Wilson, P. W. *General Evangeline Booth of the Salvation Army.* New York: Chas. Scribner's Sons, 1948.

Wisbey, Herbert Andrew, Jr. *Soldiers Without Swords: A History of the Salvation Army in the United States.* New York: Macmillan Co., 1956.

11 *Manual of Rules,* pp. 65—72.

SECTION VI
Scandinavian Bodies

Evangelical Covenant Church of America

The majority of the Swedish immigrants who came to this country during the second half of the nineteenth century had been members of the Swedish state church and upon their arrival in America quite naturally united with the Swedish Augustana Synod, which had maintained fraternal relations with the Lutheran state church in Sweden. An appreciable number of immigrants, however, came from the free churches or from mission societies of Sweden which had all but seceded from the Lutheran state church after the great revival of the nineteenth century, which, in turn, had been fed by German Pietism, Herrnhuterism, and Methodism.[1] The Swedish immigrants coming from the mission societies organized independent congregations, or "mission" churches. In 1873 a number of these societies, especially in Illinois, united and formed the Swedish Lutheran Mission Synod, and in the following year others organized the Ansgarius Synod. Since the work of these two bodies was identical, they united in 1855 as the Swedish Evangelical Mission Covenant of America. In 1957 the present name was adopted. The Covenant Church is in reality no more than a voluntary union of congregations without a specific or binding creedal statement. According to its constitution, the Covenant congregations accept the Holy Scriptures as God's Word and as the only rule of faith, creed, and conduct. They claim to be determined to perpetuate their evangelical freedom of thought and worship by avoiding both an unevangelical modernism and the rigidity of confessional orthodox fundamentalism.[2]

In accord with its historic origin in Sweden the Covenant Church stresses the following "covenant principles":

1. The necessity of spiritual life, which is described as

a personal and vital relationship to Christ as the Savior. This means to know and love and trust and obey Him. It is a commitment of life itself. This relationship is a sunny reality that puts a new halo on every phase of life. The Bible describes it as a new birth, a new creation, a resurrection from the dead. It is a partaking of the divine nature. Christ makes all things new.

2. The essential unity of all true Christians, which

means admitting into the church all who are recognized as believers and barring from active church membership all others. Minor differences regarding issues on which sincere Christians disagree must not divide us. Even at their best, human creeds and codes are fragmentary. Unity and uniformity are not synonymous.

[1] Nathaniel Franklin, *Covenant Church Membership.* (Chicago: Covenant Book Concern), p. 13. Cp. Gösta Hök, "Herrnhutische Theologie in schwedischer Gestalt," *Uppsala Universitets Arsskrift,* 1950.

[2] Franklin, pp. 15, 20. Cp. also Danal C. Frisk, *What Christians Believe* (Chicago: Covenant Press, 1951). *Yearbook,* 1952, Evangelical Covenant Church.

Without distinguishing the church in the strict and in the wider sense one writer states:

> The door to the church must be sufficiently wide to admit all true believers, but not wide enough to admit the unbelieving world. The proper place for a boat is in the water, but woe to the boat if the water comes in and fills the boat. And the proper place for a church is in the world, but woe to the church if the unregenerate world comes in and fills the church.

3. Consecrated living in every area of life.

4. An urgent missionary imperative.

Evangelical Free Church of America

This body represents a merger of the Swedish Evangelical Free Church and the Evangelical Free Church Association, formerly the Norwegian and Danish Evangelical Free Church Association. This merger was effected in 1950.

When the Swedish Covenant Church was organized in 1885, a number of mission congregations declined to join the union and organized the Swedish Evangelical Free Mission, later changed to Swedish Evangelical Free Church, and more recently to Evangelical Free Church of America. It allows still greater liberty in doctrine than the Covenant Church, permitting its ministers to have their own convictions concerning such doctrines as the atonement, Baptism, and Holy Communion. The only requisite for church membership is "conversion" and "the Christian life." Baptism is usually administered by immersion.[3]

[3] On the Scandinavian bodies see also Karl A. Olsson, "The Evangelical Mission Covenant Churches and the Free Churches of Swedish Background," in Vergilius Ferm, ed., *The American Church of the Protestant Heritage* (New York: Philosophical Library, 1953), pp. 249—76.

Unionizing Churches

Introduction

The attempts to merge denominations usually stem from one of two motives: (1) the desire to remove at least some of the schisms in visible Christendom by uniting those churches which have a common historical, cultural, and doctrinal background; (2) the belief that the restoration of the apostolic church requires the complete eradication of denominational names and creeds. The first type of unionism is predicated on the premise that the church can best fulfill her mission by external union. The advocates of this principle overlook the fact that history has established beyond a doubt that church unions without doctrinal unity have strengthened neither the merging bodies nor Christendom as a whole.[1] The Moravian church adopted as its principle the unionistic motto: "In essentials unity, in nonessentials liberty, in all things charity." But this church, the oldest of the Protestant churches, has remained numerically small and relatively unimportant. The Evangelical and Reformed Church exhibited no phenomenal growth during the twenty-three years of its existence prior to its merger into the United Church of Christ.

The same is true of the United Church of Canada, a Congregational-Presbyterian-Methodist merger, and of Community churches. The last-named usually are undenominational or federated churches in local areas. The leaders of the World Council of Churches seem to favor the continuance of denominational distinctions without denominational separations until the time when all Christian denominations unite in "true unity." The continuance of the separate denominational organizations is even encouraged on the ground that each group has a distinct contribution to make and that a premature organizational union would despoil Christendom of the diversity of gifts which is a potential of a divided, though unseparated, church.

The first motive for union takes the *status quo* of divided Christendom for granted and hopes to remove the divisions by mergers. The second motive usually operates with an extreme form of Biblicism. However, it usually considers the New Testament unity of the holy Christian church as organizational and identifies the church with one visible organization.[2]

NOTE: For key to abbreviations see Appendix C; for Bibliography, the end of the section.

[1] Engelder, et al., *Pop. Symb.*, p. 16 ff. Th. Hoyer, "Union Movements in the Church," *Proceedings of the Evangelical Lutheran Synodical Conference* (St. Louis: C. P. H., 1938), pp. 10—49. The Prussian Union, the merger of Lutherans and Reformed brought about through a royal edict, sapped the lifeblood of the German Lutheran church wherever and as long as this unnatural union existed.

[2] Neve, *Ch. and Sects*, p. 377, distinguishes between conservative and comprehensive unions. But according to C. Meusel, *Kirchliches Handlexikon* (Leipzig: Justus Naumann, 1887), s. v. "Union," this nomenclature applies to German, not to American, church conditions.

Denominational names or creeds, extra-Biblical forms of cultus and polity, ecclesiastical nomenclature, are said to be inherently sinful because they are not prescribed in the New Testament. Known also as the Restoration Movement, this type of unionism hopes to restore the fourfold original characteristics of the New Testament church: its unity, by a visible unity of all Christians in one body; its apostolicity, by following only those practices expressly sanctioned by the apostles; its catholicity, by removing all denominational divisions; its holiness, by emphasizing deeds, not formulated creeds. This type of unionism, represented chiefly in the young churches of America, was a part of the expanding American frontier at the turn of the nineteenth century. It is represented in such groups as the Disciples of Christ, the Churches of Christ, Christians, and the General Convention of Christian Churches (now a part of the United Church of Christ). The Plymouth Brethren and one group of Churches of God (Winebrennerians) resemble the Christians in some aspects.

SECTION I

Moravians

The oldest among the union Churches is the Moravian church. Its history goes back to the work of John Huss and Jerome of Prague, martyred in 1415 and 1416 respectively. In 1457 the followers of Huss and Jerome formed an association at Kunwald, withdrew from the Bohemian national church, and ten years later organized the "Brethren of the Law of Christ," also known as the *Unitas Fratrum*. The distinctive features of this organization were: (1) the earnest desire to organize the serious-minded laymen as separate groups, to act as a leaven within the established national church, and, in particular, to supplant the perfunctory worship of the state church with a service patterned after that of the apostolic church; (2) its consistent opposition to all formulated creeds and its resultant latitu-dinarianism. The first synod (1457) declared that "a godly life is essential as evidence of saving faith and is of greater importance than the dogmatic formulation of creeds in all details so as to be binding upon all." [3]

At the beginning of the Lutheran Reformation the Brethren numbered about 400 parishes with 200,000 members, had their own catechism and hymnal, operated printing presses, and even had their own bishops. Luther repeatedly conferred with them,[4] but they preferred the Bucerian-Reformed type of theology. During the succeeding decades the Roman Catholic Counter Reformation almost exterminated the *Unitas*. Only a small group, "a hidden remnant," carefully observed the *Unitas* principles and continued the episcopate "in the secret hope of a resuscitated *Unitas*."

---

[3] E. de Schweinitz and A. Schultze, p. 4. For a sympathetic appreciation of John Huss, see Matthew Spinka, ed., *Advocates of Reform from Wyclif to Erasmus* (Philadelphia: The Westminster Press, 1953), pp. 187 to 195.

[4] Cp. Luther, W. A., VI, 454—457, and Koestlin, I, 635 ff. (See P. III, Bibliog.)

The resuscitation of the *Unitas Fratrum* occurred a century later. In 1722 Christian David revived the principles of the original *Unitas* and led the Neisser family to the estate of Count Zinzendorf in Saxony, where the Brethren established a colony called Herrnhut, i. e., the Lord's watch. Soon several hundred Bohemians, Moravians, Lutheran Saxons, and a sprinkling of Reformed settled in the Moravian colony and willingly adopted the same distinctive features which had characterized the original Unity, namely, a fellowship based on piety rather than on doctrine. The mystical and Pietistic tendencies of the Moravians appealed to Zinzendorf, the godchild of the Pietist Jakob Spener. The Moravians considered themselves a leaven in a society which was Christian in name only. To carry out this ideal, the Herrnhut colony retained "the ordinances and statutes received from the fathers, which had made this church an instrument in promoting the spiritual life of its living members, in quickening the dead, in confirming the feeble and wavering, and in correcting the obstinate and insincere." [5] Zinzendorf supported the Pietistic principle of establishing a "little church within the church." He added rules and statutes to govern the entire conduct of the members of this religious community and purposed to present, as far as possible, "the communion of saints, a living communion of Jesus Christ in the fellowship of faith and the observance of God's commandments." [6] Zinzendorf hoped to make the *Unitas* "a grand association upon the basis of experimental religion and practical piety." [7] His plan was to create throughout the world, primarily among the Germans of America, "little retreats, cut off from the world, for the promotion of personal spirituality and the development of a holy brotherhood," with little or no regard for doctrinal matters. Zinzendorf viewed dissenting creeds only as so many "modes of teaching." The Augsburg Confession was adopted as the confessional standard merely to satisfy the demands of the government, which was Lutheran. Zinzendorf at first did not desire to organize a distinct religious body. But the Herrnhut group became a separate denomination when it reassumed the old official name, *Unitas Fratrum*, and when in 1735 the episcopacy, "which had been wonderfully preserved, was transferred upon David Nitzschmann by Daniel Jablonski and Christian Sitkovius." Zinzendorf became the second bishop, and under his aggressive leadership the body was officially recognized in Germany and England and began its farflung mission endeavor, organizing "religious communities governed by laws having for their object a total separation from the sinful follies of the world." The body soon became known as the Moravian Church.

The missionary zeal prompted the Moravians to send a group of colonists to Savannah in 1734, where the two Wesleys became acquainted with the exclusive polity and Pietistic tendencies of the Herrnhuters. At the same time a settlement was started at Philadelphia, at the invitation of George Whitefield, which was later transferred to Bethlehem, Nazareth, and Lititz, Pa. In these colonies the members were grouped according to age and station into separate "choirs" under the supervision of one or more elders. The Moravians immediately entered upon an aggressive missionary program, not for the expansion of their denomination, but professedly to set

[5] Fabricius, IV, 4.

[6] Ibid., p. 2.

[7] *Moravian Manual*, p. 31.

before all Christendom the pattern of a "pure church." In 1843 the American communities of Moravians discontinued the "choir" system and became a regular denomination.[8]

Doctrinal Position

Unionism and Pietism are the two distinctive doctrinal characteristics of the Moravian church.

1. The Moravians, "in common with all Christendom, adhere to the doctrines contained in the Apostles' Creed and further recognize that the chief doctrines of the Christian faith are clearly set forth in the first twenty-one articles of the Augsburg Confession," without in the least binding the consciences, "especially in those countries where the Augsburg Confession has not the same authority as in Germany."[9] The principle "In essentials unity, in nonessentials liberty, in all things charity," prompts them to seek "unity in variety" and to express the heart of the Gospel in various forms.[10] Moravians believe that the peculiar mission of their church is to effect a higher and living unity by unifying the divergent points of view among Christians as far as these can be traced to the Scriptures. Moravians teach that the personal, mystical union with Christ is the living force of Christianity, and they offer the hand of fellowship to everyone who accepts this basis, though he may incline to the Lutheran or the Reformed position, believing that "only one thing is needful, namely, to love our Lord in sincerity and to live to His glory."[11]

2. The Moravians have always placed great emphasis upon personal and emotional piety. In his endeavor to popularize the Halle Pietism, Zinzendorf was carried to an extreme mystical subjectivism. The Brethren have not followed their leader in his sentimental extravagance. They are nevertheless definitely committed to the principle that "the aim of the church is to constitute a living church in which every individual is a true Christian." Moravians believe that the peculiar purpose of their church is to keep its members "in constant confidential intercourse with Christ . . . and to carry the new life of the regenerate child forward towards its maturity and its perfection in eternity." To foster the continual intimate communion of the pardoned sinner with the Savior, Moravians stress the observance of disciplinary measures and the diligent use of spiritual exercises. While many of the specific rules and ordinances, e. g., the choir system, daily services, the communal life to exclude all sinful follies, the brethren's, sisters', and widows' houses under a spiritual superintendent, have been abrogated in all but the Continental European colonies, yet "every church is bound to confess adherence to a printed code of regulations embodying its discipline."[12]

The peculiar type of Moravian piety has manifested itself in the group's theology and cultus. One would expect the Moravians to be strong advocates of legalism, since they stress the observance of rules in the interest of developing and accentuating pious and sentimental

---

[8] Ibid., p. 44. — The *Losungen,* daily Scripture texts and brief meditations, prepared by the Moravians, are widely and favorably known.

[9] *Moravian Manual,* p. 84.

[10] Resolutions of 1909, Fabricius, IV, 74.

[11] Sovocol, pp. 88, 425. See also Josef Dobias, "Ecumenical Motifs in the Theology of the 'Unity of Bohemian Brethren,'" in *Ecumenical Review,* XII (1959/1960), 455—470.

[12] Cp. *Catechism,* p. 125; *Synodal Results,* 1914; *Manual,* pp. 88 f., 111, 43 ff.

love of the Redeemer. In theory they are strictly antinomian, rejecting, in the final analysis, the preaching of the Law both to the unconverted sinners and to the Christians. They claim to make the "bloody merit of Jesus" the beginning, middle, and end of their sermons, their hymns, their liturgy. The preaching of Christ's death is said to work contrition, conversion, and sanctification. Their missionaries are instructed not to preach the Law, but to "proclaim the bloody sacrifice of Jesus to the heathen to convince them of the damnableness of idolatry." [13] The goal of Christian preaching and instruction among the Moravians is to know and love Jesus as a personal Friend in whose company and presence one experiences a deep religious peace and joy. To attain this aim, the sinner dare not resist the divine call addressed to him in the preaching of Christ, but, awakened to a deep sense of his misery, he must throw himself into the arms of the Savior, lay hold of Christ's redemption, and consecrate himself to Christ.[14] The emphasis which Moravians place on the believer's mystical union with Christ, more specifically the atoning Savior, is evident from their views regarding the sacraments. Infant baptism is not regarded as the sacrament of initiation, but merely as a public testimony that the child is to be reared in the nurture of the Lord. The Lord's Supper is considered an opportunity for self-examination, for renewing the union with the Lord, and for an expression of the bond of fellowship.[15]

Their peculiar type of piety is manifest also in the Moravian cultus. To confirm the believer's joy and love in the Savior, they place great importance on outward means, such as liturgically attractive services, the rite of confirmation, numerous festivals, special gatherings for the respective ages and classes of members, Bible classes, song services, love feasts, and especially the regular Sunday services. The Christian Sunday is said to be founded upon the completion of the first and the second creation, i. e., the resurrection of Christ, and therefore all distractions are proscribed on Sunday. The emphasis which Moravians have always placed upon emotional religion has made this church rich in its liturgy and hymnody.[16]

Moravian polity can be described as democratic, though the general supervision of the congregations rests with the provincial synods. The Moravians claim to be the oldest Protestant episcopal church, tracing the episcopal successions to Matthias von Kunwald, in 1467, though the authority of the bishops

[13] Fabricius, pp. 9, 55. The Moravian antinomianism, known also as "blood theology," was offensive to John Wesley and one of the reasons for his early departure from Herrnhut.

[14] *Manual*, p. 87 ff. Sovocol, p. 452.

[15] Fabricius, p. 22. The congregation is always represented at sick communions to indicate formally that the Lord's Supper is primarily a *Gemeinschaftsmahl*.

[16] Zinzendorf "wrote over 2,000 hymns, some of them good, most of little merit, and some excessive in their emotionalism, bordering on irreverence." Two of his hymns are in *The Lutheran Hymnal:* No. 371, "Jesus, Thy Blood and Righteousness"; No. 410, "Jesus, Lead Thou On." Cp. W. G. Polack, *Handbook to The Lutheran Hymnal* (St. Louis: C. P. H., 1946), p. 603. James Montgomery "wrote 400 hymns, of which 100 are still in common use. A perusal of almost any English evangelical hymnbook will probably reveal more hymns by this gifted and consecrated man than by any other author, excepting only Isaac Watts and Charles Wesley." Fourteen of his hymns are in *The Lutheran Hymnal* — Nos. 2, 35, 59, 136, 149, 159, 454, 455, 484, 490, 504, 516, 616, 635. Cp. Polack, p. 548.

is very limited. The general synod, with headquarters in Herrnhut, deals with matters of faith and discipline and governs the foreign mission work.

Though the Moravians have remained a small body, they have exerted considerable influence. They were pioneers in mission work, and they have always emphasized the need of thorough Christian training.[17]

The foregoing applies to the *Moravian Church in America (Unitas Fratrum)*.

The *Unity of the Brethren* (as the former *Evangelical Unity of the Czech-* *Moravian Brethren in North America* has been known since 1959) "is a child of the old *Unitas,* founded in Bohemia, 1457." Since the Edict of Toleration, 1781, granted religious liberty to Lutherans and Reformed, but not to the *Unitas,* the Brethren temporarily united with these tolerated churches and at the same time retained the distinctive features of the ancient *Unitas.* In 1850 a number of such members in the Lutheran and Reformed churches of Czechoslovakia emigrated to Texas. Their doctrinal position is very close to that of the Moravians.[18]

BIBLIOGRAPHY

PART VI   SECTION I

De Schweinitz, E., and A. Schultze. *The Moravians and Their Faith.* Bethlehem, Pa.: Moravian Book Shop, 1930.

Fabricius, C. *Corpus Confessionum.* Berlin and Leipzig: W. De Gruyter, 1931. Contains history, confessional standards, ritual, hymns, synodal results, etc.

Langton, Edward. *History of the Moravian Church: The Story of the First International Protestant Church.* London: George Allen and Unwin, 1956.

Moravian Manual, The, publ. by authority of the Provincial Synod of the American

Moravian Church, North, Bethlehem, Pa.: Moravian Book Shop, 1901.

Sovocol, L. R. "The Moravians and Their Religious Philosophy," *Bibliotheca Sacra,* LXXXVIII, 440 ff.

Weinlick, John R. "The Moravian Church," in Vergilius Ferm, ed., *The American Church of the Protestant Heritage.* New York: Philosophical Library, 1953. Pp. 7 to 21.

———. *Count Zinzendorf.* New York: Abingdon Press, c. 1956.

[17] Goethe and Schleiermacher could not deny their early Moravian background.

[18] This information was supplied by the Rev. Joseph Hegar of Hus Memorial School, Temple, Tex.

SECTION II

The United Church of Christ

In June 1957 the General Council of Congregational and Christian Churches and the Evangelical and Reformed Church united to form the United Church of Christ. The last meetings of the constituent bodies were held in 1958 and the first General Synod of the United Church of Christ met in July 1959. The constitution of the new body was approved in 1960 and is to be presented for formal acceptance at the 1961 General Synod in Philadelphia. The merger has been described as "in some ways the most significant union that has taken place in our country, since it has united two denominations of very different backgrounds and polity, and has done so in such a way as deliberately to invite and encourage further union with other bodies." The new union has begun informal talks with united churches in India, Germany, Canada, and other parts of the world, with a view to exploring "the future witness of interconfessional united churches in general ecumenical conversations." [1]

Precisely because the United Church of Christ is so new, however, the best approach to understanding it must proceed by reviewing the history of the four streams of tradition that it combines: (1) the Congregational tradition and (2) the Restorationist "Christian" tradition that merged in 1931 to produce the General Council of Congregational and Christian Churches; and (3) the German Evangelical-United tradition

and (4) the German Reformed tradition that were fused in 1934 into the Evangelical and Reformed Church.

Congregationalism

During the sixteenth century the Protestants in England were divided into four parties: the Anglicans, the Puritans, the Congregationalists, and the Separatists.[2] In theology the last three groups were largely in agreement. The point at issue between them pertained to the New Testament concept of *ecclesia* or the local congregation. The Puritans recognized the Established Church as the properly constituted church; the perfectionist Separatists, however, insisted that the term *ecclesia* applied only to "an organized brotherhood of converted believers in a specific locality," fully autonomous and responsible only to Christ.[3] Another difference concerned the endeavor to purify the Anglican church of all Romanizing tendencies. The Puritans wanted to remain within the church to purify it from within, whereas the Separatists held that the Established Church was so corrupt that separation from it was mandatory. But under the reign of Queen Elizabeth such separation or nonconformity was severely punished. Under the spiritual leadership of Robert Browne and John Robinson, many Separatists found a haven of refuge in Holland. Here Ames and Jacob converted Robinson from Sep-

---

[1] Keith R. Bridston, "Survey of Church Union Negotiations 1957 to 1959," *Ecumenical Review*, XII (1959/1960), 255.

[2] See p. 228, n. 7, above.

[3] Schaff, *Creeds*, I, 826 f., esp. p. 827, n. 1.

aratism to Congregationalism. The various groups of exiles were united in maintaining the basic premises of Calvinistic theology.[4] At the same time the differences between the Congregationalists and the perfectionist Separatists became increasingly serious and divisive. The former emphasized the supremacy and sovereignty of the local congregation. The latter went a step farther and insisted on the supremacy and competency of the individual conscience, which caused them to advocate a so-called "believers' baptism" and to reject infant baptism.[5]

BRITISH CONGREGATIONALISM

The distinctive characteristic and basic principle of English Separatism was developed chiefly by Robert Browne. In his opinion the church is a congregation of experiential believers in Christ in a specific locality. The pattern of the apostolic church allows each local group of Christians to govern itself. However, it is not to do so according to the laws of the state, but solely according to the rules and regulations which the Bible lays down for each congregation. Browne recognized no other leadership than that of "the Spirit of the living Christ." He believed that the people must be free to worship God as their conscience dictates and to establish only such offices and enact only such laws as best suit their purposes and conform to the New Testament pattern.[6]

But Ames, Jacob, and after his con-version, Robinson saw that the principle of complete autonomy of the local congregation might readily lead to extreme spiritism or "ecclesiastical atomism." Therefore they endeavored to establish a form of fellowship which would unite the individual congregations without infringing upon their independence. Theoretically English Congregationalism had "two taproots, independency and fellowship, on the basis of the Puritan or Calvinistic faith. . . . It is a compromise between pure Independency and Presbyterianism." [7] In practice, however, English Congregationalism moved toward independency. Strictly speaking, Congregationalism has no interest in creeds and confessional standards as a means to unite separate congregations. Nevertheless, British Congregationalism has adopted the Savoy Declaration — essentially the same doctrinal statement as the Westminster Confession, except that they differ in the article dealing with church government.

AMERICAN CONGREGATIONALISM

In 1620 the first band of Pilgrim Congregationalists founded the colony at Plymouth, Mass., and organized the first Congregational church upon American soil. It is significant that John Robinson, the spiritual father of the Pilgrims, had dispatched them from England with these words: "The Lord has more light and truth to break forth out of His holy Word." In America Congregationalism developed somewhat differently than in

---

[4] In a symposium under the title "The Witness of the Churches of the Congregational Order" (*Christendom*, Autumn, 1940, p. 481 f.), R. A. Ashworth, Charles Clayton Morrison, and Douglas Horton, representing respectively the Baptists, the Disciples, and the Congregationalists, show that there is a basic similarity among these three groups and that the points of difference are relatively unimportant. Accordingly the early Congregationalists and Baptists, and later the Disciples, consistently follow the principle of the sovereignty of the local congregation in determining matters of faith and life.

[5] See "The Baptist Churches," P. IV, Sec. VI.

[6] Fagley, *Congr. Ch.*, pp. 6, 47.

[7] Schaff, loc. cit.

England, largely because of the pioneering spirit of the frontiersmen and the peculiar needs of the isolated colonists. These differences are chiefly twofold: (1) In England Congregationalism moved more and more toward independency; in America both independency and fellowship were fully preserved and yet successfully fused. (2) In England Congregationalism remained relatively loyal to the theology of the Savoy Declaration; in America independency led to an ever greater emancipation from doctrinal control.

HISTORY

1. The Pilgrim Fathers who settled at Plymouth were Congregationalists; whereas the Puritans who nine years later founded nearby Salem, and the group which in 1639 settled at New Haven, Conn., were Presbyterians. In theology the Congregationalists and Presbyterians were in accord, both having adopted the Westminster theology. The "Bay People" at Salem had come directly from England, while the "Plymouth People" had come via the Netherlands. The two groups were brought into intimate contact when the Pilgrim Fathers at Plymouth were called upon to aid the neighboring Puritans at Salem during an epidemic in 1630. In subsequent meetings, arranged by Governor Endicott at Salem and the physician Dr. Fuller at Plymouth, they discovered their agreement in doctrine and in 1648 jointly adopted the Cambridge Platform. This document, the charter of American Congregationalism, not only preserves the principles of independency and fellowship, but also unites them in a practical way.[8] Indeed, American Congregationalists always cherished both principles. On the one hand, they laid great emphasis on independency, which has been described as follows:

> The individual Christian is regarded as responsible directly to God and as having immediate access to God by many pathways, but pre-eminently through Jesus Christ. . . . He is subject to his own conscience as led by the Spirit of God. . . . As does the individual Christian, so the church [congregation] enjoys full freedom. . . . Each church [congregation] enjoys full autonomy. It elects its officers, determines its own Constitution and By-Laws, formulates or adopts its own covenant or mutual obligations, and, if one is desired, its statement of beliefs and principles. The local congregation exercises all power of admitting or excluding members, regulates the forms of its worship, determines the corporate life, sets for itself the tasks of Christian service which it

[8] The Cambridge Platform (1648) states: "Although Churches be distinct, and therefore may not be confounded one with another: and equal, and therefore have not dominion one over another: yet all the churches ought to preserve church communion one with another, because they are all united unto Christ, not only as a mystical, but as a political Head; whence is derived a communion suitable thereunto. . . . Synods orderly assembled, and rightly proceeding according to the pattern, Acts 15, we acknowledge as the ordinance of Christ: and though not absolutely necessary to the being, yet many times, through the iniquity of men, and perverseness of times, necessary to the well-being of churches, for the establishment of truth, and peace therein. . . . It belongeth unto Synods and counsels, to debate and determine controversies of faith, and cases of conscience. . . . Not to exercise Church-censures in way of discipline, nor any other act of church-authority or jurisdiction. . . . The Synod's directions and determinations, so far as consonant to the word of God, are to be received with reverence and submission. . . ." Walker, *Cr. and Platf.*, pp. 229—234. The same author (*History*, III, 153—63) gives a detailed account of the discussion leading up to the adoption of the Cambridge Platform. It is significant that this confession accepts the Westm. Conf., with the exception of the sections on church polity.

will undertake. Ultimate authority in all of its own interests resides in the whole body of the membership of each church, not in the officers or boards of the local congregation, not in any ecclesiastical body exterior to the church.[9]

On the other hand, they attached great significance to the principle of fellowship. This principle required individuals and local congregations constantly to check their own findings by the experiences of others. The bond which united the members of the local congregation, and to some extent the several congregations, was "the fellowship in common thinking and common aspirations." Modern Congregationalists expressed this principle as follows:

> The Christian is bound to respect the rights of others, to learn of others, to check his conscience by the conscience of others. . . . He recognizes the obligation under Christ of joining himself with other Christians to constitute the Church [congregation], in which he finds instruction, guidance, and inspiration, and to whose discipline he freely submits himself by a sacred covenant.[10]

The two marks of American Congregationalism were therefore independency and fellowship. In the fusion of these two principles Congregationalism manifested its strength and its weakness: its strength inasmuch as it placed great responsibility on the individual, its weakness inasmuch as it was unable to control doctrinal aberrations and encouraged theological liberalism.

2. Within the orbit of independency and fellowship Congregationalism was always impelled to free itself from what it considered theological and dogmatical bondage. Modern Congregationalists formulated their concept of fellowship thus:

> The Congregational Christian churches have from their inception refused to build their fellowship about any center save the living God, who reveals himself in Christ. Forms of church government, creeds, and rituals have to be used by human beings to express to each other the meaning of that God-centered fellowship. Every good form in the Church must therefore (a) witness to God and (b) conform to the apperceptions of those who would understand and profit by it. Congregational Christians have never gone to the extreme of denying the place of forms, but they have resolutely resisted the use of any particular one as sacrosanct. They have striven constantly toward the universal, which includes all particular forms. The form of their government, their theology, and their liturgical practice is hospitable to all forms by which Christians, whatever their denomination, point toward God. It is this quality which makes them the interdenominational denomination. Their fellowship is not exclusive, but inclusive. The two great sacraments mean induction into and nourishing communion in the universal fellowship of all who love and serve the Lord Jesus.
>
> They look toward people of faiths other than Christian with a somewhat simi-

---

[9] Burton, *Manual*, pp. 1, 2. Fagley, p. 47; cp. W. Horton, Pref., p. XIX. — For an answer to the question: What is the difference between the sovereignty of the congregation in Congregationalism and such sovereignty in other bodies, particularly in the Lutheran church, see Neve, *Churches and Sects*, p. 401. Traditional Congregationalist theory held that all other forms of church organization are contrary to the Scriptures, while Lutheranism holds that various forms of church organization are permissible.

[10] Burton, *Manual*, p. 3. See also Walker, *Cr. and Platf.*, p. 203 ff., and "Changes in Theology Among American Congregationalists," *Journal of Theology*, X, 204—18. Sweet, *Rel. in Col. Am.*, ch. iii. See also Emil Oberholzer, Jr., *Delinquent Saints: Disciplinary Action in the Early Congregational Churches of Massachusetts* (New York: Columbia University Press, 1956).

lar attitude. Congregational Christians would say of them that when their lives fundamentally witness to the living God of love, who is in Jesus Christ, they are essentially, if not formally, Christians.[11]

Under this concept of fellowship, Congregationalists asserted, they maintained their religious independence. In the words of modern Congregationalists:

> [They] have never delivered up their freedom to ecclesiastical authorities of any kind, whether individuals, minorities, or majorities; nor have they submitted their conscience to the powers of the State. So they remain a creative, not an imitative nor a servile community. To exercise freedom in behalf of the creative Spirit of God is, they believe, to escape slavery to tradition, to forms of all sorts, important as forms and traditions are in their place. The "freedom of the Christian man," as they understand it, does not mean irreverence for human statutes or divine commands, but the right to judge all external injunctions, in the last resort, by the inward light and leading of God's free Spirit.[12]

Congregationalism was not anti-creedal. It was noncreedal. It insisted that creeds dare not be invested with a binding character, but that liberty must be granted to each local church to formulate and adopt its own confession, or, if it so desired, not to have a creed at all. Historic Congregationalism was not indifferent to heresies, as its history proves. But fellowship as conceived in Congregationalism was no guarantee that independency, or individual freedom, would not eventuate in theological anarchy. The Congregational churches were totally impotent to deal with doctrinal aberrations because each local church was considered *iure divino* the final authority to establish its own doctrinal platform.[13] The peculiar blending of independency and fellowship in Congregationalism explains the fact that there is a straight line from the strict Calvinistic theology of the Pilgrim Fathers to religious liberalism, widespread among modern Congregationalists. Foster, a Congregationalist, stated quite correctly:

> Liberalism has been with them [the Congregational Churches] a matter of internal necessity. It has been their great good fortune to be free churches, free from ecclesiastical control and free in the association of like-minded men zealous for the truth and determined to know it ever more perfectly. They are historically innovators, from Scrooby to Plymouth, and from Boston to Providence. They have always been looking for more light, and they have been eager to follow it. The great, closely organized churches, like the Presbyterian and Episcopalian, cannot pass through a course of peaceful evolution of doctrine. Their only method is revolution. Hence the work of leadership has fallen upon these churches, whose natural American aggressiveness has been touched and hallowed by a longing for a deeper experience of religion and for an ever-increasing understanding of its fundamental principles.[14]

Though Congregationalism seemed to have deviated radically from the religious position of its founding fathers, it nevertheless remained loyal to its two basic principles of independency and fellowship.

In establishing the formal principle — the source of doctrine — one must keep in mind that the local congregation was

---

[11] *A Statement of Faith*, adopted at Grand Rapids, 1944, quoted in Horton, *Our Chr. Faith*, p. 58.

[12] Ibid., p. 70.

[13] F. E. Mayer, "The Rise of Liberal Theology in Congregationalism," *C. T. M.*, XV (1944), 649 ff.

[14] Foster, *Modern Movement*, pp. 14, 15.

sovereign and fixed the confessional standard by the light which it possessed at a given time. As a result, the material principle — the central doctrine — would change as the local congregation obtained further light in its independency and in its fellowship with other likeminded congregations. Congregationalists adopted a number of platforms over the years. However, these are not to be viewed as static confessions, but rather as indicating the points of emphasis at a given period and the general direction in which Congregationalists were moving theologically. To understand the spirit of Congregationalism one must study it in the light of its theological controversies and its reactions to political, social, and economic changes. In short, one must take note of the progressive development of its theology and practice as reflected in its history.

THE THEOLOGICAL DEVELOPMENT IN CONGREGATIONALISM

Probably no American denomination experienced so many doctrinal upheavals without losing its denominational identity as Congregationalism did. Later Congregationalism can best be understood in the light of doctrinal controversies that gave point and emphasis to the basic principles of its developed theology.

Social Covenanting and the Democratic Principle. One of the basic tenets of the early Congregational churches was the teaching that the local congregation constituted a group of experiential believers who were obligated to co-operate by a social covenant. The Mayflower Compact, adopted by the Plymouth colonists on November 11, 1620, reads in part as follows:

We covenant with the Lord and with one another and do bind ourselves in the plans of God to work together in all His ways according as He is pleased to reveal Himself unto us in His blessed Word of truth.[15]

Each signer of the compact agreed to take such part in the work of the local congregation and manifest such an attitude toward the other members as would most fully develop the spiritual life of all. Social covenanting is in reality the application of Calvin's theocratic principle to life in New England. This principle had several significant implications.

1. It led to the halfway-covenant theory. Only those persons could enter the covenant and be regarded as members of the ecclesiastico-political community who could point to a definite religious experience. It was seriously questioned whether others were eligible for membership in the congregation and even in the political society. More disconcerting still was the question whether the children of such parents were entitled to Baptism. The majority held that only children of covenant members may be baptized. Solomon Stoddard, however, advocated a compromise, known as the "halfway covenant." According to this device the unconverted children of covenant parents were said to be "halfway" in the covenant, and their children, in turn, by virtue of the grandparents' covenant relation, were entitled to Baptism. The halfway-covenant relation, however, did not entitle them to partake of the Lord's Supper nor to exercise the franchise.[16]

2. Social covenanting implied the close integration of the ecclesiastical and the civil life, symbolized in New England villages by erecting both the courthouse and the church in the public

---

[15] Walker, *Hist. of Congr. Ch.,* p. 66 f.

[16] Ibid., pp. 170—82; Foster, *Gen. Hist.,* pp. 31—43.

square. The Puritan New Haven colony in 1639 adopted a statement which reflects the ideals of Calvin's theocracy:

> That the Scriptures do hold forth a perfect rule for the direction and government of all men in all duties which they are to perform to God and man as well in the government of the family and commonwealth as in the matters of the Church.[17]

Congregationalism was the state religion in the New England colonies, and only members of the church could vote. In some colonies the salaries of the ministers were paid out of the state treasury as late as 1834.[18] Religious tolerance was virtually unknown. The early Congregationalists came to America in search, not of a general religious freedom, but of a religious freedom in which they could carry out unhampered their own religious ideals.[19] Intolerance manifested itself, e. g., in the trial of Roger Williams for his strong opposition to any ecclesiastical or political enslavement of an individual. Mrs. Anne Hutchinson was tried because of her leanings toward mysticism, and the Quakers subsequently were tried and banished, and some were executed, because they rejected the rites and ceremonies of the church, particularly Baptism and the Lord's Supper. In 1692 the New England Congregationalists were actively engaged in the persecution of the alleged practice of witchcraft in Salem.[20] It seems paradoxical that the adherents of such principles would play a prominent part in shaping the political philosophy expressed in the preamble to the Declaration of Independence. True, the Congregational churches could advocate complete religious liberty as little as their Presbyterian brethren, since in their opinion the "Second" Commandment definitely proscribes the toleration of heresies. Nevertheless the principles underlying social covenanting emphasize the doctrines of natural right, the social contract, the right of resistance. The Covenanters declared that these doctrines are contained in the divine Law which was engraved into man's heart before it was written in the Bible, or as one Congregational minister expressed it: "This voice of Nature is the voice of God." In this sense, then, the *vox populi est vox Dei.*[21] The Congre-

---

[17] Fagley, *Congr. Ch.*, p. 13. Sweet, *The Story of Rel.*, pp. 76—78; *Rel. in Col. Am.*, I, 81—115.

[18] Complete disestablishment did not come in New Hampshire until 1817, in Connecticut until 1818, and in Massachusetts until 1834. Cf. Walker, *Hist. of Congr. Ch.*, p. 236. In this connection, see James Fulton Maclear, " 'The True American Union' of Church and State: The Reconstruction of the Theocratic Tradition," *Church History*, XXVIII (1959), 41—62, and Jerald C. Brauer, "The Rule of the Saints in American Politics," ibid., XXVII (1958), 240—255.

[19] Early Congregationalism is a case study for the theory that significant social and ecclesiastical revolts have been inaugurated by the socially or economically disinherited. When the state or the hierarchy usurped power to suppress the people, then the masses arose in protest either by rejecting such authority and power entirely, like the Mennonites, or by claiming such powers for themselves, like the English Separatists.

[20] Cf. James Truslow Adams, *The Founding of New England* (Boston: Little, Brown and Co., 1926), pp. 163—74 and 452, where the author refers to C. W. Upham, *History of Witchcraft and Salem Village*, Boston, 1867. Cf. "What We Do Not Owe the Pilgrim Fathers," *Theol. Monthly*, VIII (May, 1928), 152.

[21] Alice M. Baldwin, *The New England Clergy and the American Revolution* (Durham, N. C.: Duke University Press, 1928), p. 15, esp. also chs. ii—v. This is a well-documented study.

gationalists of the 18th century, heirs of the cumulative effect of the long disputes on covenanting, advocated a constitutional, if not a democratic, form of government. The ideal of the separation of church and state was also strongly advocated by Jonathan Edwards, who was an ardent advocate of the principles enunciated by Augustine in the *City of God*. Edwards held that the church is greater than the state and operates in a sphere entirely different from that of the state. He considered state control over religion an intolerable anomaly.[22]

The Liberalizing Tendencies of the New England Theology. During the first century of their history the Congregational churches spent much energy in discussing civic and moral questions, the eradication of heresies, and the rights of halfway-covenant members. At the end of this period spirituality was at a low ebb. Under the leadership of Jonathan Edwards (1703–1758) and George Whitefield the Great Awakening swept through the New England States in 1734 and again in 1740 to 1741.[23] The Great Awakening left an unmistakable imprint on the Congregational churches, particularly in two respects.

1. During its early history Congregationalism had manifested a deep interest in civic well-being, in broad philanthropic plans, and in the promotion of education.[24] The Great Awakening, however, made the spiritual ministry of the church the first great duty in the life of the churches. The ideal of living "spiritually" rather than legalistically by code was first fostered during the Great Awakening, and in varying degrees it became thereafter a characteristic of Congregational faith and life.[25] For the Congregationalist spiritual living thus came to mean

that a Christian finds his freedom by dedicating himself to the service of God and man. Even the most menial service is not servitude to the Christian, who remembers how his Lord girded Himself with a towel and washed the disciples' feet; it is a free expression of his gratitude for the generous way he has been treated and an attempt to pass on to others the talents and benefits which have been given him. Some of this service naturally takes the form of miscellaneous "good turns" that we do to those we chance to meet by the way, or whose need of help comes home to us closely; but the major part of it ought to be related to some specific "calling," through which we serve God and society in a manner peculiar to ourselves, though not without guiding precedents and traditions. . . . Jesus summarized

---

[22] See Qualben (P. III, Bibliog.), *Luth. Ch. in Col. Am.*, p. 443. Anson Phelps Stokes (Bibliog., Sec. VI), *Ch. and St.*, I, 219 and 241, where he strictly limits Edwards' influence on religious liberty to this point.

[23] For a history and critique of the Great Awakening see Henry Kalloch Rowe, *History of Religion in the United States* (New York: Macmillan Co., 1928). Sweet, *Revivalism in America* (New York: Charles Scribner's Sons, 1944), ch. iv. Frank G. Beardsley, *A History of American Revivals* (New York: American Tract Society, 1904), ch. iii. Edwin Scott Gaustad, *The Great Awakening in New England* (New York: Harper & Brothers, 1957). Ralph G. Turnbull, *Jonathan Edwards the Preacher* (Grand Rapids: Baker Book House, 1958). Carl J. C. Wolf, ed., *Jonathan Edwards on Evangelism* (Grand Rapids: Wm. B. Eerdmans Publishing Co., 1958). C. C. Goen, "Jonathan Edwards: A New Departure in Eschatology," *Church History*, XXVIII (1959), 25—40, which describes Edwards as "America's first major postmillennial thinker." — See also the definitive edition of the *Works of Jonathan Edwards* (New Haven: Yale University Press, 1957—) under the general editorship of Perry Miller.

[24] Harvard was founded in 1637 and Yale in 1701.

[25] Fagley, *Congr. Ch.*, p. 21.

the great requirement [what we must do to be "saved"] in a memorable phrase, many times repeated in various forms in the Gospels: "If any man will come after Me, let him deny himself and take up his cross daily and follow Me. For whosoever will save his life shall lose it; but whosoever will lose his life for My sake, the same shall save it." (Luke 9:23, 24.) In other words, if you would know complete freedom, give yourself unreservedly to the only cause that will never disappoint you, the only Master who will never enslave you. Go "all out" for that cause and that Leader and the gracious God who calls you through them. Pray to that God to purge you of all the sins and weaknesses that make you an unfit instrument for His purposes; to remake you according to the new pattern shown in Christ; to guide and sustain you by His Spirit for the doing of His will in some special way that answers to the unique talents He has given you.[26]

2. The Great Awakening, with its strong appeal to the sinner's will and emotions, is diametrically opposed to Calvin's emphasis on the sovereign will of God. During the Great Awakening Calvinism and Arminianism met in sharp antithesis. Edwards and his followers were determined to defend the Calvinistic ideal of the sovereignty of God and at the same time to find a theological and philosophical basis for maintaining human responsibility without yielding to the Arminian view of free will.[27] In 1754 Edwards wrote his famous treatise *Careful and Strict Enquiry into the Modern Prevailing Notions of Freedom of the Will*.[28] Edwards maintained against Arminianism that human freedom implies no more than the natural power to act in accordance with the choice of the mind; that man, however, has nothing to do with the origin of the inclinations, that man will always act in conformity with the strongest inclination, determined by what man considers to be the "highest good." At the same time, in defense of a modified Calvinism, Edwards held that man cannot determine the direction of his choice. From this inability he inferred that while man has by nature the full power to serve God, he cannot do so until God reveals Himself to man as the Highest Good. On the other hand, the wicked person must be condemned because his actions flow from his own choice, though the direction which he chooses is not determined by him. Man acts by his own choice and inclination according to what he considers the highest good.[29] In his treatise on *The Nature of True Virtue* (1765) Edwards held that virtue is essentially benevolence, which always seeks "the highest Good of Being in general." God as the infinitely perfect Being is the Object of the highest love or benevolence. The actual exercise of such benevolence will bring an appreciation and a perception of spiritual joy

---

[26] Walter Horton, pp. 76—78.

[27] The long history of the New England theology, from Edwards to Finney of Oberlin is adequately described in Foster, *The Gen. Hist.* Cp. also Walker, *Hist. of Congr. Ch.*, ch. viii. For a good biography of Edwards see Ola E. Winslow, *Jonathan Edwards* (New York: Macmillan Co., 1940).

[28] Republished by Leavitt & Co., London, 1851. — On Edwards as a philosopher, see Harvey G. Townsend, ed., *The Philosophy of Jonathan Edwards from His Private Notebooks* (Eugene: University of Oregon Publications, 1955).

[29] Foster, *Gen. Hist.*, pp. 62—81. Walker, *Hist. of Congr. Ch.*, p. 283 ff. In spite of his philosophical attempt, Edwards was unable to harmonize Calvinistic determinism and human responsibility. Even his "federal headship" theory is no solution of the problem.

and beauty which no other experience can equal. Self-love is hostile to true virtue, and virtue must therefore oppose it and take satisfaction in its punishment.

The main points of the New England theology may be summarized under four points: (1) Man has a natural ability to serve God, and his failure to do so lies in the lack not of power, but of *inclination*. It is therefore not necessary for man to wait for an experience of religion, for a man who desires to know God may seek Him; and through repentance, prayer, and right living he will experience God's forgiving love. (2) Self-forgetful love is the essence of the religious life (3) Divine action both to save and to punish man flows from God's wise benevolence for the manifestation of divine glory.[30] This view led to the New England, or governmental, theory of the atonement, similar to the rectoral theory developed by Hugo Grotius. The New England theology minimized the value of Christ's passive obedience and viewed justification primarily as man's union with Christ, whereby man shares Christ's active obedience.[31] (4) Edwards and his school sought to foster among the Calvinists an emotional type of Christian character based on an immediate communion between God and the human soul. This endeavor is reflected in such Congrega-

tional leaders as Timothy Dwight (1752 to 1817) and Charles Finney (1792 to 1875), the great revivalist and later president of Oberlin College.[32] While subsequent doctrinal and moral interests so occupied the Congregationalists that the New England theology has not been an issue for almost a century, the Edwardsian type of thinking has deeply influenced and to a large extent molded the theological pattern of much of Congregationalism.

The Unitarian Controversy and the Beginning of Denominational Consciousness. During the early decades of the 18th century some Congregationalists in eastern Massachusetts held Arminian and Arian views. In their endeavor to combat the Edwardsian Calvinism and particularly the excesses of the Great Awakening and subsequent revivals, they more and more openly denied the total depravity of man, questioned the doctrine of eternal punishment, advocated Arianism, and in their preaching dwelt on man's moral duties and the cultivation of virtues. All but one of Boston's fourteen congregations, Harvard University, and the stronger churches in eastern Massachusetts had adopted Arminianism and Unitarianism by the end of the 18th century. With the election of the Unitarian Henry Ware as Hollis professor of divinity at Harvard in 1805

[30] Even such a mediating Calvinist as Samuel Hopkins, prominent among the New England theologians, when arguing that the chief virtue of man is disinterested, wholly unselfish love, says: "It is not for the glory of God that all should be saved, but most for His glory that a number should be damned; otherwise all would be saved. We will, therefore, now make a supposition, which is not an impossible one, viz., that it is most for God's glory and for the universal good that you should be damned; ought you not to be willing to be damned on the supposition that God could not be glorified by you in any other way?" Quoted by Foster, *Gen. Hist.*, p. 157.

[31] On Hugo Grotius see R. S. Franks, *The History of the Doctrine of the Work of Christ* (London: Hodder and Stoughton, n. d.), II, 48 ff.; on Edwards, ibid., pp. 182—89.

[32] See the exhaustive and sympathetic biography by Richard E. Day, *Man of Like Passions, the Life Story of Charles G. Finney* (Grand Rapids: Zondervan Publ. House, 1942). Foster, *Modern Movement*, ch. x; *New Engl. Theology*, ch. xv.

the cleavage between the Trinitarians and anti-Trinitarians became so wide that an actual separation and the organization of the Unitarian body resulted.[33]

The loss to the Unitarians of some 100 influential churches, of Harvard University, and of rich legacies spurred the Congregationalists to re-examine and to embrace anew the basic religious tenets of their forefathers. Andover Seminary was founded in 1808 to train Congregational pastors well versed in strict Calvinistic theology.[34] The most significant result of the Unitarian defection was the awakening of a Congregational denominational consciousness. Since 1708 no general meeting of Congregational churches had been held until 1852, when representatives of churches from all parts of the country met at Albany. The National Council of Congregational Churches was formed — a significant departure from the former church polity —

the Plan of Union with the Presbyterians was abolished,[35] the way was paved for the adoption of a common confession,[36] and an aggressive program of missionary expansion was inaugurated to establish new Congregational churches, especially in the Central and Western States.

The Rise and Spread of Liberal Theology in Congregationalism. Liberal theology, also in Congregationalism, has been eclectic and has drawn on many sources, such as German empiricism and higher criticism, English transcendentalism and evolutionism, Austrian psychologism, and American pragmatism. But the very genius of Congregationalism is such that it has produced more leaders in the modernist movement than any other American church body.[37] From Robert Browne, John Robinson, and William Brewster down to the present, Congregationalists have often spoken of themselves as "seekers." They believe

[33] Walker, *Hist. of Congr. Ch.,* pp. 329—46; Foster, *Modern Movement,* ch. x. See "Unitarian Universalist Association," below.

[34] After three quarters of a century, however, this school became involved in the Universalist controversy and finally adopted liberal theology. For an interesting account of the issues involved see D. D. Williams, *The Andover Liberals, a Study in American Theology* (Morningside Heights, N. Y.: King's Crown Press, 1941).

[35] For this plan see Sec. VI, "Presbyterianism." The Congregationalists claim that in the preceeding years this plan had been responsible for loss to the Presbyterians of some 2,000 churches. Cp. Sweet, *Rel. on Am. Fr.,* III, 13—42.

[36] Historically the Congregational churches were opposed in principle to a "denominational" creed, since they maintained that the establishment of a creed is a matter of the individual local church. Generally speaking, the early Congregationalists agreed to the doctrinal statement contained in the Savoy Declaration, and also later Congregationalists expressed their approval of it, notably in the conventions at Saybrook in 1708 and at Boston in 1865. Later Congregationalists, however, came to feel that a typically American statement of belief, or "platform," should be drafted and approved. As a result, the "Statement of Doctrine" was adopted at Boston in 1885. It can be found in Schaff, *Creeds,* III, 911—15, and in the Kansas City Platform of 1913, reprinted below.

[37] Liberal theology will be discussed later in a separate chapter. Here reference will be made only to the contributions which Congregational theologians made to the rise and spread of modernism. Among the many studies in this field the following are suggested: Foster, *Modern Movement;* E. T. Thompson, *Changing Emphases in American Preaching* (Phila.: Westminster Press, 1943); W. Walker, "Changes in Theology Among American Congregationalists," *Journal of Religion,* X, 204—18; F. E. Mayer, "Rise of Lib. Theol." (see fn. 13).

that their contribution to Christianity is that they meet today's needs in today's ways by today's unfettered judgment.

Horace Bushnell, an eminent Congregational preacher (1802–1876),[38] is sometimes called the father of American modernism. His major controversial publications show his liberal theology in four areas.

1. In his *Christian Nurture,* published in 1847, he maintained that man is morally good by nature and that conversion is therefore not — as the revivalists of his day maintained — an act of divine grace wrought in an emotional experience, but rather a normal psychological development of personality under the proper environment.

2. Bushnell held that the creedal statements concerning the Trinity must be interpreted as a trinity of manifestations. In his *God in Christ,* published in 1849, he maintained that the ecclesiastical term "Trinity" must be interpreted so that the Deity is brought to the inner man as a living power.

3. Against the naturalism of his day Bushnell in 1858 published *Nature and the Supernatural,* in which he argued that the natural and the supernatural are actually coeternal factors in God's economy and that the supernatural is no more than God's activity in repairing the damage which is caused by the laws of the natural realm. Man possesses these supernatural powers in his own personality, and he need therefore not yield to the temptations of his evil and natural environment. The ecclesiastical terms "creation," "inspiration," "incarnation," "reconciliation," and "miracles" are merely expressions for God's activities as Rectifier, Redeemer, Regenerator, in which, however, God does not suspend any laws of nature.

4. Bushnell's departure from the historic position of Calvinistic theology becomes apparent most patently in his *The Vicarious Sacrifice, Grounded in Principles of Universal Obligation,* published in 1866. In this book he developed the moral-influence theory of the atonement in accord with his modalistic Sabellianism. He held that during His earthly life Christ was the manifestation of God's moral or regenerative power, which is now active through the Spirit. This moral power or regenerative consciousness of sin leads to repentance and establishes the at-one-ment with God.[39]

Bushnell had prepared the way for liberal theology in the Congregational churches. While his immediate associates, especially Theodore T. Munger and James M. Whiton, ultimately joined the Unitarians, the majority of liberal Congregational pastors and professors continued their membership in the Congregational churches. Through their sermons and publications they developed liberal theology in four major areas.

1. On the basis of Darwin's evolutionary hypothesis liberal theology maintained the possibility of man's evolving morally and spiritually to such an extent that he ultimately would reach perfection and in his quest for God ultimately would find God within himself. The divine-immanence theory was the final stage in the conclusions to which the evolutionary hypothesis had led the liberal theologians.[40]

---

[38] See Barbara M. Cross, *Horace Bushnell: Minister to a Changing America* (Chicago: The University of Chicago Press, 1958).

[39] In *The Vicarious Sacrifice* Bushnell retains the traditional terminology, but fills it with an entirely different meaning.

[40] Cf., e. g., John Fiske, *The Destiny of Man Viewed in the Light of His Origin,* Boston, 1884 (see H. Burnell Pannill, *The Religious Faith of John Fiske* [Durham: Duke University Press, 1957], 195—200); Newman Smyth,

2. In accord with German higher criticism the liberals discarded the inerrancy and finality of the Bible. The Bible was studied inductively, i. e., the theologians endeavored to recapture the culture of each portion of the Bible, examine the religious experiences recorded, and interpret them in the light of modern needs.[41]

3. The criterion for final truth must be sought in its pragmatic value.[42]

4. The message of the church is a social gospel. Influenced in part by the evolutionary hypothesis — the human race is a social unit of potentially good men — in part by an entirely worldly concept of the kingdom of Christ according to Ritschl's view, and in part by the interest in the new social studies, the liberal theologians maintained that the purpose of Christianity is to "Christianize" all social institutions so that man may become perfect in a perfect society.[43]

Twentieth Century Congregationalism. In our own century Congregationalism continued to demonstrate that it could allow great latitude in formulating doctrinal beliefs. To quote:

> Congregationalism stands for the liberty of the human spirit. Its birthright is one of freedom from all tyranny, either doctrinal or ecclesiastical. The individual is free from the despotism of the local church; the local church is free from the dominion of bishops or ecclesiastical assemblies; the churches in their association in groups are free from compelling authority of larger groups or of their representatives, either national or international. It is as free as it can be and still possess the genius of organization and the power of co-operative activity.[44]

Since there was no official statement of general belief, one person's summary was considered as good as another's. A number of attempts were made by individuals to summarize the beliefs generally

The Place of Death in Evolution, 1897 (a synopsis of this treatise is given in Henry Sloane Coffin, *Religion Yesterday and Today* [Nashville: Abingdon-Cokesbury, 1940], p. 22); Washington Gladden, *How Much Is Left of the Old Doctrines?* 1899. See Foster, *Modern Movement,* p. 156. Gaius Glenn Atkins, *The Procession of the Gods* (New York: Richard R. Smith, 1930), though representing the comparative religions school, proceeds on the theory that there has been a continuous growth of man's understanding of God in keeping with the evolutionary process.

[41] Lyman Abbott was the chief exponent of this view, esp. in his *The Evolution of Christianity,* 1892 (see Foster, p. 94 ff.), and in the theological publication the *Outlook.* Cp. also Abbott's contribution to the symposium *The Atonement in Modern Religious Thought,* 2d ed. (London: James Clark & Co., 1902), pp. 89—103, as well as Ira V. Brown, *Lyman Abbott, Christian Evolutionist: A Study in Religious Liberalism* (Cambridge: Harvard University Press, 1953).

[42] Henry C. King, president of Oberlin College, was the chief systematician of the liberal theology. Cp. Foster, *Modern Movement,* ch. x.

[43] Cp. Charles Howard Hopkins, *The Rise of the Social Gospel in American Protestantism* (New Haven: Yale University Press, 1940), p. 126 ff.; Henry C. King, *Theology and Social Consciousness;* cp. Foster, p. 173 ff.; Washington Gladden, *Tools and the Man* (Boston: Houghton Mifflin & Co., 1893), esp. ch. i; *In His Steps: What Would Jesus Do?* tendential novel by the Congregationalist minister Charles M. Sheldon, popularized the social Gospel.

[44] W. E. Barton, *The New Congregational Handbook,* 1922, p. 25, quoted from Neve, pp. 408, 409.

held by Congregationalists.[45] The statement of belief contained in the Kansas City Platform, adopted by the National Council in 1913, was widely accepted:

Preamble. The Congregational churches of the United States, by delegates in National Council assembled, reserving all the rights and cherished memories belonging to this organization under its former constitution and declaring the steadfast allegiance of the churches composing the Council to the faith which our fathers confessed, which from age to age has found its expression in the historic creeds of the Church Universal and of this communion, and affirming our loyalty to the basic principles of our representative democracy, hereby set forth the things most surely believed among us concerning faith, polity, and fellowship.

Faith. We believe in God the Father, infinite in wisdom, goodness, and love; and in Jesus Christ, His Son, our Lord and Savior, who for us and for our salvation lived and died and rose again and liveth evermore; and in the Holy Spirit, who taketh of the things of Christ and revealeth them to us, renewing, comforting, and inspiring the souls of men. We are united in striving to know the will of God as taught in the Holy Scriptures and in our purpose to walk in the ways of the Lord, made known or to be made known to us. We hold it to be the mission of the Church of Christ to proclaim the Gospel to all mankind, exalting the worship of the true God and laboring for the progress of knowledge, the promotion of justice, the reign of peace, and the realization of human brotherhood. Depending, as did our fathers, upon the continued guidance of the Holy Spirit to lead us into all truth, we work and pray for the transformation of the world into the kingdom of God, and we look with faith for the triumph of righteousness and the life everlasting.

Polity. We believe in the freedom and responsibility of the individual soul and the right of private judgment. We hold to the autonomy of the local church and its independence of all ecclesiastical control. We cherish the fellowship of the churches united in district, State, and national bodies for counsel and cooperation in matters of common concern.

The Wider Fellowship. While affirming the liberty of our churches and the validity of our ministry, we hold to the unity and catholicity of the Church of Christ and will unite with all its branches in hearty cooperation and will earnestly seek, so far as in us lies, that the prayer of our Lord for His disciples may be answered that they all may be one.[46]

Toward mid-century a definite departure from the liberalism of the early decades of this century became noticeable. In 1942 a fellowship of Congregational pastors who frankly described themselves as neo-orthodox and Trinitarian was organized under the name *Christus Victor.* The great spiritual restlessness of our times tended to produce also among the Congregationalists a deep concern for theological matters. There was a marked reaction to the "theological irresponsibility" held to be characteristic of Congregationalists. Instead one author sensed

a new sense of the importance of a clearly defined faith for the life of the Church. . . . [Congregationalism, he said] will not abandon its habitual free-

---

[45] F. L. Fagley, Associate Secretary of Congregational and Christian Churches, submitted such a summary in *Congr. Ch.,* pp. 61—66. Walter Horton, *Our Chr. F.,* pp. 127—37, presented the Congr. beliefs from the point of view of his theological orientation. Horton is the author of *Realistic Theology* (New York: Harpers, 1935). For a synopsis of Horton's theology cp. Wieman and Meland, *American Philosophies of Religion* (New York: Willett Clark & Co., 1936), ch. x.

[46] *Census,* 1936, I, 523.

dom from creedal authoritarianism, and it will continue to cultivate the critical interpretation of Christianity which the "modern" theological leaders have begun. But by means of that historical understanding of the Christian life which liberalism has made possible, it will open itself to a fresh encounter with the Bible and the message of the Reformation. Thus it will deepen its faith and come to reassert a Christocentricism that will enable it to align itself with the genius of historic Congregationalism and, at the same time, with the spirit of the new ecumenical Christianity.[47]

The "Christian" Tradition

The first merger of real significance in which the Congregationalists participated was the merger with the General Convention of Christian Churches.[48] The General Convention, formerly the American Convention, traced its origin to the anticreedal movement inaugurated during the early decades of the nineteenth century and culminating in the formation of the Churches of Christ and the Disciples. During the Civil War the Churches of Christ, also known as "Christian" churches, divided over the slavery question. The Southern Churches of Christ are known for their opposition to the introduction of any innovations which they consider extra-Biblical; for example, the use of instrumental music in public worship and modern means of raising money. Generally speaking, one might say that theologically they are conservative. The Northern Christian

Churches with headquarters at Dayton, Ohio — not to be identified with Disciples of Christ — rejected not only the traditional creedal terminology, e. g., "Trinity," "Deity of Christ," but also the doctrines expressed in these terms. Their test for church fellowship was "Christian character," not any theological belief. Baptism was optional, though baptism by immersion was frequently urged upon the members as a matter of duty. They were even known as "Baptist Unitarians."[49]

The General Council of Congregational and Christian Churches

It was this group of Christian Churches which in 1931 effected a merger with the Congregational Churches. The merger posed no problems, since neither group was asked to deviate from its historic position.

The resulting General Council of Congregational and Christian Churches was, strictly speaking, not a denomination, but, as the name clearly indicated, a general council of like-minded local congregations. One of the basic principles of both merging bodies was the belief that the term "church" was applicable only to a local group united by a voluntary covenant and completely autonomous and self-governing. The terms "Congregational Church" and "Christian Church" were used to designate only the local church, or congregation, never the state or national association. The local churches usually

---

[47] Wilhelm Pauck, "What Is Disturbing Congregationalists?" *Christian Century*, June 7, 1944, p. 690 f.

[48] The Evangelical Protestant Conference of Congregational Churches, which came into existence in 1911 by a merger of the German Evangelical Protestant Ministers' Association and the German Evangelical Ministers' Conference, united with the Congregational churches in 1925. This group of German extraction was known for its extreme liberalism, rationalism, Unitarianism.

[49] The rather involved historical development of the Christian Churches and the Disciples is treated later. For a brief description of their Unitarian orientation see W. E. Garrison and A. T. De Groot, *The Disciples of Christ* (St. Louis: The Christian Board of Publication, 1948), pp. 87—92.

united in a state organization and in a national or general council, but neither the one nor the other exercised any authority over the local congregation. On the local or congregational level the individual congregations continued, in keeping with their historic origin, either as Congregational or as Christian Churches.

The general missionary and educational activities were conducted through two national organizations with an interlocking agency. Each local congregation was granted great doctrinal freedom. At the reception of members into fellowship of the local congregation the recitation of the following covenant was recommended:

> We are united in striving to know the will of God as taught in the Holy Scriptures, and in our purposes to walk in the ways of the Lord, made known or to be made known to us. We hold it to be the mission of the Church of Christ to proclaim the gospel to all mankind, exalting the worship of the one true God and laboring for the progress of knowledge, the promotion of justice, the reign of peace, and the realization of human brotherhood. Depending as did our fathers upon the continued guidance of the Holy Spirit to lead us into all truth, we work and pray for the transformation of the world into the kingdom of God; and we look with faith for the triumph of righteousness and the life everlasting.[50]

These statements were so latitudinarian that liberal as well as conservative theologians could regard them as consonant with the basic theological principles of both groups.

When the long-awaited merger of the Congregational and Christian Churches and the Evangelical and Reformed Church under the name of the United Church of Christ took place at Cleveland in 1957,[51] some local churches refused to enter the new body and proceeded to form two new Congregational-Christian groups: the *National Association* of *Congregational-Christian Churches* (organized at Detroit in 1955) and the *Conservative Congregational-Christian Conference.*

The Reformed Church in the United States [52]

The first larger Lutheran territory in Germany to adopt a modification of Calvinism was the Palatinate.

The Elector Frederick III, desiring to end the controversy concerning the Lord's Supper between the orthodox Lutherans and the Cryptocalvinists, had as head of his provincial church approved the *Variata* of 1540, whose vague article on the Real Presence could satisfy both Lutherans and Calvinists. In 1563 the Elector, who had converted to Calvinism three years before, introduced the Heidelberg Catechism, prepared by Ursinus and Olevianus, the former a student of Melanchthon, the latter of Calvin. The Heidelberg Catechism, though containing some Lutheran elements, was predominantly Reformed and very instrumental in shaping the theological characteristics of the German Reformed churches.

The aftermath of the Thirty Years' War, the devastation of the Rhineland by Louis XIV of France (1689), and other factors prompted large numbers of Germans from the Palatinate to seek economic, political, and religious secu-

---

[50] Burton, *Manual,* p. 96.

[51] On the basis for the union see Douglas Horton, "Now the United Church of Christ," *The Christian Century,* LXXIV (June 12, 1957), 731 to 734; and Harold E. Fey, "Born of the Spirit," ibid. (July 10, 1957), 837 to 839.

[52] On the European background of the Reformed church, particularly the significance of the Heidelb. C., see P. IV, secs. II, III, IV.

rity in America, especially in Pennsylvania. By 1725 such large numbers of West Germans — also some Swiss — had settled in America that the need for systematic religious work was keenly felt. John Philip Boehm, a former schoolteacher, was ordained by the authority of the Classis of Amsterdam at New York in 1729, and soon became the recognized leader, especially during the chaotic conditions precipitated by the mystic Henry Antes. Taking advantage of the religious dissensions among the settlers, this mystic hoped to unite the Lutherans, the Reformed, and the Moravians in the "Congregation of God in the Spirit," representing an extreme type of mysticism or inspirationism. Boehm helped to settle the chaotic conditions among the Reformed, as Henry Melchior Muehlenberg, who arrived in America in 1742, did among the Lutherans.[53] In 1746, Michael Schlatter, as official representative of the Reformed church of Holland, inaugurated a program of orderly and effective work by uniting the separate German Reformed church as a *coetus*, the Dutch equivalent of presbytery or synod. He was instrumental in raising considerable amounts of money in Holland, also in Scotland, and in enlisting a number of younger ministers for America. Though composed exclusively of Germans and some Swiss, this church was under the jurisdiction of the Dutch church until 1793, when it became independent and assumed the name German Reformed church. During the Great Revival of

1800, when emotional preaching, prayer meetings, and revivalistic excesses supplanted Christian indoctrination in many sections of the church, several ministers of the Reformed church likewise substituted revivals for instruction in the Heidelberg Catechism. Under the leadership of Philip W. Otterbein and John Winebrenner two groups seceded from the Reformed church: the former to organize the United Brethren Church and the latter the General Eldership of the Churches of God. No other secessions occurred in this church body, though serious friction was occasioned by the introduction of the English language, the attempts to bring about a union with the Lutherans,[54] the demand for total abstinence, and especially the rise of the Mercersburg theology, which emphasized the objective sacramental and liturgical factors rather than the subjective, revivalistic, and rationalistic elements so congenial to the American frontiersman of the early decades of the nineteenth century. Though the peculiar emphases of the Mercersburg theology at first appeared foreign to Reformed thinking and caused considerable dissent, the new theology became an important factor in the subsequent doctrinal development of the Reformed church, especially in its liberalism, which demanded a constant re-examination of the church's creedal statements in the light of alleged new insights arising from the so-called cumulative experience of Christians and the scientific research of Biblical scholars.[55] Because

---

[53] Horstmann and Wernecke, p. 36.

[54] S. S. Schmucker, of the General Synod, in the *American Lutheran Church* (Springfield: Harbaugh and Butler, 1851), advocated union between the Lutherans and the German Reformed. In some areas both denominations used *Das gemeinschaftliche Gesangbuch.*

[55] Richard E. Wentz, "Mercersburg and the United Church," *The Christian Century*, LXXV (1958), 687—688. George W. Richards, "The Mercersburg Theology — Its Purpose and Principles," *Church History*, XX (1951), 43—55. Luther J. Binkley, *The Mercersburg Theology* (Lancaster, Pa.: Franklin and Marshall College, 1953). John W. Nevin and Philip Schaff, professors at Mercersburg (Pennsylvania) Seminary during the mid-

of its peculiar genius the Reformed church experienced a normal growth in spite of these dissensions. In 1863, the tercentenary of the Heidelberg Catechism, the previously autonomous Eastern Synod and Ohio Synod united, adopting the name the Reformed Church in the United States. A group of German Reformed from Lippe-Detmold and a colony of Swiss Reformed had settled in Wisconsin and ultimately united with the Reformed Church, as did also two small groups of Hungarian Reformed.

The theological position of the Reformed church in Germany at the time of its establishment and during its early history in America resembled the theology of the Dutch Reformed church more than that of the Lutheran church. However, it did not follow the Dutch church in its theocentric and legalistic orientation. On the contrary, the German branch of the Reformed church — in Europe as in America — reflects the mediating theology of some of Melanchthon's disciples and the "practical" Christianity of the Heidelberg Catechism. Unionism and Pietism always go hand in hand, and the watchword of both is "Deeds, not creeds." Nevin states:

> It [The Heidelberg Catechism] is always closely related in origin and constitution to the Lutheran Confessions. . . . It is only in the German Church that the two

great divisions of the Protestant Evangelical faith have seemed able, to this day, to understand one another at all, in their principal differences, so as to preserve clearly either their own contradiction or agreement in its true ground. In the Palatinate all hinged on the Eucharistic question and, in the case of this question, on the mode, not the fact of Christ's Real Presence in the Sacrament. . . . The Heidelberg Catechism was designed to interpret rather than contradict the Augsburg Confession; to explain the sense in which it was held by the Church in the Palatinate. . . . The Augsburg Confession as explained by Melanchthon and signed by Calvin is abundantly broad enough for both Catechisms; and on this platform the whole German Church (in America), if still true in any measure to its original life, might well stand shoulder to shoulder and hand in hand in the Lord's Work.[56]

The Evangelical Synod of North America

Many German Reformed theologians have held that the only really significant point of difference between Luther and Zwingli concerned the mode of Christ's presence in Holy Communion. In their opinion Luther and Zwingli

> had worked so hard to make their respective systems compatible with the

dle of the nineteenth century, espoused a mediating type of theology — somewhat according to the thought patterns of Schleiermacher — hoping not only to reconcile the separate Christian denominations, but also to harmonize Christian dogma with the conclusions of philosophy and to integrate religion with culture. Nevin in particular adopted some of the basic Christological views of Schleiermacher and strongly advocated the theory that the unity of all Christendom can be achieved solely by the mystical fellowship of believers with Christ, a mystical union which would require a higher form of Christian life than had thus far been evident in the church. The historian Schaff, later professor at Union Theological Seminary (1870 to 1893), was under suspicion of entertaining the Romanizing tendencies of Anglo-Catholicism, because he espoused certain liturgical trends in the interest of his peculiar type of ecumenism. Schaff was very active in the founding of the ecumenical Evangelical Alliance (1846), and he popularized the Moravian principle: "In essentials unity; in doubtful points freedom; in all things love."

56 John W. Nevin, *History and Genius of the Heidelb. C.*, quoted by Horstmann and Wernecke, p. 110 f.

Word of God and reasonable to the human mind that they were loath to give up their fundamental schemes. . . . The fury of the theologians (during the Crypto-Calvinistic controversy) made the Word of God almost as scarce as it had been prior to the Reformation, while the disagreement was of a personal opinion only, since Christ does not give any explanation of the part that bread and wine take in the bestowal of the blessings of His Last Supper. Why endeavor to clear up a process left a mystery by the Son of God Himself? [57]

German Reformed leaders, who did not agree with Luther's declaration to the Sacramentarians: "You have a different spirit," repeatedly attempted, notably in 1717, to unite the Lutherans and the Reformed on the basis of the *Variata* edition of the Augsburg Confession. During the period of rationalism and the Napoleonic Wars many Germans felt that the cause of Christianity in Germany could be preserved only by a merger of the two Reformation churches. In 1817 King Frederick William III of Prussia issued the proclama-

tion which gave formal and legal status to the Evangelical Church, a union of the Lutheran and the Reformed churches without doctrinal and confessional agreement. The king and his chief theological adviser, Friedrich Schleiermacher, placed purity of life into an entirely false relation to purity of doctrine by so emphasizing subjective and personal piety that the doctrinal differences between the Lutheran and the Reformed confessions appeared to be entirely irrelevant.[58]

During the opening decades of the previous century several groups from the German Evangelical church emigrated to Missouri — in part because of Gottfried Duden's glowing description of this state — and settled within a fifty-mile radius of St. Louis. In 1840, H. Garlichs, Louis Nollau, G. Wall, and several other pastors perfected an association according to the principles underlying the Prussian Union. These pastors adopted the following doctrinal statement:

---

[57] D. Irion, pp. 13—15.

[58] The union was at first accepted without protest, inasmuch as the confessional status of an individual person, a local congregation, or a provincial church was left intact. But the compulsory introduction of the new Agenda (1830), which clearly taught the Reformed doctrine of the Real Presence, brought forth many protests against the Union, esp. in Silesia, where the Old Prussian Luth. church — Breslau Synod — was organized. The Union was in reality abortive, since it did not unite the two existing churches, but merely added a third, the Evangelical, or United, Church. Cp. Meusel, VII, 4 ff. For a detailed study of the entire movement and its many implications see A. G. Rudelbach, *Reformation, Luthertum und Union* (Leipzig: B. Tauchnitz, 1839), esp. chs. v—xiii. In 1948 the twenty-eight provincial churches — Lutheran, Reformed, and Evangelical — formed the *Evangelische Kirche in Deutschland* (EKiD). Some hoped that this organization might prove to be the culmination of the Union established in 1817. However, the Lutheran confessional upsurge caused the confessional lines between Lutherans and Reformed again to be drawn more sharply. At present seven of the provincial churches are Evangelical, but with a strong percentage of Lutherans; twelve are Lutheran; two are expressly Reformed; seven are confessionally more or less indifferent union churches. Joachim Beckmann, *Kirchliches Jahrbuch,* 1945—1948 (Gütersloh: C. Bertelsmann Verlag, 1950), pp. 454 to 470. Cp. also Stewart Herman, *The Rebirth of the German Church* (New York: Harper & Bros., 1946). In passing it should be mentioned that the charters of several universities in Lutheran provinces demand that the state provide a chair in Reformed theology.

The German Evangelical Church Association of the West, as a part of the Evangelical Church, defines the term Evangelical Church as denoting that branch of the Christian Church which acknowledges the Holy Scriptures of the Old and New Testaments as the Word of God, the sole and infallible guide of faith and life, and accepts the interpretations of the Holy Scriptures as given in the symbolical books of the Lutheran and Reformed Churches, the most important being the Augsburg Confession, Luther's and Heidelberg Catechisms, in so far as they agree; but where they disagree, the German Evangelical Association of the West adheres strictly to the passages of Holy Scripture bearing on the subject and avails itself of the liberty of conscience prevailing in the Evangelical Church.[59]

During the subsequent years a number of similar organizations were effected, and in 1877 these various synods, being united in principle concerning doctrine and polity, formed the German Evangelical Synod of North America. Though there was at no time an organic union with the Evangelical church of Prussia, the Evangelical Synod received moral and financial support from the state churches of Germany, and especially from the Basel, the Berlin, and the Barmen mission societies. These societies espoused the unionistic and pietistic principles of the Prussian Union, and its emissaries implanted these trends upon the Evangelicals in America. Unionism and a "practical Pietism" seem to have been the chief characteristics of the Evangelical Synod.

The Evangelical Synod consistently took the position that a broad and latitudinarian spirit should make it possible for Lutherans and Reformed to dwell together in unity and to treat the so-called points of difference as nonessentials. The confessional consciousness which has characterized the Lutheran church was always more or less foreign to the Evangelical Synod. It maintained that every denomination which accepts Jesus has equal "right of membership in the body of Christ," and only that spirit is truly ecumenical which relegates "relatively unimportant and inconsequential matters to a sphere where they will not render impossible the consummation of a great spiritual, even if not organic, union that all Christendom, with a few notable exceptions, is striving for." [60] In its basic premise the Evangelical Synod held that there are no really distinctive elements in the Lutheran and the Reformed churches, at least not so distinctive as to warrant separate organizations. Frequently the statement was made that the only point

---

[59] Carl Schneider, *The German Church on the Frontier*, ch. iii. — According to S. S. Schmucker, who shared the views of the Evangelicals, the pastors who founded the *Kirchenverein* should have joined the General Synod (Lutheran). Ibid., p. 131, fn. 51. Wall preached the funeral sermon for Pastor O. H. Walther, one of the Saxon Lutherans. Ibid., p. 104.

[60] D. Irion, I, 39 f. When C. F. W. Walther warned against the unionistic tendencies of the amended constitution of the Evangelical Church (*Der Lutheraner*, I, 42 ff.), Nollau declared in *Ein Wort für die gute Sache der Union*: "Is it not possible for us (Lutherans and Evangelicals) to labor conjointly? Let us fight with united front against the real, the most dangerous enemy, against unbelief!" Alb. Muecke, p. 106 ff. In 1880 Prof. E. Otto of Eden Theological Seminary was charged with too liberal an attitude, and in his defense he stated that the tension between a conservative and a liberal element was only beneficial. Synod granted that a certain freedom of doctrine ought to obtain, but it insisted that such freedom must remain within the bounds of "synodical consciousness" [*Gesamtbewusstsein der Synode*], and that Christian doctrine must be taught according to the principles of positive religion. Ibid., p. 200 f.

of divergence between the two bodies concerns the manner of the Real Presence of Christ in the Lord's Supper. The Lutherans, however, uniformly denied this contention, insisting that the difference lies in fundamental principles.[61]

The former Evangelical Synod espoused, in the second place, the Reformed emphasis on the purity of life as the heart of Christianity. In its Catechism the Evangelical Synod described conversion and regeneration as "the beginning of a new life within us . . . the turning from the broad way of a sinful life and entering into the narrow way of a godly life." The real function of the church is therefore conceived of as the extension of "the rule of God in the hearts and lives of men according to the Sermon on the Mount." Membership in the Holy Christian church is established by personal piety rather than by faith. It is said that the church, though still below its ideal, will ultimately reach its goal "when Christian principles will be established in every relation of life" and when "all Christians stand together in their emphasis of the essential teachings."

The two basic trends, latitudinarianism and Pietism, progressively widened the chasm between the theological orientation of the Evangelical Synod and the Lutheran church and simultaneously helped to draw the Evangelical Synod and the Reformed Church more closely together, since their theological premises were practically identical. At the same time Evangelical theology inclined more and more toward liberalism, on the principle that the church's prime purpose is to preach a gospel of moral and social salvation.[62]

The Evangelical and Reformed Church

The European cultural and theological backgrounds of the Evangelical Synod and the Reformed Church and their American historical developments were so much alike that a merger of these churches posed no particular problem. The experiences at the Stockholm Conference on Life and Work (1925) prompted several leading members of the Evangelical Synod to persuade their body to appoint a commission to work for the union of their body with the Moravian and Reformed churches. The Reformed Church had already initiated proceedings to effect a merger with the United Brethren, who had seceded from the parent body under Otterbein. This group in turn had begun negotiations with the Evangelical Church, the so-called "Albright" Brethren. By 1929 the "Plan of Union" for the merger of the Reformed Church, the Evangelical Synod, and the United Brethren in Christ was adopted by these three bodies. In seven short articles the Plan of Union set forth the doctrinal position of the new body. Articles Six

---

[61] In his controversy with Zwingli concerning the Real Presence Luther pointed out that much more was at stake than the question whether the words of institution were to be taken literally or symbolically. In Luther's judgment the denial of the sacramental presence of Christ's body and blood was predicated on the denial of the doctrine of the personal union of Christ. Cp. "Lord's Supper," P. II, Sec. IV.

[62] Both H. Richard and Reinhold Niebuhr were born and reared in the Evangelical Synod and continued to maintain their connections with it. — At the annual convocations of Eden Theological Seminary outspoken liberal theologians have served as lecturers. — In 1921 a Commission on Christianity and Social Problems was created to gather information on economic conditions and in co-operation with the Federal Council to suggest measures to remove social and moral wrongs and to "Christianize the present social order." Horstmann and Wernecke, p. 102 f.

and Seven are significant inasmuch as they seem to indicate the distinctive theological character of the negotiating bodies.

6. In the fellowship of the Universal Church, in loyalty to the fundamental doctrines of the Faith revealed in the Holy Scriptures, and in the name of the Father, the Son, and the Holy Spirit, we proclaim the saving gospel of the Divine Love in Christ, through whom alone are offered and by faith in whom are appropriated the forgiveness of sins, reconciliation with God, the resurrection from the dead, and life eternal; and we work and pray for the coming of the kingdom of God throughout the world.

7. We believe that the divine plan for mankind includes a social order in harmony with the ideals and spirit of Jesus Christ; that the triumph of the kingdom of God in its present aspect would mean not only its establishment in the hearts of men individually, but in a world in which righteousness and brotherhood would prevail; and that a primary duty of the Church is to give positive witness that the Christian principles of justice and love should have full expression in all human relationships.[63]

This proposed merger did not materialize.[64] Instead of the tri-denominational merger only the Evangelical Synod and the Reformed Church finally united in 1934 under the name of Evangelical and Reformed Church. The final merger of all boards and commissions was not completed until 1940. However, Central Theological Seminary of the Reformed Church at Dayton was im-

mediately merged with Eden Seminary of the Evangelical Synod at Webster Groves, Mo.

The doctrinal position of the Evangelical and Reformed Church was set forth in its Constitution as follows:

The Holy Scriptures of the Old and New Testaments are recognized as the Word of God and the ultimate rule of Christian faith and practice.

The doctrinal standards of the Evangelical and Reformed Church are the Heidelberg Catechism, Luther's Catechism, and the Augsburg Confession. They are accepted as an authoritative interpretation of the essential truth taught in the Holy Scriptures.

Whenever these doctrinal standards differ, ministers, members, and congregations, in accordance with the liberty of conscience inherent in the gospel, are allowed to adhere to the interpretation of one of these confessions. However, in each case the final norm is the Word of God.

In its relation to other Christian communions the Evangelical and Reformed Church shall constantly endeavor to promote the unity of the Spirit in the bond of peace.[65]

The theological emphases in these confessional writings were of such a divergent nature that one could subscribe simultaneously to all three only if he makes full use of the latitudinarian principle which the Constitution granted.

The theological orientation of this church appears from its textbooks for religious instruction.[66] The leitmotiv is the believer's pious and consecrated life.

---

[63] Pamphlet published by the Joint Committee at Dayton, Ohio, Feb. 7, 1929.

[64] The Reformed Church discontinued negotiations, in the main because at the time they were more interested in a proposed union among churches of the Presbyterian-Reformed family. Horstmann and Wernecke, p. 115 ff.

[65] *Constitution,* loc. cit.

[66] *My Confirmation,* loc. cit. This was a rather formidable textbook and manual for confirmation instruction. While not an "official" document approved by the entire church, it was representative of this church's theological orientation.

Thus the doctrine of the Trinity is said to mean

> that Christians believe in one God, who as Father made all things, as Son showed Himself clearly to men in order to lead them away from their sins into a full life, and as Spirit is even now at work in the world and in our own hearts.[67]

Concerning Christ's work *My Confirmation* suggests the following answer to the question: "What can Jesus mean to me?"

> Through Him we can find the way to live . . . to find God . . . be saved from sin to an endless life of goodness and happiness. . . . In the first place, Jesus saves us from our sins and leads us to a better, fuller life by helping us to find the way of life. . . . He shows what we ought to be. He also [in the second place] saves us by helping us to find God. . . . Jesus shows us how much God loves us, even when we have done wrong. He shows us God's love by His teachings and His life, but most of all by His death upon the cross. There we see how much He loved us. And since God is like Him, that is the way God loves . . . and suffers when we do wrong. . . . [This] is the atonement. . . . Through Him the world can be saved from sin to goodness and happiness. . . . Jesus "can" mean all this to us . . . as we come to know Him, love Him, and follow Him as Lord and Master.[68]

The section of the manual which described man and his natural condition was presented in terms of the modernist theory of the fatherhood of God and brotherhood of man. And the explanation of the Second Article of the Creed read in part:

> I believe that He is God's only-begotten Son. All of us are sons of God, but He alone is so fully and completely God's Son that I can know what the Father is like by looking at Him.[69]

The Christian life, which received the major emphasis throughout the confirmation manual, was described as "to live as nearly as possible as Jesus did. . . . It is to trust God, to care for others, to master oneself, to seek the kingdom of God as Jesus did." [70] The kingdom of God was seen as largely future, but sure to come as "more and more people accept God's rule in their lives . . . more and more kindness and sympathy; less and less hatred and poverty and war and cruelty." [71]

In polity the Evangelical and Reformed Church was presbyterian. The congregational judicatories were the consistory, or church council, and a spiritual council. The denominational judicatories were the Synod, which met annually in spring for legislative business and in the fall as a workers' conference, and

---

[67] Ibid., p. 24 f.

[68] Ibid., pp. 34, 35. Of the twenty-five lesson units in the manual only one is devoted to the person and work of Christ, but four to the Christian way of life. The reason for this disproportionate distribution of subject matter is said to have been the fact that otherwise not all areas could have been adequately treated. (P. 141.)

[69] Ibid., p. 42; cp. p. 36.

[70] Ibid., p. 44 ff. It is significant that there is no reference to the motivation for the Christian life that Luther gives in the exposition of the Second Article or that the A. C. gives in Art. VI, though the church's constitution professes adherence to these two confessions. The Lutherans who take these confessions at face value maintain that any admonition to a Christian life outside this frame of reference is moralism.

[71] Ibid., p. 62 ff. This description of the kingdom of God is not far from Albrecht Ritschl's concept of the kingdom as a moral and ethical force in society.

the General Synod, which met every three years and enacted legislation for the entire body.

In 1944 the Evangelical and Reformed Church approved the necessary steps leading to a merger with the Congregational and Christian Churches.[72] At the time, many Congregationalists expressed their misgivings concerning the proposed merger. The very liberal spirits among them held that the general run of theology in the Evangelical and Reformed Church was still too conservative. Others feared that cultural and social differences would preclude a real integration of the two groups. Still another group objected on the ground that the proposed merger would inevitably lead to centralization of ecclesiastical government.[73] In spite of this opposition, however, the merger took place in 1957, subject to subsequent approval by the requisite number of local groups in each merging body.

At its first General Synod at Oberlin, Ohio, in July 1959 the United Church of Christ adopted the following Statement of Faith, stipulating, however, that each individual church was free to adopt or not to adopt it, as the church might see fit:

We believe in God, the Eternal Spirit, Father of our Lord Jesus Christ and our Father, and to his deeds we testify:

He calls the world into being, creates man in his own image, and sets before him the ways of life and death.

He seeks in holy love to save all nations from aimlessness and sin.

He judges men and nations by his righteous will declared through prophets and apostles.

In Jesus Christ, the man of Nazareth, our crucified and risen Lord, he has come to us and shared our common lot, conquering sin and death and reconciling the world to himself.

He bestows upon us his Holy Spirit, creating and renewing the Church of Jesus Christ, binding in covenant faithful people of all ages, tongues, and races.

He calls us into his Church to accept the cost and joy of discipleship, to be his servants in the service of men, to proclaim the Gospel to all the world and resist the powers of evil, to share in Christ's baptism and eat at his table, to join him in his passion and victory.

He promises to all who trust him forgiveness of sin and fullness of grace, courage in the struggle for justice and peace, his presence in trial and rejoicing, and eternal life in his kingdom which has no end.

Blessing and honor, glory and power be unto him. Amen.[74]

In December 1960, in a sermon delivered in Grace Protestant Episcopal Cathedral, San Francisco, Calif., just before the opening of the biennial assembly of the National Council of the Churches of Christ in the U. S. A., Dr. Eugene Carson Blake, Stated Clerk of the United Presbyterian Church in the U. S. A., boldly proposed the extension of the union represented by the United Church of Christ to the United Presbyterian Church in the U. S. A., the Protestant Episcopal Church in the U. S. A., and The Methodist Church, with a view to the eventual union of all Christians. The unofficial proposal has evoked mixed reactions from representatives of the bodies immediately concerned.[75]

---

[72] Reprinted in *C. T. M.*, XX (1949), 784.

[73] In 1949 several Congregational churches filed suit in New York to prevent the union, and the state Supreme Court granted an injunction. But in December 1953 the state Court of Appeals ruled that civil courts were without jurisdiction in this case. This and other litigation impeded the consummation of the merger.

[74] Reprinted from *The Christian Century*, LXXVI (1959), 846.

[75] The sermon, together with the statement made in the same service by Protestant Episcopal Bishop James A. Pike of California, is reprinted in

BIBLIOGRAPHY

PART VI   SECTION II

Atkins, G. G. and Fagley, F. L. *History of American Congregationalism.* Boston: Pilgrim Press, 1942.

Bainton, R. H. "Congregationalism, the Middle Way," *Christendom,* V, 345—54.

Burton, Charles E. "The Congregational and Christian Churches," *Census Report,* 1936, II¹, 519.

———. *Manual of Congregational and Christian Churches.* Boston: Congregational Publ. Co., 1936.

Deems, Mervin M. "The Congregational Christian Churches," in Vergilius Ferm, ed., *The American Church of the Protestant Heritage.* New York: Philosophical Library, 1953, pp. 167—83.

Dunn, David. "The Evangelical and Reformed Church," in Vergilius Ferm, ed. *The American Church of the Protestant Heritage.* New York: Philosophical Library, 1953. Pp. 295—309.

———, Paul N. Crusius, Josias Friedli, et al. *A History of the Evangelical and Reformed Church.* Philadelphia: Christian Education Press, 1961.

Evangelical Catechism. St. Louis: Eden Publ. House, 1929.

Fagley, F. L. *Congregational Churches.* Boston: Pilgrim Press, 1925.

Foster, F. H. *A Genetic History of the New England Theology.* University of Chicago Press, 1907.

———. *The Modern Movement in American Theology.* New York: Fleming H. Revell Co., 1939.

Freeman, Elmer S. "What Do We Congregationalists Do Now?" *Religion in Life,* 1951, p. 265 ff.

Horstmann, J. H., and H. H. Wernecke. *Through Four Centuries.* St. Louis: Eden Publ. House, 1938. A popular historical sketch.

Horton, Douglas. *Congregationalism, a Study in Church Polity.* London, 1952.

Horton, Walter M. *Our Christian Faith, Congregationalism Today and Tomorrow.* Boston: Pilgrim Press, 1945.

Irion, Andr. *Erklärung des Kl. Evang. Katechismus.* St. Louis: Aug. Wiebusch u. Sohn, 1870.

Irion, D. *Evangelical Fundamentals.* St. Louis: Eden Publ. House, 1929.

Maurer, Oscar E. *Manual of the Congregational Christian Churches.* Boston: Pilgrim Press, 1952.

Miller, Perry. *The New England Mind from Colony to Province.* Cambridge: Harvard University Press, 1953.

Muecke, A. *Geschichte der Ev. Synode.* Saint Louis: Eden Publ. House, 1915.

My Confirmation: A Guide for Confirmation Instruction. St. Louis: Eden Publ. House, 1942.

Neve, J. L. *The Lutherans in Movements for Church Union.* Phila.: Luth. Publ. House, 1921.

Schneider, Carl E. *The German Church on the Frontier: The Story of the Evangelical Synod, 1840—1866.* St. Louis: Eden Publ. House, 1939.

Sweet, W. W. *Religion in Colonial America.* New York: Chas. Scribner's Sons, 1942.

———. "The Congregationalists," *Religion on the American Frontier, 1783—1850.* University of Chicago Press, 1939, Vol. III.

———. *The Story of Religion in America.* New York: Harper & Bros., 1930.

Walker, Williston. *A History of the Congregational Churches* ("American Church History Series"). Vol. III. New York: The Christian Literature Co., 1894.

———. *The Creeds and Platforms of Congregationalism.* New York: Charles Scribner's Sons, 1893.

The Christian Century, LXXVII (1960), 1508—1511. James Hastings Nichols, "Merger for Metropolitan Mission," *The Christian Century,* LXXVIII (1961), 617—619, offers a realistic appraisal of the Blake proposal's prospects.

SECTION III

The United Church of Canada

The United Church of Canada came into being in 1925 by a merger of the Canadian Methodist, Congregationalist, and some Presbyterian churches.[1] The merging churches consider themselves to be of the historic stream of the Christian church, affirming their faith in Holy Scripture of the Old and the New Testament as the primary source and ultimate standard of faith and life, accepting the ancient creeds and particularly maintaining allegiance to the doctrinal position of the standards adopted by the Presbyterian Church in Canada, the Congregational Union of Ontario and Quebec, and by the Methodist Church. The Twenty Articles adopted in 1925 avoid those points in doctrine which have always separated anthropocentric Arminians and theocentric Calvinists.[2] In 1940 a Statement of Faith, consisting of twelve articles, was presented to the General Council of the U. C. C. These articles are not sufficiently specific and can be interpreted in either the conservative or the liberal tradition. In explaining the article on the Scriptures the leading theologians clearly disavow the radical views of the comparative religions school, which sees in every form of ethnic religion a self-disclosure of God as authentic as that of the Scriptures. Currently the Barthian view of the Scriptures seems to prevail among the U. C. C. theologians.[3] Article IV of the Statement

---

[1] The census of 1931 shows that many Presbyterian churches in eastern Canada did not join the merger. This is another instance where a merger increased the number of denominations instead of reducing them. The Baptist churches refused to enter into the merger because they are on principle opposed to any ecclesiastical organization. The Anglican church, while sympathetic to the movement, did not join the union because of its position regarding the apostolic succession. Negotiations for an agreed basis of union between the Anglican Church of Canada and the United Church conducted since the forties reached a stalemate in 1958 but are being continued with little likelihood of early success (Keith R. Bridston, "Survey of Church Union Negotiations 1957—1959," *Ecumenical Review*, XII [1959/1960], 252—253).

[2] It seems that the Articles of Faith are considered, at least by some of the leaders, a historic statement rather than a real doctrinal affirmation. The *Basis of Union* states that candidates for the ministry must be in substantial agreement with the Twenty Articles. Not a few of the leaders in the United Church have espoused Liberalism. J. N. Sturk, *passim.*

[3] Dow, pp. 171, 173, 180 ff. The Barthians so overemphasize the Word (John 1:1) behind the Word (John 5:38), the creative, dynamic Word, or the Logos, that they not only distinguish between the personal Word and the written Word, but completely separate them. They contend that since the Word of God always comes to man as a living and dynamic personal Word, there is a personal encounter between God and man, and something must happen. This statement raises the question whether God speaks to men in an "objective" Word today. Is the Word only *Deus loquens* or also *Deus locutus?* What relevance has the written Word, or any word of God, to me outside my own subjective experience? Is it really the Word of God?

declares that "knowing God as Creator and Father, as Redeemer in Christ, and as Holy Spirit working in us, we confess our faith in the Trinity." This statement, however, is given a modalistic interpretation. There is not a Trinity of persons, but a threefold manifestation of God, just as when an actor appears now as a soldier, now as a king, and now as a judge. Paul is said to have experienced the Trinity when in his father's home he learned to know God as the Lawgiver, on the road to Damascus as the outreaching Love, and finally in his ministry as the sustaining Spirit.[4]

The exposition of the Article concerning the person of Christ is in terms of modern kenoticism, if not even in terms of the Ritschlian "moral union," i. e., the union of the divine and human in Christ consists merely in this, that His will was completely attuned to the Father's will. U. C. C. theologians maintain that the phrase "God was in Christ" was Paul's way of saying that it is impossible to disengage the perfect life and ministry of Christ from God's revelation of His graciousness and love. In this sense the Word was made flesh.[5] The reconciliation which Christ effected is described as follows:

It is only suffering love, such as we have in Christ crucified, that can serve as a reconciling power. Suffering in the place of others and for others; suffering that is endured for the sake of lifting others to a higher plane of life; suffering that is sacrificial in its very nature, is

the strongest reconciling force in the world of man.[6]

In describing the work of Christ on the cross some of the leaders in the U. C. C. seem to lean toward the Grotian rectoral theory of the Atonement and even toward the Bushnell concept of the moral influence theory. They maintain that in the fourth word on the cross Christ could not have meant that He was actually experiencing the wrath of God, since God cannot be a prisoner of His own laws of retribution and demand the payment of a satisfaction. In this cry Christ would have us see, first, God's vindication of the moral order which He has established for the world, and, second, man's inhumanity to Christ and the true nature of our own sins, that thus we may be led to true repentance and the ultimate conquest of our sins. Christ's resurrection is a sign of this ultimate victory, when man's deepest evil will be transmuted into God's highest purpose.[7] In Article X of the *Basis of Union* faith in Christ is said to be "a saving grace whereby we receive Him, trust in Him, and rest upon Him alone for salvation." This evangelical statement is somewhat obscured in the official expositions where faith is described as "the personal self-committal of a man to the gracious unseen power that is revealed in Jesus," or "as loyalty to Him and His way of life, absolute commitment to Him in life and death, that tests the reality and sincerity of our faith."[8] There is bound to be confusion

---

4 Lockhead, p. 11. Dow, pp. 77—80.

5 Ibid., p. 36 ff.

6 Chalmers, p. 22.

7 Dow, pp. 115—31.

8 Chalmers, p. 10. Late in 1959 a brochure was published by the 43 theologians comprising the Committee on Christian Faith of the United Church of Canada, A. G. Reynolds, ed., *Life and Death: A Study of the Christian Hope.* The Church's General Council approved it as "worthy of study in the church." Some controversy was evoked by the fact that the study suggests a place or condition of probation after death and before the soul's entry into heaven. It also looks with favor on prayers for the dead, both memorial and intercessory. (*The Christian Century,* LXXVI [1959], 1288.)

and unclarity in describing justifying and saving faith, in fact, all the great Scriptural concepts, when there is no clarity concerning the nature of Christ's person and work, as is the case in the official writings explaining the theology held in the U. C. C. There are voices in the U. C. C. which deplore the creedless and liberal position of the leading theologians.[9]

The U. C. C. found a *modus vivendi* in polity to satisfy the three merging bodies, each with a basically different form of church government. The pastoral charge consisting of one or more local congregations constitutes the basic unit of organization — this satisfies the Congregationalists. The Presbytery, the Conference, and the General Council are the governing courts, patterned after the church polity prevalent among Presbyterians and Methodists.

BIBLIOGRAPHY

PART VI

Chalmers, R. G. *Our Living Faith,* an Interpretation of the Faith of U. C. C. Toronto, Can.: Board of Evangelism and Social Service, the United Church of Canada, Wesley Bldg., 1949.

Dow, John. *This Is Our Faith,* an Exposition of the Statement of Faith of U. C. C. Toronto, Can.: Board of Evangelism and Social Service, the United Church of Canada, Wesley Bldg., c. 1943.

SECTION III

Lockhead, Arthur W. *A Companion to the Catechism.* Toronto, Can.: Board of Evangelism and Social Service, the United Church of Canada, Wesley Bldg., c. 1945.

Sturk, J. N. *The Looting of a Legacy.* Winnipeg: Berean Bible & Tract Depot, 1931.

Walsh, H. H. *The Christian Church in Canada.* Toronto: Ryerson Press, 1956.

SECTION IV

Interdenominational Churches

Federated, Community and Independent Churches

Federated Churches are congregations "in which two or more denominational units conduct local affairs in common but maintain their separate denominational affiliation."[1]

Community Churches are described as follows:

In some cases denominational churches have broadened the terms of membership to include all professing Christians . . . giving them the privilege of continuing their benevolent contributions to their several boards. In these churches

---

[9] Cp. *The United Church Observer,* July 15, 1951, p. 11.

[1] Benson Y. Landis, ed., *Yearbook of American Churches,* 29th ed. (New York: NCCCUSA, 1960), p. 53. The census report does not use the term "community church."

it is possible to be a Christian without being a denominationalist. . . .

In other communities an independent church has been organized broad enough to include all denominations. No one is asked to give up any religious opinion or loyalty already formed. The only new thing in such a situation is the new spirit of toleration of religious opinion.[2]

Independent Churches.[3] It is impossible to determine what these churches teach, because every local congregation is autonomous and because in every local unit there may be and usually are several groups of divergent denominational background. The 1936 Census listed a body known as *Independent Negro Churches,* about which current information is not available.

The International Ministerial Federation, an association of ordained ministers, was incorporated in 1937 to serve interdenominational, nondenominational, and community churches.

Independent Fundamental Churches of America

As its title indicates, this group of churches has two distinctive characteristics: (1) opposition to every form of sectarian denominationalism and espousal of the spiritual unity of believers and their sovereignty; (2) complete withdrawal from the modernist churches and a militantly aggressive evangelistic program.[4]

The organization was effected at Cicero, Ill., in 1930 with a view to uniting such independent churches and groups as had severed their relations with their denominations on account of modernist inroads and to enabling these independent groups to establish closer fellowship and a more effective defense of the Gospel. The constitution provides specifically that all members, churches, or groups must sever every denominational connection, since this association is only a "Christian Fellowship" and totally independent of any denomination. The argument is that only such an antidenominational position meets the requirements of 1 Cor. 1:11-13; 3:19, whereas denominationalism breeds pride of name, pride of creed as the final standard of truth, pride of denominational machinery. In short, because the modernist trends were an accidental concomitant in some denominations, this group sought the remedy in completely discarding every denominational affiliation. This appears to be a case of pouring the child out with the bath water. To the charge that this association is a denomination, only under an-

---

[2] O. E. Jordan, *What Is a Community Church?* (Park Ridge, Ill.), p. 2.

[3] The Census Report lists the Independent Churches in three categories:

1. Community, union, nondenominational, interdenominational churches which represent the movement of the consolidation of small or weak churches, esp. in rural communities.

2. Independent missions or Sunday schools which were established by Christian workers on undenominational lines.

3. Denominational congregations which for one or several reasons fail to unite with their denominations, e. g., independent Lutheran, Baptist, Methodist congregations. *Census,* 1936, II, 689, 738.

[4] The information on this group of churches was supplied by the IFCA, 542 S. Dearborn, Chicago, Ill. Fundamentalism has been an unorganized trend to combat modernism. While the Independent Fundamental Churches hold many doctrines in common with fundamentalists, the two must be kept distinct, since fundamentalism is a trend and the fundamentalists, by and large, remained in their respective denominations.

other name, the adherents reply that it is not a church, does not function as a denomination, cannot own property.

In spite of the opposition to denominationalism the constitution requires every member to subscribe to sixteen basic articles of faith, such as the complete inerrancy, verbal inspiration, and absolute authority of Holy Scripture; the theanthropic person of Christ and His vicarious atonement; man's total depravity and the Holy Spirit's regenerating power; dispensationalism and the imminent premillennial coming of Christ. The constitution, however, specifically rejects the teaching of entire holiness and the restoration of the charismatic gifts, especially tongues speaking.[5]

A strong Calvinistic trend is evident, especially in the creedal statement "Once saved, you are secure in Christ forever." However, this tenet seems to be tinged with the Wesleyan emphasis on the believer's joy in his salvation.

SECTION V

The Disciples and the Churches of Christ

The Disciples

The Disciples, who in 1957 formally took "The International Convention of Christian Churches (Disciples of Christ)" as their corporate name, originated in the Restoration Movement, a nineteenth century effort to restore the "one, holy, catholic, and apostolic church" on a nondenominational and noncreedal basis.[1]

In some of its phases the movement was extremely unionistic; in other respects, intensely literalistic and separatistic. In fact, its extreme Biblicism has proved to be divisive, and the Disciples instead of uniting all Christians have become responsible for new divisions in the church.[2] The following groups represent the Restoration Movement today: The

---

[5] This statement is no doubt intended to avoid any false identification. Both the Holiness-Pentecostal and the Independent churches are made up largely of former Baptists and Methodists. Though the Independent Fundamental churches agree on some points with the Holiness bodies (cp. the Creed of Nazarene Church), they, according to the official constitution, adopted in 1930 and amended in 1948, specifically repudiate any Pentecostal leanings.

[1] George Calixt envisioned a possible reunion of all Christendom on the basis of the *consensus quinquesaecularis,* or the creeds of the first five centuries. The American Restoration Movement went beyond the ideals of Calixt and hoped to do away with all creeds. Garrison and De Groot, p. 175 f.

[2] Alfred T. De Groot, *The Ground of Divisions Among the Disciples of Christ* (Priv. ed., distr. by Univ. of Chicago Libraries, 1939), pp. 3, 12. Prof. W. E. Garrison, like De Groot a member of the Disciples, states that the controversies resulting from the Restoration Movement have split the Disciples into six hostile and exclusive groups. W. E. Garrison, *Religion,* p. 297. Garrison quotes an unpublished manuscript by C. C. Klingman and comments: "This enumeration of divisions must not be taken too seriously. It pictures the schisms of that extreme right wing of the Disciples [The Churches of Christ]." The extreme literalism and false Biblicism which accompanied the Restoration Movement is illustrated in the controversy

Christian Union, the Churches of Christ, and the Disciples of Christ. Within these more or less clearly delineated groups there are internal divisions designated by the terms "progressives" and "conservatives." The entire movement is usually and popularly associated with the group known as Disciples. (The General Convention of Christian Churches also grew out of the Restorationist Movement, but it has now been absorbed into the United Church of Christ.)

The nomenclature commonly employed by these groups causes difficulty. It must be kept in mind that these groups specifically disclaim to be a denomination and wish to be known merely as a movement to restore the sovereignty of the local congregation. There is little or no denominational organization, at best a state, national, or international convention of like-minded congregations or, in some instances, of individual pastors and laymen. On national or state lines the adherents of the restoration movement have divided, one party being known as "Disciples" and the other as "Churches of Christ." Locally the Disciples usually call their congregation "Christian Church." When speaking of a group of their churches, the "Churches of Christ" use such terms as "Churches in Christian Union" or "Christian Churches." The local name is usually "Church of Christ."

HISTORY

The Disciples constitute the largest church body indigenous to America.[3] It came into being at the turn of the nineteenth century, when the religious atmosphere was such as to assure, from the very start, the rapid expansion of this movement. The recently gained religious liberty, the impact of French rationalism, which questioned all dogmatic statements, the rapid expansion of the American frontier with its corollary of doctrinal indifference, were factors favorable to the development of a unionistic, non-creedal, congregational church movement. Almost simultaneously four distinct movements arose in widely scattered areas under the leadership of Abner Jones, Barton Stone, Thomas and Alexander Campbell, and Walter Scott. These four movements finally merged to form the various Christian Churches.

THE EARLY PERIOD

The New England Restoration Movement. Abner Jones, a New England Baptist, is usually considered the first successful "restorationist."[4] Protesting at

between two so-called restored churches — one in Edinburgh and the other in New York. The one maintained that according to 1 Tim. 2:1 the public service must be opened with prayer; the other contended that on the basis of Psalm 100 this priority must be given to the hymn. Garrison, *Am. Rel. M.*, pp. 24—27.

[3] There were two restorationist movements in Scotland — the one under John Glas and Robert Sandeman in the first half of the eighteenth century, and the other under the Haldane brothers. Both movements were protests against the alleged assumption of ecclesiastical authority and attempts to restore the pattern of the New Testament church. There is little evidence that these movements had any specific bearing on their American counterpart. Glas observed the weekly Communion service, a distinctive feature of modern Disciples; Sandeman's definition of faith in Locke's thought-patterns seems to predate the Disciples' view that faith is an intellectual acceptance of the Scriptural evidence of Christ rather than the personal assurance of God's grace in Christ. Garrison and De Groot, pp. 46—50.

[4] The Methodist James O'Kelly protested against the assumption of dictatorial powers by the Methodist bishops, seceded from the Methodists in 1792, organized the Republican Methodist Church. The principles he

first against the Five Points of Calvinism, he ultimately rejected the use of any creed as a test for fellowship, every denominational name, all ecclesiastical terms. However, Jones rejected not only the terms "Trinity" and "deity of Christ," but also the doctrines thereby expressed. Because of their evident Unitarianism the New England "Christians" were generally known as Evangelical Unitarians, or Unitarian Baptists. They organized as the General Convention of Christian Churches, merged with the Congregational churches in 1931, and are now a part of the United Church of Christ.

Barton Stone and the Kentucky Revival. From his contacts with "New School" Presbyterianism Barton W. Stone acquired two principles which ultimately made him the recognized leader of the Restoration Movement in the middle Southeast. For one thing, he believed that Christians should stress only those elements which all Christians hold in common and suppress all divisive doctrines and practices.[5] With James McGready, Stone favored the Arminian type of theology and was a strong advocate of the revival system.[6] In fact, Stone became the moving spirit in the Kentucky Revival, which finally centered in Stone's parish at Cane Ridge, about thirty miles northeast of Frankfort, Ky., and which for its psychological phenomena, its religious frenzy, and its "holy exercises" is unique in revivalism.[7] The revival reached its climax in August, 1801, when preachers from several denominations addressed the 20,000 who had gathered at Cane Ridge. The "holy exercises" soon disappeared.[8] But the leaders — Presbyterians, Methodists, Baptists — feeling that the revival had clearly demonstrated that deeds are more important than creeds, held that the church must rise above denominational distinctions and creedal differences. The proponents of these views became subject to disciplinary action by their respective church bodies. Thereupon they withdrew and banded together under the name "Christians" and soon attracted many followers in northern Kentucky and southwestern Ohio. Before long they became established in all the Central States. The autonomy of the local congregation and the spiritual competence and independence of the laity became the watchword of

announced were later adopted by the Disciples: No creed but the Bible; no denominational name; no ranks in the ministry. Garrison and De Groot, pp. 85—87. Many Disciples apparently do not regard Jones as being in their historic tradition.

[5] William Garrett West, *Barton Warren Stone: Early American Advocate of Christian Unity* (Nashville: Disciples of Christ Historical Society, 1954). In 1956 the College of the Bible at Lexington, Kentucky, republished Stone's *History of the Christian Church in the West,* a somewhat bland and superficial account of the beginnings of the movement which Stone led. — *The Christian Congregation* (see p. 323 above) is also related to the Stone movement.

[6] McGready helped found the Cumberland Presbyterian Church.

[7] There are several studies that deal with the phenomena of this revival. Frank G. Beardsley, *The History of Christianity in America* (New York: American Tract Society, 1938), p. 99 ff.; Sweet, *Revivalism,* p. 122 f.; Richard MacNemar, *The Kentucky Revival: A Short History of the Late Extraordinary Outpouring of the Spirit of God in the Western State of America* (Cincinnati, 1807. Repr., New York, 1846), p. 27.

[8] The only people who seem to have capitalized on these phenomena were the Shakers, who gained a few of the leaders as members. Sidney Rigdon, one of Joseph Smith's companions, was first associated with Campbell. For Rigdon's and Campbell's influence among the Mormons see G. A. Arbaugh, *Revelation in Mormonism* (Univ. of Chicago Press, 1932), p. 9 ff.

this group of Christians.[9] They held that the spirit of the New Testament left no room for any attempt to formulate a statement concerning even such central doctrines as the Trinity or the person and work of Christ.[10]

The Campbells. Thomas and Alexander Campbell became the spiritual fathers of the Disciples.[11] Thomas Campbell, a member of the Irish Seceder Presbyterian Church, inclined toward the union principles of Hugo Grotius, the "covenant" theology of John Coccejus, the Restoration principles of John Glas, and especially the principles of tolerance espoused by John Locke's *Letters Concerning Toleration.* In 1807, at the age of forty-five, he became pastor of a Seceder Presbyterian Church in western Pennsylvania. After a short time he was severely censured because he advocated open Communion, questioned the binding character of the Westminster Confession, and ignored the ecclesiastical regulations concerning parish lines. In consequence of this censure and as a protest against it, Campbell on August 17, 1809, formed the "Christian Association of Washington County, Pa.," near the Ohio State line, and published the "Declaration and Address," still considered the theological *magna carta* of the Disciples. The Declaration states that the Christian Association is founded for the "sole purpose of promoting simple evangelical Christianity far from

the admixture of human opinions." The Address contains thirteen propositions, which are substantially the following:

1. "The church of Christ upon earth is essentially, intentionally, and constitutionally one."

2. Congregations locally separate ought to be in fellowship with one another.

3. Nothing ought to be an article of faith, a term of Communion, or a rule for the constitution and management of the church except what is expressly taught by Christ and His apostles.

4. "The New Testament is as perfect a constitution for the worship, discipline, and government of the New Testament church, and as perfect a rule for the particular duties of its members, as the Old Testament was for the Old Testament church."

5. The church can give no new commandments where the Scriptures are silent.

6. Inferences and deductions from the Scriptures may be the true doctrine, but they dare not be made binding on the consciences of Christians.

7. Creeds may be useful for instruction but must not be used as tests of fitness for membership in the church.

8. Full knowledge of all revealed truth is not necessary to entitle persons to membership, "neither should they, for this purpose, be required to make a profession more extensive than their knowledge." Realization of their need of salvation, faith in Christ as Savior,

---

[9] The details of this somewhat intricate history are carefully traced in Garrison and De Groot, ch. v. "The Last Will and Testament," published in 1804 by Stone and four fellow Presbyterian pastors, is the first formal document setting forth the principles of theology and polity of the Churches of Christ. Cp. ibid., p. 109 f.

[10] Stone disavowed the Trinity because in his view it was not a revealed doctrine. He seems to have favored a modalist theology and an Arian Christology. He held the vicarious atonement to be contrary to reason, to Holy Scripture, and to civil law. God sent Christ to reconcile men to God, not God to man. "The Holy Spirit," said Stone, "means power or energy of God, never a third person in the deity." Garrison and De Groot, pp. 117—23; Garrison, *Am. Rel. M.,* p. 93.

[11] Hence "Campbellites," a nickname to which they object strenuously for reasons of principle.

and obedience to Him are all that is necessary.

9. All who are thus qualified should love one another as brothers and be united.

10. "Division among Christians is a horrid evil."

11. Divisions have been caused, in some cases, by neglect of the expressly revealed will of God; in others, by assuming authority to make human opinions the test of fellowship or to introduce human inventions into the faith and practice of the church.

12. All that is needed for the purity and perfection of the church is that it receive those, and only those, who profess faith in Christ and obey Him according to the Scriptures, that it retain them only so long as their conduct is in accord with their profession, that ministers teach only what is expressly revealed, and that all divine ordinances be observed as the New Testament church observed them.

13. When the church adopts necessary "expedients," they should be recognized for what they are and should not be confused with divine commands, so that they will give no occasion for division.[12]

In 1810 his son Alexander joined him and soon became the leader of the new movement, with headquarters at Brush Run, thirty miles southwest of Pittsburgh. Being refused membership in the Presbyterian church, the Brush Run congregation united with an association of Particular, or Calvinistic, Baptists. But during the subsequent two decades several points of disagreement arose, which culminated in a separation in 1830. During this period Alexander Campbell urged two points which have given direction and emphasis to the distinctive message of the Disciples down to the present: the peculiar stress upon the significance of the New Testament and the definition of the nature and function of faith. In his "Sermon on the Law" (1816) he took the view that the Christian system differs fundamentally from the Old Testament. He held that the first covenant was designed only for the Jews and was entirely abrogated when Christ in His divine Messiahship established a new covenant, the obligations of which are contained in the New Testament. From this fact Campbell argued that the heart of the Christian religion as well as the true basis for Christian union is undivided loyalty to the sole authority of Christ under the new covenant.[13] Campbell arrived at his definition of faith by way of Locke's theory of knowledge. Campbell and his followers maintained — and this is still a central point in the Disciples' message — that faith is not a supernaturally wrought trust in God, but rather an intellectual testing and accepting of the basic principles of the moral order of salvation presented by Christ in the New Testament. Obedience to Christ, the Messiah, is the essence of faith and hence also the only and all-sufficient basis for New Testament fellowship.[14] After his separation

---

[12] Quoted in Garrison, *Am. Rel. M.*, pp. 70—72. Cp. also Garrison and De Groot, pp. 145—53.

[13] The idea of successive covenants was first advanced by John Coccejus of Holland to escape the logical necessity of Calvin's divine decrees. In Coccejus' plan the two covenants diverge in Adam's fall when he lost the divine image. Campbell placed the distinction between the two at the coming of Chirst. Ainslee, p. 77 ff. Heinrich Heppe, *Reformed Dogmatics,* trans. G. T. Thomson (London: Geo. Allen and Unwin Ltd., 1950), chs. xiii, xvi.

[14] Garrison and De Groot, pp. 168, 181 ff., and *passim.* R. Frederick West, "Campbell's Defense of Revealed Religion," *Religion in Life,* Winter, 1947—48, p. 82. The salient points of Campbell's theology are contained

from the Baptists in 1830 he entered into fellowship with Stone. Although he had many things in common with Stone, there were also divisive differences between the two men. Stone was an outspoken Unitarian and Arian. Campbell, at least in his later years, repudiated Unitarianism.[15] Stone preferred the all-inclusive name "Christians," while Campbell, in deference to the members of other Christian denominations, had selected the name "Disciples." In 1833 most of the churches which followed Stone and Campbell united and while, strictly speaking, these congregations constituted a "movement," they gradually took on more and more the character of a denomination. In the interest of a more efficient missionary and educational program Campbell supported

the demand for the formation of a national convention, though he could find no apostolic direction for such a procedure. The first national convention of the Disciples met at Cincinnati in 1849. Though the Disciples seemingly lack the usual tools for an aggressive mission program — strictly speaking, the Convention of Disciples is not a denomination, but only a loose association of congregations — they experienced a phenomenal growth. An important factor in this growth is the success these people had in the publication of periodicals. It has been said that the Disciples do not have bishops, but editors. Campbell was the editor of the *Christian Baptist* from 1823 to 1830 and of the *Millennial Harbinger* from 1830 to 1866. Campbell believed in a "symbolic millennium," whose chief

in his *The Christian System*, 1836, in which he states that belief in the one fact, that Jesus is the Messiah, and submission to the one institution of Baptism, is sufficient for salvation. In the *Millennial Harbinger* he describes the Christian as one who believes that Jesus of Nazareth is the Messiah, the Son of God, repents of his sins, and obeys Him in all things according to his measure of knowledge of His will. Garrison, *Am. Rel. M.*, p. 103 f.

15 He condemned the New England Christians for their outspoken Unitarianism. In his debate with Rice (1843) he did indeed condemn the use of creeds, but he insisted that he was upholding the doctrines professed in the ecumenical creeds. Garrison and De Groot, pp. 231 f., 264 f. Campbell has frequently been charged with Unitarianism on the basis of statements made in *The Christian System*, e. g., pp. 20 f. and 24 f., and in the debate with Rice. The following quotations from the Campbell-Rice debate show that it is extremely difficult to determine Campbell's position:

CAMPBELL: [Peter's confession, Matthew 16] is the whole revelation of the mystery of the Christian constitution — the full confession of the Christian faith. All that is peculiar to Christianity is found in these words. [P. 822.]

RICE: Mr. C., I believe, professes to believe in the true and proper divinity of Christ. But if we ask Barton W. Stone, a prominent teacher in the same church, concerning his character, he will tell us that the Son of God existed before the creation of the world, but not from eternity; and consequently, he makes him only an exalted creature. If Mr. C. believes in the divinity of Christ, there is an infinite difference between his faith and that of Mr. Stone. [P. 829.]

CAMPBELL: But Unitarianism is also preached amongst us. So says Mr. Rice. If so, I know it not. For my part, I know and acknowledge no man as a brother preaching Unitarianism amongst us. I say again that I neither know of any such person, nor do I acknowledge any such person as a fellow-laborer with me. [P. 847. Campbell, however, accepted any heretic if the heretic would call his "error" merely an opinion and would promise not to teach it openly.]

characteristic was the complete restoration of the New Testament church as the sure sign that Christ had been universally accepted as Messiah.[16]

Walter Scott and the Disciples' Message. In 1822 Walter Scott, a follower of the extremely literalistic Haldane restorationists, became associated with Campbell. Scott reduced the Christians' message to simple factual statements in accordance with the Lockean principle of epistemology. Predominant in his thinking was the conviction that faith is not some form of emotional assurance, but rather the acceptance of the demonstrable truth of Christ's Messiahship. He held that the only effective manner of presenting the Gospel was by way of five approaches: (1) hearing and accepting the evidence for Christ's Messiahship; (2) repentance of personal and actual sin; (3) submission to Baptism as the condition for (4) God's liberation from the guilt, penalty, and dominion of sin and for (5) God's bestowal of the Holy Spirit and eternal life. Like other Disciples, Scott was averse to the religious frenzy of the ordinary revival and maintained that the Christian message is for the intellect, not the emotions. He inaugurated an evangelistic program which took for granted the absolute authority of the New Testament, man's rational ability to understand the New Testament's demands, and man's moral ability to fulfill them. The primary reason for the rather phenomenal growth of the Disciples is no doubt the fact that the Disciples demand no more for Christian fellowship than the acceptance of Christ's Messiahship, repentance of personal sins, and baptism by immersion.[17]

THE MODERN PERIOD

During the early part of their history the Disciples and the Christians represented the extreme wing of perfectionism and Pentecostalism. After the first generation, and especially the second, a decided change took place, which manifested itself in two directions.

RICE [quoting Campbell from his book *Christianity Restored*]: We will acknowledge all as Christians who acknowledge the Gospel facts and obey Jesus Christ. . . . We will have neither Unitarians nor Trinitarians. How can this be? Systems make Unitarians and Trinitarians. Renounce the system, and you renounce its creatures. . . . What is a Unitarian? One who contends that Jesus Christ is not the Son of God. Such a one has denied the faith, and therefore we reject him. . . . If he will ascribe to Jesus all Bible attributes, names, works, and worship, we will not fight with him about scholastic words. But if he will not ascribe to Him everything that the first Christians ascribed, and worship and adore Him as the first Christians did, we will reject him, not because of his private opinions, but because he refuses to honor Jesus as the first converts did. . . . In like manner we will deal with a Trinitarian. If he will ascribe to the Father, Son, and the Holy Spirit, all that the first believers did, and nothing more, we will receive him — but we will not allow him to apply scholastic and barbarous epithets to the Father, the Son, or the Holy Spirit. If he will dogmatize and become a factionist, we reject him — not because of his opinions, but because of his attempting to make a faction, or to lord it over God's heritage. [P. 867. Cp. below, Note 30.]

16 Garrison and De Groot, pp. 253—60. Among the many periodicals published by the Disciples, as individuals or as a society, probably none was so well known as *The Christian Century* under Charles Clayton Morrison's editorship. It is now an undenominational organ.

17 Garrison and De Groot, ch. ix. The Disciples and the Churches of Christ together are the sixth largest Christian denomination, exceeded only by the Roman Catholics, Baptists, Methodists, Lutherans, and Presbyterians.

A large portion of the members became known as "progressive," inasmuch as in their theology they increasingly disavowed all forms of emotionalism and leaned toward intellectualism and in church polity adopted modern methods. Others within the body became known as "conservative." Whereas the "progressives" seemed to deviate from the strong emphasis given to some of the early Christian principles, the conservatives exaggerated those views. They considered them the basic principles of their movement and became increasingly literalistic and separatistic.[18] The Disciples successfully avoided the strife and contention which the slavery question caused in other denominations. Nevertheless, immediately after the Civil War, they were disturbed by controversies which divided them into two camps, the "progressives" and the "conservatives," and ultimately — about 1900 — into two bodies, the Disciples and the Churches of Christ.[19] The controversies revolved about the assumption of pastoral powers by preachers, open Communion, instrumental music in public worship, and the establishment of mission societies. Those who took liberal views with regard to these questions were called "progressives" and can be said to represent what is known today as the Disciples. With the beginning of the nineteenth century higher criticism and liberal theology found many exponents among the Disciples. Since the days of Campbell the Disciples have been students of the New Testament and in their theological work have laid emphasis on Biblical interpretation rather than on systematic theology. The introduction of higher criticism into Disciples' circles caused a considerable stir and resulted in serious tensions between the conservatives, or fundamentalists, and the progressives, or liberals. In this conflict the inherent weakness of the Disciples' anticreedalism became very evident, and the conservatives were

[18] There is involved a significant sociological factor, observable again and again in the history of the smaller religious bodies. Sweet makes the following observation:

> With the rapid changes in the cultural, economic, social, and religious climate which took place in the United States following the Civil War, the revivalistic emphasis among the evangelical churches rapidly declined. Education, refinement, and dignity now characterized the ministry of an increasing number of Methodists, Baptists, and Disciples. . . . Outside the Southern Baptists the revivalistic techniques have largely disappeared among the large evangelical churches. The waning of revivalism among these large bodies has been one of the principal reasons for the emergence of numerous revivalistic sects, most of them stressing holiness and premillennialism. Appealing largely to the people of the lower economic and cultural level of American society, they flourished as never before during the period of the great depression and the First and Second World Wars. The very fact that they have increased so rapidly in the last several years would seem to indicate that they are supplying needs in reaching a certain class of people which, at the present time at least, seem beyond the power of the middle-class churches either to reach or supply. Methodism, once a great religious ferment, largely among the poor, has now become an upper-middle-class church. Once it was proud to be called the poor man's church; now it boasts of its colleges and universities, its great endowments and tremendous corporate power. Much the same thing is true of the Northern Baptists and in a more limited degree of the Disciples. The Episcopalians, the Presbyterians, and the Congregationalists are still more "upper-class." [*Am. Ch.*, pp. 55—58.]

[19] Garrison and De Groot, ch. xv. Garrison, *Am. Rel. M.*, ch. viii.

stymied in every attempt to check liberalism.[20]

Though the Disciples have been advocates of the union of all Christiandom, they have healed not so much as one division in the Christian church. On the contrary they have caused divisions even in their own communion.[21] They have been very active in modern ecumenical efforts, notably the founding of the Federal Council of Churches and, more recently, the National Council of the Churches of Christ and the World Council of Churches. The proposed mergers, at first with the Congregationalists and later with the Baptists, failed, mainly because of divergent opinions on baptismal regeneration.[22]

THE DOCTRINAL POSITION

THE FORMAL AND MATERIAL PRINCIPLES

The Disciples consider the formulation of creedal statements as contrary to the letter and the spirit of the New Testament. As a result there is a great diversity of doctrinal opinion in this body, and — as the preceding historical section shows — it is well-nigh impossible to present the Disciples' doctrinal position. Nevertheless there are a few sign-posts which indicate the direction of theological thinking among the Disciples. Since these directives, whether or not they are called creeds, have all the characteristics of formal creedal statements, they are regarded as creeds by those who wish to examine the Disciples' system of theology. When Campbell in the *Christian System* set forth the immutably ordained "facts, precepts, promises, ordinances, and doctrines" of the Christian institution, he wrote a creed, even though he did not demand a formal subscription to it. And the more than two dozen "interpretations" of the Disciples' message set forth the *credo*, the religious convictions, of the Disciples. And a statement of this sort is precisely what everybody else calls a creed.[23]

The Disciples insist that their formal principle, or their source of religious truth, is the Bible. Some Disciples declare that the divinely inspired books of both Testaments are all-sufficient and final in all matters of faith and life.[24] Disciples think that they have escaped the pitfalls of the Reformation principle of private interpretation because they have attempted to set up a consensus of interpretation as the means of attaining

---

[20] Cp. Cole, ch. vii. Some Disciples distinguish even three groups, the conservatives supported by the *Christian Standard;* a middle-of-the-road group, the progressives, represented by the *Christian Evangelist;* and the extreme liberal element, whose spokesman was *The Christian Century* until it became an undenominational paper. The Disciples' Divinity House at the University of Chicago, under Dean Edward S. Ames and Prof. Herbert L. Willett, spearheaded the liberal movement. See Van Meter Ames, ed., *Beyond Theology: The Autobiography of Edward Scribner Ames* (Chicago: The University of Chicago Press, 1959).

[21] Frederick W. Burnham, "What Is Disturbing the Disciples?" *Christian Century,* May 17, 1944, p. 616 ff., attempts to analyze this problem.

[22] The progressives declare that there are no barriers to such a merger. Cp. *Christian Century,* June 22, 1949. The *Watchman Examiner* (Baptist) contained several articles maintaining the opposite.

[23] When Campell published *The Christian System,* he did not escape the charge of inconsistency for having published the "Campbellite Creed." Garrison and De Groot, p. 224. Cp. also p. 575.

[24] Stephen J. Corey, president of the United Christian Missions Society, in *Census,* II, 541.

unity in Christ while retaining freedom of thought and action.[25] Indeed, the Disciples have always been known for a Bible-centered training of their ministers. Their Bible colleges have only recently introduced courses in systematic theology, and these are still given from the exegetical standpoint.[26] But obviously the material principle, the central core of the Disciples' message, determines their approach to the Bible. Briefly the core proclamation of the Disciples can be said to be "Christian union." The schisms in the church are alleged to be a grim witness of the fratricidal struggles which Christ came to erase. In a divided Christian church love is marred, life is weakened, and the conversion of the world is hindered. Scripture with all its ordinances is to implement selfless love among Christians.[27] Other religious emphases seem to serve only to undergird this central message. Whether they stress the obedience to Christ's Messiahship, the rejection of creeds, an intelligent interpretation of faith, the necessity of moral

character for membership, the Disciples never lose sight of their central idea. The basic principle with its several implications and emphases has been summarized in various ways. One summary reads as follows:

(1) A catholic confession that Jesus is the Christ over against creedal declarations; (2) a catholic name for all believers, such as Christian, Disciple of Christ, etc.; (3) a catholic book of authority, the Holy Scriptures, emphasizing especially the New Testament; (4) a catholic mode of baptism, immersion of the penitent believer; and (5) a catholic observance of the Lord's Supper to which all persons of all communions are invited on an equality of fellowship.[28]

This basic, or material, principle is reflected in the theology, the cultus, and the polity of the Disciples.

CARDINAL CHRISTIAN DOCTRINES

Of God. Disciples speak of "the revelation of God in a threefold personality of Father, Son, and Holy Spirit, as set

---

25 R. C. Snodgrass, *That for Which We Stand,* a tract published by First Christian Church, Amarillo, Tex.

26 The charter of Bethany College, founded by Campbell in 1840, specifies that not theology, but only religion — the common-sense philosophy of John Locke — be taught in the training of pastors. Edward S. Ames, *The Disciples of Christ* (a tract), p. 27 f.

27 Ainslie, *Message,* p. 20 f.

28 Ibid., p. 26. Another statement, presented by Stephen J. Corey and published in *Census,* II, p. 542, reads as follows:

1. Feeling that "to believe and do none other things than those enjoined by our Lord and His Apostles must be infallibly safe," they aim "to restore in faith and spirit and practice the Christianity of Christ and His Apostles as found on the pages of the New Testament."

2. Affirming that "the sacred Scriptures as given of God answer all purposes of a rule of faith and practice, and a law for the government of the church, and that human creeds and confessions of faith spring out of controversy and, instead of being bonds of union, tend to division and strife," they reject all such creeds and confessions.

3. They place especial emphasis upon the "Divine Sonship of Jesus, as the fundamental fact of Holy Scripture, the essential creed of Christianity, and the one article of faith in order to baptism and church membership."

4. Believing that in the Scriptures "a clear distinction is made between the law and the gospel," they "do not regard the Old and New Testaments as of equally binding authority upon Christians," but that

forth by the Apostles." [29] There seems to be no doubt that not a few Disciples have repudiated not only the term Trinity but also the doctrine. This repudiation need not be surprising, since the Trinitarian doctrine is without any religious relevance unless it is accepted in its soteriological setting. The Disciples' theology, when its central motif of the "good life" is taken seriously, has no interest in the deity of Christ and considers the Trinity a metaphysical abstraction. It is more than passing strange that among their voluminous writings the Disciples can point to no book dealing with this doctrine, except Stone's early writings against it. One is inclined to assume that modalism is commonly espoused. At any rate, the Disciples have refused to put their views into creedal forms.[30] The Disciples entertain divergent views concerning the person and work of Christ. The conservatives speak of the

> divine glory of Jesus Christ as the Son of God, His incarnation, doctrine, miracles, death as a sin offering, resurrection, ascension, and coronation . . . the

"the New Testament is as perfect a constitution for the worship, government, and discipline of the New Testament church as the Old was for the Old Testament church."

5. While claiming for themselves the New Testament names of "Christians," or "Disciples," "they do not deny that others are Christians or that other churches are Churches of Christ."

6. Accepting the divine personality of the Holy Spirit, through whose agency regeneration is begun, they hold that men "must hear, believe, repent, and obey the gospel to be saved."

7. Repudiating any doctrine of "baptismal regeneration," and insisting that there is no other prerequisite to regeneration than confession of faith with the whole heart in the personal living Christ, they regard baptism by immersion "as one of the items of the original divine system," and as "commanded in order to the remission of sins."

8. Following the apostolic model, the Disciples celebrate the Lord's Supper on each Lord's day, "not as a sacrament, but as a memorial feast," from which no sincere follower of Christ of whatever creed or church connection is excluded.

9. The Lord's day with the Disciples is not a Sabbath, but a New Testament institution, commemorating our Lord's resurrection, and consecrated by apostolic example.

10. The Church of Christ is a divine institution; sects are unscriptural and unapostolic. The sect name, spirit, and life should give place to the union and co-operation that distinguished the church of the New Testament.

[29] Corey, ibid.

[30] Garrison and De Groot, p. 537. In his debate with Rice, Campbell said:

[At Pentecost] a new manifestation of the Divinity became necessary. Hence the development of a plurality of existence in the Divine nature. The God of the first chapter of Genesis is the Lord God of the second. Light advances as the pages of human history multiply until we have God, the Word of God, and the Spirit of God clearly intimated in the law, the prophets, and the Psalms. But, it was not until the Sun of Righteousness arose — till the Word became incarnate and dwelt among us — till we beheld His glory as that of an only-begotten of the Father, full of grace and truth; it was not till Jesus of Nazareth had finished the work of atonement on the hill of Calvary — till he had brought life and immortality to light, by his revival and resurrection from the sealed sepulchre of the Arimathean senator; it was not till he gave a commission to convert the whole world, that the development of the divine Sonship of Jesus as the fundamental fact of Holy Scripture, the essential creed of Christianity.[31]

The progressives entertain the most radical views concerning Christ. And yet both profess to be united in their loyalty to Christ, the Messiah, and in their obedience to His revelation in the New Testament. The endeavor to unite all Christians externally under Christ supersedes the questions whether the Scriptural terms given to Christ are only honorific or descriptive of His metaphysical nature, whether Christ's work consists primarily in His vicarious atonement or in His teaching ministry.[32] Also there is no uniform teaching concerning the Holy Spirit. Some accept His divine personality, others speak of the Holy Spirit merely as a third manifestation of the Trinity.[33]

Of Man. The Disciples' doctrine of man is in the Arminian and Semi-Pelagian tradition. The doctrine of man's total depravity is said to be unworthy of God and man. Disciples argue further that Christians could never constitute a vital fellowship of love if man were by nature depraved and his every impulse vitiated by self-love.[34] Since the days of Campbell and Scott the Disciples have insisted that conversion is a moral change which occurs when man intelligently examines the evidences for Christ's Lordship. In antithesis to the Baptist and Methodist emphasis on the miraculous, supernatural activity of the Holy Spirit and the Christian's "religious experience," Disciples have likened conversion to the naturalization of an alien. The validity of citizenship rests upon the conscious and intelligent fulfillment of the stipulated requirements and not upon the alien's emotions.[35] The Dis-

Father, and of the Son, and of the Holy Spirit was fully stated and completed. Since the descent of the Holy Spirit, on the birthday of Christ's church — since the glorious immersion of the 3000 triumphs of the memorable Pentecost, the church has enjoyed the mysteries and sublime light of the Father, and of the Son, and of the Holy Spirit, as one Divinity. [*Debate*, p. 615.]

Cp. also *American Church History Series*, XII, 119; Campbell, *Chr. System*, p. 8. Campbell did not make acceptance of the doctrine of the Trinity an issue in fellowship, since he regarded "loyalty to Christ" evident in faith and works the one essential bond of fellowship. Those Lutherans who do not recognize the validity of Unitarian Baptism have insisted on rebaptism in the case of "Christians" asking for membership, on the assumption that all "Christians" are Unitarian. This charge seems to be true only of the New England "Christians," with whom even Campbell would not enter into fellowship because of their outspoken Unitarianism. Stone also entertained similar anti-Trinitarian views, whereas Campbell did not. Garrison and De Groot, pp. 91, 216, 264. In the final analysis the official doctrinal position can be ascertained only by investigating the local congregation's position.

[31] *Census*, II, 541 f.

[32] Ames, pp. 28 f., 34 (above, fn. 26). The extensive Christological literature of the Disciples deals with Christ's Lordship, character, and teaching, rather than with Christology proper. Garrison and De Groot, p. 537.

[33] Campbell used the neuter gender in reference to the Holy Spirit, *Chr. System*, p. 24, but cp. also p. 20.

[34] A. W. Fortune, *Christian Evangelist*, a Disciples' weekly, July 1, 1945, p. 11. E. S. Ames, pp. 20, 39.

[35] Snodgrass, p. 11 (fn. 25, above). Ames, p. 21. Campbell, *Chr. System*, p. 94. — This teaching that faith is an act of the intellect was most fully developed by W. Scott, who followed John Locke rather closely.

ciples describe faith, then, primarily as obedience to Christ's Lordship, not as the personal assurance and acceptance of God's pardoning grace.

Law and Gospel. The Disciples say that the distinction between Law and Gospel is one of the prime requisites for Christian fellowship. The Disciples' distinction between Law and Gospel does not, however, imply the distinction between God's proclamation of His wrath and the message of His grace in Christ. The Disciples consider the entire Old Testament as Law. Since Campbell's famous "Sermon on the Law," they maintain that the Old Covenant has been completely and entirely abolished and the New Testament put into its place. The Old Testament contained the blueprint for the tabernacle and its services. The New Testament contains the blueprint and all specifications for the Christian church. The great program which the Disciples have envisioned for themselves is the "restoration" of the church to its original status under the perfect constitution, or body of laws and regulations prescribed by Christ, the Messiah.[36]

The Sacraments. With reference to the sacraments the Disciples have developed views which are distinct from those held by other Reformed bodies. They have employed terminology which seems to imply baptismal regeneration.

The Disciples, however, expressly "repudiate any doctrine of baptismal regeneration." They say that "Baptism is for the remission of sins; together with faith and repentance it constitutes the condition upon which God will grant remission (or regeneration), the gift of the Holy Spirit, and eternal life."[37] They teach the necessity of Baptism, not as a means of grace, with regenerating efficacy, but as a sacred act which Christ prescribed for His church. According to most Disciples, Baptism is one of the three indispensable acts which determine one's membership in the one holy catholic church. Baptism by immersion is an act of obedience to Christ, and as such it is necessary for the remission of sins and salvation.[38] Likewise the celebration of the Lord's Supper every Sunday is made mandatory as man's act of obedience to Christ's original plan.

Cultus and Church Polity. The basic and central point of the Disciples' theology becomes most apparent in its cultus and church polity. Some maintain that nothing is permissible in the worship of the New Testament church unless Christ or His apostles have expressly commanded it; others say that only such things are permissible as are not expressly forbidden. The latter view prevails today and accounts for the fact that the Disciples show greater latitude than the Christian Churches toward in-

---

[36] In Presbyterianism, whose theology both Campbells had espoused for many years, the Westm. Conf. and Church-adopted regulations form the constitution. In like manner the Disciples consider the New Testament as the constitution of the church. — In his debates on Baptism, immersion, and observance of Sunday, Campbell maintained that these New Testament ordinances dare not be established by analogy from the Old Covenant. They are entirely distinct and must be observed as items of the New Covenant.

[37] S. J. Corey, p. 542. Garrison and De Groot, p. 204, cp. also p. 557. Campbell, *Chr. System,* p. 171.

[38] F. D. Kershner, *Christian Baptism* (Commission on Christian Union of the Disciples of Christ, 1912). In recent years some of the "progressives" have advocated "open membership," that is, reception of Christians from other communions even if they have not been immersed. Garrison and De Groot, p. 432 ff. — On "Immersion" see "Baptists," P. IV, Sec. VI.

novations in the worship of the congregation, architecture of their edifices, and in the organization of various societies for the furtherance of their missionary, educational, and publicational programs.

Evaluation. In evaluating the movement one is constrained to say that a peculiar legalism or intellectual moralism is one of the chief characteristics. This is manifest in the Disciples' watchword that an upright character and love of God and man is the final test of fellowship. Paradoxically the movement is characterized by both a unionistic and a separatistic spirit. On the one hand, the movement is not interested in doctrinal theology, but only in right living, and is thus willing to reduce the basis for fellowship to the least common denominator. On the other hand, in its demands for church fellowship, it has assumed an extremely literalistic concept of the New Testament. Frequently by its very narrow interpretations it has excluded itself from Christian fellowship and has fallen into separatism.

In 1957 the Cleveland Convention of the Disciples authorized a "10-year program of acquaintance with the United Church of Christ." Disciples delegates participated in the United Church of Christ commissions which drafted the latter body's statement of faith and constitution, and co-operative endeavors in student work, federated churches, ministers' institutes, and similar activities are already in progress.

The Restorationist Movement spread to Canada at a very early date. Since 1922 the *All-Canada Committee of the Churches of Christ (Disciples)* has directed the affairs of the denomination in Canada.

Churches of Christ

HISTORY

A gradual and almost imperceptible separation took place among the Disciples. The conservatives alleged that the progressives among the Disciples had departed from the platform of the original Christians under Campbell, Stone, and Scott. The issues were deeply significant to the "conservatives," but their antidenominational principle prevented them from declaring a formal and actual division. Nevertheless, by the beginning of the twentieth century, a separation between the "conservatives" and the "progressives" among the Disciples had taken place. However, when in 1906 the census of religious bodies for the first time listed the Churches of Christ as distinct and separate from the Disciples, it indicated what was a denominational division on paper only, rather than in fact. Notwithstanding the complete lack of any type of organizational and denominational apparatus, these churches show remarkable strength, especially in Texas, Tennessee, and Arkansas.

The controversies which led to the division between the Disciples and the Churches of Christ were occasioned by such problems as lie in the realm of *adiaphora*. One area of difference was the assumption of pastoral powers by some preachers, the use of the distinctive title "Reverend" instead of "elder," and the government of the local church by the pastor alone rather than by a plurality of elders. The Churches of Christ are very emphatic in claiming that according to the New Testament a local church must be ruled by elders and not by the pastor. The majority forbid even membership in pastoral associations. A second controversy originated over the group's attitude toward open Communion. The conservatives argued that open Communion is sinful, not because the New Testament has forbidden it, but because it has not been commanded. However, no questions so disturbed the Disciples and so directly led to the separation as the introduction of instrumental music into the services and the establishment of missionary societies. Some of the antiorganists went so far as to condemn the pro-organists as insulters of the authority of Christ and as defiant and impious innovators who were destroying the simplicity and purity of the ancient and apostolic order. They held that instrumental music is not, like a tuning fork, a mere aid to singing, but itself an act of divine worship and that this type of worship, since nowhere prescribed, is inherently sinful. Forced to admit that God is pleased when saints and angels use musical instruments in their divine heavenly worship, they nevertheless asserted that God denies to men in the flesh this form of worship, just "as we deny our immature children many pleasures which mature people may enjoy." The establishment of mission societies to which the members are asked to pay annual dues was condemned by the conservatives not only because of its "money basis," but also because they could find no directive in the New Testament for such a procedure.[39]

Strictly speaking, there has not been — in fact, there cannot be — a denominational division into two bodies. The Disciples do not wish to be known as a denomination, since denominational divisions are in their opinion inherently sinful. Still less do the Churches of Christ want to be a denomination. The Churches of Christ are merely a group of independent, autonomous, unattached local congregations, and they seem to represent the most extreme form of congregationalism among all Christian church bodies.[40]

SEPARATE BODIES

The Christian Union sprang up in 1864, when several local unions, or federations, of Christian and Disciples churches in Ohio, Indiana, and Missouri banded together as Churches of Christ in Christian Union. The genetic history and the basic theological tenets of this group of churches are essentially those of the Restoration Movement.[41] In the organizational meeting the following seven points were adopted as Christian Union principles: (1) the oneness of the church of Christ; (2) Christ the only Head; (3) the Bible the only rule of faith and practice; (4) good fruits the only condition of fellowship; (5) Christian union without controversy; (6) each local church governs itself; (7) partisan political preaching discountenanced.[42] The only test of fellowship is Christian character, and nothing else is required

---

[39] The controversies which led to the separation among the Disciples are described in great detail in Garrison and De Groot, ch. xv. Cp. also Leslie C. Thomas of the Churches of Christ, *Census*, 1936, II, 469. The Churches of Christ state that prior to 1849 the writings of Alexander Campbell represented their position on some of these controverted questions. They find it very difficult to explain why Campbell changed his mind in 1849 and what reasons prompted him to support the establishment of the first national convention.

[40] There are said to be five distinct camps within the Churches of Christ. These camps hold divergent views concerning Sunday schools, colleges, the one cup, the proper sequence of the items of worship prescribed in Acts 2:42, and premillennialism. De Groot, *The Grounds for Divisions*, private edition (Univ. of Chicago Libraries, 1939), pp. 8—10.

[41] J. Clevenger, ed., *Life History of J. V. B. Flack* (Excelsior Springs, Mo., 1912).

[42] H. Rathbun and A. C. Thomas, *Christian Union and Bible Theology* (Excelsior Springs, Mo., 1911), p. 146. Cp. also p. 143.

as a condition of fellowship. The right of private interpretation of the Scriptures and the autonomy of every local congregation loom large in this organization.[43]

Churches of Christ in Christian Union (Ohio). This small group separated from the parent body, described in the preceding section, in 1909, primarily because of the doctrine of "entire sanctification." In general the group maintains the basic principles of the original restoration movement. However, it seems to come very close to the Holiness bodies, whose four basic principles — regeneration, entire sanctification as a second divine act of grace distinct from regeneration, divine healing, the premillennial coming of Christ — it espouses.[44]

The Social Brethren. This is a very small body organized in 1867 by a number of persons in Illinois as a result of disagreements as to interpretations of Scripture and points of decorum prevalent in the various denominations to which they belonged. They agreed to form a separate body and to formulate rules of conduct which they believed to be in accordance with God's Word.

BIBLIOGRAPHY

PART VI   SECTION V

Adams, Hampton. *Why I Am a Disciple of Christ.* New York: Thomas Nelson and Sons, c. 1957.

Ainslie, Peter. *The Message of the Disciples to the Union of the Church.* New York: Fleming H. Revell Co., 1913.

Campbell, Alexander. *Debate with N. L. Rice.* Cincinnati: Standard Publ. Co., 1917.

———. *The Christian System in Reference to the Union of Christians and the Restoration of Primitive Christianity.* Cincinnati: Central Book Concern, 1835.

Cole, S. G. "The 'Restoration Movement' in the Disciples' Denomination," *The History of Fundamentalism.* New York: Richard R. Smith, 1931, pp. 132—62.

Garrison, W. E. *An American Religious Movement.* St. Louis: Bethany Press, 1945.

——— and De Groot, Alfred T. *The Disciples* of Christ: A History. St. Louis: Christian Board of Publication, 1948.

Lindley, D. Ray. *Apostle of Freedom.* Saint Louis: Bethany Press, 1957. (A biography of Alexander Campbell)

Lunger, Harold L. *The Political Ethics of Alexander Campbell.* St. Louis: The Bethany Press, 1954.

Osborn, Ronald E. "Disciples of Christ," in Vergilius Ferm, ed. *The American Church of the Protestant Heritage.* New York: Philosophical Library, 1953. Pp. 389 to 412.

Thomas, Cecil K. *Alexander Campbell and His New Version.* St. Louis: The Bethany Press, 1958.

West, Earl. "Churches of Christ," in Vergilius Ferm, ed., op. cit. Pp. 415—31.

Whitley, Oliver Reed. *Trumpet Call of Reformation.* St. Louis: Bethany Press, 1959.

[43] Cp. J. W. Hyder, secretary of the Christian Union General Council, Excelsior Springs, Mo., in *Census,* 1936, II, 370.

[44] F. E. Terry, ibid., p. 472.

SECTION VI

Plymouth Brethren

The Plymouth Brethren

The Plymouth Brethren (also known as Darbyites) is the popular designation for a number of independent movements which originated in England and Ireland during the early decades of the nineteenth century as a protest against the secularization of religion, a result of the intimate relation between church and state. The movement was popularized by John N. Darby (1800–1882), who became the recognized leader of an "assembly of brethren" at Plymouth, England. Hence the name Plymouth Brethren, to distinguish them from other Brethren. By his learning and personal magnetism, coupled with tireless zeal, Darby gained many adherents, e. g., the Biblical scholar Tregelles, George Mueller, the founder of orphanages, William Kelley, H. C. Mackintosh. Darby's early contacts with an extreme form of ecclesiasticism undoubtedly created in him an aversion to all creeds, to denominationalism, and particularly to an ordained ministry, and crystallized his conviction that the pristine purity of the apostolic church can be attained only if the spiritual and heavenly nature of the church is properly emphasized, if the New Testament "gifts and offices" are recognized, and if the premillennial coming of Christ is duly stressed. Darby was the recognized leader of the Brethren movement until 1848. But his egotism and dogmatism, together with the highly developed individualism of the members, unchecked by ecclesiastical

organization or denominational creeds, led to various schisms. The Brethren may be roughly divided into "open" and "exclusive" members. The points of cleavage among the various groups arose, for the most part, from divergent opinions with regard to fellowshiping teachers and members whose doctrine or life was not fully in accord with what the Brethren regarded as Scripture teaching. Since it is fundamental with the Brethren to refuse to adopt "human" or sectarian names and to use only such names as "are common to all Christians," the separate groups, now eight in the United States, can only be designated as Group I, II, etc. The cause of the divisions among them lies in their inability to agree in matters of discipline and do not affect the doctrinal position of the various groups.

The Plymouth Brethren say that they acknowledge no creeds. Nevertheless they all accept historic Calvinism, especially the distinctive Calvinistic doctrine of final perseverance.[1]

The distinctive feature in the theology of the Plymouth Brethren is their doctrine of the church. Carried away by their anticreedalism and antidenominationalism, they so emphasize the heavenly character and essential unity of the church that they speak of the "invisible membership in the church." At the same time they stress the external and visible unity of the church and say that the unity between Christ and the believers was intended to be visible. The

---

[1] Instead of creeds the Brethren have published a tract: *What Do You Believe?* Cp. also *Census,* II, 292.

communion of saints is described as "a united company, i. e., there is, and ought to be, one church composed of believers and including all believers . . . for membership in any sect, denomination, or party is a denial of the divine truth of the 'one body.'" According to the Brethren, the union of believers with the glorified Christ is the specific work of the Holy Ghost, which was inaugurated at Pentecost.[2] They hold that the church is the total number of believers. But at the same time they seem to teach that this is an empirical and statistical reality. They ignore the fact that in the outward association hypocrites may always be mingled with the Christians, and therefore they apply all Scriptural characteristics of the true church to the so-called visible church. The central thought seems to be that the unity of the true church must be visible and demonstrable.[3]

The Brethren believe that such a visible unity of the church requires the exercise of a threefold discipline: (1) preventive — to make sure that the candidate for reception really believes on Jesus Christ; (2) corrective — to cleanse the church of incipient evil; and (3) preservative — to put away the false professors and evil men.[4]

Further, they affirm that the Holy Spirit personally and immediately presides in the local assembly and that its decisions are "the righteous judgments of the Holy Ghost." The reception of members into the body of Christ and the excommunication of evil men are said to take place under the direct "presidency" of the Holy Spirit. Obviously this theory has caused the Brethren much difficulty, since they must grant the possibility that an assembly may not have been under the guidance of the Holy Spirit. One answer is that during the New Testament dispensation "the Holy Ghost is forming the church as a chaste virgin to Christ, whereas the marriage will not take place until Christ will present her to Himself as a glorious church, without spot, at His second coming."[5]

And, third, the inamissibility of grace and impossibility of defection is probably the Brethren's strongest argument for their conception of the church's unity as a visible and external unity. They say that he who under the Spirit's guidance has once been "formed into the body of Christ" can never fall away, as that would be "a break in the chain of the sovereign electing love of God" and "the body of Christ would be imperfect forever." Eternal life is said to be given as a free gift immediately upon the sinner's conversion and never to be lost; but the believer's labor and service may not stand the test of the Judgment (1 Cor. 3:15). A fourfold reward will be given according to the degree of faithfulness, to wit, the crown of incorruption, of righteousness, of life, and of glory. The elect are admonished to strive for the highest of the four rewards.[6]

---

2 Pickering, p. 109 f. Cp. Ridout, *passim*

3 Pickering, p. 116, fn.

4 Ridout, pp. 80—89.

5 Ibid., pp. 98 ff., 12 f. The first split among the Brethren came when other assemblies put the Plymouth assembly under the ban because one man there was suspected of heresy. The Bristol assembly objected to this procedure and received some Plymouth members. This started a chain reaction, other assemblies condemned Bristol, and ultimately some assemblies put into the ban all assemblies which did not condemn both Plymouth and Bristol. (Clark, *Small Sects*, p. 182.)

6 Pickering, p. 95; see also pp. 83, 85. *Straight Paths,* 9 f.

In their effort to restore the primitive Christian church as a fellowship of elect under the direct guidance of the Holy Spirit, they have repudiated not only any denominational organization but also every form of the ministry. They assert that since the Spirit is present in the church, i. e., in the local congregation, any established and fixed ministerial order would be "a usurpation of the prerogatives of the Holy Ghost." They teach that "when a company is gathered for worship, all should be left to the Spirit to use whom He may choose in prayer, praise, or exhortation." They believe that the Head will supply His body with the necessary gifts without the intervention of seminaries, bishops, or congregations and that the Holy Ghost will introduce the New Testament gifts, to wit, evangelists, pastors, and teachers to the church according to necessity.[7] The rejection of any fixed ministerial order is supported by their doctrine of verbal inspiration, according to which they hold that conversion is exclusively the work of the Holy Spirit's Word.[8] A high form of spiritualism or "enthusiasm" characterizes the Brethren, as is manifest in their refusal to adopt any ritual or form of worship. They "find the great occasion for worship in the breaking of bread on every Sabbath as a memorial of the Savior's dying love." The meetings for the breaking of bread are held in private homes (Acts 2:46), since "the very thought of an earthly sanctuary is foreign to the genius of Christianity."[9] They accept only "believers' baptism," or adult baptism by immersion, because they hold "that Baptism is the symbol of the identification of the believer with Christ in His burial and resurrection."[10] The emphasis on the spiritual or heavenly character of Christ's church is no doubt reflected in their extreme premillennialism. They contend that at His first coming Christ will translate the living and resurrected saints out of this world, which He will purge by a judgment preparatory to the millennium, the period when Israel and the nations will rule the world. The church, however, will always be in heaven, for the purpose of Christ is to present the church as a glorious church.[11]

Among the Brethren, as among all other anticreedal groups, there are two apparently contradictory trends. On the one hand the Brethren have entertained a great divergence of teachings on fundamental Christian doctrines, especially concerning the person and work of Christ. On the other hand they have been plagued by schisms over purely administrative problems so minute that it is difficult to define the difference. And there seems to be no end of divisions.[12]

[7] Pickering, p. 107. Ridout, pp. 7, 55—69.

[8] Pickering, p. 16.

[9] Ridout, p. 111.

[10] Pickering, p. 122.

[11] Ibid., pp. 180, 197.

[12] Clark, *Small Sects*, p. 183 f. — The points which separate the eight bodies are given in *Census*, II, 298 ff. Cp. Mead, p. 45. Like others, the author found it difficult to obtain information from members on the ground that the respective person would speak only for himself.

BIBLIOGRAPHY

PART VI   SECTION VI

Bass, Clarence B. *Backgrounds to Dispensationalism: Its Historical Genesis and Ecclesiastical Implications.* Grand Rapids, Mich.: Wm. B. Eerdmans Publishing Co., c. 1960. Contains a careful critical evaluation of the theology of John Nelson Darby.

Carroll, H. K. *The Religious Forces of the United States.* "American Church History Series," Vol. I. New York: The Christian Literature Co., 1893.

Pickering, H. *The Believer's Blue Book.* London: Pickering and Inglis, n. d.

Ridout, S. *The Church and Its Order According to Scripture.* New York: Loizeaux Bros., n. d.

Straight Paths. St. Louis: Faithful Words Publ. Co., n. d.

Tracts. New York: Bible Truth Depot.

SECTION VII

General Eldership of the Churches of God in North America

In many respects this group of Churches of God resembles the Restoration Movement, especially in rejecting formal creeds and insisting on calling "Bible things" by "Bible names" only. The founder of this group of Churches of God is John Winebrenner (1797 to 1860), a minister in the German Reformed Church in Harrisburg, Pa. He was censured by his church when he resorted to the highly emotional forms of revivalism and charged his own church with perfunctory observance of its religious rites and ceremonies. In 1825 Winebrenner withdrew from the Reformed church and with six like-minded men organized in 1830 the General Eldership of the Church of God. The term "general eldership" is said to

be the Bible name for the presbytery. In 1896 the wording "Church of God" was changed to "Churches of God"; and these churches are now usually known by this name. However, to distinguish them from other Churches of God, we designate them either "General Eldership of Churches of God" or "Churches of God (General Eldership)."[1]

In theology this group resembles other groups of restoration churches in maintaining that the only cure for anti-Scriptural sectarianism is the restoration of the pristine purity of the apostolic church. These churches hold that it is inherently sinful to use any non-Biblical names in designating a church, any denominational creeds as tests of fellowship, and any man-made forms as aids

---

[1] S. G. Yahn, *History of the Church of God* (Harrisburg, Pa.: Central Publ. House, 1926), p. 68. There are several groups known as "Church of God." The body with headquarters at Anderson, Ind., is a Holiness body; others are typical Pentecostalists. Clark (*Small Sects*, p. 81 f.) lists the Winebrennerian group with the perfectionist bodies.

to worship or church government. They will therefore never call the local church by any other name than the allegedly Biblical name "The Church of God at —" Being anticreedal, they grant to every individual the right of private interpretation. Nevertheless they embodied the "leading matters of faith, experience, and practice" in the *Twenty-Seven Points of 1849* and in the *Doctrinal Statement of 1925*.[2] These documents prove that their theology is not the traditional German Reformed, but the typically Arminian theology, with its emphasis on man's moral freedom and on the necessity of good works and a virtuous life for salvation. They believe that the "church of God" at a specific locality is a visible communion of believers from which all sinners are excluded. With a view to restoring the cultus and polity of the apostolic church, they insist on observing the three ordinances instituted by

Christ — foot washing, Baptism, and the Lord's Supper. In these three rites Christians are said to commemorate the three fundamental facts in Christ's mission: His humiliation by the rite of foot washing, His death by the Lord's Supper, His burial and resurrection by baptismal immersion. Their literalistic interpretation of the New Testament impels them to receive the Lord's Supper in a sitting posture and only at night. The church government is presbyterian, similar to that in vogue in the Reformed church. Each local Church of God elects an elder and a deacon, who, together with the pastor, constitute the local church council. "The eldership," said to be divinely instituted, is composed of one teaching and one ruling elder from each local church in a given area. It is similar to the presbytery in the Reformed churches. The various "elderships" constitute the "General Eldership."[3]

SECTION VIII

National David Spiritual Temple of Christ Church Union (Incorporated) of the U. S. A.

This body was founded by David William Short in 1921, partly in protest against every form of denominationalism, partly on the premise that all the New Testament charismatic gifts are the permanent possession of the true church, and chiefly on the assumption that the church is guided directly by the Holy Spirit.

---

[2] Yahn, ch. xii.

[3] J. O. Weigle, secretary of this body, in *Census Report*, II, 484 f.

PART SEVEN

The Enthusiastic or Inner Light Bodies

SECTION I

The Mennonites

In this section all those churches are to be discussed which have emphasized the Inner Light, or the theory of the immediacy of the Holy Spirit's operation. This classification includes the Mennonites, the Quakers, and several small groups of Inspirationists. In the opinion of some, the Mennonites and the Brethren properly belong to the Baptist family. They do in Continental Europe, but not in the United States.[1]

EARLY HISTORY

The Mennonites usually trace the origin of their church body to the establishment of an Anabaptist congregation at Zurich in 1525.[2] However, the later Mennonites did not espouse the weird theological aberrations and radical social ideas advocated by individual Anabaptists. Denk was a pantheist; Sattler,

primarily a moralist; Hutter stressed chiliasm; Hubmaier was an iconoclastic, legalistic Biblicist; Muenzer advocated the utmost asceticism; some leaders denied the Trinity and the deity of Christ; others taught the restoration of all things. Still others demanded complete separation of the church from the world and withdrew from participation in the social, economic, and political affairs of life, believing themselves to be the "community of saints" to usher in the millennium. As a utopian and chiliastic scheme the Anabaptist movement collapsed in the cataclysmic disorders under Jan van Leyden and the catastrophe at Muenster in 1535. Nevertheless the basic premise of the early Anabaptists, a pietistic mysticism or a mystic asceticism, was perpetuated both in Switzerland by the

NOTE: For key to abbreviations see Appendix C; for Bibliography, the end of the section.

[1] See Neve, *Ch. and Sects*, ch. x.

[2] See Fritz Blanke, *Brothers in Christ: The History of the Oldest Anabaptist Congregation, Zollikon, near Zurich, Switzerland*, trans. Joseph Nordenhaug (Scottdale: Herald Press, c. 1961). The early Anabaptist movement has undergone a number of reappraisals in recent years. See Guy F. Hershberger, ed., *The Recovery of the Anabaptist Vision: A Sixtieth-Anniversary Tribute to Harold S. Bender* (Scottdale: Herald Press, 1957); Hans Hillerbrand, "Anabaptism and the Reformation: Another Look," *Church History*, XXIX (1960), 404—423; George Huntston Williams, "Studies in the Radical Reformation (1517—1618): A Bibliographical Survey of Research since 1939," ibid., XXVII (1958), 46—69, 124—160; Lowell H. Zuck, "Anabaptism: Abortive Counter-Revolt within the Reformation," ibid., XXVI (1957), 211—226. For representative selections from the works of sixteenth-century Anabaptist and Mennonite leaders, see Part One of George Huntston Williams and Angel M. Mergal, ed., *Spiritual and Anabaptist Writers* (Philadelphia: The Westminster Press, 1957).

Swiss Brethren and in Holland by the Mennonites.

Menno Simons (1492–1559), a Roman priest from 1516 until 1536, embraced the Anabaptist doctrine in 1536, affiliated himself with the more conservative members of the Anabaptists, was rebaptized by Obbe Philips, and spent the remainder of his life gathering the remnants of the Muenster catastrophe and organizing the scattered and leaderless Anabaptists into orderly congregations.[3] Menno Simons systematized the doctrinal tendencies of the earlier Anabaptists and developed a strict and definite church discipline. He pursued his aims with such firmness and zeal that the Anabaptists soon became known by his name. The Swiss Anabaptists, known as *Täufer*, and the Dutch Mennonites were exposed to bitter persecution because of their doctrine of nonresistance. These persecutions, however, rather aided their cause by uniting them internally and compelling them to seek refuge in Austria, southern Russia, Germany, and finally in America. The first colony of Mennonites in America was organized in Germantown, under the guidance and with the aid of William Penn, in 1683. In the following decades many Swiss Mennonites emigrated from southern Germany to America, and in the seventies of the nineteenth century large groups of German and Swiss Mennonites came from southern Russia to the United States and Canada.[4] In spite of the many migrations the majority of the Mennonites have retained their ancestral customs and language.

Following the bitter persecutions of the early years they tended to become lax in their religious life and discipline. Jacob Ammon, or Amen, whence the adjective "Amish," became the recognized leader of the faction which insisted on a literalistic interpretation of 1 Cor. 5: 9-11. By 1698 a definite break occurred between the so-called Amish people and the Mennonites.[5] In the two succeeding centuries both groups experienced numerous schisms concerning the question of the ban, but the two main bodies reunited at the close of the nineteenth century. The American Mennonites may be grouped as follows: (1) the Old Order Amish, representing the most conservative; (2) the General Conference of the Mennonites of North America, the most liberal; and (3) the Mennonite Church (the fusion of the original Mennonites and the main body of the Amish movement), forming the central party.[6] The differences between the sixteen divisions concern practice rather than doctrine. Some of the points of difference are too small to be grasped by anyone not in direct contact with the group.

THE DOCTRINAL POSITION

Though the Mennonites entertain widely divergent doctrinal views, they are all agreed on certain basic theological principles, summarized in the eighteen articles of the 1632 Dordrecht (Dort) Confession of Faith.[7]

---

[3] Horsch, I, pp. 185—209. See also Hans J. Hillerbrand, "Menno Simons: Moulder of a Tradition," *The Christian Century*, LXXVIII (1961), 107—109; Ralph L. Moellering, "Attitudes Toward the Use of Force and Violence in Thomas Muentzer, Menno Simons, and Martin Luther: A Comparative Study with Reference to Prevalent Contemporary Positions," *C. T. M.*, XXXI (1960), 405—427.

[4] Sweet, *Rel. in Col. Am.*, p. 213 ff. See also E. K. Francis, *In Search of Utopia: The Mennonites in Manitoba* (Glencoe: The Free Press, 1955).

[5] C. Henry Smith, *The Mennonites* (Berne, Ind.: Mennonite Book Concern, 1920), p. 237 f.

[6] See chart in *Yearbook of American Churches*, 1933, p. 175.

[7] Horsch, p. 246 f. For synopsis see *Census*, II, 1003.

The Formal Principle. According to Mennonite theology, the source of Christian knowledge is the Bible, but at the same time the true understanding of saving truth is said to come from a mystical experience of Christ. This is "enthusiasm" or, better still, mysticism.[8] The *Brevis Confessio* of 1580 declares:

> Christ must be known and believed according to the spirit in His exaltation . . . so that the form and image of Christ is developed in us, that He manifests Himself to us, dwells in us, teaches us, completes the miracles in us according to the spirit which He performed while in the flesh, heals us of the sickness of our spirit, blindness, impurity, sin, and death, nourishes us with heavenly food, and makes us partakers of His divine nature, so that by His power the old man in us is crucified and we arise to a new life, experiencing the power of His resurrection.[9]

The Mennonites lay great emphasis on the immediate operation of the Holy Spirit, who is said to "guide the saints into all truth."[10] The Holy Spirit is viewed as "the inner word" enabling the Christians to understand the Scriptures. Mennonites insist that without this inner word, or inner light, Holy Scripture is a dead letter and a dark lantern.[11]

The Material Principle. The central doctrine can probably most appropriately be called "mystical pietism." The pronounced mystical spiritualism, which seems to dominate the entire doctrinal system, manifests itself most patently in the great Mennonite emphasis upon the outward purity of the church. Mennonites frequently claim affinity to the Novatians, Paulicians, Albigenses, Waldenses, and similar movements, because these stressed abstinence from the world and advocated a life of self-abnegation. The Mennonites believe that the church must be a visible organization of regenerated persons and that it must be kept holy by the strict exercise of the ban.

Mystical pietism invariably becomes the mother of a strange paradox: complete tolerance of conflicting and even mutually exclusive doctrinal views and violent dissensions in matters of cultus. This paradox we find also among the Mennonites. The Mennonite camp offers shelter to "enthusiasts" of the Quaker type; to Socinians, who deny the doctrine of the Trinity and teach that personal piety is the essence of Christianity; to Pelagians and Arminians, to spiritualists and mystics; and to Quietists, who saw in faith an intense consciousness of God without a definite knowledge concerning God. And on the other hand they rent their body asunder over the language question and split a congregation over the question whether the second band of suspenders constitutes a forbidden luxury.

MENNONITE THEOLOGY AND PRACTICE

The core idea of the Mennonites is personal holiness, to be achieved by a mystical pietism and to manifest itself

---

[8] Sometimes a distinction is made between "enthusiasm" and mysticism as sources of religion. "Enthusiasm" is said to denote a coming down of the deity and speaking directly to man; "mysticism" the alleged ecstatic condition in which man ascends to and enters into union with the deity. Both forms of spiritualism were present among the Anabaptists. Cp. Tschakert, p. 132 ff. (see P. III, fn. 4).

[9] Herman Schyn, *Historia Mennonitarum,* p. 193 ff., quoted by Tschakert, loc. cit., (see fn. 8).

[10] Funk, p. 151 ff.

[11] Horsch, *Geschichte der Mennonitengemeinden,* quoted in Guenther, p. 108.

in the outward purity of the church. This basic principle seems more or less reflected in the eighteen articles of the Dordrecht Confession. Article V speaks of the New Testament or the Gospel only as the Law of Christ, "in which the whole counsel and will of God are comprehended." [12] An extreme form of legalism characterizes the entire Mennonite theology. Whenever the "Gospel" is equated with the "new Law," the doctrines of Christ's theanthropic person and vicarious work become of secondary significance. This fact may account for the vagueness with which many early Mennonites treated the doctrine of the Trinity and Christ's eternal Sonship. [13]

A theological system which consistently teaches a way of salvation by personal piety cannot take original sin and guilt seriously. The early Mennonites were in the tradition of Semi-Pelagianism. Concerning the doctrine of sin the Waterland Confession denies that Adam's fall brought guilt or punishment upon his descendants. The Confession of Dordrecht and later doctrinal statements avoid this matter entirely. True, *A Statement of Christian Doctrine*, Art. VI, declares that "man in his fallen estate is estranged from God . . . is utterly unable of himself to return to righteousness, even his mind and conscience being defiled." But it is difficult to determine how far this statement is accepted in the light of the older confessions. [14]

In Mennonite theology the mystical union of the believer with Christ is considered the cause and not the effect of justification. Regeneration is viewed as a moral transformation.

> As man is inclined to all unrighteousness, therefore the first doctrine of the New Testament is repentance and amendment of life. . . . Without faith, the new birth, and a change or renewal of life, neither Baptism, Eucharist, community, nor any other external ceremonies can help us to please God or receive any consolation or promise of salvation from Him. [15]

Mennonites say that we are saved by faith, but faith is continually identified with obedience. "All men without distinction, if as obedient children they would through faith fulfill, follow, and live according to [God's counsel], He has declared His true and rightful heirs." Obedience to Christ's Law (the Gospel), to the will of God, to my Lord — these are ever-recurring phrases. The work of Christ is said to consist primarily in giving us a new law. The Dort Confession states expressly that Christ finished His work before His suffering and death and that by His death He confirmed and sealed the new testament which He had established and left it to His followers as an everlasting testament. [16] Faith is therefore primarily obedience and not the "hand" which appropriates Christ's complete redemptive activity. Justification is not viewed as a forensic act, but is continually identi-

---

[12] As to New Testament finality and Christ as the New Testament Lawgiver see Wenger, *Glimpses*, p. 162 ff.

[13] The Mennonites held that Christ brought His flesh and blood from heaven. Cp. F. C., Th. D., XII, 25. The Conf. of Dort avoids the phrase "conceived by the Holy Ghost." The Doctrinal Statement, adopted by the Mennonites in 1921, however, employs the Chalcedonian terminology.

[14] For the Mennonite doctrine of sin see Menno Simons, II, 312 ff.

[15] *Dort Conf.*, Art. VI; reproduced in Daniel K. Cassel, *Geschichte der Mennoniten* (Phila.: J. Kohler, 1890), p. 18 f.

[16] Ibid. In Mennonite theology Law and Gospel are identified as essentially "one and the same truth." There is but "one God; so there is but one truth, for God Himself is the truth." Philip, *Enchiridion*, p. 160 f.

fied with sanctification. A summary of Mennonite theology reads:

> The law of Christ is contained in the Gospel, by obedience to which alone humanity is saved. Repentance and conversion, or complete change of life, without which no outward obedience to Gospel requirements will avail to please God, is necessary to salvation. All who have repented of their sins and believed on Christ as the Savior, and in heart and life accept His commandments, are born again. As such they obey the command to be baptized with water as a public testimony of their faith, are members of the church of Jesus Christ, and are incorporated into the communion of saints on earth.[17]

And the catechism states that the ground of justification in Mennonite theology is not the "Christ for us," but the "Christ in us," for man is justified through the Lord Jesus alone, of whose righteousness we must become partakers through faith which works by love.

In accord with its strong mystical trends Mennonite theology views the sacraments merely as symbols. Baptism, usually performed by affusion, is said to be a "sign of a spiritual birth, an incorporation into the [visible] church." Mennonites consider Baptism only "an evidence that we have established a covenant with Christ," an action which requires conscious reflection. Therefore the Mennonites reject infant baptism and demand the rebaptism of adults who have received infant baptism. The Lord's Supper is said to "represent to us how Christ's holy body was sacrificed on the cross" and "to remind us of the use of Christ's death and to exhort us to love one another." Foot washing is observed as a sign of true humiliation and of the purification of the soul.[18]

The central core of Mennonite theology appears most clearly in the description of the nature and function of the church. While the doctrinal statements apparently acknowledge a distinction between the invisible and the visible church, the Dordrecht Confession ascribes all the Scriptural characteristics of the invisible church to the visible church and declares: "We confess a visible church of God, consisting of those . . . who are united with God in heaven and incorporated into the communion of saints on earth." (Art. VIII.) Mennonites maintain that a local congregation is a true church only if it is totally free from open sinners.[19] The marks of the church are said to be "her evangelical faith, doctrine, love, godly conversation, pure walk and practice, observance of the true ordinances of Christ." In order to make sure that outward piety will be properly observed, the Dort Confession teaches "that, as the church cannot exist and prosper nor continue in its structure without offices and regulations, therefore the Lord Jesus has Himself appointed His offices and regulations" (Art. IX). These offices are said to be three: those of bishop, minister, and almoner. Mennonites strictly observe certain rules of excommunication, "so that what is pure may be separated from that which is impure." Among the strict Mennonites a banned person must be "shunned and avoided by all the members of the church, whether it be in eating or drinking or other such social matters" (Dordrecht Confession, Art. XVII). Believing themselves to be "the communion of saints," the Mennonites are very separatistic, "withdraw themselves from the sinful world," forbid marriage with an unbeliever, even with a non-Mennonite, in some instances excommunicating a member who does not marry "amongst the chosen generation."

---

[17] *Census,* II, 1003.

[18] Cp. *Shorter C.,* 17:21, Dort Conf., X, XI.

[19] Wenger, *Glimpses,* p. 170 f.

The Mennonites are probably best known today because of their traditional stand on nonresistance. The Mennonites hold that the Christian Gospel cannot be a part of the administrative or civil powers. When demanding oaths, inflicting capital punishment, or waging wars, the civil powers are said to be acting under the Old Testament dispensation or under human laws. But since these matters are contrary to Christ's teachings, the Mennonites will render obedience to the "government of the world" only in those things "which do not militate against the Law, will, and commandments of God." [20]

In their Biblicism and legalism the Mennonites classify as sinful many practices which other devout Christians consider adiaphora. They forbid all forms of luxury, the specified items varying as the degree of legalism varies. Some still forbid the use of automobiles, telephones, modern furniture, higher education, use of buttons, wearing of any but somber clothes. Membership in secret societies, any form of litigation, the use of force, are forbidden. Women are obliged to wear "the devotional covering" in public worship. The Mennonites have established an enviable record through their honesty, integrity, industry, and other civic virtues.

THE SEVERAL BODIES

The American Mennonites may be grouped into three main bodies: (1) the Old Order Amish, which under the leadership of Jacob Ammon used 1 Cor. 5:9-11 as the basis for their extreme separatism and legalism; (2) the General Conference of the Mennonites of North America, considered the most progressive; (3) the Mennonite Church, a fusion of original Mennonites and the main body of the Amish movement, usually considered the central party.

The Mennonite Church goes back to the first Mennonite immigrants, who came to Pennsylvania in 1683. It has also absorbed three conferences of the former Amish Mennonite Church. It is most closely identified with the history given in the preceding paragraphs. This is the largest body.

The General Conference Mennonite Church was organized in 1860 in the hope of uniting at least the majority of the Mennonites. They differ from other bodies in not demanding a "devotional covering" for the women, nor do they insist on foot washing. They urge an educated ministry and mission work. In 1945 the former Central Conference united with this body.

The Hutterian Brethren, followers of Jacob Huter, constitute a very small communistic group.[21] They use a peculiar dialect of German in their services and homes.

The Conservative Mennonite Conference is more liberal in its interpretation of the rules concerning worship and attire than other Amish groups. Until 1954

---

[20] *Dort, Confession* of 1632, XIII. For Mennonite doctrines of nonresistance and nonconformity see Horsch, "The Mennonite Church and Non-Resistance," *Mennonite Q. Review,* I (1927, July and Oct.), esp. p. 15 ff.

[21] Remotely related to the Hutterian Brethren is a group of three communities in the East — Woodcrest, N. Y., Oak Lake, Pa., and Evergreen, Conn. — operated by the *Society of Brothers,* a communal movement founded in 1920 by Eberhard Arnold of Königsberg, Prussia, which currently has branches in Germany, England, Paraguay, Uruguay, and, since 1954, in the United States. See Hans Zumpe, "Die Bruderhof-Gemeinschaft," in Lydia Präger, ed., *Frei für Gott und die Menschen: Evangelische Bruder- und Schwesternschaften der Gegenwart in Selbstdarstellungen* (Stuttgart: Quell-Verlag, c. 1959), pp. 68—89.

this body was known as the Conservative Amish Mennonite Church.

The Old Order Amish Mennonite Church broke with the less separatistic party in the Amish movement. It strictly adheres to the old customs concerning the ban, attire, and language. There have been divisions in this body caused by differences concerning the ban. It opposes any organized church activity, also centralized schools.

The Church of God in Christ (Mennonite) was organized by John Holdemann in 1859, who believed himself called by God to re-establish and maintain the strict observance of the ban. They shun the banned, refuse to fellowship other denominations, condemn the taking of interest on loans. Through the influence of Russian Mennonites these practices have been modified.

The Old Order Mennonite Church (Wisler) is a fusion of a number of groups under the leadership of Jacob Wisler, who condemned certain "innovations," e. g., Sunday school, evening meetings, the use of English.

The Reformed Mennonite Church was organized by John Herr in 1812, in protest against the laxity among some Mennonites.

The Evangelical Mennonite Church, formerly the *Defenseless Mennonites,* seceded from the Old Order Amish on the ground that the need of a definite experience of conversion was not sufficiently emphasized.

The Evangelical Mennonite Brethren, formerly the *Conference of Defenseless Mennonites,* are of Russian origin.

The United Missionary Church, formerly the *Mennonite Brethren in Christ,* stresses entire sanctification, divine healing, and millennialism. In 1955 it adopted a more strongly centralized form of government.

The Beachy Amish Mennonite Churches, which withdrew from the Old Order Amish Mennonite Church in the years following 1923, hold services in meeting-houses and permit their members to use modern conveniences.

The Mennonite Brethren Church of North America (Schellenberger Brüdergemeinde) is also of Russian origin.

The Krimmer Mennonite Brethren Conference traces its origin to separations which took place in the Crimea as a protest against supposed laxity. They agree doctrinally with the other Mennonites except that they insist on baptism by immersion, one group among them baptizing backward, another forward.

There are also a number of churches which have withdrawn from the Conservative Mennonite Conference and the Old Order Amish Mennonite Church without affiliating with another conference.

BIBLIOGRAPHY

PART VII

SECTION I

Bender, Harold S., and C. Henry Smith, ed. *The Mennonite Encyclopedia.* Scottdale: Mennonite Publishing House, c. 1955 to 1959. 4 vols.

Funk, John F. *The Mennonite Church and*

Her Accusers. Elkhart, Ind.: Mennonite Publ. Co., 1878.

Herschberger, Guy F. *War, Peace, and Nonresistance.* Scottdale, Pa.: Herald Press, 1944.

———. *The Mennonite Church in the Second World War.* Scottdale, Pa.: Herald Press, 1951. The author discusses the work of the "Old" Mennonite Church only.

Horsch, John. "Mennonites in Europe." *Mennonite History.* Vol. I. Scottdale, Pa.: Mennonite Publ. House, 1950.

Kaufman, Gordon D. *The Context of Decision: A Theological Analysis.* New York: Abingdon Press, c. 1961.

Littell, Franklin Hamlin. *The Anabaptist View of the Church: A Study in the Origins of Sectarian Protestantism.* Boston: The Beacon Press, 1958.

Mennonite Confession of Faith and Shorter Catechism. Scottdale, Pa.: Herald Press, 1927.

Philip, Dietrich. *Enchiridion, or Handbook, of the Christian Doctrine and Religion.* Elkhart, Ind.: Mennonite Publ. Co., 1910.

Simons, Menno. *Complete Works.* 2 Vols. Elkhart, Ind.: Mennonite Book Concern, 1941. The most recent edition is: *The Complete Writings of Menno Simons (c. 1496 to 1561),* trans. Leonard Verduin, ed. John Christian Wenger (Scottdale: Herald Press, 1956).

Wenger, John C. *Glimpses of Mennonite History and Doctrine.* Scottdale, Pa.: Herald Press, 1947.

———. *Doctrines of the Mennonites.* Scottdale, Pa.: Herald Press, 1950.

———. "The Mennonites," in Vergilius Ferm, ed. *The American Church of the Protestant Heritage.* New York: Philosophical Library, 1953. Pp. 51—66.

———. *Introduction to Theology.* Scottdale: Herald Press, 1954.

SECTION II

The Brethren Churches

The Church of the Brethren

There are several distinct groups of Brethren, all of which arose, at least in part, as a result of anticreedal inclinations. This was true of the Plymouth Brethren, founded by the Calvinist John Darby in England; and of the United Brethren, established by the Arminian Philip Otterbein in Pennsylvania. Anticreedalism, to a large extent, likewise gave rise to the Brethren groups known as Dunkers, or German Baptists, frequently associated with the Baptists; and to the River Brethren, usually associated with the Mennonites. The two last-named groups are considered by many to be a part of the large Baptist family. However, "enthusiasm" and pietism are more specifically characteristic of the Brethren than the theological emphases of the Calvinist Baptists.

HISTORY

In 1708 Alexander Mack, a student of Francke at Halle, founded an organization at Schwarzenau in Western Germany to put into practice some of the principles which he and others had drawn from German Pietism. At the organizational meeting the eight charter members were baptized by trine immersion and hence came to be known as *Täufer, Tunkers, Dunkers, Dompelaars,* German Baptists. One of the basic principles of this small group was complete freedom in all religious matters. They were opposed to any compulsory oath of allegiance and to all participation in war. They protested against every form of mingling of church and state and every type of religious oppression. These views found many adherents throughout the Rhine Valley. Naturally, these views were considered dangerous to society, and the new group was exposed to such severe persecution that in 1719 they sought an asylum in Germantown, Pa., and by 1729 virtually all the Brethren had emigrated from Germany. In their new home they retained their European dialect and customs, and their American neighbors frequently thought them to be backward, separatistic, and even uncultured. The last charge is not wholly in accord with the facts. Christian Saur, one of their members, for instance, operated a highly successful publishing business.[1] Like the Quakers, and to a small extent the Mennonites, the Brethren have been in the limelight more than their numerical strength would warrant, because they have uncompromisingly maintained their historic position of nonresistance.[2]

DOCTRINAL POSITION

The central message of the Brethren has been formulated as follows:

> Jesus came into the world to reveal the Father and to demonstrate a manner of Christlike living; He came to save mankind and to give men an abundant life beginning here and lasting forever. [Brethren] want to live as completely as possible the life which Christ demonstrated and taught.[3]

Christ's work is described very largely as the giving of the new Law, so that the Brethren view as the heart of Christianity the meticulous observance of the new Law as contained in the New Testament. In their interpretation of the New Testament the Brethren tend in the direction of an extreme literalism. The Brethren usually present the Christian life as revealed in the New Testament under five ideals: (1) They stress the "good life" and insist that Christian faith can be set forth only in Christian living. Since the New Testament constitutes the new Law, it is presumptuous for Christians to have any creedal statements. (2) They extol the brotherhood. Christ has laid down the principle for this brotherhood in the New Testament, especially in the Sermon on the Mount and in Matthew 18. In brief, the brotherhood is said to center in the reconciliation of man to man to lead to the elimination of all social distinctions, and to sustain man's reconciliation with God. (3) They seek peace, and peace means more than mere nonresistance in time of war. The Brethren profess to be opposed to every form of religious oppression. Viewed from their angle, pedobaptism is a form of oppression, since the administration of the rite of baptism without the infant's knowledge and consent is an act of religious coercion. They recognize only "believers' baptism." The Brethren aver that the great ideal of peace makes it impossible for them to engage in any litigation before "pagan courts." Brethren, however, are permitted to participate in such government activities as are not inherently sinful. (4) The Brethren deem total abstinence from liquor and tobacco to be an essential of the Christian life and a prerequisite for the Holy Spirit's indwelling in the believer. (5) They strive for the simple life, that is, the greatest simplicity in their entire mode of living and a conscientious avoidance of all luxury.

These basic principles are reflected in the cultus of the Brethren. They hold

---

[1] For a history of this body see Brumbaugh. Cp. also Carroll, loc. cit. (P. VI, Sec. VI, Bibliog.). Sweet, *Story of Rel. in Am.*, p. 153 f.; *Rel. in Col. Am.*, p. 217 ff.

[2] Herschberger, *War*, loc. cit. (Bibliog., Sec. I, above). The Brethren practically stand for the same things as do the Mennonites.

[3] A tract: *Church of the Brethren*, p. 12. The Church of the Brethren, 22 S. State Street, Elgin, Ill., supplied a number of helpful tracts.

that Christ instituted four ordinances: Believers' baptism by trine immersion; the complete Lord's Supper, including foot washing and the love feast; the anointing of the sick; and the imposition of hands on Christian workers. These ordinances are said to be "teaching and worship techniques," whereby man can learn more clearly the principles which undergird the kingdom of God. Some groups still observe the ancient customs, such as the "holy kiss" and the devotional head covering for women.

The Several Bodies

The Church of the Brethren (Conservative Dunkers) is the largest and the best-known of the Brethren bodies. Its history and doctrinal position has been outlined above. It has experienced several defections, notably the one under Conrad Beissel. The Brethren Commission developed a relatively large program of physical reconstruction in Europe after World War II. Since 1958 threefold immersion is no longer required as a condition of membership in the Church of the Brethren.[4] The Evangelical United Brethren Church has been carrying on conversations with the Church of the Brethren looking toward closer co-operation between the two denominations.

The Brethren Church (Ashland, Ohio) withdrew from the Church of the Brethren in 1881.

The Brethren Church (Progressive) separated from the main body in 1882 because in their opinion the simplicity of life was overstressed and the conferences had too much authority.

The Old German Baptist Brethren (Old Order Dunkers) strictly adhere to the old customs and are opposed to formal religious education, organized mission work, membership in secret societies, and a salaried ministry.

The Church of God (New Dunkards) is a very small body. It was founded in 1848 on the ground that the only rightful name for the church is the Bible-approved name "Church of God."

River Brethren

The congregations — they preferred the term brotherhoods — of Swiss Mennonites established in 1752 near the Susquehanna River in Lancaster County, Pa., and augmented by some Lutherans and Baptists in 1770, are known as River Brethren, because the strongest among the brotherhoods was known as the "brotherhood down by the river." Some think that the name arose from their practice of baptizing in the river. Their theology and practice follow the Mennonite pattern very closely.

The River Brethren are represented by three small groups. (1) *Brethren in Christ*, who adhere to an austere type of Mennonite theology. (2) *The Old Order*, or *Yorker River Brethren*, organized in 1843 as a protest against other Brethren's moral laxity, manifested in part, by the erection of churches. (3) *The United Zion Church*, which split off under Matthias Brinser in 1855.

---

[4] *The Christian Century*, LXXVIII (1961), 832. The German Seventh-Day Baptists, founded in 1728 by Conrad Beissel, Mack's early associate, and established in 1732 at Ephrata, Pa., as a communistic colony with Sabbatarian, ascetic, and celibate views, united with a similar group of English Baptists.

BIBLIOGRAPHY

PART VII

SECTION II

Bittinger, Desmond W. "The Church of the Brethren," in Vergilius Ferm, ed. *The American Church of the Protestant Heritage.* New York: Philosophical Library, 1953. Pp. 279—92.

Brumbaugh, M. G. *A History of German Baptist Brethren in Europe and America,* 1899.

Durnbaugh, Donald F., ed. *European Origins of the Brethren: A Source Book on the Beginnings of the Church of the Brethren* in the Early Eighteenth Century. Elgin: The Brethren Press, 1958.

Eby, Kermit, *For Brethren Only.* Elgin: The Brethren Press, 1958.

Kent, Homer A., Sr. *250 Years Conquering Frontiers: A History of the Brethren Church.* Winona Lake: Brethren Missionary Herald Co., 1958.

Mallott, F. *Studies in Brethren History.* Elgin: Brethren Publishing House, 1954.

SECTION III

The Quakers

The Quaker concept of the Inner Light presupposes not only that God is immanent in the world and in man and thus knowable directly and immediately, but also that man is inherently capable of the divine nature. The Quakers thus embrace both "enthusiasm" and mysticism.[1] The very heart of their religion is the conviction that man lives in vital contact with God and that the stream of divine light flowing into man should become active in and through him for the good of his fellow men.[2]

History of Quakerism in England (1647—1689)

Quakerism has well been called the most protestant movement in Protestantism. For the Quakers, even more than the Baptists, have consistently applied the principle of the sovereignty and competence of every human soul.

Religious life was at a very low ebb in England during the middle of the seventeenth century. The Established Church seemed to be content with out-

---

[1] In this text the term "enthusiasm" is employed to denote the religious theory that divine revelation comes to man directly; that in one of several ways God conveys to man His will immediately as by inspiration, an inner light, a vision. "Mysticism" is used in the commonly accepted meaning, *viz.,* that after a series of highly ecstatic and deeply depressing experiences, the soul finally wings its way upward to a full union with God. In the former, God, as it were, comes down to man; in the latter, man ascends to God.

[2] Cp. Russell, pp. 48—53.

ward religiosity and dead formalism. The majority of the Puritans sought religion in an intellectual approach to the Five Points of Calvinism, observed a strict and literal interpretation of the Old Testament, and followed a fixed moral code. The reaction against this deplorable condition manifested itself in the rise of such sects as the Anabaptists, the Familists (family of love), the Brethren of the Free Spirit, the Behemists, adherents of the German mystic Jacob Boehme, the Mennonites, the pantheistic Ranters, the Seekers.[3] All these groups were highly emotional and advocated some form of "enthusiasm" and/or mysticism. Some of them had discontinued the liturgy and the use of the sacraments and some lapsed into bizarre and even immoral abuses.

George Fox (1624–1690) was a product of this age of contradictions. He said he had, at the age of 11, a deep religious experience. This experience seems to have made him extremely rigorous in his personal life. At the age of 19 he became deeply depressed, partly because the life of the majority of the Puritan clergy was inconsistent with their profession, partly because of the brutalities of the English Civil War (1642–1649), and, in general, man's inhumanity to man grieved him. This gloom was no doubt aggravated by the pessimism of Calvinistic theology, in which he had been reared. He insisted that in his unsuccessful quest for an answer to his questions he had heard a voice: "There is one, even Jesus Christ, that can speak to thy condition." This experience, sometime in 1647, led him to believe that God is willing and ready to share His truth and love with all men by a direct and immediate indwelling; that all men have inherently the capacity to open their lives fully to God and to live in His power. Fox immediately proclaimed his doctrine of the soul's immediate communion with God and shortly found many adherents among the Seekers, the Familists, and the Anabaptists or General Baptists, and even among the extremely individualistic Ranters, who in turn had much in common with the "Brethren of the Free Spirits," a pantheistic, highly emotional, and even anarchistic sect.

Neither Fox nor his early followers made any attempt to set forth their message in any set of theological propositions. They considered Christianity to be the religious experience of a new life. Nevertheless, they had a definite and quite well-established theological principle — the "Inner Light." Fox was a mystic, and all his adherents were exponents of some form of mysticism.[4] Many mystics find the ultimate religious authority in the individual's own experience. Fox describes this authority in his own case. He says:

> Now the Lord God opened to me by His invisible power that every man was enlightened by the divine light of Christ, and I saw it shine through all; and they that believed in it came out of condemnation to the light of life, and became children of it; but they that hated it, and did not believe in it, were condemned by it, though they made a profession of Christ. . . . I was sent to turn people from darkness to the light, that they might receive Jesus Christ.[5]

---

[3] Thomas Edwards, writing in 1646, listed 199 errorists, heresies, etc. Russell, p. 14.

[4] On mysticism in general, see Rudolf Otto, *Mysticism East and West: A Comparative Analysis of the Nature of Mysticism*, trans. Bertha L. Bracey and Richenda C. Payne (New York: Meridian Books, 1957 [c. 1932]), and Evelyn Underhill, *Mysticism: A Study in the Nature and Development of Man's Spiritual Consciousness*, 12th ed. (New York: Meridian Books, 1955 [c. 1930]).

[5] Quoted by Russell, p. 48. The theory of the Inner Light had three significant theological implications for the early Quakers: (1) God is

The principle of the Inner Light made of the Quakers ardent advocates of moral and social reform. They unflinchingly maintain every man's divine potentialities and, as a concomitant of this tenet, the absolute equality of all men. Their mystical experience seems to have provided the dynamic to oppose every social institution which threatened to negate their basic convictions. The Quakers were among the first to advocate the abolition of slavery, capital punishment, war, and inhumane treatment of the insane. They fought such conditions as seemed to favor pauperism and its many ills.

On the other hand, the principle of the Inner Light prompted them to speak disparagingly of the clergy, the sacraments, the churches ("steeple houses"). Not infrequently they interrupted the clergyman in his sermon. They refused to pay the tithe on the principle that the ministry must be free. Because they believed everyone to be endowed with the same Inner Light, they refused to recognize any social rank. They held that the show of deference by any gesture, such as doffing the hat, or by a formal address, such as the plural form of "you," was a denial of the absolute equality of all men. They opposed the taking of oaths on the ground that it would imply a double standard of truthfulness. Their opposition to war was founded on the principle that under no condition does man have the right to take the life of one endowed by the Inner Light. In their fanatical opposition to the clergy, to all titles, the oath, military service, the early Quakers provoked the combined hostility of the civil and ecclesiastical rulers and of the people in general. No other sect of modern history has been subjected to such severe persecution: 13,258 were imprisoned, fined, or mutilated; 360 perished in prisons, and 219 were banished.[6] The followers of Fox called themselves Children of Light or Friends. But because occasionally they quaked and trembled in their religious services, they were commonly called Quakers.[7]

The early Quakers made no attempt to present their views in systematic form. But later such men as Robert Barclay, William Penn, Isaac Pennington, George Whitehead, formulated them. The copious anti-Quaker literature [8] compelled the Quakers to prepare a correspondingly large amount of apologetic literature. Outstanding among these, and still held in high regard, is Barclay's *Apology for the True Christian Divinity,* 1678.[9] Barclay received his early training from strict Calvinists. Later he studied in Paris under Roman Catholic scholastic tutors. His own theological point of

immanent in man and therefore can be known only by an inward experience; (2) all men, pagan or Christian, are potentially God's children and are equally endowed by nature with the ability to respond to God; (3) the truth is never a fixed datum, but grows with the experience of the Inner Light. These principles are diametrically opposed to historic Calvinism. They are, however, in full accord with Schleiermacherian theology.

6 Schaff, *Creeds,* I, 682. Cp. Russell, p. 106 ff.

7 One theory is that Judge Bennett first used the term Quaker when Fox bade the Court to tremble at God's Word. Russell, p. 31.

8 Smith's *Bibliotheca anti-Quakeriana,* 1725, lists 1,200 titles. See Russell, p. 167.

9 Though Barclay's *Apology* is still highly esteemed by many Quakers, not all modern Quakers adopt his anti-Trinitarianism nor his view that men receive the Inner Light only by an act of God's grace. In the opinion of many modern Quakers this view implies that man is essentially depraved. Cp. Russell, p. 178 ff.

view seems to have been a *via media* between the uncontrolled individualism of the Ranters and the absolute authoritarianism of the Roman Catholic church. In his *Apology* he deals primarily with those points in which he differs fundamentally with Calvin. His method is somewhat scholastic, especially in his use of the Scriptures, reason, and the Fathers. He no doubt appealed to this threefold source to satisfy the Protestants, the Socinians, and the Roman Catholics. His most significant contribution to Quaker thought is undoubtedly the theory that the Inner Light is primarily a corporate experience. As many candles augment the chief light, so he said every individual Inner Light increases the effectiveness and brightness of the cumulative Inner Light.

The Establishment of Quakerism in America

In spite of Colonial laws against the entry of Quakers, and in spite of bitter persecutions, especially in the New England Colonies, from 1660 onward, Quakers came in relatively large numbers to New England, New York, New Jersey, Maryland, and several other States.[10] These widely scattered Quakers were brought into closer relation through the visit of George Fox in 1672 and 1673. Two significant events removed the pressure from the persecuted. The first was the establishment of Pennsylvania under a charter. Penn's so-called "holy experiment" in applied Quakerism made his colony a haven for persecuted Quakers. The second significant event was the

adoption of the Act of Toleration by Parliament in 1689, which granted the Quakers surcease from persecution. But as the period of martyrdom ended, an era of lethargy set in.

During the second period of Quaker history, known as the Age of Quietism, 1691—1827, Quaker thinking passed through radical changes. It moved toward mystical quietism [11] and toward evangelicalism. Various reasons are given for this complete change in theological orientation. Undoubtedly the Wesleyan movement and the Edwards revival played a prominent role, since these movements emphasized the reality of a divinely wrought religious experience. Toward the end of the 18th century many Quakers became interested in the works of medieval and Roman Catholic mystics and contemplatives, and these may have had some influence in the shaping of Quaker quietism.[12] Probably the strongest factor in the change of Quaker thought was the result of the sudden relief from the horrors of persecution, the comparative ease of witnessing, and their more settled way of life. Quaker quietism manifested itself in the first place in the adoption of "The Discipline." The Quakers were no longer crusaders. On the contrary, they were inclined to withdraw from the world and its ways and to place themselves under rules and regulations so strict that they became indeed a "peculiar" people. The "discipline" is designed to govern every possible phase of Quaker life, whether it be that of the individual, or of the family, or of the corporate

10 Cp. Sweet, *Rel. in Col. Am.* The first recorded visit of a Quaker to America was that of Ann Austin and Mary Fisher, who came to Massachusetts from Barbados in 1656, only to be promptly deported.

11 Quietism — at least as it was developed among the Quakers — presumes that man is by nature morally corrupt and incapable of religious good. He can do nothing to achieve his mystical union with God, but must remain absolutely silent and inactive if he is to hear God's voice.

12 For example, the *Imitatio Christi* and Mme. Guyon. Cp. Russell, p. 232 ff.

body.[13] Quaker quietism evinced itself, in the second place, in the Quakers' deep humanitarian and philanthropic interests. On all sides the basic concepts of God's love and man's dignity were challenged. It seems that in the "silent meeting" the quietist became particularly sensitive to his fellow's pains and sufferings as well as to his own personal responsibility to alleviate such sufferings.[14] This realization was the beginning of the flowering of Quaker philanthropy, apparent in many social reforms.[15]

More significant than the Quakers' shift toward quietism was the gradual infiltration of evangelicalism,[16] which manifested itself in the emphasis they placed on such doctrines as the plenary inspiration and absolute authority of the Bible, man's total depravity, the theanthropic person and work of Christ, the need of personal religious experience. The early Quakers had considered the Biblical record of the historical events as having merely symbolic meaning. The evangelicals, however, followed the Protestant tradition and accepted them as soteriological facts. Evangelicalism had gained such a definite foothold that the Philadelphia Yearly Meeting in 1806 changed its "discipline" to the effect that henceforth the denial of the deity of Christ or the authenticity of the Bible was made a cause for excommunication.[17] This change was a radical departure from the position of historic Quakerism and inevitably led to serious controversies.

The matter came to a head when a group of men under the leadership of Elias Hicks (1748–1830) charged that the elders "controlled the meetings," introduced a speculative theology, set up and fixed a standard of dogmatical opinions, a "yoke of enforced orthodoxy," and even introduced the so-called "evangelical" movement, patterned after the Methodist revivalistic methods. The organization of Sunday schools, Bible institutes, and Bible societies was viewed, especially by Hicks, as a deviation from the original Quaker principles. Elias

---

[13] It is difficult to establish how much the Herrnhuters and the Wesleyans influenced the Quakers in adopting the respective "disciplines." But it is a fact that the similarity between Quakerism and Wesleyanism is more than incidental.

[14] *Russell,* p. 251 ff.

[15] In prison reform Elizabeth Fry has made an outstanding contribution. For Quaker influence on educational reform see Paul Monroe, *Founding of the American Public School System, A History of Education in U. S.* (New York: Macmillan, 1940), ch. iv. T. Woody, *Early Quaker Education in Pennsylvania* (New York: Teachers College, Columbia Univ., 1920).

[16] Evangelicalism is frequently associated with the rise of Bible societies and worldwide mission endeavors, which came into being largely as a result of the various revivals during the opening decade of the 19th century.

[17] Russell, p. 296. To the consternation of the "conservative Quakers," the 1879 yearly Ohio meeting adopted the following Declaration of Faith:

We do not believe that there is any principle or quality in the soul of man, innate or otherwise, which, even though rightly used, will ever save a single soul; but that it pleased God by the foolishness of preaching to save them that believed; and the Holy Spirit is sent to convince the ungodly of sin, who, upon repentance towards God, and faith in Jesus Christ, who died for us, are justified by His blood; and we repudiate the so-called doctrine of the inner light, or the gift of a portion of the Holy Spirit in the soul of every man, as dangerous, unsound, and unscriptural.

Hicks himself entertained many liberal views. He denied the Trinity, disavowed the doctrines of the imputation of Adam's sin and guilt, and, of course, of Christ's righteousness.[18] He rejected as unnecessary for experiencing the Inner Light any such external means as the Bible, the ministry, or even the historic Christ. When his "unsoundness" was dealt with as an infraction of discipline, Hicks separated and in 1827 organized the Religious Society of Friends. Not all his followers embraced his anti-Trinitarian views, but all agreed with Hicks that the Inner Light is supreme and that Quakers must have the right to entertain divergent statements concerning theological belief. Someone has said that in this separation the orthodox took the Quaker theology, and the Hicksites the Quaker religion, and each side got what it wanted.[19]

A further division was occasioned by the theology of the English Quaker Joseph John Gurney (1788–1846). He was a convinced evangelical and a dogmatic authoritarian. After Gurney's visit to America with a letter of recommendation from the London Meeting, Quakers began progressively to introduce the pastoral office, to employ a new approach to the Scriptures, to adopt creedal statements, and even to introduce Baptism. The antievangelicals gathered about John Wilbur (1774–1856). They laid great emphasis upon the Inner Light, paid little heed to the "historic Christ," were afraid of any "creaturely or artificial activity," and held their meetings largely in silence. Since then

most American Quakers are divided among three groups: the Conservative Friends (Wilburites); the General Conference (Hicksites), forming the extreme left wing; and the Five Years Meeting of Friends, who occupy middle ground and constitute the largest body.[20]

During the modern period of Quaker history, comprising roughly the last 100 years, the Quakers have experienced several notable shifts of emphasis, both in practice and in theology. The influences of the Finney and Moody revivals were deeply felt among the Quaker evangelicals. In some sections these evangelicals introduced the "mourner's bench," testimonial meetings, and Bible reading in the meetings for worship. In some sections of Quakerism the pastoral system has replaced the spirit-prompted testimony of early Quakerism, and the meeting house has been rebuilt to allow for a pulpit. Today many Quaker meetings differ little from the public worship services of some Protestant churches. The past century has also witnessed several attempts to reunite the various branches of Quakerism. There has also been a remarkable outreach on the part of the Quakers, especially in the fields of education and humanitarianism. Their efforts to alleviate the suffering of the two wars have been outstanding. It also appears that their former aloofness has disappeared to a marked degree. The two World Wars have compelled also Quakers to rethink their historic peace position, since they realize that "total pacifism" is impossible in the modern world. Some Friends are genuinely dis-

---

[18] Cp. Russell, ch. 23. See also Bliss Forbush, *Elias Hicks: Quaker Liberal* (New York: Columbia University Press, 1956).

[19] The "nicknames" are obnoxious to Quakers. They usually designate their group by the name of the street where the annual meeting takes place. Thus the Orthodox group in Philadelphia was long known as "Meeting at Fourth and Arch Streets," and the Hicksite group as "Yearly Meeting at Race Street." The two merged in 1955.

[20] The very "orthodox" Primitive Quakers are almost nonexistent today.

turbed because they doubt that they have the spiritual resources necessary to meet the needs of the contemporary world.[21]

The Quakers represent many types of theology, ranging from fundamentalism to liberalism. A reaction has been at work for some decades against evangelicalism with its emphasis on revivalism, Biblical and theological authoritarianism, as well as against that form of quietism which spurned every form of scholarly investigation, whether in the field of science, philosophy, or theology. The outstanding American Quaker in the liberal movement was Rufus M. Jones (1863–1948), who espoused a theology which may be called "rational mysticism."[22] It is difficult to determine whether Quakerism in America today is predominantly fundamentalistic or modernistic, for the theory of the Inner Light is still the distinguishing feature of Quakerism.

Theology

THE THEOLOGICAL PRINCIPLE

The Quakers have refrained from stating their beliefs in creeds or affirmations. They acknowledge the historic value of the ecumenical creeds but refuse to be bound by any creed. Creeds are said to be below the rich reality of the truth itself.[23] This anticreedal position is fully in accord with the basic Quaker principle "that God communicates with every spirit He has made; that He never leaves Himself without a witness in the heart of man; and that the measure of light thus given increases by obedience."[24] God is said to endow every human spirit with His own Spirit, which no outward authority can replace. If, as is frequently the case, diversity of doctrine does appear, the individual Quaker is counseled to "compare his conception of the truth with the individual and collective experience of his

---

[21] Pendle Hill, a "Quaker center for advanced religious and social studies" at Wallingford, Pa., is publishing pamphlets on current moral, social, and political problems. Cp. Henry J. Cadbury, "What is Disturbing the Quakers?" *Christian Century*, Aug. 16, 1944, p. 945 ff.

[22] The thinking of Rufus Jones was grounded primarily in spiritual monism rather than in supernaturalism. The latter assumes that there is a sharp barrier between the lower realm and the higher realm and that this barrier can be punctuated only from above. Spiritual monism, however, holds that there is only one realm, with God at the center, permeating and pervading everything. Wieman and Meland, *American Philosophies of Religion* (New York: Willett, Clark and Co., 1936), loc. cit.

[23] In the *Reply of Society of Friends to the Statement Issued by the Lausanne Conference*, 1927, the Quakers acknowledged the historic value of creeds, but refused to be bound by any of them. The Hicksites state in their *Book of Discipline* that "each person must seek individual guidance and follow his own conception of God" (p. 8). Edward B. Rawson says: "If I were to describe doctrinal Christianity, I should not tell what Fox or Hicks believed, not what I believed yesterday. I should tell what I believe today and refer to other Friends, who believe something else, for the rest of it." *First-Day Lessons*, Senior Course, No. 2 (1916), a Hicksite publication. Written creeds are said to stultify and arrest thinking processes and are viewed as "shackles of a priest-devised theology." Even the conservative Orthodox Friends, whose strong evangelicalism suggests an interest in creedal formulations, declare: "We adopt no fixed statement of faith because God is continually disclosing fresh revelations of His truth as men are able to receive it." *Faith and Practice*, XV (see Bibliog., below).

[24] Caroline E. Stephen, quoted in *Principles of Quakerism*, p. 34 ff.

fellow men, especially as expressed in the life of Jesus." [25]

The early Quakers hesitated to describe or define this "Inner Light" because they considered it so supreme in guiding the individual that they spurned the use of any empirical means to determine religious matters, including the description of Inner Light. Barclay held "the things which properly relate unto God and Christ cannot be known or discerned by any lower or baser thing than the Spirit of God," hence not by written word or vocal ministry. This "Inner Light" is not man's conscience, which can be defiled, while the "Inner Light" cannot; nor man's reason, which hinders rather than promotes man's salvation; nor any other faculty of man's mind, but a real spiritual substance which "the soul is capable of apprehending, subsisting even in the hearts of wicked men." [26]

THEOLOGICAL EMPHASES

THE TRINITY

It appears that the issues of the Trinitarian and Christological controversies of the early Christian church were revived in new forms by the early Quakers, but throughout their history the Quakers have found it difficult to state their position on these doctrines clearly. Barclay defines the Inner Light as "the light which lighteth every man" (John 1:9; 12:36); as the "seed" (Matt. 13:18, 19; Col. 1:23); as "the spiritual, heavenly principle in which God as Father, Son, and Holy Ghost dwells." He also speaks of it as the "Gospel, the inward manifestation of God in man, the inward power and life, which preacheth glad tidings in the hearts of all men," by which God invites, calls, exhorts, strives with, every man in order to save him. And then again Barclay seems to identify the Inner Light with Christ, when he says: "God operates in the creature by His own eternal power and word, so that no creature has access unto Him but in and by the Son." This seems to be very close to the *logos spermatikos* theory of the early Apologists, who held that Christ had appeared to all men prior to His incarnation and outside the Gospel.[27] But apparently Barclay does not identify the "Inner Light" with the Personal Word of the Gospel According

---

[25] *Book of Discipline*, p. 727. Cp. also Faith and Practice, XII, XIV.

[26] Barclay, Thesis II, proposition 6, p. 39; V, 16, 14. Cp. *Principles of Quakerism*, pp. 30, 33.

[27] The problem of "inner illumination" goes back to Justin Martyr, who, in his *Apologetics*, attempted to find a common meeting ground for the pagan philosopher and the Christian. He held that the Logos in John was present in the Greek philosophers as *logos spermatikos*, the divine reason and the source of moral ethics. Similarly many scholastics held that men like Aristotle received a knowledge of the truth through the Logos. Luther and his followers rejected this view as being diametrically opposed to the *sola Scriptura* principle. The Evangelist in John 1:9 does not mean to imply that the Logos is the "Inner Light" of every man who was born, but rather means to emphasize that the Logos is the only *source*. The very next verse reads: "Yet the world knew Him not" (v. 10). John's conception of human nature leaves little room for any pantheistic mysticism. Cp. John 3:6, 19; 8:23 f., 44 f.; 15:19. Man must confront the Logos as the crucified Christ. Cp. 3:14; 6:53; 14:3 ("prepare"). Therefore, in the view of the total Gospel and its purpose (20:31), the Quaker interpretation of John 1:9 is untenable. For further grammatical and exegetical study of John 1:9 cp. Edwyn Clement Hoskyns, *The Fourth Gospel*, 2d ed. by Francis Noel Davey (London: Faber and Faber Limited, 1947), p. 145; Moulton, *Grammar of the N. T. Greek*, I, 227; II, 452; B. F. Westcott, *The Gospel According to St. John* (Grand Rapids, Mich.: Wm. B. Eerdmans Publ. Co., 1950), pp. 6, 7.

to St. John, for the early Quakers moved in anti-Trinitarian concepts, at best in dynamic Monarchianism.[28]

It is almost impossible to determine where the early Quakers stood on the two doctrines which the Athanasian Creed considers absolutely essential to salvation, the doctrine of the Trinity and Christology. Nor is it easy to determine the modern Quakers' position.

On the one hand, Barclay uses terminology which seems to indicate a Trinitarian leaning. He states:

> Jesus is the Mediator betwixt God and man; for having been with God from all eternity, being Himself God, and partaking in time of the human nature, through Him the goodness and love of God are conveyed to mankind. . . . By this Light we understand a spiritual, heavenly principle, in which God as Father, Son, and Spirit dwells . . . and some call this (indwelling Seed) the spiritual body of Christ, the flesh and blood of Christ, which came down from heaven, of which all saints feed and are nourished into eternal life.[29]

But, on the other hand, neither Barclay nor the early Quakers were outspoken Trinitarians. It seems that they by and large considered the Logos of John 1 not as a self-subsistent Person but as the divine operative Force, which somehow united itself with the person of Jesus. The principle of the "Inner Light" has apparently relegated all else to the background. Barclay states that "the Inner Light is never separated from God nor Christ; but wherever it is, God and Christ are as wrapped up therein." The Hicksites describe the Inner Light as "the Father's own divine spirit, which became so wholly Jesus' own that His teaching, example, and sacrificial life are the complete revelation in humanity of the will of God." And even the Orthodox Friends, who frequently approach evangelical terminology, virtually endorse Barclay's definition of the "Inner Light" as a power issuing from God, for they declare: "We have benefit unto salvation by (the historic) Christ as well as by the light within, they being one." Carl Heath calls Christ the "expression or creativeness of God" and speaks of the "seed, word, light, or Christ," as the animating, living, bursting power of the indwelling God.[30]

The modern Quakers are divided. The Hicksites refuse to define the doctrine of God, but the Orthodox Friends are likely to have definite Trinitarian convictions and unqualifiedly to confess the deity of Christ.[31]

---

[28] Barclay states that God is not divisible into parts and therefore cannot be crucified. *Ap.*, Prop. VI, § 13. In *The Sandy Foundation Shaken* William Penn radically criticized the doctrine of the Trinity and was promptly imprisoned; and Isaac Pennington had recourse to ancient Apollinarianism, the theory that the pre-existent Christ became for a season the divine Soul of the human Jesus. Grubb, pp. 12—14; Russell, p. 175 f.

[29] *Ap.*, Prop. II, § 5; VI, 13. This teaching, as Rufus M. Jones points out, is identical with the Christology of Caspar Schwenkfeld. Grubb, p. 14.

[30] *Ap.*, Prop. V, § 13. *Book of Discipline*, p. 7. *Principles of Quakerism*, pp. 38, 39. *Woolman Tracts*, No. 1. (See Pennsburg Leaflets, Bibliog.)

[31] In *Popular Symbolics* I classified the Quakers among the anti-Trinitarian bodies. Members of the orthodox branch called my attention to the position of the "evangelicals," who since 1800 are to all intents and purposes a Trinitarian Reformed body. Otherwise the Society of Friends could not be a member of the National Council, which has consistently refused to receive the Unitarians and Universalists. As to the theological change see Grubb, ch. iii: "The Evangelical Movement and the Society of Friends," pp. 58—96.

THE DOCTRINE OF MAN AND HIS SALVATION

The "Inner Light" theory has determined the Quakers' views concerning God's relation to the sinner and the sinner's capacity for self-salvation. Quakers believe that

the personal consciousness of God in the soul of every man has led to a fuller recognition of the dignity and value of every human soul.

And, again,

As we become conscious of the inner light and submit to its leadings, we are enabled to live in conformity to the will of our heavenly Father. . . . The application of love to the whole life is the core of the Christian Gospel.[32]

The early Quakers were charged with virtually identifying themselves with Christ by their theory of the indwelling Christ. This charge is not valid, for Barclay said, on the one hand, that the Divine Seed, the Christ, dwells in man mediately, not immediately, and, on the other, that

Adam's posterity is fallen, degenerate, and dead and that all their imaginations are evil perpetually and whatever good any man doth proceeds not from his nature, but from the seed of God in him.[33]

But this utter inability to take a step in the right direction is not considered a damnable condition in itself, nor as guilt, until one actually consents to it. When the Divine Seed visits, enlightens, and reproves him, man has the capacity to be obedient to the Light and to convert himself. Although this seed is said to be in all men, even in those who finally reject it, yet Barclay explains why the seed does not work effectively in all, by the simile of the sun, which benefits living creatures, but putrefies a carcass.[34]

According to the early Quakers Christ's work consisted of two parts. The first part has been "performed for us in Christ's crucified body and has put man into the capacity [i. e., possibility of receiving] of salvation and conveys to man a measure of the power which was in Christ and which is able to counterbalance, overcome, and root out the evil seed." The second part is the redemption within us, when the capacity for justification becomes active and when "we witness and possess real, true, and inward redemption from the power and prevalency of sin and are truly redeemed and justified." "The death of Christ was a most certain declaration of God's free grace. This was not for the pacifying of God, but of men's conscience as to past sins," declared Penn. By showing man God's love in His propitiatory sacrifice, "Christ reconciled the world, i. e., removed the enmity in man," and therefore "Friends reject the idea of God as an offended Deity whose wrath needs to be appeased by such a sacrifice."

Generally speaking, Quakers maintain that it would be improper to speak of God's "wrath," since such speech would imply that, to remove sin, God would have to destroy the sinner. That has been too long and too often man's foolish and vain way of attempting to solve the tensions in his personal, social, and international relations. Man employs the tools of wrath in his attempt to right the wrong, viz., war and capital punishment. God uses only the way of love to correct man. And Quakers hold that this should also be man's way of dealing with society's sins and crimes.[35]

Barclay and his followers teach that justification is not a divine forensic act, but a moral transformation which en-

[32] *Faith and Practice*, XII. *Book of Discipline*, p. 7.
[33] *Ap.*, Prop. IV, § 2.
[34] *Ap.*, Prop. IV, § 4; Prop. V., § 18. Cp. Russell, pp. 178 f., 229 ff.
[35] *Ap.*, Prop. VII, § 3. Prop. VII, § 6. *Principles of Quakerism*, pp. 56, 57. See esp. Grubb, *Quaker Thought*, ch. v: "The 'Wrath' of God," pp. 114 to 124.

ables the believer to overcome all evil by the force of love and to produce the works of righteousness. The believer's real righteousness is not an imputed, but a self-acquired holiness.[36]

It was only natural that this principle soon developed into perfectionism.[37] Penn states:

The function of the living Word is to bring into harmonious relation and use all the faculties and activities of the soul so that the whole being becomes divinely naturalized.

And Barclay declares that

when the pure and holy birth is fully brought forth, the body of sin and death come to be crucified and removed. Such hearts are free from actual sinning and in that respect holy. Such an increase and stability in truth may be attained in this life, from which there can be no total apostasy.[38]

And George Fox reports that in an experience which he had in 1648, at twenty-four, he was transported as it were into Paradise and there knew nothing but pureness, being renewed into the image of Jesus Christ and restored to Adam's original state of holiness.

MEANS OF GRACE

Since the rise of evangelicalism there is no longer full unanimity among Quakers concerning the significance of the Bible, the place of the ministry, the relevance of the sacraments. Nevertheless the basic premise remains, that is, that the "Inner Light" is sufficient to effect salvation even where there is no acquaintance with the historical facts of Christianity. Barclay taught that Scripture cannot be considered the principal ground of all truth, for the Spirit is the first and principal Leader, nor can the Bible ever properly be called the Word of God. The Scriptures are said to be a record of the revelations which the divine Spirit gave from time to time, and they dare not be substituted for the Spirit, who gave them forth, or for Christ, or for the Inner Light. Pennington says: "The immediate word of the Lord, spoken and declared at this day, is of no less authority than it was in His servants by whom the Scriptures were given forth." John Woolman reports that he was moved to spend some time with the Indians if haply he might receive some instruction from them. Quakers so highly exalt the Inner Light that they do not hesitate to claim that the Inner Light, when rightly used, will lead to Biblical conclusions, since both, their own experiences and those of the men recorded in the Scriptures, emanate from the same divine Spirit. Quakers motivate their urging of the private reading of the Bible by stating that it gives an interesting account of "the progressive development from the primitive conceptions of an early religion to the culminating gospel of forgiveness, love, and brotherhood as taught and lived by Jesus." But even the Orthodox Friends, many of whose churches have a professional ministry and who maintain Bible schools, "refrain from attributing to the Scriptures themselves saving power, infallible guidance, and authoritative finality." Nor is the Bible read in the regular meetings for worship, for it is said that "such an exercise may be easily abused by unqualified persons and disturb the spirit of prayer in the meetings." [39]

[36] *Ap.*, Prop. VII, § 3.

[37] See the excellent study on the perfectionism of the early Quakers in Flew, pp. 280—92.

[38] *Ap.*, Prop. VIII; Prop. IX. Cp. also Pentecostals with regard to entire sanctification. Barclay's idea of perfection agrees essentially with John Wesley's.

[39] *Ap.*, Prop. III. *Book of Discipline*, pp. 25, 26. *Faith and Practice*, p. 19 *Principles of Quakerism*, pp. 17, 35, 68 ff., 115.

This is not to say that Quakers believe that salvation is possible without some knowledge of Christ. Their contention is that the oral preaching of Christ's work is unnecessary, since Enoch, Job, and other Old Testament believers had a knowledge of Christ's death without the outward Word. Barclay claims that "heathen who never heard of Christ's death, but, being sensible of their loss, are also sensible to the power and salvation of Christ." For as poison is effective destructively and medicine recuperatively, although the recipient does not know their names and natures, thus also not only sin, but also the unconscious "experimental knowledge of Christ's death" is said to be effective in the heathen. Caroline E. Stephen says: "The light of Christ is through obedience to that light, even while in ignorance of its source, purifying the hearts of many who name not His name." [40]

Quakers consider the Christian sacraments to be mere rituals, without any intrinsic significance. Any event in life is considered sacramental if it is truly an outward sign of an inward grace. Water baptism is said to be at best but a symbol of the baptism with fire and the Holy Ghost. The Lord instituted the Last Supper only to admonish His disciples to remember Him "as oft" as they celebrated the Passover. Some Quakers say that all work and worship, in short, the whole Christian life, is a sacrament of communion with Jesus Christ. [41]

WORSHIP AND CULTUS

In the traditional view of Quakers there is no place for the office of the ministry. Anyone who believes himself called immediately by the Spirit is granted the right and duty to speak. Many Quakers still espouse the "silent meeting," when a group of Quakers meditate in complete silence and, if none is moved to speak, each departs refreshed by this "corporate worship." In the worship meetings no hymns are sung or prayers recited, because "there may not be a corresponding spontaneous inner experience." [42] Some Quakers, however, employ the forms commonly used in the services of other churches, such as the office of the ministry and Sunday schools.

ETHICS

"The belief in the immediate manifestation of the light to all men has led to a fuller recognition of the dignity and value of every human soul." This was the principle which prompted the early Quakers to oppose war, slavery, capital punishment, oaths, secret societies, litigation, and to reject all honorary titles. The early Quakers discouraged their members from holding public office, since such connections might compel them to act counter to their principles. In the modern era they have taken a lively interest in philanthropy and have been pioneers in several movements for the uplift of society. Their honesty, thrift, sincerity, and simplicity have been proverbial. Modern Quakers state that "Jesus has shown us how the sense of God as our common Father may permeate the whole of life. He has shown us that all final solutions of human problems are in terms of personal relationship and mutual understanding." [43]

[40] *Ap.*, Prop. V, § 24. Prop. V, § 26. *Principles of Quakerism*, p. 48.

[41] *Faith and Practice*, pp. 13—16. Brinton, p. 15 ff.

[42] Ibid., ch. iii.

[43] The Quaker *Book of Discipline* contains detailed instructions to the members of the society on their conduct in business, in their social life, and in their respective homes. Quakers seem to be seriously determined to

CHURCH POLITY

Quakers speak of two types of meetings, one for worship, which meets weekly, and the second for business. The basic unit for business is the local or monthly meeting. The next administrative group is the quarterly meeting, to which the monthly meeting sends its "minutes"; the final unit is the yearly or general meeting. This carries on the work which the individual monthly or quarterly meetings cannot undertake. Quakers do not decide questions by a majority vote. The clerk "gathers the sense of the meeting," reads this "minute," and the meeting validates it by unanimous approval.[44]

THE SEPARATE BODIES

The Five Years Meeting of Friends. This is the largest body and is also known as Orthodox Friends. The Five Years Meeting — roughly the equivalent of "General Convention" in other bodies — meets every five years. It comprises the majority of "yearly meetings" of the American Quakers. This branch is a member of the National Council of Churches of Christ.

The Oregon Yearly Meeting of Friends Church and the *Religious Society of Friends, Kansas Yearly Meeting,* have withdrawn from the Five Years Meeting and are now independent bodies.

Religious Society of Friends (General Conference). This body comprises six "yearly meetings." It was founded in 1827 by Elias Hicks, who represented the most liberal elements in Quakerism. *The Philadelphia Yearly Meeting of the Religious Society of Friends,* a 1955 union of the Race Street and Arch Street Yearly Meetings, is affiliated with this group.

Religious Society of Friends (Conservative). This group was founded in 1845 by John Wilbur by way of protest against the introduction of a creed and doctrinal terminology as a "substitute for the inner experience."

The Central Yearly Meeting of Friends is a small evangelical and fundamental body with societies in Indiana, Arkansas, Michigan, and Ohio.

Other bodies are the *Ohio Yearly Meeting of Friends Church (Independent)* and the *Pacific Yearly Meeting of Friends.*

The Canadian Yearly Meeting of the Religious Society of Friends unites the Quakers of Canada.

BIBLIOGRAPHY

PART VII   SECTION III

Anscombe, Francis C. *I Have Called You Friends: The Story of the Quakers in North Carolina.* Boston: The Christopher Publishing House, 1959.

Barclay, Robert. *Apology of the True Christian Divinity.* First edition, 1678. Various editions.

Berry, William Eugene. "The Society of

develop a very intimate fellowship among the members, equivalent almost to a large family. The meeting, for example, claims the right to sanction a marriage if "parental consent has been withheld on grounds which seem to the meeting insufficient." *Faith and Practice,* p. 37.

[44] Brinton, loc. cit.

Friends in America (Quakers)," in Vergilius Ferm, ed. The American Church of the Protestant Heritage. New York: Philosophical Library, 1953. Pp. 225—46.

The Book of Discipline. Phila.: Yearly Meeting at Race Str., 1927. (Hicksites)

Brinton, Howard H. Guide to Quaker Practice. Wallingford, Pa.: Pendle Hill, n. d.

Eleg-Olofsson, Leif. The Conception of the Inner Light in Robert Barclay's Theology. Lund: C. W. K. Gleerup, 1954.

Faith and Practice: Handbook of the Society of Friends. Phila.: Friends' Book Store, 1926.

Flew, R. Newton. "Quakerism." The Idea of Perfection in Christian Theology, Ch. XVII. London: Oxford U. Press, 1934.

Fosdick, Harry E. Rufus Jones Speaks to Our Time. A Quaker's Permanent Message to the World. New York: Macmillan, 1951.

Grubb, Edward. Quaker Thought and History. New York: Macmillan, 1924.

Jacob, Caroline N. Builders of the Quaker Road. Chicago: Henry Regnery Co., 1953.

Jones, Rufus M. The Faith and Practice of Quakers. New York: Macmillan, 1927.

———. Spiritual Reformers in the Sixteenth and Seventeenth Centuries. London: Macmillan and Co., 1914.

———. Studies in Mystical Religion. London: Macmillan and Co., 1909.

———. The Flowering of Mysticism. New York: Macmillan, 1939.

———. The Later Period of Quakerism. London, 1921. (2 vols.)

———. The Story of Geo. Fox. New York: Macmillan, 1919.

———. The Quakers in Action. New York: Macmillan, 1929.

Nickalls, John L. Journal of George Fox. Cambridge Univ. Press, 1952.

Noble, Vernon. The Man in Leather Breeches. New York: Philosophical Library, 1953.

Russell, Elbert. The History of Quakerism. New York: Macmillan, 1942.

Thomas, A. C. A History of the Friends in America. 5th ed. Phila.: J. C. Winston, 1919.

Van Etten, Henry. George Fox and the Quakers. Trans. E. Kelvin Osborn. New York: Harper and Brothers, c. 1959.

Vipont, Elfrida. The Story of Quakers Through Three Centuries, 2 ed. London: The Bannisdale Press, 1960.

SECTION IV

The Amana Church Society

The Amana Society [1] became well known primarily as one of the few successful experiments in communism. However, the Amana Church Society was originally not organized as a communistic group; nor is communism today an essential and basic principle of the society. The Inspirationists, as they were first known, were pietistic mystics. The "enthusiastic" principles of the Camisards, or "French prophets," found fertile soil in Western Germany during the early years of the eighteenth century. John F. Rock and Eberhard Gruber, teaching that God deals directly and immediately with man, gained many adherents in Hesse. In 1714 these two men with their followers formed the Community of True Inspiration. They protested against what they termed the dogmatism and ritualism of the Lutheran church. They refused to render military

[1] Also known as the "Community of True Inspiration."

service. The heart of their faith was that divine inspiration — hence the name *Inspirierten* — and direct revelation had been given to their spiritual leaders as truly as it had been granted to Moses. In his extended missionary journeys Rock tried less to organize a new sect than to lead, as he declared, the church to a purer Christianity by following the directions which the Lord was giving to His inspired prophet Rock. But the society began to disintegrate when the supposed revelations diminished or led to unusual excesses and when Zinzendorf, in order to repudiate the charge of being partly responsible for the extravagant theories, renounced Rock. With the latter's death, in 1749, the gift of inspiration was held to have ceased.

In 1817 Christian Metz and Barbara Heinemann laid claim to the gift of inspiration. They gained adherents especially in Wuerttemberg, but their opposition to war and the oath brought them into conflict with the government. But, in spite of persecution, Metz in particular was successful in strengthening the remnants of the first Inspiration movement. He planned to settle the Inspirationists on large estates where they could share a simple life as a congregation and ultimately also practice the community of goods. But the civil authorities made their continued stay in Germany virtually impossible. In 1842 the society purchased land near Buffalo, N. Y., and called the settlement Ebenezer. The original plan was to hold the land in common, each sharing the real estate and the profits proportionately according to his investment. When this policy was found impracticable, absolute communism was introduced.

By 1854 the society had outgrown its quarters and began its westward trek, settling twenty miles west of Iowa City,

at a place which they named Amana, i. e., "Remain true." According to the articles of incorporation of 1859, communism was made obligatory not for temporal or pecuniary purposes or as the solution of social problems, but as a means of performing more effectively the duties incident to a truly Christian life. In 1932, however, communism was abolished, and all civil affairs, all farms, all businesses, as well as good will, were taken over by a corporation known as the Amana Society, whereas all ecclesiastical matters were placed into the hands of the Amana Church Society.[2]

The Community of True Inspiration has adopted the following confessional statement:

We believe in God the Father, the almighty Creator of the heavens, and of earth, and of all that is visible and invisible, and in His only-begotten Son, the Lord Jesus Christ, the Mediator and Savior of the world, the Word, who was in the beginning with God, the light of the world, who was made flesh, God of God and Son of man, sent unto the world, that whosoever believeth in Him should not perish; who suffered great agony, was crucified, died and shed His blood for the remission of sin. And also in God the Holy Ghost, who proceeds from the Father and Son, who is equally adored and honored, who has spoken and operated through the prophets of old, and who even now speaks and operates audibly through the instruments of true inspiration, and hidden inwardly, through the heart and conscience towards repentance and renewal of heart, teaching denial of ungodliness, and worldly lusts, and to live soberly, righteously and godly in the present world. We acknowledge and avow a holy, universal Christian Church, and a communion of saints, and all people of every nation who fear God and work righteousness are accepted with Him. We believe in the remission of sin, the

---

[2] *A Brief History,* pp. 1—26.

resurrection of the body, and in life blessed and everlasting.[3]

The society does not observe baptism with water, on the ground that the substance of this sacrament is spiritual regeneration and a baptism in the spirit. The rite of confirmation is observed at the age of fifteen. The celebration of the Lord's Supper in connection with foot washing *(Liebesmahl)*, formerly observed biennially, seems virtually to have been discontinued. The strict rules against participation in warfare have been rescinded, and those against taking oaths have been relaxed. Some of the older members still observe the traditional regulations imposing simplicity of dress, housing, and amusement. The retention of the German language in congregational worship is meeting with opposition.[4] The government of the church in the various colonies as well as the public worship is in charge of twenty-six elders.

BIBLIOGRAPHY

PART VII

SECTION IV

Anon. *A Brief History of the Amana Society.* Amana, Iowa, 1918.

Shambough, Bertha. "Amana That Was and Amana That Is." *The Palimpsest,* XVII (1936), pp. 149—84. Publ. by Hist. Soc. of Iowa. Reprint June, 1950.

SECTION V

The Schwenkfelder Church

Caspar Schwenkfeld (1490–1561), a Silesian nobleman, occupies a peculiar and isolated position among the mystics and spiritualists of the Reformation period. Luther's opposition to Rome's ceremonialism appealed to Schwenkfeld, and he became a stanch supporter of the Lutheran Reformation in Silesia. By 1525, however, he definitely broke with the Wittenberg theologians because Luther, in his opinion, in emphasizing the doctrine of justification, did not sufficiently stress sanctification. He believed in the immediacy of the Spirit; and prompted by his mysticism, he rejected the Word and the sacraments as means of grace.

Schwenkfeld's theology is predicated on the premise that a subjective experience of the love and grace of God is

---

[3] Ibid., p. 28 ff. Since the death of Christian Metz (1867) and Barbara Heinemann Landmann (1883) no one has claimed the gift of inspiration. The writings of these departed prophets are read in the regular services.

[4] Information supplied by the Rev. Enno Schuelke of Williamsburg, Iowa.

the essence of Christianity. This experience, said Schwenkfeld, cannot be engendered in man through the means of grace or any other means, since the Holy Spirit can enter the soul of the believer solely through the "eternal Word." In 1525 Schwenkfeld endeavored to mediate between the Lutherans and the Zwinglians by proposing a highly speculative conception of the essence and purpose of the Lord's Supper. He declared that in the words of institution the body of Christ is Christ Himself and that the sacramental eating is a mystical partaking of Christ as food of the soul. Thus the food, he said, is really "bread," for it is the nature of bread to nourish the body. This controversy undoubtedly helped Schwenkfeld to crystallize his peculiar notions concerning the person of Christ. Since, according to his views, God will bestow His grace through no creaturely means, since God uses the body of Christ to convey His love to man, therefore, so Schwenkfeld concluded, Christ's human nature was not created, but born of the Father out of the Virgin and therefore capable of deification and "glorification." This theory of a complete deification of Christ's human nature is the most complete form of Eutychian monophysitism. Controlled by this central idea, Schwenkfeld held the following: Man is incomplete until God's love and grace fill him. God's ethical essence must become man's property. This divine righteousness is conveyed to the believer by the "Eternal Word," the "glorified or deified human nature of Christ." Faith is the soul's

mystical union with the absolute God and His ethical righteousness, and therefore justification cannot be the imputation of Christ's perfect obedience, but the union with the "glorified reigning King in heaven." [1]

Because the adherents of Schwenkfeld were definitely opposed to a regular church organization, they could not obtain recognition nor immunity during the unsettled times of the sixteenth and seventeenth centuries. Bitter persecutions finally prompted about 200 members of the small Schwenkfeldian remnant to emigrate to Pennsylvania in 1734. They continued their exclusiveness and emphasized leading "a quiet and peaceable Christian life according to the will of Christ in all meekness and lowliness as the quiet in the land and being true and faithful in their spiritual as well as their temporal calling." Since 1895 they no longer object to the bearing of arms, joining secret societies, and rendering an oath; but they still observe the rigorous rules of church discipline and emphasize experimental religion. The Schwenkfelders believe that it is the duty of their churches "to mediate the higher social virtues and moral ideals (which they have inherited from their more exclusive ancestors) to those that shall come after them." Although they number only six churches, they support a school of higher learning at Perkiomenville, Pa., and maintain a publishing house, which is currently publishing a critical edition of Schwenkfeld's voluminous writings.

[1] Cp. *The Lutheran Confessions*, F. C., XII.

BIBLIOGRAPHY

PART VII   SECTION V

Brecht, Samuel Kriebel, ed. *The Genealogical Record of the Schwenkfelder Families . . . Who Fled . . . to Pennsylvania in the Years 1731—1737*. New York: Rand, McNally and Co., 1923.

Corpus Schwenckfeldianorum. 17 vols. Pennsburg, Pa.

Hoffmann, Franz. *Caspar Schwenkfelds Leben u. Lehren*. Part I. Berlin: Erste Städtische Realschule, 1897.

Jones, Rufus M. *Spiritual Reformers in the Sixteenth and Seventeenth Centuries*. London: Macmillan and Co., 1914.

Kadelbach, Oswald. *Ausführliche Geschichte Kaspar v. Schwenkfelds und der Schwenkfelder*. Laubau: M. Baumeister, 1860.

Maier, Paul L. *Caspar Schwenckfeld on the Person and Work of Christ*. St. Louis: Concordia Seminary School for Graduate Studies, 1959.

Schultz, Selina Gerhard. *Caspar Schwenckfeld von Ossig (1489—1561)*. Norristown: The Board of Publication of the Schwenckfelder Church, 1946.

Who Are the Schwenckfelders? Pennsburg, Pa., 1923.

PART EIGHT

The Millennial Groups

SECTION I

The Millennial Trends

Premillennialism

Chiliasm is the belief that Christ will establish a glorious kingdom in this world.[1] Mankind has, of course, always hoped for a golden age. After the oppression of the intertestamental period, Jewish hopes ran high that the Messiah would liberate them from the Roman bondage and establish a glorious kingdom.[2] At first even the disciples held chiliastic views, and many of the early Christian writers such as Irenaeus, Tertullian, and Methodius were outspoken chiliasts.[3] Eras of economic and social pressures, moral decline, war, or great

NOTE: For key to abbreviations see Appendix C; for Bibliography, the end of the section.

[1] "Millennialism" is derived from the Latin *mille* and *annus*, and "chiliasm" from *chilias*, each meaning one thousand years.

[2] The Jewish views current at the time of Christ concerning the Messianic hope of Israel shed new light on the Savior's parables concerning the Kingdom. See A. Edersheim, *Life and Times of the Messiah* (London: Longmans, Green & Co., 2d ed., 1886; 29th impression. Grand Rapids: Wm. B. Eerdmans), I, 160 ff.

[3] Chiliasm has its roots in the postexilic eschatological views of the Jewish rabbis. The rabbis of this period were greatly influenced by the millennial views of Zoroastrianism, through their immediate contact with the Persian magis in the Babylonian Captivity and their later correspondence with them. During the intertestamental period the apocryphal literature reveals growth of the millennial concept, i. e., the kingdom of the Messiah was to be on the earth for Israel. Cp. *The Apocrypha and Pseudepigrapha of the Old Testament*, ed. R. H. Charles (Oxford: Clarendon Press, 1913), I, 131, 197, 529; II, 478, etc. Also H. Maldwyn Hughes, *The Ethics of Jewish Apocryphal Literature* (London: Robert Culley), pp. 104, 307, etc. William Foxwell Albright, *From the Stone Age to Christianity* (Baltimore: Hopkins Press, 1940), pp. 287—88. Because of this influential and prevalent millennial interpretation of the last things, plus the fact of persecutions and the current concept of Christ's early return, the church during the first centuries was plagued with chiliast movements and propaganda, even among its soundest theologians. Papias (d. 170) was an outspoken chiliast. The millennial doctrine is also found in the *Shepherd of Hermas* (1, 3); *Didache* (10, 16); Justin, *Dial.* (80, 81); Irenaeus, *Adv. Haereses* (5, 32 ff.); Tertullian, *Adv. Marcionem* (3, 24); Lactantius, *Divinae Institutiones* (7:20 ff.); Methodius, *Conviv.* (9, 1, 5). Both the Ebionites and the Montanists were crass chiliasts, the latter teaching that Christ would return and establish the New Jerusalem at Pepuza in Phrygia. In the Eastern church it was the Alexandrian school that dealt the chiliastic movement the death blow; in the West it was Augustine, in his *De civitate Dei* (XX, 7, 9). Chiliasm was condemned in the testimonies of Dionysius (d. 265), Jerome (d. 420), Gregory of Nyssa (d. 400), John of Damascus

religious upheavals usually produce waves of chiliastic preaching, frequently motivated by distressing conditions and the belief that only a divine cataclysm can remedy matters.

There are two types of millennialism. The one holds that Christ's second coming will occur after (post) the millennium, hence "postmillennialism." This type ignores the Scriptural teaching that mankind will increasingly be afflicted by wars, disorders, catastrophes, etc. The other type believes that Christ will return before (prae) the millennium, during which He will visibly rule on earth, hence "premillennialism." This type has a relatively large following.

THE RISE OF MODERN PREMILLENNIALISM

Probably the present emphasis on premillennialism is due in no small measure to a reaction against liberal theology. Modernists had all but removed eschatology from their message. Fundamentalism countered by making eschatology a center emphasis of the Christian message. Furthermore, modernists had stressed the necessity of reinterpreting the Bible in terms of modern psychology and sociology. As a result practically everything in the Scriptures was questioned or given a symbolical meaning. Many fundamentalists went to the opposite extreme and advocated a literalism so strict that they would brook no figurative language whatever. Many

conservative pastors and laymen in the Presbyterian and Baptist churches became ardent advocates of premillennialism. All the Fundamentalist Associations as well as the Holiness and Pentecostal groups have written premillennialism into their creed. The catastrophic World Wars, and particularly the emergence of the State of Israel, stimulated interest in the imminence of Christ's second coming. The formation of the World Council of Churches in 1948 brought about a close interchange of thought between the European continent, with its pessimistic approach of apocalypticism, and the American continent, with its optimistic outlook of premillennialism.[4]

Frequently premillennialism and dispensationalism are regarded as identical, but the fact is that while all dispensationalists are premillennialists, not all premillennialists are dispensationalists. They indeed have many points in common, particularly this, that they interpret the Old Testament Messianic prophecies alike. Nevertheless the underlying premises of the two systems vary so fundamentally that fairness to both requires a separate discussion of each.

THE PREMISES OF PREMILLENNIALISM

A large number of fundamentalists interpret Revelation 20 very literally and teach that Christ will personally rule in glorious splendor over His enemies for a period of a thousand years. The mil-

(d. 752), and Theophylact (d. 1107). At the synod of Rome, 383, Damasus condemned the error of chiliasm. Some of the above-named patristic fathers are commonly appealed to by present-day chiliasts to substantiate the orthodoxy of their views. But it is an interesting fact that chiliasm seldom appeared in the primitive church except in the company of other errors, Cp. V. A. W. Mennicke, "Notes on the History of Chiliasm," *C. T. M.*, XIII (March, 1942), 200, also 192—207; Hastings, *Encyc. of Religion and Ethics*, V, 388; *New Schaff-Herzog Encyc.*, VII, 374—378. For a general introduction to the history of chiliasm see Kromminga, loc. cit.

4 Cp. the studies published for discussion at the Second World Assembly of the World Council of Churches at Evanston, Ill., in 1954 under the title *The Christian Hope and the Task of the Church* (New York: Harper & Brothers, 1954), especially the "Report of the Advisory Commission on the Main Theme of the Second Assembly: 'Christ — the Hope of the World.'"

lennial reign of Christ, say the premillennialists, is a doctrine which is taught not only in the mysterious Book of Revelation, but also in other books of the Bible. It runs, in fact, through both Testaments.[5] The first premise of premillennialism is that all prophecies concerning the establishment of the Messianic kingdom must be literally fulfilled. On the basis of Psalm 2, Psalm 110, Isaiah 11, Dan. 7:13, 14, and especially 2 Sam. 7:12, the premillennialist believes that God will unfailingly establish the throne of David. Since it has not as yet been re-established, this event is still in the future. Jesus must come as the promised King of the earth, the Messiah of Israel, and the One who will bring to this earth the long-looked-for ideal conditions — that era of good will, that time of peace, that time of blessedness, for which all mankind has been waiting.[6]

A second premise of some (but not all) premillennialists is that there is a fundamental difference between the kingdom of God, or of heaven, and the kingdom of Christ, the former being the holy Christian church, and the latter Christ's visible and earthly kingdom with Jerusalem as its center. Many premillennialists hold that Christ Himself at first expected to establish this kingdom, the throne of David, but that when He met with the insurmountable opposition of the Jews, He abandoned His plan. He now proclaimed only the nearness of the kingdom of God, the establishment of the church, and was willing to postpone the establishment of His earthly kingdom until His second coming.[7]

A third premillennial premise is that only two of the three purposes of Israel have so far been fulfilled. Israel has produced the Messiah and given us the Bible. However, Israel was also to be a light unto the Gentiles (Is. 43:12; 66:19). This third purpose Israel cannot fulfill until it is converted. This notion accounts for the fact that the conversion of Israel plays so large a part in modern premillennialism.[8]

The fourth premise is that the Lord, visibly present, will by an act of His sovereign power so transform mankind

---

[5] Cp. Francis Pieper, *Christian Dogmatics* (St. Louis: C. P. H., 1953), III, 520—25. F. C. G. Schumm, *Essay on Revelation*, Chapter 20 (St. Louis: C. P. H., 1915). Benjamin B. Warfield, "The Millennium and the Apocalypse," *Biblical Doctrines* (New York: Oxford Univ. Press, 1929), p. 643 ff. R. C. H. Lenski, *Interpretation of St. John's Revelation* (Columbus: Luth. Book Concern, 1935). In 1 Thess. 4:16, a passage which those who interpret Revelation 20 literally often cite to support their doctrine of a millennium, St. Paul speaks only of believers, and the adverb "first" contrasts the resurrection of the dead believers with the transfiguration of the living believers. There is no basis whatsoever for the assumption that St. Paul is here contrasting a first resurrection, one of believers, to a second resurrection, one of unbelievers, 1,000 years later. Cp. John 5:28, 29.

[6] Brownville, p. 32.

[7] This premise leads to many strange views; for example, that the Sermon on the Mount is primarily for the future kingdom, the kingdom of Christ. Barnhouse, ch. iii, p. 47. In ch. v, "Christ's Great Crisis," Barnhouse says John's statement: "He came unto His own, and His own received Him not, but as many as received Him" (John 1:11), is the key which unlocks more doors than any other in the New Testament. The word "but" is like a watershed which divides a continent. When Israel refused His royal sovereignty, there was a right-about-face which set Him on the path that would lead to the cross. (P. 64 f.) See Brownville, pp. 36—38, 136.

[8] Brownville, p. 73 ff.

that it will accept His Lordship. In the millennium Christ will be the Center of every man's religious life, and every sphere of his activity will be related to Christ. The influence and sovereignty of Christ will be so universal that even the harness of the horses will bear the stamp "Holiness unto the Lord" (Zech. 14:20).[9]

The final premise is that the millennium is an earthly kingdom of universal blessings. It must be earthly because in it swords will be changed into plowshares, and plowshares — so we are told — obviously do not belong in heaven. Rom. 8:18-23 is said to refer to the removal of the curse resting upon the dumb creatures, which the premillennialists say are so constituted that they cannot enjoy their glorious liberation in heaven. All the prophecies clothed in figurative language are given a very literalistic interpretation; for example, "the plowman shall overtake the reaper," "the mountains shall drop sweet wine," "the desert shall blossom as the rose," "the parched ground shall become a pool," "highways shall be built which shall be called 'the way of holiness,'" "the myrtle tree shall replace the briar," "the wolves and the lambs shall sleep together."' In brief, the millennium is pictured as a real utopia, and mankind's personal, domestic, social, political, economic problems shall all have been solved. There shall be nothing in God's holy mountain to hurt or to destroy, because "the earth shall be full of the knowledge of the Lord as the waters cover the sea" (Is. 11:1-13).[10] And the splendor will be universal, for every knee shall bow before Christ and acknowledge Him as the King of kings. This is inferred from 1 Cor. 15:24-28, which is said to teach that Christ at

one time, that is, during the millennium, must have possessed the universal kingdom if He is to surrender it after the final Judgment.

THE EVENTS OF THE MILLENNIAL PERIOD

There is no agreement among premillennialists as to the interpretation of the alleged premillennial Scripture references. Seemingly all are agreed that according to Holy Scripture at least five major events will occur in the millennium.

1. The millennial period will be ushered in by Christ's invisible return to remove the believers from this earth during the "great tribulation." In the "first resurrection" the dead believers will be raised, and the living believers will be transfigured (1 Thess. 4:16; Phil. 3:20; 1 Cor. 15:51, 52). Then all the quickened and transfigured saints will be removed from this world, or "raptured" out of it, not only to escape the imminent tribulation (Luke 21:36), but chiefly to be presented to Christ as the pure bride after the long betrothal of the New Testament period (1 Cor. 11:2; Eph. 5:25-27) and to be married to the Lamb (Rev. 19:7).

2. After the church has been removed to heaven, the great tribulation, a period of seven years (Dan. 9:26, 27), will come upon the Jewish nation (Daniel 12; Luke 21:25, 26; Acts 15: 13-17). In the "midst of the week" (Dan. 9:27), that is, after three and a half years, Antichrist will be revealed (2 Thess. 2:3; Rev. 11:3-7), and God's wrath will be poured upon the nations so copiously (Ps. 2:1-3) that Israel will accept Christ (Zech. 12:10-14; 13:6, 9).

3. Thereupon the revelation of Christ can take place, for Israel has accepted

---

[9] Erl Olsen, "God's World of Tomorrow," *Bibl. S.*, 1940, p. 103 ff. This premise is fully in accord with historic Calvinism's view of the sovereignty of God and its social implications.

[10] Ibid.

Christ, and He can establish His millennial kingdom (2 Thess. 1:7, 8; Zech. 2:10; 14:4; Matt. 24:29, 30; 2 Thess. 1:7; esp. Is. 59:20). Christ will gather all nations to judge them by their treatment of "His brethren," the Jews, and will destroy the great nations. (Matt. 25:31 ff.) This is the "first judgment," which takes place at the beginning of the millennium and has only one standard — man's attitude toward the Jews. Antichrist will be destroyed (Ezek. 38:39).

4. The millennium will now be established. Together with the Jews, Christ will usher in the era in which all the Messianic prophecies will be literally fulfilled. Toward the end of the millennium, Satan will be loosed for a season (Rev. 20:7-10), and make an assault with the rebels against Christ, only to be utterly destroyed.[11]

5. The end of the millennium will witness the "second resurrection" (John 5:29; Dan. 12:2); to be followed by the "Judgment at the great white throne" (Rev. 20:11-15). Hell and death will be destroyed (Rev. 20:14; 1 Cor. 15:26), and God will make a new heaven and a new earth (Is. 66:22).

AMILLENNIALISM VS. PREMILLENNIALISM

Amillennialists believe that the premillennialists are at basic variance with the Scriptures on the following points.[12]

1. Premillennialists frequently resort to a very arbitrary interpretation. For example, in 1 Cor. 15:24, the adverb "then" is made to represent the 1,000 years of the millennium.

2. A basic distinction is made between the kingdom of God and the kingdom of Christ, whereas modern studies show conclusively that this distinction is untenable.[13]

3. The premillennialists believe that the church will be a church of splendor during the millennium, whereas Scripture presents the church as covered or hidden by the cross until the end of time.

4. Premillennialism pictures the Antichrist primarily as the opponent of the Jews rather than as the adversary of Christ.

5. There is no Scriptural support for the two resurrections.

6. The exalted Christ is pictured as warring against the powers of evil in real battle array. This conception is contrary to His state of glorious exaltation.

7. The conversion of Israel by a display of Christ's glory and splendor contradicts both the doctrine of the means of grace and an unbiased interpretation of Rom. 11:25, 26.[14]

8. Premillennialism is in constant peril of removing soteriology from the center of Christian doctrine and substituting an earthly eschatology for it.

---

[11] Here the interpretations vary greatly. Some hold that the raptured saints will return with Christ after their seven-year sojourn in heaven. Cp. Blackstone, pp. 74, 191. Some hold that Armageddon takes place during the "week" or seven years of tribulation; others, during the closing days of the millennium. The attempts to identify Gog, Magog, and Rosh have led to some strange historical aberrations. Cp. Graebner, p. 46 ff.

[12] Most of the points apply also to dispensationalism. Cp. Engelder, "Notes on Chiliasm," *C. T. M.,* VI (1935), 161—173, 241—254, 321—335, 401—413, 481—496. Also his "Dispensationalism Disparaging the Gospel," ibid., VIII (1937), 649—666. *Pop. Symb.,* p. 373. Mayer, *Dispensationalism,* pp. 89—94.

[13] Cp. Gerhard Kittel, *Theologisches Wörterbuch zum Neuen Testament* (Stuttgart: W. Kohlhammer, 1933), Ib, 581 ff.

[14] Victor Bartling, "All Israel Shall Be Saved, Rom. 11:26," *C. T. M.,* XII (1941), pp. 641—52.

Dispensationalism

Though dispensationalism shares all the points discussed in the previous section, it differs sharply from the majority of premillennialists. Dispensationalism is predicated on the theory that the history of the world is divided into dispensations, "periods of time during which man is tested in respect to obedience to some specific revelation of the will of God." [15] Modern dispensationalists differ from their predecessors chiefly in their insistence that there are seven dispensations, or seven different periods in which God has given a specific revelation to man. They teach that all time is divided into seven eras. The history of the world is said to be a perfect counterpart of the creation week. As the creation week comprised six days of labor — each with a specific task — and one day of rest, so the history of mankind runs through six dispensations — each with its specific revelation and particular obligations — and one period of Sabbath rest, or the millennium. Israel's religious calendar is said to be built on the "sacred seven": a week of seven days, a "week" of seven weeks from Passover to Pentecost, a "week" of seven months from the Passover to the Atonement, another "week" of seven years ending with the sabbatical year, and finally the grand period of a "week" of "seven years" ending in the fiftieth year as the jubilee year. The typical dispensationalists find the holy "seven" in the seventy weeks of Daniel, in the sevenfold name of God, in the seven churches of Asia. The dispensationalists believe that upon this rock of the sacred seven they can confidently base their conclusion that as there is a week of days, a week of weeks, a week of months, a week of years, so there must also be a week of aeons or dispensations. [16] The unprejudiced student of Holy Scripture soon gains the impression that dispensationalism attempts to force Scripture into a preconceived frame of reference. [17]

[15] Scofield, *Ref. Bible*, comment on Gen. 1:3. Dispensationalism is nothing new. In modern times the theory of dispensationalism has been popularized by John Nelson Darby of the Plymouth Brethren; by James Brookes in his *Maranatha* of 1870; by the Keswick prophetic conferences since 1878; by the Scofield Bible with its elaborate notes and charts; and by Blackstone, *Jesus Is Coming*, which was sent gratis to all Protestant pastors in 1916. Both Allis and Bass (see Bibliogr.) discuss in some detail the dispensationalism of Darby and Scofield.

[16] Blackstone, p. 39. Blackstone based his theory of seven aeons in part on Lev. 26:18, 21, 24, 28, completely overlooking the fact that the English phrase "seven times" in the reference has nothing to do with seven aeons, but is an adverb denoting "sevenfold."

[17] A typical example of dispensational interpretation follows: John 1:19 to 2:1 is said to show that even the first week of Christ's ministry is a prophecy of the entire work of redemption. On Thursday John identifies himself as the representative of the Old Testament prophets. Friday is the day of humiliation, when John points out Christ as the Lamb of God. The Sabbath foreshadows the formation of the church. On Sunday (v. 43) Jesus gathers Philip and Nathaniel as the witnessing remnant (Zech. 12:10). On Monday and Tuesday Christ traveled to Cana, and nothing happened, which typifies the 2,000 years of the New Testament church, the kingdom of mystery. Wednesday is the customary wedding day for Jews, and Christ appropriately comes to Cana, where the bridal couple lacked wine, the emblem of joy. His presence at the marriage and furnishing of the wine symbolizes the wedding of the Lamb and the millennial period of joy. Graham Gilmer, "A Week in the Life of Christ," *Bibl. S.*, XCVI (1939), 42.

The "prophetic" day as denoting a period of 1,000 years (2 Peter 3:8) plays a prominent part in dispensationalism. However, individual dispensationalists make different computations. Some hold that a "prophetic day" is exactly 1,000 sun years and that the six "days" of labor, i. e., 6,000 years, are about at an end. Others hold that the "prophetic" days may be of varying duration, the sixth "day," for example, already extending over 1,900 years. Nor are they agreed as to the distinctive features which mark the beginning and the close of each dispensation. Many seem to maintain that the emphasis in each dispensation rests upon its concluding catastrophe, because the creation days are measured as "evening and morning," that is, first darkness, then the light. Others hold that the new revelation is the important factor. The majority seem to combine both emphases and hold that every dispensation with its peculiar revelation ends with a catastrophe, because God was unable to deal successfully with mankind on the basis of the knowledge given to man during that specific dispensation. They have developed the following scheme:

1. The era of innocence in the Garden of Eden ended with Adam's fall.

2. The era in which God governed man solely by his conscience and the little revelation which he had taken from Paradise ended with the Flood.

3. The period of human government which was established by the introduction of capital punishment (Gen. 9:6) ended with the destruction of Sodom.

4. The era of the patriarchs who had not as yet received the promise (Heb. 11:13) closed with the destruction of Pharaoh's hosts in the Red Sea.

5. The Mosaic era is the history of Israel beginning with the giving of the Law and ending with the crucifixion of Christ.

6. The Christian, or Mystery, era began with Pentecost and will end with the great tribulation, the judgment of the nations, and the destruction of the Antichrist.

7. The era of Manifestation, or of the Great Rest, is ushered in with the "first resurrection," the glorious manifestation of Jesus to His brethren, and will end with the destruction of Satan and the Judgment at the White Throne. Thereupon will follow eternal life for the believers and eternal condemnation for the unbelievers.[18]

Chief among the differences between premillennialism and dispensationalism is that the latter is exclusively Jewish. The dispensationalists hold that God's purposes as revealed in the Bible are twofold: (1) He is related to the earth, with earthly people and earthly objectives, culminating in the history and glorification of the Jewish race. (2) He is related to heaven, with heavenly people and heavenly objectives, namely, the Christian church of the Sixth Dispensation.[19] Dispensationalists hold that the establishment of the Davidic throne was temporarily halted to allow for the establishment of the church. This New Testament church is called a "parenthesis church," for it is placed between the Old Testament and the millennium. Just before the millennium the church will have been "raptured," or taken out of this world, and God will deal exclu-

[18] Another rather popular division follows: (1) the Adamic Covenant, Gen. 3:14—19; (2) the Noahitic Covenant, Gen. 8:20—9:27; (3) the Abrahamic Covenant, Gen. 15:18; (4) the Palestinian Covenant, Deut. 30:1-10; (5) the Davidic Covenant, 2 Sam. 7:16; (6) the New Covenant, Jer. 31:34; (7) the Millennial Covenant.

[19] Chafer, p. 448.

sively with the children of Israel. Then He will fulfill the promises given to Abraham that he and his descendants are to possess the land. And God will carry out His plan regardless of Israel's obedience or disobedience.[20]

AMILLENNIALISM AND DISPENSATIONALISM

The amillennialists differ fundamentally from dispensationalists.

1. The amillennialists believe that in all history the Gospel is the only means and the all-sufficient means for converting men; the dispensationalists hold that in each dispensation God uses a different means to accomplish His purpose.

2. Amillennialists hold that dispensationalism is predicated on an entirely false philosophy of history. They hold that the church, not Israel, is the center of the history of the world. The theory is preposterous that the church is a "parenthesis" in history, a sort of discursive activity of God, who temporarily set aside His real goal, the establishment of the Messianic kingdom. The amillennialists disavow the dispensationalists' distinction between the "prophetic church" of Peter and the "mystery church" of Paul: the former, a "Satanic counterfeit," to be spewed out; the latter, the mystery church, to be taken out

of the world during the millennium. Such a theory gives the church a position secondary to Judaism. The amillennialists can find no warrant in the Scriptures that the Cross of Christ as the focal point of history should be supplanted by the establishment of an Abrahamic promise dealing with so many square miles of land.[21]

3. Dispensationalism tends to disparage the Gospel. This is a sharp criticism in view of the fact that all dispensationalists are fundamentalists. However, according to Scofield, there is "not a ray of grace nor a drop of blood in the millennium." The Sermon on the Mount, which the Jews rejected during Christ's earthly sojourn, will be established as the constitution of the future kingdom. The Gospel is said to be only an "interim" revelation.[22]

4. Amillennialists believe that Eph. 2:11-22; Gal. 3:27-29, and the Epistle to the Hebrews militate against the idea that the Old Testament cultus will be re-established. The amillennialists believe that the sacrificial offerings cannot be reinstituted during the millennium to serve as a memorial looking back to the cross, as dispensationalists assert, because they were only the shadow of the things to come (Col. 2:17) and have forever been abolished by Christ's redemptive work.

[20] Chafer states that Israel was given the opportunity to enter Canaan at Kadesh two years after they had left Egypt. This was an opportunity of grace, which Israel spurned. Thereupon it was compelled to journey for 38 years, when the people again came to Kadesh. Now Israel had no choice, but was compelled by God to enter Canaan. The symbolical meaning of this occurrence is said to be that the two years correspond to the years of Israel's exile. The first encampment at Kadesh is said to correspond to Christ's work among Israel during His first coming and Israel's rejection of Christ. The 38 years are symbolic of the New Testament era. At the end of this era Israel will again be confronted by Christ, and at this time Israel will not be able to refuse Christ's sovereignty. Chafer, p. 403. Barnhouse, p. 47.

[21] See Allis, pp. 90 ff., 104 ff., 251.

[22] See Allis, pp. 233, 277.

BIBLIOGRAPHY

PART VIII   SECTION I

Premillennialism

Barnhouse, Donald Grey. *His Own Received Him Not.* New York: Fleming H. Revell Co., 1933.

Brownville, C. G. *Romance of the Future.* New York: Fleming H. Revell Co., 1938.

Feinberg, Chas. *Premillennialism or Amillennialism?* Grand Rapids: Zondervan Publishing House, 1936.

Graebner, Theodore. *War in the Light of Prophecy.* St. Louis: C. P. H., 1942.

Hamilton, Floyd. *Basis of Millennial Faith.* Grand Rapids: Wm. B. Eerdmans, 1942.

Kik, J. Marcellus. *Revelation Twenty, An Exposition.* Philadelphia: The Presbyterian and Reformed Publishing Co., 1955.

Kromminga, D. H. *The Millennium in the Church.* Grand Rapids: Wm. B. Eerdmans, 1945.

Masselink, William. *Why Thousand Years?* Grand Rapids: Wm. B. Eerdmans, 1930.

Murray, George L. *Millennial Studies.* Grand Rapids: Baker Book House, 1948.

Simpson, A. B. *The Fourfold Gospel.* Harrisburg, Pa.: Christian Alliance Publ. Co., 1925. Ch. iv.

Dispensationalism

Allis, Oswald T. *Prophecy and the Church.* Phila.: Presb. and Ref. Publ. Co., 1945. An incisive critique of the premises on which dispensationalism is based. Cp. *C. T. M.,* XVII (1946), p. 89 ff.

Bass, Clarence B. *Backgrounds to Dispensationalism: Its Historical Genesis and Ecclesiastical Implications.* Grand Rapids: Wm. B. Eerdmans Publishing Co., 1960.

Bibliotheca Sacra, a theological quarterly published by Dallas (Texas) Theological Seminary. Vol. CVII (1950) contained the following articles dealing with phases of dispensationalism:

Evans, W. Glyn. "Will Babylon Be Restored?" p. 335.

Payne, Homer Lemuel. "Contemporary Amillennial Literature," p. 103.

Scofield, C. I. "The Times of the Gentiles," p. 343.

Unger, Merrill F. "Ezekiel's Vision of Israel's Restoration," p. 51.

Walvoord, John F. "Amillennialism as a Method of Interpretation," p. 42.

———. "Amillennialism as a System of Theology," p. 154.

———. "Amillennial Soteriology," p. 281.

———. "Amillennial Ecclesiology," p. 420.

Woychuk, N. E. "Life in Heaven," p. 227.

Blackstone, W. E. *Jesus is Coming.* Chicago: Moody Press, 1916.

Chafer, L. C. "Dispensationalism." *Bibl. S.,* Oct.—Dec., 1936.

Engelder, Theodore. "Dispensationalism Disparaging the Gospel." *C. T. M.,* VIII (Sept. 1937), pp. 649—666.

Kraus, C. Norman. *Dispensationalism in America: Its Rise and Development.* Richmond: John Knox Press, 1958.

Scofield, C. I. *The Scofield Reference Bible.* New York: Oxford Univ. Press, American Branch, 1909.

Walvoord, John F. "Israel's Restoration." *Bibl. S.,* CII (1945), 405—416.

Whiting, Arthur B. "The Rapture of the Church." *Bibl. S.,* CII (1945), 360—372, 490—499.

SECTION II

The Catholic Apostolic Church

The Catholic Apostolic Church

The distinctive doctrine of the two groups known as the Catholic Apostolic Church and the New Apostolic Church is the fantastic theory that the Lord's second coming cannot take place without the existence of the twelvefold apostolate. The momentous events of the closing years of the eighteenth century, especially the French Revolution, had aroused the deep conviction in many that the time of the Lord's second coming had arrived. However, the premillenarians associated as the Catholic Apostolic Church believed that the church was not ready for His coming. Therefore they insisted upon praying for a revival of the gifts which had marked the early Christian church. All the troubles of the church, the many heresies of the ancient and modern church, the many schisms and divisions, the indifference, the decline of morals, and the large number of defections were said to be due to the absence of the apostolate and of the charismatic gifts, especially the gift of prophesying, including an authoritative teaching office.[1] Edward Irving (1792–1834), an unusually gifted pulpit orator and pastor of a Presbyterian congregation in London, gave a large place in his sermons to the hope of an early restoration of the charismatic gifts and of the early return

of Christ. About 1830 a number of ecstatic phenomena were viewed as the restoration of the gift of prophecy. The contents of these prophecies were said to indicate the Lord's early return and the church's duty to prepare for it. According to Irving's interpretation of Acts 1:11; 1 Thess. 4:15; Matt. 28:20, etc., the Lord's return can take place only during the time of apostles, and therefore a "visible active apostolate, identical with the former apostolate established in the early church," was considered indispensable to the church. In 1835 twelve men, including John Cardale and Henry Drummond, after being designated by the prophets of the movement, were solemnly ordained apostles. As such they assumed the right to take up every doctrinal question, every form of worship or of church government which was in dispute, and to settle these questions by their "apostolic authority." When their letters to the ecclesiastical and secular rulers of virtually the entire Christian world remained unheeded, the "apostles" ordained "angels" (evangelists) and commissioned them to organize churches in all Christian nations after the pattern of the apostolic church. London, with its seven churches (patterned after the seven churches of Asia Minor), was the center of the movement.[2]

[1] This movement is frequently considered the historical antecedent of modern Pentecostalism.

[2] Schaff says: "This movement is one of the unsolved enigmas of church history. It combines a high order of piety and humility of individual members with astounding assumptions, which, if well founded, would require the submission of Christendom to the authority of its inspired apostles." *Creeds,* I, 908. Cp. the statement prepared by Andrews in Schaff, I, 911.

The Irvingites believe that "the twelve apostles were the twelve spiritual canals going forth from the Great Apostle, Jesus Christ, so that through their doctrines and decrees they would make it possible for the Holy Spirit to flow through the ordinances of the church and through the laying on of hands to bestow the Holy Spirit upon every member, to lead and direct all persons in whom the various gifts of the Holy Spirit became manifest, and thus to prepare the church as a pure virgin and to lead her to the Lord when He appears." Since this can be done only through "apostles," the twelvefold apostolate must be present in the end dispensation. The New Apostolic Church went so far as to say that without twelve apostles the body of Christ is incomplete and crippled. All the charismatic gifts with which the first apostles were endowed are said to have been given to the office. For this reason the "apostles" in the dispensation immediately preceding Christ's coming are believed to "have direct mission from the Lord, so that He could speak through them and make known His will through them."[3]

The centrality of the apostolate in their doctrinal system has a tremendous effect on every tenet of the Christian. In their view the Bible in its normative character and even in its efficacy is dependent upon "living apostles, prophets, who rule the communities with their instructions and dispense the blessings prescribed in the Bible."[4] They say that "the Lord did not complete the work of His redemption in the early church, but will effect a thorough redemption from eternal death and destruction through the present office of grace. Through the apostolate a thorough transformation of mankind to the image of Christ is to be effected."[5] Like the later Pentecostals, the Irvingites seem to place greater emphasis on the work of the Spirit than on the work of Christ. They say that Christ had no advantage of His Godhead in His earthly life, but did everything as man; upheld, guided, and energized by the Holy Ghost. The work of the Holy Ghost, beginning with Pentecost, consists of glorifying Jesus through His body, the church, which is constantly in need of supernatural gifts, visions, and dreams if it would properly glorify Jesus.

Three sacraments — Baptism, Communion, and Sealing — are said to be absolutely necessary as the means to unite redeemed humanity with the body of Christ. The Eucharist is considered the center of all worship. "As the antitype of the priestly act of Melchizedek" it is observed as a sacrifice of praise by the "priests" for the congregation with a great deal of ritualism patterned after the daily sacrifice of the Old Testament. Tithing is part of the Eucharistic service. The holy Sealing, also called baptism with the Holy Ghost, or holy anointing, is the "dispensing and reception of the Holy Spirit, the bestowal of citizenship in the heavenly Jerusalem, the security of redemption and future glory," and cannot be received "through faith alone," but "only through the laying on of hands by 'the apostles.'"[6] According to the New Apostolic Church, the sacraments can be applied also to the dead who through no fault of their own could not come to the knowledge of the truth during their life. The theory is that the departed apostles continue the work of preaching which Christ began at His descent into hell. The departed are brought to the living apostles by the perfected saints and angels, and thus

---

[3] *Apostles or Not?* pp. 11, 24, 48.

[4] Ibid., p. 53.

[5] *The New Apostolic Office*, pp. 26, 24.

[6] Ibid., pp. 17, 19.

there is salvation after death if the living apostles can perform the sacraments on some living person as a substitute for the departed individual. Only the "apostles," who claim to be directly called by the Holy Ghost, have the Office of the Keys and the power to forgive sins. It is their exclusive right and duty to supply the several congregations with bishops, priests, and deacons, the agents to convey God's grace and bring Christ's body to the stature of His fullness. The Irvingites are strict millennialists and believe themselves to be the 144,000 (Rev. 14:1-5), who are sealed with the Holy Ghost.

The fact that the Lord did not return during the lifetime of the "twelve apostles" greatly disturbed the Irvingites. The last of the divinely chosen "apostles" died in 1901. Some attributed the nonappearance of Christ to the fact that these "apostles" were unable to prepare the church, even as the first apostles did not succeed in preparing the church for Christ's second coming. Others maintain that the deceased apostles continue their activities in behalf of the church, and they are awaiting further direction from the Lord.

New Apostolic Church of North America. The origin and early history of this German branch of the Catholic Apostolic Church is identical with that of the parent body in England. The division arose when in 1862 Bishop Schwarz of Hamburg asserted that the Spirit appointed a priest named Preuss as an additional apostle. While the original body teaches that no new apostles have been called since about 1840, the New Apostolic Church believes that as there were more than twelve apostles in the first church, e. g., Paul, Barnabas, so there may also be more than twelve apostles in the end dispensation. The chief apostle *(Stammapostel)* is considered the visible head of the church on earth. His importance to the present church is said to be far greater than that of the first apostles. Indeed, his work for the church is virtually placed on a par with Christ's.

The group developed a great activity in Germany, where its headquarters are at Frankfurt-am-Main. It has established itself also in American cities with a large German population. Its doctrines are essentially those of the parent body.

BIBLIOGRAPHY

PART VIII

SECTION II

Andrews, W. W., in Ph. Schaff, *Creeds of Christendom.* (See P. II, Bibliog.)

Apostles or Not in the 20th Century? Chicago, 1930.

Miller, Edward. *The History and Doctrines of Irvingism.* London: C. K. Paul and Co., 1878.

New Apostolic Office. Chicago, 1930.

Oliphant, Mrs. M. O. W. *The Life of E. Irving.* London, 1865.

Shaw, P. E. *The Catholic Apostolic Church, Sometimes Called Irvingite, A Historical Study.* New York: King's Crown Press.

SECTION III

Adventism

The Adventists seem to regard struggle, a continuous *apokalyptisches Wetterleuchten,* as the basic cosmic principle, and to believe that the history of mankind will end with the victory of the forces of good over the forces of evil, culminating in the liberation of the disinherited and in the final punishment of their oppressors.[1] Adventism usually assumes that when society will have reached the depth of moral decline, a divine cataclysm will put an end to the wickedness of the world, and Christ will establish a kingdom of righteousness on this earth. There have been several great outbursts of apocalypticism, or Adventism, notably Montanism, the Anabaptist movements of the Reformation, and the several Adventist movements at the beginning of the 19th century.[2]

Time setting is frequently a concomitant of Adventism. Modern time setters usually argue that since the exact date of important catastrophes has been foretold, it is only reasonable to assume that the date of the greatest and the final cataclysm has also been prophesied in the Scriptures.[3] This type of thinking is represented most fully in the several Adventist bodies. In other Adventist bodies, e. g., Jehovah's witnesses, Adventism is so completely overshadowed by other points of emphasis that they must be treated in separate sections.

THE HISTORY

The most significant Adventist movement of the nineteenth century was initiated by William Miller (1782 to 1849), a farmer of Low Hampton, N. Y. After his conversion in 1816 he became a licensed Baptist preacher and devoted himself diligently to the study of the Bible, particularly to its apocalyptic and prophetic sections. From these he said he had learned that the millennium would be established at a relatively early date. On the basis of his computations he ventured even to predict the exact date of Christ's second coming. Miller held that the cleansing of the sanctuary (Dan. 8:13, 14) is prophetic language describing Christ's second advent. He held that the Temple, i. e., the earth, would be desecrated for 2,300 days, which, according to Num. 14:34, denote so many years. He arrived at the following computation:

The desolation of the Holy Place was to continue for 2,300 "prophetic days," or 2,300 years. The *terminus a quo* of this period is 457 B. C., when the commandment to rebuild Jerusalem was given (Dan. 9:24, 25). 2300 − 457 = 1843. Therefore the end of the desolation and the cleansing of the sanctuary, i. e., Christ's advent, would occur "between March 21, 1843, and March 21,

---

[1] Cp. Clark, *Small Sects,* ch. ii.

[2] "Millennium" in *New Schaff-Herzog Encyc.,* III, 374—78. As to views of the S. D. A., see Froom, *The Prophetic Faith of Our Fathers,* Vol. IV.

[3] E. g., the Flood, 120 years (Gen. 6:3); the destruction of Pharaoh's host in the Red Sea after Israel's bondage (Gen. 16:15, 16; Ex. 13:40); the complete overthrow of the Canaanites at the end of Israel's 40 years' wandering (Num. 14:33); the death of Christ at the conclusion of seventy weeks (Dan. 9:24). Graebner, *Prophecy,* pp. 38 ff., 46 ff. Cp. Sec. I, above.

1844." Miller predicated his computation on the correctness of the date 457 B. C., his *terminus a quo*. He said that the 69 weeks (483 "days," i. e., years) and the 70 weeks (490 "days," or years) of Dan. 9:24, 25 support the date 457 B. C., inasmuch as they refer respectively to Christ's baptism, A. D. 26–27, and Saul's conversion in A. D. 33–34. Christ's death occurred in the midst of the seventieth week, i. e., three and a half "days," or years, before Saul's conversion. Subtracting the 26 from 483, or 33 from the 490, one arrives at 457 B. C., the year in which, according to Ezra 7:11-26, the king issued the command to rebuild Jerusalem.[4]

In 1831 Miller began to lecture in the interest of his Adventism and time setting, and he is said to have gained at least 50,000 followers from various Protestant denominations. No attempt was made to organize this interchurch movement into a denomination. When the dates passed without the expected event taking place, Miller expressed his sincere disappointment, and there was great dismay in the ranks of the Adventists. However, at a camp meeting at Exeter, N. H., a number of leading Adventists advanced the theory that the "midnight cry" of Matt. 25:6, 7 shows that a delay in the coming of the Bridegroom was to be expected. This delay was due to a miscalculation on Miller's part, who had failed to observe that the commandment to rebuild Jerusalem was issued after the seventh month of 457 B. C. and that, according to the Jewish calendar, the 2,300 years would be accomplished October 22, 1844. The enthusiasm and religious fervor reached even greater heights than previously.[5]

After this second disappointment the majority renounced the Adventist faith and returned to their respective churches. Some of the leading Adventists, however, believed that though the computation of the "2,300 days" had been correct, the description of the nature of the event had been false. Hiram Edson and O. R. L. Cozier stated that according to Heb. 8:1, 2 the sanctuary spoken of in Dan. 8:13, 14 is in heaven and not on the earth, as Miller had assumed. This new interpretation temporarily rallied the Adventist group. But gradually basically divergent opinions concerning the Sabbath and the immortality of the soul caused several divisions. Of these the most significant is the one which led to the organization of the Seventh-day Adventists.[6]

The Seventh-day Adventists

A group of Miller's followers, under the leadership of Joseph Bates, James White, and his wife, Ellen G. White, at first were stanch supporters of William Miller's views.[7]

During the morning devotions in a home of a friend in Portland, Maine, Mrs. White, as she averred, had a vision which vindicated the discredited Adventists. She saw a narrow path lead-

---

[4] Loughborough, ch. iii.

[5] There is no foundation for the fanciful stories that the followers of Miller had prepared "ascension robes," nor for the alleged cases of insanity and suicide as a result of the bitter disappointment. Francis D. Nichol, "The Seventh-day Adventists" in *Encyc. Brit.;* same author, "The Growth of the Millerite Legend," *Church History,* XXI (1952), 296—313.

[6] Loughborough, ch. v. For a more recent parallel, see Leon Festinger, Henry W. Riecken and Stanley Schachter, *When Prophecy Fails* (Minneapolis: University of Minnesota Press, c. 1956).

[7] Ellen G. White, nee Harmon, of Portland, Maine (1827—1915), reportedly had visions and revelations from the age of 17 throughout her life. As a result her followers consider her voluminous writings as quasi-inspired.

ing to the heavenly Jerusalem. Only Adventists were walking on this path, guided by an angel and admonished by him to keep their eyes fixed upon Jesus. This allegedly cheering vision left Mrs. White totally exhausted, just as Daniel had no strength left after his vision (Dan. 10:8, 17-19). In another vision Mrs. White saw the significance of the messages of the three angels in Rev. 14:6 ff., especially of the third angel. The essence of this revelation was three-fold: (1) the hour of God's judgment had come in 1843–44; (2) Babylon, that wicked city, fell when the Adventists left the regular denominations; (3) a warning is issued against worshiping the beast, the Antichrist, who introduced Sunday in place of the Sabbath (Dan. 7:25). Mrs. White held that it was the duty of the Seventh-day Adventists to announce to the nations the impending doom proclaimed by the third angel, to warn against worshiping the beast and his image, to impress on all their obligation to observe the commandments of God, particularly the Sabbath.

Throughout their history the adherents of Mrs. White have featured their twin message: observance of the seventh day and the imminence of Christ's second coming. This intimate relation between these two proclamations is said to explain the name the Seventh-day Adventists adopted in 1860. In order to propagate their witnessing work more effectively they organized the General Conference, with headquarters at Battle Creek, Mich., in 1863. Since 1903 their headquarters have been at Takoma Park, a suburb of Washington, D. C. The Seventh-day Adventists (frequently abbreviated as S. D. A.) have developed an activity that is out of proportion to their numerical strength. They conduct mission work in virtually all parts of the world; are engaged in a tremendous publication program; support a large educational system on the elementary, secondary, and collegiate levels. The funds for this extensive program of church work are provided by a tithe, generously supplemented with freewill offerings.

THE THEOLOGICAL PRINCIPLES

The Seventh-day Adventists are non-creedal. The Statement of Faith, published annually in their *Yearbook*, is affirmed to be based entirely on the Bible. Individuals may therefore hold varying theological views.[8] But they are all agreed on the formal and material principles of their theology. The formal principle, i. e., the source of religious truth, is said to be the Scriptures alone. Seventh-day Adventists seem to be the most fundamental of fundamentalists in their extreme literalism. The reason for their refusal to accept creeds is that "the Bible contains a sufficient rule for faith, morals, and practices." But they also maintain that the truth of the Gospel is "a growing, dynamic thing that must not be shackled by the cold formularies of men."[9] It is rather difficult to harmonize these two views. It is still more difficult to reconcile their teaching that "the Bible contains an all-sufficient revelation of God's will to men" with their assertion that "the gift of prophecy together with other gifts of the Spirit should be manifested in the Church in every age." They believe, for instance, that Mrs. White possessed the gift of prophecy and received messages of instruction for the church from time to time by the direct

---

[8] Guenther, pp. 130, 134 (cp. Index, p. 449, for complete list of references). Cp. *What Do Seventh-Day Adventists Believe?* Reprinted in *C. T. M.*, IV (1933), 212 ff.

[9] A. L. Baker, an Adventist leader, in Julius A. Weber, *Religions and Philosophies in the U. S.* (Los Angeles: Wetzel Publ. C., 1931), p. 144.

inspiration of the Holy Spirit.[10] Mrs. White evidently was an "enthusiast," i. e., she held the theory of the immediacy of the Spirit's revelation. She believed that while in the Word we have clearer lines of the great work of atonement, yet the listening ear can hear and understand the communications of God through the things of nature. The same author declared that even the heathen not only have heard God's voice in nature, but also have been touched by the Holy Ghost and are recognized as God's children.[11]

In view of this notion one is constrained to ask why these Adventists uphold the verbal inspiration of the Bible. The answer seems to be in accord with the central thought of their theology, summarized in the message of the three angels of Rev. 14:6 ff. They believe that the purpose of the Bible is to tell us

> how sin began and how it will finish. It tells us how the world was created by the fiat of the Almighty and how it will end, because of sin, in flaming destruction; thereafter to be re-created in its pristine beauty to become the home of the redeemed throughout the ages to come. . . . This (Dan. 2:44) is one of the passages of Scripture which so greatly move the soul of Seventh-Day Adventists; for it emphasizes with dramatic forcefulness the leadership of God in human affairs, His lordship of the nations, His knowledge of the course of history, and the certainty of His ultimate triumph over all the forces of evil.[12]

The doctrine of verbal inspiration enables them to interpret the prophecies in a very literal sense, especially the prophecies in Daniel and Revelation, which tell with dramatic forcefulness

that God will assume leadership in human affairs and will ultimately triumph over all the forces of evil. Their approach to the Bible is determined very largely by their central theological principle: loyalty to the Ten Commandments, especially to the "Fourth" Commandment to keep holy the Sabbath. They affirm that when they understood that the keeping of the Sabbath was mandatory upon all generations, the Bible became a new book to them. Now they see truth in it, they say, which previously had been hidden to them. Likewise the belief in a reappearance or millennial coming of Christ has deeply influenced their attitude toward Holy Scripture. These two doctrines constitute the theology of the Seventh-day Adventists. In reality, the material principle of their theology is legalism, for their two chief doctrines have changed the Gospel message into Law and erased the distinction between Law and Gospel. "In the Law is embodied the same principle as in the Gospel." In other words, the Gospel is in essence the message that Christ has shown that true religion does not consist in systems, rites, or creeds, but in "genuine goodness" and that He is holding the investigative judgment according to the "Ten Principles."[13] It is true that the Adventist publications abound in statements which beautifully set forth the vicarious atonement of Christ and the saving function of faith. One writer states:

> Crowning His revelation of the love of God, Jesus went at last to the cross. There, as the one perfect Representative of the race, His divine and human natures inseparably blended, having throughout His earthly life lived in blameless obedience to His own eter-

---

10 H. E. Rogers, *Census*, II, 24.

11 White, *Steps*, pp. 89, 92; *Desire*, p. 638.

12 Maxwell, loc. cit.

13 White, *Desire*, pp. 497, 608.

nal law of righteousness, He offered up a complete, perfect, and all-sufficient sacrifice for the sins of men.[14]

But such statements must be read in the context of Adventist theology. In evangelical terminology faith is understood to be the means whereby believers appropriate Christ's substitutionary redemption. Adventists say that faith takes hold of Christ's divine power, "inducting the believing into the covenant relationship where the Law of God is written on his heart, and through the enabling power of the indwelling Christ his life is brought into conformity with the divine precepts." [15]

The believer's mystical union with Christ is said to result in man's moral transformation. Mrs. White declares that Christ's work consisted first and foremost in showing that man could keep the Law of God, for "Christ came to reshape the sin-marred character of man after the pattern of His divine character and to make it beautiful with His own glory." [16]

This legalistic spirit of Adventism manifests itself in the two distinctive tenets of Seventh-day Adventism — the permanent obligation of the Sabbath law and the imminent return of Christ. These two doctrines they find in the third angel's message, and for its proclamation they believe themselves to have been raised by God.

They [the early Adventists] saw the law of God in its true relation to the Gospel; they heard the challenge to preach "the commandments of God, and the faith of Jesus" to all the world. . . . In 1844 the Sabbath truth, long trodden under foot, was raised to its proper place, and, with the advent truth [Christ's imminent return] marched into all the world! [17]

THE SABBATH LAW

In Mrs. White's theology the observance of the seventh day was the heart of God's message to man. She supported this doctrine with alleged visions. In one she saw Jesus raising the lid of the ark in the heavenly sanctuary and displaying a heavenly counterpart of Moses' two tables. The "Fourth" Commandment was surrounded by a halo indicating its superiority over the other commandments.[18]

In support of this view the Seventh-day Adventists adduce Ex. 31:12, 13 and Ezek. 20:12, 20, where the Sabbath is called God's seal, and call the Sabbath a device by which God indicates His ownership. According to Rev. 7:2, 3, God will place His seal upon the forehead of His servants, which means, say the Seventh-day Adventists, they that keep the Sabbath. But the beast, Rev. 14:9 ff., will attempt to put his seal on those who ultimately will be tormented. The seal of the beast, according to Dan. 7:25, is the change from the Sabbath to Sunday. For the Seventh-day Adventists life's most important issue is the correct

---

[14] Maxwell, p. 19.

[15] *Fundamental Beliefs*, p. 8.

[16] White, *Desire*, pp. 38 ff., 296, 308, 458, 763, 310, 123, 604; *Steps*, pp. 11, 26, 68, and *passim*.

[17] Maxwell, p. 87; White, *Desire*, ch. xxix.

[18] In their enthusiasm to elevate the Sabbath Law above every other commandment some have gone as far as to say that Jerusalem is the center of the only true divine worship; the Temple is the center of Jerusalem; the Law is the center of the Temple; and the Sabbath is the center of the Law. In support of this assertion they say that of 497 words which make up the Decalog in its English form (A. V.) the word "is" of the Sabbath commandment ("This *is* the Sabbath of the Lord") is the 249th word, or exactly in the center of the Decalog. Cp. Milton C. Wilcox, *The Lord's Day*, p. 28.

choice between acceptance of God's seal (Sabbath) or the beast's sign (Sunday). The Sabbath is said to be God's seal that He is the Creator of the universe and Christ's sign that He has power to save in the new creation. On the other hand, keeping the Sabbath is man's sign to accept God's work to save man from sin through Christ.[19] Those who insist on observing the Sunday thereby indicate their allegiance to the beast, the express opponent of God. The beast of Dan. 7:25, which changes times, is said to be none other than the pope.[20]

Adventists believe that they have been raised for the express purpose of proclaiming that God requires all men to observe the Sabbath. The Sabbath has become a major *raison d'être*, a justification for their existence.[21] Their arguments for the universally binding character of the Sabbath law revolve about three points: (1) it is part of the moral law, (2) was given at the creation, and (3) was not abrogated in the New Testament.

They hold that the Sabbath is a part of the moral law and is therefore universally binding. They argue as follows: The Sabbath commandment is part of the Decalog; the Decalog is the Law of God; God's Law is true; therefore heaven and earth shall pass away, but God's Law can never pass away (Matt. 5: 17-19). To be consistent, the Seventh-day Adventists, in conformity with the

"Second Commandment," should discontinue the elaborate use of religious paintings in their publications. There is no Scripture nor other evidence that the commandment to worship on the exact seventh day of the week — or even one day out of seven — is part of the universal moral law. The counterargument that the ancient pagan nations worshiped the sun is not valid, since the pagan sun worshipers did not observe one day out of seven — a basic demand of the Sabbath law. Furthermore, the commandment to observe the Sabbath Day does not flow from the holiness of God nor from love of our neighbor as do other commandments. After all, Christians observe this commandment, not by resting from labor one day in seven, but by sanctifying every day through the Word of God and by giving their servants an opportunity for the needed bodily rest.[22]

The Sabbath law is said to be universally binding, secondly, because it was instituted at the creation of the world and concerns all men. The Seventh-day Adventists argue that by resting on the first seventh day of time the Lord instituted the Sabbath and now demands that men observe each succeeding seventh day. It is, of course, very doubtful whether there has been an exact sequence of seven-day or 168-hour cycles since Creation. Joshua's "long day" would somehow have to be accounted

---

[19] John L. Shuler, *The Seal of God and the Mark of the Beast.* (Tract 33)

[20] In their literature they have vehemently attacked the Roman church, but only because in their opinion Sunday was established by this church. They completely by-pass such unscriptural innovations of the Roman church as are based solely upon "tradition." That the papacy is the beast of Dan. 7:25 is said to be clearly revealed in Rev. 13:17, 18, where the number (name) of the beast is given as 666. They arrive at this number thus: The pope allegedly calls himself *Vicarius Filii Dei.* The Latin letters I, V, L, C, D have the numerical values 1, 5, 50, 100, 500. The letters in the Pontiff's title (V, I, C, I, V, I, L, I, I, D, I) total 666.

[21] White, *Desire,* ch. xxix. The modern Adventists have published much literature on the Sabbath question.

[22] See Luther's exposition of the Third Com. in the Large C.

for, likewise the international dateline. These objections are dismissed with the statement that God is just and that since He gave the Sabbath law, He has also preserved unbroken the cycle of seven days so that each recurring Sabbath is in a perfect multiple of seven days since the first Sabbath at the end of the creation week.

The Seventh-day Adventists are vehemently opposed to the almost universally accepted and Scriptural thesis that the Sabbath in its ceremonial aspects was given only to the Jews. From the Sacred Record it is apparent that the Sabbath was unknown to the Jews before God gave the Decalog on Mount Sinai (Ex. 16:21 ff.); that the observance of the Sabbath was to remind Israel of God's creation (Lev. 23:2, 3) and especially of their deliverance from bondage in the land of Egypt (Deut. 5:15); that God made His covenant only with Israel as His peculiar and distinct people (Ex. 31:13; Ezek. 20:12, 20). The Jewish Sabbath was in reality a figure, or symbol, to remind Israel of the coming of the Messiah (Col. 2:16, 17). When Christ came, the figure foreshadowing His coming was no longer necessary. To continue the observance of the Sabbath as did the Jews is tantamount to a denial that Christ has already come to free us from the demands, threats, and dominion of the Law. If the Sabbath law is universally binding, then the penalty for transgression, death by stoning, is also universally applicable.

The Seventh-day Adventists argue in the third place that Christ and the apostles observed the Sabbath and that its abrogation and the substitution of the Sunday for the Sabbath is the work of the Antichrist, the beast, the papacy. The facts are that Christ and the apostles restate all Commandments of the Decalog except the Sabbath law; and that the early Christian church, long before the rise of the papacy, observed the Sunday and not the Sabbath.[23]

The Seventh-day Adventists resemble the Judaizing teachers of St. Paul's day who were determined to subjugate the Gentile Christians to the Mosaic law of circumcision and observing Jewish festivals, the Sabbath in particular. The Seventh-day Adventists hold that the Ten Commandments, as given on Mount Sinai, govern the entire universe and embrace the whole duty of man. They believe that Is. 58:13, 14 must be taken literally and that if observed literally, it will also literally bring the blessings of happiness and prosperity promised by Isaiah to all who keep the correct "seventh day," the Sabbath, from Friday evening until Saturday evening.[24] In the interest of their legalistic theology they employ an approach to the Scriptures entirely different from that of evangelical Christians, who make the most of the Christian liberty so beautifully described by St. Paul in Galatians.[25] Christ's claim of Lordship over the Sabbath (Matt. 12:8), which evangelical Christians have understood in the light of Col. 2:16, 17 and Gal. 4:10, 11, is said by the Adventists to establish the continuance rather than the abrogation of the Sabbath. They say that through the

---

[23] Cp. Justin Martyr, "Dialogue with Trypho," *Ante-Nicene Fathers,* ed. Roberts and Donaldson (New York: Christian Literature Co., 1896), I, 203 ff.; the Epistle of Barnabas, ibid., I, 146—47; and Tertullian "Against Marcion," ibid., III, 362 ff.; IV, 112. Cp. Schaff, *History,* I, 478 f.

[24] Maxwell, p. 56 f., White, *Desire,* p. 289.

[25] St. Paul shows that the "gospel" of the Judaizers is inferior to the Gospel of Christ (2 Cor. 3:7-11); in fact, is no Gospel at all. Cp. Gal. 3:17-22; 4:8-11. He calls the compulsory observance of specific days "beggarly elements" (Gal. 4:9).

Sabbath Christ established Himself as Lord inasmuch as the Sabbath observance recognizes Him as the Creator, the Reconciler, and the Head of the church. His followers, on the other hand, by keeping the Sabbath are sanctified and made a part of Israel.[26]

A legalistic spirit permeates the entire Adventist theology. They hold that in the Law is embodied the same principle as in the Gospel, that religion does not consist in systems, rites, or creeds, but in genuine goodness, that man must punctiliously observe the Old Testament laws and regulations.[27] The Old Testament tithing system is made mandatory for all Adventists; in fact, they go beyond the Old Testament tithing laws. They insist that their members dress in modest and dignified apparel, partly because they do not want to conform to the world in any way and partly because they believe that their bodies are temples of the Holy Ghost. This belief, moreover, prompts them not only to abstain from intoxicant drink, tobacco, and all forms of narcotics, but also to observe the dietary laws of the Old Testament. Seventh-day Adventists are not strict vegetarians. It is somewhat difficult to determine whether the dietary laws of the Adventists are based upon the Old Testament prescriptions or on the theory that healing can be accomplished through correct dieting. At any rate, dieting has become one of the chief characteristics of Seventh-day Adventism.[28]

Legalism inevitably leads to perfectionism. Adventists believe that the basic purpose of the plan of salvation is to deliver man from the penalty and power of sin and to restore within him the Law of the image of his Maker. This statement is, of course, truly evangelical, unless it is understood to mean that the purity of the church consists primarily in righteousness of its members and not in the holy perfection which Christ won for sinners by His holy life and innocent death and which faith appropriates.[29]

CHRIST'S IMMINENT RETURN

The second great message for the proclamation of which the Adventists believe themselves raised up by God is the second coming of Christ. In connection with this message they have developed a peculiar eschatology which comprises a number of rather unique and singular ideas.

They maintain first that Christ must cleanse the sanctuary before He can come again. The Adventists are convinced that Christ began the cleansing of the sanctuary in 1844, the year which Miller had identified correctly, though he was mistaken as to the nature of the "cleansing of the sanctuary." On the basis of an alleged vision of Ellen White the Seventh-day Adventists maintain that the cleansing of the sanctuary is taking place in heaven and that it consists in Christ's investigative judgment. The standard by which He is said to judge is the Decalog, particularly the "Fourth" Commandment. It is a fundamental belief of Seventh-day Adventists that

the true sanctuary, of which the tabernacle on earth was a type, is the temple of God in heaven, of which Paul speaks in Hebrews 8 and onward, and of which

---

[26] White, *Desire*, p. 288.

[27] Ibid., pp. 608, 497.

[28] See Baker in Weber (fn. 9, *supra*), p. 139; White, *Ministry*, loc. cit. Adventists believe that proper dieting is essential for healing and that healing is a complementary function of the Gospel. In the many Adventist sanatoria all patients must submit to their principles of dieting.

[29] Maxwell, pp. 60, 63.

the Lord Jesus, as our great High Priest, is minister; and that the priestly work of our Lord is the antitype of the work of the Jewish priests of the former dispensation; that this heavenly sanctuary is the one to be cleansed at the end of the 2,300 days of Dan. 8:14; its cleansing being as in the type, a work of judgment, beginning with the entrance of Christ as the High Priest upon the judgment phase of His ministry in the heavenly sanctuary foreshadowed in the earthly service of cleansing the sanctuary on the Day of Atonement. This work of judgment in the heavenly sanctuary began in 1844. Its completion will close human probation.[30]

During the cleansing of the sanctuary the Adventists are to proclaim the message of the three angels (Rev. 14:6 ff.) and thereby to prepare the world for the second coming of Christ.[31] The Adventist theory concerning cleansing the sanctuary has very serious implications for the doctrine of Christ's work. It denies that Christ's death on the cross is the complete redemption from sin. The adherents of Mrs. White hold strange views with respect to Christ's atoning work. The ceremonies of the Great Day of Atonement are said to be antitypical of Christ's work from the first Good Friday until 1844. The Old Testament priests daily entered the Holy of the Temple to offer sacrifices and plead for pardon. Only once a year did the high priest enter the Holy of Holies, the sanctuary, with the blood of the first goat to sprinkle the mercy seat. Thereupon the high priest placed the sins of the people upon the second goat, the scapegoat, which was driven into the wilderness (Azazel) to symbolize that the sins for which the first goat had been sacrificed had been completely removed from the people (Lev. 16:1-10).[32] The Seventh-day Adventists say that on October 22, 1844, Christ, according to Heb. 8:1 ff., entered the Holy of Holies in the heavenly sanctuary to begin the "investigative" judgment of all men's conduct, especially as to their attitude toward the Decalog. Upon completion of this investigation Christ will come forth bringing the sins of the people with Him to place them upon Satan, the antitype of the goat for Azazel. As this goat was destroyed in the wilderness, so Satan, the tempter and the instigator of man's sin, and all the wicked will be annihilated, and with them the sins of the righteous will be forever destroyed. In conformity with the belief that the investigative judgment did not begin until 1844, and that its final result will not be made known until the second coming, Adventists hold that no man is judged at his death, but must await the judgment of his soul until the cleansing of the sanctuary is completed. Prior to this event the souls are neither in bliss nor in condemnation, but in a state of unconsciousness, a doctrine known as soul sleep, or psychopannychism.[33] Related to the theory of the soul sleep, but of

---

[30] *Fundamental Beliefs,* § 14. Mrs. White says that this investigative judgment takes place according to the Law, according to one's light and character (*Great Contr.,* chs. xxv and xxviii, esp. pp. 467 ff., 516).

[31] Some early Seventh-day Adventists advocated the so-called shut-door theory, teaching that those who failed to heed the Adventist message would have no opportunity for redemption. See D. M. Canright, p. 103 ff.

[32] Cp. A. Edersheim, *The Temple* (New York: James Patt, 1881), pp. 263—88.

[33] In reply to the statement that the malefactor on the cross (Luke 23:43) entered Paradise immediately, the Adventists declare the text in our English Bible is falsely punctuated and should read: "Verily, I say unto thee today: Thou, etc."; not: "Verily, I say unto thee: Today, etc."

much greater significance, is the theory that man's soul is mortal, that immortality and eternal life come only through the Gospel, and that they are bestowed upon believers only at the second coming of Christ. The Adventists insist that the doctrine of man's essential mortality is the only possible way to relieve God of the stigma of everlastingly torturing the wicked. They teach that all the wicked will be totally annihilated at the second coming of Christ. This doctrine that Christ has won immortality for believers is said to give full honor to Christ and His vicarious death.[34]

A second distinctive feature of their eschatology concerns the purpose of Christ's second coming. While they have abstained from predicting the exact time of the second advent, they nevertheless attempt to explain practically all current events as the literal fulfillment of some prophecy and as indicating the nearness of Christ's second coming, when the rulers of this world will have to yield their scepter to Jesus Christ and when, according to Dan. 7:27, the Most High will establish His kingdom.

The sequence of events at the second coming of Christ is described as follows: The voice of Christ will call forth from their graves the just of all the ages; the living righteous will be translated. At this point all the just, both the living and the resurrected, having been approved in the preceding investigative judgment, will ascend with Jesus to heaven to receive their reward and will spend 1,000 years with Christ in heaven. The living unjust will be consumed and destroyed by the glory of Christ's coming. The earth will be desolate and uninhabited for 1,000 years, except for Satan, who will bear the sins of men on this uninhabited earth during the millennium.

At the end of the millennial period Christ will descend to the earth for the "second resurrection," when He will raise and judge the wicked dead. Under the leadership of Satan these will assault the Lord and the holy city, but final judgment will be pronounced upon them, and they together with Satan, the "sin-bearer," will be totally annihilated through a consuming fire. In this fire the earth will be regenerated and purified from the effect of Satan's curse. The purified and regenerated earth then becomes the eternal home of the redeemed. In this home there is to be no pain, no sin, and every creature will give praise to God.[35]

In taking this position, Seventh-day Adventists feel that they are not simply one more cult or sect among many but that they are the contemporary counterparts of the medieval dissenters, such as the Waldenses, the Wycliffites, and the Hussites. They also claim the Reformers, as well as the Baptists and the Wesleyans, as their spiritual ancestors, but hold that the sixteenth-century Reformation was "arrested" and needs to be completed by a total repudiation of all the innovations and departures from what they regard as apostolic faith and practice.

The Local Church. In its government the Seventh-day Adventist local

---

[34] See Baker, p. 144 (cp. fn. 9, 28).

[35] See *Fundamental Beliefs*, pars. 20—22; *Census*, II, 28. White, *Great Contr.*, p. 658. Jehovah's witnesses resemble the Adventists on some points, and the millennial events as taught by these two groups are sometimes mistakenly regarded as identical. It seems that the millennial views of the Adventists are more closely related to premillennialism, while those of Jehovah's witnesses are starkly mundane. Many Adventists believe that this earth in its purified and perfected state will be man's future home; others present the future world in terminology which would seem to point to a heaven distinct from this world.

church is congregational and usually supervised by one or more elders. In larger city congregations the charge is committed to a pastor. The main effort is directed toward the development of new churches and the establishment of missions in foreign lands. Members are received upon baptism by immersion, upon giving the pledge to keep the Sabbath, to obey the dietary laws, and to eschew tobacco and liquor. They observe the custom of footwashing prior to the celebration of the Lord's Supper. The Seventh-day Adventists insist on absolute separation of church and state. Seventh-day Adventists interpret the "Sixth" Commandment to forbid participation in war. Nevertheless they have been very active in alleviating the suffering incident to war.

Other Adventist Bodies

The Advent Christian Church. The prediction of Jonathan Cummings that Christ would return in 1853–54 aroused the criticism of the majority of the Millerites, who after the sad experiences in 1844 had given up the attempt of fixing the date of Christ's return. It was hoped that when Cummings' prophecy had proved false, the rift would be healed. But by this time his belief in the mortality of the world and the extinction of the wicked had definitely fixed a breach between his followers and the original Millerites. His doctrines are essentially the same as those of the Seventh-day Adventists, except that he taught that Sunday must be observed instead of the Jewish Sabbath. In 1855 Cummings organized the Advent Christian Church, whose distinctive doctrines include the following: Man was created

for immortality, but through sin forfeited his birthright. All the dead are unconscious. The righteous are to receive immortality and the unrighteous to suffer complete extinction at Christ's second coming. Salvation is free to all who in this life accept it, on the condition that they turn from sin, repent, believe, and consecrate themselves. At Christ's second coming sin will be abolished in this world. The earth will become the home of the redeemed.[36]

The Church of God (Adventist) agrees essentially with the Seventh-day Adventists, except that Mrs. White is not recognized as a prophetess and no church name is considered permissible save "Church of God." [37]

The Life and Advent Union, a very small body, is closely related to the Advent Christian Church, differing only on minor eschatological questions, e. g., the wicked dead shall not be raised at all; Christ's second coming is near, since the millennium — a period of religious persecution — is already past.

The Church of God of the Abrahamic Faith represents a merger of the former Brethren of the Abrahamic Faith, Restitutionist, Age-to-Come Adventists, and similar associations. They differ from the other Adventists in believing that the kingdom of God will be established with Jerusalem as its capital, the believers to be joint rulers with Christ.

The Primitive Advent Christian Church is a small body which developed out of the Advent Christian Church.

The United Seventh Day Brethren is a very small body resulting from the merger in 1947 of two independent Sabbatarian premillennial churches.

---

[36] *Declaration of Principles,* 1900.

[37] The doctrines are set forth in forty articles in the tract "What the Church of God Believes and Why" (Stanberry, Mo.).

BIBLIOGRAPHY

PART VIII

SECTION III

Bird, Herbert S. *Theology of Seventh-day Adventism.* Grand Rapids: Wm. B. Eerdmans Publishing Co., 1961. A conservative Protestant appraisal.

Brueggemann, H. C. *The Seventh-Day Adventists* (tract). St. Louis: C. P. H., 1951.

Canright, D. M. *The Life of E. G. White.* Cincinnati: Standard Publ. Co., 1919. — A critical evaluation of the entire movement by a former adherent.

Davies, Horton. *Christian Deviations.* New York: Philosophical Library, 1954. Chapter v.

Froom, Le Roy E. *The Prophetic Faith of Our Fathers,* 1946—1954. Four vols.[38]

———. "Seventh-day Adventists," in Vergilius Ferm, ed. *The American Church of the Protestant Heritage.* New York: Philosophical Library, 1953. Pp. 371—86.

Herndon, Booton. *The Seventh Day: The Story of the Seventh-day Adventists.* New York: McGraw-Hill Book Co., c. 1960.

Jemison, T. H. *Christian Beliefs: Fundamental Biblical Teachings for Seventh-day Adventist College Classes.* Mountain View, Calif.: Pacific Press Publishing Association, c. 1959.

Life and Health (a monthly health journal).[38]

Loughborough, J. N. *Rise and Progress of Seventh-Day Adventists.*[38]

Martin, Walter R. *The Truth About Seventh-day Adventism.* Grand Rapids: Zondervan Publishing House, 1960.

Maxwell, A. S. *Your Friends, the Seventh-Day Adventists.*[38]

Mitchell, David. *Seventh-day Adventists.* New York: Vantage Press, 1958.

Nichol, F. D. *Ellen G. White and Her Critics,* 1951.[38]

Review and Herald (a weekly).[38]

Seboldt, Roland H. A. *What Is Seventh-day Adventism?* St. Louis: Concordia Publishing House, c. 1959.

Seventh-day Adventists Answer Questions on Doctrine: An Explanation of Certain Major Aspects of Seventh-day Adventist Belief.[38]

Signs of the Times ("interpretation of current events in the light of prophecy").[38]

White, Ellen G. *The Great Controversy Between Christ and Satan.*[38]

———. *The Desire of Ages.*[38]

———. *The Ministry of Healing.*[38]

———. *Steps to Christ.*[38]

SECTION IV

Communistic Millennial Bodies

United Society of Believers (Shakers)

The Shaker Society is in part an outgrowth of the fanatical preaching of the Camisards, or the "French prophets," who advocated spiritualism and asceticism. More directly it grew out of a Quaker revival under Jane Wardley in Manchester, England. The parents of Ann Lee were among the first converts of these "Shaking Quakers." Claiming a di-

[38] Published by the Review and Herald Publ. Assn., Takoma Park, Washington, D. C.

vine commission, Ann Lee and a small group immigrated to America in 1774 and settled at Watervliet, near Albany, N. Y., in 1776. Joseph Meacham, a Baptist, became a convert to the doctrines of Ann Lee and in 1780 organized the first Shaker communistic society at New Lebanon, where a religious revival of a highly ecstatic nature, with many "prophecies" of Christ's immediate return, had taken place. Ann Lee, now known as "Mother" Lee, traveled extensively, trying to organize societies on the basis of her doctrines after the pattern of the communistic society of New Lebanon. She gained adherents in New York, Connecticut, and Massachusetts. In 1805 the activities of the society were extended to Kentucky, Ohio, and Indiana, and it is reported to have numbered 5,000 members at one time. In 1874 there were 58 groups, with about 2,500 souls, controlling 100,000 acres of land. In 1905 the society had dwindled to 1,000 members. In 1930 they claimed about 100 adult members and 40 boys and girls, and in 1950 only a handful remained. The Shaker movement, also known as Alethianism, is historically important for its own sake and for its influence in the development of spiritualism and theosophy. Through Ann Lee, considered by spiritualists one of the best mediums, the highest Spirit is said to have conveyed the most important message to mankind. "Mother Ann" initiated one of history's most successful experiments in religious communism and one lasting for over a century. The Shakers are well known for several further peculiarities. Their worship is highly ecstatic, consisting chiefly in singing and dancing and they say that they possess the gifts of speaking in tongues and of performing healings. An exami-

nation of their religious tenets reveals that they deny every specific Christian doctrine — the deity of Christ, the authority of Scriptures, the Trinity, the vicarious atonement, and the resurrection of the body.[1]

The underlying principle of Shakerism is a strange form of dualism. Ann Lee taught that since Adam and Eve as male and female are essentially made in the image of God, God must exist as the eternal Father and Mother. As such they are said to be the parents of all human and angelic beings, who of course necessarily then are also male and female. The dualism is extended even to the plant and mineral kingdoms.[2] The ideal human society is therefore a sort of socialism in which all constitute a spiritual family patterned after the natural family. Ann Lee advocated the complete equality of sexes in all departments of life. Though Ann Lee placed such great emphasis on the two sexes, she considered celibacy one of the basic requisites of a virtuous life. It was her belief that the root of all human depravity is the uncontrolled sexual relation originating from the "act of Adam and Eve in Paradise." Therefore

> the object of Shaker life is self-conquest, salvation from all wrongdoing, to be utterly rid of the carnal life and will. . . . It is to die to the corrupt, passionate animal life of the world that we may be resurrected in the pure and angelic societies. . . . The highest spiritual attainments can be acquired only by virgin chastity and continence and the total crucifixion of the passions and appetites of the carnal mind.[3]

Marriage is said to be at variance with the "spiritual life," and Shakers contend that only the children of the world will marry. The natural inclina-

---

[1] Evans.

[2] Ibid., p. 103. The theory of the duality of sexes in the deity is prominent in some theosophical cults.

[3] Hollister, p. 3.

tions created by God are considered so unholy that if "these lustful passions are not overcome in this world," they will increase in hell and actually constitute the torment of the damned. Where the "generating spirit" of God has created a new soul, there will be hatred of father, mother, etc., i. e., the procreative faculties and their results.[4]

Shakers believe that the history of the world is divided into four major cycles, each with its countless smaller cycles, with its own heaven and hell, and with its progressive revelation of the Deity. The first cycle is said to have reached its culmination under Noah, when the Deity revealed itself as the Spirit; the second, under Moses when God became known as Jehovah. The third cycle reached its culmination under Jesus, through whom the Christ was revealed. But since Jesus was a male, He could reveal only the Father. The last cycle reached its culmination when Ann Lee, whose spiritual parents were the male and female in Christ, revealed the Mother Spirit, or the love of Christ. Mother Ann, as the female counterpart of Jesus, the bride of Jesus (cp. Psalm 45), and the mother of all spiritual things, is worthy of the same honor as Jesus.

Indian Shakers

Genetically unrelated to the Ann Lee movement are two syncretistic groups among various American Indian tribes of the Pacific Northwest, each of which calls itself the *Indian Shaker Church* and claims to represent the continuation of a body organized in 1910 to perpetuate the teachings which a Skokomish Indian by the name of John Slocum, reportedly a baptized Roman Catholic, allegedly received from God in 1881

during the interim between his apparent death and resuscitation. The total membership is estimated at about 2,000. The polity of the church is episcopal.[5]

Christian Catholic Church

This body was founded at Chicago in 1896 by John Alexander Dowie, a Congregational preacher who had been ordained in Australia in 1871. He began to practice divine healing, came to America in 1881, and built Zion Tabernacle in Chicago in 1893. He assumed in 1901 the title "Elijah the Restorer" and in 1904 advanced to "First Apostle."

In 1899 the organization was established at Zion City, north of Chicago, as a communistic sect with a theocratic government, and conducted business enterprises which have had a value of millions. In 1906 Dowieism claimed 17 branches, 35 ministers, and 5,865 members. A missionary campaign in New York proved a failure and broke Dowie's influence. Accused of immorality and mismanagement of funds, he was deposed in 1906 and died in 1907. Wilbur Glenn Voliva, his son-in-law, became his successor. The movement has failed to spread, though a few missionaries are still at work. It teaches baptism by immersion, the millennium, tithing as an obligation, and abstinence from pork. The apostolate is regarded as a mark of the true church "throughout the Christian dispensation." The salvation of Jesus Christ eliminates sin from the spirit, from the soul, and from the body. In its later stages the cult advocated an extreme chiliasm, which included the setting of dates. Voliva, unlike Dowie, taught the plenary inspiration of the Bible but interpreted the Bible in a very literalistic way.

---

[4] Ibid., p. 15.

[5] H. G. Barnett, *Indian Shakers: A Messianic Cult of the Pacific Northwest* (Carbondale: Southern Illinois University Press, 1957), is a very complete study of the Indian Shaker movement.

The House of David

The House of David is a communal religious colony established by Benjamin Purnell in 1903 at Benton Harbor, Mich. Little is known of Purnell's activities prior to this time. In 1895 he professed to have received a revelation that he was the last of the seven messengers mentioned in Rev. 8:6; 11:15. Joanna Southcotte was alleged to be the first of them.[6] Purnell proclaimed that it was his mission to gather the 144,000 true Israelites, the remnant of the twelve tribes of Israel, 12,000 from each tribe, who alone had the promise of immortality of the body. Purnell said that man is endowed with body, soul, and spirit. Only those who are on the narrow way, the 144,000, will save their bodies, souls, and spirits, while those on the broad way save only their souls, which at the resurrection will be united with their spirits. At his first coming Christ procured salvation for the souls of Jews and Gentiles; but at the second coming, when the remnant, the 144,000, will be gathered together, Christ will provide for the resurrection and the immortality of their bodies.[7]

Purnell assumed that the glory of Christ's transfigured body consists in perfect immortality. The "bride of Christ," the 144,000, who alone are the sons of God, will be fashioned like the glorious body of Christ. The rest of mankind can at best become like angels and receive immortality only for the soul. Their bodies, according to Eccl. 12:7, will return to dust. Purnell denied the eternity of damnation on the as-sumption that *sheol* means annihilation. The 144,000 are obligated to keep the Law of Christ, especially two command-ments. The first is that the 144,000 must conform their bodies to Christ's body, Phil. 3:21. From Rev. 1:14 it is evident that Christ wore long hair. Paul's state-ment in 1 Cor. 11:4 is brushed aside with the explanation that St. Paul states ex-pressly that nature teaches man to cut his hair, and from Rom. 8:7 it is said to be clear that any teaching of nature is *eo ipso* false. The second chief com-mandment demands absolute vegetarian-ism. They hold that the Fifth (Sixth) and Seventh (Eighth) Commandments forbid all killing and every stealing of life (Gen. 1:29; 9:4, 5). They maintain further that since there is no death in the millennium (Rev. 21:4), there will be only vegetarians in God's perfected world.

Since its inception the colony has been on a communal, or communistic, basis. All converts turn their property over to the colony. In 1923 a number of disillusioned members brought suit to have their property restored to them. The ensuing litigation brought such im-moral practices to light as to shock the nation. Benjamin Purnell died at the height of the scandal.

Today the community continues on the original communal basis. A board of directors conducts the spiritual and temporal affairs. All converts turn their property over to this board and con-tribute their services without monetary compensation. According to its cata-log, the colony appears to be a success financially.

[6] Joanna Southcotte (1750—1814) made the startling announcement that as the bride of the Lamb, though already past sixty years of age, she had miraculously conceived the "Second Shiloh." The birth, however, failed to materialize.

[7] When Purnell died in 1927, his followers believed that he would be shortly resurrected, and his body, carefully embalmed, was exhibited for two years.

BIBLIOGRAPHY

PART VIII   SECTION IV

Andrews, Edward Deming. *The People Called Shakers: A Search for the Perfect Society.* New York: Oxford University Press, 1953.

Evans, F. W. *Compendium of Origin, History, Principles,* etc. 1853.

Hollister, A. G. *Mission of Alethian Believers.* 1899.

Melcher, Marguerite F. *The Shaker Adventure.* Princeton: Princeton Univ. Press, 1941.

Weber, Everett. *Escape to Utopia: The Communal Movement in America.* New York: Hastings House, 1959.

SECTION V

The Church of Jesus Christ of Latter-Day Saints

The Founding of Mormonism

Mormonism is never satisfied with doing things halfway. As a socio-religious experiment it established not merely a local colony but a great agricultural, industrial, and financial empire. Mormonism has gone beyond every other modern religious group as to the type and extent of its alleged revelations. Its priesthood is in a class by itself in regard to both its origin and its authority. The Mormons have a doctrinal system so peculiar and bizarre that it seems well-nigh incomprehensible; a secrecy in their temple rites so close that a non-Mormon — even an ordinary Mormon — cannot penetrate it; a zeal and bigotry for the spreading of Mormonism unmatched by any other denomination.

Joseph Smith (1805–1844), founder of Mormonism, reports that during a revival meeting in 1820 at Palmyra, N. Y., he was greatly disturbed by the interdenominational conflict between Methodists, Baptists, and Presbyterians, that upon his direct inquiry of God for guidance in selecting the true church, he was told by two transfigured persons not to unite with any church. Joseph Smith avers that three years later the angel Moroni in a vision informed him that he had been selected to translate *The Book of Mormon,* written in a strange language on golden plates hidden by Moroni over 1,000 years ago on Mount Cumorah, near Palmyra. But it was not until September 22, 1827, that Moroni instructed him to remove the plates and to begin the translation. Meantime several attempts were made, it was said, to force Smith to reveal the hiding place, but on pain of eternal destruction Smith was to show the plates to no one. With the mysterious spectacles Urim and Thummim, Smith and Oliver Cowdery undertook the translation and prepared copy for the printer. Both men purported to have received a vision in May, 1829, which ordained them as priests of Aaron. Shortly after this, Peter, James, and John, they said, bestowed upon Smith also the priesthood of Melchizedek. With the completion of *The Book of Mormon* and the re-establishment of the priesthood, Smith and five others on April 6, 1830, organized the Church of Christ under the immediate direction of the Holy Spirit, who guided them in their appointment of various officers.[1] The new church grew with surprising rapidity. The many doctrinal and organizational problems of the new church were settled by the special revelations given to Smith. The church established headquarters at Kirtland, Ohio, in 1831, as a socio-religious organization. But because of poor management the experiment proved to be a failure. Thereupon the majority of Smith's followers moved to Independence, Mo. Here, according to a revelation given to Joseph Smith, the Mormons were to build during the millennium a temple for Americans, and the Jews would erect a temple at Jerusalem for Europeans and Asiatics. A clash between the natives, "the Gentiles," and the Mormons was inevitable because of their revolutionary views on social questions, especially polygamy. As a result the Mormons were forced to leave Independence and established Nauvoo, Ill., which prospered tremendously and at one time was the largest city in Illinois. However, charges of polygamy, riot, and treason were preferred against Joseph Smith and his younger brother Hyrum.

During the trial at Carthage, Ill., both men were shot to death by a mob while imprisoned. Smith's early and unexpected death found the young organization without adequate leadership, and several divisions took place. Brigham Young, the president of the Apostles, was chosen as Smith's successor by the majority. Under his leadership most of the Mormons settled at Salt Lake City, where they established a socio-religious empire. Young deserves the title "empire builder." The beehive *(deseret)* has quite appropriately been chosen as the Mormon emblem.[2]

The Doctrinal System

THE MORMON PHILOSOPHY OF LIFE

The philosophical foundation of Mormonism is predicated on two basic premises: "First, the eternal existence of a living personal God and the preexistence and eternal duration of mankind as His literal offspring; and, second, the placing of man upon the earth as an embodied spirit to undergo the experiences of an intermediate probation." These basic premises seem to permeate all Mormon thinking and give the key to the peculiar tenets and practices of Mormonism.[3]

THE SOURCE OF DOCTRINE

There are few modern religious cults for the understanding of which the question concerning the source of doctrine is so vital as in Mormonism. This is due

---

[1] *The Prophet Joseph Smith Tells His Own Story,* a pamphlet published at Salt Lake City. G. B. Arbaugh brings rather conclusive proof that the new church was organized by Sidney Rigdon rather than by Joseph Smith.

[2] Cp. any good history of Mormonism, e. g., Fisher. On the Mormon economic experiments, see Leonard J. Arrington, *The Great Basin Kingdom* (Cambridge: Harvard University Press, 1958).

[3] James E. Talmage, quoted in Howells, p. 55. It is, of course, impossible to determine whether Smith developed his theological system with these basic premises in mind. In fact, it is more than likely that the original leaders of this church developed their thoughts gradually and that later leaders expanded and systematized them.

to the fact that Mormonism claims three sources of revelations: the Bible, *The Book of Mormon*, the progressive revelations.

Mormons say they accept the Bible as the Word of God so far as it is correctly translated.[4] They consider the Bible a record of the historical events that took place in the Eastern world.

Also *The Book of Mormon* is accepted as the Word of God and is said to be the record of the events that took place on the Western continent as they were recorded by Mormon and delivered to his son Moroni, who made the golden records in "Reformed Egyptian" hieroglyphics.[5] The first part of *The Book of Mormon* deals with the history of Jared's descendants, who supposedly came to America after the confusion of tongues at Babel. Owing to internecine warfare, these people became extinct about 600 B.C. But a certain Ether recorded their history on 24 golden plates and hid them. These were later found by Moroni. The second portion of *The Book of Mormon* purports to record the history of Lehi and his family, who emigrated from Jerusalem to America about 600 B.C., the time the Jaredites disappeared. The descendants of his son Nephi were pious, built large cities, and developed a very highly advanced culture. According to *The Book of Mormon* Jesus appeared among the Nephites after His ascension, established the church among them, and inaugurated the golden age of the Nephites. The descendants of Laman, however, were wicked, insisted on walking in the nude, and ultimately became Indians. In the struggle between the two races the Nephites became extinct about A. D. 385; however, not before Moroni had completed the work of his father Mormon in recording all the events that had taken place on the Western continent.[6]

As was to be expected, a tremendous controversy arose between Mormons and non-Mormons — and has not abated — as to the genuineness of this allegedly divine book. The Mormons vigorously defend Smith's story as to the origin of *The Book of Mormon*, since the entire structure of Mormonism rests upon the genuineness of this book. Mormons declare that the sacred character of the plates forbade their display as a means of satisfying idle curiosity. Nevertheless several men of reputable character are said to have examined them.[7] The opponents of Mormonism have advanced several theories as to the origin of this book. The most commonly accepted is that a Presbyterian clergyman named Spaulding had written a historic novel concerning the origin of the American Indians; that Sidney Rigdon saw the manuscript in the printing shop of his employers, Patterson and Hopkins, took

---

[4] Art. VIII of the Mormon Thirteen Articles of Faith.

[5] Smith said that the name is partly English (*more*) and partly Egyptian (*mon*, that is, good). Arbaugh, p. 48. Mormons are told that Ps. 85:11 foretold the two great events in Mormon history: the finding of *The Book of Mormon*, buried on Cumorah ("Truth shall spring out of the earth") and the establishment of the priesthood by heavenly agents ("Righteousness shall look down from heaven"). Richards and Little, p. 102.

[6] See Talmage, pp. 273—95; 497—504. A colored skin was the punishment visited on the Lamanites and Lemuelites for warring against the Nephites, according to *The Book of Mormon*. A Utah State Advisory Committee to the U. S. Commission on Civil Rights in 1959 saw this tenet partly to blame for the sorry condition of nonwhites in Utah. *Time*, April 13, 1959.

[7] Talmage, pp. 269—71. But the reliability of some of the eleven witnesses has been challenged. Cp. Arbaugh, p. 41 ff. Shook, esp., p. 115.

it, enlarged and edited it, and prepared it for publication. This theory merits support, for Rigdon was a Campbellite minister, and *The Book of Mormon* contains many references to Campbellite theology, which had gained a following only a short time before the publication of *The Book of Mormon*.[8] The Mormon contention that *The Book of Mormon* is genuine cannot meet the test of literary criticism. The author moves in the phraseology of the King James Version of the Bible, written 1,200 years later, employs such dogmatical terms as the atonement of Christ, which did not come into use until much later; alludes to the leading theological controversies of the early nineteenth century, particularly the questions which were raised by the rise of the Disciples' theology; refers to such current events as the anti-Masonic excitement caused by the murder of William Morgan; mentions animals which were introduced to America from Europe long after the book supposedly had been written.[9]

Less known as a source of doctrine but nevertheless important is *The Pearl of Great Price*, which contains Smith's translations of the Bible, the Book of Moses, and the Book of Abraham. The Book of Moses is an interpolation between Genesis 5:21 and 23 and contains alleged visions of Moses. Among these

are visions that the devil organized Masonry to mislead men. Cain calls himself a "Master Mahan," that is, a master of the great secret which enabled him to murder and to kill.[10] The Book of Abraham is interesting, inasmuch as it contains passages in support of plural marriage.[11]

But more important than the Bible and *The Book of Mormon* as sources of religious knowledge are the direct revelations to be given to the leaders of Mormonism. The revelations which Joseph Smith said he had received were published by him under the title *Doctrines and Covenants*. The Mormons are willing to stake everything on the genuineness of the revelations received by Joseph Smith.[12] According to Mormon belief, the revelations given to the lawful successors of the priesthood of Melchizedek are as significant as those given to Smith. Mormons teach that God will yet reveal many great and important things pertaining to the kingdom of God.[13]

In their proselytizing work the Mormon missionaries affirm that in asking anyone to accept *The Book of Mormon* they demand no more than do the Christians when they ask for wholehearted acceptance of the Bible. In fact, say the Mormons, their source book of religion is intended specifically for the

---

[8] Arbaugh, pp. 21, 31—44.

[9] Cp. Sheldon, pp. 49—82. Arbaugh, pp. 45—56.

[10] Some see in this passage a reference to the murder of the anti-Mason William Morgan and Smith's opposition to Masonry. Later on, however, the Mormons patterned their cults and ritual after that of the Masonic Order. Cp. Schumann.

[11] Cp. Arbaugh, chs. viii, x, xi.

[12] Richards and Little, p. 100: "If he were not sent of God, the pretentions of the Latter-Day Saints to be the true Gospel Church are without foundation." *Doctrines and Covenants* is arranged in 133 chapters or sections, each subdivided into a number of "verses." These revelations cover practically all the peculiar doctrines which Joseph Smith introduced, including also the practice of polygamy in Sec. 132. Cp. also Arbaugh, pp. 88—101.

[13] Art. IX of the Thirteen Articles of Faith. See esp. Talmage, ch. xvi, pp. 296—313.

inhabitants of the American continent, while the Bible is intended for those of the Eastern continent. It must be kept in mind, Mormons argue, that the authenticity of the Bible and, for that matter, of any other alleged religious source, is not demonstrable by rational argumentation. The acceptance of the authority of the Bible — no less than the acceptance of the Koran or the revelation given to Smith — is wholly a matter of faith. However, there is a difference — one that makes all the difference in the world. It is that, in the case of the Bible, faith rests upon the divine-human person of Christ, while in the case of all other alleged divine writings it rests upon a human person. Christians believe that Jesus Christ is the eternal Son of God, who alone can reveal the divine wisdom to man (John 1:1-18); that He has spoken through the Prophets of the Old Testament (1 Peter 1:11); and that in Him God has given us the final revelation (Heb. 1:1, 2). Christians believe furthermore that Christ has spoken so clearly and with such finality that His followers are not to look for additional revelations, for the Sacred Scriptures, or the Bible, are the inspired, inerrant, and all-sufficient revelation of God to man.[14]

The Theological Emphases

The many unique and peculiar views of Mormonism make their theological system seem complicated. But this is not the case; for Mormon theology, briefly stated, teaches that man, an eternally pre-existent soul, is placed upon earth in order to gain "the remission of his sins" through obedience to the laws and regulations laid down by the priesthood and ultimately that he reaches perfection by a continual advance and eternal progress. In the interest of this central doctrine the Mormons have developed their theology and worship.[15]

Concerning God. Article I reads: "We believe in God, the eternal Father, and the Son, Jesus Christ, and the Holy Ghost." This seems to be a trinitarian confession. But it is not trinitarian, not even theistic. For (1) Mormonism denies the doctrine of the Trinity as is evident from its rejection of the deity of Christ and the personality of the Holy Spirit. Mormons distinguish between Elohim, the Father, and Jehovah Jehovah, so the Mormons teach, is the name for Jesus in His prenatal state, or the executive of the Father, or the firstborn of the spirit children of Elohim. It is somewhat confusing when Mormons say that Elohim is the "literal" parent of Christ, who is also Jehovah, or Jesus, or even the Father. According to a revelation given to the first presidency and the council in June, 1916, the Father and the Son are said to be in the form and stature of perfect men, each having a tangible body pure and perfect and attended by a transcendent glory, a body of flesh and bone; the Holy Spirit, however, is said to be not a body of flesh

---

14 Cp. John 5:39; 8:31, 32; 17:17, 20; 10:35; 16:13, 14; Luke 16:29, 31; Acts 17:11; 20:27; 1 Cor. 14:3; Gal. 1:8; 1 Tim. 6:3, 4; 2 Tim. 3:15-17; Heb. 1:12; 2 Peter 1:19, 21. The question is not whether both the Bible and the *Book of Mormon* are sources of religion, but whether *The Book of Mormon* contains teachings not contained in the Bible or even contrary to the Bible.

15 The most comprehensive and clearest exposition of Mormonism is Talmage, *A Study of the Articles of Faith,* in which the author expounds the Thirteen Articles of Faith accepted by Mormons. From this study it clearly appears that Mormons understand the Christian terminology in a completely different way from the way that the historic Christian churches understand it.

and bone, but "a personage of spirit."[16] (2) The Salt Lake City branch of Mormons has espoused the theory of a plurality of gods. Many Mormon leaders state that they have found numerous references in *The Book of Mormon* and Smith's *Doctrines and Covenants* to substantiate the theory that God is plural. In a word, they teach polytheism. In his revelation concerning plural marriages, Joseph Smith, speaking of the implications of celestial marriage, says that they shall be gods to whom all things, including the angels, will be subject.[17] Polytheism is central in the theology of the Mormons. The Salt Lake City Mormons hold that as God is eternally progressive and has advanced from His original manhood, so also man progresses according to the Mormon maxim: "As man is, God once was; as God is, man may be."[18] The Mormon doctrine concerning God

is involved and extremely confusing. Sometimes it speaks of two, 144,000, or even more gods; sometimes, of a Supreme Being distinct from Jehovah and Elohim. This confusion may account for the strenuous objection which modern Mormons raise against the charge that they have ever held the Adam-god theory.[19]

Concerning Man. Mormonism has a very high regard for man's spiritual ability. It considers man to be a preexistent disembodied soul procreated by God and temporarily embodied in order to pass through a time of probation. By teaching that man cannot be punished for any but his own actual sins, Mormonism denies the doctrine of original sin.[20]

Man is said to be able to reach perfection. To this end he must pass through a threefold probationary period:

[16] Cp. Talmage, p. 465 ff. Joseph Smith had received a similar revelation: the Father has a body of flesh and bone as tangible as man; the Son also; but the Holy Ghost has not a body of flesh and bone but is a personage of spirit. Were it not so, the Holy Ghost could not dwell in us. *Doctrines and Covenants*, 130:22.

[17] *Doctrines and Covenants*, 132:20; esp. 76:58. Richards and Little, pp. 170—72, state that the 144,000 (Rev. 14:1) are gods, for they have the Father's name written on their forehead.

[18] Talmage, p. 430.

[19] Cp. Talmage, p. 564 ff. There is no doubt that Brigham Young introduced the Adam-god doctrine. In *Journal of Discourses*, I, 50, he said: "Adam is our father and our god, and the only god with whom we have to do." And again: "How many gods there are I do not know. There never was a time when there were not gods and worlds." Ibid., VII, 333. In a sermon preached in the Tabernacle, April 9, 1852, Brigham Young said: "When our father Adam came into the Garden of Eden, he came into it with a celestial body. He is our father and god, and the only god with whom we have to do." Quoted in Braden, p. 440. This view may also account for the fact that the earlier Mormons attributed phallic powers to God, i. e., they viewed God as procreating spiritual children just as human parents procreate physical children. It seems that the Adam-god theory no longer plays a role in Mormonism.

[20] Art. II, Talmage, p. 474 ff. They hold a theory concerning Adam's fall which makes his fall a virtue rather than a curse. They say: Adam received the commandments to tend the Garden and to multiply and fill the earth. When Eve fell into sin and was about to be cast out of Paradise, Adam had to break one or the other commandment, and he chose to break the lesser, namely, to tend the Garden, in order to fulfill the greater commandment of filling the earth. In other words: "Adam fell that man might be." Richards and Little, pp. 3—5. Talmage, pp. 68—70.

in his pre-existence, in his incarnation, and after death. In this respect Jesus was like any other man and also had to pass through a threefold probationary period.[21] Mormons believe in universal salvation. To them the term "eternal damnation" does not mean that the individual will be eternally damned, but that as long as there is sin to be punished, there will be a hell.

Christ's Work. The atonement in which the Mormons profess to believe is in reality nothing more than the provision that man might be obedient to the laws and ordinances of the Gospel.[22] The chief work of Christ is that by His resurrection to immortality He opened the way for man to work out his salvation after death. The Mormon doctrine of the atonement is very hazy. It seems to center in the theory that while in their pre-existent state spirits are immortal, they become mortal during their embodiment; but through the atonement they will regain the lost immortality and the ability to complete their probationary period.[23]

The Mormon Heaven. According to the measure of his obedience man will be crowned, it is alleged, with celestial, terrestrial, or telestial glory. The first degree of glory is for those who have merited the highest honors of heaven; the second, for those whose works do not quite come up to the standard; and the third for such as have not as yet received the Gospel of Christ, but will become acquainted with Christ after death. In short, heaven is an eternal advancement along different lines, for eternity is progressive and perfection relative, in accord with the essential feature of God's being, which is associated with the power of eternal increase.[24]

The Priesthood. Like a red thread the demand to obey the laws and ordinances of the "Gospel" runs through Mormon philosophy. The first principles and ordinances of the Gospel are said to be faith in the Lord Jesus Christ, repentance, Baptism by immersion for the remission of sins, laving on of hands for the gift of the Holy Ghost. These first principles require obedience to a divinely established priesthood, which alone has the right to lay on hands, to preach the Gospel, and to administer its ordinances. Faith is said to recognize God's existence and His claims upon man and to make man willing to suffer in order to reach the goal of perfection. Repentance is said to consist in the recognition of God's authority and man's respect for God's Law.[25] The Mormon system is built on a twofold priesthood: the Aaronic priesthood, bestowed by John the Baptist on Smith and Cowdery, and the Melchizedek priesthood, given to Smith under the direction of Peter, James, and John. With this twofold priesthood the church is said to be endowed with the keys and powers to perform its threefold work: to prosecute the work of gathering conferred by Moses, to exercise authority over the living and the dead conferred by Elijah, and to dispense the promise of blessings for all generations by the Mormons conferred through Elijah. Prior to the re-

21 Talmage, p. 192 f. Talmage holds that the knowledge of good and evil is essential for man's advancement, p. 53. Smith teaches that obedience to the "laws of the Gospel" will lead to godhood. *Doctrines and Covenants,* 76:51—58.

22 See *Articles of Faith,* Art. III. Richards and Little, pp. 8—11.

23 Talmage, pp. 87, 476—79.

24 Talmage, pp. 91, 92; 406—9.

25 Articles III, IV, and V. See Talmage, pp. 96—116. Richards and Little, pp. 19—31.

establishment of the twofold priesthood in the spring of 1829 there was no church, because there was no priesthood to perform the rites and ordinances necessary for man's perfection.[26]

Marriage for Time and Eternity. The Mormon doctrine concerning marriage has probably been the most controversial point in their entire system. They hold that marriage is ordained of God that the earth might fulfill its purpose. Without marriage even salvation seems to be incomplete.[27] Mormonism distinguishes between temporal and eternal, or celestial, marriages. In the Mormon philosophy of life the significance of marriage is greatly exaggerated. Regarding the marriage for time the Mormon argument runs about as follows: Man is created in the image of God. Since God is said to be the Father of spirits, there must of necessity be a mother of spirits. Since man was created in the image of God, the male must like God become a father and the female a mother.

Polygamy, which was advocated by Joseph Smith and practiced by the early Mormons in Salt Lake City, is only a consistent application of some of Mormonism's basic principles. It is problematic whether polygamy was introduced that men might obey the "Gospel" and provide as many bodies as possible for the pre-existent souls or whether the theory of the pre-existence of souls was set up to justify the practice of polygamy.[28]

It seems that the celestial marriage is of even greater importance than the marriage for time. Mormonism regards marriage as an eternal relationship of the sexes. But, say the Mormons, an eternal relationship can be established only by an authority which comes directly from God, namely, the order of Melchizedek. The celestial marriage can be performed only by special rites, and only such as are considered worthy to enter the secret chambers of the temple may contract this marriage.[29] In reply to the argument that there are no marriages "in the resurrection" (Matt. 22:30), the Mormons say: "True, no marriages will be performed in heaven. They can be performed only upon earth. But they shall continue throughout eternity." [30]

Baptism for the Dead. The Mormons believe that the spirit of man is an intelligent being both before and after its embodiment and that the disembodied spirit can learn and progress after death toward the celestial perfection. But the

---

[26] *Doctrines and Covenants,* 13:27; 112:30 ff.; 107:40—52; 84:6-14; 84:35-39. The various rites are performed in the secret chambers of the temple. The secrecy which surrounds the Mormon temple rites may account for the rise of several ugly stories about Mormonism, esp. the doctrine known as the "blood atonement," or the execution of those who fail to be obedient to the priesthood. Cp. Sheldon, p. 123 ff.

[27] *Doctrines and Covenants,* 49:15-17.

[28] *Doctrines and Covenants,* No. 132. Polygamy is no longer practiced except in isolated cases. It must be kept in mind that the president of the church, Wilford Woodruff, October 6, 1890, discontinued polygamy, not because he considered it wrong, but because he deemed it inexpedient. His statement reads: "My advice to the Latter-Day Saints is to refrain from contracting marriage forbidden by the law of the land." See *Doctrines and Covenants,* p. 256 f.

[29] *Doctrines and Covenants,* 124:30—40. Cp. Talmadge, pp. 444—46.

[30] It seems that a woman's resurrection is dependent upon her being sealed to a husband at whose command she will come forth out of the grave on Judgment Day, and that the plurality of wives for the celestial estate is to guarantee the woman's eternal bliss.

disembodied spirit cannot reach perfection without baptism by water. Obviously spirits cannot be baptized. However, a living descendant may stand proxy for a departed ancestor, provided such a spirit is obedient to the "Gospel," which he heard "in prison" from Christ or hears from a departed member of the priesthood. Through his proxy the departed spirit receives the ordinances of the priesthood as if he personally were being baptized. Like all other rites all ordinances for and on behalf of the dead are administered only in the temple. Only approved Mormons are admitted.[31]

The priesthood imposes many rules and regulations concerning tithing, dietary regulations, and the manifold missionary endeavors. The young men are expected to spend two years in doing missionary work, and the zeal which they manifest is indeed most exemplary.

The Millennium. Basic for the Mormon eschatology is the assumption that during the millennium two cities are to be established: Jerusalem for the Jews and Zion for the ten tribes of Israel.[32] In general the Mormons follow the Adventist millennial pattern. They hold that the millennium will be ushered in when the Jews accept Christ as their personal Redeemer and return to Jerusalem. Christ will reign personally in Zion (Independence, Mo.), where He will establish a perfect theocracy and administer both kingdoms — the Jerusalem and Zion kingdoms — under one authority. During the millennium perfect peace, righteousness, and length of life will prevail. Toward the close of the millennium Satan will attempt in vain to establish his power. At the conclusion of this period the earth will be "celestialized" so that men may reach their foreordained perfection and ultimately become the literal offspring of the Deity.[33]

Ecclesiastical Polity. The church is divided into "stakes of Zion," and these are subdivided into "wards." The church is governed by the "First Presidency," the president and two other high priests, which shares its authority with "the Council of the Twelve." Next in authority is the "Presiding Quorum of Seventy." A presiding bishop and two counselors have jurisdiction over the other bishops and the various organizations of the lower priesthood.

As a religious system Mormonism is a mixture of theosophy, spiritism, and elements of paganism, under a thin veneer of Christian terminology. As a philosophy it is slightly materialistic and approaches Islam. Mormonism has emphasized education and reached a high level of culture. As a social experiment in mutual helpfulness it has been highly successful. The Mormon church has consistently grown numerically, and today its activities extend over the entire world.[34] True, there have been many internal differences, but Mormonism has thus far been able to overcome them.

Divisions in Mormonism

The unexpected death of Joseph Smith was responsible for the rise of several separations, several men claiming to be his rightful successor.

By far the largest branch of Mormonism is *The Church of Jesus Christ of Latter-Day Saints* with headquarters

---

31 Talmage, pp. 145—53. A. G. Moseley, "Baptized for the Dead," *Review and Expositor*, Vol. 49, No. 1 (Jan., 1952), pp. 57—61.

32 *Doctrines and Covenants*, 45:64 f.; 84:5, 31. The Salt Lake City Mormons say that Is. 2:2, 3 led them to select the Rocky Mountain Valley as their temporary abode. See Talmadge, p. 513.

33 See Talmage, chs. xviii—xxi, pp. 328—94.

34 Cp. *Census*, 1936, II, 814.

at Salt Lake City. The above account applies to this group.

The Reorganized Church of Jesus Christ of the Latter-Day Saints, with headquarters at Independence, Mo., proclaims itself to be the true successor of the church founded by Joseph Smith. The leaders, direct descendants of Joseph Smith, specifically denounced Brigham Young's assumption of the leadership, and they have always protested against his espousal of polygamy and the theory of the plurality of gods. This branch declares that it has preserved unbroken the teachings of Joseph Smith and that it subscribes to the Thirteen Articles of Faith formulated by him. They say that they lay special emphasis on the principles of stewardship and are particularly interested in the development of a social consciousness which views the possession of property only as a stewardship for social ends, not as a means for private gain. This means that everyone must strive to develop his own capabilities for service to the good of all, particularly for the good of the needy. They hold that there is only one God; that Jesus is the Son of God, who came that we might have a more abundant life by making His teachings the basis for right living in every area of human life. They claim the "lineal right" of

office, i. e., only the descendants of Joseph Smith are recognized as the legitimate officers of the church. This branch is relatively strong in the Midwest.[35]

The Church of Christ (Temple Lot) was organized in Bloomington, Ill., by a small group who held that Sidney Rigdon had dedicated the Temple Lot (almost three acres) in Independence, Mo., as the site which, according to the Lord's revelation, was to become the center of the priesthood of God during the "restoration." In 1867 they returned to Independence, Mo., and in spite of much opposition purchased the Temple Lot. They seem to spend their energy in maintaining their legal right to this small plot of ground. They repudiate the Salt Lake City group's teaching on Baptism of the dead, polygamy, and the elevation of man to godhood.

The *Church of Jesus Christ* is divided into two separate groups, both of which denounce Brigham Young's leadership and his migration to Utah, his advocacy of polygamy, polytheism, and Baptism for the dead. One group is known as the Bickertonites, after William Bickerton, who organized it in Pennsylvania in 1867. The other group, known as the Cutlerites, was organized in 1853 by Alphaeus Cutler, who believed that the temple was to be built at Nauvoo, Ill.

BIBLIOGRAPHY

PART VIII

SECTION V

1. Mormon sources published by Deseret Book Co., Salt Lake City, Utah

McGavin, Elmer Cecil. *How We Got the Book of Mormon.* 1961.

Messages of Inspiration: Selected Addresses of the General Authorities of The Church of Jesus Christ of Latter-day Saints. 1957.

Richards, Franklin D., and Little, James A. *A Compendium of the Doctrines of the Gospel.* 1925.

Smith, Joseph. *The Book of Mormon.* Ed. of 1906.

———. *The Doctrines and Covenants.* Ed. of 1926.

[35] Ibid., p. 822.

———. *The Pearl of Great Price.* Ed. of 1929.

Talmage, James E. *Articles of Faith.* 14th ed., 1925.

2. Other Sources

Anderson, Nels. *Deseret Saints, the Mormon Frontier in Utah.* Chicago: University of Chicago Press, 1942.

Arbaugh, G. B., *Revelation in Mormonism.* Chicago: Univ. of Chicago Press, 1932.

———. *Gods, Sex, and Saints: The Mormon Story.* Rock Island: Augustana Press, 1957.

Braden, Chas. S. *These Also Believe.* New York: Macmillan Co., 1949. Ch. xiii: "Mormonism."

Brodie, Fawn M. *No Man Knows My History, the Life Story of Joseph Smith.* New York: Alfred A. Knopf, 1945.

Davies, Horton. *Christian Deviations.* New York: Philosophical Library, 1954. Ch. vii.

Fisher, Vardis. *Children of God.* New York: Harper & Brothers, 1939.

Hill, Marvin S. "The Historiography of Mormonism," in *Church History,* XXVIII (1959), 418—428.

Mulder, William. *Homeward to Zion: The Mormon Immigration from Scandinavia.* Minneapolis: University of Minnesota Press, c. 1957.

——— and A. Russell Mortensen, eds. *Among the Mormons: Historic Accounts by Contemporary Observers.* New York: Alfred A. Knopf, 1958.

O'Dea, Thomas F. *The Mormons.* Chicago: University of Chicago Press, 1957.

Schumann, F. E. *Is This the Church of Jesus Christ?* St. Louis: C. P. H., 1943. Tract.

Sheldon, Henry C. *The Fourfold Test of Mormonism.* Nashville: Abingdon Press.

Young, Kimball. *Isn't One Wife Enough?* New York: Henry Holt and Co., 1954.

SECTION VI

Jehovah's Witnesses

History

The movement now known as Jehovah's witnesses was initiated by Charles T. Russell in 1872. Russell, a Congregational layman, was seriously troubled by the doctrine of the eternal duration of hell and subsequently by doubts about the reliability of Holy Scripture. He credited the Adventists with restoring his faith in the doctrine of inspiration and with removing his doubts. Their theories concerning the imminence of Christ's second coming and the total annihilation of the wicked appealed to him. Russell expanded tne Adventist view and soon gained a large following by his lectures "Photo Drama of Creation" and "Millions Now Living Shall Never Die." The circulation of his publications allegedly reached a total of over 13,000,000. The *Divine Plan of the Ages* alone had a circulation of 5,000,000. His popularity was so great that even his divorce could not diminish it or impede the growth of his cult.[1]

Russell was a dispensationalist. He held that God will provide a period in the history of the world in which conditions will be so favorable that man can merit divine blessings through his good conduct.[2] Russell divided the history of the world into three great dis-

---

[1] The movement is known also as the International Bible Students Association, the Millennial Dawn, the Watchtower Bible and Tract Society.

[2] Russell's dispensationalism differs from that of the premillennialists. Cp. Sec. I. Like Adventism, Russellism maintains that man's sharing in the "new earth" is predicated on his effort to keep God's laws. — Present-day Jehovah's witnesses do not accept everything that Russell taught.

pensations. In each of these man had, or will have, the opportunity by obedience to God's Law to merit for himself the right to live in this world forever. From Heb. 2:5 Russell inferred that angels had charge of the first "world" but that God ended this dispensation with the Flood because the angels were unable to subdue the evil angels. In the second "world," or dispensation, said Russell, Satan rules as the unchallenged power, having subjected all things to his dominion until his destruction in 1914. In that year, we are informed, God was to establish the "third world," with ideal conditions, making it easy for man to acquire the right for continued life and happiness.[3] Russell was somewhat perplexed when in 1914 there came World War I instead of the anticipated "third world," mankind's golden age. This "error" was soon corrected, however; for in 1914 — so the new theory goes — Satan was cast out of heaven, and only the invisible part of God's organization, the church, was established in heaven.

Russell died in 1916, and Joseph F. Rutherford became his successor. Under his leadership the society reached worldwide influence and today is active in every part of the world. Upon Rutherford's death in 1942 Nathan H. Knorr succeeded him.[4] The affairs of the society are now managed by a board, and its very profitable publications appear anonymously.

Few modern sects have been so active, so bold in propagandizing, so provocative in their methods, so indifferent to controversy and persecution, as Jehovah's witnesses. Each member believes himself called and ordained as

---

[3] *Studies in Scripture*, I, 219—44. Russell considered the dates 1874, the year in which he published his first book, and 1914 of tremendous importance for the third "world." He computed that the "second world" would end in 1914. But he arrived at this date by a roundabout route and a rather arbitrary manipulation of dates. According to Dan. 12:12, Russell said, the end of the world must come 1,335 years after some important event which was unknown until discovered by Russell, namely, the conquest of the Ostrogoths and the establishment of the papacy in the year 539. By adding 539 and 1,335 Russell arrived at the year 1874, in which he calculated Christ must have returned invisibly. If someone challenged the accuracy of the date 539 and the significance of the alleged events in that year, Russell would answer that according to Dan. 7:7, 8 and 12:7 the rule of the papacy was limited to "a time" (i.e., a year), "times" (i.e., two years), and "dividing of time" (i.e., half a year); in other words, to three and a half years. In prophecy a "time" is 360 days, "three and a half times" are 1,260 "prophetic days," or 1,260 calendar years. Accordingly, the papacy would extend 1,260 years forward from its founding in 539 and therefore come to an end in 1799. In 1799, according to Russell, Daniel 11:40, 41, and particularly 12:4 were fulfilled in the founding of Bible societies, which led to increased knowledge, and the invention of new modes of travel, which enabled many to run to and fro. Thus Russell thought he had demonstrated the accuracy of the date 1874. But in order to arrive at the year 1914, he had to take another step in his computation. He said therefore that God granted a period of forty years for the Jewish harvest, from Pentecost to Jerusalem's destruction, in which Israel's remnant was gathered. Likewise there must be a period of forty years for the Christian harvest, in which the Christian remnant would be forewarned and thus forearmed. The main dates in Russel's calendar are: the establishment of the papacy in 539; the end of the papacy in 1799; Christ's invisible return to this world in 1874; the end of the second and the beginning of the third "world" in 1914. Cp. Mayer, *Jehovah's Witnesses*, p. 31 ff.

[4] For a biography of Knorr, see Cole, *Jehovah's Witnesses*, 210—212.

a witness of Jehovah and a member of "a society of ministers," which precludes making a distinction between clergy and laity.[5] "Ministers" — without distinction of sex — are divided into Publishers, who give their leisure time to "field work," and Pioneers, who devote at least 100 hours (in the case of Special Pioneers, 160 hours) a month to their ministry, and receive a stipend in return.

Doctrinal System

THE CENTRAL MESSAGE

At first glance the central message of Jehovah's witnesses seems to be in substantial harmony with that of the historic Christian churches. It reads:

God made man perfect; man sinned and was sentenced to death; God promised to redeem him; he who will be the redeemer must also be the Messiah and the "seed" of promise, through which the blessings shall come to the people; this redeemer must be a perfect man who must give his life as a ransom price for mankind; no man on earth could meet these requirements; the obedient and faithful Son of Jehovah, the Logos, was sent from heaven to earth, being begotten by the power of Jehovah and born as a perfect man-child; he grew to manhood's estate; he suffered death as a sin-offering; he was raised from the dead and ascended on high; at the end of the world he returns to establish his kingdom; the time has come for the Jews to be restored to Palestine; the blessing of the people will be restitution; and the time for the comfort of Israel is here, because her warfare has ended.[6]

However, this statement must be understood in the light of the central theory, which can be summarized as follows: Jehovah created this world to be the everlasting home of man on condition that man prove his obedience to Jehovah. Lucifer, the lord of the visible world, however, became disobedient and challenged Jehovah to put a creature on this earth who would not blaspheme and reproach Him. Thereupon Jehovah created man and gave Lucifer, or Satan, permission to do everything in his power to tempt man to blaspheme Jehovah, so that it would become evident that man can keep the laws of Jehovah's theocracy. Of course, at the present time Satan is still ruling the world, and only comparatively few are able to recognize the claims of the Lord Jehovah. But Satan's dominion will soon be destroyed, and God's theocracy will be established. Mankind will be obedient. This world will be under Jehovah's everlasting kingdom. God's original purpose in creating the world will be realized. Jehovah's witnesses believe that they have been raised to announce the early establishment of God's theocracy.[7]

SOURCE OF DOCTRINE

Jehovah's witnesses maintain that they accept the Bible as the divinely inspired Word of God and the only source of their doctrines.[8] But they ignore all the basic principles of Bible interpretation employed by the Christian church.

1. To prove a specific point, Jehovah's witnesses often completely ignore the context. To prove that Satan is to

---

[5] This contention sometimes presented a troublesome problem to selective service boards in determining the right of the individual member to claim exemption as a clergyman. See Cole, pp. 200—206.

[6] Rutherford, *Life*, p. 226.

[7] Cp. Russell, *Theocracy*, p. 2.

[8] Rutherf., *Deliverance*, p. 10; *Creation*, pp. 124, 47—49. Rutherford quoted Scriptures extensively in his writings. Some of his books are almost half full of direct Scripture quotations.

have every opportunity to deceive men so that through his ultimate destruction God's glory may be enhanced, they quote Ex. 9:16: "For this cause have I raised thee up, for to show in thee My power." But this refers to Pharaoh, not to Satan. Ignoring the context of Gen. 9:4, they place all blood transfusions under the divine ban.[9] On the basis of Jer. 10:3 f. they condemn Christmas trees as a pagan custom.

2. They allegorize the Scriptures, especially many Old Testament stories. To prove their theory that Satan's empire consists of a visible and an invisible part and that Satan completely tyrannizes man, they point to Babylon built on both sides of Euphrates. The temple representing Satan's invisible empire, they say, was built on one side of the Euphrates, whereas the palace, symbolic of the visible part of Satan's organization, was on the other side of the river. The river Euphrates, coming from the Garden of Eden, to them represents humanity, which is obstructed and tyrannized on each side by Satan's twofold organization.[10] Jehovah's witnesses find a mandate to announce the doom of the world by means of the radio in Job. 38:35: "Canst thou send lightnings, that they may go and say unto thee, Here we are?"[11] The use of sound trucks for their witnessing and the resultant disturbance of the peace of the neighborhood the witnesses regard not only as justified but also as obligatory, for they identify themselves with the locusts which in the prophecy of Joel are said to climb in through the windows. Because of their fierce opposition to the Government in 1918 many Jehovah's witnesses were mobbed and imprisoned. Rutherford found this persecution prophesied in the piercing of the Savior's feet. He allegorized: "The faithful witnesses since Pentecost constitute the body of Christ. The early martyrs are represented by Christ's pierced hands and the latter by His pierced feet."[12]

3. On the basis of their interpretation of Dan. 12:9 they assert that the Bible will remain a dark book and its symbolism unintelligible without their instruction. They declare that no one understood the Book of Job until Rutherford explained that the three friends represent the three allies of Satan, the religious, the political, and the commercial powers. Christ's coming to the Temple is said to symbolize Rutherford's identifying himself in 1922 as the elder of Rev. 7:13 f., who alone knew the nature of the "great multitude," which even Russell had not understood.[13]

4. The witnesses subject all Scripture and all Christian doctrines to human reason. They deny the existence of hell, because in their opinion hell is repugnant to reason, justice, and love. They teach that this world will be inhabited by a "rejuvenated" mankind, because it is unreasonable to assume that God could not carry out His original plan to populate the world with a perfect society.[14]

---

[9] *Time,* May 12, 1952.

[10] Rutherf., *Prophecy,* p. 114.

[11] Rutherf., *Life,* p. 303.

[12] Cp. Russell, *Theocracy,* p. 41.

[13] Rutherf. *Creation,* p. 122; *Harp of God,* pp. 18—20; *Life,* p. 228. *Theocracy* (tract), p. 33.

[14] Rutherf., *Creation,* pp. 47—49. Witnesses usually appeal to Is. 1:18, "Come, let us reason together." But they completely ignore the fact that the word "reason" does not refer to man's rationalistic activity, but rather to a discussion between two persons.

Jehovah's witnesses maintain that the standard translations of the Bible contain grave errors. In 1950 they began the publication of the *New World Translation* of the Bible, a translation prepared especially for the "new world." This world, according to 2 Peter 3:13, will have no uninspired human traditions to darken and nullify the divine Word or to propagate the misleading influence of "religious traditions" rooted in paganism, such as the elimination of the name "Jehovah" and the use of the creature terms *theos* and *kyrios* (god and lord).[15]

But it is not a mere idiosyncrasy when the witnesses demand that the Supreme Being be called by no other name than Jehovah. It is a basic theological principle with them. They claim that such names as "God" and "Lord" were introduced into the Septuagint (the Greek translation of the Old Testament prepared in the third and second centuries before Christ), into the New Testament, and subsequently into all translations, to displace the doctrine of Jehovah's sole supremacy and to introduce the doctrines of the Trinity and the deity of Christ. The Supreme Being alone may be called Jehovah; Christ may be called lord and god (small letters), but never Jehovah. The witnesses always protest violently when members of the Christian churches point out the fact that "Jehovah," which occurs nearly 7,000 times in the Old Testament, is regularly translated in the Septuagint with *theos* and *kyrios* (God and Lord) and that the Bible therefore ascribes the name "Jehovah" to Jesus Christ. The Preface to the *New World Translation,* however, states that someone has tampered with all the Septuagint manuscripts and deliberately substituted the Greek words *theos* and *kyrios* for the Hebrew tetragrammaton JHWH. They base this assertion on the version of the Septuagint prepared by Aquila A. D. 128. True, in one out of nearly 7,000 instances this version uses the Hebrew form of JHWH. It must, however, be observed that Aquila's version was written more than 2–300 years after the original Septuagint; that Aquila uses the Hebrew from JHWH only once; that he uses archaic Hebrew letters. The witnesses insist that someone also tampered with the New Testament by substituting *theos* and *kyrios* for the "divine name JHWH." Their argument is based on the theory that Matthew originally wrote his Gospel in Aramaic — an undemonstrated assumption — and used the name JHWH, whereas later writers introduced other names for God to replace the distinctive name "Jehovah" and to introduce the doctrine of the Trinity.[16]

15 Foreword, *New World Translation,* p. 7. When the witnesses insist that only the name "Jehovah" dare be used, they ignore the following: (a) The Hebrew alphabet originally had signs only for consonants, none for vowels. Only very late were vowels added to the consonants by means of a point system. (b) The most common name for God in the Hebrew is the tetragrammaton JHWH, a four-lettered word without vowels. It is quite certain that the Hebrews pronounced it "Yahweh" and not "Jehovah." (c) From a false sense of reverence the Hebrews did not utter the divine name, but substituted *Adonai,* my Lord. The unwarranted and linguistically impossible form of "Jehovah" is a medieval combination of the four consonants in JHWH and the vowels of "Adonai." (d) The significant thing is not a particular sound, but the meaning of the name. God's names are a description of God, and God explains His divine name in Ex. 3:14 as "I Am Who I Am," or simply as "I Am." (e) God Himself ascribes many other names to Himself, such as "Elohim" and the "Holy One."

16 Ibid., pp. 11—19.

The *New World Translation* sets forth other distinctive views which are essential to the entire doctrinal structure of the witnesses' message. It is a version that lends support to the denial of doctrines which the Christian churches consider basic, such as the co-equality of Jesus Christ with the Father, the personhood of the Holy Spirit, and the survival of the human person after physical death. It teaches the annihilation of the wicked, the nonexistence of hell, and the purely animal nature of man's soul.[17]

THEOLOGICAL EMPHASES

The Doctrine of God. Jehovah's witnesses emphatically deny the doctrine of the Trinity. Rutherford states:

The doctrine of the "trinity" finds no support whatsoever in the Bible, but, on the contrary, the Bible proves beyond all doubt that it is the Devil's doctrine, fraudulently imposed upon men to destroy their faith in Jehovah God and His gracious provision for the redemption and regeneration of the human race. Therefore it definitely appears that the doctrine of the so-called "holy trinity" is another of Satan's lies.[18]

The doctrine of the Trinity involves the idea of three gods of equal rank, says Rutherford, and is therefore inconsistent with a theocracy, for the very essence of a theocracy requires that man dare be obedient to only one, the Lord Jehovah. Since the name Jehovah is never ascribed to Christ nor to the Holy Spirit, the latter, says Rutherford, cannot share with Jehovah the obedience due Him alone.[19]

The terminology employed in describing the person of Christ is very confusing. Christ is called the Son of God, and yet He is only a god (with a small letter).[20] Jehovah's witnesses describe the Word *(Logos)* as God's spokesman, His chief executive, the first to understand God's "divine plan," God's administrator of the theocracy.[21] But they expressly deny the equality of Christ with the Father, so clearly taught in John 10:30, with the arbitrary assertion that the unity is not one of essence, but of purpose. In other words, it is only a moral or mystical union, which unites all believers with God.[22]

Jehovah's witnesses reject the deity

---

[17] Cp. *Report of International Assembly of Jehovah's Witnesses,* August 6, 1950, p. 2, and *Foreword,* p. 22 f.

[18] Rutherf., *Riches,* p. 188.

[19] Russell, *Theocracy,* p. 6; Rutherf., *Riches,* p. 141.

[20] The *New World Translation* reproduces John 1:1: "The Word was a god," and v. 18: "the only-begotten god who is in the bosom position with the Father." In the Appendix, p. 773 f., the translators state: "Every honest person will have to admit that John's saying that the Word, or 'Logos,' was divine is not saying that he was the God with whom he was. . . . It does not identify him as one and the same as God." Jehovah's witnesses stake their argument on the false and unscholarly assumption that when St. John uses the article with *theos,* he refers to Jehovah; but when he omits it, *theos* denotes only a glorious creature. Cp. Bruce M. Metzger, *Jehovah's Witnesses and the Divine Name* (a pamphlet), Princeton Theological Book Store, 1953. But more important still is the fact that St. John wrote his Gospel for the express purpose of proving that Jesus Christ is the Son of God (John 20:31). Why do the witnesses not follow the example of Thomas and say in the words of the *New World Translation:* "My Lord and my God" (capital *G!*), and esp. 1 John 5:20: . . . "his Son Jesus Christ. This is the true God and life everlasting" (again capital *G*)?

[21] Rutherf., *Theocracy,* p. 8; *Creation,* pp. 12—14; *Deliverance,* pp. 15, 114; *Harp of God,* pp. 18, 98, 99.

[22] Russell, *Theocracy,* p. 9; Rutherf., *Riches,* p. 182.

and even the personality of the Holy Spirit. They say that the "holy spirit" is only the power of God, thus depersonalizing the Holy Spirit.[23] Jehovah's witnesses imagine that they are obedient to Is. 45:5 (God will tolerate none besides Himself) by impugning the true deity of the Son and the Holy Spirit.

Jehovah's Theocracy and Satan's Empire. Jehovah's witnesses teach that according to Is. 45:18 and similar promises God will give man this world as an everlasting inheritance on condition that man remain loyal to the laws of God's theocracy.[24] Jehovah's witnesses hold that at the present time it is extremely difficult for man to live as a member of God's theocracy, because Satan has established his powerful empire in direct opposition to God's theocracy. God had originally, the witnesses believe, created the Logos and Lucifer as His representatives, the Logos to have charge of Jehovah's invisible kingdom, while Lucifer as man's lord and ruler of the world was to represent Jehovah in the visible organization of the theocracy. But Lucifer became jealous and planned to establish his throne on such a firm foundation that

he would be equal to God.[25] Lucifer, who became Satan or the devil, decided to tempt Adam to eat of the forbidden tree and then to urge him to eat of the tree of life immediately. Thus man would become immortal, and God could not carry out His threat of destroying Adam for disobedience nor fill the world with rational human beings who would be forever obedient to God.[26] When Eve yielded to Satan's temptation, Adam was confronted with the following dilemma: Should he remain in the Garden sinless, but also childless, or should he eat of the forbidden tree and with Eve populate the world? He chose the latter.[27]

Rutherford says Jehovah did not immediately destroy Satan, but accepted the challenge in order to give Satan full opportunity to prove his boast.[28]

Satan's empire is said to be this present evil world (Gal. 1:4), consisting of a visible and invisible part. As prince and god of this world Satan organized the visible part of his empire by founding the churches, the great capitalistic organizations, and the world empires. Through these three forces Satan has

---

[23] Rutherf., *Deliverance,* p. 150, *Harp of God,* p. 198. Throughout the *New World Translation* the name is printed in lower case; thus: "The undeserved kindness of the Lord Jesus Christ and the love of God and sharing in the *holy spirit* be with you all" (2 Cor. 13:14). — Jehovah's witnesses seem to make much of the fact that in Greek the word "spirit" ($\pi\nu\epsilon\tilde{\upsilon}\mu\alpha$) is in the neuter gender and therefore, so they argue, cannot refer to a person. This caused the translators of the *New World Translation* considerable difficulty in the Savior's "last discourses," esp. John 14:15 ff., where the Savior uses the masculine gender word Paraclete ($\pi\alpha\varrho\acute{\alpha}\varkappa\lambda\eta\tau\sigma\varsigma$). The *New World Translation* in the interest of its denial of the Trinity translates: "He [the Father] will give you another helper . . . the spirit of the truth, which the world cannot receive, because it [the world] neither beholds it [the helper] nor knows it." The translation of John 14:26 reads: "The helper, the holy spirit . . . that one will teach, etc." But in a footnote the translators add: " 'That one' is in the masculine gender to agree with 'helper.' " Cp. John 16:8.

[24] Rutherf., *Creation,* pp. 47 f., 60.

[25] The proof for this statement is sought in Ezek. 28:12 f., although this text clearly refers to the king of Tyre, not to Satan.

[26] Rutherf., *Riches,* p. 172 f.

[27] Rutherf., *Deliverance,* p. 32; *Creation,* p. 61; *Harp of God,* pp. 36, 116. Cp. Section on Mormonism, fn. 20.

[28] Rutherf., *Salvation,* p. 16; *Riches,* p. 165 f.; *Life,* p. 80 f.

introduced "religion" into the world, whereby he ensnared and enslaved mankind. "Religion," according to Rutherford, was established when Satan told Adam and Eve that they would not die. With the invention of the "lie of man's immortality," Satan not only became the father of lies and man's murderer, but he also defamed God, to whom alone belongs immortality.[29] The witnesses maintain that the great tragedy of history is that through the triple alliance, the ecclesiastical, political, and commercial powers, Satan has forced mankind to practice religion. Babylon, the mother of harlots, is married to Satan and is the symbol of all religious powers and ecclesiastical rulers. Egypt was primarily a commercial nation and became exceedingly rich under the Pharaohs. But the devil saw to it that the heathen priests, i. e., "religion," remained the dominant force. Assyria was the symbol of political power, and its history shows how politicians support Satan's kingdom, i. e., religion, for their own gain. And bringing this allegorical interpretation down to present times, Rutherford says:

> In these latter times the three elements, under the supervision of the Devil, have united in forming the most subtle and wicked world power of all time. They operate under the title of Christendom, which is a fraudulent and blasphemous assumption that they constitute Christ's kingdom on earth.[30]

The witnesses refuse to bear arms, to salute the flag, or to participate in the affairs of the secular government, not because of any pacifist views, but because they consider the present political powers allies of Satan.[31] These will shortly be abolished and Jehovah will establish His theocracy. Then man will be able to throw off the triple shackles of Satan: the snares of religion, the tyranny of governments, the oppression of business. Then man can prove his integrity toward God and His chief executive officer, Christ, and through full loyalty to Jehovah mankind will procure for itself the right to live a life of liberty and happiness in this world.

The Fall of Adam and Its Consequences. The witnesses hold that under God's theocratic rule in Paradise all was peace and happiness. But Lucifer's rebellion and Adam's fall ended this happy state of affairs. Man lost his right to live, and after his short span of life he will go down into oblivion and extinction, since no imperfect man can

---

[29] Rutherf., *Riches,* p. 179 f.; *Religion,* p. 22.

[30] Rutherf., *Deliverance,* p. 53. Cp. *Prophecy,* pp. 124 ff., 259. *Religion,* pp. 17, 23, 169. Commenting on Rev. 16:13 (three unclean spirits, like frogs, shall come out of the mouth of the dragon), Rutherford asserted that this was partially fulfilled when President Franklin Delano Roosevelt, the politician, invited the capitalist Myron C. Taylor and representative churchmen to work for peace. Croaking like frogs, the leaders of Satan's triple empire boasted of having effected a close relationship between religion, politics, and finance. The most vituperative attacks have been directed against the Roman hierarchy, since in the opinion of the witnesses the political, commercial, and the ecclesiastical elements of Satan's "visible organization" are combined in the papacy to defame Jehovah by establishing religion in violation of God's theocratic rule.

[31] Rutherf., *Salvation,* p. 260 ff. The "powers" in Rom. 13:1 ff. are said to be God's theocracy and Christ, God's chief executive, who beareth the sword. Jehovah's witnesses pay taxes because the chief executive of the theocracy has commanded such payments. It appears incongruous that Jehovah would command His subjects to support His sworn enemies, the political organizations, the "instruments of Satan."

claim the right of life. Two basic teachings of the witnesses take their rise here.

1. The witnesses brand the doctrine of man's immortality as "Satan's lie" and make it the essence of all "religion." If man's soul were immortal, they argue, then God would not be able to execute His threat that the soul which sins must die; in other words, God would cease to be almighty.[32] They say that the soul cannot be immortal, since it is only the animal faculty to breathe and move.[33]

2. Jehovah's witnesses deny categorically that there is an eternal punishment for sin. They declare:

All the prophets of God taught that *sheol,* the grave, and hell are one and the same condition, referring to the condition of death. The Jews knew that the Scriptures taught that all in their graves are dead, unconscious, and know nothing. Eccl. 9:5, 10; Ps. 115:17.[34]

The witnesses say that God would be unjust if He first threatened death as the penalty for Adam's sin and then later added the punishment of eternal torments to the original threat. And again:

There could be no eternal torment of any of God's creatures except by God's will. A reasonable, loving God could not torment any of his creatures. A Creator that would put in operation a system of endless torment would be a fiend and not a reasonable God.[35]

The Restoration of the Right to Live. It is frequently assumed that the witnesses hold a doctrine of atonement according to "the traditional Christian idea." Rutherford states:

God has provided salvation by and through his Son, Christ Jesus; that the lifeblood of the man Jesus poured out at Calvary is the purchase price of sinful man, which price purchased all the right that Adam lost for his offspring; that such purchase price was presented in heaven and paid over to God as a sin offering in behalf of as many as do believe on the Lord Jesus Christ; that such was done and performed by Christ Jesus in obedience to God's will; that Christ Jesus, having paid over the ransom price, is the owner of all men, and all receive the benefit thereof who believe and obey; that life everlasting is the gift of Jehovah God through Jesus Christ, our Lord, because salvation belongs to Jehovah, and Christ Jesus is his means of administering the same; that there is no other means of gaining life; that no man can gain life or receive life everlasting unless he believes God and believes on the Lord Jesus Christ and asks for salvation by making an unconditional agreement to do the will of God.[36]

This statement must be examined in the light of the central principle: the theocracy. 1. The witnesses hold that man requires a redeemer to regain the

---

[32] Rutherf., *Creation,* p. 51.

[33] The Scriptures declare that man survives physical death, Matt. 10:28; that death entered the world through man's sin, Rom. 5:12; 6:23; that man's dust returns to the earth and the spirit to God, Eccl. 12:7; that the torments of hell are eternal (Matt. 25:41, 46; Mark 9:48; cf. also Dan. 12:2). Rutherford states that Heb. 11:5 actually means that Enoch saw no one die and that the word "graves" in John 5:38 denotes monuments or memorials. In other words, the resurrection consists in no more than raising the memory of the departed or resurrecting the "right to life." Rutherf., *Salvation,* p. 142 f.

[34] Lewis W. Spitz, *Our Church and Others* (St.Louis: C. P. H., c. 1960), p. 138, suggests that "Russell's objection to the Calvinistic doctrine of predestination of the wicked to eternal damnation made him turn to the Adventist denial of hell."

[35] Rutherf., *Harp of God,* p. 62 f. Cp. *New World Translation,* Appendix, p. 772.

[36] Rutherf., *Salvation,* p. 199.

right to live which Adam lost for himself and his posterity, so that under more favorable conditions man can prove his obedience to the theocracy. 2. Only a life of perfect obedience — not death — could regain the right to live. 3. It was as man, and as man only, that Jesus earned the right to live. If Jesus had been more than man, even if He had been only an angel, His obedience would have been of no value to man, for God requires a life for a life.[37] Jesus is said to have ransomed mankind in the following manner: By His perfect obedience He earned the right to life for this world; but the Father and the Son offered Jesus [note the distinction between the Son and Jesus] immortality of the soul if He would sacrifice His hard-earned right to life and die as a sinner. Thus Jesus regained for all men the lost right to life.[38] In this ransom work Jesus was assisted by the 144,000. The witnesses teach that according to Eph. 5:32 the mystical body of Christ consists of Jesus as the head and of the 144,000 as the body. Like Jesus these 144,000 sacrificed their right to live in this world, earned through their perfect obedience to Jehovah's theocracy, and like Jesus these — and these alone — will receive immortality of the soul.[39]

The Establishment of the Theocracy. The witnesses believe that Jehovah placed His King, Christ Jesus, on the throne in 1914 and that the kingdom of the new world is already in operation, at least in heaven. It is their conviction that they have been commissioned to gather in the "other sheep," not in tens of thousands, but in hundreds of thousands, lest they be destroyed when the "second world," this present social order with its three allies of Satan, the capitalistic system, religious organizations,

---

[37] Ibid., pp. 170, 172.

[38] In *Deliverance*, p. 159, Rutherford writes:

The perfect man Jesus, while he remained alive, could not provide a ransom price. He must now convert his perfect human life into an asset of value, which asset would be sufficient to release man from judgment and from the condemnation resulting from that judgment. He must lay down his human life that the value thereof might be presented to divine justice instead or in place of that which Adam had forfeited, to the end that Adam and his race might have an opportunity to live. Otherwise stated, Jesus must make his human life thereto a legal tender for the payment of Adam's debt.

It is in their denial of Christ's deity that the witnesses deviate from the Christian faith. Their entire Christology is hazy and confusing. Rutherf., *Salvation*, pp. 172, 176.

When that equivalent, to wit, the perfect human life of Jesus and the right thereto, is presented to Jehovah God in heaven, it constitutes and constituted the purchase price of all the rights which Adam's offspring had lost by reason of Adam's sin. Therefore Christ Jesus' receiving life as a spirit creature and paying over his right to life as a human creature made him by right of purchase the owner of every one of Adam's offspring that would comply with God's requirements, to wit: have faith in God and in Christ Jesus, and meet the rules subsequently made to govern all who take that step of faith. The ransom sacrifice of the Lord Jesus Christ is a price exactly corresponding to what Adam lost; but it is not a substitute for Adam, nor was it given for the purpose of satisfying justice but was given as a purchase price. [Ibid., p. 228 f.]

[39] Rutherf., *Harp of God*, p. 18; *Creation*, pp. 66, 245.

and dictatorial governments, will go out of existence.[40]

Jehovah's witnesses are "daters." They find the following timetable prophesied in the Bible for the establistment of the theocracy:

1914: Satan was expelled from heaven and started World War I. Jehovah established the invisible part of His organization in heaven.[41]

1918: The year of persecution following the "quiet years" (1916–1918) was typified by the dumbness of Ezekiel (24:27). (Russell had died in 1916, and his followers were imprisoned as "conscientious objectors.")

1919: The beginning of the "Lord's strange work" (Is. 28:21) of fearlessly condemning the "religionists."

1925: Rutherford sounded the trumpet to end the prophetic seventy jubilee years.[42]

1926: Rutherford sounded the fifth trumpet of Rev. 9:1.

1927: Rutherford sounded the trumpet of the sixth angel, Rev. 9:13.

1935: Rutherford correctly identifies the 144,000 as those witnesses who were found worthy to establish God's rule.

?: Battle of Armageddon (Rev. 16:16)

and the establishment of Jehovah's reign on earth.

On the basis of such passages as Ps. 110:5, 6; Ezek. 35:6-8; Zech. 14:16-19; Zeph. 3:8; Joel 3:2, 14; Rev. 16:14-16; 19:14, 15; 12:1-9, the witnesses foresee the following events: Satan will marshal all his visible forces, the commercial, political, and ecclesiastical powers, against Jehovah. They will come with tanks, planes, cannons; priests, politicians, capitalists, from every nation will go forth into the "Valley of Threshing." The faithful witnesses will occupy the mountainsides to watch Christ, the invisible field marshal of Jehovah, strike down Satan's armies with the flail of destruction. All the weapons of war will be consumed, all organizations of a political, ecclesiastical, or commercial nature, being Satan's instruments, will be destroyed. Christ Jesus will bind Satan, who, by introducing "religion" and the doctrines of the Trinity and immortality, had deceived the nations for a long time. And now the honor of Jehovah has been vindicated, for now God can establish His theocracy, and mankind will be able to become obedient to Jehovah and serve Him and His King, Christ Jesus.[43]

---

[40] *Yearbook*, 1952, p. 33. This "quiet and invisible coming" of Christ is said to be taught in the Greek word *parousia*. The common English versions render this word with "coming," and the church has always used it as one of the terms for Christ's return in glory. Russell, Rutherford, and the *New World Translation* render *parousia* with "presence." Cp. Appendix, pp. 779, 780. *Parousia* can mean both "presence" and "coming." Used of Christ in the New Testament lexicographers agree that it almost always means "the Messianic Advent of the Transfigured One as Judge at the end of this age." Walter Bauer, *Griechisch-deutsches Wörterbuch zu den Schriften des Neuen Testaments*, 5th ed. (Berlin: Alfred Töpelmann, 1958), 1249. See also Henry George Liddel and Robert Scott, eds., *A Greek-English Lexicon*, 9th ed. by Henry Stuart Jones and Roderick McKenzie (Oxford: Clarendon Press, 1940), 1343, and Albrecht Oepke's article on *parousia, pareimi* in Gerhard Friedrich, ed. *[Kittel's] Theologisches Wörterbuch zum Neuen Testament*, V (Stuttgart: W. Kohlhammer, [1954]), 856—869.

[41] Russell had calculated thus: Christ, who came invisibly in 1874, allowed a period of 40 years for the "Gentile harvest," as the Jews had been granted 40 years respite between A. D. 30 and 70. See above, and cp. Mayer, *Jehovah's Witnesses*, pp. 30—36.

[42] Rutherf., *Life*, pp. 166—70.

[43] Rutherf., *Religion,* pp. 337—57.

The Church. Actually the witnesses have no doctrine of the church. In accord with their central idea of God's theocracy the witnesses divide mankind of the "third world" into four distinct groups.

The first group consists, of the 144,000, the "great mystery class," or the "bride of Christ," who by their obedience have earned immortality. They constitute the "body of Christ," or the church. Not all of the 144,000 have already become immortal. A "remnant" on earth is commissioned by Jehovah to proclaim the good news of the kingdom. Not all Jehovah's witnesses belong to the relatively small number of 144,000, who alone will receive the "divine nature," i. e., immortality.

The Scriptures plainly tell us that the quality of immortality belongs originally only to Jehovah. 1 Timothy 6:16. Immortality will be given as a great reward to faithful Christians, the 144,000 and to none other of the human race. 2 Peter 1:4; 1 Peter 1:3, 4; Romans 2:7; Revelation 2:10. We may be sure that a man does not seek that which he already possesses; and the Apostle Paul plainly says: "Seek for . . . immortality." And again he says to those who will be faithful Christians: "This mortal must put on immortality." 1 Corinthians 15:53. If a soul, a man, were already immortal, he could not subsequently put on immortality. No one of the human race will ever be made immortal except the faithful Christians. God has a different reward for others who are obedient to him.[44]

In the theocracy Christ (i. e., Jesus and the 144,000) will form the invisible, the spiritual, part of God's organization.[45]

The second class comprises the Old Testament believers. These indeed gained God's approval, but because Christ had not as yet deposited His ransom in heaven, they could not obtain an incorruptible inheritance, or immortality. Their reward will be the "looked-for city" (Heb. 11:40), the government of Jehovah, in which they will form the visible part of God's theocracy, even as the 144,000 constitute the invisible part.[46]

The third group is called the Jonadab class, also the "multitude," or the "other sheep," or the "people of good will," who defend, protect, and assist Jehovah's witnesses.[47]

The fourth class will not come into being until the theocracy has been fully established. It consists of those who will have the opportunity to prove their integrity in Jehovah's theocracy.[48]

---

[44] Rutherf., *Harp of God,* p. 41 ff.

[45] Rutherf., *Harp of God,* pp. 191, 200 f.

[46] Rutherford erected a pretentious residence in San Diego for Abel, Noah, Abraham, David, and many others. This *Beth Sarim* (House of Princes) was intended to serve as headquarters for God's theocracy (Rutherf., *Salvation,* p. 311 f.). It was sold in 1948.

[47] Ibid., pp. 316, 319.

[48] Ibid., p. 356. Corresponding to this division of mankind into four classes, there are said to be four resurrections. In the "first resurrection" the 144,000 are made members of the royal house of Jehovah in heaven. The second, or the "better resurrection" (Heb. 11:35), is for the Old Testament faithful men. Those of the great multitude who die before Armageddon will see the "third resurrection." The fourth resurrection is the "resurrection of the unjust." All those who had no opportunity to obey God's theocracy during their first life will take part in this general resurrection, which will occur progressively during the millennium. Not all will be raised. Adam had his chance and failed. Men like Judas and the Pharisees will not be raised from their graves, since the word "grave"

The New Heaven and the New Earth. Christ will be the king of Jehovah's theocracy. But contrary to all other millennial theories the witnesses teach that Christ cannot rule visibly, for "Christ," that is, Jesus and the 144,000, have given up their right to live on the earth, have become immortal, and are spiritual. The visible government of the theocracy will be in the hands of the Old Testament princes near San Diego, Calif. The "great multitude, which cannot become spiritual and immortal, will have the important task of "finishing the earth" according to God's system of laws and the "new covenant," consisting primarily in such dietary laws as will enable mankind to obtain health and through health ultimately prosperity and bliss.[49] There will be no death, Rev. 21:4; infant mortality will be wiped out completely, for, according to Rutherford's interpretation of Is. 65:17-20, every babe will "fill its years," which means that it will grow to maturity.

After the theocracy has been firmly established, God will progressively raise all the "unjust," those who completely ignored God's theocracy during their earthly existence. They will now receive a second chance under the most favorable conditions. If they are obedient, they will earn the right to live in this world for "ages to come." [50] If, however, they fail to make good during the period of probation, they will go to gehenna,

the place of entire destruction and annihilation. Each man will be given 100 years of probation, as foretold Is. 65:20: "The sinner being an hundred years shall be accursed."

It is one of God's basic laws that man must prove his integrity under trial, says Rutherford, and therefore God will once more release Satan for a period to test man. Afterwards Satan will be destroyed.

According to Rutherford, the millennium will be the glorious "third world," in which every individual will enjoy perfect health [51] and the "rejuvenated earth" will provide for mankind security, international peace, economic justice, a perfect utopia under God's theocracy.[52]

In 1918 a number of Russell's followers severed their membership in the International Bible Students Association. In their opinion the majority did not follow their late leader's extreme pacifism. This group, known as Elijah Voice Society, espoused all the doctrines proclaimed by "Pastor" Russell and held in especially high regard the posthumously published *The Finished Mystery*. This volume maintains an extreme form of pacifism, which was disavowed by a large segment of the witnesses during the national emergency in 1918.[53]

The Servants of Yah, with headquarters in Brooklyn, New York, is a group reportedly formed by dissident Jehovah's witnesses.

means "God's remembrance," and it is not reasonable to assume that God would remember Judas. Only such as were ignorant of God's theocratic law will be raised for a second chance.

[49] Rutherf., *Deliverance*, pp. 311—18, 337.

[50] Ibid., p. 327.

[51] Ibid., pp. 339—42.

[52] Rutherf., *Harp of God*, p. 352.

[53] Cp. *Battle of Armageddon*, tract published by Elijah Voice Society, Seattle, Wash., 1928.

BIBLIOGRAPHY

PART VIII

SECTION VI

Primary Sources

The Watchtower Bible and Tract Society, Brooklyn, N. Y., publishes and distributes the literature of Jehovah's witnesses.

The Watchtower, announcing Jehovah's kingdom, and *Awake*, biweeklies.

Writings of Charles Taze Russell:
Studies in the Scriptures (7 vols.), also known as *Millennial Dawn: The Divine Plan of the Ages*. Vol. VII, *The Finished Mystery*, was published posthumously. Some contemporary witnesses contend that it does not set forth Russell's views. They challenge any statement from this book when used against Jehovah's witnesses. Cp. *Report of International Assembly*, 1950, p. 15.

Writings of Joseph F. Rutherford include many books and pamphlets. The following books seemed most significant for an objective appraisal of the tenets held by Jehovah's witnesses: *The Harp of God*, 1921 (the most comprehensive exposition of Rutherford's beliefs); *Deliverance*, 1926; *Creation*, 1927; *Life*, 1929; *Prophecy*, 1929; *Riches*, 1936; *Salvation*, 1939; *Religion*, 1940.

Yearbook of Jehovah's Witnesses, published annually since 1933.

Among the numerous tracts the following set forth most clearly the aims and objectives of Jehovah's witnesses:

Conspiracy Against Democracy, 1940; *Judge Rutherford Uncovers the Fifth Column*, 1940; *The Theocracy*, 1941, the best synopsis of the witnesses' message; *End of Axis Powers*, 1941.

Anonymous publications since Rutherford's death: *The Truth Shall Make You Free*, 1943; *Let God Be True*, 1946; *This Means Everlasting Life*, 1950; *New World Translation of the Christian Greek Scriptures*, 1950, revised 1951; *New World Translation of the Hebrew Scriptures*, 1953—. This translation is of utmost significance to the witnesses, inasmuch as it supports their distinctive teachings, more particularly their denial of such Christian doctrines as the Trinity, the personhood of the Holy Spirit, the survival of human beings after physical death, the existence of hell.

Secondary Sources

Bach, Marcus. *They Have Found a Faith*. Indianapolis: Bobbs-Merrill Co., 1946.

Braden, Chas. S. *These Also Believe*. New York: The Macmillan Co., 1949.

Clark, Elmer T. *The Small Sects in America*. Nashville: Cokesbury Press, 1937.

Cole, Marley. *Jehovah's Witnesses: The New World Society*. New York: Vantage Press, 1955.

Davies, Horton. *Christian Deviations*. New York: Philosophical Library, 1954. Ch. vi.

Engelder, Theodore, et al. *Popular Symbolics*. St. Louis: C. P. H., 1934.

Ferguson, Charles W. *The Confusion of Tongues*. Garden City: Doubleday, Doran & Co., 1928.

Graebner, Theodore. *War in the Light of Prophecy*. St. Louis: C. P. H., 1941.

Martin, Walter R., and Norman H. Klann. *Jehovah of the Watchtower*. New York: The Truth Publ. Society, 1953. Now published in Grand Rapids, Mich: Zondervan Publishing House.

Mayer, F. E. *Jehovah's Witnesses*. Revised ed. St. Louis: C. P. H., 1957.

Metzger, Bruce M. "The Jehovah's Witnesses and Jesus Christ," *Theology Today*, X (April, 1953), 65—86.

Pike, Edgar Royston. *Jehovah's Witnesses*. New York: Philosophical Library, 1954.

Stroup, Herbert H. *Jehovah's Witnesses*. New York: Columbia Univ. Press, 1945.

Van Baalen, Jan Karel. *The Chaos of Cults*, 2d ed. Grand Rapids: Wm. B. Eerdmans Publ. Co., 1956.

SECTION VII

Anglo-Israelism

Anglo-Israelism, known as British-Israelism in England, is strictly speaking, not a religion, but, according to its leaders, a movement to establish the absolute reliability of the Bible by demonstrating that God's promises to Abraham are fulfilled in the Anglo-Saxon race. The theological tenets of the Anglo-Israelites are those featured by the various fundamentalist bodies. They advocate a Biblicism of the extreme type and interpret the Bible in a thoroughly literalistic manner.[1]

The Anglo-Israelites state that the express purpose of their movement is to convince the infidels of the divine inspiration, the absolute authority, and the complete reliability of the Bible. Anglo-Israelism argues thus: God promised to Abraham a perpetual nation. There must be a nation not only of Jews but of the Ten Tribes as well somewhere today. This nation is found in the Anglo-Saxon race. The main objective of Anglo-Israelism is therefore to furnish proof that Britain and America constitute the Ten Tribes and thereby to establish incontrovertibly the "divine inspiration" of the Sacred Record. A few examples will be given to indicate the method of interpretation used by Anglo-Israelites. Judah's son, Zarah, the first Israelite to migrate to England, became the head of England's royal house. To prove this contention, the Anglo-Israelites point to Gen. 38:28 ff. and the preponderant use of scarlet-colored tape in British documents. Dan was Jacob's "restless" son, and his descendants in their westward trek left traces along their journey by such names as Dardanelles, Danube, Rhodan-us (Rhone), Dunkirk, Denmark, London. A third westward migration was organized under Jeremiah and Baruch, who brought with them the stone on which Jacob slept, at present the coronation stone in Westminster Abbey. Gradually representatives of all tribes came to England. The word *British* is explained etymologically as a contraction of the Hebrew words *berith* (covenant) and *ish* (man) and *Britain* of *berith* and *ain* (land) [?]. Manasseh in particular represents the United States, since he was really the father of the "thirteenth tribe" and America was discovered on the 13th of October; thirteen colonies united; the first navy had thirteen ships; the number "13" plays a significant role in the Great Seal; and there are even 13 letters in *E pluribus unum.* The "Great Pyramid" at El Gizeh in Egypt also plays a role in their calculations.

---

[1] They still use the "seven times" argument of W. E. Blackstone, who saw in the "seven times" of Lev. 26:18 ff. seven aeons instead of the adverb "sevenfold." The Anglo-Israelites argue that a time is a "prophetic year," representing 360 years, and seven "times" signify 2,520 years. Samaria was punished "seven times," beginning in 720 B. C. and ending 2,520 years later, in 1801, the year when the United Kingdom was formed. Judah's captivity is said to have begun in 604 B. C. and ended in 1917, when Israel was freed from Turkish oppression. Cp. Braden, p. 391.

BIBLIOGRAPHY

PART VIII   SECTION VII

Braden, Chas. S. *These Also Believe.* (New York: Macmillan, 1949), ch. xi.

Davies, Horton. *Christian Deviations.* New York: Philosophical Library, 1954. Chapter viii.

Destiny. A monthly published by Destiny Publishers, Haverhill, Mass.

National Message. A weekly published by British Israel World Federation, London, England.

PART NINE

Interdenominational Trends and Organizations

SECTION I

Modernism

Modernism represents the school of thought in modern Protestant theology which proceeds on the premise that all religious beliefs must be examined scientifically. It denies that religious doctrines should find a priori acceptance. All "sacred writings," inclusive of the Christian Scriptures, all dogmatical terminology, and all religious practices, modernists think, must be subjected to a critical examination. They will accept nothing unless its moral and religious values have been firmly established. Modernists have employed the so-called empirical method, considering it the only valid criterion by which any religious statement is to be judged.

Modernism therefore is a method rather than a system of religion. At best, its tenets constitute an eclectic religious philosophy. Modernism originated early in the 19th century and came into full bloom in America a century later.

Modernism is rooted in the soil of four types of liberal theology, which are represented by Friedrich D. Schleiermacher, Albrecht Ritschl, the Wellhausen-Baur school, and Ernst Troeltsch. American psychologism, empiricism, pragmatism, and social consciousness brought modernism to its full development.[1]

Genetic History of Modernism

The theologian who more than any other influenced religious thought during the past century is Friedrich D. Schleiermacher (1768—1834). His great influence is largely due to the fact that he has become, probably unwittingly, the father of modern empiricism. He thought the purpose of theology is to describe and interpret religious, more specifically Christian, experience. He considered the feeling of absolute dependence upon God (das fromme Gottesbewusstsein) the essence of religion. A thorough examination of this religious experience, he believed, shows that in every action we are totally dependent on something beyond us.[2] Schleiermacher, a pantheistic mys-

NOTE: For key to abbreviations see Appendix B; for bibliography, the end of each section.

[1] On principle the author discusses only those trends which have a direct bearing on the theological development in the various denominations. For this reason he does not include in this text a presentation of the several religio-philosophical systems, such as humanism, Communism, etc., nor does he include the deistic principles basic to many of the fraternal secret orders. Cp. Engelder et al., *Popular Symbolics* (St. Louis, Mo.: C. P. H., 1934), pp. 427—435, 459—461. Theodore Graebner, *Handbook of Organizations* (St. Louis, Mo.: C. P. H., 1948).

[2] In *Die Reden,* 1799 (trans. John Oman, London, 1893), addressed to the rationalists of his day, Schleiermacher attempted to prove the existence of God and man's dependence on God. Through Coleridge Schleiermacher's theology was introduced to the English-speaking world. Cp. Mackintosh, chs. ii, iii. Like Goethe, Schleiermacher had been trained in the Moravian atmosphere.

tic, thought that every man in his own religious feelings can discover this ultimate, universal, all-controlling reality. Thus he finds the source of religious truth in the Christian consciousness. According to Schleiermacher, Christian experience reveals three basic facts: to wit, man's sinfulness, the divine gracious pardon, and the divine redemption. He retained the traditional Christian terminology and seemingly moved in Christian thought patterns. In reality, however, he had broken completely with the orthodoxy of preceding centuries. First of all, Schleiermacher introduced a new methodology. He has provided for modernistic theology the basic philosophical principle by developing the empirical method into a positive and constructive system of interpreting religion.[3] Second, his theological method, i. e., reliance on human experience, does away with the finality of the Christian religion. Schleiermacher admits that up to his time the Christian religion had offered the best god-consciousness, but it is possible, he said, that some non-Christian or a composite religion can serve this purpose better than Christianity. In his theology everything is relative. God and the divine attributes must be described in concepts which satisfy our needs and meet the demands of our own "god-consciousness." Accordingly, each of his modernistic successors has drawn his own picture — or caricature — of God and made such a god as best suits his own needs. According to Schleiermacher, sin is relative. It is, at best, a struggle between the spiritual and natural will, a mere tension in man, not rebellion against God. These tensions man can best overcome in the Christian community. Schleiermacher

therefore views Christ not as rendering a substitutionary satisfaction for man's sins, but merely as a satisfactory substitution *(keine stellvertretende Genugtuung, sondern nur genügende Stellvertretung).*

Albrecht Ritschl and his school left an indelible impact on a number of American theological students who later played a prominent part in the formation of modernistic theology; for instance, Arthur Cushman McGiffert, William Adams Brown, and Shailer Mathews. The Ritschlian impact on American theology is twofold. First of all, Ritschl's value-judgment theory suited the American temperament, which has a bias for pragmatic philosophy. Ritschl thought that as the historian must determine the historicity of an event *(Seinsurteil),* so the theologian must determine its ethical and moral value *(Werturteil).* Accordingly the theologian must determine the religious, ethical, and spiritual value of all historically accepted truths, such as the attributes of God, the cross of Christ, the doctrine of the Trinity, man's fall into sin. Since, so Ritschl argued, none of these actually improve man morally, they have no theological relevance. Ritschl's new standard of determining religious truth was of tremendous significance for the emergence of American liberalism. But probably even more significant was his doctrine that Christ's work consisted primarily in establishing the kingdom of God on earth as an ethical society. This theory gave rise to the social gospel.[4]

The third prop of modernism is the German school of higher criticism, which denied the divine inspiration and absolute inerrancy of the Bible. The basic

---

[3] Burtt, p. 302.

[4] Mayer, "Ritschl's Theology," *C. T. M.,* XV (1944), 145—157. Cp. also Adolf Harnack, *What Is Christianity?* trans. by Thomas Bailey Saunders (New York: Harper & Bros., c. 1957). F. H. Foster, ch. vii. Mackintosh, p. 142 ff. Knudson, p. 132 ff.

principle of this school was that the Bible is a collection of human documents subject to the same literary criticism as other human writings. This fact, the advocates of higher criticism maintain, demands (1) the recapture of the particular situation in which each book of the Bible was written; (2) the fixing of the original purpose and distinctive message of each respective book; and (3) the determination of the relevance of the recorded experiences, particularly those of Jesus, for modern man. The unique position of the Bible was said to be due to its ability to guide men to religious experiences higher than those achieved by any other collection of sacred writings.[5]

Probably the most influential factor in developing modernism came from the school of comparative religions. Throughout Christianity's long history it has always been maintained that all ethnic religions are the result of a degenerating process; in other words, that man lost his original correct concept of God, religion, worship; that according to Rom. 1:18 ff. man progressively deteriorated as he deviated from the truth. But this radically liberal school of German theologians[6] asserted that if there is a biological evolution upward and forward, there must also be a constant spiritual, moral, religious development toward higher goals. They discarded the study of theology and advocated in its stead the study of anthropology, philosophy, psychology of religion, and sociology. In this way they hoped to find the laws which govern the alleged evolutionary growth of religious and spiritual concepts. This school operated with four basic assumptions: (1) As in a mountain range, so in all religions there is one basic principle. But as the various peaks attain varying heights through one or the other physical phenomenon, so there are various levels of religious insights effected by the divergent social, cultural, climatic, geographic, or other environmental factors. But no religion, not even the Christian religion, can claim any finality. (2) The basis of all religion is worship. The religious practices of the lowest kind of ethnic people are considered just as pious and helpful as the worship of the Christian congregation. (3) The only standard of religious truth is the completely satisfying life. (4) All religious concepts or terms are phrased in such well-known symbols as "Father," "Redeemer," "fellowship," "patriotism," "Nirvana," "Messiah." The term "Christ" likewise is simply a symbol, and the historicity of Jesus is not essential for the Christian religion. The term "Christianity" is merely a symbol for a way of worship and could just as well be expressed in the symbol "Paulianity."[7]

The philosophy of comparative religions, popularized in America at the

---

[5] The *International Standard Bible Encyclopedia* was published under the general editorship of James Orr (Chicago: Howard-Severance Co., 1915) to counteract the impact of higher criticism.

[6] Ernst Troeltsch, 1865—1923, is probably the most significant representative of this school of thought. Cp. *Der Historismus und seine Probleme.* Mackintosh, ch. vi; xix. J. L. Neve and O. W. Heick, *History of Christian Thought,* Vol. II, ch. viii, pp. 155—64.

[7] Garnett, *Realistic Philosophy of Religion,* offers a usable synopsis of the views held by Durkheim, Maret, Westermarck, Rudolf Otto, concerning the origin of religion. Albert Schweitzer, *The Quest for the Historical Jesus* (London: Adam & Charles Black, 1911). Cp. Mackintosh, ch. vi. Samuel Zwemer, *The Origin of Religion* (Nashville: Cokesbury Press, 1935), tries to provide a refutation of the theories of the school of comparative religions.

World's Fair of 1893,[8] soon found its way into several prominent theological schools which had previously added the psychology of religion as a "new theological science" to their curriculum. Like the school of comparative religions, the American religious psychologists attempted to explain man's normal and abnormal psychological behavior in terms of religious concepts.[9] It was agreed that all religions are good; that none is perfect; that, for the Western mind, Christianity seems to be the best, but does not satisfy the Eastern mind; that it ill becomes the American missionary to attempt the pagan's conversion to Christianity; that the missionary's task consists merely in comparing Christian, Buddhistic, Shintoistic, and Islamic views, with the idea of enlarging each religious culture.[10]

Modernism came into being as these four strains of European thought were molded into a theological system congenial to a relatively large group of American theologians, especially in the Congregational, Baptist, Methodist, and Disciples churches.[11] Congregationalism furnished the richest soil for liberal theology. Here since the days of Horace Bushnell the attempt was made to harmonize the "new science" and theology.[12] The Disciples did much to popularize the theories of higher criticism, largely because of their one-sided emphasis on Biblical study to the exclusion of all dogmatical formulations. The Baptists and Methodists were primarily responsible for the rise of the social gospel. Walter Rauschenbusch of Colgate Rochester Seminary, a Baptist institution, and to a less degree Shailer Mathews of the Divinity School of the University of Chicago, originally also a Baptist school, were the chief exponents of the social gospel. The Methodist church was the first officially to adopt a social creed and to make the preaching of the social message the heart and core of the church's message.[13]

[8] See Frank T. Neely, *Neely's History of the Parliament of Religions and Religious Congresses at the World's Columbian Exposition* (Chicago: Neely, c. 1893).

[9] Gaius Glenn Atkins, *The Procession of the Gods* (New York: Richard R. Smith, Inc., 1930). Shailer Mathews, *The Growth of the Idea of God* (New York: Macmillan, 1931). A. Eustace Haydon, *Biography of the Gods* (New York: Macmillan, 1941). Smith, pp. 116—39, "Psychology of Religion."

[10] See the report, *Re-Thinking Missions: A Laymen's Inquiry* (New York: Harper & Bros., 1932).

[11] P. IV, Secs. VI, VII; P. V, Sec. I; P. VI, Sec. V.

[12] The Congregational theologians were the first to grant religious status to Darwin's theory. John Fiske, in *Destiny of Man*, attempted to explain evolution in terms of theological concepts. It is difficult to determine the impact of Karl Marx's *Manifesto* on the liberalism of the Congregational church. Cp. Carlton J. H. Hayes, *A Generation of Materialism (1871—1900)* (New York: Harper & Bros., 1941), esp. p. 135 ff.

[13] Walter Rauschenbusch, through his *Christianizing the Social Order* (New York: Macmillan, 1913), and through his classroom activity, became the "father of the social gospel." In his opinion the means of grace are a permanent job and a deed to a house. Industrial accidents handicap the wage earner, deprive his family of many necessities, frequently lead to crime, and thus retard and even block all social progress. Therefore the church's task in the industrial area is to Christianize the social order. Rauschenbusch thus summarized his theology: On Mount Carmel Elijah's challenge was, the God who answers by fire is God; Charles Haddon Spurgeon's challenge was, The God who answers with orphanages, let

Nature of Modernism

Modernism is a method, not a creed. Modernists are united in their approach to the theological problem, but not in their conclusions.[14] They assert that they are motivated by the attempt to modernize Christian thinking by reinterpreting the church's rich dogmatical heritage in the light of modern man's insights, interests, and needs. Accordingly they attempt to recapture the religious experience out of which the classic doctrines of the church have developed and to restate them in terms of modern man's religious experience.[15] Thus modern man will fill with new meaning such Biblical terms as revelation, grace, the kingdom of heaven, and such terms as Trinity, inspiration, atonement, deity of Christ, justification.

To reach this goal, modernism has adopted the empirical or scientific method. Modernism, then, insists that it never starts with an a priori truth nor ever reaches the final truth. The empirical method flatters man, for it elevates the individual to the position where he and he alone by his own religious experience determines his theological premises and findings. But this method, by its very nature, confounds man, leads him to uncertainty and finally to despair. It is in the very nature of the modernistic method that men arrive at greatly varying and even contradictory conclusions. The variance among modernists is one in degree only, depending on one of three factors.[16]

1. Modernists vary in the degree of their radicalism. Some have taken the non-theistic position of humanism, which states: "Man is the measure of all things, he is the captain of his own soul and the master of his own destiny." [17]

2. Modernists differ according to the type of religious experience on which the individual bases his theology. This accounts for the fact that one group of modernists may be typical mystics and another such militant foes of every form of capitalism, such ardent advocates of social salvation, that they come to be suspected as "fellow travelers."

3. Modernists vary with the philosophical bases adopted by the various groups.[18]

Him be God. But in the present social crisis labor exclaims: The God who answers with low food prices, let Him be God. Cp. C. H. Hopkins, loc. cit. Also Mayer, "Liberal Theology and the Reformed Churches," *C. T. M.*, XV (1944), 798; Benson Y. Landis, ed., *A Rauschenbusch Reader* (New York: Harper & Brothers, 1957).

14 Aubrey, p. 25 ff.

15 For examples of the Modernist's approach to the Bible see Harry Emerson Fosdick, *The Modern Use of the Bible* (New York: Macmillan, 1924).

16 Cp. Burt, p. 331 ff.

17 See William P. King, *Humanism, Another Battle Line* (Nashville: Cokesbury Press, 1931). Elias Andrews, *Modern Humanism and Christian Theism* (Grand Rapids: Zondervan, 1939). Arthur Dakin, *Man the Measure* (Princeton Univ. Press, 1939). Burtt, ch. ix, pp. 350—408. Mayer, "Modern Humanism," *C. T. M.*, XII (May, 1941), 362—70.

18 Wieman and Meland, loc. cit., have grouped the modernistic and liberal theologians into four main categories based upon four systems of theology. 1. Supernaturalism, represented by neo-orthodoxy, or the dialectical theologians. 2. Idealism, represented by absolutists, modern mystics, and personalists. 3. Romanticism, represented by ethical intuitionists and aesthetic naturalists. 4. Naturalism, embraced by various types of theists and religious humanists.

Theological Emphases

The findings of modernism on the basis of religious experience differ very sharply and basically from the historic position of Calvinism or Arminianism.[19]

1. For modernism the source and criterion of truth and the standard of religious values are man's own experiences. The Bible is considered unique only because it contains the most advanced religious experiences of God, especially Jesus' experience of His oneness with the Father.[20]

2. The universe is a cosmic order which strictly observes all biological and more particularly all psychological laws, thus enabling man to grow morally toward a unified and integrated personality.

3. Such growth toward a perfect personality involves "faith in God," or, better still, dependence on some mundane factor, for example, one's environment, the laws of nature, one's psychological make-up. The concepts of God and of faith will vary according to each individual's experience. One will speak of faith as reliance on the Absolute; another, as the committal to the ultimate Reality; a third, as trust in the personality-evolving Process.

4. The ultimate goal of all religious experiences is said to be a fully developed personality. With such a personality a person is "saved," that is freed from all fears, inhibitions, complexes, etc.[21] In modernism sin is no more than a barrier to becoming an integrated personality. Redemption from sin is the conquest of the psychologically disturbing factors in one's personality and the acquisition of such a life plan as will bring poise, serenity, and self-control. Up until the present time no one has so successfully obtained this "redemption" as Jesus, who is therefore rightly called the Son of God.

5. An integrated personality cannot be developed in a society in which injustices and economic insecurity prevail. Therefore it is the duty of the Christian society to transform all social institutions according to the spirit of Jesus.[22]

6. The modernist finds it difficult to report any religious experiences which would warrant a definite statement concerning the immortality of the soul. Some modernists have ventured the opinion that inasmuch as the power which has created a unified personality is more real and more active than the factors which would destroy it, one may assume that personalities will endure beyond the grave.[23]

The Decline of Modernism

Modernism has lost its former optimistic confidence in the supposed omni-

---

[19] Liberal theology has not succeeded in making extensive inroads into any branch of the Lutheran church in America.

[20] This theory, also known as divine immanence, is the keystone of modernism. It has been characterized as man's delusion that he hears the voice of God when he shouts at the top of his voice in a dark room.

[21] Of the various types of modern religious philosophy personalism, as advocated by Borden Parker Bowne, Albert C. Knudson, and later by Edgar Sheffield Brightman, has proved to be very attractive for many of the modernists. The main cause of personalism's attractiveness is the assumption that since only a person can serve as a personality factor, God must be a person. Cp. Methodist Church, P. V., Sec. 1. See Wieman and Meland, pp. 133—45. Arthur Carl Piepkorn, "The Finite-Infinite God of Edgar Sheffield Brightman," *C. T. M.*, XXV (1954), 28 ff.

[22] See "Social Creed of the Churches," P. V., Sec. I.

[23] See Burtt, pp. 345—47.

competence of science. The theological scientists learned by bitter experience that, strictly speaking, there is no deductive science, since every man invariably turns to induction. They have learned, furthermore, that the scientist dare not trust what he knows as "natural laws," because these are not absolute, not always prescriptive, but usually only descriptive. This statement is true because no scientist ever has all the facts and therefore cannot be entirely objective in describing the laws nor their effects, particularly the laws which govern human behavior. Moreover, science cannot investigate the whole realm of nature or the interrelation of the various phenomena, least of all in the realm of psychology.[24] In short, modernism's chief instrument came close to undermining irreparably the very foundation of its own structure.[25]

Although liberalism has not ceased to exist, it exhibits both the chastening marks of the times and the influence of more realistic theologies.

BIBLIOGRAPHY

PART IX   SECTION I

Aubrey, E. E. "Modernism" in *Present Theological Tendencies*. New York: Harper & Bros., 1936. Ch. ii.

Burtt, Edwin A. "Modernism" in *Types of Religious Philosophy*. New York: Harper & Bros., 1939. Ch. viii.

Bushnell, Horace. *The Vicarious Sacrifice*. New York: Charles Scribner's Sons, 1866.

DeWolf, L. Harold. *The Case for Theology in Liberal Perspective*. Philadelphia: The Westminster Press, 1959.

Ferm, Vergilius, ed. *The Protestant Credo*. New York: Philosophical Library, 1953.

Ferré, Nels F. S. *Searchlights on Contemporary Theology*. New York: Harper & Bros., c. 1961.

Fiske, John. *The Destiny of Man*. Boston: Houghton Mifflin Co., 1884.

Fosdick, Harry E. *Shall the Fundamentalists Win?* (Tract)

Foster, F. H. *The Modern Movement in American Theology*. New York: Fleming Revell Co., n. d.

Foster, G. B. *The Finality of the Christian Religion*. University of Chicago Press, 1906.

Hopkins, C. H. *The Rise of the Social Gospel in American Protestantism*. New Haven: Yale Univ. Press, 1940.

Horsch, John. *Modern Religious Liberalism*. Scottdale, Pa.: Mennonite Publ. House, 1921.

Kepler, Thomas S. *Contemporary Religious Thought*. New York: Abingdon-Cokesbury, 1941.

————. *Contemporary Thinking About Jesus*. New York: Abingdon-Cokesbury, n. d.

Knudson, Albert C. *Present Tendencies in Religious Thought*. Nashville: Abingdon-Cokesbury, 1924.

[24] Antonia Aliotta, *The Idealistic Reaction Against Science* (New York: The Macmillan Co., 1914). Arthur Sears Eddington, *The Nature of the Physical World* (New York: The Macmillan Co., 1929). Karl Heim, *Die Wandlung im naturwissenschaftlichen Weltbild* (Stuttgart: Furche-Verlag, 1951).

[25] See the series of 34 statements by liberal theologians in answer to the question "How My Mind Has Changed," published in *The Christian Century*, 1939, and compare it with the subsequent decennial series of 1949 and 1959/1960.

Mackintosh, H. R. *Types of Modern Theology.* New York: Charles Scribner's Sons, 1937. Chs. i—vi.

Mathews, Shailer. *The Faith of Modernism.* New York: The Macmillan Co., 1924.

Mayer, F. E. "The Rise of Liberal Theology in Congregationalism," *Concordia Theological Monthly,* XV (1944), pp. 649—66.

McGiffert, A. C. *The Rise of Modern Religious Ideas.* New York: The Macmillan Co. 1915.

Roberts, David E., and Henry P. Van Dusen, eds. *Liberal Theology.* New York: Charles Scribner's Sons, 1943.

Smith, Gerald Birney, ed. *Religious Thought in the Last Quarter Century.* Univ. of Chicago Press, 1927.

Vanderlaan, Eldred C. *Fundamentalism vs. Modernism.* New York: H. W. Wilson Co., 1925. An anthology of leading fundamentalists and modernists.

Wieman, Henry Nelson, and Bernard Meland. *American Philosophies of Religion.* New York: Willett, Clark and Co., 1936.

Williams, D. D. "The Perplexity and Opportunity of Liberal Theology in America," *Journal of Religion,* XXV (July 1945).

SECTION II

Fundamentalism

The term "fundamentalism" denotes the interdenominational movement in the Reformed churches which attempted to stem the tide of the rationalistic modernism of the nineteenth century and early decades of the present century. When modernistic theologians had gained control of many influential positions on denominational boards and in theological seminaries and were able to propagate their views, the conservatives among the Baptists, Presbyterians, Methodists, Christians, organized to combat liberal theology. The new organization first came to public notice through the publication in 1909 of twelve volumes entitled *The Fundamentals.* The cost of publishing these books was defrayed through the generosity of two laymen, Lyman and Molton Stewart, who also established the Los Angeles Bible Institute and a fund for the promotion of conservative doctrines throughout the world.

The Fundamentals received an enthusiastic welcome by Protestant ministers. They stirred up strong action for the preservation of the historic faith of Protestantism and in the defense of the old Gospel of the fathers. In this way fundamentalism had mobilized its forces for a long and bitter battle against modernism, which threatened to make of Christianity a Christless and man-centered religion. The energy of fundamentalism was directed toward two objectives: "Conservatives directed their energies to gain control of evangelicalism for the purpose of reinstating Christian orthodoxy; they also undertook reformative measures beyond the church with a view to checking the standards of secular culture and substituting the principles of the historic faith." [1]

Other factors aided in the systematic organization of the conservative forces in the battle against modernism. Summer Bible conferences were directed toward the re-establishment of the principles of the ancient Gospel and against the "scientific" attitude and the social gospel of modernism. A number of

[1] Cole, p. 623.

interdenominational and undenominational seminaries (notably Moody Bible Institute, Wheaton College, and Dallas Theological Seminary) were established for the preservation of traditional Christianity. A vigorous crusade against modernism was carried on through polemical literature. Finally, a number of interdenominational organizations were organized to conduct a militant program against modernistic theology.[2]

Fundamentalists are ardent supporters of the strict orthodox doctrines of Christianity, particularly those which are susceptible to rational attacks, such as the inerrancy and authority of Scripture, the deity of Christ, the virgin birth, miracles, the atonement, resurrection, and the glorious return of Christ. However, in their zeal to preserve and defend traditional Christianity against the inroads of rationalism, they went to indefensible extremes.

In their reaction against the principle of modernism that the Bible is subject to the same literary criticism as every human document, many conservatives in the Reformed bodies resorted to a theory of mechanical inspiration and extreme literalism, which brought discredit upon fundamentalism. From its inception modernism tended to be this-worldly. Prompted in part by its literalism but chiefly by its opposition to modernism, the majority of fundamentalists espoused premillennialism; some, dispensationalism.[3]

Today conservative Protestant theology has entered into a postfundamentalist phase.[4]

BIBLIOGRAPHY

PART IX   SECTION II

Cole, Stewart G. *History of Fundamentalism.* New York: Richard R. Smith, 1931.

Carnell, Edward John. *The Case for Orthodox Theology.* Phila.: The Westminster Press, 1959.

Furniss, Norman F. *The Fundamentalist Controversy, 1918—1931.* New Haven: Yale University Press, 1954.

Hebert, Gabriel. *Fundamentalism and the Church.* Phila.: The Westminster Press, 1957.

Henry, Carl F. H. *Evangelical Responsibility in Contemporary Theology.* Grand Rapids: Wm. B. Eerdmans Publishing Co., 1957.

———, ed. *Contemporary Evangelical Thought.* Great Neck: Channel Press, c. 1957.

———, ed. *Revelation and the Bible: Contemporary Evangelical Thought.* Grand Rapids: Baker Book House, 1958.

Kik, J. Marcellus. *Ecumenism and the Evangelical.* Phila.: Presbyterian and Reformed Publishing Co., 1958.

[2] The Christian Fundamentals League, with headquarters at Los Angeles, and the World's Christian Fundamentals Association, with headquarters at Minneapolis. The Independent Fundamental Churches of America, with headquarters at Cicero, Ill., are discussed in P. VI, Sec. IV. — The revivalism of the early twentieth century reflected a thoroughly fundamentalist theology: see, for instance, William G. McLoughlin, Jr., *Billy Sunday Was His Real Name* (Chicago: The University of Chicago Press, 1955).

[3] See section on Premillennialism. Some fundamentalists militantly support capitalism on religious grounds (Matt. 20:1-6).

[4] See, for instance, Arnold W. Hearn, "Fundamentalist Renascence," *The Christian Century,* LXXV (1958), 528—530, and Edward John Carnell, "Post-Fundamentalist Faith," ibid., LXXVI (1959), 971.

Machen, J. G. *Christianity and Liberalism.* New York: The Macmillan Co., 1930.

Stott, John R. W. *Fundamentalism and Evangelism.* Grand Rapids: Wm. B. Eerdmans Publishing Co., 1959.

Tenney, Merrill C., ed. *The Word for This* Century: *Evangelical Certainties in an Era of Conflict.* New York: Oxford University Press, 1960.

Vanderlaan, Eldred C. *Fundamentalism vs. Modernism.* New York: H. W. Wilson Co., 1925.

SECTION III

Neo-Orthodoxy

The term "neo-orthodoxy" seems to designate a frame of mind rather than a theological system. It arose when liberal theology flourished in America during the period of prosperity before and after World War I. In Europe, the cradle of liberalism, men had lost their former faith in human progress, in reason's unlimited resources, and in the omnicompetence of science. At the conclusion of World War I the Europeans, especially the Germans, saw the vanity of their self-made gods, discarded the scientific method as totally unfit for solving religious problems, and even doubted the value of human reason in guiding men morally and spiritually. The Europeans found themselves in a moral and spiritual vacuum. This vacuum was filled to a very large extent by the rise of dialectical theology under the brilliant leadership of the Barthian school.[1]

The principles of dialectical theology are clearly enunciated in the Barmen Theological Declaration of 1934, a confessional statement designed to unite the Lutherans and the Reformed of Germany during the hectic days of the *Kirchen-kampf,* when the German church clashed with the Nazi philosophy. Under Karl Barth's guidance the drafters of this document attempted to set forth the principles of a dynamic and existential theology. According to the Declaration, such a theology does not ask the various denominations regarding their confessional status, but directs the church to the "present" Christ, who speaks in and through the church, to an encounter with Christ and a resultant crisis, to the acceptance of Christ's absolute sovereignty in the secular and spiritual realms, and to complete submission to Christ in both areas by all. Many regarded the adoption of this Declaration as an epochal event and as a theological watershed.[2]

In America the turn toward some form of supranaturalism began in the late twenties. In those days and later disillusionment was spreading, in part because of the depression, in part because of the catastrophe of World War II, but mostly because of the fear of the consequences of a possible atomic warfare. Men felt that the old optimistic

---

[1] Cp. H. Rolston, *A Conservative Looks to Barth and Brunner* (Nashville: Cokesbury Press, 1933), p. 17 f. Herman Sasse: "In Karl Barth liberal theology brought forth its own conqueror. He could overcome liberal theology because he was bone of its bone and flesh of its flesh." *Here We Stand* (New York: Harper & Bros., 1938), p. 155.

[2] Wilhelm Niesel, *Das Evangelium und die Kirchen: Ein Lehrbuch der Symbolik* (Neukirchen: Verlag des Erziehungsvereins), 1953, pp. 5—19.

liberalism was totally inadequate. The faith to which they turned was termed, for want of a better name, neo-orthodoxy. This new theological term may denote a number of theological concepts. In its strictest sense the term is applied to the theology of Karl Barth and Emil Brunner. In a wider sense it includes men like Karl Heim, Paul Tillich, Reinhold Niebuhr, the neosupernaturalism of John Oman, the conservatism of Edwin Lewis, the Christian realism of Walter Horton and John Bennett. Sometimes it is used in a sense wide enough to include the Neoplatonism of Dean Inge.

Neo-orthodoxy manifests the theological temper at the middle of the twentieth century in at least four significant areas.

1. Modernism had attempted to erase completely the line of demarcation between God and man. It saw in man a potential God, and believed to hear in man's voice the voice of God. But neo-orthodoxy has in varying degrees fixed a gulf between God and man. God is viewed as the Wholly Other.

2. The shibboleth of liberalism is that man is forever going upward and onward. Neo-orthodoxy holds that man is self-centered and therefore tyrannical, bent on destroying others, even at the risk of self-destruction. Man is evil. He is not on his way onward and upward by inherent power. Sin has again been taken more seriously. A change for the better cannot be brought about by man's own efforts, but only through God's grace.[3] Man must repent of his inherent egocentricity and trust that divine mercy, even through a cataclysm, will help him to solve his problems.

3. The Fatherhood of God is the central plank in liberalism's platform. Since Schleiermacher's day, God was pictured as a kind deity whose one and only attribute is love or forbearance. But "realistic theology" points to the socially and economically disinherited, to the underprivileged, to the tragedies in concentration camps, and sees behind it all a God not only of love but of judgment as well. As a result the social Gospel of liberal theology has had to make room for a message of sin and divine pardon.

4. Reason is the chief theological instrument in liberalism, but neo-orthodoxy in varying degrees holds that there are supranatural truths, which lie beyond the reaches of reason. Some think that divine revelation as it is given in the Bible is essential to the Christian faith; others — and they seem to be in the majority — hold that the record of the Bible itself is not the revelation, but that man must seek for the revelation behind the "revelation."

However, neo-orthodoxy, in at least four areas, is closer to liberalism than may appear at first glance. Like liberalism, neo-orthodoxy believes that theology dare not be stymied by doctrinal formulations, since theology is only a method which assures man of continued growth in his theological understanding. — In its attempt to return to the orthodox view on original sin neo-orthodoxy goes to the opposite extreme and finds the ground and cause of sin in the very constitution of man. This finding, strangely enough, brings neo-orthodoxy back into the fold of liberal theology. — Like liberalism, neo-orthodoxy in

---

[3] Cp. esp. Niebuhr, Vol. I, chs. v, vi. E. Brunner, probably more than any other neo-orthodox theologian, has expounded the paradox in the current view of man, stressing on the one hand man's terrific egocentricity (*cor incurvatum in se*) and, on the other, the noble aspirations of man, who still has the divine image. The neo-orthodox anthropology endeavors to combine human finitude with self-transcendence. Cp. E. Brunner, *Man in Revolt*, trans. Olive Wyon (New York: Scribner's, 1939), esp. p. 172 ff.

the final analysis maintains an optimistic view concerning the destiny of the world. True, neo-orthodox theologians seemingly hold a very pessimistic view. Both the European and the American neo-orthodox theologians, however, view eschatology as the fulfillment of the Creator's purpose chiefly in terms of a this-worldly readjustment of the universe. — And finally, like liberalism, neo-orthodoxy accepts the principles of higher criticism. Many of its exponents accept the Biblical account as divine revelation on the theory that the Biblical language is cast into symbolic language behind which the real truth is hidden. Barth and the American dialectical school favor the principles of higher criticism, and some have remained in the tradition of the Baur-Tübingen school. The process of acclimatization to the American situation is still going on.

BIBLIOGRAPHY

PART IX   SECTION III

Ahlstrom, Sidney E. "Continental Influence on American Christian Thought since World War I," *Church History*, XXVII (1958), 256—272.

Barth, Karl. *Die kirchliche Dogmatik*. Zurich: Evangelischer Verlag, 1939—. English translation: *Church Dogmatics*. New York: Charles Scribner's Sons, 1946—.

Brunner, Emil. *The Christian Doctrine of God*. Phila.: Westminster Press, c. 1950.

————. *The Christian Doctrine of Creation and Redemption*. Phila.: The Westminster Press, 1952.

————. *Eternal Hope*. London: Lutterworth Press, 1954.

————. *I Believe in the Living God: Sermons on the Apostles' Creed*. Trans. John Holden. Phila.: The Westminster Press, c. 1960.

Davies, D. R. *On to Orthodoxy*. New York: The Macmillan Co., c. 1949.

————. *Reinhold Niebuhr, Prophet from America*. New York: The Macmillan Co., 1945.

DeWolf, L. Harold. *The Religious Revolt Against Reason*. New York: Harper & Bros., 1949.

Engelder, Theodore. "Principles and Teachings of Dialectical Theology." *C. T. M.*, VIII (1936), *passim*.

Ferré, Nels F. S. *Searchlights on Contemporary Theology*. New York: Harper & Bros., c. 1961. Chapters 8 and 9.

Halverson, Marvin P., ed. *A Handbook of Christian Theology*. New York: Living Age Books, 1958.

Harland, Gordon. *The Thought of Reinhold Niebuhr*. New York: Oxford University Press, 1960.

Hazelton, Roger. *New Accents in Contemporary Theology*. New York: Harper & Brothers, 1960.

Hordern, William. *A Layman's Guide to Protestant Theology*. New York: The Macmillan Co., 1955.

————. *The Case for a New Reformation Theology*. Phila.: The Westminster Press, 1959.

Horton, Walter Marshall. *Christian Theology: An Ecumenical Approach*. Revised ed. New York: Harper & Brothers, c. 1958.

Kegley, Charles W., and Robert W. Bretall, ed. *Reinhold Niebuhr: His Religious, Social and Political Thought*. New York: The Macmillan Co., 1956.

Kroner, Richard. *The Primacy of Faith*. New York: The Macmillan Co., 1943.

Lewis, Edwin. *A New Heaven and a New Earth*. New York: Cokesbury Press, 1941.

———. *The Biblical Faith and Christian Freedom.* Phila.: Westminster Press, 1953.

Niebuhr, Reinhold. *The Nature and Destiny of Man.* 2 vols. New York: Charles Scribner's Sons, 1941 and 1943.

Otwell, John H. "Neo-Orthodoxy and Biblical Research," *Harvard Theological Review,* April, 1950. (Cp. *C. T. M.,* XXI [1950], 707—9).

Soper, David Wesley. *Major Voices in American Theology.* Phila.: The Westminster Press, 1953.

———. *Men Who Shape Belief.* Phila.: The Westminster Press, 1955.

Williams, Daniel Day. *What Present-Day Theologians Are Thinking.* Revised edition. New York: Harper & Bros., 1959.

SECTION IV

Ecumenical Theology

The term "ecumenical theology" has several connotations. It denotes first of all the theology of the universal church as it is enshrined and expressed in the ecumenical, or universal, creeds of the church. Frequently, however, the term has been used to denote a least common denominator in Christian theology on the basis of which all sectors of visible Christendom may unite.[1] Two objectives in particular have prompted the endeavor to unite all churches without doctrinal unity: a powerful church and a common front against the enemy. Therefore periods of great enthusiasm as well as periods of persecution have given rise to attempts to develop an ecumenical theology.[2]

The present-day attempt to devise an "ecumenical theology" is responsible for the several movements which cul-minated in the organization of the World Council of Churches.[3] Probably never before in modern history have such determined efforts been made by so many churchmen to establish this so-called "ecumenical theology." It appears that in formulating theological statements which would find general approval, theologians followed these postulates:

1. It is necessary to recognize and accept the proper perspective in doctrine; in other words, to distinguish clearly between primary and secondary doctrine.

2. The "universal church" is not merely an ideal but a reality.

3. Ecumenical theology must have a focal point, a central doctrine, as the leitmotif of theology.

4. Having grown out of specific life situations, all Christian doctrines are

---

[1] George Calixt, known as the champion of modern unionism, or syncretism, advocated a union of all denominations on the creedal formulations of the first five centuries, *quinquesaecularis consensus.*

[2] At the beginning of the 19th century the church experienced a period of revivalism accompanied by a wave of doctrinal indifference. As a result churches of divergent theological views united in the formation of missionary and Bible societies. Shortly afterward secularism swept the world and the various denominations set aside all doctrinal differences to meet jointly a "common foe" in the Evangelical Alliance of 1846. Macfarland, *Steps Toward the World Council,* ch. i.

[3] Sec. VI, below.

determined, modified, or accentuated by a continuous life experience.[4]

The assumption seems to be correct that the doctrines of God, man, Christ, sin, redemption, the church, and the kingdom of God are of prime importance in modern ecumenical theology. But it is also true that there is no agreement concerning these doctrines in the creedal statements of the various churches and among the individual theologians. At first glance it may appear as if ecumenical theology today had found the key which will open the door to a common faith, for in Christ the church is said to have the entire Christian truth. Many profess that their guide in arriving at an ecumenical theology is the central fact that God reveals Himself in Christ, or that Christ is the living Word through which God speaks to His church. However, it must be kept in mind that among ecumenical theologians "Christ" Himself is subject to a variety of interpretations. Ecumenical theology seems to run the danger of supplementing the central facts of Christian revelation with a human interpretation of these facts. At any rate, it seems passing strange that that portion of the constitution of the World Council has been challenged which restricts membership to such denominations as confess "Our Lord Jesus Christ as God and Savior."[5]

Ecumenical theology seeks Christian unity not so much in doctrinal agreement as rather in a diversity of theological opinions and in the sharing of divergent views and worship. A denomination inclined to favor a contemplative and mystical theology would have an opportunity to share in the religious experience of an activistic communion; the nonliturgical churches would be enriched by the liturgy of other communions; the anticreedal denominations would profit from the strongly confessional groups in the "oneness with Christ."[6] And this type of fellowship is said to equip all the churches to fight and conquer the common enemy of the church. Ecumenical theology is said to be the instrument to effect a spiritual change that will widen the range of the various denominations and ultimately establish a world-wide brotherhood. Such an ecumenical brotherhood is expected to solve the problems which arise from the diversity of races and cultures and merge all Christians into one unit. This merging does not necessarily mean that all denominations will ultimately unite and form a supraracial, supranational denomination, since each denomination with its divergent views will make a contribution to the whole.[7] In short, ecumenical theology does not strive for a universal denomination, but for a universal church in which the richness of the Christian faith will come to life in diversity rather than in conformity.

The impacts of World War II brought about a tremendous readjustment in the-

---

[4] Lewis Matthews Sweet, "Toward an Ecumenical Theology," *Christendom*, Vol. VI, No. 1, p. 377 ff., has been very helpful to the author in developing his conception of "ecumenical theology."

[5] Cp. Clarence T. Craig, "Christological Foundation of World Council of Churches," *Christendom*, IX, 13—22.

[6] The men who advocated an out-and-out "ecumenicity" advocated that the World Council be organized along geographic lines and do away completely with any denominational blocs. The Lutherans, esp. the participating American Lutherans, protested vigorously against such a plan, and in accord with their Lutheran consciousness advocated the organization of the World Council along denominational lines.

[7] See Daniel J. Fleming, *Bringing Our World Together* (New York: Charles Scribner's Sons, 1946), Preface.

ological thought, especially in two directions. In the first place, the continental, racial, national isolationism was making room for a "one-world" concept. Denominationalism was considered in large areas as part and parcel of the former provincialism, which was doomed in the modern world. Many believed that a composite ecumenical theology could do away with denominations completely or at least reduce denominationalism to a status in which each denomination would retain its denominational emphasis but also recognize as legitimate the views of every other. In the second place, the former voices of modernistic theologians have been silenced to a large degree by the sobering effects of the war. After the war the conservative theologians seemed to be much more influential in the forming of an ecumenical theology than liberal theologians.[8] In formulating doctrine ecumenical theology has given much thought to the place that is to be assigned to the Bible.[9]

Ecumenical theology began to take more definite shape after the "third" meeting of the Commission on Faith and Order (formerly the World Conference) in 1952 at Lund. The tendency seems to be to combine Christocentric with ecclesiocentric theology. One statement adopted at Lund reads as follows:

In His eternal love the Father has sent His Son to redeem creation from sin and death. In Jesus Christ God's Son became man. By word and deed He proclaimed on earth the arrival of God's kingdom, bore away the sins of the world on the Cross, rose again from the dead, ascended into heaven, the throne of His kingdom, at the right hand of God. At Pentecost God poured out His Spirit upon the Church, giving all who believe in Jesus Christ the power to become God's children. Through the indwelling of His Spirit Jesus Christ dwells in the midst of His Church. As Lord and King He will come again to judge the quick and the dead and to consummate the eternal kingdom of God in the whole creation.[10]

In our work we have been led to the conviction that it is of decisive importance for the advance of ecumenical work that the doctrine of the Church be treated in close relation both to the doctrine of Christ and to the doctrine of the Holy Spirit. We believe that this must occupy a primary place in the future work of this movement, and we so recommend to the Faith and Order Commission and to its working committee.[11]

The centrality of the doctrine of the church in ecumenical theology becomes quite evident in the omnibus volume published after the Amsterdam meeting in 1948.[12] One of the most difficult problems confronting ecumenical theology is a satisfactory description of the nature and the function of the church. At Amsterdam the theologians agreed on the following statements, to be submitted to the churches for further study:

A. We all believe that the church is God's gift to men for the salvation of

---

[8] O. S. Tomkins, "Implications of the Ecumenical Movement," *Ecumenical Review*, Oct., 1952, p. 20.

[9] See Wolfgang Schweitzer, "The Bible and the Church's Message to the World," *Ecumenical Review*, II (1949/1950), 123—132, and the World Council of Churches symposium *Biblical Authority for Today*, ed. Alan Richardson and Wolfgang Schweitzer (Phila.: Westminster Press, 1951).

[10] *Ecumenical Review*, V (1952/1953), 67.

[11] Ibid., p. 69.

[12] See Bibliog. Cp. particularly Herklots, *A Pilgrimage to Amsterdam;* Edm. Schlink, "Die Kirche in Gottes Heilsplan," *Theologische Literaturzeitung*, November, 1948, republished as "The Church and the Churches," *Ecumenical Review*, I (1948/1949), 150—168.

the world; that the saving acts of God in Jesus Christ brought the church into being; that the church persists in continuity throughout history through the presence and the power of the Holy Spirit.

Within this agreement, we should continue, in obedience to God, to try to come to a deeper understanding of our differences in order that they may be overcome. These concern:

1. The relation between the old and new Israel and the relation of the visible church to "the new creation" in Christ. It appears from our discussion that some of our differences concerning the church and the ministry have their roots here.

2. The relation, in the saving acts of God in Christ, between objective redemption and personal salvation, between Scripture and tradition, between the church as once founded and the church as Christ's contemporary act.

3. The place of the ministry in the church and the nature of its authority and continuity, the number and interpretation of the sacraments, the relation of Baptism to faith and confirmation, the relation of the universal to the local church, the nature of visible unity and the meaning of schism.

B. We believe that the church has a vocation to worship God in His holiness, to proclaim the Gospel to every creature. She is equipped by God with the various gifts of the Spirit for the building up of the Body of Christ. She has been set apart in holiness to live for the service of all mankind, in faith and love, by the power of the crucified and risen Lord and according to His example, by faith, in the eternity of the Kingdom of God and waiting for the consummation when Christ shall come again in the fullness of His glory and power.

Within this agreement also, we should continue, in obedience to God, to try to come to a deeper understanding of our differences in order that they may be overcome. These concern:

1. The relation between the Godward vocation of the church in worship and her manward vocation in witness and service.

2. The degree to which the Kingdom of God can be said to be already realized within the church.

3. The nature of the church's responsibility for the common life of men and their temporal institutions.[13]

A second problem is the church's witness to God's design in the disorder of mankind. At Amsterdam the purpose of God was formulated as follows:

> The purpose of God is to reconcile all men to Himself and to one another in Jesus Christ, His Son. That purpose was made manifest in Jesus Christ — His incarnation, His ministry of service, His death on the Cross, His resurrection and ascension. It continues in the gift of the Holy Spirit, in the command to make disciples of all nations, and in the abiding presence of Christ with His church. It looks forward to its consummation in the gathering together of all things in Christ. Much in that purpose is still hidden from us. Three things are perfectly plain:
>
> All that we need to know concerning God's purpose is already revealed in Christ.
>
> It is God's will that the Gospel should be proclaimed to all men everywhere.
>
> God is pleased to use human obedience in the fulfillment of His purpose.[14]

Some of the theologians in the ecumenical movement see it as the function of the church to act in order to remedy the disorder of society. This disorder is due to the crises of our age as they come to the surface in the clash between capitalism and labor, in the unequal distribution of the world's goods, in the social

---

[13] *Man's Disorder and God's Design*, I, 206. See also Conrad Bergendoff, *The One Holy Catholic Apostolic Church: The Hoover Lectures 1953* (Rock Island: Augustana Book Concern, 1954).

[14] Ibid., II, 212.

and economic insecurity, and similar situations. The church must resolve the resultant tensions by freeing mankind from racial prejudices and by bringing about a full recognition of the worth of the individual.[15]

Ecumenical theologians have tried to find the answer to the many problems growing out of the international disorder. They believe that war is contrary to the will of God and that therefore Christians must critically examine every governmental action which would tend to create an international tension and must demand that human rights and fundamental freedom be encouraged, especially the freedom of religious worship and assembly.[16]

BIBLIOGRAPHY

PART IX

SECTION IV

Baillie, Donald, and John Marsh, eds. *Intercommunion*. New York: Harper & Bros., 1952.

Bell, G. K. A., ed. *Documents on Christian Unity, Fourth Series: 1948—1957*. London: Oxford University Press, 1958.

Bilheimer, Robert S. *The Quest for Christian Unity*. New York: Association Press, 1952.

Bradshaw, Marion J. *Free Churches and Christian Unity: A Critical View of the Ecumenical Movement*. Boston: The Beacon Press, 1954.

Bridston, Keith R. "Survey on Church Union Negotiations 1957—1959," *Ecumenical Review*, XII (1959/1960), 231—260.

The Christian Hope and the Task of the Church (Evanston Assembly volume). New York: Harper & Bros., 1954.

Douglass, H. Paul. *A Decade of Objective Progress in Church Unity*. New York: Harper & Bros., 1937.

Ecumenical Review, a quarterly published by the World Council of Churches in the interest of ecumenical theology. Founded in 1948.

Edwall, Pehr, Eric Hayman, and William D. Maxwell. *Ways of Worship*. New York: Harper & Bros., 1952.

Flew, R. Newton, ed. *The Nature of the Church*. New York: Harper & Bros., 1952.

Herklots, H. G. G., and H. S. Leiper. *Pilgrimage to Amsterdam*. New York: World Council of Churches, 1947.

Horton, Walter. *Contemporary Continental Theology*. New York: Harper & Bros., 1938. Ch. iv.

Man's Disorder and God's Design, "The Amsterdam Assembly Series." New York: Harper & Bros., 1948.

Pauck, Wilhelm. "The Prospect of Ecumenical Theology Today," *Journal of Religion*, XXV (1945), 79.

Rouse, Ruth, and Stephen Charles Neill. *A History of the Ecumenical Movement 1517—1948*. Phila.: The Westminster Press, 1954.

Söderblom, N. *Christian Fellowship*. New York: Fleming H. Revell, 1923. Esp. Ch. iv.

Van Dusen, Henry P. "Reunion and Revival," *Christendom*, X (Winter 1945), p. 32.

---

[15] Ibid., III, 189—97.

[16] Ibid., IV, 215—23. See "The Declaration of Religious Liberty," pp. 225—28. Cp. also Herklots, chs. v—vii; Fey, p. 15 ff.

SECTION V

Moral Re-Armament

Buchmanism, or Moral Re-Armament (MRA),[1] was founded by Frank N. Buchman, a graduate of Mount Airy (Lutheran) Theological Seminary and member of the Lutheran Ministerium of Pennsylvania. He says that he was deeply moved by a simple sermon in an English village church and led to believe that the great facts of the Christian life are confession of sins, restitution, sharing, changing lives. His experiences as a Y. M. C. A. secretary had convinced him that the individual approach to men is a most effective way of dealing with people's spiritual problems. To set the stage for such an individual approach, he introduced the house-party technique, by which, in an informal setting and in a spirit of cameraderie, one man can lead another to confess his sins and ultimately to change his life.[2] The first house party of significance was held in 1921 at Oxford for Oxford and Cambridge university students. Later, teams of workers carried the Buchmanite principles to practically every European country, the U. S. A., China, India, South America, Australia. Diplomats, industrial magnates, members of royalty, accepted the Buchmanite principles that a world religion of absolute love, honesty, purity, unselfishness, would usher in a period of universal peace. While Hitler plotted to make war, Buchman in May 1938, proclaimed that the moral re-armament of the nations would abolish war.[3] With the outbreak of the war, Buchmanism became discredited in large areas. Since the war it has experienced a rather remarkable comeback and is using the former technique to proclaim its essential points.[4]

The heart and core of Buchman's philosophy of life may be stated in four principles: confession, surrender, guidance, sharing. There are no theological statements on such vital Christian truths as the person and work of Christ. The movement claims to be "applied Christianity," but apparently its concept of Christianity revolves solely about what man can do for a moral re-armament of the individual, the group, and the

[1] The original designation, Oxford Group Movement, was ultimately discarded because of its similarity to the Oxford, or Tractarian, movement. Buchmanism is also known as First Century Christian Fellowship, because those who have accepted the Buchmanite principles form a local "fellowship" (congregation) supposedly after the pattern of the early Jerusalem fellowship.

[2] From the beginning Buchman held many of his house parties at the better hotels and resorts as part of his program to win over people of influence and position.

[3] Cp. *Booktab* (Winter 1943).

[4] In 1946 the Buchmanites bought a 700-room hotel at Caux, near Geneva. Diplomats, industrialists, theologians (e. g., Emil Brunner), financiers, have attended house parties here. *Christian Century*, Jan. 15, 1947, p. 76. The MRA owns Island House, a large hotel on Mackinac Island, where house parties are held continuously during the summer months.

world. An English philosopher summarizes Buchmanism as follows:

> Let God change you, guide you in everything along the lines of absolute purity, honesty, unselfishness, and love, and use you to bring others to Him. When man listens, God speaks. When man obeys, God acts. When men change, nations change.[5]

The first principle is confession. An unconfessed sin works havoc with man's spiritual life. The "worker" must prevail upon the individual to confess whatever sin stands between him and God. The Buchmanite holds that everyone is nursing some secret sin which must be brought to light by facing Christ's fourfold standard of absolute honesty, purity, selflessness, love. This must be followed by four steps: to hate, forsake, confess, and repair sin. This process is called the "change," conversion. The "groupers" tend to approach sins very atomistically.

Surrender is the second principle. It implies complete surrender of the will to Christ and may even imply an entire change of one's whole life plan. Surrender, or conversion, means

> a complete experience of Jesus Christ; and the degree to which any of us is truly converted is measured by our likeness to the lives and experiences of the disciples.[6]

The groupers insist that a halfhearted allegiance does not satisfy Christ, and it cannot satisfy the serious-minded grouper. Their slogan is: "Surrender as much as you know of yourself to as much as you know of Christ." This counsel means that though the surrender may be genuine, yet it is never complete, since man always holds back something.

Direct guidance is said to follow surrender. During the "quiet time" the grouper is told to pray. In Buchmanite parlance prayer implies both talking and listening to God. As an acrostic the word *p-r-a-y* means "Powerful radiograms *a*lways *y*ours." During this period the grouper awaits directions from God as to the activity of the day, the plans for the future, the purchases to be made, journeys to be undertaken, etc.[7]

Sharing is the fourth principle. The Buchmanites distinguish between the sharing for confession and the sharing for witness. The basic idea is that one or the other, or both, are required to change another's life. To lead one's fellow man to confess his sin, it may become necessary for the grouper to give a frank confession of his own sin in order to remove every inhibition in the other person. The sharing for witness is the public testimony of the grouper's own changed life, the moral re-armament which he has experienced, the restitution he has made. All this is considered important in "changing" other people's lives.

In its emphasis on sincere devotion, personal mission work, religious meditation, Buchmanism is a rebuke to institutionalized religion and to a mere external religiosity. The dynamics for its alleged moral re-armament, however, is often not the Christ-centered faith of the Scriptures, but anthropocentric philosophy of man's own devising.

---

[5] Philip Leon, p. 14.

[6] Samuel M. Shoemaker, *Twice-Born Ministers* (New York: Fleming H. Revell, 1929), p. 10 f.

[7] The grouper is advised to write down the directions, since, as says a Chinese proverb, the weakest ink is stronger than the best memory. Next the grouper will check his guidance for the day with that given to others, inquiring especially whether the direction goes counter to the highest standards of our belief, to Christ's revelations in the Bible, to our real duties. Finally, the grouper must carry out the order for the day, "even if it involves a trip to Timbuctu."

BIBLIOGRAPHY

PART IX   SECTION V

Bach, M. *They Have Found a Faith.* Indianapolis: Bobbs-Merrill, 1946. Ch. v.

Braden, Charles S. *These Also Believe.* New York: The Macmillan Co., 1949. Ch. xii.

Clark, Walter H. *The Oxford Group: Its History and Significance.* Bookman Associates, 1951.

Davies, Horton. *Christian Deviations.* New York: Philosophical Library, 1954. Ch. ix.

Leon, Philip. *The Philosophy of Courage.* New York: Oxford Univ. Press, 1939.

Murray, Robert. *Group Movements Throughout the Ages.* New York: Harper & Bros., 1936. Final chapter.

Russell, J. A. *For Sinners Only.* New York: Harper & Bros., 1932.

Schwehn, W. W. *What Is Buchmanism?* St. Louis: C. P. H., 1940.

Williamson, Geoffrey. *Inside Buchmanism.* New York: Philosophical Library, 1954.

SECTION VI

National Council of the Churches of Christ in the United States of America (NCCCUSA)

The NCCCUSA is the merger, effected December, 1950, in Cleveland, of twelve interdenominational agencies.

The Federal Council was organized in 1908 by twenty-five Protestant denominations representing 26,000,000 people. Its purpose was to promote a spirit of fellowship, service, and co-operation among the churches. Through the forty years of its history the leaders of the organization were outspoken advocates of liberal theology and its social gospel. Its leaders wholeheartedly supported and expanded the social creed adopted by the Methodist church.

The Foreign Missions Conference was formed in 1893. It united in planning and action some 122 boards and agencies of the United States and Canada and represents 66 Protestant denominations and 30,000,000 Christians.

The Home Mission Council of N. A. was a merger in 1940 of the Council of Women of Home Missions and the Home Missions Council. Both had their beginning in 1908, and represented 23 denominations in many areas of American life.[1]

The Missionary Education Movement was begun as the Young People's Missionary Movement, a co-operative agency of 23 denominations. It published missionary and educational materials, conducted training schools and conferences, etc.

The United Council of Church

---

[1] See Robert T. Handy, *We Witness Together: A History of Cooperative Home Missions* (New York: Friendship Press, 1956).

Women (1941) aimed to integrate the entire program of the church into building Christian communities.

The International Council of Religious Education was organized to stimulate and improve religious education by research projects and publications.

Church World Service, Inc., has served as the agency for physical relief in stricken areas throughout the world.

Other agencies were the Protestant Council of Higher Education; United Stewardship Council; Interseminary Commission; Protestant Film Commission; Protestant Radio Commission.

It was felt in many circles of the Protestant churches that the aims and objectives of these separate agencies could be best fulfilled if one organization with properly constituted boards and committees were brought into being. The plans for the merger of the twelve agencies were slow in taking shape, because so many divergent interests had to be satisfied. In spite of every effort the organizational structure of the Council appears very complex because of the multitude of departments, divisional units, commissions, and committees. The National Council functions through four major divisions, each one responsible for one of the broad areas of Christian activity: The Division of Christian Life and Work; the Division of Christian Education; the Division of Home Missions; the Division of Foreign Missions.

The National Council's program [2] is indicated in the 1952 "Letter to Christian America":

1. The Gospel must be proclaimed to all people. Evangelism . . . is the church's primary task. It is not sufficient that the gospel be preached in established places of worship. It is necessary that it be taken to the people.

2. The necessity of integrating religion into our public schools, so that they will not decay into secularism, without, however, any violation of the principle of the separation of church and state.

3. The Council considers it as its duty to sensitize the conscience of the nation . . . that no group of citizens shall arrogate to itself perpetual rights and privileges which it denies others.

A serious basic weakness of the National Council, inherited from the Federal Council, is the lack of theological concern among some of the member bodies. This manifests itself from time to time in extreme forms of unionism and in a misunderstanding of Christ's kingdom in terms which seem to match the objectives of the United Nations. Yet at Denver in 1952 the leaders declared:

The National Council of Churches, composed of thirty communions, with a membership of 35 million people, is not itself a church but a council of churches. Neither is it a superchurch, and does not aspire to become one. . . . The council does, however, afford a unique medium whereby churches meet together, worship together, think, plan and act together. We are, above all, churches of Christ. The constitution-tie which binds us together is our common allegiance to Him as our divine Lord and Savior. Jesus Christ, crucified and risen, who is for all of us the one and only Head of the church, drew us together and holds us together, in unswerving loyalty to himself and to one another, and leads us to seek an ever greater unity.[3]

Some of the accomplishments of the Council will serve to illustrate its program: the completion of the Revised Standard Version of the Bible; completion of the resettlement of 52,000 dis-

---

[2] *The National Council Outlook,* published by the Council at 475 Riverside Drive, New York 27, N. Y., is the official monthly publication.

[3] From "Letter to Christian America," issued by the General Assembly of the National Council of Churches, Denver, 1952.

placed persons; an increasing impact upon the American public through news services, radio, and television; the co-ordinated effort against the appointment of a U. S. ambassador to the Vatican; concerted action to counteract the infiltration of secularism into the public schools. The prominence given to social problems is evident in the pronouncements which the National Council has made on such matters as these: displaced persons; emergency food for India; conscientious objectors; gambling and public morals; the technical assistance program and the churches; the peace treaty with Japan; approval of Article 13 of the draft of the International Covenant of Human Rights; universal military training; and the problem of drug addiction.[4]

SECTION VII

The American Council of Christian Churches

The American Council of Christian Churches was organized in direct opposition to the Federal Council by the Rev. Carl McIntire of Collingswood, N. J., September 17, 1941. The ACCC has designated itself to be the voice of Christians.[1] Its stated purpose is "to enable evangelical Christians to accomplish tasks that can better be done in co-operation than separately, including joint witness to the glorious testimony to precious souls against denials or distortions of the historic Christian faith." The church bodies behind this new organization were initially the Bible Protestant and the Bible Presbyterian churches. The organization very emphatically states its main purpose is to unite its members' testimony against the National Council of Churches. They charge that this body has not been true to the Gospel, has "injected itself into political and economic life, and has promoted theories hardly to be distinguished from downright Communism." They challenge the National Council's assertion that it is the most effective and most representative spokesman for the Protestant churches in America. In particular, the American Council protests against the policy of the broadcasting companies to appoint the National Council as the agent to distribute the free time allotted for religious broadcasts. It objects as vehemently to the tacitly accepted principle that the National Council is to be recognized as the agent to deal with the Federal Government.

The American Council is outspokenly and sometimes even militantly fundamentalist. The preamble to its Constitution reads:

WHEREAS, It is the duty of Christian believers to make common testimony to

---

[4] For the objectives of the National Council see the Constitution, Art. II.

[1] Prominent among the original founders of the American Council were Dr. J. O. Buswell of the National Bible Institute; Mr. Ernest Gordon of the *Sunday School Times;* Dr. Wm. Houghton of the Moody Bible Institute; Rev. F. J. Meldau, editor of *Christian Victory;* Rev. J. Davis Adams, president of Philadelphia School of the Bible. The information in this sketch is based on the pamphlet *About the American Council* (The American Council of Christian Churches, 340 West 55th Street, New York, N. Y.)

their glorious faith . . . to these truths among others equally precious: the full truthfulness, inerrancy, and authority of the Bible, which is the Word of God; the holiness and love of the one sovereign God, Father, Son, and Holy Spirit; the true deity and sinless humanity of our Lord Jesus Christ, His virgin birth, His atoning death, "the just for the unjust," His bodily resurrection, His glorious coming again; salvation by grace through faith alone; the oneness in Christ of those He has redeemed with His own precious blood; and the maintenance in the visible church of purity of life and doctrine.

The member churches emphasize above all else the inerrancy of the Bible. Some are extremely literalistic, especially in their advocacy of premillennialism. They oppose the ideologies of modern social movements, as they were adopted and espoused by many leaders of the Federal Council. Officially they do not interfere with the economic nor the political convictions of their individual members.[2] The authorized departments are evangelism, information and publication, home missions, foreign missions, Christian education, and radio. Membership can be by a denomination (synod or association), by a local church, or by an individual Christian. But none can hold membership simultaneously in the National Council.

SECTION VIII

The National Association of Evangelicals for United Action (EUA)

The American Council of Christian Churches had hoped to unite all fundamentalists in an anti-Federal Council organization. But some leading fundamentalists did not share the theological views of leaders in ACCC nor their bitter opposition to the Federal Council.[1] They organized as the Evangelicals for United Action (EUA) in St. Louis, Mo., April, 1942, not so much to oppose the Federal Council as rather to supplement its program. Though the leaders represent the fundamental wing of Protestantism, they have — unlike the leaders of ACCC — retained their membership in the various major denominations now belonging to the National Council.

Their purpose is to oppose from within the liberal elements in their respective denominations. The reason for organizing a third interdenominational agency is summarized in the Preamble to the Constitution:

> WHEREAS, There is no existing organization which adequately represents or acts for a very large proportion of our evangelical Protestant constituency; and WHEREAS, We realize that in many areas of Christian endeavor the organizations which now purport to be the representatives of Protestant Christianity have departed from the faith of Jesus Christ, we do now reaffirm our unqualified loyalty to this Gospel. . . . And in this loyalty to the evangelical

[2] Though they make this statement, they nevertheless attack socialism, Communism, and other forms of economic polity, while they defend capitalism.

[1] For a summary and comparison of the ACCC and the Evangelicals see *C. T. M.*, XIV, 143—46.

Christian faith and opposition to all apostasy, we do hereby unite our testimony.[2]

The Evangelicals' principles for united action are based on fundamentalistic doctrines, though broad in scope. They profess to be fully dedicated to the truth, yet attempt to frame their definition of orthodoxy in the simplest possible terms.[3] According to its constitution, the EUA confesses the infallibility of the Bible, the Trinity, the deity of Christ, the vicarious atonement, the personality and work of the Holy Spirit, and the personal return of Christ.[4] The

activities of the Evangelicals are in the same areas as those of other interdenominational groups: Relation to the government, use of radio, evangelism, home and foreign missions, Christian education, etc. As the American Council, so EUA protested the Federal Council's exclusive control of allotting the networks' free radio time for religious broadcasts. They maintained that the many divisions in Protestantism — especially the conservatives — could not be properly represented by the Federal Council and its successor, the National Council.

SECTION IX

The World Council of Churches

Historical Genesis

The World Council of Churches grew out of three inter- and supradenominational movements and programs of activities:

A. Movements that aimed at co-ordination of existing church work and promoted co-operation to avoid overlapping and rivalry. E. g., the World Student Christian Federation and the International Missionary Council.

B. Movements that aimed at bringing Christian conscience to bear on the practical and contemporary problems of the world. E. g., the World Alliance for International Friendship through the Churches, and the Universal Christian Council for Life and Work.

C. Movements that aimed directly at the discussion of the doctrinal disagreements underlying the disunion of Christendom. E. g., the World Conference on Faith and Order.[1]

---

[2] *Evangelical Action,* compiled and edited by the Executive Committee (Boston: United Action Press, 1942), p. 101—2. In it W. W. Ayer states: [The Federal Council is] strong and competent in certain religious fields or religious activities, but does not represent the great body of evangelical Christians in faith and doctrine. I would not deny the Federal Council its proper existence, but I feel that it does not represent me in many of its programs and pronouncements. [Ibid., p. 43.]

[3] S. W. Paine of Houghton College, New York, ibid., p. 59. The following Fundamentalists took an active part in organizing EUA: Dr. H. J. Ockenga of Boston (president); the Rev. R. T. Davis, secretary of African Inland Mission; Dr. W. W. Ayer, Calvary Baptist Church, New York; Dr. W. H. Houghton, president of Moody Bible Institute.

[4] Ibid., pp. 101—6. See also James DeForest Murch, *Cooperation Without Compromise: A History of the National Association of Evangelicals* (Grand Rapids: Wm. B. Eerdmans Publishing Co., 1956).

[1] Hodgson, p. 8.

1. The International Missionary Council, after several preliminary meetings, was organized at Lake Mohonk, N. Y., in 1921.[2] This organization has played an important part in the life of a large segment of Protestantism. It held meetings at Jerusalem in 1925 and at Madras in 1938.[3]

2. The Universal Christian Council for Life and Work was initiated jointly by the Federal Council of Churches; the World Alliance for International Friendship through the Churches; the British Conference on Christian Politics, Economics, and Citizenship (COPEC); and the Church of Sweden, with the hearty support of the Swedish government and the ecclesiastical statesman, Archbishop Nathan Söderblom. At its first meeting in Stockholm, 1925, this interdenominational agency deliberately by-passed all doctrinal issues and devoted itself to a "solution of the contemporary social and international problems." However, at the second meeting at Oxford in 1937 attention was given to some theological issues.[4]

3. The World Conference on Faith and Order came into being largely in response to an invitation of the Prot-estant Episcopal Church, issued at the urging of Bishop Brent, asking "representatives of all Christian bodies throughout the world which accept our Lord Jesus Christ as God and Savior [to participate in a conference] for the consideration of questions pertaining to Faith and Order of the Church of Christ."[5] The leaders in this movement, e. g., Adolf Deissmann, realized that it was impossible to avoid the theological issues which separated the churches. The invitation to a conference on Faith and Order stated specifically that the purpose of the meeting was a discussion of the differences on Faith and Order, i. e., the creed and the ministry, but that no church should lose its own individuality or independent sovereignty, nor would any church be expected to ratify the findings of this Conference.[6] The first meeting was held at Lausanne, 1927. The theological basis for membership included "all who accept the Lord Jesus Christ as God and Savior" and who acknowledge the ecumenical creeds of the church as the acceptable doctrinal statement of the Conference. The Conference set forth its message to the world in a lengthy statement.[7] The second meeting was held in 1937 at

---

[2] Brown, pp. 54, 55. For the resolutions on organization of the Continuation Committee of the World Missionary Conference at Edinburgh, 1910, see ibid., pp. 206, 207. See also *World Missionary Conference* (New York: Fleming H. Revell Co., 1913), 9 vols. For an excellent history of the IMC see Hogg, esp. p. 15 ff. For the contents of the agreements see Slosser, pp. 256, 257.

[3] See Brown, pp. 213—16 for the basis of the IMC's message, and Hogg, pp. 378—82, for the present Constitution. After protracted and delicate negotiations, the integration of the IMC — although not without some losses — into the World Council of Churches is in prospect.

[4] Brown, pp. 64, 82, 83. Cf. Slosser, p. 294. Hodgson, p. 13 f. For the official reports of the Stockholm Conferences see Bell and Oldham.

[5] Oldham, p. 15. Cp. H. N. Bate, ed., *Faith and Order: Proceedings of the World Conference, Lausanne* (Garden City, N. Y.: Doubleday, Doran and Co., 1928), p. vii; also see Bishop Brent in *Report of the Preliminary Meeting at Geneva*, p. 19. Hodgson, p. 16.

[6] Brown, pp. 51, 83.

[7] Cp. Bate (fn. 5, above), pp. 461—63; also see Brown, pp. 101, 110.

Edinburgh,[8] just prior to the Oxford meeting of the Council on Life and Work. Later, at the organizational meeting of the World Council of Churches in 1948 the Council on Faith and Order became the Commission on Faith and Order; and as such it functions somewhat independently within the World Council. It had its third meeting as the Council, and its first as the Commission, at Lund in 1952. The North American Faith and Order Conference on "The Nature of the Unity We Seek," held at Oberlin, Ohio, in September 1957 under the auspices of the World Council of Churches, was marked by the emergence of a strongly Biblical theology and achieved a somewhat unexpected degree of unanimity among the participants on many, though by no means all, issues. It helped to shift the attention of the delegates from the traditional American pattern of interdenominational co-operation to a recognition of the immediate relevance of the theological issues involved in the quest for unity.[9]

In the opinion of the leaders the 1937 meetings showed that a merging of the Life and Work (Stockholm) and the Faith and Order (Lausanne) movements was highly desirable. They realized the difficulties of a possible merger, because of the basic differences in the purpose and plan of each. The former organization concerned itself chiefly with the moral and social problems which confronted the world as a result of the maladjustments of human society, but it sought also to remove the provincial isolationism which was universal prior to World War I. The other movement dealt primarily with doctrinal matters and the vexing problems growing out of the divergent views on the ministry. Life and Work took it upon itself to issue pronouncements and to express opinions concerning world problems and current issues. Faith and Order, however, prided itself on its independent structure. It passed no resolutions that would subject a church to a doctrinal agreement. It permitted only statements of faith and doctrine from the various branches of the church to be presented.[10]

Specific steps leading to the formation of the World Council were (1) the meeting of the Committee of Thirty-five at Westfield College, London, England, in July, 1937;[11] and (2) the meeting of

---

[8] After Brent's death William Temple succeeded Bishop Brent in 1929 as chairman of the Continuation Committee. For the summary of events that took place from 1927 to 1937 cp. Leonard Hodgson, ed., *The Second World Cohference on Faith and Order* (New York: Macmillan Co., 1938), pp. 1—14. For a report of the Edinburg Conference see ibid., p. 224 ff., Brown, p. 115 ff. *The Report of the Second World Conference on Faith and Order* was published by the Secretariat, Nov., 1937, in New York. A number of excellent studies, prepared by various commissions for the Edinburgh meeting, were subsequently published by Harper & Bros. and distributed by the Continuation Committee. See also R. Newton Flew, ed., *The Nature of the Church* (New York: Harper & Bros., 1952), pp. 233—337.

[9] See the articles and reports on the Oberlin meeting in the *Ecumenical Review*, X (1957/1958), 121—181, as well as the official report (see Bibliog. below) and the symposium edited by J. Robert Nelson, *Christian Unity in North America* (St. Louis: The Bethany Press, c. 1958).

[10] The Faith and Order movement, dealing primarily with theological problems, had no occasion to establish and finance an organization, whereas Life and Work had a centralized office and full-time secretariat at Geneva.

[11] An early practical step was taken in May, 1933, when, at Archbishop Temple's invitation, ten ecumenical leaders conferred informally at the archiepiscopal palace at Bishopthorpe, York. Each held an important place in the movement of which he was a member: Dr. J. H. Oldham and Dr. Wil-

the special advisory conference to aid the Committee of Fourteen at Utrecht in May, 1938, whose chief task was to formulate a provisional constitution for a projected Council of the Churches of the World. This document was to be a witness to the historic (Trinitarian) faith of the church and an instrument which would deprive no church of its specific interests or interpretations.[12] The organizational meeting, scheduled for 1941, had to be postponed until 1948, when it was held in Amsterdam. The Second World Assembly was held in Evanston, Illinois, in 1954. The Third World Assembly is to meet in New Delhi, India, in 1961, when the Inter-national Missionary Council is to be formally integrated into the World Council of Churches.

Nature and Purpose

The World Council of Churches is a "fellowship of churches which accept our Lord Jesus Christ as God and Savior." [13] At the organizational meeting all sections of Christendom, except the Roman Catholic church, were repre-sented.[14] The World Council presents a new attempt and an unprecedented approach to the problem of interchurch relationships.[15] It is confronted with pe-culiar problems, the most difficult of

liam Paton represented the International Missionary Council; Dean H. N. Bate and the Archbishop of York (William Temple) — Faith and Order; Dr. Samuel McCrea Cavert and William Adams Brown — Life and Work; Bishop Valdemar Ammundsen and Henry Louis Henriod — the World Alli-ance; Charles Guillon and Dr. W. A. Visser 't Hooft — the Youth Move-ment. Cp. Brown, pp. 134, 138—44. Brown records the interesting note that it was Dr. Samuel McCrea Cavert (Life and Work) who first suggested the name "World Council of Churches."

[12] Membership was opened to all historically Trinitarian churches in the phrase "which accept our Lord Jesus as God and Savior." Cp. Brown, p. 146; *Christendom*, IX, 13—22. Hodgson makes the pertinent comment that "everyone at this meeting demanded the acceptance of the Nicene Faith as the basis of the Council . . . and that no one present voiced the modernist liberalism which would have been prominent a quarter of a century earlier" (*Ecum. Movement*, p. 33).

[13] The Constitution of the World Council, as drafted by the Com-mittee of Fourteen in 1937, was adopted with only a few minor changes in 1948. The Central Committee of the Council is urging the New Delhi Assembly to adopt a new version: "A fellowship of churches which confess the Lord Jesus Christ as God and Savior according to the Scriptures and therefore seek to fulfill together their common calling to the glory of the one God, Father, Son and Holy Spirit."

[14] Though invited, the Roman Catholic church's position that there is only one church made it impossible for the pope to permit participation in any conference which places other churches on a par with the Church of Rome. See P. II, Sec. VI. There were, however, unofficial gatherings of Roman theologians with some of the Protestant theologians during the Amsterdam Conference in 1948. Cp. Hodgson, p. 44. For statements of the Roman reaction to the World Council see *Ecumenical Review*, II (1949/1950), 296—298.

[15] "Unlike certain earlier efforts, the World Council is not to consist of a series of periodic conferences. It is to be a continuing body, functioning regularly in behalf of its member churches, drawing strength from their varied outlooks and interests, and in turn seeking to guide toward deeper mutual understanding and a more united apprehension of God's will for His churches in these days." Bennett, *Man's Disorder*, p. 5.

which is formulating a definition that would account for the various ecclesiologies of its member churches. The leaders have found it necessary to state as explicitly what the World Council is not as what it is.

The World Council claims to be a council, not a church, not the world church, nor the one holy catholic and apostolic church of the creeds. Its avowed purpose is

> to bring the churches into living contact with each other and to promote the study and discussion of the issues of Church unity. By its very existence and its activities the Council bears witness to the necessity of a clear manifestation of the oneness of the Church of Christ. But it remains the right and duty of each Church to draw from its ecumenical experience such consequences as it feels bound to do on the basis of its own convictions.[16]

From the various discussions and reports it is apparent that varied ecclesiologies are probably the greatest theological barrier to real union of churches.[17] While the Council stands for church unity, it recognizes that among its member churches there are great divergences in the way the unity of the church is to be understood. But the leaders insist that no one of these conceptions expresses the ecumenical theory around which the World Council is formed.

The Constitution lists the functions of the World Council as follows:

1. To carry on the work of the two world movements, for Faith and Order and for Life and Work.

2. To facilitate common action by the Churches.

3. To promote co-operation in study.

4. To promote the growth of ecumenical consciousness in the members of all Churches.

5. To establish relations with denominational federations of world-wide scope and with other ecumenical movements.

6. To call world conferences on specific subjects as occasion may require, such conferences being empowered to publish their own findings.[18]

To define the positive assumptions which underlie the World Council of Churches, the Central Committee in its 1950 message emphasized the following points:

1. Conversation, co-operation and common witness of the Churches must be based on the common recognition that Christ is the Divine Head of the Body.

2. Though the New Testament unity is not one of churches with each other, the fact is that there can only be one Church of Christ.

3. The member Churches recognize that the membership of the Church of Christ is more inclusive than the membership of their own Church body. They seek, therefore, to enter into living contact with those outside their own ranks who confess the Lordship of Christ. Therefore the task is to seek fellowship with all those who, while not members of the same visible body, belong together as members of the mystical body. And the ecumenical movement is the place where this search and discovery takes place.

---

[16] *The Church, the Churches and the World Council of Churches* (A statement commended to the churches for study and comment by the Central Committee of the Council, meeting at Toronto, July, 1950), p. 7.

[17] Ibid., p. 8. It is readily understood that it is impossible to find a "golden mean" among the strongly hierarchical system and highy sacramental worship of Eastern Orthodoxy, the highly "democratic" form of Baptist church government, and the "enthusiastic" and uninhibited type of worship of some Reformed bodies.

[18] American office of the World Council of Churches is located at 475 Riverside Drive, New York 27, N. Y.

4. The member churches of the World Council consider the relationship of other churches to the holy catholic church which the creeds profess as subject for mutual consideration. Nevertheless, membership in the Council does not imply that each church must regard the other member church as church in the true and full sense of the word.

5. The member churches of the World Council recognize in other churches elements of the true church. . . . They consider that this mutual recognition obliges them to enter into a serious conversation with one another in the hope that these elements of truth will lead to the recognition of full truth and to unity based on the full truth.

6. The member churches of the Council are willing to consult together in seeking to learn of the Lord Jesus Christ what witness He would have them bear to the world in His name. That is, the purpose is "that the world may believe" and that the church may "testify that the Father has sent the Son to be the Savior of the world."

7. A further practical implication of common membership in the World Council is that the member churches should recognize their solidarity with one another, render assistance to one another in case of need, and refrain from such actions as are incompatible with brotherly relationships.

8. The member churches enter into spiritual relationships through which they seek to learn from one another and to give help to one another in order that the Body of Christ may be built up and that the life of the churches may be renewed.

BIBLIOGRAPHY

PART IX

SECTION IX

Bate, H. N., ed. *Faith and Order (Proceedings of the World Conference, Lausanne, August 3—21, 1927).* Garden City, N. Y.: Doubleday, Doran and Co., 1928.

Bell, G. K. A. *The Stockholm Conference on Life and Work,* 1925.

Brown, William Adams. *Toward a United Church.* New York: Charles Scribner's Sons, 1946.

The Christian Hope and the Task of the Church (Evanston Assembly volume). New York: Harper & Bros., 1954.

The Church, the Churches, and the World Council (a statement commended to the churches for study and comment by the Central Committee of the Council, meeting at Toronto, Ontario, July, 1950). New York: World Council of Churches, 1950.

Cushman, Robert E. "Impressions of the Lund Conference," *Religion in Life.* Nashville, Tenn., XXII (1953), 230—42.

D'Espine, Henri. "The Role of the World Council of Churches in Regard to Unity," *Ecumenical Review,* XIII (1960/1961), 14—23.

Hodgson, Leonard. *The Ecumenical Movement.* Sewanee, Tenn.: Univ. Press, 1951.

———, ed. *The Second World Conference on Faith and Order.* New York: The Macmillan Co., 1938.

Hogg, William Richey. *Ecumenical Foundations.* New York: Harper & Bros., 1952.

Kennedy, James W. *Venture of Faith.* New York: Morehouse-Gorham Co., 1948.

Macfarland, Charles S. *Steps Toward the World Council.* New York: Fleming H. Revell Co., 1938.

Lee, Robert. *The Social Sources of Church Unity: An Interpretation of Unitive Forces and Movements in American Protestantism.* Nashville: Abingdon Press, 1960.

Man's Disorder and God's Design, "Amsterdam Assembly Series." New York: Harper & Bros., 1948.

Minear, Paul Sevier, ed. *The Nature of the Unity We Seek: Official Report of the North American Conference on Faith and Order.* St. Louis: Bethany Press, 1958.

Nichols, James H. *Evanston: An Interpretation.* New York: Harper & Bros., 1954.

Oldham, J. H. *The Story of the Oxford Conference* (Official Report), 1937.

Rouse, Ruth, and Charles Stephen Neill, eds. *A History of the Ecumenical Movement 1517—1948.* Phila.: The Westminster Press, 1954.

Slosser, G. J. *Christian Unity, Its History and Challenge.* New York: E. P. Dutton, 1929.

The Story of the World Council of Churches. New York: World Council of Churches, c. 1948.

Tomkins, Oliver S., ed. *The Third World Conference on Faith and Order, Lund, 1952.* London: SCM Press, 1953.

Visser 't Hooft, W. A. "What Is the World Council of Churches?" *Christendom*, IV, 1, Winter, 1939, pp. 21—31.

———, ed. *The First Assembly of the World Council of Churches.* New York: Harper & Bros., 1949.

———, ed. *The Evanston Report.* New York: Harper & Bros., 1955.

———. "The Super-Church and the Ecumenical Movement," *Ecumenical Review*, X (1957/1958), 365—385.

SECTION X

The International Council of Christian Churches

The International Council of Christian Churches was organized at Amsterdam in 1948, a few days prior to the formation of the World Council of Churches, by representatives of 61 Protestant bodies from 29 countries. They contend that the modernistic leadership of the WCC necessitates a strong fundamentalist organization. In particular the International Council charges the WCC with disloyalty to the Scriptures, with an "inclusivistic" policy which permits joint participation with the Eastern and the Roman churches and fellowship of believers and unbelievers, liberal and orthodox. They interpret the World Council's program of action as lacking a true spiritual character and being in essence a worldly social order following the Communistic economic principles. In summary, they say: "In the light of the apostasy, the social disorder, and the drive for Communism, the Christian people must make their choice. . . . The call to all Bible believers is to separation from apostasy and to fellowship in a true Christian denomination." [1] Its total membership is extremely small.

[1] *What Is the Difference?* a pamphlet published by the International Council of Christian Churches, International Headquarters, Singel 386, Amsterdam, The Netherlands. Cp. also *An International Council of Christian Churches,* prepared and released by The American Council of Christian Churches, 15 Park Row, New York 7, N. Y. See "Message to the First Assembly of the World Council of Churches from the ICCC," Minutes of the First Congress of the ICCC, pp. 33—85; David Hedegård, *Ecumenism and the Bible* (Amsterdam: The International Council of Churches, 1954), the original of which was entitled *Söderblom, påven och det stora avfallet* [*Söderblom, the Pope, and the Great Apostasy*] Örebro: Evangeliipress, 1954).

Anthropocentric and Anti-Trinitarian Bodies

SECTION I
Unitarian Universalist Association

The Unitarian Universalist Association will come into being formally in May 1961. The union of the Unitarian Association and the Universalist Church of America, first proposed as far back as 1931, was formally agreed to in 1958, confirmed by delegates of both bodies in 1959, and ratified in 1960.

For the understanding of this new body, a knowledge of the background of the two uniting groups is essential.

Unitarianism

Historically the term "Unitarianism" denotes the theory of the divine unipersonality as opposed to the church's faith in the Trinity and the deity of the incarnate Christ. The term, however, fails to characterize modern Unitarianism. American Unitarians have accepted the name only under protest, since they view their movement not so much as a denial of the Trinity as rather an attempt to practice religion on the highest plane of an ethical intellectualism, wholly free from ecclesiasticism.

Modern Unitarianism often is traced to the work of Faustus Socinus (1539 to 1604). He organized the scattered elements of anti-Trinitarians in Poland and Transylvania into an officially recognized body and formulated a dogmatical system based largely on the literary bequest of his uncle Laelius.[1] But by 1658 the Socinians were expelled from Poland "as dissenters from the religion, and not as dissenters only concerning the religion." Socinianism was thereby dissolved as an organization, with the exception of a small group in Transylvania which had been organized by the nonadorantist Franciscus Davidis in 1568. It still has some 170 churches.

According to the Rakovian Catechism, written under Socinus' direction and published in 1605, the essence of Christianity consists in fulfilling God's will as revealed in the Bible and approved by reason. Man is viewed as fully capable of working out his spiritual destiny. The doctrine of the Trinity is considered irrational. Christ is said to be essentially only human, but

NOTE: For key to abbreviations see Appendix B; for bibliography, the end of each section.

[1] There were several Unitarians prior to Socinus, such as the German Anabaptists Denk and Hetzer, the Dutch mystic Campanus, the Italian freethinkers Blandrata, Garibaldo, and Gentile (executed in Bern, 1556). Notably Michael Servetus (executed in Geneva, 1553) is held in high esteem by many Unitarians because of his Sabellian view. See Allen, p. 72; Roland H. Bainton, *Hunted Heretic* (Boston: Beacon Press, 1953); John Farquhar Fulton, *Michael Servetus, Humanist and Martyr* (New York: Herbert Reichner, 1953). On Polish Socinianism, see Stanislas Kot, *Socinianism in Poland: The Social and Political Ideas of the Polish Antitrinitarians in the Sixteenth Century*, trans. Earl Morse Wilbur (Boston: Starr King Press, c. 1957).

to have been endowed with divine powers because of His blameless life. His work consisted primarily in revealing God's commandments and promises. Socinianism, though using such Biblical terms as grace, justification, faith, is a system of works-righteousness.[2]

The Socinian theological system was not tolerated in Continental Europe, and even in England, where it was introduced by John Biddle (1615–1662), it met with bitter persecution. The Long Parliament declared the profession of Socinianism a felony, and Elizabeth and James I ordered the execution of a number of Socinians. But late in the eighteenth century many Anglican and Nonconformist clergymen held Socinian, or, to use their term, Unitarian views. The leaders in the Unitarian movement were Theophilus Lindsey, who opened the first Unitarian chapel in 1778, and Joseph Priestley (1733–1804). Averse to organizing a separate denomination, Priestley preferred to propagate his Unitarian ideas through the organized church.[3] James Martineau (1805–1885), successively Presbyterian, Nonconformist, and Unitarian preacher, became the recognized leader after the formal organization of the British and Foreign Unitarian Association in 1825.

American Unitarianism developed primarily within New England Congregationalism. Three causes may be mentioned why the Congregational church, with its highly Calvinistic theology, could offer such fertile soil for Unitarian principles. 1. The Calvinistic Christology often tends toward a Nestorian view which brings the two natures of Christ only into a nominal union, hence no union at all. From denying the communication of divine attributes to the human nature it was but a step to excluding the entire Christ from the divine attributes. 2. The early Congregational churches were nondogmatic in their original charters, "recognizing as the tribunal of last appeal not church authority or creeds, but the direct guidance of the Spirit of Truth, present to the individual mind, which is ever the invitation to free thought and the motive of doctrinal advance."[4] 3. A number of historical events helped to crystallize the early doctrinal indifference into moral intellectualism. While the descendants of the Pilgrim Fathers retained the rugged morality of their an-

[2] The Roman Catholic historian J. A. Moehler brands Socinianism as the antipode of Roman Catholicism and as belonging among the offshoots of Protestantism. *Symbolism,* p. 479 ff. The origin of Socinianism, however, must be sought in a number of movements which antedate the Reformation. A comparison of Roscellin's nominalistic argumentation for his tritheism with Socinus' deductions in the interest of his Unitarianism show the affinity of the latter to the medieval theologians and philosophers. Walch, *Streitigkeiten ausserhalb der lutherischen Kirche* (Jena: Joh. Meyers, 1736), IV, 24. Socinianism may be defined as a mixture of Scotist Pelagianism (denial of original sin and definition of faith as obedience), of the critical Humanism of the Renaissance (reason is the supreme arbiter in all matters of religion), and of certain pre-Reformation vulgar heresies. See also Tschackert, *Entstehung der luth. u. ref. Kirchenlehre,* pp. 460—76.

[3] These early Unitarians were opposed by orthodox theologians, notably by the Baptist Andrew Fuller (1754—1815), whose *Calvinistic and Socinian Systems Examined and Compared as to Their Moral Tendency* (London, 1794) is a very able refutation of Unitarianism.

[4] Allen, p. 171. In the covenants, or constitutions, of these early churches more emphasis was placed upon conduct than upon doctrine. Thus King's Chapel in Boston, the first Anglican church to be built in the city (1688—1689) and the first Boston church to become Unitarian, continues to exist under its original charter and covenant.

cestors, they refused to affiliate with the church until they could point to a definite "religious experience." Since the Reformed teach that children of Christian parents are members of the church by birthright, the question arose whether children of non-Christians were admissible to Baptism. The Halfway Covenant (1662) admitted the children of baptized, though noncommunicant, parents to Baptism on the condition that the parents accepted the main truths of the Gospel "by intellectual belief" and promised to walk under the discipline of the church. Solomon Stoddard's sermon of 1707 vigorously supported this covenant, advocated the admission to full membership in the church of such as led blameless lives, though unconverted, and thereby encouraged moral intellectualism and furthered the spiritual decline in pew and pulpit. The Great Awakening under the elder Edwards (1735–1745) abrogated the Halfway Covenant and temporarily halted the spiritual decline. But the reaction from the excesses of this great revival resulted in a renewed interest in Arminianism, liberalism, and Unitarianism. Arian ministers filled a large number of Congregational pulpits without perceptible inward commotion. Ebenezer Gay, James Freeman, Lemuel Briant, Charles Chauncy, Jonathan Mayhew, and William Bentley, among many others, had quietly, but effectively permeated Congregationalism with rationalism. It is said that at the end of the eighteenth century, twelve out of Boston's fourteen Congregational churches had Arian, that is, Unitarian, preachers.

The election in 1805 of the liberal Henry Ware as divinity professor at Harvard prompted the conservative Congregationalists to dissolve any fellowship with the liberal group, and by 1819 the liberals had become a distinct denomination known as Unitarians. In 1825 they formed the American Unitarian Association. The organization was weakened by internal strife. There were primarily three schools of thought. These were led respectively by (1) William Ellery Channing (1780–1842), the real founder of American Unitarianism, an Arian;[5] (2) Ralph Waldo Emerson (1803–1882), a pantheist and idealist who represented the extreme left wing of Unitarianism; (3) Theodore Parker (1810–1860), a radical theologian in the spirit of the emerging German liberalism.[6] The inward strife was somewhat allayed, and a great denominational consciousness developed, when H. W. Bellows organized the National Conference in 1865. In recent decades the Unitarians have endeavored to propagate their teachings more energetically.[7] Nevertheless the Unitarian Association remained numerically small. A creedless religion based on personal commitment to high ethical ideals, Unitarianism has attracted many statesmen and educators. As a liberal movement it has many spiritual brethren in the Reformed churches. As a result there are undoubtedly more Unitarians outside than inside the Unitarian fellowship.[8]

[5] Channing crystallized Unitarian thinking in his "Baltimore Sermon," preached in 1819 at the installation of Jared Sparks. Cp. Allen, p. 195 ff. See Arthur W. Brown, *Always Young for Liberty: A Biography of William Ellery Channing* (Syracuse: Syracuse University Press, 1956), and David P. Edgell, *William Ellery Channing: An Intellectual Portrait* (Boston: Beacon Press, 1955).

[6] Cp. his sermon "The Transient and the Permanent," 1841, published as a tract by Unitarian Press.

[7] See Laile E. Bartlett, *Bright Galaxy: Ten Years of Unitarian Fellowships* (Boston: Beacon Press, 1960).

[8] The Unitarian church is barred from membership in the National Council of the Churches of Christ because of its avowed anti-Trinitarianism.

Unitarians have no formal creed. Their doctrinal position must be gleaned from the writings of Priestley, Channing, Charles Eliot, Ralph Waldo Emerson, Theodore Parker, and others. These writings again must be compared with the opinions of modern Unitarians, published in tracts and booklets by the American Unitarian Association.[9] Nevertheless Unitarians have definite basic beliefs:

1. Individual freedom of belief may be viewed as fundamental. Unitarianism "does not believe that truth is ever fixed. . . . The Unitarians prefer to give their allegiance to certain immutable principles recognized by all ages and all religions, such as the brotherhood of man, perfectibility of man, presence of certain laws of justice, goodness, mercy." Channing described spiritual liberty as follows: "I call that mind free which does not cower to human opinion (including the Bible) and which respects itself too much to be the slave or the tool of the many or the few." A modern Unitarian states: "The basic difference lies in this: We conceive religion to be an attitude, an inner experience, not a body of doctrines. We believe that any true religion grows within a man, that it sums up his loyalties, his choices, his ideals, his disillusionments, his aspirations. This we have tested among ourselves for many centuries and have validated. Inevitably it rules out creeds." The "enthusiasm of freedom" is said to be the dynamic of Unitarianism. But it is difficult to find an incentive for mis-

sion work in Unitarian principles. Japanese Christianity, they assert, cannot possibly be the same as the Christianity of America; and our missionaries can do no more than indicate the simple lines of the teaching of Jesus and then to leave them to fill in the picture according to Japanese thought; people unite, they say, like mountains, at the roots of thought and separate at the peaks.[10] This opinion determines the Unitarian's attitude toward the Bible. He holds that all truth is God's truth, whether of pagan or Christian origin, and that such truth is infallible and a revelation of the divine if it encourages culture of the human soul and develops the human mind. And again:

> To none of these [tribal traditions, one man's visions, revelations of an institutionalized Church, or even a library of 66 books written over a period of 1,000 years by inspired men] will the Unitarian abdicate the Authority which he possesses. . . . The final test is: Do they [Buddha, Christ, Confucius, Amos] contravene his Reason, Common Sense, and Experience?[11]

2. The Unitarians have given high priority to their second basic assumption — the Fatherhood of God. This term symbolizes, according to Charles Eliot, "the best human combination of justice, tenderness, and infinite sympathy." A modern Unitarian states:

> God represents the highest and noblest principles, a spirit which lives in and illuminates every human soul and which shapes life toward lofty goals. Whether or not the Deity is described as a defi-

---

[9] Where two numerals occur, the first identifies the tract or booklet as published for free distribution by the American Unitarian Association.

[10] *What Is Liberal Religion?* p. 2; *Five Bases of Unitarian Advance*, p. 3. Cp. 248, p. 4. At the other end are a minority who "consider themselves Catholic Christians . . . and who do not have the slightest desire to separate from the mainstream of Christianity." See Ronald M. Mazur, "Unitarians and the Dialogue," *The Christian Century*, LXXVIII (1961), 205—208.

[11] 100, p. 13 f.; 493, p. 3. *Ten Elements of the Unitarian Religion.*

nite personality, as a transforming spirit, or as an abstract ideal rests upon the individual judgment of each member of the faith. Whatever the conception, it is a strong faith which impels Unitarians to regard service to others, that all may be uplifted in enduring brotherhood, as a primary outflowing of this divine spirit.[12]

The Fatherhood of God is said to be incompatible with the Trinitarian belief, especially when it is maintained that man's salvation depends on the theanthropic person and work of Christ. The Unitarians say that Jesus may be called divine — we are all divine — but not God; the Virgin Birth is only a poetic legend; Christmas commemorates the victory of light over darkness; and Easter is a symbol of the immortality of the soul.[13] The vicarious atonement is said to do an injustice to God and to man, since a Creator who needs propitiation is not Jesus' merciful Father, but a monster. If God be God, He will not bargain with Himself.[14] Man is able to maintain his own "at-one-ment." Salvation is by character, and man must realize his inherent divine possibilities.[15]

3. The third basic assumption is the perfectibility of man. Unitarians believe

> that human nature is imperfect, but not inherently bad; that it has been appointed to man to rise by slow degrees out of low conditions and not that we are the degenerate descendants of perfect ancestors in some remote past.

The incarnation of Christ is said to have dispelled the foolish notion that every child is the result of "evil lust," since Christ's purity demonstrated clearly that "every child has three par-

ents — his father, his mother, and the Father in heaven."[16]

According to Unitarians, the supreme test of religion is so to improve man that he will be a credit to God and society.

> Unitarianism is the religion of faith in man. When man sins he is denying the essential divinity of his own conscience, for he knows that his innermost spirit is in disagreement with the external act. Instead of being fundamentally sinful man has an upsurging moral and spiritual nature of such positive strength and courage that, when coupled with the underlying spiritual forces of the universe, he can meet and solve his own problems. The soul of every man possesses a spark of the divine. No man stands condemned. Given the freedom to guide himself according to the best that religion can teach, in the light of his own conscience man can gain ultimate victory over himself.[17]

And again

> Within man lie infinite power and possibility. It is, as a great modern poet has said, "The God-root within man." Here lies the source of courage and hope, the promise of all future progress, the sign and seal of man's divine origin and destiny, the guarantee of his ultimate victory over all that now thwarts his hopes and degrades his true nature. . . . There is, however, a third way of looking at human life and human history. This theory recognizes the part in life which chance plays in the actual course of events, and it also recognizes that God is the sovereign ruler of the universe; but it places the primary responsibility for human progress upon man himself, and it affirms the real possibility of man's consciously learning how to direct his own destiny so as

---

[12] *Introducing Unitarianism*, p. 15.

[13] 11, p. 4; 2, p. 38 f.; *Unitarian Answers*, pp. 15—17; *Unitarian Belief*, p. 48 ff.

[15] 248, p. 47.

[15] 248, p. 47.

[16] 11, p. 7; 316, p. 11.

[17] 375, p. 16 f.

to achieve increasingly the dreams and ideals which he cherishes.[18]

4. The brotherhood of man is held to be one of the universals of all religions. It is said to prompt Unitarians to see in their fellow man not only an animal a little higher than anthropoids, but also a creature only a little lower than angels. Thus Unitarians claim to espouse the only workable kind of human relations, based on the equality of all persons and all peoples.

5. The final assumption is salvation by character.

The test of religion is what happens to us inwardly, spiritually, and the way we conduct ourselves outwardly, socially. In the refinement of character lies more hope for the salvation of the world than in all the pronouncements of theologians. . . . There is no other group in this country today which is trying more fervently than the liberal church to motivate people and to get them to do what must be done in our time.[19]

Asked what meaning worship can have for Unitarians, since they have discarded the traditional concepts of the Christian church, the Unitarians answer that the only purpose of any form of worship is to change the attitude of the worshiper, not to please God. Believing that the Protestant form of corporate worship may enrich man's entire experience, Unitarians manifest a growing desire to enrich their services of worship through use of the common heritage of religious literature, music, and art.[20]

Universalists

"Universalism" as a theological term denotes the belief that God will ultimately save all people, since, as is supposed, a just and loving God cannot permit the universe to end in dualism. Universalism, known also as apocatastasis, or restoration of all things, is based on a false interpretation of Acts 3:21, Rom. 5:18, and similar passages. Isolated cases of this doctrine can be traced through the entire history of the Christian church.[21]

The Universalists did not become a distinct denomination until 1785, when John Murray (1741—1815) gathered the exponents of universalism as a distinct society at Oxford, Mass., under the name of the "Independent Christian Society, commonly called Universalists." As a religious body the Universalists are distinctly American and are largely confined to the American continent. The only doctrinal bond that united the early leaders of this organization was their opposition to the Scriptural doctrine of hell and eternal retribution. On other

---

[18] 351, pp. 17, 23.

[19] 492, p. 6.

[20] 351, p. 41.

[21] In some sections of conservative Protestantism the theory of universalism has been vigorously defended. Cp. Theodore Engelder, "The Hades Gospel" and "The Argument in Support of the Hades Gospel," *C. T. M.*, XVI (1945), 293—300, 374—396. Barth bases the restoration of all things on the premise that Christ as all men's Representative is the Elect, i. e., both to reprobation and adoption. In Christ the double election centers and ends. There is no reprobation or election outside Christ. There are not two groups, one elect to salvation, the other to reprobation, since Christ Himself was the object of God's act of reprobation and salvation. *Kirchliche Dogmatik*, Zurich, 1946, II, 2, pp. 157, 462 ff., 325, 528. Paul Althaus is representative of a large number of theologians who maintain that all those who did not have an opportunity to hear and accept Christ in this world will get a second opportunity in Hades (*Christliche Wahrheit*, II, 265), or that all divine wrath is only God's love in disguise, p. 491 ff.

doctrines there was wide divergence. Murray inclined toward Calvinism, holding that all men are depraved through their actual participation in Adam's sin. He based the doctrine of universalism on the theory that God's grace made Christ the actual Head of the human race, in whom all were punished for their sins. Therefore all will obtain eternal salvation. Murray's doctrine has been called an "improved Calvinism." For while accepting the Calvinistic theory that God decreed the salvation of only the elect, he stated that all men are elect. However, Elhanan Winchester (died 1797), a strict Arminian, taught that an adequate punishment for every sin was necessary. He believed that the unbelievers and rebels shall be purified by the final conflagration and that at last all men and angels shall enjoy universal bliss.[22] In 1790 the Philadelphia Universalists adopted a doctrinal statement which accepted the Scriptures as containing "a revelation of perfections and the will of God and the rule of faith and practice" and professed faith in one God and in Christ as a mediator and in the Holy Ghost.[23]

Hosea Ballou (1771–1852) became the recognized theological leader at the beginning of the nineteenth century and led the Universalists into Unitarian channels of theological thought. There is an old quip that the Unitarians teach that man is too good to be eternally damned; the Universalists, that God is too good to damn man eternally.[24] How-ever, this quip is no longer applicable. In his *Treatise on the Atonement* (1805) Ballou said that Christ's atonement was a moral, not a legal work, a reconciliation of man with God, not of God with man; that Christ did no more in His death than to demonstrate God's loving interest in the moral cure of the human soul; that God cannot punish arbitrarily and the wages of sin cannot be an aimless torment and a wicked vengeance; that all punishment for sin must be corrective. Ballou advocated the "death and glory" theory, so called by his opponents because he held that death brings the unconverted sinner to repentance by changing the soul's environment. The radical views of Ballou led to a secession in 1831 and to the formation of the Massachusetts Association of Universal Restorationists, which, however, was dissolved in 1841. The majority of Universalists ignored the divergent views concerning the length and severity of punishment for sin and were agreed that "the horizon of eternity will not, relatively, either largely or for a long time, be overcast by the clouds of sin and punishment." [25]

The original and basic tenet of Universalism, the restoration of all things, has progressively received less and less emphasis. Gradually the Universalists have become Unitarians. In 1899 the Universalists adopted the following five points, not as a creed, but as a sign indicating the direction of their thinking: (1) the universal Fatherhood of God;

---

[22] Fisher, p. 33 f. Eddy, p. 442.

[23] Eddy, p. 414.

[24] Unitarianism and Universalism are concurrent movements. Both have deeply influenced Congregational theology and indirectly helped to develop New England theology. Universalism undoubtedly was a protest against the excessive emphasis which the Jonathan Edwards school and the Andover Creed placed upon the sovereignty of God as related to everlasting punishment. Fisher, p. 48 ff. Frank Hugh Foster, *A Genetic History of the New England Theology* (Chicago: University of Chicago Press, 1907), ch. xi. Daniel Day Williams, *The Andover Liberals* (New York: King's Crown Press, 1941), pp. 50—53.

[25] Adopted by Boston Universalists in 1878, quoted in Eddy, p. 460 ff.

(2) the spiritual authority and leadership of His Son; (3) the trustworthiness of the Bible as containing a revelation from God; (4) the certainty of just retribution for sin; and (5) the final harmony of all souls with God.

Modern Universalists are strongly anthropocentric in their religious thinking. "We hold," one of their modern leaders says, "to confidence in the moral potentialities of man, and in salvation as a matter of human co-operation with God in organizing life so that the rude instincts which are our biological heritage may become habits of a co-operative society animated by love." [26]

The essence of the Universalist fellowship is expressed in the "Great Avowal," ratified in 1935. According to this declaration Universalists believe in

> God as eternal and all-conquering Love, in the spiritual leadership of Jesus, in the supreme worth of every human personality, in the authority of truth known or to be known, and in the power of men of good will and sacrificial spirit to overcome all evil and progressively establish the Kingdom of God. [27]

A Universalist leader says:

> Universalism's message is based squarely upon: (1) the primacy of man; (2) the unity of the human family; and (3) the universality of truth. And this is God's own message, its truth inscribed on every page of man's recorded rise.
>
> Universalism is the philosophy and religion of the all-inclusive. The whole is greater than its parts. It interprets life in terms of universals and unities, levels barriers, abjures prejudice, renounces all that sets man against his fellow man, endeavors to integrate humanity into one harmonious co-operating society.

Universalism is found wherever men work together for a better world, embraces all religions, works with science to create a finer, happier world.

> Universalism is being reborn. It is a "one world" faith in the making. It must come because without it the world cannot continue, except on the present path which leads toward suicide. Universalism is a reconciling, unifying faith; more than a negative protest against errors of the past, more than a mere social credo. It is a faith broad enough and deep enough to command the loyalty of all men. It means a "way of life," and a way of life means a way of behaving. [28]

Radical Liberalism is expressed in the following statement:

> Universalists today consider all religions, including Christianity, expressions of human spiritual aspirations; the Bible a marvelous work of man, not the miraculous handiwork of the gods; Jesus, a Spiritual Leader, not a Divine Savior; man's fate in human hands, not superhuman clutches; faith, the projection of known facts into the unknown, not blind creedal acceptance; the supernatural merely the natural beyond man's present understanding, not a violation of nature's laws. [29]

Most Universalists regard Baptism and the Lord's Supper as "sacred symbols."

The Unitarians and the Universalists produced a joint hymnal in 1937.

In 1953 the Council of Liberal Churches (Universalist-Unitarian) was set up as the first step toward the "federal union" of these two denominations. But in 1955 this plan was superseded when delegates to a joint meeting of the General Conference of the American

---

[26] Robert Cummins, in Vergilius Ferm, ed., *The American Church of the Protestant Heritage* (New York: Philosophical Library, 1953), p. 337.

[27] *Census*, II, p. 1658.

[28] Statement by Robert Cummins, general superintendent of the Universalist Church of America, in the tract *Universalism*.

[29] Statement by Brainerd Gibbons, president of the Universalist Church, 1952—1953.

Unitarian Association and the General Assembly of the Universalist Church of America voted to create a Commission to explore the possibility of an early organic merger of the two bodies.

In the united body, each church is free to retain its present name, and the independence and autonomy of local congregations is guaranteed. Ministers will be called and ordained by local churches, but the Association will grant fellowship. The overall policy-setting and directing body is to be an annual General Assembly.

No minister, church, or member is constitutionally required to subscribe to any particular interpretation of religion or to any particular religious belief or creed. The basic tenet is "religious liberalism" as distinct from a specifically Christian or a secular liberalism. The name of Jesus is not mentioned in the statement of purpose, which, as finally adopted, reads: "To cherish and spread the universal truths taught by the great prophets and teachers of humanity in every age and tradition, immemorially summarized in the Judeo-Christian heritage as love to God and love to man." [30]

A group of Universalists, organized as the Committee for Continuing Universalist Churches and committed to the retention of "Christian philosophy," has refused to enter the merged body.

BIBLIOGRAPHY

PART X   SECTION I

Allen, Joseph H. *American Church History Series.* Vol. X. New York: The Christian Literature Co., 1894.

Buehrer, Edwin T. "Unitarianism," in Vergilius Ferm., ed., *The American Church of the Protestant Heritage.* New York: Philosophical Library, 1953. Pp. 149—63.

Channing, William Ellery. *Unitarian Christianity and Other Essays,* ed. Irving H. Bartlett. New York: The Liberal Arts Press, c. 1957.

Cole, Alfred S. *Our Liberal Heritage.* Boston: Beacon Press, 1951.

Crompton, Arnold. *Unitarianism on the Pacific Coast: The First Sixty Years.* Boston: Beacon Press, c. 1957.

Cummins, Robert. "The Universalist Church of America," in Vergilius Ferm, ed., *The*

American Church of the Protestant Heritage. New York: Philosophical Library, 1953. Pp. 333—49.

Eddy, R. *American Church History Series.* X. New York: The Christian Literature Co.

Fisher, L. B. *Which Way?* A Study of Universalists and Universalism. Boston: Universalist Publishing House, 1921.

Mendelsohn, Jack. *Why I Am a Unitarian.* New York: Thomas Nelson and Sons, c. 1960.

Parke, David B., ed. *The Epic of Unitarianism: Original Writings from the History of Liberal Religion.* Boston: Starr King Press, 1957.

Wright, Conrad. *The Beginnings of Unitarianism in America.* Boston: The Beacon Press, 1954.

[30] *The Christian Century,* LXXVI (1959), 1356—1358; LXXVII (1960), 730—732.

SECTION II

The Church of the New Jerusalem (Swedenborgians)

As a religious body Swedenborgianism is in a class by itself. It has marked Socinian, Unitarian, Arminian, and millennial characteristics, though it also differs sharply from these in their historical manifestations. Since it is probably best known for the founder's claim to have had access to the spirit world, it is often classified with the Spiritualists. But it holds little in common with Spiritualism.

Emanuel Swedenborg (1688–1772), the son of Sweden's distinguished Lutheran Bishop Jesper Svedberg, had gained an enviable reputation as a scientist. But at the age of fifty-five he resigned his position to devote himself to the revelations allegedly given to him of the things in the heavens and below the heavens. He declared that he had been commanded to relate what he had seen. To him, he boasted, it had been revealed in the spirit world that the church had become sensual in its philosophy, its doctrines, and its Scriptural interpretation; but the "Lord had opened to him the spiritual sense of the Word" and he was to reform the church and to bring down the "new Jerusalem" prophesied in Revelation. He had been especially endowed, he said, to receive and to publish the doctrines of this "New Church."

In order that he might gain a clear vision of the new doctrine, he asserted, he had been permitted to hold open intercourse with the spirits of every class and to become familiar with their character and surroundings. For this same purpose he had held, he furthermore maintained, many conversations with angels, devils, with Luther, Melanchthon, and Calvin.[1]

The New Church insists that in its teachings the Bible is concerned with spiritual things only, not with scientific matters. Whenever the Bible refers to historical, natural, scientific matters, it uses such terminology only symbolically. Basic for understanding the Bible is the "science of correspondence," a universal relation between the material and the spiritual world.[2] This is the key to open the deeper and spiritual meaning of the Scriptures. According to Swedenborg, the mundane sun has his counterpart in "divine wisdom" of the spirit world; the three degrees of atmosphere (aura, ether, and air) have their correspondence in the three grades of the heavenly angels. Swedenborg applied this "science of correspondence" in his interpretation of Holy Scripture, not only in such well-known analogies as Christ as the Light and the Vine, but also in every statement of those books of the Bible which he considered inspired. By way of illustration: Swedenborg stated that no one had known what is meant by the clouds of heaven (Matt. 24:30), since everyone believed that Christ was to come in them personally. But by applying the law of correspondence one can see that in the literal sense the word denotes physical clouds, but in its spiritual sense it denotes those theologians who insist upon the literal meaning and who have obscured the "sun of the

---

[1] Swedenborg, *True Christian Religion*, Nos. 188; 776—798.

[2] Barrett, *The Question*, p. 66 ff.

divine wisdom," the interior, or spiritual, sense of the word. But the "Lord," i. e., the "New Church," was brought down from heaven when it was given to Swedenborg, ca. 1757, to know the "holiness contained in every sentence and in every word and, in some places, in the very letters." [3]

The Swedenborgians profess belief in plenary inspiration. But they state expressly that such inspiration applies only to the spiritual sense hidden in the geographical names, the historical data, the lists of various animals, the records of human accomplishments and failures. It is only by applying the law of correspondence that one learns to know that the trees, groves, and orchards mentioned in the Bible designate intelligence, wisdom, knowledge, and that the sheep, goat, calf, or ox signify innocence, charity, and natural affection. The rediscovery of this science, "which had been hidden from the days of Job to Swedenborg," is considered the beginning of the New Jerusalem, or the second coming of Christ, prophesied in Revelation. That person is said to be a member of the "New Church" whose "understanding is elevated into the light of heaven, wishes to see the truth, and with his interior thoughts approaches the Lord directly. He will shun 'faith,' and his understanding having been opened, he will see wonderful things." [4]

According to Swedenborg, the Trinity is not of persons, but of great essentials, being represented in the Scriptures as Father, Son, and Holy Ghost. The trinity of soul, body, and mind in man is a replica of the divine Trinity and constitutes God's image in man. The essence of man is his soul; the body is the covering for the soul during the natural life; and the mind manifests itself in various operations. Likewise the "esse" of God is invisible, infinite, and is commonly called the Father. But to redeem man, the divine "esse" had to assume tangible form. According to Swedenborg, this incarnation was accomplished in the same manner as in human generation, for as the soul is from the father and the body from the mother, so also the Lord (the *Logos,* the Son) had His life, His soul, from the "Father," or the divine "esse." Since the divine cannot be divided, therefore the divine of the Father was itself the Son's soul and life. In other words: "God sent Himself into the world as the Son of God in the human form received from His mother." But "that a son of God was born from eternity, descended, and assumed the human may be compared to the fables of the ancients," and "such a doctrine was unknown before the Council of Nicaea." Likewise it is the same divine "esse" when the Scriptures speak of the Holy Ghost, "who is, properly speaking, the divine truth and the Word and in this sense the Lord Himself." [5]

Swedenborgianism denies the necessity of the vicarious atonement, not only because "no first person demands satis-

---

[3] *True Christian Religion,* Nos. 85; 191; 776.

[4] Ibid., No. 200, *Apocalypse Revealed,* No. 914. The Swedenborgians teach that the Word of God, contained in the Bible, is not written like any other book and cannot be subjected to the same methods of criticism; that it is plenarily dictated by the Lord Himself, inspired as to every word and letter, and, like nature itself, a divine symbol; that besides the literal sense adapted to men it contains a spiritual sense adapted to angels; that these senses are connected with each other by the great law of correspondence, in accordance with which the universe itself was created in the beginning; and that in letter and spirit it contains the rule of life for angels and men. *Census,* II, 429.

[5] *True Christian Religion,* Nos. 169; 695; 103; 82 f.; 92; 102; 171; 176 f. Barrett, p. 23 ff.

faction from a second," but also because sin is treated only as a moral disease and disorder, which needed rectifying. Swedenborg's theory of the atonement is as follows: God's very essence is order. There is always a correct relation between divine attributes and works; e. g., God employs His omnipotence only for the extension of good. This same divine order is also in man; but man is able not only to live according, but also contrary to divine order. The spiritual sense of Adam's ejection from Eden is that in the course of many generations the human race became completely immersed in selfishness and sin; that these wicked men took their malignant feelings into the spiritual world and thus became devils; and as they increased in numbers, they filled also the world of the good spirits, causing confusion and disorder in the realm of the spirits of departed believers or angels. Swedenborg said that his revelations clearly indicated that a new doctrine of the atonement must replace the old one. Since the union between the world of spirits and the world of men is the same as that between a man's body and his soul, man cannot be redeemed unless his counterpart in the spirit world is first redeemed or restored to order.[6] In order to put the heaven in order and subjugate the evil spirits, the Infinite assumed the sinful human and in the tangible and finite form of man submitted to the manifold temptations of the devils, including the great temptation on the cross, and by victoriously withstanding the temptations, He removed the power of evil over good and brought men and angels back to order.

Swedenborg teaches that salvation consists in the "unition" (reciprocal conjunction) between God and man. But in such a unition the human would be consumed by the divine, had not the Lord Himself glorified humanity and united it with the divine in the God-Man, or Man-God. Christ did this when in the acts of redemption He successively laid aside His human quality, which was only a covering for His soul and which He had received only from His mother. By submitting to and overcoming all temptations He ceased to be Mary's son (John 2:3, 4; 19:26, 27). Swedenborgianism holds that man, who was originally created in the image of God, must now be recreated in the image of Christ's glorification. Like Christ man must endure and overcome temptations and bring the external into "at-one-ment" with the spiritual. According to the Official Book of Worship, the one God, Jehovah, the Creator, came to earth to endure temptation, even to the Passion of the cross, to overcome the hells and to deliver man. He glorified the humanity, uniting it with the divinity, and so became the Redeemer of the world.[7] Swedenborgian literature speaks of saving faith, but not in the concept of the *sola fide* of the Lutheran Reformation.[8] Swedenborg's concept of justification by faith has been summarized as follows:

> Divine Love is ever ready to flow into human hearts, but it can flow in only in the degree in which we come to see our evils in the light of truth and shun their indulgence. . . . Divine forgiveness is a voluntary turning from moral evil. . . . [Faith is] the means whereby con-

---

[6] *True Christian Religion*, Nos. 132—134; 52 ff.; 95 ff.; 118 ff. Barrett, pp. 38—56.

[7] The Creed in *Book of Worship*, p. 673; cp. Barrett, p. 40 ff.

[8] Swedenborg said that this doctrine had so intoxicated the present clergy that they could not see the most essential thing of the church. From his several journeys into the spirit world he knew that until 1758 Luther's spirit tenaciously held to *sola fide*, but as a result of Swedenborg's instruction he renounced it entirely. *T. C. R.*, No. 796. Cp. No. 98.

junction with the Lord is effected, by which is salvation. To believe in Him is to have confidence that He saves; and because no one can have such confidence unless he lives well, therefore godly living also is understood by believing.[9]

Swedenborg's eschatological views are fully in accord with his basic premise. There is no resurrection of the body, for death is putting off the material body, never to be resumed, and man rises again in a spiritual body. But very few people become altogether fitted for heaven — or for hell — in this world. Therefore the spirits are led from one society to another and explored as to whether or not they are willing to receive the truths of heaven. If not, they are sent into societies which have conjunction only with hell. But their association with devils will not appear obnoxious to them, just as robbers do not appear morally deformed to a robber; in fact, the wicked spirits will enjoy hell as the crow enjoys the carcass and the hog the mire. Swedenborg's concept of heaven is in reality a relatively perfect earth, with beautiful cities, a perfect society in various organizations, heat and light to suit our wishes, etc. The second coming of Christ occurred about 1757, when Swedenborg received the doctrine of the "New Church." [10]

The New Church observes the sacraments of Baptism and the Lord's Supper. Infant baptism is followed by confirmation. Its church polity is quasi-episcopal.

1. The "New Church" is represented in this country by the *General Convention of the New Jerusalem in the U. S. A.* It regards Swedenborg as a divinely illumined seer and his law of correspondence as the key to the divinely authorized exposition of the spiritual sense of Sacred Scripture and a truthful disclosure of the facts, phenomena, and laws of the spiritual world.

2. *The General Church of the New Jerusalem* is a very small body. It differs from the parent organization in believing that Swedenborg was not only divinely illumined, but also divinely inspired.

BIBLIOGRAPHY

PART X

SECTION II

Barrett, B. F. *The Science of Correspondences Elucidated*, 1883.

———. *The Question What Are the Doctrines of the New Church?* Germantown, Pa.: Swedenborg Publ. Association, 1909.

Official Book of Worship. Boston: General Convention of New Jerusalem, 1912.

Smyth, Julian K. *Gist of Swedenborg.* Phila.: J. B. Lippincott, 1920.

Swedenborg, Emanuel. *Complete Works.* Boston: Houghton, Mifflin Co., 1907.

Vrooman, Hiram. *Science and Theology Coordinated* (Pamphlet). Chicago: Swedenborg Philosophical Center, n. d.

[9] Barrett, p. 43 f. Cp. Articles of Faith in *Book of Worship*, p. 685 f. *True Christian Religion*, Nos. 611—614.

[10] Barrett, pp. 115 ff., 142. *Arcana coelestia*, No. 519.

SECTION III

Christadelphians

The Christadelphian body originated in the United States through the labors of John Thomas, M. D., about the year 1848. However, the name "Christadelphians" (Christ's brethren) was not adopted until the Civil War compelled them to justify their religious objections to war. Dr. Thomas identified himself at first with the Disciples. Later he separated from them in part because he was an anti-Trinitarian, but chiefly because he advocated a conditional immortality and a coarse millenarianism. Contending that historic Christendom had become apostate, he organized autonomous *ecclesiae,* or local societies, to be governed by ruling, or serving, brethren.

Christadelphians teach dynamic monarchianism. They state: "There is but one God, the Father. The Spirit is the effluence, or power, of God, the spirit of God in official manifestation." Jesus is "not the Second Person, but the manifestation of the one eternal Creator. By His spirit effluence the Father begot Jesus, who therefore during the days of His weakness had two sides: Deity and humanity. The man was the Son, whose existence dates from the birth of Jesus; the Deity dwelling in Him was the Father." [1]

The central idea in Christadelphian theology seems to be the theory of conditional immortality. The premise of this theory is that man has only a body, not a body and a soul. Christadelphians think that the words "soul" or "spirit" are merely designations "expressing a variety of aspects in which a living creature can be contemplated." Because of sin the total man is mortal, not only his body in distinction from his soul. The doctrine of the immortality of the soul is rejected as a pagan fiction. Immortality is attainable only "in connection with, and as a result of, the resurrection, or the change, of the body." Christ's work was "not to die and appease the wrath of an offended Deity," but "to acquire immortality by His resurrection." "The righteousness of God is declared in the death of every sinner, but stops short at the grave. The object in the case of Christ was to go beyond the grave — to abolish death." Immortality is said to be a "quality brought within reach by Christ in the Gospel and will be attained on condition of believing the Gospel and obeying the divine commandments." Christadelphians claim immortality only for those who believe the Gospel. They teach that the wicked "will be put out of existence by divine judgment with attendant circumstances of shame and suffering." They condemn "the theory of hell and eternal torments." The devil is said to be no more than "the Scriptural personification of sin in the flesh." The Christadelphians, unlike some other annihilationists, teach that the "unfaithful" shall be resurrected to be destroyed at Christ's second coming, but the "irresponsible of mankind, those who never heard the Gospel . . . will pass away in death and never see the light of resurrection." [2]

The Christadelphians believe that

---

[1] *A Declaration,* pp. 19—22.

[2] *A Declaration,* p. 24 ff., esp., pp. 29, 38, 24, 42, 47 ff. *Bible Finger Posts,* pp. 100—104, 241. Jannaway, *Satan's Biography.*

the kingdom to be established at Christ's second coming "will be a divine political dominion on the earth, established on the ruins of all existing kingdoms." This kingdom will be the kingdom of Israel restored, with Jerusalem as the residence of the Lord Jesus, who, as the promised Son of David, will be the supreme Ruler. This kingdom will last one thousand years. Sin and death will continue among mankind, though in a milder form, until Christ surrenders His su-premacy to the Father. Then a second judgment will take place, resulting in the consignment of the rejected to de-struction and in the immortalization of the approved, who shall inhabit the earth forever.[3]

Admission to fellowship is contingent on profession of faith in these doctrines and on baptism by immersion as an act of obedience. The autonomous local *ecclesiae* elect the "serving brethren," who serve gratuitously.

BIBLIOGRAPHY

PART X

SECTION III

Bible Finger Posts. (Sixty topics discussed.) Birmingham, Eng.: Office of *The Christa-delphian,* 1919.

A Declaration of the Truth Revealed in the Bible. Birmingham, Eng.: C. C. Walker, 1928.

Jannaway, F. G. *Satan's Biography.* London: Maran-atha Press, n. d.

Thomas, J. *Elpis Israel.* 11th ed., 1924. 350 Greenwood St., Worcester, Mass.

SECTION IV

American Ethical Union

This union is a movement inaugu-rated by Dr. Felix Adler in 1876 to "assert the supreme importance of the ethical factor in all the relations of life" and to interpret "religion more in keep-ing with the thought and demands of daily living." Societies have been formed in New York, Chicago, Philadelphia, St. Louis, Brooklyn, Boston (now de-funct), Westchester (N. Y.), Los An-geles, and San Francisco. In 1952 the first International Congress on Human-ism and Ethical Culture was held in Amsterdam "to demonstrate that there is a thoroughly ethical alternative to traditional religion." Julian Huxley of England, Wm. H. Kilpatrick of New York, Jules Romains of France, and Gil-bert Murray of England are the officers of this congress. In their attitude toward Christianity they seem to overlook the fact that a set of denials is in reality a confession and make the statement that,

> without denying belief in God, or Jesus, or the Bible, they yet stand for absolute

---

[3] *A Declaration,* pp. 4—17. This view is much like the theory advo-cated by Jehovah's witnesses.

neutrality on all theological and philosophical doctrines, demanding of no one who seeks their fellowship either acceptance or denial of any species of belief.

One of the leaders has formulated the basic tenets as follows:

1. No one — no institution, no church, no philosophy — has final answers on the over-arching questions regarding God, immortality, and prayer. No position in relation to these areas is finally demonstrable and, accordingly, no movement should be founded upon any authoritative deliverances about them. . . .

2. Every person should count as a person. . . . By this we mean that human relations should be such as to encourage and stimulate the distinctive qualities in every human being.

3. Genuine concern with developing the distinctive qualities of others is the inescapable means of one's own growth.

4. The social technique for implementing these first three tenets is drawing people together to work for matters of common concern, for whenever people of diverse backgrounds and interests can be so brought together, ethical objectives will be advanced.*

SECTION V

Judaism

Traditional Judaism

Traditional Judaism considers the history of the world as a preparation for the Messianic age. It is said to be a living force in world civilization, a vital element in solving the problems of human life, and fully equipped to facilitate the ushering in of the Messianic age. Judaism is not a system of laws, in spite of the well-nigh countless laws and regulations, but it is a way of life to prepare for the coming of the Messiah. The pious Jew is taught to view the morning ablutions as paying respect to the body, which is the reflection of the Deity. Because breakfast is considered an act of worship, it must be preceded by the ceremonial washing of the hands. The activities of every day, every week, every month, are somehow made to have religious significance. Religious rites and ceremonies govern and control the Jew's entire life. The rabbis give a great deal of thought to turn apparently burdensome rites into meaningful religious ceremonies.[1]

The Jewish way of life, with its countless prescriptions and prohibitions, is based on the Torah, which, strictly speaking, is the Law as given in the Pentateuch, with its 613 precepts. The Talmud contains the Mishnah and Mid-

---

* Jerome Nathanson, leader of New York Society, in the pamphlet *Our Common Ground.*

[1] A good example is the meaning of the Sabbath for the devout Jew. He is told that after spending six days under the tyranny of space, on the seventh he must become attuned to holiness in time. On the Sabbath he celebrates time, transcendent things, not space. He turns from the results of creation to the mystery of creation. Abraham J. Heschel, *The Sabbath, Its Meaning for Modern Man* (New York: Farrar, Straus & Co., 1951), pp. 10, 59, 98. Admittedly it is impossible for the Jew to observe all the laws of the Torah. Cp. Louis Finkelstein, "Judaism," in Sperry, *Religion and Our Divided Denominations.*

rash, Rabbinic interpretations and ethical maxims.[2] Jewish beliefs in the form of dogmatical statements are so broad and, with a few minor exceptions, so universal that almost every philosopher, and certainly every liberal theologian, can accept them.[3]

All types of Judaism have the following three points in common: 1. *The Unity of God.* The Jewish religion wants to be strictly monotheistic and unipersonal. It rejects the dualism of the East and the doctrine of the Trinity of the West. 2. *The World and Man.* Jews believe that the world is a unit and that it is good. The world is ruled by everlasting wisdom, and there is no room in the universe for evil; nor is there inherent sinfulness in man. Man is capable of perfection, is endowed with freedom of the will, and has been created in God's own image. 3. *The Future of Mankind and Israel.* The ultimate aim of history is the perfection of humanity through the unfolding of the divine power in man. Judaism teaches that under the Servant of the Lord, described in Isaiah, this earth will become a social order of human perfection and bliss.[4]

In matters concerning "the way of life" American Jewry is divided.

1. *Orthodox Judaism or Torah-True Judaism.*[5] With other forms of Judaism, Orthodoxy holds that there is no way to God except through loyalty to the divine laws. But Orthodoxy, more so than other forms of Judaism, maintains that this goal can be achieved only by being true to the Torah. According to Orthodoxy, the Torah is a revelation of the Fatherhood of God and the brotherhood of man. More specifically, the Torah reveals that God has chosen the Jews to be His peculiar people to teach the world truth, justice, and love. Thus the Torah is said to be the regulating factor in Jewish life from the cradle to the grave and the power pervading every phase of life. It aims to prevent sin rather than to forgive, and contains many "fences" so that in Jewish life there may be a minimum of opportunity for evil and a maximum for good. Thus the Torah becomes the means whereby a faithful Jew merits many blessings and finally receives immortality as a reward.

The majority of Orthodox Jews believe that the Messianic prophecies will be fulfilled by a personal Messiah under whom all Israel will return to the land of Canaan and re-establish the Old Testament worship. In the meantime the Orthodox Jews observe as meticulously

[2] The Talmud is the collection of the text (*Mishnah*) and the commentary (*Gemara*) of Jewish civil and canonical law. These laws and explanations were committed to writing between 30 B. C. and A. D. 250.

[3] Rabbi Maimonides, in the twelfth century, formulated the Jewish beliefs in the following articles: The belief in (1) God's existence and creative power; (2) unity; (3) incorporeality; (4) timelessness; (5) approachableness through prayer; (6) prophetic inerrancy; (7) the superiority of Moses to all other prophets; (8) Moses' authorship of the Torah; (9) the immutability and finality of the Law; (10) divine providence; (11) divine justice; (12) the coming of the Messiah; (13) the resurrection and human immortality. — A contemporary Jewish philosopher-theologian who has exerted a great deal of influence on contemporary liberal Protestant thought is Martin Buber (b. 1878). See Malcolm L. Diamond, *Martin Buber: Jewish Existentialist* (New York: Oxford University Press, 1960); Maurice S. Friedman, *Martin Buber: The Life of Dialogue* (Chicago: The University of Chicago Press, 1955); and Will Herberg, *Four Existentialist Theologians* (Garden City: Doubleday and Co., 1958), 171—253.

[4] H. S. Linfield, *Census*, 1936, II, 763 f.

[5] See Rabbi Leo Jung, "Orthodox Judaism," in *Judaism*, ed. Opher.

as possible the countless ceremonies, prayers, and festivals.[6]

2. *Reform Judaism* seeks to solve two problems confronting the American Jew: (1) How can he reconcile Jewish beliefs with modern thought? (2) How can he observe Jewish ceremonies in modern society? The Orthodox Jew maintains that God has given only one revelation — the Torah. The Reform Jew, however, maintains that God reveals Himself progressively. Therefore he denies the absolutely binding character of the Torah. He believes that Judaism has a universal message aiming at the union and perfection of mankind under the sovereignty of God. It holds that the one living God rules the world through law and love and is the indwelling Presence of the world. Endowed with moral freedom, man seeks fellowship with God by striving after holiness, righteousness, and goodness and by showing proper consideration for his fellow man. There is virtually no difference between the tenets of Reformed Judaism and those of liberal theology.[7] Reform Judaism maintains that since God is an ethical Being, He can have only the qualities of love, mercy, and justice. There can be no idea of vengeance in God. God cannot ever punish a sinner unless it is to cure him. Man must worship God, not through ceremonies, but through his life of love, justice, and righteousness. Man's soul, a fragment of the divine spirit, must return to God. Reform Judaism speaks of a social immortality in the sense that, for example, the humble ditchdigger obtains immortality in the increased sanitary service which his work has provided for a community.[8]

3. *Conservative Judaism.* This relatively new movement within Jewry endeavors to hold a mediating position between Orthodox and Reform Jews. It seeks to preserve the ideals and values of both. With the Orthodox Jews it maintains its belief in the Torah, observes the dietary laws, and uses the Hebrew language. Like Reform Judaism, it attempts to reconcile the ancient truths and practices with modern culture.[9]

[6] Prominent are the regulations governing the kosher foods. Kosher meats, for example, are slaughtered according to a ritual known as *shehitah*, a method to kill the animal quickly and painlessly.

[7] The *National Conference of Christians and Jews* seeks to work for the unity of the human race by removing racial prejudice. This organization, composed of Jews, Protestants, and some Roman Catholics, maintains that God is the Father of all; that all are brothers; that all religions have the same common principles; that Christianity is really the outgrowth of Judaism; and that therefore any form of anti-Semitism is at the same time a blow against Christianity.

One of the paragraphs of the "basic convictions" reads:

We believe in one God, Creator and Sustainer of the Universe. Though we have varying views as to the nature and content of God's more direct revelation, we hold that He also manifests His being, power, wisdom, and love through His works and especially in the mind, will and personality of man.

We believe that the mind of man reflects, though imperfectly, the mind of God, and we reject, as a betrayal of human dignity, all attempts to explain man in merely material terms.

From literature supplied by headquarters, 381 Park Ave., New York, N. Y..

[8] Issermann, op. cit. Cp. also "Columbus Platform," a statement of beliefs adopted by Reform Jews, May 27, 1937.

[9] Cp. Finkelstein, "Judaism," in Sperry, loc. cit., and (by the same author) "The Beliefs and Practices of Judaism," *Religious Digest*, Sept., 1941, pp. 84—95.

4. *Reconstructionism.* According to M. M. Kaplan, a number of Jews are interested in a complete reorganization of the entire Jewish life. Its thrust is in the direction of religious naturalism.[10]

5. *Zionism.* Some Jews treat Zionism as a purely political matter, whereas others regard it as a religious problem. Theo. Herzl, who espoused Zionism for political reasons, was instrumental in establishing the Basel program, which crystallized in the Balfour Declaration of 1917. Currently the majority of Jews view Zionism as a religious movement. They theorize that Judaism is a universal religion and can indeed retain its universal character in America, but that it can develop more freely in a country where it is the dominant, in fact, the only culture. If therefore Palestine, they argue, can maintain itself as the homeland for the majority, or at least a great number, of Jews, Jewish life throughout the world will thereby be enriched. The Reform Jews were opposed to Zionism because they feared that it would have the very opposite effect. Today the majority of harassed Jews deem the preservation of Palestine as a haven for Jews imperative.[11]

The non-Jewish observer finds it very difficult to trace the many interrelations and separations among Judaism. Jewish thought in America is shaped to a large extent by a number of rabbinical schools.

Rabbi Isaac Elehonan Theological Seminary of New York and Hebrew Theological College of Chicago train Orthodox rabbis.

The Hebrew Union College of Cincinnati, Ohio, founded in 1875, and its affiliate, the Jewish Institute of Religion, founded in 1950, in New York, serve Reform Judaism.

The Jewish Theological Seminary in New York, patterned after the world-renowned Jewish school of Breslau, serves Conservative Judaism.[12]

The synagog, in charge of the rabbi, is the complete and autonomous unit. There are usually three classes of members: corporate members, the pewholders, and those who pay for a seat at the high services.

BIBLIOGRAPHY

PART X   SECTION V

Agus, Jacob B. *Modern Philosophies of Judaism.* New York: Behrman House, 1942.

Glaser, Nathan. *American Judaism.* Chicago: The University of Chicago Press, c. 1957.

Gordis, Robert. *Judaism for the Modern Age.* New York: Farrar, Strauss, and Cudahy, 1955.

Hedenquist, Göte, ed. *The Church and the Jewish People.* London: Edinburgh House Press, 1954.

Herberg, Will. *Protestant — Catholic — Jew: An Essay in American Religious Sociology.* Garden City: Doubleday and Co., 1955. Esp. Ch. viii.

[10] Cp. Mead *(Gen. Bibliog.),* p. 106, and Jack L. Cohen, *The Case for Religious Naturalism: A Philosophy for the Modern Jew* (New York: The Reconstructionist Press, c. 1958).

[11] See Opher, p. 53; Finkelstein, in Sperry, p. 81 ff.

[12] Cp. "A Trumpet for All Israel," *Time,* Oct. 15, 1951, p. 52 ff.

Issermann, Ferdinand M. *This Is Judaism.* Willet, Clark & Co., 1944.

Opher, Ahron, ed. *Judaism.* A symposium published in mimeographed form. 2d ed. New York: National Council of Jewish Women, 1952.

Sperry, W. L. *Religion and Our Divided De-* nominations. Cambridge: Harvard Univ. Press, 1945. Ch. iv., by Louis Finkelstein.

Williams, J. Paul. *What Americans Believe and How They Worship.* New York: Harper & Bros., 1952. Ch. xi.

Jewish Encylopedia. Isidore Singer, ed. New York: Funk & Wagnalls, 1907.

PART ELEVEN

Egocentric or Healing Cults

The "New Thought" cults, sometimes described merely as mental healing cults, attribute the attainment of wholeness in mind and body to right mental attitudes. They hold in varying degrees that thought is potent, if not omnipotent. Because of his divine origin and divine goal man is said to have at his command an unlimited reservoir of divine powers for the solution of any and every problem of life. Some of these cults emphasize the healing of the body; others widen the scope of blessings to include virtually everything the human heart desires: health, friends, a perfectly integrated personality, wealth, immortality. Mind is the key to the storehouse of every treasure.

Theologically they are extremely anthropocentric or, more accurately, egocentric.[1] Philosophically they are related to New England transcendentalism, or new thought. There is hardly any doubt that the modern mental healing cults owe their origin in part to such philosophers as William E. Channing, Ralph Waldo Emerson, Theodore Parker, Margaret Fuller. New England transcendentalism ascribed tremendous power to the human mind and advocated a type of immanentism which is in reality pantheism. Transcendentalism is very much akin to Oriental Hindu thought which aims to erase the distinction between God and man and wants man to regard himself as possessing divine capabilities.[2]

Another stream of thought which greatly influenced the various healing cults was supplied by Phineas P. Quimby of Portland, Maine. He accomplished some startling healing cures, which he attributed to mental healing. He believed that he had discovered the healing method employed by Christ and could heal by changing the mind of the patient or by establishing truth in the place of error.[3]

There are numerous healing cults. Since some are small or of local interest only, it is impossible to classify all of them. They can most conveniently be treated under four groups:

[1] "Egocentric" seems most descriptive. Elmer Clark in *Small Sects in America*, p. 233, employs this epithet. Some writers, e. g., Braden, p. 130 ff., use the generic term "New Thought" to classify these cults.

[2] For New England transcendentalism see Vernon Louis Parrington, *Main Currents in American Thought* (New York: Harcourt, Brace & Co., 1927—1930), II, 379—85. Joseph L. Blau, *Men and Movements in American Philosophy* (New York: Prentice-Hall, Inc., 1952), p. 110 ff. Herbert W. Schneider, *A History of American Philosophy* (New York: Columbia Univ. Press, 1946), p. 159 ff. W. G. Muelder and Laurence Sears, *The Development of American Philosophy* (Boston: Houghton Mifflin Co., 1940), p. 111 ff. Also for a more specific study on James Marsh, Caleb Henry, and Fredric Henry Hedge, see Ronald Vale Wells, *Three Christian Transcendentalists* (New York: Columbia Univ. Press, 1943).

[3] Quimby has become a controversial figure. Many assert that Mrs. Mary Baker Eddy copied her system from Quimby, but the Christian Scientists deny this assertion and maintain that she alone is responsible for Christian Science. Cp. the biographies of Mrs. Eddy, also Ernest Holmes, *Mind Remakes Your World* (New York: Dodd, Mead & Co., 1944), p. xii.

1. Christian Science, founded with the publication of *Science and Health* in the year 1875;
2. Unity School of Christianity, established by the Fillmores in the year 1889;
3. New Thought, given organizational character in the first national convention of some 18 related groups.
4. Such movements as I Am, Father Divine, and Psychiana.

SECTION I

Christian Science

History

Among the several women of the 19th century who founded new religions, none has become so controversial a figure as Mrs. Mary Baker Glover Patterson Eddy (1821–1910), the founder of the Church of Christ (Scientist). Ordinarily one is less interested in the person and more in the tenets of one who pretends to have founded a new religion. This observation does not hold true in the case of Mrs. Eddy. Practically all members of Christian churches who have studied Mrs. Eddy's religious system believe that her theories are so preposterous and her writings so confused that there must have been serious psychological maladjustments in her personal life. Her followers, on the other hand, reject such views and consider Mrs. Eddy as their inerrant teacher and inspired leader.[4] Concerned about their ecclesiastical or-

ganization, they naturally will reject all unsavory charges against Mary Baker Eddy's personal life.[5]

Unprejudiced and trustworthy students of Mrs. Eddy's life have shown that her private life was not of a kind to inspire confidence in her as a religious leader. From early childhood she was sickly, highly emotional, and subject to fits of hysteria. Her education was very limited. She was a domineering, quarrelsome, and extremely self-centered woman. At times she was suspicious of her intimate friends, even of her only son, and seemingly could get along with no one but herself. Even in early youth she had "visions," and throughout her life she remained highly superstitious. In 1862 she met Phineas P. Quimby of Portland, Maine, who held that sickness was due to erroneous thinking and pointed to marvelous cures

[4] Some have so extravagantly overrated Mrs. Eddy as to see in her a sort of deity. She claimed the title "Mother Mary" for herself.

[5] They are determined to suppress any publication which in their opinion discredits the Christian Science movement, and they make every effort to have writers accept their side of the story. The attempt to suppress the Dakin biography is a good case in point. The Christian Science Committee on Publication carefully scrutinizes all publications in which references are made to Christian Science. If any statement discreditable to the opinions of Christian Scientists is found, they will courteously ask the author to make changes in subsequent editions and will gratuitously submit their own literature. The author experienced this procedure in connection with his *American Churches* (St. Louis: C. P. H., 1946). Cp. Braden, p. 181 ff.

he had effected by using "Christ's method of healing." One cannot readily determine the exact relation between Mrs. Eddy and Quimby. Nor can one easily prove the truth or falsity of the charge that Mrs. Eddy not only copied Quimby's method, but also plagiarized Quimby's manuscript in her book *Science and Health.* In the opinion of some, Mrs. Eddy merely adapted Quimby's system to her own ends. The Christian Scientists deny this charge.[6] Mrs. Eddy contended that the discovery of Christian Science did not occur until after Quimby's death in 1866, when she fell on the ice and injured herself to such an extent that recovery seemed to be out of the question. She asserts that she turned quite accidentally to Matt. 9:2 and there learned to heal herself by right thinking. This experience, she said, marked the discovery of divine metaphysical healing, for then she gained the scientific certainty that all

[6] See ibid., p. 185 ff., where the relevant material is made available for a quick overview, esp. also as regards the source of Mrs. Eddy's philosophical references. In ch. vii of Dakin's biography of her, Quimby's influence on *Science and Health* is investigated, and ch. vii deals with the source of the philosophy presented in her writings. Bates and Dittemore take up the same question in ch. xv, and pp. 386 and 387 show in parallel columns the great similarity between quotations by Mrs. Eddy and quotations found in *Philosophic Nuggets* (p. 386 f.). The officially approved biography by Miss Wilbur (ch. viii) gives the impression that the "Quimby manuscript" was really written by Mrs. Eddy — not Quimby — during the years when she was in "contact" with Quimby. Dr. Powell, an approved biographer, follows the same line of thought as Miss Wilbur.

In 1936, the Rev. Walter M. Haushalter, minister of the Christian Temple (Disciples of Christ), Baltimore, published an essay entitled *Mrs. Eddy Purloins from Hegel.* It reproduced, with some supplementary material, a manuscript entitled *The Metaphysical Religion of Hegel.* The thesis of the book is that the manuscript is a "lengthy and learned treatise" on Hegelianism in the handwriting of Francis Lieber (1800—1872), a German-American encylopedist, political economist, and constitutional historian; that the treatise originated in 1865; that it came into the hands of Mrs. Eddy in 1866; and that she used its language verbatim "to the equivalent of thirty-three pages of *Science and Health*" in setting forth the chief doctrinal points of her system. In 1945 Haushalter published his *Validation of the Lieber-Hegel-Eddy Source Document,* as he called the treatise, and asserted that the validation of the document — currently in the custody of the Princeton Theological Seminary Library — had been "done by a group of American university professors and documentary experts." But in his critical biography, *Francis Lieber, Nineteenth Century Liberal* (Baton Rouge: Louisiana State University Press, 1947), Frank Freidel expressed the opinion that "the authenticity of the document seems open to serious doubt" and did not make use of it in his book. His reasons were the apparent disparity between the handwriting of Lieber and that of the manuscript; the marked similarity of the handwriting of the manuscript and the "Mary Baker" endorsement; the fact that none of the thousands of authentic Lieber letters mention the alleged recipient of the covering letter of the document, Hiram Crafts; and that the "phrasing and concepts of the letter and essay are not characteristic of Lieber" (p. 420). More recently, Conrad Henry Moehlman, in *Ordeal by Concordance* (New York: Longmans, Green & Co., 1955), has classed the documents with the Cotton Mather forgery purporting to give details of a "scheme to bag Penn" and other "literary inventions accepted 'on faith' by Americans and Europeans alike in the nineteenth and twentieth centuries" (pp. 11; 150 f.). He presents evidence that the essay in question was written after 1887 (p. 128) and that none of the three signatures involved (two allegedly Lieber's, one that of "Mary Baker") could be demonstrated to be authentic (pp. 34 f., 42 f.; 143).

causation is Mind and every effect a mental phenomenon.[7]

During the following years she gained several adherents, and in 1875, at the age of 54, she published *Science and Health with Key to the Scriptures*. In 1879 she organized the Church of Christ (Scientist) at Boston. In 1881 she opened the Massachusetts Metaphysical College, which for 12 lessons in healing charged a fee of $300. In 1889 she retired from leadership of the local Boston church and devoted her time to the mother church and to writing. She amassed a fortune estimated at above $2,000,000. The discoverer of Christian Science remained a slave of superstitious fears throughout her life, particularly of "animal magnetism." She attributed the death of her third husband to mental arsenic poisoning administered from a distance by one of her enemies. Mrs. Eddy had so thoroughly organized the mother church that her death in 1910 made little difference in its management.

Doctrinal System

Christian Science, usually viewed as a philosophy, as a theology, and as a healing cult, must be examined from these three points of view.

An objective examination of her system as theology depends on her answer to two questions: (1) What is the formal principle, i. e., the source, of her theology? (2) What is the material principle, i. e., the central core of her message?

SOURCE OF DOCTRINE

Mrs. Eddy insists that the source of her doctrine is Sacred Scripture. She says that the divinely inspired Bible was her sole teacher, her only authority and guide, in the "straight and narrow way of truth." [8] The fact is that Mrs. Eddy considered the Bible a dark book which cannot be understood without "the key of David" (Rev. 3:7). Mrs. Eddy supplied this "key to the Scriptures" in the appendix to her textbook *Science and Health*. This appendix is a glossary in which she gives the metaphysical or spiritual interpretation of the "material" terms used in the Bible, and her definitions of the "spiritual" meaning are said to be the original meaning of these Biblical terms.[9] A good example of how her "key to the Scriptures" completely distorts the Scriptures is her version of

---

[7] Mrs. Eddy, *Retrospection*, pp. 24, 38.

[8] *Science and Health*, Preface, pp. viii, 126, 497.

[9] The glossary covers 20 pages, pp. 579—99. We append some definitions as given by Mrs. Eddy.

    Adam. Error; a falsity; the belief in "original sin," sickness, and death; a belief in intelligent matter, nothingness; the first god of mythology; the opposite of Spirit and His creations; material belief, opposed to the one Mind, or Spirit; a product of nothing as the mimicry of something; an unreality as opposed to the great reality of spiritual existence and creation; an inverted image of Spirit; the image and likeness of what God has not created, namely, matter, sin, sickness, and death.

    Children. The spiritual thoughts and representatives of Life, Truth, and Love.

    Christ. The divine manifestation of God, which comes to the flesh to destroy incarnate error.

    Church. The structure of Truth and Love; whatever rests upon and proceeds from divine Principle.

    Creator. Spirit; Mind, intelligence; the animating divine Principle

two of Christendom's best-loved texts — the 23d Psalm and the Lord's Prayer.[10] By no stretch of the imagination can the Christian Scientists claim the Bible as the source of their theology.

In reality Mrs. Eddy's *Science and Health* is the source of religious truths in the Christian Science church. She maintained that while the Bible is full of mistakes, her book contains the real, unadulterated truth; that it is the perfect Word of God inspired without error by the Holy Ghost. She prescribed the specific section from her book and the specific sections from the Bible which are to be read in the public services on each Sunday of the year. Of the textbook itself she says:

> I should blush to write a *Science and Health with Key to the Scriptures* as I have, were it of human origin, and I, apart from God, its author; but as I was only a scribe echoing the harmonies of heaven in divine metaphysics, I cannot

of all that is real and good, self-existent Life, Truth, and Love; the opposite of matter and evil, which have no Principle.

Death. An illusion, the lie of life in matter; matter has no life, hence it has no real existence. Mind is immortal.

Euphrates (river). Divine Science encompassing the universe and man.

God. The great I AM; Principle; Mind; Soul; Spirit; Life; Truth; Love.

Hell. Mortal belief; error.

Jacob. A corporeal, mortal, embarrassing duplicity, repentance, sensualism. Inspiration.

Jesus. The highest human corporeal concept of the divine idea, rebuking and destroying error and bringing to light man's immortality.

Man. The compound idea of infinite Spirit.

Matter. Mythology; mortality; another name for mortal mind; illusion; intelligence, substance, and life in non-intelligence and mortality; sensation in the sensationless; mind originating in matter; that of which immortal Mind takes no cognizance; that which mortal mind sees, feels, hears, tastes, and smells only in belief.

Mind. The only I, for Us; the only Spirit, Soul, divine Principle, Substance, Life, Truth, Love; the one God.

Mortal Mind. Nothing claiming to be something, for Mind is immortal; error creating other errors; sensation is in matter, which is sensationless.

Mother. God; divine and eternal Principle; Life, Truth, and Love.

Salvation. Life, Truth, and Love understood and demonstrated as supreme over all sin; sin, sickness, and death destroyed.

Wine. Inspiration; understanding. Error; fornication; temptation; passion.

10 "Divine Love is my Shepherd. . . . Love restores my soul (spiritual sense). . . . I will dwell in the house (the consciousness) of love forever." (*Science and Health,* p. 578.) "Our Father-Mother God, all harmonious, Adorable One, Thy kingdom is come; Thou art ever-present. Enable us to know, — as in heaven, so on earth, — God is omnipotent, supreme. Give us grace for today; feed the famished affections; and Love is reflected in love; and God leadeth us not into temptation, but delivereth us from sin, disease, and death. For God is infinite, all-power, all Life, Truth, Love over all, and All." (*Science and Health,* pp. 16, 17). — She seems to have been familiar with that phase of Hindu philosophy which imagines that there is a male and a female part in God and regards the female as the real origin of all being. Ann Lee of the Shakers held a similar view.

be super-modest in my estimate of the Christian Science textbook.[11]

In the final analysis Mrs. Eddy's formal principle is philosophy. The central core of her system is akin to the philosophy of idealism. But also a number of other philosophical systems come to the surface, so that her system is in reality a conglomeration of various and variant philosophical systems.

Idealism in the form of New England transcendentalism was the most significant factor in the development of her system.[12] Idealism holds that true reality does not exist in the material world, but in the Absolute. Only the original idea, as Plato maintains, not the object, has true reality. Berkeley, Hume, Hegel, and Kant further developed the idea that all things which exist have being only as images of our perception. New England transcendentalism, as advocated by individuals like Ralph Waldo Emerson, William Ellery Channing, W. R. Trine, and especially by Margaret Fuller, believes that the human spirit is God's light. Without adequate criticism Mrs. Eddy adopted as the foundation of her religious system the conclusions which the transcendentalists tried to establish on philosophical grounds. Someone has said that Mrs. Eddy gave a new meaning to old terms and thus became more obscure than the idealists, since she completely discounted the testimony of the senses. In this way she actually

opened the door to arbitrary subjectivism.[13] But, worse still, when she identified the universe and Divine Mind, Mrs. Eddy unwittingly espoused pantheism.[14]

It has been stated, and not without cause, that there are strong elements of Gnosticism and Manichaeism in Christian Science. Mrs. Eddy stresses again and again that there is only one Cause, only one Divine Principle, outside of which everything is error. Nevertheless she ascribes sin, sickness, and death to mortal mind, which can only mean that she believes in two causes, in two conflicting powers in the world, the one the source of good, and the other the source of evil. And that is a basic principle of ancient Manichaeism.

Some find mysticism in Mrs. Eddy's system, in the sense that man by progressively stripping off the corporeal will enter into union with God. By teaching that man is a divine thought, Mrs. Eddy actually identifies God with man and advocates a form of pantheistic mysticism that is held in Hinduism. Whether or not Mrs. Eddy was familiar with Hindu philosophy is debatable, but more than a marked similarity is obvious. In Hindu philosophy matter is unreal; the only reality is the Cosmic Soul or Mind. Since all is illusory, man's highest ideal is to reach complete union with the Cosmic Impersonal Soul. The source of Mrs. Eddy's religion, her formal prin-

---

[11] *Christian Science Journal*, Jan., 1901, quoted by Wittmer, p. 27. Cp. Schaff-Herzog Encycl., X, 297. In the English-German edition she states that the one side should "contain the divinely inspired English version" (Preface, p. ii). In her opinion *Science and Health* is indispensable to every Scientist because it is the voice of Truth and registers the revealed Truth uncontaminated by human hypotheses. *Science and Health*, p. 456 f. Cp. Braden, p. 209.

[12] This has often been questioned on the ground that Mrs. Eddy, an uneducated woman, could not have come under the influence of idealism. Miss Wilbur, pp. 148—58, has shown that she became well acquainted with New England transcendentalism through a certain H. S. Craft.

[13] Bellwald, p. 68f.

[14] In *Christian Science vs. Pantheism* Mrs. Eddy strenuously objects to the charge of teaching pantheism.

ciple, is not the Christian revelation in Sacred Scripture, but the philosophical system expounded in her writings.

THE CENTRAL MESSAGE

In keeping with *Science and Health*, her material principle, the core of her message, may be formulated as follows: God is the only Being, the Absolute Cause, the Principle of everything, and man is only a divine reflection of God, a divine thought. The purpose of Christian Science is to teach man to cast off the error that man is subject to human limitations and to believe that he is divine thought. Mrs. Eddy expresses this material principle in four "self-evident" and "mathematically proved" propositions. These are said to be self-evident, since they are reversible, i. e., they can be read forward or backward, and since in divine metaphysics, as well as in mathematics, inversion proves a proposition correct (e. g., $2 \times 2 = 4$ or $4 \div 2 = 2$).

1. "God is All-in-All." This thesis means that God is Divine Principle. He is the Author and Cause of everything. Whatever exists is only a reflection of God; in fact, is really God. Man and God are coexistent and eternal. If man were separated from God and only for a moment did not reflect the idea of God, Divine Mind would be childless, i. e., be no Father.[15]

2. "God is good. Good is Mind." This statement means that only what God, Mind, Principle, etc., thinks really exists. The only reality is Divine Mind.

... There can be but one Mind, because there is but one God; and if mortals claimed no other Mind and accepted no other, sin would be unknown. We can have but one Mind if that one is infinite. We bury the sense of infinitude, when we admit that, although God is infinite, evil has a place in this infinity, for evil can have no place, where all space is filled with God.[16]

3. "God, Spirit, being all, nothing is matter"; in other words, Mind is Good, and Good is Mind. Man is only Mind, Idea, inseparably united with God. The real man, the image, thought, and reflection of Divine Mind, is holy (475), immortal (476), incapable of sinning (480). "The man of God's creating is wholly spiritual, incorporeal, and immortal." [17]

4. "Life, God, omnipotent Good, deny death, evil, sins, disease." That God, or Divine Mind, is all, and that there can be no matter, is established by a syllogism:

Major proposition: Opposites cannot coexist;

Minor proposition: Mind and matter are opposites.

Conclusion: Mind and matter cannot coexist. Everything is Mind. There is no room for matter.

There is no life, truth, intelligence, nor substance in matter. All is infinite Mind and its infinite manifestation, for God is All-in-All, Spirit is immortal Truth; matter is mortal error. Spirit is the real

---

[15] God is the creator of man, and, the divine Principle of man remaining perfect, the divine idea or reflection, man, remains perfect. Man is the expression of God's being. If there ever was a moment when man did not express the divine perfection then there was a moment when man did not express God, and consequently a time when Deity was unexpressed — that is, without entity. If man has lost perfection, then he has lost his perfect Principle, the divine Mind. If man ever existed without this perfect Principle or Mind, then man's existence was a myth. (*Science and Health*, pp. 258, 259.)

[16] Ibid., p. 469.

[17] Ibid., pp. 475, 476, 480.

and eternal; matter is the unreal and temporal. Spirit is God, and man is His image and likeness. Therefore man is not material; he is spiritual.[18]

THEOLOGICAL IMPLICATIONS

God. Mrs. Eddy defines God as

the only Life, substance, Spirit, or Soul, the only intelligence of the universe. . . . Spirit is divine Principle [the first cause], and divine Principle is Love and Love is Mind . . . God is Mind. . . . God is divine Life. . . . God is All-in-All. Nothing possesses reality except the Divine Mind. . . . Everything in God's universe expresses Him. . . . There is no other self-existence. . . . He fills all space. . . . Hence all is Spirit and spiritual.[19]

Mrs. Eddy fails to state in unequivocal terms that she believes in the personality of God. In her terminology God is Mind, Spirit, Soul, Principle [First Cause], Life, Truth, Love.[20]

Not only does she reject the "theory of three persons in one God" as suggesting polytheism, but she also personifies the divine attributes. Instead of the Christian Trinity she maintains that

Life, Truth, and Love constitute the triune Person called God — that is, the triply divine Principle, Love. They represent a trinity in unity, three in one, — the same essence, though multiform in office: God the Father-Mother; Christ the spiritual idea of sonship; divine Science or the Holy Comforter. These three express in divine Science the threefold, essential nature of the infinite. They also indicate the divine

Principle of scientific being, the intelligent relation of God to man and the universe.[21]

The name "Father-Mother" is said to indicate His tender relationship to His spiritual creation and man's divine origin.[22]

Mrs. Eddy's concept of the Second Person is very vague. In her glossary "Christ" is no more than Truth, the divine manifestation of God to destroy error, and the Divine Idea to heal man. Jesus, whom she sharply separates from Christ, is said to be that human person who more than anyone else presented the Christ or the Divine Idea. The impersonal idea of Truth and the personal presentation of this Idea by Jesus of Nazareth is said to be expressed by the duality of natures in Christ.[23]

Mrs. Eddy understood the Third Person, the Comforter, to be "Divine Science," "the Pentecostal Power," "the Christian Science system of healing." [24]

Man. In her glossary she defines man as the "compound idea of infinite spirit; the spiritual image and likeness of God; the full representation of Mind." Man is a reflection of God. As the mirror reflects the image, so man is an eternal, perfect personal reflection or image of God. When and as God thinks — which goes on continuously — man is in existence. God and man are to be identified, for they are co-existent, co-eternal, co-perfect, co-sinless, co-immortal. Man, the reflection, is everything which Divine Mind is. One Christian Scientist

[18] Ibid., p. 468.

[19] Ibid., p. 330.

[20] Cp. Qu. What is God? Ibid., p. 465.

[21] Ibid., pp. 256, 331.

[22] Ibid., p. 256. This dual concept of God is of Hindu origin and is a prominent feature in theosophy and several New Thought groups, e. g., Father Divine, School of Livable Christianity.

[23] Ibid., pp. 332, 361, 473. Cp. Glossary.

[24] Ibid., pp. 55, 46 f.

summarizes the basic anthropological doctrine of Christian Science as follows:

> Accepting the premise that God, the Creator of all, is perfect and that man is made in God's likeness, then it inevitably follows that man, the son of God, is as perfect in a degree as God Himself. This solves the problem completely.[25]

Mrs. Eddy says that "the only reality of sin, sickness, or death is the awful fact that unrealities seem real to human belief." To get rid of sin means that one must free himself of the error that any reality is real, in brief, to deny its existence.[26]

The Atonement. There is no need of divine redemption and atonement in Christian Science. Mrs. Eddy does not need the divine-human Savior, the God-Man, and therefore denies the deity of Jesus and the personality of the pre-existent Logos. She describes the "spiritual conception" of Christ as follows:

> The Virgin-mother conceived this idea of God, and gave to her ideal the name of Jesus — that is, Joshua, or Savior.

> The illumination of Mary's spiritual sense put to silence material law and its order of generation, and brought forth her child by the revelation of Truth, demonstrating God as the Father of men. The Holy Ghost, or divine Spirit, overshadowed the pure sense of the Virgin-mother with the full recognition that being is Spirit. The Christ dwelt forever an idea in the bosom of God, the divine Principle of the man Jesus, and woman perceived this spiritual idea, though at first faintly developed.[27]

A modern Christian Science writer describes the virgin birth of Christ as follows:

> This spiritually minded maiden gained so clear a concept of God as the Father of all that she was enabled to bear the Christ Child, the Babe of Bethlehem, born in a stable and cradled in a manger.[28]

Mrs. Eddy categorically denies Christ's vicarious atonement. She teaches that no matter how great the sacrifice, it would be insufficient to pay the debt of sin and that the material blood of Jesus could be no more efficacious to cleanse from sin when it was shed upon the tree than when it was flowing in His veins.[29]

She maintains:

> That God's wrath should be vented upon His beloved Son, is divinely unnatural. Such a theory is man-made. The atonement is a hard problem in theology, but its scientific explanation is, that suffering is an error of sinful sense which Truth destroys, and that eventually both sin and suffering will fall at the feet of everlasting Love.[30]

The at-one-ment is accomplished when man shows in his life that he has part in Divine Mind.[31] For Christian Scientists Christ is not the Savior, but the Way-Shower, the "Christ-Comforter," who would demonstrate to men how to apply spiritual truth in order that man can free himself of all error and

---

[25] Gilmore, p. 96. Cp. *Science and Health,* p. 469 f.

[26] *Science and Health,* pp. 339, 472, 480.

[27] Ibid., p. 29.

[28] Gilmore, p. 4. One of Mrs. Eddy's followers declared she had conceived a child spiritually. Mrs. Eddy, however, stated that she knew only one case in which a woman claimed agamogenesis and that this woman was later cured of incipient insanity by a Christian Science practitioner. (*Science and Health,* p. 68.)

[29] Ibid., pp. 23, 25.

[30] Ibid., p. 23.

[31] Ibid., pp. 19, 53.

learn the truth regarding all reality. In other words,

> Not because Jesus was crucified are mortals redeemed from sin, relinquished of their false beliefs based upon a material existence. Rather is redemption won through the understanding of God, of man as the child of God made in His image, and of the regenerating Christ ever at hand to lead all who are willing and obedient into the haven of perfect being. This is the way of salvation.[32]

Mrs. Eddy thinks that the foundation of all mortal discord is man's false notion that he exists separate and distinct from the Divine Mind. But when in his egotism man imagines that he is an individual personality with a corporeal body, man actually elevates himself to the stature of a creator. He has forgotten that Divine Mind is the only Principle, of which man is the eternal reflection.[33]

Science of Healing. In the light of this proposition, it is clear what Christian Scientists mean by healing. Strictly speaking, Christian Science does not teach bodily healing from sickness. There is no room for prayer healing in this system — it denies the efficacy of prayer — nor for mind-healing, since there is no basis for the idea of suggestion. Mortal mind, Christian Science insists, cannot possibly heal, since it is the Cause of the error of disease. The "healing" method of Christian Scientists consists in "demonstrating" the principle that there is no matter; that everything is Divine Mind, which is perfect, sinless, and incapable of sickness or death. Mrs. Eddy believed that the time is coming when mortal mind will forsake its corporeal, structural, and material belief and in its stead accept the spiritual fact that man is indestructible and eternal and therefore incapable of sickness.

The cause of all accidents and diseases is no more than the mistaken mental belief that man is subject to the power of sickness. Accidents, sickness, and hereditary diseases are unknown to God; they are no more than pictures which mortal mind has painted on the body [?]. Unless this erroneous picture is destroyed by Truth, it will end in what people call death. For "as in Adam [evil] all die, so in Christ [Truth] all shall be made alive." In other words, when according to the principles of Christian Science a person unites his mind with the Divine Mind, the erroneous pictures of accidents, diseases, evil, failures, unhappiness, sin, and death will disappear as readily as a chimera, a bad dream.[34]

Up to now no Christian Scientist has succeeded in mastering the Science that death is simply the error of mortal mind. In fact, this error may even continue in "heaven," for no man, not even the Son, only the Father, knows when the period

---

[32] Gilmore, p. 51. Cp. p. 7. In His crucifixion and resurrection Jesus demonstrated the practical meaning of Truth and solved the great problem of Being. In the grave Jesus met and mastered the power of mind over matter. He demonstrated to the apostles by His resurrection and subsequent ascension that solely by Christian Science and without recourse to medicine, surgery, and hygiene, man can conquer and vanquish every material obstacle. (*Science and Health*, pp. 44—46.)

[33] Ibid., ch. ix, "Creation," Gilmore states: "The sons of God have never entered upon or passed a material experience; else man would have literally fallen from his original high estate" (p. 56).

[34] *Science and Health*, pp. 286, 379 ff. Cp. Glossary, under "Death." In ch. xii, pp. 362—442, Mrs. Eddy discusses the method of "healing" by demonstrating the principle of Christian Science, esp. in the section "Mental Treatment Illustrated," p. 410 ff. Christian Science practitioners frequently apply absent healing, since space is said to be no obstacle to the mind. *Science and Health*, p. 179.

will come that Science has perfectly and completely overthrown the corporeal sense.[35] For the time being Christian Scientists endeavor to ignore completely the so-called experience of death, as was done by the *Christian Science Monitor* in making no mention of the death of former President Franklin Delano Roosevelt.

Prayer. There is no room for prayer in Christian Science, since God and man are really one. A prayer to God could at best be a monolog. Petitionary prayers are considered as absolutely futile, since Divine Mind is immutably right and knows what to do without our petitions, and prayers of praise would be foolish and insulting attempts to give God information on something He knows.[36]

Ethics. Most critics of Christian Science are convinced that Mrs. Eddy advocated a principle which, if consistently applied, must undermine all ethics. Mrs. Eddy took the position that if a person is unable to divest his mind of an error, he may temporarily entertain a less grievous misconception in order to silence and overcome a worse one. As long as a person labors under the double error that he becomes hungry and that food will still his hunger, he may with impunity suppress the former and more serious error by the second and lesser error. This standard enables Christian Scientists to use home remedies and medical care and even to engage the services of the undertaker.[37] Christian Science holds that, to conquer false beliefs, one must be willing ultimately to give up such errors, even if for a time they are highly cherished. One of these is the belief that the estate of matrimony is necessary. A Christian Science writer states:

> Adultery is primarily a mental state that is to be eliminated by the abandonment of belief in a physical mortal as man. In the Kingdom, God's children neither marry nor are given in marriage, for each child of God is complete in his own selfhood as the likeness of all the deific qualities.[38]

EVALUATION

1. As a philosophy Christian Science aims to demonstrate the nonexistence of all material things and thereby to establish for man an atmosphere of perfect serenity, happiness, and contentment,

---

[35] Ibid., p. 77.

[36] Ibid., ch. i, "Prayer."

[37] In his deathbed Lord Lothian, England's ambassador to the U. S. A. and a Christian Scientist, summoned a physician in order — so the news agency reported — to avoid the legal complications, if no properly signed death certificate were available. — The author heard an accredited Christian Science lecturer give a glowing account of the instantaneous cure of a child's whooping cough. Then he paused and said to the ushers: "Isn't it very warm here? I wonder whether we could have some fresh air." For a faintly humorous incident that illustrates the legal complications of such a faith as Christian Science, see I. H. Rubenstein, *Contemporary Religious Jurisprudence* (Chicago: Waldain Press, 1948), pp. 67, 68.

[38] Gilmore, p. 91 f. In ch. iii of *Science and Health* (Marriage) Mrs. Eddy speaks in very strong terms of the sanctity and chastity of marriage. She regards marriage as the legal and moral provision for the generation of mankind, but adds significantly that the time will come when the corporeal sense of creation will be cast out to make room for the fact of spiritual creation. (P. 56.) In 1906, at the dedication of the Boston mother church, she applied the word "legalized lust" to marriage. Quoted by Riley, *The Faith, the Falsity, and the Failures of Christian Science* (New York: Fleming H. Revell, 1925), p. 145. Snowden, pp. 107 ff., 159 ff., 171.

though "mortal mind" seems to aver the very opposite. God is the only Divine Principle, the Cause of everything. He is pure Being, and there is room for absolutely nothing but Pure Mind. It is perfect, good, and there can be no evil, no troubles, no sickness, no sin, no death. In Science man "is neither young nor old. He has neither birth nor death." Mortal existence is merely a dream. It is an error to think that there is such a thing as matter.

But, one asks, if matter is nonexistent and only "a sensation in the sensationless," how can there be any sense of perception? How can there be any knowledge at all? How can man know that there is a Divine Mind? Mrs. Eddy's basic premise defies all principles of the idealist philosophers, none of whom have denied the reality of matter as Christian Science does.

If there is mortal mind, as Mrs. Eddy supposes, and if this mortal mind is the cause of the error of evil, sin, sickness, death; then there are, after all, two principles, not one, and Mrs. Eddy actually teaches the very thing she so strenuously denies.

2. Christian Science proclaims itself to be the final interpretation of the Christian religion. The heart of the Christian religion is that salvation is God's gracious gift to man for Christ's sake. In this respect the Christian religion is diametrically opposed to all ethnic religions, each of which advocates some type of autosoterism, self-salvation.[39] But even the lowest form of ethnic religion realizes and teaches that man must do something to save himself from sin and for the service of God. In this sense Christian Science cannot be considered a religion at all. In terms of the concept of religion Christian Science might be summarized thus: An abstract idea (Christ or Truth) has freed the error of mortal mind (the human body) from another error of mortal mind (sin) by a third error of mortal mind (the death of Jesus).

3. A superficial acquaintance with Christian Science leads one to believe that it is predominantly a healing cult. Mrs. Eddy has disavowed this supposition, on the ground that there can be no healing because there is no sickness.[40] The purpose of Christian Science is not to heal from bodily sickness, but to teach men by demonstration that the only reality of sin, sickness, and death is the awful fact that unrealities seem to be real; that bodily diseases, accidents, and death proceed from mortal mind; that Divine Mind, which is eternal, will ultimately get rid of all mortal errors. The basic philosophic premise of the seeming reality of unrealities has led Mrs. Eddy to the following conclusion:

> The less mind there is manifested in matter, the better. When the unthinking lobster loses it claw, the claw grows again. If the Science of Life were understood, it would be found that the senses of Mind are never lost and that matter has no sensation. Then the human limb would be replaced as readily as the lobster's claw — not with an artificial limb, but with the genuine one. Any hypothesis which supposes life to be in matter is an educated belief. In infancy this belief is not equal to guiding the hand to the mouth; and as consciousness develops, this belief goes out — yields to the reality of everlasting Life." [41]

---

[39] Cp. Paul Althaus, *Christliche Wahrheit*, I, 170 ff. F. E. Mayer, "Solus Christus," *C. T. M.*, XII (1951), 676.

[40] See *Science and Health*, ch. vi, "Science, Theology, and Medicine"; ch. xviii, "Fruitage" (reports of her "healings").

[41] *Science and Health*, p. 489. Herbert Wyrick, *Seven Religious Isms* (Grand Rapids: Zondervan Publ. House, 1940), p. 49, comments on this subject as follows: "It did not seem to occur to Mrs. Eddy that while

Most adherents of Christian Science were attracted to it primarily as a healing cult. As such, like all forms of miraculous, faith, divine, or mental healing, it deals successfully with certain physical disturbances.[42] It is therefore subject to the same criticism as faith healing, with this difference: Christian Science knows of no draft in which a person can catch a cold, no infectious diseases, no epidemics. A Christian Scientist, then, made free by "Truth," will take no precautionary measures, such as vaccination and quarantines; nor can he show sympathy, since both the suffering and the sufferer are unreal. Christian Science boasts that it is the correct interpretation of the Christian religion and a philosophical science of knowing and healing. But an unbiased examination of the claim reveals the fact that Christian Science is neither Christian nor scientific.

Somewhat related to Christian Science is the *Church of Revelation,* a small body organized in 1930 at Long Beach, Calif., to provide for spiritual, mental, and bodily healing.

BIBLIOGRAPHY

PART XI

SECTION I

Bates, Ernest S., and Dittemore, John V. *Mary Baker Eddy.* New York: Alfred A. Knopf, 1932.

Beasley, Norman. *The Cross and the Crown: The History of Christian Science.* New York: Duell, Sloan, and Pearce, 1952.

———. *The Continuing Spirit.* New York: Duell, Sloan, and Pearce, c. 1956.

Bellwald, A. M. *Christian Science and the Catholic Faith.* New York: Macmillan Co., 1922.

Braden, Charles S. *These Also Believe.* New York: Macmillan Co., 1949. Ch. v.

———. *Christian Science Today: Policy, Power, Practice.* Dallas: Southern Methodist University Press, 1958.

Coombs, J. V. *Religious Delusions.* Cincinnati: Standard Publ. Co., 1914.

Coppage, L. J. *Christian Science in the Light of Reason.* Cincinnati: Standard Publ. Co., 1914.

Dakin, Edward F. *Mrs. Eddy, the Biography of a Virginal Mind.* New York: Chas. Scribner's Sons, 1930. The Christian Scientists have endeavored to suppress this biography as being unfair to Mrs. Eddy.

the lobster's claw grows again, the lamb's tail does not. But this is accounted for, no doubt, by the proposition that the less of mind in matter the better. The lobster gets his claw again because he has so little mind; the lamb does not get his tail, and the man does not get his leg, because each has too much mind. The only hope then for the one-legged man is to become a lunatic or a lobster!"

[42] Cp. Riley (fn. 38), pp. 249—55. See Pentecostal healings, P. V, Sec. III. On divine healing, cp. Horatio W. Dressen, *The Quimby Manuscripts* (New York: Crowell Co., 1921). For a general history see Carl J. Scherzer, *The Church and Healing* (Phila.: Westminster Press, 1950), esp. p. 147 ff. Arno Clemens Gaebelein, *The Healing Question* (New York: Our Hope Publication Office, 1925). For a textbook on healing see Charles Fillmore, *The Science of Being and Christian Healing* (Kansas City, Mo.: Unity Tract Society, 1909). For an argument for divine healing see J. W. Byers, *The Grace of Healing* (Moundsville, W. Va.: Gospel Trumpet Publ. Co., 1899).

Davies, Horton. *Christian Deviations.* New York: Philosophical Library, 1954. Ch. iii.

Eddy, Mary Baker. *Science and Health with Key to the Scriptures.* Many editions. Boston: Christian Science Publ. Society.

———. *Retrospection and Introspection.* Boston: Chr. Sc. Publ. Soc.

———. *Truth vs Error.* Boston: Chr. Sc. Publ. Soc.

Ferguson, Chas. *The New Book of Revelations.* Garden City, N. Y.: Doubleday Doran and Co., 1929. Ch. ix.

Gilmore, Albert F. *The Christ at the Peace Table.* New York: Prentice-Hall, Inc., 1943.

Haldeman, I. M. *Christian Science in the Light of Holy Scripture.* New York: Fleming Revell, 1909.

Powell, Lyman P. *Mary Baker Eddy.* New York: Publ. by author, 1930. Though written by an Episcopalian, it is highly endorsed by the Christian Science Board.

Sadler, William S. *The Mind at Mischief.* New York: Funk & Wagnalls Co., 1929.

Snowden, James. *The Truth About Christian Science.* Phila.: Westminster Press, 1921.

Steiger, Henry W. *Christian Science and Philosophy.* New York: Philosophical Library, 1948.

Van Baalen, Jan K. *Chaos of Cults,* 2d ed. Grand Rapids: Wm. B. Eerdmans Publ. Co., 1956. Ch. v.

Wilbur, Sibyl. *The Life of Mary Baker Eddy.* Boston: Chr. Sc. Publ. Soc., 1938. This is the official biography.

Wittmer, George W. *Christian Science in the Light of the Bible.* St. Louis: C. P. H., 1949.

Wyckoff, H. *The Nonsense of Christian Science.* New York: Fleming H. Revell, 1921.

Christian Science Journal. Boston: Chr. Sc. Publ. Soc., a monthly. Founded 1883.

Christian Science Sentinel. Boston: Chr. Sc. Publ. Soc., a weekly. Founded 1895.

SECTION II

Unity School of Christianity

Unity School of Christianity, located on a beautiful estate near Kansas City, Mo., is one of the country's best-known healing cults. The leaders declare that they founded Unity not as a separate denomination, but as a help in teaching men, whether they belong to a church or not, to use the eternal truth taught by the Master. Though the movement has taken on all characteristics of a separate denomination, the bulk of activity still remains in the Kansas City center, and especially in the department known as Silent Unity. Here requests for help in time of sickness, business crisis, family problems, and various forms of troubles are received, and "affirmations" (prayers) are made in behalf of the petitioner. No special fees are set, but gifts are accepted. Unity Center claims over two million readers for its various publications.

In 1887 Myrtle Fillmore was cured from what was believed to be an attack of tuberculosis by a Christian Science practitioner. She and her husband Charles accepted some Christian Science principles, but differed basically with Mrs. Eddy in her denial of the reality of matter. The Fillmores were closer to New Thought than to Christian Science and at the same time distinct from both in some of the major points. Unity, as they called the movement which they organized, is extremely eclectic. It has garnered its material from many sources.[1]

The underlying thought or the basic principle of Unity is the theory that thought is omnipotent. Unity affirms that when man knows how to employ this omnipotent power, he will have healing for his body, complete freedom from any distressing thought, and ultimate perfection. Specifically Unity holds the following views:

1. Like Christian Science, Unity teaches that the Bible veils its metaphysical meanings under the names of persons, towns, rivers. In reality, Fillmore's *Metaphysical Dictionary of the Bible* is a glorification and deification of man's power.[2] In Unity literature Bible stories are allegorized. For example, Dives and Lazarus become a sort of schizophrenic person, Dives representing the outer, self-indulgent part of man, and Lazarus the undeveloped psychic or spiritual body. The story itself is said to show how each · one can overcome his own split personality.

2. Unity describes God in a terminology very similar to that of Christian Science. God is said to be Principle, Law, Being, Mind, Spirit, All-Good, Omnipotent, Omniscience, Unchangeable, Creator, Father, Cause, and Source of all that is.[3] Unity personifies the divine attributes in true mystical pantheism. The Trinity is no more than "Mind, Idea, Expression, or Thinker, Thought, and Action." [4]

---

[1] Marcus Bach, p. 246, states that the Fillmores apparently have covered the entire field of metaphysical and mystical speculation and received rare insights into "the transcendent truths of reality" from various fields. Unity has elements of Quakerism (Inner Light), of Christian Science (healing), of Theosophy (reincarnation), of Rosicrucianism (cosmic unity), of Spiritism (the astral or physical self), of Hinduism (idealism).

[2] A few samples from the dictionary will demonstrate the egocentric character of Unity:

Bethesda is the point in consciousness where we feel the flow of the cleansing life of Spirit.

Bethlehem symbolizes the abiding place of substance. It indicates the nerve center at the pit of the stomach, through which universal substance joins the refined or spiritualized chemical products of the body substance. Through this center are gradually generated the elements that go to make up the electrical body of the Christ man.

Jerusalem means habitation of peace. In man it is the abiding consciousness of spiritual peace, which is the result of continuous realizations of spiritual power tempered with spiritual poise and confidence.

Jesus is the I in man, the self, the directive power, raised to divine understanding and power — the *I Am* identity. Jesus represents God's idea of man in expression; Christ is that idea in the absolute. Christ is the divine-idea man. — Christ is the one complete idea of perfect man in Divine Mind. He is the embodiment of all divine ideas: intelligence, life, love, substance, and strength. . . . The cosmic man, or grand man of the universe, often referred to by religious mystics, is the Christ, and the Christ is the higher self of man.

Mind (is) God — the universal principle of causation, which includes all principles (first causes).

Thought is the process in mind by which substance is acted on by energy, directed by intelligence. Thought is the movement of ideas in mind. Thought control is established by aligning the thoughts with the mind of Christ, bringing every thought into a harmonious relation to eternal, unchangeable principles.

[3] Quoted from Charles Fillmore, *Christian Healing*. Braden, p. 156.

[4] *Metaphysical Dictionary*, under "Trinity."

3. Man is viewed as an embryonic divine being, the son of God filled with Christ consciousness. In reality, in Unity man takes the place of God, for God is said to be a spirit, not a being or person. God is the creative Energy, the Cause of all things, intangible, the thing that we call Life. And the individual must assert that he is life, that he is Christ, that he is a manifestation of God.[5]

4. According to the Unity school of thought, there is no need of salvation. George Fillmore is quoted as saying that the "superconsciousness of Christ" in man has mastery and dominion over all conditions of mind and body. Jesus is an example of what man can become. He was the result of the series of incarnations through which He reached the highest peak of consciousness, and through this superconsciousness, His real self, He redeemed His body. In like manner all men can redeem and transform their bodies into the Christ consciousness. This true spiritual body will replace the physical body, and man will ultimately come to be what Jesus Christ was here on earth.[6]

5. Unity does not deny the reality of sin and sickness, as does Christian Science. Unity believes that health is the natural and sickness the unnatural condition of man. Our illnesses are said to be the result of our sin. When the sinning state of mind is forgiven and the right state of mind is established, man is also automatically restored to his natural wholeness. The body is said to be shocked to death by the violent voltage of the unwise mind. Strife, anger, and hate generate currents of thought which burn out the connection in the gland just as a high current burns out the fuse. And when the lights go out, death of the body sets in. Therefore a person must constantly make the "affirmation": "I am an intelligent person with the intelligence of Christ," until it becomes a part of his consciousness. This "affirmation" and the good thoughts will generate an entirely new element and produce good microbes in a person's body, which will destroy the evil microbes caused by our evil thoughts.[7]

6. Instead of addressing prayers of praise and supplications to God, the ad-

---

[5] Bach, p. 234. In *The Twelve Powers of Man* Fillmore states that the twelve apostles represent the twelve specific powers which each man possesses and which each one must develop in order to reach human perfection. He states that according to phrenology spirituality is located in the top of the head. This is represented by Jesus, the I Am or central entity. Each of the apostles is said to represent one of the twelve powers located in various parts of the body, such as the loins, root of the tongue, navel, pit of the stomach. These powers are: faith (Peter), strength (Andrew), judgment (James), love (John), power (Philip), imagination (Bartholomew), understanding (Thomas), will (Matthew), order (James the Less), zeal (Simon), renunciation (Thaddeus), life conserver (Judas). Quoted from Braden, p. 168 f.

[6] Braden, p. 160 ff.; Bach, p. 250. In its statement of faith, Unity declares: "We believe that the dissolution of spirit, soul, body, caused by death, is annulled by rebirth of the same spirit and soul in another body here on earth. We believe the repeated incarnations of man to be a merciful provision of our loving Father to the end that all may have opportunity to obtain immortality through regeneration as did Jesus." Quoted by Van Baalen, p. 83.

[7] Based on quotations from Unity literature quoted by Braden, p. 165 ff. Unity holds that there is a thought cause for every ill. The cross-eyed person has an inner crossing of a thought. Selfishness closes the ears and results in deafness. An unforgiving state of mind causes hardening of the

herent of Unity "makes affirmations." In Unity parlance he paraphrases the Twenty-third Psalm in the following "affirmation": "The Lord is my Master; My credit is good, and He maketh me to lie down in the consciousness of omnipresent abundance." Whatever a man wants he can have by continuously affirming that he has it. Similarly, by constantly denying all those things which he does not wish to come into his life, he can ward them off. In Unity there is no worship of a merciful and saving God. Its suggested daily "meditations" are no more than a form of human self-glorification, *autolatria,* idolatry.[8]

BIBLIOGRAPHY

PART XI

SECTION II

Bach, Marcus. *They Have Found a Faith.* Indianapolis: Bobbs-Merrill Co., 1946. Ch. viii.

Braden, Chas. S. *These Also Believe.* Macmillan Co., 1949. Ch. iv.

Fillmore, Charles. *The Twelve Powers of Man.* Kansas City, Mo.: Unity Center, 1943.

————. *Metaphysical Dictionary of the Bible.* Kansas City, Mo.: Unity Center, 1944.

Fillmore, Lowell, ed. *Weekly Unity.* Kansas City, Mo.: Unity Center.

Van Baalen, J. K. *Chaos of Cults.* 2d ed. Grand Rapids: Wm. B. Eerdmans Publ. Co., 1956.

arteries. Bitterness is the cause of gall stones. *Divine Remedies,* quoted in Bach, p. 233 f. Contrariwise, there is also a thought cause to cure every ill. Fillmore states that he discovered how to send spiritual impulses to any part of his body. He said that through the daily "affirmations of health" he released the necessary electronic forces to grow new tissues in his leg bone to replace those destroyed by tuberculosis.

8 The following is an example of "affirmations" for each day of the week from *Weekly Unity:*

Sunday. The Son of God is now manifesting His nature through me, and I offer no resistance to His divine will. — Monday. Divine order is now being established in the affairs of men through the power of Jesus Christ, backed by the substance of many good men's prayers. — Tuesday. In Truth there is but one presence and one power in the universe. No man can change this truth. — Wednesday. The peace prayers that are being offered by people of many faiths and creeds are joining their forces to save the world. — Thursday. The earth is the Lord's, and it is filled with His glory and goodness. There is no room left in it for evil. — Friday. I refuse to believe in the power of evil. I ally myself with the power of God Almighty. — Saturday. There is healing power in the unity of the spirit of man with God.

SECTION III

New Thought

"New Thought" is used as both a generic and a specific term. As a generic term it denotes the idealistic thought patterns usually associated with transscendentalism of the Concord school, which has close affinities with Plato, Neoplatonism, and the Vedanta philosophy of India. New Thought believes in the omnipresence and immanence of the Divine. It teaches a progressive conquest of human ills by re-establishing the harmony between the divine and the human spirit. Currently the term "New Thought" is usually employed with reference to about a score of metaphysical cults associated in the National New Thought Alliance, formed in 1895.

New Thought resembles Christian Science and Unity in both its historical origin and its doctrine. It maintains the same omnipotence of mind. It shares virtually the same views concerning the Father-Mother Godhead. But, unlike Christian Science, it does not deny the reality of matter or suffering. Like Unity, New Thought teaches that there are healing forces at work within us, to which man surrenders himself. New Thought has been summarized by its adherents as follows: (1) God's power and activity are universally accessible. (2) Man is the highest creation — son or idea — of his loving Father-Mother (God). (3) There is no evil ·or error. What appears to be (d)evil or error is the product of man's mortal mind, working negatively, in reverse to the will of God, without understanding His creative laws. . . . (4) Jesus Christ is not only our Exemplar but also, in a larger sense, the perfect-man Idea existing eternally in the divine Mind. . . . (5) The exaltation of right thinking is the means of attaining the divine life.[1]

An early New Thought author states that the great central fact in human life is man's coming into a conscious vital realization of his oneness with the infinite life. In the degree in which man opens himself to this divine inflow, he has changed himself from mere man into God-man. Since man is in essence the same as the Infinite Spirit, he possesses spiritual thought forces of creative power. When man uses his latent divine power, he can change "dis-ease into ease-harmony; suffering and pain into abounding health and strength." To achieve this goal, man must constantly keep a high ideal of health and harmony before his mind, must constantly affirm and repeat about his health what he would wish to be true, always concentrate on thoughts of health, never dwell on his ailment. Furthermore, since man is essentially divine, the fullness of truth is said to reside within every man. He therefore requires no Bible as the source of truth and revelation, but can trust his Inner Guide. New Thought is acclaimed by its followers as the system that assures to man perfect self-sufficiency inasmuch as it teaches him the art of using his tremendous latent powers.[2]

---

[1] Mrs. B. M. Peters, the founder of the Radiant Life Truth Center, in *Christ Heals Today*. The summary is taken from a review of her book by O. E. Buchholz, *Interpretation*, Jan., 1949, p. 116 f.

[2] Trine, pp. 16, 18, 25, 56, 84, 86, 106, 183 ff.

New Thought literature has progressively placed less emphasis on bodily healing and more on "mental and spiritual hygiene." The advocates of New Thought say that it is more important to keep well than to be restored to health. In New Thought, as in Unity, man makes use of the latent infinite powers by constantly negating what he considers to be undesirable and affirming what he desires for himself. Through "affirmation" everything is said to be available to man. In 1917 the New Thought Alliance adopted at St. Louis the "Affirmations" which are herewith given in full.

We affirm the freedom of each soul as to choice and as to belief, and would not, by the adoption of any declaration of principle, limit such freedom. The essence of the New Thought is TRUTH, and each individual must be loyal to the Truth as he sees it. The windows of his soul must be kept open at each moment for the higher light, and his mind must be always hospitable to each new inspiration.

We affirm the Good. This is supreme, universal, and everlasting. Man is made in the image of the Good, and evil and pain are but the tests and correctives that appear when his thought does not reflect the full glory of this image.

We affirm health, which is man's divine inheritance. Man's body is his holy temple. Every function of it, every cell of it, is intelligent, and is shaped, ruled, repaired, and controlled by mind. He whose body is full of light is full of health. Spiritual healing has existed among all races in all times. It has now become a part of the higher science and art of living the life more abundant. We affirm the divine supply. He who serves God and man in the full understanding of the law of compensation shall not lack. Within us are unused resources of energy and power. He who lives with his whole being and thus expresses fullness, shall reap fullness in return. He who gives himself, he who knows, and acts in his highest knowledge, he who trusts in the divine return, has learned the law of success.

We affirm the teaching of Christ that the Kingdom of Heaven is within us, that we are one with the Father, that we should judge not, that we should love one another, that we should heal the sick, that we should return good for evil, that we should minister to others, that we should be perfect even as our Father in Heaven is perfect. These are not only ideals, but practical, everyday working principles.

We affirm the new thought of God as universal Love, Life, Truth, and Joy, in whom we live, move and have our being, and by whom we are held together, that His mind is our mind now, that realizing our oneness with Him means love, truth, peace, health, and plenty, not only in our own lives, but in the giving out of these fruits of the Spirit to others.

We affirm these things, not as a profession, but practice, not in one day of the week, but in every hour and minute of every day, sleeping and waking, not in the ministry of the few, but in a service that includes the democracy of all, not in words alone, but in the innermost thoughts of the heart expressed in living the life. By their fruits ye shall know them.

We affirm Heaven here and now, the life everlasting that becomes conscious immortality, the communion of mind with mind throughout the universe of thought, the nothingness of all error and negation, including death, the variety of unity that produces the individual expression of the One Life, and the quickened realization of the indwelling God in each soul that is making a new heaven and a new earth.

We affirm that the universe and we are spiritual beings. . . . To attain this we must be clean, honest, and trustworthy.[3]

---

[3] Quoted in Atkins, *Modern Religious Cults*, p. 228, also in Braden, p. 136 f.

The following bodies are associated in the New Thought Alliance and presumably hold the tenets as outlined above:

Absolute Science Center
Center of Religious Education
Chapel of Truth
Christian Assembly
Christian Science Liberals
Church of Advanced Thought
The Church of Divine Science (see below)
Church of the Healing Christ
Church of Truth
Fellowship of Divine Truth
Fellowship of Universal Design
Home of Truth
Institute of Man
Institute of Religious Thought
Metaphysical School of Health
New Thought
New Thought Temple
Radiant Life Fellowship
Unity Church of Truth
Unity Metaphysical Center
Unity Truth Centers [4]

The Church of Divine Science was founded by three sisters in Denver in 1898. God is said to be impersonal, the Universal Mind, the first Cause and Source of everything. This God Presence is everywhere as omnipotent and omniscient power. Man is the expression of God and in perfect unity with Perfect Life, Love, Intelligence, and Substance. Man is in reality a creative force and therefore never in need of petitionary prayer. Prayer is merely an affirmation of man's infinite faculties.[5]

In addition to the above, the following groups are treated in this section,

since they have borrowed heavily from New Thought. But this list is incomplete, for it is impossible to obtain information on all the groups, some of which are represented by no more than one center.

The Aquarian Ministry was started in 1918 by George and Louise Brownell at Santa Barbara, Calif., to heal the sick and to show the value of right thinking in building a grand and noble life structure for one's self. The name is taken from Aquarius, a sign of the zodiac.[6]

In 1923 the *Biosophical Institute* was founded in New York City by Frederick Kettner.

The Boston Home of Truth was organized in Boston in 1891 by Annie Mix Militz.

The Peace Mission Movement of Father Divine.[7] Little is known of Father Divine's early life, who, in his own words, "wasn't born. He combusted on the corner of 42d Street and Lennox."

From the many titles given to Father Divine by his followers it is evident that they regard him as a divine being. They address him as King of the Universe, God Almighty, Source of Salvation, King of Peace, Power House of Redemption, the Almighty, the Holy Magnetic Body of God, and by dozens of similar titles. Father Divine has nowhere actually called himself God. But, in speaking of his mission, he states that since the Spirit of God was not sufficient to guide men, therefore the body of God has come, and the Word was made flesh so that God would be more perfectly visualized. He states that his condescension to the Earth plane was as a member of the

---

[4] See Braden, p. 128.

[5] Information supplied by the headquarters of the movement in Denver, Colo.

[6] Clark, *Small Sects*, p. 232.

[7] The material here presented is based largely on Father Divine's *New Day*, published at Newark, N. J.: New Day Publ. Co. Braden, ch. i, pp. 1—77, and Bach (Sec. II, above), pp. 162—188, have been of great assistance.

Negro race, not because he is of a special race, creed, or color, but because the Negroes are the most needy. Father Divine ascribes divine works to himself, promises his adherents physical immortality, claims to control the political events of the entire world, and calls himself the "Reincarnature of America Political Documents."

New Thought and theosophy play a large part in Father Divine's philosophy. Following New Thought, Father Divine teaches that man can redeem himself by concentrating on perfection while on this material plane. By putting on the Divine Mind in place of the mortal mind, man will gain victory over sin and death. In Father Divine's system, reincarnation is called the "materialization of the spiritual," in other words, the body is only a reflection, a "tangibilization, a visibilization of man's mental and spiritual being." When the outer man passes on, the inner man — a replica — continues with features somewhat like Christ's in that body, only that Christ is both Father and Mother in that body.

The kingdom joys are said to be available now in the presence of Father Divine. All members of Father Divine's colonies are said to have God through a thorough regeneration, which was possible because each one has a "fertile egg" (the Christ within you), which will lead to the personification of perfection. A rather large number of genuine moral transformations have taken place. According to Father Divine, the atonement is an expression of the interracial character of his movement. In the final analysis, his religious concepts are also his ideals of Americanism, with the em-

phasis on the civil rights program and on the elimination of all distinctions of race, color, and religion — a movement which would ultimately result in a universal creedless, classless society.

No statistics are available on the membership of the movement. The source of Father Divine's income is a mystery.[8]

The Fellowship of Divine Truth was founded in 1934 by "Hilarion, The Master of Wisdom," in Philadelphia.

The I Am Movement. This movement, inaugurated by Mr. and Mrs. Guy Ballard,[9] is a weird conglomeration of Hinduism, Mazdaism, Theosophy, Spiritism, New Thought. Ballard affirmed that he was an accredited messenger of a group of spirits known as "The Ascended Masters," including Christ, Moses, and especially St. Germain. He said that St. Germain appeared to him on Mount Shasta, in California, gave him a drink of "creamy liquid," and imparted to him the secrets of the Mighty I Am Presence. These are: Man is ignorant of his immanent divine resources, but by strict discipline man can learn to control his thoughts and emotions and thus find the key to the inexhaustible supply of all that man needs. St. Germain further revealed to Ballard that every individual has a "Mighty I Am," controlling influence, which (or who) is ready to help man release his dormant powers as soon as man makes the "call." When contact has been established with the "Mighty I Am," a purple light cleanses man from his former embodiments. It seems that Ballard believed that ordinarily a series of reincarnations are required before

---

[8] Chester E. Belstrem of Minneapolis has sent out literature with the heading "Attach Yourself to God in Spirit, in Mind, in Body, Harmonize with God." He invites people to visit Father Divine and assure themselves of the blessings which can come to men through Father's Divine's Peace Mission.

[9] Ballard died in 1940. Mrs. Ballard and her son Donald are carrying on the work. The material is chiefly from the author's files. Braden, ch. vii, pp. 257—307, presents a good study of this movement.

man reaches perfection, but not when the body is cleansed perfectly by the heavenly light. If, however, the purple flame is extinguished, further migrations will be necessary. Ballard seems to have believed that he had completed the round of reincarnations and that he had become an individualized Identity of the Eternal and had reached immortality.

There is no room for prayers in the I Am Movement. Instead of prayers the Ballards issue "decrees." For a time they opened their public meetings by shouting "decrees" against five destructive agencies at work in America: spy activity, Communism, labor agitation, dope activity, and war. Ballard claimed that through his contact with St. Germain, the patron saint of American politics, he destroyed by his decree a fleet of submarines which threatened the Pacific coast.[10]

Psychiana. The late Frank B. Robinson of Moscow, Idaho, claimed to be "the Prophet of God, born for the express purpose of revealing the power of the Spirit of God." He supposed himself to be the medium through which the world was to be made conscious of the Presence of God and the inexhaustible supply of material wealth available for every situation in life.[11]

The School of Livable Christianity maintains that Christ is the aggregation of God principles, identified in the consciousness of man. Man is a consciousness uniting in male and female qualities. God, Christ, and man constitute the three degrees of the Word, celestial, spiritual, and natural, respectively. . . . Man is the throne of God, from which the unfolding God-qualities are projected into the race and into the universe. . . . Christianity is predicated upon certain principles of being. There are seven principles, corresponding to the seven days (actions) of creation. These are wisdom, love, substance, understanding, will, life, and truth. . . . The oneness of these seven is Christ. Christ is the qualities of God identified in consciousness, by which spiritual man is revealed.[12]

Anthroposophy. Modern anthroposophy, developed by Rudolf Steiner of Germany, makes its appeal to the intelligentsia. It is a philosophical attempt to construct a metaphysical world view which will give a noble, almost divine, aspect to all branches of science and thus give meaning to life. At the same time anthroposophy tries to satisfy the intellectual's search for "the deeper wisdom" by initiating him into the occult wisdom of the Gnostics and theosophists and by promising that he will find the key to release his inner dormant divine powers.[13]

---

[10] The St. Louis *Post-Dispatch*, Dec. 18, 1940. On one occasion Ballard decreed to possess a necktie in a show window, but the "master" in another town had already decreed it for himself.

[11] *Psychiana Lessons*, published at Moscow and sold by Psychiana, are advertised as imparting the art of contacting the Divine Power for anything one might desire. Braden, ch. ii; Bach, ch. iv. It seems that the work continues in spite of the founder's death.

[12] Ida Mingle, quoted in Guenther, *Pop. Symb.*, p. 472 f.

[13] Ernst Emmert, "Die lutherische Kirche und die Anthroposophie," *Jahrbuch des M. Luther Bundes*, 1949/50, p. 126 ff. See also the Epilogue by A. P. Shepherd and Mildred Robertson Nicoll in Rudolf Steiner, *The Redemption of Thinking: A Study in the Philosophy of Thomas Aquinas*, trans. by Shepherd and Nicoll (London: Hodder and Stoughton, 1956). Anthroposophy has been introduced into this country since World War II, but it has not gained much of a following.

BIBLIOGRAPHY

PART XI   SECTION III

Braden, Chas. S. *These Also Believe.* New York: Macmillan Co., 1949. Ch. iii.

Dresser, Horatio W. *A History of the New Thought Movement.* New York: Thomas Y. Crowell Co., 1919.

Holmes, Ernest. *Mind Re-Makes Your World.* New York: Dodd, Mead & Co., 1944.

————. *New Thought Terms and Their Meanings.* New York: Dodd, Mead & Co., 1942.

Peters, Blanche Marie. *Christ Heals Today.* Hobson Book Press, 1947.

Trine, Ralph W. *In Tune with the Infinite.* New York: Dodd, Mead & Co., 1897.

Esoteric and Miscellaneous Groups

SECTION I

Theosophy

Theosophy has been called the "apostate child of spiritism mixed with Buddhism." Spiritism and theosophy both venture into the spirit world: spiritism through a medium, theosophy through man's own clairvoyant powers.

Theosophical principles are prominent in such metaphysical cults as New Thought, Psychiana, Father Divine's Peace Mission, and the Unity School. Some theosophical views, especially the theory that man will have an opportunity to continue his moral and spiritual development after death, appeal to liberal theology.

Theosophists state that theosophy is not a religion, but an attempt to fuse Eastern and Western philosophy. Its adherents hope to form a nucleus of the universal brotherhood of man without distinction of race, creed, sex, or color; to encourage the study of comparative religions, philosophies, and sciences; and to investigate the unexplained laws of nature and the power in man.[1] Today theosophy is less a philosophical movement than a religious phenomenon, represented in a fairly large number of organized cults.

Modern theosophy — not to be confused with the theosophy of such mystics as Jacob Boehme — was introduced to America by Madame Helena P. Blavatsky (1851—1891), who came to New York from India in 1872. Associated at first with the spiritists, she met Henry Olcott, with whom she organized the Theosophical Society in 1875. After Olcott's death in 1907, Mrs. Annie Besant (1847—1933), wife of an Anglican clergyman, an atheist and a divorcee, became the leader. Theosophy professes to study the secret wisdom of all the great adepts and masters — Moses, Confucius, Homer, Brahman, Serapis. These secrets are supposedly found in Hinduism, Buddhism, spiritualism, Egyptian hermeticism, and occultism. Theosophists say that their research has revealed two basic truths: (1) the hidden forces in nature show that God is immanent, and (2) the latent powers in man show that man is perfectible.

THE COSMIC FORCE

Theosophy teaches that not only physical but also metaphysical forces are constantly active in the universe. Modern science is said to demonstrate that the old ideas of matter are no longer tenable. It is supposed to be more reasonable to accept the thesis of theosophy that an invisible world occupies the same space as the visible world. Theosophists teach that different grades of matter can readily interpenetrate each other and occupy the same space, just as water interpenetrates a sponge in such a way

NOTE: For key to abbreviations see Appendix C; for Bibliography, the end of the section.

[1] *Information About Theosophical Society*, a tract published at Wheaton, Ill.

that both occupy the same space. An invisible world of very subtle matter is said to exist, unaffected by the visible matter, within, and around, and throughout the visible world. Theosophy professes to know that there are many forms of rare grades of this invisible matter which surround the visible world in an ascending series of various strata. Theosophists also assert that they have gained the know-how to enter this metaphysical or spiritual world directly by clairvoyant or clairaudient powers and to draw inexhaustible information from this rarefied spiritual and metaphysical world. According to some theosophists, there are seven distinct worlds or planes of this kind:

(1) a divine, (2) a monadic, (3) a spiritual, (4) an intuitional, (5) a mental, (6) an emotional, or astral, and (7) a physical world.[2]

In these metaphysical or spiritual worlds the theosophists find God at work. They hold that

All nature is but an expression of a supreme being; that God is not a being apart from life and matter, from men and other creatures, but that which exists is God in manifestation; that every human being is part of the supreme being . . . in short that the consciousness of the supreme being permeates every atom of matter and that in the most literal way we live and move and have our being in God.[3]

Theosophy sees no more in God than an impersonal, pantheistic activity, "wave after wave pushing its way up through matter." Man is said to exert a tremendous influence on this pantheistic cosmic force. As man's good or evil thoughts and actions will ultimately be reflected in the lines of his face, so men's actions are impressed upon the subtle and invisible matter surrounding the visible world. And these impressions

will remain, because — says theosophy — matter is eternal. Every emotion somehow modifies the matter that will constitute man's invisible body on another plane and will have a deep effect on the character of the "consciousness" which ultimately will dwell in the invisible world.

Theosophy maintains that man is fully equipped to investigate these God-forces of the universe operative in the various planes. Since all nature is but an expression of the Supreme Being; since God is never apart from life and matter; and since man himself helps to shape the forces known as God, he must also be in a position to investigate these forces active in the various forms of matter, whether it be the present or past world, the visible or invisible world.

MAN'S PERFECTIBILITY

Theosophy holds that man has three bodies at the same time, and each must be developed on its particular level until it reaches perfection. The three forms are described as the physical body of activity, the astral body of emotions, and the mental body of thought. The gradual evolution of each form can take place only by a series of reincarnations. In reply to those who deny the Hindu teaching of reincarnation, theosophists state that daily experiences demonstrate the "fact" of reincarnation. A child prodigy is said to be the result of the cumulative experiences gathered in many previous incarnations. "Masculine women" are unfortunate persons who have returned in the form of the opposite sex. Love at first sight, sudden friendships, familiar scenes are explained on the basis of reincarnation. Ordinarily the evolutionary process whereby man reaches perfection is extremely slow and requires many reincarnations. Some the-

[2] See Braden, p. 246.

[3] *What Theosophy Is,* a tract by L. W. Rogers.

osophists hold that in its existence of 18,000,000 years the cosmos has gone through endless cycles.[4] Likewise each individual has gone through long periods of time slowly evolving before he even reached the human stage, and then he must go through many reincarnations in the mental, astral, and physical body, until he comes to a full understanding of the higher world developed in him.

In each incarnation the inexorable law of karma is at work, or the principle that as a man sows, so shall he reap. Man will be advanced or retarded in his evolutionary process as the soul stores up good or evil effects in each existence. The law of karma leaves no room for mercy. One wonders whether there is even justice. For man has no clear recollection of any wrong done in the previous existence, and yet he is being chastised now for that wrong. Nor is he conscious of the good done by him for which he is being advanced.[5]

THE ROAD TO PERFECTION

Yoga plays a large part in theosophy. The swamis and the yogis present yoga as the path that leads to union of the individual with the Cosmic Soul. Royal Yoga, the highest form of yoga, has eight branches; four prescribe physical, and four mental exercises. They are the following:

1. The observances of moral principles, both positive and negative, whereby man frees his soul from all fear and bondage. Liberation from the body is considered essential.

2. Correct posture leads to poise and calm, the prerequisite for the practice of meditation.

3. Breath is the life force. Through proper breathing the individual develops clairvoyant powers.

4. Breath control leads to such concentration that one becomes completely oblivious to the surrounding world.

5. In concentration the yogi can focus his mind upon any object at will.

6. This leads to meditation, an unbroken flow upon the object of one's concentration.

7. The mind loses consciousness of the material world and makes a direct contact with the Ultimate.

8. In this state, man is free from all misery, enters into the realm of the Divine Presence, and makes an actual experience of God.[6]

Nirvana is the ultimate goal of man and the consummation of the many earth rounds. According to some, Nirvana is absolute and final annihilation. According to others, it is such a complete union of the individual souls with the Cosmic Soul that the individual loses his own personality. According to still others, Nirvana is the graduation from the many earthly incarnations into the realm of endless progress by a higher form of evolution.

[4] Madam Blavatsky advanced and popularized the theory that on the lost continents of Atlantis, so vividly described by Plato, and of Lemuria in the Indian Ocean the world's wisdom of the past 60,000,000 years is deposited. Cp. *Time*, Sept. 8, 1952, p. 91.

[5] Buddhism presents life as a wheel in 'control of the lords of karma. Man is viewed as a helpless pawn in the clutches of these cruel lords.

[6] This report is based on notes taken at a lecture at Vedanta Center, St. Louis, February 25, 1940. Many of the yogis operating in the American hotel parlors are frauds. Under their manipulations many middle-aged women were driven to the point of insanity. Compare Steiner, p. 145; Engelder et al., *Popular Symbolics*, p. 467 f. For a sympathetic account see Ernest Wood, *Great Systems of Yoga* (New York: Philosophical Library, 1954).

SOURCES OF THEOSOPHICAL WISDOM

There are several sources of information from which the theosophists receive what they call their knowledge.

1. The mahatmas are said to be the great accomplished teachers: Buddha, Hermes, Zoroaster, Orpheus, and Jesus. During his earthly sojourn each mahatma contributes as much knowledge as the race at that specific time can endure. Christ has already made five appearances, and His sixth appearance was expected in the form of Krishnamurti, Mrs. Besant's protégé.

2. The astral records are said to be a complete record of every thought and action in a person's life, indelibly inscribed in the atmosphere surrounding our material and physical world. The careful study of one's own and other people's record will lead to a better understanding of life's purposes.

3. As a result of his various reincarnations man acquires intuitive powers which enable him to delve directly and immediately into the depths of the wisdom of the world. In his search for the wisdom of the ages man is aided by latent occult powers, particularly clairvoyance. This power is merely the extension of one's normal vision to penetrate areas which because of their higher and more subtle vibrations are closed to the material and physical eyesight.

4. Yoga is said to be another means of access to the reservoir of wisdom. The great universal truths are said to be in the air, and yoga shows the seeker how by proper breathing he can make contact and establish rapport with the great life principle.

Theosophy appeals to man's inherent egocentricity and self-righteousness, because it is a system of self-development, of character building, of self-purification and illumination. It does away entirely

with the Christian doctrines of sin, atonement, the grace of God, forgiveness, heaven. Theosophy professes to make men see their power over every circumstance in life, compelling even the wrong to serve them. In theosophy man is the captain of his soul, the master of his destiny. He is a fragment of divinity temporarily clothed in matter.

It must be pointed out also that theosophy, like spiritism, holds views which may lead to conclusions in support of sexual promiscuity. The theosophist theory is that in its pre-existent state the soul is bisexual, both male and female; that at the time of birth, however, a separation of the two occurs. Since the two are eternally equal and complemental, they are restless while separated in the material world and tend to draw towards each other. Accordingly only a "soul marriage," the union of these original complemental sex principles, is a true marriage. If by chance the two affinities meet in this world, the conventional marriage must be set aside and permit the two affinities to cleave to each other.

The Various Theosophical Groups

There is a fairly large number of metaphysical, healing, and psychological bodies that owe a great deal to theosophy, such as Psychiana, Father Divine's Peace Mission, the I Am Movement, Unity School. But since other trends of thought, particularly New Thought, predominate in these groups, they have been listed under New Thought rather than under theosophy. It was impossible to establish a complete list of the bodies which profess to be theosophical. This impossibility is due to the fact that some groups are of a purely local nature, and others have had only a short existence because of brushes with the law. Still others seem to find it convenient to change their post office address occasionally.[7] The first three groups follow quite closely the principles described above.

The Theosophical Society in America, with headquarters in Wheaton, Ill., was originated by Madam Blavatsky and Col. Olcott in 1875 at New York.

The Theosophical Society has its headquarters at Covina, Calif.

The United Lodge of Theosophists has its headquarters at Los Angeles, Calif.

The Vedanta Society asserts that the Vedas contain the foundation of all creeds and explain the eternal and universal laws governing all spiritual life. The world's various religions are viewed only as so many aspects and phases of Vedanta. The followers of Vedanta maintain that man is essentially pure, blissful, immortal, and that they are masters of the various methods by which man can exercise his ability to be the master of his own destiny and ultimately to reach divine perfection.

The Self-Realization Fellowship was founded by Paramhansa Yogananda in the United States in 1920, two years after he had founded the *Yogoda Sat-Sanga Society* in India. With branches in eight states and two Canadian provinces, this organization seeks to interpret the spiritual ideas of Hindu religion for Westerners and offers its adherents healing of mind, body and soul.

Rosicrucianism, the Ancient and Mystical Order Rosae Crucis. The modern Rosicrucians declare that they are the rightful successors of the Rosicrucian Order. This order flourished during the Middle Ages. Its members claimed to possess occult powers and practiced alchemy and astrology.[8] The Rosicrucians insist that they have access to all the knowledge which men have acquired in former centuries, including also the records deposited on the lost continents of Atlantis and Lemuria. In these documents — many of which are said to be in the Rosicrucian library at San Jose — the Rosicrucians have found the key with which each one can choose such a program for himself as will lead to his own perfection. Rosicrucianism purports to teach people to meet successfully every problem of life by demonstrating that the "kingdom of God is within everyone," i. e., everyone is a royal king, a powerful dictator, since all the powers of the universe are in his body. Understanding fully the highest consciousness of God as taught by Rosicrucianism, its adherents are able to do more than any other group of men, no matter how large they are. Where two or three are gathered together in the consciousness of their powers, "Christ" is in the midst of them, and they are able to create mentally the things considered essential for their happiness.[9]

Church of Illumination.[10] According

---

[7] Steiner, p. 143 f. — The list of separate groups in this section was established on the basis of information gleaned from E. T. Clark, *The Small Sects;* Engelder and others, *Popular Symbolics;* Chas. Braden, *These Also Believe; The Yearbook of the Churches;* Census, *Religious Bodies,* 1936; the author's files.

[8] The Rosicrucians, with headquarters at Oceanside, Calif., affirm that this order was founded in the 13th century. The branch known as AMORC, founded by H. W. Spencer Lewis, has its headquarters at San Jose, Calif.

[9] See the article "Rosicrucianism," *Encyclopaedia Britannica* (1950 ed.), XIX, 559—560.

[10] The material for the following sketch is taken from R. Swinburne Clymer, *The Teachings of the Masters,* and *Manual, Order of Service and Ritual* (Quakertown, Pa.: Philosophical Publ. Co., c. 1952). Clymer is

to its constitution, the Church of Illumination teaches that there is a divine spark in man, that is, man's soul, which is part of the Father, or Cosmic Soul; that man must put forth every effort to bring his body into consciousness, known as man's individualization or illumination; that the purpose of this church is to enlighten humanity to reach the high and noble purpose of the soul's illumination. Much is made of the order of Melchizedek, said to be the small body of seekers throughout the ages, including Moses, the Nazarene, the Egyptian Hermetics, the Greek philosophers, the Hindu monks, and today the Illuminate. R. Swinburne Clymer charges that formal religions have failed on three points: (a) They are concerned only about the welfare of the soul and ignore completely the importance of the body; (b) they have led men into slavery by teaching man to depend on someone else (e. g., God's grace), instead of assuming responsibility himself; (c) they have taught man to rely on a divine power for his regeneration, whereas only man himself can awaken the *Christos* spark, the inherent "Christic" principles.[11] The Church of Illumination teaches a system of self-salvation. The Nazarene obtained the cosmic consciousness by living according to an exact law. He became the Son of God by making use of His inherent native ability. Likewise man today must work out his own regeneration if he is to become a son of God. In accord with theosophical principles the Church of the Illumination

teaches that as long as the soul is buried under the deep debris of past and present sins, it is "unconscious" and unable to reach immortality. But the soul can awaken its inherent *Christos* consciousness and thus obtain immortality and divine sonship.[12] Since not everyone can reach immortality in one earthly existence, reincarnation is provided for the soul which has failed to learn its lesson. For most people death is only a graduation from one class to the next. It is the opening of a new opportunity to achieve complete Christlikeness or divine sonship.[13]

The manual for the order of services prescribes a liturgy for Baptism and the Lord's Supper, two forms for marriage, and several forms of funeral services, and various chants (e. g., one for the "awakened soul"). This group holds some views in common with Anglo-Israelism. The Egyptian Hermetic wisdom, the secrets of the Holy Grail, the magnificence of Solomon's Temple, and other phases of the "secret wisdom" are said to be reflected in the early history of the Republic, in our American Constitution, and especially in the Great Seal.[14]

The Liberal Catholic Church. This body was formed in 1915. While it claims to possess Old Catholic orders, theologically it has nothing in common with the Old Catholicism of the Jansenists and Döllinger. The Liberal Catholic Church is a theosophical group. The well-known theosophist Leadbeater

listed as "Director General, Church of Illumination, Supreme Grand Master of International Confederation of Initiates, also of the Merged Occult Fraternities, which comprise: The Priesthood of Aeth, the Rosicrucian Order, the Secret Schools, the Hermetic Brotherhood, Fraternitas Rosae Crucis, Temple of the Rosy Cross, the Order of the Magi, Sons of Isis and Osiris, Illuminatae Americanae."

11 Clymer, *The Teachings of the Masters*, p. 7.

12 Ibid., pp. 37, 40, 96—98, 221.

13 Ibid., pp. 103—105, 119, 127.

14 Ibid., pp. 50—57, 189. Cp. Anglo-Israelism, P. VIII, Sec. VII.

became the leading spirit in the Liberal Church.[15]

In truly theosophical fashion all historic religions are said to be divinely inspired, and the members are not required to profess any doctrine or creed. It seems that the only bond which unites the members is a common ritual. Its concept of God is pantheistic. Though the Trinitarian formula is used, the Trinity is viewed merely as a symbol to denote the threefold activity of an impersonal God. The divinity of Christ is said to be unfolded in man until all become a perfect man measuring up to the fullness of Christ. In fact, the ultimate goal of man is to obtain a complete oneness with God. All specifically Christian doctrines are categorically denied. Man is reputedly a spark of the divine fire and will go through incarnations until he ultimately reaches a perfect union with God. The creed of the Liberal Catholic is summarized in these words:

> We believe that God is Love, and Power, and Truth, and Light; that perfect justice rules the world; that all His sons shall one day reach His feet, however far they stray. We hold the Fatherhood of God, the brotherhood of man; we know that we do serve Him best when best we serve our brother man. So shall His blessing rest on us and peace forevermore. Amen.[16]

The Church of the Radiant Light, also known as the Royal Fraternity of Master Metaphysicians, is established at Oakdale, Long Island, on the old Vanderbilt estate. James B. Schaefer, the founder, attempted to prove his metaphysical powers by promising immortality to a young girl which the group had adopted. Because of fraudulent practices Schaefer was sentenced to Sing Sing.

Institute of Mentalphysics was begun by Edward J. Dingle of Los Angeles, who believed himself to be a reincarnation to impart the wisdom of the great mystics of Tibet.

The Temple of Yahweh, founded by Joseph Jeffers in 1946, teaches that there is power in the "vibrations" involved in the use of the Hebrew name Yehweh. With his fraudulent practices Jeffers seems to have often run afoul of the law.[17]

Church of Truth Universal, AUM.[18] The initials AUM do not denote an organization but are said to be the prehistoric word for God or the "pulsating conscious-life-action," the union with the Cosmic Soul, the at-one-ment.[19] The leader of the group, Nina Bounier, claims to have received the universal truth by direct inspiration. In their literature there are references to the Aquarian Ministry, to the Yahwe Yogoda, and especially to the basic teachings of theosophy. The AUM holds that man, a divine fragment, can learn to unlock the hidden powers within himself. Every person has an "atman" who has lost his way in the great illusion, but has finally completed the circle and obtained union with the Cosmic Soul and the right to live in the great AUM.

---

[15] Braden, ch. viii.

[16] Engelder, et al., *Popular Symbolics,* p. 208.

[17] Clark, *Small Sects,* pp. 227—228. Views held by Anglo-Israelism seem to be entertained by this cult.

[18] The description is based on tracts and booklets published by this body at Highway Islands, Calif.

[19] In a pamphlet the AUM published the correspondence between the Rev. E. W. Miller and the committee of the Revised Standard Version. The AUM group protested against the omission of the name Jehovah from the English translation, on the ground that the use of the name Jehovah is essential to true worship.

The Brotherhood of the White Temple was founded by Maurice Doreal, who maintains that his spirit journeys to Tibet for consultation with the mystics.[20]

The Brotherhood of Light, established at Los Angeles, claims to teach mediumship, astrology, spiritism, alchemy, divination, and character reading.[21]

The Order of the Cross was founded by J. Todd Ferrier, who declared that he had accumulated a wealth of source material, especially those teachings of Jesus which are contained only in the *Logia* of Jesus — chiefly His teachings on reincarnation and the unjust taking of both animal and human life.[22]

The Institute of Religious Science and School of Philosophy, with headquarters at Los Angeles, asserts that it leads to the understanding of man's physical, mental, and spiritual nature.

Mayan Temple, with headquarters in Brooklyn, contends that it has restored the religious principles and practices of prehistoric Mayas. They consider reincarnation and the continuity of life a scientifically established fact.[23]

Buddhist Churches of America are made up chiefly of Japanese Buddhists belonging to the Jodo Shinshu sect.

Appendix: The following groups claim to be religious organizations, but there is reasonable doubt that they actually have a significant following.

Humanity Benefactor Foundation of Detroit was founded by Alfred Lawson and is also known as Lawsonamy. This system probably follows the pattern of New Thought as much as that of theosophy. Lawson teaches that God has decreed that mankind must move to new heights of intelligence by following the basic law of Lawsonomy, a system which, as Lawson promises, will teach his followers to cleanse their mind of all falsities and develop their reasoning.

The Life Study Fellowship is a mail-order scheme of offering help through prayer and theosophical philosophy.

The Altruist Church professes to be founded on a realistic conception of God and asserts that God created both good and evil and gave man the power to choose what he wants.

The Assemblies of Yahweh and of Messiah, the members of which are called *Yahwists,* lay stress on the correct pronunciation of the Holy Name of God, deny the Trinity, keep the Sabbath, baptize by immersion, hold premillennial views.[24]

Mazdaznan Philosophy was founded by Ottoman Zar Adust Hanish (a Swiss by the name of Hanisch), who insisted that he had revived the old system of Zoroastrian philosophy. The cult professes to possess the older and more comprehensive system of body and mind culture, consisting in correct dieting, correct breathing, sexual hygiene, prenatal education. Ultimate perfection is obtained through a series of reincarnations.

The Metaphysical School of Health holds the basic theosophical views concerning the manifold nature of man, the bisexual character of God, and attributes all diseases to wrong thinking.

The Fellowship of the Order of Christian Mystics was founded by Dr. and Mrs. F. Homer Curtis, who profess to have contact with higher spiritual creatures of mankind and predict that shortly the great spiritual world teacher, Avatar, will appear.

The Modern Church, purports to combine all religious thought contained in

---

[20] Clark, *Small Sects,* pp. 234, 228.

[21] Engelder et al, *Popular Symbolics,* p. 469.

[22] Braden, p. 470.

[23] *Census,* II, 1273; Clark, *Small Sects,* p. 234.

[24] Haig M. Mardirossian, *The Rules of Faith* (Kansas City: Faith Scriptural Truths, n. d.) and *The Forgotten Faith of the True Worshippers* (New York: Vantage Press, 1958). The author identifies himself as a V. Y. M. *(Verba Yahweh Minister).*

Brahmanism, Buddhism, Judaism, Moham-medanism, and Christianity and now presented in the teachings of theosophy, spiritualism, and New Thought.

The Fellowship Following Buddha is a group which supports Dwight Goddard of Thetford, Vt., in his efforts to circulate the Buddhist scriptures and to enable the few "homeless brothers" (Buddhist monks) to practice the path of Buddha.

Maha Bhodi Society of America, with headquarters in New York, teaches that desire and evil are synonymous and that happiness can be attained only by eradicating all evil desire. This is done through following closely the eightfold Royal Yoga path.

BIBLIOGRAPHY

PART XII

SECTION I

Braden, Chas. S. *These Also Believe.* Ch. vi.

Davies, Horton. *Christian Deviations.* New York: Philosophical Library, 1954. Ch. ii.

Leadbeater, Chas. W. *Outline to Theosophy.* Los Angeles: Theosophical Book Concern, 1916.

————. *Textbook of Theosophy.* Los Angeles: Theosophical Publ. Co., 1918.

Radhakrishnan, Sarvepelli, and A. Charles Moore. *A Source Book in Indian Philosophy.* Princeton: Princeton University Press, 1957.

Sloan, M. E. *Modern Theosophy.* St. Paul: The Way Press.

Steiner, Lee R. *Where Do People Take Their Troubles?* Boston: Houghton Mifflin Co., 1945. Ch. vii.

Tracts furnished by Theosophical Press, Wheaton, Ill.

Van Baalen, Jan K. *The Chaos of Cults,* 2d ed. Grand Rapids: Eerdmans, 1956.

Wood, Ernst. *The New Theosophy.* Chicago: Theosophical Press, 1929.

SECTION II

Spiritualism

Spiritism, usually spoken of as spiritualism, has attracted a very large following because it professes to draw aside the curtain which hides the future from man.[1] Spiritism believes that the disembodied spirits are reservoirs of highly desirable and essentially valuable information conveyed from the spirit world to the physical world through specially endowed mediums. Spiritism has a three-fold appeal: (1) the theory that the disembodied spirits are very benevolent and eager to help men still in the body, especially their former close associates; (2) the alleged ability and willingness of disembodied spirits to describe the world beyond the grave, which will naturally attract many who are concerned

---

[1] There are many superstitious means which people employ to gain an insight into the future, such as astrology, the horoscope, palmistry, numerology, necromancy. M. C. Poinsat, *The Encyclopedia of Occult Sciences* (New York: Robert M. McBride and Co., 1939).

about their own future in the hereafter; (3) spiritistic mediums promise to establish a pleasant rapport with departed loved ones.[2] For that reason spiritism usually experiences an upsurge during times of war.

Nature of Spiritualism

Spiritism is frequently viewed primarily as a psychic phenomenon. It is that. But it is also a religious movement and claims the ability to comfort people and prepare them for the life to come. Modern spiritism parades under the name spiritualism and must therefore be examined as both a psychic and a religious phenomenon.

A PSYCHIC PHENOMENON

The rise of modern spiritualism is frequently associated with the peculiar psychic phenomena displayed by the Fox sisters at Hydesville, N. Y. The spiritualists, however, say that the "Hydesville rappings" and "Rochester knockings" could never have produced modern spiritualism. They maintain that modern spiritualism owes its origin to the writings of Andrew Jackson Davis and that the movement was fully established March 31, 1848.[3] Nevertheless the various psychic phenomena play a prominent part in any and every form of spiritism, or spiritualism. The psychic experiments performed by the mediums in the séances are usually classified as of two kinds: the physical and the mental. Among the physical phenomena the

most common are rappings, the Ouija board, table tipping, slate writing, spirit photography, levitation (raising bodies into the air), penetration (the passing of bodies through walls and curtains), materialization (the spirits assume human form), telekinesis (the moving of heavy objects without any visible means). Among the mental phenomena the following are most frequently used: The platform method (at the request of one in the audience the medium reveals a message from the spirit world); automatic writing (the supposed message from the spirit is written by the medium in a state of trance); clairvoyance, clairaudience, clairsentience (a supersensory faculty to see, hear, and feel the vibrations in the spirit world); transpeaking (the medium discusses topics beyond her ordinary knowledge and sometimes in terminology foreign to her); healing through magnetic and hypnotic powers.

Spiritists point out that spiritualism as a religion neither stands nor falls with the various psychic phenomena. Whether in a given case the phenomena are genuine or fraudulent is difficult to decide. According to Holy Scripture, the devil can perform many inexplicable phenomena and grossly deceive men. The Scriptures contain many injunctions against, and severe condemnations of, every form of spiritism. Several psychic research societies have investigated the various psychic phenomena of spiritism, and it seems that only a few mediums are above suspicion. Even Sir Arthur

[2] In this regard modern spiritism differs fundamentally from spirit worship in many of the ethnic religions. Cp. Samuel M. Zwemer, *The Origin of Religion* (Nashville, Tenn.: Cokesbury Press, 1935). Theodore H. Robinson, *An Outline Introduction to the History of Religion* (London: Oxford Univ. Press, 1926). Edmund Soper, *The Religions of Mankind* (New York: Abingdon Press, 1921), pp. 45—80. Robert E. Speer, *Christianity and Non-Christian Religions* (West Medford, Mass.: Central Committee on United Study of Missions, 1911).

[3] See *Census*, II, 1599. Emanuel Swedenborg is often considered the founder of modern spiritism. However, Swedenborg holds views so different from those of spiritism that Swedenborg's Church of the New Jerusalem must be treated separately.

Conan Doyle, the well-known spiritist, admitted that it is impossible to determine whether "spirits" are bona fide or not. Houdini duplicated practically all of the phenomena of the séance.[4]

A RELIGIOUS SYSTEM

As a religious system spiritualism must be characterized as a complete denial of every Christian truth: the fall of man; the theanthropic person of Christ — He is merely a medium; the doctrine of the atonement; the final and decisive character of death; the existence of hell. Spiritualism teaches a form of self-salvation.[5]

1. According to the spiritualists, God is a pantheistic deification of nature and the natural phenomena.

2. Man is said to consist of body, soul, and spirit. The spirit is the personal life proceeding from God. It establishes the union of each man with the Eternal Spirit, the impersonal Intelligence of the Universe, and with every other man in a great "brotherhood of men." The soul is the life of the physical body. The physical body, the covering of the soul, is discarded at death. Then the soul, also known as the astral body, becomes the "body of the spirit." Spiritualists view death as the liberation of the soul and the spirit and the entrance into an unlimited existence. Since the rate of vibrations of the body is lower than that of the spirit world, only the mediums, with their sensitive eyes and ears, can sense these higher vibrations and close the wide gap between the spiritual and material world. Like theosophy, spiritualism holds that man's eternal spirit is bisexual. Shortly before birth, they say, this bisexual spirit is split into its male and female parts, and the one is embodied in a male and the other in a female body. The desire for a reunion of these spiritual mates persists, they think, even during the earthly marriage if it is not consummated between the bisexual mates of the pre-existent spirit. The reunion of the separated mates will occur, it is said, in the "summerland," where the spirit will be freed from all bodily inhibitions.

3. The spiritualists deny the significance and the importance of death. Life

---

[4] Van Baalen, p. 19; Henry J. Trienzenberg, *Spiritism* (Grand Rapids: Zondervan Publ. House). See Bach, on his experiences at Chesterfield, Ind., pp. 97—121.

[5] The National Spiritualistic Association subscribes to the following principles:

We believe in Infinite Intelligence; and that the phenomena of nature, both physical and spiritual, are the expression of Infinite Intelligence.

We affirm that a correct understanding of such expressions and living in accordance with them constitute the true religion; that the existence and personal identity of the individual continue after the change called death; and the communication with the so-called dead is a fact scientifically proved by the phenomena of Spiritualism.

We believe that the highest morality is contained in the Golden Rule: "Whatsoever ye would that others should do unto you, do ye also unto them."

We affirm the moral responsibility of the individual, and that he makes his own happiness or unhappiness as he obeys or disobeys Nature's physical and spiritual laws.

We affirm that the doorway to reformation is never closed against any human soul, here or hereafter. [*Census,* 1936, II, 1600 f. The main tenets of the Progressive Spiritual Church are listed, p. 165 f.]

after death is the continuation of this life, and both the ills and the blessings of this life are said to continue on the various levels in the spirit world. As a rule spiritualists speak of seven such levels. The first two are for the unrepentant wicked. Then there is the "summerland," the counterpart of the earthly existence. The fourth level is reserved for the philosophers, the fifth for the contemplative spirits. The sixth is the love sphere, and the seventh the Christ sphere.

4. The spiritualists believe that the spirit world is a counterpart of the visible world, only more beautiful and perfect. To enter the spirit world, the soul must be free from the evil which it had in the body. Spiritualists hold that there is salvation after death, that both punishments and rewards will continue after death, that hell is only a remedial agency, and that by his own efforts man will ultimately reach perfection. In theosophy the path to perfection is a series of earthly reincarnations; in spiritualism perfection is attained by a continuous evolutionary process after death.

5. The organized spiritualistic associations have regular services for worship, some even observing the Christian sacraments. But it is impossible to worship an impersonal God or pray to an abstract concept.[6]

Spiritualistic Association

The National Spiritualist Association of Churches is the oldest of the several groups. The present organization attributes its origin to the principles enun-

ciated by Andrew Jackson Davis and published by him three years before psychic phenomena of the Fox sisters caused so much commotion. The religious tenets of modern spiritualism are practically identical with those developed by Davis. Spiritualists maintain that the subsequent psychic experiments only support the principles set forth by Davis. *The Spiritualist Manual* contains the ritual for public worship as well as for the marriage, baptism, and funeral services. This body has a threefold ministry: ordained clergymen, licentiates, and mediums.[7]

The National Spiritual Alliance of the U. S. A. was founded by G. Tabor Thompson in 1913 at Lake Pleasant, Mass. Its main tenet is the belief that mediums with a high degree of sensitivity to spirit influence have demonstrated that there is an eternally progressive life after death.[8]

The International General Assembly of Spiritualists was organized for the purpose of chartering spiritualist churches.

In 1937 the *International Constitutional Church* was founded in Los Angeles by C. E. Kelso.[9]

Universal Psychic Science was established in 1942 by J. Bertram Gerling at Rochester, N. Y.[10]

In 1944 *the Federation of Spiritual Churches and Associations* was formed at Bloomington, Ill., to bring together all spiritualistic bodies in order to make as strong an impact on the religious scene as possible.[11]

---

6 Cp. Graebner, p. 112.

7 *Census,* 1936, II, 1600.

8 Ibid., p. 1610.

9 Braden, p. 332 f.

10 Ibid., p. 333 f.

11 Ibid., p. 334 f.

BIBLIOGRAPHY

PART XII

SECTION II

The Spiritualist Manual. Washington, D. C.: National Spiritualist Association.

Atkins, G. G. *Modern Religious Cults and Movements.* New York: Fleming H. Revell Co., 1923.

Bach, Marcus. *They Have Found a Faith.* Indianapolis: Bobbs-Merrill, 1946. Ch. iv.

Biederwolf, William Edward. *Spiritualism.* Chicago: Glad Tidings Publ. Co., n. d.

Braden, Charles S. *These Also Believe.* New York: Macmillan Co., 1949. Ch. ix.

Coombs, J. V. *Religious Delusions.* Cincinnati: Standard Publ. Co., 1904.

Davies, Horton. *Christian Deviations.* New York: Philosophical Library, 1954. Ch. iv.

Graebner, Theo. *Spiritism, a Study of Its Phenomena and Religious Teachings.* St. Louis: C. P. H., 1919.

Hill, J. A. *Spiritualism, Its History, Phenomena, and Doctrine.* Garden City, N. Y.: Geo. H. Doran & Co., 1919.

Lawton, George S. *The Drama of Life After Death.* New York: Henry Holt & Co., 1932.

Leaf, Horace. *What Is This Spiritualism?* Garden City, N. Y.: George H. Doran & Co., 1919.

Longaker, F. C. *Some Counterfeit Religions.* Phila.: Lutheran Board of Publication, 1916.

Repplier, Agnes. *Saints or Spirits.* New York: Paulist Press, 1920.

Sadler, Wm. S. *The Mind at Mischief.* New York: Funk & Wagnalls Co., 1929.

Steiner, Lee. *Where Do People Take Their Troubles?* Boston: Houghton Mifflin Co., 1945. Ch. vii.

Stoodart, J. T. *The Case Against Spiritualism.* Garden City, N. Y.: George H. Doran & Co., 1919.

Van Baalen, Jan K. *The Chaos of Cults.* 2d ed. Grand Rapids: Eerdmans, 1956.

SECTION III

Unclassified Sects

The Bahai Faith

Many Shiite Moslems [1] of Persia 150 years ago believed that soon a reincarnation of the twelfth Imam (prophet) would occur. In 1819 Mirza Ali Muhammad, who claimed to be the "Bab" (gate) and the forerunner of the Imam, was born. His successor, Mirza Hussein Ali, called himself Baha'u'llah (Glory of God) and the last and the greatest of "God's manifestations." The Bahais (followers of this new prophet) believe that the last dispensation of the history of the world began May 23, 1844. Baha'u'llah is considered to be the fulfillment of the prophecies of the Old Testament concerning the coming of the Messiah. [2]

[1] It is rather difficult to classify Bahaism. Since Moslem ideas seem to predominate in this syncretistic movement, some have classified it with Islamic cults.

[2] Esslemont, p. 261 ff.

The new prophet is spoken of as a divine manifestation, and his writings, which are quoted profusely in Bahai literature, are said to be divine.

The basic principles may be summarized as follows: The world is a continuous divine emanation. Man is the product of a long process of evolution. Death is merely the new birth, through which the soul enters into a larger life, there to continue its growth until it reaches such perfection as to enter the presence of God. The body serves only as a temporary housing for the soul. These basic principles are usually presented under various concepts of unity.

1. The "unity of thought" is listed first and is said to teach that a pantheistic, impersonal God is the only source of everything. Since God is all in all, there is no room for evil. Evil is but the absence of good or the lesser degree of good, but never a positive thing.[3]

2. The "unity of truth and prophecy" is maintained on the basis that there can be only one truth, a living and progressive revelation, which all men of all ages, races, and creeds have a right to investigate. The ancient prophets, such as Christ and Moses, had not as yet reached full and complete knowledge of the truth. This privilege was reserved for the son of Baha'u'llah, Abdul Baha, who is held in so high an esteem that while the Bahais grant the right to search the wisdom independently, only Abdul Baha's interpretation is accepted as correct.[4]

3. The "unity of religion" is said to be expressed in the nonagon temple at Wilmette, Ill. In Bahai symbolology, "nine" is the number of perfection, and this temple with its nine sides and nine doors is said to express fully that in Bahaism all religions are merged.

4. The "unity of mankind" is based on the premise that a spiritual power breathed in this age into the soul of humanity shall remove every cause of difference, misunderstanding, discord, disagreement. There should be no idle rich and no idle poor; compulsory education is advocated; both sexes are to have equal opportunity; and an auxiliary international language should be adopted and be taught in all schools to bring men into closer fellowship. In the interest of universal peace a universal league of nations should be established.[5] Their literature contains a rather detailed plan to establish full equality among individuals, creeds, races, and nations.[6]

5. The phrase "unity of two worlds" expresses the Bahai theory that both the embodied and disembodied human beings are united and that there is a constant and inevitable communion between the two. The living are to love, help, and pray for the dead; those who are advanced in the unity of the two worlds are to help the undeveloped souls.

6. The "unity of religion and science" is predicated on the basis that since truth is one, there can be no conflict between religion, on the one hand, and science and reason on the other.[7]

---

[3] Ibid., p. 237.

[4] Ibid., p. 144 f.

[5] Horace Holly in *Census*, II, 1936, 80 f.

[6] Esslemont, ch. ix, 164—212.

[7] In a review of William M. Miller, *Bahaism* (New York: Fleming H. Revell), W. E. Garrison states that the position of the Bahais is precisely the same as that of liberal and socially minded Christians. They stand for independence in searching for the truth, oneness of the human race, international peace, conformity of religion to science and reason, and a total absence of ecclesiastical authority. *The Christian Century*, Dec. 9, 1931, p. 1,559.

Islam

The Moslem population of North America now exceeds 80,000. Most of these people are immigrants from Islamic countries or their descendants, but about 7,000 — chiefly Harlem Negroes — are converts.

The first Moslem mosque in the United States was built in Detroit in 1922; the oldest mosque still in existence was erected in Cedar Rapids, Iowa, in 1935. Currently there are twelve mosques in North America, associated in the Islamic Federation of the United States and Canada.[8]

The Ahmadiyya Movement in Islam originated in India and accepts the basic tenets of Islam. It says that Christ did not die on the cross, but swooned and was released. Afterwards He went to India, where He spent forty years in teaching and preaching.

The Moorish Science Temple of America is fully organized but is restricted exclusively to the Negro race. Timothy Drew in 1913 organized this group on the principle that the Christian religion is divisive of the races while the Islamic creed erases the color barrier and gives proper status to the Negro people, Moorish Americans. They hold that Christianity is for the white race whereas the Moslem faith is for the colored races. They are vegetarians, pray thrice daily, wear beards, proscribe smoking and drinking, observe Friday as their Sabbath.[9]

Temples of Islam. Although this fanatically antiwhite and anti-Christian movement has adopted Islamic features it has no genetic connection with the other Moslem movements in this country. The movement, which exploits the inequities of the American social system had, it was estimated, some 50 "temples" and some 70,000 adherents in 1960. The leader is Elijah Muhammad, a Baptist minister's son who was born Elijah Poole. Converts to the movement are taught in the doctrinal instruction given to them to "keep up prayer, spend of what Allah has given in the cause of truth, speak truth despite circumstances, love the brother or sister believer as oneself, be kind, kill no one whom Allah has not ordered killed, worship no God but Allah, never [to] be the aggressor but always defend yourself if attacked." [10]

Dukhobors

This is a fanatical sect of Russians who settled in Canada at the beginning of this century. They were persecuted in Russia under the Czarist regime because they refused to bear arms. The Canadian government granted them exemption from military and civil service. These "wrestlers with the Spirit" hold many strange views. Spirit-led members, they say, are free from sinning. Christ was human, and His soul reappears intermittently in living people. Strict vegetarianism is incumbent upon all, since the slaughtering of animals is considered sinful. Some refuse to use beasts of burden for heavy farm work and do it themselves. Strictly communistic, they ordinarily remain within their self-sufficient colonies. But on occasion they will

---

[8] See Nadim Makdisi, "The Moslems of America," *The Christian Century,* LXXVI (1959), 969—971.

[9] Braden, p. 469; Fausset, ch. v.

[10] Alex Haley, "Mr. Muhammad Speaks," *Reader's Digest,* XXXIX, 4 (March 1960), 100—105. See also Nat Hentoff, "Elijah in the Wilderness: Temples of Islam," *Reporter,* Aug. 4, 1960, 37—40, and ibid., Sept. 29, 1960, 10; C. E. Lincoln, *The Black Muslims in America* (Boston: Beacon Press, 1961).

leave their colonies to stage religious processions accompanied by weird exercises, sometimes bordering on the insane. The most fanatical will discard all clothing and conduct their pilgrimage in the nude as a sign of protest against whatever action of the government at the time met with their disapproval.

Peter Verigin is revered as the last of the many Messiahs who are said to have appeared among the Dukhobors. He acquired large Canadian holdings for his sect, but under his son the wealth accumulated for the communistic groups seems to have been lost. The society is divided into three parties, the Sons of Freedom representing the most extreme party.

BIBLIOGRAPHY

PART XII

SECTION III

Bach, Marcus L. *Shoghi Effendi.* Englewood Cliffs: Hawthorn Books, 1958.

Esslemont, J. E. *Baha'u'llah and the New Era,* rev. ed. New York: Bahai Publ. Committee, 1937.

Fausset, A. H. *Black Gods of the Metropolis.* Phila.: Univ. of Pa. Press, 1944.

Ferraby, John. *All Things Made New: A Comprehensive Outline of the Bahá'í Faith.* New York: The Macmillan Co., 1958.

Grossmann, Hermann. "Die Ausbreitung und gegenwärtige Aktivität der Bahá'í-Religion, insbesondere in Amerika und Europa," *Zeitschrift für Religions- und Geistesgeschichte,* X (1958), 386—399.

Wright, J. C. F. *Slava Bohu, The Story of the Dukhobors.* New York: Farrar and Rinehart, 1940. Presents the history and beliefs of this group in great detail.

Appendix

APPENDIX A

Glossary of Dogmatic Terminology

Adiaphora: Activities and especially ceremonies which are neither commanded nor forbidden in Scripture and whose use or non-use is a matter of choice.

Anthropocentrism: The assumption that man is the author, center, and ultimate end of his temporal and eternal bliss.

Anthropology: The doctrine of man.

Antinomianism: The teaching that in the Gospel dispensation the Law has no place in preaching either to the unconverted or to the converted.

Apocalypticism: The attempt to interpret literally the prophetic and figurative portions of the Bible depicting some catastrophe, especially the end of the world.

Apocatastasis: The theory that ultimately all sinful beings will be restored to God.

Apotheosis: The deification of a human being.

Baptism of Desire: In Roman Catholic theology an act of love made by an unbaptized person with the desire to do everything required for his salvation; it remits all sin and its eternal punishment.

Biblicism: In its good sense it denotes thorough acquaintance with the Bible. As conventionally used it is a literal use of the Bible which ignores context, figures of speech, and principles of interpretation.

Catholic: (a) Universal, the entire Christian church; (b) Frequently but incorrectly applied to the Roman Catholic Church.

Charismatic Gifts: Special spiritual endowments to edify the church, such as the ability to expound the Scriptures, or such unusual gifts as the ability to speak in unknown tongues.

Chiliasm: Known also as millennialism. It is the belief that a period of 1,000 years in which holiness will be triumphant will precede the end of the world.

Consubstantiation: The view that in the Eucharist the body and blood of Christ are substantially and permanently united with the consecrated bread and wine.

Creationism: The theory that each human soul is created by a special divine act.

Cultus: The system of worship observed by a given body of Christians.

Dualism: (a) The belief that man's body and soul always act as two independent elements, in contrast to the view that the total person is engaged in every act; (b) The theory that two opposing forces, one good, the other evil, govern the universe.

Dulia: The veneration or homage given to the saints in the Greek and Roman Catholic churches in distinction from *latria,* which is given to God alone.

Ecclesiology: The doctrine of the church.

Ecumenical: The term denotes universality. It is applied to the creeds adopted by all Christendom, to the councils approved by the whole church, and to the recent movement which attempts to bring all denominations into a united fellowship.

Egocentric: Considering everything only in relation to oneself.

Empiricism: The philosophical theory which claims that the only source of knowledge is experience and which rejects all supernatural revelation.

Encyclical: A prelate's circular letter, especially a letter of the pope addressed to all Roman Catholic bishops on matters of doctrinal, moral, and social interest.

Enthusiasm: (a) The belief that God still reveals Himself directly to man by a special act outside His revelation in Holy Scripture; (b) The theory that human reason, intuitive knowledge, or religious experience are valid sources and criteria of truth.

Eschatology: The doctrines dealing with the end of this world and with the world to come.

Ex opere operato: The Roman Catholic teaching that sacramental grace is caused by the validly performed sacramental sign and is not conferred on the ground of the subjective activity of the recipient, although the subjective disposition of the recipient is an indispensable precondition of the communication of grace.

Ex opere operantis: The Roman Catholic teaching that the minister or recipient must meet the prescribed conditions before he can validly administer or worthily use a sacrament or sacramental.

Fides explicita: The Roman Catholic term for faith when it is based on the knowledge of divine truth.

Fides formata: The Roman Catholic term which denotes that faith can justify only because it is active in good works.

Fides implicita: The Roman Catholic term for a faith which is not acquainted explicitly with the teachings of the church.

Filioque: The doctrine that the Holy Spirit proceeds eternally from both the Father and the Son.

Forensic Justification: The doctrine that God by a judicial act declares the sinner righteous.

Formal Principle: The source from which all teaching is derived and the standard by which it is judged.

Genus majestaticum: The doctrine that in our Lord's Incarnation all His divine attributes were communicated to the human nature, without an essential change in either nature.

Hamartiology: The doctrine of sin.

Iconoclast: One who breaks icons or religious symbols; one who is opposed to the use of images in the church.

Impeccability: The doctrine that during His earthly life Christ, the God-Man, could not sin.

Inner Light: A divine Presence alleged to be in the soul which enlightens and guides it.

Inspiration, Verbal: The teaching that the Holy Spirit gave to the writers of Scripture the content and the fitting word, so that Scripture in its originals is the inerrant Word of God.

Latitudinarianism: Tolerance of variations in religious belief or doctrine; approval of freedom and difference of doctrine and belief.

Latria: In Roman Catholic theology the worship due to God alone, in distinction from the veneration or homage given to saints, *dulia.*

Legalism: The belief that observance of the Ten Commandments or of humanly established laws will gain merit and eternal life.

Literalism: The interpretation of Holy Scripture according to the letter and ignoring all figurative language or the specific situation in which statements occur.

Material Principle. The central thought of a respective theological system.

Modalism: The error that there is only one person in the Deity, who manifests Himself in three ways — as Father, Son, and Holy Spirit.

Monarchianism: The theory that God is one in person as well as in nature.

Monergism: The doctrine that God alone is the author of man's salvation.

Monophysitism: The teaching that Christ's human and divine natures were fused into one nature.

Mysticism: The belief that one can attain direct knowledge of God and divine truth through insight or intuition in a way different from ordinary sense perception.

Neoplatonism: A mixture of Greek philosophy and Oriental speculations. It holds that there are three emanations from God, the last, including the human body, being material and evil. The soul must free itself from the evil matter of the body by ascetic practices.

Orders: (a) The various ranks of the ministry, especially in episcopal churches; (b) The conferring of the ministry, ordination.

Pedobaptism: Infant baptism.

Pelagianism: The theory advanced by Pelagius that by nature man is in a state of moral indifference but that by his free will he can develop powers to do good.

Pentecostalism: The belief that the special gifts of Pentecost, especially the gift to speak in unknown tongues, are bestowed upon the church as a permanent blessing.

Polity: The specific form of church government.

Postmillennialism: The theory that Christ will return to the earth visibly after the millennium.

Premillennialism: The theory that Christ will return visibly prior to the millennium.

Real Presence: The doctrine that the true and essential body and blood of Christ are present, distributed, and received in the Sacrament of the Altar by all communicants.

Sacerdotalism: The teaching that ordination confers special powers and rights necessary for the exercise of the ministry.

Sacramentalism: The attitude which attaches great importance to the sacraments.

Scholasticism: The theological method employed in the Middle Ages to support the doctrines of the church by reason and logic.

Septuagint (LXX): The Greek version of the Old Testament begun about 270 B. C. According to tradition, it was the work of seventy-two scholars.

Sola fide: The doctrine that God forgives the sinner without any merit on his part when he believes that he is included in Christ's complete redemption.

Sola gratia: The Gospel doctrine that God pardons believers without any merit of their own, solely by grace for Christ's sake.

Sola Scriptura: The doctrine that the Sacred Scriptures contain everything that a person needs to believe for his salvation.

Soteriology: The doctrine of man's redemption and salvation.

Subjectivism: The theory that the individual is the source and critic of all religious truths on the basis of his own knowledge and experience.

Synergism: The view that in his conversion man in some degree co-operates with the Holy Spirit by alleged inherent spiritual powers.

Theanthropic: Term to denote that the incarnate Christ is both God and man.

Theocentric: The term applies to a theology which makes God the absolute center and source of all action.

Theopoiesis: The process whereby the Christian is transformed and participates in the divine nature (2 Peter 1:4) by grace.

Traducianism: The belief that human souls are propagated by generation, just as the body is.

Transubstantiation: The Roman Catholic doctrine that through the consecration in the Lord's Supper the substance of the bread and wine are changed into substance of the body and blood of Christ and that only the accidents and appearances of the earthly elements remain.

Tritheism: The theory that the three divine persons are three gods.

Una sancta: The one holy Christian church referred to in the Apostles' Creed.

Unionism: Joint religious work and worship across denominational lines without doctrinal unity and with evident denial of the divine truth.

Venial Sin: In Roman Catholic theology such sins as are forgiven without sacramental confession in distinction from mortal sin.

Vulgate: Jerome's translation of the Bible into Latin at the end of the fourth century; the revision of 1592 is the official text of the Roman Catholic church.

APPENDIX B

Statistics

Except as noted, the following statistics on religious bodies in the continental United States are taken from the edition for 1961 of the *Yearbook of American Churches: Information on All Faiths in the U. S. A.* (New York: National Council of the Churches of Christ in the U. S. A.), issued October 1960. These statistics are printed here with the publisher's permission. We omit all groups of less than 50,000 but include over 98% of all religiously affiliated Americans. Except where another year is indicated, the statistics are for the end of the calendar year 1959 or for a fiscal year ending in 1959. The membership shown is inclusive in terms of the respective denomination's definition of member (all baptized persons, including infants, in the case of the Roman Catholic church, the Protestant Episcopal church, and the Lutheran church; all full members in the case of most Protestant bodies; all Jews in communities having congregations in the case of the Jewish congregations; all persons in the respective nationality or cultural group in the case of Eastern Orthodoxy).

Apostolic Overcoming Holy Church of God (1956)	75,000
Armenian Orthodox Church of America	125,000
Assemblies of God	505,703

Baptist:

American Baptist Association	647,800
American Baptist Convention (1957)	1,555,360
Baptist General Conference of America	68,930
Conservative Baptist Association of America	275,000
Free Will Baptists	200,000
General Association of Regular Baptist Churches	130,612
General Baptists	55,637
National Baptist Convention of America (1956)	2,688,799
National Baptist Convention of the U. S. A., Inc. (1958)	5,000,000
National Baptist Evangelical Life and Soul Saving Assembly of the U. S. A. (1951)	57,674

National Primitive Baptist Convention of the U. S. A. (1957)	80,983
North American Baptist Association	330,265
North American Baptist General Conference	50,455
Primitive Baptists (1950)	72,000
Southern Baptist Convention	9,485,276
United Baptists (1955)	63,641
United Free Will Baptist Church (1958)	100,000
Christian and Missionary Alliance	59,644
Christian Churches (Disciples of Christ), International Convention	1,801,414
Church of Christ, Scientist (1936)	268,915
Church of God in Christ	382,679
Church of the Brethren	201,219
Church of the Nazarene	300,771
Churches of Christ	2,007,650

Churches of God:

Church of God (Anderson, Ind.)	135,294
Church of God (Cleveland, Tenn.)	162,794
The Church of God (Queens Village, N. Y.)	74,209

Eastern Orthodox:

American Carpatho-Russian Orthodox Greek Catholic Church	100,000
Bulgarian Eastern Orthodox Church	80,000
Greek Archdiocese of North and South America	1,200,000
Romanian Orthodox Episcopate of America	50,000
Russian Orthodox Church Outside Russia (1951)	55,000
Russian Orthodox Greek Catholic Church of America (1957)	755,000
Serbian Eastern Orthodox Church	250,000
Syrian Antiochian Orthodox Church	115,000

Ukrainian Orthodox Church of the U. S. A.	84,400
Evangelical Covenant Church of America	59,396
Evangelical United Brethren Church	749,788
Federated Churches (1936)	88,411
Friends, Five Years Meeting of	68,399
Independent Fundamental Churches of America	90,000
International Church of the Four-square Gospel (1958)	79,012
International General Assembly of Spiritualists (1956)	164,072
Jehovah's witnesses	239,418
Jewish Congregations (1954)	5,500,000

Latter Day Saints:

Church of Jesus Christ of Latter-day Saints	1,457,735
Reorganized Church of Jesus Christ of Latter-day Saints	152,408

Lutheran:

American Lutheran Church	2,194,505
Augustana Evangelical Lutheran Church	596,147
Lutheran Free Church	82,595
The Lutheran Church — Missouri Synod	2,304,692
United Lutheran Church in America	2,369,263
Wisconsin Evangelical Lutheran Synod	342,993
Mennonite Church	72,138

Methodist:

African Methodist Episcopal Church (1951)	1,166,301
African Methodist Episcopal Zion Church	780,000
Christian Methodist Episcopal Church (1951)	392,167
Free Methodist Church of North America	55,568
The Methodist Church	9,815,460
Moravian Church in America (Unitas Fratrum)	60,470
North American Old Roman Catholic Church	71,521

Pentecostal:

Pentecostal Assemblies of the World, Inc. (1958)	50,000
Pentecostal Church of God of America, Inc. (1958)	103,500
Pentecostal Holiness Church, Inc.	51,688
United Pentecostal Church, Inc. (1958)	160,000
Polish National Catholic Church of America (1958)	271,316

Presbyterian:

Cumberland Presbyterian Church	87,263
Presbyterian Church in the U. S.	889,196
United Presbyterian Church in the U. S. A.	3,145,733
Protestant Episcopal Church (1958)	3,126,662

Reformed:

Christian Reformed Church	236,145
Reformed Church in America	219,770
Roman Catholic Church	40,871,302
Salvation Army	253,061
Seventh-day Adventists	311,535
Syrian Orthodox Church of Antioch	50,000
Triumph the Church and Kingdom of God in Christ	71,089
Unitarian Universalist Association	178,457
United Church of Christ	2,223,732

APPENDIX C

Abbreviations Used in Text

A. C. = Augsburg Confession
ALC = American Lutheran Church
Ap. = Apology of the A. C.
Art. = Article

Bibliogr. = Bibliography
B. C. = *Book of Concord*
B. of Disc. = *Book of Discipline*
Brit. = Britannica

C. = Catechism
Cambr. = Cambridge
Cath. = Catholic
Ch. = Church, chapter
Com. = Commandment
Conf. = Confession
Congr. = Congregation
C. P. H. = Concordia Publishing House
C. R. = *Corpus Reformatorum*
C. T. M. = *Concordia Theological Monthly*

ed. = edition, editor
ELC = Evangelical Lutheran Church
Encyc. = Encyclopedia
Ep. = Epitome of F. C.

F. C. = Formula of Concord
fn. = footnote

Heidelb. C. = Heidelberg Catechism
Hist. = History, Historical

IMC = International Missionary Council
Inst. = Institutes
Introd. = Introduction

Large C. = Large Catechism
Luth. = Lutheran

Mod. = Modern

Op. sel. = *Opera selecta*
org. = organize

P. = Part
Phila. = Philadelphia
Pop. Symb. = *Popular Symbolics*
Pref. = Preface
Publ. = Publishing

Q. = Quarterly
Qu. = Question

S. A. = Smalcald Articles
S. D. A. = Seventh-day Adventists
Sec. = Section
Sec. Pet. = Second Petition
Small C. = Small Catechism
Syst. = Systematic

theol. = theology
Th. D. = Thorough Declaration of F. C.
trans. = translated

ULCA = United Lutheran Church in America
Univ. = University

W. A. = Weimar Ausgabe (ed.) of Luther's Works
Westm. = Westminster Confession

Abbreviations Used in Index

A. C. C. = American Council of Christian Churches
Adv. = Adventists
Am. = Amana
Anab. = Anabaptists
Arm. = Arminianism

Bap. = Baptists
Buch. = Moral Re-Armament (Buchmanism)

Cal. = Calvinism
Chil. = Chiliasm
Christa. = Christadelphians

Chr. Sc. = Christian Science
Con. = Congregationalism (see United Church of Christ)

Disc. = Disciples of Christ
Disp. = Dispensationalism

E. and R. = Evangelical and Reformed Church (see United Church of Christ)
E. C. = Eastern Orthodox Catholic churches
Ecu. = Ecumenical movement
Ep. = Protestant Episcopal Church
E. U. B. = Evangelical United Brethren

Fund. = Fundamentalism

Gen. El. = General Eldership
Gl. = Glossary

H. of D. = House of David
Hol. Bod. = Holiness bodies

Irv. = Irvingites, Catholic Apostolic Church

Jud. = Judaism
J. W. = Jehovah's witnesses

L. C. = Lutheran church

Menn. = Mennonite
Meth. = Methodist
Mil. = Millennialism
Mod. = Modernism
Mor. = Moravians
Morm. = Mormons, or Latter-day Saints

N. C. C. = National Council of the Churches of Christ in the U. S. A.
Neo. = Neo-Orthodoxy
N. Th. = New Thought

O. C. = Old Catholic

Pen. = Pentecostalism
Plym. = Plymouth Brethren
Prem. = Premillennialism
Pres. = Presbyterian

Qua. = Quakers

R. C. = Roman Catholic
Ref. = Reformed churches

S. A. = Salvation Army
S. D. A. = Seventh-day Adventist
Schw. = Schwenkfelder
Sha. = Shaker
Spi. = Spiritism
Swed. = Swedenborgian

Theo. = Theosophy

U. C. Can. = United Church of Canada
U. C. C. = United Church of Christ
Unit. Univ. = Unitarian Universalist Association

W. C. C. = World Council of Churches

Index

INDEX